PROGRAMMED

STATISTICS

(Questions-Answers)

PROGRAMMED STATISTICS (Questions-Answers)

FIFTH EDITION

B L AGARWAL
Formerly-Professor & University Head
Department of Statistics and Mathematics
Rajasthan College of Agriculture
Udaipur, Rajasthan

Committed to Educate the Nation

NEW AGE

Publishing Globally

IN INDIA

NEW AGE INTERNATIONAL (P) LIMITED, PUBLISHERS

LONDON • NEW DELHI

Bangalore • Chennai • Cochin • Guwahati • Hyderabad • Kolkata • Mumbai

Visit us at www.newagepublishers.com

Published by New Age International (P) Ltd., Publishers
First Edition: 2003
Fifth Edition (*in two colours*) : 2024

GLOBAL OFFICES

- **New Delhi** **NEW AGE INTERNATIONAL (P) LIMITED, PUBLISHERS**
7/30 A, Daryaganj, New Delhi-110002, (INDIA), **Tel.:** (011) 23253472, 23253771
E-mail: contactus@newagepublishers.com • Visit us at www.newagepublishers.com

- **London** **NEW AGE INTERNATIONAL (UK) LTD.**
27 Old Gloucester Street, London, WC1N 3AX, UK
E-mail: info@newacademicscience.co.uk • Visit us at www.newacademicscience.co.uk

BRANCHES

- **Bangalore** 37/10, 8th Cross (Near Hanuman Temple), Azad Nagar, Chamarajpet, Bangalore- 560 018
Tel.: (080) 26756823, **E-mail: bangalore@newagepublishers.com**

- **Chennai** 26, Damodaran Street, T. Nagar, Chennai-600 017, **Tel.:** (044) 24353401
E-mail: chennai@newagepublishers.com

- **Cochin** CC-39/1016, Carrier Station Road, Ernakulam South, Cochin-682 016
Tel.: (0484) 4051304, **E-mail: cochin@newagepublishers.com**

- **Guwahati** Hemsen Complex, Mohd. Shah Road, Paltan Bazar, Near Starline Hotel
Guwahati-781 008, **Tel.:** (0361) 2513881, **E-mail: guwahati@newagepublishers.com**

- **Hyderabad** 105, 1st Floor, Madhiray Kaveri Tower, 3-2-19, Azam Jahi Road, Near Kumar Theater
Nimboliadda Kachiguda, Hyderabad-500 027, **Tel.:** (040) 24652456
E-mail: hyderabad@newagepublishers.com

- **Kolkata** RDB Chambers (Formerly Lotus Cinema) 106A, 1st Floor, S N Banerjee Road
Kolkata-700 014, **Tel.:** (033) 22273773, **E-mail: kolkata@newagepublishers.com**

- **Mumbai** 142C, Victor House, Ground Floor, N.M. Joshi Marg, Lower Parel, Mumbai-400 013
Tel.: (022) 24927869, 24915415, **E-mail: mumbai@newagepublishers.com**

- **New Delhi** 22, Golden House, Daryaganj, New Delhi-110 002, **Tel.:** (011) 23262368, 23262370
E-mail: sales@newagepublishers.com

C-23-11-13836

Printed in India at Parmanand Offset, Delhi.
Typeset at Blue Birds Graphics, Delhi.

NEW AGE INTERNATIONAL (P) LIMITED, PUBLISHERS
7/30 A, Daryaganj, New Delhi-110002
Visit us at **www.newagepublishers.com**
(CIN: U74899DL1966PTC004618)

Dedicated

to

my brother

Dr. S.P. Agarwal

Scientist Emeritus

Preface to the Fifth Edition

Previous editions of ***Programmed Statistics*** have already proven their worth for the last two decades in the area of statistics as one of the most successful books. The book has excelled in presenting the fundamentals of statistics to students, teachers and examinees in the form of questions-answers and objective type of questions.

On the statistical front, there have been continuous developments during the last decade, especially due to easy access to personnel computers (PC) and moreover the availability of computer software packages such as SPSS and SAS. All these advances have increased the interest and scope of multivariate statistical methods involving theory and multivariate data analysis. A number of professional and traditional programs in statistics have included courses on multivariate distributions, tests and analytical procedures.

To fulfill the requirement of the present day courses some important terms have been added in this book which will enable the readers to understand the complexities of the multivariate statistical concepts in a cozy manner.

This is a user-friendly book for all examinations, viva-voce, interviews etc.

BASANT LAL AGARWAL

Preface to the First Edition

In this progressive age of cut throat competition, a scholar is required to have a detailed knowledge and deeper insight of the subject to get an edge over his colleagues in pursuit of higher studies. Thus, a student would like to acquire maximum information in minimum time which is an uphill task because most of the available books are exhaustive and time-consuming. An examinee is also confronted with the lack of knowledge about the nature of questions and their precise answers.

In order to circumvent these difficulties, the author has ventured to scribe this book – *Programmed Statistics (Questions – Answers)* – so that the students of statistics could accumulate sufficient knowledge about the subject matter in a short span of time, and may also abreast themselves with the nature of questions and their exact answers. For brevity and clarity, "short essay-type" and, "fill in the banks" type questions have been setup. The former explains the core of the topic to enable the reader to answer many more related questions, and the latter brushes up their knowledge. In Section-C of each chapter, "multiple choice type questions" will enable a reader to test his grasp over the topics, and answer correctly any objective type questions in any examination. It is expected that a thorough study of this book will enable the readers to accurately answer most of the questions pertaining to each topic covered in this book.

The answer to each question is also provided at the end of each chapter so that a reader has not to run from pillar to post to ascertain whether his answer is correct or not. For some questions, hints are also given alongwith the answer so that the book proves to be self sufficient for an inquisitive mind, and the topics covered in this book.

Since a wide range of topics have been covered in this book, the readers may restrict their studies to the chapters according to their requirement, and not necessarily go through all the chapters. The mathematics derivations of formulae have been kept out as they do not form the part of competitive examinations, applied and professional statistics. In this way, the book will serve all types of examinees except those who appear in traditional type of examinations in mathematical statistics.

Suggested reading contains all those books which can be of immense help to the examinees who want greater details on any topic. The author has no hesitation to accept that any chapter does not contain as much details as a whole book on a topic does. The background of this book is, *Basic Statistics* by the author himself but the present book contains much more material as it does not confine to a few syllabi. The book, *Programmed Statistics (Questions – Answers)* has a wide coverage of topics in conceptual as well as descriptive manner.

The author will be failing in his duty if he does not acknowledge, all those who have helped him in writing this book. First of all, I thank Mr. A. Machwe, Managing Director, and Shri H.S. Paplai, General Manager, New Age International (P) Limited, Publishers New Delhi, who at the very outset agreed to publish a book on a new pattern to fulfil the pressing need of the present day examinees. Another person, who deserves gratitude, is my reverend brother, Dr. S.P. Agarwal, M.V. Sc., Ph.D., Scientist Emeritus, who not only encouraged and inspired me for writing this book but has also gone through the whole manuscript and corrected it at best. There has been lot of cooperation from my colleagues and friends who helped me whenever asked for. Last but not the least my wife Mrs. Kanak Lata Agarwal, M.A., B.T. deserves appreciation for her patience, perseverance, sustenance and help. This book would have not been a reality but for her cooperation. The author is also thankful to all those who have helped directly or indirectly in completing this book.

The author shall be grateful for any suggestions made by the readers towards the improvement of the book. Any reader sending 100 questions with new theme which are found fit for inclusion' in the book, will be gratefully acknowledged by name.

BASANT LAL AGARWAL

Contents

Chapter 8 Bivariate Random Variable and Distributions 163–183

Chapter 9 Sampling Methods 184–213

Chapter 22 Multivariate Statistical Methods 630–668

CHAPTER 1

Statistics in General

SECTION A

Short Essay Type Questions

Q. 1. *Define statistics as given by Sir R.A. Fisher.*

Ans. Sir R.A. Fisher defined statistics as, "The science of statistics is essentially a branch of applied mathematics and may be regarded as mathematics applied to observational data."

Q. 2. *Give the definitions of statistics given by A.L. Bowley, Lovitt, W.A. Wallis and H.V. Roberts and C.H. Meyers.*

Ans. The definitions given by statisticians named in the question are quoted below:

A.L. Bowley:

(*i*) Statistics is the device for abbreviating and classifying the statements and making clear the relations.

(*ii*) Statistics is the science of measurement of social phenomenon regarded as a whole in all its manifestations.

(*iii*) Statistics is the numerical statement of facts in any department of enquiry, placed in relation to each other.

Lovitt: Statistics is the science which deals with the collecting, classifying, presenting, comparing and interpreting numerical data collected to throw light on any sphere of enquiry.

W.A. Wallis and H.V. Roberts: (*i*) Statistics is not a body of substantive knowledge, but a body of methods obtaining knowledge.

(*ii*) Statistics is a body of methods for making wise decision in the face of uncertainty.

Cecil H. Meyers: (*i*) Statistics may be defined as a science of numerical information which employs the processes of measurement and collection, classification, analysis, decision-making and communication of results in a manner understandable and verifiable by other.

(*ii*) A statistician is a practitioner of the art and science of statistics.

Q. 3. *Give the statements given by A.L. Bowley and William A. Spurr and Charles P. Bonini.*

Ans. A.L. Bowley: Great numbers are not counted correctly to a unit, they are estimated.

William A. Spurr and Charles P. Bonini: Not all numbers are statistical, Logarithms, for instance, are mere abstract numbers. Statistical data are concrete numbers, which represent objects.

Q. 4. *Quote statements about statistics made by A.E. Waugh, A.L. Boddington, Whipple, Tippet, W.I. King, Marshall, Yule and Kendall, R.A. Fisher, A.M. Mood, Disraeli and Darrel Huf.*

Ans. A.E. Waugh: The purpose of statistical methods is to simplify great bodies of numerical data.

A.L. Boddington: The essence of statistics is not mere counting but comparison.

Whipple: Statistics enables one to enlarge his Horizon.

L.H.C. Tippet:

(*i*) Planning is the order of the day and without statistics planning is inconceivable.

(*ii*) Statistics is both a science and an art.

W.I. King:

(*i*) The science of statistics is a most useful servant, but only of great value to those who understand its proper use.

(*ii*) The science of statistics is the method of judging collective, natural or social phenomena from the results obtained by the analysis of enumeration or collection of estimates.

Marshall: Statistics are the straw out of which I like every other economist have to make bricks.

Yule and Kendall: Statistics is not a science, it is a scientific method.

R.A. Fisher: Statistics is a branch of applied mathematics which specialises in data.

A.M. Mood: Statistics provides tools and techniques for research workers.

Disraeli: There are three kinds of lies – lies, damned lies and statistics.

Darrel Huf: A well wrapped statistics is better than Hitlers biglie it misleads, yet it cannot be pinned on you.

Q. 5. *Which definition of statistics is considered to be the best?*

Ans. The definition of statistics given by R.A. Fisher is considered to be the best and most exact.

Q. 6. *Give in a few words the statistical perspective.*

Ans. Statistical perspective is the invaluable compendium which gather all the facts, figures, objective survey and fascinating remembrances to a assimilable record.

Q. 7. *Mention main divisions of statistics.*

Ans. Following are the main divisions of statistics:

(*i*) *Mathematical or theoretical statistics:* It covers development of statistical distributions, experimental designs, sampling designs, etc.

(*ii*) *Statistical methods or functions:* It covers collection, tabulation, analysis and interpretation of data, etc.

(*iii*) *Descriptive statistics:* Classification and diagrammatic representation of data.

(*iv*) *Inferential statistics:* To draw conclusion about population on the basis of sample drawn from it.

(*v*) *Applied statistics:* It mainly covers population, census, national income, production, business statistics, industrial statistics, quality control, biostatistics, etc.

Q. 8. *What are the limitations of statistics?*

Ans. Broadly the limitations of statistics are:

(*i*) Statistics deals with quantitative data only. Even qualitative information is converted into numerical data by the method of ranking, scoring or scaling.

(*ii*) Statistics is true on an average only.

(*iii*) Statistics deals with the masses, not an individual. No statistics is applicable for a single observation.

(*iv*) Statistical results are correct in a general sense. They are always subject to certain amount of error.

(*v*) Statistics is only a means to draw conclusions about masses or population but not a panacea to all sort of problems.

(*vi*) Statistics can be misused in many ways.

Q. 9. *What are different types of investigations?*

Ans. There are two types of investigations, namely:

(*i*) investigation through census method.

(*ii*) investigation through sample methods.

Q. 10. *What does census method imply?*

Ans. Census method means to include each and every unit or object of the population under reference for enquiry or observation. For example, to know the national income, we have to include every individual or unit which contributes towards the national income.

Q. 11. *What is meant by investigation through sample method?*

Ans. In sample method, an investigator has to select some units from the population about which conclusions have to be drawn and take observations on the selected units. The results obtained from sample values are applicable to the population as a whole. For instance, to know the average age at marriage, an investigator selects an adequate number of married couples and arrive at an average age of marriage which is considered to be the average age of marriage for the whole population.

Q. 12. *What are four main functions of statistics?*

Ans. Four main functions of statistics are:

(*i*) Collection of data;

(*ii*) Presentation of data;

(*iii*) Analysis of data; and

(*iv*) Interpretation of results.

Q. 13. *Give different methods of collection of data.*

Ans. Following are the methods of collection of data:

(*i*) Direct personal enquiry method;

(*ii*) Indirect oral investigation;

(*iii*) By filling of schedules;

(*iv*) By mailed questionnaires;

(*v*) Information from local agents and correspondents;

(*vi*) By old records; and

(*vii*) By direct observational method.

Q. 14. *Name two kinds of statistical data and describe them in brief.*

Ans. Two kinds of statistical data are:

(*i*) *Primary data:* Primary data are those which are collected from the units or individuals directly and these data have never been used for any purpose earlier.

(*ii*) *Secondary data:* The data, which had been collected by some individual or agency and statistically treated to draw certain conclusions. Again the same data are used and analysed to extract some other information, are termed as secondary data.

Q. 15. *What are the requisites of a reliable data?*

Ans. The requisites of a reliable data are:

(*i*) It should be complete;

(*ii*) It should be consistent;

(*iii*) It should be accurate; and

(*iv*) It should be homogeneous in respect of unit of information.

Q. 16. *What precautions should be taken in the planning of a statistical survey?*

Ans. Following precautions are to be taken in the planning of a survey:

(*i*) *Purpose:* First a clear-cut objective of the survey should be spelled out.

(*ii*) *Scope of survey:* Different aspects to be covered to achieve the fixed objectives should clearly be explained.

(*iii*) *Definition of terms:* All the terms involved in a survey should be defined without ambiguity so that no unit is likely to fall in more than one category.

(*iv*) *Stating the hypothesis:* Hypothesis to be tested from the data collected by way of survey should be laid down in accordance with the objectives of the survey.

Q. 17. *Give briefly the characteristics of a good questionnaire or a schedule.*

Ans. Characteristics of a good questionnaire or a schedule are:

(*i*) Number of questions should be such that it extracts all information required for the report.

(*ii*) Each question should have almost all alternative answers.

(*iii*) The question should be clear and without any ambiguity.

(*iv*) All questions should be mutually exclusive in nature.

(*v*) Some very personal questions be avoided.

(*vi*) Questionnaire or schedule should not be very lengthy and time-consuming.

Q. 18. *Name five fields where statistics is inevitable.*

Ans. Broadly five fields where statistics is inevitable can be named as follows:

(*i*) Scientific research;
(*ii*) Economic analysis;
(*iii*) Planning;
(*iv*) Business and commerce; and
(*v*) Forecasting and projection.

Q. 19. *Mention different kinds of statistical investigations.*

Ans. Different kinds of statistical investigations are:

(*i*) Surveys or experiments;
(*ii*) Surveys through census or sample enquiry;
(*iii*) Confidential or open enquiry;
(*iv*) Direct or indirect enquiry;
(*v*) Original or repetitive enquiry;
(*vi*) Regular or ad hoc enquiry; and
(*vii*) Limited or extensive enquiry.

Q. 20. *What is an absolute biased error?*

Ans. When the figures are rounded straight way to the nearest lowest unit of rounding or to the nearest highest unit of rounding, the difference between actual and estimated (rounded) values in the two cases are called biased errors. For example, if we round the value 357 to the nearest 100, the nearest lower value is 300 and nearest higher value is 400.

In case I, Absolute biased error = 357 – 300 = 57.

In case II, Absolute biased error = 357 – 400 = – 43.

If there are two or more values in a set, the sum of absolute errors is taken.

Q. 21. *What is an absolute unbiased error?*

Ans. If the values are rounded as per the rules of rounding, *i.e.*, a given value is rounded to nearest lower value of the unit of rounding in case it is less than half of the unit of rounding and to next higher value of the unit of rounding if it is more than half of the unit of rounding, it is called unbiased error. The difference between the actual value and the estimated (rounded) value is called absolute unbiased error. If, there are two or more values in a set, then the sum of the absolute unbiased error is taken.

Q. 22. *How do you estimate an average unbiased absolute error (A.E.)?*

Ans. The Formula is,

Average A.E. (unbiased) = Average error × $\sqrt{n}$

where, n = Number of items in the set and Average error = The mean of the minimum and maximum values which are likely to be left over or increased in the process of rounding. For example, if we are rounding a value to the nearest 100, the chances are that the lowest value which may be left out is 0 and maximum value which may be added is 50. Hence, the average error is (0 + 50)/2 = 25.

Q. 23. *Enunciate the law of statistical regularity.*

Ans. The law states that a reasonably large number of items selected at random from a large group of items will, on the average, be representative of the large group or population. This law is governed by the theory of probability.

Q. 24. *State the law of inertia of large numbers.*

Ans. The law of inertia states that the large aggregates are more stable than small ones. According to Professor A.L. Bowley, great numbers and averages resulting from them, such as we always obtain measuring social phenomena have a great inertia.

Q. 25. *What is the law of persistence of small number?*

Ans. The law of persistence of small numbers states that the ratio of the small number of items having some distinguished characteristics to the total number of units in the population remains constant even though the population size is immensely increased.

Q. 26. *Give an example of the law of persistence of small numbers.*

Ans. Suppose a school admits all good students. Even then some students will be of poor intelligence. The ratio of such students to the total number of students will remain the same even if the number of students in the school is doubled, trebled, etc.

Q. 27. *State the law of decreasing variation.*

Ans. Law of decreasing variation indicates that the variation in a sample tends to reduce as the sample size increases.

Q. 28. *How is the law of decreasing variation helpful in sample surveys?*

Ans. It is the law of decreasing variation which puts an investigator on sound footing to decide about the adequate sample size which is a true representative of the population.

Q. 29. *What do you understand by approximation of values or figures?*

Ans. To express a value or figure to a round figure which is easy to write and understand is called approximation. This is mostly done from convenience point of view. It helps in comparison of values tremendously.

Q. 30. *Give different methods of approximation with a brief description.*

Ans. Different methods of approximation are:

(*i*) *By adding figure:* In this methods the given value of figure is always increased to next higher value of unit of rounding. For instance, a value 21,357.4 will be approximated to 21,358 up to unit place, 21,360 up to tenth place, 21,400 up to hundredth place and 22,000 up to thousandth place.

(*ii*) *By discarding figures:* It is a process just reverse to the adding figures. In this method, the given value is decreased to next lower value of unit of rounding. For example, the value 21,357.4 is approximated to 21,357 up to unit place, 21,350 up to tenth place, 21,300 up to hundredth place and 21,000 up to thousandth place.

(*iii*) *Approximation to the whole number:* This method is also known as rounding of figures and is an usually accepted method. This method is the best one as it minimises the error of approximation. In this method, a value is raised to the next higher value of the unit of rounding if it is more than half of the unit of rounding and is left over if it is less than half of the unit of rounding.

Q. 31. *What are different sources of statistical errors?*

Ans. Following are the four sources of statistical errors:

(*i*) Errors of origin;

(*ii*) Errors of inadequacy;

(*iii*) Errors of manipulation; and

(*iv*) Errors of interpretation.

Q. 32. *Explain briefly the possible error.*

Ans. In rounding of values to the nearest of units, tens or hundreds or thousands, etc., a value less than half of the unit of rounding is left over and greater than half of the unit of rounding is increased to the next higher unit. Thus, the possible error is $\pm$ 1/2 $\times$ unit of rounding. For example, if the number 23 is rounded to the nearest ten, its value is 20 and possible error is $\pm$ 5. Hence, the value will lie between 20 $\pm$ 5, *i.e.*, between 15 and 25.

Q. 33. *What are different sources of primary data?*

Ans. Data obtained from original experiments or surveys, *i.e.*, the data collected by investigators or enumerators is known as primary data. Also the census data, data released in the Reserve Bank of India bulletins, data published by other authorities in original form are considered as primary data.

Q. 34. *What are different sources of secondary data?*

Ans. Published thesis, research papers, project reports, summarised census report, monthly abstracts of CSO and different publications of trade and commerce associations, etc., are the various sources of secondary data.

Q. 35. *What kind of deficiencies of data are checked through editing?*

Ans. Data are edited to remove mainly four deficiencies which are:

(*i*) Completeness of data;

(*ii*) Consistency of data;

(*iii*) Accuracy of data; and

(*iv*) Homogeneity of data.

SECTION B

Fill in the Blanks

Fill in the suitable word(s) or phrase(s) in the blanks:

1. The statement, "Not all numbers are statistical; logarithms for instance, are merely abstract numbers. Statistical data are concrete numbers, which represents objects", was given by ________ and ________ .
2. "Great numbers are not counted correctly to a unit, they are estimated", is the statement of ________ .
3. The definition, "Statistics is the science which deals with the collection, classification and tabulation of numerical facts as the basis for explanation, description and comparison of phenomena", was given by ________ .
4. "Statistics is a body of methods for making wise decisions in the face of uncertainty" is the definition of statistics given by ________ and ________ .
5. Statistics is both, a ________ and an ________ .
6. The credit of the statement, "A statistician is a practitioner of the art and science of statistics" goes to ________ .
7. "The purpose of statistical methods is to simplify great bodies of numerical data" is the statement given by ________ .
8. The definition, "The essence of statistics is not mere counting but comparison", was given by ________ .
9. The statement, "Statistics enables one to enlarge his horizon", goes in the name of ________ .
10. The statement, "Planning is the order of the day and without statistics planning is inconceivable" was given by ________ .
11. The author of the statement, "The science of statistics is a most useful servant, but only of great value to those who understand its proper use", was due to ________ .
12. Statistics can prove ________ .
13. Use of statistical methods is most dangerous in the hands of ________ .
14. The statement, "On average a factory labour has become younger in 1991 as compared to 1981", is ________ .
15. Statistics deals with only ________ .
16. Statistical analysis helps in the ________ of results.
17. Statistics is not applicable to ________ observation.
18. Not a ________ but data are the subject-matter of statistics.
19. Statistics are numerical ________ of facts, but all numerical statements are not ________ .
20. By statistics we mean quantitative data affected to a marked extent by ________ of causes. (*Yule and Kendall*)
21. Statistics does not study ________ .
22. Statistics is not a science, its a ________ .
23. Statistics are the straw out of which I like every other economist, have to make ________ . (*Marshall*)
24. Statistics is the arithmetic of human ________ .
25. Planning on the basis of inadequate and inaccurate statistics is ________ than no planning at all. (*Third-Five-Year Plan, Planning Commission*).
26. Statistics is liable to be ________ .
27. The data collected from published reports is known ________ data.
28. Data obtained by conducting a survey is called ________ data.
29. Before analysis, the data should be ________ .

30. __________ units are better than arbitrary units.

31. __________ are used in a mailed enquiry method.

32. Mailed enquiry method cannot by adopted if the respondents are __________ .

33. In personal enquiry method, the response is better than __________ method.

34. Pretesting is essential for preparing a good __________ or __________ .

35. Population figures published by the Census Commissioner are __________ data.

36. Mistakes and statistical errors are __________ .

37. If a quantity is such that all errors tend to be in the same direction, they are called __________ errors.

38. The errors caused by the carelessness of the investigators are called __________ errors.

39. Formula for the estimation of biased absolute error is __________ .

40. Formula for the estimation of unbiased absolute error is __________ .

41. Biased relative error can be estimated by the formula __________ .

42. Unbiased relative error can be estimated by the formula __________ .

43. A survey in which information is collected from each and every individual of the population is known as __________ .

44. Assigning number digits to various responses whether quantitative or qualitative is called __________ .

45. A figure 16,318.7 rounded to the nearest tenth place is __________ .

46. The figure 32,627 rounded to the nearest hundredth place is __________ .

47. The figure 32,627 approximated to the thousandth place by the method of discarding figure is __________ .

48. The figure 45,067 approximated to thousandth place by the method of adding figure is __________ .

49. The figure 13.85 rounded to one decimal place is __________ .

50. The figure 13.75 rounded to one decimal place is __________ .

51. Government cannot do proper planning without the help of __________ .

52. Observations collected through surveys or experiments are classified as __________ .

53. To know the area under cultivation of wheat, the appropriate type of investigation is __________ .

54. To know the average yield of a crop, an appropriate investigation type will be __________ .

55. The compendium which gathers all the facts and fascinating memories in a assimilable record is known as __________ .

SECTION C

Multiple Choice Questions

Select the correct alternative out of given ones:

1. The statement, "Statistics is both a science and an art", was given by:

(*a*) R.A. Fisher
(*b*) Tippet
(*c*) L.R. Connor
(*d*) A.L. Bowley

2. Who stated that statistics is a branch of applied mathematics which specialises in data?

(*a*) Horace Secrist
(*b*) R.A. Fisher
(*c*) Ya Lun Chou
(*d*) L.R. Connor

3. The word 'statistics' is used as:
(*a*) Singular
(*b*) Plural
(*c*) Singular and plural both
(*d*) None of the above

4. "Statistics provides tools and techniques for research workers", was stated by:
(*a*) John I. Griffin
(*b*) W.I. King
(*c*) A.M. Mood
(*d*) A.L. Boddington

5. Out of various definitions given by the following workers, which definition is considered to be most exact?
(*a*) R.A. Fisher
(*b*) A.L. Bowley
(*c*) M.G. Kendall
(*d*) Cecil H. Meyers.

6. Who stated that there are three kinds of lies: lies, damned lies and statistics?
(*a*) Mark Twin
(*b*) Disraeli
(*c*) Darrell Huff
(*d*) None of the above

7. Who gave the statement, "A well wrapped statistics is better than Hitler's 'biglie', it misleads, yet it cannot be pinned on you."
(*a*) Mark Twain
(*b*) W.A. Neiswanger
(*c*) Darrell Huff
(*d*) G.W. Snedecor

8. Which of the following represents data?
(*a*) A single value
(*b*) Only two values in a set
(*c*) A group of values in a set
(*d*) None of the above

9. Statistics deals with:
(*a*) qualitative information
(*b*) quantitative information
(*c*) both (*a*) and (*b*)
(*d*) none of (*a*) and (*b*)

10. Statistical results are:
(*a*) cent per cent correct
(*b*) not absolutely correct
(*c*) always incorrect
(*d*) misleading

11. If 'a' is the actual value and 'e' is its estimated value, the absolute error is:
(*a*) $a - e$
(*b*) $|a - e|$
(*c*) a/e
(*d*) $(a - e)/e$

12. If 'a' is the actual value and 'e' is its estimated value, the formula for relative error is:
(*a*) a/e
(*b*) $(a - e)/e$
(*c*) $|a - e|/e$
(*d*) $(a - e)/a$

13. Data taken from the publication, '*Agricultural Situation in India*' will be considered as:
(*a*) primary data
(*b*) secondary data
(*c*) primary and secondary data
(*d*) neither primary nor secondary data

14. Mailed questionnaire method of enquiry can be adopted if respondents:
(*a*) live in cities
(*b*) have high income
(*c*) are educated
(*d*) are known

15. The statement, "Designing of an appropriate questionnaire itself wins half the battle", was given by:
(*a*) A.R. Ilersic
(*b*) W.I. King
(*c*) H. Huge
(*d*) H. Secrist

16. Statistical data are collected for:
(*a*) collecting data without any purpose
(*b*) a given purpose
(*c*) any purpose
(*d*) none of the above

17. Relative error is always:
(*a*) positive

(*b*) negative
(*c*) positive and negative both
(*d*) zero

18. Statistical error refers to:
(*a*) Original value – Approx. value
(*b*) Actual value – Estimated value
(*c*) $\dfrac{\text{Actual value} - \text{Estimated value}}{\text{Estimated value}}$
(*d*) $\dfrac{\text{Actual value} - \text{Estimated value}}{\text{Actual value}}$

19. Method of complete enumeration is applicable for:
(*a*) knowing the production
(*b*) knowing the quantum of export and import
(*c*) knowing the population
(*d*) all of the above

20. A statistical population may consist of:
(*a*) an infinite number of items
(*b*) a finite number of items
(*c*) either of (*a*) and (*b*)
(*d*) none of (*a*) and (*b*)

21. Which of the following example does not constitute an infinite population?
(*a*) Population consisting of odd numbers
(*b*) Population of weights of newly born babies
(*c*) Population of heights of 15-year-old children
(*d*) Population of head and tails in tossing a coin successively.

22. Which of the following can be classified as hypothetical population?
(*a*) All labourers of a factory
(*b*) Female population of a country
(*c*) Population of real numbers between 0 and 100
(*d*) Students of the world

23. A study based on complete enumeration is known as:
(*a*) ample survey
(*b*) pilot survey
(*c*) census survey
(*d*) none of the above

24. If the actual value of a unit is 415 and its estimated value is 400, the absolute error is:
(*a*) – 15
(*b*) 15
(*c*) 0.0375
(*d*) – 0.0361

25. If the estimated value of an item is 50 and its actual value is 60, the relative error is:
(*a*) – 20
(*b*) 0.16
(*c*) 1.2
(*d*) 0.20

26. Who originally gave the formula for the estimation of errors?
(*a*) L.R. Connor
(*b*) W.I. King
(*c*) A.L. Bowley
(*d*) A.L. Boddington

27. Boddington gave the formula for the estimation of errors of the type:
(*a*) Absolute error biased
(*b*) Absolute error unbiased
(*c*) both (*a*) and (*b*)
(*d*) neither (*a*) nor (*b*)

28. Boddington's formula for estimation of absolute error (A.E.) unbiased is:
(*a*) Total A.E./ $\sqrt{n}$
(*b*) Average A.E. × $\sqrt{n}$
(*c*) Total A.E./n.
(*d*) Average A.E. × n (n = No. of items)

29. Boddington's formula for estimation of relative error is:
(*a*) Total A.E. $\sqrt{n}$
(*b*) Average A.E./n
(*c*) $\dfrac{\text{Average A.E.} \times n}{e}$
(*d*) $\dfrac{\text{Average A.E.} \times \sqrt{n}}{e}$

[e = estimated value]

30. Bowley's formula for absolute unbiased error is:

(*a*) $\frac{1}{\sqrt{n}}$ (Average A.E.)

(*b*) $\frac{2}{3\sqrt{n}}$ (Average A.E.)

(*c*) $\frac{2\sqrt{n}}{3}$ (Average A.E.)

(*d*) $\frac{3}{2\sqrt{n}}$ (Average A.E.)

31. Statistical results are:

(*a*) absolutely correct
(*b*) not true
(*c*) true on average
(*d*) universally true

32. The statistical law(s) based on trial and error methods is/are:

(*a*) law of statistical regularity
(*b*) law of inertia of large numbers
(*c*) both laws (*a*) and (*b*)
(*d*) none of the laws (*a*) and (*b*)

33. The figure 32,64,616.8 approximated to the tenth place by the method of discarding figure is:

(*a*) 32,64,615.8
(*b*) 32,64,616
(*c*) 32,64,620
(*d*) 32,64,610

34. The figure 32,64,616.8 approximated to the tenth place by adding figure is:

(*a*) 32,64,615
(*b*) 32,64,616
(*c*) 32,64,620
(*d*) 32,64,610

35. The figure 26,476 approximated to the hundredth place by discarding figure is:

(*a*) 26,400
(*b*) 26,500
(*c*) 27,000
(*d*) 25,000

36. The figure 47,616 approximated to hundredth place by adding figure is:

(*a*) 47,630
(*b*) 47,620
(*c*) 47,700
(*d*) 47,600

37. The figure 43,572.6 approximated to the thousandth place by discarding figure is:

(*a*) 43,500
(*b*) 43,000
(*c*) 44,000
(*d*) 44,500

38. The value 43,572.6 approximated to the thousandth place by adding figure is:

(*a*) 43,500
(*b*) 43,000
(*c*) 44,000
(*d*) 44,600

39. The figure 45,986 approximated to the ten thousandth place by the method of discarding figure is:

(*a*) 40,000
(*b*) 46,000
(*c*) 45,500
(*d*) 45,000

40. The figure 45,986 approximated to ten thousandth place by the method of adding figure is:

(*a*) 50,000
(*b*) 46,000
(*c*) 40,000
(*d*) none of the above

ANSWERS

Section B

1. William A. Spurr and Charles P. Bonini **2.** A. L. Bowley **3.** Lovitt **4.** W.A. Wallis and H.V. Roberts **5.** science, art **6.** C.H. Meyers **7.** A.E. Waugh **8.** A.L. Boddington **9.** Whipple **10.** Tippet **11.** W.I. King **12.** anything **13.** inexperts **14.** acceptable **15.** quantitative data **16.** interpretation **17.** single **18.** datum **19.** statements; statistics **20.** multiplicity **21.** individuals **22.** scientific method **23.** bricks **24.** welfare **25.** worse **26.** misused **27.** secondary **28.** primary **29.** edited **30.** Physical **31.** Questionnaires **32.** illiterate **33.** mailed enquiry **34.** schedule; questionnaire **35.** primary **36.** not same **37.** biased **38.** unbiased **39.** Average A.E. × No. of items **40.** Average A.E. × $\sqrt{\text{No. of items}}$ **41.** Biased A.E./Estimated value **42.** $\frac{\text{Unbiased A.E.}}{\text{Estimated value}}$ **43.** census survey **44.** coding **45.** 16,320 **46.** 32,600 **47.** 32,000 **48.** 46,000 **49.** 13.8 **50.** 13.8 **51.** statistics **52.** primary data **53.** census method **54.** sample method **55.** statistical perspective.

Section C

1. (*b*)	**2.** (*b*)	**3.** (*c*)	**4.** (*c*)	**5.** (*a*)
6. (*b*)	**7.** (*c*)	**8.** (*c*)	**9.** (*b*)	**10.** (*b*)
11. (*b*)	**12.** (*c*)	**13.** (*b*)	**14.** (*c*)	**15.** (*c*)
16. (*b*)	**17.** (*c*)	**18.** (*b*)	**19.** (*d*)	**20.** (*c*)
21. (*c*)	**22.** (*c*)	**23.** (*c*)	**24.** (*b*)	**25.** (*d*)
26. (*d*)	**27.** (*c*)	**28.** (*b*)	**29.** (*d*)	**30.** (*b*)
31. (*c*)	**32.** (*c*)	**33.** (*d*)	**34.** (*c*)	**35.** (*a*)
36. (*c*)	**37.** (*b*)	**38.** (*c*)	**39.** (*a*)	**40.** (*a*)

SUGGESTED READING

1. Agarwal, B.L., *Basic Statistics*, New Age International Publishers, New Delhi, 8th edition, 2024.
2. Gupta, B.N., *Statistics*, Sahitya Bhawan, Agra, 3rd edition, 1978.
3. Harvey, J.M., *Sources of Statistics*, Clive Bingley, 1969.
4. McCarthy, P.J., *Introduction to Statistical Reasoning*, McGraw-Hill Book Company, New York, 1957.
5. Monroney, M.J., *Facts from Figures*, Penguin Books, Baltimore, 1959.
6. Reichman, W.J., *Use and Abuse of Statistics*, Penguin Books, Baltimore, 1961.
7. Simpson, G. and Kafka, F., *Basic Statistics*, Oxford & IBH, Calcutta, 3rd edition, 1971.
8. Anderson, T. and Sclove, S., *An Introduction to the Statistical Analysis of Data*, Houghton Mifflin, Boston, 1978.

CHAPTER 2

Classification, Tabulation and Frequency Distribution

SECTION A

Short Essay Type Questions

Q. 1. *What is meant by classification?*

Ans. Classification is the process of arranging things or items in groups or classes according to their resemblance and affinities and give expression to the units of attributes that may subsist amongst the diversity of individuals.

Q. 2. *What are the modes of classification?*

Ans. Different modes of classification are:

(*i*) *Geographical classification:* Classification is according to place, area or region.

(*ii*) *Chronological classification:* It is according to the lapse of time, e.g., monthly, yearly, etc.

(*iii*) *Qualitative classification:* Data are classified according to the attributes of the subjects or items, e.g., sex, qualification, colour, etc.

(*iv*) *Quantitative classification:* Data are classified according to the magnitude of the numerical values, e.g., age, income, height, weight, etc.

Q. 3. *What are the objectives of classification?*

Ans. Broadly, there are six objectives of classification:

(*i*) To present the facts in a simple manner.

(*ii*) To highlight items which possess or do not possess certain attributes or qualities.

(*iii*) To provide help in making comparison between items.

(*iv*) To find out mutual relationship between certain measures and their effects.

(*v*) To present the data in a manner which is suitable for further treatment.

(*vi*) To provide basis for tabulation.

Q. 4. *What do you understand by qualitative classification?*

Ans. It is the classification on the basis of certain attributes or some qualities of items which cannot be measured quantitatively.

Q. 5. *Describe in brief different kinds of classification.*

Ans. Different types of classification are:

(*i*) Classification according to attributes.

(*ii*) Simple or two-fold or dichotomous classification.

(*iii*) Multiple classification.

(*iv*) Quantitative classification, *i.e.*, the classification according to variate values.

Q. 6. *What do you understand by multifactor classification?*

Ans. Classification criteria based on two or more factors (attributes) is known as multifactor classification. In this type of classification, first the data are classified into two or more classes on the basis of one factor. For each component classification, further classification is done on the basis of second factor and so on.

Q. 7. *What do you understand by open end(s) in group data?*

Ans. If in grouped classes, the lower limit of the beginning class is not specified and/or the upper limit of the highest (last) class is not specified, it is known as grouped data with open end class(es).

Q. 8. *What are different characteristics of classification? Describe each characteristic in five lines.*

Ans. Different characteristics of classification are:

(*i*) *Exhaustive:* The classes should be such that they cover every item of the set, *i.e.*, they should also be complete and non-overlapping. For instance, for marital status the classes should be married, unmarried, widow, widower, divorcee, deserted.

(*ii*) *Stability:* Classification should be uniform or standardised so that the results are comparable at different occasions or in different studies.

(*iii*) *Flexibility:* Classification should be amenable according to different situations or requirements of study.

(*iv*) *Homogeneity:* The units of measurement of all classes should be same. Also like units only be accommodated in one class.

(*v*) *Suitability:* Classification be done according to the objective of the study only. For instance, to study the financial status of people, it will be useless to classify them according to their skin colour or their hair colour, etc.

(*vi*) *Arithmetic accuracy:* The sum of number of units in all classes should be equal to the total number of units. Also in case of observations, the sum of observations in all classes should be equal to the sum of all observations.

Q. 9. *How can one determine the number of classes for a frequency distribution?*

Ans. In quantitative classification, the number of classes depends upon the class interval. So a formula was suggested by H.A. Sturges to determine the class interval and also the number of classes. The formula is,

$$i = \frac{L - S}{1 + 3.322 \log_{10} n}$$

where,

i = Class interval

L = Largest observation

S = Smallest observation

and n = Total number of observations in the set.

Also, the denominator, $1 + 3.322 \log_{10} n$ is equal to the number of classes.

Q. 10. *Describe in brief the grouping error.*

Ans. If the classes are formed in such a way that the frequencies are evenly distributed throughout the class interval, it is justified to assume that the frequencies are centered at the mid-value of the class. But in cases where such an assumption is not valid, it leads to error which is known as grouping error. Grouping error affects the accuracy of the results.

Q. 11. *Clarify the difference between exclusive and inclusive class intervals.*

Ans. Following are the differences between exclusive and inclusive class intervals:

(*i*) In exclusive class intervals, the upper limit of a class is the lower limit of the next class. Also the upper limit of a class is not included in that class.

(*ii*) In inclusive class intervals the upper limit of a class instead is not the lower limit of the next class. The lower limit is generally greater by unit measurement.

(*iii*) In inclusive method, both the limits of a class are included.

(*iv*) To simplify the calculation procedure, inclusive classes are converted into exclusive classes.

(*v*) Inclusive classes approach is suitable in case of data given in whole numbers. In rest of the cases exclusive class approach is suitable.

Q. 12. *If mid-values of the classes are known, how can the classes be formed?*

Ans. Find the difference between two consecutive mid-values. Subtract half of the difference from the mid-value and again add it to the mid-value. The values obtained on subtracting and adding half of the difference are the lower and upper limits of the class of which the mid-value has been used. If m is the mid-value of a class and i is difference between two consecutive mid-values, the lower and upper class limits are $\left(m - \frac{i}{2}\right)$ and $\left(m + \frac{i}{2}\right)$, respectively.

Q. 13. *Illustrate exclusive and inclusive class intervals.*

Ans. In exclusive class intervals uppers limit of the class is not included, e.g., in the class 10-20 those values are included which are 10 or more and less than 20. Similarly in the inclusive class intervals, both the limits of a class are included. The classes may be of the type, 5 – 5.99, 10 – 14.99, etc.

Q. 14. *Distinguish between real limits and apparent class limits of a distribution in grouped data.*

Ans. If the distribution is for a discrete variable, the real and apparent class limits are same, e.g., 5-10, 11-16, 17-22, ... since there is no recorded value between 10 and 11, 16 and 17, etc.

But if the class intervals are exclusive, in that case either the upper limit or the lower limit is to be excluded since the value can be included in one class only. For instance, let the classes be 5-10, 10-15, 15-20, etc. Suppose the upper limits are excluded. In that case, the real limits are 5-9, 10-14, 15-19, etc. Of course, there is no point in between 9 and 10, 14 and 15, etc. If the lower limits are excluded, the real limits are 6-10, 11-15, 16-20, etc.

Q. 15. *What do you understand by tabulation?*

Ans. It is the process of presenting data collected through survey, experiment or record in rows and columns so that it can more easily be understood and can be used for further statistical analysis.

Q. 16. *What are different parts of a standard table?*

Ans. There are five parts of a table:

(*i*) Title, (*ii*) Captions and stubs, (*iii*) Body; (*iv*) Prefatorial and (*v*) Source note.

Q. 17. *What are the objectives of tabulation of data?*

Ans. The objectives of tabulation are:

(*i*) To clarify the object of investigation.

(*ii*) To reduce complexity of data

(*iii*) To economise space

(*iv*) To depict the relation among data if it exists.

(*v*) To facilitate analysis of data.

Q. 18. *What are the requisites of a standard table?*

Ans. Requisites of a standard table are:

(*i*) It should be suitable for the purpose.

(*ii*) Clarity and completeness of table is necessary.

(*iii*) Table should be of adequate size.

(*iv*) Units of measurements should be specified.

(*v*) Logical arrangement of items.

(*vi*) Totals and sub-totals be given.

Q. 19. *What are the main purposes of tabulation?*

Ans. The main purposes of tabulation are:

(*i*) To present the haphazard data in simple and concised manner.

(*ii*) To save space.

(*iii*) To show the trend of data, if any.

(*iv*) To facilitate comparison of data.

(*v*) To detect errors and omissions of data, if any.

(*vi*) To facilitate the process of statistical analysis.

(*vii*) To know the source of data.

Q. 20. *What is the difference between classification and tabulation?*

Ans. Classification is meant for arranging the data into characteristics or groups where each group has the number of item attached to it. In case of variables, it is given in the form of frequency distribution.

Tabulation is the logical and systematic arrangement of data in rows and columns. In a table, data may be presented in modified form as well, e.g., in per cent, proportion, total or average values, etc.

Q. 21. *What is an original table (classification table)?*

Ans. In an original table, the data are presented in the same form in which they are collected.

Q. 22. *What is a derivative table?*

Ans. In a derivative table the data are not presented in its original form but the values based on original observations are presented. For instance, totals for different classifications, the means, percentage, ratios or proportions, etc., are presented in a derivative table.

Q. 23. *Distinguish between frequency and cumulative frequency.*

Ans. *Frequency:* Number of times a variate value is repeated is called its frequency.

Cumulative frequency: This is the number of observations corresponding to less than (more than) or equal to a specified value.

Q. 24. *Differentiate between a time series and a spatial series.*

Ans. (*i*) Time series is an ordered data arranged in sequence of time period. Time periods may be weekly, monthly, yearly, quinquennially, decadal, etc. Time series is also known as *historic series*. (*ii*) Spatial series is one in which the data are arranged according to the place or space. The place or space may be localities, cities, states, countries, etc.

Q. 25. *Explain briefly the stem and leaf display of data.*

Ans. It is a method of presentation of data in which each value is divided into two parts. One part consists of one or more leading digits as stem and remaining of the digits as leaf.

SECTION B

Fill in the Blanks

Fill in the suitable word(s) or phrase(s) in the blanks:

1. Classification is the ________ of facts that are distinguished by some significant ________ .
2. For a good classification, the class should be ________ and ________ .
3. Classification can be done according to ________ .
4. Quantitative classification leads to ________ .
5. Yearwise recording of data of food production will be called ________ classification.
6. The census data published for citywise population in India will be known as ________ classification.
7. The data recorded according to standard of education like illiterate, primary, secondary, graduate, technical, etc., will be known as ________ classification.
8. Distribution of families according to their size will be classified as ________ classification.
9. The difference between the upper and lower limit of a class is called ________ .
10. The average of the upper and lower limits of a class is known as ________ .
11. There is a general assumption that the class frequency is centered at the ________ of the class.
12. Departure from the assumption that the frequencies are evenly distributed over the class interval leads to ________ error.
13. Formula for determining the number of classes was given by ________ .
14. H.A. Sturges formula for determining the number of classes is ________ .
15. Number of classes depend on ________ .
16. H.A. Sturges formula for finding out the class interval is ________ .
17. The number of classes and class interval for the distribution of marks from 0 to 100 of 50 students of a class should be ________ and ________ respectively.

18. Class boundaries are also sometimes called ________ limits.

19. Mid-values of the classes are also called ________ .

20. Frequency density of a class is the frequency ________ of class.

21. In the mid-value of a class interval is 20 and the difference between two consecutive mid-values in 5, the class limits are ________ and ________ .

22. An arrangement of data in rows and columns is known as ________ .

23. Tables help in ________ of data.

24. Tabulation makes the data easily ________ .

25. Tabulation follows ________ .

26. ________ facts cannot be presented in the form of a table.

27. A general purpose table is also known as ________ or ________ table.

28. A general table is a ________ of a large amount of data.

29. The table which do not present the data but the results of analysis are called ________ tables.

30. Headings of the columns of a table are known as ________ .

31. Headings of the rows of a table are called ________ .

32. The portion of the table in which data are presented is designated as ________ of a table.

33. The manner in which the frequencies are distributed according to variate values is known as ________ .

34. Frequency distributions are often constructed with the help of ________ .

35. Relative frequency is the ratio of a frequency to the ________ of the distribution.

36. Percentage frequency is the ________ multiplied by 100.

37. Frequencies added successively in an ordered series giving the number of items up to that value are called ________ .

38. A frequency distribution with upper limits of classes and corresponding cumulative frequencies is known as ________ type distribution.

39. A frequency distribution with lower limits of classes and corresponding cumulative frequencies is known as ________ type distribution.

40. The graphs of less than type and more than type distributions intersect at ________ .

41. A grouped series, in which either the lower limit of the first group or the upper limit of the last group is missing or both, is called an ________ .

42. A series arranged in accordance with each and every observation is known as ________ .

43. The distribution of frequencies according to individual variate values is called ________ distribution.

44. A series of data with exclusive classes along with the corresponding frequencies is called ________ distribution.

45. Given the following frequency distribution, fill in the missing frequencies:

Class intervals	*Frequency*	*Cumulative Frequency*
10–20	5	5
20–30	10	15
30–40	12	–
40–50	–	–
50–60	7	–
60–70	4	52

SECTION C

Multiple Choice Questions

Select the correct alternative out of given ones:

1. Numerical data presented in descriptive form are called
   (*a*) classified presentation
   (*b*) tabular presentation
   (*c*) graphical presentation
   (*d*) textual presentation
2. Whether classification is done first or tabulation?
   (*a*) Classification follows tabulation.
   (*b*) Classification precedes tabulation.
   (*c*) Both are done simultaneously.
   (*d*) No criterion.
3. For the mid-values given below,
   25, 34, 43, 53, 61, 70
   The first class of the distribution is:
   (*a*) 24.5-34.5
   (*b*) 25-34
   (*c*) 20-30
   (*d*) 20.5-29.5
4. In an exclusive type distribution, the limits excluded are:
   (*a*) lower limits
   (*b*) upper limits
   (*c*) either of the lower or upper limit
   (*d*) lower limit and upper limits both
5. A series showing the sets of all distinct values individually with their frequencies is known as:
   (*a*) grouped frequency distribution
   (*b*) simple frequency distribution
   (*c*) cumulative frequency distribution
   (*d*) none of the above
6. A series showing the sets of all values in classes with their corresponding frequencies is known as:
   (*a*) grouped frequency distribution
   (*b*) simple frequency distribution
   (*c*) cumulative frequency distribution
   (*d*) none of the above
7. If the number of students in a school is 200 and maximum and minimum marks earned are 90 and 10 respectively, for the distribution of marks, the class interval (rounded) is:
   (*a*) 10
   (*b*) 9
   (*c*) 12
   (*d*) none of the above
   [Given $\log_{10} 2 = 0.3010$, $\log_{10} 3 = 0.4771$]
8. If the lower and upper limits of a class are 10 and 40 respectively, the mid-points of the class is:
   (*a*) 25.0
   (*b*) 12.5
   (*c*) 15 0
   (*d*) 30.0
9. In a grouped data, the number of classes preferred are:
   (*a*) minimum possible
   (*b*) adequate
   (*c*) maximum possible
   (*d*) any arbitrarily chosen number
10. Class interval is measured as:
    (*a*) the sum of the upper and lower limit
    (*b*) half of the sum of lower and upper limit
    (*c*) half of the difference between upper and lower limit
    (*d*) the difference between upper and lower limit.
11. The class interval of the continuous grouped data

    10–19
    20–29
    30–39
    40–49
    50–59

    is:
    (*a*) 9 (*b*) 10 (*c*) 14.5 (*d*) 4.5
12. A grouped frequency distribution with uncertain first or last classes is known as:

(*a*) exclusive class distribution
(*b*) inclusive class distribution
(*c*) open end distribution
(*d*) discrete frequency distribution

13. The distribution,

Values	*Frequency*
Less than 5	5
Less than 10	12
Less than 15	21
Less than 20	27
Less than 25	31
Less than 30	33

is of the type:
(*a*) inclusive class type
(*b*) exclusive class type
(*c*) discrete type
(*d*) none of the above

14. Data can be well displayed or presented by way of:
(*a*) stem and leaf display
(*b*) cross classification
(*c*) two or more dimensional table
(*d*) all of the above

15. A simple table represents:
(*a*) only one factor or variable
(*b*) always two factors or variables
(*c*) two or more number of factors or variables
(*d*) all of the above

16. A complex table represents:
(*a*) only one factor or variable
(*b*) always two factors or variables
(*c*) two or more factors or variables
(*d*) all of the above

17. The headings of the rows given in the first column of a table are called:
(*a*) stubs
(*b*) captions
(*c*) titles
(*d*) prefatory notes.

18. The column heading of a table are known as:
(*a*) sub-titles
(*b*) stubs
(*c*) reference notes
(*d*) captions

19. The series,

Place	*No. of accidents per day*
Delhi	10
Kolkata	15
Mumbai	18
Chennai	17
Indore	7

is of the type:
(*a*) Spatial
(*b*) Geographical
(*c*) Industrial
(*d*) Time series

20. The series,

Year	*Production of food (M. Tonnes)*
1987	160
1988	168
1989	170
1990	172
1991	174
1992	176

is categorised as:
(*a*) individual series
(*b*) continuous series
(*c*) discrete series
(*d*) time series

21. The income of five persons is as follows:

Person	*Income (₹/Month)*
Mr. A	1,700
Mr. B	2,300
Mr. C	7,000
Mr. D	8,500
Mr. E	5,400

The above series is of the type:
(*a*) Individual series
(*b*) Discrete series
(*c*) Continuous series
(*d*) Time series

22. The series,

Marks	*No. of students*
20–30	5
30–40	14
40–50	24
50–60	12
60–70	9
70–80	2

is of the type:

(*a*) Discrete series
(*b*) Continuous series
(*c*) Individual series
(*d*) none of the above

23. A frequency distribution can be:

(*a*) discrete
(*b*) continuous
(*c*) both (*a*) and (*b*)
(*d*) none of (*a*) and (*b*)

24. In an individual series, each variate value:

(*a*) has same frequency
(*b*) has frequency one
(*c*) has varied frequency
(*d*) has frequency two

25. Which of the following statements is true?

(*a*) An individual series is a particular case of discrete series
(*b*) An individual series is a particular case of continuous series
(*c*) An individual series is a special case of discrete and continuous series
(*d*) There is nothing like individual series

26. Frequency of a variable is always:

(*a*) in percentage
(*b*) a fraction
(*c*) an integer
(*d*) none of the above

27. The data given as, 5, 7, 12, 17, 79, 84, 91 will be called as:

(*a*) a continuous series
(*b*) a discrete series
(*c*) an individual series
(*d*) time series

28. The following frequency distribution

x	12	17	24	36	45	48	52
f	2	5	3	8	9	6	1

is classified as:

(*a*) continuous distribution
(*b*) discrete distribution
(*c*) cumulative frequency distribution
(*d*) none of the above

29. In an ordered series, the data are:

(*a*) in ascending order
(*b*) in descending order
(*c*) either (*a*) or (*b*)
(*d*) neither (*a*) or (*b*)

30. The following frequency distribution,

Classes	*Frequency*
0–10	3
0–20	8
0–30	14
0–40	20
0–50	25

is known as:

(*a*) continuous frequency distribution
(*b*) discrete frequency distribution
(*c*) cumulative distribution in more than type
(*d*) cumulative distribution in less than type

31. The following frequency distribution,

Classes	*Frequency*
0–15	17
0–10	8
0–5	3

is classified as:

(*a*) cumulative distribution in less than type
(*b*) cumulative distribution in more than type
(*c*) discrete frequency distribution
(*d*) cumulative frequency distribution

32. Classification is applicable in case of:

(*a*) quantitative characters
(*b*) qualitative characters
(*c*) both (*a*) and (*b*)
(*d*) none of the above

ANSWERS

Section B

1. grouping; characteristics (attributes) **2.** exhaustive; mutually exclusive **3.** attributes **4.** frequency distribution **5.** Chronological **6.** geographical **7.** qualitative **8.** quantitative **9.** class interval **10.** mid-value **11.** mid-value **12.** grouping **13.** H.A. Sturges **14.** $1 + 3.322 \log_{10} n$ **15.** class interval **16.** $(L - S)/(1 + 3.322 \log_{10} n)$ where L = largest value, S = smallest value and n = No. of values **17.** 7 and 15 **18.** mathematical **19.** class marks **20.** per unit **21.** 17.5 and 22.5 **22.** tabulation **23.** analysis **24.** understandable **25.** classification **26.** Qualitative **27.** primary; reference **28.** repository **29.** specific purpose **30.** captions **31.** stubs **32.** body **33.** frequency distribution **34.** tally marks **35.** total frequency **36.** relative frequency **37.** cumulative frequency **38.** less than **39.** more than **40.** median **41.** open end series **42.** individual series **43.** discrete frequency **44.** continuous frequency **45.** freq = 14; as, cu-freq-27, 41, 48.

Section C

1. (*d*)	2. (*b*)	3. (*d*)	4. (*c*)	5. (*b*)
6. (*a*)	7. (*b*)	8. (*a*)	9. (*b*)	10. (*d*)
11. (*b*)	12. (*c*)	13. (*b*)	14. (*d*)	15. (*b*)
16. (*c*)	17. (*a*)	18. (*d*)	19. (*b*)	20. (*d*)
21. (*a*)	22. (*b*)	23. (*c*)	24. (*b*)	25. (*a*)
26. (*c*)	27. (*c*)	28. (*b*)	29. (*c*)	30. (*d*)
31. (*b*)	32. (*c*).			

SUGGESTED READING

1. Agarwal, B.L., *Basic Statistics,* New Age International Publishers, New Delhi, 8th edition, 2024.
2. Devore, J.L., *Probability and Statistics for Engineering and the Sciences,* Brooks/Cole Publishing Co., California, 1982.
3. Gupta, C.B., *An Introduction to Statistical Methods,* Vikas Publishing House, Delhi, 8th edn., 1978.
4. Kenny, J.F. and Keeping, E.S., *Mathematics of Statistics,* Part I, D. Von Nostrand Co., New York, 1951.
5. Sancheti, D.C. and Kapoor, V.K., *Statistics,* Sultan Chand & Sons, New Delhi, 7th edn., 1991.
6. Shukla, M.C. and Gulshan, S.S., *Statistics,* Sultan Chand & Co., New Delhi, 1970.
7. Simpson, G. and Kafka, F., *Basic Statistics,* Oxford & IBH, Calcutta, 3rd Indian print, 1971.

CHAPTER 3

Diagramatic and Graphical Representation

SECTION A

Short Essay Type Questions

Q. 1. *What are the advantages of diagramatic representation of data?*

Ans. Following are the advantages of diagramatic representation of data:

(*i*) Diagrams give a bird's-eye view of complex data.

(*ii*) They have long lasting impression.

(*iii*) Easy to understand even by a common man.

(*iv*) They save time and labour.

(*v*) They facilitate comparison.

Q. 2. *Give the names of diagrams which are one-dimensional.*

Ans. Bar diagrams and line diagrams are one-dimensional. Different types of bar diagrams are:

(*i*) simple bar diagram

(*ii*) multiple bar diagram

(*iii*) sub-divided or component bar diagram

(*iv*) percentage bar diagram.

Q. 3. *Name diagrams which are two-dimensional.*

Ans. Rectangles, circles and pie diagrams are two-dimensional diagrams.

Q. 4. *What are the diagrams categorised under three-dimensional diagrams?*

Ans. Cubes, cylinders and spheres are categorised as three-dimensional diagrams.

Q. 5. *What types of diagram are known as non-dimensional diagrams?*

Ans. Pictograms are known as non-dimensional diagrams.

Q. 6. *What do you understand by bar diagram and a sub-divided bar diagram?*

Ans. A bar diagram represents the magnitude of a single factor according to time periods, places, items, etc. But when the magnitude of the factor is given with its sub-factors, each bar is further sub-divided into components in proportion to the magnitude of the sub-factors.

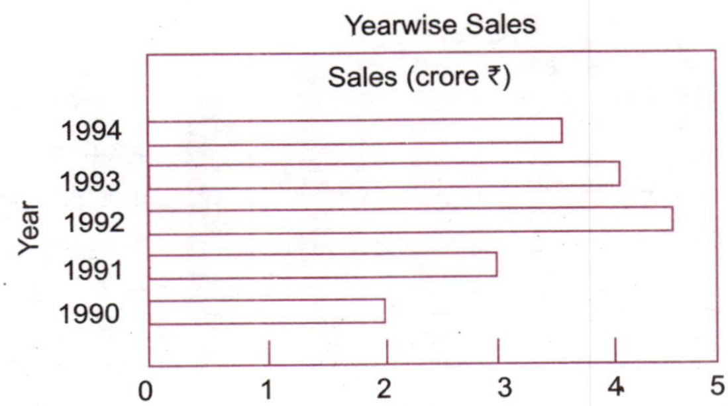

Fig. 3.1. Bar diagram

Such a diagram is known as sub-divided bar diagram.

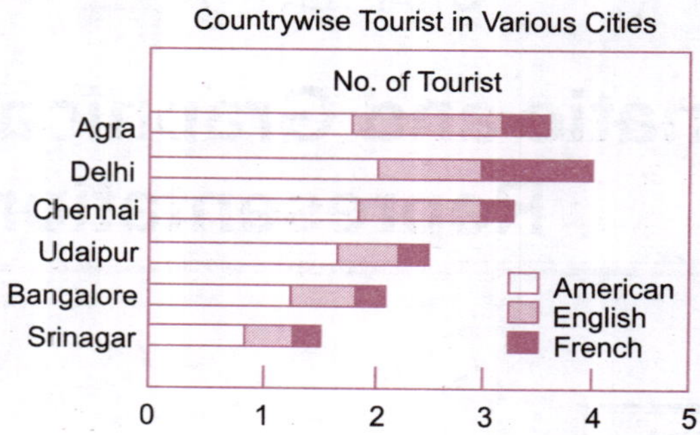

Fig. 3.2. Sub-divided bar diagram

Q. 7. *When do you prefer a multiple bar diagram (compound bar diagram)?*

Ans. To depict a number of related factors for comparison in various years or at a number of places, multiple bar diagrams are preferable.

Q. 8. *What is a multiple bar diagram?*

Ans. In a multiple bar diagram, adjoining bars are drawn according to the number of factors and their heights in proportion to the values of the factors in the same order for each period or place. Each bar of a group is shown by different patterns or colours to make them easily distinguishable and this pattern is retained in all the groups. A constant distance is maintained between groups of bars drawn for periods or places. Such a diagram is known as multiple or compound bar diagram (Fig. 3.3).

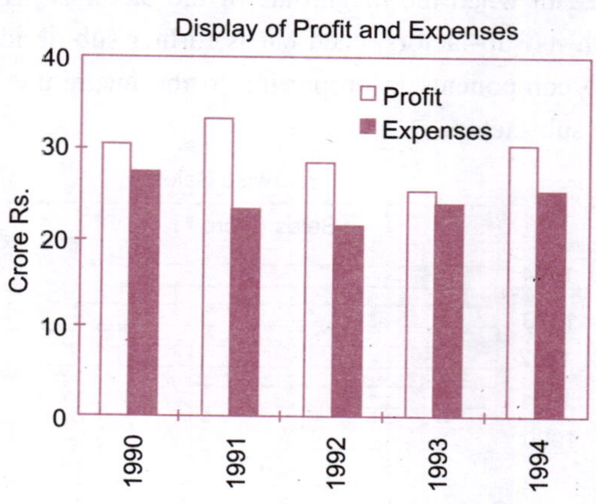

Fig. 3.3. Multiple bar diagram

Q. 9. *What do you understand by deviation bar diagram?*

Ans. Deviation bar diagrams are suitable to show the net deviations during various years or according to different countries or places, etc. In the deviation bar diagrams, positive deviations are shown to the right side of the base line and negative deviations are shown to the left side of the same base line. For instance, the gaps between imports and exports, profit and loss in different years or from different countries can be very well displayed through deviation bar diagrams (Fig. 3.4).

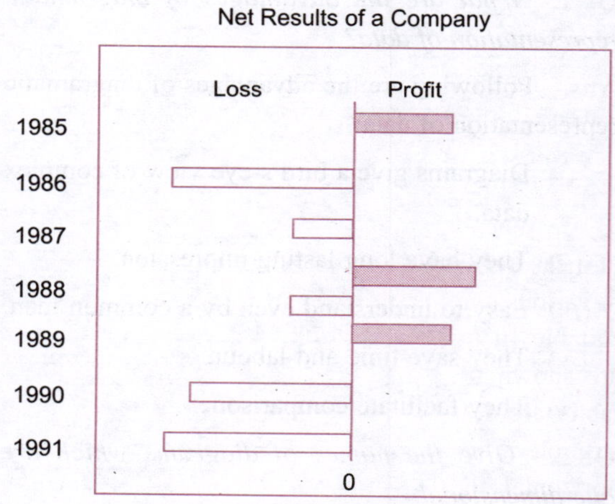

Fig. 3.4. Deviation bar diagram

Q. 10. *Write a short note on duo-directional bar diagrams.*

Ans. Duo-directional bar diagrams are used to exhibit the two aspects of a single factor at a glance given for different periods or places. In this type of diagram, one part of the bar remains above the base line and the other below the base line. The heights of the bars below and above the line are in proportion to the values of the two aspect separately whereas the bar as a whole represents the factor. For example, we want to show the price of certain item in different years. The price consists of two parts, the cost and the profit. So profit may be taken above the line and cost below the line. It is a sort of sub-divided bar diagram (Fig. 3.5).

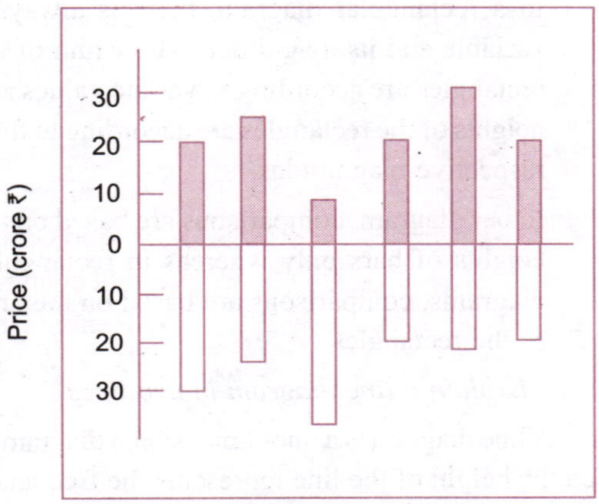

Fig. 3.5. Duo-directional bar diagram

Q. 11. *Write a brief note on paired bar diagram.*

Ans. When two related factors having different units of measurements are to be displayed for comparison in various periods or places, paired bar diagrams are suitable. In this diagram usually, the periods or places are shown in a strip and horizontal bars for each factor are drawn to the right and left of the vertical strip or vertical bars are drawn below and above the horizontal strip. For instance, area and production of paddy in different years in India can be very well displayed through a paired bar diagram (Fig. 3.6).

Q. 12. *What are sliding bar charts? Explain in brief.*

Ans. Sliding chart is a bilateral chart in which two components of a factor are represented by two parts of the bar. One part is on the left and the other is on the right of the base line. The scale may be the absolute numbers or in percentages. Such a chart is suitable in situations such as a numbers arrested in a criminal case or patients operated for different diseases. What percentage or number of suspects have been cleared and what are still under trial? How many patients are cured and how many of them still

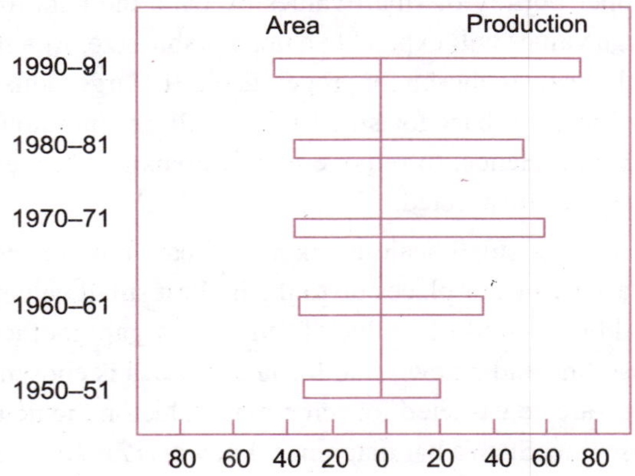

Fig. 3.6. Paired bar diagram

suffer? The two components can be better displayed by a sliding bar diagram. The base line may be representing the type of operations, kind of court cases, etc. The percentage or numbers in the two components, cured and not cured, cases cleared and not cleared may be changing from time to time. For each type of operation crime (factor), a separate sliding bar will be drawn.

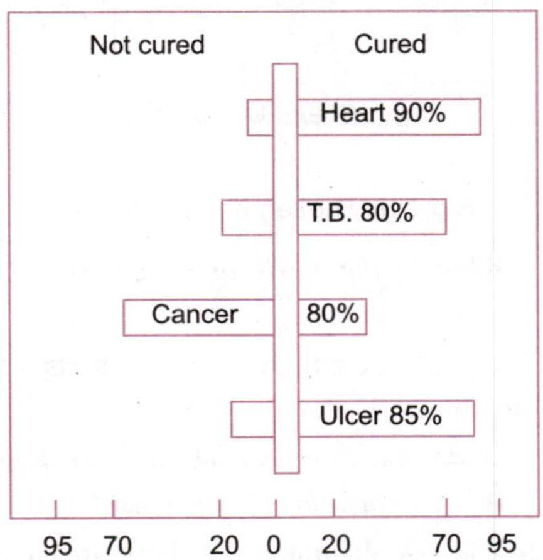

Fig. 3.7. Sliding bar chart

Q. 13. *What is a broken bar diagram?*

Ans. Often an investigator comes across cases where some figures are very large as compared to others. In this situation, if the scale is chosen for proper portray of small values by bars, the bars for large values will expand to a unpalatable size. Again, if the scale is chosen for proper display of large values by bars, the bars for small value will become non-existent. Hence, to remove this discrepancy, broken bars are constructed.

First, a small scale is taken and bars are erected at all periods or places up to the highest small values and/or a round off value. Then with a gap another base line and a new scale for large values is chosen. Bars are constructed for remaining value on the new base line. Such a bar diagram is known as *broken bar diagram*. These diagrams be interpreted very carefully to avoid any wrong conclusions.

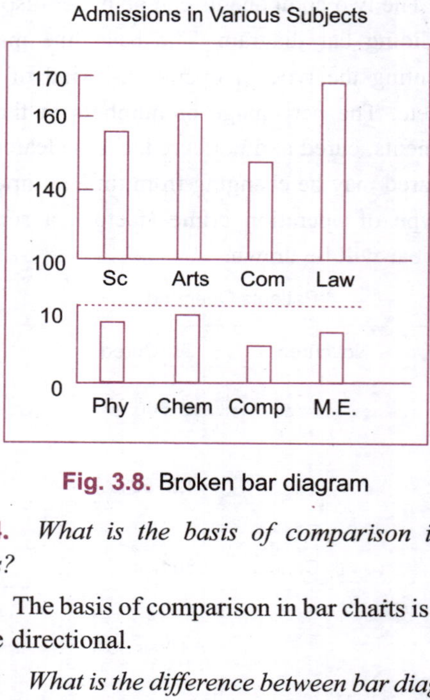

Fig. 3.8. Broken bar diagram

Q. 14. *What is the basis of comparison in bar charts?*

Ans. The basis of comparison in bar charts is linear or one directional.

Q. 15. *What is the difference between bar diagrams (charts) and column charts (diagrams)?*

Ans. In the bar diagrams, the bars are arranged horizontally on a vertical base line, whereas in the column charts, bar are arranged vertically on a horizontal base line.

Q. 16. *What are the differences between a bar diagram and a rectangular diagram?*

Ans. The differences are:

(*i*) In bar diagram, all bars are of equal width.

(*ii*) The width of bars in bar diagram is chosen arbitrarily for qualitative characters like places, states, countries, etc., or according to the equal class intervals.

(*iii*) In a rectangular diagram, there is always a variable and its magnitude. The width of the rectangles are according to variate values and heights of the rectangles are according to their respective magnitudes.

(*iv*) In bar diagram, comparisons are based on the heights of bars only whereas in rectangular diagrams, comparisons are based on the area of the rectangles.

Q. 17. *Explain a line diagram in two lines.*

Ans. A line diagram is a one-dimensional diagram in which the height of the line represents the frequency corresponding to the value of the item or a factor.

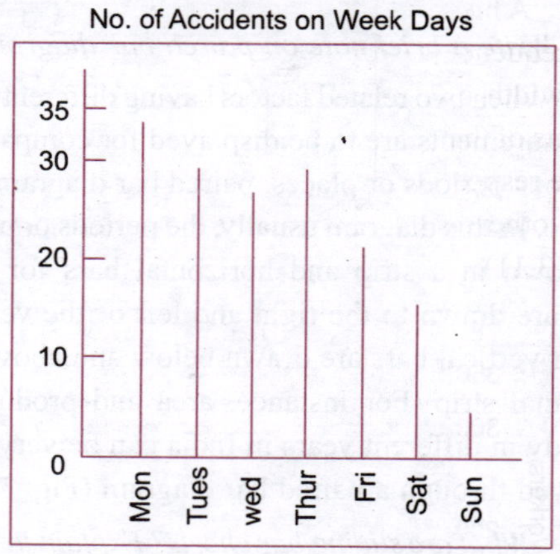

Fig. 3.9. Line diagram

Q. 18. *Explain in brief a pie-chart.*

Ans. A pie-chart is a circular diagram which is usually used for depicting the components of a single factor. The circle is divided into segments which are in proportion to the size of the components. They are shown by different patterns or colours to make them attractive (Fig. 3.10).

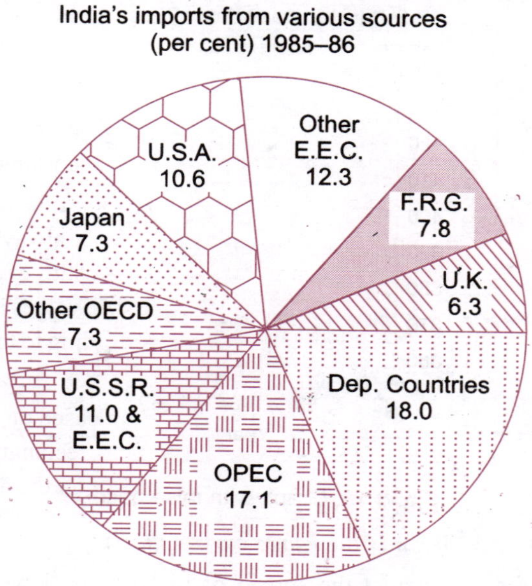

Fig. 3.10. Pie-chart

Q. 19. *Explain a histogram.*

Ans. A histogram is a bar diagram which is suitable for frequency distributions with continuous classes. The width of all bars is equal to class interval and heights of the bars are in proportion to the frequencies of the respective classes. In this diagram, bars touch each other but one bar never overlaps the other (Fig. 3.11).

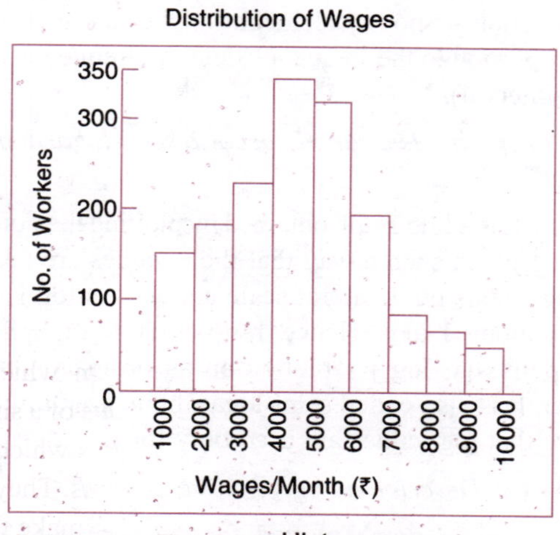

Fig. 3.11. Histogram

Q. 20. *Can there be a gap between rectangles or blocks in a histogram?*

Ans. As a rule, in a histogram there is no gap between rectangles or blocks. But a gap is possible if the frequency of a group is zero. In that case, the height of the block is zero which creates a gap.

Q. 21. *Describe a frequency polygon.*

Ans. When the mid-points of the tops of the adjacent bars of a histogram are joined in order, then the graph of lines so obtained is called a frequency polygon.

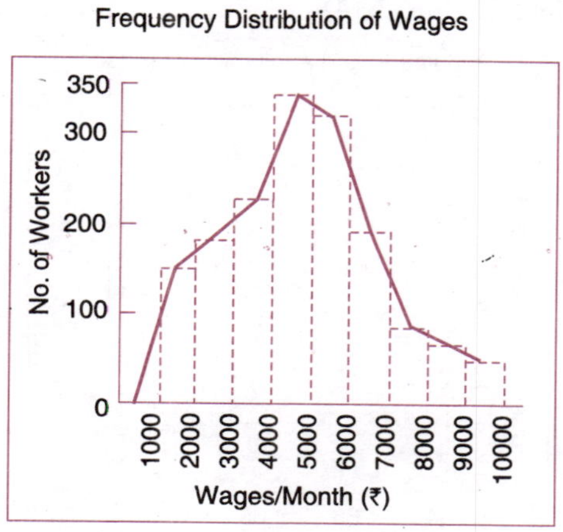

Fig. 3.12. Frequency polygon

Q. 22. *Discuss a frequency curve in brief.*

Ans. A frequency curve is a graphical representation of frequencies corresponding to their variate values by a smooth curve. A smoothened frequency polygon represents a frequency curve.

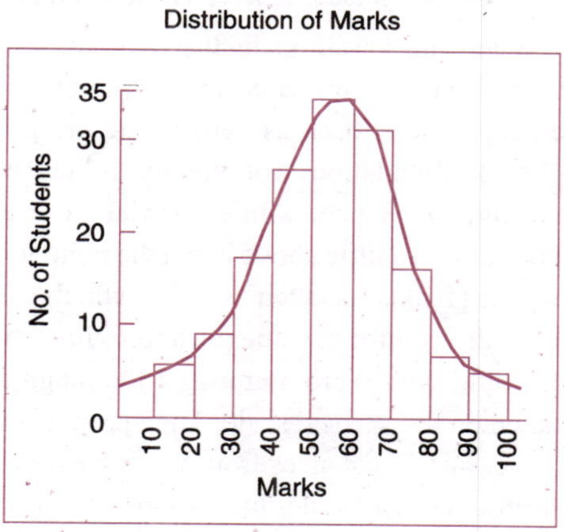

Fig. 3.13. Frequency curve

Q. 23. *What do you understand by a graph?*

Ans. A graph is a display of points and lines. In a graph of paired values (x, y), so called the co-ordinates of a point, are plotted on a graph paper by suitably choosing the scales along X-axis (abscissa) and Y-axis (ordinate). The plotted points are joined by straight lines in their sequence of occurrence. The figure so obtained is called a graph. The graph depicts the trend, fluctuations, variability, etc., very prominently (Fig. 3.14).

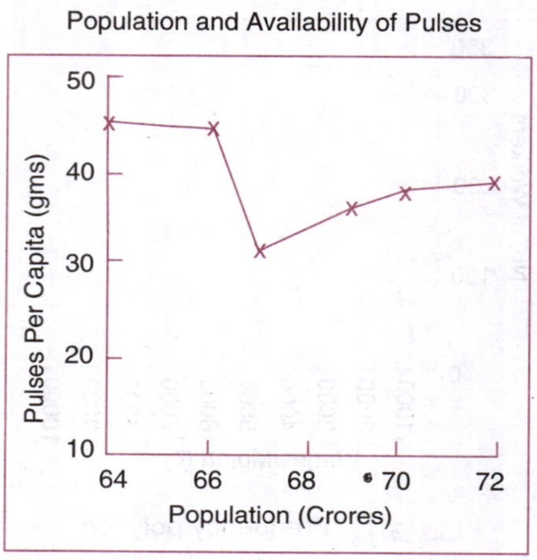

Fig. 3.14. Graph

Two or more graphs made on the same graph paper having a common scale along X-axis and Y-axis facilitate the comparison of data tremendously.

Q. 24. *What is a false line in reference to a graph?*

Ans. When the variation in the magnitudes of a variable is small as compared to the variate values, the vertical scale chosen as zero at the origin fails to depict the fluctuation prominently as desired by the investigator. Hence, a line parallel to abscissa (X-axis) is drawn a little above it and the point joining the ordinate (Y-axis) is taken as origin which usually represents the minimum value (an approximate value by discarding figure) from amongst the magnitudes to be taken on the vertical scale. Then proper scale is chosen measuring distances from this false base line. Such a process makes the fluctuations conspicuous. The graph so obtained is called *gee whiz* graph. False line on the graph is usually shown by a sawtooth line.

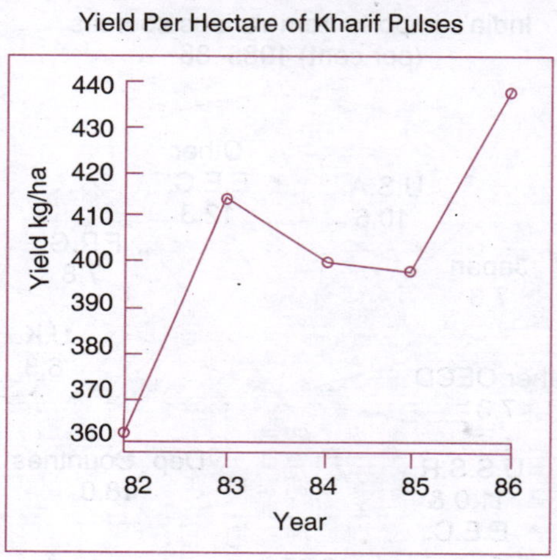

Fig. 3.15. Graph with false base

Q. 25. *What is the range curve (chart)?*

Ans. To depict the spread of highest and lowest values of a time series, the band formed by the line graphs of highest and lowest values is known as *range curve.* Range curve can also be represented through bar segments drawn at each period which are of magnitudes of the differences between highest and lowest values. These bars start from the lowest price and go up to the highest value.

Q. 26. *How do you draw a histogram when the widths of all classes are not equal?*

Ans. When widths of all classes of a frequency distribution are not equal, heights of the bars are taken in proportion to the frequency density (frequency per unit interval).

Q. 27 (a) *What is a ratio chart or a semi-logarithmic graph?*

Ans. It is a line graph obtained by plotting the points $(x, \log y)$ in such a way that the x-values are taken along X-axis on a natural scale and values $\log y$ are taken along Y-axis. Hence, ratio chart is a graph of the points $(x, \log y)$ plotted on an ordinary graph paper. It is also called semi-logarithmic graph in the sense that log-values are used only for y.

Q. 27 (b) *Describe an ogive curve in brief.*

Ans. It is a graph plotted for the variate values and their corresponding cumulative frequencies of a frequency distribution. Its shape is just like elongated

S. An ogive curve is prepared either for more than type or less than type distribution.

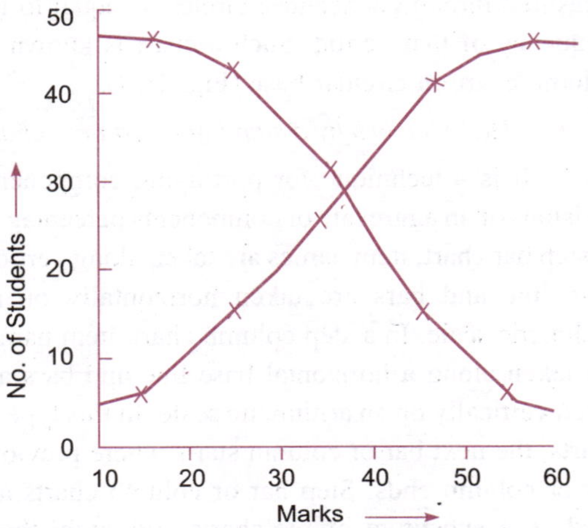

Fig. 3.16. Ogive curve

Q. 28. *What are the uses of ogive curve?*

Ans. Ogive curve is useful in finding out quartiles, deciles, percentiles, etc.

Q. 29. *At what point the ogives for more than type and less than type distribution intersect?*

Ans. The ogives for more than type and less than type distributions intersect at the median.

Q. 30. *Explain briefly a Lorenz curve.*

Ans. Lorenz curve is a special type of cumulative frequency curve which is used to portray the data to indicate whether a factor is equally distributed in relation to the other factor for certain segment of the population. It was originally developed by M.O. Lorenz and is named after him.

Q. 31. *How can one draw a Lorenz curve?*

Ans. Following steps are involved while drawing a Lorenz curve:

1. The variate values giving information about the segment of population are ignored.
2. Cumulative totals for the magnitudes or frequencies of the two other factors are found out separately.
3. Cumulative totals are expressed as percentage of their respective grand totals.
4. Paired cumulative percentages are plotted on a graph paper choosing same scale along axes from 0 to 100.
5. Plotted points are joined by a smooth free hand curve. This curve always starts from the origin and terminates at the end point (100, 100) (Fig. 3.17).

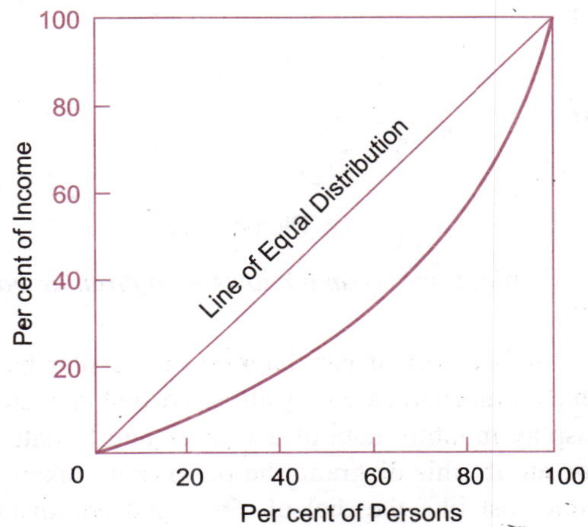

Fig. 3.17. Lorenz curve

Q. 32. *What is the importance of the Lorenz curve?*

Ans. In case of equal distribution of both the factors in the segment of population, the graph will be a straight line. But the Lorenz curve farther from straight line shows the inequality of distribution of two factors.

Q. 33. *How are the data portrayed by pictograms?*

Ans. In pictograms, the data are displayed by the pictures of the items to which the data pertain. A single picture represents a fixed number. For example, the population is shown by man, milk production by milk cans, fleets of aeroplane by the pictures of aeroplanes, etc.

Population of India in 1993 is 89.6 crore. This can be shown by a pictogram having the pictures of nine men, each man representing 10 crore. Pictograms are the least satisfactory type of diagrams. They are inaccurate too. Even then they are preferred by novice and dilettante people. Display of data through pictograms was initiated by Dr. Otto Neurath in 1923 (Fig. 3.18).

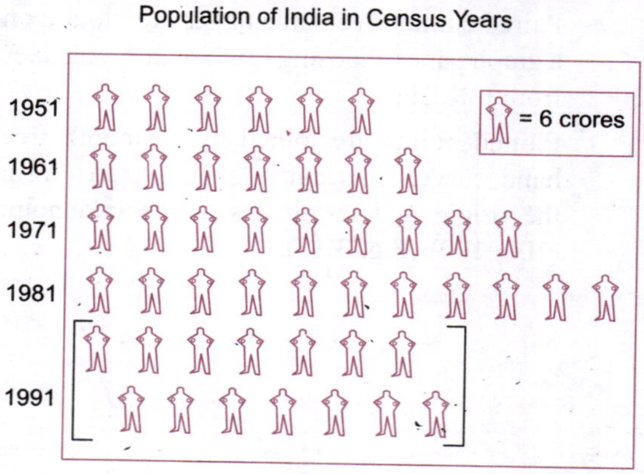

Fig. 3.18. Pictograms

Q. 34. *What are column charts with circular base line?*

Ans. It is a sort of bar diagram on circular base. Such column charts are very attractive and appealing to display monthly data of a year or hourly data of a day, etc. In this diagram, the periods are taken on a circle just like the dial of clock and equidistant concentric circles represent certain frequency. For instance, let the inner circle represent a frequency equal to 10, the second circle would represent 20 and so on. Columns (bars) are drawn on each period of the circular dial whereas the length of the column, measured through concentric circles, is equal to the frequency of that period. Such a chart is known as column chart on circular base (Fig. 3.19).

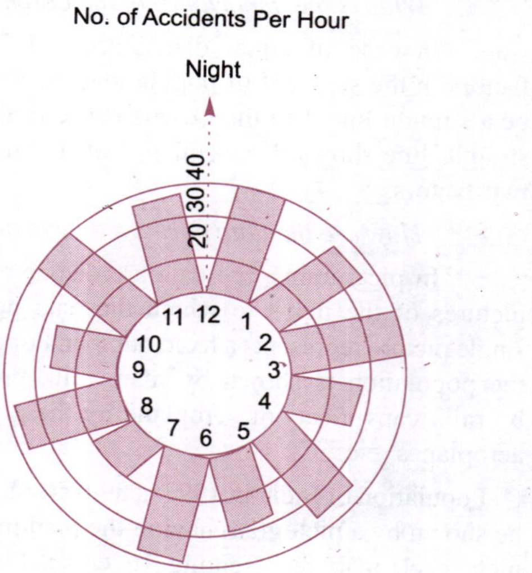

Fig. 3.19. Column chart on circular base

Q. 35. *Describe briefly a step bar or column chart.*

Ans. It is a technique for portraying components divisions of an aggregate or components percentages. In step bar chart, item names are taken along vertical base line and bars are taken horizontally on an arithmetic scale. In a step column chart, item names are taken along a horizontal base line and bars are taken vertically on an arithmetic scale. In this type of charts, the next bar or column starts where previous bar or column ends. Step bar or column charts are used as a substitute of pie-charts, although, these charts are not as appealing as the pie-charts.

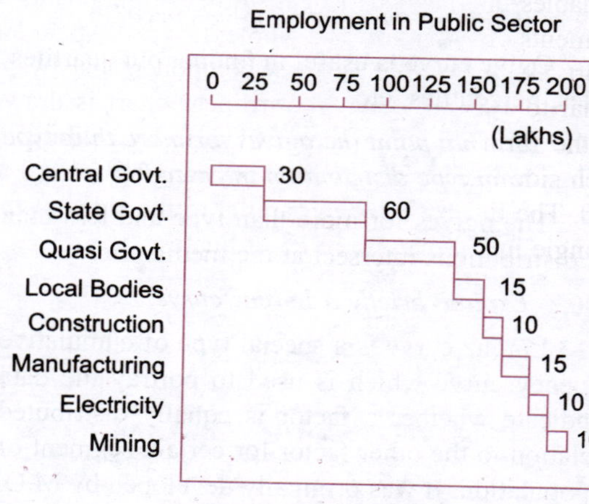

Fig. 3.20. Step bar chart

Q. 36. *What are overlapping bar or column charts?*

Ans. These are digression designed multiple bar or column charts. In this type of charts, one column (bar) penetrates into the next column (bar) by half of its width. Each column or bar is shown by different patterns or colours. Of course, such charts save space as the spread of group of columns or bars is sizeably reduced (Fig. 3.21).

All India Production (M. Tonnes)

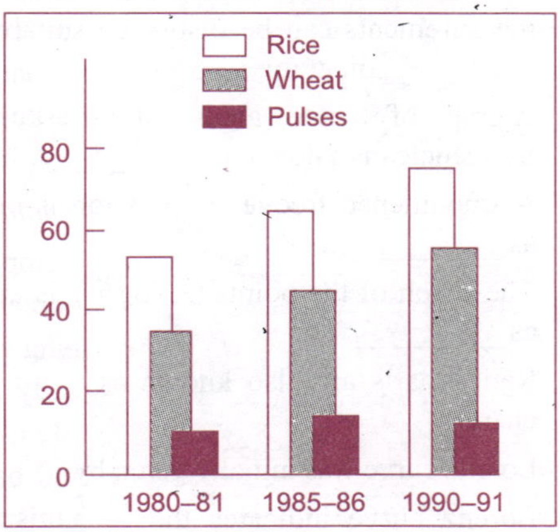

Fig. 3.21. Overlapping bar chart

Q. 37. *Write six lines about trilinear chart.*

Ans. The trilinear charts enables to display three variables simultaneously in the form of components or elements of a quantity as a whole. It is a 100 per cent chart, *i.e.*, the sum of the three components is always equal to 100 per cent. The trilinear chart is drawn in the form of a equilateral triangle by calibrating each side in percentage divisions ranging from 0 to 100. The lines are drawn parallel to the sides of the triangle in the manner of co-ordinates.

Q. 38. *How do you define a chart, diagram or graph?*

Ans. It is technique for portraying numerical facts through dots, lines, areas, volumes, other geometrical forms and symbols.

Q. 39. *What are the advantages of charts, diagrams and graphs?*

Ans. Charts, diagrams and graphs facilitate the presentation of quantitative values in a simple and easily understandable form. They facilitate comparison and analysis of data. Graphs in particular show fluctuations, trends and relationships between the variables. In comparison to tables and textual forms, charts and graphs are better and easily understood by a commoner.

Q. 40. *What factors are responsible for the choice of a chart, diagram and graph?*

Ans. The main factors responsible for the choice of a chart or graph are:

(1) Objective of the display of data.
(2) Type of data.
(3) Size of chart or graph.
(4) Audience for whom a chart or graph is prepared.
(5) Funds available.
(6) Predilection of the scientist.

SECTION B

Fill in the Blanks

Fill in the suitable word(s) or phrase(s) in the blanks:

1. Diagrams are another form of _________ .
2. It is comparatively easier to understand _________ than numerical figures.
3. The ogives of less than type and more than type distributions intersect at _________ .
4. Histogram and historigram are _________ .
5. In a histogram bars _________ each other.
6. A histogram is _________ for geographical classification.
7. Frequency polygon can be drawn with the help of _________ .
8. _________ diagram can be sketched for geographical series.
9. Sub-divided bar diagram depicts the distribution of _________ of a factor.
10. Paired bar diagrams are suitable for the data of two related factors having _________ units of measurements.
11. _________ bar diagram is suitable for showing the differences between budget

provisions and actual expenditure of PWD in the last ten years.

12. Histograms can be drawn only for __________ distributions.

13. Pie-chart is always __________.

14. Squares are __________ dimensional diagrams.

15. Cylinders are __________ dimensional diagrams.

16. Pictograms are __________ dimensional diagrams.

17. A straight line in a graph indicates the __________.

18. A zigzag graph shows the __________ of a series.

19. The heights of bars with unequal class intervals are proportional to __________.

20. In rectangular diagrams, comparison is based on __________ of the rectangles.

21. Line diagram is suitable when there are __________ variate values in the frequency distributions.

22. Multiple bar diagram has a __________ of bars for each year or place.

23. When more than one factor is to be displayed for comparison during various years, __________ bar diagram is suitable.

24. Two related factors having different units of measurements can be displayed suitably by __________ diagram.

25. A graph of variate values and corresponding frequencies is known as __________.

26. A smoothened frequency polygon is known as __________.

27. The graph of the points $(x, \log y)$ is known as __________.

28. Ratio charts are also known as __________ charts.

29. Lorenz curve was initially given by __________.

30. Lorenz curve indicates the __________ of distributions of two factors of a population.

31. When Lorenz curve turns out to be a straight line, it's concluded that the two factors have __________ distribution.

32. More the distance of Lorenz curve from the line of equal distribution, more is the __________ in the distributions of two factors.

33. Pictograms are __________ satisfactory.

34. Pictograms were originated by __________.

35. Column charts on circular base are just like __________.

36. There is no zero base line in a semi-logarithmic graph since __________.

SECTION C

Multiple Choice Questions

Select the correct alternative out of given ones:

1. Charts and graphs are the presentation of numerical facts by means of:
   (*a*) points and lines
   (*b*) area and other geometrical forms
   (*c*) symbols
   (*d*) all of the above

2. Graphs and charts facilitate:
   (*a*) comparison of values
   (*b*) to know the trend
   (*c*) to know relationship
   (*d*) all of the above

3. The purpose served by diagrams and chart is:
   (*a*) simple presentation of data
   (*b*) to avoid tabulation
   (*c*) to avoid textual form
   (*d*) all of the above

4. Choice of a particular chart depends on:

(*a*) the purpose of study
(*b*) the nature of data
(*c*) the type of audience
(*d*) all of the above

5. Rectilinear co-ordinate chart is also referred as:
(*a*) Cartesian co-ordinate graph
(*b*) rectangular graph
(*c*) both (*a*) and (*b*)
(*d*) none of (*a*) and (*b*)

6. Trilinear chart is used to portray simultaneously:
(*a*) two variables
(*b*) three variables
(*c*) four variables
(*d*) any number of variables

7. The shape of a trilinear charts is that of a:
(*a*) cone
(*b*) cube
(*c*) equilateral triangle
(*d*) pyramid

8. Which of the followings is a one-dimensional diagram?
(*a*) Bar diagram
(*b*) Pie-chart
(*c*) Cylinder
(*d*) A graph

9. Which of the followings is not a two-dimensional diagram?
(*a*) Square diagram
(*b*) Multiple bar diagram
(*c*) Rectangular diagram
(*d*) Pie-chart

10. Which of the following statement is not correct?
(*a*) The bars in a histogram touch each other
(*b*) The bar in a column chart touch each other
(*c*) There are bar diagrams which are known as broken bar diagrams
(*d*) Multiple bar diagrams also exist

11. Non-dimensional diagrams are also known as:
(*a*) cubes
(*b*) spheres
(*c*) pictograms
(*d*) all of the above

12. Which of the statement is correct?
(*a*) Histograms and historigrams are similar in look
(*b*) Cube and square diagrams are similar in look
(*a*) Pie-chart and ogives
(*b*) none of the above

13. Ogive curve occur for:
(*a*) more than type distribution
(*b*) less than type distribution
(*c*) both (*a*) and (*b*)
(*d*) none of (*a*) and (*b*)

14. In an ogive curve, the points are plotted for:
(*a*) the values and frequencies
(*b*) the values and cumulative frequencies
(*c*) frequencies and cumulative frequencies
(*d*) none of the above

15. A semi-logarithmic graph or ratio chart is obtained by plotting the points:
(*a*) $\{x, y\}$
(*b*) $\{\log x, \log y\}$
(*c*) $\{x, \log y)$
(*d*) $\{x, \log y/x\}$

16. Ogives for more than type and less than type distributions intersect at:
(*a*) mean
(*b*) median
(*c*) mode
(*d*) origin

17. When the values are large in magnitude in a chronological series and variation amongst values is small, a graph is better drawn by choosing:
(*a*) a false base line
(*b*) wide scale
(*c*) narrow scale
(*d*) none of the above

18. In a bar diagram, the base line is:
(*a*) horizontal
(*b*) vertical
(*c*) false base line
(*d*) any of the above

19. In a column chart, the base line is:
(*a*) horizontal
(*b*) vertical
(*c*) at an angle of 45°
(*d*) false base line

20. In a column chart, bars are:
(*a*) horizontal
(*b*) vertical
(*c*) slanting
(*d*) none of the above

21. In a bar diagram, the bars are:
(*a*) horizontal
(*b*) vertical
(*c*) slanting
(*d*) none of the above

22. In case of frequency distribution with classes of unequal widths, the heights of bars of a histogram are proportional to:
(*a*) class frequency
(*b*) class intervals
(*c*) frequencies in percentage
(*d*) frequency densities

23. Yearwise production of rice, wheat and maize for the last ten years can be displayed by:
(*a*) simple column chart
(*b*) subdivided column chart
(*c*) broken bar diagram
(*d*) multiple column chart

24. Profit and loss of a firm during various years can be displayed through:
(*a*) simple bar diagram
(*b*) duo-directional bar diagram
(*c*) deviation bar chart
(*d*) multiple bar diagram

25. When for some countries, the magnitudes are small and for other, the magnitudes are very large, to portray the data, it is preferred to construct:
(*a*) deviation bar diagram
(*b*) duo-directional bar diagram
(*c*) broken bar diagram
(*d*) any of the above

26. With the help of histogram we can prepare:
(*a*) frequency polygon
(*b*) frequency curve
(*c*) frequency distribution
(*d*) all of the above

27. Historigram is suitable for:
(*a*) time series data
(*b*) chronological distribution
(*c*) none of (*a*) or (*b*)
(*d*) both (*a*) and (*b*)

28. When we have the number of court cases of different categories and information about number of cases settled, the information can be better portrayed through:
(*a*) sliding bar diagram
(*b*) histogram
(*c*) paired bar diagram
(*d*) column chart

29. To show the maximal and minimal values in a time series, the suitable chart is:
(*a*) deviation bar diagram
(*b*) range curve
(*c*) historigram
(*d*) all of the above

30. With the help of ogive curve, one can determine:
(*a*) median
(*b*) deciles
(*c*) percentiles
(*d*) all of the above

31. Lorenz curve is an indicator for the distribution of two factors:
(*a*) being equal
(*b*) being unequal
(*c*) both (*a*) and (*b*)
(*d*) neither (*a*) nor (*b*)

32. Greater the distance of Lorenz curve from the line of equal distribution:
(*a*) more is the inequality
(*b*) less is the inequality
(*c*) has to tell nothing about inequality
(*d*) none of the above

33. Pictograms are:
(*a*) very accurate
(*b*) least accurate

(*c*) mostly used
(*d*) scientifically correct

34. Pictograms are generally used by:
(*a*) cartographers
(*b*) dilettante
(*c*) scientist
(*d*) all the above

35. Pictograms are suitable for the data in:
(*a*) counts
(*b*) intervals
(*c*) fraction
(*d*) none of the above

36. Pictograms are shown by:
(*a*) dots
(*b*) lines
(*c*) circles
(*d*) pictures

37. In a column chart on circular base, bars are:
(*a*) vertical
(*b*) horizontal
(*c*) slanting
(*d*) curved

38. If there is an increase in a series at constant rate, the graph will be a:
(*a*) convex curve
(*b*) parabola
(*c*) concave curve
(*d*) a straight line from left bottom to right top

39. If there is a decrease in a series at constant rate, the graph will be a:
(*a*) hyperbola
(*b*) a straight line from left top to right bottom
(*c*) a convex curve
(*d*) none of the above

40. A semi-logarithmic graph of a series increasing by a constant amount will be a:
(*a*) straight line at angle of 45°
(*b*) a convex upward curve
(*c*) a concave upward curve
(*d*) a convex downward curve

41. The suitable chart to emphasise the difference between two time series, of which one is at a higher level, is:
(*a*) range chart
(*b*) deviation bar chart
(*c*) paired bar diagrams
(*d*) band chart

42. When there is a pronounced skewness, the desirable scale to plot the frequency distribution is:
(*a*) arithmetic scale
(*b*) multiple scale
(*c*) logarithmic scale
(*d*) any of the above

43. When there are a large number of values in an individual series, preference for portraying the data goes to:
(*a*) bar diagram
(*b*) column chart
(*c*) line chart
(*d*) scatter diagram

44. An alternative chart to pie-chart is:
(*a*) step bar diagram
(*b*) rectangular chart
(*c*) sphere
(*d*) none of the above

45. The graph of the successive points of a distribution joined by straight lines in statistical terminology is known as:
(*a*) frequency distribution
(*b*) frequency curve
(*c*) trend
(*d*) cumulative distribution curve

46. A deviational or bilateral chart with 100 per cent component columns is also known as:
(*a*) duo-directional chart
(*b*) floating column chart
(*c*) sub-divided column chart
(*d*) range chart

47. Pie-chart represents the components of a factor by:
(*a*) percentages
(*b*) angles
(*c*) sectors
(*d*) circles

48. The immigration and outmigration of people in a number of countries and also the net migration can be better displayed by:

(a) duo-directional column chart
(b) gross-deviation column chart
(c) net deviation column chart
(d) range chart

49. Common form of rectilinear co-ordinate graph is:
(a) band chart
(b) surface chart
(c) stratum chart
(d) all the above

50. An arithmetic chart can:
(a) have only one amount scale
(b) have multiple amount scale
(c) be without any amount scale
(d) none of the above

51. It is necessary to find commutative frequencies in order to draw a/an:
(a) histogram
(b) frequency polygon
(c) ogive curve
(d) column chart

52. If we plot the points of a less than type or more than type frequency distribution, the shape of graph is:
(a) ogive curve
(b) scatter diagram
(c) zigzag curve
(d) parabola

53. Histogram is suitable for the data presented as:
(a) continuous grouped frequency distribution
(b) discrete grouped frequency distribution
(c) individual series
(d) all the above

54. A histogram can be drawn for the distribution with unequal class intervals by considering:
(a) class frequency
(b) height of bars proportional to class intervals
(c) height of bars proportional to frequency density
(d) all of the above

55. In a histogram with equal class intervals, heights of bar are proportional to:
(a) mid-values of the classes
(b) frequencies of respective classes
(c) either (a) or (b)
(d) neither (a) nor (b)

56. The data relating to the number of registered allopathic and homeopathic doctors in six different states can be most appropriately represented by diagram:
(a) line graph
(b) histogram
(c) pie-diagram
(d) double bar diagram

57. Histogram can be used only when:
(a) class intervals are equal or unequal
(b) class intervals are all equal
(c) class intervals are unequal
(d) frequencies in class interval are equal.

58. The most appropriate diagram to represent the data relating to the monthly expenditure on different items by a family is:
(a) histogram
(b) pie-diagram
(c) frequency polygon
(d) line graph

59. The gross income, taxes and net income of a manufacturer during different years can better be represented by:
(a) deviation bar diagram
(b) broken bar diagram
(c) paired bar diagram
(d) duo-directional bar diagram

60. Proportion of males and females in India in different occupations in the year 2000 can most properly be represented by:
(a) sliding bar diagram
(b) deviation bar diagram
(c) sub-divided bar diagram
(d) multiple bar diagram

ANSWERS

Section B

1. tabulation **2.** diagrams **3.** median **4.** not same **5.** touch **6.** not suitable **7.** histogram **8.** Bar **9.** Components **10.** different **11.** Deviation **12.** continuous frequency **13.** circular **14.** two **15.** three **16.** non **17.** trend **18.** fluctuations **19.** frequency densities **20.** area **21.** too many **22.** group **23.** multiple **24.** paired bar **25.** frequency polygon **26.** frequency curve **27.** ratio chart **28.** semi-logarithmic **29.** M.O. Lorenz **30.** inequality **31.** equal **32.** variability **33.** least **34.** Dr. Otto Neurath **35.** bar diagrams **36.** log 0 = – ∞

Section C

1. (*d*)	**2.** (*d*)	**3.** (*d*)	**4.** (*d*)	**5.** (*c*)
6. (*b*)	**7.** (*c*)	**8.** (*a*)	**9.** (*b*)	**10.** (*b*)
11. (*c*)	**12.** (*a*)	**13.** (*c*)	**14.** (*b*)	**15.** (*c*)
16. (*b*)	**17.** (*a*)	**18.** (*b*)	**19.** (*a*)	**20.** (*b*)
21. (*a*)	**22.** (*d*)	**23.** (*d*)	**24.** (*c*)	**25.** (*c*)
26. (*d*)	**27.** (*d*)	**28.** (*a*)	**29.** (*b*)	**30.** (*d*)
31. (*b*)	**32.** (*a*)	**33.** (*b*)	**34.** (*b*)	**35.** (*a*)
36. (*d*)	**37.** (*c*)	**38.** (*d*)	**39.** (*b*)	**40.** (*b*)
41. (*d*)	**42.** (*c*)	**43.** (*c*)	**44.** (*a*)	**45.** (*b*)
46. (*b*)	**47.** (*c*)	**48.** (*b*)	**49.** (*d*)	**50.** (*b*)
51. (*c*)	**52.** (*a*)	**53.** (*a*)	**54.** (*c*)	**55.** (*b*)
56. (*d*)	**57.** (*b*)	**58.** (*b*)	**59.** (*d*)	**60.** (*a*)

SUGGESTED READING

1. Agarwal, B.L., *Basic Statistics,* New Age International Publishers, New Delhi, 8th edition, 2024.
2. Calvin, F.S. and Stanton, E.S., *Handbook of Graphics Representation,* John Wiley & Sons, New York, 2nd edn., 1979.
3. Devore, J.L., *Probability and Statistics for Engineering and the Sciences,* Brooks/Cole Publishing Co., California, 1982.
4. Gupta, C.B., *An Introduction to Statistical Methods,* Vikas Publishing House, Delhi, 8th edn., 1978.
5. Kenny, J.F. and Keeping, E.S., *Mathematics of Statistics,* Part I, D. Von Nostrand Co., New York, 1951.
6. Sancheti, D.C. and Kapoor, V.K., *Statistics,* Sultan Chand & Sons, New Delhi, 7th edn., 1991.
7. Shukla, M.C. and Gulshan, S.S., *Statistics,* S. Chand & Co., New Delhi, 1970.
8. Simpson, G. and Kafka, F., *Basic Statistics,* Oxford & IBH, Calcutta, 3rd Indian print, 1971.

Chapter 4

Measures of Central Tendency

SECTION A

Short Essay Type Questions

Q. 1. *What do you understand by measure of central tendency?*

Ans. It is a single value within the range of data which represents a group of individual values in a simple and concise manner so that the mind can get a quick understanding of the general size of the individuals in the group. Since the value lies within the range of data, it is known as a measure of central tendency (value).

Q. 2. *Quote the statements about central values given by John I. Griffin, R.A. Fisher and A.L. Bowley.*

Ans. The statements of the prominent statisticians about the central values are:

John I. Griffin: An average may be thought of as a measure of central value.

R.A. Fisher: The inherent inability of human to grasp in its entirely a large body of numerical data compels us to seek relatively few constants that will adequately describe the data.

A.L. Bowley: Averages are statistical constants which enable us to comprehend in a single effort the significance of the whole.

Q. 3. *Name different measures of central values.*

Ans. Different measures of central values are:

(*i*) Arithmetic mean; (*ii*) Geometric mean; (*iii*) Harmonic mean, (*iv*) Median; (*v*) Mode; (*vi*) Quartiles, (*vii*) Octiles; (*viii*) Deciles; (*ix*) Percentiles, etc.

Q. 4. *What are the properties of a good measure of central tendency?*

Ans. The desired properties of a good measure of central tendency are:

(*i*) It should be based on all observations of a set of values.

(*ii*) It should be rigorously defined.

(*iii*) It should be easily computable.

(*iv*) It should be least affected by extreme values.

(*v*) It should fluctuate least from sample to sample drawn from the same population.

Q. 5. *What are the major classifications of averages?*

Ans. Major classifications of averages are:

(*i*) Mathematical averages—arithmetic mean, geometric mean, harmonic mean.

(*ii*) Positional averages—median, mode, quartiles, quintiles, octiles, deciles, percentiles.

(*iii*) Commercial averages—moving average, progressive average, composite average.

Q. 6. *What are the functions of averages?*

Ans. Various functions of averages are:

(*i*) It presents a simple and concised picture of large and complicated set of data.

(*ii*) It makes possible and easier to compare two or more groups of data.

(*iii*) It provides a study of different groups of data.

(*iv*) It facilitates the interpretation of data.

(*v*) It helps in taking decisions. For example, one can tell whether the income of a family is above or below the average income.

Q. 7. *What are the limitations of an average in general?*

Ans. The general limitations of an average are:

(*i*) A mean represents a group as a whole, not an individual.

(*ii*) Often an average is a value which does not exist in the set of data.

(*iii*) Sometimes an average gives a value which is not feasible, e.g., average size of a family is 3.62.

(*iv*) An average is incapable to throw any light on the constitution of the series.

Q. 8. *Define arithmetic mean (average).*

Ans. Arithmetic mean (A.M.) of a set of data may be defined as the sum of the values divided by the number of values in the set. Its formula is, A.M. = $\Sigma x_i/N$ for $i = 1, 2, 3, ..., N$.

Q. 9. *What are the merits of arithmetic mean?*

Ans. Merits of arithmetic mean are:

(*i*) It is easy to calculate.

(*ii*) It is rigidly defined.

(*iii*) It is based on all observations.

(*iv*) Observations are not to be arranged in order.

(*v*) It provides sound basis for comparison of two series.

(*vi*) It can be calculated if partial calculations are available.

(*vii*) It is less susceptible to sampling fluctuations.

(*viii*) It is most suitable for further algebraic treatment.

Q. 10. *What are the demerits of arithmetic mean?*

Ans. Demerits of arithmetic mean are:

(*i*) It is too much affected by extreme values.

(*ii*) Mostly it does not correspond to any value of the set of observations.

(*iii*) It cannot be calculated for frequency distribution with open end classes.

(*iv*) It does not convey any information about the spread or trend of data.

(*v*) It is not a suitable measure of central value in case of highly skewed distribution.

Q. 11. *Prove that the sum of deviations from mean is zero.*

Ans. Suppose $x_1, x_2, ..., x_n$ are n observations in a set. The sum of deviations from mean $\bar{x}$ is $\sum_{i=1}^{n}(x_i - \bar{x})$.

$$\sum_{i=1}^{n}(x_i - \bar{x}) = \sum_{i=1}^{n}x_i - \sum_{i=1}^{n}\bar{x} = \sum_{i=1}^{n}x_i - n\bar{x}$$

$$= \sum_{i=1}^{n}x_i - \sum_{i=1}^{n}x_i = 0$$

Q. 12. *Give the formula for calculating mean of a set of values from coded data.*

Ans. The formula for calculating mean from coded data is,

$$\bar{x} = a + \frac{\sum_{i=1}^{k} f_i x_i'}{\sum_{i=1}^{n} f_i} \times c$$

where, a is the constant value which is subtracted from each observation and c is a constant which divides each value obtained after subtracting a.

Also f_i is the frequency of the value x_i and $x_i' = (x_i - a)/c$.

Q. 13. *What is the effect of change of origin and scale on arithmetic mean?*

Ans. Arithmetic mean is increased or decreased by the constant value added or subtracted from each observation respectively. Also it is $\frac{1}{c}$ time of the original mean if each observation is divided by c and c times the original mean if each observation is multiplied by c.

Q. 14. *What is the difference between sample mean and population mean?*

Ans. Population mean is based on the values of each and every item of the population, whereas sample mean is based on the values of items selected in the sample from the population. If we have a random sample, then the sample mean is an estimate of population mean.

Q. 15. *There are (n + 1) observations in a sample. If $\bar{x}_1$ is the mean of the first n numbers and $\bar{x}_2$ is the mean of the last n numbers, prove that*

$$\bar{x}_2 = \bar{x}_1 + \frac{1}{n}(x_{n+1} - x_1)$$

Ans. **Proof:** By Formula,

$$\bar{x}_1 = \frac{1}{n}(x_1 + x_2 + \ldots + x_n)$$

$$\bar{x}_2 = \frac{1}{n}(x_2 + x_3 + \ldots + x_{n+1})$$

$$= \frac{1}{n}(x_1 + x_2 + x_3 + \ldots + x_n + x_{n+1} - x_1)$$

$$= \frac{1}{n}(x_1 + x_2 + \ldots + x_n) + \frac{1}{n}(x_{n+1} - x_1)$$

$$= \bar{x}_1 + \frac{1}{n}(x_{n+1} - x_1)$$

Q. 16. *Express weighted mean in brief.*

Ans. If $x_1, x_2, \ldots, x_k$ are the values having weights $w_1, w_2, \ldots, w_k$ respectively, the weighted mean,

$$\bar{x} = \frac{w_1x_1 + w_2x_2 + \ldots + w_kx_k}{w_1 + w_2 + \ldots + w_k}$$

Q. 17. *What would be the weighted mean of n natural numbers if weights are the corresponding numbers?*

Ans. Using the formula, the weighted mean

$$\bar{x} = \frac{1.1 + 2.2 + \ldots + n.n}{1 + 2 + \ldots + n}$$

$$= \frac{1^2 + 2^2 + \ldots n^2}{1 + 2 + \ldots + n}$$

$$= \frac{n(2n+1)(n+1)/6}{n(n+1)/2}$$

$$= \frac{2n+1}{3}$$

Q. 18. *What is a moving average?*

Ans. In this type of average, we get a series of averages out of a series of data. In this we take a fixed number of beginning items and find its average. To get the next average, delete the first item of the previous group and add next one item of the series to it and find its average. Continue this process till all the values are exhausted. This gives a series of averages. For example, suppose there are five items, a, b, c, d, e in the series. Taking three items in a group, the moving averages will be, $\frac{a+b+c}{3}, \frac{b+c+d}{3}, \frac{c+d+e}{3}$.

Q. 19. *Where do you utilise moving averages?*

Ans. Moving averages are utilised mostly in the analysis of time series data to know the trend.

Q. 20. *What do you understand by progressive average?*

Ans. In progressive average, we find out the average of the first two periods value and then go on adding the value for the third, fourth, fifth period, etc., and calculate the averages of three, four, five, etc., periods successively. Such averages are called *progressive averages*. For example, if a, b, c, d and e are the values of five successive periods, the progressive averages are:

$$\frac{a+b}{2}, \frac{a+b+c}{3}, \frac{a+b+c+d}{4}, \frac{a+b+c+d+e}{5}.$$

Q. 21. *For what purposes the progressive averages are utilised?*

Ans. Progressive averages are used to know the average profits in the starting years of commercial institutions.

Q. 22. *What is meant by composite average?*

Ans. The average of the averages of different series is known as composite average. The formula is,

$$\text{Composite average} = \frac{\text{Sum of the averages of individual series}}{\text{Number of series}}$$

Q. 23. *What is combined or pooled mean?*

Ans. The mean of the data that would be obtained by combining the values of all individual samples.

Q. 24. *Give the formula for finding out the combined (pooled) mean of three samples when their means and sample sizes are given.*

Ans. Suppose $\bar{x}_1, \bar{x}_2, \bar{x}_3$ are three sample means base on n_1, n_2 and n_3 observations respectively.

Formula for the pooled or combined mean is,

$$\bar{x}_{123} = \frac{n_1\bar{x}_1 + n_2\bar{x}_2 + n_3\bar{x}_3}{n_1 + n_2 + n_3}$$

Pooled mean is the mean obtained on combining all samples, considered as a single sample.

Q. 25. *Elucidate trimmed mean.*

Ans. Suppose we want a 10 per cent trimmed mean, then the mean of the observations by excluding 10 per cent smallest and 10 per cent largest observations is known as 10 per cent trimmed mean. Not necessarily 10 per cent trimmed mean has to be found out, it can be any other chosen percentage which is considered suitable.

Q. 26. *In a frequency distribution, the mid-value of the first class is 10 and each class has equal class intervals. The cumulative frequencies of the classes are 3, 18, 37, 40 and 45. Give the original frequency distribution and find its mean.*

Ans. The first class will be (10 – 2.5) to (10 + 2.5), *i.e.*, 7.5 – 12.5. The second class will be 12.5 – 17.5 and so on. Their corresponding frequencies will be 3, (18 – 3), (37 – 18), (40 – 37) and (45 – 40), *i.e.*, 3.15, 19, 3 and 5. Hence the frequency distribution is:

Classes	Frequency
7.5–12.5	3
12.5–17.5	15
17.5–22.5	19
22.5–27.5	3
27.5–32.5	5

In the above distribution, the mid-values of the classes are: 10, 15, 20, 25, 30 respectively. Hence, the mean μ of the distribution is,

$$\mu = \frac{10 \times 3 + 15 \times 15 + 20 \times 19 + 25 \times 3 + 30 \times 5}{3 + 15 + 19 + 3 + 5}$$

$$= \frac{860}{45}$$

$$= 19.11$$

Q. 27. *Define geometric mean.*

Ans. Geometric mean is the nth root of the product of n values of a set of observations. By formula,

$$G = (x_1, x_2, ..., x_n)^{1/n}.$$

Q. 28. *What are the merits of geometric mean?*

Ans. Merits of geometric mean are:

(*i*) It is least affected by extreme values.

(*ii*) It is based on all observations of the set.

(*iii*) It is suitable for further algebraic treatment.

Q. 29. *What are the demerits of the geometric mean?*

Ans. Demerits of the geometric mean are:

(*i*) Its calculation is somewhat complicated.

(*ii*) It cannot be calculated if any of the value in the set is zero.

(*iii*) If any one or more values are negative, either geometric mean will not be calculable or an absurd value will be obtained.

Q. 30. *For what type of data geometric mean is the most appropriate measure of location?*

Ans. It is appropriate for averaging the ratios of change, for average of proportions, etc.

Q. 31. *Where geometric mean is considered to be the best average theoretically?*

Ans. Geometric mean is considered most suitable average for index numbers.

Q. 32. *If G_1 is the geometric mean of n_1 observations $x_1, x_2, ..., x_{n_1}$ and G_2 is the geometric mean of n_2 observations $y_1, y_2, ..., y_{n_2}$ and let G be the geometric mean of all $(n_1 + n_2)$ observations, prove that,*

$$\log G = \frac{1}{n_1 + n_2}\{n_1 \log G_1 + n_2 \log G_2\}$$

Ans. By formula, geometric mean of $(n_1 + n_2)$ observations is,

$$G = (x_1 \cdot x_2 \dots x_{n_1} \cdot y_1 \cdot y_2 \dots y_{n_2})^{1/n_1 + n_2}$$

$$\therefore \quad \log G = \frac{1}{n_1 + n_2} \log (x_1 \cdot x_2 \dots x_{n_1} \cdot y_1 \cdot y_2 \dots y_{n_2})$$

$$= \frac{1}{n_1 + n_2} \{\log (x_1 \cdot x_2 \dots x_{n_1}) + \log (y_1 \cdot y_2 \dots y_{n_2})\}$$

$$= \frac{1}{n_1 + n_2} \left\{ \sum_{i=1}^{n_1} \log x_i + \sum_{j=1}^{n_2} \log y_j \right\}$$

We know, $\log \text{G.M.} = \frac{1}{n} \sum_i \log x_i$

or $\sum_i \log x_i = n \log \text{G.M.}$

$$\therefore \quad \log G = \frac{1}{n_1 + n_2} \{n_1 \log G_1 + n_2 \log G_2\}$$

Q. 33. *Explain briefly the inverse property of geometric mean.*

Ans. If $\overline{x}_G$ is the geometric mean of $x_1, x_2, \dots, x_n$, the geometric mean of the inverse of the observations $1/x_1, 1/x_2, \dots, 1/x_n$ is $1/\overline{x}_G$. This is known as inverse property of geometric mean.

Q. 34. *The arithmetic mean of two numbers is 10 and their geometric mean is 8. Find the numbers.*

Ans. Suppose the two numbers are x_1 and x_2. Then by formula,

$$\text{A.M.} = \frac{x_1 + x_2}{2} = 10$$

and $$\text{G.M.} = \sqrt{x_1 \cdot x_2} = 8$$

$$\therefore \quad (x_1 + x_2) = 20 \text{ and } x_1 x_2 = 64$$

$$(x_1 - x_2)^2 = (x_1 + x_2)^2 - 4x_1 x_2$$

$$= 400 - 4 \times 64 = 144$$

$$\therefore \quad (x_1 - x_2) = +12$$

Solving $x_1 + x_2 = 20$

and $x_1 - x_2 = 12$,

we get $x_1 = 16, x_2 = 4$

Hence, the numbers are 16 and 4.

Q. 35. *Define harmonic mean and give the formula for harmonic mean.*

Ans. Harmonic mean is the inverse of the arithmetic mean of the reciprocals of the observations of a set. The formula for harmonic mean is,

$$\text{H.M.} = \frac{f_1 + f_2 + \dots + f_k}{\frac{f_1}{x_1} + \frac{f_2}{x_2} + \dots + \frac{f_k}{x_k}}$$

$$= \frac{\Sigma_i f_i}{\Sigma_i (f_i / x_i)} \quad \text{for } i = 1, 1, \dots, k$$

where, f_1 is the frequency of x_i for $i = 1, 2, \dots, k$.

Q. 36. *What are the merits of harmonic mean?*

Ans. Merits of harmonic mean are:

(*i*) It is based on all observations of a set.

(*ii*) It is a good mean for a highly variable series.

(*iii*) It gives more weightage to the small values and less weightage to the large values.

(*iv*) It is better than weighted mean since in this, values are automatically weighted.

Q. 37. *What are the demerits of harmonic mean?*

Ans. Demerits of harmonic mean are:

(*i*) Its calculation is complicated.

(*ii*) If any value is zero, it cannot be calculated.

(*iii*) Its value is generally not a member of the series.

Q. 38. *Can we use coding while calculating geometric mean or harmonic mean?*

Ans. We cannot use coding in geometric mean or harmonic mean as no easy expression is available which relates the mean of coded data to the mean of the original data.

Q. 39. *How will you calculate mean in case of a continuous frequency distribution?*

Ans. To calculate the mean of a continuous frequency distribution, first find the mid-values of the classes and use them as variate values. Then use the formula for the weighted mean with frequencies as weights.

Q. 40. *Given two values x_1 and x_2, prove that*

$$A.M. \geq G.M. \geq H.M.$$

Ans. We know,

$$\text{A.M.} = \frac{x_1 + x_2}{2}, \text{ G.M.} = \sqrt{x_1 x_2},$$

$$\text{H.M.} = \frac{2x_1 x_2}{x_1 + x_2}$$

Again, $\left(\sqrt{x_1} - \sqrt{x_2}\right)^2 \geq 0$

or $x_1 + x_2 - 2\sqrt{x_1 x_2} \geq 0$

or $\frac{x_1 + x_2}{2} \geq \sqrt{x_1 x_2}$

$\therefore$ A.M $\geq$ G.M.

Again, $x_1 + x_2 \geq 2\sqrt{x_1 x_2}$

or, $(x_1 + x_2)\sqrt{x_1 x_2} \geq 2\left(\sqrt{x_1 x_2}\right)^2$

or $(x_1 + x_2)\sqrt{x_1 x_2} \geq 2x_1 x_2$

or $\sqrt{x_1 x_2} \geq \frac{2x_1 x_2}{x_1 + x_2}$

or G.M. $\geq$ H.M.

$\therefore$ A.M. $\geq$ G.M. $\geq$ H.M.

Q. 41. *Express geometric mean in terms of arithmetic mean and harmonic mean.*

Ans. The relation between geometric mean, arithmetic mean and harmonic mean is,

$$\text{G.M.} = \sqrt{\text{A.M.} \times \text{H.M.}}$$

Q. 42. *Express harmonic mean in terms of geometric mean and arithmetic mean.*

Ans. The expression for harmonic mean relating to geometric mean and arithmetic mean is,

$$\text{H.M.} = (\text{G.M.})^2/\text{A.M.}$$

Q. 43. *For what type of values harmonic mean is suitable?*

Ans. Harmonic mean is suitable when the values are pertaining to the rate of change per unit time such as speed, number of items produced per day, contracts completed per year, etc. In general, harmonic mean is suitable for time, speed, rates, prices, etc.

Q. 44. *Define quadratic mean.*

Ans. The square root of the arithmetic mean of the square of numbers of a set is known as quadratic mean.

Q. 45. *When do you prefer a quadratic mean than a mean.*

Ans. When one has some negative numbers in a set, quadratic mean is preferable than any other mean. The reason being that considering the sign of negative numbers, the mean value is considerably reduced. If the signs of negative numbers are ignored, the mean thus obtained depends on an algebraic lie. But the quadratic mean is devoid of the mathematical abuse and has the same scale and units as the original values.

Q. 46. *Comment on the value of quadratic mean as compared to arithmetic mean.*

Ans. Generally the quadratic mean is greater than the arithmetic mean. The reason being that the difference between a number and its square increases exponentially as the number gets larger. Hence, the square root of the average of squared numbers results into a higher value than arithmetic mean of original numbers.

Q. 47. *Find the arithmetic mean (A.M.) and quadratic mean (Q.M.) for the following set of values and comment on the mean values.*

X :	2	3	5	8	12

Ans.

$$\text{A.M.} = \frac{2+3+5+8+12}{5}$$

$$= 6.0$$

Sum of squares of numbers,

$$\Sigma X^2 = 4 + 9 + 25 + 64 + 144 = 246$$

$$\text{A.M. of squared numbers} = \frac{246}{5} = 49.2$$

$$\text{Q.M.} = \sqrt{49.2} = 7.0143$$

Q.M. is greater than A.M. as is expected on the basis of our theoretical knowledge.

Q. 48. *Where do you make use of quadratic mean in general?*

Ans. Quadratic mean is absolutely utilized in finding the standard deviation of a set of data. As a matter of fact, the standard deviation is nothing but the quadratic mean of the deviations from data mean.

Q. 49. *What do you understand by median?*

Ans. It is a most preferable measure of location for asymmetric distributions. Median is the value of the variable that divides the ordered set of values into two equal halves. 50 per cent values are to the left of the median and 50 per cent are to the right of the median.

Q. 50. *What are the points in favour of median?*

Ans. Points in favour of median are:

(*i*) Median is not influenced by extreme values because it is a positional average.

(*ii*) Median can be calculated in case of distribution with open end intervals.

(*iii*) Median can be located even if the data are incomplete.

(*iv*) Median can be located even for qualitative factors such as ability, honesty, etc.

(*v*) Median can be located visually in case of discrete series.

Q. 51. *What are the demerits of median?*

Ans. Following are the demerits of median:

(*i*) A slight change in the series may bring drastic change in median value.

(*ii*) In case of even number of observations or continuous series, median is an estimated values other than any value in the series.

(*iii*) It is not suitable for further mathematical treatment except its use in mean deviation.

(*iv*) If we know the median of various groups, then the combined median cannot be found out by any formula like mean.

Q. 52. *How will you calculate median in case of ungrouped data?*

Ans. To calculate median of ungrouped data, following steps be followed:

(*i*) Arrange the data in order.

(*ii*) For an individual or discrete series of N items, the value corresponding to $(N + 1)/2^{\text{th}}$ item is the median value when N is odd.

(*iii*) When N is even, median is the average of $\frac{N}{2}^{\text{th}}$ and $\left(\frac{N+2}{2}\right)^{\text{th}}$ items.

Q. 53. *Give the interpolation formula for calculating median of grouped series.*

Ans. For grouped data, the formula for median with usual rotation is,

$$M_d = L_0 + \frac{N/2 - c}{f} \times I$$

where, L_0 = Lower limit of the median class

c = Cumulative frequency just above the median class

f = Frequency of the median class

I = Class interval

Q. 54. *What is the impact of extreme values of a set on median?*

Ans. Median is not affected by the extreme values of a set.

Q. 55. *What is the apparent difference between mean and median?*

Ans. The basic difference between mean and median is that of point of balance.

The mean balances the differences from itself *i.e.*, $\sum_i (x_i - \bar{x}) = 0$.

The median balances number of items *i.e.*, the number of values in a series exceeding the median is same as the median exceeds.

Q. 56. *Discuss mode in brief.*

Ans. The variate value x having maximum frequency in a distribution is known as its mode.

Q. 57. *What was said about the mode by Ya Lun Chou?*

Ans. Ya Lun Chou statement about mode is, "The mode is that value of a series which appears most frequently than any other."

Q. 58. *Can there be more than one mode of a distribution ?*

Ans. Some distributions have equal peaks and hence mode is not necessarily unique. There will be as many modes of distribution as the number of peaks in it.

Q. 59. (*a*) *How would you calculate mode of a grouped frequency distribution?*

Ans. For frequency distribution with classes in

ascending order, the formula for calculating the mode is,

$$M_0 = L_0 + \frac{\Delta_1}{\Delta_1 + \Delta_2} \times I$$

$$= L_0 + \frac{f_0 + f_{-1}}{2f_0 - f_{-1} - f_{+1}} \times I$$

where, the class having the maximum frequency is known as model class.

L_0 = Lower limit of the modal class

I = Class interval

Δ_1 = Difference of modal frequency from its preceding class frequency

Δ_2 = Difference of modal frequency from its following class frequency.

In the second formula,

L_0 and I are same above.

f_0 = Modal class frequency

f_{-1} = Frequency of the preceding class

f_{+1} = Frequency of the following class.

Q. 59. **(*b*)** *How would you find out the mode of a discrete frequency distribution?*

Ans. It can be determined merely by inspection. The value having maximum frequency is the mode of the distribution.

Q. 60. *How can one locate mode graphically in case of grouped data?*

Ans. Prepare a histogram. Consider a bar having maximum height and the bars to the left and right adjoining to it. Join the top left corner of the highest bar to the top left corner of the right side bar and top right corner of the highest bar to the top right corner of the bar to its left. The abscissa value of the point of intersection of the joining lines is the mode.

Q. 61. *Discuss quartiles and their importance.*

Ans. Three variate values of the variable, say x, which divide the series (frequency) into four equal parts are called quartiles for the corresponding distribution of x. There are three quartiles namely Q_1, Q_2 and Q_3. Q_1 is called the lower quartile and Q_3, the upper quartile. 25 per cent values are less than Q_1 and 25 per cent values are larger than Q_3 and the rest 50 per cent values lie between Q_1 and Q_3. Q_2 divide the series into two equal parts and hence it is the same as median.

As regards their importance, quartiles are widely used in economics and business. They are also helpful in determining the shape of a distribution.

Q. 62. *Give the formula for calculating the quartiles, of a continuous distribution.*

Ans. Formula for calculating i^{th} quartile (i = 1, 2, 3) for a continuous distribution having K-classes is,

$$Q_i = l_0 + \frac{\frac{iN}{4} - c}{f} \times I$$

where, Q_i = i^{th} quartile which is to be calculated

l_0 = Lower limit of the ith quartile class

N = Total of all frequencies

c = Cumulative frequency of the class just above the quartile class

f = Frequency of the quartile class

I = Class interval.

Q. 63. *Discuss deciles in brief.*

Ans. The variate values which divide the series (frequency) into ten equal parts are called deciles. Hence, there are in all nine deciles denoted by D_1, D_2, ..., D_9: The items before D_1 and after D_9 are 10 per cent. Also, the number of items that lie between any two deciles is also 10 per cent. D_5, the fifth decil divides the series into halves and hence, it is the same as median.

Q. 64. *Give the formula for finding the deciles of a continuous distribution.*

Ans. The formula for calculating deciles of a continuous distribution is,

$$D_i = l_0 + \frac{\frac{iN}{10} - c}{f} \times I$$

for i = 1, 2, ..., 9.

All notation can be decoded by replacing the word quartile by decile as in the formula for quartiles.

Q. 65. *Describe percentiles in brief.*

Ans. The values of the variable x which divide its distribution into 100 equal parts are called percentiles. There are in all 99 percentiles and are denoted by $P_1, P_2, ..., P_{99}$ respectively. Area between any two percentiles, before P_1 and after P_{99} is 0.01, *i.e.*, it represents $\frac{1}{100}$ part of the population. 50th percentile is same as median.

Q. 66. *Give the formula for calculating percentiles of a continuous distribution.*

Ans. Formula for calculating i^{th} percentile is,

$$P_i = l_0 + \frac{\frac{iN}{100} - c}{f} \times I$$

for $i = 1, 2, ..., 99.$

All notation can be decoded as for quartiles by replacing the word quartile by percentile.

Q. 67. *How to determine quartiles, deciles and percentiles in case of a discrete series?*

Ans. *Quartiles*: The values of the variable x corresponding to $\left(\frac{N+1}{4}\right)^{th}, \left(\frac{N+1}{2}\right)^{th}$ and $\frac{3(N+1)}{4}$th items of an ordered discrete series are the values of Q_1, Q_2 and Q_3 respectively. The position of the required item can easily be adjudged with the help of cumulative frequencies.

Deciles: Similar to quartiles, the values of the variable x corresponding to $\frac{i(N+1)}{10}$th item for $i = 1, 2, ..., 9$ of an ordered discrete series is D_i. The position of $\frac{i(N+1)}{10}$th item can be located with the help of cumulative frequencies.

Percentiles: Just like deciles, the value of the variable x corresponding to $\frac{i(N+1)}{100}$th item for $i = 1, 2, ..., 99$ of an ordered series is P_i. $\frac{i(N+1)}{100}$th item in the series can easily be placed with the help of cumulative frequencies.

SECTION B

Fill in the Blanks

Fill in the suitable word(s) or phrase(s) in the blanks:

1. "The statement, "An average may be thought of as a measure of central value," was given by ________ .
2. The statement, "The inherent inability of human to grasp in its entirely a large body of numerical data compels us to seek relatively few constants that will adequately describe the data," was given by ________ .
3. "Averages are statistical constants which enable us to comprehend in a single effort the significance of the whole", was stated by ________ .
4. Measures of central tendency are also known as ________ or ________ .
5. Arithmetic mean is very much affected by ________ .
6. Any mean is based on ________ values of a set.
7. An average ________ the data.
8. In an open end distribution ________ cannot be determined.
9. If 5 is subtracted from each observation of a set, then the mean of the observation is reduced by ________ .
10. If each value of a set is divided by 10, the mean of observations is ________ of the mean of the original observations.

11. The mean of the values 11, 12, 13, 14 and 15 is _________ .

12. The mean of 8 numbers is 15. Afterwards a new number 24 is added. The mean of the nine numbers is _________ .

13. The sum of the deviations from mean is _________ .

14. The average income of a person on working for the first five days of the week is ₹ 35 per day and if he works for the first six days of the week, his average income per day is ₹ 40. Then, his income for the sixth day is _________ .

15. A factory employs 5 persons in the first week of the month and pays ₹ 25 per day per person. In the second week he employs 8 persons and pays ₹ 30 per day per person. In the third week he employs 7 persons and pays ₹ 25 per day per person. The average payment per day per person by the employer is _________ .

16. Weighted mean is more _________ than unweighted mean.

17. In case of 15 per cent trimmed mean, only _________ per cent observations are utilised.

18. The arithmetic mean of n natural numbers from 1 to n is _________ .

19. Sum of squares of the deviations from mean is always _________ .

20. The geometric mean of four numbers 2, 4, 8 and 64 is _________ .

21. If $x_1, x_2, ..., x_n$ and $y_1, y_2, ..., y_n$ are the variate values of two variables X and Y and their geometric means are G_1 and G_2 respectively, then the geometric mean of (x_i/y_i) is _________.

22. Geometric mean cannot be calculated if any value of the set is _________ .

23. Geometric mean is suitable when the values are given as _________ or _________ .

24. If arithmetic mean of certain values is 9 and their geometric mean is 6, then the harmonic mean is _________ .

25. If the harmonic mean of the two numbers a and b is 5 if $a = 5$, then b is _________ .

26. Harmonic mean is suitable as an average for finding out the _________ .

27. If the two observations x_1 and x_2 are such that $x_1 = -x_2$, their harmonic mean is _________ .

28. The relation between A.M., G.M. and H.M. is _________ .

29. The variate value in a series which divides the series into halves is called _________ .

30. The sum of the absolute deviations taken from median is _________ .

31. The median of the series 3, 18, 7, 20, 11, 12, 9, 17, 22 is _________ .

32. Median is _________ for each and every distribution.

33. Two ogives, the one less than type and the other more than type, intersect at _________ .

34. Median is a more suited average for grouped data with _________ classes.

35. The variate value having maximum frequency in a frequency distribution is called _________.

36. The mode of the distribution of values 5, 7, 9, 9, 8, 5, 6, 8, 7, 7, 5, 7, 9, 2, 7 is _________ .

37. _________ and _________ are least affected by the extreme values as a measure of central tendency.

38. Out of all the measures of central tendency _________ is the only measure which is not unique.

39. _________ is not appropriate for further algebraic treatment as a measure of central value.

40. The distribution which has only one mode is called _________ .

41. The distribution having two modes is called _________ .

42. If the frequencies in distribution have ups and downs, the mode is determined by the method of _______ .

43. In an individual or discrete series $\left(\frac{N+1}{4}\right)^{th}$ item is known as first _________ .

44. Second quartile is same as ________ .

45. Third quartile and ________ percentile are same.

46. Second quartile and ________ decile are equal.

47. The decile which precedes 72th percentile is ________ .

48. The percentage of values which lie between P_{30} and P_{56} is ________ .

49. 25th percentile is same as ________ quartile.

50. Sixth decile is same as ________ percentile.

51. Percentage of values lying between first and sixth decile is ________ .

52. Percentage of values which are greater than 66th percentile is ________ .

53. In a frequency distribution fourth decile and ________ percentile are same.

54. The relation between second quartile Q_2, sixth decile D_6 and 80th percentile is ________ .

55. Median is same as ________ decile.

56. Median is same as ________ percentile.

57. Percentiles (quartiles, deciles) are always in ________ order.

58. The variate values which divide a series into five equal parts are called ________ .

59. If in a series, 20 per cent values are greater than 75, then ________ = 75.

60. If in a discrete series 30 per cent values are less than 35, then ________ decile = 35.

61. If in a discrete series 75 per cent values are greater than 20, then ________ quartile = 20 or ________ percentile = 20.

62. The general name for quartile, quintiles, octiles, deciles and percentiles is ________ .

63. The statement, "The mode is that value of a series which appears most frequently than any other", was given by ________ .

64. The relation between first quartile and 25th percentile is ________ .

65. The relation between 4th decile and 45th percentile is ________ .

66. Percentage of values that lie between tenth and eighty fifth percentile is ________ .

67. The number of types of statistical facts are ________ or ________ .

68. For a symmetrical distribution, median in terms of quartiles is ________ .

69. Geometric mean is ________ of the arithmetic mean of logarithmic values of a variable.

70. Harmonic mean is ________ of the arithmetic mean of the reciprocal of the observations of a data set.

71. Quadratic mean is preferred most, if the data set contains some ________ number.

72. If a variable takes some non-negative values $x_1, x_2, ..., x_n$, then the inequality that holds between H.M., G.M. and A.M. is ________ .

73. Quadratic mean has ________ scale and units as that of original observation.

74. The application of quadratic mean is evidently found in ________ .

75. The mean of 20 observations is 7. If each observation is multiplied by 3 and then 5 is added to it, then the mean of the new data set is ________ .

76. The mean of a set of 10 observations is 4. Another set of 20 observations is added to it which makes the mean of the combined set equal to 6. The mean of second set is ________ .

77. If $2y - 6x = 6$ and the mode of y is 66, then the mode of x is ________ .

78. An average is that value of a distribution which represents ________ .

79. No average can be regarded as ________ for all times and all data.

80. Mode is ________ defined.

SECTION C

Multiple Choice Questions

Select the correct alternative out of given ones:

1. Mean is a measure of:
   (*a*) location (central value)
   (*b*) dispersion
   (*c*) correlation
   (*d*) none of the above
2. Which of the following is a measure of central value?
   (*a*) Median
   (*b*) Standard deviation
   (*c*) Mean deviation
   (*d*) Quartile deviation
3. Which of the following represents median?
   (*a*) First quartile
   (*b*) Fiftieth percentile
   (*c*) Sixth decile
   (*d*) None of the above
4. If a constant value 50 is subtracted from each observation of a set, the mean of the set is:
   (*a*) increased by 50
   (*b*) decreased by 50
   (*c*) is not affected
   (*d*) zero
5. If a constant 5 is added to each observation of a set, the mean is:
   (*a*) increased by 5
   (*b*) decreased by 5
   (*c*) 5 times the original mean
   (*d*) not affected
6. If each observation of a set is multiplied by 10, the mean of the new set of observations:
   (*a*) remains the same
   (*b*) is ten times the original mean
   (*c*) is one-tenth of the original mean
   (*d*) is increased by 10
7. If each value of a series is multiplied by 10, the median of the coded values is:
   (*a*) not affected
   (*b*) 10 times the original median value
   (*c*) one-tenth of the original median value
   (*d*) increased by 10
8. If each value of a series is multiplied by 10, the mode of the coded values is:
   (*a*) not affected
   (*b*) one-tenth of the original modal value
   (*c*) 10-times of the original modal value
   (*d*) 100-times of the original modal value
9. If each observation of a set is divided by 2, then the mean of new values:
   (*a*) is two times the original mean.
   (*b*) is decreased by 2.
   (*c*) is half of the original mean
   (*d*) remains the same
10. Which of the following relations among the location parameters does not hold?
    (*a*) Q_2 = median
    (*b*) P_{50} = median
    (*c*) D_5 = median
    (*d*) D_6 = median
11. If the grouped data has open end classes, one cannot calculate:
    (*a*) median
    (*b*) mode
    (*c*) mean
    (*d*) quartiles
12. Geometric mean of two observations can be calculated only if:
    (*a*) both the observations are positive
    (*b*) one of the two observations is zero
    (*c*) one of them is negative
    (*d*) both of them are zero
13. Geometric mean is better than other means when,
    (*a*) the data are positive as well as negative
    (*b*) the data are in ratios or percentages
    (*c*) the data are binary
    (*d*) the data are on interval scale
14. Geometric mean is a good measure of central value if the data are:

(*a*) categorical
(*b*) on ordinal scale
(*c*) in ratios or proportions
(*d*) none of the above

15. Harmonic mean is better than other means if the data are for:
(*a*) speed or rates
(*b*) heights or lengths
(*c*) binary values like 0 and 1
(*d*) ratios or proportions

16. The correct relationship between A.M., G.M. and H.M. is:
(*a*) A.M. = G.M. = H.M.
(*b*) G.M. ≥ A.M. ≥ H.M.
(*c*) H.M. ≥ G.M. ≥ A.M.
(*d*) A.M. ≥ G.M. ≥ H.M.

17. Extreme value have no effect on:
(*a*) average
(*b*) median
(*c*) geometric mean
(*d*) harmonic mean

18. Geometric mean of two numbers $\frac{1}{16}$ and $\frac{4}{25}$ is:
(*a*) $\frac{1}{10}$
(*b*) $\frac{1}{100}$
(*c*) 10
(*d*) 100

19. Expenditure during first five months of a year is ₹ 96 per month and during last seven months is ₹ 120 per month. The average expenditure per month during whole year is:
(*a*) ₹ 108 per month
(*b*) ₹ 110 per month
(*c*) ₹ 100 per month
(*d*) ₹ 216 per month

20. Average strength of eleven members = 11.0. Average strength of the first six members = 10.5. Average strength of the last six members = 11.5.
The average strength of the sixth member is:
(*a*) 10.5
(*b*) 11.5
(*c*) 11.0
(*d*) 10.0

21. The average of the 7 numbers 7, 9, 12, *x*, 5, 4, 11 is 9. The missing number *x* is:
(*a*) 13
(*b*) 14
(*c*) 15
(*d*) 8

22. The mean proportion of 0.16 and 0.01 is:
(*a*) 0.4
(*b*) 0.17
(*c*) 0.085
(*d*) 0.04

23. A train covered the first 5 km of its journey at a speed of 30 km/h and next 15 km at a speed of 45 km/h. The average speed of the train was:
(*a*) 35 km/h
(*b*) 40 km/h
(*c*) 32 km/h
(*d*) 42 km/h

24. The second of the two samples has 50 item with mean 15. If the whole group has 150 items with mean 16, the mean of the first sample is:
(*a*) 18.0
(*b*) 15.5
(*c*) 16.5
(*d*) none of the above

25. For a group of 100 candidates, the mean was found to be 40. Later on it was discovered that a value 45 was misread as 54. The correct mean is:
(*a*) 40.50
(*b*) 39.85
(*c*) 39.80
(*d*) 39.91

26. A distribution consists of three groups having 40, 50 and 60 items with means 20, 26 and 15 respectively. The mean of the distribution is:
(*a*) 20
(*b*) 18

(*c*) 22
(*d*) 25

27. The average age of 50 students in a bus is 20 years. When the age of conductor is included, the average age is increased by one year. The age of the conductor is:
(*a*) 51
(*b*) 55
(*c*) 71
(*d*) 50

28. The average of five numbers is 40 and the average of another four numbers is 50. The average of all numbers taken together is:
(*a*) 44.44
(*b*) 45.00
(*c*) 45.55
(*d*) 90.00

29. The average temperature of two cities on first six days of a week is same. The temperature dropped in one city all of a sudden on the seventh day of the week. The average weekly temperature of the two cities differed by 0.5°C. The difference between the six days average daily temperature of two cities and the seventh day temperature of the other city is:
(*a*) 2.5
(*b*) 3.0
(*c*) 3.5
(*d*) 2.0

30. What percentage of values is greater than 3rd quartile?
(*a*) 75 per cent
(*b*) 50 per cent
(*c*) 25 per cent
(*d*) 0 per cent

31. What percentage of values is less than 3rd decile?
(*a*) 30 per cent
(*b*) 70 per cent
(*c*) 40 per cent
(*d*) none of the above

32. What percentage of values lies between 5th and 25th percentiles.
(*a*) 15 per cent
(*b*) 30 per cent
(*c*) 75 per cent
(*d*) none of the above

33. There were 25 teachers in a school whose mean age was 30 years. A teacher retired at the age of 60 years and a new teacher was appointed in his place. The mean age of teachers in the school was reduced by one year. The age of the new teacher was:
(*a*) 25 years
(*b*) 30 years
(*c*) 35 years
(*d*) 40 years

34. If the A.M. of a set of two observations is 9 and its G.M. is 6. Then the H.M. of the set of observations is:
(*a*) 4
(*b*) $3\sqrt{6}$
(*c*) 3
(*d*) 1.5

35. The A.M. of two numbers is 6.5 and their G.M. is 6. The two numbers are:
(*a*) 9, 6
(*b*) 9, 5
(*c*) 7, 6
(*d*) 4, 9

36. If M_d, Q, D and P stand for median, quartile, decile and percentile respectively, then which of the following relation between them is true?
(*a*) $M_d = Q_2 = D_6 = P_{50}$
(*b*) $M_d = Q_3 = D_5 = P_{75}$
(*c*) $M_d = Q_2 = D_4 = P_{50}$
(*d*) $M_d = Q_2 = D_5 = P_{50}$

37. Which of the following relation is true between 3rd decile and 30th percentile?
(*a*) $D_3 = P_{70}$
(*b*) $D_3 = P_{50}$
(*c*) $D_3 = P_{30}$
(*d*) $D_7 = P_{30}$

38. Which of the deciles are less than first quartile?
(*a*) D_1 and D_3

(*b*) D_1 and D_2
(*c*) D_2 and D_3
(*d*) None of the above

39. In a factory there are 60 per cent labourers. 30 per cent scribes and 10 per cent executives. On average, the salary of a labourer is ₹ 1600 p.m, of a scribe ₹ 3000 p.m and that of an executive ₹ 8000 p.m. The average salary of a employee in the factory is:
(*a*) ₹ 4200 p.m
(*b*) ₹ 1166 p.m
(*c*) ₹ 2660 p.m
(*d*) None of the three

40. The mean of seven observations is 8. A new observation 16 is added. The mean of eight observations is:
(*a*) 12
(*b*) 9
(*c*) 8
(*d*) 24

41. If the sum of N observations is 630 and their mean is 42, then the value of N is:
(*a*) 21
(*b*) 30
(*c*) 15
(*d*) 20

42. If the two observations are 10 and –10, then their harmonic mean is:
(*a*) 10
(*b*) 0
(*c*) 5
(*d*) ∞

43. If the observations are 5 and –5, their geometric mean is:
(*a*) 5
(*b*) –5
(*c*) 0
(*d*) none of the above

44. If the two observations are 20 and –20, their arithmetic mean is:
(*a*) 10
(*b*) 20
(*c*) 0
(*d*) none of the above

45. Can a quartile, a decile and a percentile be the median?
(*a*) Only quartile but not decile and percentile
(*b*) Quartile and decile but not percentile
(*c*) Decile and percentile but not quartile
(*d*) Quartile, decile and percentile, all the three

46. When all the observations are same, then the relation between A.M., G.M. and H.M. is:
(*a*) A.M. = G.M. = H.M.
(*b*) A.M. < G.M. < H.M.
(*c*) A.M. < H.M. < G.M.
(*d*) G.M. < A.M. < H.M.

47. The percentage of values used in case of 10 per cent trimmed mean is:
(*a*) 40 per cent
(*b*) 60 per cent
(*c*) 80 per cent
(*d*) 20 per cent

48. The average of $2n$ natural numbers from 1 to $2n$ is:
(*a*) $(n + 1)/2$
(*b*) $(2n + 1)/2$
(*c*) $n(n + 1)/2$
(*d*) $n(2n + 1)/2$

49. A man goes from his house to his office at the speed of 20 km/h and returns from his office to home at the speed of 30 km/h. His mean speed is:
(*a*) 24 km/h
(*b*) $10\sqrt{6}$ km/h
(*c*) 25 km/h
(*d*) none of the above

50. Mode is that value in a frequency distribution which possesses:
(*a*) minimum frequency
(*b*) maximum frequency
(*c*) frequency one
(*d*) none of the above

51. The value of the variable corresponding to the highest point of a frequency distribution curve represents:
(*a*) mean

(*b*) median
(*c*) mode
(*d*) none of the above

52. A frequency distribution having two modes is said to be:
(*a*) unimodal
(*b*) bimodal
(*c*) trimodal
(*d*) without mode

53. If modal value is not clear in a distribution, it can be ascertained by the method of:
(*a*) grouping
(*b*) guessing
(*c*) summarising
(*d*) trial and error

54. Shoe size of most of the people in India is No. 8. Which measure of central value does it represent?
(*a*) mean
(*b*) second quartile
(*c*) eighth decile
(*d*) mode

55. In a discrete series having $(2K + 1)$ observations, median is:
(*a*) K^{th} observation
(*b*) $(K + 1)^{th}$ observation
(*c*) $(K + 2)/2^{th}$ observation
(*d*) $(2K + 1)/2^{th}$ observation

56. The median of the variate values 11, 7, 6, 9, 12, 15, 19 is:
(*a*) 9
(*b*) 12
(*c*) 15
(*d*) 11

57. The median of the variate values 48, 35, 36, 40, 42, 54, 58, 60 is:
(*a*) 40
(*b*) 41
(*c*) 44
(*d*) 45

58. To find the median (mode), it is necessary to arrange the data in:
(*a*) ascending order
(*b*) descending order
(*c*) ascending or descending order
(*d*) any of the above

59. For a grouped data, the formula for median is based on:
(*a*) interpolation method
(*b*) extrapolation method
(*c*) trial and error method
(*d*) iterative method

60. Which of the measure of central tendency is not affected by extreme values?
(*a*) mode
(*b*) median
(*c*) sixth decile
(*d*) all of the above

61. The middle value of an ordered series is called:
(*a*) 2nd quartile
(*b*) 5th decile
(*c*) 50 percentile
(*d*) all of the above

62. Formula for directly calculating the mean $\bar{X}$ of an individual series is:

(*a*) $\bar{X} = \dfrac{\Sigma X}{N}$

(*b*) $\bar{X} = \dfrac{\Sigma fX}{N}$

(*c*) $\bar{X} = A + \dfrac{\Sigma dx}{n}$ where $dx = X - A$

(*d*) $\bar{X} = A + \dfrac{\Sigma dx}{N}$ where $dx - X - A$

63. Formula for calculating the mean of an individual series by short-cut method is:

(*a*) $\bar{X} = \dfrac{\Sigma X}{N}$

(*b*) $\bar{X} = \Sigma fX/N$

(*c*) $\bar{X} = A + \dfrac{\Sigma dx}{N}$

(*d*) $\bar{X} = A + \dfrac{\Sigma fdx}{N}$

64. Formula for calculating the mean of a discrete series by direct method is:

(*a*) $\bar{X} = \Sigma X / \Sigma f$

(*b*) $\bar{X} = \Sigma_i f_i X_i / \Sigma_i f_i$

(*c*) $\bar{X} = A + \Sigma_i f_i dx_i / \Sigma f_i$

(*d*) none of the above

65. Formula for calculating the mean of a discrete series by short-cut method is:

(*a*) $\bar{X} = \Sigma X / \Sigma f$

(*b*) $\bar{X} = \Sigma f_x / \Sigma f$

(*c*) $\bar{X} = A + \Sigma\, dx / \Sigma f$

(*d*) $\bar{X} = A + \dfrac{\Sigma f\, dx}{\Sigma f}$

66. ₹ 600 per day are paid on a research farm to its 50 daily paid labourers. A worker gets five unpaid holidays in a month. The average income of a daily paid labourer is:

(*a*) ₹ 250 p.m

(*b*) ₹ 300 p.m

(*c*) ₹ 350 p.m

(*d*) ₹ 400 p.m

67. The variate values which divide a series (frequency distribution) into five equal parts are called:

(*a*) quintiles

(*b*) quartiles

(*c*) octiles

(*d*) percentiles

68. The variate values which divide a series (frequency distribution) into four equal parts are called:

(*a*) quintiles

(*b*) quartiles

(*c*) deciles

(*d*) percentiles

69. The variate values which divide a series (frequency distribution) into ten equal parts are called:

(*a*) quartiles

(*b*) deciles

(*c*) octiles

(*d*) percentiles

70. The variate values which divide a series (frequency distribution) into 100 equal parts are known as:

(*a*) octiles

(*b*) quartiles

(*c*) percentiles

(*d*) deciles

71. The variate values which divide a series (frequency distribution) into eight equal parts are known as:

(*a*) quartiles

(*b*) quintiles

(*c*) deciles

(*d*) octiles

72. The number of partition values in case of quartiles is:

(*a*) 4

(*b*) 3

(*c*) 2

(*d*) 1

73. The number of partition values in case of quintiles cannot exceed:

(*a*) 4

(*b*) 3

(*c*) 2

(*d*) 1

74. For deciles, the total number of partition values are:

(*a*) 5

(*b*) 8

(*c*) 9

(*d*) 10

75. For percentiles, the total number of partition values are:

(*a*) 10

(*b*) 59

(*c*) 100

(*d*) 99

76. The second decile divides the series in the ratio:

(*a*) 1 : 1

(*b*) 1 : 2

(*c*) 1 : 4
(*d*) 2 : 5

77. Eightieth percentile divides a frequency distribution in the ratio:
(*a*) 4 : 1
(*b*) 4 : 5
(*c*) 3 : 1
(*d*) 3 : 2

78. The first quartile divides a frequency distribution in the ratio:
(*a*) 4 : 1
(*b*) 1 : 4
(*c*) 3 : 1
(*d*) 1 : 3

79. Fourth octile divides a frequency distribution in the ratio:
(*a*) 1 : 1
(*b*) 1 : 2
(*c*) 1 : 3
(*d*) 1 : 4

80. The first quartile is also known as:
(*a*) median
(*b*) lower quartile
(*c*) mode
(*d*) third decile

81. The third quartile is also called:
(*a*) lower quartile
(*b*) median
(*c*) mode
(*d*) upper quartile

82. In case of weighted mean, the accuracy or utility of the mean:
(*a*) decreases
(*b*) increases
(*c*) is unaffected
(*d*) none of the above

83. In certain situations weighted mean and unweighted mean can:
(*a*) be equal
(*b*) never be equal
(*c*) both (*a*) and (*b*)
(*d*) neither (*a*) and nor (*b*)

84. Weighted mean is more accurate if we use:
(*a*) estimated weights
(*b*) arbitrary weights
(*c*) real weights
(*d*) any of the above

85. If .3, .5, .8, .7, and 1.5 are the respective weights of the values 10, 15, 20, 25 and 30, then the weighted mean is:
(*a*) 20.0
(*b*) 23.42
(*c*) 16.58
(*d*) none of the above

86. If for a discrete series, the assumed mean $A = 50$, $\Sigma f\,dx = 45$ for $dx = x - A$, $\Sigma f = 12$, then the mean of the series is:
(*a*) 46.25
(*b*) 7.92
(*c*) 49.17
(*d*) 53.75

87. The mean of the following discrete series (frequency distribution),

x:	7	12	16	22	25
f:	4	5	8	3	2

is:
(*a*) 16.40
(*b*) 15.09
(*c*) 20.80
(*d*) none of the three

88. If for an individual series, assumed mean, $A = 25$, $\Sigma\, dx = -21$ for $dx = X - A$ and $N = 7$ then the mean of the series is:
(*a*) 20
(*b*) 21
(*c*) 22
(*d*) 6.57

89. Given the following less than type frequency distribution of income per month,

Income (₹) less than	*No. of persons*
1500	100
1250	80
1000	70
750	55
500	32
250	12

the median class of income is:
(*a*) 750–1000

(*b*) 1000–1250
(*c*) 250–500
(*d*) 500–750

90. For the distribution given in question 89, the modal class is:
(*a*) 250–500
(*b*) 500–750
(*c*) 750–1000
(*d*) none of the above

91. For the distribution given in question 89, the upper quartile class is:
(*a*) 500–750
(*b*) 750–1000
(*c*) 1000–1250
(*d*) 1250–1500

92. For the distribution given in question 89, the sixth decile class is:
(*a*) 500–750
(*b*) 750–1000
(*c*) 1000–1250
(*d*) 1250–1500

93. For the distribution given in question 89, 30th percentile class is:
(*a*) 250–500
(*b*) 500–750
(*c*) 750–1000
(*d*) none of the above

94. Given the following frequency distribution of income of employees,

Income ₹/month	*No. of employees*
0–250	12
250–500	20
500–750	23
750–1,000	15
1,000–1,250	10
1,250–1,500	20

The median income of employees is:
(*a*) 625.00
(*b*) 760.00
(*c*) 695.65
(*d*) none of the above

95. For the frequency distribution given is question 94, the mode of the distribution is:
(*a*) 23
(*b*) 666.66
(*c*) 513.33
(*d*) 568.18

96. For the grouped data given in question 94, the third quartile is:
(*a*) 1,200
(*b*) 1,125
(*c*) 1,183.33
(*d*) none of the above

97. Sixth decile of the continuous frequency distribution given in question 94 is:
(*a*) 833.33
(*b*) 1,000.00
(*c*) 70.00
(*d*) none of the above

98. 20th percentile of the grouped data given in question 94 is:
(*a*) 250
(*b*) 350
(*c*) 500
(*d*) 550

99. The more than type frequency distribution of age of the patients on a particular day in a hospital is as given below.

Age (years)	*No. of patients*
> 10	152
> 20	128
>30	113
> 40	77
> 50	36
> 60	22
> 70 and up to 80	5

the 50th percentile class is:
(*a*) 30–40
(*b*) 40–50
(*c*) 50–60
(*d*) none of the above

100. For the more than type distribution given in question 99, the modal class is:
(*a*) 30–40
(*b*) 40–50
(*c*) 50–60
(*d*) none of the above

101. For the more than type distribution given in question 99, the first quartile class is:
(*a*) 30–40
(*b*) 40–50
(*c*) 50–60
(*d*) none of the above

102. In the ascending series of question 99, fourth decile class is:
(*a*) 30–40
(*b*) 40–50
(*c*) 50–60
(*d*) none of the above

103. The mode of the more than type distribution given in question 99 is:
(*a*) 37.78
(*b*) 41.56
(*c*) 42.56
(*d*) none of the above

104. The median (second quartile) of the more than type distribution given in question 99 is:
(*a*) 37.33
(*b*) 40.00
(*c*) 40.24
(*d*) 50.00

105. The seventh decile of the cumulative distribution of question 99 is:
(*a*) 42.34
(*b*) 48.78
(*c*) 57.66
(*d*) 47.66

106. Thirtieth percentile of the more than type distribution of question 99 is:
(*a*) 31.83
(*b*) 53.50
(*c*) 30.88
(*d*) none of the above

107. The upper quartile of the distribution given in question 99 is:
(*a*) 50.00
(*b*) 49.51
(*c*) 45.00
(*d*) 41.00

108. If we plot the more than type and less than type frequency distributions of the same set of data, their graphs intersect at the point which is known as:
(*a*) median
(*b*) mode
(*c*) mean
(*d*) none of the above

109. Mean of a set of values is based on:
(*a*) all values
(*b*) 50 per cent values
(*c*) first and last value
(*d*) maximum and minimum value

110. Which mean is most affected by extreme values?
(*a*) Geometric mean
(*b*) Harmonic mean
(*c*) Arithmetic mean
(*d*) Trimmed mean

111. The measure of central value which cannot be calculated with open end classes in case of grouped data is:
(*a*) median
(*b*) arithmetic mean
(*c*) mode
(*d*) third quartile

112. Harmonic mean gives more weightage to:
(*a*) small values
(*b*) large values
(*c*) positive values
(*d*) negative values

113. Harmonic mean gives less weightage to:
(*a*) positive values
(*b*) negative values
(*c*) small values
(*d*) large values

114. For further algebraic treatment geometric mean is:
(*a*) suitable
(*b*) not suitable
(*c*) sometimes suitable
(*d*) none of the above

115. For further algebraic treatment harmonic mean is:
(*a*) suitable
(*b*) not suitable

(*c*) sometimes suitable
(*d*) none of the above

116. For a highly variable series, the most suitable mean is:
(*a*) arithmetic mean
(*b*) geometric mean
(*c*) harmonic mean
(*d*) none of the above

117. The percentage of values in a set of values which are less than (more than) the median value is:
(*a*) 100 per cent
(*b*) 75 per cent
(*c*) 50 per cent
(*d*) 25 per cent

118. The percentage of values of a set which is beyond the third quartile is:
(*a*) 100 per cent
(*b*) 75 per cent
(*c*) 50 per cent
(*d*) 25 per cent

119. The percentage of data of a set which are to the left of seventh decile is:
(*a*) 30 per cent
(*b*) 50 per cent
(*c*) 70 per cent
(*d*) 90 per cent

120. The percentage of data of a set which is to the right of ninetieth percentile is:
(*a*) 0 per cent
(*b*) 10 per cent
(*c*) 90 per cent
(*d*) 80 per cent

121. In a class test, 40 students out of 50 passed with mean marks 6.0 and the overall average of class marks was 5.5. The average marks of students who failed were:
(*a*) 2.5
(*b*) 3.0
(*c*) 4.8
(*d*) 3.5

122. Seven persons gambled sitting on a table. Four persons lost on an average ₹ 55 whereas the other three gained on an average ₹ 70. Is the information worth believing?
(*a*) Yes
(*b*) No
(*c*) Not certain
(*d*) None of the above

123. The average marks of section A are 65 and that of section B are 70. The average of both the sections combined is 67. The ratio of number of students of sections A to B is:
(*a*) 1 : 3
(*b*) 2 : 3
(*c*) 3 : 1
(*d*) 3 : 2

124. The partition value which divide a series into two equal parts is known as:
(*a*) second quartile
(*b*) third quintile
(*c*) fourth octile
(*d*) sixth deciles

125. In a distribution, the value around which the items tend to be most heavily concentrated is called:
(*a*) mean
(*b*) median
(*c*) third quartile
(*d*) mode

126. Geometric mean can be used to find out:
(*a*) population growth
(*b*) growth rate of GNP
(*c*) both the above
(*d*) none of (*a*) and (*b*)

127. Formula for the combined geometric mean 'GM_{12}' of two series of sizes n_1 and n_2 and their G.M.'s GM_1 and GM_2 respectively is:

(*a*) $GM_{12} = \dfrac{n_1 \log GM_1 + n_2 \log GM_2}{n_1 + n_2}$

(*b*) $GM_{12} = \dfrac{n_1 \times GM_1 + n_2 \times GM_2}{n_1 + n_2}$

(*c*) $GM_{12} = \dfrac{GM_1 \log n_1 + GM_2 \log n_2}{n_1 + n_2}$

(*d*) $GM_{12} = \text{Antilog}\left(\dfrac{n_1 \log GM_1 + n_2 \log GM_2}{n_1 + n_2}\right)$

128. Sum of the deviations about mean is:
(*a*) zero
(*b*) minimum
(*c*) maximum
(*d*) one

129. Sum of the absolute deviations about median is:
(*a*) zero
(*b*) maximum
(*c*) minimum
(*d*) one

130. Sum of square of the deviations about mean is:
(*a*) maximum
(*b*) minimum
(*c*) zero
(*d*) none of the above

131. Histogram is useful to determine graphically the value of:
(*a*) mean
(*b*) median
(*c*) mode
(*d*) all of the above

132. Graphically partition values can be determined with the help of:
(*a*) frequency polygon
(*b*) bar diagram
(*c*) line diagram
(*d*) ogive curve

133. The suitable measure of central tendency for qualitative data is:
(*a*) mode
(*b*) arithmetic mean
(*c*) geometric mean
(*d*) median

134. Two series having the same mean, median and mode may:
(*a*) have same values
(*b*) not have same values
(*c*) both (*a*) and (*b*)
(*d*) none of (*a*) and (*b*)

135. Weighted mean gives a higher value than unweighted mean if:
(*a*) all the items have equal weights
(*b*) larger items have higher weights and small items have lower weights.
(*c*) larger items have lower weights and smaller items have higher weights
(*d*) none of the above

136. In a frequency distribution with open ends, one cannot find out:
(*a*) mean
(*b*) median
(*c*) mode
(*d*) all of the above

137. The average of n observations $x_1, x_2, ... x_n$ is M. If x_1 is replaced by x', then the new average is:
(*a*) $M - x_1 + x'$
(*b*) $\frac{M - x_1 x'}{n}$
(*c*) $\frac{(n-1)M - x_1 + x'}{n}$
(*d*) $\frac{nM - x_1 + x'}{n}$

138. In case of 15 per cent trimmed mean, the percentage of observations utilised is:
(*a*) 15 per cent
(*b*) 30 per cent
(*c*) 85 per cent
(*d*) none of the above

139. If for values of X, A.M. = 25, H.M. = 9, then the G.M. is:
(*a*) 17
(*b*) 15
(*c*) 5.83
(*d*) 16

140. The second quartile of the following set of data, 0, 1, –1, –2, 6, 4, 5, 8, 12, 10, 11 is:
(*a*) 4
(*b*) 5
(*c*) 6
(*d*) 8

141. The measure of central tendency which remains unaltered by extreme observations is:
(*a*) mean
(*b*) mode

(*c*) harmonic mean

(*d*) geometric mean

142. The mean of the squares of first eleven natural numbers is:

(*a*) 46

(*b*) 23

(*c*) 48

(*d*) 42

143. The point of intersection of two cumulative frequency curves provides:

(*a*) mean

(*b*) mode

(*c*) median

(*d*) first quartile

144. The percentage of items in a frequency distribution lying between upper and lower quartiles is:

(*a*) 80 per cent

(*b*) 40 per cent

(*c*) 50 per cent

(*d*) 25 per cent

145. A person has been deputed to find the average income of factory employees. To provide a correct picture of average income, he should find out:

(*a*) geometric mean

(*b*) weighted mean

(*c*) progressive mean

(*d*) arithmetic mean.

146. To know the trend of a time series data, preferable type of average is:

(*a*) progressive average

(*b*) moving average

(*c*) weighted mean

(*d*) quadratic mean.

147. If we know the mean values and number of units of various groups, then one mean value for all the groups can be obtained by finding out:

(*a*) geometric mean

(*b*) weighted mean

(*c*) pooled mean

(*d*) progressive mean

148. In a frequency distribution of a large number of values, the mode is:

(*a*) largest observation

(*b*) smallest value

(*c*) observation with maximum frequency

(*d*) maximum frequency of an observation

149. The relation between quadratic mean (Q.M.) and arithmetic mean (A.M.) is:

(*a*) Q.M. = A.M.

(*b*) Q.M. > A.M.

(*c*) Q.M. < A.M.

(*d*) Q.M. ≠ A.M.

150. A set of values contains a few negative values. The average of set can better be measured by:

(*a*) arithmetic mean

(*b*) geometric mean

(*c*) progressive mean

(*d*) quadratic mean

151. If $y = 3x + 6$ and mode of y is 66, then the mode of x is:

(*a*) 66

(*b*) 21

(*c*) 60

(*d*) 204

152. If $y = 2x - 11$ and median of y is 49, then the median of x is:

(*a*) 87

(*b*) 60

(*c*) 30

(*d*) 49

153. The geometric mean of 3, 6, 24, 48 is:

(*a*) 12

(*b*) 18

(*c*) 20

(*d*) 16

ANSWERS

Section B

1. John I. Griffin **2.** R.A. Fisher **3.** A.L. Bowley **4.** typical value, summary measure **5.** extreme values **6.** variate **7.** summarises **8.** mean **9.** 5 **10.** $\frac{1}{10}$th **11.** 13 **12.** 16 **13.** zero **14.** ₹ 65 **15.** ₹ 27 **16.** accurate **17.** 70 **18.** $(n + 1)/2$ **19.** minimum **20.** 8 **21.** Antilog (G_1/G_2) **22.** zero **23.** ratio; proportions **24.** 4 **25.** 5 **26.** average speed **27.** infinity **28.** G.M. $= \sqrt{\text{A.M.} \times \text{H.M.}}$ **29.** median **30.** minimum **31.** 12 **32.** unique **33.** median **34.** open end **35.** mode **36.** 7 **37.** Median; mode **38.** mode **39.** Mode **40.** unimodal **41.** bimodal **42.** grouping **43.** Quartile **44.** median **45.** 75th **46.** fifth **47.** D_7 **48.** 26 per cent **49.** lower or first **50.** 60th **51.** 50 percent **52.** 34 per cent **53.** 40th **54.** $Q_2 < D_6 < P_{80}$ **55.** fifth **56.** fiftieth **57.** ascending **58.** quintiles **59.** P_{80} **60.** third **61.** first; twenty-fifth **62.** fractiles **63.** Ya Lun Chou **64.** $Q_1 = P_{25}$ **65.** $D_4 < P_{45}$ **66.** 75 per cent **67.** numerical; analytical **68.** $(Q_1 + Q_3)/2$ **69.** antilog **70.** reciprocal **71.** negative **72.** H.M. ≤ G.M. ≤ A.M. **73.** same **74.** standard deviation **75.** 26 **76.** 7 **77.** 21 **78.** entire data **79.** best **80.** not rigidly.

Section C

1. (*a*) **2.** (*a*) **3.** (*b*) **4.** (*b*) **5.** (*a*)
6. (*b*) **7.** (*b*) **8.** (*c*) **9.** (*c*) **10.** (*d*)
11. (*c*) **12.** (*a*) **13.** (*b*) **14.** (*c*) **15.** (*a*)
16. (*d*) **17.** (*b*) **18.** (*a*) **19.** (*b*) **20.** (*c*)
21. (*c*) **22.** (*d*) **23.** (*b*) **24.** (*c*) **25.** (*d*)
26. (*a*) **27.** (*c*) **28.** (*a*) **29.** (*a*) **30.** (*c*)
31. (*a*) **32.** (*d*) **33.** (*c*) **34.** (*a*) **35.** (*b*)
36. (*d*) **37.** (*c*) **38.** (*b*) **39.** (*c*) **40.** (*b*)
41. (*c*) **42.** (*d*) **43.** (*d*) **44.** (*c*) **45.** (*d*)
46. (*a*) **47.** (*c*) **48.** (*b*) **49.** (*a*) **50.** (*b*)
51. (*c*) **52.** (*b*) **53.** (*a*) **54.** (*d*) **55.** (*b*)
56. (*d*) **57.** (*d*) **58.** (*d*) **59.** (*a*) **60.** (*d*)
61. (*d*) **62.** (*a*) **63.** (*c*) **64.** (*b*) **65.** (*d*)
66. (*b*) **67.** (*a*) **68.** (*b*) **69.** (*b*) **70.** (*c*)
71. (*d*) **72.** (*b*) **73.** (*a*) **74.** (*c*) **75.** (*d*)
76. (*c*) **77.** (*a*) **78.** (*d*) **79.** (*a*) **80.** (*b*)
81. (*d*) **82.** (*b*) **83.** (*a*) **84.** (*c*) **85.** (*b*)
86. (*d*) **87.** (*b*) **88.** (*c*) **89.** (*d*) **90.** (*b*)
91. (*c*) **92.** (*b*) **93.** (*a*) **94.** (*c*) **95.** (*d*)
96. (*b*) **97.** (*a*) **98.** (*b*) **99.** (*b*) **100.** (*b*)
101. (*d*) **102.** (*a*) **103.** (*d*) **104.** (*c*) **105.** (*d*)
106. (*a*) **107.** (*b*) **108.** (*a*) **109.** (*a*) **110.** (*c*)
111. (*b*) **112.** (*a*) **113.** (*d*) **114.** (*b*) **115.** (*b*)
116. (*c*) **117.** (*c*) **118.** (*d*) **119.** (*c*) **120.** (*b*)
121. (*d*) **122.** (*b*) **123.** (*d*) **124.** (*a*) **125.** (*d*)
126. (*c*) **127.** (*d*) **128.** (*a*) **129.** (*c*) **130.** (*b*)
131. (*c*) **132.** (*d*) **133.** (*d*) **134.** (*c*) **135.** (*b*)
136. (*a*) **137.** (*d*) **138.** (*d*) **139.** (*b*) **140.** (*b*)
141. (*b*) **142.** (*a*) **143.** (*c*) **144.** (*c*) **145.** (*b*)
146. (*b*) **147.** (*c*) **148.** (*c*) **149.** (*b*) **150.** (*d*)
151. (*b*) **152.** (*c*) **153.** (*a*).

SUGGESTED READING

1. Agarwal, B.L., *Basic Statistics*, New Age International Publishers, New Delhi, 8th edition, 2024.
2. Freud, J.E., *Modern Elementary Statistics*, Prentice-Hall of India, New Delhi, 1981.
3. Goon, A.M., Gupta, M.K. and Dasgupta, B., *Fundamentals of Statistics*, Vol. I, the World Press, Calcutta, 1977.
4. Gupta, S.C. and Kapoor, V.K., *Fundamentals of Mathematical Statistics*, Sultan Chand & Sons, New Delhi, 8th edition, 1983.
5. Hoel, P.G. and Jessen, R.J., *Basic Statistics for Business and Economics*, John Wiley, New York, 1982.
6. Joseph, F. Healey, *Statistics*, Thomson Wadsworth, 2004.
7. Meter, J., Wasserman, W. and Whitmore, G.A., *Applied Statistics*, Allyn and Bacon, London, 1982.
8. Ostle, B., *Statistics in Research*, Oxford & IBH, Calcutta, 1966.
9. Sellers, G.R. and Vardeman, S.B., *Elementary Statistics*, Saunders College Publishing, New York, 1982.
10. Wine, L.R., *Beginning Statistics*, Winthop Publishers, Cambridge, 1976.

CHAPTER 5

Measures of Dispersion, Skewness and Kurtosis

SECTION A

Short Essay Type Questions

Q. 1. *What do you understand by dispersion of a set of values?*

Ans. Experience tells that in many situations, the spread of values is different but their central values are same. All the more, a central value provides no information about the scattering of values in a set of data. Hence, certain measures are evolved which reflect on the scattering of values in numerical terms are known as measures of dispersion.

Q. 2. *Quote the statements about the term dispersion given by (i) Reigleman, (ii) W.I. King, (iii) Spiegel, (iv) B.C. Brookes and W.F.L. Dick, (v) A.L. Bowley.*

Ans. The statements given by various workers are as follows:

(*i*) **Reigleman:** Dispersion is the extent to which the magnitude or qualities of the items differ, that is the degree of diversity.

(*ii*) **W.I. King:** The term dispersion is used to indicate the facts that within a given group, the items differ from another in size or in other words there is a lack of uniformity in their size.

(*iii*) **Spiegel:** The degree to which numerical data tend to spread about an average value is called the variation or dispersion of data.

(*iv*) **B.C. Brookes and W.F.L. Dick:** Dispersion or spread is the degree of the scatter or variation of the variable about a central value.

(*v*) **A.L. Bowley:** Dispersion is the measure of the variation of the items.

Q. 3. *Name different measures of dispersion.*

Ans. Following are the different measures of dispersion:

(*i*) Range, (*ii*) Interquartile range and quartile deviation, (*iii*) Mean deviation, (*iv*) Median absolute deviation, (*v*) Variance (*vi*) Standard deviation, and (*vii*) Coefficient of variation.

Q. 4. *In what manner, John I. Griffin, C.T. Clark and L.L. Schkade defined measures of dispersion.*

Ans. The definitions given by the statisticians named in the question are as given below:

John I. Griffin: A measure of variation or dispersion describes the degree of scatter shown by the observations and is usually measured as an average deviation about some central value or by any order statistic.

Clark and Schkade: Measures of dispersion are measures of scatter about an average.

Q. 5. *What are requisites of a good measure of dispersion?*

Ans. Main requisites of an ideal measure of dispersion can be given as follows:

(*i*) It should be based on all the observations.

(*ii*) Its unit should be same as the unit of measurement of items.

(*iii*) It should be rigidly defined.

(*iv*) It should follow general rules of mathematics.

(*v*) It should not be subjected to complicated and tedious calculations.

Q. 6. *What are the uses of dispersion?*

Ans. Main uses of dispersion are:

(*i*) It tells about the reliability of a measure of central value.

(*ii*) It makes possible to compare two series of data in respect of their variability.

(*iii*) Measure of dispersion provides the basis for the control of variability.

(*iv*) It has a wide application in almost all fields of statistics.

Q. 7. *Define range.*

Ans. The difference between the largest and smallest values of a set of data is called its range. Range is shown as lowest value – largest value.

Q. 8. *Give the merits of range.*

Ans. Merits of range are:

(*i*) It is the easiest measure of dispersion.

(*ii*) It can always be found out visually *i.e.*, it involves no calculations.

(*iii*) It is one of the largely used measure of dispersion.

Q. 9. *Give demerits of range.*

Ans. Demerits of range are:

(*i*) It depends on two extreme values of a series. Thus, it gives no information about the observations lying between smallest and largest values.

(*ii*) It is highly susceptible to sampling fluctuations.

(*iii*) It is not suitable for further mathematical treatment.

(*iv*) Addition or deletion of a single value may change the entire complex of range.

Q. 10. *Define coefficient of range.*

Ans. It is a pure number given as the ratio of difference between the largest and smallest values to the sum of the largest and smallest values of a set of data. Numerically, coefficient of range is $(L - S)/(L + S)$. Lesser the coefficient of range, better it is.

Q. 11. *Express interquartile (I.Q.) range.*

Ans. It is equal to the difference between the upper and lower quartiles. Symbolically, it is equal to $(Q_3 - Q_1)$. This measure of dispersion tells about the range of the middle 50 per cent values of a set of data. In this measure, lower 25 per cent and upper 25 per cent values are excluded. It is not a good measure of dispersion as it tells nothing about the dispersion of values around average. It hardly fulfils any of the requisites of a good measure of dispersion.

Q. 12. *Define percentile range.*

Ans. The difference between 90th percentile (P_{90}) and 10th percentile (P_{10}) is called percentile range. It is denoted as $P_{90} - P_{10}$. Its value is same as $D_9 - D_1$ where D_9 and D_1 denote 9th and 1st deciles. This measure is more useful in education.

Q. 13. *Define quartile deviation (Q.D.) and give its important features.*

Ans. It is half of the interquartile range, *i.e.*, $(Q_3 - Q_1)/2$. It is an absolute measure of dispersion. Hence, to compare two series, a relative measure known as coefficient of quartile deviation is given which is symbolically expressed as $(Q_3 - Q_1)/(Q_3 + Q_1)$.

Q. 14. *For a symmetrical distribution, how can one determine the upper and lower quartiles with the help of quartile deviation?*

Ans. For a symmetrical distribution, the upper and lower quartiles can be determined by the formula $(Q_2 + Q.D.)$ and $(Q_2 - Q.D.)$ respectively.

Q. 15. *What are the good points of quartile deviation?*

Ans. Following are the good points of quartile deviation:

(*i*) It is easy to calculate and understand.

(*ii*) It can be calculated in case of open end frequency distributions as well.

(*iii*) It is not affected by 25 per cent upper and 25 per cent lower extreme values.

Q. 16. *Throw light on mean deviation (M.D.).*

Ans. Range and quartile deviations are positional measures of dispersion, whereas, mean deviation is a measure of dispersion which is based on all values of a set of data. It is defined as the average of the absolute deviations taken from an average usually, the mean, median or mode. It is denoted by δ. To clarify whether the average used in mean deviation is mean, median or mode, a suffix is attached to δ such as δ_{M}, δ_{Md} or δ_{Mo}.

The formula for calculating mean deviation of n observations $X_1, X_2, ..., X_n$ is,

$$\delta = \frac{1}{n}\sum_i |X_i - A|$$

for $\quad i = 1, 2, ..., n$

Also A may be any chosen constant out of mean, median and mode.

For a frequency distribution in which the variate value x_i occurs f_i times ($i = 1, 2, ..., k$), the formula for mean deviation is,

$$\delta = \frac{1}{n}\sum_i f_i |X_i - A|$$

where $\sum_i f_i = n$ and A as defined above.

Here, it is worth emphasizing that mean deviation is minimum about the median. That is why median is commonly used as an average value about which the mean deviation is calculated.

Q. 17. *Discuss coefficient of mean deviation.*

Ans. Mean deviation has the same unit of measurement as that of the variable x. If two series have different units of measurement, the series cannot be compared. Hence, for comparing any two series, a unitless measure is given known as *coefficient of mean deviation.* It is the ratio of mean deviation to the average 'A' used in calculating it. Its formula is,

$$\text{Coeff. of M.D.} = \frac{\text{Mean deviation}}{A} \times 100$$

It is multiplied by 100 to express coefficient of mean deviation in percentage.

Q. 18. *Write the merits of mean deviation.*

Ans. Following are the merits of mean deviation:

1. It utilizes all the observations of the set.
2. It is simple to calculate and understand.
3. It is least affected by extreme values.

Q. 19. *Mention the demerits of mean deviation.*

Ans. Following are the demerits of mean deviation:

1. The foremost weakness of mean deviation is that in its calculation negative differences are considered positive without any sound reasoning.
2. It is not amenable to further algebraic treatment.
3. It cannot be calculated in case of open end(s) frequency distribution.

Q. 20. *Define and discuss variance.*

Ans. The average of the square of the deviations taken from mean is called variance. The population variance is generally denoted by σ^2 and its estimate (sample variance) by s^2. For N population values $X_1, X_2, ..., X_N$ having the population mean μ, the population variance,

$$\sigma^2 = \frac{1}{N}\sum_i (X_i - \mu)^2$$

for $\quad i = 1, 2, ..., N$

where $\quad \mu = \Sigma_i X_i / N$

An estimate of σ^2 based on n sample values $x_1, x_2, ..., x_n$, the sample variance,

$$s^2 = \frac{1}{n-1}\sum_i (x_i - \bar{x})^2$$

for $\quad i = 1, 2, ..., n$

and $\quad \bar{x} = \Sigma_i x_i / n.$

For a frequency distribution of sample values $x_1, x_2, ..., x_k$ having frequencies $f_1, f_2, ..., f_k$ respectively. The sample variance,

$$s^2 = \frac{1}{n-1}\sum_i f_i (x_i - \bar{x})^2$$

$$= \frac{1}{n-1}\left\{\sum_i f_i x_i^2 - \frac{(\sum_i f_i x_i)^2}{n}\right\}$$

where $\quad n = \sum_i f_i \quad$ for $i = 1, 2, ..., k$

Q. 21. *Discuss merits and demerits of variance.*

Ans. It possesses all the requisites of a good measure of dispersion except that its unit is square of the unit of measurement of variate values. Hence, many times it becomes difficult to actually adjudge the magnitude of variation. Also variance is sensitive to extreme values. Variance is the backbone of statistics.

Q. 22. *Mean deviation is minimum while taking the deviations from median. Then why do we take sum of square of deviations from mean while calculating the variance?*

Ans. Deviations from mean are used for variance because sum of squares of deviations from mean is minimum.

Q. 23. *How does variance is affected by the change of origin and scale?*

Ans. Variance is independent of change of origin, but is affected by the change of scale. If each observation of a data set is multiplied by c, then the variance of new data set, is c^2 times the variance of original data.

Q. 24. *What is the difference between absolute and relative dispersion?*

Ans. If the unit of a measure of dispersion is in same terms as that of the observations of a series, it is called *absolute measure of dispersion,* e.g., height in cm, weight in kg., income in rupees, etc. In this case two series, having different units of dispersion, cannot be compared. Hence, for comparison of two series having different units of measurement, one requires an unit less measure of dispersion. Such measures are termed as *relative measures or coefficient of* dispersion. For this, a measure of dispersion is usually divided by mean used in its calculation and multiplied by 100. This provides the measure expressed in percentage which is fit for comparison of any two or more series.

Q. 25. *Define and describe in brief standard deviation.*

Ans. The positive square root of the variance is called standard deviation. The idea of standard deviation was first given by Karl Pearson in 1893.

Symbolically,

$$\sigma = \sqrt{\sigma^2}$$

and $\quad s = \sqrt{s^2}$

It fulfils all the requisites of a good measure of dispersion except that it is sensitive to extreme values. That is why it is known as standard deviation.

Q. 26. *Explain median absolute deviation (MAD).*

Ans. Standard deviation is affected by extreme values. Hence, the median absolute deviation is an alternative measure of dispersion. Median absolute deviation is defined as the median of the absolute deviation taken from median. It is seldom used as it is not easily amenable to further algebraic treatment. Moreover, it is not involved in distribution function. The formula for median absolute deviation is,

$$\text{MAD} = \text{Median}\ | X_i - X_{M_d} |$$

Q. 27. *Comment on the variances of median and sample mean based on a sample of size n from a normal population having variance σ^2.*

Ans. Variance of sample median for samples of size n from a normal population is $\pi\ \sigma^2/2n$ which is greater than the variance of sample mean $\bar{x}$ which is equal to σ^2/n.

Q. 28. *How variability is indicated by a measure of dispersion?*

Ans. Lesser the value of a measure of dispersion, more is the degree of nearness of observations. It is also an indicator of homogeneity of values of a series.

Q. 29. *What are the different names given to standard deviation?*

Ans. Standard deviation is also known as *mean error, mean square error or root mean square deviation from mean.*

Q. 30. *What is the effect of adding or subtracting a constant 'c' from each observation of a set on variance or standard deviation?*

Ans. The variance or standard deviation remains the same as they are independent of change of origin.

Q. 31. *Standard deviation is equivalent to what type of mean?*

Ans. As a matter of fact, standard deviation is nothing but the quadratic mean of the deviations from data mean.

Q. 32. *Why are mean deviation (M.D.) and standard deviation (S.D.) not calculated using the same average?*

Ans: Mean deviations and standard deviation are not calculated using the same average because M.D. is minimum when the deviations are taken from median whereas mean square deviation is least when deviations are measured from mean.

Q. 33. *Give the formula for standard deviation of a population of first n natural numbers.*

Ans. The formula for standard deviation (σ) of first n natural numbers is

$$\sigma = \sqrt{\frac{1}{12}(n^2 - 1)}$$

Q. 34. *How is variance affected if each observation of a set is divided by a constant 'd'?*

Ans. The variance of the new set of values will be $\frac{1}{d^2}$ times the original value of variance.

Q. 35. *How is variance affected if each observation of a set is multiplied by 'd'?*

Ans. The variance of the transformed set of values will be d^2 times the variance of the original set of values.

Q. 36. *What is coefficient of variation and its importance?*

Ans. Coefficient of variation (C.V.) is the ratio of the standard deviation and the mean. Usually it is expressed in percentage. The formula for coefficient of variation is,

$$\text{C.V.} = \frac{\text{S.D.}}{\text{mean}} \times 100$$

It is a relative measure and is most suitable to compare any two series. As we know, the size of measure of dispersion also depends on the size of measurement. Hence, it is very appropriate measure of dispersion to compare two series which differ largely in respect of their means. All the more, a series or a set of values having lesser coefficient of variation as compared to the other is more consistent.

Q. 37. *How can the variance of two groups or series of data can be combined (pooled)?*

Ans. Suppose σ_1^2, σ_2^2; $\bar{X}_1$, $\bar{X}_2$ and N_1, N_2 are the variances, means and sizes of two groups of values respectively. Also let $\bar{X}_{12}$ be their combined mean. The combined variance of two groups is given by the formula.

$$\sigma_{12}^2 = \frac{N_1\{\sigma_1^2 + (\bar{X}_1 - \bar{X}_{12})^2\} + N_2\{\sigma_2^2 + (\bar{X}_2 - \bar{X}_{12})^2\}}{N_1 + N_2}$$

$$= \frac{N_1(\sigma_1^2 + d_1^2) + N_2(\sigma_2^2 + d_2^2)}{N_1 + N_2}$$

where, $\bar{X}_1 - \bar{X}_{12} = d_1$ and $\bar{X}_2 - \bar{X}_{12} = d_2$. The formula for combined variance can be extended to any number of groups.

Q. 38. *What is the advantage of combined variance?*

Ans. Many times we know the means and variances of individual series or groups of data of known sizes. Then for some statistical analysis, their pooled variance is required. By the formula for pooled variance, it can easily be obtained without original data. Also a lot of time and labour is saved.

Q. 39. *Define and discuss moments in brief.*

Ans. r^{th} moment may be defined as the average of the rth exponent of the deviations of the variate values of a series about mean, r^{th} moment about an arbitrary mean 'a' is given as

$$\mu_r = E\,(x - a)^r$$

for $r = 1, 2, ..., r$

where, E stands for expectation. Mathematical expectation has been discussed in Chapter 7. Read it from there. For a series having N values X_1, X_2, ..., X_N, the rth moment about an arbitrary origin 'a' is given as.

$$\mu_r^a = \frac{1}{N}\sum(X_i - a)^r$$

for $i = 1, 2, ..., N$.

If $a = 0$, the moment is known as r^{th} raw (simple) moment and is given as

$$\mu'_r = \frac{1}{N}\sum X_i^r$$

Again, if $a = \mu$, the rth moment is known as central (absolute) moment and its formula is,

$$\mu_r = \frac{1}{N}\sum(x_i - \mu)^r$$

It is interesting to reveal that an algebraic relation between μ_r^a, μ'_r and μ_r can easily be established. It helps in determining one when others are known.

Q. 40. *What are the uses and importance of moments?*

Ans. Each frequency distribution is specified by its moments especially the first and second moments. They also help in determining the shape of a distribution since skewness and kurtosis are usually measured with the help of moments. Mean and variance are nothing but first and second moments respectively. In practice, moments of order higher than fourth are rarely required.

Q. 41. *What is known as probable error?*

Ans. Two-thirds of the standard deviation is known as probable error. It is also equal to quartile deviation. Symbolically,

$$\text{P.E.} = \frac{2}{3}\sigma$$

$$= \text{Q.D.}$$

Q. 42. *What does empirical relations exist between quartile deviation, mean deviation and standard deviation?*

Ans. Relation between Q.D., M.D. and S.D. is,

$$\text{Q.D.} = \frac{5}{6}\text{M.D.} = \frac{2}{3}\text{S.D.}$$

or $\quad 6 \text{ Q.D.} = 5 \text{ M.D.} = 4 \text{ S.D.}$

Q. 43. *Give an empirical relation between range, standard deviation, quartile deviation and mean deviation.*

Ans. The empirical relation between range, standard deviation, quartile deviation and mean deviation is as follows:

$$R = 6 \text{ S.D.} = 9 \text{ Q.D.} = \frac{15}{2}\text{M.D.}$$

Q. 44. *Give relations of the first four central moments with the raw moments.*

Ans. The relations of the first four moments μ_1, μ_2, μ_3 and μ_4 with the raw moments μ'_1, μ'_2, μ'_3 and μ'_4 are:

$$\mu_1 = 0$$

$$\mu_2 = \mu'_2 - \mu'^2_1$$

$$\mu_3 = \mu'_3 - 3\mu'_2\,\mu'_1 + 2\mu'^3_1$$

$$\mu_4 = \mu'_4 - 4\mu'_3\,\mu'_1 + 6\mu'_2\,\mu'^2_2 - 3\mu'^4_1$$

Q. 45. *Write the relations of the first four moments about the arbitrary mean 'a' and raw moments.*

Ans. Four moments about the arbitrary mean 'a' *i.e.*, in terms of raw moments can be expressed as:

$$\mu_1^a = \mu'_1 - a = \mu - a$$

$$\mu_2^a = \mu'_2 - 2a\,\mu'_1 + a^2$$

$$\mu_3^a = \mu'_3 - 3a\,\mu'_2 + 3a^2\,\mu'_1 - a^3$$

$$\mu_4^a = \mu'_4 - 4a\,\mu'_3 + 6a^2\,\mu'_2 - 4a^3\,\mu'_1 + a^4$$

Q. 46. *What will be the effect of coding (change of origin and scale) of data on moments?*

Ans. Let a constant value c is subtracted from each variate value and then divided by h, *i.e.*, the coded value $d = \frac{X - c}{h}$. Then, the raw moments can be determined by the following relations:

$$\mu'_1 = \left(\frac{1}{N}\sum_i f_i d_i\right) \times h$$

$$\mu'_2 = \left(\frac{1}{N}\sum_i f_i d_i^2\right) \times h^2$$

$$\mu'_3 = \left(\frac{1}{N}\sum_i f_i d_i^3\right) \times h^3$$

$$\mu'_4 = \left(\frac{1}{N}\sum_i f_i d_i^4\right) \times h^4$$

where, there exists k variate values $X_1, X_2, ..., X_k$ having frequencies $f_1, f_2, ..., f_k$ respectively and for $i = 1, 2 ..., k$. Also $\Sigma f_i = N$.

The relations show that there is no effect of change of origin on the moments but the scale factor appears in multiplication if each value after subtracting c is divided by h. Once we know the raw moments, we can find the central moments using the relations between two types of moments.

Q. 47. *What are the special advantages of standard deviation?*

Ans. The special advantages of standard deviation are:

(*i*) Standard deviation carries great importance in sampling methods.

(*ii*) It is least sensitive to sampling fluctuations.

(*iii*) With the help of standard deviation, it is possible to ascertain the area under the normal curve.

(*iv*) It has great utility in testing of hypotheses which other measures of dispersion hardly do.

Q. 48. *What is meant by skewness?*

Ans. Lack of symmetry of tails (about mean) of a frequency distribution curve is known as skewness. Symmetry of tails means that the frequency of the points at equal distances on both sides of the centre of the curve on X-axis is same. Also, the area under the curve at equidistant intervals on both sides of the centre is also equal. Departure from symmetry leads to skewness. It is adjudged by the elongation of the right and left tails of the curve.

Q. 49. *What is positive and negative skewness?*

Ans. If the left tail of the frequency curve is more elongated than right tail, it is known as negative skewness and a reverse situation leads to positive skewness.

Q. 50. *What purpose is served by measuring skewness?*

Ans. Measure of skewness indicates to what extent and in what direction the distribution of a variable differs from symmetry of a frequency curve. The curve may have positive or negative skewness. Both positive and negative skewness can never occur simultaneously.

Q. 51. *What changes occur in the position of mean, median and mode in case of positive and negative skewness?*

Ans. In a negative skew curve, the mean and median are pulled to the left whereas in a positive skew curve, the mean and median are pulled to the right. Also it should be kept in mind that median always lies in between mean and mode.

Q. 52. *How can we know about skewness?*

Ans. Skewness can be known by two methods given below:

(*i*) Graphically

(*ii*) By mathematical measures.

Q. 53. *Describe graphical method of detecting skewness.*

Ans. Draw a frequency curve by plotting the points for variate values and corresponding frequencies. Judge by naked eyes whether the tails of the curve are symmetrical or not. If not symmetrical, the curve is skew. Positive skewness depends whether the right tail is more elongated than left tail. For negative skewness, a reverse situation exists.

Graphical method is just enough to know about

skewness. But it does not give the idea about the extent of skewness. Further slight skewness cannot be detected by naked eyes.

Q. 54. *Give different formulae for measuring skewness α_3.*

Ans. Different formulae for measuring skewness are:

(*i*) Bowley's formula for measuring skewness in terms of quartiles is:

$$\alpha_3 = \frac{Q_3 + Q_1 - 2Q_2}{Q_3 - Q_1}$$

In many books measure of skewness is denoted by J or S_k.

(*ii*) Kelley gave the formula in terms of percentiles and deciles.

Kelley's absolute measures of skewness are,

$$S_k = P_{90} + P_{10} - 2P_{50}$$
$$= D_9 + D_1 - 2D_5$$

These formulae are not practically used. Instead, it is measured as coefficient of skewness which is given as,

$$S_k = \frac{P_{90} + P_{10} - 2P_{50}}{P_{90} - P_{10}}$$
$$= \frac{D_9 + D_1 - 2D_5}{D_9 - D_1}$$

Kelley's formulae are seldom used.

(*iii*) Karl Pearson's measure of skewness,

$$\alpha_3 = \frac{\text{Mean} - \text{Mode}}{\text{S.D.}}$$

(*iv*) Karl Pearson's formula for a wide class of frequency distributions in terms of moments is,

$$\beta_1 = \frac{\mu_3^2}{\mu_2^3}$$

β_1 gives only the measure of skewness but not the direction of skewness. So another measure γ_1 is defined as,

$$\gamma_1 = \sqrt{\beta_1} = \frac{\mu_3}{\mu_2^{3/2}} = \alpha_3$$

Q. 55. *How do you interpret the value of measure of skewness?*

Ans. If the measure of skewness is zero, it means that the frequency curve is symmetrical. Hence, for a symmetrical curve $\beta_1 = \alpha_3 = \gamma_1 = 0$ which implies that $Q_3 + Q_1 = 2Q_2$; $P_{90} + P_{10} = 2P_{50}$; $D_9 + D_1 = 2D_5$; mean = Median = Mode. Also, $\mu_3 = 0$.

Again, if the value of S_k, γ_1 or α_3 is positive, it leads to positive skewness. In this situation, the frequency curve has elongated right tail. A negative value of S_k, γ_1, or α_3 leads to negative skewness and the frequency curve has a long tail on the left as compared to the right tail. Greater the magnitude of S_k, γ_1, or α_3 more is the skewness.

Q. 56. *For a moderately skew distribution, what relation between mean, median and mode exists?*

Ans. For a moderately skew distribution, the relation between mean, median and mode is,

$$\text{Mean} - \text{Mode} = 3\ (\text{Mean} - \text{Median})$$

Q. 57. *What do you understand by Kurtosis?*

Ans. Kurtosis means bulginess. Kurtosis relates to the peakedness of a frequency curve as compared to a normally peaked curve. If a frequency distribution curve is more peaked or flat than a normally peaked curve then it is called a *Kurtic curve.* This property of bulginess is called *Kurtosis.*

If a frequency curve is more peaked than normal then it is called a *leptokurtic* curve and if it is less peaked than normal, it is called *platykurtic curve.* In terms of Kurtosis, a normally peaked curve is known as *mesokurtic curve.*

Q. 58. *Kurtosis is adjudged around which measure of central tendency?*

Ans. Kurtosis is adjudged around mode of the frequency distribution.

Q. 59. *How can one know about Kurtosis?*

Ans. Kurtosis can be perceived simply by looking a frequency distribution curve. But such a perception becomes difficult if the curve is slightly kurtic.

To overcome this difficulty of subjective judgement, it is mathematically measured as the ratio of fourth moment to the square of the second moment.

Symbolically,

$$\beta_2 = \frac{\mu_4}{\mu_2^2}$$

Q. 60. *How to ascertain Kurtosis with the help of β_2?*

Ans. If the value of β_2 is more than 3, the curves is leptokurtic and if less than 3, the curve is platykurtic. For a mesokurtić curve, $\beta_2 = 3$.

Q. 61. *What are standard measures of skewness and kurtosis given by Karl Pearson?*

Ans. Karl Pearson gave two convenient quantities as gamma measures defined as

$$\gamma_1 = \sqrt{\beta_1} = \frac{\mu_3}{\mu_2^{3/2}}$$

and

$$\gamma_2 = \beta_2 - 3 = \frac{\mu_4 - 3\mu_2^2}{\mu_2^2}$$

If γ_1 is negative, the frequency curve is negatively skew and if positive, the curve possesses positive skewness. Whereas β_1 gives only the magnitude but not direction.

Again, if $\gamma_2 > 0$, the curve is leptokurtic, if $\gamma_2 < 0$ the curve is platykurtic. When $\gamma_2 = 0$, the curve is mesokurtic or we can say, there is no Kurtosis.

Q. 62. *What is the purpose of measuring skewness and Kurtosis?*

Ans. Two measures namely, skewness and Kurtosis determine the shape of the frequency curve which obviously reflects on the type of distribution.

Q. 63. *What is the role of averages, measures of dispersion, skewness and Kurtosis?*

Ans. Averages, measures of dispersion, skewness and Kurtosis are complementary to each other in understanding frequency distribution.

Q. 64. *Why mean deviation and standard deviation are not calculated using the same average?*

Ans. The same average is not used in calculating mean deviation and standard deviation because mean deviation is minimum about median and standard deviation is minimum about mean as the sum of squares of the deviations from mean is minimum.

Q. 65. *What is Sheppard's correction?*

Ans. W.F. Sheppard pointed out that in case of continuous frequency distributions at the time of calculating moments, it is presumed that frequencies are centred at the mid-points of the class intervals. Such a presumption introduces some error in the calculation of moments. Hence, he suggested some corrections in various moments. These corrections are known as Sheppard's correction. They are as follows:

Corrected $\mu_1 = \mu_1$ (no correction needed)

Corrected $\mu_2 = \mu_2 - \frac{I^2}{12}$ (I is the class interval)

Corrected $\mu_3 = \mu_3$ (no correction needed)

Corrected $\mu_4 = \mu_4 - \frac{I^2}{2}\mu_2 + \frac{7}{240}I^4$

Corrections for higher order moments than fourth can be seen in a textbook if needed.

Q. 66. *What are first and second coefficient of skewness.*

Ans. The coefficients of skewness $\alpha_3 = \sqrt{\beta_1} = \gamma_1$ are the first coefficient of skewness. Another measure of skewness which is mainly useful for measuring slight skewness is known as moment coefficient of skewness and is given by the formula,

$$\text{Moment coeff. of skewness} = \frac{\sqrt{\beta_1}\,(\beta_2 + 3)}{2(5\beta_2 - 6\beta_1 - 9)}$$

where β_1 and β_2 are already given.

Moment coefficient of skewness is known as *second coefficient of skewness.*

Q. 67. *Can second coefficient of skewness be used to determine the mode?*

Ans. Yes, mode can be determined by the second coefficient of skewness using the relation,

$$\text{Mode} = \frac{\sqrt{\beta_1}\,(\beta_2 + 3)\sigma}{2(5\beta_2 - 6\beta_1 - 9)}$$

$$= -\text{ Second coeff. of skewness} \times \text{S.D.}$$

SECTION B

Fill in the Blanks

Fill in the suitable word(s) or phrase(s) in the blanks:

1. The statement, "The term dispersion is used to indicate the facts that within a group, the items different from one another in size or in other words, there is lack of uniformity in their size" was given by _________ .
2. "Dispersion is the extent to which the magnitudes or qualities of the items differ that is the degree of diversity" is the statement about dispersion given by _________ .
3. The definition, "Dispersion is the measure of the variation of the items" was given by _________ .
4. "Dispersion or spread is the degree of the scatter or variation of the variable about a central value" is the definition of dispersion given by _________ .
5. _________ defined dispersion as, "The degree to which numerical data tend to spread about an average value is called the variation or dispersion of the data."
6. Dispersion was explained as, "measures of dispersion are measures of scatter about an average" by _________ .,
7. _________ definition of dispersion is "A measure of variation or dispersion describes the degree of scatter shown by the observations and is usually measured as an average deviation about some central value or by an order statistic."
8. Measure of dispersion which utilises only two observations is _________ .
9. _________ is the measure of dispersion which utilises only extreme values.
10. Coefficient of range is the _________ measure of dispersion.
11. Inter-quartile range is equal to _________ .
12. Percentile range is given as _________ .
13. Percentile range in terms of deciles is given as _________ .
14. Mean deviation is based on _________ .
15. Mean deviation is minimum about _________ .
16. Mean deviation suffers with the lacuna that it considers all differences _________ .
17. Coefficient of mean deviation about a central value '*c*' is given as _________ .
18. The formula for calculating mean deviation about median for a discrete frequency distribution is _________ .
19. Standard deviation is the _________ of variance.
20. Other names of standard deviation are _________ .
21. Best measure of dispersion is _________ .
22. Measure of dispersion suitable for comparing any two series is _________ .
23. The relation between variance and standard deviation is _________ .
24. _________ the value of coefficient of range, better it is.
25. _________ deviation can be obtained in case of open end intervals.
26. Quartile deviation is not affected by _________ per cent extreme values.
27. Quartile deviation is a _________ measure of dispersion.
28. The relation, $2Q_2 = Q_3 + Q_1$ holds in case of _________ distribution.
29. Mean deviation is calculated by considering _________ deviations.
30. _________ is highly susceptible to sampling fluctuations.
31. Measures of dispersion tell about _________ of central value.
32. Interquartile range is _________ of quartile deviation.

33. Median absolute deviation is the ________ of the absolute deviations taken from median.

34. ________ moment represents variance.

35. The relation between probable error and standard deviation is ________ .

36. The ratio of quartile deviation to mean deviation is ________ .

37. The ratio of quartile deviation to standard deviation is ________ .

38. The moments about mean are called ________ moments.

39. Moments about origin zero are called ________ moments.

40. Moments of odd order about mean for a symmetric distribution are ________ .

41. Sheppard's correction adjusts the error due to consideration of frequencies located at ________ of the class intervals.

42. For a symmetric distribution coefficient of skewness is ________ .

43. $\alpha_3 \sqrt{\beta_1}$ and γ_1 are ________ coefficients of skewness.

44. Moment coefficient of skewness is called ________ coefficient of skewness.

45. Measure of central tendency which can be determined with the help of second coefficient of skewness is ________ .

46. In case of normal distribution, mean, median and mode are ________ .

47. Less is the coefficient of variation, ________ consistent is the series.

48. The relation between β_2 and γ_2 is ________.

49. For a leptokurtic curve, the relation between μ_4 and μ_2 is ________ .

50. For a mesokurtic curve, β_2 equal to ________ .

51. For a platykurtic curve is γ_2 is ________ .

52. For a platykurtic curve, the relation between second and fourth moment is ________ .

53. β_1 gives the measure of skewness but ________ .

54. Kurtosis means ________ of the frequency curve.

55. Skewness means ________ of the frequency distribution curve.

56. Sum of squares of the deviations from mean is ________ .

57. The relation that holds between percentiles in case of symmetric distribution is ________ .

58. For a symmetric distribution 1st, 5th and 9th deciles are connected as ________ .

59. The relation of third central moment with raw moments is ________ .

60. There is ________ effect of change of origin on the values of moments.

61. Change of scale ________ the value of moments.

62. ________ can be calculated about an arbitrary origin.

63. With the help of a measure of dispersion, namely, ________, area under the normal curve can be determined.

64. Karl Pearson's formula for measure of skewness is ________ .

65. If the coefficient of Kurtosis is equal to 3, the frequency curve is ________ .

66. If the coefficient of Kurtosis is greater than 3, the distribution is ________ .

67. If the mean, mode and standard deviation of a distribution are 48, 38 and 10 respectively, the distribution is ________ skew.

68. If for an asymmetric distribution, the mean, median and S.D. are 25, 15 and 10, respectively the distribution is ________ skew.

69. If $\beta_1 = 0$ and $\beta_2 = 3$, it is known as frequency ________ curve.

70. Mean is not equal to ________ in case of skew distribution.

71. For a symmetric distribution, upper and lower quartiles are equidistant from ________ .

72. If skewness is negative, the mean is ________ mode.

73. For moderately skew distribution, the relation between mean, median and mode is ________ .

74. Mean deviation can never be ________ .

75. For calculating variance, deviations are taken from ________ .

76. Coefficient of variation is usually expressed in ________ .

77. Graphical method of measuring dispersion is through ________ .

78. It is necessary to ________ the data before a Lorenz curve is drawn.

79. Coefficient of mean deviation and coefficient of variation are ________ .

80. If quartile deviation of a series is 30 and median is 45, the coefficient of mean deviation is ________ .

81. If mean deviation is 16 and mean 30, the coefficient of variation is ________ per cent.

82. If quartile deviation of certain items is 20 and mean is 50, the coefficient of variation is ________ per cent.

83. If team A has mean score 7 and variance 25, team B has mean score 6 and variance 9, ________ is more consistent.

84. Standard deviation is a ________ order measure of dispersion.

85. Range is a ________ order measure of dispersion.

86. In any distribution mean deviation is ________ standard deviation.

87. ________ the distance of Lorenz Curve from the line of equal distribution, the greater is the variability in the series of values.

88. The average of squared deviations from mean is called ________ .

89. A measure of dispersion is a measure of reliability of an ________ .

90. If a distribution has, mean = 7.5, mode = 10 and skewness $\alpha = -0.5$, the variance is ________ .

91. If the maximum value in a series is 60 and coefficient of range 0.5, the minimum value of the series is ________ .

92. Formula for coefficient of mean deviation is ________ .

93. The standard deviation of the five observations 5, 5, 5, 5, 5 is ________ .

94. Mean deviation is always ________ quartile deviation.

95. The sum of squares of deviations taken from mean 40 for 9 sample observations is 288. The coefficient of variation is ________ .

96. The sum of the deviations from median 24 for 12 observations is 72, the coefficient of mean deviation is ________ .

97. Range of a set of values is 16 and its minimum value is 21, the maximum value is ________ .

98. If mean and standard deviation of 8 observations in a sample are 9 and 4 and that of second sample of size 4 are 15 and 3, the combined variance of the two samples is ________ .

99. For a highly skewed distribution, the best measure of central value is ________ .

100. If the mean of a distribution is 15 and variance = 25. Also given that $\beta_1 = 1$, the third moment about origin is ________ .

101. Variance of median for a sample of size n from a normal population is ________ .

102. Standard deviation utilises ________ mean.

103. Variance of sample median is ________ than the variance of sample mean.

104. The inequality that holds between arithmetic mean (A.M.) and standard deviation (S.D.) is ________ .

105. Standard deviation of first n natural numbers is ________ .

106. The measure of central tendency about which Kurtosis is marked is ________ .

107. Standard deviation gives more weight to _________ values.

108. Standard deviation is useful in finding the descriptive measures like _________ and _________ of a distribution.

109. Variation in data can graphically be perceived by _________ .

110. If the sum of deviations from median is not zero, then a distribution will be _________ .

111. If the frequencies on either side of mode are not similarly distributed, the frequency distribution curve will be _________ .

112. Measure of skewness provides the _________ and _________ of asymmetry present in a distribution.

113. Measure of Kurtosis shows the degree of _________ of a frequency distribution curve.

114. Standard deviation of two values X_1 and X_2 is equal to _________ .

115. Change of origin and scale of values for a set makes the calculation of standard deviation _________ .

SECTION C

Multiple Choice Questions

Select the correct alternative out of given ones:

1. Which of the following is not a measure of dispersion?

(*a*) mean deviation
(*b*) quartile deviation
(*c*) standard deviation
(*d*) average deviation from mean

2. Which of the following is a unitless measure of dispersion?

(*a*) standard deviation
(*b*) mean deviation
(*c*) coefficient of variation
(*d*) range

3. Which one of the given measures of dispersion is considered best?

(*a*) standard deviation
(*b*) range
(*c*) variance
(*d*) coefficient of variation

4. For comparison of two different series, the best measure of dispersion is:

(*a*) range
(*b*) mean deviation
(*c*) standard deviation
(*d*) none of the above

5. Correct formula for mean deviation from a constant A of a series in which the variate values $x_1, x_2, ..., x_k$ have frequencies $f_1, f_2, ..., f_k$ respectively is:

(*a*) $\frac{1}{N}\sum_i (f_i x_i - A)$

(*b*) $\frac{1}{N}\sum_i f_i (x_i - A)$

(*c*) $\frac{1}{N}\sum_i | f_i (x_i - A)|$

(*d*) $\frac{1}{N}\sum_i | f_i x_i - \overline{A}|$

where $i = 1, 2, ..., k$ and $\sum_i f_i = N$

6. Correct formula for variance of n sample observations $x_1, x_2, ..., x_n$ is:

(*a*) $\frac{1}{n-1}\sum_i (x_i - \overline{x})^2$

(*b*) $\frac{1}{n-1}\left(\sum_i x_i^2 - \overline{x}^2\right)$

(*c*) $\frac{1}{n}\sum_i (x_i - \overline{x})^2$

(*d*) $\frac{1}{n}\sum_i x_i^2 - \bar{x}^2$

7. The correct relation between variance and standard deviation (S.D.) of a variable X is:

(*a*) S.D. = $[\text{Var}(X)]^2$

(*b*) S.D. = $[\text{Var}(X)]^{1/2}$

(*c*) S.D. = Var (X)

(*d*) none of the above

8. Formula for coefficient of variation is:

(*a*) $\text{C.V.} = \frac{\text{S.D.}}{\text{Mean}} \times 100$

(*b*) $\text{C.V.} = \frac{\text{Mean}}{\text{S.D.}} \times 100$

(*c*) $\text{C.V.} = \frac{\text{Mean} \times \text{S.D.}}{100}$

(*d*) $\text{C.V.} = \frac{100}{\text{Mean} \times \text{S.D.}}$

9. Out of all measures of dispersion, the easiest one to calculate is:

(*a*) standard deviation

(*b*) range

(*c*) variance

(*d*) quartile deviation

10. Formula for range (R) of a set of values X_1, X_2, ..., X_n is:

(*a*) $R = X_{\min} - X_{\max}$

(*b*) $R = |X_{\min} - X_{\max}|$

(*c*) $R = X_{\max} - X_{\min}$

(*d*) $R = X_n - X_1$

11. Formula for coefficient of range of the set of observations X_1, X_2, ..., X_n is:

(*a*) $\text{coeff. of range} = \frac{X_{\max} - X_{\min}}{X_{\max} + X_{\min}}$

(*b*) $\text{coeff. of range} = \frac{X_{\max} + X_{\min}}{X_{\max} - X_{\min}}$

(*c*) $\text{coeff. of range} = \frac{X_{\max}}{X_{\min}}$

(*d*) $\text{coeff. of range} = \frac{X_{\max} - X_{\min}}{X_{\max}}$

12. Coefficient of quartile deviation is given by the formula:

(*a*) $\text{coeff. of Q.D.} = \frac{Q_3 + Q_1}{Q_3 - Q_1}$

(*b*) $\text{coeff. of Q.D.} = \frac{Q_3 + Q_1}{Q_1 - Q_3}$

(*c*) $\text{coeff. of Q.D.} = \frac{Q_3 - Q_1}{Q_1 - Q_3}$

(*d*) $\text{coeff. of Q.D.} = \frac{Q_3 - Q_1}{Q_3 + Q_1}$

13. For a symmetrical distribution, M_d ± Q.D. covers:

(*a*) 25 per cent of the observations

(*b*) 50 per cent of the observations

(*c*) 75 per cent of the observations

(*d*) 100 per cent of the observations

M_d = Median and Q.D. = Quartile deviation

14. Quartile deviation or semi-interquartile deviation is given by the formula:

(*a*) $\text{Q.D.} = \frac{Q_3 + Q_1}{2}$

(*b*) Q.D. = $Q_3 - Q_1$

(*c*) Q.D. = $(Q_3 - Q_1)/2$

(*d*) Q.D. = $(Q_3 - Q_1)/4$

15. Mean deviation is minimum when deviations are taken from:

(*a*) mean

(*b*) median

(*c*) mode

(*d*) zero

16. Sum of squares of the deviations is minimum when deviations are taken from:

(*a*) mean

(*b*) median

(*c*) mode

(*d*) zero

17. If a constant value 5 is subtracted from each observation of a set, the variance is:

(*a*) reduced by 5

(*b*) reduced by 25

(*c*) unaltered

(*d*) increased by 25

18. If each observation of a set is divided by 10, the S.D. of the new observations is:

(*a*) $\frac{1}{10}$ th of S.D. of original obs.

(*b*) $\frac{1}{100}$ th of S.D. of original obs.

(*c*) not changed

(*d*) 10 times of S.D. of original obs.

19. If each value of a set is divided by *c*, then the variance (s^2) of the original sample values from coded values $dx_1, dx_2, ..., dx_n$ is obtained by the formula:

(*a*) $s^2 = \frac{1}{n-1}\sum_i (dx_i - \bar{dx})^2 \times c$

(*b*) $s^2 = \frac{1}{n-1}\sum_i (dx_i - \bar{dx})^2 \times c^2$

(*c*) $s^2 = \frac{1}{n-1}\sum_i (dx_i - \bar{dx})^2 \times \frac{1}{c}$

(*d*) $s^2 = \frac{1}{n-1}\sum_i (dx_i - \bar{dx})^2 \times \frac{1}{c^2}$

20. Which of the following formula for standard deviation of a frequency distribution is not correct?

(*a*) $\sigma = \sqrt{\frac{1}{N}\sum_i f_i(x_i - \bar{x})^2}$

(*b*) $\sigma = \sqrt{\frac{1}{N}\sum_i f_i x_i^2 - \bar{x}^2}$

(*c*) $\sigma = \sqrt{\frac{1}{N}\sum_i f_i x_i^2 - \left(\frac{\Sigma_i f_i x_i}{N}\right)^2}$

(*d*) $\sigma = \sqrt{\frac{1}{N}\left(\sum_i f_i x_i\right)^2 - \frac{\Sigma_i f_i x_i}{N}}$.

where $\Sigma_i f_i = N$ and other notations are as usual.

21. If a constant '*c*' is subtracted from each observation and then divided by *d*, then the formula for variance of frequency distribution having *k* groups is:

(*a*) $\sigma^2 = \left[\frac{1}{N}\sum_{i=1}^{k} f_i x_i'^2 - \left(\frac{\sum_{i=1}^{k} f_i x_i'}{N}\right)^2\right] \times d^2$

(*b*) $\sigma^2 = \frac{1}{N-1}\left[\sum_{i=1}^{k} f_i(x_i' - \bar{x}')^2\right] \times d^2$

(*c*) $\sigma^2 = \left[\frac{1}{N}\sum_{i=1}^{k} f_i x_i'^2 - \frac{\left(\sum_{i=1}^{k} f_i x_i'\right)^2}{N}\right] \times d^2$

(*d*) none of the above

where $x_i' = \frac{x_i - c}{d}$ and $N = \sum_i f_i$

22. The empirical relationship between quartile deviation (Q.D.) and standard deviation in normal distribution is:

(*a*) 3 Q.D. = 2 S.D.

(*b*) 4 Q.D. = 3 S.D.

(*c*) 6 Q.D. = 5 S.D.

(*d*) 5 Q.D. = 4 S.D.

23. The relationship between mean deviation (M.D.) and standard deviation is:

(*a*) 3 M.D. = 2 S.D.

(*b*) 5 M.D. = 4 S.D.

(*c*) 6 M.D. = 5 S.D.

(*d*) M.D. = S.D.

24. The empirical relation between quartile deviation (Q.D.) and mean deviation (M.D.) from mean is:

(a) 3 Q.D. = 5 M.D.
(b) 6 Q.D. = 3 M.D.
(c) 5 Q.D. = 6 M.D.
(d) 6 Q.D. = 5 M.D.

25. An empirical relation between standard deviation, mean deviation about mean and quartile deviation is:
(a) 4 S.D. = 6 M.D. = 5 Q.D.
(b) 4 S.D. = 5 M.D. = 6 Q.D.
(c) 6 S.D. = 5 M.D. = 4 S.D.
(d) 5 S.D. = 4 M.D. = 6 Q.D.

26. The empirical relation between range (R) and standard deviation is:
(a) $R = 3$ S.D.
(b) $R = 2$ S.D.
(c) $R = 6$ S.D.
(d) $R = 4$ S.D.

27. An empirical relationship between range and quartile deviation about mean is:
(a) $R = 4$ Q.D.
(b) $R = 9$ Q.D.
(c) $R = 6$ Q.D.
(d) none of the above

28. An empirical relation between range and mean deviation is:
(a) $R = 10$ M.D.
(b) $2R = 5$ M.D.
(c) $3R = 5$ M.D.
(d) $2R = 15$ M.D.

29. Which measure of dispersion ensures highest degree of reliability?
(a) Range
(b) Mean deviation
(c) Quartile deviation
(d) Standard deviation

30. Which measure of dispersion ensures lowest degree of reliability?
(a) Range
(b) Mean deviation
(c) Quartile deviation
(d) Standard deviation

31. There are two populations consisting of N_1 and N_2 units, having means $\overline{X}_1$ and $\overline{X}_2$, variances σ_1^2 and σ_2^2 respectively. Let their pooled mean be $\overline{X}_{12}$. Also, supposing $\overline{X}_1 - \overline{X}_{12} = d_1$ and $\overline{X}_2 - \overline{X}_{12} = d_2$. The formula for pooled variance is:

(a) $\sigma^2 = \dfrac{N_1(\sigma_1^2 + d_1^2) + N_2(\sigma_2^2 + d_2^2)}{N_1 + N_2}$

(b) $\sigma^2 = \dfrac{N_2(\sigma_1^2 + d_1^2) + N_1(\sigma_2^2 + d_2^2)}{N_1 + N_2}$

(c) $\sigma^2 = \dfrac{N_1\sigma_1^2 + N_2 d_1^2 + N_2\sigma_2^2 + N_1 d_2^2}{N_1 + N_2}$

(d) $\sigma^2 = \dfrac{N_2\sigma_1^2 + N_1\sigma_2^2 + N_1 d_1^2 + N_2 d_2^2}{N_1 + N_2}$

32. Average wages of workers of a factory are ₹ 550.00 per month and the standard deviation of wages is 110. The coefficient of variation is:
(a) C.V. = 30 per cent
(b) C.V. = 15 per cent
(c) C.V. = 500 per cent
(d) C.V. = 20 per cent

33. If the mean deviation of a distribution is 20.20, the standard deviation of the distribution is:
(a) 15.15
(b) 25.25
(c) 30.30
(d) none of the above

34. If the mean and standard deviation of A and B are as, $\overline{X}_A = 15.0$, $\overline{X}_B = 20.0$ and $\sigma_A^2 = 25$ and $\sigma_B^2 = 16$, which of the two series is more consistent?
(a) Series A
(b) Series B
(c) Series A and B are equally consistent
(d) None of the above

35. If the standard deviation of a distribution is 15, the quartile deviation of the distribution is:

(a) 15.0
(b) 12.5
(c) 10.0
(d) none of the above

36. If the quartile deviation of a series is 60, the mean deviation of this series is:
(a) 72
(b) 48
(c) 50
(d) 75

37. In a discrete set of values, the correct relation between mean deviation and standard deviation is:
(a) M.D. > S.D.
(b) M.D. < S.D.
(c) M.D. ≤ S.D.
(d) M.D. ≥ S.D.

38. If the first 25 per cent observations of a series are 20 or less and last 25 per cent observations of a series are 50 or more, the quartile deviation (semi-interquartile deviation) is:
(a) 25
(b) 35
(c) 15
(d) 30

39. The mean and standard deviation of a set of values are 25 and 5, respectively. If a constant value 5 is added to each value, the coefficient of variation of the new set of values is:
(a) 250 per cent
(b) 600 per cent
(c) 20 per cent
(d) 16.6 per cent

40. If the mean of a series is 10 and its coefficient of variation is 40 per cent, the variance of the series is:
(a) 4
(b) 8
(c) 12
(d) none of the above

41. Which of the following measures of dispersion can attain a negative value?
(a) Range
(b) Mean deviation
(c) Standard deviation
(d) Variance

42. A set of values is said to be relatively uniform if it has:
(a) high dispersion
(b) zero dispersion
(c) little dispersion
(d) negative dispersion

43. The mean and standard deviation of a set of values from a normal distribution are 66 and 4, respectively. The range in which almost 95 per cent values lie is:
(a) 62 to 70
(b) 62 to 74
(c) 58 to 74
(d) 66 and 74

44. The measure of dispersion which ignores signs of the deviations from a central value is:
(a) range
(b) quartile deviation
(c) standard deviation
(d) mean deviation

45. Which measure of dispersion is least affected by extreme values?
(a) Range
(b) Mean deviation
(c) Standard deviation
(d) Quartile deviation

46. Which measure of dispersion is most affected by extreme values?
(a) Range
(b) Mean deviation
(c) Standard deviation
(d) Quartile deviation

47. Range of a set of values is 65 and maximum value in the series is 83. The minimum value of the series is:
(a) 74
(b) 9
(c) 18
(d) none of the above

48. If the minimum value in a set is 9 and its range is 57, the maximum value of the set is:
(*a*) 33
(*b*) 66
(*c*) 48
(*d*) none of the above

49. If the values of a set are measured in cm, the unit of variance will be:
(*a*) no unit
(*b*) cm
(*c*) cm^2
(*d*) cm^3

50. Which measure of dispersion has a different unit other than the unit of measurement of values?
(*a*) Range
(*b*) Mean deviation
(*c*) Standard deviation
(*d*) Variance

51. The average of the sum of squares of the deviations about mean is called:
(*a*) variance.
(*b*) absolute deviation
(*c*) standard deviation
(*d*) mean deviation

52. Quartile deviation is equal to:
(*a*) interquartile range
(*b*) double the interquartile range
(*c*) half of the interquartile range
(*d*) none of the above

53. Which measure of dispersion can be calculated in case of open end intervals?
(*a*) Range
(*b*) Standard deviation
(*c*) Coefficient of variation
(*d*) Quartile deviation

54. Which one property out of the following does not hold good in case of standard deviation?
(*a*) It is distorted by extreme values
(*b*) It is not very sensitive to sampling fluctuations as compared to other measures.
(*c*) It is a unitless measure of dispersion
(*d*) It is a most used measure of dispersion

55. If each value of a series is divided by 5, its coefficient of variation is reduced by:
(*a*) 0 per cent
(*b*) 5 per cent
(*c*) 10 per cent
(*d*) 20 per cent

56. If each value of a series is multiplied by 10, the coefficient of variation will be increased by:
(*a*) 5 per cent
(*b*) 10 per cent
(*c*) 15 per cent
(*d*) 0 per cent

57. If a constant value 10 is subtracted from each value of a series, the coefficient of variation will be:
(*a*) decreased in comparison to original value
(*b*) increased in comparison to original value
(*c*) same as original value
(*d*) none of the above

58. If each value of a series is multiplied by a constant '*c*', the coefficient of variation as compared to original value is:
(*a*) increased
(*b*) decreased
(*c*) unaltered
(*d*) zero

59. If each value of a set is divided by a constant '*d*', the coefficient of variation will be:
(*a*) same as original value
(*b*) less than original value
(*c*) more than original value
(*d*) none of the above

60. For a positive skewed distribution, which of the following inequality holds?
(*a*) Median > Mode
(*b*) Mode > Mean
(*c*) Mean > Median
(*d*) Mean > Mode

61. For a negatively skewed distribution, the correct inequality is:
(*a*) mode < median
(*b*) mean < median

(c) mean < mode
(d) none of the above

62. For a positive skewed frequency curve, the inequality that holds is:
(a) $Q_1 + Q_3 > 2Q_2$
(b) $Q_1 + Q_2 > 2Q_3$
(c) $Q_1 + Q_3 > Q_2$
(d) $Q_3 - Q_1 > Q_2$

63. For a negatively skewed frequency distribution curve, the third central moment,
(a) $\mu_3 > 0$
(b) $\mu_3 < 0$
(c) $\mu_3 = 0$
(d) μ_3 does not exist

64. For a symmetrical distribution, the coefficient of skewness:
(a) $\alpha_3 = 1$
(b) $\alpha_3 = 3$
(c) $\alpha_3 = 0$
(d) $\alpha_3 = -1$

65. For a leptokurtic frequency curve, the measure of Kurtosis,
(a) $\alpha_4 = 0$
(b) $\alpha_4 = -3$
(c) $\alpha_4 < 1$
(d) $\alpha_4 > 3$

66. In case of a positive skewed distribution, the relation between mean, median and mode that holds is:
(a) median > mean > mode
(b) mean > median > mode
(c) mean = median = mode
(d) none of the above

67. If a moderately skewed distribution has mean 30 and mode 36, the median of the distribution is:
(a) 30
(b) 28
(c) 32
(d) none of the above

68. If a moderately skewed distribution has mean 40 and median equal to 30, the mode of the distribution is:
(a) 10
(b) 35
(c) 20
(d) zero

69. First and third quartiles of a frequency distribution are 30 and 75. Also its coefficient of skewness is 0.6. The median of the frequency distribution is:
(a) 40
(b) 39
(c) 38
(d) 41

70. If the mean, standard deviation and coefficient of skewness of a frequency distribution are 60, 45 and –0.4, respectively, the mode of the frequency distribution is:
(a) 80
(b) 82
(c) 78
(d) 68

71. For a moderately skew distribution, the empirical relation between mean (M), median (M_d) and mode (M_0) is:
(a) $3(M - M_0) = M - M_d$
(b) $3(M_d - M) = M_0 - M$
(c) $3(M - M_d) = M - M_0$
(d) $2(M_0 - M) = 3(M_d - M)$

72. If the first quartile Q_1 =15 and third quartile Q_3 = 25, the coefficient of quartile deviation is:
(a) 4
(b) 1/4
(c) 5/3
(d) 3/5

73. If the first quartile Q_1 = 20 and third quartile Q_3 = 50, the quartile deviation is:
(a) 35
(b) 15
(c) 2.5
(d) 0.8

74. For a negatively skewed distribution, the correct relation between mean, median and mode is:

(a) mean = median = mode
(b) median < mean < mode
(c) mean < median < mode
(d) mode < mean < median

75. If the mode of a frequency distribution M_0 = 16 and its mean $\bar{X}$ = 16, the median of the distribution is:
(a) zero
(b) 16
(c) 32
(d) 8

76. In case of positive skewed distribution, the extreme values lie in the
(a) left tail
(b) right tail
(c) middle
(d) anywhere

77. The extreme values in a negatively skewed distribution lie in the:
(a) middle
(b) right tail
(c) left tail
(d) whole curve

78. The relation between variance and standard deviation is:
(a) variance is the square root of standard deviation
(b) standard deviation is the square of the variance
(c) variance is equal to standard deviation
(d) square of the standard deviation is equal to variance

79. Which of the following statements is true for a measure of dispersion?
(a) Mean deviation does not follow algebraic rule.
(b) Range is a crudest measure.
(c) Coefficient of variation is a relative measure.
(d) All the above statements

80. For a set of values:
(a) mean deviation is always less than standard deviation
(b) mean deviation is always greater than standard deviation
(c) mean deviation is always equal to standard deviation
(d) none of the above

81. Variance of the following frequency distribution,

Classes	*Frequency*
2–4	2
4–6	5
6–8	4
8–10	1

is approximately equal to:
(a) 2.5
(b) 2.9
(c) 5.0
(d) none of the above

82. For the data given is question 81, mean deviations about median is:
(a) 1.43
(b) 1.00
(c) 2.43
(d) 6

83. Coefficient of variation for the data given in question 81 is:
(a) 48.33 per cent
(b) 206.90 per cent
(c) 195.17 per cent
(d) 30.03 per cent

84. The range of values for the frequency distribution given in question 81 is:
(a) 2
(b) 10
(c) 8
(d) 6

85. For the data given in question 81, the coefficient of quartile deviation is:
(a) 4.385
(b) 0.228
(c) 2.6
(d) 11.4

86. The range of the set of values, 15, 12, 27, 6, 9, 18, 21 is:
(a) 21
(b) 4.5
(c) 0.64
(d) 3

87. The coefficient of range for the values given in question 86 is:
(*a*) 1.571
(*b*) 4.500
(*c*) 0.636
(*d*) 0.222

88. The coefficient of skewness of a series *A* is 0.15 and that of series *B* 0.062. Which of the two series is less skew?
(*a*) Series *A*
(*b*) Series *B*
(*c*) No decision
(*d*) None of the above

89. If the coefficient of Kurtosis γ_2 of a distribution is zero, the frequency curve is:
(*a*) leptokurtic
(*b*) platykurtic
(*c*) mesokurtic
(*d*) any of the above

90. If for a distribution, coefficient of Kurtosis $\gamma_2 < 0$, the frequency curve is:
(*a*) leptokurtic
(*b*) platykurtic
(*c*) mesokurtic
(*d*) any of the above

91. The value of coefficient of Kurtosis β_2 can be:
(*a*) less than 3
(*b*) greater than 3
(*c*) equal to 3
(*d*) all of the above

92. The standard deviation of a set of values will be:
(*a*) positive when the values are positive
(*b*) positive when the values are negative
(*c*) always positive
(*d*) all of the above

93. Sum of square of the deviations is minimum when the deviations are taken from:
(*a*) mean
(*b*) median
(*c*) mode
(*d*) an arbitrary value.

94. The relationship between the variance of median [*V* (med)] and variance of mean [*V* (mean)] of a normal population is:
(*a*) *V* (med) < *V* (mean)
(*b*) *V* (med) = *V* (mean)
(*c*) *V* (med) > *V* (mean)
(*d*) 1.57 *V* (med) = *V* (mean)

95. Kurtosis in frequency distribution is adjudged around:
(*a*) second quartile
(*b*) arithmetic mean
(*c*) quadratic mean
(*d*) mode.

96. The variance of first *n* natural numbers is:
(*a*) $(n^2 + 1)/12$
(*b*) $(n + 1)^2/12$
(*c*) $(n^2 - 1)/12$
(*d*) $(2n^2 - 1)/8$

97. If a random variable *X* has mean 3 and standard deviation 5, then the variance of a variable $Y = 2X - 5$ is:
(*a*) 45
(*b*) 100
(*c*) 15
(*d*) 40

98. Kurtosis and skewness of a frequency distribution curve are bound by the relation:
(*a*) they always coexist
(*b*) either of the two can exist alone
(*c*) their measures are always positive
(*d*) their measures are always negative.

99. All values in a sample are same. Then their variance is:
(*a*) zero
(*b*) one
(*c*) not calculable
(*d*) all of the above

100. Calculation of pooled variance of two series of sizes n_1 and n_2 requires:
(*a*) means of individual series
(*b*) variances of individual series
(*c*) pooled mean
(*d*) all of the above

ANSWERS

Section B

1. W.I. King **2.** Reigleman **3.** A.L. Bowley **4.** B.C. Brookes and W.F.L. Dick **5.** Speigel **6.** C.T. Clark and L.L. Schkade **7.** John I. Griffin **8.** range **9.** Range **10.** relative **11.** $Q_3 - Q_1$ **12.** $P_{90} - P_{10}$ **13.** $D_9 - D_1$ **14.** all observations **15.** median **16.** positive **17.** δ_c/c **18.** $\Sigma f \mid X - M_d \mid / \Sigma f$ **19.** +ve square root **20.** mean error; mean square error; root mean square deviation from mean **21.** standard deviation **22.** coefficient of variation **23.** S.D. = + $\sqrt{\text{variance}}$ **24.** Lesser **25.** Quartile **26.** 50 **27.** positional **28.** symmetric **29.** absolute **30.** Range **31.** reliability **32.** twice **33.** median **34.** Second **35.** P.E.= $\frac{2}{3}\sigma$ **36.** 5 : 6 **37.** 2 : 3 **38.** central **39.** raw **40.** zero **41.** mid-points **42.** zero **43.** first **44.** second **45.** mode **46.** equal **47.** more **48.** $\gamma_2 = \beta_2 - 3$ **49.** $\mu_4 > 3\mu^2_2$ **50.** three **51.** less than zero **52.** $3\mu_2^2 > \mu_4$ **53.** not direction **54.** bulginess **55.** asymmetry **56.** minimum **57.** $P_{90}+P_{10}=2P_{50}$ **58.** $D_9+D_1=2D_5$ **59.** $\mu_3=\mu_3'-3\mu_2'\mu_1' + 2\mu_2'^3$ **60.** no **61.** affects **62.** Moments **63.** standard deviation **64.** (mean-mode)/S.D. **65.** mesokurtic **66.** leptokurtic **67.** positive **68.** positive **69.** normal **70.** mode **71.** median (second quartile) **72.** less than **73.** mean – mode = 3 (mean – median) **74.** negative **75.** mean **76.** percentage **77.** Lorenz curve **78.** cumulate **79.** not same **80.** 0.8 **81.** 66.66 **82.** 60 per cent **83.** team *B* **84.** second **85.** first **86.** less than **87.** More **88.** variance **89.** average value **90.** 25 **91.** 20 **92.** $\left(\frac{1}{n}\sum f \mid X - A \mid \Big/ A\right)$ **93.** zero **94.** greater than **95.** 15 per cent **96.** 0.25 **97.** 37 **98.** 21.66 **99.** median **100.** 4625 **101.** $\pi\,\sigma^2/2n$ **102.** quadratic **103.** greater **104.** A.M. ≥ S.D. **105.** $\sqrt{(n^2-1)/12}$ **106.** mode **107.** extreme **108.** skewness; Kurtosis **109.** Lorenz curve **110.** skewed **111.** skewed or asymmetrical **112.** magnitude; direction **113.** convexity **114.** $(X_1 \sim X_2)/2$ **115.** easier or simpler.

Section C

1. (*d*)	2. (*c*)	3. (*a*)	4. (*d*)	5. (*c*)
6. (*a*)	7. (*b*)	8. (*a*)	9. (*b*)	10. (*c*)
11. (*a*)	12. (*d*)	13. (*b*)	14. (*c*)	15. (*b*)
16. (*a*)	17. (*c*)	18. (*a*)	19. (*b*)	20. (*d*)
21. (*a*)	22. (*a*)	23. (*b*)	24. (*d*)	25. (*b*)
26. (*c*)	27. (*b*)	28. (*d*)	29. (*d*)	30. (*c*)
31. (*a*)	32. (*d*)	33. (*b*)	34. (*b*)	35. (*c*)
36. (*a*)	37. (*b*)	38. (*c*)	39. (*d*)	40. (*d*)
41. (*a*)	42. (*c*)	43. (*c*)	44. (*d*)	45. (*d*)
46. (*a*)	47. (*c*)	48. (*b*)	49. (*c*)	50. (*d*)
51. (*a*)	52. (*c*)	53. (*d*)	54. (*c*)	55. (*a*)
56. (*d*)	57. (*b*)	58. (*c*)	59. (*a*)	60. (*d*)
61. (*c*)	62. (*a*)	63. (*b*)	64. (*c*)	65. (*d*)
66. (*b*)	67. (*c*)	68. (*a*)	69. (*b*)	70. (*c*)
71. (*c*)	72. (*b*)	73. (*b*)	74. (*c*)	75. (*b*)
76. (*b*)	77. (*c*)	78. (*d*)	79. (*d*)	80. (*a*)
81. (*b*)	82. (*a*)	83. (*d*)	84. (*c*)	85. (*b*)
86. (*a*)	87. (*c*)	88. (*b*)	89. (*c*)	90. (*b*)
91. (*d*)	92. (*c*)	93. (*a*)	94. (*c*)	95. (*d*)
96. (*c*)	97. (*b*)	98. (*b*)	99. (*a*)	100. (*d*).

SUGGESTED READING

1. Agarwal, B.L., *Basic Statistics,* New Age International Publishers, New Delhi, 8th edition, 2024.
2. Freud, J.E., *Modern Elementary Statistics,* Prentice-Hall of India, New Delhi, 1981.
3. Goon, A.M., Gupta, M.K. and Dasgupta, B., *Fundamentals of Statistics,* Vol. I, the World Press, Calcutta, 1977.
4. Gupta, S.C. and Kapoor, V.K., *Fundamentals of Mathematical Statistics,* Sultan Chand & Sons. Delhi, 8th edn., 1983.

5. Hoel, P.G. and Jessen, R.J., *Basic Statistics for Business and Economics,* John Wiley, New York, 1982.
6. Meter, J., Wasserman, W. and Whitmore, G.A., *Applied Statistics,* Allyn and Bacon, London, 1982.
7. Ostle, B., *Statistics in Research,* Oxford & IBH, Calcutta (now Kolkata), 1966.
8. Sancheti, D.C. and Kapoor, V.K., *Statistics,* Sultan Chand & Sons, 7th edn., 1991.
9. Sellers, G.R. and Wardeman, S.B., *Elementary Statistics,* Saunders College Publishing, New York, 1982.
10. Walker, H.M. and Lev, J., *Elementary Statistical Methods,* Holt Rinehart and Winston, New York, 1969.
11. Wine, L.R., *Beginning Statistics,* Winthop Publishers, Cambridge, 1976.

CHAPTER 6

Elementary Probability

SECTION A

Short Essay Type Questions

Q. 1. *Give in brief the concept of probability.*

Ans. There are a number of events in day-to-day life about which one is not sure whether it will occur or not. But one is always curious to know what chance is there for a happening or event to occur. For instance, one may be interested to estimate whether it will rain today or not, one would like to evaluate his chance of winning for head in a definite number of tosses, what is the chance that there are four aces in one hand in a game of cards among four players, etc. The numerical evaluation of chance factor of an event is known as probability.

Q. 2. *Define an event and give its two examples.*

Ans. An event is the collection of possible outcomes which are favourable to an happening out of total outcomes which may be enumerable or denumerable.

Consider a statistical experiment which may consist of finite or infinite number of trials whereas each trial results into an outcome such as tossing three coins at a time or tossing a coin three times. We shall have in all eight outcomes. If we consider the birth weight of children, it will consist of an infinite number of outcomes. The totality of all possible outcomes of an experiment is called *sample space* and is denoted by Ω. At the same time, the collection of all outcomes favourable to a phenomenon or happening is called an *event* and is denoted by *E, A, B, C*, etc. In the experiment of tossing a coin thrice, the sample space consists of eight points and each point of the sample space is usually denoted by ω_i (i = 1, 2, ...). The sample space,

$$\Omega = \text{HHH HHT HTH HTT THH THT TTH TTT}$$

$$= \omega_1 \quad \omega_2 \quad \omega_3 \quad \omega_4 \quad \omega_5 \quad \omega_6 \quad \omega_7 \quad \omega_8$$

Event *E:* there are at least two heads, consists of four points,

$$\text{HHH HHT HTH THH}$$

$$\omega_1 \quad \omega_2 \quad \omega_3 \quad \omega_5$$

Again, event *A:* there is no head, consists of only one point, *i.e.*,

$$\text{TTT} \equiv \omega_8$$

Q. 3. *Define complementary event, and give an example.*

Ans. An event $\bar{A}$ is said to be complementary to an event A in Ω if $\bar{A}$ consists of all those points which are not in A. In tossing a coin three times, Ω consists of eight points $\omega_1, \omega_2, \ldots, \omega_8$. The event '$A$' that there is no head consists of the point ω_8. The event $\bar{A}$, complementary to A, that there is at least one head consists of the seven points, $\omega_1, \omega_2, \omega_3, \omega_4, \omega_5, \omega_6$ and ω_7.

Q. 4. *Define a simple or elementary event.*

Ans. An event having only one sample point is called simple or elementary event. In the experiment of tossing three coins at a time, the event 'A' that all the coins turn up with heads consists of only one point HHH. Hence, A is a simple event. As a matter of fact each outcome of an experiment is a simple event.

Q. 5. *Define equal events.*

Ans. Two events A and B are said to be equal if $A \subset B$ and $B \subset A$. This statement implies that all the points of A are also the points of B and vice-versa.

Q. 6. *What do you understand by transitivity of events?*

Ans. If A, B and C are three events such that $A \subset B$ and $B \subset C$, it implies that $A \subset C$. Such a property of events is known as transitivity of events.

Q. 7. *Define compound event.*

Ans. An event which is not simple or elementary is called a compound event. Every compound event can be uniquely represented by the union of a set of elementary events.

Q. 8. *Discuss mutually-exclusive or disjoint events.*

Ans. Events are said to be mutually exclusive if the occurrence of one precludes the occurrence of others. For example, in tossing a coin, the events head and tail are mutually-exclusive events since if the coin falls with head upside, tail cannot turn up and vice-versa. In other words, two events A and B are said to be mutually-exclusive if there is no point in common in between the points belonging to A and B. Consider the trial of tossing a coin thrice. Let the event A is that there are two heads in three tossings of a coin. Event A has points: HHT, HTH, THH. Again let the event B be that there are at least two tails. Event B has points: HTT, THT, TTH, TTT. There is no common point amongst the events A and B. Hence, A and B are mutually-exclusive events. All the more, two distinct elementary events are always disjoint.

Q. 9. *What do you understand by primary events?*

Ans. Mutually-exclusive and exhaustive events defined over a sample space Ω usually constitute primary events.

As a matter of fact each outcome of a conceptual or statistical (random) experiment is an event. All such events are called primary events. For example, in throwing of a die, six possible outcomes 1, 2, 3, 4, 5 and 6 spots turning upside of a die constitute primary events.

Q. 10. *What is a derived event?*

Ans. Two or more events joined by the conjunction 'or' are called derived events. For two events A and B, the event A or B ($A \cup B$) is a derived event.

Q. 11. *Explain unision of events.*

Ans. Unision of two events A and B means the event which relates to the occurrence of A or B or both. It is denoted by $A \cup B$ (A union B). For instance, in tossing a coin three times, suppose the event A: there is at least one head and one tail. Event A will consist of the six points,

	HHT	HTH	HTT	THH	THT	TTH
i.e.,	ω_2	ω_3	ω_4	ω_5	ω_6	ω_7

Again suppose the event B: there are at least two heads.

Event B has four points, HHH, HHT, HTH, THH
ω_1 ω_2 ω_3 ω_5

The event $A \cup B$ (A or B) will consist of the points

$$\omega_1, \omega_2, \omega_3, \omega_4, \omega_5, \omega_6, \omega_7$$

It contains all the points of A and B taken only once. The idea of unision of two events can be extended to any number of events.

Q. 12. *Discuss intersection of events.*

Ans. Intersection of two events A and B leads to an event which conforms to the occurrence of A as well as B. Hence, it consists of those points which are common to A and B. It is denoted as $A \cap B$ (A intersection B). In the example given in Question No. 11, the event $A \cap B$ consists of the points,

HHT, HTH, THH
ω_2 ω_3 ω_5

Event $A \cap B$ consists of three points only. The idea of intersection of two events can be extended to any number of events.

Q. 13. *What is meant by an impossible event?*

Ans. An event which is certain not to occur is called an impossible event. It is denoted by the empty set ϕ. For example, the event A that in two throws of a die, the sum of the spots is one. Event A is an impossible event as in two throws of a die, the sum of spots has to be at least two.

Further the intersection of two mutually-exclusive events is always an impossible event.

Q. 14. *What do understand by exhaustive (partition) set of events?*

Ans. A set of disjoint events $A_1, A_2, \ldots, A_n$ is said to be exhaustive if the union of A_i's ($i = 1, 2, \ldots, n$) is the sample space, *i.e.*, $\bigcup_{i=1}^{n} A_i = \Omega$. This implies that every point of the sample space belongs to one and only one of the A_i's. In throwing a die, the spots 1, 2, 3, 4, 5 and 6 are exhaustive events.

Q. 15. *Give classical (Laplacian, mathematical) definition of probability.*

Ans. If Ω is a sample space having N points which arises out of all possible equally likely and independent outcomes of a random experiment and n points in Ω are favourable to an event A, the probability of the event A is given as,

$$P(A) = \frac{n}{N}$$

where $0 \le n \le N$.

This is also known as a **priori probability**.

Q. 16 *What are the properties of classical probability of an event A?*

Ans. Properties of $P(A)$ are:

(*i*) Probability is a pure number, *i.e.*, it has no unit.

(*ii*) $0 \le P(A) \le 1$, *i.e.*, probability can never be negative and cannot exceed unity (one).

(*iii*) It is a relative measure.

(*iv*) If $A_1, A_2, \ldots, A_k$ are k mutually exclusive and exhaustive events in the sample space Ω then

$$\sum_{i=1}^{k} P(A_i) = 1 \rightarrow P(\Omega) = 1.$$

(*v*) $P(\phi) = 0$, *i.e.*, probability of an impossible events is zero.

(*vi*) If $A \subset B$, $P(A) \le P(B)$ and if $B \subset A$, $P(A) \ge P(B)$.

(*vii*) If $A + \bar{A} = \Omega$, $P(A) + P(\bar{A}) = P(\Omega) = 1$ or

$P(\bar{A}) = 1 - P(A)$.

(*viii*) If $A \subset B$, $P(B\bar{A}) = P(B) - P(A) = P(B - A)$.

Q. 17. *Narrate addition theorem of probability.*

Ans. If A and B are two arbitrary (possible) events in the sample space Ω, the probability of the union of A and B is governed by the law,

$$P(A \cup B) = P(A) + P(B) - P(A \cap B)$$

The formula for probability of union of two events can be extended to any number of events. For three arbitrary events A, B and C in Ω, the probability of their union is given as,

$$\begin{aligned} P(A \cup B \cup C) = {} & P(A) + P(B) + P(C) \\ & - P(A \cap B) - P(A \cap C) \\ & - P(B \cap C) + P(A \cap B \cap C). \end{aligned}$$

Q. 18. *Enunciate demerits of classical probability.*

Ans. Classical probability approach cannot be adopted if any of the following situation exists:

(*i*) If it is not possible to enumerate all possible outcomes. For example, the sample space of all even numbers, total number of male births, etc.

(*ii*) If the outcomes are not independent.

(*iii*) If the total number of outcomes is infinite.

(*iv*) If each and every outcome is not equally likely.

Q. 19. *If two events A and B are mutually exclusive, what shall be the probability of their union?*

Ans. If two events A and B are mutually exclusive, $P(A \cap B) = 0$ and hence,

$$P(A \cup B) = P(A) + P(B)$$

Q. 20. *Define independent events.*

Ans. Two events A and B are said to be independent if the occurrence of one does not affect the occurrence of the other.

Q. 21. *Define pairwise independent events.*

Ans. If $A_1, A_2, \ldots, A_k$ are k events, they are said to be pairwise independent iff,

$$P(A_i \cap A_j) = P(A_i)\, P(A_j) \qquad \forall \quad i \neq j$$

where $i, j = 1, 2, \ldots, k$.

Q. 22. *If A and B are independent events, how about the independence of their complements $\bar{A}$ and $\bar{B}$?*

Ans. If A and B are independent, their complements are also independent, *i.e.*,

if $\quad P(A \cap B) = P(A)P(B)$

then $\quad P(\bar{A} \cap \bar{B}) = P(\bar{A})\, P(\bar{B})$

$$= [1 - P(A)]\, [1 - P(B)]$$

Also $\quad P(A \cup B) = 1 - P(\bar{A} \cap \bar{B})$

$$= 1 - P(\bar{A})\, P(\bar{B})$$

Q. 23. *State multiplicative law of probability.*

Ans. If two events A and B are independent, the probability of their product (intersection) is equal to the product of their individual probabilities. Notationally,

$$P(AB) = P(A \cap B) = P(A)\, P(B)$$

This law can be extended to any number of events. For three independent events A, B and C,

$$P(ABC) = P(A \cap B \cap C) = P(A)\, P(B)\, P(C).$$

Q. 24. *Give concept and definition of statistical (empirical) probability.*

Ans. The definition of statistical probability goes after the name of Richard Von Mises. Many deficiencies of classical definition could be removed by introducing the relative frequency approach. If N is infinite or equilikelyness cannot be guessed, statistical definition is more appropriate. The definition is, "If out of a large number of trials, only n are conducted under essentially homogeneous and identical conditions resulting into n outcomes. Out of n outcomes k are favourable to an event A, the probability of A is,

$$P(A) = \lim_{n \to \infty} \left(\frac{k}{n}\right)$$

Here n is never infinity but the relative frequency $\left(\frac{k}{n}\right)$ stabilises as n is fairly large.

This definition removes some of the deficiencies of classical probability. But n is always finite in physical experiments. Hence, it is not definite that such a limit always exists.

Q. 25. *Explain conditional probability.*

Ans. Many times the information is available that an event has occurred and one is required to find out the probability of occurrence of another event B utilising the information about A. Such a probability is known as conditional probability and is denoted by $P(B \mid A)$, *i.e.*, the probability of the event B given A. For example, suppose we know that a newly born baby will be a male (A) then one is interested to know the probability of a strile birth (B), *i.e.*, we want to calculate $P(B \mid A)$. The formula is,

$$P(B \mid A) = \frac{P(A \cap B)}{P(A)}$$

If A and B are independent, then

$$P(B \mid A) = \frac{P(A \cap B)}{P(A)}$$

$$= \frac{P(A)\, P(B)}{P(A)} = P(B)$$

Q. 26. *Give the multiplication rule for the simultaneous occurrence of two events A and B.*

Ans. Using the rule of conditional probability, the relations for simultaneous occurrence of A and B can be established as follows:

$$P(A \text{ and } B) = P(A)\, P(B \mid A)$$

$$P(B \text{ and } A) = P(B)\, P(A \mid B)$$

Q. 27. *If A, B and C are three events, how can you express the probability of simultaneous events A, B and C.*

Ans. Using the property of conditional probability, the relation for the simultaneous occurrence of events *A*, *B* and *C* is,

$$P(A \cap B \cap C) = P(A)\, P(B \mid A)\, P(C \mid A \text{ and } B)$$

Q. 28. *Discuss Bayes' probability and give formula for its calculation.*

Ans. Bayes' probability is also known as *inverse probability*. The idea of inverse probability was given by Sir Thomas Bayes in 1763 which was reprinted in *Biometrika* in the year 1958. The problem of inverse probability arises when we have an outcome and we want to know the probability of its belonging to a specified trial or population out of many alternative trials or populations. To be more specific, let us consider three urns containing white (W), black (B) and red (R) balls as follows:

URN I : 2W, 3B and 4R balls.

URN II : 3W, 1B and 2R balls.

URN III : 4W, 2B and 5R balls.

Two balls are drawn from a urn and they happen to be one while and one red balls. Now the interest lies to know the probability that the balls are drawn from Urn III. Such a probability is Bayes' probability. Bayes' theorem can be stated as follows:

If $E_1, E_2, \ldots, E_k$ are *k* mutually exclusive events defined in $\mathfrak{B}$ (a collection of events), each being a subset of the sample space Ω such that $\bigcup_{i=1}^{k} E_i = \Omega$ and $P(E_1) > 0$ for $i = 1, 2, \ldots, k$ and if *A* is any arbitrary event which is associated with E_i's such that $P(A) > 0$, we can evaluate probabilities $P(A \mid E_1)$ for $i = 1, 2, \ldots, k$. In Bayes' approach we have to find out the probability of E_i given that *A* has occurred, *i.e.*, $P(E_i \mid A)$. This is also known as *posteriori* probability Bayes' formula for posteriori probability is,

$$P(E_i \mid A) = \frac{P(A|E_i)\, P(E_i)}{\sum_{i=1}^{k} P(A \mid E_i)\, P(E_i)}$$

Q. 29 *Calculate the probability for the example given in Question 28.*

Ans. Let E_1, E_2 and E_3 be the events the Urn I, II and III are selected, respectively, and *A* be the event that out of two selected balls, one is white and the other is red.

Probabilities of selecting a urn are,

$$P(E_1) = \frac{1}{3},\ P(E_2) = \frac{1}{3} \text{ and } (E_3) = \frac{1}{3}$$

Probability of selecting 1W and 1R ball from Urn I is,

$$P(A \mid E_1) = \frac{{}^2C_1 \times {}^4C_1}{{}^9C_2}$$

$$= \frac{2 \times 4 \times 2}{9 \times 8} = \frac{2}{9}$$

similarly from Urn II is,

$$P(A \mid E_2) = \frac{{}^3C_1 \times {}^2C_1}{{}^6C_2}$$

$$= \frac{3 \times 2 \times 2}{6 \times 5} = \frac{2}{5}$$

and from Urn III is,

$$P(A \mid E_3) = \frac{{}^4C_1 \times {}^5C_1}{{}^{11}C_2}$$

$$= \frac{4 \times 5 \times 2}{11 \times 10} = \frac{4}{11}$$

Now the Bayes' probability that ball drawn belong to Urn III is,

$$P(E_3 \mid A) = \frac{P(A|E_3)\, P(E_3)}{\sum_{i=1}^{3} P(A|E_i)\, P(E_i)}$$

$$= \frac{4/11 \times 1/3}{\left(\frac{2}{9} \times \frac{1}{3} \times \frac{2}{5} \times \frac{1}{3} + \frac{4}{11} \times \frac{1}{3}\right)}$$

$$= \frac{45}{122}$$

Q. 30. *What is D'Alembert's paradox?s*

Ans. D'Alembert considered the tossing of two coins. He argued that there are three possible cases namely, (*i*) both heads, (*ii*) both tails, (*iii*) one head and one tail.

He concluded that the probability of getting one head and one tail is 1/3. As a matter of fact, the actual probability of getting one head and one tail in two tosses of a coin is 1/4. This is known as D'Alembert's paradox which has arisen due to the difficulty of deciding equally likely alternatives.

SECTION B

Fill in the Blanks

Fill in the suitable word(s) or phrase(s) in the blanks:

1. Classical probability concept was given by ________.
2. Probability is attached only to ________.
3. There can be established one to one correspondence between events and ________.
4. Events may be simple as well as ________.
5. Two events are mutually exclusive if there is ________ in between them.
6. Intersection of two mutually exclusive events is a ________ event.
7. An event consisting of only one point is called an ________ event.
8. Laplace's probability cannot be calculated if the total number of outcomes is ________.
9. Mathematical probability cannot be calculated if the outcomes are ________.
10. Mathematical probability is also known as ________ probability.
11. Classical probability is not calculable if the ________ number of outcomes is not countable.
12. An event which cannot occur is known as ________ event.
13. Two events A and B are equal if ________.
14. The set of union of disjoint events $A_1, A_2, \ldots, A_n$ such that $\sum_{i=1}^{n} A_i = \Omega$ is called ________ event.
15. If an event is such that its points belong to either of the two sets A and B, the set is the ________ of A and B.
16. If an event consists of only those points which are in A as well as in B, the event represents the ________ of A and B.
17. The idea of relative frequency for calculating probability was given by ________.
18. The probability based on the concept of relative frequency is called ________ probability.
19. In statistical probability n is never ________.
20. An event of the type A or B is a ________ event.
21. Totality of all possible outcomes of a random experiment is called ________.
22. Probability can never be less than ________.
23. Probability can never be greater than ________.
24. Probability of the sample space Ω is equal to ________.
25. Probability of an event is never ________.
26. Probability can vary from ________.
27. The need for probability was originally felt in ________.
28. If two events are independent, the probability that both will occur together is equal to the ________ of their individual probabilities.
29. Addition theorem will be applicable only when the various events belong to the ________.
30. Probability can be expressed as ________.

31. Multiplication theorem is applicable only if the events are _________ .

32. When all possible outcomes are included, they are known as _________ cases.

33. If $B \subset A$, the relation between $P(A)$ and $P(B)$ is _________ .

34. If $B \subset A$, the probability $(A\bar{B})$ is _________.

35. If A and B are two events, the $P(A \cap \bar{B})$ is _________.

36. If A and B are two events, the $P(\bar{A} \cap B)$ is _________.

37. $P(A \cup B)$ can be expressed by the _________ law of probability.

38. If two events A and B are disjoint, the $P(A \cup B) =$ _________ .

39. If out of three events A, B and C, the events A and B are mutually exclusive, the formula for $P(A \cup B \cup C)$ is _________ .

40. If the A and B are independent, then $(A \cap B)$ is _________ .

41. If the events A and B are independent, then $P(B \mid A) =$ _________ .

42. For any three events A, B and C, $P(A + B/C) =$ _________.

43. For any three events A, B and C, $P(AB \mid C) + P(A\bar{B} \mid C) =$ _________.

44. For any two events A and B, $P(AB) =$ _________ .

45. If A and B are independent, then $P(A \mid B) =$ _________ .

46. If $P(A \cap B) = P(A)\,P(B)$, the events A and B are _________ .

47. If A, B and C are pairwise independent events, the probability, $P(A \cap B \cap C)$ _________ or _________ or _________ .

48. If an event A is independent of the events B, $B \cup C$ and $B \cap C$, then $P(A \cap C) =$ _________.

49. If an event A is independent of the events B, $B \cup C$ and $B \cap C$, the events A and C are _________.

50. If $A \subset B$, then $P(A \mid C)$ _________ $P(B \mid C)$.

51. For any two events A and B the probability, $P[(A \cap B) \cup (\bar{A} \cap B)] =$ _________.

52. If $P(A) = p_1$, $P(B) = p_2$ and $P(A \cap B) = p_3$, then

(*a*) $P(\bar{A} \cup \bar{B}) =$ _________ .

(*b*) $P(\bar{A} \cap B) =$ _________ .

(*c*) $P(\bar{A} \cap \bar{B}) =$ _________ .

(*d*) $P(\bar{A} \cup B) =$ _________.

(*e*) $P(A \mid B) =$ _________.

53. For any two events A and B, the probability $P(A \mid B) + P(\bar{A} \mid B) =$ _________ .

54. Bayes' probability is also known as _________ probability.

55. In Bayes' probability we calculate _________ probability.

56. For any two arbitrary events A_1, A_2 and given that an event B has already occurred, the expanded form of $P(A_1 \cup A_2 \mid B)$ is _________.

57. Suppose A and B are two events. Event B has occurred and it is known that $P(B) < 1$ then $P(A \mid \bar{B}) =$ _________ .

58. If A_1 and A_2 are mutually exclusive events then $P(A_1 \mid A_1 \cup A_2) =$ _________ .

59. If $\bar{A}$ is the complement of A, the probability of the complement of $\bar{A}$ using involution law is _________ .

60. If A and B are two events, the probability of the complement of their union using Demorgan's (dualization) law is _________ .

61. If A and B are two events, the probability of

the complements of their intersection using Demorgans or dualization law is ________.

62. In tossing a fair coin turning up of head and tail are ________ outcomes.

63. The turning up of spots, 1, 2, 3, 4, 5 and 6 in rolling of a die are ________ and ________ events.

64. The probability of obtaining a total of 8 in a single throw of two dice is ________.

65. If A is an arbitrary event, then $P(A/A)$ = ________.

66. For any two arbitrary events A and B, $P(\bar{A} \mid B)$ = ________.

67. For any given event C, $P(\phi \mid C)$ = ________.

68. For any two events A and B, $P(A \cup \bar{B})$ = ________.

69. For any two events A and B, $P(\bar{A} \cap \bar{B})$ = ________.

70. If two events A and B are mutually exclusive and $P(A) = \frac{1}{3}$, $P(B) = \frac{1}{2}$, then

(*i*) Probability that either A or B will occur is ________.

(*ii*) Probability that neither A nor B will occur is ________.

(*iii*) Probability that A and B both will occur is ________.

71. Making use of the multiplication theorem, the expression for $P(A \cap B \cap C \cap D)$ is ________.

72. If no outcome of an experiment is expected to occur more frequently then others, the outcomes are ________.

73. If an event is not simple, it is a ________ event.

74. The outcomes of a statistical experiment which result in the happening of an event are called ________.

75. If two events are not independent, they are obviously ________.

76. Probability interpreted as a measure of degree of belief of an individual is called ________.

77. Assigning of equal probabilities to all the elementary events of a statistical experiment is called ________ of probabilities.

78. If $P(A \cap B) = P(A)\ P(B)$, $P(A \cap C) = P(A)\ P(C)$ and $P(B \cap C) = P(B)\ P(C)$, the events A, B and C are ________.

79. If a class has 60 per cent boys and 40 per cent girls and the probability of getting first class of a girl is 0.30 and that of a boy getting first class is 0.25, the probability of a randomly chosen student getting first class is ________.

80. If A and B are two mutually exclusive and exhaustive events and $P(B) = 2P(A)$, then $P(A)$ = ________.

SECTION C

Multiple Choice Questions

Select the correct alternative out of given ones:

1. The outcome of tossing a coin is a:
(*a*) simple event
(*b*) mutually exclusive event
(*c*) complementary event
(*d*) compound event

2. Classical probability is measured in terms of:
(*a*) an absolute value
(*b*) a ratio
(*c*) absolute value and ratio both
(*d*) none of the above

3. Probability can take values

(*a*) $-\infty$ to ∞
(*b*) $-\infty$ to 1
(*c*) -1 to 1
(*d*) 0 to 1

4. Probability is expressed as:
(*a*) ratio
(*b*) proportion
(*c*) percentage
(*d*) all of the above

5. Two events are said to be independent if:
(*a*) each outcome has equal chance of occurrence
(*b*) there is no common point in between them
(*c*) one does not affect the occurrence of the other
(*d*) both the events have only one point

6. If *A* and *B* are two events which have no point in common, the events *A* and *B* are:
(*a*) complementary to each other
(*b*) independent
(*c*) mutually exclusive
(*d*) dependent

7. Classical probability is also known as:
(*a*) Laplace's probability
(*b*) mathematical probability
(*c*) a priori probability
(*d*) all of the above

8. Each outcome of a random experiment is called:
(*a*) primary event
(*b*) compound event
(*c*) derived event
(*d*) all of the above

9. If *A* and *B* are two events, the probability of occurrence of either *A* or *B* is given as:
(*a*) $P(A) + P(B)$
(*b*) $P(A \cup B)$
(*c*) $P(A \cap B)$
(*d*) $P(A)\ P(B)$

10. If *A* and *B* are two events, the probability of occurrence of *A* and *B* simultaneously is given as:
(*a*) $P(A) + P(B)$
(*b*) $P(A \cup B)$
(*c*) $P(A \cap B)$
(*d*) $P(A)\ P(B)$

11. The limiting relative frequency approach of probability is known as:
(*a*) statistical probability
(*b*) classical probability
(*c*) mathematical probability
(*d*) all of the above

12. The definition of statistical probability was originally given by:
(*a*) De Moivre
(*b*) Laplace
(*c*) Von-Mises
(*d*) Pascal

13. The definition of a priori probability was originally given by:
(*a*) De Moivre
(*b*) Laplace
(*c*) Von-Mises
(*d*) Feller

14. If it is known that an event *A* has occurred, the probability of an event *E* given *A* is called:
(*a*) empirical probability
(*b*) a priori probability
(*c*) posteriori probability
(*d*) conditional probability

15. Probability by classical approach has:
(*a*) no lecunae
(*b*) only one lecuna
(*c*) only two lecunae
(*d*) many lecunae

16. Classical probability is possible in case of:
(*a*) unequilikely outcomes
(*b*) equilikely outcomes
(*c*) either unequilikely or equilikely outcomes
(*d*) all of the above

17. An event consisting of those elements which are not in *A* is called:
(*a*) primary event
(*b*) derived event
(*c*) simple event

(*d*) complementary event

18. The probability of all possible outcomes of a random experiment is always equal to:

(*a*) infinity

(*b*) zero

(*c*) one

(*d*) none of the above

19. The probability of the intersection of two mutually exclusive events is always:

(*a*) infinity

(*b*) zero

(*c*) one

(*d*) none of the above

20. The individual probabilities of occurrence of two events *A* and *B* are known, the probability of occurrence of both the events together will be:

(*a*) increased

(*b*) decreased

(*c*) one

(*d*) zero

21. If $E_1, E_2, \ldots. E_n$ is a countable sequence of events such that $E_i \supset E_{i+1}$ for $i = 1, 2, \ldots.$ then:

(*a*) $\lim_{n \to \infty} P(E_n) = 0$

(*b*) $\lim_{n \to \infty} P(E_n) = \infty$

(*c*) $\lim_{n \to \infty} P(E_n) = 1$

(*d*) $\lim_{n \to \infty} P(E_n) =$ impossible value

22. If A_1, A_2 and A_3 are three mutually exclusive events, the probability of their union is equal to:

(*a*) $P(A_1)\, P(A_2)\, P(A_3)$

(*b*) $P(A_1) + P(A_2) + P(A_3) - P(A_1\, A_2\, A_3)$

(*c*) $P(A_1) + P(A_2) + P(A_3)$

(*d*) $P(A_1)\, P(A_2) + P(A_1) \times P(A_3) + P(A_2)\, P(A_3)$

23. If A_1, A_2 and A_3 are three independent events, the probability of their joint occurrence is equal to:

(*a*) $P(A_1)\, P(A_2)\, P(A_3)$

(*b*) $1/P(A_1)\, P(A_2)\, P(A_3)$

(*c*) $P(A_1) + P(A_2) + P(A_3)$

(*d*) $P(A_1 \cap A_2) + P(A_1 \cap A_3) + P(A_2 \cap A_3)$

24. If two events *A* and *B* are such that $A \subset B$ and $B \subset A$, the relation between $P(A)$ and $P(B)$ is:

(*a*) $P(A) \leq P(B)$

(*b*) $P(A) \geq P(B)$

(*c*) $P(A) = P(B)$

(*d*) none of the above

25. If *A* is an event, the conditional probability of *A* given *A* is equal to:

(*a*) zero

(*b*) one

(*c*) infinite

(*d*) indeterminate quantity

26. If $A \subset B$, the probability, $P(A/B)$ is equal to:

(*a*) zero

(*b*) one

(*c*) $P(A)/P(B)$

(*d*) $P(B)/P(A)$

27. If $B \subset A$, the probability $P(A/B)$ is equal to:

(*a*) zero

(*b*) one

(*c*) $P(A)/P(B)$

(*d*) $P(B)/P(A)$

28. If two events *A* and *B* are such that $A \subset B$, the relation between the conditional probabilities $P(A/C)$ and $P(B/C)$ is:

(*a*) $P(A/C) = P(B/C)$

(*b*) $P(A/C) > P(B/C)$

(*c*) $P(A/C) < P(B/C)$

(*d*) all of the above

29. For any two events A and B, $P(A - B)$ is equal to:

(*a*) $P(A) - P(B)$

(*b*) $P(B) - P(A)$

(*c*) $P(B) - P(AB)$

(*d*) $P(A) - P(AB)$

30. If an event B has occurred and it is known that $P(B) = 1$, the conditional probability $P(A/B)$ is equal to:

(*a*) $P(A)$

(*b*) $P(B)$

(*c*) one

(*d*) zero

31. If A and B are any two mutually exclusive events, the $P(A/A \cup B)$ is equal to:

(*a*) $P(A)/[P(A) + P(B)]$

(*b*) $P(A \cup B)/[P(A) + P(B)]$

(*c*) $P(B)/P(A \cup B)$

(*d*) none of the three

32. If A and B are two independent events, then $P(\bar{A} \cap \bar{B})$ is equal to:

(*a*) $P(\bar{A})\, P(\bar{B})$

(*b*) $1 - P(A \cup B)$

(*c*) $[1 - P(A)]\, [1 - P(B)]$

(*d*) all of the above

33. If $E_1, E_2, \ldots, E_n$ are n mutually exclusive events such that $P(E_j) \neq 0$ for $j = 1, 2, \ldots, n$ and A is an arbitrary event contained in $\cup\, E_j$ with $P(A) > 0$ and has been observed, the probability of a particular event E_j given A is given by the formula

(*a*) $P(E_j \mid A) = \dfrac{P(E_j)\, P(A \mid E_j)}{\sum_j P(E_j)}$

(*b*) $P(E_j \mid A) = \dfrac{P(E_j)\, P(A \mid E_j)}{\sum_j P(E_j)\, P(A \mid E_j)}$

(*c*) $P(E_j \mid A) = \dfrac{P(A \mid E_j)}{\sum_j P(A \mid E_j)}$

(*d*) none of the above

34. If A and B are two events such that AB and $A\bar{B}$ are two mutually exclusive and exhaustive events in which the event A can occur, then

(*a*) $P(A) = 1$

(*b*) $P(A) = P(AB) + P(A\bar{B})$

(*c*) $P(A) = P(\bar{A}) + P(A\bar{B})$

(*d*) $P(A) = P(\bar{A}B) + P(A\bar{B})$

35. If k toffees are distributed at random among n children, the probability that a child will receive exactly r toffees is:

(*a*) $\dfrac{kc_r (n-1)^{n-r}}{n^k}$

(*b*) $\dfrac{kc_r (k-1)^{k-r}}{k^n}$

(*c*) $\dfrac{kc_r (n-1)^{r}}{n^k}$

(*d*) $\dfrac{kc_r (n-1)^{n-r}}{k^n}$

36. The idea of posteriori probabilities was introduced by

(*a*) Pascal

(*b*) Peter and Paul

(*c*) Thomas Bayes

(*d*) M. Loe've

37. In a city, 60 per cent read newspaper A, 40 per cent read newspaper B and 30 per cent read newspaper C, 20 per cent read A and B, 30 per cent read A and C, 10 per cent read B and C. Also 15 per cent read papers A, B and C. The percentage of people who do not read any of these newspapers is:

(*a*) 65 per cent

(*b*) 15 per cent

(*c*) 45 per cent

(*d*) none of the above

38. If a bag contains 4 white and 3 black balls. Two draws of 2 balls are successively made, the probability of getting 2 white balls at first draw and 2 black balls at second draw when the balls drawn at first draw were replaced is:

(*a*) 3/7

(*b*) 1/7

(*c*) 19/49

(*d*) 2/49

39. In question 38, if the balls are not replaced after the first draw, the probability of 2 white balls at first draw and 2 black balls at second draw is:

(*a*) $\frac{3}{35}$

(*b*) $\frac{13}{35}$

(*c*) $\frac{1}{2}$

(*d*) none of the above

40. In tossing three coins at a time, the probability of getting at most one head is:

(*a*) 3/8

(*b*) 7/8

(*c*) 1/2

(*d*) 1/8

41. There is 80 per cent chance that a problem will be solved by a statistics student and 60 per cent chance is there that the same problem will be solved by the mathematics student. The probability that at least the problem will be solved is:

(*a*) 0.48

(*b*) 0.92

(*c*) 0.10

(*d*) 0.75

42. The probability of two persons being borned on the same day (ignoring date) is:

(*a*) 1/49

(*b*) 1/365

(*c*) 1/7

(*d*) none of the above

43. An urn contains 5 red, 4 white and 3 black balls. The probability of three balls being of different colours when the ball is replaced after each draw is equal to:

(*a*) 3/144

(*b*) 4/144

(*c*) 5/144

(*d*) 1

44. In question 43, the probability of three balls being drawn in the order red, white and black when the balls are not replaced after each draw, is equal to:

(*a*) 1/22

(*b*) 5/144

(*c*) 60/144

(*d*) none of the above

45. An urn *A* contains 5 white and 3 black balls and *B* contains 4 white and 4 black balls. An urn is selected and a ball is drawn from it, the probability, that the ball is white, is:

(*a*) 9/8

(*b*) 9/16

(*c*) 5/32

(*d*) 5/16

46. From a pack of 52 cards, two cards are drawn at random. The probability that one is an ace and the other is a king is:

(*a*) 2/13

(*b*) 1/169

(*c*) 16/169

(*d*) 8/663

47. Two dice are rolled by two players *A* and *B*. *A* throws 10, the probability that *B* throws more than *A* is:

(*a*) 1/12

(*b*) 1/6

(*c*) 1/18

(*d*) none of the above

48. The data reveals that 10 per cent patients die in a particular type of operation. A doctor performed 9 operations and all of them survived. Whether the 10th patient on being operated:

(*a*) will survive

(*b*) will die

(*c*) may survive or die

(*d*) none of the above

49. There are two groups of students consisting of 4 boys and 2 girls; 3 boys and 1 girl. One student is selected from both the groups. The probability of one boy and one girl being selected is:

(*a*) 1/9

(*b*) $\frac{5}{12}$

(*c*) 1

(*d*) none of the above

50. In a shooting competition, Mr. *X* can shoot at the bull's eye 4 times out of 5 shots and Mr. *Y*, 5 times out of six and Mr. *Z*, 3 times out of 4 shots. The probability that the target will be hit at least twice is:

(*a*) 107/120

(*b*) 47/120

(*c*) 1/2

(*d*) none of the above

51. There are two bags. One bag contains 4 red and 5 black balls and the other 5 red and 4 black balls. One ball is to be drawn from either of the two bags. The probability of drawing a black ball is:

(*a*) 1

(*b*) 16/81

(*c*) 1/2

(*d*) 10/81

52. Three dice are rolled simultaneously. The probability of getting 12 spots is:

(*a*) 1/8

(*b*) 25/216

(*c*) 1/12

(*d*) none of the above

53. Given that $P(A) = \frac{1}{3}$, $P(B) = \frac{1}{4}$, $P(A \mid B) = \frac{1}{6}$, the probability $P(B \mid A)$ is equal to:

(*a*) 1/4

(*b*) 3/4

(*c*) 1/8

(*d*) none of the above

54. From the probabilities given in question 53, the probability, $P(B \mid \bar{A})$ is equal to:

(*a*) 1/16

(*b*) 15/24

(*c*) 15/16

(*d*) 5/16

55. A number is selected randomly from each of the two sets

1, 2, 3, 4, 5, 6, 7, 8

2, 3, 4, 5, 6, 7, 8, 9

The probability that the sum of the numbers is equal to 9 is:

(*a*) 8/91

(*b*) 7/72

(*c*) 14/81

(*d*) 7/64

56. A bag contains 3 white and 5 red balls. Three balls are drawn after shaking the bag. The odds against these balls being red is:

(*a*) 5/28

(*b*) 5/8

(*c*) 15/64

(*d*) 3/5

57. A bag contains 3 white, 1 black and 3 red balls. Two balls are drawn from the well shaked bag. The probability of both the balls being black is:

(*a*) 1

(*b*) zero

(*c*) 1/7

(*d*) none of the above

58. The chance of winning the race of the horse *A* in Durby is $\frac{1}{5}$ and that of horse *B* is $\frac{1}{6}$. The probability that the race will be won by *A* or *B* is:

(*a*) 1/30

(*b*) 1/3

(*c*) 11/30

(*d*) none of the above

59. Four cards are drawn from a pack of 52 cards. The probability that out of 4 cards being 2 red and 2 black is:

(*a*) 325/833
(*b*) 46/833
(*c*) 234/574
(*d*) none of the above

60. The probability of Mr. *R* living 20 years more is $\frac{1}{5}$ and that of Mr. *S* is $\frac{1}{7}$. The probability that at least one of them will survive 20 years hence is:
(*a*) 12/35
(*b*) 1/35
(*c*) 13/35
(*d*) 11/35

61. For a 60 year old person living up to the age of 70, it is 7 : 5 against him and for another 70 year old person surviving up to the age of 80, it is 5 : 2 against him. The probability that one of them will survive for 10 years more is:
(*a*) 5/42
(*b*) 49/84
(*c*) 59/84
(*d*) none of the above

62. If 7 : 6 is in favour of *A* to survive 5 years more and 5 : 3 in favour of *B* to survive 5 years more, the probability that at least one of them will survive for 5 years more is:
(*a*) 35/104
(*b*) 12/26
(*c*) 21/26
(*d*) 43/52

63. The chance of Ram to stand first in the class is $\frac{1}{3}$ and that of Abdul is $\frac{1}{5}$. The probability that either of the two will stand first in the class is:
(*a*) 1/15
(*b*) 8/15
(*c*) 7/15
(*d*) none of the above

64. The probability of throwing an odd sum with two fair dice is:
(*a*) 1/4
(*b*) 1/16
(*c*) 1
(*d*) 1/2

65. The probability that there is at least one spot in two rollings of a die is:
(*a*) 13/36
(*b*) 5/18
(*c*) 11/36
(*d*) 1/18

66. The probabilities of Mr. *J* and Mr. *M* not living for one more year are $\frac{1}{9}$ and $\frac{1}{7}$ respectively. The probability of living one more year of either one or both is:
(*a*) 20/21
(*b*) 62/63
(*c*) 14/63
(*d*) 5/21

67. A group consists of 4 men, 3 women and 2 boys. Three persons are selected at random. The probability that 2 men are selected is:
(*a*) 3/28
(*b*) 7/28
(*c*) 5/28
(*d*) 5/14

68. The probability that a leap year will have 53 Sundays is:
(*a*) 1/7
(*b*) 2/7
(*c*) 2/53
(*d*) 52/53

69. With a pair of dice thrown at a time, the probability of getting a sum more than that of 9 is:
(*a*) 5/18
(*b*) 7/36
(*c*) 5/6
(*d*) none of the above

70. If the chance of *A* hitting a target is 3 times out of 4 and of *B* 4 times out of 5 and of *C* 5 times out of 6. The probability that the target will be hit in two hits is:
(*a*) 19/24
(*b*) 23/30

(c) 47/120
(d) none of the above

71. A consignment of 15 record players contains 4 defectives. The record players are selected at random one by one and examined. The ones examined are not put back. The probability that the 9th piece examined is the last defective one is:
(a) 24/455
(b) 8/195
(c) 96/195
(d) none of the above

72. The chance that doctor A will diagnose a disease X correctly is 60 per cent. The chance that a patient will die by his treatment after correct diagnosis is 40 per cent, and the chance of death by wrong diagnosis is 70 per cent. A patient of doctor A, who had disease X, died. The probability that his disease was diagnosed correctly is:
(a) 6/25
(b) 7/25
(c) 6/7
(d) 6/13

73. An urn contains four tickets marked with numbers 112, 121, 211, 222 and one ticket is drawn at random. Let A_i (i = 1, 2, 3) be the event that i^{th} digit of the number of the ticket drawn is 1. Are the events A_1, A_2 and A_3:
(a) mutually exclusive
(b) dependent
(c) independent
(d) pairwise independent

74. In Question 73, are the events A_1, A_2 and A_3:
(a) dependent
(b) independent
(c) mutually exclusive
(d) none of the above

75. An urn contains 5 yellow, 4 black and 3 white balls. Three balls are drawn at random. The probability that no black ball is selected is:
(a) 1/66
(b) 7/55
(c) 2/9
(d) none of the above

76. A bag contains 3 white and 5 red balls. A game is played such that a ball is drawn, its colour is noted and replaced with two additional balls of the same colour. The selection is made three times, the probability that a white ball is selected at each trial is:
(a) 7/64
(b) 21/44
(c) 105/512
(d) 9/320

77. Given that $P(A) = \frac{1}{3}$, $P(B) = \frac{3}{4}$ and $P(A \cup B) = \frac{11}{12}$, probability, $P(B/A)$ is:
(a) 1/6
(b) 4/9
(c) 1/2
(d) none of the above

78. If A, B and C are three events such that $P(A) = 0.3$, $P(B) = 0.4$, $P(C) = 0.5$ and $P(AB') = 0.2$, $P(BC) = 0.3$, $P(A'B'C') = 0.3$, $P(AB \mid C') = 0.1$, the probability, $P(B' \mid C')$ is equal to:
(a) 3/5
(b) 4/5
(c) 1/5
(d) none of the above

79. Given the probability in question 78, the probability $P(A \mid B)$ is equal to:
(a) 1/4
(b) 1/2
(c) 1/3
(d) none of the above

80. If four whole numbers are taken at random and multiplied, the chance that the first digit in their product is 0, 3, 6 or 9 is:
(a) $(2/5)^3$
(b) $(1/4)^3$
(c) $(2/5)^4$
(d) $(1/4)^4$

81. A can hit a target 2 times in 5 shots, B 3 times in 5 shots and C 4 times in 5 shots. They fire a volley (each try once to hit the target). The probability that two shots hit is:
(*a*) 24/125
(*b*) 67/125
(*c*) 121/125
(*d*) 58/125

82. There are four coins in a bag. One of the coins has head on both sides. A coin is drawn at random and tossed five times and fell always with head upward. The probability that it is the coin with two head is:
(*a*) 3/128
(*b*) 1/4
(*c*) 32/35
(*d*) none of the above

83. One of the two events is certain to happen. The chance of one event is one-fifth of the other. The odds in favour of the other is:
(*a*) 1 : 6
(*b*) 6 : 1
(*c*) 5 : 1
(*d*) 1 : 5

84. One of the two events must happen; given that the chance of one is one-fourth of the other. The odd in favour of the other is:
(*a*) 1 : 3
(*b*) 1 : 4
(*c*) 1 : 5
(*d*) none of the above

85. A coin is tossed six times. The probability of obtaining heads and tails alternately is:
(*a*) 1/64
(*b*) 1/2
(*c*) 1/32
(*d*) none of the above

86. The odds in favour of certain event are 5 : 4, and odds against another event are 4 : 3. The chance that at least one of them will happen is:
(*a*) 15/63
(*b*) 51/63
(*c*) 47/63
(*d*) none of the above

87. A and B start in a ring with ten other persons. If the arrangement of 12 persons is at random, the chance that there are exactly three persons between A and B is:
(*a*) 1/66
(*b*) 2/11
(*c*) 4/11
(*d*) none of the above

88. Three houses were available in a locality for allotment. Three persons applied for a house. The probability that all the three persons applied for the same house is:
(*a*) 1/3
(*b*) 1/9
(*c*) 1/27
(*d*) 1

89. In the problem of Question 88, the probability that each of the three applied for a different house is:
(*a*) 1/9
(*b*) 1/27
(*c*) 1
(*d*) 2/9

90. A speaks truth 4 times out of five and B speaks truth 3 times out of four. They agree in the assertion that a white ball has been drawn from a bag containing 10 balls of different colours. The probability that a white ball was really drawn is:
(*a*) 3/50
(*b*) 1/27
(*c*) 1/1350
(*d*) 81/82

91. In the problem of Question 90, if the bag contains 1 white and 9 red balls, the probability of one white ball being drawn is:
(*a*) 4/7
(*b*) 3/50
(*c*) 9/200
(*d*) none of the above

92. If A tells truth 4 times out of 5 and B tells truth 3 times out of 4. The probability that both expressing the same fact contradict each other is:
(*a*) 1/20

(b) 3/20
(c) 1/5
(d) none of the above

93. The probability of drawing a white ball in the first draw and again a white ball in the second draw with replacement from a bag containing 6 white and 4 blue balls is:
(a) 2/10
(b) 6/10
(c) 36/100
(d) 1/3

94. A fair coin is tossed repeatedly unless a head is obtained. The probability that the coin has to be tossed at least four times is:
(a) 1/2
(b) 1/4
(c) 1/6
(d) 1/8

95. Out of 20 employees in a company, five are graduates. Three employees are selected at random. The probability of all the three being graduates is:
(a) 1/64
(b) 1/125
(c) 1/114
(d) none of the above

96. In the problem of question 95, the probability that at least one of them is a graduate is:
(a) 11/114
(b) 137/1368
(c) 137/228
(d) none of the above

97. (Parzen) In answering a question on a multiple choice test, an examinee either knows the answer with probability p or he guesses with probability $(1 - p)$. Let the probability of answering the question correctly be 1 for an examinee who knows the answer and $\frac{1}{m}$ who guesses (m being the number of multiple choice alternatives). Suppose an examinee answer a question correctly. The probability that he really knows the answer is:
(a) $\frac{mp}{1+mp}$
(b) $\frac{mp}{1+(m-1)p}$
(c) $\frac{(m-1)p}{1+(m-1)p}$
(d) none of the above

98. A machine part is produced by three factories A, B and C. Their proportional production is 25, 35 and 40 per cent, respectively. Also, the percentage defectives manufactured by three factories are 5, 4 and 3, respectively. A part is taken at random and is found to be defective. The probability that the selected part belongs to factor B is:
(a) 28/503
(b) 4/11
(c) 14/276
(d) none of the above

99. A card is drawn from a well shuffled pack of 52 cards. A gambler bets that it is either a heart or an ace. What are odds against his winning this wet?
(a) 9 : 4
(b) 4 : 9
(c) 35 : 52
(d) 1 : 3

100. If one card is selected at random from 100 cards numbered as 00, 01, …, 99. Suppose x and y are the sum and product of the digits on the selected card. If i is a whole number, the probability $P(x = i/y = 0)$ is equal to:
(a) $\frac{1}{19}$
(b) 1/50
(c) 19/100
(d) none of the above

101. Two dice, each numbered 1 to 6, are thrown together. Consider two events A and B given by
A – even number of the first die

B – number on the second die is greater than 4, then $P(A \cup B)$ is:

(*a*) 2/3
(*b*) 1/6
(*c*) 1/2
(*d*) 3/4

102. An unbiased coin is tossed four times. The probability that the number of heads exceeds the number of tails is:

(*a*) 1/12
(*b*) 3/4
(*c*) 3/8
(*d*) 5/16

103. If $P(A|B) = \frac{1}{4}$ and $P(B|A) = \frac{1}{3}$, then $P(A)/P(B)$ is equal to:

(*a*) 3/4
(*b*) 7/12
(*c*) 4/3
(*d*) 1/12

104. For two events E_1, E_2, if $P(E_1) = 1/2$, $P(E_2) = \frac{1}{3}$, $P(E_1 \cup E_2) = \frac{2}{3}$, then $P(E_1 \cap E_2)$ is equal to:

(*a*) 1/4
(*b*) 1/6
(*c*) 2/5
(*d*) 1/3

105. For two events A_1 and A_2, if $P(A_1) = \frac{2}{3}$, $P(A_2) = \frac{3}{8}$ and $P(A_1 \cap A_2) = \frac{1}{4}$, then A_1 and A_2 are:

(*a*) mutually exclusive but not independent
(*b*) mutually exclusive and independent
(*c*) independent but not mutually exclusive
(*d*) not mutually exclusive and not independent

106. In a library there are 40 per cent mathematics books and remaining 60 per cent science books. It is known that 2 per cent of the mathematics books are in Hindi and 1 per cent of science books are in Hindi. If one book is taken out at random and is found to be in Hindi, the probability that it is a science book is:

(*a*) 2/9
(*b*) 3/7
(*c*) 6/13
(*d*) 1/4

107. Take four identical marbles. On the first write symbols A_1, A_2, A_3. On each of the other three write A_1, A_2, A_3 respectively. Put the four marbles in an urn and draw one at random. Let E_i denotes the event that the symbol A_i appears on the drawn marble. Then which of the four statements is true for this problem?

(*a*) $P(E_1) = P(E_2) = P(E_3) = \frac{1}{4}$

(*b*) $P(E_1E_2) = P(E_2E_3) = P(E_1E_3) = \frac{1}{4}$

(*c*) $P(E_1E_2E_3) = \frac{1}{8}$

(*d*) all of the above.

108. For a post in a factory, husband and wife both applied. The probability of selection of a male is $\frac{1}{5}$ and that of a female is $\frac{1}{3}$. The probability of selection of only one of them is:

(*a*) 2/15
(*b*) 4/15
(*c*) 8/15
(*d*) 2/5

109. Consider a family of three children. Also assume that all possible distributions of children have same probabilities. Let H be the event, 'the family has children of both the sexes' and A be the event, 'there is at most one girl'. Then the events H and A are:

(*a*) mutually exclusive
(*b*) complementary events
(*c*) independent events
(*d*) exhaustive events.

110. In a certain residential suburb, 70 per cent of all households subscribe to the metropolitan newspaper, 60 per cent subscribe to the local evening paper and 40 per cent households subscribe to both the papers. The probability that a household selected at random subscribes to one of the two newspapers is:

(*a*) 0.3
(*b*) 0.5
(*c*) 0.9
(*d*) 0.2

ANSWERS

Section B

1. Laplace **2.** event **3.** sets **4.** compound **5.** no common point **6.** null **7.** elementary **8.** infinite **9.** not equally likely **10.** a priori **11.** total **12.** null or impossible **13.** $A \subset B$ and $B \subset A$ **14.** exhaustive **15.** union **16.** intersection **17.** Von Mises **18.** statistical or empirical **19.** infinite **20.** derived **21.** sample space **22.** zero **23.** one **24.** one **25.** negative **26.** 0 to 1 **27.** gambling **28.** product **29.** same sample space **30.** ratio or fraction or percentage **31.** independent **32.** exhaustive **33.** $P(A) \geq P(B)$ **34.** $P(A) - P(B)$ or $P(A - B)$ **35.** $P(A) - P(A \cap B)$ **36.** $P(B) - P(A \cap B)$ **37.** additive **38.** $P(A) + P(B)$ **39.** $P(A) + P(B) + P(C) - P(A \cap C) - P(B \cap C)$ **40.** $P(A) \times P(B)$ **41.** $P(B)$ **42.** $P(A|C) + P(B|C) - P(AB|C)$ **43.** $P(A|C)$ **44.** $P(A)P(B|A)$ or $P(B)P(A|B)$ **45.** $P(A)$ **46.** independent **47.** $P(A)\ P(B)\ P(C|A \cap B)$ or $P(A)\ P(C)\ P(B|A \cap C)$ or $P(B)\ P(C)\ P(A|B \cap C)$ **48.** $P(A)\ P(C)$ **49.** independent **50.** $\leq$ **51.** $P(A) + P(B) - 2P(A \cap B)$ **52.** (*a*) $1 - p_3$ (*b*) $p_2 - p_3$ (*c*) $1 - p_1 - p_2 + p_3$ (*d*) $1 - p_1 + p_3$ (*e*) $\frac{p_3}{p_2}$ **53.** 1 **54.** inverse **55.** posteriori **56.** $P(A_1 | B) + P(A_2 | B) - P(A_1A_2 | B)$ **57.** $[P(A) - P(AB)]/[1 - P(B)]$ **58.** $P(A_1)/[P(A_1) + P(A_2)]$ **59.** $P(A)$ **60.** $P(\bar{A} \cap \bar{B})$ **61.** $P(\bar{A} \cup \bar{B})$ **62.** exhaustive **63.** mutually exclusive; exhaustive **64.** $\frac{5}{36}$ **65.** 1 **66.** $1 - P(A/B)$ **67.** zero **68.** $1 - P(A \cap B)$ **69.** $1 - P(A \cup B)$ **70.** (*i*) 5/6 (*ii*) 1/6 (*iii*) 0 **71.** $P(A)\ P(B|A)\ P(C|A \cap B)\ P(D|A \cap B \cap C)$ **72.** equally likely **73.** Compound **74.** favourable cases **75.** dependent **76.** subjective probability **77.** natural assignment **78.** pairwise independent **79.** 0.27 **80.** 1/3

Section C

1. (*a*)	**2.** (*b*)	**3.** (*d*)	**4.** (*d*)	**5.** (*c*)
6. (*c*)	**7.** (*d*)	**8.** (*a*)	**9.** (*b*)	**10.** (*c*)
11. (*a*)	**12.** (*c*)	**13.** (*b*)	**14.** (*d*)	**15.** (*d*)
16. (*b*)	**17.** (*d*)	**18.** (*c*)	**19.** (*b*)	**20.** (*b*)
21. (*a*)	**22.** (*c*)	**23.** (*a*)	**24.** (*c*)	**25.** (*b*)
26. (*c*)	**27.** (*b*)	**28.** (*c*)	**29.** (*d*)	**30.** (*a*)
31. (*a*)	**32.** (*d*)	**33.** (*b*)	**34.** (*b*)	**35.** (*a*)
36. (*c*)				

37. (*b*) [Hint: $P(A \cup B \cup C) = 0.85$, and required percentage = 100 – 85 = 15 per cent]

38. (*d*) $\left[\text{Hint: } P(2W) = \frac{^4C_2}{^7C_2} = \frac{2}{7},\ P(2B) = \frac{^3C_2}{^7C_2} = \frac{1}{7},\ P(2W \text{ and } 2B) = \frac{2}{7} \times \frac{1}{7} = \frac{2}{49}\right]$

39. (*a*) $\left[\text{Hint: } P(2W) = \frac{2}{7},\ P(2B) = \frac{^3C_2}{^5C_2} = \frac{3}{10},\ P(2W \text{ and } 2B) = \frac{2}{7} \times \frac{3}{10} = \frac{3}{35}\right]$

40. (*c*) $\left[\text{Hint: } \Omega = 8 \text{ points}, E = \text{HTT, THT, TTH, TTT}, P(E) = \frac{4}{8} = \frac{1}{2}\right]$

41. (*b*) [Hint: $P(E) = 0.8 + 0.6 - 0.8 \times 0.6 = 0.92$]

42. (*c*) $\left[\text{Hint: } P(E) = 7\left(\frac{1}{7} \times \frac{1}{7}\right) = \frac{1}{7}\right]$

43. (*c*) $\left[\text{Hint: } P(E) = \frac{5}{12} \times \frac{4}{12} \times \frac{3}{12} = \frac{5}{144}\right]$

44. (*a*) $\left[\text{Hint: } P(E) = \frac{5}{12} \times \frac{4}{11} \times \frac{3}{10} = \frac{1}{22}\right]$

45. (*d*) $\left[\text{Hint: } P(E)=\frac{1}{2}\left(\frac{5}{8}+\frac{4}{8}\right)=\frac{9}{16}\right]$

46. (*d*) $\left[\text{Hint: } P(E)=\frac{^4C_1 \times {^4C_1}}{^{52}C_2}=\frac{8}{663}\right]$

47. (*a*) [Hint: Ω = 36 points, E: (6, 6), (6, 5), (5, 6), $P(E)=\frac{3}{36}=\frac{1}{12}$]

48. (*c*)

49. (*b*) $\left[\text{Hint: } P(E) = \left(\frac{^4C_1 \times {^1C_1}}{^6C_1 \times {^4C_1}}\right)+\left(\frac{^2C_1}{^6C_1}\times\frac{^3C_1}{^4C_1}\right)=\frac{5}{12}\right]$

50. (*a*) $\left[\text{Hint : } P(E)=\frac{4}{5}\times\frac{5}{6}\times\frac{1}{4}+\frac{4}{5}\times\frac{1}{6}\times\frac{3}{4} +\frac{1}{5}\times\frac{5}{6}\times\frac{3}{4}+\frac{4}{5}\times\frac{5}{6}+\frac{3}{4}=\frac{107}{120}\right]$

51. (*c*) $\left[\text{Hint : } P(E)=\frac{1}{2}\left(\frac{5}{9}+\frac{4}{9}\right)=\frac{1}{2}\right]$

52. (*b*) [Hint: Ω = 6 × 6 × 6 points, E = (1, 5, 6), (1, 6, 5) …, (6, 4, 2), (6, 5, 1) = 25 points, $P(E)=\frac{25}{216}$]

53. (*c*) $\left[\text{Hint : } P(B/A)=\frac{P(A/B)\,P(B)}{P(A)}=\frac{1}{8}\right]$

54. (*d*) $\left[\text{Hint : } P(B/\bar{A})=\frac{[1-P(A/B)]\,P(B)}{1-P(A)}=\frac{5}{16}\right]$

55. (*d*) [Hint: Ω = 64 points, E = (1, 8), (2, 7), (3, 6), (4, 5), (5, 4), (6, 3), (7, 2), $P(E)=\frac{7}{64}$]

56. (*a*) $\left[\text{Hint: } P(E)=\frac{^5C_3}{^8C_3}=\frac{5}{28}\right]$

57. (*d*) [Hint: Impossible event]

58. (*c*) $\left[\text{Hint: } P(E)=\left(\frac{1}{5}+\frac{1}{6}\right)=\frac{11}{30}\right]$

59. (*a*) $\left[\text{Hint: } P(E)=\frac{^{26}C_2 \times {^{26}C_2}}{^{52}C_4}=\frac{325}{833}\right]$

60. (*d*) $\left[\text{Hint: } P(E)=\frac{1}{5}+\frac{1}{7}-\frac{1}{5}\times\frac{1}{7}=\frac{11}{35}\right]$

61. (*b*) $\left[\text{Hint: } P(E)=\frac{5}{12}+\frac{2}{7}-\frac{5}{12}\times\frac{2}{7}=\frac{49}{84}\right]$

62. (*d*) $\left[\text{Hint: } P(E)=\frac{7}{13}+\frac{5}{8}-\frac{7}{13}\times\frac{5}{8}=\frac{43}{52}\right]$

63. (*b*) $\left[\text{Hint: } P(E)=\frac{1}{3}+\frac{1}{5}=\frac{8}{15}\right]$

64. (*d*) [Hint: Ω = 36 points, E = 18 pairs of odd sum, $P(E)=\frac{18}{36}=\frac{1}{2}$]

65. (*c*) [Hint: Ω 36, pairs E = first throw 1 and second throw 2, 3, 4, 5; 6 or 1st throw 2, 3, 4, 5, 6 and 2nd throw 1 or both the throws 1, 1. E = 11 points $P(E)$ = 11/36]

66. (*b*) $\left[\text{Hint: } P(E)=\frac{8}{9}+\frac{6}{7}-\frac{8}{9}\times\frac{6}{7}=\frac{62}{63}\right]$

67. (*d*) $\left[\text{Hint: } P(E)=\frac{^4C_2 \times {^3C_1}}{^9C_3}+\frac{^4C_2 \times {^2C_1}}{^9C_3}=\frac{5}{14}\right]$

68. (*b*) [Hint: A leap year has 366 days, *i.e.*, 52 week and 2 days. 52 Sundays are sure. 53rd Sunday may be on the remaining two days. The possible pairs of days are (S, M), (M, T), (T, W), (W, Th), (Th, F) (F, Sat), (Sat, S) . E = (S, M) and (Sat, S) . $P(E)$ = 2/7]

69. (*d*) [Hint: Ω = 36 pairs, E = (4, 6) (6, 4), (5, 5), (5, 6), (6, 5) and (6, 6). $P(E)$ = 6/36 = 1/6]

70. (*c*) $\left[\text{Hint: } P(E)=\frac{3}{4}\times\frac{4}{5}\times\frac{1}{6}+\frac{3}{4}\times\frac{1}{5}\times\frac{5}{6} +\frac{1}{4}\times\frac{4}{5}\times\frac{5}{6}=\frac{47}{120}\right]$

71. (*b*) [Hint: A – 3 defectives out of 1st eight examined record players B – 9th piece is defective. $P(A) = \binom{4}{3}\binom{11}{5}\Big/\binom{15}{8}$, $P(B/A) = \frac{1}{7}$, $P(A \cap B) = P(B/A)\,P(A) = 8/195$]

72. (*d*) [Hint: E_1: disease X is correctly diagnosed by doctor A, E_2: Patient having disease X dies.

$$P(E_1) = 0.6,\ P(\bar{E}_1) = 0.4,\ P(E_2/E_1) = 0.4,$$

$$P(E_2/\bar{E}_1) = 0.7$$

$$P(E_1/E_2) = \frac{P(E_2/E_1)\,P(E_1)}{P(E_2/E_1)\,P(E_1) + P(E_2/\bar{E}_1)\,P(\bar{E}_1)} = \frac{6}{13}\Bigg]$$

73. (*d*) [Hint: $P(A_1) = P(A_2) = P(A_3) = \frac{1}{2}$, $(A_1 \cap A_2) = \frac{1}{4} = P(A_1)P(A_2)$. Similarly, $P(A_2 \cap A_3) = P(A_2)\,P(A_3)$ and $P(A_1 \cap A_3) = P(A_1)P(A_3)$.

Also $P(A_1 \cap A_2 \cap A_3) = 0$]

74. (*d*)

75. (*b*) $\left[\text{Hint: } P(E) = \binom{8}{3}\Big/\binom{12}{3} = \frac{14}{55}\right]$

76. (*a*) [Hint: $P(E_1\, E_2\, E_3) = P(E_1)P(E_2/E_1)$

$$P(E_3 \mid E_1\, E_2) = \frac{3}{8} \times \frac{5}{10} \times \frac{7}{12} = \frac{7}{64}\Bigg]$$

77. (*c*) $\left[\text{Hint: } P(A \cap B) = \frac{1}{3} + \frac{3}{4} - \frac{11}{12} = \frac{1}{6},\right.$

$$\left. P(B/A) = \frac{1/6}{1/3} = \frac{1}{2}\right]$$

78. (*b*) $\left[\text{Hint: } P(B'/C') = \frac{P(B'/C')}{P(C')} = \frac{P(B' \cup C')}{P(C')}\right.$

$$\left. = \frac{0.6 + 0.5 - 0.7}{1 - 0.5} = \frac{4}{5}\right]$$

79. (*a*) [Hint: $P(AB') = P(A) - P(AB) = 0.1$, $P(A/B) = 0.1/0.4 = 1/4$]

80. (*c*) [Hint: There are ten digits from 0 to 9 in which a product can end. Problem of any given digit to be the first digits is $\frac{4}{10} = \frac{2}{5}$ for the given event,

$$P(E) = \frac{2}{5} \times \frac{2}{5} \times \frac{2}{5} \times \frac{2}{5} = \left(\frac{2}{5}\right)^4\Bigg]$$

81. (*d*) $\left[\text{Hint: } P(E) = \frac{2}{5} \times \frac{3}{5} \times \frac{1}{5} + \frac{2}{5} \times \frac{4}{5} \times \frac{2}{5} + \frac{3}{5}\right.$

$$\left. \times \frac{3}{5} \times \frac{4}{5} = \frac{58}{125}\right]$$

82. (*c*) [Hint: Prob. of selecting a coin having both head = 1/4 and it has all five heads = $\frac{1}{4} \times 1 \times 1 \times 1 \times 1 \times 1 = \frac{1}{4}$. Problem of selection of a coin having head and tail = 3/4 and it falls with five heads = $\frac{3}{4} \times \left(\frac{1}{2}\right)^5 = \frac{3}{128}$.

$$P(E) = \frac{1/4}{1/4 + \dfrac{3}{128}} = \frac{32}{35}\Bigg]$$

83. (*d*) $\left[\text{Hint: } p_1 = x,\ p_2 = \frac{x}{5},\ x + \frac{x}{5} = 1,\right.$

$$\left. x = \frac{5}{6},\ p_2/p_1 = \frac{1/6}{5/6} \text{ or } p_2 : p_1 = 1:5\right]$$

84. (*b*)

85. (*c*) [$P(E) = P(\text{HTHTHT}) + P(\text{THTHTH})$

$$= \left(\frac{1}{2}\right)^6 + \left(\frac{1}{2}\right)^6 = \frac{1}{32}\Bigg]$$

86. (*c*) $\left[\text{Hint: } P(E_1) = \frac{5}{9},\ P(\bar{E}_2) = \frac{3}{7},\ P(E_1 \cup \bar{E}_2)\right.$

$$\left. = \frac{5}{9} + \frac{3}{7} - \frac{5}{9} \times \frac{3}{7} = \frac{47}{63}\right]$$

87. (*b*) [Hint: Let A be at 12th place, $P(A) = 1/12$. B can be at 4th or 8th places out of remaining 11 places. $P(B) = \frac{2}{11}$. Also A can be at any of the 12 places. Therefore, $P(E) = \frac{1}{12} \times \frac{2}{11} \times 12 = \frac{2}{11}$]

88. (*b*) $\left[\text{Hint: } P(E) = 3 \times \left(\frac{1}{3}\right)^3 = \frac{1}{9}\right]$

89. (*d*) $\left[\text{Hint: } P(E) = \frac{3P_3}{3^3} = \frac{2}{9}\right]$

90. (*d*) [Hint: Prob. of their true assertion that a white ball is drawn = 3/50. Chance of *A* statement being wrong = $\frac{1}{9} \times \frac{1}{5} = \frac{1}{45}$ and that of *B* being wrong $= \frac{1}{9} \times \frac{1}{3} = \frac{1}{27}$. Prob. of *A* and *B* to agree in false statement that a white ball is drawn $= \frac{1}{45} \times \frac{1}{27} \times \frac{9}{10} = \frac{1}{27 \times 50}$. $P(E)$
$$= \frac{3/50}{3/50 + \frac{1}{27 \times 50}} = \frac{81}{82}$$]

91. (*a*) $\left[\text{Hint: } P(E) = \frac{3/50}{\frac{3}{5} + \frac{9}{10} \times \frac{1}{5} \times \frac{1}{9}} = \frac{4}{7}\right]$

92. (*d*) $\left[\text{Hint: } P(E) = \frac{4}{5} \times \frac{1}{4} + \frac{1}{5} \times \frac{3}{4} = \frac{7}{20}\right]$

93. (*c*) $\left[\text{Hint: } P(E) = \frac{{}^6C_1 \times {}^6C_1}{{}^{10}C_1 \times {}^{10}C_1} = \frac{36}{100}\right]$

94. (*b*) [Hint $P(E) = P(TTTH) + P(TTTTH) + P(TTTTTH) + \ldots$
$$= \frac{1}{8} + \frac{1}{16} + \frac{1}{32} + \ldots = \frac{1/8}{1 - 1/2} = \frac{1}{4}$$]

95. (*c*) [Hint: $P(E) = {}^5C_3/{}^{20}C_3 = 1/114$]

96. (*c*) $\left[\text{Hint: } P(E) = \frac{1}{20c_3}[{}^5C_1 \times {}^{15}C_2 + {}^5C_2 + {}^{15}C_1 + {}^5C_3] = \frac{137}{228}\right]$

97. (*b*) [Hint: A_1 – Examinee knows the answer,
A_2 – Examinee guesses the answer,
B – Answers correctly.
$$P(A_1/B) = \frac{P(A_1)P(B/A_1)}{P(A_1)P(B/A_1) + P(A_2)\,P(B/A_2)}$$
$$= \frac{p \times 1}{p \times 1 + \frac{1-p}{m}}$$]

98. (*b*) [Hint: $P(E) =$
$$= \frac{35/100 \times 4/100}{\frac{35}{100} \times \frac{4}{100} + \frac{25}{100} \times \frac{5}{100} + \frac{40}{100} \times \frac{3}{100}} = \frac{4}{11}$$]

99. (*a*) [Hint: *A* – card is heart, *B* – card is ace
$$P(A) = \frac{1}{4},\ P(B) = \frac{1}{13},\ P(A \cap B) = \frac{1}{52}.$$
$$P(A \cup B) = \frac{4}{13} = p,\ q = \frac{9}{13},\ q : p = 9 : 4$$]

100. (*c*) [Hint: E = 00, 01, 02, 03, 04, 05, 06, 07, 08, 09, 10, 20, 30, 40, 50, 60, 70, 80, 90 = 19 points Ω = 00, 01, …, 99 = 100 points, $P(E)$ = 19/100]

101. (*b*) **102.** (*d*) **103.** (*a*) **104.** (*b*) **105.** (*c*)
106. (*b*) **107.** (*b*) **108.** (*d*) **109.** (*c*) **110.** (*c*)

SUGGESTED READING

1. Agarwal, B.L., *Basic Statistics,* New Age International Publishers, New Delhi, 8th edition, 2024.
2. Bhat, B.R., *Modern Probability Theory,* Wiley Eastern Ltd., Publishers, New Delhi, 2nd edn., 1995.
3. Chung, K.L., *Elementary Probability Theory with Stochastic Processes,* Springer Verlag, Berlin, 1975.
4. Feller, W., *An Introduction to Probability Theory and its Applications,* Vols. I & II, John Wiley & Sons, New York, 1966.
5. Finetti, B. D., *Theory of Probability,* Translated by Antonio Machi and Adrian Smith, John Wiley & Sons, New York, 1974.
6. Fish, M. *Probability Theory and Mathematical Statistics,* John Wiley & Sons, New York, 1963.

7. Gottinger, H.W., *Elements of Statistical Analysis,* Walter de Gruyter, Berlin, 1980.

8. Haight, F.A., *Applied Probability,* Plenum Press, New York, 1981.

9. Lindgren, B.W. and McElrath, G./W., *Introduction to Probability and Statistics,* The MacMillan Company, New York, 1959.

10. Loe've, M., *Probability Theory and Mathematical Statistics,* John Wiley & Son, New York, 1963.

11. Mises, R.V., *Probability, Statistics and Truth,* George Allen and Unwin, New York, 1957.

12. Parzen, E., *Modern Probability Theory and its Applications,* John Wiley & Sons, New York, 1960.

13. Rahman, N.A., *Practical Exercises in Probability and Statistics, Charles Griffin,* London, 1972.

14. Rohatgi, V.K., *An Introduction to Probability Theory and Mathematical Statistics,* Wiley Eastern Ltd., Publishers, New Delhi, 1993.

15. Uspensky, J.V., *Introduction to Mathematical Probability,* Tata McGraw Hill, Delhi, 1965.

CHAPTER 7

Random Variable, Mathematical Expectation and Probability Distributions

SECTION A

Short Essay Type Questions

Q. 1. *Define a random variable and give its examples.*

Ans. A rule that assigns a real number to each outcome (sample point) of a random experiment is called a random variable (r.v.). It is governed by a function of the variable. Hence, a random variable is a real valued function $X(x)$ of the elements of the sample space Ω where x is an element of Ω. Further, the range of the variable will be a set of real values. For example, in tossing a coin, $x = 1$, if the coin falls with head, and $x = 0$ if the coin falls with tail. The height of persons can be given by $X(x) = X$, the height measured in centimeters or inches. A random variable is usually denoted by any of the capital Latin letters $X, Y, Z, U, V, \ldots$.

Q. 2. *Discuss different types of variables with examples.*

Ans. There are two types of random variables namely (*i*) discrete random variable, (*ii*) continuous random variable.

(*i*) A random variable, say x, which can take a finite number of values in an interval of the domain, is called *discrete random variable.* For example, if we toss a coin, the variable can take only two values 0 and 1 assigned to tail and head respectively, *i.e.*,

$$X(x) = \begin{cases} 0 \text{ if } x \text{ is } T \\ 1 \text{ if } x \text{ is } H \end{cases}$$

In rolling of a die, only six values of the variable X, *i.e.*, 1, 2, 3, 4, 5 and 6 are possible. Hence, the variable X is discrete. Here the variable,

$$X(x) = \{x : x = 1, 2, 3, 4, 5 \text{ and } 6\}$$

(*ii*) A random variable X, which can take any value in its domain or in an interval or the union of intervals on the real line is called *Continuous random variable.* For a continuous variable, the probability of a point x is zero, *i.e.*, $P(X = x) = 0$. But the probability is ascribable in an interval. For instance, the weight of middle-aged people in India lying between 40 kg and 150 kg is a continuous variable. Notationally,

$$X(x) = [x : 40 \leq x \leq 150]$$

The maximum breaking strength 250 kg of a wire is a continuous variable. Notationally,

$$X(x) = [x : 0 \leq x \leq 250]$$

Q. 3. *What are the important properties of a random variable?*

Ans. The properties of a random variable are:

(*i*) If X is a random variable and a, b are any two constants, $aX + b$ is also a random variable.

(*ii*) If X is a random variable, X^2 is also a random variable.

(*iii*) If X is a random variable, $1/X$ is also a random variable.

(*iv*) If X and Y are two random variables defined over the same space, $X + Y$, $X - Y$, aX, bY or $aX + bY$ are also random variables where a and b are any two constants except that a and b both are not zero.

(*v*) If $X_1, X_2, \ldots, X_n$ are n random variables, $U_n = \max (X_1, X_2, \ldots, X_n)$ and $V_n = \min (X_1, X_2, \ldots, X_n)$ are also random variables.

Q. 4. *What do you understanding by a distribution function?*

Ans. A function $F_X(x)$ of a random variable X for a real value x giving the probability of the event $(X \leq x)$ is called a *cumulative distribution function* (c.d.f.) or simply *distribution function.* Symbolically,

$$F_X(x) = P(X \leq x)$$

Obviously X lies in the interval $(-\infty, x)$.

Q. 5. *What are the properties of a distribution function?*

Ans. Some important properties of distribution function are:

(*i*) If a and b are two constant values such that $a < b$ and F is the distribution function, then $P(a \leq X \leq b) = F(b) - F(a)$.

(*ii*) If $F(x)$ is the distribution function of a monovariate X, then $0 \leq F(x) \leq 1$.

(*iii*) If $X < Y$, then $F(x) < F(y)$.

(*iv*) If $F(x)$ is the distribution function of a monovariate X, then

$$F(-\infty) = \lim_{x \to -\infty} F(x) = 0$$

$$F(\infty) = \lim_{x \to \infty} F(x) = 1$$

Q. 6. *What is a probability mass function (p.m.f.) or discrete probability distribution?*

Ans. If $X_1, X_2, \ldots$ are the variate values in the sample space Ω of a single dimensional variable X with probabilities of occurrence $p_1, p_2, \ldots$ respectively, *i.e.*, $p_i = P(X = x_i) = p(x_i)$ such that $p(x_i) \geq 0 \ \forall \ i$ and $\sum_{\text{all } x_i \varepsilon \Omega} p(x_i) = 1$, $p(x)$ is called the *probability mass function* and $F(x)$ the *probability distribution function* of the random variable x where,

$$F(x) = \sum_{\text{all } (i;\, x \leq x_i)} p(x_i)$$

The function $F(x)$ is also called the *step function* and its graph is just like staircase having a jump of magnitude p_i at each i taken along abscissa.

Q. 7. *What is meant by probability density function?*

Ans. If X is a continuous variable and $f_X(x)$ is a continuous function of X, $f_X(x)\, dx$ gives the probability of the event that X lies in the interval

$$\left(x - \frac{1}{2}dx\right) \text{and} \left(x + \frac{1}{2}dx\right)$$

i.e. $$\left(x - \frac{1}{2}dx \leq x \leq x + \frac{1}{2}dx\right),$$

$f_X(x)$ or simply $f(x)$ is called *probability density function* (p.d.f.) or simply *density function.* It is also known as *frequency function* because it also gives the proportion of units lying in the interval $\left(x - \frac{1}{2}dx\right)$ and $\left(x + \frac{1}{2}dx\right)$. When the probability, which is the area under *probability density curve* within the interval, is multiplied by the total number of units in the population, this gives the actual number of units in the prescribed interval. If x has the range $[\alpha, \beta], f(x) \geq 0 \forall x \ \varepsilon[\alpha, \beta]$, then $\int_{\alpha}^{\beta} f(x)\, dx = 1$. Also for any two values (a, b).

$$p = \int_a^b f(x)\,dx = F(b) - F(a)$$

Q. 8. *Define and discuss mathematical expectation.*

Ans. *Definition:* The expected value of a random variable is simply the long run average of this variable over an indefinite number of samples.

If X is a discrete random variable that takes on the values $x_1, x_2, \ldots, x_n$ with probability $p_1, p_2, \ldots, p_n$, respectively, the expected value of X is given as,

$$E(X) = \sum_{i=1}^{n} p_i x_i \quad \text{where} \sum_{i=1}^{n} p_i = 1$$

In general, the expected value of a function $H(x)$ of X is,

$$E\{H(x)\} = \sum_{\text{all } x_i} H(x)\,p(x)$$

Again, if X is a continuous random variable with p.d.f. $f(x)$, the expected value of X is,

$$E(X) = \int_a^b x f(x)\,dx\ ;\ a \le x \le b.$$

$E(X)$ is also known as *theoretical average value.* If $g(x)$, a function of X is also a continuous variable and $E[g(x)]$ exists, then

$$E[g(x)] = \int_a^b g(x) f(x)\,dx$$

Mathematical expectation is extremely used to find out the moments of a distribution and has great importance. Moments have already been discussed in Chapter 5.

Q. 9. *Give some important results of mathematical expectation.*

Ans. Following are some of the important results on mathematical expectation:

(*i*) $E(X) = \sum_{\text{all } x_i} p_i x_i = \frac{1}{N} \sum_{\text{all } x_i} x_i = \mu_1 = \mu$

(mean) where each x_i has probability $\frac{1}{N}$.

If X be a continuous r.v.,

$$E(X) = \int x f(x)\,dx = \mu$$

Further, $E(x - \bar{x}) = 0$ where $\bar{x}$ is sample mean and $E(\bar{x}) = \mu$.

(*ii*) $E(X - \mu)^2 = \sum_{\text{all } x_i} p_i (x_i - \mu)^2$

$$= \frac{1}{N} \sum_{\text{all } x_i} (x_i - \mu)^2 = \mu_2 \text{ (variance)}$$

or if X be a continuous r.v.,

$$E(X - \mu)^2 = \int (x - \mu)^2 f(x)\,dx = \mu_2$$

(*iii*) If $X_1, X_2, \ldots, X_n$ are n random variables, then $E(X_1 + X_2 + \ldots + X_n) = E(X_1) + E(X_2) + \ldots + E(X_n)$

It is known as *addition theorem* of expectation.

(*iv*) If $X_1, X_2, \ldots, X_n$ are n independent random variables, then

$$E(X_1 X_2 \ldots X_n) = E(X_1)\,E(X_2) \ldots E(X_n)$$

(*v*) Expectation of a constant is the constant itself, *i.e.*, $E(c) = c$ where c is a constant.

(*vi*) If c is a constant, then

$$E(cX) = cE(X)$$

Again, if a and c are two constants, then

Also $E(aX + c) = aE(X) + c$

and $V(aX + c) = a^2 V(X)$

(*vii*) If X and Y are two random variables, c_1 and c_2 are two constants, then

$$E(c_1 X + c_2 Y) = c_1 E(X) + c_2 E(Y)$$

(*viii*) If $X \le Y$, $E(X) \le E(Y)$.

(*ix*) If X and Y are two random variables, the covariance between X and Y is given as,

$$\text{cov}(X, Y) = E[\{X - E(X)\}\{Y - E(Y)\}]$$
$$= E(XY) - E(X)\,E(Y).$$

If X and Y are independent, $\text{cov}(X, Y) = 0$

(*x*) If X_1 and X_2 are two random variables, then

$$V(X_1 + X_2) = V(X_1) + V(X_2) + 2\text{ cov }(X_1, X_2)$$

Also $$V(c_1X_1 + c_2X_2) = c_1^2V(X_1) + c_2^2V(X_2) + 2c_1c_2\text{ cov }(X_1, X_2)$$

(*xi*) If X_1 and X_2 are two random variables, then

$$V(X_1 - X_2) = V(X_1) + V(X_2) - 2\text{ cov }(X_1, X_2)$$

Also $$V(c_1X_1 - c_2X_2) = c_1^2V(X_1) + c_2^2V(X_2) + 2c_1c_2\text{ cov }(X_1, X_2)$$

Q. 10. *State Cauchy-Schwartz inequality on expectation.*

Ans. Cauchy-Schwartz inequality states that if X and Y are two random variables taking real values then

$$E[(XY)^2] \leq E(X^2)\, E(Y^2)$$

Q. 11. *State Jenson's inequality on expectation.*

Ans. If ϕ is a continuous and convex function and X is a random variable having finite mean μ, *i.e.*, $E(X) = \mu$, then

$$E[\phi(x)] \geq \phi[E(x)]$$

In case ϕ is a continuous and concave function,

$$E[\phi(x)] \leq \phi[E(x)]$$

Q. 12. *State Gurland's inequality on expectation.*

Ans. If ϕ and ψ be two continuous monotone functions of a variable X which are both non-decreasing or both non-increasing and also their expectations exist, then

$$E[\phi(x)\,\psi(x)] \geq E[\phi(x)]\, E[\psi(x)]$$

It implies $E(X^2) \geq [E(X)]^2$, provided X takes non-negative values. Also if one of them is non-increasing and the other is non-decreasing, then

$$E[\phi(x)\,\psi(x)] \leq E[\phi(x)]\, E[\psi(x)]$$

Q. 13. *Define moment generating function (m.g.f.) and its usage.*

Ans. Moment generating function $M_X(t)$ of a random variable X having probability function $f(x)$ is

$$M_X(t) = E(e^{tx}).$$

For a discrete distribution,

$$M_X(t) = E(e^{tx}) = \sum_{\text{all } x} e^{tx} f(x)$$

and for continuous distribution,

$$M_X(t) = E(e^{tx}) = \int e^{tx} f(x)\, dx$$

Moment generating function is used to find the moments of a distribution. The rth moment about origin is the coefficient of $t^r/r!$ in the expansion of $M_X(t)$.

Note: A m.g.f. may exist without the existence of moments.

Q. 14. *Define characteristic function (c.f.) and give its importance.*

Ans. The characteristic function of a random variable X having the probability function $f(x)$ is given as,

$$\phi_X(t) = E(e^{itx})$$

For a discrete distribution,

$$\phi_X(t) = \sum_{\text{all } x} e^{itx} f(x)$$

and for a continuous distribution,

$$\phi_X(t) = \int e^{itx} f(x)\, dx$$

The greatest importance of characteristic function is that it exists for each and every distribution whereas moment generating function does not exist for every distribution.

Secondly, once we know the characteristic function, we can identify the distribution.

Also, characteristic function is as good as moment generating function in finding out the moments of a distribution. r^{th} moment about the origin is the coefficient of $\frac{(it)^r}{r!}$ in the expansion of $E(e^{itx})$.

Properties

If X and Y are two independent variables and a, b any two real constants, then

$$M_{aX+bY}(t) = M_{aX}(t) \cdot M_{bY}(t)$$

when $a = b = 1$, $M_{X+Y}(t) = M_X(t) \cdot M_Y(t)$

Similarly, $\phi_{aX+bY}(t) = \phi_{aX}(t) \cdot \phi_{bY}(t)$

if $a = b = 1$, $\phi_{X+Y}(t) = \phi_X(t) \cdot \phi_Y(t)$

This is known as the additive or reproductive property.

Q. 15. *Describe in brief probability generating function (p.g.f.).*

Ans. If X is non-negative integer-valued variate, the probability generating function of X is,

$$G_X(t) = E(t^x) = \sum_{\text{all } x} P(X = x)t^x \quad 0 \le t \le 1$$

$$= \sum_{\text{all } x} p(x)t^x$$

$G_X(t)$ is known as p.g.f. since the coefficient of t^x in $E(t^x)$ is $p(x)$.

Probability generating function is closely related to moment generating function as by replacing t in p.g.f. by e^t, we obtain m.g.f. For example, the m.g.f. of binomial distribution is $(q + pe^t)^n$ and p.g.f. is $(q + pt)^n$. Similarly in case of Poisson distribution,

$$M_X(t) = e^{\mu(e^t - 1)} \quad \text{whereas} \quad G_X(t) = e^{\mu(t-1)}.$$

Probability generating function also holds the *additive property*. If X and Y are two independent variates, the p.g.f. of the sum of variates is equal to the product of p.g.f's of individual variates, *i.e.*,

$$G_{X+Y}(t) = G_X(t) \times G_Y(t).$$

If $X_1, X_2, \ldots, X_n$ are i.i.d, then

$$G_{X_1 + X_2 + \ldots X_n}(t) = [G_X(t)]^n$$

If X is an integer valued variable, p.g.f. can be used to find the moments of the distribution.

Q. 16. *Describe in brief the uniform distribution.*

Ans. A discrete variable X is said to follow *discrete uniform distribution* if its probability function is,

$$P(X = x) = p(x)$$

$$= \frac{1}{n} \quad \text{for} \quad x = 1, 2, \ldots, n$$

$$= 0 \text{ otherwise}$$

For example, the outcomes of rolling a fair die or drawing cards successively from a well shuffled deck of cards follow uniform distribution. In this distribution, probability at every point remains the same.

Q. 17. *Give Bernoulli distribution and its properties.*

Ans. A random variable X, marked by only two values 1 and 0 or 1 and –1 with probability of occurrence p and q ($q = 1 - p$) respectively where $P(x = 1) = p$ and $P(x = 0) = q$, is called a Bernoulli variate and its distribution is called *Bernoulli distribution*. The probability distribution of x is,

$$f(x) = p^x q^{1-x}$$

where $0 \le p \le 1$ and $x = 0$ or 1.

The only parameter of Bernoulli distribution is p.

Properties

(*i*) Mean of Bernoulli distribution is p.

(*ii*) Variance of Bernoulli distribution is pq.

(*iii*) Moment generating function of Bernoulli distribution is $(q + p\,e^t)$.

(*iv*) An experiment with two possible outcomes classified as success A and failure $\bar{A}$ is called a *Bernoulli trial* if the $P(A)$ remains the same at repeated trials. For instance in tossing a fair coin again and again, the probability of falling the coin with head upside remains $\frac{1}{2}$. Hence it is a Bernoulli trial.

Q. 18. *Delineate Binomial distribution and its important features.*

Ans. Binomial distribution was invented by James Bernoulli which was posthumously published in 1713. Let n (finite) Bernoulli trials be conducted with probability 'p' of a success and 'q' of a failure. The probability of x successes out of n Bernoulli trials is given by

$$f(x) = \binom{n}{x} p^x q^{n-x}$$

where $x = 0, 1, 2, \ldots, n$

$0 \le p \le 1$, and $p + q = 1$

A dichotomous r.v., X having the probability mass function $f(x) = \binom{n}{x} p^x q^{n-x}$ is said to follow *Binomial distribution* and is usually denoted as $b(n, p)$ or $b(x; n, p)$. The probability function $\binom{n}{x} p^x q^{n-x}$ is the $(x + 1)^{th}$ term in the binomial expansion of $(q + p)^n$.

Important features

(*i*) If $n = 1$, the binomial distribution reduces to Bernoulli distribution. Hence, seldom Bernoulli distribution is known as *point binomial.*

(*ii*) Binomial distribution has two parameters n and p.

(*iii*) Mean of binomial distribution is np.

(*iv*) Variance of binomial distribution is npq.

(*v*) The moment generating function of binomial distribution is $(q + pe^t)^n$.

(*vi*) Characteristic function of $b(n, p)$ is $(q + pe^{it})^n$.

(*vii*) The first four moments with their relation to cumulants are:

$$\mu = \kappa_1, = np, \mu_2 = \kappa_2 - npq,$$
$$\mu_3 = \kappa_3 = npq(q-p)$$
$$\mu_4 = \kappa_4 + 3\kappa_2^2 = npq[1 + 3pq(n-2)].$$

(*viii*) The measure of skewness, $\beta_1 = \frac{(1-2p)^2}{npq}$ or $\gamma_1 = \frac{1-2p}{\sqrt{npq}}$. The value of β_1 indicates that binomial distribution is positively skewed if $p < \frac{1}{2}$ and symmetrical if $p = \frac{1}{2}$.

(*ix*) $\beta_2 = 3 + \frac{1-6pq}{npq}$ or $\gamma_2 = \frac{1-6pq}{npq}$. The value of measure of kurtosis 'β_2' reveals that as the number of trials $n \to \infty$, the distribution tends to mesokurtic.

(*x*) Recurrence formula for binomial distribution is,

$$p(x = x + 1) = p(x = x)\ \frac{n-x}{x+1} \cdot \frac{p}{q}$$

This formula is very helpful in calculating the probability of the consecutive successes.

(*xi*) If $X \sim b(n_1, p)$ and $Y \sim b(n_2, p)$, then $X + Y \sim b(n_1 + n_2, p)$. This property is known as *additive* or *reproductive* property of binomial distribution.

(*xii*) If $Y \sim b(y; n, p)$, the variable $X = Y/n$, the ratio of number of successes to the total number of trials n, is called a *relative* or *Pseudo* binomial variate.

Q. 19. *In five tossings of a fair coin find the chance of getting 3 heads.*

Ans. $P(3 \text{ heads}) = \binom{5}{3}\left(\frac{1}{2}\right)^3\left(\frac{1}{2}\right)^2 = \frac{5}{16}$.

Since $p = \frac{1}{2}, q = \frac{1}{2}$.

Q. 20. *A machine produces 10 per cent defective items. Ten items are selected at random. Find the probability of not more than two items being defective.*

Ans. $P(X \le 2) = \sum_{x=0}^{2} \binom{10}{x}\left(\frac{1}{10}\right)^x\left(\frac{9}{10}\right)^{10-x}$

$$= \binom{10}{0}\left(\frac{1}{10}\right)^0\left(\frac{9}{10}\right)^{10-0} + \binom{10}{1}\left(\frac{1}{10}\right)^1\left(\frac{9}{10}\right)^{10-1} + \binom{10}{2}\left(\frac{1}{10}\right)^2\left(\frac{9}{10}\right)^{10-2} = \left(\frac{24}{9}\right)\left(\frac{9}{10}\right)^{10}$$

Q. 21. *The chances of a bomber hitting the target and missing the target are 3 : 2. Calculate the probability that the target will be hit at least once in five sorties.*

Ans. $P(X \ge 1) = \sum_{x=1}^{5} \binom{5}{x}\left(\frac{3}{5}\right)^x\left(\frac{2}{5}\right)^{5-x}$

or $P(X \geq 1) = 1 - P(x = 0)$

$$= 1 - \left(\frac{2}{5}\right)^5 = \frac{3093}{3125}.$$

Q. 22. *Explicate Poisson distribution and its properties.*

Ans. Poisson distribution was discovered by a French Mathematician-cum-Physicist, Simeon Denis Poisson in 1937. He derived it as a limiting case of binomial distribution. If a dichotomous variable X is such that the constant probability p of success for each trial is very small and the number of trials n is indefinitely large and $np = \mu$ is finite, the probability of x successes is given by the probability mass function,

$$P(X = x) = \frac{e^{-\mu}\,\mu^x}{x\,!} \quad \text{for } x = 0, 1, 2, \ldots$$

$$= 0 \quad \text{otherwise.}$$

It is denoted by $P(x;\ \mu)$.

Some of the example of Poisson variate are:

(*a*) No. of deaths in a city due to suicides.

(*b*) No. of defective items in a box of 100 items.

(*c*) No. of plane accidents per week.

Main properties of Poisson distribution are:

(*i*) Poisson distribution has only one parameter 'μ'.

(*ii*) Mean of Poisson distribution (variate) is μ.

(*iii*) Variance of Poisson distribution (variate) is also μ. This is the only distribution of which the mean and variance are equal.

(*iv*) Moment generating function of Poisson distribution is $e^{\mu(e^t - 1)}$.

(*v*) Characteristic function of Poisson distribution is $e^{\mu(e^{it} - 1)}$.

(*vi*) First three moments of Poisson distribution (variate) are equal, *i.e.*, $\mu_1 = \mu_2 = \mu_3 = \mu$ and $\mu_4 = \mu + 3\mu^2$.

(*vii*) All the cumulants are equal, *i.e.*, $\kappa_1 = \kappa_2 = \kappa_3 = \kappa_4 = \mu$.

(*viii*) The measure of skewness, $\beta_1 = \frac{\mu_3^2}{\mu_3^2} = \frac{\mu^2}{\mu^3} = \frac{1}{\mu}$ or $\gamma_1 = \frac{1}{\sqrt{\mu}}$.

(*ix*) Measure of kurtosis, $\beta_2 = \frac{\mu_4}{\mu_2^2} = \frac{1}{\mu} + 3$ or $\gamma_2 = \frac{1}{\sqrt{\mu}}$. These measures show that Poisson distribution is positively skewed and leptokurtic.

(*x*) For a Poisson variate X with mean μ, the recurrence relationship between $P(X = x)$ and $P(X = x + 1)$ is,

$$P(X = x + 1) = P(X = x) \cdot \frac{\mu}{x+1}$$

(*xi*) If n is large ($n \to \infty$) and p small in a binomial distribution such that np remains constant say, μ, the binomial distribution tends to Poisson distribution $\frac{e^{-\mu}\,\mu^x}{x\,!}$

(*xii*) Independent Poisson variates possess additive (reproductive) property. This property ensures that the sum of independent Poisson variates is also a Poisson variate. If X_1, X_2, ..., X_n are $P(x_1;\ \mu_1)$, $P(x_2;\ \mu_2)$, ..., $P(x_n;\ \mu_n)$, respectively, then $(X_1 + X_2 + \ldots + X_n)$ is $P(\Sigma\, x_i;\ \mu_1 + \mu_2 + \ldots + \mu_n)$.

(*xiii*) If X and Y are two Poisson variates with means μ and λ respectively, the conditional distribution of X given $(X + Y)$ is binomial.

(*xiv*) If X_1 and X_2 are two independent Poisson variates distributed as $P(x_1;\ \mu_1)$ and $P(x_2;\ \mu_2)$ respectively, $(X_1 - X_2)$ is not a Poisson variate. This property of Poisson variates is known as the *subtractive* property.

Q. 23. *A gear manufacturing company expects that the chance of a gear being defective is* $\frac{1}{200}$. *The gears are supplied in boxes of 10 gears. Find the probability that there are two defective gears in a box of 10 gears. Also calculate the number of boxes containing two defective pieces out of 10,000 boxes.*

Ans. Since the probability of a gear being defective (X) is small, the variate follows Poisson distribution.

The mean, $\mu = 10 \times \frac{1}{200} = 0.05$

$$P(x = 2) = \frac{e^{-0.05}(0.05)^2}{2!}$$

From the table $e^{-0.05} = 0.9512$

$$P(x = 2) = \frac{0.9512 \times 0.0025}{2}$$

$$= 0.0012$$

No. of boxes having two defective pieces out of 10,000 boxes is,

$$n = 0.0012 \times 10{,}000 = 12.$$

Q. 24. *It has been found that on an average the number of mistakes per typed page of a typist is 1.5. Find the probability that there are 3 or less mistakes.*

Ans. Given that $\mu = 1.5$

The variable (no. of mistakes) follow Poisson distribution.

Thus,

$$P(X \leq 3) = e^{-1.5}\left\{\frac{(1.5)^0}{0!} + \frac{(1.5)^1}{1!} + \frac{(1.5)^2}{2!} + \frac{(1.5)^3}{3!}\right\}$$

From the table $e^{-1.5} = 0.2231$

$$P(X \leq 3) = 0.2231\ (1 + 1.5 + 1.125 + 0.5625)$$

$$= 0.9342$$

Q. 25. *If a Poisson variate X is such that $P(x = 1) = P(x = 2)$, Work out $P(x = 4)$.*

Ans. Using the recurrence formula for Poisson distribution.

$$P(x = 2) = P(x = 1)\ \frac{\mu}{1+1}$$

or $\mu = 2$

$$\therefore \quad P(x = 4) = \frac{e^{-2}(2)^4}{4!}$$

From the table $e^{-2} = 0.1353$

$$P(x = 4) = \frac{0.1353 \times 16}{24}$$

$$= 0.09$$

Q. 26. *Explain Negative binomial distribution and its properties.*

Ans. In sampling procedure, seldom the sample size is not fixed but is determined as the sample size required to achieve r successes. (This is known as inverse sampling.) Obviously n^{th} individual will always be possessing $(r - 1)$ successes. A random variable X, the number of failures before the rth success occurs in a random experiment which results either in a success or a failure is said to follow a negative binomial distribution and its probability function with probability p of a success and q that of a failure is given by

$$p_X\{nb(x;\ r,\ p)\} = \binom{x+r-1}{r-1} p^r q^x$$

for $x = 0, 1, 2, \ldots,$

$r \geq 0;\ 0 \leq p < 1$

$$\text{Also, } p_X\{nb(x;\ r,\ p)\} = \binom{-r}{x} p^r q^x$$

$$\because \quad \binom{x+r-1}{r-1} = \binom{-r}{x}(-1)^x$$

Negative binomial distribution is also known as *Pascal's distribution.*

Properties of negative binomial distribution

(*i*) Number of successes is fixed and number of trials is a random variable.

(*ii*) Its means is $r(1 - p)/p$.

(*iii*) Its variance is $r(1 - p)/p^2$.

(*iv*) The frequency curve is *J*-shaped with maximum frequency at $n = 1 + \frac{r-1}{p}$.

(*v*) Moment generating function of $nb(x;\ r,\ p)$ is $(Q - Pe^t)^{-r}$ where $p = \frac{1}{Q}, q = \frac{P}{Q}$ or $Q - P = 1$.

(*vi*) Recurrence relationship between negative binomial probabilities $f(x + 1)$ and $f(x)$ is

$$f(x+1) = q \cdot \frac{x+r}{x+1} f(x)$$

(*vii*) Central moments and cumulants of $nb(x; r, p)$ are:

$$\mu_1 = \kappa_1 = rP,\ \mu_2 = \kappa_2 = rPQ,$$
$$\mu_3 = rPQ(Q+P)$$

and
$$\mu_4 = \kappa_4 + 3\kappa_2^2 = rPQ(1+6PQ) + 3r^2P^2Q^2$$
$$= rPQ(1 + 6PQ + 3rPQ)$$

(*viii*) Pearson's coefficients of skewness are:

$$\beta_1 = \frac{\mu_3^2}{\mu_2^3} = \frac{(Q+P)^2}{rPQ} \quad \text{or} \quad \gamma_1 = \frac{Q+P}{\sqrt{rPQ}}$$

β_1 or γ_1 are always positive hence negative binomial distribution is positively skewed.

(*ix*) Pearson's coefficient of kurtosis are:

$$\beta_2 = \frac{\mu_4}{\mu_2^2} = \frac{1+6PQ}{rPQ} + 3$$

or
$$\gamma_2 = \frac{1+6PQ}{rPQ}$$

The value of $\beta_2 > 3$ or $\gamma_2 > 0$, reveals that negative binomial distribution is leptokurtic.

Q. 27. *A marker is to continue shooting at the target until he hits the target 6 times. The probability that he hits the target on any shooting is 0.4. Calculate the probability that the marker will have to shoot 9 times.*

Ans. Since the number of successes is fixed, we will use negative binomial distribution. In the given problem,

$$r + x = 9,\ r = 6, \quad \therefore\ x = 3$$

Also
$$p = 0.4,\ q = 1 - 0.4 = 0.6$$

Thus, using negative binomial probability,

$$P(x=3) = \binom{x+r-1}{r-1} p^r q^x$$

$$= \binom{9-1}{6-1} (0.4)^6\,(0.6)^3$$

$$= \binom{8}{5} (0.4)^6\,(0.6)^3$$

$$= 0.0495$$

Q. 28. *Elucidate Geometric distribution and give its properties.*

Ans. If there are a number of trials such that the probability of success '*p*' at each trial remains the same, the probability that there are *x* failures before the first success is given by $p.q^x$. Hence, a random variable *X* which can take only positive integer values is said to follow geometric distribution if its probability mass function is

$$f(x) = P(X = x) = p\,.\,q^x$$

for $x = 0, 1, 2, \ldots$ and $0 \le p \le 1$

= 0 otherwise.

It is usually denoted as geom. (*p*).

Since the probabilities of the events $x = 0, 1, 2$, etc., are in geometric progression, it is named as geometric distribution.

Also it is a particular case of negative binomial distribution for $r = 1$.

The waiting time *X* follows geometric distribution.

Properties of geometric distribution:

(*i*) The mean of geometric distribution is q/p.

(*ii*) The variance of geometric distribution is q/p^2.

(*iii*) Moment generating function of geometric distribution is $p/(1 - qe^t)$.

(*iv*) $x = 0$ is the mode of geometric distribution.

(*v*) Median of geometric variate is $-\log 2/\log(1-p)$.

(*vi*) Recurrence formula for geometric distribution is $p(x + i) = qp(x)$.

(*vii*) If an event '*E*' has not occurred before the time *k*, then $Y = X - k$ is the additional time required for *E* to occur. The distribution of $Y = t$ for $X \ge k$ is pq^t which is independent of *k*. Since the distribution of *Y* is independent of *k*, the waiting time *k* is forgotten. This property of geometric distribution is known as the *lack of memory or memoryless* property of geometric distribution. This shows that shifting of origin does not affect the geometric distribution.

Q. 29 *A man rolls a fair die again and again until he obtains a 5 or 6. Calculate the probability that he will require 5 throws.*

Ans. Given that $P = \frac{1}{3}, q = \frac{2}{3}$.

The number of failures before a success = 4.

The variable x follows geom (1/3) distribution.

Hence,

$$P(x = 5 \text{ or } 6) = \frac{1}{3}\left(\frac{2}{3}\right)^4 = \frac{16}{243}$$

Q. 30. *Give Polya's distribution.*

Ans. If we put in negative binomial probability function the value of r and p as,

$$r = \frac{1}{\beta}, p = \frac{1}{1+\beta\mu}, q = \frac{\beta\mu}{1+\beta\mu}$$

$$f(x) = P(X - x) = \binom{-r}{x}\left(\frac{1}{1+\beta\mu}\right)^{1/\beta}\left(\frac{\beta\mu}{1+\beta\mu}\right)^x$$

or $$f(x) = \frac{(1+\beta)(1+2\beta)+\ldots+\{1+\beta(x-1)\}}{x!} \times \left(\frac{1}{1+\beta\mu}\right)^{1/\beta}\left(\frac{\beta\mu}{1+\beta\mu}\right)^x$$

for $x = 0, 1, 2, \ldots$

This form of Polya's distribution has only two parameters β and μ.

If in Polya's probability function, we put $\beta = 1$, $f(x)$ reduces to,

$$f(x) = \left(\frac{1}{1+\mu}\right)\left(\frac{\mu}{1+\mu}\right)^x$$

since $\frac{2, 3, \ldots, x}{x!} = 1$

which is another form of geometric distribution with $p = \frac{1}{1+\mu}$.

Q. 31. *Explain Hypergeometric distribution and give its characteristics.*

Ans. Suppose N individuals of a population can be categorised either a success (S) and a failure (F) and it contains k successes and obviously $(N-k)$ failures. Let a sample of n elements be drawn at random without replacement. In this process successive trials (draws) are dependent. Suppose x is the number of successes in the sample. The variable X follows hypergeometric distribution and its probability mass function is given as,

$$f(x) = p(X = x) = \frac{\binom{k}{x}\binom{N-k}{n-x}}{\binom{N}{n}}$$

For $p = \frac{k}{N}, f(x) = \frac{\binom{Np}{x}\binom{Nq}{n-x}}{\binom{N}{n}}$

for $x = 0, 1, 2 \ldots, n$

and $n \le k$

It has three parameters, N, K, n, and is usually denoted as H.G. $(x; N, K, n)$.

Characteristics of hypergeometric distribution:

(*i*) The mean of H.G. $(x; N, K, n)$ is np where $p = \frac{K}{N} \cdot N$ is not necessarily large.

(*ii*) The variance of hypergeometric distribution is $\left(\frac{N-n}{N-1}\right)npq$, where $q = 1 - p$.

or $\text{var}(X) = \frac{N-n}{N-1} \cdot \frac{nk}{N} \frac{N-k}{N}$.

(*iii*) Recurrence formula between $f(x+1)$ and $f(x)$ for H.G. $(x; N, K, n)$ is,

$$f(x+1) = \frac{n-x}{x+1} \frac{k-x}{N-k-n+x+1} f(x)$$

(*iv*) Hypergeometric distribution tends to binomial distribution if $N \to \infty$ and $\frac{K}{N} \to p$.

(*v*) Characteristic function of hypergeometric distribution does not yield a convenient form to be worked out for moments. The hypergeometric distribution provides an example of a distribution for which the characteristic function is virtually useless while obtaining the moments of the distribution. However, the method of moments may be fruitful.

Q. 32. *Give the example of a distribution for which characteristic function is useless for obtaining the moments.*

Ans. The hypergeometric distribution provides an example of a distribution for which characteristic function is virtually useless while obtaining the moments of the distribution. However, the method of factorial moments may be useful.

Q. 33. *In an international film festival, a panel of 11 judges was formed to judge the best film. At last two films F_A and F_B were considered to be the best where the opinion of judges got divided. Six judges were in favour of F_A whereas five in favour of F_B. A random sample of five judges was drawn from the panel. Find the probability that out of five judges, three were in favour of film F_A.*

Ans. It can be calculated with help of hypergeometric probability in the following manner:

In the given problem,

$$N = 11, K = 6, N - K = 5, n = 5, x = 3$$

$$P(x = 3) = \frac{\binom{6}{3}\binom{5}{2}}{\binom{11}{5}}$$

$$= \frac{100}{231}$$

Q. 34 *Describe briefly the multinomial distribution.*

Ans. Suppose there are k distinct classes. Let the probability that X_i observations fall in the ith class is p_i the probability,

$$P(X_1 = x_1, X_2 = x_2, ..., X_K = x_K / \Sigma x_i = n) \quad \text{for } i = 1, 2, ..., k.$$

is given by

$$f(x_1, x_2, ..., x_k) = \frac{n!}{x_1!x_2!...x_k!} p_1^{x_1} p_2^{x_2} \cdots p_k^{x_k}$$

Subject to the condition, $\Sigma p_i = 1$

Then $f(x_1, x_2, ..., x_k)$ is the probability function of multinomial distribution. It has parameters n and $p_1, p_2, ..., p_k$.

This distribution reduces to binomial distribution when there are only two classes.

Q. 35. *What is meant by continuous distribution?*

Ans. We know that a continuous variable (variate) will have continuous distribution. A variate X which can take any value in an interval (a, b), *i.e.*, $a \le X \le b$ of arithmetic continuum is a continuous variable. The probability density function $f(x)$ of the random variable X in the interval (a, b) is defined as,

$$f(x) = \begin{cases} 0 & \text{if } x < a \\ \phi(x) & \text{if } a \le x \le b \\ 0 & \text{if } x > b \end{cases}$$

Also $f(x)$ always possesses the following *properties*:

(*i*) $f(x) \ge 0$.

(*ii*) The total density (probability) in its entire range is equal to unity, *i.e.*,

$$\int_a^b f(x)\,dx = 1$$

It implies that the total area under the frequency curve is always unity.

(*iii*) The distribution function of X is given as,

$$P(X \le x) = F(x) = \int_{-\infty}^{x} f(x)\,dx.$$

(*iv*) $\int_a^b f(x)\,dx = F(b) - F(a)$ for $a \le x \le b$

(*v*) $F(-\infty) = 0$ and $F(+\infty) = 1$

(*vi*) For a continuous distribution with p.d.f. $f(x)$ where $a \le X < b$, the following relations hold.

(*a*) The mean, $\mu = E(X) = \int_a^b x f(x)\,dx$

(*b*) The median $Md = \int_a^{Md} f(x)\, d_x$

$$= \int_{Md}^{b} f(x)\, dx = 1/2$$

(*c*) The variance, $\mu_2 = E(X^2) - \{E(X)\}^2$

where $E(X^2) = \int_a^b x^2 f(x)\, dx$

(*d*) The geometric mean G,

$$\log G = \int_a^b \log x\, f(x)\, dx$$

(*e*) The Harmonic mean H,

$$\frac{1}{H} = \int_a^b \frac{1}{x} f(x)\, dx$$

(*f*) The mode is the solution of $f'(x) = 0$ and $f''(x) < 0$ provided the derivatives, $f'(x)$ and $f''(x)$ exist.

(*g*) The point of inflection of a continuous frequency curve $y = f(x)$ is obtained by putting $f''(x) = 0$ and verifying $f'''(x) \neq 0$ provided second and third derivatives exist.

(*h*) The mean deviation about a constant A,

$$M.D_A = \int_a^b |x - A|\, f(x)\, dx$$

(*i*) The moment generating function,

$$M_X(t) = \int_a^b e^{tx} f(x)\, dx$$

(*j*) The cumulant generating function,

$$\kappa_X(t) = \log M_X(t)$$

(*k*) i^{th} quartile Q_i ($i = 1, 2, 3$) is obtained by the relation,

$$\int_a^{Q_i} f(x)\, dx = \frac{i}{4}$$

(*l*) i^{th} decile D_i ($i = 1, 2, \ldots, 9$) is obtained by the relation,

$$\int_a^{D_i} f(x)\, dx = \frac{i}{10}$$

(*m*) i^{th} percentile P_i ($i = 1, 2, \ldots, 99$) is obtained by the relation

$$\int_a^{P_i} f(x)\, dx = \frac{i}{100}$$

(*n*) r^{th} raw moment,

$$\mu_r' = \int_a^b x^r f(x)\, dx$$

(*o*) r^{th} central moment,

$$\mu_r = \int_a^b (x - \mu)^r f(x)\, dx$$

Q. 36. *Discuss a continuous uniform or Rectangular distribution and its properties.*

Ans. A random variable X is said to follow continuous uniform or rectangular distribution in an interval (a, b) if its density function is constant over the entire range of the variable X. Its functional form is,

$$f(x) = \begin{cases} \dfrac{1}{b-a} & \text{if } a \le x \le b \\ 0 & \text{otherwise} \end{cases}$$

It is denoted as $U(a, b)$. If $X \sim U(0, 1), f(x) = 1$. The distribution function of the variable $X \sim U(a, b)$ is,

$$F(x) = \begin{cases} 0 & \text{if } -\infty < x < a \\ \dfrac{x-a}{b-a} & \text{if } a \le x \le b \\ 1 & \text{if } b < x < \infty \end{cases}$$

Properties of rectangular distribution:

(*i*) Its mean is equal to $\dfrac{b+a}{2}$.

(*ii*) All the moments of odd order are zero.

(*iii*) Its variance, $\mu_2 = \dfrac{(b-a)^2}{12}$.

(*iv*) Its fourth central moment, $\mu_4 = \dfrac{(b-a)^4}{80}$.

(*v*) Median of rectangular distribution is $\dfrac{b+a}{2}$.

(*vi*) Mean deviation about mean, $M.D_{\bar{x}} = \dfrac{b-a}{4}$.

(*vii*) Measure of Skewness, $\beta_1 = 0$ or $\gamma_1 = 0$.

(*viii*) Measure of Kurtosis, $\beta_2 = \dfrac{9}{5}$ or $\gamma_2 = \beta_2 - 3 = -\dfrac{6}{5}$. Pearson's coefficients β_1 and β_2 reveal that rectangular distribution is symmetrical and platykurtic.

(*ix*) Moment generating function of rectangular distribution, $M_X(t) = \dfrac{e^{th} - e^{ta}}{t(b-a)}$.

(*x*) Characteristic function of rectangular distribution, $\phi_X(t) = \dfrac{e^{itb} - e^{ita}}{it(b-a)}$.

(*xi*) Mode does not exists as the probability at each point in the interval (a, b) remains the same.

(*xii*) If X and Y are independently and identically distributed (i.i.d.) rectangular or uniform $U(0, 1)$, the distribution of the variates $(x + y)$, $(x - y)$, xy and x/y are as follows:

$$f(x+y) = \begin{cases} x+y & 0 \le x+y \le 1 \\ 2-(x+y), & 1 \le x+y \le 2 \end{cases}$$

$$f(x-y) = \begin{cases} x-y+1, & -1 \le x-y \le 0 \\ 1-(x-y), & 0 \le x-y \le 1 \end{cases}$$

$$f(xy) = -\log(xy),\ 0 < xy < 1$$

$$f(x/y) = \begin{cases} 1/2, & 0 \le x/y < 1 \\ y^2/2x^2, & 1 < x/y < \infty \end{cases}$$

(*xiii*) If a variable $X \sim U(0, 1)$, then the variable $y = -2 \log X$ is distributed as χ^2 with 2 d.f.

(*xiv*) Let $X_1, X_2, \ldots, X_n$ be i.i.d. random variables with distribution $U(0, 1)$, then the variable $y = -2 \sum_{i=1}^{n} \log x_i$ or $y = 2 \log\left(1 \Big/ \prod_{i=1}^{n} X_i\right)$ is distributed as χ^2 with $2n$ d.f.

Q. 37. *When is a variable said to follow exponential distribution? What are the properties of exponential distribution?*

Ans. A continuous random variable X is said to follow exponential distribution if for any positive value λ, it has the probability density function,

$$f(x) = \lambda\, e^{-\lambda x} \text{ for } \lambda > 0,\ x > 0$$

This is usually denoted as Expo (λ). λ is known as the parameter of exponential distribution.

The distribution function of exponential variate X is

$$F(x) = \begin{cases} 1 - e^{-\lambda x}, & \text{if } x > 0 \\ 0, & \text{otherwise} \end{cases}$$

The length of time interval between successive occurrences of events follow exponential distribution provided the number of occurrences in fixed time interval follow Poisson distribution. The variate, elapsed time between two calls at a telephone switch board follows exponential distribution. This plays an important role in the theory of reliability.

The well known properties of exponential distribution are:

(*i*) Mean of exponential distribution is $1/\lambda$.

(*ii*) Variance of exponential distribution is $1/\lambda^2$.

(*iii*) Moments of all order exist. The first four central moments are:

$$\mu_1 = \frac{1}{\lambda},\ \mu_2 = \frac{1}{\lambda^2},\ \mu_3 = \frac{2}{\lambda^3},\ \mu_4 = \frac{9}{\lambda^4}$$

If $\lambda > 1$, mean > variance. If $\lambda < 1$, mean < variance, if $\lambda = 1$, mean = variance.

(*iv*) The relationship between central moments and cumulants are:

$$\mu_1 = \kappa_1,\ \mu_2 = \kappa_2,\ \mu_3 = \kappa_3 \text{ and } \mu_4 = \kappa_1 + \kappa_2^2$$

(*v*) Pearson's measure of skewness, $\beta_1 = 4$ or $\gamma_1 = \sqrt{\beta_1} = 2$.

(*vi*) Pearson's measure of Kurtosis, $\beta_2 = 9$ or $\gamma_2 = \beta_2 - 3 = 6$.

The values of β_1 or γ_1 and β_2 or γ_2 clearly reveal that exponential distribution is positively skewed and is leptokurtic.

(*vii*) The median of exponential distribution is $\frac{1}{\lambda}$.

(*viii*) Moment generating function,

$$M_X(t) = \left(1 - \frac{t}{\lambda}\right)^{-1}$$

(*ix*) Characteristic function, $\phi_X(t) = \left(1 - \frac{it}{\lambda}\right)^{-1}$

(*x*) It also possesses the memoryless property just like geometric distribution.

Q. 38. *What is the probability density function of Laplace or double exponential distribution? Also give its properties.*

Ans. A random variable X is said to follow Laplace or double exponential distribution with parameters λ and μ if its probability density function,

$$f(x) = \frac{1}{2}\lambda e^{-\lambda|x-\mu|}$$

for $-\infty < x < \infty$, $\lambda > 0$ and $\mu < \infty$.

It is denoted as $L(\mu, \lambda)$.

If $\mu = 0$,

$$f(x) = \frac{1}{2}\lambda e^{-\lambda|x|}$$

for $-\infty < x < \infty$, $\lambda > 0$.

and is denoted as $L(\lambda)$.

The variate standing for the longest lasting object out of a large number of apparently identical objects follows double exponential distribution.

Properties of double exponential distribution

(*i*) The mean of double exponential distribution is μ.

(*ii*) The variance of double exponential distribution is $\frac{2}{\lambda^2}$.

(*iii*) First four central moments of double exponential distribution and their relations with cumulants are:

$$\mu_1 = \kappa_1 = \mu,\ \mu_2 = \kappa_2 = \frac{2}{\lambda^2},\ \mu_3 = \kappa_3 = 0$$

$$\mu_4 = \kappa_4 + 3\kappa_2^2 = \frac{24}{\lambda^4}.$$

(*iv*) Measure of skewness, $\beta_1 = 0$ or $\gamma_1 = \sqrt{\beta_1} = 0$.

(*v*) Measure of skewness, $\beta_2 = 6$ or $\gamma_2 = \beta_2 - 3 = 3$. The values of β_1 and β_2 *vis-a-vis* γ_1 and γ_2 ensure that double exponential distribution is symmetrical but is leptokurtic.

(*vi*) Moment generating function of double exponential distribution is $e^{\mu t} \cdot \frac{\lambda^2}{\lambda^2 - t^2}$

(*vii*) Its characteristic function is $e^{i\mu t} \cdot \frac{\lambda^2}{\lambda^2 + t^2}$

(*viii*) Interquartile range $(Q_3 - Q_1)$ of double exponential distribution is $\frac{2}{\lambda}$ log 2.

Q. 39. *Discuss elaborately normal distribution and its characteristics.*

Ans. Normal distribution was first discovered by De-Moivre in 1733 and was also known to Laplace in 1774. Later it was derived by Kark Friedrich Gauss in 1809 and used it for the study of errors in astronomy. Anyhow, the credit of normal distribution has been given to Gauss and is often called Gaussion distribution. Normal distribution is the maximally used probability distribution in the theory of statistics.

A random variable X is said to follow a normal distribution with mean μ and variance σ^2, if its probability density function is

$$f_X(x; \mu, \sigma^2) = \frac{1}{\sigma\sqrt{2\pi}} e^{-\frac{1}{2\sigma^2}(x-\mu)^2}$$

for $-\infty < x < \infty$

$-\infty < \mu < \infty$ and $\sigma > 0$

The variate X is said to be distributed normally with mean μ and variance σ^2 and is denoted as $X \sim N(\mu, \sigma^2)$. If $\mu = 0$ and $\sigma = 1$, then

$$f_X(x) = \frac{1}{\sqrt{2\pi}} e^{-\frac{1}{2}x^2}$$

Here, X is said *standardized normal variate* and is denoted as $X \sim N(0, 1)$. Also, p.d.f. $f_X(x)$ is called standardized normal distribution. If $X \sim N(\mu, \sigma^2)$ and we make a transformation, $Z = \frac{X-\mu}{\sigma}$, the distribution of Z is a standardized normal distribution as $Z \sim N(0, 1)$ irrespective of the values of μ and σ^2 in the distribution of X. Z is also called *standard normal deviate.* We can write, $f(z) = \frac{1}{\sqrt{2\pi}} e^{-\frac{1}{2}z^2}$.

Also, $\int_{-\infty}^{\infty} f(z)\, dz = 1$. The area under the standard normal curve between the ordinates at $z = 0$ and $z_1 = \phi(z)$ is given as,

$$\phi(z) = \int_0^{z_1} f(z)\, dz.$$

Also $\phi(z) = \phi(-z)$

Area under the normal curve have been tabulated and can be obtained from appendix Table IV provided in the book entitled, *Basic Statistics* by B.L. Agarwal or any other textbook.

Characteristics of the normal distribution:

(*i*) The normal distribution curve is bell-shaped and is symmetrical about the line $x = \mu$.

(*ii*) The mode of the normal curve lies at the point $x = \mu$.

(*iii*) The area under the normal curve within its range $-\infty$ to ∞ is always unity, *i.e.*,

$$\frac{1}{\sigma\sqrt{2\pi}} \int_{-\infty}^{\infty} e^{-\frac{1}{2\sigma^2}(x-\mu)^2} dx = 1$$

(*iv*) On either side of the line $x = \mu$, the frequency decreases more rapidly within the range $(\mu \pm \sigma)$ and get slower and slower as we depart farther from the point μ on either side. The area under the normal curve beyond the distance $\pm 3\sigma$ is only 0.27 per cent which is very small. As a matter of fact, the area under the normal curve within the range $\mu \pm \sigma$ is 0.6826, in the range $\mu \pm 2\sigma$ is 0.9544 and within the range $\mu \pm 3\sigma$ is 0.9973. The fact that 99.73 per cent items are covered within the range $\mu \pm 3\sigma$ of a normal distribution. It gives rise to the large number theory. Hence, for a sample of size $n \geq 30$, the distribution is taken as normal. The area under standard normal curve, bounded by the line $Z = \pm 1.96$ is 0.95, *i.e.*, 95 per cent. Since the normal curve is symmetrical, 2.5 per cent area lies on the left tail and 2.5 per cent on the right tail beyond the points $z = -1.96$ and $z = 1.96$, respectively.

(*v*) Mean = Median = Mode.

(*vi*) The normal curve is unimodal.

(*vii*) All odd order moments of the normal distribution are zero.

(*viii*) The first raw moment, *i.e.*, mean = μ. Also $\mu_2 = \sigma^2$, $\mu_3 = 0$, $\mu_4 = 3\sigma^4 = 3\mu_2^2$.

(*ix*) Measure of skewness, $\beta_1 = \frac{\mu_3^2}{\mu_2^2} = 0$

or $\gamma_1 = \sqrt{\beta_1} = 0$.

(*x*) Measure of Kurtosis, $\beta_2 = \frac{\mu_4}{\mu_2^2} = 3$

or $\gamma_2 = \beta_2 - 3 = 0$.

The value of β_1 and β_2 clearly reveal that the normal curve is symmetrical and mesokurtic.

(*xi*) Quartile deviation, Q.D. $= \frac{Q_3 - Q_1}{2} = \frac{2}{3}\sigma$.

(*xii*) The mean deviation about mean, M.D.$_\mu$

$$= \frac{1}{\sigma\sqrt{2\pi}} \int_{-\infty}^{\infty} |x-\mu|\, e^{-\frac{1}{2\sigma^2}(x-\mu)^2} dx$$

$$= \sqrt{\frac{2}{\pi}}\sigma = \frac{4}{5}\sigma.$$

(*xiii*) The maximum probability say, Max $[p(x)]$ of the normal curve occurs at the point $x = \mu$ whereas,

$$\text{Max}[p(x)] = \frac{1}{\sigma\sqrt{2\pi}}$$

As σ increases, $p(x)$ decreases and the curve becomes more and more flat and *vice-versa.*

(*xiv*) The moment generating function of the normal distribution, $N(x; \mu, \sigma^2)$ is

$$M_X(t) = \frac{1}{\sigma\sqrt{2\pi}} \int_{-\infty}^{\infty} e^{tx} e^{-\frac{1}{2\sigma^2}(x-\mu)^2} dx = e^{\mu t + \frac{1}{2}\sigma^2 t^2}$$

(*xv*) Characteristic function of the normal distribution, $N(x; \mu, \sigma^2)$ is

$$\phi_X(t) = \frac{1}{\sigma\sqrt{2\pi}} \int_{-\infty}^{\infty} e^{itx} e^{-\frac{1}{2\sigma^2}(x-\mu)^2} dx = e^{i\mu t - \frac{1}{2}\sigma^2 t^2}$$

(*xvi*) The points of inflexion of the normal curve are given by $x = \mu \pm \sigma$ and at this point

$$f(x) = \frac{1}{\sigma\sqrt{2\pi}} e^{-1/2}$$

(*xvii*) If $X_1, X_2, \ldots, X_n$ are n independent random variables distributed normally with mean $\mu_1, \mu_2, \ldots, \mu_n$ and variances $\sigma_1^2, \sigma_2^2, \ldots, \sigma_n^2$ respectively, the sum $(X_1 + X_2 + \ldots + X_n)$ is distributed with mean, $(\mu_1 + \mu_2 + \ldots + \mu_n)$ and variance, $(\sigma_1^2 + \sigma_2^2 + \ldots + \sigma_n^2)$.

(*xviii*) If X and Y are two normal variates such that $X \sim N(0, 1)$ and $Y \sim N(0, 1)$, the variate X/Y follow Cauchy distribution.

Q. 40. *What is the importance of standard normal curve?*

Ans. The importance of standard normal curve lies in the fact that one has not to tabulate probability (areas) under the curve between two lines $x = a$ and $x = b$ for different value of μ and σ. Only one table of areas prepared for the standard normal curve is sufficient as for this curve, the mean $\mu = 0$ and S.D., $\sigma = 1$.

Q. 41. *Throw light on the importance of normal distribution.*

Ans. Normal distribution is most important amongst all known distributions due to the facts that:

(*i*) Most of the discrete distributions such as binomial, Poisson, etc., tend to normal distribution as n increases, *i.e.*, $n \to \infty$.

(*ii*) Almost all sampling distributions like t, χ^2, F, etc., for their large degrees of freedom conform to normal distribution.

(*iii*) Users convenience is another reason for wide adoptability of normal distribution.

(*iv*) One of the greatest reason behind the extensive use and application of normal distribution lies in most celebrated theorem known as *central limit theorem*. The theorem states that.

If $X_1, X_2, \ldots, X_n$ is a random sample of size n from any population with mean μ and variance σ^2, the distribution of sample mean $\bar{x}\left(\bar{x} = \frac{\Sigma x_i}{n}\right)$ is asymptotically normal, with mean μ and variance σ^2/n, as $n \to \infty$.

(*v*) Many variables which are not normally distributed can be normalised through suitable transformation(s).

Q. 42. *If a r.v. $X \sim N(40, 5^2)$, find the probabilities for the values of X specified as (i) $32 < X \leq 50$ (ii) $|X - 40| > 5$ (iii) $X \leq 25$ (iv) $X \geq 44$ (v) $45 \leq X \leq 50$ (vi) $31 \leq X \leq 35$.*

Given the areas $\phi(z)$ from 0 to Z:

z	0.8	1.0	1.6	1.8	2.0	3.0
$\phi(z)$	0.28814	0.34134	0.35543	0.46407	0.47725	0.49865

Ans.

(*i*) $z_1 = \frac{32-40}{5} = -1.6,\ z_2 = \frac{50-40}{5} = 2.0$

$\phi(z_1) = 0.35543,\ \phi(z_2) = 0.47725$

$P(32 \leq x \leq 50) = 0.47725 + 0.35543 = 0.83268$

(*ii*) $P(|x - 40| > 5) = P\left(\left|\frac{x-40}{5}\right| > \frac{5}{5}\right)$

$= P(|z| > 1)$
$= 2P(z > 1)$
$= 2(0.5 - 0.34134)$
$= 0.31732$

(*iii*) $P(x \le 25) = P\left(\frac{x-40}{5} \le \frac{25-40}{5}\right)$
$= P(z \le -3)$
$= P(|z| \le 3)$
$= 0.5 - \phi(|-3|)$
$= 0.5 - 0.49865$
$= 0.00135$

(*iv*) $P(x \ge 44) = P\left(\frac{x-40}{5} \ge \frac{44-40}{5}\right)$
$= P(z \ge 0.8)$
$= 0.5 - \phi(0.8)$
$= 0.5 - 0.28814$
$= 0.21186$

(*v*) $P(45 \le x \le 50)$
$= P\left(\frac{45-40}{5} \le \frac{x-40}{5} \le \frac{50-40}{5}\right)$
$= P(1 \le z \le 2)$
$= \phi(2) - \phi(1)$
$= 0.47725 - 0.34134$
$= 0.13591$

(*vi*) $P(31 \le x \le 35)$
$= P\left(\frac{31-40}{5} \le \frac{x-40}{5} \le \frac{35-40}{5}\right)$
$= P(-1.8 \le Z \le -1)$
$= \phi(-1.8) - \phi(-1)$
$= \phi(1.8) - \phi(1)$
$= 0.46407 - 0.34134$
$= 0.12273$

Q. 43. *If a variable $X \sim N(5, 4)$ and $P\{|x-5| > c\} = 0.01$, find c.*

$$\left[\text{Given} \int_0^{2.58} \frac{1}{\sqrt{2\pi}} e^{-1/2z^2}\, dz = 0.495\right]$$

Ans. $P\left\{\left|\frac{x-5}{2}\right| > \frac{1}{2}c\right\} = 0.01$

$$P\left(|z| > \frac{1}{2}c\right) = 0.01$$

$$2P(Z > 2.58) = 0.01$$

$\therefore \qquad \frac{1}{2}c = 2.58$

or $\qquad c = 5.16$

Q. 44. *If $f(x) = ce^{-(x^2-6x+9)/32}$, $-\infty < x < \infty$ represents a normal distribution, find the value of c, the mean and the variance of the distribution.*

Ans. We can write,

$$f(x) = ce^{-\frac{1}{2}\left(\frac{x-3}{4}\right)^2}$$

By comparing $f(x)$ with normal p.d.f.

$$\frac{1}{\sigma\sqrt{2\pi}} e^{-\frac{1}{2}\left(\frac{x-\mu}{\sigma}\right)^2}$$

we find, $\mu = 3$, $\sigma = 4$, and $c = \frac{1}{4\sqrt{2\pi}}$. Thus, $\sigma^2 = 4$.

Q. 45. *Give the outline of lognormal distribution and its properties.*

Ans. A positive continuous random variable X is said to follow lognormal distribution if the variable $\log_e x$ has normal distribution with mean μ and variance σ^2. Notationally, $\log_e x \sim N(\mu, \sigma^2)$. The probability density function of lognormal distribution is

$$f_X(\log_e x; \mu, \sigma^2) = \frac{1}{\sigma x\sqrt{2\pi}} e^{-\frac{1}{2\sigma^2}(\log_e x - \mu)^2}$$

It has two parameters μ and σ^2.

The hourly median power of radio signals received and transmitted between two places follow lognormal distribution.

If $\mu = 0$, $\sigma = 1$,

$$f_X(\log_e x) = \frac{1}{x\sqrt{2\pi}} e^{-\frac{1}{2}(\log_e x)^2}$$

In this particular case when $\log_e x \sim N(0, 1)$, the distribution is called logarithmico normal distribution.

Properties of lognormal distribution:

(*i*) Mean of X for lognormal distribution is $e^{\mu+\frac{1}{2}\sigma^2}$.

(*ii*) Its variance is $e^{2(\mu+\sigma^2)} - e^{2\mu+\sigma^2}$

(*iii*) Measure of skewness $\gamma_1 > 0$. It means that lognormal distribution curve is positively skewed.

(*iv*) Measure of Kurtosis $\gamma_2 > 3$. It manifests that lognormal distribution curve is leptokurtic.

(*v*) If X and F are independent lognormal variates distributed as $N(\mu_1, \sigma_1^2)$ and $N(\mu_2, \sigma_2^2)$, the variate $(X + Y)$ is distributed as lognormal with mean $(\mu_1 + \mu_2)$ and variance $(\sigma_1^2 + \sigma_2^2)$. The variate $(X - Y)$ is distributed as lognormal with mean $(\mu_1 - \mu_2)$ and variance $(\sigma_1^2 - \sigma_2^2)$.

(*vi*) The distribution of the variates XY and X/Y is also lognormal.

Q. 46. *Enunciate Cauchy distribution.*

Ans. A continuous random variable X is said to have Cauchy distribution if its probability density function is

$$f_X(x) = \frac{1}{\pi\beta\left\{1+\left(\frac{x-\alpha}{\beta}\right)^2\right\}}$$

for $-\infty < x < \infty$

$-\infty < \alpha < \infty$ and $\beta > 0$.

It has two parameters α and β. Notationally, this distribution is denoted as $C(\alpha, \beta)$. If $\alpha = 0, \beta = 1$, then

$$f_X(x) = \frac{1}{\pi(1+x^2)}$$

Here the variable $X \sim C(0, 1)$.

Properties of Cauchy distribution:

(*i*) Moment generating function of Cauchy distribution does not exist.

(*ii*) Its mean does not exist.

(*iii*) Its variance does not exist.

(*iv*) Characteristic function of Cauchy distribution is $e^{i\alpha t - \beta|t|}$.

(*v*) Cauchy distribution curve is unimodal and has its maximum at the point $x = \alpha$.

(*vi*) Cauchy distribution curve has two points of inflexion, $\left(\alpha + \frac{1}{\sqrt{3}}\beta\right)$ and $\left(\alpha - \frac{1}{\sqrt{3}}\beta\right)$.

(*vii*) If X and Y are two independent Cauchy variates distributed as $X \sim C(\alpha_1, \beta_1)$ and $Y \sim C(\alpha_2, \beta_2)$, their sum $(X + Y)$ is also a Cauchy variate distributed as $C(\alpha_1 + \alpha_2, \beta_1 + \beta_2)$.

(*viii*) If $X_1, X_2, \ldots, X_n$ are n i.i.d. Cauchy variates distributed as $X_i \sim C(\alpha, \beta)$ for $i = 1, 2, \ldots, n$, the mean $\bar{x} = \frac{1}{n}\Sigma x_i$ is also a Cauchy variate distributed as $C(\alpha, \beta)$.

Q. 47. *Elucidate beta distribution of first kind.*

Ans. A continuous random variable X with parameters m and n is said to possess beta distribution of first kind. If the probability density function of the variable X is

$$f_X(x) = \begin{cases} \frac{1}{B(m,n)} x^{m-1}(1-x)^{n-1} & m > 0, n > 0 \\ & 0 \le x \le 1 \\ 0 & \text{otherwise} \end{cases}$$

It is denoted as $\beta_1(m, n)$.

The distribution function of beta distribution of first kind is

$$F_X(x) = \frac{1}{B(m,n)} \int_0^x x^{m-1}(1-x)^{n-1}\,dx$$

for $m, n > 0$

$0 \le x < 1$

The cumulative distribution function $F_X(x)$ is also known as *incomplete beta function.*

Properties of beta distribution of first kind:

(*i*) The mean of beta distribution of first kind is $\frac{m}{(m+n)}$.

(*ii*) Its variance is $\frac{mn}{(m+n)^2 (m+n+1)}$.

(*iii*) The third and fourth central moments of beta distribution of first kind are:

$$\mu_3 = \frac{2mn(n-m)}{(m+n)^3 (m+n+1)(m+n+2)}$$

and

$$\mu_4 = \frac{3mn\{mn(m+n-6)+2(m+n)^2\}}{(m+n)^4 (m+n+1)(m+n+2)(m+n+3)}$$

(*iv*) Measure of skewness,

$$\beta_1 = \frac{4(m-n)^2 (m+n+1)}{mn(m+n+2)^2}$$

(*v*) Measure of Kurtosis,

$$\beta_2 = \frac{3(m+n+1)\{mn(m+n-6)+2(m+n)^2\}}{mn(m+n+2)(m+n+3)}$$

(*vi*) Mode of beta distribution of first kind depends on the values of m and n.

If $m < 1$, $x = 0$ is the modal value.

If $n < 1$, $x = 1$ is the modal value.

If $m < 1$, $n < 1$, both hold good simultaneously, beta distribution of first kind is bimodal. One mode occurs at $x = 0$ and the other at $x = 1$. If $m = 1$, $n = 1$, then $f(x) = 1$ for $0 < x < 1$. In such a situation each of $x \varepsilon (0, 1)$ is mode.

If $m = 1$, $n > 1$, $x = 0$ is the mode.

If $m > 1$, $n = 1$, $x = 1$ is the mode.

If $m > 1$, $n > 1$, $x = \frac{m-1}{m+n-2}$ is the mode.

(*vii*) Characteristic function of beta distribution of first kind is $\frac{1}{B(m,n)} \sum_{j=0}^{\infty} \frac{(it)^j}{j!} B(m+j, n)$.

(*viii*) The harmonic mean of $\beta_1 (m, n)$ is

$$H = \frac{m-1}{(m+n-1)}$$

(*ix*) If $X \sim \beta_1 (m, n)$ and $Y \sim \beta_I (p, q)$ are independent variates such that $p + q = m$, the variate XY is distributed as $\beta_I (p, n + q)$.

Q. 48. *Explicate beta distribution of second kind.*

Ans. A continuous random variable X with parameters m and n is said to follow beta distribution of second kind if its probability density function is

$$f_X(x) = \begin{cases} \frac{1}{B(m,n)} \frac{x^{m-1}}{(1+x)^{m+n}}, & \text{for } m, n > 0,\ 0 < x < \infty \\ 0 & \text{otherwise} \end{cases}$$

It is generally denoted as $\beta_{II}(m, n)$.

The distribution function of beta distribution of second kind is

$$F_X(x) = \begin{cases} \frac{1}{B(m,n)} \int_0^x \frac{u^{m-1} du}{(1+u)^{m+n}} & \text{for } m, n > 0,\ 0 < x < \infty \\ 0 & \text{otherwise} \end{cases}$$

Main features of beta distribution of second kind:

(*i*) Its mean is $\frac{m}{n-1}$.

(*ii*) Its variance is $\frac{m(m+n-1)}{(n-1)^2 (n-2)}$.

(*iii*) The harmonic mean of $\beta_{II}(m, n)$ is $\left(\frac{m-1}{n}\right)$.

(*iv*) Characteristic function of beta distribution of second kind is

$$\frac{1}{\Gamma m \, \Gamma n} \sum_{k=0}^{\infty} \frac{(it)^k}{k!} \Gamma(m+k)\, \Gamma(n-k)$$

Note: As a matter of fact, both beta type I and type II distribution are same except in respect of range. Beta type I has range (0, 1) and beta type II has range $(0, \infty)$.

Q. 49. *When does a variable follow gamma distribution and what are its properties?*

Ans. A positive random variable X is said to follow gamma distribution with parameters n and α if and only if its probability density function is

$$f_X(x;\alpha,n)=\begin{cases}\dfrac{\alpha^n}{\Gamma n}e^{-\alpha x}x^{n-1} & \text{for } x>0 \text{ and } n,\alpha>0\\ 0 & \text{otherwise}\end{cases}$$

It is generally denoted by $\gamma(\alpha, n)$ or gam (α, n).

If $\alpha = 0$, the gamma distribution is simply denoted as $\gamma(n)$.

The cumulative distribution of gamma variate X is

$$F_X(x)=\begin{cases}\dfrac{\alpha^n}{\Gamma n}\displaystyle\int_0^x e^{-\alpha u}u^{n-1} & \text{for } x>0\\ 0 & \text{otherwise}\end{cases}$$

It is also sometimes called *incomplete gamma function.*

Properties of gamma distribution:

(*i*) Mean of gamma distribution is $\dfrac{n}{\alpha}$.

(*ii*) Variance of gamma variate is $\dfrac{n}{\alpha^2}$.

(*iii*) If $\alpha < 1$, var. > mean; if $\alpha > 1$, var. < mean and if $\alpha = 1$, variance = mean.

(*iv*) Moment generating function of gamma distribution

$$M_X(t)=\left(\frac{\alpha}{\alpha-t}\right)^n \text{ or } \left(1-\frac{t}{\alpha}\right)^{-n}$$

(*v*) First-four central moments and their relationship with analogous cumulants are:

$$\mu_1=\kappa_1=\frac{n}{\alpha},\ \mu_2=\kappa_2=\frac{n}{\alpha^2},\ \mu_3=\kappa_3=\frac{2n}{\alpha^3}$$

$$,\ \mu_4=\kappa_4=3\kappa_2^2=\frac{(6n+3n^2)}{\alpha^4}.$$

(*vi*) Pearson's coefficients of skewness are, $\beta_1 = \dfrac{4}{n}$ or $\gamma_1 = \sqrt{\beta_1} = \dfrac{2}{\sqrt{n}}$.

(*vii*) Pearson's coefficients of Kurtosis are, $\beta_2 = 3 + \dfrac{6}{n}$, or $\gamma_2 = \beta_2 - 3 = \dfrac{6}{n}$.

Since $\gamma_1 > 0$, it ratifies that the gamma frequency curve is positively skewed. Further $\beta_2 > 3$ or $\gamma_2 > 0$ clearly indicate that gamma distribution is leptokurtic.

(*viii*) Characteristic function of gamma distribution is $\left(\dfrac{\alpha}{\alpha-it}\right)^n$ or $\left(1-\dfrac{it}{\alpha}\right)^{-n}$.

(*ix*) If $X_1, X_2, ..., X_k$ and k i.i.d. $\gamma(\alpha, n_i)$ variates for $i = 1, 2, ..., k$, the sum of the variates, $X_1 + X_2 + ... + X_k$ is also a gamma variate with parameters α and $\Sigma\, n_i$ *i.e.*, $\gamma(\alpha, \Sigma\, n_i)$. It is known as *additive* or *reproductive* property of gamma variate.

(*x*) As $n \to \infty$, gamma distribution tends to normal distribution. It is called the *limiting form* of gamma distribution.

(*xi*) If $X \sim \gamma(\alpha, n)$, the mode of gamma distribution, is $\dfrac{n-1}{\alpha}$ for $n > 1$. Again if, $n < 1$, the mode is 0.

(*xii*) If in gam (α, n), $n = 1$, the gamma distribution is same as exponential distribution.

(*xiii*) If $X \sim \gamma(\alpha, n)$, $E(\sqrt{X}) = \dfrac{\Gamma\left(n+\frac{1}{2}\right)}{\Gamma\alpha\,\Gamma n}$.

(*xiv*) If X and Y are two gamma variates distributed as $\gamma(n_1)$ and $\gamma(n_2)$ respectively, then

(*a*) The variable $(X + Y) \sim \gamma(n_1 + n_2)$.

(*b*) The variable $\dfrac{X}{X+Y}$ is distributed as $\beta_I(n_1 + n_2)$.

(*c*) The variate $\dfrac{X}{Y}$ is distributed as $\beta_{II}(n_1, n_2)$.

Q. 50. *Give a brief description of Logistic distribution.*

Ans. The logistic distribution of a continuous variable X is given in the form of cumulative distribution function (c.d.f.) which is

$$F_X(x; \alpha, \beta) = \frac{1}{1+e^{-\frac{(x-\alpha)}{\beta}}}$$

for $-\infty < \alpha < \infty$; $\beta > 0$.

The model tolerance levels in bioassays follows logistic distribution.

Properties of logistic distribution

(*i*) Its mean is α.

(*ii*) Its variance is $\frac{\pi^2 \beta^2}{3}$.

(*iii*) Logistic distribution curve is symmetrical.

Q. 51. *Give concisely Paretò distribution.*

Ans. A continuous random variable X which has probability density function

$$f_X(x; x_0, \theta) = \frac{\theta}{x_0}\left(\frac{x_0}{x}\right)^{\theta+1}$$

for $x > 0$; $\theta > 0$

is said to follow Pareto distribution.

The income of people exceeding a certain limit x_0 follows Pareto distribution. It has found its application in modelling problems.

Properties of Pareto distribution

(*i*) Mean of Pareto distribution is $\frac{\theta x_0}{\theta - 1}$ for $\theta > 1$.

(*ii*) Variance of Pareto distribution is

$$\frac{\theta x_0^2}{\theta - 2} - \left(\frac{\theta x_0}{\theta - 1}\right)^2 \text{ for } \theta > 2.$$

(*iii*) Moment generating function of Pareto distribution does not exist.

Q. 52. *Give briefly Weibull distribution.*

Ans. Weibull distribution was discovered by Swedish physicist Wallodi Weibull in 1939. A continuous random variable X is said to follow Weibull distribution if its probability density function

$$f_X(x; \alpha, \beta) = \frac{\alpha}{\beta^\alpha} x^{\alpha-1} e^{(-x/\beta)^\alpha}$$

for $x > 0$, $\alpha, \beta > 0$.

This distribution has two parameters α and β. It has application in reliability theory. Corrosion, weight loss of an alloy, tensile strength of a metal follow Weibull distribution.

Properties of Weibull distribution:

(*i*) Weibull distribution has mean $\beta\Gamma\left(1+\frac{1}{\alpha}\right)$.

(*ii*) Weibull distribution has variance

$$\beta^2\left[\Gamma\left(1+\frac{2}{\alpha}\right) - \left\{\Gamma\left(1+\frac{1}{\alpha}\right)\right\}^2\right]$$

Q. 53. *Give the concept of circular distributions.*

Ans. When a distribution is absolutely continuous with respect to lebesgue measure on the circumference of a unit circle and it can be represented by a density function $f(x)$ where the random variable X refers to an angle measured from a chosen direction satisfying,

$$f(x) \geq 0$$

subject to,

$$\int_0^\pi f(x)\,dx = 1;\ 0 \leq x \leq 2\pi$$

Such families of distributions are known as circular distributions.

Q. 54. *Give a brief account of the Pearsonian system of distributions.*

Ans. Karl Pearson gave various types of distributions through differential equation:

A density function $f_X(x)$ which satisfies the differential equation with constants a, b_0, b_1 and b_2,

$$\frac{1}{f_X(x)}\frac{d}{dx} f_X(x) = \frac{x-a}{b_0 + b_1 x + b_2 x^2}$$

is said to belong to Pearsonian system of distribution density function. A number of the distributions studied so far belong to the Pearsonian system of distributions. For instance, gamma distribution belong to the Pearsonian type III distribution. Normal distribution belongs to the Pearsonian zero type distribution.

Q. 55. *What do you understand by sampling distribution?*

Ans. Sampling distribution describes the manner in which a statistic or a function of statistics, which is/are a function(s) of the random sample variate values $x_1, x_2, \ldots, x_n$, will vary from one sample to another of the same size.

Some popular and useful sampling distributions are χ^2, t, z and F.

Q. 56. *Explicate the Chi-square distribution and give its properties.*

Ans. The chi-square distribution was first discovered by Helmert in 1876 and later independently by Karl Pearson in 1900..

If X is N (0, 1) variate, then X^2 is known as the Chi-square variate. If $X \sim N(\mu, \sigma^2)$, then the standard normal deviate $Z = \left(\frac{x-\mu}{\sigma}\right) \sim N(0, 1)$ and Z^2 is distributed a Chi-square (χ^2) with 1 degree of freedom (d.f.). If $X_1, X_2, \ldots, x_n$ are n independent variates distributed as $N(\mu_i, \sigma_i^2)$, then

$$\sum_{i=1}^{n} Z_i^2 = \sum_{i=1}^{n}\left(\frac{x_i-\mu}{\sigma_i}\right)^2$$

is distributed as Chi-square with n d.f. The probability density function of the Chi-square distribution is,

$$f(\chi^2) = \frac{1}{2^{\frac{n}{2}}\,\Gamma\frac{n}{2}}\, e^{-\chi^2/2}(\chi^2)^{\frac{n}{2}-1}$$

$$0 \le \chi^2 < \infty.$$

The Chi-square can be expressed in terms of sample variance (s^2) also. If $x_1, x_2, \ldots, x_n$ is a random sample[1] of size n from a normal population, the quantity $\frac{ks^2}{\sigma^2}$ is distributed as Chi-square with k d.f.

where $s^2 = \frac{1}{n-1}\sum_{i=1}^{n}(x_i - \bar{x})^2$ and $k = n - 1$. σ^2 is the population variance of the population from which the sample has been drawn. The probability density function of Chi-square distribution is

$$f(\chi^2) = \frac{1}{2^{k/2}\,\Gamma\, k/2}\, e^{-\chi^2/2} \cdot (\chi^2)^{k/2-1}$$

$$0 \le \chi^2 \le \infty.$$

Chi-square is gamma $\left(\frac{1}{2}, \frac{k}{2}\right)$ or $\chi^2 \sim$ gam $\left(\frac{1}{2}, \frac{k}{2}\right)$.

Chi-square distribution has only one parameter n or k as the case may be, which stands for the degrees of freedom of χ^2.

Properties of the Chi-square distribution

Properties have been expressed taking the first p.d.f. of χ^2 having n d.f.:

(*i*) Mean of the Chi-square distribution is n.

(*ii*) Variance of the Chi-square distribution is $2n$.

(*iii*) Mode of the Chi-square distribution curve lies at the point $\chi^2 = n - 2$.

(*iv*) Moment generating of the Chi-square distribution is $(1 - 2t)^{-n/2}$.

(*v*) Characteristic function of the Chi-square distribution is $(1 - 2it)^{-n/2}$.

(*vi*) First four central moments and their relation with cumulants are:

$$\mu_1 = \kappa_1 = n,\ \mu_2 = \kappa_2 = 2n,\ \mu_3 = \kappa_3 = 8n,$$

$$\mu_4 = \kappa_4 + 3\kappa_2^2 = 48n + 12n^2$$

(*vii*) Measure of skewness, $\beta_1 = \frac{8}{n}$ or γ_1

$$= \sqrt{\beta_1} = 2\sqrt{\frac{2}{n}}.$$

(viii) Measure of Kurtosis, $\beta_2 = 3+\frac{12}{n}$ or

$$\gamma_2 = \beta_2 - 3 = \frac{12}{n}$$

The values of β_1 and β_2 lead us to conclude that the χ^2-distribution curve has positive skewness since $\beta_1 > 0$, χ^2-distribution curve is leptokurtic as $\beta_2 > 3$.

(ix) Pearson's coefficient of skewness, $S_k = \frac{\text{mean} - \text{mode}}{\text{S.D.}}$ is $\left(\frac{2}{n}\right)^{1/2}$. This also leads to the conclusion that Chi-square distribution curve has positive skewness.

(x) The Chi-square distribution curve with 1 or 2. d.f. is hypebolic in shape whereas for $n > 2$, the curve is unsymmetrical bell-shaped.

(xi) Recurrence relation between r^{th} and $(r-1)^{th}$ raw moment of the Chi-square distribution is,

$$\mu'_r = (n + 2r - 2)\mu'_{r-1}$$

(xii) Recurrence relation between central (absolute) moments of the Chi-square distribution is,

$$\mu_{r+1} = 2r(\mu_r + n\mu_{r-1}) \text{ for } r \geq 1.$$

(xiii) If $X_1, X_2, \ldots, X_k$ are k independently distributed Chi-square variates such that $X_i \sim \chi^2_{ni}$ (for $i = 1, 2, \ldots, k$) $\sum_{i=1}^{k} X_i$ is also a Chi-square variate with Σn_i d.f. This is known as *additive* or *reproductive property of Chi-square.*

(xiv) If X and Y are two independently distributed Chi-square variates such that $X \sim \chi^2_{n_1}$ and $Y \sim \chi^2_{n_2}$ the variate $(X - Y) \sim \chi^2_{n_1 - n_2}$ for $n_1 > n_2$.

(xv) If $X \sim \chi^2_{n_1}$, $X + Y \sim x_{n_1 + n_2}$, then $Y \sim \chi^2_{n_2}$.

(xvi) If $X \sim \chi^2_{n_1}$, $Y \sim \chi^2_{n_2}$ and $(X + Y) \sim \chi^2_{n_1 + n_2}$, the Chi-square variates X and Y are independent.

(xvii) If n is large, then $\lim_{n\to\infty} \chi^2_n \to N(n, 2n)$. This is known as the limiting property of the Chi-square.

(xviii) Points of inflexion of the Chi-square distribution curve are

$$x = (n-2) \pm \{2(n-2)\}^{1/2}$$

(xix) Points of inflexion of the Chi-square distribution curve are equidistant from its mode.

(xx) If $X \sim \chi^2_{n_1}$ and $Y \sim \chi^2_{n_2}$ are independent Chi-square variates, the distribution of the quotient (X/Y) is beta distribution of type II, *i.e.*, $X/Y \sim \beta_{II}\left(\frac{n_1}{2}, \frac{n_2}{2}\right)$.

(xxi) If $X \sim \chi^2_{n_1}$ and $Y \sim \chi^2_{n_2}$ are two independent Chi-square variates, the distribution of the quotient $X/(X + Y)$ is beta distribution of type I *i.e.*, $\frac{X}{X+Y} \sim \beta_I\left(\frac{n_1}{2}, \frac{n_2}{2}\right)$

(xxii) If all $X_i \sim N(0, 1)$ for $i = 1, 2, \ldots, n$, $\Sigma X_i^2 \sim \chi^2_n$. But if X_i's are distributed normally with unit variance and non-zero means, *i.e.*, $X_i \sim N(\mu_i, 1)$. The distribution of ΣX_i^2 is known as *non-central Chi-square* (χ'^2) with non-centrality parameter λ where $\lambda = \frac{1}{2}\Sigma\mu_i^2$. We denote $\chi'^2 = \chi'^2_{(n, \lambda)}$.

(xxiii) The Chi-square distribution is used to test whether a hypothetical value σ_0^2 of the population variance is true or not.

(xxiv) χ^2 is used to make a *test* of *goodness* of *fit*.

(xxv) χ^2 is used to test the *independence* of *attributes*.

(xxvi) χ^2 is used to test the validity of a hypothetical ratios.

(xxvii) χ^2 is used to test the homogeneity of several population variances.

(xxviii) χ^2 is used to test the equality of several population correlation coefficients.

Q. 57. *What statistic is known as Pearson's Chi-square statistic?*

Ans. In a frequency distribution of large sample

having k classes such that the frequency of the ith-class is f_i, the statistic $\sum_{i=1}^{k} \frac{(f_i - np_i)^2}{np_i}$ is distributed as Chi-square with $(k - 1)$ d.f. where np_i is the expected frequency corresponding to the observed frequency f_i and p_i is the probability that a sample observation x_i belong to the ith-class. Also $\Sigma f_i = n$.

Q. 58. *What is a Chi-distribution?*

Ans. The positive square root of χ_n^2 is called the Chi-distribution, *i.e.*, $+\sqrt{\chi_n^2} = \chi_n$. The mean of Chi-distribution is $\sqrt{n}$.

Q. 59. *Define and discuss student's t-distribution.*

Ans. Student's t is defined as the deviation of sample mean from its population mean expressed in terms of standard error.

The credit of t-distribution goes to W.S. Gosset who published it in 1908 in research paper entitled, "The probable error of the mean". Professor R.A. Fisher defined t as the ratio of a normal variate $X \sim N(0, 1)$ and the square root $\sqrt{y/v}$, where $y \sim \chi_n^2$ and v is the degree of freedom of χ^2, *i.e.*, $t = X\Big/\sqrt{\frac{Y}{v}}$.

The two approaches result into the same t-distribution. Student's t is extremely used in the theory and application of statistics.

Let $x_1, x_2, \ldots, x_n$ be a random sample drawn from a normal distribution having mean μ and standard deviation σ (unknown). The statistic $\sqrt{n}(\bar{x} - \mu)/s$ is distributed as student's – t with $(n - 1)$ d.f.^{2}, where $\bar{x}$ is the sample mean and s, the sample standard deviation. Thus, student's t-statistic is,

$$t = \frac{\bar{x} - \mu}{s/\sqrt{n}}$$

where, $$s^2 = \frac{1}{n-1}\sum_{i=1}^{n}(x_i - \bar{x})^2$$

The probability density function of student's t with $v\,(= n - 1)$ d.f. is

$$f_v(t) = \frac{1}{\sqrt{v}\,\beta\left(\frac{1}{2}, \frac{v}{2}\right)\left(1 + \frac{t^2}{v}\right)^{(v+1)/2}}$$

$$= \frac{\Gamma\left(\frac{v+1}{2}\right)}{\sqrt{v}\,\sqrt{\pi}\,\Gamma\frac{v}{2}}\left(1 + \frac{t^2}{v}\right)^{-(v+1)/2}$$

$$-\infty < t < \infty$$

since $$\beta\left(\frac{1}{2}, \frac{v}{2}\right) = \frac{\Gamma\left(\frac{v+1}{2}\right)}{\Gamma\frac{v}{2}\sqrt{\pi}} \text{ and } \Gamma\frac{1}{2} = \sqrt{\pi}$$

Properties of student's *t*-distribution:

(*i*) t-distribution is symmetrical about the origin since $f(t) = f(-t)$.

(*ii*) All moments of odd order are zero, *i.e.*, $\mu'_{2r+1} = 0$.

(*iii*) The mean of t-distribution is zero.

(*iv*) The variance of t-distribution is $\frac{n}{n-2}$ for $n > 2$.

(*v*) The third moment $\mu'_3 = 0$ also $\mu_3 = 0$.

(*vi*) The fourth central moment

$$\mu_4 = \frac{3n^2}{(n-2)(n-4)} \text{ for } n > 4.$$

(*vii*) Measure of skewness, $\beta_1 = 0$.

(*viii*) Measure of Kurtosis, $\beta_2 = \frac{3(n-2)}{(n-4)}$ for $n > 4$.

This reveals that t-distribution is symmetrical about mean and is leptokurtic because $\beta_2 > 3$ as $\left(\frac{n-2}{n-4}\right) > 1$.

$$\text{Also } \lim_{n\to\infty}\beta_2 = \lim_{n\to\infty}\frac{3\left(1 - \frac{2}{n}\right)}{\left(1 - \frac{4}{n}\right)} = 3.$$

The limiting value of $\beta_2 = 3$. Hence, this

shows that for large n, t_n is approximately $N(0, 1)$. In practice $n > 30$ is considered as large. Some workers take $n \geq 50$ as large.

(*ix*) Mode of t-distribution lies at the origin $t = 0$.

(*x*) Points of inflexion of t-distribution are

$$\pm\left(\frac{n}{n+2}\right)^{1/2}$$

(*xi*) Moment generating function of t-distribution does not exist.

(*xii*) Recurrence formula for even order moments of t-distribution is:

$$\mu_{2r} = \frac{n(2r-1)}{(n-2r)}\mu_{2r-2} \text{ for } n > 2r$$

(*xiii*) The maximum height of distribution curve is $\dfrac{1}{\sqrt{n-1}\,\beta\left(\frac{1}{2}, \frac{n-1}{2}\right)}$ at the point $t = 0$.

(*xiv*) If $n = 2$, the probability density function reduces to $\dfrac{1}{\pi(1+t^2)}$ which is the standard Cauchy distribution. Hence, t with 1 d.f. reduces to Cauchy distribution.

(*xv*) Probability tables for t-distribution can be prepared for various d.f. and different value of $t = t_0$. Fisher and Yates prepared tables for $P_F = P(t > t_0)$. William Gosset prepared tables for $P_S = P(t \leq t_0)$. By little manipulation it can be shown that $P_F = 2(1 - P_S)$. t-tables are prepared for various d.f. for direct usage in statistical inference which are extremely useful and extensively used.

(*xvi*) t-distribution is used to test whether the sample mean conforms to a specified value of population mean or not.

(*xvii*) t-distribution provides the facility of testing the equality of two population means based on sample means.

1. Random sample has been discussed in Chapter 9.
2. Degrees of freedom has been defined in Chapter 10.

(*xviii*) The significance of correlation coefficient and regression coefficient is tested by student-t.

(*xix*) Significance of partial correlation coefficient is also tested by student-t.

(*xx*) If $X \sim N(\delta, 1)$ and $Y \sim \chi^2$ with n d.f. are two independent variates, the distribution of the statistic

$$t' = X/\sqrt{Y/n}$$

is known as non-central t variate and is said to follow non-central t-distribution with n d.f. and non-centrality parameter δ. Non-central t-distribution is seldom needed to develop the power function of certain tests concerning normal population.

Q. 60. *Define Fisher's z-statistics and discuss z-distribution appropriately.*

Ans. Sir R.A. Fisher in 1925 defined a statistic which is based on the ratio of two sample variances. Suppose the variances of two random samples based on sizes n_1 and n_2 drawn from two normal populations are s_1^2 is defined as s_2^2 respectively. Fisher's z-statistic is defined as

$$z = \frac{1}{2}\log_e\left(\frac{s_1^2}{s_2^2}\right)$$

or

$$\frac{s_1^2}{s_2^2} = e^{2z}$$

Putting

$$\frac{s_1^2}{s_2^2} = F,$$

$$F = e^{2z}.$$

The letter F is the first letter of Fisher's name as a mark of respect given to him by G.W. Snedecor. Probability density function of Fisher's z-distribution is,

$$f_F(z) = \frac{2\nu_1^{\nu_1/2}\,\nu_2^{\nu_2/2}}{\beta\left(\frac{\nu_1}{2}, \frac{\nu_2}{2}\right)} \frac{e^{\nu_1 z}}{(\nu_2 + \nu_1 e^{2z})^{\frac{\nu_1+\nu_2}{2}}}$$

$$-\infty < z < \infty$$

where $\nu_1 = (n_1 - 1)$, $\nu_2 = (n_2 - 1)$

ν_1 and ν_2 are called the degrees of freedom of Fisher's z-distribution.

Properties of Fisher's *z*-distribution:

(*i*) It is highly skew distribution.

(*ii*) *z*-distribution is a family of distributions for different values of ν_1 and ν_2.

(*iii*) The mean of *z*-distribution is $\frac{1}{2}\left(\frac{1}{\nu_2}-\frac{1}{\nu_1}\right)$.

(*iv*) The variance of *z*-distribution is

$$\frac{1}{2}\left(\frac{1}{\nu_1}+\frac{1}{\nu_2}+\frac{1}{\nu_1^2}+\frac{1}{\nu_2^2}\right)$$

(*v*) The third moment,

$$\mu_3 = \frac{1}{2}\left\{\left(\frac{1}{\nu_2^2}-\frac{1}{\nu_1^2}\right)+\frac{1}{2}\left(\frac{1}{\nu_2^3}-\frac{1}{\nu_1^3}\right)\right\}.$$

(*vi*) The fourth moment,

$$\mu_4 = \left(\frac{1}{\nu_2^3}+\frac{1}{\nu_1^3}\right)+3\left(\frac{1}{\nu_2^4}+\frac{1}{\nu_1^4}\right)+3\mu_2^2$$

(*vii*) Moment generating function of *z*-distribution is,

$$M_z(t) = \left(\frac{\nu_2}{\nu_1}\right)^{t/2}\frac{\Gamma\left(\frac{\nu_1+t}{2}\right)\Gamma\left(\frac{\nu_2-t}{2}\right)}{\Gamma\frac{\nu_1}{2}\Gamma\frac{\nu_2}{2}}$$

(*viii*) Characteristic function of *z*-distribution is,

$$\phi_z(t) = \left(\frac{\nu_2}{\nu_1}\right)^{it/2}\frac{\Gamma\left(\frac{\nu_1+it}{2}\right)\Gamma\left(\frac{\nu_2-it}{2}\right)}{\Gamma\frac{\nu_1}{2}\Gamma\frac{\nu_2}{2}}$$

(*ix*) *z*-distribution tends to normal with mean $\frac{1}{2}\left(\frac{1}{\nu_2}-\frac{1}{\nu_1}\right)$ and variance $\frac{1}{2}\left(\frac{1}{\nu_1}+\frac{1}{\nu_2}\right)$ when ν_1 and ν_2 are large.

Q. 58. *What is Snedecor's F and F-distribution?*

Ans. G.W. Snedecor founded *F*-statistics as the ratio of two sample variances and prepared *F*-tables in 1934. Suppose there are two samples of sizes n_1 and n_2 from normal populations $N(\mu_1, \sigma_1^2)$ and $N(\mu_2, \sigma_2^2)$ respectively. Suppose s_1^2, s_2^2, are the sample variances respectively.

We know,

$$\frac{\nu_1 s_1^2}{\sigma_1^2} \sim \chi_1^2 \text{ where } \nu_1 = (n_1-1)$$

and

$$\frac{\nu_2 s_2^2}{\sigma_2^2} \sim \chi_2^2 \text{ where } \nu_2 = (n_2-1)$$

The ratio,

$$\frac{s_1^2/\sigma_1^2}{s_2^2/\sigma_2^2} = \frac{\chi_1^2/\nu_1}{\chi_2^2/\nu_2}$$

$$= F_{\nu_1, \nu_2}$$

If we have to test $\sigma_1^2 = \sigma_2^2$, under this hypothesis

$$\frac{s_1^2}{s_2^2} = F_{\nu_1, \nu_2}$$

From the above expression, it is evident that the ratio of two independent Chi-squares *vis-a-vis* the ratio of two independent variances is distributed as *F.* ν_1 and ν_2 are called the d.f. of *F*-distribution. As a norm larger sample variance is taken in the numerator. The probability density function of *F*-distribution is

$$f_{\nu_1,\nu_2}(F) = \frac{\left(\frac{\nu_1}{\nu_2}\right)^{\nu_1/2}}{\beta\left(\frac{\nu_1}{2},\frac{\nu_2}{2}\right)}\frac{F^{\frac{\nu_1}{2}-1}}{\left(1+\frac{\nu_1}{\nu_2}F\right)^{\frac{\nu_1+\nu_2}{2}}}$$

$$0 \le F < \infty$$

F-distribution has two parameters ν_1 and ν_2.

Properties of *F*-distribution:

(*i*) *F*-distribution extends along abscissa from 0 to ∞.

(*ii*) *F*-distribution curve wholly lies in the first quadrant.

(*iii*) Shape of the curve depends on the d.f. ν_1 and ν_2.

(*iv*) F-distribution curve is a positive skew curve and is highly positively skewed when ν_2 is small ($\nu_2 < 5$).

(*v*) The curve is unimodal and its mode is at the point $F = \nu_2 (\nu_1 - 2)/\nu_1 (\nu_2 + 2)$ for ($\nu_1 \geq 3$). The mode is always less than unity.

(*vi*) Mean of F-distribution is $\nu_2/(\nu_2 - 2)$ for $\nu_2 \geq 3$.

(*vii*) Variance of F-distribution is

$$\frac{2\nu_2^2(\nu_1 + \nu_2 - 2)}{\nu_1(\nu_2 - 2)^2 (\nu_2 - 4)} \quad \text{for } \nu_2 > 4$$

(*viii*) Moment generating function of F-distribution does not exist.

(ix) There exists a very useful relation between F-values having interchanged d.f., *i.e.*,

$$F_{\alpha; (\nu_1, \nu_2)} = \frac{1}{F_{1-\alpha; (\nu_2, \nu_1)}}$$

or $$P\{F_{\nu_1, \nu_2} \geq c\} = P\left\{F_{\nu_2, \nu_1} \leq \frac{1}{c}\right\}$$

This is known as the reciprocal property of F-distribution.

(*x*) If X_1 and X_2 are two variables having the density function $f(x) = e^{-x}$ $(0 < x \infty)$, the variate X_1/X_2 follows F-distribution.

(*xi*) If $X \sim F(\nu_1, \nu_2)$, the variable $\nu_1 X/(\nu_2 + \nu_1 X)$ is distributed as beta distribution of type I, *i.e.*, $\beta_I\left(\frac{\nu_1}{2}, \frac{\nu_2}{2}\right)$ and the variable $\nu_1 F/\nu_2$ is distributed as $\beta_{II}\left(\frac{\nu_1}{2}, \frac{\nu_2}{2}\right)$.

(*xii*) If $\nu_1 = 1$ and $\nu_2 \to \infty$, $\sqrt{F_{1,\infty}} \sim N(0, 1)$.

(*xiii*) If $\nu_1 = 1$ and $\nu_2 \to \infty$, $F_{1,\infty} = \chi_1^2$

(*xiv*) If t has ν d.f. and F has $(1, \nu)$ d.f., $t_\nu^2 = F_{1,\nu}$

(*xv*) If t has ∞ d.f., $\chi_1^2 = t_\infty^2$.

(*xvi*) The two points of inflexion of the F-distribution are equidistant from its mode.

(*xvii*) F-distribution is used to test the equality of two population variances.

(*xviii*) F-distribution is entirely used in analysis of variance.

(xix) F-distribution is applied to test the equality of several regression coefficients.

(*xx*) F-distribution is used to test the equality of several population means.

(*xxi*) If χ_1^2 is a non-central χ^2 with ν_1 d.f. and non-centrality parameter λ and χ_2^2 is a central χ^2 with ν_2 d.f., the distribution of $\frac{\chi_1^2/\nu_1}{\chi_2^2/\nu_2}$ is F' which is known as non-central F.

SECTION B

Fill in the Blanks

Fill in the suitable word(s) or phrase(s) in the blanks:

1. A discrete variable can take a _________ number of values within its range.

2. A continuous variable can take any value within its _________.

3. If a fair coin is tossed three times, the probability function $p(x)$ of the number of heads x is _________ .

4. A fair coin is tossed three times. If x denote the number of heads and y denotes the number of head runs of two or three heads, the probability function of the variable $Z = x + y$ is _________.

5. If a discrete random variable has the probability function as,

x:	0	1	2	3	4	5	6	7	8
$p(x)$:	k	$2k$	$3k$	$5k$	$5k$	$4k$	$3k$	$2k$	k

then the value of k is equal to ________ and $E(x)$ = ________ .

6. If the probability density function of a variable x is defined as,

$$f(x) = cx(2 - x) \qquad 0 \le x < 2$$

then the value of c ________ .

7. If p.d.f. of a variable x is defined as,

$$f(x) - \frac{3}{4}x(2 - x), \qquad 0 < x < 2$$

then the median of the distribution is ________ .

8. The probability density function $f(x)$ cannot exceed ________.

9. If a random variable X possesses the following function:

x:	+3	+2	+1	0	−1	−2	−3
$p(x)$:	0.1	0.2	$3k$	k	$2k$	0	0.1

then

(*a*) the value of K is ________ .

(*b*) the mean of X is ________ .

(*c*) the variance X is ________ .

10. If $p(x) = \frac{x}{12}$ for $x = 1, 2, 3, 4, 5, 6$

$= 0$ otherwise.

then

(*a*) $P(x = 2 \text{ or } 3)$ = ________

(*b*) $P\left\{\left(\frac{1}{2} < x < \frac{5}{2}\right) x > 1\right\}$ = ________

11. The function $f(x) = x^2;\ -1 < x < 1$

$= 0$ otherwise

is a possible ________ .

12. If $f(x)$ is the p.d.f. of x; $a \le x \le b$ then

(*a*) the mean μ_1 is equal to ________ .

(*b*) the logarithm of the geometric mean, $\log G$ = ________.

(*c*) the harmonic mean of x, $\frac{1}{H}$ = ________.

(*d*) the expected value of x^2, *i.e.*, $E(x^2)$ ________.

(*e*) the variance of x, *i.e.*, $V(x)$ = ________.

(*f*) the mean deviation about mean μ, *i.e.*, M.D. = ________.

(*g*) the median of the frequency distribution, M = ________.

(*h*) i^{th} quartile of the frequency distribution for = 1, 2, 3, *i.e.*, Q_i = ________.

(*i*) i^{th} decile of the frequency distribution for i = 1, 2, ..., 9, *i.e.*, D_i = ________.

(*j*) i^{th} percentile of the frequency distribution for i = 1, 2, …, 99, *i.e.*, P_i = ________ .

13. If $f(x)$ is a p.d.f. of a variable X defined as,

$$f(x) = cx,\ 1 \le x \le 2$$
$$= c,\ 2 \le x \le 3$$
$$= 0 \text{ otherwise}$$

then the value of c is ________.

14. If the exponential distribution is given as,

$$f(x) = e^{-x},\ 0 \le x \le \infty$$

then

(*a*) the mean of the distribution is ________.

(*b*) the variance of the distribution ________.

(*c*) the third moment of the distribution is ________ .

(*d*) Pearson's constant β_1 = ________:

15. If the probability density function of a variable x is given as,

$$f(x) = \frac{x}{a^2} e^{-x^2/2a^2},\ 0 \le x \le \infty$$

then the variance of the distribution is ________.

16. If a random variable X has the p.d.f.

$$f(x) = 3x,\ 0 < x < 1$$
$$= 0 \text{ otherwise}$$

then the p.d.f. of $y = 4x + 3$ is ________ .

17. If x has a rectangular distribution

$$f(x) = \frac{1}{4},\ -2 \le x \le 2.$$

then p.d.f. $g(y)$ of a variable $y = \sin x$ is ________ .

18. The distribution of a random variable x in the range [0, 2] is defined by

$$f(x) \neq x^3,\ 0 < x \leq 1$$
$$= (2-x)^3,\ 1 < x \leq 2$$

then the mean of the distribution $f(x)$ is ________ .

19. If ce^{-ax} is a p.d.f. for $0 < x < \infty$, the value of c is equal to ________ .

20. The mean of binomial distribution $b(n, p)$ is ________ and its variance is ________ .

21. The mean of the binomial distribution is ________ than its variance.

22. If the mean and variance of binomial distribution are 2 and 1 respectively, the $P(x \leq 1)$ is equal to ________ .

23. If on an average the rain falls on ten days in a month (30 days), the probability that the rain will fall on two days of the week is ________ .

24. In a police control room there are on an average 3 calls per 10 minute interval. The probability of receiving 4 calls in a 10 minute interval is ________ .

25. If the probability of a rocket hitting the target is $\frac{1}{2}$ and the rockets are being launched one after the other, then the probability that the 10th launch being the 5th hit on the target is ________ .

26. Shifting of origin does not affect the ________ distribution.

27. Mean and variance of geometric distribution are ________ .

28. Under shifting of time origin in geometric distribution, the p.d.f. remain the same. This property is known as ________ .

29. The mode of the geometric distribution.

$$f(x) = \left(\frac{1}{2}\right)^x$$

for $x = 1, 2, 3, \ldots$ is ________ .

30. In case of geometric variate x, the variance of x is always ________ mean of x.

31. Negative binomial distribution $nb(r, p)$ reduces to geometric distribution when ________ .

32. Polya's distribution reduces to geometric distribution when ________ .

33. In hypergeometric distribution, the probability of successive draws (trails) are ________ .

34. The probability of a success changes from trial to trial in ________ .

35. The number of trials in hypergeometric distribution is ________ .

36. Hypergeometric distribution reduces to binomial distribution when ________ .

37. If the rectangular distribution, $f(x) = \frac{1}{b-a}$, $a \leq x \leq b$, the mean and the median of the distribution are ________.

38. Rectangle distribution is ________ .

39. Mode of the rectangular distribution ________.

40. Mean deviation about mean in case of rectangular distribution is ________ .

41. Variance of rectangular distribution is equal to ________ .

42. Moment generating function for rectangular distribution ________ .

43. If the random variable x has the rectangular distribution with p.d.f., $f(x) = \frac{1}{\theta}$, $0 < x \leq \theta$, then

(*a*) the mean of the distribution is ________.

(*b*) the variance of the distribution is ________.

(*c*) the third central moment is equal to ________.

(*d*) the fourth central moment is ________.

(*e*) the coefficient of skewness is ________.

(*f*) The coefficient of Kurtosis is ________.

44. The number of Parameter(s) involved in exponential p.d.f. is/are ________ .

45. The tails of the exponential distribution curve are ________ .

46. The exponential distribution is ________ peaked than normal.

47. If $x \sim$ Expo (λ), variable $y = e^{-\lambda x}$ has ________ distribution.

48. The variance of $L(\lambda)$ is ________ the variance of Expo (λ).

49. The distribution curve of double exponential distribution in respect of its bulginess is ________ .

50. Semi-interquartile range of double exponential distribution is ________ .

51. If $X \sim N(\mu, \sigma)$, the standard normal deviate is distributed as ________ .

52. The maximum height of the normal curve lies at the point ________ .

53. The p.d.f. at the point of inflexion of the normal curve is ________ .

54. If $X_1, X_2, ..., X_n$ are i.i.d. normal variates with mean μ and variance σ^2, the variable $\sum_{i=1}^{a} X_i$ is distributed as ________ .

55. If $X_1, X_2, \ldots, X_n$ are i.i.d. $N(\mu, \sigma^2)$, the variable $\bar{x}$ is distributed as ________.

56. The normal distribution curve is (*a*) ________ (*b*) ________ (*c*) ________.

57. For a normal distribution, quartile deviation, mean deviation and standard deviation are in the ratio ________.

58. For a normal distribution $N(\mu, \sigma^2)$, the mean deviation from mean is ________ .

59. For a normal frequency, the odd order moment μ_{2r+1} are equal to ________ .

60. The moment generating function of the normal distribution $N(\mu, \sigma^2)$ is ________ .

61. The characteristic function of the normal distribution $N(\mu, \sigma^2)$ is ________ .

62. If $X \sim N(\mu_1, \sigma_1^2)$ and $Y \sim N(\mu_2, \sigma_2^2)$, the variable $X + Y$ is distributed as ________ .

63. If $X \sim N(12.5, 3.5^2)$ and $Y \sim N(8.5, 2.5^2)$, the variable $X + Y$ is distributed as ________ .

64. If the income X (rupees) of people is distributed normally with mean $\mu = 500$ and S.D. $\sigma = 200$, the percentage of people having the income:
Given,

z:	0.50	1.00	1.25
$\phi(z)$	0.19146	0.19146	0.39435
z:	1.50	2.25	2.50
$\phi(z)$	0.43319	0.48778	0.49379

(*a*) more than ₹ 1000 is ________.
(*b*) less than ₹ 250 is ________.
(*c*) between ₹ 400 and 600 is ________.
(*d*) between ₹ 200 and 400 is ________.
(*e*) between ₹ 700 and ₹ 950 is ________.

65. In the problem number 64, if the total number of workers in a factory is 500, the number of employees having income.
(*a*) more than ₹ 1000 is ________.
(*b*) less than ₹ 250 is ________.
(*c*) between ₹ 400 and 600 is ________.
(*d*) between ₹ 200 and 400 is ________.
(*e*) between ₹ 700 and ₹ 950 is ________.

66. The mean of lognormal distribution is ________.

67. The variance of lognormal distribution is ________.

68. The right tail of lognormal distribution is ________.

69. Lognormal distribution curve is ________ peaked than normal curve.

70. If $X_1 \sim \log - N(\mu_1, \sigma_1^2)$ and $X_2 \sim \log - N(\mu_2, \sigma_2^2)$, the distribution of X_1/X_2 is ________ .

71. If $X_1 \sim \log - N(\mu_1, \sigma_1^2)$ and $X_2 \sim \log - N(\mu_2, \sigma_2^2)$ the distribution of $(X_1 - X_2)$ is ________.

72. If $X_1, X_2, \ldots, X_n$ are n observations on log-normal variate $X \sim f(x; \mu, \sigma^2)$, the geometric mean $G = (x_1, x_2, \ldots, x_n)^{1/n}$ has ________ distribution.

73. The probability density function of a Cauchy variate X with parameters 2 and 5 is ________.

74. Mean of Cauchy distribution is ________.

75. Variance of Cauchy distribution is ________.

76. Moment generating function of Cauchy distribution is ________.

77. If $X \sim C$ (5, 4), the maximum of Cauchy distribution lies at the point ________.

78. ________ moments of Cauchy variate exist.

79. If $X \sim C$ (2, 1), the mode of the Cauchy distribution lies at the point ________.

80. If $X_1, X_2, \ldots, X_n$ are i.i.d. $C(\alpha, \beta)$, their mean, $\bar{X}$ is distributed as ________.

81. If X and Y are standard normal variates, the variable X/Y has the distribution ________.

82. If X and Y are i.i.d. variates and X/Y is C (0, 1), X and Y ________ necessarily normal.

83. If $X \sim \beta_I(\alpha, \beta)$, the variate X follows U (0, 1) for the values of α and β as ________.

84. Mean of distribution $\beta_I(\alpha, \beta)$ is ________.

85. Mean of distribution $\beta_{II}(\alpha, \beta)$ is ________.

86. The shape of beta distribution curve depends on the values of ________.

87. If a random variable $X \sim \gamma(n, \alpha)$, the relation between mean and variance is ________.

88. As regards the position of tails, gamma distribution curve has ________.

89. As regards the peakedness, gamma distribution curve is ________.

90. If $X \sim \gamma(n_1)$ and $Y \sim \gamma(n_2)$, the variable $X + Y$ is distributed as ________.

91. If $X \sim \gamma(n_1)$ and $Y \sim \gamma(n_2)$, the variable $X/(X + Y)$ is distributed as ________.

92. The cumulative distribution function of gamma distribution is also known as ________.

93. If X follows logistic distribution with parameter α and β, the variance of the distribution is independent of ________.

94. The tails of the logistic distribution curve are ________.

95. Pareto distribution has application in ________.

96. Weibull distribution has application in ________.

97. The variable like ________ follows Weibull distribution.

98. If X is a binomial variate with parameters $n = 25$, and $p = 0.2$. The probability $P\{x < \mu_x - 2\sigma_x\}$ is ________.

99. If X is a binomial variate with parameters n and p, the distribution of the variable $Y = (n - X)$ is a ________ variate with parameters ________.

100. If a variable X follows Poisson distribution with $P(x = 1) = P(x = 2)$, the probability $P(x = 1 \text{ or } 2)$ is ________.

101. If X is a Poisson variate with $P(x = 1) = P(x = 2)$, the mean of the Poisson variate is equal to ________.

102. The normal curve is symmetrical about mean 50 and 5 per cent values are greater than 70. The standard S.D. of the distribution is ________. [Given that $\phi(1.64) = 0.05$].

103. The standard deviation of a Poisson variate is 2, the mean of the Poisson variate is ________.

104. The shape of Chi-square distribution curve with d.f. 1 is ________.

105. If the Chi-square distribution has 10 d.f., the relation between μ_3' and μ_2' is ________.

106. If the Chi-square has 8 d.f., the relation between μ_3, μ_2 and μ_1 is ________.

107. In a way the Chi-square distribution is equivalent to ________.

108. If χ_1^2 and χ_2^2 are two independent Chi-square variates with d.f. n_1 and n_2, respectively, then

(*a*) the distribution of χ_1^2/χ_2^2 is ________

(*b*) the distribution of $\dfrac{\chi_1^2/n_1}{\chi_2^2/n_2}$ is ________.

(*c*) the distribution of $(\chi_1^2 + \chi_2^2)$ is ________.

(*d*) the distribution of $\dfrac{\chi_1^2}{\chi_1^2 + \chi_2^2}$ is ________.

(*e*) the distribution of $(\chi_1^2 - \chi_2^2)$ is ________.

109. The mean of the Chi-square distribution is ________ of its variance.

110. The third moment of the Chi-square distribution is ________ of its variance.

111. Pearson's coefficient of skewness for Chi-square distribution curve is ________.

112. The Chi-square distribution curve for d.f. 3 or more is always ________.

113. If the d.f. n for Chi-square are large, the Chi-square distribution tends to ________.

114. The positive square root of χ_n^2 follow ________ distribution.

115. The mean of the Chi-square distribution with n d.f. is ________.

116. If the variates $X_i (i = 1, 2, \ldots, n)$ are distributed as $N(\mu, 1)$, the variate $\Sigma\chi_i^2$ is distributed as ________.

117. If $x_1, x_2, \ldots, x_n$ is a random sample from a population $N(\mu, \sigma^2)$, the distribution of $\dfrac{\Sigma(x_i - \bar{x})^2}{\sigma^2}$ is ________.

118. If $X_1, X_2, \ldots, X_n$ are n i.i.d. expo (λ) variates, the distribution of $2\lambda\Sigma X_i$ is ________.

119. Pearson's Chi-square statistic for K classes is

120. t_n-distribution tends to normal if ________.

121. t-distribution curve in respect of tails is always ________.

122. Measure of Kurtosis for t-distribution curve cannot be defined if ________.

123. t-distribution curve as regards its peak is always ________.

124. Maximum height of t-distribution curve is ________.

125. t-distribution with 1 d.f. reduces to ________.

126. Equality of two population means can be tested by ________.

127. Significance of Pearson's correlation coefficient can be tested by ________.

128. Independence of two attributes can be tested by ________.

129. Whether a given frequency distribution follows an specified distribution or not can be tested by ________.

130. The population variance σ^2 has a hypothetical value 25 or not can be tested by ________.

131. If $X \sim N(0, 1)$ and $Y \sim \chi_n^2$, the statistic $\dfrac{\sqrt{n}X}{\sqrt{Y}}$ is distributed as ________.

132. The ratio of two sample variances is distributed as ________.

133. The relation between Fisher's z and Snedecor's F is ________.

134. The mean of z-distribution is ________.

135. Mode of F-distribution is always ________ unity.

136. Moment generating function of F-distribution ________.

137. Reciprocal property of F-distribution leads to the relation ________.

138. For distributions F_{ν_1, ν_2} and $\chi_{\nu_1}^2$, and $\nu_2 \to \infty$, the relation between F and χ^2 is ________.

139. If the d.f. for χ^2 are large, the χ^2-distribution tends to ________ distribution.

140. If s^2 is the variance of a sample of size n from a population $N(\mu, \sigma^2)$, the statistic $\dfrac{(n-1)s^2}{\sigma^2}$ is distributed as ________.

141. If x_1 and x_2 be a random sample from a population $N(1, 1)$, the variate $\dfrac{x_1 - x_2}{\sqrt{2}}$ is distributed as ________.

142. Beta type I and beta type II distributions are same excepting in respect of _________ .

143. Characteristic function is not useful to workout the moments in case of _________ distribution.

144. If a variate $X \sim \gamma(\alpha, 1)$, the distribution of X is same at that of _________ distribution.

145. If a variate $Y \sim b(y; n, p)$, variate Y/n is known as _________ variate.

146. A variable X representing the angles and satisfying the condition $\int_0^\pi f(x)\,dx = 1$ for $f(x) \geq 0$ and $0 \leq x \leq \pi$ follows _________ distribution.

147. The parameters of a multinomial distribution having k classes and n observations are _________.

148. The variable $y = -2 \log x$ for $X \sim U(0, 1)$ is distributed as Chi-square with _________ d.f.

149. The variable $Y = -2 \sum_{i=1}^{n} \log X_i$, where X_i are i.i.d. $U(0, 1)$, follows _________ distribution.

150. A distribution having always mean and standard deviation equal is _________ .

SECTION C

Multiple Choice Questions

Select one correct alternative out of given ones:

1. Two random variables X and Y are said to be independent if:

(*a*) $E(XY) = 1$
(*b*) $E(XY) = 0$
(*c*) $E(XY) = E(X)\,E(Y)$
(*d*) $E(XY)$ = any constant value

2. If X and Y are two random variables such that their expectations exist and $P(x \leq y) = 1$, then

(*a*) $E(X) \leq E(Y)$
(*b*) $E(X) \geq E(Y)$
(*c*) $E(X) = E(Y)$
(*d*) none of the above

3. If X and Y two independent variables and their expected values are $\bar{X}$ and $\bar{Y}$ respectively, then

(*a*) $E\{(X - \bar{X})(Y - \bar{Y})\} = 0$
(*b*) $E\{(X - \bar{X})(Y - \bar{Y})\} = 1$
(*c*) $E\{(X - \bar{X})(Y - \bar{Y})\} = C$ (constant)
(*d*) all of the above

4. If X is a random variable with its mean $\bar{X}$, the expression $E(X - \bar{X})^2$ represents:

(*a*) the variance of X
(*b*) second central moment
(*c*) both (*a*) and (*b*)
(*d*) none of (*a*) and (*b*)

5. If X and Y are two random variables, then

(*a*) $E\{(XY)^2\} = E(X^2)E(Y^2)$
(*b*) $E\{(XY)^2\} = E(X^2\,Y^2)$
(*c*) $E\{(XY)^2\} \geq E(X^2)\,E(Y^2)$
(*d*) $E\{(XY)^2\} \leq E(X^2)\,E(Y^2)$

6. The outcomes of tossing a coin three times are a variable of the type:

(*a*) continuous random variable
(*b*) discrete random variable
(*c*) neither discrete nor continuous random variable
(*d*) discrete as well as continuous random variable

7. The height of persons in a country is a random variable of the type:

(*a*) continuous r.v.
(*b*) discrete r.v.
(*c*) neither discrete nor continuous r.v.
(*d*) continuous as well as discrete r.v.

8. If X and Y are two random variables with means $\bar{X}$ and $\bar{Y}$ respectively, then the expression

$$E\left[(X-\bar{X})(Y-\bar{Y})\right]$$

is called:

(a) variance of X
(b) variance of Y
(c) cov (X, Y)
(d) moments of X and Y

9. If X is a random variable, $E(e^{tx})$ is known as:
(a) characteristic function
(b) moment generating function
(c) probability generating function
(d) all of the above

10. If X is a random variable, the $E(t^x)$ is known as:
(a) characteristic function
(b) moment generating function
(c) probability generating function
(d) the xth moment

11. If X is a random variable with mean μ, the $E(X-\mu)^r$ is called:
(a) variance
(b) r^{th} raw moment
(c) r^{th} central moment
(d) none of the above

12. If X is a random variable, $E(e^{itx})$ is known as:
(a) characteristic function
(b) moment generating function
(c) probability generating function
(d) all of the above

13. If $X_1, X_2, \ldots, X_n$ be a sequence of mutually independent random variables where X_i can take only positive integral values and

$$S_m = \sum_{i=1}^{m} X_i (m \leq n),\ S_n = \sum_{i=1}^{n} X_i,\ E(X) = \mu > 0$$

then

(a) $E\left(\frac{S_m}{s_n}\right) = 1$
(b) $E\left(\frac{S_m}{s_n}\right) = 0$
(c) $E\left(\frac{S_m}{S_n}\right) = \frac{m}{n}$
(d) $E\left(\frac{S_m}{S_n}\right) = \infty$

14. If X is a random variable which can take only non-negative values, then
(a) $E(X^2) = [E(X)]^2$
(b) $E(X^2) \geq [E(X)]^2$
(c) $E(X^2) \leq [E(X)]^2$
(d) none of the above

15. If X is a random variable having its p.d.f. $f(x)$, the $E(X)$ is called:
(a) arithmetic mean
(b) geometric mean
(c) harmonic mean
(d) first quartile

16. If X is a random variable and $f(x)$ is its p.d.f., $E\left(\frac{1}{X}\right)$ is used to find:
(a) arithmetic mean
(b) harmonic mean
(c) geometric mean
(d) first central moment

17. If X is a random variable and its p.d.f. is $f(x)$, $E(\log x)$ represents:
(a) arithmetic mean
(b) geometric mean
(c) harmonic mean
(d) logarithmic mean

18. If X and Y are two random variables, the covariance between the variables $aX+b$ and $cY+d$ in terms of COV(X, Y) is:
(a) COV$(aX+b, cY+d)$ = COV (X, Y)
(b) COV$(aX+b, cY+d)$ $= abcd \times$ COV (X, Y)
(c) COV$(aX+b, cY+d)$ $= ac$ COV $(X, Y) + bd$
(d) COV$(aX+b, cY+d) = ac$ COV (X, Y)

19. If X, Y and Z are three random variables, then

(*a*) COV $(X + Y, Z)$ = COV (X, Z) + COV (Y, Z)

(*b*) COV $(X + Y, Z)$ = COV (X, Z, YZ)

(*c*) COV $(X + Y, Z)$ = COV (X, Y, Z)

(*d*) COV $(X + Y, Z) = 0$

20. If X is a random variable and r is an integer, then $E(X^r)$ represents:

(*a*) r^{th} central moment

(*b*) r^{th} factorial moment

(*c*) r^{th} raw moment

(*d*) none of the above

21. For Bernoulli distribution with probability p of a success and q of a failure, the relation between mean and variance that holds is:

(*a*) mean < variance

(*b*) mean > variance

(*c*) mean = variance

(*d*) mean ≤ variance

22. The outcomes of an experiment classified as success A or $\bar{A}$ failure will follow a Bernoulli distribution if:

(*a*) $P(A) = \frac{1}{2}$

(*b*) $P(A) = 0$

(*c*) $P(A) = 1$

(*d*) $P(A)$ remains constant in all trials.

23. The mean and variance of a binomial distribution are 8 and 4, respectively. Then, $P(X = 1)$ is equal to:

(*a*) $\frac{1}{2^{12}}$

(*b*) $\frac{1}{2^4}$

(*c*) $\frac{1}{2^6}$

(*d*) $\frac{1}{2^8}$

24. If for a binomial distribution, $b(n, p)$, $n = 4$ and also $P(X = 2) = 3P(X = 3)$, the value of p is:

(*a*) $\frac{9}{11}$

(*b*) 1

(*c*) $\frac{1}{3}$

(*d*) none of the above

25. If for a binomial distribution $b(n, p)$, mean $= 4$, variance $= \frac{4}{3}$, the probability, $P(X \geq 5)$ is equal to:

(*a*) $\left(\frac{2}{3}\right)^6$

(*b*) $\left(\frac{2}{3}\right)^5\left(\frac{1}{3}\right)$

(*c*) $\left(\frac{1}{3}\right)^6$

(*d*) $4\left(\frac{2}{3}\right)^6$

26. An experiment succeeds twice as often as it fails. The chance that in the next six trials, there shall be at least four successes is:

(*a*) $\frac{240}{729}$

(*b*) $\frac{489}{729}$

(*c*) $\frac{496}{729}$

(*d*) none of the above

27. A manufacturer produces switches and experiences that 2 per cent switches are defective. The probability that in a box of 50 switches, there are at most two defective is:

(*a*) $2.5\, e^{-1}$

(*b*) e^{-1}

(*c*) $2\, e^{-1}$

(*d*) none of the above

28. If $X \sim b\left(3, \frac{1}{2}\right)$ and $Y \sim b\left(5, \frac{1}{2}\right)$, the probability of $P(X + Y = 3)$ is:
(*a*) 7/16
(*b*) 7/32
(*c*) 11/16
(*d*) none of the above

29. If X and Y are two Poisson variates such $X \sim P(1)$ and $Y \sim P(2)$, the probability, $P(X + Y < 3)$ is:
(*a*) e^{-3}
(*b*) $3e^{-3}$
(*c*) $4e^{-3}$
(*d*) $8.5e^{-3}$

30. If X is a binomial variate with its mean $\mu = 4$ and third moment $\mu_3 = 4.8$, the value of Pearson's constant β_1, is:
(*a*) 2/3
(*b*) 5/6
(*c*) 0
(*d*) none of the above

31. If $X \sim b(n, p)$, the distribution of $Y = (n - X)$ is:
(*a*) $b(n, 1)$
(*b*) $b(n, x)$
(*c*) $b(n, p)$
(*d*) $b(n, q)$

32. A family of parametric distribution in which mean is equal to variance is:
(*a*) binomial distribution
(*b*) gamma distribution
(*c*) normal distribution
(*d*) Poisson distribution

33. A family of parametric distributions in which mean is always greater than its variance is:
(*a*) binomial distribution
(*b*) geometric distribution
(*c*) both (*a*) and (*b*)
(*d*) neither (*a*) nor (*b*)

34. A family of parametric distributions having mean <, =, > variance is:
(*a*) gamma distribution
(*b*) exponential distribution
(*c*) logistic distribution
(*d*) all of the above

35. The family of parametric distributions which has mean always less than variance is:
(*a*) beta distribution
(*b*) lognormal distribution
(*c*) Weibull distribution
(*d*) negative binomial distribution

36. The family of parametric distributions, for which the mean and variance does not exist, is:
(*a*) Polya's distribution
(*b*) Cauchy distribution
(*c*) negative binomial distribution
(*d*) normal distribution

37. A family of parametric distributions which has mean always less than its variance is:
(*a*) negative binomial distribution
(*b*) Polya's distribution
(*c*) beta distribution of second kind
(*d*) hypergeometric distribution

38. The family of parametric distributions for which moment generating function does not exist is:
(*a*) student *t*-distribution
(*b*) Pareto distribution
(*c*) *F*-distribution
(*d*) all of the above

39. The distribution possessing the memoryless property is:
(*a*) gamma distribution
(*b*) geometric distribution
(*c*) hypergeometric distribution
(*d*) all of the above

40. The distribution in which the probability at each successive draw varies is:
(*a*) hypergeometric distribution
(*b*) geometric distribution
(*c*) binomial distribution
(*d*) discrete uniform distribution

41. In hypergeometric distribution, H.G. (N, k, n), if $N \to \infty$, $\frac{k}{N} \to p$, the hypergeometric distribution reduces to:
(*a*) binomial distribution

(*b*) geometric distribution
(*c*) normal distribution
(*d*) none of the above

42. Negative binomial distribution, $nb\ (x; r, p)$ for $r = 1$ reduces to:
(*a*) binomial distribution
(*b*) Poisson distribution
(*c*) hypergeometric distribution
(*d*) geometric distribution

43. The distribution for which the mode does not exist is:
(*a*) normal distribution
(*b*) *t*-distribution
(*c*) continuous rectangular distribution
(*d*) *F*-distribution

44. For a normal curve, the Q.D., M.D. and S.D. are in the ratio
(*a*) 5 : 6 : 7
(*b*) 10 : 12 :15
(*c*) 2 : 3 : 4
(*d*) none of the above

45. The mode of the geometric distribution $\left(\frac{1}{2}\right)^X$ for $X = 1, 2, ...$ is:
(*a*) 1
(*b*) 0
(*c*) 1/2
(*d*) does not exist

46. The moment generating function of Bernouli distribution is:
(*a*) $(q + pe^t)^n$
(*b*) $(q + pe^t)^{-n}$
(*c*) $(q + pe^t)$
(*d*) $(q + pe^{-t})$

47. If $X \sim N(\mu, \sigma^2)$, the points of inflexion of normal distribution curve are:
(*a*) $\pm \mu$
(*b*) $\mu \pm \sigma$
(*c*) $\sigma \pm \mu$
(*d*) $\pm \sigma$

48. If $X \sim N(\mu, \sigma^2)$, the maximum probability at the point of inflexion of normal distribution is:
(*a*) $\frac{1}{\sqrt{2\pi}} e^{1/2}$
(*b*) $\frac{1}{\sqrt{2\pi}} e^{-1/2}$
(*c*) $\frac{1}{\sigma\sqrt{2\pi}} e^{-1/2}$
(*d*) $\frac{1}{\sqrt{2\pi}}$

49. An approximate relation between Q.D. and S.D. of normal distribution is:
(*a*) 5 Q.D. = 4 S.D.
(*b*) 4 Q.D. = 5 S.D.
(*c*) 2 Q.D. = 3 S.D.
(*d*) 3 Q.D. = 2 S.D.

50. An approximate relation between M.D. about mean and S.D. of a normal distribution is:
(*a*) 5 M.D. = 4 S.D.
(*b*) 4 M.D. = 5 S.D.
(*c*) 3 M.D. = 3 S.D.
(*d*) 3 M.D. = 2 S.D.

51. Pearson's constants for a normal distribution with mean μ and variance σ^2 are:
(*a*) $\beta_1 = 3, \beta_2 = 0, \gamma_1 = 0, \gamma_2 = -3$
(*b*) $\beta_1 = 0, \beta_2 = 3, \gamma_1 = 0, \gamma_2 = 0$
(*c*) $\beta_1 = 0, \beta_2 = 0, \gamma_1 = 0, \gamma_2 = 3$
(*d*) $\beta_1 = 0, \beta_2 = 3, \gamma_1 = 0, \gamma_2 = 3$

52. The area under the standard normal curve beyond the lines $z = \pm 1.96$ is:
(*a*) 95 per cent
(*b*) 90 per cent
(*c*) 5 per cent
(*d*) 10 per cent

53. *X* is a binomial variate with parameters *n* and *p*. If $n = 1$, the distribution of *X* reduces to:
(*a*) Poisson distribution
(*b*) binomial distribution itself
(*c*) Bernoulli distribution
(*d*) discrete uniform distribution

54. If a random variable *X* has the following probability distribution:

x:	− 1	− 2	1	2
Prob:	$\frac{1}{3}$	$\frac{1}{6}$	$\frac{1}{6}$	$\frac{1}{3}$

then the expected value of X is:

(a) 3/2
(b) 1/6
(c) 1/2
(d) none of the above

55. A box contain 12 items out of which 4 are defective. A person selects 6 items from the box. The expected number of defective items out of his selected items is:

(a) 2
(b) 3
(c) 3/2
(d) none of the above

56. If X is a normal variate with mean 20 and variance 64, the probability that X lies between 12 and 32 is:

(a) 0.4332
(b) 0.1189
(c) 0.7475
(d) 0.5

$$\left[\begin{array}{lll}\text{Given:} \quad Z: & -1.0 & 1.5 \\ \phi(z): & 0.3143 & 0.4332\end{array}\right]$$

57. For the normal variate X in Q. No. 56, the percentage of items between 24 and 44 is:

(a) 30.72
(b) 19.27
(c) 69.02
(d) 30.98

$$\left[\begin{array}{lll}\text{Given:} \quad Z: & 0.5 & 3.0 \\ \phi(z): & 0.1915 & 0.4987\end{array}\right]$$

58. If Z is a standard normal deviate, the proportion of items lying between $Z = -0.5$ and $Z = -3.0$ is:

(a) 0.4987
(b) 0.1915
(c) 0.3072
(d) 0.3098

59. If X is a normal variate representing the income in ₹ per day with mean = 50 and S.D. = 10. If the number of workers in a factory is 1200, then the number of workers having income more than ₹ 62.00 per day is:

(a) 462
(b) 138
(c) 738
(d) none of the above

[Given: $z = 1.2$, $\phi(z) = 0.3849$]

60. Assuming the distribution of diameters of shafts normal with mean = 5 and S.D. = 0.05. The tolerance limit of shafts is 4.90 to 5.10 cm. In a consignment of 200 shafts, the number of shafts out of tolerance limits is:

(a) 5
(b) 191
(c) 9
(d) 20

[Given: $z = 2.0$, $\phi(z) = 0.4772$]

61. Assuming that the height of students is distributed as $N(\mu, \sigma^2)$. Out of a large number of students, 5 per cent are above 72 inches and 10 per cent are below 60 inches. The mean and S.D. of the normal distribution are:

(a) $\mu = 0, \sigma = 1$
(b) $\mu = 65, \sigma = 5$
(c) $\mu = 66, \sigma = 4$
(d) $\mu = 65, \sigma = 4$

$$\left[\begin{array}{ll}\text{Given:} \quad \phi(z_1) = 0.45, & z_1 = 1.64 \\ \phi(z_2) = 0.40, & z_2 = 1.28\end{array}\right]$$

62. Probability mass function for a binomial distribution with usual notations is:

(a) $\binom{n}{X} p^n q^{n-X}$

(b) $\binom{n}{X} p^n q^X$

(c) $\binom{n}{X} p^{n-X} q^X$

(d) none of the above.

63. With usual notations, the probability of hypergeometric variate X is given as:

(a) $\binom{k}{X}\binom{N-k}{n-X}\Big/\binom{N}{X}$

(b) $\binom{n}{k}\binom{N-k}{n-X}\Big/\binom{N}{n}$

(c) $\binom{k}{X}\binom{N-k}{n-X}\Big/\binom{N}{n}$

(d) $\binom{n}{X}\binom{N-k}{n-X}\Big/\binom{N}{n}$

64. The probability mass function for the negative binomial distribution with parameters r and p is:

(a) $\binom{X+r-1}{r-1}p^r q^X$

(b) $\binom{-r}{X}(-1)^X p^r q^X$

(c) $\binom{-r}{X}p^r(-q)^X$

(d) all of the above

65. Negative binomial distribution reduces to Polya's distribution if we substitute:

(a) $r = \frac{1}{\beta}, p = \frac{1}{1+\beta\mu}$

(b) $r = \beta, p = 1 + \beta\mu$

(c) $r = \frac{1}{\beta}, p = 1+\beta\mu$

(d) all of the above

66. In the Polya's distribution

$$p(X) = \binom{-r}{X}\left(\frac{1}{1+\beta\mu}\right)^{1/\beta}\left(\frac{\beta\mu}{1+\beta\mu}\right)^X$$

if we put $\beta = 1$, Polya's distribution reduces to:

(a) negative binomial distribution

(b) geometric distribution

(c) Poisson distribution

(d) none of the above

67. If $X \sim N(5, 1)$, the probability density function for the normal variate X is:

(a) $\frac{1}{5\sqrt{2\pi}}e^{-\frac{1}{2}\left(\frac{X-1}{5}\right)^2}$

(b) $\frac{1}{\sqrt{2\pi}}e^{-\frac{1}{2}\left(\frac{X-1}{5}\right)^2}$

(c) $\frac{1}{5\sqrt{2\pi}}e^{-\frac{1}{2}X^2}$

(d) $\frac{1}{\sqrt{2\pi}}e^{-\frac{1}{2}(X-5)^2}$

68. If $X \sim N(8, 64)$, the standard normal deviate Z will be:

(a) $Z = \frac{X-64}{8}$

(b) $Z = \frac{X-8}{64}$

(c) $Z = \frac{X-8}{8}$

(d) $Z = \frac{8-X}{8}$

69. The characteristic function of the normal distribution of a normal variate $X \sim N(\mu, \sigma^2)$ is:

(a) $e^{\mu t - \frac{1}{2}\sigma^2 t^2}$

(b) $e^{-i\mu t + \frac{1}{2}\sigma^2 t^2}$

(c) both (a) and (b)

(d) none of (a) and (b)

70. The probability density function for beta type II distribution with parameters $\alpha, \beta > 0$ is:

(a) $\frac{X^{\alpha-1}}{(1+X)^{\alpha+\beta}}$ for $X > 0$

(b) $\frac{1}{B(\alpha,\beta)}\cdot\frac{X^{\beta-1}}{(1+X)^{\alpha+\beta}}$ for $0 \le X \le 1$

(c) $\frac{1}{B(\alpha,\beta)} \cdot \frac{X^{\alpha-1}}{(1+X)^{\alpha+\beta}}$ for $0 \le X \le \infty$

(d) $\frac{1}{B(\alpha,\beta)} \cdot \frac{X^{\alpha-1}}{(1-X)^{\alpha+\beta}}$ for $0 < X < \infty$

71. The probability density function for beta distribution of first kind with parameters m, $n > 0$ is:

(a) $\frac{1}{B(m,n)} X^{m-1} (1+X)^{n-1}; 0 < X < 1$

(b) $\frac{1}{B(n,m)} X^{m-1} (1-X)^{n-1}; 0 < X < 1$

(c) $\frac{1}{B(m,n)} X^{m-1} x^{n}; 0 < X < 1$

(d) $\frac{1}{B(m,n)} X^{m-1} (1-X)^{n-1}; 0 < X < 1$

72. If X is a Poisson variate with parameter μ, the moment generating function of Poisson variate is:

(a) $e^{\mu t-1}$

(b) $e^{\mu(e^t-1)}$

(c) $e^{\mu(e^{it}-1)}$

(d) $e^{i\mu(e^t-1)}$

73. The characteristic function of the binomial distribution for the binomial variate $X \sim b(n, p)$ is:

(a) $(q + pe^{it})$

(b) $(p + qe^{it})^n$

(c) $(p + qe^{t})^n$

(d) $(q + pe^{it})^n$

74. If $X \sim$ Expo (5), the probability density function of X is:

(a) $5e^{-5X}$ for $X > 0$

(b) e^{-5X} for $X > 0$

(c) $5e^{-X}$ for $X > 0$

(d) $\frac{1}{5}e^{-5x}$ for $X > 0$

75. The characteristic function of Laplace exponential distribution $L(\lambda)$ is:

(a) $e^{\mu t} \frac{\lambda^2}{\lambda^2 + t^2}$

(b) $e^{i\mu t} \frac{\lambda^2}{\lambda^2 - t^2}$

(c) $e^{i\mu t} \frac{\lambda^2}{\lambda^2 + t^2}$

(d) $e^{\mu t} \frac{\lambda^2}{(\lambda^2 - t^2)}$

76. The probability density function for Laplace variate $X \sim L(\mu, \lambda)$ is:

(a) $\frac{1}{2} e^{-\lambda|X-\mu|}$

(b) $\frac{1}{2} \mu e^{-\lambda|X-\mu|}$

(c) $\frac{1}{2} \lambda e^{\lambda|X-\mu|}$

(d) $\frac{1}{2} \lambda e^{-\lambda|X-\mu|}$

77. Laplace distribution curve in respect to tails is:

(a) not skewed

(b) positive skewed

(c) negatively skewed

(d) not definite

78. Laplace distribution curve with regard to peakedness is:

(a) more peaked than normal

(b) less peaked than normal

(c) adequately peaked

(d) depends on the values of its parameters

79. The moment generating function for geometric distribution with parameter p is:

(a) $p(1 - qe^t)$

(b) $p(1 - qe^{it})$

(c) $p/(1 - qe^{it})$

(d) $p/(1 - qe^t)$

80. The distribution function of a continuous uniform distribution of a variable X lying in the interval (a, b) is:

(*a*) $\frac{1}{b-a}$

(*b*) $\frac{X-a}{b-a}$

(*c*) $\frac{b-a}{X-a}$

(*d*) $\frac{X-b}{b-a}$

81. If $X \sim C(-2, 3)$, the probability density function of the variate X is:

(*a*) $\frac{1}{3\pi\left\{1-\left(\frac{X+2}{3}\right)^2\right\}}$ for $-\infty < X \leq \infty$

(*b*) $\frac{1}{\pi\left\{1+\left(\frac{X+2}{3}\right)^2\right\}}$ for $-\infty < X \leq \infty$

(*c*) $\frac{1}{3\pi\left\{1+\left(\frac{X+2}{3}\right)^2\right\}}$ for $-\infty < X < \infty$

(*d*) all of the above

82. The characteristic function of the Cauchy distribution $X \sim C(\alpha, \beta)$ is:

(*a*) $e^{i\alpha t - \beta t}$

(*b*) $e^{\alpha t - i\beta t}$

(*c*) $e^{i(\alpha t - \beta t)}$

(*d*) $e^{i\alpha t - \beta |t|}$

83. If $X_1, X_2, ..., X_n$ are n i.i.d. $C(\alpha, \beta)$ variates, the mean of X_i's is distributed as:

(*a*) $C\left(\frac{\alpha}{n}, \frac{\beta}{n}\right)$

(*b*) $C\left(\alpha, \frac{\beta}{\sqrt{n}}\right)$

(*c*) $C(\alpha, \beta)$

(*d*) $C(n\,\alpha, n\,\beta)$

84. The probability density function of a random variable X distributed as $\gamma(n)$ is:

(*a*) $\frac{1}{\Gamma n} X^{n-1} e^{-X}$

(*b*) $\Gamma n X^{n-1} e^{X}$

(*c*) $\frac{1}{\Gamma n}(1-X)^{n-1} e^{-X}$

(*d*) $\frac{1}{\Gamma n} X^{n-1} e^{-1/X}$

85. The characteristic function of the distribution $\gamma(\alpha, n)$ is:

(*a*) $\left(1-\frac{it}{\alpha}\right)^{-n}$

(*b*) $\left(\frac{\alpha}{\alpha - it}\right)^{n}$

(*c*) $\left(\frac{1}{1-\frac{it}{\alpha}}\right)^{n}$

(*d*) any of the above

86. If X and Y are two gamma variate $\gamma(n_1)$ and $\gamma(n_2)$, the distribution of $\frac{X}{Y}$ is:

(*a*) $\beta_I(n_1, n_2)$

(*b*) F_{n_1, n_2}

(*c*) $\beta_{II}(n_1, n_2)$

(*d*) $\gamma(n_1 + n_2)$

87. The characteristic function of beta distribution of first kind, *i.e.*, $\beta_I(\alpha, \beta)$ is:

(*a*) $\frac{1}{B(\alpha, \beta)} \sum_{j=0}^{\infty} (it)^j B(\alpha + j; \beta)$

(*b*) $\frac{1}{B(\alpha, \beta)} \sum_{j=0}^{\infty} \frac{(it)^j}{j!} B(\alpha, \beta + j)$

(c) $\frac{1}{B(\alpha, \beta)} \sum_{j=0}^{\infty} \frac{t^j}{j!} (\alpha + j, \beta)$

(d) $\frac{1}{B(\alpha, \beta)} \sum_{j=0}^{\infty} \frac{(it)^j}{j!} (\alpha + j, \beta)$

88. If X is a r.v., the probability density function of the variable $\log_e x \sim N(\mu, \sigma^2)$ is:

(a) $\frac{1}{\sigma\sqrt{2\pi}} e^{-\frac{1}{2\sigma^2}(\log_e x - \mu)^2}$

(b) $\frac{1}{X\sqrt{2\pi}} e^{-\frac{1}{2\sigma^2}(\log_e x - \mu)^2}$

(c) $\frac{1}{\sigma X\sqrt{2\pi}} e^{-\frac{1}{2\sigma^2}(\log_e x - \mu)^2}$

(d) any of the above

89. If $\log_e x \sim N(\mu_1, \sigma_1^2)$ and $\log_e y \sim N(\mu_2, \sigma_2^2)$, the variable $(\log_e x - \log_e y)$ is distributed as:

(a) $N(\mu_1 - \mu_2, \sigma_1^2 - \sigma_2^2)$

(b) $N(\mu_1 - \mu_2, \sigma_1^2 + \sigma_2^2)$

(c) $N(\mu_1, \sigma_1^2) - N(\mu_2, \sigma_2^2)$

(d) none of the above

90. The variance of the logistic distribution function given as $1/[1 + e^{-\frac{(X-\alpha)}{\beta}}]$ is:

(a) $\frac{\pi\beta^2}{\alpha^2}$

(b) $\frac{\pi^2\alpha^2}{\beta^2}$

(c) $\frac{\pi^2\beta^2}{\alpha^2}$

(d) $\frac{\pi^2\beta^2}{3}$

91. The mean of the Pareto distribution $f(X; X_0, \theta)$ is:

(a) $\frac{X_0}{\theta - 1}$ for $\theta > 1$

(b) $\frac{\theta X_0}{\theta - 1}$ for $\theta > 1$

(c) $\frac{\theta}{X_0 - 1}$ for $X_0 > 1$

(d) none of the above

92. The variance of the Pareto distribution $f(x; X_0, \theta)$ is:

(a) $\frac{\theta X_0^2}{\theta - 2}$ for $\theta > 2$

(b) $\left(\frac{\theta X_0}{\theta - 1}\right)^2$ for $\theta > 1$

(c) $\frac{\theta X_0^2}{\theta - 2} - \left(\frac{\theta X_0}{\theta - 1}\right)^2$ for $\theta > 2$

(d) $\frac{\theta X_0}{\theta - 2} - \left(\frac{\theta X_0}{\theta - 1}\right)^2$ for $\theta > 2$

93. The mean of Weibull distribution with parameters $\alpha, \beta > 0$ is:

(a) $\beta\Gamma\left(1 + \frac{1}{\alpha}\right)$

(b) $\alpha\Gamma\left(1 + \frac{1}{\alpha}\right)$

(c) $\alpha\Gamma\left(1 + \frac{1}{\beta}\right)$

(d) $\Gamma\left(\alpha + \frac{1}{\beta}\right)$

94. The variance of the Weibull distribution will parameters α, β is given as:

(a) $\beta^2\Gamma\left(1+\frac{2}{\alpha}\right)-\beta^2\left(\Gamma\left(1+\frac{1}{\alpha}\right)\right)^2$

(b) $\beta^2\left[\Gamma\left(1+\frac{2}{\alpha}\right)-\left(\Gamma\left(1+\frac{1}{\alpha}\right)\right)^2\right]$

(c) $\beta^2\Gamma\left(1+\frac{2}{\alpha}\right)-\left(\beta\Gamma\left(1+\frac{1}{\alpha}\right)\right)^2$

(d) all of the above

95. Student's t-distribution was given by:

(a) G.W. Snedecor

(b) R.A. Fisher

(c) W.S. Gosset

(d) none of the above

96. Student's t-distribution curve is symmetrical about mean, it means that:

(a) odd order moments are zero

(b) even order moments are zero

(c) both (a) and (b)

(d) none of (a) and (b)

97. If $X \sim N(0, 1)$ and $Y \sim \chi^2/n$, the distribution of the variate $X/\sqrt{Y}$ follows:

(a) Cauchy's distribution

(b) Fisher's t-distribution

(c) student's t-distribution

(d) none of the above

98. The p.d.f. of student's t-distribution based on the random sample $X_1, X_2, \ldots, X_n$ from a population $N(\mu, \sigma^2)$ is:

(a) $\dfrac{1}{B\left(\frac{1}{2}, \frac{n-1}{2}\right)}\left(1+\dfrac{t^2}{n-1}\right)^{-n/2}$

(b) $\dfrac{1}{\sqrt{n-1}\,B\left(\frac{1}{2}, \frac{n-1}{2}\right)}\left(1+\dfrac{t^2}{n}\right)^{-\frac{n+1}{2}}$

(c) $\dfrac{1}{\sqrt{n-1}\,B\left(\frac{1}{2}, \frac{n}{2}\right)}\left(1+\dfrac{t^2}{n-1}\right)^{-\frac{n}{2}}$

(d) $\dfrac{1}{\sqrt{n-1}\,B\left(\frac{1}{2}, \frac{n-1}{2}\right)}\left(1+\dfrac{t^2}{n-1}\right)^{-\frac{n}{2}}$

99. The degrees of freedom for students-t based on a random sample of size n is:

(a) $n - 1$

(b) n

(c) $(n - 2)$

(d) $\dfrac{n-1}{2}$

100. If the sample size $n = 2$, the student's t-distribution reduces to:

(a) normal distribution

(b) F-distribution

(c) Cauchy distribution

(d) none of the above

101. If n, the sample size is larger than 30, the student's t-distribution tends to:

(a) normal distribution

(b) F-distribution

(c) Cauchy distribution

(d) Chi-square distribution

102. The points of inflexion of t-distribution are:

(a) $\pm\sqrt{\dfrac{n}{n+1}}$

(b) $\pm\left(\dfrac{n}{n-2}\right)^{1/2}$

(c) $\pm\left(\dfrac{n}{n+2}\right)^{1/2}$

(d) $\pm\sqrt{\dfrac{n+2}{n}}$

103. Maximum height of the student's t-distribution curve at the point $t = 0$ is:

(a) $\dfrac{1}{B\left(\frac{1}{2}, \frac{n-1}{2}\right)}$

(b) $\dfrac{1}{\sqrt{n-1}\, B\left(\frac{1}{2}, \frac{n-1}{2}\right)}$

(c) $\dfrac{1}{\sqrt{n-1}\, B\left(\frac{1}{2}, \frac{n}{2}\right)}$

(d) $\sqrt{n-1}\, B\left(\frac{1}{2}, \frac{n-1}{2}\right)$

104. For $n > 4$ and $n < 30$, the t-distribution curve with regard to peakedness is:

(a) mesokurtic
(b) platykurtic
(c) leptokurtic
(d) bimodal

105. t-distribution is used to test:

(a) the validity of a postulated value of population mean
(b) to test the significance of sample correlation coefficient
(c) to test the equality of two population means
(a) all of the above

106. The value of statistic t to test a hypothetical value 20 of population mean from a sample of size 10 having its mean = 18.5 and variance = 1.21 is:

(a) – 3.71
(b) – 11.16
(c) 3.71
(d) – 4.31

107. A random sample of 17 items from a heap of machine parts gives a mean of 42 and S.D. = 6.25. The value of statistic t to test the hypothesis that the population mean = 38 is:

(a) 2.64
(b) 6.6
(c) 2.56
(d) none of the above

108. If $Z_1, Z_2, \ldots, Z_n$ are n i.i.d. variates, the distribution of $\sum_{i=1}^{n} Z_i^2$ is:

(a) student-t^2
(b) χ^2 with n d.f.
(c) χ^2 with $(n - 1)$ d.f.
(d) all of the above

109. The probability density function of the sum of squares of independent n normal variates $N(0, 1)$ is:

(a) $\dfrac{1}{2^{n/2}\, \Gamma\frac{n-1}{2}} e^{-\chi^2/2} (\chi^2)^{n-1}$

(b) $\dfrac{1}{2^{n/2}\, \Gamma\frac{n}{2}} e^{-\chi^2/2} (\chi^2)^{\frac{n-1}{2}}$

(c) $\dfrac{1}{2^{n/2}\, \Gamma\frac{n}{2}} e^{-\chi^2/2} (\chi^2)^{\frac{n}{2}-1}$

(d) $\dfrac{1}{2^{n}\, \Gamma\frac{n}{2}} e^{-\chi^2} (\chi^2)^{\frac{n}{2}-1}$

110. The relation between the mean and the variance of χ^2 with n d.f. is:

(a) mean = 2 variance
(b) 2 mean = variance
(c) mean = variance
(d) none of the above

111. Chi-square distribution curve in respect of symmetry is:

(a) negatively skew
(b) symmetrical
(c) positively skew
(d) any of the above

112. Chi-square distribution curve with regard to bulginess is:

(a) mesokurtic
(b) leptokurtic
(c) platykurtic
(d) not definite

113. Moment generating function of the Chi-square distribution is:

(a) $(1 - 2it)^{n/2}$

(*b*) $(1-2t)^{n/2}$
(*c*) $(1-2it)^{-n/2}$
(*d*) $(1-2t)^{-n/2}$

114. Mode of the Chi-square distribution with n d.f. lies at the point:
(*a*) $\chi^2 = m - 1$
(*b*) $\chi^2 = n$
(*c*) $\chi^2 = n - 2$
(*d*) $\chi^2 = 1/(n-2)$

115. The points of inflexion of the Chi-square distribution curve lie at the points:
(*a*) $(n-2) \pm (n-2)^{1/2}$
(*b*) $(n-2) \pm \{2(n-2)\}^{1/2}$
(*c*) $(n-2) \pm 2(n-2)^{1/2}$
(*d*) $\left\{\frac{n}{2(n-2)}\right\}^{1/2}$

116. If X and Y are distributed as χ^2 with d.f. n_1 and n_2, respectively, the distribution of the variate X/Y is:
(*a*) $\beta_I\left(\frac{n_1}{2}, \frac{n_2}{2}\right)$
(*b*) $\beta_{II}\left(\frac{n_1}{2}, \frac{n_2}{2}\right)$
(*c*) χ^2 with d.f. $(n_1 - n_2)$
(*d*) none of the above

117. If $X \sim \chi^2_{n_1}$, and $Y \sim \chi^2_{n_2}$, the distribution of the variate $(X - Y)$ is:
(*a*) $\beta_I\left(\frac{n_1}{2}, \frac{n_2}{2}\right)$
(*b*) $\beta_{II}\left(\frac{n_1}{2}, \frac{n_2}{2}\right)$
(*c*) χ^2 with $(n_1 - n_2)$ d.f.
(*d*) all of the above

118. If X and Y are both Chi-square variate with d.f. n_1 and n_2 respectively, the distribution of the variate $X/(X+Y)$ is:
(*a*) $\beta_I\left(\frac{n_1}{2}, \frac{n_2}{2}\right)$
(*b*) $\beta_{II}\left(\frac{n_1}{2}, \frac{n_2}{2}\right)$
(*c*) χ^2 with $\left(\frac{n_1 - n_2}{2}\right)$ d.f.
(*d*) none of the above

119. Pearson's Chi-square with usual notations f_i, p_i and n for k classes in a frequency distribution is:
(*a*) $\chi^2 = \sum_{i=1}^{k} \frac{(f_i - np_i)^2}{np_i}$
(*b*) $\chi^2 = \sum_{i=1}^{k} \frac{f_i^2}{np_i} - n$
(*c*) both (*a*) and (*b*)
(*d*) none of (*a*) and (*b*)

120. In throwing a fair die 90 times, the number of times, the spots 1, 2, ..., 6 appeared upside were as follows:

No. of spots:	1	2	3	4	5	6
Frequency:	12	16	14	20	18	10

The value of Pearson's Chi-square for the given frequency distribution is:
(*a*) 0.31
(*b*) 4.66
(*c*) 1.20
(*d*) none of the above

121. The variate $\sqrt{\chi^2_n}$ will be distributed as:
(*a*) Fisher's t with n d.f.
(*b*) Gamma distribution
(*c*) exponential distribution
(*d*) Chi-distribution

122. If $X_i \sim \chi^2_{n_i}$ for $i = 1, 2, \ldots, n$, the distribution of the variate $\sum_{i=1}^{n} X_i$, is:
(*a*) normal distribution
(*b*) Chi-distribution
(*c*) χ^2 distribution with $\Sigma\, n_i$ d.f.
(*d*) none of the above

123. Chi-square distribution is useful to test the:

(*a*) independence of attributes

(*b*) equality of several population correlation coefficients

(*c*) equality of several population variances

(*d*) all of the above

124. Chi-square distribution is used for the test of:

(*a*) goodness of fit

(*b*) hypothetical value of population variance

(*c*) both (*a*) and (*b*)

(*d*) neither (*a*) nor (*b*)

125. The shape of Chi-square distribution curve for χ^2 with d.f. 1 or 2 is:

(*a*) a parabola

(*b*) a hyperbola

(*c*) a J-shaped curve

(*d*) a bell-shaped curve

126. The Chi-square distribution is said to be a non-central Chi-square if:

(*a*) If each of X_i is not distributed as $N(0, 1)$ in ΣX_i^2 for $i = 1, 2, ..., n$.

(*b*) If the variate $X_i \sim N(\mu_i, 1)$ for $i = 1, 2, \ldots, n$.

(*c*) both (*a*) and (*b*)

(*d*) none of (*a*) and (*b*)

127. If each of $X_i \sim N(\mu_i, 1)$, for $i = 1, 2, \ldots, k$, the non-centrality parameter λ for non-central Chi-square distribution is:

(*a*) $\lambda = \sum_{i=1}^{k} \mu_i$

(*b*) $\lambda = \sum_{i=1}^{k} \mu_i^2$

(*c*) $\lambda = \frac{1}{n} \sum_{i=1}^{k} \mu_i^2$

(*d*) $\lambda = \frac{1}{2} \sum_{i=1}^{k} \mu_i^2$

128. If the d.f. n for the Chi-square distribution tend to infinity, the Chi-square distribution tends to:

(*a*) Fisher's t-distribution with n d.f.

(*b*) normal distribution with mean n and variance $2n$

(*c*) both (*a*) and (*b*)

(*d*) none of (*a*) and (*b*)

129. The relation between statistics t and χ^2 is:

(*a*) $t_1^2 = \chi_\infty^2$

(*b*) $t_n^2 = \chi_1^2$

(*c*) $t_\infty^2 = \chi_1^2$

(*d*) $t_1^2 = \chi_1^2$

130. Fisher's z-statistic in terms of two sample variances is expressed as:

(*a*) $z = \log_{10}\left(\frac{s_1^2}{s_2^2}\right)$

(*b*) $z = \frac{1}{2}\log_{10}\left(\frac{s_1^2}{s_2^2}\right)$

(*c*) $z = \log_e\left(\frac{s_1^2}{s_2^2}\right)$

(*d*) $z = \frac{1}{2}\log_e\left(\frac{s_1^2}{s_2^2}\right)$

131. The probability density function of Fisher's z with d.f. k_1 and k_2 is:

(*a*) $\dfrac{2k_1^{k_1/2}\, k_2^{k_2/2}}{B\left(\frac{k_1}{2}, \frac{k_2}{2}\right)} \dfrac{e^{k_1 z}}{\left(k_2 + k_1 e^{2z}\right)^{\frac{k_1+k_2}{2}}}$

(*b*) $\dfrac{2k_1^{k_1/2}\, k_2^{k_2/2}}{B\left(\frac{k_1}{2}, \frac{k_2}{2}\right)} \dfrac{e^{k_1 z}}{\left(k_1 + k_2 e^{2z}\right)^{\frac{k_1+k_2}{2}}}$

(*c*) $\dfrac{2k_1^{k_2/2}\, k_2^{k_1/2}}{B\left(\frac{k_1}{2}, \frac{k_2}{2}\right)} \dfrac{e^{k_2 z}}{\left(k_2 + k_1 e^{2z}\right)^{\frac{k_1+k_2}{2}}}$

(*d*) none of the above

132. Moment generating function of Fisher's z-distribution with d.f. k_1 and k_2 is:

(a) $\left(\frac{k_2}{k_1}\right)^{t/2} \frac{\Gamma\left(\frac{k_1+t}{2}\right)\Gamma\left(\frac{k_2+t}{2}\right)}{\Gamma\frac{k_1}{2}\Gamma\left(\frac{k_2-t}{2}\right)}$

(b) $\left(\frac{k_2}{k_1}\right)^{t/2} \frac{\Gamma\left(\frac{k_1+t}{2}\right)\Gamma\left(\frac{k_2-t}{2}\right)}{\Gamma\frac{k_1}{2}\Gamma\frac{k_2}{2}}$

(c) $\left(\frac{k_2}{k_1}\right)^{t} \frac{\Gamma\left(\frac{k_1+k_2t}{2}\right)}{\Gamma\frac{k_1}{2}\Gamma\frac{k_2}{2}}$

(d) $\left(\frac{k_2}{k_1}\right)^{t/2} \frac{\Gamma\left(\frac{k_1+t}{2}\right)\Gamma\left(\frac{k_2+t}{2}\right)}{\Gamma\left(k_1+\frac{k_2}{2}\right)}$

133. z-distribution with d.f. k_1 and k_2 has mean equal to:

(a) $\frac{1}{2}\left(\frac{1}{k_1}+\frac{1}{k_2}\right)$

(b) $\frac{1}{2}(k_1+k_2)$

(c) $\frac{1}{2}\left(\frac{1}{k_2}-\frac{1}{k_1}\right)$

(d) $2\left(\frac{1}{k_2}-\frac{1}{k_1}\right)$

134. The variance of Fisher's z-distribution with d.f. k_1 and k_2 is:

(a) $\frac{1}{2}\left(\frac{1}{k_1}+\frac{1}{k_2}-\frac{1}{k_1^2}\right)$

(b) $\frac{1}{2}\left(\frac{1}{k_1}+\frac{1}{k_1^2}-\frac{1}{k_2}-\frac{1}{k_2^2}\right)$

(c) $\frac{1}{4}\left(\frac{1}{k_1}+\frac{1}{k_2}+\frac{1}{k_1^2}+\frac{1}{k_2^2}\right)$

(d) $\frac{1}{2}\left(\frac{1}{k_1}+\frac{1}{k_2}+\frac{1}{k_1^2}+\frac{1}{k_2^2}\right)$

135. When d.f. k_1 and k_2 are large, the z-distribution tends to:

(a) normal distribution

(b) F-distribution

(c) χ^2-distribution

(d) none of the above

136. Fisher's z is closely related to:

(a) Helmert χ^2

(b) Snedecor's F

(c) Fisher's t

(d) all of the above

137. The relation between Snedecor's F and Fisher's z is:

(a) $z = \frac{1}{2}\log_e(F)$

(b) $F = e^{2z}$

(c) both (a) and (b)

(d) none of (a) and (b)

138. F-distribution was invented by:

(a) R.A. Fisher

(b) G.W. Snedecor

(c) W.S. Gosset

(d) all of the above

139. The variate F with usual notations is defined as:

(a) $F = \frac{\chi_1^2/\nu_1}{\chi_2^2/\nu_2}$

(b) $F = \frac{s_1^2}{s_2^2}$

(c) e^{2z}

(d) all of the above

140. The parameters of F_{ν_1,ν_2}-distribution are:

(a) ν_1 and ν_2

(b) s_1^2 and s_2^2

(*c*) χ_1^2 and χ_2^2

(*d*) 0 and ∞

141. The range of F-variate is:

(*a*) $-\infty$ to ∞

(*b*) 0 to 1

(*c*) 0 to ∞

(*d*) $-\infty$ to 0

142. The probability density function of F with usual notations is:

(*a*) $\dfrac{(\nu_2/\nu_1)^{\nu_2/2}}{B\left(\frac{\nu_1}{2}, \frac{\nu_2}{2}\right)} \dfrac{F^{\nu_1/2-1}}{\left(1+\frac{\nu_1}{\nu_2}F\right)^{\frac{\nu_1+\nu_2}{2}}}$

(*b*) $\dfrac{(\nu_1/\nu_2)^{\nu_2/2}}{B\left(\frac{\nu_2}{2}, \frac{\nu_1}{2}\right)} \dfrac{F^{\nu_1/2-1}}{\left(1+\frac{\nu_1}{\nu_2}F\right)^{\nu_1+\nu_2}}$

(*c*) $\dfrac{(\nu_1/\nu_2)^{\nu_2/2}}{B\left(\frac{\nu_2}{2}, \frac{\nu_1}{2}\right)} \dfrac{F^{\nu_1/2-1}}{\left(1+\frac{\nu_2}{\nu_1}F\right)^{\nu_1+\frac{\nu_2}{2}}}$

(*d*) none of the above

143. F-distribution curve in respect of tails is:

(*a*) negative skew

(*b*) positive skew

(*c*) symmetrical

(*d*) any of the above

144. F_{ν_1, ν_2} distribution curve becomes highly positive skew when:

(*a*) ν_1 is less than 5

(*b*) ν_2 is less than 5

(*c*) any of ν_1 and ν_2 is less than 5

(*d*) ν_2 is greater than 5

145. The mode of F-distribution curve for $\nu_1, \nu_2 \geq 3$ lies at the point:

(*a*) $F = \dfrac{\nu_2(\nu_1 - 2)}{\nu_1(\nu_2 + 2)}$

(*b*) $F = \dfrac{\nu_1(\nu_2 - 2)}{\nu_2(\nu_1 + 2)}$

(*c*) $F = \dfrac{\nu_1(\nu_2 - 2)}{\nu_2(\nu_1 - 2)}$

(*d*) $F = \dfrac{(\nu_1 + 2)\,\nu_1}{(\nu_2 + 2)\,\nu_2}$

146. Mean of the F-distribution with d.f. ν_1 and ν_2 for $\nu_2 \geq 3$ is:

(*a*) $\dfrac{\nu_2}{\nu_1 - 2}$

(*b*) $\dfrac{\nu_1}{\nu_2 - 2}$

(*c*) $\dfrac{\nu_1}{\nu_1 - 2}$

(*d*) $\dfrac{\nu_2}{\nu_2 - 2}$

147. Second central moment of the F_{ν_1, ν_2}-distribution is given by the formula:

(*a*) $\dfrac{2\nu_2^2(\nu_1 + \nu_2 - 2)}{\nu_2(\nu_2 - 2)^2\,(\nu_2 - 4)}$

(*b*) $\dfrac{2(\nu_1 + \nu_2 - 2)\,\nu_2^2}{\nu_2(\nu_2 - 2)\,(\nu_2 - 4)}$

(*c*) $\dfrac{2\nu_2(\nu_1 + \nu_2 - 2)}{\nu_2(\nu_2 - 2)\,(\nu_2 - 4)}$

(*d*) $\dfrac{2\nu_2^2(\nu_1 + \nu_2 - 2)}{\nu_1(\nu_2 - 2)^2\,(\nu_2 - 4)}$

148. Moment generating function of F-distribution is:

(*a*) $\left(1 + \dfrac{\nu_1}{\nu_2} e^{tF}\right)^{\nu_2 - 1}$

(*b*) $\left(1+\frac{\nu_2}{\nu_1}Fe^{t}\right)^{\frac{\nu_1+\nu_2}{2}-1}$

(*c*) $\left(1+\frac{\nu_2}{\nu_1}e^{tF}\right)^{\nu_1/2-1}$

(*d*) does not exist

149. The reciprocal property of F_{ν_1,ν_2} -distribution can be expressed as:

(*a*) $F_{1-\alpha;\nu_2,\nu_1}=\frac{1}{F_{\alpha;\nu_1,\nu_2}}$

(*b*) $P\left(F_{\nu_1,\nu_2}\geq C\right)=P\left(F_{\nu_2,\nu_1}\leq\frac{1}{C}\right)$

(*c*) both (*a*) and (*b*)

(*d*) neither (*a*) nor (*b*)

150. If $X \sim F(m, n)$, the variable $\frac{nX}{n+mX}$ follows the distribution:

(*a*) $\beta_{II}(m, n)$

(*b*) $\beta_{II}\left(\frac{m}{2},\frac{n}{2}\right)$

(*c*) $\beta_{I}\left(\frac{m}{2},\frac{n}{2}\right)$

(*d*) $\beta_{I}(m, n)$

151. If $X \sim F(m, n)$, the variable $\frac{m}{n}X$ is distributed as:

(*a*) $\beta_{II}(m, n)$

(*b*) $\beta_{II}\left(\frac{m}{2},\frac{n}{2}\right)$

(*c*) $\beta_{I}\left(\frac{m}{2},\frac{n}{2}\right)$

(*d*) $\beta_{I}(m, n)$

152. The relation between student's-*t* and *F*-distribution is:

(*a*) $F_{1,1}=t_n^2$

(*b*) $F_{n,1}=t_1^2$

(*c*) $t_\infty^2=F_{1,n}$

(*d*) none of the above

153. The non-central *F*-distribution is defined as:

(*a*) The ratio of two non-central χ^2

(*b*) The ratio of a central-χ^2 and a non-central χ^2 divided by their corresponding d.f.

(*c*) The ratio of a central-χ^2 and a non-central χ^2

(*d*) all of the above

154. *F*-distribution is applied for:

(*a*) testing the equality of two population variances

(*b*) for testing the equality of two or more population means

(*c*) for testing the equality of several regression coefficients

(*d*) all of the above

155. The distribution having the m.g.f. $\frac{1}{(3-2e^t)}$ can be identified as:

(*a*) negative binomial distribution

(*b*) geometric distribution

(*c*) exponential distribution

(*d*) none of the above

156. The given probability function,

$$f(X)=\frac{1}{2^X}\text{ for } X=1, 2, 3,...$$

represents:

(*a*) Bernoulli distribution

(*b*) Poisson distribution

(*c*) Geometric distribution

(*d*) All of the above

157. The characteristic function of a distribution is given as:

$$e^{i\mu t}\left(1+\frac{t^2}{\lambda^2}\right)^{-1}$$

By identicality, the distribution for which it stands is:

(*a*) Exponential distribution
(*b*) Poisson distribution
(*c*) Cauchy distribution
(*d*) Double exponential distribution

158. Normal distribution was invented by:

(*a*) Laplace
(*b*) De-Moivre
(*c*) Gauss
(*d*) All of the above

159. If a variate $X \sim \beta_I(m, n)$ where $m < 1$ and $n < 1$, the beta distribution is:

(*a*) bimodal with its mode at the points $X = 0$ and $X = 1$
(*b*) unimodal with its mode at the point $X = 1$.
(*c*) unimodal with its mode at the point $X = 0$
(*d*) mode does not exist

160. If a variate $X \sim \beta_I(m, n)$ where $m > 1, n > 1$, the mode lies at the point:

(*a*) $\dfrac{m}{m+n-2}$
(*b*) $\dfrac{m-1}{m+n-1}$
(*c*) $\dfrac{m-1}{m+n-2}$
(*d*) $\dfrac{m}{m+n}$

161. If a beta variate $X \sim \beta_I(m, n)$ where $m = 1$ and $n > 1$ the mode lies at the point:

(*a*) $X = 1$
(*b*) $X = 0$
(*c*) both (*a*) and (*b*)
(*d*) none of (*a*) and (*b*)

162. If a beta variate $X \sim \beta_I(m, n)$ where $m = 1$, $n = 1$, the mode lies at the point(s):

(*a*) $X = 1$
(*b*) $X = 0$
(*c*) both (*a*) and (*b*)
(*d*) none of (*a*) and (*b*)

163. The abbreviation i.i.d. stands for:

(*a*) independent and identically distributed
(*b*) identically and independently distributed
(*c*) both (*a*) and (*b*)
(*d*) none of (*a*) and (*b*)

164. If a variate $X \sim \gamma(\alpha, 1)$, the p.d.f. of X is same as that of:

(*a*) Chi-square distribution
(*b*) Exponential distribution
(*c*) Normal distribution
(*d*) Weibull distribution

165. If the moment generating function of a distribution is $(q + pe^t)^n$, the variance of the distribution is:

(*a*) $2n$
(*b*) pq
(*c*) npq
(*d*) pq/n

166. The distribution for which the moment generating function does not exist but moments exits is:

(*a*) Pareto distribution
(*b*) *t*-distribution
(*c*) *F*-distribution
(*d*) all of the above

167. The distribution of which the characteristic function is not useful in finding the moments is:

(*a*) negative binomial distribution
(*b*) hypergeometric distribution
(*c*) geometric distribution
(*d*) none of the above

168. Pearson's coefficient of skewness for the negative binomial distribution

$$\binom{-r}{X} p^r (-q)^X \text{ is:}$$

(*a*) $\dfrac{(p+q)^2}{rpq}$
(*b*) $\dfrac{(P+Q)^2}{rpq}$ where $p = \dfrac{1}{Q}, q = \dfrac{P}{Q}$

(*c*) $\frac{(P+Q)^2}{PQ}$

(*d*) $\frac{(P+Q)^2}{rPQ}$

169. The name of the distribution having the characteristic function $(e^{itb} - e^{ita})/it\,(b - a)$ is:

(*a*) continuous rectangular distribution

(*b*) discrete rectangular distribution

(*c*) normal distribution

(*d*) none of the above

170. If $X \sim b(n_1, p_1)$ and $X_2 \sim b(n_2, p_2)$ the sum of the variates $(X_1 + X_2)$ is distributed as:

(*a*) Hypergeometric distribution

(*b*) Binomial distribution

(*c*) Poisson distribution

(*d*) none of the above

171. If X_1 and X_2 are two independent Poisson variates with parameters λ_1 and λ_2 respectively, the variable $(X_1 + X_2)$ follows:

(*a*) binomial distribution with parameters $(\lambda_1 + \lambda_2)$

(*b*) Poisson distribution with parameter $(\lambda_1 + \lambda_2)$

(*c*) either of (*a*) and (*b*)

(*d*) neither of (*a*) and (*b*)

172. The skewness of a binomial distribution will be zero if:

(*a*) $p < \frac{1}{2}$

(*b*) $p > \frac{1}{2}$

(*c*) $p = \frac{1}{2}$

(*d*) $p < q$

173. If a variable $Y \sim b(Y; n, p)$ the variable Y/n is called:

(*a*) a relative variate

(*b*) a pseudo variate

(*c*) both (*a*) and (*b*)

(*d*) none of (*a*) and (*b*)

174. Binomial distribution tends to Poisson distribution when:

(*a*) $n \to \infty, p \to 0$ and $np = \mu$ (finite)

(*b*) $n \to \infty, p \to \frac{1}{2}$ and $np \to \mu$ (finite)

(*c*) $n \to 0, p \to 0$ and $np \to 0$

(*d*) $n \to 15, p \to 0$ and $np \to 0$

175. If for a normal distribution, $Q_1 = 54.52$ and $Q_3 = 78.86$, the median of the distribution is:

(*a*) 12.17

(*b*) 39.43

(*c*) 66.69

(*d*) none of the above

176. A discrete random variable has probability mass function

$p(x) = kq^x p;\ p + q = 1;\ x = 2, 3, 4, \ldots$

The value k should be equal to,

(*a*) $1/q^2$

(*b*) $1/p$

(*c*) $1/q$

(*d*) $1/pq$

177. If a discrete random variable takes on four values – 1, 0, 3, 4 with probabilities 1/6, k, 1/4 and $1 - 6k$, where k is a constant, then the value of k is:

(*a*) 1/3

(*b*) 2/9

(*c*) 1/12

(*d*) 5/24

178. Let X be a continuous random variable with probability density function,

$$\begin{aligned} f(x) &= kx;\ 0 \le x \le 1 \\ &= k;\ 1 \le x \le 2 \\ &= 0;\ \text{otherwise} \end{aligned}$$

The value of k is equal to:

(*a*) 1/4

(*b*) 2/3

(*c*) 2/5

(*d*) 3/4

179. For the distribution function of a random variable X, $F(5) - F(2)$ is equal to:

(*a*) $p\,(2 < x < 5)$
(*b*) $p\,(2 \leq x < 5)$
(*c*) $p\,(2 \leq x \leq 5)$
(*d*) $p\,(2 < x \leq 5)$

180. If a continuous random variable X has probability density function,

$$f(x) = \frac{1}{3}\,;\ -1 \leq x \leq 0$$
$$= \frac{2}{3}\,;\ 0 \leq x \leq 1,$$

then $E(X^2)$ is equal to:

(*a*) 1/9
(*b*) 2/3
(*c*) 5/12
(*d*) 1/3

181. If binomial random variable has mean = 4 and variance = 3, then its third central moment μ_3 is:

(*a*) 1/2
(*b*) 5/2
(*c*) 3/2
(*d*) 7/4

182. A Poisson random variable has $\mu_4 = 2$, the value of its mean is:

(*a*) 1/3
(*b*) 2/3
(*c*) 1/4
(*d*) 3/4

183. A negative binomial variate has probability mass function,

$$f(x) = \binom{n+x-1}{x} q^x\, p^n;\ x = 0, 1, 2, \ldots$$

with its mean = 2 and variance = 3. The value of p is equal to

(*a*) 2/3
(*b*) 1/3
(*c*) 1/4
(*d*) 3/4

184. A random variable has uniform distribution over the interval [–1, 3]. This distribution has variance equal to:

(*a*) 8/5
(*b*) 4/3
(*c*) 13/4
(*d*) 9/2

185. For an exponential distribution with probability density function,

$$f(x) = \frac{1}{2} e^{-x/2};\ x \geq 0,$$

its mean and variance are:

(*a*) $\left(\frac{1}{2}, 2\right)$
(*b*) $\left(2, \frac{1}{4}\right)$
(*c*) $\left(\frac{1}{2}, \frac{1}{4}\right)$
(*d*) (2/4)

186. If a variable x has probability density function,

$$f(x) = \frac{1}{\Gamma\alpha\beta^{\alpha}} x^{\alpha-1} e^{-x/\beta};\ x \geq 0$$

then its variance is:

(*a*) $\alpha\beta^2$
(*b*) $\alpha^2\beta$
(*c*) $\alpha^2\beta^2$
(*d*) α/β^2

187. A normal random variable has mean = 2 and variance = 4. Its fourth central moment μ_4 will be:

(*a*) 16
(*b*) 64
(*c*) 80
(*d*) 48

188. If a random variable X has mean 3 and standard deviation 5, then, the variance of the variable $Y = 2X - 5$ is,

(*a*) 25
(*b*) 45
(*c*) 100
(*d*) 50

189. The moment generating function of a random variable X is,

$$M_x(t) = \frac{2}{5} + \frac{1}{3}e^{2t} + \frac{4}{15}e^{3t}$$

The expected value of X is,

(*a*) 22/15
(*b*) 9/5
(*c*) 17/15
(*d*) 11/5

190. A random variable X is distributed as $F_{(4,7)}$, the mode of the distribution is:

(*a*) 7/6
(*b*) 21/10
(*c*) 7/18
(*d*) 8/21

191. If X_1 and X_2 are two independent χ^2-variates, which of following has also χ^2-distribution?

(*a*) $X_i/(X_1 + X_2)$
(*b*) $X_1 + X_2$
(*c*) X_1/X_2
(*d*) X_2/X_1

192. If X_1 and X_2 are two random variables having the same probability density function $f(x) = e^{-x}$ where $x > 0$, the variable X_1/X_2 follows:

(*a*) χ^2-distribution
(*b*) t-distribution
(*c*) F-distribution
(*d*) β_I-distribution

193. The distribution χ_1^2 is equivalent to the distribution:

(*a*) $F_{1, \infty}$
(*b*) $F_{1, 0}$
(*c*) $F_{\infty, 1}$
(*d*) $F_{1, 1}$

194. If X_1 and X_2 are two independent χ^2-variates with n_1 and n_2 d.f. respectively, then the variable X_1/X_2 is distributed as:

(*a*) $F_{(n_1, n_2)}$
(*b*) $F_{(n_1/2, n_2/2)}$
(*c*) $\gamma(n_1/n_2)$
(*d*) $\beta_{II(n_1/2, n_2/2)}$

195. If X_1 and X_2 are two gamma variates distributed as $\gamma(n_1)$ and $\gamma(n_2)$ respectively, which of the following has $\beta_I(n_1, n_2)$ distribution?

(*a*) $X_1/(X_1 + X_2)$
(*b*) $X_1 + X_2$
(*c*) X_1/X_2
(*d*) $X_1 - X_2$

196. If X_1 and X_2 have $\gamma(n_1)$ and $\gamma(n_2)$ distributions respectively, then the variable X_1/X_2 is distributed as:

(*a*) $\beta_I(n_1, n_2)$
(*b*) $\beta_{II}(n_1, n_2)$
(*c*) $F(n_1, n_2)$
(*d*) none of the above

197. Let X has F-distribution with (n_1, n_2) d.f. The distribution of $1/X$ will be:

(*a*) t-distribution with n_2 d.f.
(*b*) F-distribution with $\left(\frac{1}{n_1}, \frac{1}{n_2}\right)$ d.f.
(*c*) F-distribution with (n_2, n_1) d.f.
(*d*) χ^2 distribution with n_1 d.f.

198. Let $X \sim F(n_1, n_2)$ then the variable $Y = 1\Big/\left(1 + \frac{n_1}{n_2}X\right)$ follows the distribution:

(*a*) $\beta_I\left(\frac{n_2}{2}, \frac{n_1}{2}\right)$
(*b*) $\beta_{II}\left(\frac{n_2}{2}, \frac{n_1}{2}\right)$

(*c*) $F\left(\frac{1}{n_1}, \frac{1}{n_2}\right)$

(*d*) $F_{(n_2, n_1)}$

199. Let $X \sim N(\mu, \sigma^2)$, then the central moments of odd order are:

(*a*) one

(*b*) zero

(*c*) infinite

(*d*) positive

200. Let X be a random variable $U(0, 1)$, then the variable $y = -2 \log X$ follows:

(*a*) Lognormal distribution

(*b*) Gamma distribution

(*c*) Chi-square distribution

(*d*) Exponential distribution

201. The number of parameters in a multinomial distribution having k classes and n observations is:

(*a*) $n + 1$

(*b*) $k + 1$

(*c*) $n - k$

(*d*) $n + k$

202. The variable $y = -2 \log x$, where x is distributed as $U(0, 1)$, follows:

(*a*) F-distribution

(*b*) t-distribution

(*c*) χ^2-distribution

(*d*) exponential distribution

203. The distribution type of the variable $y = -2 \sum_{i=1}^{n} \log X_i$ is same as that of the variable:

(*a*) $-2 \log X_i$

(*b*) $2 \log\left(\prod_{i=1}^{n} X_i\right)^{-1}$

(*c*) both (*a*) and (*b*)

(*d*) neither (*a*) nor (*b*)

204. The variable $Y = -2 \sum_{i=1}^{n} \log X_i$, where all X_i are i.i.d. $U(0, 1)$, follows:

(*a*) χ^2-distribution with n d.f.

(*b*) χ^2-distribution with $2n$ d.f.

(*c*) lognormal distribution

(*d*) circular distribution

205. A variable X with moment generating function $M_X(t) = \left(\frac{2}{3} + \frac{1}{3}e^t\right)$ is distributed with mean and variance as:

(*a*) mean $= \frac{2}{3}$, variance $= \frac{2}{9}$

(*b*) mean $= \frac{1}{3}$, variance $= \frac{2}{9}$

(*c*) mean $= \frac{1}{3}$, variance $= \frac{2}{3}$

(*d*) mean $= \frac{2}{3}$, variance $= \frac{1}{9}$

206. If a distribution has moment generating function $M_X(t) = (2 - e^t)^{-3}$, then the distribution is:

(*a*) geometric distribution

(*b*) hypergeometric distribution

(*c*) binomial distribution

(*d*) negative binomial distribution

207. If X is a standard normal variate, then $\frac{1}{2}X^2$ is a gamma variate with parameters:

(*a*) $1, \frac{1}{2}$

(*b*) $\frac{1}{2}, 1$

(*c*) $\frac{1}{2}, \frac{1}{2}$

(*d*) 1, 1

208. If the moment generating function of a random variable X is $\left(\frac{1}{3} + \frac{2}{3}e^t\right)$, then X is a:

(*a*) Bernoulli variate
(*b*) Poisson variate
(*c*) binomial variate
(*d*) negative binomial variate

209. If a variable X has the p.d.f., $f(x) \frac{1}{4} \cdot xe^{-x/2}$ for $x > 0$, then the variable X is distributed as:
(*a*) gamma variate
(*b*) Chi-square variate
(*c*) both (*a*) and (*b*)
(*d*) neither (*a*) nor (*b*)

210. If a variable X has the p.d.f., $f(x) \frac{1}{4} \cdot xe^{-x/2}$ for $0 \le x < \infty$, then the distribution has mean and variance as:
(*a*) mean = 2, variance = 4
(*b*) mean = 1/2, variance = 1/4
(*c*) mean = 4, variance = 2
(*d*) mean = 4, variance = 8

211. If a Poisson distribution is such that $P(X=2) = P(X=3)$, then the variance of the distribution is:
(*a*) 9
(*b*) 3
(*c*) 6
(*d*) $\sqrt{3}$

212. As σ increases, the shape of the normal curve becomes:
(*a*) more and more constrict
(*b*) more and more flat
(*c*) asymmetrical
(*d*) symmetrical

213. Binomial distribution approximated to normal distribution is adequate for large n if:
(*a*) $\frac{1}{n}\left(\sqrt{\frac{q}{p}} + \sqrt{\frac{p}{q}}\right) > 0.3$
(*b*) $\frac{1}{n}\left(\sqrt{\frac{P}{q}} - \sqrt{\frac{q}{p}}\right) < 0.3$
(*c*) $\frac{1}{\sqrt{n}}\left(\sqrt{\frac{q}{p}} - \sqrt{\frac{p}{q}}\right) < 0.3$
(*d*) $\frac{1}{\sqrt{n}}\left(\sqrt{\frac{q}{p}} - \sqrt{\frac{p}{q}}\right) = 0.3$

ANSWERS

Section B

1. finite **2.** domain **3.** $\begin{matrix} x: & 0 & 1 & 2 & 3 \\ p(x): & \frac{1}{8} & \frac{3}{8} & \frac{3}{8} & \frac{1}{8} \end{matrix}$ **4.** $\begin{matrix} z: & 0 & 1 & 2 & 3 & 4 \\ p(z): & \frac{1}{8} & \frac{3}{8} & \frac{1}{8} & \frac{2}{8} & \frac{1}{8} \end{matrix}$ **5.** $\frac{1}{26}$ and $E(x) = 3.96$ **6.** $\frac{3}{4}$ **7.** 1

8. unity **9.** (*a*) 0.1 (*b*) 0.5 (*c*) 2.85 **10.** (*a*) $\frac{5}{12}$ (*b*) $\frac{2}{11}$ **11.** p.d.f. **12.** (*a*) $E(X) = \int_a^b xf(x)\,dx$ (*b*) $\log G = \int_a^b \log x f(x)\,dx$ (*c*) $\frac{1}{H} = \int_a^b \frac{1}{x} f(x)\,dx$ (*d*) $E(X^2) = \int_a^b x^2 f(x)\,dx$ (*e*) $\mu_2 = \int_a^b x^2 f(x)\,dx - \left\{\int_a^b xf(x)\,dx\right\}^2$

(*f*) M.D. $= \int_a^b |x - \mu|\, f(x)\,dx$ (*g*) $\int_a^M f(x)\,dx = \int_M^b f(x)\,dx = \frac{1}{2}$ (*h*) $\int_a^{Q_i} f(x) = \frac{i}{4}$ (*i*) $\int_a^{D_i} f(x)\,dx = \frac{i}{10}$

(*j*) $\int_a^{P_i} f(x)\,dx = \frac{i}{100}$ **13.** 0.4 **14.** (*a*) 1 (*b*) 1 (*c*) 2 (*d*) 4 **15.** 1 **16.** $\frac{3}{16}(y-3)$ **17.** $\frac{1}{4\sqrt{1-y^2}}$ **18.** $\frac{1}{2}$

19. (*a*) **20.** *np*; *npq* **21.** greater than **22.** $\frac{5}{16}$ **23.** $\frac{224}{729}$ **24.** $\frac{27}{8}e^{-3}$ **25.** $\frac{63}{512}$ **26.** geometric **27.** related

28. lack of memory **29.** 1 **30.** greater than **31.** $r = 1$ **32.** $\beta = 1$ **33.** dependent **34.** hypergeometric distribution

35. fixed **36.** $N \to \infty$ and $\frac{k}{N} \to p$ **37.** equal **38.** symmetrical **39.** does not exist **40.** $\frac{b-a}{4}$ **41.** $\frac{(b-a)^2}{12}$ **42.** exist **43.** (*a*) $\frac{\theta}{2}$ (*b*) $\frac{\theta^2}{12}$ (*c*) 0 (*d*) $\frac{\theta^4}{80}$ (*e*) 0 (*f*) $\frac{9}{5}$ **44.** one **45.** symmetrical **46.** more **47.** $U(0, 1)$ **48.** twice **49.** leptokurtic **50.** $\frac{1}{\lambda}\log 2$ **51.** $N(0, 1)$ **52.** $X = \mu$ **53.** $\frac{1}{\sigma\sqrt{2\pi}}e^{-1/2}$ **54.** $N(n\,\mu,\ n\,\sigma^2)$ **55.** $N\left(\mu, \frac{\sigma}{\sqrt{n}}\right)$ **56.** (*a*) unimodal (*b*) not skewed (*c*) Mesokurtic **57.** 10 : 12 : 15 **58.** $\sigma\sqrt{\frac{2}{\pi}}$ or $\frac{4}{5}\sigma$ **59.** zero **60.** $e^{\mu t + \frac{1}{2}\sigma^2 t^2}$ **61.** $e^{i\mu t - \frac{1}{2}\sigma^2 t^2}$ **62.** $N(\mu_1 + \mu_2, \sigma_1^2 + \sigma_2^2)$ **63.** $N(21.0, 18.5)$ **64.** (*a*) 0.62% (*b*) 10.56% (*c*) 38.29% (*d*) 24.17% (*e*) 29.63% **65.** (*a*) 3 (*b*) 53 (*c*) 191 (*d*) 121 (*e*) 148 **66.** $e^{\mu + \frac{1}{2}\sigma^2}$ **67.** $e^{2\mu + \sigma^2}\, e^{\sigma^2 - 1}$ **68.** elongated **69.** more **70.** lognormal **71.** $\log - N(\mu_1 + \mu_2, \sigma_1^2 + \sigma_2^2)$ **72.** $\log - N\left(\mu, \frac{\sigma^2}{n}\right)$ **73.** $1\Big/\left[5\pi\left\{1 + \left(\frac{X-2}{5}\right)^2\right\}\right]$ **74.** not existing **75.** not existing **76.** non-existing **77.** $X = 5$ **78.** No **79.** $X = 2$ **80.** $C(\alpha, \beta)$ **81.** $C(0, 1)$ **82.** are not **83.** $\alpha = 1, \beta = 1$ **84.** $\frac{\alpha}{\alpha + \beta}$ **85.** $\frac{\alpha}{\beta - 1}$ **86.** α and β **87.** mean = $\alpha \times$ variance **88.** positive skewness **89.** leptokurtic **90.** $\gamma(n_1 + n_2)$ **91.** $B_I(n_1, n_2)$ **92.** incomplete gamma function **93.** α **94.** symmetrical **95.** modelling problem **96.** reliability theory **97.** corrosion **98.** $(0.8)^{25}$ **99.** binomial; n and q **100.** $4e^{-2}$ **101.** 2 **102.** $\sigma = 12.2$ **103.** 4 **104.** hyperbolic **105.** $\mu'_3 = 14\mu'_2$ **106.** $\mu_3 = 4(\mu_3 + 8\mu_1)$ **107.** gamma distribution **108.** (*a*) $\beta_2\left(\frac{n_1}{2}, \frac{n_2}{2}\right)$ (*b*) *F*-distribution with d.f. (n_1, n_2) (*c*) χ^2 will d.f. $(n_1 + n_2)$ (*d*) $\beta_1\left(\frac{n_1}{2}, \frac{n_2}{2}\right)$ (*e*) χ^2 with $(n_1 - n_2)$ d.f. **109.** half **110.** four times **111.** $\left(\frac{2}{n}\right)^{1/2}$ **112.** leptokurtic **113.** normal distribution **114.** Chi **115.** n **116.** non-central Chi-square **117.** Chi-square with $(n - 1)$ d.f. **118.** Chi-square with $2n$ d.f. **119.** $\sum_{i=1}^{k} \frac{(f_i - np_i)^2}{np_i}$ **120.** $n \to \infty$ **121.** symmetric **122.** $n \le 4$ **123.** leptokurtic **124.** $1\Big/\sqrt{n-1}\, B\left(\frac{1}{2}, \frac{n-1}{2}\right)$ **125.** Cauchy distribution **126.** *t*-test **127.** *t*-test **128.** χ^2-test **129.** χ^2-test **130.** χ^2-test **131.** Fisher's-*t* **132.** Snedecor's-*F* **133.** $F = e^{2z}$ **134.** $\frac{1}{2}\left(\frac{1}{\nu_2} - \frac{1}{\nu_1}\right)$ **135.** less than **136.** oes not exist **137.** $F_{\alpha;\,\nu_1\,\nu_2} = \frac{1}{F_{1-\alpha;\,\nu_2\,\nu_1}}$ **138.** $\nu_1 F = \chi^2$ **139.** normal **140.** χ^2 with $(n - 1)$ d.f. **141.** $N(0, 1)$ **142.** range **143.** hypergeometric **144.** exponential **145.** Pseudo binomial **146.** circular distribution **147.** $n, p_1, p_2, \ldots, p_k$ **148.** n **149.** Chi-square **150.** exponential distribution

Section C

1. (*c*) 2. (*a*) 3. (*a*) 4. (*c*) 5. (*d*) 111. (*c*) 112. (*b*) 113. (*d*) 114. (*c*) 115. (*b*)
6. (*b*) 7. (*a*) 8. (*c*) 9. (*b*) 10. (*c*) 116. (*b*) 117. (*c*) 118. (*a*) 119. (*c*) 120. (*b*)
11. (*c*) 12. (*a*) 13. (*c*) 14. (*c*) 15. (*a*) 121. (*d*) 122. (*c*) 123. (*d*) 124. (*c*) 125. (*b*)
16. (*b*) 17. (*b*) 18. (*d*) 19. (*a*) 20. (*c*) 126. (*c*) 127. (*d*) 128. (*b*) 129. (*c*) 130. (*d*)
21. (*b*) 22. (*d*) 23. (*a*) 24. (*c*) 25. (*d*) 131. (*a*) 132. (*b*) 133. (*c*) 134. (*d*) 135. (*a*)
26. (*c*) 27. (*a*) 28. (*b*) 29. (*d*) 30. (*b*) 136. (*b*) 137. (*c*) 138. (*b*) 139. (*d*) 140. (*a*)
31. (*d*) 32. (*d*) 33. (*c*) 34. (*d*) 35. (*d*) 141. (*c*) 142. (*d*) 143. (*b*) 144. (*b*) 145. (*a*)
36. (*b*) 37. (*a*) 38. (*d*) 39. (*b*) 40. (*a*) 146. (*d*) 147. (*d*) 148. (*d*) 149. (*c*) 150. (*c*)
41. (*a*) 42. (*d*) 43. (*c*) 44. (*b*) 45. (*a*) 151. (*b*) 152. (*d*) 153. (*b*) 154. (*d*) 155. (*b*)
46. (*c*) 47. (*b*) 48. (*c*) 49. (*d*) 50. (*a*) 156. (*c*) 157. (*d*) 158. (*d*) 159. (*a*) 160. (*c*)
51. (*b*) 52. (*c*) 53. (*c*) 54. (*b*) 55. (*a*) 161. (*b*) 162. (*d*) 163. (*a*) 164. (*b*) 165. (*c*)
56. (*c*) 57. (*a*) 58. (*c*) 59. (*b*) 60. (*c*) 166. (*d*) 167. (*b*) 168. (*d*) 169. (*a*) 170. (*b*)
61. (*d*) 62. (*d*) 63. (*c*) 64. (*d*) 65. (*a*) 171. (*b*) 172. (*c*) 173. (*c*) 174. (*a*) 175. (*c*)
66. (*b*) 67. (*d*) 68. (*c*) 69. (*d*) 70. (*c*) 176. (*a*) 177. (*c*) 178. (*b*) 179. (*c*) 180. (*d*)
71. (*d*) 72. (*b*) 73. (*d*) 74. (*a*) 75. (*c*) 181. (*c*) 182. (*b*) 183. (*a*) 184. (*b*) 185. (*d*)
76. (*d*) 77. (*a*) 78. (*a*) 79. (*d*) 80. (*b*) 186. (*a*) 187. (*d*) 188. (*c*) 189. (*a*) 190. (*c*)
81. (*c*) 82. (*d*) 83. (*c*) 84. (*a*) 85. (*d*) 191. (*b*) 192. (*c*) 193. (*a*) 194. (*d*) 195. (*a*)
86. (*c*) 87. (*d*) 88. (*c*) 89. (*b*) 90. (*d*) 196. (*b*) 197. (*c*) 198. (*a*) 199. (*b*) 200. (*c*)
91. (*b*) 92. (*c*) 93. (*a*) 94. (*d*) 95. (*c*) 201. (*b*) 202. (*c*) 203. (*c*) 204. (*b*) 205. (*b*)
96. (*a*) 97. (*b*) 98. (*d*) 99. (*a*) 100. (*c*) 206. (*d*) 207. (*a*) 208. (*a*) 209. (*c*) 210. (*d*)
101. (*a*) 102. (*c*) 103. (*b*) 104. (*c*) 105. (*d*) 211. (*b*) 212. (*b*) 213. (*c*)
106. (*d*) 107. (*a*) 108. (*b*) 109. (*c*) 110. (*b*)

SUGGESTED READING

1. Agarwal, B.L., *Basic Statistics,* New Age International Publishers, New Delhi, 8th edition, 2024.
2. Crammer, H., *Mathematical Methods of Statistics,* Princeton University Press, Princeton, 1958.
3. Ferguson, T.S., *Mathematical Statistics,* Academic Press, New York, 1967.
4. Hogg, R.V. and Craig, A.T., *Introduction to Mathematical Statistics,* Amerind Publishing Co., New Delhi, 3rd edn., 1972.
5. Johnson, N.L. and Kotz, S.M., *Discrete Distributions,* John Wiley & Sons, New York, 1970.
6. *Continuous Univariate distribution—1, 2,* John Wiley & Sons, New York, 1970.
7. Kendall, M.G. and Stuart, A., *An Advanced Theory of Statistics,* Vol. 1, Charles Griffin, London, 1958.
8. Mood, A.M., Graybill, F.A. and Boes, D.C., *Introduction to the Theory of Statistics* (International Student Edition), McGraw-Hill, Kogakusha, Tokyo, 1974.
9. Rao, C.R., *Linear Statistical Inference and its Applications,* Wiley Eastern Ltd., Publishers, New Delhi, 1974.
10. Rohatgi, V.K., *An Introduction to Probability Theory and Mathematical Statistics,* Wiley Eastern Ltd., Publishers, New Delhi, 1993.
11. Wilks, S.S., *Mathematical Statistics,* John Wiley & Sons, Toppan, 1962.

CHAPTER 8

Bivariate Random Variable and Distributions

SECTION A

Short Essay Type Questions

Q. 1. *What do you understand by bivariate random variable?*

Ans. In many situations, a scientist has to measure more than one factor or character at a time on the same item or some adjutant items. These measurements may have different units of measurements and moreover the range or the domain of the variables may also be different. If two variables are studied simultaneously in respect of their distribution, then they are known as bivariate random variable. Two or more variables studied concurrently with regard to their distributions are known in general *multivariate studies.* The variables may be discrete or continuous or the *mixture* of the two. But in this chapter, we have dealt with the situations when both the variables are either discrete or continuous. Just like univariate variables, the two variables have also various distributions. Their properties have also been studied which behave differently than univariates because of the impact of one variable over the other. The variables should be defined over the same sample space. In this situation, the variables can be jointly discrete or jointly continuous. Here, we are dealing with two-dimensional spaces or planes.

Q. 2. *Define bivariate discrete random variable and give an illustration.*

Ans. A random variable (X, Y) is said to be a two-dimensional discrete random variable if it can take only a countable number of points (x, y) in a two-dimensional space. The random variable (X, Y) is also said to be *joint discrete random variable.*

As for illustration, let us consider an experiment of tossing a coin three times and take the variable X as the number of tails in first tossing and Y the number of heads in three tosses. In this problem our bivariate random variable is the ordered pair (X, Y). Also both the variables X and Y are discrete. The possible outcomes are:

HHH, HHT, HTH, HTT, THH, THT, TTH, TTT. The pairs of variate values (x, y) are,

(x, y) : (0, 3), (0, 2), (0, 2), (0, 1), (1, 2), (1, 1), (1, 1), (1,0).

Q. 3. *Define bivariate continuous random variable.*

Ans. A two-dimensional random variable (X, Y) is called a bivariate continuous random variable if there exists a function $f(x, y) \geq 0$ such that for $-\infty < x, y < \infty$, the distribution function $F(x, y)$ of (X, Y) is given as

$$F(x, y) = \int_{-\infty}^{x}\int_{-\infty}^{y} f(u, v)\, du\, dv$$

The function $f(x, y)$ is called the joint probability density function of (X, Y).

As an example, the age X of husband and age Y of wife at marriage when treated jointly, they represent the bivariate continuous random variable.

Q. 4. *Explain joint distribution function. What are its properties?*

Ans. Let X and Y be two random variables defined over the same probability space. The joint *cumulative distribution function* (c.d.f.) of X and Y is denoted by $F_{X, Y}(x, y)$ and is defined as the $P(X \le x, Y \le y)$ for all (x, y) in the $X - Y$ plane. Its domain is just the $X - Y$ plane. Cumulative distribution function is often known as *distribution function* only.

Properties of joint distribution function:

(*i*) $\lim_{\substack{x \to \infty \\ y \to \infty}} F(x, y) = F(\infty, \infty) = 1.$

(*ii*) $\lim_{x \to -\infty} F(x, y) = F(-\infty, y) = 0$ for all y.

(*iii*) $\lim_{y \to -\infty} F(x, y) = F(x, -\infty) = 0$ for all x.

(*iv*) $F(x, y)$ is right continuous in each argument, *i.e.*, $\lim_{h \to 0} F(x + h, y) = \lim_{h \to 0} (x, y + h) = F(x, y)$.

(*v*) $P(x_1 \le x \le x_2, y_1 < y \le y_2) = F(x_2, y_2) - F(x_1, y_2) - F(x_2, y_1) + F(x_1, y_1) \ge 0.$

(*vi*) $0 \le F(x, y) \le 1.$

Q. 5. *Discuss joint discrete density (probability mass) function.*

Ans. The joint density function of X and Y is said to be discrete if there exists a non-negative function $p(x, y)$ such that it vanishes everywhere except at a finite or countably infinite number of mass points. The joint probability distribution describes the relationship between x and y and assigns probabilities to all possible outcomes (x, y). Thus,

$p(x, y) = P(X = x, Y = y)$ for all x, y in the $X - Y$ plane. $p(x, y)$ is called the joint probability mass function (p.m.f.). Some writers use $f(x, y)$ in place of $p(x, y) \cdot p(x, y)$ holds the following properties:

(*i*) $p(x_i, y_j) \ge 0$ for all i, j

(*ii*) $F(x, y) = \sum_{x_i \le x} \sum_{y_i \le y} p(x_i, y_j)$

(*iii*) $\sum_{i} \sum_{j} p(x_i, y_j) = 1$ for $i, j = 1, 2,...$

Q. 6. *Explain joint probability density function of the continuous random variables X and Y.*

Ans. A function $f_{X, Y}(x \cdot y)$ is a continuous function of x, y which gives the joint probability distribution of X and Y such that the probability of the variates falling within the infinitesimal rectangular region bounded by the lines $x \pm \frac{1}{2}dx$ and $y \pm \frac{1}{2}dy$ is expressed as $f_{X, Y}(x, y)\, dx,\, dy$. This function is called the joint probability density function (p.d.f.). Symbolically,

$$P\left(x - \frac{1}{2}dx \le X \le x + \frac{1}{2}dx,\; y - \frac{1}{2}dy \le Y \le y + \frac{1}{2}dy\right) = f_{X,Y}(x, y)\, dx\, dy$$

Often the suffix X, Y to f is omitted.

Q. 7. *Define marginal probability functions.*

Ans. If X and Y are joint discrete random variables with probability function $p(x, y)$, the individual distribution of either X or Y is called the marginal distributions of X or Y and/or denoted as $p_X(x)$, and $p_Y(y)$, respectively. Thus,

$$p_X(x) = P(X = x) = \sum_{y} p(x, y) = \sum_{y} p(X = x, Y = y)$$

Similarly,

$$p_Y(y) = P(Y = y) = \sum_{x} p(x, y) = \sum_{x} p(X = x, Y = y)$$

Q. 8. *Define marginal probability density function.*

Ans. If X and Y are jointly continuous random variables and their joint p.d.f. is $f_{X, Y}(x, y)$, the marginal probability density function of the variable X is given as:

$$f_X(x) = \int_{-\infty}^{\infty} f_{X,Y}(x, y)\, dy$$

Similarly, the marginal probability density function of the variable Y is given as:

$$f_Y(y) = \int_{-\infty}^{\infty} f_{X,Y}(x, y)\, dx$$

Q. 9. *What do you understand by conditional random variable?*

Ans. If (X, Y) is a bivariate random variable, the consideration of the variable Y for given value of X is known as the conditional variable Y for given X and is denoted as $Y \mid X = x$ or $Y \mid x$.

Similarly, the conditional X for given Y can be defined and denoted as $X \mid Y = y$ or $X \mid y$.

Q. 10. *Define conditional probability mass function.*

Ans. Let X and Y be two discrete random variables with their p.m.f. $p_{X,Y}(x, y)$. The conditional probability mass function of Y given X usually denoted as $p_{Y|x}(y \mid x)$ or $p(y \mid x)$ is defined as the ratio of the joint probability mass function to the marginal probability of X, *i.e.*,

$$p_{Y|x}(y \mid x) = \frac{p_{X,Y}(x, y)}{p_X(x)}$$

Similarly, the conditional probability mass function of X given Y can be given as.

$$p_{X|y}(x \mid y) = \frac{p_{X,Y}(x, y)}{p_Y(y)}$$

Also, the conditional discrete distribution function,

$$F_{Y|x}(y \mid x) = \sum_{y_j \le y} p_{Y|x}(y_j \mid x) = P(Y \le y \mid X = x)$$

and

$$F_{X|y}(x \mid y) = \sum_{x_i \le x} p_{X|y}(x_i \mid y) = P(X \le x \mid Y = y).$$

Note: The suffix X, Y or $Y \mid x$ or $X \mid y$ with p or F is often not indicated.

Q. 11. *Define conditional probability density function.*

Ans. If X and Y are two bivariate continuous random variables and their joint p.d.f. is $f_{X,Y}(x, y)$, the conditional probability density function of Y given $X = x$ is given as,

$$f_{Y|x}(y \mid x) = \frac{f_{X,Y}(x, y)}{f_X(x)} \quad \text{for } f_X(x) > 0$$

where $f_X(x)$ is the marginal p.d.f. of X and is undefined at points where $f_X(x) = 0$.

Similarly, the conditional p.d.f. of X given $Y = y$ is given as,

$$f_{X,y}(x \mid y) = \frac{f_{X,Y}(x, y)}{f_Y(y)} \quad \text{for } f_Y(y) > 0$$

where $f_Y(y)$ is the marginal p.d.f. of Y and is undefined at the points where $f_Y(y) = 0$.

Q. 12. *Explain independence of two random variables.*

Ans. If X and Y are two random variables and their joint p.d.f. is $f_{X,Y}(x, y)$, the variables X and Y are independent if and only if (*iff*),

$$f_{X,Y}(x, y) = f_Y(y) \cdot f_X(x)$$

for all values, x, y of X and Y.

In terms of conditional distributions,

$$f_{Y|x}(y \mid x) = \frac{f_{X,Y}(x, y)}{f_X(x)} = \frac{f_X(x) \cdot f_Y(y)}{f_X(x)} = f_Y(y)$$

Similarly,

$$f_{X|y}(x \mid y) = f_X(x).$$

Also,

$$f_{X,Y}(x, y) = F_X(x)\, F_Y(y).$$

The definition of independence remains as such for discrete case except that one has to call $f_{X,Y}(x, y)$ as joint probability mass function and $f_Y(y)$ and $f_X(x)$ as marginal probability mass function. Also, instead of f for density function, one may use p for mass functions, *i.e.*, one may use $p_{X,Y}(x, y)$, $p_X(x)$ and $p_Y(y)$ instead of $f_{X,Y}(x, y)$, $f_X(x)$ and $f_Y(y)$ respectively.

Q. 13. *What do you understand by conditional expectation?*

Ans. Let X and Y be two random variables having joint p.d.f. $f_{X,Y}(x, y)$ and their marginal p.d.f.'s be

$f_X(x)$ and $f_Y(y)$. The conditional expectation of $Y \mid X = x$ is given as,

$$E(Y \mid x) = y\int_{-\infty}^{\infty} y\frac{f_{X,Y}(x, y)}{f_X(x)}\,dy$$

where $f_X(x) > 0$.

Similarly, the conditional expectation of $X \mid Y = y$ is given as,

$$E(X \mid y) = \int_{-\infty}^{\infty} x\frac{f_{X,Y}(x, y)}{f_Y(y)}\,dx \quad \text{for } f_Y(y) > 0.$$

For discrete random variables X and Y, the conditional expectation of Y given X is given as,

$$E(Y \mid x) = \sum_j y_j \frac{p_{ij}}{p_i} \quad \text{for } p_i > 0$$

$$= \sum_j y_j\, p(j \mid i)$$

Similarly, $$E(X \mid y) = \sum_i x_i \frac{p_{ij}}{p_j} \quad \text{for } p_j > 0$$

where, $$p_{ij} = P(X = x_i, Y = y_j),$$
$$p_i = P(X = x_i),\ p_j = P(Y = y_j)$$

Q. 14. *Give properties of conditional expectation.*

Ans.

(*i*) $E\{E(Y \mid x)\} = E(Y)$

(*ii*) $E(XY \mid x) = XE(Y \mid x)$

(*iii*) $E(XY) = E\{XE(Y \mid x)\}$

(*iv*) If X and Y are independent, then $E(XY) = E(X)\,E(Y)$. But the converse is not true.

(*v*) $E(Y \mid X = x)$ is called the regression curve of Y on X.

(*vi*) $E(X \mid Y = x)$ is called the regression curve of X on Y.

(*vii*) The conditional expectation of a function $g(x, y)$ of X, Y is,

$$E[g(x,y) \mid X = x] = \int_{-\infty}^{\infty} g(x, y)\, f_{Y|x}(y \mid x)\,dy$$

when X, Y are continuous.

or,

$$E[g(x, y) \mid Y = y] = \int_{-\infty}^{\infty} g(x, y)\, f_{X|y}(x \mid y)\,dx$$

when X, Y are continuous.

Also, $$E[g(x, y) \mid X = x] = \sum_j g(x, y_j)\frac{p_{ij}}{p_i}$$

when X, Y are discrete.

$$E[g(x, y) \mid Y = y] = \sum_i g(x_i, y)\frac{p_{ij}}{p_j}$$

when X, Y are discrete. If X and Y are independent, then

$$E[\phi_1(x)\,\phi_2(y)] = E[\phi_1(x)]\,E[\phi_2(y)]$$

Q. 15. *Give conditional variance.*

Ans. The conditional variance of a variable Y given $X = x$ is denoted by $V(Y \mid X = x)$ and is defined as,

$$V(Y \mid X = x) = E(Y^2 \mid X = x) - [E(Y \mid X = x)]^2$$

Q. 16. *Express variance of a variable X in terms of conditional variances.*

Ans. If X and Y are two random variables having their joint p.d.f. $f(x, y)$, then the variance of X in terms of conditional variance is,

$$V(X) = E[V(X \mid y)] + V[E(X \mid y)]$$

Q. 17. *Discuss covariance between two variables X and Y. What are its properties?*

Ans. Covariance between two variables X and Y is defined,

$$\text{cov}(X, Y) = E[\{X - E(x)\}\{Y - E(y)\}]$$
$$= E[(X - \mu_X)(Y - \mu_Y)]$$
$$= E(XY) - \mu_X \mu_Y = \sigma_{XY}$$

Properties of covariance:

(*i*) Covariance between two variables is a measure of strength and direction of association between two variables.

(*ii*) Covariance tends to measure the linear relationship of X and Y.

(iii) If the variates X and Y are independent, the cov (X, Y) is zero.

(iv) The magnitude of cov (X, Y) does not indicate much towards the linear relationship between X and Y as it is subject to the variances of X and Y.

(v) If cov $(X, Y) = 0$, it means that the variables X and Y are uncorrelated but not necessarily independent.

Q. 18. *Define conditional covariance.*

Ans. If X, Y and Z are three random variables, the covariance between X and Y given $Z = z$ is,

$$\text{cov}(X, Y \mid z) = E[\{(X - E(X \mid z)\} \{Y - E\{Y \mid z)\} \mid z]$$

Q. 19. *Express covariance between two variables for a given third variable in terms of conditional covariances.*

Ans. If X, Y and Z are three random variables, the covariance between X and Y for a given value of Z in terms of conditional covariances is,

$$\text{cov}(X, Y) = E[\text{cov}(X, Y \mid z)] + \text{cov}[E(X \mid z)\, E(Y \mid z)]$$

Q. 20. *Define joint moment generating function for bivariate random variables.*

Ans. If X and Y are two random variables having the joint p.d.f. $f(x, y)$, then their joint moment generating function (m.g.f.) $M_{X, Y}(t_1, t_2)$ is defined as,

$$M_{X, Y}(t_1, t_2) = E(e^{t_1 x + t_2 y})$$

$$= \int_{-\infty}^{\infty} \int_{-\infty}^{\infty} e^{t_1 x + t_2 y} f(x, y)\, dx\, dy$$

Q. 21. *Define joint raw moments for bivariate distribution.*

Ans. The $(r, s)^{\text{th}}$ moment of the variables X and Y about the origin is called the raw moment of bivariate distribution and is given as,

$$\mu'_{r, s} = E(X^r Y^s)$$

Also $\mu'_{r, 0} = E(X^r)$ and $\mu'_{0, s} = E(Y^s)$

for $r, s = 0, 1, 2, 3, \ldots$

Q. 22. *Define joint central moments for the bivariate distributions.*

Ans. The $(r, s)^{\text{th}}$ moment about the means μ_X, μ_Y of (X, Y) is called the central moment of bivariate distribution and is obtained as,

$$\mu_{r, s} = E\{(X - \mu_X)^r (Y - \mu_Y)^s\}$$

for $r, s = 0, 1, 2, \ldots$

Also,

$$\mu_{1, 0} = E(X - \mu_X) = 0;\ \mu_{0, 1} = E(Y - \mu_Y) = 0;$$

$$\mu_{2, 0} = E\{(X - \mu_X)^2\} = \sigma_X^2;$$

$$\mu_{0, 2} = E\{(Y - \mu_Y)^2\} = \sigma_Y^2;$$

$$\mu_{11} = E\{(X - \mu_X)(Y - \mu_Y)\} = \text{cov}(X, Y)$$

Q. 23. *Explicate bivariate normal distribution and its properties.*

Ans. The bivariate continuous random variables (X, Y) with population means μ_X and μ_Y, population variances σ_X^2 and σ_Y^2 respectively and constant ρ, which is known as the population correlation coefficient between X and Y, are said to follow *bivariate normal distribution* if their probability density function is:

$$f_{X, Y}(x, y) = \frac{1}{2\pi\sigma_X\sigma_Y\sqrt{1-\rho^2}} \times e^{-\frac{1}{2(1-\rho^2)}\left[\left(\frac{x-\mu_X}{\sigma_X}\right)^2 - 2\rho\left(\frac{x-\mu_X}{\sigma_X}\right)\left(\frac{y-\mu_Y}{\sigma_Y}\right) + \left(\frac{y-\mu_Y}{\sigma_Y}\right)^2\right]}$$

for $-\infty < \mu_X, \mu_Y < \infty, < \sigma_X^2, \sigma_Y^2 > 0$ and $0 \le \rho \le 1$.

Bivariate normal distribution is sometimes named after its inventors as *Gaussian, Laplace-Gauss* and *Bravais*.

Bivariate normal distribution has five parameters namely, μ_X, μ_Y, σ_X^2, σ_Y^2 and ρ.

If we put $\frac{x-\mu_X}{\sigma_X} = u$ and $\frac{y-\mu_Y}{\sigma_Y} = v$, then

$$g(u, v) = \frac{1}{2\pi(1-\rho^2)} e^{-\frac{1}{2(1-\rho^2)}(u^2 - 2\rho uv + v^2)}$$

This is known as the standardised bivariate normal distribution with parameters (0, 0, 1, 1, ρ).

Latest definition: *A* random vector (*X*, *Y*) is said to possess bivariate normal distribution if for any two constants *a* and *b*, $Z = aX + bY$ is a normal variate.

Bivariate normal distribution is denoted as BVN $(\mu_X, \mu_Y, \sigma_X^2, \sigma_Y^2, \rho)$.

Properties of bivariate normal distribution:

(*i*) Moment generating function of bivariate normal distribution. If $(X, Y) \sim \text{BVN}(\mu_X, \mu_Y, \sigma_X^2, \sigma_Y^2, \rho)$ is given as,

$$M_{X,Y}(t_1, t_2) = E(e^{t_1x + t_2y})$$

$$= \int_{-\infty}^{\infty}\int_{-\infty}^{\infty} e^{t_1x + t_2y} f(x, y)\, dx\, dy$$

$$= e^{t_1\mu_X + t_2\mu_Y + 1/2(t_1^2\sigma_X^2 + t_2^2\sigma_Y^2 + 2\rho t_1t_2\sigma_X\sigma_Y)}$$

If $(X, Y) \sim \text{BVN}(0, 0, 1, 1, \rho)$, then

$$M_{X,Y}(t_1, t_2) = e^{1/2(t_1^2 + t_2^2 + 2\rho t_1t_2)}$$

If *X* and *Y* are independent, *i.e.*, if ρ = 0, then

$$M_{X,Y}(t_1, t_2) = M_X(t_1)\, M_Y(t_2)$$

$(r, s)^{\text{th}}$ moment about the origin is,

$$\mu'_{r,s} = \text{coeff. of } \frac{t_1^r t_2^s}{r!\,s!} \text{ in } M_{X,Y}(t_1, t_2)$$

$$\mu'_{1,0} = \int_{-\infty}^{\infty}\int_{-\infty}^{\infty} xf(x, y)\, dx\, dy$$

$$= \int_{-\infty}^{\infty} xf_X(x)\, dx$$

$$= \mu_X$$

Similarly, $\mu'_{01} = \mu_Y$

$(1, 1)^{\text{th}}$ moment about mean is,

$$\mu_{11} = \int_{-\infty}^{\infty}\int_{-\infty}^{\infty} (x - \mu_X)(y - \mu_Y) f(x, y)\, dx\, dy$$

$$= \text{cov}(X, Y)$$

$$\mu_{2,0} = \int_{-\infty}^{\infty} (x - \mu_X)^2 f_X(x)\, dx$$

Similarly, $\mu_{0,2} = \int_{-\infty}^{\infty} (y - \mu_Y)^2 f_Y(y)\, dy$

Also, the correlation coefficient between *X* and *Y*,

$$\rho_{XY} = \frac{\mu_{11}}{\sqrt{\mu_{2,0}\,\mu_{0,2}}}$$

(*ii*) Marginal distribution *X* if $(X, Y) \sim \text{BVN}(\mu_X, \mu_Y, \sigma_X, \sigma_Y, \rho)$ is given as,

$$f_X(x) = \frac{1}{\sqrt{2\pi}\sigma_X} e^{-\frac{1}{2}\left(\frac{X - \mu_x}{\sigma_x}\right)^2}$$

Similarly, the marginal distribution of *Y* is,

$$f_Y(y) = \frac{1}{\sqrt{2\pi}\sigma_y} e^{-\frac{1}{2}\left(\frac{Y - \mu_y}{\sigma_y}\right)^2}$$

Marginal density describes the probability density of one variable ignoring the other.

(*iii*) Conditional distribution of *Y* given *X* for the BVN $(\mu_x, \mu_y, \sigma_X^2, \sigma_Y^2, \rho)$ distribution is,

$$f_{y|x}(y \mid x) = \frac{1}{\sqrt{2\pi}\sigma_y\sqrt{1-\rho^2}}$$

$$e^{-\frac{1}{2(1-\rho^2)\sigma_Y^2}\left\{(y - \mu_Y) - \rho\frac{\sigma_Y}{\sigma_X}(x - \mu_X)\right\}^2}$$

for $-\infty < y \leq \infty$.

The right hand expression is the probability density function of the univariate normal distribution of *Y* with mean $\mu_Y + \rho\frac{\sigma_Y}{\sigma_X}(x - \mu_X)$ and variance $\sigma_Y^2(1 - \rho^2)$. In other words, the mean of the conditional distribution of Y given X,

$$E(Y \mid x) = \mu_Y + \rho \frac{\rho_Y}{\sigma_X}(x - \mu_X)$$

and $V(Y \mid x) = \sigma_Y^2 (1 - \rho^2)$

Similarly, the conditional distribution of X given Y is,

$$f_{X|y}(x \mid y) = \frac{1}{\sqrt{2\pi}\sigma_X \sqrt{1-\rho^2}}$$

$$e^{-\frac{1}{2(1-p^2)\sigma_X^2}\left\{(x-\mu_X)-\rho\frac{\sigma_X}{\sigma_Y}(y-\mu_y)\right\}^2}$$

The conditional distribution of X given Y has mean,

$$E(X \mid y) = \mu_X + \rho \frac{\sigma_X}{\sigma_Y}(y - \mu_Y)$$

and variance, $V(X \mid y) = \sigma_X^2 (1 - \rho^2)$

The conditional density of a variate describes the probability of a variable when the value of the other variable is known.

(*iv*) If $(X, Y) \sim N(0, 0, 1, 1, \rho)$, the correlation between X^2 and Y^2 is ρ^2.

(*v*) The surface $z = f(x, y)$ is called *normal correlation surface* or *bivariate normal density surface*.

(*vi*) For bivariate normal distributions, elliptical contours can be used for densities in $X - Y$ plane. The exponent of e in bivariate normal function describes the densities in $X - Y$ plane.

(*vii*) If (X, Y) are bivariate normal variates with joint p.d.f. $f(x, y)$, the $E(Y \mid x)$ is a function of x and is defined as the regression of Y on X. Similarly $E(X \mid y)$ is a function of y and is defined as the regression of X on Y.

(*viii*) If the regression of Y on X is linear, it is not necessary that the regression of X on Y is also linear.

(*ix*) If the regression of X and Y is linear, it does not imply that the regression of Y on X is linear.

(*x*) If $(X, Y) \sim$ BVN $(\mu_X, \mu_Y, \sigma_X^2, \sigma_Y^2, \rho)$, the distribution of the variable,

$$Z = \frac{(X - \mu_X)/\sigma_X}{(Y - \mu_Y)/\sigma_Y}$$

follows Couchy distribution with parameters ρ and $\sqrt{1-\rho^2}$, *i.e.*, $Z \sim C\left(\rho, \sqrt{1-\rho^2}\right)$ and the modal value of Z is ρ.

Again if,

$$Z = \frac{X - \mu_X}{Y - \mu_Y}$$

then $Z \sim C\left(\rho\frac{\sigma_X}{\sigma_Y}, \frac{\sigma_X}{\sigma_Y}\sqrt{1-\rho^2}\right)$ and its modal value is $\rho\frac{\sigma_X}{\sigma_Y}$.

(*xi*) In case of bivariate random variable (X, Y) it is possible that each of the marginal distribution of X and Y is normal but their joint distribution is not bivariate normal.

(*xii*) If (X, Y) follows bivariate normal distribution, then X and Y are independent only if the correlation between them is zero, *i.e.*, $\rho = 0$.

(*xiii*) For the standard BVN distribution (0, 0, 1, 1, ρ), the recurrence relation between moments is,

$$\mu_{r,s} = (r + s - 1)\rho\mu_{r-1,s-1} + (r-1)(s-1) \times (1-\rho^2)\mu_{r-2,s-2}$$

(*xiv*) If in the given BVN distribution with parameters $(\mu_X, \mu_Y, \sigma_X^2, \sigma_Y^2, \rho)$, $\sigma_X = \sigma_Y$ and $\rho = 0$ the density function is known as *circular normal*.

(*xv*) If in the BVN $(\mu_X, \mu_Y, \sigma_X^2, \sigma_Y^2, \rho)$ distribution, $\sigma_X \neq \sigma_Y$ and $\rho = 0$ the bivariate normal distribution is known as *elliptical* normal distribution.

(*xvi*) For a standardised bivariate normal distribution, *i.e.*, $(U, V) \sim \text{BVN}(0, 0, 1, 1, \rho)$, the values of various moments are as follows:

$$\mu_{0,0} = 1; \quad \mu_{1,1} = \rho; \quad \mu_{2,2} = 1 + 2\rho^2;$$
$$\mu_{3,3} = 3\rho(3 + 2\rho^2)$$
$$\mu_{1,2} = \mu_{2,1} = 0; \mu_{1,3} = \mu_{3,1} = 3\rho;$$
$$\mu_{1,4} = \mu_{4,1} = 0; \mu_{2,3} = \mu_{3,2} = 0;$$
$$\mu_{1,5} = \mu_{5,1} = 5\rho; \mu_{2,4} = \mu_{4,2} = 3(1 + 4\rho^2)$$

(*xvii*) If (X_i, Y_i) are BVN $(\mu_1, \mu_2, \sigma_1^2, \sigma_2^2, \rho)$ for $i = 1, 2, \ldots n$, then $(\bar{X}, \bar{Y})$ is distributed as

$$\text{BVN}\left(\mu_1, \mu_2, \frac{\sigma_1^2}{n}, \frac{\sigma_2^2}{n}, \rho\right).$$

Q. 24. *Consider an experiment of tossing a coin thrice. Also take the variate X as the number of tails appearing first time and Y the number of heads appearing in three tosses, i.e., X can take values 0, 1 and Y can take values 0, 1,2, 3. In this experiment, the bivariate values (x, y) for the sample space HHH, HHT, HTH, HTT, THH, THT, TTH, TTT are (0, 3), (0, 2), (0, 2), (0, 1), (1, 2), (1, 1), (1, 1), (1, 0). Let p be the constant probability of occurrence of each sample point. The probabilities for each (x, y) values can be presented in the following two way Table:*

X \ Y	0	1	2	3	Total
0	0	p	2p	p	4p
1	p	2p	P	0	4p
Total	p	3p	3p	P	8p

For bivariate distribution given in the above table find the values of (i) E(X), (ii) E(Y), (iii) E(X + Y), (iv) cov (X, Y) (v) var (Y | X = 1), (vi) V(X | Y = 2) (vii) P(X | Y = 2) (viii) P(Y | X = 1), (ix) P(X = 1, Y = 2), (x) P(Y = 3 | X = 0) (xi) P (X = 1 | Y = 1).

Ans. We know that the sum of probabilities is equal to 1. Hence, $8p = 1$ or $p = \frac{1}{8}$

(*i*) $E(X) = 0 \times 4p + 1 \times 4p = 4p = 4 \times \frac{1}{8} = \frac{1}{2}$

(*ii*) $E(Y) = 0 \times p + 1 \times 3p + 2 \times 3p + 3 \times p$

$$= 12p = \frac{12}{8} = \frac{3}{2}$$

(*iii*) $E(X + Y) = E(X) + E(Y) = \frac{1}{2} + \frac{3}{2} = 2.0$

(*iv*) $\text{cov}(X, Y) = E(XY) - E(X)E(Y)$

$$E(XY) = \sum_{i;j} (x_i y_j)\, p_{ij}$$

$$= (0 \times 0)\,0 + (0 \times 1)\,p + (0 \times 2)\,2p + (0 \times 3)\,p + (1 \times 0)\,p + (1 \times 1)\,2p + (1 \times 2)\,p + (1 \times 3)0$$

$$= 4p = \frac{1}{2}$$

$$\therefore \quad \text{cov}(X, Y) = \frac{1}{2} - \frac{1}{2} \times \frac{3}{2} = -\frac{1}{4}$$

(*v*) $V(Y \mid X = 1) = E(Y^2 \mid X = 1) - \{E(Y \mid X = 1)\}^2$

$$E(Y^2 \mid X = 1) = \sum_y \frac{y^2}{P} \frac{p(1, y)}{P(x=1)}$$

$$= \frac{0 \times p + 1 \times 2p + 4 \times p + 9 \times 0}{4p}$$

$$= \frac{3}{2}$$

$$E(Y \mid X = 1) = \frac{\sum_y yp(1, y)}{P(X=1)}$$

$$= \frac{0 \times p + 1 \times 2p + 2 \times p + 3 \times 0}{4p}$$

$$= 1$$

$$V(Y \mid X = 1) = \frac{3}{2} - (1)^2 = \frac{1}{2}$$

(vi) $V(X \mid Y = 2) = E(X^2 \mid Y = 2) - \{E(X \mid Y = 2)\}^2$

$$E(X^2 \mid Y = 2) = \frac{\sum_x x^2\, p(x, 2)}{P(Y = 2)}$$

$$= \frac{0 \times 2p + 1 \times p}{3 \times p} = \frac{1}{3}$$

$$E(X \mid Y = 2) = \frac{\sum_x x\, p(x, 2)}{P(Y = 2)}$$

$$= \frac{0 \times 2p + 1 \times p}{3 \times p} = \frac{1}{3}$$

$$V(X \mid Y = 2) = \frac{1}{3} - \left(\frac{1}{3}\right)^2 = \frac{2}{9}$$

(vii) $$P(X \mid Y = 2) = \frac{\sum_x p(x, 2)}{P(Y = 2)}$$

$$= \frac{2p + p}{3p} = 1$$

(viii) $$P(Y \mid X = 1) = \frac{\sum_y p(1, y)}{P(X = 1)}$$

$$= \frac{p + 2p + p + 0}{4p} = 1$$

(ix) $$P(X = 1 \mid Y = 2) = \frac{P(1, 2)}{P(Y = 2)} = \frac{p}{3p} = \frac{1}{3}$$

(x) $$P(Y = 3 \mid X = 0) = \frac{P(0, 3)}{P(X = 0)} = \frac{p}{4p} = \frac{1}{4}$$

(xi) $$P(X = 1 \mid Y = 1) = \frac{P(1, 1)}{P(Y = 1)} = \frac{2p}{3p} = \frac{2}{3}$$

Q. 25. *Given the joint distribution of (X, Y) as BVN (3, 4, 16, 25, 0.8), find (i) $P(5 < X < 9 \mid Y = 6)$ (ii) $P(-3 < Y < 3 \mid X = 5)$.*

Z:	0.3	1.0	1.97	3.0
Given $\phi(z)$:	0.11791	0.34134	0.47558	0.49865

Ans. (i) We know that the conditional distribution of X given Y has mean $\mu_X + \rho\frac{\sigma_X}{\sigma_Y}(y - \mu_Y)$ and variance $\sigma_X^2(1 - \rho^2)$.

$$\therefore \quad E(X \mid Y + 6) = 3 + 0.8 \times \frac{4}{5}(6 - 4) = 4.28$$

and $$V(X \mid y) = 16(1 - 0.8^2) = 5.76$$

Using conditional mean and variance,

$$P(5 < X < 9 \mid Y = 6)$$

$$= P\left(\frac{5 - 4.28}{2.4} < \frac{X - 4.28}{2.4} < \frac{9 - 4.28}{2.4}\right)$$

$$= P(0.3 < Z < 1.97)$$

$$= \phi(1.97) - \phi(0.3)$$

$$= 0.47558 - 0.11791$$

$$= 0.35767$$

(ii) The conditional distribution of Y given X has mean $\mu_Y + \rho\frac{\sigma_Y}{\sigma_X}(x - \mu_X)$ and variance $\sigma_Y^2(1 - \rho^2)$.

$$\therefore \quad E(Y \mid X = 5) = 4 + 0.8 \times \frac{5}{4}(5 - 3) = 6.0$$

$$V(Y \mid X = 5) = 25\,[1 - (0.8)^2] = 9.0$$

Using conditional mean and variance,

$$P(-3 < Y < 3 \mid X = 5)$$

$$= P\left(\frac{-3 - 6}{3} < \frac{Y - 6}{3} < \frac{3 - 6}{3}\right)$$

$$= P(-3 < Z < -1)$$

$$= \phi \mid (-3) \mid - \phi \mid (-1) \mid$$

$= 0.49865 - 0.34134$

$= 0.15731$

Q. 26. *If (X, Y) ~ BVN (3, 6, 16, 25, ρ) and P (1 < X < 5 | Y = 6) = 0.724 then find the values of ρ.*

[Given: ϕ(1.09) = 0.36214]

Ans. $E[X \mid Y = 6] = \mu_X + \rho \frac{\sigma_X}{\sigma_Y}(y - \mu_Y)$

$$= 3 + \rho \cdot \frac{4}{5}(6 - 6) = 3.0$$

$$V(X \mid Y = 6) = \sigma_X^2(1 - \rho^2)$$

$$= 16(1 - \rho^2)$$

$P(1 < X < 5 \mid Y = 6)$

$$= P\left(\frac{1-3}{4\sqrt{1-\rho^2}} < \frac{X-3}{4\sqrt{1-\rho^2}} < \frac{5-3}{4\sqrt{1-\rho^2}}\right)$$

$$= P\left(\frac{-2}{4\sqrt{1-\rho^2}} < Z < \frac{2}{4\sqrt{1-\rho^2}}\right)$$

$$= \frac{1}{\sqrt{2\pi}} \int_{-1/2\sqrt{1-\rho^2}}^{+1/2\sqrt{1-\rho^2}} e^{-1/2z^2}\, dz = 0.724$$

$$= \frac{2}{\sqrt{2\pi}} \int_{0}^{+1/2\sqrt{1-\rho^2}} e^{-1/2z^2}\, dz = 0.724$$

$$= \frac{1}{\sqrt{2\pi}} \int_{0}^{+1/2\sqrt{1-\rho^2}} e^{-1/2z^2}\, dz = 0.362$$

Using the area under the standard normal curve,

$$\phi(1.09) = 0.362$$

$$\therefore \quad 1.09 = \frac{1}{2\sqrt{1-\rho^2}}$$

or $\quad \rho = 0.89$

SECTION B

Fill in the Blanks

Fill in the suitable word(s) or phrase(s) in the blanks:

1. The distribution of two or more variables taken simultaneously is a _________ problem.
2. The multivariate random variables should be defined over the same _________ .
3. The marks X and Y secured by examinees in Physics and Chemistry will follow _________ normal distribution.
4. Joint cumulative distribution function, $F_{X,Y}(x, y)$ = _________ .
5. The cumulative distribution function $F(x, y)$ lies between _________ and _________ .
6. $P(a \le X \le b, c \le Y \le d)$ in terms of cumulative distribution function is equal to _________ .
7. Joint probability mass function $p(x, y)$ = _________ .
8. The relation between joint cumulative distribution function $F(x, y)$ and joint probability mass function $p(x, y)$ is _________.
9. The value of the expression $\sum_{\text{all } i} \sum_{\text{all } j} p(x_i, y_j)$ is always _________ .
10. If $p(x, y)$ is the joint probability mass function, the marginal probability function $p_X(x)$ is equal to _________ .
11. Let $p(x, y)$, $p_X(x)$ and $p_y(y)$ be the joint and marginal probability mass functions of the random variables X and Y. The conditional probability mass function $p_{Y \mid x}(y \mid x)$ = _________ .
12. The conditional discrete distribution function $F_{X \mid y}(x \mid y)$ is equal to _________ .
13. Let the joint probability density function of two random variables X and Y is $f(x, y)$. The

marginal probability density function $f_Y(y)$ = ________.

14. The conditional probability density function $f(Y \mid x)$ of Y given $X = x$ can be found out by the formula ________ .

15. $E(Y \mid x)$ is called the ________ of Y on X.

16. The expression for conditional variance of a variable Y for a given value of $X = x$ is ________ .

17. The variance of a variable X in terms of the conditional variance of Y given $X = x$ is ________.

18. If two variables X and Y are independent, then $E(XY)$ = ________.

19. If X and Y are two independent variables, then $f_{X,Y}(x, y)$ = ________.

20. If X and Y are two independent variables, the conditional distribution of X given $Y = y$, *i.e.*, $f_{X \mid y}(x \mid y)$ = ________.

21. If X, Y and Z are three random variable, the covariance between X, Y for a given value of Z, *i.e.*, cov $(X, Y \mid Z)$ = ________.

22. If X, Y and Z are three random variates, the covariance between X and Y in terms of conditional covariance, *i.e.*, cov (X, Y) = ________.

23. If two variables X, Y with joint p.d.f. $f_{X,Y}(x, y)$ are independent, the joint moment generating function $M_{X,Y}(t_1, t_2)$ = ________.

24. Given a joint bivariate normal distribution of X, Y as BVN $(\mu_X, \mu_Y, \sigma_X^2, \sigma_Y^2, \rho)$, the marginal distribution $f_X(x)$ = ________.

25. For conditional distribution $f_{X \mid Y}(x \mid y)$, the mean = $E(X \mid y)$ = ________.

26. If $X, Y \sim$ BVN $(0, 0, 1, 1, \rho)$, the correlation coefficient between X^2 and Y^2 is equal to ________.

27. If (X, Y) are distributed as BVN $(\mu_X, \mu_Y, \sigma_X^2, \sigma_Y^2, \rho)$, the variable $Z = \dfrac{X - \mu_X}{Y - \mu_Y}$ follows ________.

28. If the regression of Y on X is linear, it is ________ that the regression of X on Y is linear.

29. For a bivariate normal distribution $f(x, y)$, the surface $z = f(x, y)$ is called ________

30. For a bivariate normal density surface of the joint random variables X and Y is given as ________.

31. $(r, s)^{th}$ moment of the joint random variables having the joint p.d.f. $f(x, y)$ are given as ________.

32. Two bivariate normally distributed variables X and Y are independent if they are ________.

33. If $f(x, y) = 4xy$, for $0 < x < 1$, $0 < y < 1$, then
    (*i*) $E(Y \mid x)$ = ________.
    (*ii*) $V(Y \mid x)$ = ________.
    (*iii*) $E(XY \mid x)$ = ________.

34. If $\rho = 0$, the joint density of a bivariate normal distribution is equal to the product of ________.

35. If X and Y are two independent random variables, $E(Y/X = x)$ ________ on x.

36. If $f(x, y) = 2(x + y)$ for $0 < x, y < 1$, then
    (*i*) marginal probability function of x = ________.
    (*ii*) $E(Y/X = x)$ ________ .

37. $P(X > Y) = 1$ implies that $E(X)$ ________ $E(Y)$.

38. If the covariance between X and Y is zero, it mean that X and Y are ________ .

39. If X and Y are independent variables, then cov (X, Y) = ________.

40. If the variables (X, Y) follows BVN (1, 2, 4, 9, 0.5) distribution, the conditional distribution of $(X \mid y = 5)$ has mean ________ and variance ________.

SECTION C

Multiple Choice Questions

Select the correct alternative out of given ones:

1. If (X, Y) is a bivariate discrete random variable, the number of values which (X, Y) can taken in the $X - Y$ plane is:
   (*a*) infinite
   (*b*) finite
   (*c*) any number of values
   (*d*) none of the above
2. $(1, 1)^{th}$ moment μ_{11} of the bivariate distribution is called:
   (*a*) Var (X, Y)
   (*b*) Var $(X) \cdot$ Var (Y)
   (*c*) cov (X, Y)
   (*d*) correlation between X, Y
3. Variance of X in a bivariate distribution of X and Y in terms of moments is represented by:
   (*a*) μ_{20}
   (*b*) μ_{02}
   (*c*) μ_{11}
   (*d*) μ_{00}
4. In rolling of two distinct dice at a time, the variable X is defined as the number greater than 2 and the variable Y as the sum of numbers of two dices is less than 10. These bivariates (X, Y) are:
   (*a*) continuous type
   (*b*) discrete type
   (*c*) continuous and discrete both
   (*d*) neither continuous nor discrete
5. The heights of fathers and their sons form bivariable variables which are:
   (*a*) continuous variables
   (*b*) discrete variables
   (*c*) pseudo variables
   (*d*) none of the above
6. If a BVN distribution with parameter $(\mu_X, \mu_Y, \sigma_X^2, \sigma_Y^2, \rho)$ is such that $\sigma_X = \sigma_Y, \rho = 0$, the distribution is known as:
   (*a*) uniform normal
   (*b*) rectangular normal
   (*c*) elliptical normal
   (*d*) circular normal
7. If in a BVN $(\mu_X, \mu_Y, \sigma_X^2, \sigma_Y^2, \rho)$ distribution, $\sigma_X \neq \sigma_Y, \rho = 0$, the distribution is named as:
   (*a*) symmetrical normal
   (*b*) uniform normal
   (*c*) elliptical normal
   (*d*) circular normal
8. If in a bivariate normal distribution of the variables X and Y, $\rho_{XY} = 0$, it implies that X and Y are
   (*a*) uncorrelated but not independent
   (*b*) uncorrelated and independent
   (*c*) independent but not uncorrelated
   (*d*) correlated and dependent
9. Bivariate normal distribution is also named as:
   (*a*) Bravais distribution
   (*b*) Laplace-Gauss distribution
   (*c*) Gaussian distribution
   (*d*) all of the above
10. Joint distribution function of (X, Y) is equivalent to the probability:
   (*a*) $P(X = x, Y = y)$
   (*b*) $P(X \leq x, Y \leq y)$
   (*c*) $P(X \leq x, Y = y)$
   (*d*) $P(X \geq x, Y \geq y)$
11. Joint cumulative distribution function $F(x, y)$ lies within the limits:
   (*a*) -1 and 1
   (*b*) -1 and 0
   (*c*) $-\infty$ and 0
   (*d*) 0 and 1

12. For the joint p.d.f. $f(x, y)$, the marginal distribution of Y given $X = x$ is given as:

(a) $\sum_{\text{all } x} f(x, y)$

(b) $\int_{-\infty}^{\infty} f(x, y)\, dx$

(c) $\int_{-\infty}^{\infty} f(x, y)\, dx\, dy$

(d) $\int_{-\infty}^{\infty}\int_{-\infty}^{\infty} f(x, y)\, dx$

13. If X and Y are independent, the cumulative distribution $F_{X, Y}(x, y)$ is equal to:

(a) $F_X(x)\, F_Y(y)$

(b) $P(X \leq x)\, P(Y \leq y)$

(c) both (a) and (b)

(d) neither (a) nor (b)

14. If X and Y are two independent variables, then

(a) $E(XY) = E(X)\, E(Y)$

(b) $\text{cov}(X, Y) = 0$

(c) $\rho_{X, Y} = 0$

(d) all of the above

15. $E(Y \mid X = x)$ is called the:

(a) regression curve of X on Y

(b) regression curve of Y on X

(c) both (a) and (b)

(d) neither (a) and (b)

16. If the joint distribution of the variables X and Y is BVN $(0, 0, 1, 1, \rho)$, the correlation coefficient between X^2 and Y^2 is equal to:

(a) 1

(b) –1

(c) ρ^2

(d) 0

17. If $f(x, y)$ is a binormal density function, then the surface $Z = f(x, y)$ is called:

(a) normal correlation surface

(b) bivariate normal density surface

(c) neither of (a) nor (b)

(d) both (a) and (b)

18. $(r, s)^{\text{th}}$ moment in a bivariate normal distribution $M_{X, Y}(t_1, t_2)$ can be found as the coefficient of:

(a) $\dfrac{t_1^r\, t_2^s}{r_s}$

(b) $\dfrac{t_1^r\, t_2^s}{\Gamma r\, \Gamma s}$

(c) $\dfrac{t_1^r\, t_2^s}{r!\, s!}$

(d) $t_1^r\, t_2^s$

19. The correlation coefficient ρ between two variables X_1 and X_2 for a bivariate population in terms of moments is:

(a) $\dfrac{\mu_{22}}{\sqrt{\mu_{20}\, \mu_{02}}}$

(b) $\dfrac{\mu_{11}}{\sqrt{\mu_{20}\, \mu_{02}}}$

(c) $\dfrac{\mu_{12}}{\sqrt{\mu_{11}\, \mu_{22}}}$

(d) $\dfrac{\mu_{11}}{\sqrt{\mu_{20}\, \mu_{02}}}$

20. If X and Y follows BVN $(\mu_X, \mu_Y, \sigma_X^2, \sigma_Y^2, \rho)$ distribution, the conditional variance $(X \mid Y = y)$ is distributed as:

(a) $N\left[\mu_X + \rho\dfrac{\sigma_X}{\sigma_Y}(y - \mu_Y), \sigma_X^2(1 - \rho^2)\right]$

(b) $N\left[\mu_X + \rho\dfrac{\sigma_Y}{\sigma_X}(x - \mu_X), \sigma_X^2(1 - \rho)\right]$

(c) both (a) and (b)

(d) neither (a) nor (b)

21. If the variable (X, Y) is BVN $(\mu_X, \mu_Y, \sigma_X^2, \sigma_Y^2, \rho)$, the variable $Z = \dfrac{(x - \mu_X)/\sigma_X}{(Y - \mu_Y)/\sigma_Y}$ follows:

(*a*) uniform continuous distribution with parameters [ρ, (1 – ρ²)]

(*b*) exponential distribution with parameters [1, ρ]

(*c*) Cauchy distribution, with parameters $\left[\rho, \sqrt{1-\rho^2}\right]$

(*d*) none of the above

22. The conditional distribution of a discrete variable Y given $X = x$ can be expressed as

(*a*) $F_{Y|x}(y \mid x) = P(Y \leq y \mid X = x)$

(*a*) $F_{Y|x}(y \mid x) = P(Y = y \mid X = x)$

(*c*) $F_{Y|x}(y \mid x) = \dfrac{P(Y \leq y \mid X \leq x)}{P(X = x)}$

(*d*) $F_{Y|x}(y \mid x) = \dfrac{P(X = x \mid Y = y)}{P(X = x)}$

23. The conditional p.d.f. of X given $Y = y$ for a joint density $f_{X,Y}(x, y)$ can be found by the formula:

(*a*) $F_{X|y}(x \mid y) = \dfrac{f_{X,Y}(x, y)}{f_X(x)}$

(*b*) $F_{X|y}(x \mid y) = F_{Y|x}(y) \cdot F_{X,Y}(x, y)$

(*c*) $F_{X|y}(x \mid y) = \dfrac{f_{X,Y}(x, y)}{f_Y(y)}$

(*d*) none of the above

24. Given the joint p.m.f. $p_{X,Y}(x, y)$, the conditional p.m.f. of Y given $X = x$ is given by the relation:

(*a*) $P_{Y/x}(y/x) = \dfrac{p_{X,Y}(x, y)}{p_Y(x)}$

(*b*) $P_{Y/x}(y/x) = p_X(x)/\, p_Y(y)$

(*c*) $P_{Y/x}(y/x) = p_Y(y)/\, p_X(x)$

(*d*) $P_{Y/x}(y/x) = \dfrac{p_{X,Y}(x, y)}{p_Y(y)\, p_X(x)}$

25. If $E(Y \mid x)$ is the conditional expectation of Y given $X = x$, the $E(XY)$ in terms of conditional expectation can be expressed as:

(*a*) $E(XY) = E(X)\, E(Y/x)$

(*b*) $E(XY) = E(Y)\, E(Y/x)$

(*c*) $E(XY) = XE(Y/x)$

(*d*) $E(XY) = E[XE(Y/x)]$

26. For any two continuous variables X and Y, if a variable Z which is a linear combination of X and Y follows normal distribution, then X and Y jointly follow:

(*a*) jointly discrete distribution

(*b*) jointly continuous distribution

(*c*) bivariate normal distribution

(*d*) circular normal distribution

27. Conditional variance of a variable X for given $Y = y$ in terms of conditional expectation can be expressed as:

(*a*) $V(X \mid Y = y) = E(Y^2 \mid X = x) - [E(X \mid Y = y)^2]$

(*b*) $V(X \mid Y = y) = [E(Y \mid X = x)]^2 - [E(X^2 \mid Y = y)]$

(*c*) $V(X \mid Y = y) = E(X^2 \mid X = x) - [E(X \mid Y = y)]^2$

(*d*) $V(X \mid Y = y) = E(X^2 \mid Y = y) - [E(X \mid Y = y)]^2$

28. If the moment generating function $M_{X,Y}(t_1, t_2)$ is $e^{1/2\,(t_1^2 + t_2^2)}$, then the variable X follows:

(*a*) standard normal bivariate distribution

(*b*) χ^2-distribution with 1 d.f.

(*c*) Cauchy distribution

(*d*) none of the above

29. Probability of the event $P(a_1 \leq X \leq a_2, b_1 \leq Y \leq b_2)$ in terms of joint cumulative distribution function $F(x, y)$ is:

(*a*) $F(a_1, b_1) - F(a_1, b_2) - F(a_2, b_1) - F(a_2, b_2)$

(*b*) $F(a_1, b_1) + F(a_2, b_2) - F(a_1, b_2) - F(a_2, b_1)$

(*c*) $F(a_1, b_2) - F(a_1, b_1) - F(a_1, b_2) + F(a_2, b_1)$

(*d*) $F(a_1, b_2) + F(a_2, b_2) + F(a_1, b_2) + F(a_2, b_1)$

30. The cumulative distribution function $F(x, y)$ of two-dimensional random variables X and Y in terms of probability is equivalent to:

(*a*) $F(x, y) = P(0 < X \leq x, 0 < Y \leq y)$

(*b*) $F(x, y) = P(-\infty < X \leq \infty, -\infty < Y \leq \infty)$

(*c*) $F(x, y) = P(-\infty < X \leq x, -\infty < Y \leq y)$

(*d*) none of the above

31. The relation of cumulative distribution function with joint p.d.f. $f(x, y)$ of two-dimensional random variables X and Y is:

(*a*) $F(x, y) = \int_{-\infty}^{\infty} \int_{-\infty}^{\infty} f(x, y)\, dx\, dy$

(*b*) $F(x, y) = \int_{0}^{\infty} \int_{0}^{\infty} F(x, y)\, dx\, dy$

(*c*) $F(x, y) = \int_{-\infty}^{x} \int_{-\infty}^{x} f(x, y)\, dx\, dy$

(*d*) $F(x, y) = \int_{-\infty}^{x} \int_{-\infty}^{y} f(x, y)\, dx\, dy$

32. If $F(x, y)$ is a non-decreasing cumulative distribution of two-dimensional random variables X and Y, then $F(x, y)$ holds the relation:

(*a*) $F(-\infty, y) = F(x, -\infty) = 0, F(\infty, \infty) = 1$

(*b*) $F(-\infty, y) = F(x, -\infty) = 1, F(\infty, \infty) = 1$

(*c*) $F(-\infty, y) = F(x, -\infty) = F(\infty, \infty) = 0$

(*d*) none of the above

33. If the joint p.d.f. of two random variables X and Y is defined as,

$$f(x, y) = x + y \text{ for } 0 \leq x, y \leq 1$$
$$= 0 \text{ otherwise}$$

then the marginal distribution of X is:

(*a*) $f_X(x) = x + \frac{1}{4}$

(*b*) $f_X(x) = x + \frac{1}{2}$

(*c*) $f_X(x) = (x + y + 1)$

(*d*) none of the above

34. A player rolls a fair die. He gets –1 point if the die turns up with 1 to 3 spots and get 1 point if the die turns up with 4 to 6 spots. In this way a variable X has two values –1 and 1. Also one gets 0 point if the die turns up with 1 spot and 1 point if the die turns up with 6 spots. In this way a second variable Y takes two values 0 and 1. The joint probability distribution is given in the following table.

X \ Y	0	1	$p_X(x)$
–1	1/6	2/6	1/2
1	2/6	1/6	1/2
$p_Y(y)$	1/2	1/2	1

For the given joint distribution, the expected value of X is:

(*a*) $E(X) = 0$

(*b*) $E(X) = \frac{1}{2}$

(*c*) $E(X) = 1$

(*d*) $E(X) = \frac{1}{4}$

35. For the problem given in Q. No. 34, the expected value of Y is:

(*a*) $E(Y) = 0$

(*b*) $E(Y) = \frac{1}{2}$

(*c*) $E(Y) = 1$

(*d*) $E(Y) = 1/4$

36. For the joint distribution given in Q. No. 34, the variance of X is:

(*a*) $V(X) = 0$

(*b*) $V(X) = 1/2$

(*c*) $V(X) = 1$

(*d*) $V(X) = \frac{1}{4}$

37. For the bivariate distribution given in Q. No. 34, the variance of Y is:

(*a*) $V(Y) = 0$

(*b*) $V(Y) = 1/2$

(*c*) $V(Y) = 1$

(*d*) $V(Y) = \frac{1}{4}$

38. For the joint distribution given in Q. No. 34, the covariance between X and Y is:

(*a*) $\text{cov}(X, Y) = 0$

(*b*) $\text{cov}(X, Y) = 1/6$

(*c*) $\text{cov}(X, Y) = -1/6$

(*d*) $\text{cov}(X, Y) = -1$

39. For the given joint distribution in Q. No. 34, the correlation between X and Y is:

(*a*) $\rho_{XY} = -1/3$

(*b*) $\rho_{XY} = -1/6$

(*c*) $\rho_{XY} = -2/3$

(*d*) $\rho_{XY} = 1/3$

40. For the problem given in Q. 34, the condition variance of X given $Y = 0$ is:

(*a*) $V(X/Y = 0) = 1/3$

(*b*) $V(X/Y = 0) = 1$

(*c*) $V(X/Y = 0) = \frac{8}{9}$

(*d*) none of the above

41. For the discrete bivariate distribution given in Q. No. 34, the conditional variance of Y given $X = 1$ is:

(*a*) $V(Y/X = 1) = \frac{1}{9}$

(*b*) $B(Y/X = 1) = \frac{2}{3}$

(*c*) $V(Y/X = 1) = \frac{2}{9}$

(*d*) none of the above

42. Following is the joint probability density function of the BVN distribution of X and Y.

$$f(x, y) = ce^{-\frac{8}{27}\{(x-7)^2 + 4(y+5)^2 - 2(x-7)(y+5)\}}$$

The parameters of BVN distribution are:

(*a*) $\mu_x = 7, \mu_y = -5, \sigma_x^2 = 36, \sigma_y^2 = 9, \rho = 0.5$

(*b*) $\mu_x = -7, \mu_y = -5, \sigma_x^2 = 6, \sigma_y^2 = 3, \rho = 1$

(*c*) $\mu_x = 7, \mu_y = 5, \sigma_x^2 = 36, \sigma_y^2 = 3, \rho = 0.5$

(*d*) none of the above

43. For the joint density function given in Q. No. 42, the value of the constant c is:

(*a*) $\frac{1}{18\sqrt{3}\pi}$

(*b*) $\frac{\sqrt{3}}{54\pi}$

(*c*) 0.0102

(*d*) all of the above

44. Given the BVN (1, 2, 9, 16, 0.5) distribution, $P(X \geq 3)$ is: [Given: $\phi(0.67) = 0.24537$]

(*a*) 0.74537

(*b*) 0.25463

(*c*) 0.24537

(*d*) none of the above

45. Given the BVN (1, 2, 9, 16, 0.5) distribution, $P(X > 2/y = 2)$ is:

[Given: $\phi(0.38) = 0.15$]

(*a*) 0.65
(*b*) 0.85
(*c*) 0.35
(*d*) 0.15

46. For a BVN (0, 0, 1, 1, 0.5) distribution, $(4, 2)^{th}$ moment is:

(*a*) $\mu_{4, 2} = \frac{15}{4}$
(*b*) $\mu_{4, 2} = 0$
(*c*) $\mu_{4, 2} = \frac{15}{2}$
(*d*) $\mu_{4, 2} = 6$

47. For a BVN $(0, 0, 1, 1, \rho)$ distribution, $(3, 1)^{th}$ moment is:

(*a*) $\mu_{3, 1} = 1 + 3\rho$
(*b*) $\mu_{3, 1} = 3(1 - \rho^2)$
(*c*) $\mu_{3, 1} = 3\rho$
(*d*) none of the above

48. If the regression of *Y* on *X* is linear, the regression of *X* on *Y* is:

(*a*) linear
(*b*) not necessarily linear
(*c*) always curvilinear
(*d*) any of the above

49. For the discrete variables *X* and *Y*, the joint probability p_{ij} is expressed as:

(*a*) $p_{ij} = P(X = x_i, Y > y_j)$
(*b*) $p_{ij} = P(X \le x_i, Y < y_j)$
(*c*) $p_{ij} = P(X \ge x_y, Y \ge y_j)$
(*d*) $p_{ij} = P(X = x_i, Y = y_j)$

50. If $f(x, y) = 3 - x - y$ for $0 \le x, y \le 1$, the marginal distribution of *X* is:

(*a*) $f_X(x) = 3 - x$
(*b*) $f_X(x) = \frac{5}{2} - x$
(*c*) $f_X(x) = 5 - \frac{x^2}{2}$
(*d*) none of the above

51. If the joint p.d.f. of *X* and *Y*, $f(x, y) = 3 - x - y$ for $0 \le x \le 1$, $0 \le y \le 1$ the marginal distribution of *Y* is:

(*a*) $f_Y(y) = \frac{5}{2} - y$
(*b*) $f_Y(y) = y - \frac{5}{2}$
(*c*) $f_Y(y) = 3 - y$
(*d*) $f_Y(y) = 3$

52. Given the joint p.d.f., $f(x, y) = 3 - x - y$ for $0 \le x, y \le 1$ the means of *X* and *Y* are:

(*a*) $\mu'_{1, 0} = \mu'_{0, 1} = \frac{15}{6}$
(*b*) $\mu'_{1, 0} = \mu'_{0, 1} = 3$
(*c*) $\mu'_{1, 0} = \mu'_{0, 1} = \frac{11}{12}$
(*d*) $\mu'_{1, 0} = \mu'_{0, 1} = 0$

53. For the joint p.d.f., $f(x, y) = 3 - x - y$ for $0 \le x, y \le 1$, the variances of *X* and *Y* are:

(*a*) $\mu'_{2, 0} = \mu'_{0, 2} = \frac{7}{12}$
(*b*) $\mu'_{2, 0} = \mu'_{0, 2} = \frac{168}{288}$
(*c*) both (*a*) and (*b*)
(*d*) none of (*a*) and (*b*)

54. The $(1, 1)^{th}$ central moment for the joint p.d.f., $f(x, y) = 3 - x - y$ for $0 \le x, y \le 1$ is:

(*a*) $\mu_{1, 1} = \frac{-1}{4}$
(*b*) $\mu_{1, 1} = 1/12$
(*c*) $\mu_{1, 1} = 0$
(*d*) none of the above

55. Given the joint p.d.f. of *X* and $Y = 3 - x - y$ for $0 \le x, y \le 1$, the correlation coefficient between *X* and *Y* is:

(*a*) $\rho_{X, Y} = \frac{-1}{2}$

(*b*) $\rho_{X,Y} = \frac{3}{7}$

(*c*) $\rho_{X,Y} = \frac{-1}{4}$

(*d*) $\rho_{X,Y} = \frac{-3}{7}$

56. The conditional distribution of X given Y for the joint p.d.f., $f(x, y) = 3 - x - y$ for $0 \le x$, $y \le 1$ is:

(*a*) $f(x \mid y) = \frac{3-x-y}{3/2-x}$

(*b*) $f(x \mid y) = \frac{\frac{5}{2}-y}{3-x-y}$

(*c*) $f(x \mid y) = \frac{3-x-y}{\frac{5}{2}-y}$

(*d*) none of the above

57. The conditional distribution of Y given X for the joint p.d.f., $f(x, y) = 3 - x - y$ for $0 \le x'$, $y \le 1$ is:

(*a*) $f(y \mid x) = \frac{3-x-y}{\frac{5}{2}-y}$

(*b*) $f(y \mid x) = \frac{3-x-y}{\frac{5}{2}-x}$

(*c*) $f(y \mid x) = \frac{\frac{5}{2}-y}{\frac{5}{2}-x}$

(*d*) all of the above

58. If the density function of bivariates X and Y is given as:

$$f(x, y) = 3xy \text{ for } 0 \le x \le 1, \quad 0 \le y \le 1,$$

the marginal distribution of X is:

(*a*) $f_X(x) = 3x$

(*b*) $f_X(x) = \frac{3}{2}x$

(*c*) $f_X(x) = \frac{3}{4}x$

(*d*) none of the above

59. For $f(x, y)$ given in Q. No. 58, the marginal distribution of Y is:

(*a*) $f_Y(y) = 3$

(*b*) $f_Y(y) = \frac{3x}{2}$

(*c*) $f_y(y) = \frac{3xy}{2}$

(*d*) $f_Y(y) = \frac{3}{2}y$

60. For $f(x, y)$ given in Q. No. 58, the mean of X is:

(*a*) $\mu'_{1,0} = \frac{3}{4}$

(*b*) $\mu'_{1,0} = \frac{1}{2}$

(*c*) $\mu'_{1,0} = 1$

(*d*) $\mu_{1,0} = 0$

61. For the BVN density $f(x, y)$ in Q. No. 58, the conditional distribution of Y given $X = x$ is:

(*a*) $f(y/x) = \frac{3}{2}y$

(*b*) $f(y/x) = 3y$

(*c*) $f(y/x) = 2y$

(*d*) $f(y/x) = y$

62. $(2, 2)^{\text{th}}$ moment of the BVN density given in Q. No. 58 is:

(*a*) $\mu_{2,2} = \frac{1}{48}$

(b) $\mu_{2,2} = \frac{1}{144}$

(c) $\mu_{2,2} = \frac{1}{4}$

(d) none of the above

63. The covariance between X, Y for the joint density function given in Q. No. 58 is:

(a) $\mu_{11} = \frac{1}{48}$

(b) $\mu_{11} = \frac{1}{144}$

(c) $\mu_{11} = \frac{1}{4}$

(d) none of the above

64. The variance of X for the joint p.d.f., $f(x, y)$ given in Q. No. 58 is

(a) $\mu_{2,0} = \frac{1}{4}$

(b) $\mu_{2,0} = \frac{1}{16}$

(c) $\mu_{2,0} = \frac{1}{8}$

(d) any of the above

65. The correlation coefficient between the variables X and Y having the joint density, $f(x, y) = 3xy$ for $0 \le x \le 1, 0 \le y \le 1$ is:

(a) $\rho_{X,Y} = \frac{1}{3}$

(b) $\rho_{X,Y} = \frac{16}{48}$

(c) $\rho_{X,Y} = \frac{2}{6}$

(d) all of the above

66. Given the joint probability mass function of X and Y be $f(x, y) = \frac{x+y}{21}$; $x = 1, 2, 3$; $y = 1, 2$ the $P(x = 3)$ is equal to:

(a) 3/7

(b) 1/9

(c) 4/9

(d) 4/7

67. Given the joint probability density function of X and Y as,

$$f(x, y) = 4xy;\ 0 \le x \le 1,\ 0 \le y \le 1$$
$$= 0;\ \text{otherwise}.$$

$P\left(0 < x < \frac{1}{2}; \frac{1}{2} \le y \le 1\right)$ is equal to

(a) 1/4

(b) 5/16

(c) 3/16

(d) 3/8

68. If (X, Y) are bivariate $N(0, 0, 1, 1, \rho)$, then the variables $(x + y)$ and $(x - y)$ are:

(a) correlated with $\rho = \frac{1}{2}$

(b) independently distributed

(c) negatively correlated

(d) none of the above

69. Let (X, Y) be jointly distributed with density function,

$$f(x, y) = \begin{bmatrix} e^{-x-y}; & 0 < x < \infty, 0 < y < \infty \\ 0 \quad ; & \text{otherwise} \end{bmatrix}$$

Then X and Y are:

(a) independent

(b) both having the mean unity

(c) both having the variance unity

(d) all of the above.

70. Let $f(x, y) = 1;\ -x < y < x,\ 0 < x < 1$

$= 0;$ otherwise

Then, the marginal density function of X is:

(a) $2x$

(b) 1

(c) $\frac{1}{2}x$

(d) $2y$

71. For two random variables X and Y, the conditional expectation $E(XY \mid x)$ is equal to:

(a) $E(Y \mid x)$

(b) $E[XE(Y \mid x)]$

(c) $XE(Y \mid x)$

(d) $E(Y)$

72. If the joint probability density function of two random variables X and Y is given as,

$$F(x, y) = x + y \text{ for } 0 \le x, y \le 1$$
$$= 0 \text{ otherwise.}$$

Then the marginal density of X is:

(a) $f_X(X) = x + 1/x$

(b) $f_X(X) = x + \frac{1}{2}$

(c) $f_X(X) = x + y + 1$

(d) $f_X(X) = x + 1$

ANSWERS

Section B

1. multivariate **2.** sample space **3.** bivariate **4.** $P(X \le x, Y \le y)$ **5.** 0 and 1 **6.** $F(a, c) + F(b, d) - F(a, d) - F(b, c)$ **7.** $P(X=x, Y=y)$ **8.** $F(x,y) = \sum_{x_i \le x} \sum_{y_i \le y} p(x_i, y_i)$ **9.** 1 **10.** $\sum_{y} p(x, y)$ **11.** $p(x,y)/p_X(x)$ **12.** $\sum_{x_i \le x} p_{X|y}(x_i \mid y)$ **13.** $\int_{-\infty}^{\infty} f(x, y)\, dx$ **14.** $f_{X,Y}(x, y)/f_X(x)$ **15.** regression curve **16.** $V(Y \mid X = x) = E(Y^2 \mid X = x) - [E(Y \mid X = x)]^2$ **17.** $V(X) = E(V(X \mid y)] + V[E(X \mid y)]$ **18.** $E(X)\,E(Y)$ **19.** $f_X(x)\, f_Y(y)$ **20.** $f_X(x)$ **21.** $E[\{X - E(X \mid Z)\}\,\{Y - E(Y \mid Z)\} \mid Z]$ **22.** $E[\text{cov}(X, Y \mid z)] + \text{cov}[E(X \mid Z)\, E(Y \mid z)]$ **23.** $M_X(t_1)\, M_Y(t_2)$ **24.** $\frac{1}{\sqrt{2\pi}\sigma_X} e^{-\frac{1}{2\sigma_X^2}(x-\mu_X)^2}$ **25.** $\mu_X + \rho \frac{\sigma_X}{\sigma_Y}(y - \mu_Y)$ **26.** ρ^2 **27.** Cauchy distribution **28.** not necessary **29.** normal correlation surface **30.** $z = f(x, y)$ **31** $\int_{-\infty}^{\infty}\int_{-\infty}^{\infty} x^r y^s f(x, y)\, dx\, dy$ **32.** uncorrelated

33. (i) 2/3 $\left[\text{Hint}: f_{Y|X}(y \mid x) = \frac{4xy}{2x} = 2y,\right.$

$$\left. E(Y|x) = \int_0^1 y \cdot 2y\, dy = \frac{2}{3}\right]$$

(ii) 1/9 $\left[\text{Hint}: E(Y^2 \mid x) = \int_0^1 y^2\, 2y\, dy = \frac{1}{2},\right.$

$$\left. V(Y \mid x) = \frac{1}{2} - \left(\frac{2}{3}\right)^2 = \frac{1}{9}\right]$$

(iii) $2x/3 \left[E(XY \mid x) = xE(Y \mid x) = \frac{2}{3}x\right]$

34. marginal densities **35.** does not depend

36. (i) $2x + 1 \left[\text{Hint}: f_x(x) = \int_0^1 2(x + y)\, dy\right.$

$$\left. = 2x(y)_0^1 + 2\left(\frac{y^2}{2}\right)_0^1 = 2x + 1\right]$$

(ii) $\frac{3x + 2}{3(2x + 1)}$

37. is greater than **38.** are not linearly related **39.** zero **40.** 2 and 3.

Section C

1. (b)	**2.** (c)	**3.** (a)	**4.** (b)	**5.** (a)
6. (d)	**7.** (c)	**8.** (b)	**9.** (d)	**10.** (b)
11. (d)	**12.** (b)	**13.** (c)	**14.** (d)	**15** (b)
16 (c)	**17.** (d)	**18.** (c)	**19.** (c)	**20.** (a)
21. (c)	**22.** (c)	**23.** (c)	**24.** (a)	**25.** (d)
26. (c)	**27.** (d)	**28.** (a)	**29** (b)	**30.** (c)
31. (d)	**32.** (a)	**33.** (b)		

34. (a) $\left[\text{Hint}: E(X) = (-1) \times \frac{1}{2} + 1 \times \frac{1}{2} = 0\right]$

35. (b) $\left[\text{Hint}: E(Y) = 0 \times \frac{1}{2} + 1 \times \frac{1}{2} = \frac{1}{2}\right]$

36. (c) $\left[\text{Hint}: V(X) = (-1)^2 \times \frac{1}{2} + (1)^2 \times \frac{1}{2} - 0 = 1\right]$

37. (*d*) $\left[\text{Hint}: V(Y) = 0 \times \frac{1}{2} + (1)^2 \times \frac{1}{2} - \frac{1}{4} = \frac{1}{4}\right]$

38. (*c*) [Hint: cov(*X*, *Y*) = *E*(*XY*) – *E*(*Y*) *E*(*X*)

$$= E(XY) = 0 \times (-1)\ \frac{1}{6} + 0 \times (1) \times \frac{2}{6} + 1 \times 1 \times \left(\frac{-2}{6}\right) + 1 \times 1 \times \frac{1}{6} = \frac{-1}{6}$$

39. (*a*) $\left[\text{Hint}: P_{XY} = \frac{-1/6}{\sqrt{1 \times 1/4}} = -\frac{1}{3}\right.$

40. (*c*) $\left[\text{Hint}: E(X^2/Y = 0) = \frac{(-1)^2 \cdot \frac{1}{6} + (1)^2 \cdot 2/6}{1/2}\right.$

$$= 1$$

$$E\ (X/Y = 0) = \frac{-1 \times \frac{1}{5} + 1 \times 2/6}{1/2} = \frac{1}{3},$$

$$\left.V(X/Y = 0) = 1 - \frac{1}{9} = \frac{8}{9}\right]$$

41. (*c*) $\left[\text{Hint}: E(Y^2/X = 1) = \frac{0 \times \frac{2}{6} + (1)^2 \times \frac{1}{6}}{1/2} = \frac{1}{3},\right.$

$$E(Y/X = 1) = \frac{0 \times \frac{2}{6} + 1 \times \frac{1}{6}}{1/2} = \frac{1}{3},$$

$$\left.V(Y/X = 1) = \frac{1}{3} - \frac{1}{9} = \frac{2}{9}\right]$$

42. (*a*) **43.** (*d*)

44. (*b*) $\left[\text{Hint}: p(X \geq 3) = P\left(\frac{X-1}{3} \leq \frac{3-1}{3}\right)\right.$

$$\left.= 0.5 - 0.24537 = 0.25463\right]$$

45. (*c*) [Hint: $\mu(X/y) = 1 + 0.5 \times \frac{3}{4}\ (2 - 2) = 1$,

$$V(X/y) = 9(1 - 0.5^2) = 6.75,$$

$$P\left(\frac{x-1}{\sqrt{6.75}} > \frac{2-1}{\sqrt{6.75}}\right) = P(Z \geq 0.385)$$

$$= 0.5 - 0.15 = 0.35]$$

46. (*d*)	**47.** (*c*)	**48.** (*b*)	**49.** (*d*)	**50.** (*b*)
51. (*a*)	**52.** (*c*)	**53.** (*c*)	**54.** (*a*)	**55.** (*d*)
56. (*c*)	**57.** (*b*)	**58.** (*b*)	**59.** (*d*)	**60.** (*b*)
61. (*c*)	**62.** (*d*)	**63.** (*a*)	**64.** (*b*)	**65.** (*d*)
66. (*a*)	**67.** (*c*)	**68.** (*b*)	**69.** (*d*)	**70.** (*a*)
71. (?)	**72.** (?)			

SUGGESTED READING

1. Anderson, T.W., *An Introduction to Multivariate Analysis,* John Wiley & Sons, Inc., New York, 1958.
2. Arora, S. and B. Lal, *New Mathematical Statistics,* Satya Prakashan, 1989.
3. Biswas, S., *Topics in Statistical Methodology,* Wiley Eastern Ltd., Publishers, New Delhi, 1991.
4. Crammer, H., *Mathematical Methods of Statistics,* Princeton University Press Princeton, 1959.
5. Fish, Marek., *Probability Theory and Mathematical Statistics,* John Wiley & Sons, Inc., New York, 1963.
6. Goon, A.M., Gupta, M.K. and Dasgupta, B., *An Outline of Statistical Theory,* Vol. I, The Word Press Pvt. Ltd., Calcutta, 1977.
7. Gupta, S.C. and Kapoor, V.K., *Fundamentals of Mathematical Statistics,* Sultan Chand & Sons, 8th edition, 1993.
8. Kendall, M.G. and Stuart, A., *The Advanced Theory of Statistics,* Charles Griffin & Company Ltd., London, Vol. I, 3rd edition, 1969 and Vol. II, 3rd edition, 1973.
9. Mood, A.M., Graybill, F and Boes, D.C., *Introduction to the Theory of Statistics,* McGraw-Hill Publishing Co., Kogakusha. 3rd edition, 1974.

CHAPTER 9

Sampling Methods

SECTION A

Short Essay Type Questions

Q. 1. *What is the need of sampling as compared to complete enumeration?*

Ans. Sampling is a part of our day-to-day life which we use advertantly or inadvertantly. For instance, a housewife takes one or two grains of rice from the cooking pan and decides whether the rice is cooked or not. A quality controller takes a few items and decides whether the lot is in accordance with the desired specifications or not. A pathologist takes a few drops of blood and tests for any change in blood of the whole body than normal. In all these situations, sampling is inevitable and gives satisfactory results.

Even in those cases where complete enumeration is possible, it is not preferred due to the facts that it is much more time consuming and expensive, requires more skilled and technical personnel, more errors are caused due to greater volume of work, measurement errors, etc.

Complete enumeration is used only for various censuses or in case of small populations.

Q. 2. *What do you understand by a population in statistical sense?*

Ans. Population is a group of items, units or subjects which is under reference of study. Population may consist of finite or infinite number of units. Population is termed as *universe* by a number of statisticians and scientists.

The inhabitants of a region, number of wheat fields in a state or district, fruit plants in a city, insects in a field, persons suffering from tuberculosis in a city, lepers in India, workers in a factory, students in an university, etc., are a few examples of finite populations. All real numbers, all stars in the sky are examples of infinite populations. Generally, the population consists of a large number of animates and inanimates. Moreover, the units or subjects constituting the population may vary from survey to survey in the same region or sphere of activity depending upon the aims and objectives of the survey.

In brief, one should very well keep in mind that statistical population is not only the human population which is usually conceived in literary sense. It is generally a group or collection of items specified by certain characteristics or defined under certain restrictions.

Q. 3. *Name different types of populations or universe and give their description summarily.*

Ans. Population can be classified into four categories namely, (*i*) Finite population (*ii*) Infinite population (*iii*) Real population (*iv*) Hypothetical population.

(*i*) *Finite population.* If the number of items or units constituting the population is fixed and limited, it is known as finite population. For instance, the workers in a factory, students in a college, etc. This usually consists of existing items.

(*ii*) *Infinite population.* If the population consists of an infinite number of items, it is called an infinite population. For example, the population of all real numbers lying between 5 and 10, the population of stars in the sky, etc.

(*iii*) *Real population.* A population consisting of the items which are all present physically is termed as real population.

(*iv*) *Hypothetical population.* The population consists of the results of repeated trials is named as hypothetical population. The tossing of a coin repeatedly results into a hypothetical population of heads and tails, rolling of a die again and again gives rise to a hypothetical population of numbers from 1 to 6, etc.

Q. 4. *In what situations sampling is inevitable?*

Ans. Sampling is inevitable in the following situations:

(*i*) When population is infinite.

(*ii*) When the item or unit is destroyed under investigation.

(*iii*) When the results are required in a short time.

(*iv*) When resources for survey are limited particularly in respect of money and trained persons.

(*v*) When area of survey is wide.

Q. 5. *What is a sample?*

Ans. Sample is a part or fraction of a population selected on some basis. Sample consists of a few items of a population. In principle a sample should be such that it is a true representative of the population. Usually a random sample is selected. If the population is reasonably homogeneous, a simple random sample is most preferred one. But the moment one starts identifying sampling units on the basis of their characteristics, it gives rise to different sampling methods.

Q. 6. *What is meant by sampling method?*

Ans. By sampling method, we mean the manner or scheme through which the required number of units are selected in a sample from a population.

Q. 7. *Mention in brief the objective of sampling.*

Ans. The foremost purpose of sampling is to gather maximum information about the population under consideration at minimum cost, time and human power. This is best achieved when the sample contains all the properties of the population.

Q. 8. *Define sampling unit and give its two examples.*

Ans. The constituents of a population which are the individuals to be sampled from the population and cannot be further subdivided for the purpose of sampling at a time are called *sampling units.* For instance, to know the average income per family, the head of the family is a sampling unit. To know the average yield of wheat, each farm owner's field of wheat is a sampling unit.

Q. 9. *What is meant by sampling frame?*

Ans. For adopting any sampling procedure it is essential to have a list or a map identifying each sampling unit by a number. Such a list or map is called sampling frame.

A list of voters, a list of households, a list of technical persons, areas in a map marked by number for soil surveys, a list of villages in a district, a list of farmer's fields, etc., are a few examples of sampling frame.

Q. 10. *Distinguish between complete enumeration and sampling study.*

Ans. In complete enumeration, each and every unit of the population is studied and results are based on all units of the population. Whereas, in sampling study only a selected number of units are studied and results based on the data of these units are supposed to yield information about the whole population.

Q. 11. *What do you understand by random sampling?*

Ans. When equal probability of selection is attached to each sampling unit at each draw, the selection procedure is known as random sampling.

Suppose, there are N units in the population, then the probability of selection of each unit is $1/N$. Also when each subsequent selection is independent of the previous selection, the selection procedure is known as simple random sampling (srs).

Q. 12. *Write a short note on the importance of random sample.*

Ans. The sampling distribution of the statistic $\bar{X}$ assuming random sampling from a population N (μ, σ) can be derived mathematically from the properties of random samples based on purely mathematical considerations. It can be shown that the sampling distribution of $\bar{X}$ is exactly $N(\mu, \sigma/\sqrt{n})$.

This result can be verified by empirical sampling experiments. So a random sample saves the labour of conducting empirical sampling experiments.

All the more, estimates obtained from random samples have highly desirable properties.

Q. 13. *Delineate the principles of sampling methods.*

Ans. There are four principles of sampling methods as described below:

(*i*) *Principle of statistical regularity:* This principle ensures that the items selected in a moderately large sample at random from a population on the average possess the characteristics of the population units.

(*ii*) *Principle of inertia of large numbers:* This law states that other things being same, as the sample size increases, the results tend to be more reliable and accurate.

(*iii*) *Principles of validity:* By the validity of a sampling design we mean that the sampling method should be such that it enables us to obtain valid estimates and tests about the parameters of the population. Probability sampling fulfils this requirement.

(*iv*) *Principle of optimisation:* This principle is related to efficiency and cost of a design. It consists of achieving a given level of efficiency at minimum cost or attaining maximum possible efficiency at fixed cost.

Q. 14. *Expound sampling and non-sampling errors.*

Ans. *Sampling error:* Mostly the population parameters are estimates through samples. In spite of the fact that one may use the best sampling method and all care is being taken in conducting the survey and obtaining the estimates for various characteristics of the population, there is always some discrepancy between the estimates and population values obtained by census studies of the sample population in the same manner. Such resulting discrepancies are termed as sampling errors. The sampling errors cannot be completely eliminated but may be minimised by choosing a proper sample of adequate size and adoping suitable method of estimation.

Non-sampling errors: Errors other than sampling errors in a survey are called *non-sampling* errors. The errors usually arise due to faulty planning, defective schedules or questionnaires, incompleteness and inaccuracy of returns, non-response, compiling errors, etc. These errors can be minimised by employing efficient investigators and supervisory staff, full coverage, better management, etc. Non-sampling errors are likely to be more widespread in complete enumeration than in a sample survey.

Q. 15. *What is purposive (subjective or judgement) sampling?*

Ans. In purposive sampling, the selection of units entirely depends on the choice of the investigator. This type of sampling is adopted when it is not possible to adopt any random procedure for selection of sampling units. For instance, a sample of patients suffering from Tuberculosis (TB) has to be drawn. Since, it is not possible to ascertain a population of TB patients, the persons turning up to TB sanitorium and having TB are selected in the sample. Such a method of sampling is known as *purposive, subjective* or *judgement sampling.* In this sampling procedure, there is no involvement of probability. That is why, it is called *subjective sampling.*

Purposive or judgement sampling is not preferred because it is not possible to determine the frequency distribution of the estimates obtained by this procedure and thus sampling error cannot be objectively determined.

Purposive sampling is highly prone to investigator's biases. Hence, purposive or judgement sampling is seldom used.

Q. 16. *Define a parameter.*

Ans. Any population constant is called a *parameter.* Out of various parameters, mean and variance are largely used besides correlation coefficient, regression coefficient, etc. In a distribution, by parameter one means those population constants which appear in probability density (mass) function.

Q. 17. *What is meant by an estimator?*

Ans. An estimator is a rule or a function of variates for estimating the population parameters. It is expressed as a function of sample variates. An estimator is itself a random variable and can have any value within its domain. For instance, the estimator for mean $\sum_{i=1}^{n} x_i/n$, which depends on the sample values x_i of a variable X. Similarly, the estimator of variance is $\sum_{i=1}^{n} (x_i - \bar{x})^2/(n-1)$.

Q. 18. *How do you distinguish between estimate and estimator?*

Ans. A particular value of an estimator from a fixed set of values of a random sample is known as *estimate.* An estimate stands for the value of a parameter. For example, sample mean $\bar{x}$ is an estimate of population mean μ and sample variance s^2 is an estimate of population variance σ^2. Whereas the functions for $\bar{x}$ and s^2 are estimators.

Q. 19. *Define the term statistic.*

Ans. A statistic is a function of observable random variables and does not involve any unknown parameter. An statistic is also a random variable but is not necessarily an estimator of a parameter. For example, student's $-t\left[t = \frac{\sqrt{n}\,(\bar{x}-\mu)}{s}\right]$ is a statistic.

Q. 20. *Give different types of sampling schemes and describe them in brief.*

Ans. There are two types of sampling schemes namely (*i*) unrestricted random sampling (*ii*) restricted random sampling.

(*i*) *Unrestricted random sampling.* In this type of sampling, each and every unit of the population has equal chance of being included in the sample. Simple random sampling is an example of unrestricted sampling.

(*ii*) *Restricted sampling.* If an investigator has any idea about the heterogeneity of sampling units, the population is divided into homogeneous groups and sample is drawn independently from each group. Such a process of sampling is known as restricted sampling. Stratified sampling, systematic sampling, multistage sampling, etc., are covered under the category of restricted sampling.

Q. 21. *Differentiate between simple random sampling with replacement and without replacement.*

Ans. If the units are selected or drawn one by one in such a way that a unit drawn at a time is replaced back to the population before the subsequent draw, it is known as *simple random sampling with replacement* (srswr). In this type of sampling from a population of size N, the probability of selection of a unit at each draw remains $1/N$. In srswr, a unit can be included more than once in a sample. Therefore, if the required sample size is n, the effective sample size is sometimes less than n due to the inclusion of one or more units more than once.

With the idea that effective sample size should be adhered to, the simple random sampling without replacement (srswor) is adopted. In this method a unit selected once is not included in the population at any subsequent draw. Hence, the probability of drawing a unit from a population of N units at r^{th} draw is $1/(N - r + 1)$.

In simple random sampling, the probability of selection of any sample of size n from a population consisting of N units remains the same, $1\Big/\binom{N}{n}$, *i.e.* Here $\binom{N}{n}$ is the number of all possible samples.

Q. 22. *Which factors are responsible for the size of a sample?*

Ans. The size of a sample depends upon the following factors:

(*i*) The purpose for which the sample is drawn.

(*ii*) The heterogeneity of the sampling units in

the population. More is the heterogeneity, larger is the size of the sample.

(*iii*) Resources available for the study in terms of time and money.

(*iv*) Number of technical persons and/or equipment available.

(*v*) Precision of estimates required is an important factor in determining the size of a sample. For greater precision usually a large sample is preferred.

Q. 23. *How can sample size be determined mathematically?*

Ans. The mathematical formula for estimating the sample size is:

$$n = \frac{(U_R \hat{s}_x)^2}{d^2}$$

where, d – The extent of difference which is desired to be detected.

U_R – Value of statistic at the reliability level R. The value of U_R is substituted from probability distribution table. If the data are selected from a normal population, then for 95 per cent reliability level, U_R = 1.96.

$\hat{s}_x$ – The standard deviation of x which is substituted from some previous study or experience.

Q. 24. *Give the formula for sample mean.*

Ans. If n sample observation are $x_1, x_2, ..., x_n$, the formula for sample mean is,

$$\bar{x} = \frac{x_1 + x_2 + ... + x_n}{n}$$

$$= \frac{1}{n}\sum_{i=1}^{n} x_i$$

Q. 25. *What formula is used to calculate the sample variance?*

Ans. If $x_1, x_2, ..., x_n$ are the observations of n sample units and $\bar{x}$ is its mean, the formula for variance is,

$$s^2 = \frac{1}{n-1}\sum_{i=1}^{n}(x_i - \bar{x})^2$$

$$= \frac{1}{n-1}\left(\sum_{i=1}^{n} x_i^2 - n\bar{x}^2\right)$$

$$= \frac{1}{n-1}\left\{\sum_{i=1}^{n} x_i^2 - \frac{(\Sigma_i x_i)^2}{n}\right\}$$

Q. 26. *How do you determine the sample mean of proportions in a dichotomous population?*

Ans. Let P be the proportion of units in category C_1 and $Q = (1 - P)$ is the proportion of units belonging to the category C_2. The estimate p of P, based on a sample of size n, can be obtained by the formula, $p = \frac{n_1}{n}$ where n_1 is the number of units in the sample belonging to the category C_1. Also $q = \frac{n_2}{n}$ where $n_2 = n - n_1$. Hence $p = 1 - q$.

Suppose the observations are coded as 1 if the unit belongs to C_1 and 0 if the unit belongs to C_2. Thus, the sample mean,

$$\bar{x} = \frac{\sum_{i=1}^{n} x_i}{n} = \frac{n_1}{n} = p$$

or $$n_1 = np = n\bar{x}$$

Q. 27. *How do you calculate the sample variance for proportions when the sample is drawn from a dichotomous population?*

Ans. With usual notations, the sample variance for proportions can be calculated by the formula,

$$s_p^2 = \frac{1}{n-1}\left(\sum_{i=1}^{n} x_i^2 - n\bar{x}^2\right)$$

$$= \frac{1}{n-1}(np - np^2)$$

$$= \frac{np}{n-1}(1 - p)$$

$$= \frac{npq}{n-1}$$

Q. 28. *Define standard error of an estimator and discuss it briefly.*

Ans. *Definition:* Standard error is the standard deviation of the sampling distribution of an estimator.

From a population of N units, $\binom{N}{n}$ samples of size n can possibly be drawn from the population. If the sampling units are distinct, each sample will give more or less a different estimate of a parameter. In this way, the estimates themselves will follow a distribution. The standard deviation of the estimates obtained from different possible samples is called standard error (S.E.). May it be the standard error of the sample mean $\bar{x}$, the standard deviation s, etc. Mostly, the standard error of mean $\bar{x}$ is calculated. Lesser is the value of the standard error, more reliable is the estimate.

Q. 29. *What is the advantage of considering standard error instead of standard deviation?*

Ans. Standard error is not much influenced by the extreme values present in the population. Moreover, it withholds all the virtues of standard deviation. All the more, the reciprocal of standard error is an index of precision of an estimator.

Q. 30. *What formula is used to find the standard error of mean?*

Ans. The formula for the standard error of sample mean $\bar{x}$ based on a sample of size n drawn from a population of N units is,

$$\text{S.E. } (\bar{x}) = s_{\bar{x}} = \sqrt{\left(\frac{1}{n} - \frac{1}{N}\right)s^2}\,.$$

where s^2 is the sample variance.

If N is large, the quantity $\frac{1}{N}$ is negligible. Hence,

$$\text{S.E. } (\bar{x}) = s_{\bar{x}} = \sqrt{\frac{s^2}{n}}$$

$$= \frac{s}{\sqrt{n}}$$

Q. 31. *Express the quantity S^2.*

Ans. S^2 is a quantity which is used in estimation of variance. It is slightly different from population variance $\sigma^2 \cdot S^2$ is expressed as,

$$S^2 = \frac{1}{N-1}\sum_{i=1}^{N}(X_i - \mu)^2$$

$$= \frac{1}{N-1}\left(\sum_{i=1}^{N} X_i^2 - N\mu^2\right)$$

Q. 32. *Express standard error of sample mean in terms of S^2.*

Ans. Standard error of sample mean in terms of S^2 is,

$$\text{S.E. } (\bar{x}) = \sqrt{\left(\frac{N-n}{N}\right)\frac{S^2}{n}}$$

Q. 33. *What is finite population correction and sampling fraction?*

Ans. The quantity $\frac{N-n}{N}$ or $\left(1-\frac{n}{N}\right)$ is known as finite population correction (f.p.c.) and it tends to unity as $N \to \infty$, *i.e.*, N is large. The quantity $\frac{n}{N}$ is known as sampling fraction. $\frac{n}{N}$ is taken as negligible if its value is 0.05 or less.

Q. 34. *How can one estimate population total and its variance?*

Ans. The population total for a variate X can be estimated by the formula,

$$\hat{X} = N\bar{x}$$

where $\bar{x}$ is the sample mean based on n sample observations and N is the total number of units in the population.

The variance of $\hat{X}$ in terms of S^2 is obtained by the formula,

$$V(\hat{X}) = N^2 V(\bar{x})$$

$$= N^2 \frac{N-n}{N} \frac{S^2}{n}$$

$$= \frac{N(N-n)}{n} S^2$$

and its estimate,

$$v(\bar{x}) = \frac{N(N-n)}{n} s^2$$

If N_1 is the number of units in a class C_1 out of N population units, the variance of the estimate $\hat{N}_1$ is

$$V(\hat{N}_1) = V(Np)$$

$$= N^2 V(p)$$

$$= N^2 \frac{N-n}{N-1} \frac{PQ}{n}$$

where $P = \frac{N_1}{N}$ and $Q = 1 - P$.

The estimated variance $v(\hat{N}_1)$ of $V(\hat{N}_1)$ can be obtained by the formula,

$$v(\hat{N}_1) = N^2 \frac{N-n}{N-1} \frac{pq}{n}$$

If N is large such that $\frac{1}{N}$ and $\frac{n}{N}$ are negligible,

$$v(\hat{N}_1) = N^2 \frac{pq}{n}$$

Also the variance of p is estimated by the formula,

$$v(p) = \frac{N-n}{N(n-1)} pq$$

If $\frac{n}{N}$ is negligible,

$$v(p) = \frac{pq}{n-1}$$

The square root of $v(p)$ will provide standard error of p, *i.e.*,

$$\text{S.E.}(p) = \sqrt{\frac{pq}{n-1}}$$

Q. 35. *What do you understand by stratified random sampling?*

Ans. Stratified sampling comes under the category of restricted sampling. In this type of sampling method first the whole population is divided into homogeneous groups under certain criterion. These groups are termed as *strata.* Then the sample is drawn randomly from each stratum independently. The estimates are calculated from the data obtained from all the strata.

Information about each individual sampling unit is rarely available. Hence, the strata are formed on some broad basis such as localities in a city, districts in a state, etc.

Q. 36. *Highlight the advantages of stratified sampling.*

Ans. Different advantages of stratified sampling can be summarised as follows:

(*i*) If the admissible error is given, small sample is needed which results into a cut of expenditure.

(*ii*) In case the cost of survey is fixed, there is reduction in error due to stratification.

(*iii*) Through stratification, it is possible to gather the information or obtain the estimates for each stratum separately and also an estimate for the whole population.

(*iv*) Stratified sampling is very convenient from organisational point of view.

(*v*) If need be, different sampling schemes can be used to draw samples from different strata. But it creates many complications and hence it is mostly avoided.

Q. 37. *Mention the exigencies of stratified sampling and describe them in brief.*

Ans. Various exigencies arise at each step or stage of stratified sampling which are listed below and discussed one-by-one.

(*i*) What should be the criterion for stratification?

(*ii*) What should be number of strata?

(*iii*) How to fix the points of demarcation between strata?

(*iv*) What should be the sample size for each stratum?

(v) What sampling procedure be adopted for sampling from each stratum?

(vi) How to find the estimate for each stratum and then to pool them to get the estimates for the population as a whole?

(i) *Criterion for stratification:* The criterion of stratification depends on the objective of the survey. For example, in opinion surveys, stratification according to educational qualifications or economic status may be a good criterion. Due to administrative and organisational convenience, localities or regions are generally taken as strata.

(ii) *Number of strata:* One should take as many strata as are necessary to maintain the homogeneity of strata. More the number of strata, better it is. But often the strata are taken as regions for which information is required separately. (For formulae, see a book on sampling.)

(iii) *Point of demarcation:* As a rule, strata be marked in such a manner that no sampling unit belongs to more than one stratum.

(iv) *Sample size for each stratum*: Since the sample size influences the estimates, it is necessary that the size of the sample for each stratum should be optimum. Determination of sample size for each stratum is known as *allocation problem.* For this, most frequently used approaches are, (*a*) proportion allocation, and (*b*) optimum allocation.

(v) *Stratumwise sampling procedure:* Most commonly used procedure is to draw a simple random sample from each stratum independently. This procedure is called *stratified random sampling*. In some cases, other procedures like probability proportional to size may be used.

(vi) *Calculation of estimates:* Different formulae are given ahead to find the estimated values of population constants.

Q. 38. *What is equal allocation?*

Ans. Under equal allocation samples of equal size are drawn from each stratum.

Q. 39. *Discuss proportional allocation in stratified sampling.*

Ans. Suppose,

N – Number of units in the population

K – Number of strata

N_j – Number of units in the jth stratum (j = 1, 2, ..., k)

n – The sample size

n_j – number of units to be selected from j^{th} stratum such that $\sum_j n_j = n$

under proportional allocations,

$$\frac{n_j}{N_j} = \frac{n}{N}$$

or

$$n_j = \frac{n}{N} N_j = nW_j$$

where

$$W_j = \frac{N_j}{N}$$

Thus proportional allocation gives a *self*-weighing sample.

Q. 40. *Discuss optimum allocation.*

Ans. The formulae for optimum allocation in various strata were derived by Tschuprow in 1923. Later J. Neyman derived them independently in 1934. That is why such an allocation is named as *Neyman* allocation.

There are three situations under which the optimum allocation is considered: (*i*) When the variance of the stratified sample mean, $V(\overline{x}_{st})$ is minimised, (*ii*) When the total cost of the survey is fixed, (*iii*) When the variance of the stratified sample mean is fixed say, $V(\overline{x}_{st}) = V_0$.

Case (*i*) – For a fixed sample size n, the optimum sample size for j^{th} stratum (j = 1, 2, ..., k),

$$n_j = n\frac{\Sigma_j W_j S_j^2}{\Sigma_j W_j S_j}$$

where S_j^2 is the variance of jth stratum. If C, C_0 and C_j are the total, overhead and cost per unit of survey in the jth stratum respectively, the optimum value of n_j which minimises the variance of $\overline{x}_{st}$ is,

$$n_j = n\frac{\left(W_j S_j/\sqrt{C_j}\right)}{\left(\Sigma_j \cdot W_j S_j/\sqrt{C_j}\right)}$$

for $j = 1, 2, ..., k$.

The formula reveals that choose a large n_j if,

(a) n is large.

(b) S_j is large *i.e.*, stratum j is more heterogeneous.

(c) C_j is small.

Case (ii) – When the cost of the survey is fixed, optimum sample size for j^{th} stratum is,

$$n_j = C_1\frac{\Sigma_j\left(W_j S_j/\sqrt{C_j}\right)}{\Sigma_j\left(W_j S_j/\sqrt{C_j}\right)}$$

for $j = 1, 2, ..., k$

and $C_1 = C - C_0$

Case (iii) – When the value of $V(\bar{x}_{st})$ is fixed say, V_0, the optimum sample size for j^{th} stratum is,

$$n_j = \frac{\left(\Sigma_j W_j S_j/\sqrt{C_j}\right)\left(\Sigma_j W_j S_j/\sqrt{C_j}\right)}{V_0 + \frac{1}{N}\sum_j W_j S_j^2}$$

Q. 41. *Give different formulae for mean and variance of stratified sample.*

Ans. Different formulae for stratum mean, variances and stratified sample means and variances are:

If x_{ij} is the ith observation in the jth stratum for $i = 1, 2, ..., N_j$ and $j = 1, 2, ..., k$ then,

(i) j^{th} stratum mean, $\bar{X}_j = \frac{1}{N_j}\sum_{i=1}^{N_j} x_{ij}$

(ii) j^{th} stratum sample mean, $\bar{x}_j = \frac{1}{n_j}\sum_{i=1}^{n_j} x_{ij}$

(iii) j^{th} stratum variance,

$$S_j^2 = \frac{1}{N_j - 1}\sum_{i=1}^{N_j}\left(x_{ij} - \bar{X}_j\right)^2$$

(iv) Sample variance of jth stratum,

$$s_j^2 = \frac{1}{n_j - 1}\sum_{i=1}^{n_j}\left(x_{ij} - \bar{x}_j\right)^2$$

(v) An unbiased estimate of population mean under stratified sampling is,

$$\bar{x}_{st} = \frac{1}{N}\sum_{j=1}^{k} N_j \bar{x}_j$$

(vi) Variance of stratified sample mean,

$$V(\bar{x}_{st}) = \frac{1}{N^2}\sum_{j=1}^{k} N_j(N_j - n_j)\frac{S_j^2}{n_j}$$

$$= \sum_{j=1}^{k} W_j^2\left(1 - \frac{n_j}{N_j}\right)\frac{S_j^2}{n_j}$$

$$= \sum_{j=1}^{k}\frac{W_j^2 S_j^2}{n_j}$$

when $\frac{n_j}{N_j}$ is negligible.

Estimated value of $V(\bar{x}_{st})$ is,

$$v(\bar{x}_{st}) = \sum_{j=1}^{k}\frac{W_j^2 s_j^2}{n_j}$$

(vii) Under proportional allocation,

$$v(\bar{x}_{st}) = \left(1 - \frac{n}{N}\right)\sum_{j=1}^{k}\frac{W_j S_j^2}{n}$$

$$= \sum_{j=1}^{k}\frac{W_j S_j^2}{n}$$

when $\frac{n}{N}$ is negligible.

Estimated value of $V(\bar{x}_{st})$ under proportional allocation is,

$$v(\bar{x}_{st}) = \sum_{j=1}^{k}\frac{W_j s_j^2}{n}$$

(*viii*) Variance of $\bar{x}_{st}$ under optimum allocation is,

$$V_{\text{Ney}}(\bar{x}_{st}) = \frac{1}{n}\left(\sum_{j=1}^{k} W_j S_j \sqrt{C_j}\right)\left(\sum_{j=1}^{k} \frac{W_j S_j}{\sqrt{C_j}}\right) - \frac{1}{N}\sum_{j=1}^{k} W_j S_j^2$$

If C_j is same for all units, then

$$V_{\text{Ney}}(\bar{x}_{st}) = \frac{1}{n}\left(\sum_{j=1}^{k} W_j S_j\right)^2 - \frac{1}{N}\sum_{j=1}^{k} W_j S_j^2$$

To have the estimated values of variance, replace S_j by s_j.

Q. 42. *How are the variances of $\bar{x}_{st}$ under random sampling, proportional allocation and Neyman allocation related with each other?*

Ans. The variances of $\bar{x}_{st}$ under random sampling, proportional allocation and Neyman allocation hold the relation,

$$V_{\text{ran}}(\bar{x}_{st}) \geq V_{\text{Prop}}(\bar{x}_{st}) \geq V_{\text{Ney}}(\bar{x}_{st})$$

This shows $V_{\text{ran}}(\bar{x}_{st})$ is largest and $V_{\text{Ney}}(\bar{x}_{st})$ is minimum.

Q. 43. *What do you understand by two-way stratification?*

Ans. Sometimes the population is stratified according to two factors, e.g., the persons are stratified according to their qualifications and monthly income. In this way, we have a two-way table and units belong to different cells or substrata. Samples are drawn from each substratum (cell) independently. Such a sampling procedure is known as two-way stratified sampling. Two-way stratification is also termed as *deep stratification.*

Further two-way stratification is generally more efficient than one way stratification. Still it is seldom used.

Q. 44. *Describe the term 'controlled selection'.*

Ans. In many situations we know that if the units of different types are not included in the sample, the estimates are most likely upward or downward biased. To avoid this situation, population is divided into various homogeneous strata and a sample is drawn from each stratum to minimise the probabilities of non-preferred samples and is thus termed as *controlled selection.*

Q. 45. *Can one make use of varying probabilities of selection in stratified sampling?*

Ans. Yes, often the units within a stratum are selected with replacement and with varying probabilities of selection.

Q. 46. *What do you understand by systematic sampling?*

Ans. When the population units occur in a deck or sequence or line and a sample of size n is to be drawn, the population is divided into n sequential groups and one unit is drawn from each group situated at equal distances.

The selection procedure is such that one unit is drawn randomly from the first group say, j^{th} unit is selected. Then select $(j + k)$, $(j + 2k)$, ..., $(j + \overline{n-1}k)^{th}$ units from the subsequent groups. Such a selection procedure is known as *linear systematic sampling*. This procedure fails if the population size N is not a multiple of n.

Q. 47. *What is the advantages of systematic sampling?*

Ans. Some of the principal advantages of systematic sampling are given below:

(*i*) The method of selection is very simple.

(*ii*) The method of selection is cheap in terms of time and money.

(*iii*) The sample is distributed over the whole population and hence all contiguous parts of the population are well represented in the sample.

(*iv*) It is easy to locate selected units and is very convenient from organisational point of view.

Q. 48. *What are the disadvantages of systematic sampling?*

Ans.

(*i*) If the variation in the units is periodic, the units at regular intervals are correlated. In this situation the sample becomes highly lopsided and hence the estimates are biased.

(*ii*) No single reliable formula is available for estimating the standard error of sample mean. A formula is good enough if the population is of the type it has been expected to, otherwise not. This is a great drawback of systematic sampling.

Q. 49. *In what situations systematic sampling is preferred over other sampling procedures?*

Ans. Systematic sampling is preferably used when the information is to be collected from cards, trees in a forest, houses in blocks, entries in a register which are in a serial order, etc.

Q. 50. *What is circular systematic sampling?*

Ans. Linear systematic sampling fails if $N \neq nk$. Circular systematic sampling was first used by D.B. Lahiri in 1952. In circular systematic sampling take $\frac{N}{n}$ as rounded to the nearest integer. Select a random number from 1 to N. Suppose the selected number is m. Now select every $(m + jk)^{th}$ unit when $m + jk < N$ and every $(m + jk - N)^{th}$ unit when $m + jk > N$ putting $j = 1, 2, ...,$ till n units are selected. Such a procedure of selection is known as *circular systematic sampling.*

Q. 51. *Give the formulae for mean and variance of systematic sample.*

Ans. Let $x_1, x_2, ..., x_n$ be the observations on n selected units of systematic sample. The mean of systematic sample,

$$\bar{x}_{sy} = \frac{1}{n}\sum_{i=1}^{n} x_i$$

The variance of $\bar{x}_{sy}$ when $N = nk$ is,

$$V(\bar{x}_{sy}) = \frac{N-1}{N}S^2 - \frac{k(n-1)}{N}S^2_{wsy}$$

Suppose x_{ij} represents the ith observation in the jth systematic sample when a number from 1 to k is selected.

In the above formula for variance of $\bar{x}_{sy}$, S^2 represents the variance between samples where,

$$S^2 = \frac{1}{N-1}\sum_{j=1}^{k}\sum_{i=1}^{n}(x_{ij} - \bar{X})^2$$

and the variance within systematic samples,

$$S^2_{wsy} = \frac{1}{k(n-1)}\sum_{j=1}^{k}\sum_{i=1}^{n}(x_{ij} - \bar{x}_j)^2$$

Also, $$\frac{N-1}{N}S^2 = \sigma^2 \text{ (Population variance)}$$

and $$\frac{k(n-1)}{N}S^2_{wsy} = \frac{1}{N}\sum_{j=1}^{k}\sum_{i=1}^{n}(x_{ij} - \bar{x}_j)^2$$

$$= \sigma^2_w \text{ (Variance within the systematic sample)}$$

$$\therefore \quad V(\bar{x}_{sy}) = \sigma^2 - \sigma^2_w$$

Hence, we conclude that variance of $\bar{x}_{sy}$ is small when the units within a systematic sample are as heterogeneous as possible.

Q. 52. *Compare systematic sampling with stratified sampling.*

Ans.

(*i*) Systematic sampling resembles stratified sampling in the sense that groups of k units look like strata but no criterion has been considered in the formation of groups that ensures homogeneity.

(*ii*) No independent samples are drawn from each group.

(*iii*) In systematic sampling we have only one sample from the whole population.

The above three points clearly reveal that systematic sampling is quite different from stratified sampling.

Q. 53. *Is the systematic sampling superior to simple random sampling and stratified sampling? Comment.*

Ans. Nothing definite can be said about the superiority of systematic sampling over simple random sampling and *vice-versa* as it depends more on the structure of the population. One may be better than the other in particular cases. The same statement holds good while comparing systematic sampling with stratified random sampling.

Q. 54. *Discuss double sampling in brief.*

Ans. Many a time, some initial information necessitated to draw a sample is not available. In that situation such information can be gathered by taking a large sample provided it is not very expensive and time consuming. Then take a sub-sample to estimate the main characters as per the objectives of the survey. Such a sampling process is known as *double sampling*. Double sampling is also called *two-phase sampling*. For example, an investigator want to draw a sample of agricultural holdings with probability proportional to size. But the areas of holdings are not known. Hence, information about each agricultural holding is collected on a large number of farmer's holdings and then a sample is selected with pps for the main survey.

Double sampling is also helpful in stratified sampling to determine the strata sizes if not known. Double sampling is also very helpful in ratio and regression methods of estimation.

Q. 55. *Describe cluster or area sampling in nutshell.*

Ans. In many situations, the sampling frame for elementary units of the population is not available, moreover it is not easy to prepare it. But the information is available for groups of elements so called *clusters*. For instance, the list of houses may be available but not the persons residing in them, list of individual farms may not be available but the list of villages is generally available. Hence, in these situations, houses or villages are known as clusters and selection has to be made of houses or villages in the sample. Such a sampling procedure is known as *cluster sampling.*

When the entire area containing the population is divided into smaller area or segments, these small areas or segments are taken as sampling units. This procedure is known as area sampling. Clusters or area segments are also known as *primary units.*

In cluster sampling, precaution should be taken that a unit should never belong to more than one cluster. Also each elementary unit of the population should definitely belong to one primary unit.

Q. 56. *In what situations the cluster sampling be preferred?*

Ans. The cluster sampling is used when:

(*i*) the sampling frame is not available and it is too expensive and time consuming to prepare it.

(*ii*) the sampling units are situated distant apart. In this situation selection of elementary units makes the survey very cumbersome. For instance, selection of farmers in a state.

(*iii*) the elementary units may not be easily identifiable and locatable. For example, the animals of certain species, the migratory populations, etc.

Q. 57. *What sampling design is used to select clusters from a population?*

Ans. Usually simple random sampling without replacement is used to select clusters or area segments from a population. But any other design can be used.

Q. 58. *Give the formulae for estimating the mean of the characteristic X under single stage cluster sampling.*

Ans. Let x_{ij} denote the ith observation in the jth cluster. Suppose,

Number of clusters $= N$

Sample size $= n.$

Suppose the number of elementary units in the jth cluster $= M_j$

Total number of elementary units in the population

$$= \sum_{j=1}^{N} M_j = M$$

The mean of jth cluster,

$$\bar{x}_j = \frac{1}{M_j} \sum_i x_{ij}$$

for $i = 1, 2, ..., M_j$ and $j = 1, 2, ..., N$

The population mean,

$$\bar{X}_c = \Sigma_j \Sigma_i x_{ij} / \Sigma_j M_j$$

$$= \frac{1}{M} \sum_j M_j \bar{x}_j$$

An estimate $\bar{x}_c$ of $\bar{X}_c$, which is unbiased but not consistent, is given as,

$$\bar{x}_c = \frac{1}{n}\sum_j M_j\, \bar{x}_j/\bar{M}$$

where $$\bar{M} = \frac{M}{N}$$

Let S_b^2 and S_w^2 denote the variance between and within clusters respectively. Now the population variance,

$$\sigma^2 = \frac{1}{NM-1}\sum_j \sum_i \left(x_{ij} - \bar{X}_c\right)^2$$

Also, $$S_b^2 = \frac{1}{N-1}\sum_j \left(\bar{X}_j - \bar{X}_c\right)^2$$

and $$S_w^2 = \frac{1}{N(M-1)}\sum_j \sum_i \left(x_{ij} - \bar{x}_j\right)^2$$

An unbiased estimate of the variance of $\bar{x}_c$ is given as,

$$v(\bar{x}_c) = \frac{N-n}{Nn} s_b^2$$

where, $$s_b^2 = \frac{1}{n-1}\sum_j (M_j\, \bar{x}_j - \bar{x}_c)^2$$

for $j = 1, 2, ..., n$

Also, an estimate of s_w^2 is,

$$s_w^2 = \frac{1}{n\,(M-1)}\sum_j \sum_i (x_{ij} - \bar{x}_j)^2$$

Since the units within a cluster are more homogeneous than those in different clusters, $S_w^2 \le S_b^2$.

Q. 59. *Comment on the efficiency of cluster sampling as compared to simple random sampling without replacement.*

Ans. The efficiency of cluster sampling as compared to simple random sampling is,

$$E = \frac{S^2}{MS_b^2}$$

where, S^2 – The variance of cluster

M – The cluster size for each cluster

S_b^2 – The difference of the total variance and within clusters variance

From the formula it is apparent that the efficiency of the cluster sampling increases:

(*i*) if the cluster size decreases.

(*ii*) if the clusters are so formed that the variation within clusters is as large as possible and between clusters is as small as possible.

Q. 60. *What are the main differences between cluster sampling and stratified sampling?*

Ans. The main differences between cluster sampling and stratified sampling are:

(*i*) In stratified sample, a sample is drawn from each stratum (cluster) whereas in cluster sampling, a cluster (stratum) is selected as such.

(*ii*) A heterogeneous cluster is more preferable whereas a homogeneous stratum is always desirable.

Q. 61. *What is multi-stage sampling?*

Ans. In single-stage cluster sampling it is costly to include every elementary unit of the selected clusters in the survey. Moreover, it appears superfluous when the clusters are homogeneous. Hence, it is better to select a sample from each selected cluster rather than surveying the clusters as a whole. Selection of a sample from each selected cluster is known as sub-sampling. Under such a sampling procedure a sample is drawn in two stages, *i.e.*, in the first stage a sample of clusters is selected, and in the second stage a sample of elementary units is drawn from each selected cluster. This kind of sampling procedure is known as *two-stage sampling*. For example, if a survey is conducted to have an estimate of crop production, one may prefer to use two-stage sampling. Select villages as first stage units and farms in the villages as second stage units.

The selection procedure can be extended to any number of stages. Hence, in general it is known as *multi-stage sampling*.

Q. 62. *Give the formulae for estimates of mean and variance in case of two-stage sampling.*

Ans. Suppose, the total number of first stage units $= N$.

No. of second stage units in i^{th} first stage unit $= M_i$ for $i = 1, 2, ..., N$.

No. of first stage units selected $= n$.

No. of second stage units selected from the hth first stage unit $= m_h$

for $h = 1, 2, ..., n$.

x_{ij} – Observation on the jth second stage unit belonging to i^{th} first stage selected unit

$\bar{X}_i$ – Mean of the ith first stage unit on the basis of per second stage unit

$\bar{x}_h$ – The estimated value of $\bar{X}_i$

$\bar{x}_s$ – Overall estimated sample mean on the basis of each second stage unit when subsampling has been done

Total number of second stage unit in the sample,

$$m = \sum_{h=1}^{n} m_h$$

i^{th} first stage unit mean,

$$\bar{X}_i = \frac{1}{M_i}\sum_{j=1}^{M_i} x_{ij}$$

for $i = 1, 2, ..., N$

Estimated value of hth first unit mean,

$$\bar{x}_h = \frac{1}{m_h}\sum_{j=1}^{m_h} x_{hj}$$

Population mean per second stage unit,

$$\bar{X} = \sum_{i=1}^{N} M_i\bar{X}_i \Big/ \sum_{i=1}^{N} M_i$$

$$= \sum_{i=1}^{N} M_i\bar{X}_i \,/\, N\bar{M}$$

where $$\bar{M} = \frac{1}{N}\sum_{i=1}^{N} M_i$$

An unbiased estimate of $\bar{X}_s$ is,

$$\bar{x}_s = \frac{1}{n\bar{M}}\sum_{i=1}^{N} M_i\bar{x}_i$$

The estimated variance of $\bar{x}_s$,

$$v(\bar{x}_s) = \left(\frac{1}{n}-\frac{1}{N}\right)s_b^2 + \frac{1}{nN}\sum_{h=1}^{N}\frac{M_i^2}{\bar{M}^2}\left(\frac{1}{m_h}-\frac{1}{M_h}\right)s_{wh}^2$$

where, $$s_b^2 = \frac{1}{n-1}\sum_{h=1}^{n}\left(\frac{M_h}{M}\bar{x}_h - \bar{x}_s\right)^2$$

and $$s_{wh}^2 = \frac{1}{m_h-1}\sum_i \left(x_{ij}-\bar{x}_h\right)^2$$

Q. 63. *Comment on two-stage sampling design.*

Ans. It has been found that two-stage sampling design is generally less efficient than single stage sampling except when the correlation between elements in the same (first) stage units is negative.

Q. 64. *Write a short note on inverse sampling.*

Ans. When the character under study rarely exists and the proportion P of units possessing the character is very small, a simple random sample without replacement does not yield satisfactory results. Hence, for getting good estimate of P. Haldane, 1946 and Finney, 1949 suggested the method of inverse sampling. In inverse sampling, the size of the sample 'n' is not fixed but selection process continues until a predecided number of units possessing the rare character or attribute has been selected in the sample.

Suppose N is the number of units in the population and P is the proportion of units possessing the rare character or attribute under study. The number of units possessing the rare character in NP. Now to estimate P, draw a sample with srswor until the sample contains m units having rare character. Let n be the total number of units selected containing m units of interest. In this type of selection, n is a random variable and follows hypergeometric distribution. An unbiased estimate of P is,

$$p = \frac{m-1}{n-1}$$

An unbiased estimate of the variance of p is,

$$s_p^2 = \frac{p(1-p)}{(n-2)}\left(1-\frac{n-1}{N}\right)$$

If $\frac{n-1}{N}$ is negligible,

$$s_p^2 = \frac{p(1-p)}{n-2}$$

Q. 65. *Give the idea of sampling with probability proportional to size (pps).*

Ans. When the units vary in size according to a measure which can influence our studies, it was considered more appropriate to select items with probabilities proportional to their size. For instance, the villages having large geographical area will be having more area under crops. Hence, a survey meant for estimating the crop production it is better that the village with larger areas be selected with probability proportional to their area.

Thus, a selection procedure in which the units are selected with varying probabilities in proportion to some measure of the size of the sampling units is known as sampling with *probability proportional to size* (pps). Under *pps* sampling larger unit has more probability of inclusion in the sample as compared to the unit of smaller size.

Q. 66. *Give the concept of non-response in brief.*

Ans. In surveys it is commonly experienced that complete data from the sampling units or respondents is not obtainable for various reasons. For example in an opinion survey, the selected family might have shifted to some other place, selected person might have died. In mailed questionnaire, many respondents do not send their replies. Such a problem of incomplete sample data due to non-availability of information from the respondents is known as the problem of non-response.

Biases are introduced in the estimates due to non-response. Hence, various methods have been evolved to tackle the problem of non-response, but the details are omitted for brevity.

To deal with the problem of non-response, one approach is to consider the population consisting of two strata, one of respondents and the other of non-respondents in a mailed questionnaire survey. A subsample is drawn from non-respondents strata and these units are interviewed personally. Two sample data are pooled to get the estimates of the population parameters. This technique was suggested by Hansen and Hurwitz in 1946.

SECTION B

Fill in the Blanks

Fill in the suitable word(s) or phrase(s) in the blanks:

1. Sampling is ________ in many situations.
2. All sampling units are present in ________ population.
3. In a ________ population all sampling units are imagined.
4. If the number of units in a population are limited, it is known as ________ population.
5. A population consisting of an unlimited number of units is called an ________ population.
6. If all the units of a population are surveyed, it is called ________.
7. The errors other than sampling errors are termed as ________.
8. The discrepancy between a parameter and its estimate due to sampling process is known as ________.
9. Any population constants is called a ________.
10. A function for estimating a parameter is called as ________.
11. A value of the estimator is an ________ of the parameter.

12. Standard deviation of all possible estimates from samples of fixed size is called ________.

13. Formula for standard error of sample mean $\bar{x}$ based on a sample of size n and with standard deviation s is ________ .

14. The list of all the items of a population is known as ________.

15. Another name of population is ________ .

16. Number of samples of size n that can be drawn out of N population units through simple random sampling without replacement is ________ .

17. The probability of selection of any one sample out of $\binom{N}{n}$ samples is ________.

18. Under simple random sampling with replacement, there can be ________ samples of size n out of N population units ($n < N$).

19. Under simple random sampling with replacement, the same item can occur ________ in the sample.

20. Formula for sample mean of n observations $x_1, x_2, \ldots, x_n$ is ________.

21. Sample variance of the variate values x_1, x_2, ..., x_n can be calculated by the formula ________.

22. The sampling procedure in which the population is first divided into homogeneous groups and then a sample is drawn from each group is called ________ .

23. Stratified sampling is appropriate when population is ________ .

24. Stratification is done in respect of certain ________.

25. Deciding the sample size for each stratum is known as ________ problem.

26. If the sample size of each stratum is in proportion to stratum size, it is called ________.

27. Stratified sampling comes under the category of ________ sampling.

28. More heterogeneous is the population, ________ is the sample size.

29. Standard error of mean in terms of S^2 is ________.

30. The quantity $\frac{N-n}{N}$ in usual notation is called ________.

31. The expression $\frac{n}{N}$ is known as ________ .

32. When the units in a sample are selected by the investigator at his will, the selection procedure is known as ________ sampling.

33. Judgement sampling is ________ used in practice.

34. For a high precision of estimates, ________ samples is required.

35. Estimator and estimate are ________ .

36. If p is the proportion of units in one category out of two categories, the variance of p can be calculated by the formula ________ .

37. Sampling fraction $\frac{n}{N}$ is negligible if it is ________.

38. Determination of sample size for each stratum subject to the cost constrained is known as ________ allocation.

39. Optimum allocation is also known as ________ allocation.

40. Estimation of sample size for a stratum subject to the prefixed value of $V(\bar{x}_{st})$ in stratified sampling is called ________ allocation.

41. Sample under proportion allocation is a ________ sample.

42. In stratified random sampling, the variance of $\bar{x}_{st}$ for a fixed total size of sample is minimum if n_j is proportional to ________ .

43. With varying cost C_j per unit in stratified random sampling, the variance of $\bar{x}_{st}$ attains the smallest value if n_j is proportional to ________.

44. Variance of $\bar{x}_{st}$ under _________ allocation is least as compared to proportional allocation.

45. $V(\bar{x}_{st})$ under proportional allocation is less than the variance $\bar{x}_{st}$ under _________ .

46. $V_{\text{prop}}(\bar{x}_{st})$ lies in between $V_{\text{opt}}(\bar{x}_{st})$ and _________.

47. The students in a college are awarded grades A, B and C. For estimating the average IQ of the college students, _________ will provide good estimate of average IQ.

48. Stratified sampling is not preferred when the population is _________ .

49. When a simple random sample is drawn from each stratum, it is known as _________.

50. When there is an infinite population, _________ is not possible.

51. When the items are perishable under investigation it is not possible to do _________.

52. When the sample of same size is drawn from each stratum, it is known as _________.

53. Population is divided into substrata or cell under _________.

54. The two-way stratification is generally _________ efficient than the one-way stratification.

55. When stratification is done to minimise the selection of non-preferred samples, it is known as _________ .

56. When the population consists of units arranged in a sequence or deck, one would prefer _________.

57. In systematic sampling, all _________ parts of the population are well represented.

58. The main advantage of systematic sampling is that it is _________ and _________.

59. The main disadvantage of systematic sampling is that _________ formula for estimating the standard error of sample mean is available.

60. When the population size N is a multiple of sample size n, _________ systematic sampling in appropriate.

61. When the population size N is not divisible by the sample size 'n', _________ systematic sampling is plausible.

62. A subsample is drawn under _________ sampling.

63. Double sampling is termed as _________ sampling.

64. Double sampling is sometimes used in _________ sampling.

65. Double sampling is useful in _________ and _________ estimation methods.

66. Cluster sampling is a good sampling technique when _________ is not available.

67. Cluster sampling is useful when sampling units are situated _________ .

68. Clusters or area segments are called _________.

69. A cluster consists of a number of _________ units.

70. In cluster sampling, the variance within clusters is _________ between cluster variance.

71. Efficiency of cluster sampling _________ as the cluster size decreases.

72. When an investigator selects firstly big size clusters and then smaller size clusters from bigger clusters and so on, the sampling method is known as _________ .

73. The two-stage sampling is better than the single-stage sampling only if the elementary units in the same unit are _________.

74. In inverse sampling, the sample size is _________.

75. If p is the estimated proportion of units having a desired attribute in inverse sampling and m, the number of units possessing it out of n units drawn in the sample, then p = _________ .

76. In inverse sampling, the proportion p of units having the desired attribute with n units drawn has variance equal to _________ .

77. If larger units have greater chance of being included in the sample and *vice-versa,* it is known as sampling with _________ .

78. Non-availability of information from the respondents is termed as the problem of _________ .

79. Sampling is _________ in all kinds of studies.

80. Sampling studies give good result if a sample is a _________ of the population.

81. For a homogeneous population, simple random sampling is _________ than stratified random sampling.

82. Systematic sample _________ be said to give more reliable results than a random sample.

83. Systematic sample _________ be said to give less reliable results as compared to a simple random sample.

84. It _________ be said that the sample mean is always more or less than population mean.

85. The population mean _________ with increase or decrease of sample size.

86. An infinite population has variance 100 and mean 96. If a random sample of 4 units is selected, the standard deviation of the sampling distribution of mean is _________ .

87. The population mean is a _________ value.

88. Precision of estimates _________ by proper stratification.

89. Sampling error may arise due to _________ selection of sample.

90. Sampling error is caused by _________ methods of analysis of data.

91. If all the units selected in the sample are not covered, it is a problem of _________.

92. Non-sampling error arise due to _________ of data.

93. Errors committed in presentation of data are categorised as _________ errors.

94. If estimates are close to their respective population parameters, the estimates are called _________ .

95. Cluster sampling ordinarily leads to the _________ of precision.

96. Cluster sampling helps to _________ cost of the survey.

97. Larger the cluster size, _________ efficient it is relative to the element as the sampling unit.

98. Two stage sampling is _________ efficient as compared to single stage sampling.

99. A sampling procedure, in which the units are selected with chance of selection in proportion to some measure of their size, is known as _________ sampling.

100. Under *pps* selection, a unit has _________ chance of being included in the sample than a unit smaller to it.

101. Estimates from random samples possess _________ properties.

102. A random sample saves the labour of conducting _________ sampling trials.

103. If a random sample of adequate size truly represents the population, then it is said to follow the principle of _________ .

104. The principle of optimisation makes one to attain a desired level of efficiency at _________ cost.

105. A sampling method resulting into reliable estimates for parameters is said to follow the principle of _________ .

106. The index of precision of an estimator is indicated by its _________ .

107. Attaining maximum efficiency in estimating for a fixed cost is a part of principle of _________.

108. As the sample size increases, the conclusions based on sample values tend to be more_________ and _________ .

109. The reciprocal of standard error is an index of _________ of an estimator.

110. The increase in sample size leading to reliability and accuracy of estimates is governed by the principle of _________ .

SECTION C

Multiple Choice Questions

Select the correct alternative out of given ones:

1. A sample consists of:
   (*a*) all units of the population
   (*b*) 50 per cent units of the population
   (*c*) 5 per cent units of the population
   (*d*) any fraction of the population
2. Sampling is inevitable in the situation(s):
   (*a*) blood test of a person
   (*b*) when the population is infinite
   (*c*) testing of life of dry battery cells
   (*d*) all of the above
3. The number of possible samples of size n out of N population units without replacement is:
   (*a*) $\binom{N}{n}$
   (*b*) $(N)_n$
   (*c*) n^2
   (*d*) $n\,!$
4. The number of possible samples of size n from a population of N units with replacement is:
   (*a*) N^2
   (*b*) n^2
   (*c*) ∞
   (*d*) $N\,!$
5. The number of all possible samples of size two from a population of 4 units as:
   (*a*) 2
   (*b*) 4
   (*c*) 8
   (*d*) 12
6. Probability of drawing a unit at each selection remains same in:
   (*a*) srswor
   (*b*) srswr
   (*c*) both (*a*) and (*b*)
   (*d*) none of (*a*) and (*b*)
7. Probability of selection varies at each subsequent draw in:
   (*a*) sampling without replacement
   (*b*) sampling with replacement
   (*c*) both (*a*) and (*b*)
   (*d*) neither (*a*) nor (*b*)
8. An unordered sample of size n can occur in:
   (*a*) n ways
   (*b*) $n\,!$ ways
   (*c*) one way
   (*d*) n^2 ways
9. Probability of any one sample of size n being drawn out of N units is:
   (*a*) $1/N$
   (*b*) n/N
   (*c*) $1/n\,!$
   (*d*) $1/\binom{N}{n}$
10. Probability of including a specified unit in a sample of size n selected out of N units is:
    (*a*) $1/n$
    (*b*) $1/N$
    (*c*) n/N
    (*d*) $\frac{N}{n}$
11. A selection procedure of a sample having no involvement of probability is known as:
    (*a*) purposive sampling
    (*b*) judgement sampling
    (*c*) subjective sampling
    (*d*) all of the above
12. When an investigator wants a sample containing m units which possess a rare attribute, the appropriate sampling procedure is:
    (*a*) srswor
    (*b*) stratified sampling
    (*c*) inverse sampling
    (*d*) all of the above

13. If larger units have greater probability of their inclusion in the sample, it is known as:
    (*a*) selection with replacement
    (*b*) selection with probability proportional to size
    (*c*) selection with constant probability
    (*d*) probability selection
14. Simple random sample can be drawn with the help of:
    (*a*) random number tables
    (*b*) chit method
    (*c*) roulette wheel
    (*d*) all of the above
15. Sampling frame is a term used for:
    (*a*) a list of random numbers
    (*b*) a list of voters
    (*c*) a list of sampling units of a population
    (*d*) none of the above
16. In simple random sampling with replacement, the same sampling unit may be included in the sample:
    (*a*) only once
    (*b*) only twice
    (*c*) more than once
    (*d*) none of the above
17. A population consisting of all the items which are physically present is called:
    (*a*) hypothetical population
    (*b*) real population
    (*c*) infinite population
    (*d*) none of the above
18. A population consisting of the results of the conceptually repeated trials is known as:
    (*a*) hypothetical population
    (*b*) finite population
    (*c*) infinite population
    (*d*) real population
19. If the items are destroyed under investigation, we have to go for:
    (*a*) complete enumeration
    (*b*) sampling studies
    (*c*) both (*a*) and (*b*)
    (*d*) neither (*a*) nor (*b*)
20. The discrepancies between sample estimate and population parameter is termed as:
    (*a*) human error
    (*b*) formula error
    (*c*) non-sampling error
    (*d*) sampling error
21. The errors in a survey other than sampling errors are called
    (*a*) formula errors
    (*b*) planning error
    (*c*) non-sampling error
    (*d*) none of the above
22. A function of variates for estimating a parameter is called:
    (*a*) an estimate
    (*b*) an estimator
    (*c*) a frame
    (*d*) a statistic
23. An estimator can possess:
    (*a*) a fixed value
    (*b*) any value
    (*c*) both (*a*) and (*b*)
    (*d*) neither (*a*) nor (*b*)
24. An estimate based on a fixed set of values of a sample always possess:
    (*a*) a single value
    (*b*) any value
    (*c*) a value equal to one
    (*d*) all of the above
25. Students-*t* is categorised as:
    (*a*) an estimate
    (*b*) an estimator
    (*c*) a statistic
    (*d*) none of the above
26. If each and every unit of a population has equal chance of being included in the sample, it is known as:
    (*a*) restricted sampling
    (*b*) purposive sampling
    (*c*) subjective sampling
    (*d*) unrestricted sampling
27. The most important factor in determining the size of a sample is:
    (*a*) the availability of resources

(*b*) purpose of the survey

(*c*) heterogeneity of population

(*d*) none of the above

28. If d is the difference to be detected, u_R the value of the statistic at reliability level R and s the S.D., the formula for the sample size n is:

(*a*) $n = \frac{U_{R^s}}{d^2}$

(*b*) $n = \left(\frac{U_{R^s}}{d}\right)^2$

(*c*) $n = \frac{U^2_{R^s}}{d^2}$

(*d*) $n = \frac{U_{R^{s^2}}}{d^2}$

29. Having sample observations $x_1, x_2, \ldots, x_n$, the formula for variance is:

(*a*) $s^2 = \frac{1}{n-1}\sum (x_i - \bar{x})^2$

(*b*) $s^2 = \frac{1}{n-1} n\bar{x}^2 \left(\sum x_i^2 - \frac{(\Sigma x_i)^2}{n}\right)$

(*c*) $s^2 = \frac{1}{n-1}\left(\sum x_i^2 - n\bar{x}^2\right)$

(*d*) all of the above

30. If the observations recorded on five sampled items are 3, 4, 5, 6, 7 the sample variance is:

(*a*) 1

(*b*) 0

(*c*) 2

(*d*) 2.5

31. If all observations in a set of observations are same, the variance of the set of values is:

(*a*) zero

(*b*) one

(*c*) infinity

(*d*) not possible to calculate

32. A sample of size n is drawn from a dichotomous population. If the sample has proportion p of items of category I and proportion q of category II, then the variance of the proportion p is:

(*a*) $s_p^2 = \frac{1}{n-1} pq$

(*b*) $s_p^2 = \frac{1}{n} pq$

(*c*) $s_p^2 = \frac{n}{n-1} pq$

(*d*) $s_p^2 = \frac{1}{n} p^2 q$

33. If a sample $x_1, x_2, \ldots, x_n$ from a dichotomous population has n_1 items of type C_1 with proportion p and n_2 items of type C_2 with proportion q. Also,

$$x_i = 1 \text{ if } x_i \in C_1$$
$$x_i = 0 \text{ if } x_i \in C_2$$

then which of given four relations does not hold good?

(*a*) $\bar{x} = p$

(*b*) $q = 1 - p$

(*c*) $q = n_2/n$

(*d*) $p = \frac{n}{n_1}$

34. Formula for standard error of sample mean $\bar{x}$ based on sample of size n having variances s^2, when population consisted of N items, is:

(*a*) s/n

(*b*) $s/\sqrt{n-1}$

(*c*) $s/\sqrt{N-1}$

(*d*) $s/\sqrt{n}$

35. Which of the following statement is true?

(*a*) More the standard error, better it is

(*b*) Less the standard error, better it is

(*c*) Standard error is always zero

(*d*) Standard error is always unity

36. Which of the following statement is not true?
(*a*) Standard error cannot be zero
(*b*) Standard error cannot be 1
(*c*) Standard error can be negative
(*d*) All of the above

37. If the sample values are 1, 3, 5, 7, 9 the standard error of sample mean is:
(*a*) S.E = $\sqrt{2}$
(*b*) S.E = $1/\sqrt{2}$
(*c*) S.E = 2.0
(*d*) S.E = 1/2

38. If we have a sample of size n from a population of N units, the finite population correction is:
(*a*) $\frac{N-1}{N}$
(*b*) $\frac{n-1}{N}$
(*c*) $\frac{N-n}{N}$
(*d*) $\frac{N-n}{n}$

39. If n units are selected in a sample from N population units, the sampling fraction is given as:
(*a*) $\frac{N}{n}$
(*b*) $1/N$
(*c*) $1/n$
(*d*) n/N

40. As a normal practice, sampling fraction is considered to be negligible if it is:
(*a*) less than 10 per cent
(*b*) less than or equal to 5 per cent
(*c*) more than 5 per cent
(*d*) more than 10 per cent

41. Stratified sampling comes under the category of:
(*a*) unrestricted sampling
(*b*) subjective sampling
(*c*) purposive sampling
(*d*) restricted sampling

42. Which of the following statements does not hold good in case of stratified sampling?
(*a*) Stratified sampling is convenient
(*b*) Stratified sampling is always good
(*c*) Enables to gather information about different stratum separately
(*d*) Reduces error for fixed cost

43. Which one problem out of the four is not related to stratified sampling?
(*a*) Fixing the criterion for stratification
(*b*) Fixing the number of strata
(*c*) Fixing the sample size
(*d*) Fixing the points of demarcation between strata

44. Regarding the number of strata, which statement is true?
(*a*) Lesser the number of strata, better it is
(*b*) More the number of strata, poorer it is
(*c*) More the number of strata, better it is
(*d*) Not more than ten items should be there in a stratum

45. Under equal allocation in stratified sampling, the sample from each stratum is:
(*a*) proportional to stratum size
(*b*) of same size from each stratum
(*c*) in proportion to the per unit cost of survey of the stratum
(*d*) all of the above

46. Under proportional allocation, the size of the sample from each stratum depends on:
(*a*) total sample size
(*b*) size of the stratum
(*c*) population size
(*d*) all of the above

47. Under proportional allocation one gets:
(*a*) an optimum sample
(*b*) a self-weighing sample
(*c*) both (*a*) and (*b*)
(*d*) neither (*a*) nor (*b*)

48. Formula for optimum sample size was derived by whom and in which year?
(*a*) Tschuprow in 1923

(*b*) J. Neyman in 1934

(*c*) Both (*a*) and (*b*)

(*d*) None of (*a*) and (*b*)

49. How many types of optimum allocation are in common use?

(*a*) One

(*b*) Two

(*c*) Three

(*d*) Four

50. With usual notations, the formula for optimum sample size n_j for the jth stratum ($j = 1, 2, \ldots, k$) for fixed total sample size n is:

(*a*) $n_j = nW_jS_j/(\Sigma_j W_j S_j^2)$

(*b*) $n_j = W_jS_j/(\Sigma_j S_j)$

(*c*) $n_j = nW_jS_j^2/(\Sigma_j W_j S_j^2)$

(*d*) $n_j = n_jW_jS_j/(\Sigma_j W_j S_j)$

51. If C, C_0 and C_j are the total, overhead and cost of survey per unit in the jth stratum resp., the optimum sample size for j^{th} stratum ($j = 1, 2, \ldots, k$) with usual notations which minimises the variance of stratified sample mean is:

(*a*) $n_j = n\dfrac{W_j S_j/\sqrt{C_j}}{\Sigma_j W_j S_j/\sqrt{C_j}}$

(*b*) $n_j = n\dfrac{W_j S_j/\sqrt{C_j}}{\Sigma_j W_j S_j/C_j}$

(*c*) $n_j = n\dfrac{W_j S_j/\sqrt{C_j}}{\Sigma_j W_j S_j/C_j}$

(*d*) $n_j = n\dfrac{W_j S_j C_j}{\Sigma_j W_j S_j C_j}$

52. To have minimum $V(\bar{x}_{st})$, one has to choose a large sample n_j using cost per unit of survey provided:

(*a*) n is fixed, S_j is small and C_j is small.

(*b*) n is small, S_j is small and C_j is large.

(*c*) n is large, S_j is large and C_j is large.

(*d*) n is large, S_j is small and C_j is small.

53. If the cost C of the survey is fixed and $C_1 = C - C_0$ where C_0 is overhead cost, optimum sample size for j^{th} stratum can be obtained by the formula:

(*a*) $n_{opt} = C_1\dfrac{\Sigma_j W_j S_j/\sqrt{C_j}}{\Sigma_j W_j S_j/C_j}$

(*b*) $n_{opt} = C_1\dfrac{\Sigma_j W_j S_j/\sqrt{C_j}}{\Sigma_j W_j S_j/\sqrt{C_j}}$

(*c*) $n_{opt} = C_1\dfrac{\Sigma_j W_j S_j\sqrt{C_j}}{\Sigma_j W_j S_j/\sqrt{C_j}}$

(*d*) $n_{opt} = C_1\dfrac{\Sigma_j W_j S_j C_j}{\Sigma_j (W_j S_j/C_j)}$

54. Formula for optimum sample size for j^{th} stratum with usual notations when the $V(\bar{x}_{st})$ is fixed and equal to V_0 is:

(*a*) $n_j = \dfrac{W_j S_j}{C_j}\dfrac{\Sigma_j W_j S_j\sqrt{C_j}}{V_0 + \Sigma_j W_j S_j^2}$

(*b*) $n_j = \dfrac{(W_j S_j/\sqrt{C_j})(\Sigma_j W_j S_j C_j)}{V_0 + \frac{1}{N}\Sigma_j W_j S_j}$

(*c*) $n_j = \Sigma_j \dfrac{W_j S_j}{\sqrt{C_j}}\dfrac{\Sigma_j W_j S_j\sqrt{C_j}}{V_0 + \frac{1}{N}\Sigma_j W_j S_j^2}$

(*d*) none of the above

55. With usual notations, the estimate of the variance of the stratified sample mean $\bar{x}_{st}$ is:

(*a*) $v(\bar{x}_{st}) = \sum_{j=1}^{k} W_j\left(1 - \dfrac{n_j}{N_j}\right)\dfrac{s_j^2}{n_j}$

(b) $v(\bar{x}_{st}) = \sum_{j=1}^{k} W_j^2 \left(\frac{N_j - n_j}{N_j}\right) \frac{s_j^2}{n_j}$

(c) $v(\bar{x}_{st}) = \frac{1}{N} \sum_{j=1}^{k} W_j \left(\frac{N_j - n_j}{N_j}\right) s_j^2$.

(d) any of the above

56. With usual notations, the estimate of the variance of $\bar{x}_{st}$ under proportional allocation is:

(a) $v(\bar{x}_{st}) = \frac{N-n}{Nn} \sum_{j=1}^{k} W_j s_j^2$

(b) $v(\bar{x}_{st}) = \left(1 - \frac{n}{N}\right) \sum_{j=1}^{k} \frac{W_j^2 s_j^2}{n_j}$

(c) $v(\bar{x}_{st}) = \left(1 - \frac{n}{N}\right) \sum_{j=1}^{k} \frac{W_j s_j}{n}$

(d) $v(\bar{x}_{st}) = \left(1 - \frac{n}{N}\right) \sum_{j=1}^{k} \frac{W_j s_j}{n_j}$

57. With usual notation, the variance of the mean $\bar{x}_{st}$ of stratified sample under Neyman allocation is:

(a) $V_{Ney}(\bar{x}_{st}) = \frac{1}{n}\left(\sum_j W_j S_j \sqrt{C_j}\right) \left(\sum_j \frac{W_j C_j}{C_j}\right) - \frac{1}{N} \sum_j W_j S_j^2$

(b) $V_{Ney}(\bar{x}_{st}) = \frac{1}{n}\left(\sum_j \frac{W_j S_j}{\sqrt{C_j}}\right)^2 - \frac{1}{N} \sum_j W_j S_j^2$

(c) $V_{Ney}(\bar{x}_{st}) = \frac{1}{n}\left(\sum_j W_j S_j \sqrt{C_j}\right)^2$

(d) $V_{Ney}(\bar{x}_{st}) = \frac{1}{n}\left(\sum_j W_j S_j \sqrt{C_j}\right) \left(\sum_j \frac{W_j S_j}{\sqrt{C_j}}\right) - \frac{1}{N} \sum_j W_j S_j^2$

58. If the cost per unit of survey is same for all units, then the formula for $V(\bar{x}_{st})$ under Neyman allocation is:

(a) $V_{Ney}(\bar{x}_{st}) = \frac{1}{n}(\Sigma W_j S_j)^2 - \frac{1}{N} \sum_j W_j S_j^2$

(b) $V_{Ney}(\bar{x}_{st}) = \frac{1}{N}\left(\sum_j W_j S_j^2\right) - \frac{1}{n} \sum_j W_j S_j$

(c) $V_{Ney}(\bar{x}_{st}) = \frac{1}{N}\left(\sum_j W_j S_j^2\right) - \frac{1}{n} \sum_j W_j S_j^2$

(d) $V_{Ney}(\bar{x}_{st}) = \frac{1}{n}\left[\left(\sum_j W_j S_j\right)^2 - \sum_j W_i S_j^2\right]$

59. Variance of $\bar{x}_{st}$ under random sampling, proportional allocation and optimum allocation hold the correct inequality as:

(a) $V_{ran}(\bar{x}_{st}) \le V_{prop}(\bar{x}_{st}) \le V_{opt}(\bar{x}_{st})$

(b) $V_{ran}(\bar{x}_{st}) \ge V_{opt}(\bar{x}_{st}) \ge V_{opt}(\bar{x}_{st})$

(c) $V_{ran}(\bar{x}_{st}) \ge V_{prop}(\bar{x}_{st}) \ge V_{opt}(\bar{x}_{st})$

(d) all of the above

60. Which of the following statement is correct?

(a) Two-way stratification can also be used

(b) Two-way stratification is usually better than one-way stratification

(c) Two-way stratification is not much used

(d) All of the above

61. If a sample is drawn from each stratum minimising the probabilities of non-preferred samples, it is known as:
(*a*) selection with proportional allocation
(*b*) controlled selection
(*c*) haphazard selection
(*d*) none of the above

62. Systematic sampling means:
(*a*) selection of n contiguous units
(*b*) selection of n units situated at equal distances
(*c*) selection of n largest units
(*d*) selection of n middle units in a sequence

63. If the number of population units N is an integral multiple of sampling size n, the systematic sampling is called:
(*a*) linear systematic sampling
(*b*) circular systematic sampling
(*c*) random systematic sampling
(*d*) all of the above

64. Circular systematic sampling is used when:
(*a*) N is a multiple of n
(*b*) N is a whole number
(*c*) N is not divisible by n
(*d*) none of the above

65. Linear and circular systematic sampling methods are equivalent if and only if
(*a*) N is a whole number
(*b*) n is a whole number
(*c*) $N = n$
(*d*) none of the above

66. Which of the following advantage of systematic sampling you approve?
(*a*) Easy selection of sample
(*b*) Economical
(*c*) Spread of sample over the whole population
(*d*) All of the above

67. Selected units of a systematic sample are:
(*a*) not easily locateable
(*b*) easily locateable
(*c*) not representing the whole population
(*d*) all of the above

68. In what situation(s) a systematic sample is more preferred than others?
(*a*) When the data are on cards
(*b*) When the items are in row
(*c*) When the items situated at equal distances are uncorrelated
(*d*) All of the above

69. A systematic sample does not yield good results if:
(*a*) variation in units is periodic
(*b*) units at regular intervals are correlated
(*c*) both (*a*) and (*b*)
(*d*) none of (*a*) and (*b*)

70. Greatest drawback of systematic sampling is that:
(*a*) one requires a large sample
(*b*) data are not easily accessible
(*c*) no single reliable formula for standard error of mean is available
(*d*) none of the above

71. Which of the following statement is correct?
(*a*) Systematic sample is superior than stratified random sample
(*b*) Simple random sample is inferior than systematic sample
(*c*) Stratified random sample is better than systematic sample
(*d*) None of the above

72. Double sampling is also known as:
(*a*) two-stage sampling
(*b*) two-phase sampling
(*c*) two-directional sampling
(*d*) all the above

73. Double sampling has its utility in:
(*a*) stratified sampling
(*b*) ratio method of estimation
(*c*) regression method of estimation
(*d*) all of the above

74. In which of the following situation(s) cluster sampling is appropriate?
(*a*) When the units are situated for apart
(*b*) When sampling frame is not available
(*c*) When all the elementary units are not easily identifiable.
(*d*) All of the above

75. What precaution(s) make(s) cluster sampling more efficient?

(*a*) By taking clusters of small size

(*b*) Choosing clusters having largest within variation

(*c*) Choosing clusters having least variation between clusters

(*d*) All of the above

76. Which of the following basis distinguishes cluster sampling from stratified sampling?

(*a*) Clusters are preferably heterogeneous whereas strata are taken as homogeneous as possible.

(*b*) A sample is always drawn from each stratum whereas no sample of elementary units is drawn from clusters.

(*c*) Small size clusters are better whereas there is no such restriction for stratum size

(*d*) All of the above

77. What distinction exists between cluster sampling and two stage sampling?

(*a*) In cluster sampling one studies each unit of the selected cluster whereas in two-stage sampling one selects a sample of elementary units from each cluster

(*b*) In two-stage sampling one draws a sample in two stages whereas in cluster sampling only a sample of clusters is selected

(*c*) Both (*a*) and (*b*)

(*d*) Neither (*a*) nor (*b*)

78. In what situation two-stage sampling is better than single-stage sampling?

(*a*) When the elements in the same stage are positively correlated

(*b*) When the elements in the same stage are negatively correlated

(*c*) When the elements in the same stage are uncorrelated

(*d*) None of the above

79. Which of the following statements is true?

(*a*) All sampling procedures involve sampling with constant probability

(*b*) There exists sampling procedure in which the units are selected with varying probability

(*c*) Every selection procedure of a sample involves probability

(*d*) All of the above

80. Non-response in surveys mean:

(*a*) non-availability of respondents

(*b*) non-return of questionnaire by the respondents

(*c*) refusal to give information by the respondents

(*d*) all of the above

81. Problem of non-response:

(*a*) has no solution

(*b*) can be solved

(*c*) is meaningless

(*d*) none of the above

82. Which of the following statements is true?

(*a*) Population mean increases with the increase in sample size

(*b*) Population mean decreases with the increase in sample size

(*c*) Population mean decreases with the decrease in sample size

(*d*) Population mean is a constant value

83. Which of the following statements does not hold good?

(*a*) An increase in sample size reduces the standard error

(*b*) An increase in sample size decreases the sampling error

(*c*) Decrease in sample size results in the reduction of population standard deviation

(*d*) The precision of an estimate depends on sample size

84. A sample of 25 units from an infinite population with standard deviation 10 results into a total score of 450. The mean of the sampling distribution is:

(*a*) 45

(*b*) 50

(*c*) 18

(*d*) 1.8

85. If population variance of an infinite population is σ^2 and a sample of n items is selected from this population, the standard error of sample mean is equal to:

(a) σ^2/n

(b) σ/n

(c) $\sigma/\sqrt{n}$

(d) σ

86. A sample of 16 items from an infinite population having S.D. = 4, yielded total scores as 160. The standard error of sampling distribution of mean is:

(a) 1

(b) 10

(c) 40

(d) none of the above

87. A population was divided into clusters and it was found that within cluster variation was less than the variation between clusters. If a sample of units was selected from each cluster, the sampling procedure used was:

(a) multistage sampling

(b) stratified sampling

(c) cluster sampling

(d) systematic sampling

88. A population is perfectly homogeneous in respect of a characteristic. What size of sample would you prefer?

(a) A large sample

(b) A small sample

(c) A single item

(d) No item

89. The selected items of a sample resulted into same values pertaining to a character. The variance of the sample is:

(a) 1

(b) 0

(c) ∞

(d) not determinable

90. A population is divided into clusters and it has been found that all items within a cluster are alike. Which of the following sampling procedures would you adopt?

(a) Simple random sampling

(b) Cluster sampling

(c) Systematic sampling

(d) Stratified sampling

91. A population of N units is divided into K strata. A sample of size n is to be selected. Let N_j the jth stratum size and n_j the sample size from it ($j = 1, 2, ..., k$). Then formula for selection of n_j under proportional allocation is:

(a) $n_j = \frac{N}{n}$

(b) $n_j = \frac{N}{N_j}$

(c) $\frac{n_j}{N_j} = \frac{n}{N}$

(d) $n_j N_j = Nn$

92. If an investigator selects districts from a state, Panchayat samities from districts and farmers from Panchayat samities, then such a sampling procedure is known as:

(a) two-stage sampling

(b) three-stage sampling

(c) cluster sampling

(d) stratified sampling

93. In sampling with probability proportional to size, the units are selected with probability in proportion to:

(a) the size of the unit

(b) the size of the sample

(c) the size of the population

(d) none of the above

94. In case of inverse sampling, the proportion 'p' of m units of interest contained in a sample of n units is:

(a) m/n

(b) $(m - 1)/n$

(c) $(m - 1)/(n + 1)$

(d) $(m - 1)/(n - 1)$

95. If the respondents do not supply the required information, this problem is known as:
(*a*) the problem of the non-response
(*b*) non-sampling error
(*c*) both (*a*) and (*b*)
(*d*) none of (*a*) and (*b*)

96. Supposing that, in cluster sampling s_w^2 represents the variance within the clusters and s_b^2 between clusters. What is the relation between s_w^2 and s_b^2?
(*a*) $s_w^2 = s_b^2$
(*b*) $s_w^2 \geq s_b^2$
(*c*) $s_w^2 \leq s_b^2$
(*d*) None of the above

97. Two stage sampling design is more efficient than single stage sampling if the correlation between units in the first stage is:
(*a*) negative
(*b*) positive
(*c*) zero
(*d*) none of the above

98. What sampling design is most appropriate for cluster sampling?
(*a*) Simple random sampling without replacement
(*b*) Simple random sampling with replacement
(*c*) Stratified random sampling
(*d*) Quota sampling

99. Circular systematic sampling was first used by:
(*a*) W.G. Cochran
(*b*) M.H. Hansen
(*c*) D.B. Lahiri
(*d*) P.C. Mahalanobis

100. A population consisting of all real numbers is an example of:
(*a*) an infinite population
(*b*) a finite population
(*c*) an imaginary population
(*d*) none of the above

101. A random sample of a reasonably large size possessing almost all properties of the population confirms to the principle of:
(*a*) inertia of large numbers
(*b*) statistical regularity
(*c*) optimisation
(*d*) Newton's first law of inertia

102. The errors emerging out of faulty planning of surveys are categorised as:
(*a*) non-sampling errors
(*b*) non-response errors
(*c*) sampling errors
(*d*) absolute error.

103. If there is a certain number of very high values in a sample, then it is preferable to calculate:
(*a*) standard deviation
(*b*) standard error
(*c*) variance
(*d*) all of the above

104. Principle of optimisation in sampling methods is related to:
(*a*) cost and efficiency of sampling designs
(*b*) validity of estimates
(*c*) asymptotic properties of estimates
(*d*) all of the above

105. Which of the following sampling designs will be categorised as non-probability sampling?
(*a*) Haphazard sampling
(*b*) Convenience sampling
(*c*) Judgement sampling
(*d*) All of the above

106. The discrepancy between estimates and population parameters is known as:
(*a*) human error
(*b*) enumeration error
(*c*) sampling error
(*d*) formula error

107. To meet requirement of the principle of validity of sampling methods, one must adopt:
(*a*) purposive sampling
(*b*) restricted sampling
(*c*) probability sampling
(*d*) any type of sampling.

108. There are more chances of non-sampling errors than sampling errors in case of:
(*a*) studies of large samples
(*b*) complete enumeration
(*c*) inefficient investigators
(*d*) all of the above

109. Increase in reliability and accuracy of results from a sampling study with the increase in sample size is known as the principle of:
(*a*) optimisation
(*b*) statistical regularity
(*c*) law of increasing returns
(*d*) inertia of large numbers

110. Sampling error can be reduced by:
(*a*) choosing a proper probability sampling
(*b*) selecting a sample of adequate size
(*c*) using a suitable formula for estimation
(*d*) all the above

111. The magnitude of the standard error of an estimate is an index of its:
(*a*) accuracy
(*b*) precision
(*c*) efficiency
(*d*) all of the above

112. For estimating the population proportion P in a class of a population having N units, the variance of the estimator p of P based on sample for size n is:
(*a*) $\frac{N}{N-1} \cdot \frac{PQ}{n}$
(*b*) $\frac{N}{N-1} \cdot \frac{PQ}{N}$
(*c*) $\frac{N-n}{N-1} \cdot \frac{PQ}{n}$
(*d*) $\frac{N-1}{N-n} \cdot \frac{PQ}{n}$

113. For estimating the population mean T, let T_1 be the sample mean under srswor and T_2 under srswr. Then:
(*a*) $\text{var}(T_1) = \text{var}(T_2)$
(*b*) $\text{var}(T_1) = 1/\text{var}(T_2)$
(*c*) $\text{var}(T_1) < \text{var}(T_2)$
(*d*) $\text{var}(T_1) \leq \text{var}(T_2)$

114. Let the standard error of an estimator T under srswor is more than the standard error of T under stratified randomly sampling. Then T under stratified sampling as compared to T under srswor is:
(*a*) more reliable
(*b*) less reliable
(*c*) equally reliable
(*d*) not comparable

115. Stratified sampling belongs to the category of:
(*a*) judgement sampling
(*b*) subjective sampling
(*c*) controlled sampling
(*d*) non-random sampling

ANSWERS

Section B

1. necessary or unavoidable **2.** real **3.** hypothetical **4.** finite **5.** infinite **6.** complete enumeration or census **7.** non-sampling error **8.** sampling error **9.** parameter **10.** estimator **11.** estimate **12.** standard error **13.** $s/\sqrt{n}$ **14.** sampling frame **15.** universe **16.** $\binom{N}{n}$ **17.** $1/\binom{N}{n}$ **18.** infinite **19.** more than once **20.** $\Sigma_i x_i/n$ **21.** $\sum_i (x_i - \bar{x})^2/(n-1)$ **22.** stratified sampling **23.** heterogeneous **24.** character or attribute **25.** allocation **26.** proportional allocation **27.** restricted **28.** larger **29.** $\sqrt{\left(\frac{N-n}{N}\right)\frac{S^2}{n}}$ **30.** finite population correction **31.** sampling fraction **32.** purposive or judgement **33.** seldom **34.** large

35. differences **36.** $\frac{n}{n-1}pq$ **37.** 5 per cent or less **38.** optimum **39.** Neyman **40.** optimum **41.** self-weighing **42.** $W_j S_j$ **43.** $N_j S_j / \sqrt{C_j}$ **44.** Neyman **45.** srswor **46.** $V_{\text{ran}}(\bar{x}_{st})$ **47.** stratified sampling **48.** homogeneous **49.** stratified random sampling **50.** complete enumeration **51.** complete enumeration **52.** equal allocation **53.** two way stratification **54.** more **55.** controlled selection **56.** systematic sampling **57.** contiguous **58.** simple; cheap **59.** no single **60.** linear **61.** circular **62.** double **63.** two phase **64.** stratified **65.** ratio; regression **66.** sampling frame **67.** far apart **68.** primary units **69.** elementary **70.** $\le$ **71.** increases **72.** multistage sampling **73.** negatively correlated **74.** not fixed or a random variable **75.** $(m-1)/(n-1)$ **76.** $\frac{p(1-p)}{n-2}\left(1-\frac{n-1}{N}\right)$ **77.** Probability proportional to size **78.** non-response **79.** not compulsory **80.** true representative **81.** better **82.** cannot **83.** can **84.** cannot **85.** remains same **86.** 5 **87.** fixed **88.** increases **89.** improper **90.** faulty **91.** non-response **92.** inadequacy **93.** non-sampling **94.** reliable **95.** loss **96.** reduce **97.** less **98.** less **99.** *pps* **100.** greater **101.** desirable **102.** empirical **103.** statistical regularity **104.** minimum **105.** validity **106.** standard error **107.** optimization **108.** accurate; reliable **109.** precision **110.** inertia of large numbers.

Section C

1. (*d*)	**2.** (*d*)	**3.** (*a*)	**4.** (*c*)	**5.** (*d*)
6. (*b*)	**7.** (*a*)	**8.** (*b*)	**9.** (*d*)	**10.** (*b*)
11. (*d*)	**12.** (*c*)	**13.** (*b*)	**14.** (*d*)	**15.** (*c*)
16. (*c*)	**17.** (*b*)	**18.** (*a*)	**19.** (*b*)	**20.** (*d*)
21. (*c*)	**22.** (*b*)	**23.** (*b*)	**24.** (*a*)	**25.** (*c*)
26. (*d*)	**27.** (*c*)	**28.** (*b*)	**29.** (*d*)	**30.** (*d*)
31. (*a*)	**32.** (*c*)	**33.** (*d*)	**34.** (*d*)	**35.** (*b*)
36. (*d*)	**37.** (*a*)	**38.** (*c*)	**39.** (*d*)	**40.** (*b*)
41. (*d*)	**42.** (*b*)	**43.** (*c*)	**44.** (*c*)	**45.** (*b*)
46. (*d*)	**47.** (*b*)	**48.** (*c*)	**49.** (*c*)	**50.** (*d*)
51. (*a*)	**52.** (*d*)	**53.** (*b*)	**54.** (*c*)	**55.** (*b*)
56. (*a*)	**57.** (*d*)	**58.** (*a*)	**59.** (*c*)	**60.** (*d*)
61. (*b*)	**62.** (*b*)	**63.** (*a*)	**64.** (*c*)	**65.** (*d*)
66. (*d*)	**67.** (*b*)	**68.** (*d*)	**69.** (*c*)	**70.** (*c*)
71. (*d*)	**72.** (*b*)	**73.** (*d*)	**74.** (*d*)	**75.** (*d*)
76. (*d*)	**77.** (*c*)	**78.** (*b*)	**79.** (*b*)	**80.** (*d*)
81. (*b*)	**82.** (*d*)	**83.** (*c*)	**84.** (*c*)	**85.** (*c*)
86. (*a*)	**87.** (*b*)	**88.** (*c*)	**89.** (*b*)	**90.** (*d*)
91. (*c*)	**92.** (*b*)	**93.** (*a*)	**94.** (*d*)	**95.** (*a*)
96. (*c*)	**97.** (*b*)	**98.** (*a*)	**99.** (*c*)	**100.** (*a*)
101. (*b*)	**102.** (*a*)	**103.** (*b*)	**104.** (*a*)	**105.** (*d*)
106. (*c*)	**107.** (*c*)	**108.** (*d*)	**109.** (*d*)	**110.** (*d*)
111. (*b*)	**112.** (*c*)	**113.** (*d*)	**114.** (*a*)	**115.** (*c*)

SUGGESTED READING

1. Agarwal, B.L., *Basic Statistics,* New Age International Publishers, 8th edition, 2024.
2. Cochran, W.G., *Sampling Techniques,* Asia Publishing House, Bombay, 1959.
3. Des Raj, *Sampling Theory,* Tata McGraw-Hill Publishing Co., Bombay, 1968.
4. Hensen, M.H., Hurwitz, W.N. and Madow, W.G., *Sampling Survey, Methods and Theory,* Vols. I & II, John Wiley & Sons, New York, 1956.
5. Kelton, G., *Introduction to Survey Sampling,* Sage Publications, New Delhi, 1983.
6. Murthy, M.N., *Sampling Theory and Methods,* Statistical Publishing Society, Calcutta, 1967.
7. Namboodiri, N.K., *Survey Sampling and Measurements,* Academic Press, New York, 1978.
8. Sudman, S., *Applied Sampling,* Academic Press, New York, 1976.
9. Sukhatme, P.V., Sukhatme, B.V., Sukhatme, S. and Ashok, C., *Sampling Theory of Surveys with Applications,* Indian Society of Agricultural Statistics, New Delhi, 1984.
10. Wilburn, A.J., *Practical Statistical Sampling for Auditors,* Marcel Dekker, New York, 1984.

CHAPTER 10

Theory of Estimation

SECTION A

Short Essay Type Questions

Q. 1. *What do you understand by estimation?*

Ans. There are a few occasions when population is studied as a whole. As a matter of fact, generally a sample is drawn from the population and population constants are determined on the basis of sample values. *Population parameters* are usually those constants which occur in the probability density or mass function or the moments or some other constants of the population like median.

We know that various sampling procedures do exist and also there are many techniques to determine the value of population constants through sample values. *The constant determined through sample observations which stands for population parameter* θ *or a function* $\tau(\theta)$ *of* θ *is called an estimate.* So, in general, we adopt $\tau(\theta)$ though $\tau(\theta)$ in many cases is equal to θ.

The choice of a technique depends on the type of the estimator *vis-a-vis* estimate and the purpose of study. The goodness of an estimator is governed by certain properties. An estimator possessing the maximum properties will be considered as a good estimator.

In general an estimator T_n will be rated as good if it differs from $\tau(\theta)$ by a small quantity ε, *i.e.*, the sampling distribution of T_n has high degree of concentration about $\tau(\theta)$. At the same time T_n will be considered as best estimator if for any other estimator T'_n, the following inequality holds.

$$P\{| T_n - \tau(\theta) | < \varepsilon\} \geq P\{| T'_n - \tau(\theta) | < \varepsilon\}$$

for all θ.

But holding of this condition is not easily feasible. Hence, one has to look for other properties of the estimator.

So in estimation theory we are concerned with the properties of estimators and methods of estimation. The merits of an estimator are judged by the properties of the distribution of estimates obtained through estimators, *i.e.*, by the properties of the sampling distribution. Further, it is emphasised that estimation is possible only if there is a random sample.

Q. 2. *Differentiate between an estimator and an estimate.*

Ans. A known function $T = t(X_1, X_2, \ldots, X_n)$ of the observable variates of a random sample $X_1, X_2, \ldots, X_n$, whose values are used to obtain the estimate of a parameter θ or a function of θ, is called an estimator. An estimator is itself a random variable. If $x_1, x_2, \ldots, x_n$ are the values of the random sample $X_1, X_2, \ldots, X_n$, the value $t(x_1, x_2, \ldots, x_n)$ of the estimator T_n is known as an estimate of the parameter θ. For example $\frac{1}{n}\sum X_i$ (i = 1, 2, ..., n) is an estimator whereas $\bar{x} = \frac{1}{n}\sum x_i$ is an estimate.

Q. 3. *Throw light on the types of estimates.*

Ans. With the help of sample observations we find a value which is taken as a value of the parameter θ. This value is termed as *point estimate.* Single estimated value is known as point estimate or simply estimate.

Also, instead of estimating a single value of a parameter from sample values, a range t_1, t_2 of numbers, which constitute an interval, determined with the help of sample values and supposed to include the parameter θ with certain confidence level $\gamma = 1 - \alpha$ is known as confidence interval. t_1 and t_2 ($t_1 < t_2$) are called the lower and upper limits of the interval estimate.

Q. 4. *Name different properties of estimators.*

Ans. Different properties of estimators *vis-a-vis* estimates are as follows:

(*i*) Consistency

(*ii*) Unbiasedness

(*iii*) Mean-squared error

(*iv*) Best asymptotically normal estimator or BAN estimators

(*v*) Efficiency

(*vi*) Sufficiency

(*vii*) Completeness

(*viii*) Minimum Variance Unbiased estimators

(*ix*) Admissibility.

Q. 5. *Define and discuss consistency of estimators in brief.*

Ans. An estimator T_n calculated from n sample variates is said to be a consistent estimator of a parameter θ if for any individual small positive quantity ε and a small positive value η there exists some N such that the following inequality holds, the estimator T_n is said to be consistent, if

$$P[\{T_n - \tau(\theta)\} < \varepsilon] < 1 - \eta \text{ for } n > N$$

Here T_n converges in probability to τ(θ) or stochastically converging to τ θ. The above definition is known as *simple consistency.* In short, T_n is said to be a consistent estimator of τ(θ) if T_n converges to τ(θ) in probability, *i.e.*,

$$T_n \xrightarrow{P} \tau(\theta)$$

Consistency is a limiting property of estimators and it reveals the behaviour of an estimator T_n as $n \to \infty$. As a simple example, $\Sigma X_i/n$, $\Sigma X_i/(n-1)$, $\Sigma X_i/(n-2)$, ... are all consistent estimators of population mean and the selection of either of them on the basis of consistency is not possible. So one has to look for other properties of T_n.

Q. 6. *What is meant by unbiasedness of estimators?*

Ans. An estimator T_n is said to be an unbiased estimator of τ(θ) if the expected value of T_n is equal to

$$E(T_n) = \tau(\theta) \text{ for all } \theta.$$

If $E(T_n) \neq \tau(\theta)$, then $E(T_n) - \tau(\theta) =$ *bias*.

In short, an estimator is unbiased if the mean of the sampling distribution of T_n is equal to τ(θ).

Also the difference $E(T_n) - \tau(\theta)$ is called the bias of the estimator T_n. Bias will be positive, if $\tau(\theta) < E(T_n)$ and negative if $\tau(\theta) > E(T_n)$.

Q. 7. *Describe the role of mean-squared error in estimation theory.*

Ans. If there are more than one unbiased estimators, the problem arises which one to choose out of the class of unbiased estimators. Not only this, one aspires that the sampling variance as well as bias should be minimum. These problems are tackled with the help of mean-squared error (m.s.e.). The mean-squared error of an estimator T_n of τ(θ) is given as,

$$\begin{aligned} \text{m.s.e.} &= E[T_n - \tau(\theta)]^2 \\ &= E[E_\theta(T_n) - \tau(\theta) + T_n - E_\theta(T_n)]^2 \\ &= E[E_\theta(T_n) - \tau(\theta)]^2 + E[T_n - E_\theta(T_n)]^2 \end{aligned}$$

$$= E_\theta[(T_n) - \tau(\theta)]^2 + E[T_n - E_\theta(T_n)]^2$$
$$= (bias)^2 + \text{var}(T_n)$$

where $E_\theta(T_n) - \tau(\theta) = \text{bias}$

Mean squared error will be minimum if T_n is an unbiased estimator of $\tau(\theta)$, *i.e.*, $E_\theta(T_n) = \tau(\theta)$ and when var (T_n) is minimum. It is an impossible task to have an estimator with least mean squared error. Hence, it is our endeavour to search for an estimator with uniformly minimum variance among the class of unbiased estimators which we call uniformly minimum variance unbiased estimator (UMVUE).

By definition, an estimator T_n based on the random sample $X_1, X_2, \ldots, X_n$ is said to be UMVUE of $\tau(\theta)$ if $E_\theta(T_n) = \tau(\theta)$ and var $(T_n) \leq$ var (T_n^*) where T_n^* is any other unbiased estimator of $\tau(\theta)$.

Q. 8. *Define mean-squared error consistency.*

Ans. Suppose $T_1, T_2, \ldots, T_n$ is a sequence of estimators of $\tau(\theta)$ based on a sample X_1, X_2, X_n, *i.e.*, $T_n = t(X_1, X_2, X_n)$. The sequence of estimators $T_1, T_2, \ldots, T_n$ is said to be mean-squared error consistent estimator of $\tau(\theta)$ if and only if

$$\lim_{n\to\infty} E_\theta \{T_n - \tau(\theta)\}^2 = 0$$

for all θ in Θ. Mean-squared error consistency implies that the estimator T_n is unbiased as well as the variance of T_n approaches to zero as n tends to infinity.

Q. 9. *State Crammer-Rao inequality for lower bound of variance of an estimator.*

Ans. Suppose $X_1, X_2, \ldots, X_n$ is a random sample from $f(x, \theta)$ and $T_n = t(X_1, X_2, \ldots, X_n)$ is an estimator of $\tau(\theta)$ based on the random sample of size n. Crammer-Rao inequality states that under the regularity conditions.

(i) $\frac{\partial}{\partial\theta} \log f(x; \theta)$ exists for all x and θ.

(ii) $\frac{\partial}{\partial\theta} \int \ldots \int \prod_{i=1}^{n} f(x_i, \theta)\, dx_1\, dx_2 \ldots dx_n$

$$= \int \ldots \int \frac{d}{\partial\theta} \prod_{i=1}^{n} f(x_i; \theta)\, dx_1\, dx_2\, \ldots, dx_n$$

(iii) $\frac{\partial}{\partial\theta} \int \ldots \int t(x_1, x_2, \ldots, x_n) \prod_{i=1}^{n} f(x_i; \theta)$

$$dx_1\, dx_2 \ldots dx_n = \int \ldots \int t(x_1, x_2, \ldots, x_n) \frac{\partial}{\partial\theta} \prod_{i=1}^{n} f(x_i; \theta)\, dx_1\, dx_2 \ldots dx_n$$

(iv) $0 \leq E\left[\left\{\frac{\partial}{\partial\theta} \log f(x_i; \theta)\right\}^2\right] < \infty$ for all θ in Θ

where Θ is the parameter space.

The variance of T_n an estimator of $\tau(\theta)$ which is differentiable with respect to θ, *i.e.*, $\tau'(\theta)$ exists, satisfies the inequality,

$$V_\theta(T_n) \geq \frac{[\tau'(\theta)]^2}{E\left[\frac{\partial}{\partial\theta} \log f(x_i; \theta)\right]^2}$$

$$\geq -\frac{[\tau'(\theta)]^2}{E\left[\frac{\partial^2}{\partial\theta^2} \log f(x_i; \theta)\right]}$$

The quantity $E\left[\frac{\partial}{\partial\theta} \log f(x_i; \theta)\right]^2$ is called the amount of information about θ in the set of random variables $X_1, X_2, \ldots, X_n$.

If $\tau(\theta) = \theta$, then $\tau'(\theta) = 1$. In this situation,

$$V_\theta(T_n) \geq -\frac{1}{E\left[\frac{\partial}{\partial\theta} \log f(x_i; \theta)\right]^2}$$

The quantity $-1/E\left[\frac{\partial}{\partial\theta} \log f(x_i; \theta)\right]^2$ is called the information limit of T_n. If $X_1, X_2, \ldots, X_n$ are n independent and identically distributed random variables, then

$$V_\theta(T_n) \geq \frac{[\tau'(\theta)]^2}{nE\left[\frac{\partial}{\partial\theta}\log f(x_i;\theta)\right]^2}$$

$$\geq -\frac{[\tau'(\theta)]^2}{nE\left[\frac{\partial^2}{\partial\theta^2}\log f(x_i;\theta)\right]}$$

It is worth noting that Crammer-Rao inequality gives the lower bound of $V_\theta(T_n)$. An estimator which attains this lower bound for all θ in Θ will be called a minimum variance bound (MVB) estimator. Crammer-Rao inequality remains valid even through the random variates $X_1, X_2, \ldots, X_n$ are discrete. C.R. Rao gave this inequality in 1945, whereas H. Crammer independently gave it in 1946. However, it had already been given by Aitken and Silverstone in 1942. Chapman Robins had also given the lower bound for the variance of T_n parallel to Crammer-Rao inequality. Chapman-Robins inequality is considered to be an improvement over Crammer-Rao inequality as it does not require stringent regularity conditions.

A. Bhattacharyya also obtained the lower bound for $V_\theta(T_n)$ in 1946 under some amended regularity conditions of Crammer-Rao inequality.

Q. 10. *Define the best asymptotically normal estimators and throw light on its implications.*

Ans. Suppose we have a sequence of estimators T_n of various sample sizes say $T_n = t_n(x_1, x_2, \ldots, x_n)$ where n indicates the size of the sample on which T_n is based. For clarity $T_1 = t_1(X_1)$, $T_2 = t_2(X_1, X_2)$, …, $T_n = t_n(X_1, X_2, \ldots, X_n)$. Also we know, the estimator 'sample mean' of population mean remains $\Sigma X_i/n$ $(i = 1, 2, \ldots, n)$ whatever may be the sample size though for varying n, we get different estimates. But out of these estimates, one would like to select one which is closest to the parameter value. Hence, a sequence of estimators $T_1, T_2, \ldots, T_n$ of $\tau(\theta)$ will be called best asymptotically normal (BAN) if and only if it satisfies the following conditions:

(*i*) The distribution of $\sqrt{n}\,[T_n - \tau(\theta)] \to N(0, \sigma)^2$ as $n \to \infty$

(*ii*) For any small quantity ε,

$$\lim_{n\to\infty} P_\theta\left[|T_n - \tau(\theta)| > \varepsilon\right] = 0 \text{ for all } \theta \text{ in } \Theta.$$

It is the same condition as for consistency.

(*iii*) If $\{T_n^*\}$ is any sequence of estimators other than $\{T_n\}$ such that,

$$\sqrt{n}\left[T_n^* - \tau(\theta)\right] \to N(0, \sigma^{*2}) \text{ as } v \to \infty,$$

Then $\sigma^{*2} \geq \sigma^2$ for all θ in Θ in an open interval.

It has been observed that reasonably good estimators are usually asymptotically normally distributed.

Since BAN estimators are consistent as well, they are sometimes given another name, *consistent asymptotically normal efficient* (CANE) estimators.

BAN estimators assimilate the limiting property as well as the property of minimum variance.

Q. 11. *Express the efficiency of an estimator.*

Ans. An unbiased estimator T_n is said to be efficient than any other estimator T_n^* of $\tau(\theta)$ if and only if,

$$V(T_n) < V(T_n^*)$$

Also the relative efficiency of T_n as compared to T_n^* is given as,

$$\text{R.E.} = \frac{V(T_n^*)}{V(T_n)}$$

Crammer gave the term *efficient estimator* to mean a *minimum variance unbiased estimator* (MVUE) or *best unbiased estimator*. Hence, MVU estimator is unbiased and also among the class of unbiased estimators it possesses minimum variance.

A MVU estimator is unique in the sense that

$$V(T_n) = V(T_n^*) \Rightarrow T_n = T_n^*$$

Q. 12. *Expatiate the concept of sufficiency of an estimator.*

Ans.

Definition 1. An estimator T_n is said to be sufficient for $\tau(\theta)$ if it provides all the information contained in the sample about the parametric function $\tau(\theta)$.

If we have a random sample $X_1, X_2,..., X_n$ from a density $f(x; \theta)$, a statistic $S = s(X_1, X_2, ..., X_n)$ (which is itself a random variable) which condenses n random variables $X_1, X_2, ..., X_n$ into a single random variable and provides as much information as the random sample $X_1, X_2, ..., X_n$ could reveal about the probability distribution characterised by $f(x; \theta)$ is known as sufficient statistics. So, the idea is that if we know the sufficient statistics, there is no need of knowing the sample values.

Definition 2. A statistic $S = s(X_1, X_2, ..., X_n)$ is sufficient for the parameter θ of a density $f(x; \theta)$ if the conditional distribution of $X_1, X_2, ..., X_n$ for a given value of $S = s$ is independent of the parameter θ.

From this definition it is clear that one cannot expect to get an information about θ from a distribution that does not contain θ.

Definition 3. This definition is known as Fisher-Neyman factorization theorem. The theorem can be stated as follows:

Let $X_1, X_2, ..., X_n$ be a random sample from a density $f(x; \theta)$. A statistic $S = s(X_1, X_2, ..., X_n)$ is said to be sufficient statistic for θ if the joint probability density function of $X_1, X_2, ..., X_n$ can be factorized as,

$$f_{X_1; X_2, ..., X_n}(x_1, x_2, ..., x_n; \theta) = g\{s(x_1, x_2, ..., x_n); \theta\} \times h(x_1, x_2, ...x_n) = g(s; \theta)\, h(x_1, x_2, ...x_n)$$

On the right hand $g(s; \theta)$ is the density function of s (the sufficient statistic) involving the unknown parameter θ and $h(x_1, x_2, ..., x_n)$ is the conditional density function $X_1, X_2, ..., X_n$ for given s and is independent of θ.

Q. 13. *Give the idea of minimal sufficient statistics.*

Ans. The idea of sufficient statistics is to condense the data to a form that provides maximum information. Hence, a sufficient statistics S will be termed as minimal sufficient statistics if the statistics for the sample $X_1, X_2, ..., X_n$ cannot be condensed any more beyond S without sacrificing the sufficiency.

Q. 14. *Define complete statistic and complete parametric families.*

Ans. Let $f(x; \theta)$ be a parametric family of univariate or multivariate distributions depending on the vector of parameter θ and $h(x)$ be any statistic independent of θ. If

$$E_i[h(x)] = \int h(x)\, f(x; \theta)\, dx$$
$$= 0 \quad \Rightarrow \quad h(x) = 0 \text{ for all } \theta,$$

then $f(x; \theta)$ is said to be complete.

The term 'complete' is appropriate in the sense that there exists no non-zero function which is orthogonal to all members of the family.

A sufficient statistics $S = s(X_1, X_2, ..., X_n)$ is said to be complete, if

$$E_\theta(S) = 0 \quad \Rightarrow \quad s = 0$$

A statistics which is unbiased and complete is necessarily unique if a MVU estimator exists.

Q. 15. *State Rao-Blackwell theorem.*

Ans. Suppose $X_1, X_2, ..., X_n$ is a random sample from the density $f(x; \theta)$ and $S = s(X_1, X_2, ..., X_n)$ is any sufficient statistic for θ of the density $f(x; \theta)$. Also let $T = t(X_1, X_2, ..., X_n)$ be any other unbiased estimator of $\tau(\theta)$. Also let there be any other statistic T_1, such that $T_1 = E(T/S = s)$. Then,

(i) T_1 is a statistic and is a function of the sufficient statistic S, *i.e.*, $T_1 = t_1(s)$.

(ii) $E_\theta(T_1) = \tau(\theta)$, *i.e.*, T_1 is an unbiased estimator of $\tau(\theta)$.

(iii) $\text{var}_\theta(T_1) \le \text{var}_\theta(T)$ for every θ.

(iv) $\text{var}_\theta(T_1) < \text{var}_\theta(T)$ for some θ.

The theorem can easily be generalised for a set of sufficient statistics $S_1 = s_1(X_1, X_2, ..., X_n)$, $S_2 = s_2(X_1, X_2,..., X_n)$ .... $S_k = s(X_1, X_2, ..., X_n)$ and also θ be a vector. The implication of the theorem is that given an unbiased estimator, another unbiased estimator T_1 which is a function of the sufficient statistics can be created which will not have greater variance than that of T.

The concepts of consistency, efficiency and sufficiency are due to R.A. Fisher.

Q. 16. *Give invariance property of estimators.*

Ans. This property relates to the coding of data. Let $X_1, X_2, \ldots, X_n$ be a random sample from the density $f(x; \theta)$ and $x_1, x_2, \ldots, x_n$ be the sample value of $X_1, X_2, \ldots, X_n$ respectively. Also θ be a vector. Then an estimator $T = t(X_1, X_2, \ldots, X_n)$ is said to be *location invariant* if and only if $t(x_1 + c, x_2 + c, \ldots, x_n + c) = t(x_1, x_2, \ldots, x_n) + c$ for all c where c is a constant value.

An estimator $T = t(X_1, X_2, \ldots, X_n)$ is said to be scale invariant if and only if $t(cx_1, cx_2, \ldots, cx_n) = ct(x_1, x_2, \ldots, x_n)$ for all c where c is a non-zero constant.

Q. 17. *When do you call an estimator admissible?*

Ans. Let $X_1, X_2, \ldots, X_n$ be a random sample from the density $f(x; \theta)$ and $T_1 = t_1(X_1, X_2, \ldots, X_n)$ and $T_2 = t_2(X_1, X_2, \ldots, X_n)$ be any two estimators for θ. The estimator T_1 is said to be a better estimator than T_2 if and only if the risks hold the inequalities,

$$R(t_1, \theta) \leq R(t_2, \theta) \text{ for all } \theta \text{ in } \Theta$$

$$R(t_1, \theta) < R(t_2, \theta) \text{ for some } \theta \text{ in } \Theta$$

t_1 will be said to be an admissible estimator if and only if there is no other estimator t_2 better than t_1. The readers should note that $R(t, \theta)$ is called the risk of taking t as an estimator of θ and is defined as the expected loss (average loss), *i.e.*,

$$R(t, \theta) = E\{l(T, \theta)\}$$

where $T = t(X_1, X_2, \ldots, X_n)$

$$R(t, \theta) = \int l(T, \theta)\, f_T(t)\, dt$$

where $f_T(t)$ is the density of the estimator T. Concept of risk is more akin to decision theoretic approach.

Q. 18. *Give the names of various methods of estimation of a parameter.*

Ans. Various methods of estimation are listed below:

1. Method of maximum likelihood
2. Least square method
3. Method of moments
4. Method of minimum Chi-square
5. Method of modified minimum Chi-square
6. Bayes' estimation procedure.

Q. 19. *Describe the method of maximum likelihood estimation.*

Ans. Maximum likelihood principle is due to R.A. Fisher in 1921.

Let $X_1, X_2, \ldots, X_n$ be n independent observations from $f(x; \theta)$ where θ is a single unknown parameter. The joint probability density function of the sample is called likelihood function (LF) and is written as,

$$L(x \mid \theta) = f(x_1, \theta)\, f(x_2, \theta) \ldots f(x_n, \theta)$$

According to maximum likelihood principle, one should take that value of estimator θ within the admissible range of θ which makes $L(x \mid \theta)$ maximum. For this, the method of maxima-minima is used. If $L(x \mid \theta)$ is differentiable *twice, i.e.,* if the first and second derivatives of $L(x \mid \theta)$ exists, put $L'(x \mid \theta) = 0$ and solve for θ. Also, for maxima check that $L''(x \mid \theta)$ is negative for a value of θ obtained by $L'(x \mid \theta)$. If so, the solution of $L(x \mid \theta)$ provides the maximum likelihood estimate of θ. In practice it is better to take logarithm of $L(x \mid \theta)$ and then differentiate and solve it. This makes the estimation process easier. If θ is a K dimensional parametric vector, *i.e.*, $\theta = (\theta_1, \theta_2, \ldots, \theta_k)$, then the estimator $(\hat{\theta}_1, \hat{\theta}_2, \ldots, \hat{\theta}_k)$, which maximise $L(x|\theta_1, \theta_2, \ldots, \theta_k)$, can be obtained by differentiating partially the log $\{L(x \mid \theta_1, \theta_2, \ldots, \theta_k)\}$, with respect to $\theta_1, \theta_2, \ldots, \theta_k$ respectively and equating them to zero. The solution of k equations provides the estimates of $\theta_1, \theta_2, \ldots, \theta_k$. Notationally,

$$\frac{\partial}{\partial \theta_1}\{\log L(x \mid \theta_1, \theta_2, \ldots, \theta_k)\} = 0$$

$$\frac{\partial}{\partial \theta_2}\{\log L(x \mid \theta_1, \theta_2, \ldots, \theta_k)\} = 0$$

$$\vdots$$

$$\frac{\partial}{\partial \theta_k}\{\log L(x \mid \theta_1, \theta_2, \ldots, \theta_k)\} = 0$$

In this way, we get k equations in k unknowns. These equations are often called the *likelihood equations.* Solving these equations one gets the maximum likelihood estimates of $\theta_1, \theta_2, \ldots, \theta_k$. To show that $\hat{\theta}$, the k-dimensional vector of estimates provides the supremum of $L(x \mid \theta)$, it is enough to show that the matrix $\left(\frac{\partial^2 \log L}{\partial \theta_i\, \partial \theta_j}\right)_{\theta=\hat{\theta}}$ is negative definite.

Q. 20. *What properties of estimators are being usually held by maximum likelihood estimators?*

Ans. In general, the following statements about the properties of maximum likelihood estimators (MLE) can be given:

(*i*) A MLE is not necessarily unique.

(*ii*) A MLE is not necessarily unbiased.

(*iii*) A MLE may not be consistent in rare cases.

(*iv*) A MLE may not be uniformly minimum variance unbiased estimator (UMVUE).

(*v*) If a sufficient statistic exists, it is a function of the maximum likelihood estimators.

(*vi*) If a minimum variance bound (MVB) unbiased estimator exists, maximum likelihood estimator provides it.

(*vii*) If $T = t(X_1, X_2, \ldots, X_n)$ is a sufficient statistics for a parameter θ and a unique MLE $\hat{\theta}$ of θ exists, $\hat{\theta}$ is a function of t. Also, if any MLE exists, MLE $\hat{\theta}$ can be found which is a function of t.

(*viii*) If $T = t(X_1, X_2, \ldots, X_n)$ is a MLE of θ and $\tau(\theta)$ is a one to one function of θ, $\tau(t)$ is a MLE of $\tau(\theta)$. This is known as *invariance property* of maximum likelihood estimator.

(*ix*) Under very general conditions, maximum likelihood estimators are consistent. Huzurbazar in 1948 showed that under regularity conditions, as sample size n tends to infinity, there exists a unique consistent maximum likelihood estimator.

(*x*) Under certain conditions, it has been observed that ML estimator is consistent but it is generally unbiased.

(xi) When maximum likelihood estimator exists, it is most efficient for large samples under the assumption that the distribution of the estimator tends to normal.

Q. 21. *A random sample of size n is drawn from a normal population $N(\mu, \sigma^2)$. Estimate μ and σ^2 by the method of maximum likelihood. Also comment on the properties of maximum likelihood estimators.*

Ans. The likelihood function,

$$\log L(x_i \mid \mu, \sigma^2) = \left(\frac{1}{\sigma\sqrt{2\pi}}\right)^n e^{-\frac{1}{2\sigma^2}\Sigma(x_i-\mu)^2}$$

To estimate μ and σ^2, we take logarithm and differentiate partially w.r.t. μ and σ^2, respectively and equate them to zero.

$$\log L = -\frac{n}{2}\log(2\pi) - \frac{n}{2}\log\sigma^2$$

$$-\frac{1}{2\sigma^2}\sum_{i=1}^{n}(x_i-\mu)^2$$

$$\frac{\partial \log L}{\partial \mu} = \frac{1}{\sigma^2}\sum_{i=1}^{n}(x_i-\hat{\mu}) = 0$$

which implies that $\sum_{i=1}^{n}(x_i-\hat{\mu}) = 0$ since $\frac{1}{\sigma^2} \neq 0$.

$$\therefore \quad \sum_{i=1}^{n} x_i - n\hat{\mu} = 0$$

or

$$\hat{\mu} = \frac{1}{n}\sum_{i=1}^{n} x_i = \bar{x}$$

Again, $$\frac{\partial \log L}{\partial \sigma^2} = \frac{-n}{2\hat{\sigma}^2} + \frac{1}{2\hat{\sigma}^4}\sum (x_i-\hat{\mu})^2 = 0$$

or $$\frac{1}{\hat{\sigma}^2}\sum_{i=1}^{n}(x_i-\bar{x})^2 = n$$

or $$\hat{\sigma}^2 = \frac{1}{n}\sum_{i=1}^{n}(x_i-\bar{x})^2$$

The ML estimate of μ is sample mean $\bar{x}$ which is *unbiased, consistent* and BAN. The estimate of σ^2 is $\frac{1}{n}\sum_{i=1}^{n}(x_i-\bar{x})^2$ which is not unbiased but consistent.

Also $\bar{x}$ is minimum variance bound estimate of μ with variance $\frac{\sigma^2}{n}$. It can be verified that ML estimators of μ and σ^2 are invariant in case of normal distribution. Also the estimators $\bar{x}$ and $\Sigma(x_i - \bar{x})/n$ are sufficient for μ and σ^2.

Q. 22. *If n_1 trials conducted are of Bernoullian type following binomial distribution, find the maximum likelihood estimate of p.*

Ans. We know that probability function of binomial distribution is

$$f(n_1, x_i) = \binom{n_1}{x_i} p^{x_i}(1-p)^{n_1-x_i}$$

for $i = 1, 2, \ldots, n$

The likelihood function,

$$L(x \mid p) = \prod_{i=1}^{n}\binom{n_1}{x_i} p^{x_i}(1-p)^{n_1-x_i}$$

Taking logarithm of both sides,

$$\log L = \sum_{i=1}^{n}\log\binom{n_1}{x_i} + \sum_{i=1}^{n} x_i \log p$$
$$+\sum_{i=1}^{n}(n_1-x_i)\log(1-p)$$

Differentiating partially w.r.t. p and equating to zero.

$$\frac{\partial \log L}{\partial p} = 0 + \sum x_i \cdot \frac{1}{\hat{p}} - \frac{nn_1 - \Sigma x_i}{1-\hat{p}} = 0$$

i.e., $$nn_1\hat{p} = \Sigma x_i$$

or $$\hat{p} = \frac{\Sigma x_i}{nn_1} = \frac{\bar{x}}{n_1}$$

It is trivial to show that $\bar{x}/n_1$ is a maximum likelihood estimate of p.

Q. 23. *If X is a Poisson variate with parameter μ, find the maximum likelihood estimate of μ.*

Ans. $$P(x;\mu) = \frac{e^{-\mu}\mu^x}{x!}$$

for $x = 0, 1, 2, \ldots, n$.

The likelihood function,

$$L(x_i \mid \mu) = \prod_{i=1}^{n}\frac{e^{-\mu}\mu^{x_i}}{x_i!}$$

for $i = 1, 2, \ldots, n$

$$\log L = \sum_{i=1}^{n}\log_e e^{-\mu} + \sum_{i=1}^{n} x_i \log\mu - \sum_{i=1}^{n}\log_e(x_i!)$$

$$= -n\mu + \sum_{i=1}^{n} x_i\log\mu - \sum_{i=1}^{n}\log_e(x_i!)$$

$$\frac{\partial \log L}{\partial \mu} = -n + \frac{\Sigma x_i}{\hat{\mu}} - 0 = 0$$

$$\therefore \quad \frac{\Sigma x_i}{\hat{\mu}} = n$$

or $$\hat{\mu} = \frac{\Sigma x_i}{n} = \bar{x}$$

Sample mean is the maximum likelihood estimate of μ.

Q. 24. *For gamma distribution $G(x; \alpha, \lambda)$ find the ML estimate of α where λ is taken to be a known constant.*

Ans. $$G(x;\alpha,\gamma) = \frac{\alpha^\lambda}{\Gamma\lambda}e^{-\alpha x}x^{\lambda-1} \quad \text{for } \alpha > 0$$

$$L(x_i \mid \alpha, \lambda) = \prod_{i=1}^{n}\frac{\alpha^\lambda}{\Gamma\lambda}e^{-\alpha x_i}x_i^{\lambda-1}$$

$$\log L = \sum_{i=1}^{n} \log \frac{\alpha^\lambda}{\Gamma\lambda} - \alpha \sum_{i=1}^{n} x_i + (\lambda - 1) \sum_{i=1}^{n} \log x_i$$

Differentiating partially w.r.t. α, we get

$$\frac{\partial \log L}{\partial \alpha} = \frac{n}{\Gamma\lambda} \frac{\lambda \alpha^{\lambda-1}}{\hat{\alpha}^\lambda} - \sum x_i + 0 = 0$$

$$\therefore \quad \frac{n\lambda}{\hat{\alpha}\Gamma\lambda} - \sum x_i = 0$$

$$\frac{n\lambda}{\hat{\alpha}\Gamma\lambda} = \sum x_i$$

or
$$\hat{\alpha} = \frac{n\lambda}{\Gamma\lambda \Sigma x_i} = \frac{\lambda}{\Gamma\lambda \bar{x}}$$

Q. 25. *Find the maximum likelihood estimate of the parameter θ of the distribution,*

$$f(x; \theta) = \frac{1}{2} e^{-|x-\theta|}$$

$$-\infty < x < \infty, -\infty < \theta < \infty$$

Ans. The likelihood function for the sample observations $x_1, x_2, \ldots, x_n$ is

$$L = \frac{1}{2} e^{-|x_1 - \theta|} \cdot \frac{1}{2} e^{-|x_2 - \theta|}, \ldots, \frac{1}{2} e^{-|x_n - \theta|}$$

$$L = \left(\frac{1}{2}\right)^n \prod_{i=1}^{n} e^{-|x_i - \theta|}$$

$$\log L = -n \log 2 - \sum_{i=1}^{n} |x_i - \theta|$$

log *L* is not differentiable w.r.t. θ. However according to ML principle log *L* has to be maximised. Log *L* is maximum when $\Sigma \mid x_i - \theta \mid$ is minimum. We know that the mean deviation about a constant θ is $\Sigma \mid x_i - \theta \mid / n$ which is minimum when θ is the median of the sample.

Therefore, when *n* is odd,

$$\hat{\theta} = \text{med}\,(x_1, x_2, \ldots, x_n)$$

when *n* is even, then

$$Y_{n/2} \le \theta \le Y_{\frac{n}{2}+1}$$

where $Y_1, Y_2, \ldots, Y_n$ are taken to be the ordered statistics.

Note: This example proves that ML estimator is not necessarily unique.

Q. 26. *Obtain the ML estimator of α and β of the uniform distribution having the probability density function,*

$$f(x; \alpha, \beta) = \frac{1}{\beta - \alpha} \quad \text{for } \alpha \le x \le b$$

$$= 0 \quad \text{otherwise.}$$

$$L = \prod_{i=1}^{n} f(x_i, \alpha, \beta)$$

$$= \prod_{i=1}^{n} \frac{1}{\beta - \alpha}$$

$$\log L = \sum_{i=1}^{n} \log \frac{1}{(\beta - \alpha)}$$

$$= -n \log(\beta - \alpha)$$

Here,
$$\frac{\partial}{\partial \alpha} \log L = \frac{n}{\beta - \alpha} = 0$$

and
$$\frac{\partial}{\partial \beta} \log L = \frac{n}{\beta - \alpha} = 0.$$

These likelihood equations fail to estimate α and β. Hence, we have to think in some other direction. Let $Y_1, Y_2, \ldots, Y_n$ be the ordered statistics. Since *x* lies between α and β, we have

$$\alpha \le Y_1 \le Y_2 \le \ldots \le Y_n \le \beta$$

Therefore,

$$\hat{a} = Y_1 \text{ and } \hat{\beta} = Y_n.$$

Q. 27. *Discuss the method of least square estimation.*

Ans. The idea of least square estimation emerges from the method of maximum likelihood itself. Consider the ML estimation of μ on the basis of a sample of size *n* from a normal population $N(\mu, \sigma^2)$

$$f(y; \mu, \alpha^2) = \frac{1}{\sigma\sqrt{2\pi}} e^{-\frac{1}{2\sigma^2}(y-\mu)^2}$$

$$L(y_i, \mu, \alpha^2) = \left(\frac{1}{\sqrt{2\pi\sigma^2}}\right)^n e^{-\frac{1}{2\sigma^2}\sum_{i=1}^{n}(y_1-\mu)^2}$$

$$\log L = -\frac{n}{2}\log_e(2\pi\sigma^2) - \frac{1}{2\sigma^2}\sum_{i=1}^{n}(y_i-\mu)^2$$

Maximising log L implies that $\Sigma(y_i - \mu)^2$ must be minimised, *i.e.*, sum of squares, $\Sigma(y_i - \mu)^2$ must be least square.

The method of least square estimation is mostly used in estimating the parameters of linear function. This very idea can be translated by considering μ itself a linear function of certain parameters β_j ($j = 1, 2, \ldots, k$) *i.e.*

$$\mu = \sum_{j=1}^{k} x_j \beta_j$$

where x_j's are some known coefficients of β_j's forming a linear function of β_j. In this situation, estimation of β_j's is in the offing.

For estimating β_j's., we have to minimise,

$$\sum_{j=1}^{k}\left(y_i - \sum_{j=1}^{k} x_j \beta_j\right)^2$$

with respect to β_j.

Q. 28. *Describe the least square method of estimation of the parameters of simple linear model.*

Ans. Consider the simple linear model,

$$Y = \beta_0 + \beta_1 X + \varepsilon$$

Let there be n paired observations $(x_1, y_1), (x_2, y_2), \ldots, (x_n, y_n)$. In the above model Y is called the dependent variable and X, the independent variable and ε is the random error. For the ith pair of observation

$$y_i = \beta_0 + \beta_1 x_i + \varepsilon_i$$

or

$$\varepsilon_i = (y_i - \beta_0 - \beta_1 x_i)$$

ε_i may be positive or negative. To avoid the problem of sign of error, square both sides and also take the sum over all pairs. Thus,

$$\sum_{i=1}^{n}\varepsilon_i^2 = \sum_{i=1}^{n}(y_i - \beta_0 - \beta_1 x_i)^2$$

To get the best estimate of β_0 and β_1, one has to minimise $\Sigma\varepsilon_i^2$, which amounts to minimising $\Sigma(y_i - \beta_0 - \beta_1 x_i)^2$. Suppose $\Sigma\varepsilon_i^2 = Q$.

The values of β_0 and β_1, which minimise Q are known as *least square estimates*. To estimate β_0 and β_1, differentiate Q partially w.r.t. β_0 and β_1 respectively and equate to zero *i.e.*

$$\frac{\partial Q}{\partial \beta_0} = 0 \text{ and } \frac{\partial Q}{\partial \beta_1} = 0$$

This gives,

$$\Sigma y_i = n\hat{\beta}_0 + \hat{\beta}_1 \Sigma x_i$$

and

$$\Sigma x_i y_i = \hat{\beta}_0 \Sigma x_i + \hat{\beta}_1 \Sigma x_i^2$$

where $\hat{\beta}_0$ and $\hat{\beta}_1$ are the estimated values of β_0 and β_1 respectively.

The two equations are known as *normal equations*. Solving these equations we obtain,

$$\hat{\beta}_0 = \bar{y} - b\bar{x}$$

$$\hat{\beta}_1 = \frac{\Sigma x_i y_i - \frac{(\Sigma x_i)(\Sigma y_i)}{n}}{\Sigma x_i^2 - \frac{(\Sigma x_i)^2}{n}}$$

Note: Method of least square estimation can be extended to multiple linear models and curvilinear models. This has been dealt with in the sequel.

Q. 29. *Throw light on the properties of least square estimates.*

Ans. Least square (LS) estimates are not so popular without reason. They possess some marvellous properties which are as follows:

(*i*) Least square estimators are unbiased in case of linear models.

(*ii*) $\hat{\beta}_0$ and $\hat{\beta}_1$ are the uniformly minimum variance unbiased estimators (UMVUEs).

(*iii*) The LS estimators $\hat{\beta}_0$ and $\hat{\beta}_1$ do not possess the asymptotically normal property.

(*iv*) The least square method is a device to obtain *best linear unbiased estimators* (BLUEs) under linear set up.

Q. 30. *Define best linear unbiased estimator.*

Ans. It has been known that sample mean is an unbiased estimate of population mean in case of finite as well as infinite populations. Also the sample mean is a linear function $a_1 x_1 + a_2 x_2 + ... + a_n x_n$ of the sample values $x_1, x_2, ..., x_n$ subject to the condition $\Sigma a_i = 1$ for $i = 1, 2, ..., n$. Linear functions of the sample values with known a_i's represented as $\Sigma a_i x_i$, such that $\Sigma a_i = 1$, are called *unbiased linear estimators.*

If one is to select an unbiased linear estimator from amongst the class of such estimators, some criteria have to be fixed. One widely accepted criterion to select one linear unbiased estimator out of all available linear unbiased estimators is to select one which has the smallest possible variance. Such a linear estimator is called *minimum variance linear unbiased estimator.* It is generally called the *best linear unbiased estimator* (BLUE). The adjective 'best' refers to minimum variance.

If an unbiased quadratic estimator of the variance σ^2 exists and it possesses the minimum variance out of the class of available unbiased quadratic estimators, it is known as *minimum variance quadratic estimator.*

Q. 31. *State Gauss-Markov theorem.*

Ans. Least square theory was put forth by Gauss in 1809 and minimum variance approach to the estimators of β_i's was propounded by Markov in 1900. Since determining of minimum variance linear unbiased estimator involves both the concepts, the theorem is known as *Gauss-Markov theorem.* It can be stated as follows:

Let y_i $(i = 1, 2, n)$ be n independent variables with mean $\sum_{j=1}^{k} \beta_j x_{ji}$ for $n > k$ and all y_i have same variance σ^2 where x_{ji} are known and linearly independent vectors. The minimum variance linear unbiased estimators of the regression coefficients β_j are $b_j (j = 1, 2, ..., k)$.

Under the terms and conditions imposed above, the minimum variance linear unbiased estimators of the regression coefficients are identically the same as the least square estimators.

The combination of the above two statements is known as Gauss-Markov theorem.

Q. 32. *Give in brief the method of moments for estimating the population parameters.*

Ans. It is the oldest method of estimating the parameters of a distribution. It was first put forward by Karl Pearson in 1894. The method of moments consists of equating the sample moments to the corresponding moments of distribution, which are the functions of the unknown parameters. Here, we equate as many sample moments as there are unknown parameters. Solving the simultaneous equations, one obtains the estimates of the moments of the population in terms of sample variates.

We know,

$$\mu'_r = E(X^r)$$

$$\mu_r = E(X - \mu)^r$$

Also,
$$\mu'_1 = E(X) = \mu_1$$

Let $X_1, X_2, ..., X_n$ be a random sample from a population $f(x; \theta_1, \theta_2, ..., \theta_k)$. Then the rth sample moment

$$\mu_r = \frac{1}{n} \sum_i (x_i - \bar{x})^r$$

Also,
$$\mu'_1 = E(X)$$

$$= \frac{1}{n} \sum_i x_i$$

$$= \bar{x}$$

Now to obtain second and higher order moments, equate

$$\mu_r = m_r \ (i = 1, 2, 3, ..., k)$$

Solving the above $(k - 1)$ equations, one gets the estimates of the population moments, which are the moments of the population distribution.

Q. 33. *Write the properties of the estimates obtained by the method of moments.*

Ans.

(*i*) Under fairly general conditions, the estimates obtained by the method of moments will have asymptotically normal distribution for large n.

(*ii*) The mean of the distribution of estimate will differ from the true value of the parameter by a quantity of order $\frac{1}{n}$.

(*iii*) The variance of the distribution of estimate will be of the type c^2/n.

(*iv*) In general, the deviation estimators obtained by the method of moments are less efficient than the maximum likelihood estimators. In particular cases, they are equivalent.

Q. 34. *Estimate the parameters* μ *and* σ^2 *of the normal distribution by the method of moments.*

Ans. Let $X_1, X_2, \ldots, X_n$ be a random sample from a normal population $N(\mu, \sigma^2)$.

We know, $m'_1 = \mu'_1 = \mu = \bar{X}$

$$\mu_2 = \mu'_2 - (\mu'_1)^2$$

$$= \frac{1}{n}\sum X_i^2 - \bar{X}^2$$

for $i = 1, 2, \ldots, n$.

$$= \frac{1}{n}\left(\sum X_i^2 - n\bar{X}^2\right)$$

$$= \frac{1}{n}\sum (X_i - \bar{X}^2)$$

Therefore, $\bar{X}$ is an unbiased estimator of μ whereas $\Sigma\left(X_i - \bar{X}\right)^2/n$ is not an unbiased estimator for σ^2.

Q. 35. *Estimate the parameter* λ *of the exponential distribution,* $f(x; \lambda) = \lambda e^{-\lambda x}$ *for* $0 \leq x \leq \infty$*, by the method of moments.*

Ans. $m'_1 = \mu'_1 = E(X)$

$$= \int_0^\infty x\lambda\, x^{-\lambda x}\, dx$$

which is a gamma integral. Hence,

$$m'_1 = \mu'_1 = \frac{\lambda\Gamma 2}{\lambda^2}$$

$$= \frac{1}{\lambda}$$

But $m'_1 = \bar{x}$. Therefore, the estimated value of λ is $\frac{1}{\bar{x}}$.

Q. 36. *Find the estimate of the lone parameter* λ *of the Poisson distribution* $\frac{e^{-\lambda}\lambda^x}{x!}$*, by the method of moments.*

Ans. Let $X_1, X_2, \ldots, X_n$ be a random sample from a Poisson distribution $P(x; \lambda)$. We know in case of Poisson distribution, its mean and variance are equal. The mean,

$$m'_1 = \mu'_1 = E(X)$$

$$= \sum_{x=0}^{n} x\frac{e^{-\lambda}\lambda^x}{x!}$$

$$= \lambda\sum_{x=0}^{n} e^{-\lambda}\frac{\lambda^{x-1}}{(x-1)!}$$

$$= \lambda = \bar{x}$$

Thus, the estimate of the parameter λ by the method of moments is the sample mean $\bar{x}$.

Q. 37. *How can one estimate the parameters of a distribution by the method of minimum Chi-square?*

Ans. The method of minimum Chi-square makes use of the Pearson's Chi-square statistic. This method can be used in case of discrete distributions or for grouped data from a continuous distribution.

Let $f_1, f_2, \ldots, f_k$ be the observed frequencies in K groups or classes and unknown probabilities that f_i elements belong to the ith group or class be $p_i(i = 1,$

2, ..., k). p's are the functions of the unknown parameters $\theta_1, \theta_2, ..., \theta_m$. Thus $p_i = p_i(\underset{\sim}{\theta})$ where $\underset{\sim}{\theta} = (\theta_1, \theta_2, ..., \theta_m)$. Suppose the total sample size is n. Therefore, $\Sigma f_i = n$. The expected frequencies are $np_1(\underset{\sim}{\theta}), np_2(\underset{\sim}{\theta}), ..., np_k(\underset{\sim}{\theta})$. We know, Pearsonian Chi-square statistic is,

$$\chi^2 = \sum_{i=1}^{k} \frac{\left[f_i - np_i(\underset{\sim}{\theta})\right]^2}{np_i(\underset{\sim}{\theta})}$$

$$= \sum_{i=1}^{k} \frac{f_i^2}{np_i(\underset{\sim}{\theta})} - n$$

Under the method of minimum Chi-square one has to choose $(\theta_1, \theta_2, ..., \theta_m)$ which minimises χ^2. This will be minimum when $np_i(\theta)$ is as close as possible to f_i. So to obtain the estimates of θ_i's, partially differentiate χ^2-statistic w.r.t. θ_i (i = 1, 2, ..., m) successively and equate them to zero. Also check that the second derivatives are non-negative, *i.e.*,

$$\frac{\partial \chi^2}{\partial \theta_i} = 0 \text{ for } i = 1, 2, ..., m$$

and $$\frac{\partial^2 \chi^2}{\partial \theta_i^2} \geq 0$$

$\frac{\partial \chi^2}{\partial \theta_i} = 0$ provides m simultaneous equations in m unknowns. Solving these m-equations for m unknown parameters, one gets the estimated values of $\theta_1, \theta_2, ..., \theta_m$ respectively.

Q. 38. *What modification in minimum-χ^2 method of estimation gives rise to the method of modified minimum Chi-square?*

Ans. Expected frequency $np_i(\underset{\sim}{\theta})$ in the denominator of χ^2-statistic causes certain difficulties. Hence, a modification has been suggested which makes the process of differentiation easier. The modified Chi-square statistic is,

$$\chi^2 = \sum_{i=1}^{k} \frac{\left[np_i(\underset{\sim}{\theta}) - f_i\right]^2}{f_i}$$

$$= \sum_{i=1}^{k} \frac{n^2 p_i^2(\underset{\sim}{\theta})}{f_i} - n$$

Rest of the procedure of modified minimum Chi-square remains same as that of minimum Chi-square.

Q. 39. *Compare the method of minimum Chi-square with maximum likelihood estimation.*

Ans.

(*i*) It is trivial to prove that for large n, the estimates obtained by the method of minimum Chi-square are almost equal to the estimates obtained by maximum likelihood method.

(*ii*) J. Berkson in 1955 showed that in particular cases, the mean square error of estimators under minimum χ^2 is smaller as compared to the mean square error of ML estimators.

Q. 40. *What properties the minimum Chi-square estimators hold?*

Ans.

(*i*) The minimum Chi-square estimators are consistent.

(*ii*) Minimum χ^2 estimators are asymptotically normal.

(*iii*) Minimum χ^2 estimators are efficient.

(*iv*) Minimum χ^2 estimators are not necessarily unbiased.

Q. 41. *Comment on the use of minimum χ^2 estimation method.*

Ans. Minimum χ^2 is rarely used in practice. It is used only when it is difficult to solve the simultaneous equations obtained under maximum likelihood estimation method.

Q. 42. *Write down the motif behind the Bayesian theory of estimation.*

Ans. In planning of any investigation or experiment

some prior information is available on the statistical properties of the variable to be studied. For instance, the type of distribution, the range of the parameters involved, etc. Heretofore, the methods of estimation did not make use of any such information. But Sir Thomas Bayes propounded the theory which makes use of the prior information to get the estimates of population parameters. The basic difference between non-Bayesians and Bayesians is that non-Bayesians consider the parameter of a population a fixed quantity, whereas Bayesians regard the parameter of a distribution a random variable.

The most important thing in the Bayesian approach is the specification of a distribution on the parametric space, which has been named as prior distribution. The specification of the prior distribution is mostly based on pragmatic grounds, *i.e.*, it is based on some previous experiment, investigation study or knowledge.

The Bayesian theory has always been a matter of controversy. Bayesians believe that it is generally very effective, whereas non-Bayesians consider it irrelevant.

Q. 43. *Present the general structure of Bayes' estimators.*

Ans. In the process of estimation so far we have a density $f(x; \theta)$ for each $\theta \varepsilon \Theta$, (the parametric space) from which a random sample $X_1, X_2, \ldots, X_n$ is drawn. Here we denote $f(x \mid \theta)$ for the conditional density of X for given value of parameter $\Theta = \theta$. Also suppose that $g(\theta)$ is a known prior distribution of θ. The density $f(x; \theta)$ in which X and Θ both are random variables and can be given as,

$$f(x; \theta) = f(x \mid \theta)\, g(\theta)$$

Using the Bayes' probability rule,

$$f(\theta \mid x) = \frac{f(x \mid \theta)\, g(\theta)}{\int f(x \mid \theta)\, g(\theta)\, d\theta}$$

The Bayesian point estimator of a parametric function $\tau(\theta)$ of θ can be obtained by the expression,

$$E[\tau(\theta)] = \int \tau(\theta)\, f(\theta \mid x)\, d\theta$$

$$\hat{\tau}(\theta) = \frac{\int \tau(\theta)\, f(x \mid \theta)\, g(\theta)\, d\theta}{\int f(x \mid \theta)\, g(\theta)\, d\theta}$$

Bayes estimator of $\tau(\theta)$ given above is under squared error loss function.

Q. 44. *Give an account of the properties of Bayes estimators.*

Ans.

(*i*) Bayes estimator is always a function of minimal sufficient statistics.

(*ii*) For large n, Bayes estimators always tend to maximum likelihood estimators, whatever may be the prior density $g(\theta)$.

(*iii*) In many cases Bayes estimators are asymptotically consistent.

(*iv*) Properties of Bayes estimators are generally given in terms of minimum risk, mean squared error, etc., which are not discussed here.

Q. 45. *Define minimax estimator.*

Ans. An estimator of which the maximum risk is less than or equal to maximum risk of any other estimator is said to be a minimax estimator. Notionally T_1 is a minimax estimator if for any other estimator T_2,

$$\sup_{\theta} R(T_1, \theta) \le \sup_{\theta} R(T_2, \theta)$$

Q. 46. *Find Bayes estimator of the parameter p of a binomial distribution with x successes out of n given that the prior distribution of p is a beta distribution with parameters* α *and* β.

Ans. The mass function,

$$f(x \mid p) = \binom{n}{x} p^x (1-p)^{n-x}$$

and $$g(p) = \frac{1}{B(\alpha, \beta)}\, p^{\alpha-1} (1-p)^{\beta-1}$$

Thus, $$f(x; p) = f(x \mid p)\, g(p)$$

Again,

$$f(p \mid x) = \frac{\binom{n}{x} p^x (1-p)^{n-x}\, p^{\alpha-1}(1-p)^{\beta-1}}{B(\alpha, \beta)}$$

$$\hat{p} = \frac{\int p \binom{n}{x} p^x (1-p)^{n-x}\, p^{\alpha-1}(1-p)^{\beta-1}\, dp}{\int \binom{n}{x} p^x (1-p)^{n-x}\, p^{\alpha-1}(1-p)^{\beta-1}\, dp}$$

$$= \frac{\int p^{x+\alpha+1-1}(1-p)^{n+\beta-x-1}\, dp}{\int p^{x+\alpha-1}(1-p)^{n+\beta-x-1}\, dp}$$

$$= \frac{B(x+\alpha+1, n+\beta-x)}{B(x+\alpha, n+\beta-x)}$$

$$= \frac{\dfrac{\Gamma(x+\alpha+1)\,\Gamma(n+\beta-x)}{\Gamma(\alpha+\beta+n+1)}}{\dfrac{\Gamma(x+\alpha)\,\Gamma(n+\beta-x)}{\Gamma(\alpha+\beta+n)}}$$

$$\therefore \quad \hat{p} = \frac{x+\alpha}{n+\alpha+\beta}$$

Q. 47. *Find Bayes estimator of the single parameter λ of the Poisson distribution when it is known that the prior distribution of λ is a gamma distribution.*

Ans. Let there be a random sample $X_1, X_2, \ldots, X_n$. As per question,

$$f(x; \lambda) = \frac{e^{-\lambda}\lambda^x}{x!} \quad \text{for } x = 0, 1, 2, \ldots, n.$$

$$g(\lambda) = \frac{\alpha^r}{\Gamma r}\lambda^{r-1}e^{-\alpha\lambda} \quad \text{for } 0 \le \lambda \le \infty$$

We know,

$$f(x; \lambda) = f(x \mid \lambda)\, g(\lambda)$$

$$= \frac{e^{-\lambda}\,\lambda^x}{x!} \cdot \frac{\alpha^r}{\Gamma r}\lambda^{r-1}\, e^{-\alpha\lambda}$$

$$E(\lambda) = \frac{\int_0^\infty \lambda \dfrac{e^{-\lambda}\,\lambda^x}{x!}\lambda^{r-1}\, e^{-\alpha\lambda}\, d\lambda}{\int_0^\infty \dfrac{e^{-\lambda}\cdot\lambda^x}{x!}\lambda^{r-1}\, e^{-\alpha\lambda}\, d\lambda}$$

$$= \frac{\int_0^\infty e^{-(1+\alpha)\lambda}\,\lambda^{(x+r+1)-1}\, d\lambda}{\int_0^\infty e^{-(1+\alpha)\lambda}\,\lambda^{x+r-1}\, d\lambda}$$

$$= \frac{\Gamma(x+r+1)/(1+\alpha)^{x+r+1}}{\Gamma(x+r)/(1+\alpha)^{x+r}}$$

$$\hat{\lambda} = \frac{x+r}{1+\alpha}$$

Q. 48. *Define Pitman's estimator for location parameter of a distribution.*

Ans. Let $X_1, X_2, \ldots, X_n$ be a random sample from a density $f(x; \theta)$ where θ is a location parameter of the distribution. Then the Pitman estimator $\hat{\theta} = t(X_1, X_2, \ldots, X_n)$ *is given by the formula,*

$$t = \frac{\int \theta \prod_{i=1}^{n} f(x_i; \theta)\, d\theta}{\int \prod_{i=1}^{n} f(x_i; \theta)\, d\theta}$$

$$= \frac{\int \theta L(x \mid \theta)\, d\theta}{\int L(x \mid \theta)\, d\theta}$$

Q. 49. *Give the properties of Pitman estimator for location which it usually holds.*

Ans.

(*i*) The Pitman estimator for location has smallest mean squared error.

(*ii*) A Pitman estimator is a function of sufficient statistics.

(*iii*) Pitman estimator is a minimax estimator on the real line.

Q. 50. *Give the expression for Pitman estimator for scale parameter of a distribution.*

Ans. Let $X_1, X_2, \ldots, X_n$ be a random sample from a density $f(x; \theta)$ where θ is a scale parameter such that $\theta > 0$. Also $f(x; \theta)$ exists for $x > 0$ and otherwise zero.

Then the Pitman estimator $\hat{\theta} = t(X_1, X_2, \ldots, X_n)$ for scale parameter can be obtained by the expression:

$$\hat{\theta} = \frac{\int \frac{1}{\theta^2} \prod_{i=1}^{n} f(x_i;\theta)\, d\theta}{\int \frac{1}{\theta^3} \prod_{i=1}^{n} f(x_i;\theta)\, d\theta}$$

$$= \frac{\int \frac{1}{\theta^2} L(x|\theta)\, d\theta}{\int \frac{1}{\theta^3} L(x|\theta)\, d\theta}$$

Pitman estimator for scale is also a function of sufficient statistics.

Q. 51. *Find the Pitman estimator of the mean μ of a normal population N (μ, 1).*

Ans. Let $X_1, X_2, ..., X_n$ be a random sample from the density $f(x; \mu, 1)$.

We know,

$$f(x; \mu, 1) = \frac{1}{\sqrt{2\pi}} e^{-\frac{1}{2}(x-\mu)^2}$$

Pitman estimator,

$$\hat{\mu} = \frac{\int \mu \left(\frac{1}{2\pi}\right)^{n/2} e^{-\frac{1}{2}\Sigma(x_i-\mu)^2} d\mu}{\int \left(\frac{1}{2\pi}\right)^{n/2} e^{-\frac{1}{2}\Sigma(x_i-\mu)^2} d\mu}$$

$$= \frac{\int \mu\, e^{-\frac{1}{2}\{\Sigma x_i^2 + n\mu^2 - 2\mu\Sigma x_i\}} d\mu}{\int e^{-\frac{1}{2}\{\Sigma x_i^2 + n\mu^2 - 2\mu\Sigma x_i\}} d\mu}$$

$$= \frac{\int \mu\, e^{\left(-\frac{n}{2}\mu^2 + \mu\Sigma x_i\right)} d\mu}{\int e^{\left(-\frac{n}{2}\mu^2 + \mu\Sigma x_i\right)} d\mu}$$

$$= \bar{x}$$

Q. 52. *Explain the general procedure for parametric interval estimation on the basis of sample drawn from continuous distributions.*

Ans. Let $X_1, X_2, ..., X_n$ be a random sample $T_1 = t_1(X_1, X_2, ..., X_n)$ and $T_2 = t_2(X_1, X_2, ..., X_n)$ be any two statistics such that $T_1 < T_2$, then the confidence limits for a parametric function $\tau(\theta)$ of θ can be obtained by the relations,

$$P_\theta\{T_1 > \tau \mid \theta\} \doteq \alpha_1$$

and $$P_\theta\{T_2 > \tau \mid \theta\} = \alpha_2$$

where α_1 and α_2 are independent of θ and are the areas of critical region on the left and right tails respectively of the probability density curve. Also $\alpha_1 + \alpha_2 = \alpha$.

The confidence interval is given as,

$$P_\theta\{T_1 \le \tau(\theta) \le T_2\} = 1 - \alpha \text{ for } \theta \in \Theta$$

where $(1 - \alpha)$ is called the *confidence coefficient* and is generally given as $(1 - \alpha)\, 100 = \lambda$ per cent.

Also the confidence interval is $(t_2 - t_1)$.

Thus, γ per cent confidence limits are t_1 and t_2.

Q. 53. *Find 95 per cent confidence limit for population mean μ of the population N (μ, σ²) in case when σ² is known.*

Ans. If $\bar{x}$ is the sample mean and $Z_{\alpha/2}$ be the critical value of the standard normal deviate Z such that 0.025 area is on the left of the lower limit and 0.025 area under the normal curve to the right of the upper limit, *i.e.*,

$$\frac{\bar{x} - \mu}{\sigma/\sqrt{n}} \ge -Z_{\alpha/2}$$

and $$\frac{\bar{x} - \mu}{\sigma/\sqrt{n}} \le Z_{\alpha/2}$$

From the first inequality we get

$$\mu \le \bar{x} + Z_{\alpha/2} \cdot \frac{\sigma}{\sqrt{n}}$$

and from second, $$\mu \ge \bar{x} - Z_{\alpha/2} \cdot \frac{\sigma}{\sqrt{n}}$$

Combining the two inequalities, we can write,

$$\bar{x} - Z_{\alpha/2} \cdot \frac{\sigma}{\sqrt{n}} \le \mu \le \bar{x} + Z_{\alpha/2} \cdot \frac{\sigma}{\sqrt{n}}$$

Thus, the confidence limits for μ are $\bar{x} \mp Z_{\alpha/2} \cdot \frac{\sigma}{\sqrt{n}}$.

Also, the confidence interval for μ is

$$\left(\bar{x} + Z_{\alpha/2} \cdot \frac{\sigma}{\sqrt{n}}\right) - \left(\bar{x} - Z_{\alpha/2} \cdot \frac{\sigma}{\sqrt{n}}\right) = 2Z_{\alpha/2} \cdot \frac{\sigma}{\sqrt{n}}$$

When the population standard deviation σ is not known, then to find the confidence limits for μ, replace $Z_{\alpha/2}$ by $t_{\alpha/2}$ and σ by its estimate s. In this situation the limits for μ are $\bar{x} \mp t_{\alpha/2} \frac{s}{\sqrt{n}}$ and confidence interval is $2t_{\alpha/2} \cdot \frac{s}{\sqrt{n}}$.

Q. 54. *Give the inequality for finding out the confidence limits for the variance σ^2 of normal population, $N(\mu, \sigma^2)$ when its mean μ is unknown.*

Ans. Let $X_1, X_2, \ldots, X_n$ be a random sample from $N(\mu, \sigma^2)$ population. Also let s^2 be the sample variance. We know that $(n-1)s^2/\sigma^2$ is distributed as χ^2 with $(n-1)$ degrees of freedom. Then we have to find out two values of χ^2 say χ_1^2 and χ_2^2 such that

$$P\left\{\chi_1^2 \le \frac{(n-1)s^2}{\sigma^2} \le \chi_2^2\right\} = \gamma$$

The values of χ_1^2 and χ_2^2 chosen in such way that,

$$P\left\{\frac{(n-1)s^2}{\sigma^2} \le \chi_1^2\right\} = P\left\{\frac{(n-1)s^2}{\sigma^2} > \chi^2\right\}$$

$$= (1-\gamma)/2 = \alpha/2$$

Such a confidence interval is referred to as *equal tails confidence interval.* Thus,

$$P\left\{\frac{(n-1)s^2}{\chi_2^2} \le \sigma^2 \le \frac{(n-1)s^2}{\chi_1^2}\right\} = \gamma$$

for $\chi_1^2 \le \chi_2^2$

For $\gamma = 0.95$, χ_1^2 and $\chi_{0.975}^2$ and $\chi_2^2 = \chi_{0.025}^2$. Thus, the confidence limits with $(1-\alpha)\,100 = \gamma$ confidence coefficient are,

$$\begin{pmatrix}\text{Lower}\\\text{limit}\end{pmatrix} L = \frac{(n-1)s^2}{\chi^2_{(1+\gamma)/2,\,n-1}}$$

and

$$\begin{pmatrix}\text{Upper}\\\text{limit}\end{pmatrix} U = \frac{(n-1)s^2}{\chi^2_{(1-\gamma)/2,\,n-1}}$$

If someone is interested to find out the confidence limits for the standard deviation σ, one way is to find out the confidence limits for σ^2 and take their under roots. So the confidence limits for σ are, $L_1 = \sqrt{L}$ and $U_1 = \sqrt{U}$. This is not an exact method but it gives quite satisfactory results.

Q. 55. *Give the formula for obtaining confidence limits for the difference between the means of two normal populations.*

Ans. Let the two normal populations be $N(\mu_1, \sigma_1^2)$ and $N(\mu_2, \sigma_2^2)$. Confidence limits for $(\mu_1 - \mu_2)$ with confidence coefficient $(1-\alpha)\,100 = \gamma$ per cent, when two samples $X_{11}, X_{12}, \ldots, X_{1n_1}$ and $X_{21}, X_{22}, \ldots, X_{2n_2}$ have been drawn from the two populations, respectively, in case when $\sigma_1^2 = \sigma_2^2$ and are unknown, can be obtained by the formula,

$$(\bar{x}_1 - \bar{x}_2) \mp t_{(1+\gamma)/2,\,(n_1+n_2-2)} \cdot s_{(\bar{x}_1 - \bar{x}_2)}$$

where,

$$s_{(\bar{x}_1 - \bar{x}_2)} = \sqrt{s_p^2\left(\frac{1}{n_1} + \frac{1}{n_2}\right)}$$

and

$$s_p^2 = \frac{(n_1-1)\,s_1^2 + (n_2-1)s_2^2}{(n_1+n_2-2)}$$

In case when $\sigma_1^2 \ne \sigma_2^2$, confidence limits for $(\mu_1 - \mu_2)$ by Cochran's approximation are:

$$(\bar{x}_1 - \bar{x}_2) \mp t^* \sqrt{\frac{s_1^2}{n_1} + \frac{s_2^2}{n_2}}$$

$$\text{where } t^* = \frac{\frac{s_1^2}{n_1} \cdot t_{\frac{1-\gamma}{2}, n_1 - 1} + \frac{s_2^2}{n_2} \cdot t_{\frac{1-\gamma}{2}, n_2 - 1}}{\frac{s_1^2}{n_1} + \frac{s_2^2}{n_2}}$$

Please note that s_1^2 and s_2^2 are the sample variances.

Q. 56. *How will you find the confidence limits for the mean of difference of paired observations?*

Ans. Let n pairs of observation on the variables X and Y be $(X_1, Y_1), (X_2, Y_2), \ldots, (X_n, Y_n)$. In this situation X and Y are said to be correlated. Also suppose $X - Y = d$. The confidence limits for the population mean difference μ_D with confidence coefficient γ can be calculated by the formula,

$$\bar{d} \mp t_{\frac{1+\gamma}{2}, (n-1)} \cdot s_{\bar{d}}$$

$$\text{where, } \quad s_{\bar{d}}^2 = \frac{1}{(n-1)}\left[\sum d_i^2 - \frac{(\Sigma d_i)^2}{n}\right]$$

for $i = 1, 2, \ldots, n$.

Q. 57. *Obtain the confidence limits for the ratio of variances of two normal populations.*

Ans. Adopting the usual notations, confidence limits for the ratio σ_1^2/σ_2^2 of variances of two normal populations with confidence coefficient γ can be given as,

$$L = \frac{s_1^2}{s_2^2} F_{\frac{1+\gamma}{2} \cdot (n_1 - 1, n_2 - 1)}$$

$$U = \frac{s_1^2}{s_2^2} F_{\frac{1-\gamma}{2} \cdot (n_1 - 1, n_2 - 1)}$$

Q. 58. *Clarify the concept of shortest confidence interval.*

Ans. We have two statistics T_1 and T_2 which are functions of sample variates $X_1, X_2, \ldots, X_n$ from a density $f(x; \theta)$ such that the area to the left of T_1 is α_1 and to the right of T_2 is α_2, both $\alpha_1, \alpha_2 > 0$ in such a way that $\alpha_1 + \alpha_2 = \alpha$. There can be an innumerable number of values of α_1 and α_2 which satisfy the condition $\alpha_1 + \alpha_2 = \alpha$ leading to an innumerable number of confidence intervals. Now the problem arises which one to choose out of countless number of confidence intervals. One widely accepted criterion is the width of the confidence interval. An interval with smaller width is better than the other having the same confidence coefficient, *i.e.*,

$$T_2 - T_1 \leq T_2' - T_1' \text{ for all } \theta \in \Theta$$

Hence, a confidence interval $(T_2 - T_1)$ which is uniformly shorter than any other confidence interval $(T_2' - T_1')$ for θ in Θ is known as the *shortest confidence interval* and is most preferred one.

It is worth pointing out that in most of the problems it is not possible to construct confidence interval of shortest width for a given confidence coefficient $1 - \alpha$. Hence, equal tail confidence intervals are generally worked out.

Q. 59. *What do you understand by confidence region?*

Ans. Sometimes an investigator aspires to extend the idea of interval estimation to more than one parameters simultaneously. For instance, one may wish to estimate the parameters μ and σ^2 of normal distribution simultaneously by some confidence region in a plane.

Suppose θ_1 and θ_2 are two parameters for which the confidence region has to be worked out. Let (t_1, t_2) and (m_1, m_2) be the statistics which are to constitute a simultaneous interval leading to the confidence region of confidence coefficient $(1 - \alpha)$ in such a way that

$$P(t_1 \leq \theta_1 \leq t_2 \text{ and } m_1 \leq \theta \leq m_2) = 1 - \alpha.$$

Practically, it is hardly possible.

Another approach is to find two statistics ω_1 and ω_2 such that,

$$P(\omega_1 \leq \theta_1^2 + \theta_2^2 \leq \omega_2) = 1 - \alpha.$$

It is also not a satisfactory proposition.

Q. 60. *What do you understand by one-sided confidence interval?*

Ans. Let $X_1, X_2, ..., X_n$ be a random sample from the density $f(x; \theta)$ and $T_1 = t_1(X_1, X_2, ..., X_n)$ be any statistic such that

$$P(t_1 \leq \theta) = 1 - \alpha \text{ for all } \theta$$

Then t_1 is known as the lower confidence bound for the parameter θ with confidence coefficient $(1 - \alpha)$. The interval $\{t_1, \theta\}$ is termed as the *lower one-sided confidence interval* for θ with confidence coefficient $(1 - \alpha)$.

Similarly, any other statistic $T_2 = t_2(X_1, X_2, ..., X_n)$ for which

$$P(t_2 \geq \theta) = 1 - \alpha \text{ for all } \theta$$

is called the upper confidence bound for θ with confidence coefficient $(1 - \alpha)$. The interval $(-\infty, T_2)$ is known as *upper one-sided confidence interval* with confidence coefficient $(1 - \alpha)$.

SECTION B

Fill in the Blanks

Fill in the suitable word(s) or phrase(s) in the blanks:

1. A sample constant representing a population parameter is known as ________.
2. An estimator T_n which is most concentrated about a parameter θ is the ________ estimator.
3. Estimation is ________ if we have a purposive sample.
4. Estimation is possible only in case of a ________.
5. An estimator is itself a ________.
6. A value of an estimator is called an ________.
7. If $X_1, X_2, ..., X_n$ be a random sample, the expression $\Sigma X_i / n$ is an ________.
8. A single value of an estimator for a population parameter θ is called its ________ estimate.
9. If an estimator T_n converges in probability to the parameteric function $\tau(\theta)$, T_n is said to be a ________ estimator.
10. $\Sigma X_j / n$ for $i = 1, 2, ..., n$ is a ________ estimator of population mean.
11. If the expected value of an estimator T_n is equal to the value of the parameter θ, T_n is said to be an ________ estimator of θ.
12. The difference between the expected value of an estimator and the value of the corresponding parameter is known as ________.
13. If T_n is an estimator of a parametric function $\tau(\theta)$, the mean square error of T_n is equal to ________.
14. For the mean square error to be minimum, bias should be ________.
15. If an unbiased estimator T_n is such that for any other unbiased estimator τ_n^*, $v(T_n) \leq v(T_n^*)$, T_n is a ________.
16. If $T_n = t_n(X_1, X_2, ..., X_n)$, an estimator of $\tau(\theta)$, is such that $\lim_{n \to \infty} [T_n - \tau(\theta)]^2 = 0$, T_n is said to be ________ consistent.
17. For discrete variable Crammer-Rao inequality ________.
18. If T_n is an estimator of a parameter θ of the density $f(x; \theta)$ the quantity $$E\left[\frac{\partial}{\partial\theta} \log f(x; \theta)\right]^2$$ is called the ________.
19. An estimator of $v_\theta(T_n)$ which attains lower bound for all θ is known as ________.
20. An inequality parallel to Crammer-Rao inequality was also given by ________.
21. Crammer and Rao gave the inequality for lower bound of $V_\theta(T_n)$ in ________ years.

22. A. Bhattacharyya inequality provides ________ of $V_\theta(T_n)$.

23. Chapman-Robins inequality is ________ than Crammer-Rao inequality.

24. Crammer gave the inequality for lower bound of $V_\theta(T_n)$ in ________.

25. C.R. Rao give the theorem for lower bound of $V_\theta(T_n)$ in ________.

26. ________ proved the theorem for lower bound of $V_\theta(T_n)$ earlier than Crammer-Rao but not published.

27. Another name of BAN estimator is ________.

28. BAN estimators possess ________ property.

29. BAN estimators have ________ variance.

30. An estimator is efficient if its variance is ________ than the variance of any other estimator.

31. Relative efficiency of an estimator T_n as compared to an estimator is T_n' given as ________.

32. If T_n and T_n^* are two estimators such that $V(T_n) = V(T_n^*)$, then ________.

33. If a statistic $T = t(X_1, X_2, \ldots, X_n)$ provides as much information as the random sample $X_1, X_2, \ldots, X_n$ could provide, then T is a ________.

34. If $T = t(X_1, X_2, \ldots, X_n)$ is a sufficient statistic for a parameter θ of the density $f(x; \theta)$ then the conditional distribution of $X_1, X_2, \ldots, X_n$ is ________ of θ for any value of $T = t$.

35. If $S = s(X_1, X_2, \ldots, X_n)$ is a sufficient statistic for θ of density $f(x; \theta)$ and $f(x_i; \theta)$ for $i = 1, 2, \ldots, n$ can be factorised as $g(s, \theta)\, h(x)$, then $s(X_1, X_2, \ldots, X_n)$ is a ________.

36. A sufficient statistic $S = s(X_1, X_2, \ldots, X_n)$ is called a ________ statistic if it cannot be condensed any more without sacrificing the criterion of sufficiency.

37. If $f(x; \theta)$ is a family of distributions and $h(x)$ is any statistic such that $E[h(x)] = 0$, then $f(x, \theta)$ is called ________.

38. An unbiased and complete statistic is compulsorily ________.

39. An unbiased and complete statistic is a ________ estimator provided MVUE exists.

40. ________ theorem states that given an unbiased estimator T, another unbiased estimator T_1, which is a function of sufficient statistics, can be formed which will not have larger variance than that of T for all parameters θ.

41. An estimator whose risk is not greater than the risk of any other estimator T of a parameter θ is called an ________ estimator.

42. Expected loss in choosing an estimator T of a parameter θ is called its ________.

43. The joint probability density function of sample variates is called ________.

44. A value of a parameter θ which maximises the likelihood function is known as ________ estimate of θ.

45. A maximum likelihood estimate is not necessarily ________.

46. If a MVB unbiased estimator exists, ________ estimator provides it.

47. A maximum likelihood estimator may be consistent but not necessarily ________.

48. If a random sample $X_1, X_2, \ldots, X_n$ is drawn from a population $N(\mu, \sigma^2)$, the maximum likelihood estimate of μ is ________.

49. If a random sample $x_1, x_2, \ldots, x_n$ is selected from a normal population $N(\mu, \sigma^2)$, the maximum likelihood estimate of σ^2 is ________.

50. Maximum likelihood estimator $\Sigma(X_i - \bar{X})^2/n$ of the variance σ^2 of a normal density $f(x; \mu, \sigma^2)$ is a ________ .

51. If $\bar{x}$ is a maximum likelihood estimator of μ of a normal population, $\bar{x}$ is a ________ .

52. For a gam (x, α, λ) distribution with λ known, the maximum likelihood estimate of α is ________.

53. Maximum likelihood estimate of the parameter θ of the distribution $f(x, \theta) = \frac{1}{2}e^{-|x-\theta|}$ is ________.

54. For a rectangular distribution $1/(\beta - \alpha)$, the maximum likelihood estimates of α and β are ________ and ________ respectively.

55. Least square method is a device to obtain a ________.

56. Linear estimators obtained by the method of least squares are ________ .

57. Linear estimators obtained by the method of least squares are ________ estimators.

58. Determining of minimum variance linear unbiased estimator is due to ________ .

59. Method of moments for estimating the parameters of a distribution was given by ________ in ________ .

60. The estimators obtained by the method of moments under general conditions are ________ for large sample size.

61. The estimators obtained by the method of moments are ________ efficient than maximum likelihood estimators.

62. The estimator of σ^2 based on a random sample $X_1, X_2, \ldots, X_n$ from a population $N(\mu, \sigma^2)$ by the method of moments is ________ .

63. The estimate of λ of a Poisson distribution $P(x; \lambda)$ based on a sample size n by the method of moments is ________ .

64. The estimate of the parameter λ of the exponential distribution $\lambda e^{-\lambda x}$ by the method of moments is ________ .

65. The estimation of a parameter by the method of minimum Chi-square utilises ________ statistic.

66. Statistics for modified minimum Chi-square differs from minimum Chi-square in respect of ________ in the statistic.

67. The estimators obtained by the method of minimum Chi-square and maximum likelihood estimators are ________ .

68. In particular cases minimum Chi-square estimators have lesser mean square error than ML estimators was proved by ________ in ________ .

69. Minimum Chi-square estimators are ________.

70. Minimum Chi-square estimators are not necessarily ________ .

71. Under Bayesian approach, the parameter of a distribution is a ________ .

72. Non-Bayesian always consider a parameter as a ________ .

73. In Bayesian approach, an investigator has always to specify ________ .

74. Prior distribution is based on some ________.

75. The density function $f(x; \theta)$ under Bayesian approach with known prior distribution $g(\theta)$ is always expressed as ________ .

76. Formula for Bayes estimator with usual notations can be expressed as ________ .

77. Bayes estimator is always a function of ________ statistics.

78. For large samples, Bayes estimators tend to ________ estimators.

79. Bayes estimators in some cases are ________ .

80. If two estimators T_1 and T_2 are such that $\sup_\theta R(T_1, \theta), \leq \sup_\theta R(T_2, \theta)$ then T_1 is said to be a ________ estimator.

81. Bayes estimator of parameter p of the binomial distribution given that the prior distribution of p is beta distribution with density $f(x; \alpha, \beta)$ is ________ .

82. If a variable X follows $P(x; \lambda)$ distribution and the prior distribution of λ is $G(x; n, \alpha)$ the Bayes estimator of λ is ________ .

83. Formula for Pitman estimator of the parameter θ of a density $f(x; \theta)$ is given by the formula ________ .

84. Pitman estimator possesses ________ mean square error.

85. Pitman estimator is a function of ________.

86. Pitman estimator is a ________ estimator.

87. Pitman estimator for location is also ________.

88. Pitman estimator for μ of a normal population $N(\mu, 1)$ is ________ .

89. Interval estimate is determined in terms of ________.

90. An interval estimate with ________ interval is best.

91. Confidence interval is specified by the ________ limits.

92. When confidence interval for two or more parameters is estimated simultaneously, then ________ is delimited.

93. Consistency ensures that the difference between the estimator T_n and the parametric function $\tau(\theta)$ ________ as n increases indefinitely.

94. The best estimator implies that the distribution of an estimator be ________ around the true parameter.

95. If t is a consistent estimator of θ, then t^2 is a ________ estimator of θ^2.

96. For the Poisson distribution $P(x; \lambda)$, $1/\bar{x}$ is a ________ estimator of λ.

97. If mean of the sampling distribution of an estimator T_n is equal to population mean, it is a ________ estimator.

98. If $E(T_n) > \theta$, the parameter value T_n is said to be ________ .

99. An unbiased estimator is not necessarily ________.

100. If $x_1, x_2, \ldots, x_n$ is a random sample from a normal population, $\Sigma(x_i - \bar{x})^2/n$ is not a ________ estimator of σ^2.

101. An estimator with smaller variance than that of another estimator is ________ .

102. If $X_1, X_2, \ldots, X_n$ is a random sample from an infinite population and S^2 is defined as $\Sigma(X_i - \bar{X})^2 / n$, $\frac{n}{n-1} S^2$ is an ________ estimator of population variance σ^2.

103. Sample standard deviation is a ________ and ________ estimator of population standard deviation.

104. If T_n is a sufficient estimator of θ of density $f(x; \theta)$, $\frac{\partial}{\partial \theta} \log L$ is a function of ________ and ________ only.

105. Let $X_1, X_2, \ldots, X_n$ be a random sample from a density $f(x; \theta)$. If $S = s(X_1, X_2, \ldots, X_n)$ is a complete sufficient statistic and $T' = t(s)$, a function of S, is an unbiased estimator of $\tau(\theta)$, T' is an ________ of $\tau(\theta)$. [*Lehmann-Scheffe theorem.*]

106. Completeness confers ________ property of an estimator.

107. The credit of factorisation theorem for sufficiency goes to ________ .

108. ________ estimator may not be unique.

109. If $X_1, X_2, \ldots, X_n$ is a random sample from the uniform distribution $f(x; \theta) = \frac{1}{\theta}$, $0 < x \le \theta$, $Y = \max(X_1, X_2, \ldots, x_n)$ is a ________ estimator of θ.

110. If X is a Poisson $(x; \lambda)$, the sufficient statistic for λ is ________ .

111. If we have a random sample of size n from a population $N(\mu, \sigma^2)$, then sample mean is ________ efficient than sample median.

112. Let there be a sample of size n from a normal population with mean μ and variance σ^2. The efficiency of median relative to the mean is ________.

113. Suppose a sample of size n is drawn randomly from a normal density $f(x; \mu, \sigma^2)$. The estimate of mean deviation about mean is a ________ estimate of σ.

114. Consistent estimators are not necessary ________.

115. An unbiased estimator need not be ________.

116. If a sufficient estimator exists, it is function of the ________ estimator.

117. An unbiased estimator of the reciprocal of the parameter of a binomial distribution is ________.

118. If a function $f(t)$ of the sufficient statistics $T = t(X_1, X_2, ..., X_n)$ is unbiased for $\tau(\theta)$ and is also unique, this is the ________ estimate.

119. If a maximum likelihood estimator exists, it is ________ among the class of such estimators.

120. If the mean $\bar{x}$ of a sample drawn from a normal population is a maximum likelihood estimator, $\bar{x}$ is a ________ estimator of population mean.

121. Sample mean is an ________ and ________ estimate of population mean.

122. In case of sampling from normal population, $N(\mu, \sigma^2)$, median is an ________ estimator of μ.

123. The variance of median tends to zero as n, the sample size tends to infinity, hence median is a ________ estimator of μ.

124. If T_1 and T_2 are two MVU estimators for $T(\theta)$, then ________.

125. If X_1, X_2, X_3 is a random sample from a population $N(\mu, \sigma^2)$ and $T_1 = (X_1 + X_2 + X_3)/3$ and $T_2 = 2X_1 + X_2 - 2X_3$ are two estimators for μ, T_1 is ________ than T_2.

SECTION C

Multiple Choice Questions

Select the correct alternative out of given ones:

1. Parameters are those constants which occur in:
(*a*) samples
(*b*) probability density function
(*c*) a formula
(*d*) none of the above

2. Estimation of parameters in all scientific investigations is of:
(*a*) prime importance
(*b*) secondary importance
(*c*) no use
(*d*) deceptive nature

3. Estimate and estimator are:
(*a*) synonyms
(*b*) different
(*c*) related to population
(*d*) none of the above

4. An estimator is considered to be the best if its distribution is:
(*a*) continuous
(*b*) discrete
(*c*) concentrated about the true parameter value
(*d*) normal

5. An estimator T_n based on a sample of size n is considered to be the best estimator of θ if:
(*a*) $P\{| T_n - \theta | < \varepsilon\} \geq P\{| T_n^* - \theta | < \varepsilon\}$

(*b*) $P\{|T_n - \theta| > \varepsilon\} \geq P\{|T_n^* - \theta| > \varepsilon\}$

(*c*) $P\{|T_n - \theta| < \varepsilon\} = P\{|T_n^* - \theta| < \varepsilon\}$ for all 0

(*d*) none of the above

6. An estimator of a parametric function $\tau(\theta)$ is said to be the best if it possesses:

(*a*) any two properties of a good estimator

(*b*) at least three properties of a good estimator

(*c*) all the properties of a good estimator

(*d*) all of the above

7. The type of estimates are:

(*a*) point estimate

(*b*) interval estimates

(*c*) estimation of confidence region

(*d*) all of the above

8. If an estimator T_n of population parameter θ converges in probability to θ as n tends to infinity is said to be:

(*a*) sufficient

(*b*) efficient

(*c*) consistent

(*d*) unbiased

9. The estimator $\Sigma X/n$ of population mean is:

(*a*) an unbiased estimator

(*b*) a consistent estimator

(*c*) both (*a*) and (*b*)

(*d*) neither (*a*) nor (*b*)

10. If $X_1, X_2, \ldots, X_n$ is a random sample from a population $N(0, \sigma^2)$, the sufficient statistic for σ^2 is:

(*a*) ΣX_i

(*b*) ΣX_i^2

(*c*) $(\Sigma X_i)^2$

(*d*) none of the above

11. If $x_1, x_2, \ldots, x_n$ be a random sample from a $N(\mu, \sigma^2)$ population, the sufficient statistic for μ is:

(*a*) $\Sigma(x_i - \bar{x})$

(*b*) $\bar{x}/n$

(*c*) Σx_i

(*d*) $\Sigma(x_i - \bar{x})^2$

12. Factorisation theorem for sufficiency is known as:

(*a*) Rao-Blackwell theorem

(*b*) Crammer-Rao theorem

(*c*) Chapman-Robins theorem

(*d*) Fisher-Neyman theorem

13. Consistency can specifically be named as:

(*a*) simple consistency

(*b*) mean-squared consistency

(*c*) simple consistency and mean squared consistency both

(*d*) all of the above

14. If the expected value of an estimator is not equal to its parametric function $\tau(\theta)$, it is said to be a:

(*a*) unbiased estimator

(*b*) biased estimator

(*c*) consistent estimator

(*d*) none of the above

15. Bias of an estimator can be:

(*a*) positive

(*b*) negative

(*c*) either positive or negative

(*d*) always zero

16. If $X_1, X_2, \ldots, X_n$ be a random sample from an infinite population where $S^2 = \frac{1}{n}\sum_i (X_i - \bar{X})^2$, the unbiased estimator for the population variance σ^2 is:

(*a*) $\frac{1}{n-1}S^2$

(*b*) $\frac{1}{n}S^2$

(*c*) $\frac{n-1}{n}S^2$

(*d*) $\frac{n}{n-1}S^2$

17. If $X_1, X_2, \ldots, X_n$ is a random sample from an infinite population, an estimator for the population variance σ^2 such as:

(*a*) $\frac{1}{n}\sum (X_i - \bar{X})^2$ is an unbiased estimator of σ^2

(*b*) $\frac{1}{n}\sum (X_i - \bar{X})^2$ is a biased estimator of σ^2

(*c*) $\sum (X_i - \bar{X})^2$ is an unbiased estimator of σ^2

(*d*) none of the above

18. If $x_1, x_2, \ldots, x_n$ be the values of random sample from a normal population $N(\mu, \sigma^2)$, $s^2 = \frac{1}{n-1}\sum (x_i - \bar{x})^2$ is a:

(*a*) unbiased estimator of σ^2

(*b*) sufficient statistics for σ^2

(*c*) mean squared error consistent estimator of σ^2

(*d*) all of the above

19. Simple consistency of an estimator T_n of $\tau(\theta)$ means:

(*a*) $P_\theta\{| T_n - \tau(\theta) | > \varepsilon\} = 1$

(*b*) $\lim_{n\to\infty} P_\theta\{|T_n - \tau(\theta)| < \varepsilon\} = 1$

(*c*) $\lim_{n\to\infty} P_\theta\{|T_n - \tau(\theta)| < \varepsilon\} = 0$

(*d*) all of the above

20. A sequence of estimators $T_1, T_2, \ldots, T_n$ of $\tau(\theta)$ is said to be a best asymptotically normal estimator if it satisfies the condition:

(*a*) $\sqrt{n}\,[T_n - \tau(\theta)] \sim N(0, \sigma^2)$ as $n \to \infty$

(*b*) T_n is consistent

(*c*) T_n has minimum variance as compared to the variance of any other estimator T_n^*.

(*d*) all of the above

21. If $X_1, X_2, \ldots, X_n$ is a random sample from a population $N(\mu, \sigma^2)$, the estimator $\frac{\Sigma X_i}{n}$ is:

(*a*) a BAN estimator for μ

(*b*) a consistent estimator for μ

(*c*) a unbiased estimator of μ

(*d*) all of the above

22. Which of the estimators are BAN estimators?

(*a*) ML estimators

(*b*) Minimum Chi-square estimators

(*c*) Both (*a*) and (*b*)

(*d*) None of (*a*) and (*b*)

23. Crammer-Rao inequality is based on:

(*a*) stringent conditions

(*b*) mild conditions

(*c*) no conditions

(*d*) none of the above

24. Regularity conditions of Crammer-Rao inequality are related to:

(*a*) integrability of functions

(*b*) differentiability of functions

(*c*) both (*a*) and (*b*)

(*d*) neither (*a*) nor (*b*)

25. Crammer-Rao inequality with regard to the variance of an estimator provides:

(*a*) upper bound on the variance

(*b*) lower bound on the variance

(*c*) asymptotic variance of an estimator

(*d*) none of the above

26. Crammer-Rao inequality is valid in case of:

(*a*) continuous variables

(*b*) discrete variables

(*c*) both (*a*) and (*b*)

(*d*) neither (*a*) nor (*b*)

27. Crammer-Rao inequality was given by them:

(*a*) jointly

(*b*) in different years

(*c*) in the same year

(*d*) none of the above

28. The denominator in the Crammer-Rao inequality is known as:

(*a*) information limit

(*b*) lower bound of the variance
(*c*) upper bound of the variance
(*d*) all of the above

29. The inequality for the lower bound of the variance of an estimator which is not based on stringent regularity conditions was given by:
(*a*) Aitken and Silverstone
(*b*) Neyman-Person
(*c*) Chapman-Robins
(*d*) none of the above

30. If $X_1, X_2, \ldots, X_n$ are *i.i.d.* variates from a density $f(x; \theta)$, then the Crammer-Rao bound on the variance of an estimator T_n of $\tau(\theta)$ is given by the equality:

(*a*) $V_\theta(T_n) \geq \dfrac{[\tau(\theta)]^2}{nE\left[\dfrac{\partial}{\partial\theta}\log f(x;\theta)\right]^2}$

(*b*) $V_\theta(T_n) \geq \dfrac{[\tau'(\theta)]^2}{nE\left[\dfrac{\partial^2}{\partial\theta^2}\log f(x;\theta)\right]}$

(*c*) $V_\theta(T_n) \geq -\dfrac{[\tau'(\theta)]^2}{E\left[\dfrac{\partial^2}{\partial\theta^2}\log f(x;\theta)\right]}$

(*d*) $V_\theta(T_n) \geq -\dfrac{[\tau'(\theta)]^2}{nE\left[\dfrac{\partial^2}{\partial\theta^2}\log f(x;\theta)\right]}$

31. The lower bound for the variance of an estimator T_n under amended regularity conditions of Crammer-Rao was given by:
(*a*) R.A. Fisher
(*b*) A. Bhattacharyya
(*c*) Silverstone
(*d*) all of the above

32. Another name of best asymptotically normal estimator is:
(*a*) minimum variance unbiased estimator
(*b*) best linear unbiased estimator
(*c*) consistent asymptotically normal efficient estimator
(*d*) all of the above

33. Mean squared error of an estimator T_n of $\tau(\theta)$ is expressed as:
(*a*) bias + $\text{var}_\theta(T_n)$
(*b*) [bias + $\text{var}_\theta(T_n)]^2$
(*c*) $(\text{bias})^2 + [\text{var}_\theta(T_n)]^2$
(*d*) $(\text{bias})^2 + \text{var}_\theta(T_n)$

34. Mean squared error of an estimator T_n of $\tau(\theta)$ is minimum only if
(*a*) bias and $\text{var}_\theta(T_n)$ both are zero.
(*b*) bias is zero and $\text{var}_\theta(T_n)$ is minimum
(*c*) bias is minimum and $\text{var}_\theta(T_n)$ is zero
(*d*) none of the above

35. Mean squared consistency of an estimator T_n of $\tau(\theta)$ implies that:
(*a*) T_n is biased but has minimum variance
(*b*) T_n is unbiased but has minimum variance
(*c*) T_n is unbiased and $\text{var}_\theta(T_n)$ tends to zero as sample size *n* tends to infinity
(*d*) T_n and $\text{var}_\theta(T_n)$ tends to zero as sample size *n* tends to infinity

36. If T_n and T_n^* are two unbiased estimators of $\tau(\theta)$ based on the random sample $X_1, X_2, \ldots, X_n$, then T_n is said to be UMVUE if and only if:
(*a*) $V(T_n) \geq V(T_n^*)$
(*b*) $V(T_n) \leq V(T_n^*)$
(*c*) $V(T_n) = V(T_n^*)$
(*d*) $V(T_n) = V(T_n^*) = 1$

37. An estimator T_n of $\tau(\theta)$ is said to be more efficient than any other estimator T_n^* of $\tau(\theta)$ if and only if

(a) var (T_n) < var (T_n^*)

(b) $\frac{\text{var}(T_n)}{\text{var}(T_n^*)} < 1$

(c) $\frac{V(T_n^*)}{V(T_n)} > 1$

(d) all of the above

38. A minimum variance unbiased estimator T_n is said to be unique if for any other estimator T_n^*,

(a) var (T_n) = var (T_n^*)

(b) var $(T_n) \leq$ var (T_n^*)

(c) both (a) and (b)

(d) neither (a) nor (b)

39. An estimator T_n is said to be a sufficient statistic for a parametric function $\tau(\theta)$ if it contained all the information which is contained in the

(a) population

(b) parametric function $\tau(\theta)$

(c) sample

(d) none of the above

40. If $X_1, X_2, \ldots, X_n$ is a random sample from a density $f(x; \theta)$ for $a < x < b$ where a and b are independent of θ, then any statistic $\hat{\theta}$ will be called a sufficient statistic if the joint probability density function $g(x_1, x_2, \ldots, x_n; \theta)$ of $X_1, X_2, \ldots, X_n$ can be expressed as:

(a) $g_1(x_i; \hat{\theta})\, g_2(\hat{\theta})$

(b) $g_1(\hat{\theta}, \theta)\, g_2(x_1, x_2, \ldots, x_n)$

(c) $g_1(\hat{\theta}, \theta)\, g_2(x_1, x_2, \ldots, x_n; \theta)$

(d) none of the above

41. Let $X_1, X_2, \ldots, X_n$ be a random sample from a density $f(x; \theta)$. A statistic $S = s(x_1, x_2, \ldots, x_n)$ is said to be a sufficient statistics if the conditional distribution of $x_1, x_2, \ldots, x_n$ given $S = s$ is:

(a) independent of s

(b) dependent of θ

(c) independent of θ

(d) all of the above

42. Let $x_1, x_2, \ldots, x_n$ be a random sample from a Bernoulli population $p^x (1-p)^{n-x}$. A sufficient statistics for p is:

(a) Σx_i

(b) Πx_i

(c) Max $(x_1, x_2, \ldots, x_n)$

(d) Min $(x_1, x_2, \ldots, x_n)$

43. Rao-Blackwell theorem enables us to obtain minimum variance unbiased estimator through:

(a) unbiased estimators

(b) complete statistics

(c) efficient statistics

(d) sufficient statistics

44. A sufficient statistics is minimal if and only if it is a:

(a) minimum sufficient statistics in a sequence of sufficient statistics.

(b) a function of every other sufficient statistics

(c) a function of UMVU estimators

(d) all of the above

45. A sufficient statistic $S = s(x_1, x_2, \ldots, x_n)$ is said to be complete for a parameter θ if:

(a) $E_\theta(S) = 0 \Rightarrow S = 0$

(b) $E_\theta(S) = 1 \Rightarrow S = 1$

(c) either (a) or (b)

(d) neither (a) nor (b)

46. If $f(x; \theta)$ is any family of parametric distribution and $g(x)$ be any function independent of θ, then $g(x)$ is a complete family if:

(*a*) $V_\theta\,[g(x)] = 0$

(*b*) $E\,[g(x)] = 0$

(*c*) $g(x; \theta) = g(x) \cdot g(\theta)$

(*d*) none of the above

47. An estimator $T_1 = t_1(x_1, x_2, \ldots, x_n)$ for θ is said to be admissible if for any other estimator $T_2 = t_2(x_1, x_2, \ldots, x_n)$ for θ, the relation is of the type:

(*a*) $R(t_1, \theta) \geq R(t_2, \theta)$

(*b*) $R(t_1, \theta) = R(t_2, \theta)$

(*c*) $R(t_1, \theta) \leq R(t_2, \theta)$

(*d*) none of the above

48. Let X be a random sample of size one from a normal population with mean 0 and variance σ^2. Then the sufficient statistics for σ^2 is:

(*a*) $|X|$

(*b*) X

(*c*) X^2

(*d*) none of the above

49. If T_1 and T_2 are two most efficient estimators with the same variance S^2 and the correlation between them is ρ, the variance of $(T_1 + T_2)/2$ is equal to:

(*a*) S^2

(*b*) ρS^2

(*c*) $(1 + \rho)\, S^2/4$

(*d*) $(1 + \rho)\, S^2/2$

50. If the sample mean $\bar{x}$ is an estimate of population mean μ, then $\bar{x}$ is:

(*a*) unbiased and efficient

(*b*) unbiased and inefficient

(*c*) biased and efficient

(*d*) biased and inefficient

51. Sample standard deviation as an estimate of population standard deviation is:

(*a*) unbiased and efficient

(*b*) unbiased and inefficient

(*c*) biased and efficient

(*d*) biased and inefficient

$$\left[\text{Hint: } \operatorname{var}(\bar{x}) = \frac{\sigma^2}{n} \text{ and var (med)} = \frac{\pi\sigma^2}{2n}\right]$$

52. Efficiency of sample mean as compared to median as an estimate of the mean of a normal population is:

(*a*) 64 per cent

(*b*) 157 per cent

(*c*) 317 per cent

(*d*) 31.5 per cent

53. If t is a consistent estimator of θ, then:

(*a*) t is also a consistent estimator of θ^2

(*b*) t^2 is also a consistent estimator of θ

(*c*) t^2 is also a consistent estimator θ^2

(*d*) none of the above

54. If T_n is a consistent estimator of θ, then e^{T_n} is a:

(*a*) unbiased estimator of e^θ

(*b*) consistent estimator of e^θ

(*c*) MVU estimator of e^θ

(*d*) none of the above

55. If $X_1, X_2, \ldots, X_n$ is a random sample from a population $p^x(1-p)^{n-x}$ for $x = 0, 1$ and $0 < p < 1$, the sufficient statistics for p is:

(*a*) $\sum_{i=1}^{n} X_i$

(*b*) $\prod_{i=1}^{n} X_i$

(*c*) both (*a*) and (*b*)

(*d*) neither (*a*) nor (*b*)

56. If $X_1, X_2, \ldots, X_n$ is a random sample from the population having the density function,

$$f(x; \theta) = \frac{1}{\sqrt{2\pi\theta}}\, e^{-\frac{1}{2}\frac{x^2}{\theta}},$$

then the maximum likelihood estimator for θ is:

(*a*) $\sqrt{\Sigma X_i^2/n}$

(*b*) $\Sigma X_i^2/n$

(*c*) $\sqrt{\Sigma X_i^2/n}$

(*d*) $\Sigma X_i^2/\sqrt{n}$

57. If $X_1, X_2, \ldots, X_n$ is a random sample from a population

$$\frac{1}{\theta\sqrt{2\pi}} e^{-x^2/2\theta^2}$$

the maximum likelihood for θ is:

(*a*) $\Sigma X_i/n$

(*b*) $\Sigma X_i^2/n$

(*c*) $\sqrt{\Sigma_i X_i^2/n}$

(*d*) $\sqrt{\Sigma X_i^2/n}$

58. The diameter of cylindrical rods is assumed to be normally distributed with a variance of 0.04 cm. A sample of 25 rods has a mean diameter of 4.5 cm. 95% confidence limits for population mean are:

(*a*) 4.5 ∓ 0.004

(*b*) 4.5 ∓ 0.0016

(*c*) 4.5 ∓ 0.078

(*d*) 4.5 ∓ 0.2

59. The monthly expenditure in excess of ₹ 2000 of the families in a locality is approximately negative exponentially distributed. A random sample of four families' per month expenditure was reported as ₹ 3000, ₹ 3500, ₹ 4500 and ₹ 5000. An estimate of the average expenditure for the given distribution of the locality is:

(*a*) 2000

(*b*) 3000

(*c*) 4000

(*d*) none of the above

60. If $T = t(X_1, X_2, \ldots, X_n)$ is a sufficient statistics for a parameter θ and an unique MLE $\hat{\theta}$ for θ exists, then

(*a*) $\hat{\theta} = t(X_1, X_2, \ldots, X_n)$

(*b*) $\hat{\theta}$ is a function of t

(*c*) $\hat{\theta}$ is independent of t

(*d*) none of the above

61. If $T = t(X_1, X_2, \ldots, X_n)$ is a MLE of θ and $T(\theta)$ is a one to one function of θ, then

(*a*) $T(t)$ is a MVU estimator of $T(\theta)$.

(*b*) $T(t)$ is a unbiased estimate of $T(\theta)$

(*c*) $T(t)$ is a MLE of $T(\theta)$

(*d*) all of the above

62. In estimating the parameters of a linear function, most commonly used method of estimation is:

(*a*) maximum likelihood method

(*b*) least square method

(*c*) method of minimum Chi-square

(*d*) method of moments

63. The set of equations obtained in the process of least square estimation are called:

(*a*) normal equations

(*b*) intrinsic equations

(*c*) simultaneous equations

(*d*) all of the above

64. Least square estimators of the parameters of a linear model are:

(*a*) unbiased

(*b*) BLUE

(*c*) UMVU

(*d*) all of the above

65. Least square estimators of the parameters of a linear model are not:

(*a*) necessarily consistent

(*b*) scale invariant

(*c*) asymptotically normal

(*d*) all of the above

66. Least square theory was propounded by whom and in which year?

(*a*) Gauss in 1809

(*b*) Markov in 1900

(*c*) Fisher in 1920
(*d*) none of the above

67. The minimum variance approach was put forth by whom and in which year?
(*a*) Gauss in 1809
(*b*) Markov in 1900
(*c*) Fisher in 1920
(*d*) all of the above

68. The credit of inventing the method of moments for estimating the parameters goes to:
(*a*) R.A. Fisher
(*b*) J. Neyman
(*c*) Laplace
(*d*) Karl Pearson

69. By the method of moments one can estimate:
(*a*) all constants of a population
(*b*) only mean and variance of a distribution
(*c*) all moments of a population distribution
(*d*) all of the above

70. Generally the estimators obtained by the method of moments as compared to ML estimators are:
(*a*) less efficient
(*b*) more efficient
(*c*) equally efficient
(*d*) none of the above

71. Method of minimum Chi-square for the estimation of parameters utilises:
(*a*) Chi-square distribution function
(*b*) Pearson's Chi-square statistic
(*c*) Contingency table
(*d*) All of the above

72. Modified minimum Chi-square differs from minimum Chi-square in respect of:
(*a*) numerator of Chi-square statistic
(*b*) denominator of Chi-square statistic
(*c*) basic approach
(*d*) none of the above

73. Mean square error of estimators obtained by the method of minimum Chi-square is:
(*a*) less than ML estimators
(*b*) more than ML estimators
(*c*) equal to ML estimators
(*d*) none of the above

74. Minimum Chi-square estimators are:
(*a*) consistent
(*b*) asymptotically normal
(*c*) efficient
(*d*) all of the above

75. Minimum Chi-square estimators are not necessarily:
(*a*) efficient
(*b*) consistent
(*c*) unbiased
(*d*) all of the above

76. Main feature of Bayes' approach in the estimation of parameter is:
(*a*) to consider the parameter a random variable
(*b*) specification of the prior distribution
(*c*) both (*a*) and (*b*)
(*d*) neither (*a*) nor (*b*)

77. The probability density function $f(x;\theta)$ in which X and Θ both are random variables can be expressed for given value of $\Theta = \theta$ and prior density $g(\theta)$ as:
(*a*) $f(x;\theta) = f(x \mid \theta)\, g(\theta)$
(*b*) $f(x;\theta) = f(x \mid \theta)\, /g(\theta)$
(*c*) $f(x;\theta) = g(\theta)\, / f(x \mid \theta)$
(*d*) none of the above

78. Bayes' approach is:
(*a*) universally accepted
(*b*) a matter of controversy
(*c*) irrelevant
(*d*) none of the above

79. Bayes estimator $\hat{\tau}(\theta)$ of a parametric function $\tau(\theta)$ of θ can be obtained by the formula with usual notations as:

(*a*) $\hat{\tau}(\theta) = \dfrac{\int \tau(\theta)\, f(x|\theta)\, d\theta}{\int f(x|\theta)\, g(\theta)\, d\theta}$

(*b*) $\hat{\tau}(\theta) = \dfrac{\int \tau(\theta)\, f(x|\theta)\, f(\theta)\, g(\theta)\, d\theta}{\int g(\theta)\, d\theta}$

(*c*) $\hat{\tau}(\theta) = \dfrac{\int \tau(\theta)\, g(\theta)\, d\theta}{\int g(\theta)\, f(x|\theta)\, d\theta}$

(*d*) $\hat{\tau}(\theta) = \dfrac{\int \tau(\theta)\, f(x|\theta)\, g(\theta)\, d\theta}{\int f(x|\theta)\, g(\theta)\, d\theta}$

80. Which of the following statements is true?

(*a*) Bayes estimator is always a function of minimal sufficient statistics

(*b*) Bayes estimators are most efficient

(*c*) Bayes estimators are always asymptotically normal

(*d*) None of the above

81. Which of the following statement is not correct?

(*a*) Bayes estimators in many cases are asymptotically consistent

(*b*) For large *n*, estimators tend to ML estimators irrespective of prior density $g(\theta)$

(*c*) Properties of Bayes estimators are given in terms of maximum risk

(*d*) Goodness of a Bayes estimator is measured in terms of mean squared error loss

82. Pitman's estimator for location parameters are generally:

(*a*) unbiased

(*b*) consistent

(*c*) a function of sufficient statistics

(*d*) none of the above

83. Pitman estimator for location usually possess:

(*a*) smallest mean square error

(*b*) asymptotic property

(*c*) a property of complete statistic

(*d*) all of the above

84. Formula for Pitman estimator for the scale parameter θ, where $L(x_i \mid \theta)$ the likelihood function for $i = 1, 2, \ldots, n$ is:

(*a*) $\hat{\theta} = \dfrac{\int \hat{\theta}\, L(x_i|\theta)\, d\theta}{\int \theta^3\, L(x_i|\theta)\, d\theta}$

(*b*) $\hat{\theta} = \dfrac{\int \frac{1}{\theta^2} L(x_i|\theta)\, d\theta}{\int \frac{1}{\theta^3} L(x_i|\theta)\, d\theta}$

(*c*) $\hat{\theta} = \dfrac{\int \frac{1}{\theta^2} L(x_i|\theta)\, d\theta}{\int \frac{1}{\theta} L(x_i|\theta)\, d\theta}$

(*d*) none of the above

85. For a fixed confidence coefficient $(1 - \alpha)$, the most preferred confidence interval for the parameter θ is one:

(*a*) with shortest width

(*b*) with largest width

(*c*) with an average width

(*d*) none of the above

86. The most pragmatic approach for determining $(1 - \alpha)$ per cent confidence interval is to find out:

(*a*) zero width confidence interval

(*b*) equal tail confidence coefficient interval

(*c*) a confidence interval such that the combined area of both the tails is equal to α

(*d*) none of the above

87. Sample median as an estimator of population mean is always:

(*a*) unbiased

(*b*) efficient

(*c*) sufficient

(*d*) none of the above

88. Confidence region tentamounts to estimation of:

(*a*) confidence interval for a parameter of a distribution

(*b*) confidence interval for two or more parameters of a population distribution

(*c*) both (*a*) and (*b*)

(*d*) neither (*a*) nor (*b*)

89. A family receives 1, 2 and 3 wrong telephone calls on three randomly selected days. Assuming that the wrong calls follow Poisson distribution, the estimate of the number of wrong calls in 6 days is:

(*a*) 6

(*b*) 12

(*c*) 36

(*d*) none of the above

90. Given the probability statement that,

$$P(4.35 \le \theta \le 15.67) = 0.90$$

which of the following statement is correct in respect of given probability statement?

(*a*) 4.35 and 15.67 are 90 per cent confidence limits

(*b*) The confidence interval is 11.32

(*c*) Probability that μ lies in the interval (4, 35, 15.67) is 0.90

(*d*) All of the above

91. If t_n is a sufficient statistic for θ based on the sample $x_1, x_2, \ldots, x_n$ the function $\frac{\partial}{\partial\theta} \text{Log } L$ is a function of:

(*a*) θ only

(*b*) t_n only

(*c*) t_n and θ only

(*d*) none of the above

92. The concepts of consistency, efficiency and sufficiency are due to:

(*a*) J. Neyman

(*b*) R.A. Fisher

(*c*) C.R. Rao

(*d*) J. Berkson

93. If $X_1, X_2, \ldots, X_n$ is a random sample from any distribution having K^{th} moment $E(X^k)$, the consistent estimator for $E(X^k)$ is:

(*a*) $\sum_{i=1}^{n} X_i^k$

(*b*) $\frac{1}{n}\sum_{i=1}^{n} X_i^k$

(*c*) both (*a*) and (*b*)

(*d*) none of (*a*) and (*b*)

94. If $\bar{x}$ is a sample mean from the binomial distribution $b(1, p)$, than

(*a*) $\bar{x}$ is a sufficient statistics for *p*

(*b*) $\bar{x}$ is an efficient statistics for *p*

(*c*) both (*a*) and (*b*)

(*d*) none of (*a*) and (*b*)

95. Formula for obtaining 95% confidence limits for the mean μ of a normal population $N(\mu, \sigma^2)$ with known σ are:

(*a*) $-1.96 \le \frac{\bar{x}-\mu}{\sigma/\sqrt{n}} < 1.96$

(*b*) $P\left(-Z_{\alpha/2} \le \frac{\bar{x}-\mu}{\sigma/\sqrt{n}} \le Z_{\alpha/2}\right) = 0.95$

(*c*) $\bar{x} \mp 1.96\frac{\sigma}{\sqrt{n}}$

(*d*) all of the above

96. If the density function of a variable *x* is,

$$f(x; \theta) = \theta e^{-\theta x}$$

for $0 < x < \infty$,

95% central confidence limits for large sample *n* are

(*a*) $\left(1 \pm \frac{1.96}{\sqrt{n}}\right)\bar{x}$

(*b*) $\left(1 \pm \frac{1.96\bar{x}}{\sqrt{n}}\right)/\,\bar{x}$

(*c*) $\left(1 \pm \frac{1.96}{\sqrt{n}}\right)/\,\bar{x}$

(*d*) none of the above

97. Formula for the confidence interval with $(1 - \alpha)$ confidence coefficient for the variance of the normal distribution, $N(\mu, \alpha^2)$, when μ is known, is given as:

(*a*) $P\left[\chi^2_{1-\alpha/2} \le \frac{ns^2}{\sigma^2} \le \chi^2_{\alpha/2}\right] = 1 - \alpha$

(*b*) $P\left[\frac{ns^2}{\chi^2_{\alpha/2}} \le \sigma^2 \le \frac{ns^2}{\chi^2_{1-\alpha/2}}\right] = 1 - \alpha$

(*c*) both (*a*) and (*b*)

(*d*) neither (*a*) nor (*b*)

98. Formula for 95% confidence limits for the variance of population $N(\mu, \sigma^2)$, when μ is unknown, is:

(*a*) $\dfrac{ns^2}{\chi^2_{(n-1)(0.025)}} \le \sigma^2 \le \dfrac{ns^2}{\chi^2_{(n-1)(0.975)}}$

(*b*) $\dfrac{ns^2}{\chi^2_{0.025}} \le \sigma^2 \le \dfrac{ns^2}{\chi^2_{0.975}}$

(*c*) both (*a*) and (*b*)

(*d*) neither (*a*) and (*b*)

99. A random sample of 16 housewives has an average body weight of 52 kg and an standard deviation of 3.6 kg. 99% central confidence limits for body weight in general are: [Given: $t_{15,\,0.01} = 2.95$]

(*a*) (54.66; 49.345)

(*b*) (52.66; 51.34)

(*c*) (55.28; 48.72)

(*d*) none of the above

100. Two samples from two normal populations having equal variances of size 10 and 12 have means 12 and 10 and variances 2 and 5 respectively. 95% confidence limits for the difference between two population means are: [Given: $t_{0.05,\,20} = 2.086$]

(*a*) (– 1.57; 5.43)

(*b*) (0.214; 3.786)

(*c*) (0.477; 3.523)

(*d*) none of the above

101. Confidence limits for the population mean difference can be found out only when:

(*a*) the observations on two variable are paired

(*b*) when the two variables are correlated

(*c*) both (*a*) and (*b*)

(*d*) neither (*a*) nor (*b*)

102. Formula for the confidence interval for the ratio of variances of two normal population involves:

(*a*) χ^2-distribution

(*b*) *F*-distribution

(*c*) *t*-distribution

(*d*) none of the above

103. Consistency of an estimator is a:

(*a*) large sample property only

(*b*) small sample property only

(*c*) property not related to sample size

(*d*) property applicable to any sample size

104. In sampling from a population having mean μ and variance σ^2, the estimator $\bar{X}_n = \dfrac{1}{n}\sum_{i=1}^{n} X_i$ be the sequence of estimators of μ, based on samples of size *n*, then $\bar{X}_n$ is:

(*a*) BAN estimator of μ

(*b*) mean-squared error consistent estimator of μ

(*c*) unbiased estimator of μ

(*d*) all of the above

105. For the exponential distribution,

$$f(x_i\, \theta) = \frac{1}{\theta} e^{-x/\theta};\ x > 0, \theta > 0\,,$$

the estimator $\Sigma\, X_i / n$, based on a sample of size *n,* is an unbiased estimator of:

(*a*) $1/\theta$

(*b*) $1/\theta^2$

(*c*) θ

(*d*) θ^2

106. For an estimator to be consistent, the unbiasedness of the estimator is:

(*a*) necessary

(*b*) sufficient

(*c*) necessary as well as sufficient

(*d*) neither necessary nor sufficient

107. For the sample mean to be an unbiased estimator of population mean, the condition of normality of population is:

(*a*) necessary but not sufficient

(*b*) necessary as well as sufficient

(*c*) sufficient but not necessary

(*d*) none of the above

108. For the distribution,

$$f(x;\ \theta) = \frac{1}{\theta};\ 0 \le x \le \theta$$

a sufficient estimator for θ, based on a sample $X_1, X_2, \ldots, X_n$ is, (*a*) $\Sigma X_i/n$

(*b*) $\sqrt{\Sigma X_i^2}$

(*c*) max $(X_1, X_2, \ldots, X_n)$

(*d*) min $(X_1, X_2, \ldots, X_n)$

109. A confidence interval of confidence coefficient $(1 - \alpha)$ is best which has:

(*a*) smallest width

(*b*) vastest width

(*c*) upper and lower limits equidistant from the parameter

(*d*) one-sided confidence interval.

110. Let $X_1, X_2, \ldots, X_n$ be a sample from density $N(\theta, \theta^2)$, then the statistic $T = (\Sigma X_i, \Sigma X_i^2)$ for θ is:

(*a*) sufficient and complete

(*b*) sufficient but not complete

(*c*) not sufficient but complete

(*d*) neither sufficient nor complete

111. The maximum likelihood estimators are necessarily:

(*a*) unbiased

(*b*) sufficient

(*c*) most efficient

(*d*) unique

112. Least square estimators under linear set up are:

(*a*) unbiased

(*b*) UMVUE's

(*c*) BLUE's

(*d*) all of the above

113. For a random sample from a Poisson population $P(\lambda)$, the maximum likelihood estimate of λ is:

(*a*) median

(*b*) mode

(*c*) geometric mean

(*d*) mean

114. For a random sample $(x_1, x_2, \ldots, x_n)$ from a population $N(\mu, \sigma^2)$, the maximum likelihood estimator of σ^2 is:

(*a*) $\frac{1}{n}\sum_i (X_i - \bar{X})^2$

(*b*) $\frac{1}{n-1}\sum_i (X_i - \bar{X})^2$

(*c*) $\frac{1}{n}\sum_i (X_i - \mu)^2$

(*d*) $\frac{1}{n-1}\sum_i (X_i - \mu)^2$

115. If the variance of an estimator attains the Crammer-Rao lower bound, the estimator is:

(*a*) most efficient

(*b*) sufficient

(*c*) consistent

(*d*) admissible

ANSWERS

Section B

1. estimate **2.** best **3.** not possible **4.** random sample **5.** random variable **6.** estimate **7.** estimator **8.** point **9.** consistent **10.** consistent **11.** unbiased **12.** bias **13.** $(\text{bias})^2 + \text{var}(T_n)$ **14.** zero **15.** UMVUE **16.** mean-squared error **17.** holds **18.** information **19.** MVB **20.** Aitken and Silverstone **21.** different **22.** lower bound **23.** better **24.** 1946 **25.** 1945 **26.** Aitken **27.** CANE **28.** limiting **29.** minimum **30.** less **31.** $V(T_n')/V(T_n)$ **32.** $T_n = T_n^*$ **33.** sufficient statistic **34.** independent **35.** sufficient statistic **36.** minimal sufficient **37.** complete **38.** unique **39.** MVU **40.** Rao-Blackwell **41.** admissible **42.** risk **43.** likelihood function **44.** maximum likelihood **45.** unbiased/consistent/unique **46.** maximum likelihood **47.** unbiased **48.** $\bar{x}$ **49.** $\Sigma(x_i - \bar{x})^2/n$ **50.** sufficient statistic **51.** sufficient statistic **52.** $\lambda/\Gamma\lambda\bar{x}$ **53.** med $(x_1, x_2, \ldots, x_n)$ **54.** smallest X; largest X **55.** BLUE **56.** unbiased **57.** UMVU **58.** Gauss-Markov **59.** Karl Pearson; 1894 **60.** asymptotically normal **61.** less **62.** $\Sigma(X_i - \bar{X})^2/n$ **63.** sample mean **64.** $1/\bar{x}$ **65.** Pearson's Chi-square **66.** denominator **67.** almost equal **68.** J. Berkson;

1955 **69.** consistent/asymptotically normal/efficient **70.** unbiased **71.** random variable **72.** fixed quantity **73.** prior distribution **74.** previous knowledge **75.** $f(x/\theta)\, g(\theta)$ **76.** $\int \tau(\theta)\, f(x\,|\,\theta) g(\theta) \Big/ \int f(x/\theta)\, g(\theta)\, d\theta$ **77.** minimal sufficient **78.** maximum likelihood **79.** asymptotically normal **80.** minimax **81.** $(x + \alpha)/(n + \alpha + \beta)$ **82.** $(x + r)/(1 + \alpha)$ **83.** $\int \theta L(x\,|\,\theta)\, d\theta \Big/ \int L(x\,|\,\theta)\, d\theta$ **84.** smallest **85.** sufficient statistic **86.** minimax **87.** location invariant **88.** $\bar{X}_n$ **89.** confidence coefficient **90.** shortest **91.** upper and lower **92.** confidence region **93.** decreases **94.** concentrated **95.** consistent **96.** consistent **97.** unbiased **98.** biased **99.** consistent **100.** unbiased **101.** more efficient **102.** unbiased **103.** biased; inefficient **104.** t_n; θ **105.** UMVUE **106.** uniqueness **107.** Fisher and Neyman **108.** Consistent **109.** consistent **110.** $\Sigma\ X_i$ **111.** more **112.** $2/\pi$ **113.** biased **114.** unbiased **115.** consistent **116.** maximum likelihood **117.** non-existent **118.** best unbiased **119.** most efficien **120.** most efficient **121.** unbiased; efficient **122.** unbiased **123.** consistent **124.** $T_1 = T_2$ **125.** better

Section C

1. (*b*)	**2.** (*a*)	**3.** (*b*)	**4.** (*c*)	**5.** (*a*)
6. (*c*)	**7.** (*d*)	**8.** (*c*)	**9.** (*c*)	**10.** (*b*)
11. (*c*)	**12.** (*d*)	**13.** (*d*)	**14.** (*b*)	**15.** (*c*)
16. (*d*)	**17.** (*b*)	**18.** (*d*)	**19.** (*b*)	**20.** (*d*)
21. (*d*)	**22.** (*c*)	**23.** (*a*)	**24.** (*b*)	**25.** (*b*)
26. (*c*)	**27.** (*b*)	**28.** (*a*)	**29.** (*c*)	**30.** (*d*)
31. (*b*)	**32.** (*c*)	**33.** (*d*)	**34.** (*b*)	**35.** (*c*)
36. (*b*)	**37.** (*d*)	**38.** (*a*)	**39.** (*c*)	**40.** (*b*)
41. (*c*)	**42.** (*a*)	**43.** (*d*)	**44.** (*b*)	**45.** (*a*)
46. (*b*)	**47.** (*c*)	**48.** (*c*)	**49.** (*d*)	**50.** (*a*)
51. (*d*)	**52.** (*b*)	**53.** (*c*)	**54.** (*b*)	**55.** (*a*)
56. (*b*)	**57.** (*d*)	**58.** (*c*)	**59.** (*a*)	**60.** (*b*)
61. (*c*)	**62.** (*b*)	**63.** (*a*)	**64.** (*d*)	**65.** (*c*)
66. (*a*)	**67.** (*b*)	**68.** (*d*)	**69.** (*c*)	**70.** (*a*)
71. (*b*)	**72.** (*b*)	**73.** (*a*)	**74.** (*d*)	**75.** (*c*)
76. (*c*)	**77.** (*a*)	**78.** (*b*)	**79.** (*d*)	**80.** (*a*)
81. (*c*)	**82.** (*c*)	**83.** (*a*)	**84.** (*b*)	**85.** (*a*)
86. (*b*)	**87.** (*d*)	**88.** (*b*)	**89.** (*b*)	**90.** (*d*)
91. (*c*)	**92.** (*b*)	**93.** (*b*)	**94.** (*c*)	**95.** (*d*)
96. (*c*)	**97.** (*c*)	**98.** (*a*)	**99.** (*a*)	**100.** (*b*)
101. (*c*)	**102.** (*d*)	**103.** (*a*)	**104.** (*d*)	**105.** (*c*)
106. (*b*)	**107.** (*d*)	**108.** (*c*)	**109.** (*a*)	**110.** (*b*)
111. (*b*)	**112.** (*d*)	**113.** (*d*)	**114.** (*a*)	**115.** (*a*)

SUGGESTED READING

1. Agarwal, B.L., *Basic Statistics*, New Age International Publishers, New Delhi, 8th edition, 2024.
2. Arora, S. and Lal, B., *New Mathematical Statistics,* Satya Prakashan, New Delhi, 1989.
3. Crammer, H. *Mathematical Methods of Statistics,* Princeton University Press, Princeton, 8th edn., 1958.
4. Goon, A.M., Gupta, M.K. and Dasgupta, B., *An Outline of Statistical Theory,* The World Press, Calcutta, 2nd edn., 1980.
5. Gupta, S.C. and Kapoor, V.K., *Fundamentals of Mathematical Statistics,* Sultan Chand, New Delhi, 9th. edn., 1994.
6. Kapur, J.N. and Saxena, H.C., *Mathematical Statistics,* S. Chand, New Delhi, 12th edn., 1984.
7. Kendall, M.G. and Stuart, A., *The Advanced Theory of Statistics,* Vol. 2, Charles Griffin, London, 3rd edn., 1973.
8. Mood, A.M, Graybill, F.A. and Boes, D.C., *Introduction to the Theory of Statistics,* McGraw Hill, Kogakusha, Tokyo, 3rd edn., 1974.
9. Saxena, H.C. and Surendran, P.U., *Statistical Interference,* S. Chand, New Delhi.
10. Wilks, S.S., *Mathematical Statistics,* John Wiley, New York, 1962.
11. Zacks, S., *The Theory of Statistical Inference,* John Wiley, New York, 1971.

CHAPTER 11

Testing Parametric Hypotheses

SECTION A

Short Essay Type Questions

Q. 1. *Write a note on the exigency of testing of hypothesis.*

Ans. There is always some contention about the value(s) of a parameter or the relationship between parameters. When parametric values are unknown, we estimate them through sample values. If the sample value is exactly the same as per our contention, there is no hitch in accepting it. And if it is far from our contention, there is no reason to accept it. But the problem arises when the sample provides a value which is neither exactly equal to the parametric value, nor too far. In that situation one has to develop some procedure(s) which enables one to decide whether to accept a contended (hypothetical) value or not on the basis of sample values. Such a procedure is known as testing of hypothesis.

There can be more than one procedure to test a hypothesis. If so, which one to choose out of many tests at hand. For this purpose, many properties of tests have been put forward. A test with maximum virtues is most preferred one. So we have to deal with hypothesis, test procedures and their properties. The theory of testing parametric statistical hypotheses was originally set forth by J. Neyman in 1928 and Karl Pearson in 1933.

Q. 2. *What is meant by the test of a statistical hypothesis?*

Ans. A statistical test of a hypothesis H is a rule or procedure which makes one to decide about the acceptance or rejection of the hypothesis H.

Q. 3. *What are the principle steps involved in statistical test?*

Ans. A statistical test mainly involves four steps:

(*i*) Evolving a test statistic

(*ii*) To know the sampling distribution of the test statistic

(*iii*) Setting of hypotheses testing conventions

(*iv*) Establishing a decision rule that lead to an inductive inference about the probable truth.

Q. 4. *What is the difference between a research or scientific hypothesis and statistical hypothesis?*

Ans. Research or scientific hypothesis is the hypothesis which a researcher postulates to meet his objectives. Whereas statistical hypothesis is a testable formulations of research or scientific hypotheses or the functional relation about the population parameter(s).

Q. 5. *Define parametric statistical hypothesis.*

Ans. A statistical hypothesis is an assertion about a parameter of a population or parameters of two or more populations. For instance, the life of the electric bulb in general, is 2,000 hours, *i.e.*, $\mu = 2000$ hours. Two bulb manufacturing processes produce bulbs of the same average life, etc., *i.e.*, $\mu_1 = \mu_2$.

In other words, a statistical hypothesis is an assertion about the distribution of one or more variables.

Q. 6. *Define null and alternative hypothesis.*

Ans. According to Fisher, any hypothesis tested for its possible rejection is called a null hypothesis and is denoted by H_0.

Alternative hypothesis is a statement about the population parameter or parameters which provides an alternative to the null hypothesis within the range of pertinent values of the parameters. It is denoted by H_1 or H_A. The idea of alternative hypothesis was propounded by J. Neyman, If H_0 is accepted, H_1 is rejected and *vice-versa*.

Q. 7. *Define simple and composite hypotheses.*

Ans. If a statistical hypothesis completely specifies a distribution, it is known as *simple hypothesis*, otherwise *composite hypothesis*. For a normal distribution $N(\mu, \sigma^2)$ with σ^2 known, the hypotheses $H_0: \mu = 20$ vs. $H_1: \mu = 30$ lead to simple hypotheses. Here H_0 and H_1, both are simple hypotheses. But generally H_1 is composite because H_1 is given as $\mu \neq \mu_0$, $\mu > \mu_0$ or $\mu < \mu_0$.

Q. 8. *Define and elaborate two types of errors in testing of hypotheses.*

Ans. There is a probability of committing an error in making a decision about a hypothesis. Hence, two types of errors are defined as follows:

First kind of error. Reject H_0 when it is true.

Second kind of error. Accept H_0 when H_1 is true. First kind of error is also named as Type I error or *rejection error*, and the second kind of error as *acceptance error*. Probability of Type I error is denoted by α and probability of Type II error by β.

Notationally,

$$P(\text{reject } H_0/H_0 \text{ is true}) = \alpha$$

$$P(\text{accept } H_0/H_1 \text{ is true}) = \beta$$

From the definitions, it is apparent that if H_0 is accepted, then only type II error is committed and if H_0 is rejected, only type I error is committed.

Let us consider a practical problem. If a medicine is administered to a few patients of a particular disease to cure them and the medicine is curing the disease, but it is claimed that it has no effect or has an adverse effect, and hence it is discontinued. *This is type I error.* On the contrary, the medicine has adverse effect and is claimed to have good effect and the treatment is continued. *This is type II error.* If we delve into the consequences of both types of errors, we find type II error is more serious than type I error. Hence, α may be relatively large than β. In view of these facts, effort is made to minimise β even for certain risk of type I error usually 0.01, 0.05 or more.

Q. 9. *Discuss power of a test and power function.*

Ans. For testing a hypothesis H_0 against H_1, the test with probabilities α and β of type I and II errors respectively, the quantity $(1 - \beta)$ is called the power of the test.

The power of the test depends upon the difference between the parameter value specified by H_0 and the actual value of the parameter. $1 - \beta$ can be expressed as a function of the true parameter, say, θ. If T is a test of H_0, the power function of T is defined as the probability of rejection of H_0 when the distribution, from which the sample is drawn, is parameterised by θ and denoted by $P_\gamma(\theta)$. In terms of second kind of error, the function $1 - \beta(\theta)$ is known as the *power function*. Whereas the function $\beta(\theta)$ is known as the *operating characteristic function* or OC function.

Q. 10. *Define and discuss the level of significance.*

Ans. The level of significance may be defined as the probability of type I error which we are ready to tolerate in making a decision about H_0. Briefly,

$$P(\text{reject } H_0/H_0 \text{ is true}) = \alpha.$$

It is our endeavour to carry out a test which minimises both types of errors. Unfortunately for a given set of observations, both the errors cannot be controlled simultaneously. Hence, it is a general practice to assign a bound to type I error and to minimise type II error. Thus, one chooses a value of α lying between 0 and 1 which is known as the level of significance.

While choosing a level of significance, one should also consider the power of a test against various alternatives. If the power of a test is too low, one should choose a higher value of α say 0.1, 0.2, 0.5, etc.

Q. 11. *Define the size of a test.*

Ans. The size of a non-randomised test is defined as the size of the critical region. Practically, it is numerically the same as the level of significance.

Q. 12. *Clarify the concept of critical region.*

Ans. Let Ω denote the sample space of observations or the potential set of data, *i.e.*, $\Omega = \{x_1, x_2, ..., x_n\}$ where $(x_1, x_2, ..., x_n)$ is a possible value of $X_1, X_2, ..., X_n$. Then sample space is specified by the test statistic under null hypothesis H_0. The space Ω is divided into two types of region, ω and $(\Omega - \omega)$. *The level of significance is the size of the critical region* ω. The critical region is also known as the *region of rejection*. The region of rejection may be situated on both the tails or on only one tail depending on the alternative hypothesis. Also the region $(\Omega - \omega)$ is called the *acceptance region*. If the value of the test statistic lies in the acceptance region, the null hypothesis H_0 is accepted and if it lies in the critical region, H_0 is rejected.

Also a critical region of size α which minimises β among all critical regions which do not exceed α is called *best critical region* (BCR).

Q. 13. *How can a decision about one-tailed and two-tailed test be taken?*

Ans. If an alternative hypothesis is such that it leads to two-sided alternatives to the null hypothesis, it is said to be a *two-tailed test*. For instance, testing $H_0: \mu = 20$ vs. $H_1 : \mu \neq 20$ leads to two-sided test as μ can be greater than 20 or less than 20. In this situation half of the area of critical region lies on the left tail and half on the right tail. If α is the area of the critical region, $\alpha/2$ is the area on both the tails.

Again, if the alternative hypothesis provides one-sided alternative to H_0, e.g., $H_0 : \mu = 20$ vs. $H_1 : \mu > 20$ or $H_1 : \mu < 20$, the critical region of size α lies only on one tail, specifically an area equal to α lies on the right tail given by $\omega : z > z_\alpha$ when H_1 is $\mu > 20$ and on the left tail when H_1 is $\mu < 20$, an area equal to α given $z < -Z_\alpha$.

Q. 14. *Distinguish between non-randomised and randomised test.*

Ans. A test T of a hypothesis H is said to be non-randomised test if the decision about the rejection or acceptance of H is based on a test statistic. H is rejected if the test statistic lies in the critical region otherwise accepted.

A randomised test is one in which no test statistics is involved. The decision about H is taken on the basis of some predicted criteria. For instance, it is decided that H_0 will be accepted if on tossing the coin falls with head and rejected if the coin fall with tail. But randomised tests are seldom used.

Q. 15. *Throw light on the role of degrees of freedom, and give its definition.*

Ans. A test statistic always involves estimates(s) of the parameter(s) under test and estimated values do depend on the sample *vis-a-vis* the sample size. Hence, number of observations plays an important role in testing of hypothesis. Also in a large number of cases, the estimate approaches the true parameter as the sample size increases. In view of these facts it becomes necessary to take into account the sample size while testing a hypothesis.

The number of independent observations in a set is called *degrees of* freedom (d.f.).

In other words, degrees of freedom may be defined as the number of observations in a set minus the number of restrictions imposed on them.

In testing of hypothesis or interval estimation, the critical value of a statistic is obtained from the table of the distribution of the test statistic for the prefixed level of significance and corresponding d.f. of the test statistic.

Q. 16. *What is a critical function?*

Ans. A function $\psi_T\{x_1, x_2, ..., x_n)$ of the sample values $x_1, x_2, ..., x_n$ where T is a test of a hypothesis

H_0 is said to be a critical function of a randomised test T if,

$$\psi_T\{x_1, x_2, ..., x_n) = P[H_0 \text{ is rejected } [(x_1, x_2, ..., x_n) \text{ is observed}]$$

On the other hand, the critical function in a non-randomised test divides the sample space into three regions, one the region of rejection, the other the region of acceptance and the third, the boundary between the region of acceptance and the region of rejection. In this situation, either the boundary is considered to be included in the region of rejection or a randomised test is applied.

Q. 17. *What do you understand by optimum test?*

Ans. A test is said to be optimum if it minimises both the errors α and β. Unfortunately, no such test is available as the reduction in one type of error causes the increase in the other. Hence, in normal practice a test which minimise β or maximises (1 – β) for a desired low level of α is considered to be an *optimum* or *best* test.

Q. 18. *Name different properties of a test.*

Ans. For comparing different tests of a hypothesis *H*, it becomes necessary to look into the properties of the tests. Main properties of the statistical non-randomised tests are as follows:

(*i*) Most powerful (MP)
(*ii*) Uniformly most powerful (UMP)
(*iii*) Unbiased
(*iv*) Uniformly most powerful unbiased (UMPU)
(*v*) Minimax
(*vi*) Admissible

Q. 19. *Define most powerful test.*

Ans. Let Ω be the sample space and ω the critical region and $\overline{\omega} = \Omega - \omega$, the acceptance region.

A test T of $H_0 : \theta = \theta_0$ vs. $H_1 : \theta = \theta_1$ (simple vs. simple) based on the sample values x: $(x_1, x_2, ..., x_n)$ is said to be a most powerful test if and only if,

$$P(x \, \varepsilon \, \omega / H_0) = \int_{\omega} L_0 \, dx = \alpha$$

and for any other test T^* of the same size α,

$$P_T(x \, \varepsilon \, \omega \mid H_1) \geq P_{T^*}(x \, \varepsilon \, \omega_1 \mid H_1)$$

where ω_1 satisfies the condition,

$$\int_{\omega_1} L_0 \, dx = \alpha$$

The critical region α satisfying the above conditions is known as the *most powerful* critical region of size α.

Q. 20. *When do you call a test uniformly most powerful?*

Ans. A test T of $H_0 : \theta = \theta_0$ vs. $H_1 : \theta \neq \theta_0$ is said to be a uniformly most powerful test of size α if,

$$P(x \, \varepsilon \, \omega \mid H_0) = \int_{\omega} L_0 \, dx = \alpha$$

and $P_T(x \, \varepsilon \, \omega \mid H_1) \geq P_T(x \, \varepsilon \, \omega_1 \mid H_1)$ for all $\theta \neq \theta_0$ where ω_1 is any other critical region such that

$$\int_{\omega_1} L_0 \, dx = \alpha$$

The critical region α satisfying the above conditions is called *uniformly most powerful* (UMP) *region.*

Q. 21. *State Neyman-Pearson lemma and give its utility.*

Ans. The lemma given by J. Neyman and E.S. Pearson provides the most powerful test for testing a simple null hypothesis against a simple alternative hypothesis.

Let $X_1, X_2, ..., X_n$ be a random sample from a density $f(x\,;\theta)$ where $\theta \, \varepsilon \, \Theta$, the parametric space. Θ consists of only two elements θ_0 and θ_1, *i.e.*, $\Theta = \{\theta_0, \theta_1\}$. Also the joint probability density function of $X_1, X_2, ..., X_n$,

$$L(x \mid \theta) = f(x_1, \theta) \, f(x_2, \theta), ..., f(x_n, \theta)$$

$L(x|\theta)$ is the likelihood function of sample observations for a parameter value of θ where $x = x_1, x_2, ..., x_n$.

If there exists a critical region ω of size α and a non-negative number K such that

$$\frac{L(x|\theta_1)}{L(x|\theta_0)} > K \text{ for every } x \in \omega$$

and $$\frac{L(x|\theta_1)}{L(x|\theta_0)} \leq K \text{ for every } x \notin \omega$$

Then ω is said to be the *best critical region* (BCR) of size α for testing $H_0 : \theta = \theta_0$ vs. $H_1 : \theta = \theta_1$.

Any test T corresponding to the BCR ω is the most powerful test of size α of the hypothesis H_0 against H_1.

Neyman-Pearson lemma helps to determine the size of type I and type II errors for the given range of x. Also it helps to find out the power and power function of a test in case of testing a simple null hypothesis against a simple alternative.

Q. 22. *Using Neyman-Pearson lemma, find the best critical region for the test of hypothesis $H_0 : \mu = \mu_0$ vs. $H_1 : \mu = \mu_1$ for the normal population $f(x; \mu, \sigma^2)$ when σ^2 is known in the cases, (i) $\mu_0 < \mu_1$ (ii) $\mu_0 > \mu_1$. Also find the power of the test.*

Ans. Let $X_1, X_2, ..., X_n$ be a random sample from the population under consideration. Adopting usual notations and using Neyman-Pearson lemma, BCR is obtained as,

$$\frac{L(x|\mu_1)}{L(x|\mu_0)} = \frac{e^{-\frac{1}{2\sigma^2}\Sigma(x_i-\mu_1)^2}}{e^{-\frac{1}{2\sigma^2}\Sigma(x_i-\mu_0)^2}} > k$$

or $$e^{-\frac{1}{2\sigma^2}\{\Sigma(x_i-\mu_1)^2-\Sigma(x_i-\mu_0)^2\}} > k$$

Taking logarithm and solving we obtain,

$$-\frac{n}{2\sigma^2}(\mu_1^2-\mu_0^2)+\frac{1}{\sigma^2}(\mu_1-\mu_0)\Sigma x_i > \log k$$

$$\bar{x}(\mu_1-\mu_0) > \frac{\sigma^2}{n}\log k+\frac{1}{2}(\mu_1^2-\mu_0^2)$$

$$\bar{x} > \frac{\sigma^2}{n(\mu_1-\mu_0)}\log k+\frac{1}{2}(\mu_1+\mu_0)$$

Case (i): When $\mu_0 < \mu_1$, BCR is determined as,

$$\bar{x} > \lambda_1$$

Case (ii): When $\mu_0 < \mu_1$, BCR is determined by,

$$\bar{x} > \lambda_2$$

where λ_1 and λ_2 are equal to the right hand of the inequality under the two situations. We know, under H_0, $\bar{x} \sim N\left(\mu_0, \frac{\sigma^2}{n}\right)$ and under H_1, $\bar{x} \sim N\left(\mu_1, \frac{\sigma^2}{n}\right)$. Using Neyman-Pearson lemma, the value of λ_1 can be obtained by the relation,

$$P(\bar{x} > \lambda_1 \mid H_0) = \frac{\sqrt{n}}{\sigma\sqrt{2\pi}}\int_{\lambda_1}^{\infty} e^{-\frac{n}{2\sigma^2}(\bar{x}-\mu_0)^2}\, d\bar{x} = \alpha \text{ and}$$

for the value of λ_2,

$$P(\bar{x} > \lambda_2 \mid H_0) = \frac{\sqrt{n}}{\sigma\sqrt{2\pi}}\int_{-\infty}^{\lambda_2} e^{-\frac{n}{2\sigma^2}(x-\mu_0)^2}\, d\bar{x} = \alpha$$

Substituting $\frac{\sqrt{n}(\bar{x}-\mu_0)}{\sigma} = Z$, the integral relation for λ_1 is

$$\frac{1}{\sqrt{2\pi}}\int_{\sqrt{n}(\lambda_1-\mu_0)/\sigma}^{\infty} e^{-\frac{1}{2}z^2}\, dz = \alpha$$

and for λ_2,

$$\frac{1}{\sqrt{2\pi}}\int_{-\infty}^{\sqrt{n}(\lambda_2-\mu_0)/\sigma} e^{-\frac{1}{2}z^2}\, dz = \alpha$$

Suppose λ_α is a value which is obtained from the table of area under standard normal curve such that the integral,

$$\frac{1}{\sqrt{2\pi}}\int_{\lambda_\alpha}^{\infty} e^{-\frac{1}{2}z^2}\, dz = \alpha$$

Therefore, by equivalence.

$$\lambda_\alpha = \frac{\sqrt{n}(\lambda_1-\mu_0)}{\sigma}$$

or $$\lambda_1 = \mu_0 + \lambda_\alpha\frac{\sigma}{\sqrt{n}}$$

Similarly, $\lambda_2 = \mu_0 - \lambda_\alpha \dfrac{\sigma}{\sqrt{n}}$

For the power of the test,

$$P(x \,\varepsilon\, \omega \mid H_1) = P(\bar{x} > \lambda_1 \mid H_1) = 1 - \beta$$

$$1 - \beta = \frac{\sqrt{n}}{\sigma\sqrt{2\pi}} \int_{\lambda_1}^{\infty} e^{-\frac{n}{2\sigma^2}(\bar{x}-\mu_1)^2} d\bar{x}$$

Now substituting $\dfrac{\sqrt{n}\,|\bar{x}-\mu_1|}{\sigma} = z,$

$$1 - \beta = \frac{1}{\sqrt{2\pi}} \int_{\sqrt{n}(\lambda_1-\mu_1)/\sigma}^{\infty} e^{-\frac{1}{2}z^2} dz$$

Putting the value of λ_1, obtained for BCR,

$$1 - \beta = \frac{1}{\sqrt{2\pi}} \int_{\sqrt{n}\left(\mu_0 + \frac{\sigma}{\sqrt{n}}\lambda_\alpha - \mu_1\right)/\sigma}^{\infty} e^{-\frac{1}{2}z^2} dz$$

$$= \frac{1}{\sqrt{2\pi}} \int_{\lambda_\alpha - \frac{\sqrt{n}}{\sigma}(\mu_1-\mu_0)}^{\infty} e^{-\frac{1}{2}z^2} dz$$

$$= \frac{1}{\sqrt{2\pi}} \int_{z_\alpha}^{\infty} e^{-\frac{1}{2}z^2} dz$$

where $z_\alpha = \lambda_\alpha - \dfrac{\sqrt{n}}{\sigma}(\mu_1 - \mu_0)$

$$= 1 - \frac{1}{\sqrt{2\pi}} \int_{-\infty}^{z_\alpha} e^{-\frac{1}{2}z^2} dz$$

$$= 1 - \phi(z_\alpha)$$

where the value of $\phi(z_\alpha)$ can be obtained from the table for the area under the standard normal curve. In a practical problem either of the two situations will occur, *i.e.*, either $\mu_0 < \mu_1$ or $\mu_0 > \mu_1$.

Q. 23. *Given the nine sample values 4.5, 6.5, 3.8, 4.2, 7.7, 8.5, 9.4, 5.3, 3.9 from a normal distribution with mean μ and variance 4. Find the best critical region for testing H_0: μ = 4 vs. H_1 : μ = 5 of size 0.05. Also calculate the power of the test.*

Ans. It is given that,

$$n = 9,\ \mu_0 = 4,\ \sigma = 2 \text{ and } \alpha = 0.05.$$

From the table, we have to search a value of λ_α such that the area on the right tail of the standard normal curve is 0.05. Therefore, $\lambda_\alpha = 1.64$. Using the same notations as in Q. No. 22,

$$\lambda_1 = \mu_0 + \frac{\sigma}{\sqrt{n}}\lambda_\alpha$$

$$= 4 + \frac{2}{3} \times 1.64$$

$$= 5.09$$

Hence the best critical region is 5.09 to ∞.

For the power of the test,

$$z_\alpha = 1.645 - \frac{3}{2}(5-4)$$

$$= 1.645 - 1.5$$

$$= 0.145$$

The power of the test,

$$1 - \beta = 1 - \phi(0.145)$$

$$= 1 - 0.05765$$

$$= 0.94235$$

Q. 24. *When a test is called a minimax test?*

Ans. A test T of $H_0 : \theta = \theta_0$ vs. $H_1 : \theta = \theta_1$ is said to be a minimax test if for any other T^*, the following inequality holds.

Max$[R(T, \theta_0), R(T, \theta_1)] \leq$ Max $[R(T^*, \theta_0), R(T^*, \theta_1]$ where $R(T, \theta)$ is the risk in using the test T when θ is the true value of the parameter. So is $R(T^*, \theta)$.

Q. 25. *Define an unbiased test.*

Ans. A test T of the null hypothesis $H_0 : \theta \,\varepsilon\, \Theta_0$ vs. $H_1 : \theta \,\varepsilon\, \Theta_1$ is said to be an unbiased test if the probability of rejecting H_0 when it is false is at least as much as the probability of rejecting H_0 when it is true, *i.e.*,

$$\sup_{\theta \varepsilon \Theta_0} P_T(\theta) \leq \inf_{\theta \varepsilon \Theta_1} P_T(\theta)$$

where $\Theta_0 \cup \Theta_1 = \Theta$ and $\Theta_0 \cap \Theta_1 = \phi$.

Here we would like to introduce a term, *unbiased critical region*. A critical region which is such that the power of a test based on it is never less than its size is called unbiased critical region and the test corresponding to it is called unbiased test. In terms of probability, the conditions for testing H_0 against H_1 for an unbiased test of size α are:

$$P\{x \varepsilon \omega \mid H_0\} \leq \alpha$$
$$P\{x \varepsilon \omega \mid H_1\} \geq \alpha$$

A test is said to be *uniformly unbiased* or *completely unbiased* if the power of the test is always greater than its size α.

Q. 26. *Define uniformly most powerful unbiased test.*

Ans. If among the class of unbiased tests, there exists a test, which is uniformly most powerful, is known as *uniformly most powerful unbiased test* (UMPUT). Neyman-Pearson called a critical region corresponding to a UMPU test, the *critical region of type* A_1. The advantage of UMPU test is that even if UMP test do not exist, UMPU test may exist.

Q. 27. *What is meant by an admissible test procedure?*

Ans. A test procedure δ is said to be admissible if there exists no other test procedure δ' whose risk for testing a hypothesis about a parameter θ is less than the risk of δ for testing the same hypothesis about θ. Notationally test procedure δ is admissible if,

$$R(\theta, \delta) \leq R(\theta, \delta') \text{ for all } \theta$$
$$R(\theta, \delta) < R(\theta, \delta') \text{ for some } \theta$$

Q. 28. *Give the names of the methods of testing of hypotheses.*

Ans. The names of different methods of testing of hypotheses are:

(*i*) Likelihood ratio test

(*ii*) Student's *t*-test

(*iii*) Normal deviate test or Z-test

(*iv*) Chi-square test

(*v*) *F*-test

(*vi*) Bayes test

(*vii*) Sequential probability ratio test (SPRT)

Q. 29. *Discuss the general approach of likelihood ratio test.*

Ans. Let $X_1, X_2, ..., X_n$ be a random sample from a density $f(x; \theta)$ where $\theta = (\theta_1, \theta_2, ..., \theta_m)$. Suppose one is interested in testing the hypothesis H_0: $\theta = \theta_0$ where $\theta_0 \varepsilon \Theta$. In likelihood ratio test we consider the likelihood functions under H_0 and under the entire parametric space. The ratio,

$$\lambda(x) = \frac{L(x \mid \theta_0)}{L(x \mid \theta)}$$

is called the *likelihood ratio*. The value of $\lambda(x)$ lies in the interval (0, 1).

The critical region for the test statistic is $\lambda(x) \leq k$, where k is determined from the distribution $g(\lambda)$ of λ to provide a test of size α, *i.e.*,

$$\int_0^k g_{H_0}(\lambda)\, d\lambda = \alpha$$

Q. 30. *Given a sample $x_1, x_2, ..., x_n$ from a normal population having mean μ and variance σ^2, test H_0 : $\mu = \mu_0$ by the method of likelihood ratio test.*

Ans. The likelihood functions under H_0 and under θ are to be written first.

We know that the maximum likelihood estimates of μ and σ^2 are,

$$\hat{\mu} = \bar{x}$$

and
$$\sigma^2 = \frac{1}{n}\sum(x_i - \bar{x})^2 = s^2$$

Likelihood function,

$$L(x \mid \hat{\mu}, \hat{\sigma}^2) = \left(\frac{1}{2\pi s^2}\right)^{n/2} e^{-\frac{1}{2}\sum\left(\frac{x_i - \bar{x}}{s}\right)^2}$$

for $i = 1, 2, ..., n$

$$= \left(\frac{1}{2\pi s^2}\right)^{n/2} e^{-n/2}$$

Under H_0, the estimate

$$\hat{\sigma}^2 = \frac{1}{n}\sum(x_i - \mu_0)^2$$

$$= \frac{1}{n}\sum(x_i - \bar{x} + \bar{x} - \mu_0)^2$$

$$= s^2 + (\bar{x} - \mu_0)^2$$

Hence under H_0, the likelihood function

$$L(x \mid \mu_0, \hat{\sigma}^2) = \left[2\pi\left\{s^2 + (\bar{x} - \mu_0)^2\right\}\right]^{-n/2} e^{-n/2}$$

The likelihood ratio,

$$\lambda = \frac{L(x \mid \mu_0, \hat{\sigma}^2)}{L(x \mid \hat{\mu}, \hat{\sigma}^2)}$$

$$= \frac{\left[2\pi\left\{s^2 + (\bar{x} - \mu_0)^2\right\}\right]^{-n/2} e^{-n/2}}{(2\pi s^2)^{-n/2} e^{-n/2}}$$

$$\lambda = \left[\frac{1}{1 + \frac{(\bar{x} - \mu_0)^2}{s^2}}\right]^{n/2}$$

or $$\lambda^{2/n} = \frac{1}{1 + \frac{t^2}{n-1}}$$

where t is student's-t with $(n - 1)$ d.f.

Therefore, λ is a monotone decreasing function of t^2. In this situation, we can use distribution of t^2 instead of λ. Rejecting 100 α per cent largest values of t^2 amounts to rejecting 100 α per cent smallest values of λ. Hence, we can use equal tail t-test. It is a UMPU test for H_0.

Q. 31. *Given a random sample $x_1, x_2, ..., x_n$ from a normal population with p.d.f. $f(x; \mu, \sigma^2)$, test H_0 : $\sigma = \sigma_0$ vs H_1 $\sigma \neq \sigma_0$ applying likelihood ratio test.*

Ans. The likelihood ratio

$$\lambda = \frac{L(x \mid \hat{\mu}, \sigma_0^2)}{L(x \mid \hat{\mu}, \sigma^2)}$$

$$= \frac{(\sigma_0\sqrt{2\pi})^{-n} e^{-\frac{1}{2\sigma_0^2}\Sigma(x_i - \bar{x})^2}}{\left(\sqrt{\frac{\Sigma(x_i - \bar{x})^2}{n}} \cdot \sqrt{2\pi}\right)^{-n} e^{-n/2}}$$

$$= n^{-\frac{n}{2}}\left[\frac{\Sigma(x_i - \bar{x})^2}{\sigma_0^2}\right]^{n/2} e^{-\frac{1}{2}\left\{\frac{\Sigma(x_i - \bar{x})^2}{\sigma_0^2} - n\right\}}$$

Suppose $$u = \frac{\Sigma(x_i - \bar{x})^2}{\sigma_0^2}$$

$$\lambda = n^{-n/2}\, u^{\frac{n}{2}}\, e^{-u/2}\, e^{n/2}$$

$$= cu^{n/2}\, e^{-u/2}$$

where c is a constant.

The critical region for the test statistic can be found by the relation,

$$u^{n/2}\, e^{-u/2} \leq k$$

Let the two roots of the above be C_1 and C_2. Then the critical regions are determined by the relations,

$$u < C_1 \text{ and } u \geq C_2$$

under H_0, the variable u is distributed as χ^2 with $(n - 1)$ d.f. and the distribution does not depend on the unspecified parameters. We can decide about H_0 by comparing the value of λ with the critical value of χ^2 for α level of significance and $(n - 1)$ d.f. If $\lambda \geq \chi^2_{\alpha,\, n-1}$, reject H_0, otherwise accept H_0.

Q. 32. *How can you apply likelihood ratio test in case of large samples?*

Ans. Suppose we want to test $H_0 : \theta = \theta_0$ where $\theta_0 \,\varepsilon\, \Theta_0$, some interval on the real line of the parametric space Θ.

Let $x_1, x_2, ..., x_n$ be a large sample of size n $(n > 30)$ and $\hat{\theta}$ be the ML estimator of θ_0. Then,

$$\lambda = \frac{L(x \mid \theta_0)}{L(x \mid \hat{\theta})}$$

If the first and second derivatives w.r.t. θ in Θ of the distribution of x exist, under H_0, $-2 \log \lambda$ is approximately distributed as χ^2 with $(n-1)$ d.f. The test may be performed in the usual manner.

Q. 33. *Describe Student's t-test.*

Ans. Student's t distribution was given and first used by W.S. Gosset in 1908. The statistician W.S. Gosset is better known by his pseudonym, *student.*

Suppose we want to test $H_0: \mu = \mu_0$ vs. $H_1: \mu \neq \mu_0$ on the basis of a small random sample $x_1, x_2, ..., x_n$ of size n $(n < 30)$ from a normal population. $N(\mu, \sigma^2)$ with σ^2 unknown for predecided level α.

Obviously it is a two tailed test.

For testing H_0, student's t statistic is,

$$t = \frac{\sqrt{n}(\bar{x} - \mu_0)}{s}, -\infty \leq t \leq \infty$$

where $$s = \sqrt{\frac{\Sigma_i (x_i - \bar{x})^2}{(n-1)}}$$

for $i = 1, 2, ..., n.$

Definition. Student's t is the deviation of estimated mean from its population mean expressed in terms of standard error. The test criteria is; reject H_0 if $t \geq t_{\alpha/2, n-1}$ or $-t_{\alpha/2, n-1}$, otherwise accept H_0.

Further, if one wants to test $H_0: \mu = \mu_0$ vs. H_1, $\mu > \mu_0$ or $\mu < \mu_0$, the test statistic remains the same. The only difference in the test procedure is that the critical value of t is only on one side.

In case of $H_1: \mu > \mu_0$, the test criteria is that reject H_0 if $t \geq t_{\alpha, n-1}$.

Q. 34. *What is a normal deviate test?*

Ans. A test of $H_0: \mu = \mu_0$ of a normal population $N(\mu, \sigma^2)$ against an alternative hypothesis H_1 can be tested by normal deviate test provided the population variance σ^2 is known or the sample drawn is large say, 30 or more. When the sample size is large enough, it is supposed that the sample variance is almost equal to population variance. The statistic Z for testing $H_0: \mu = \mu_0$ vs. $H_1: \mu \neq \mu_0$ is

$$Z = \frac{\bar{x} - \mu_0}{\sigma/\sqrt{n}}, \qquad -\infty \leq Z \leq \infty$$

where n is the sample size on which $\bar{x}$ is based. In case σ is not known and $n \geq 30$, σ is replaced by its estimated value s.

The variable $Z \sim N(0, 1)$. For the two tailed test, reject H_0 if $Z \geq Z_{\alpha/2}$ or $Z \leq -Z\alpha_{\alpha/2}$. But for a one-sided test when $H_1: \mu > \mu_0$, reject H_0 if $Z \geq Z_\alpha$ and when H_1: $\mu < \mu_0$, reject H_0 if $Z \leq -Z_\alpha$.

Q. 35. *How do you test the equality of two means of normal populations $N(\mu_1, \sigma_1^2)$ and $N(\mu_2, \sigma_2^2)$ when σ_1^2 and σ_2^2 are known?*

Ans. To test $H_0: \mu_1 = \mu_2$ vs. H_1 : or $\mu_1 \neq \mu_2$ or $\mu_1 > \mu_2$ or $\mu_1 < \mu_2$, the test statistics is

$$Z = \frac{\bar{x}_1 - \bar{x}_2}{\sqrt{\frac{\sigma_1^2}{n_1} + \frac{\sigma_2^2}{n_2}}} -\infty \leq z \leq \infty$$

where n_1 and n_2 are the sample sizes on which $\bar{x}_1$ and $\bar{x}_2$ are biased.

The decision criteria remain same as in case of one mean.

Q. 36. *What are the assumptions about t-test?*

Ans. There are five assumptions about t-test as given below:

(*i*) The random variable X follows normal distribution or the sample is drawn from a normal population.

(*ii*) All observations in the sample are independent.

(*iii*) The sample size is small, *i.e.*, less than 30 as an usual practice. Also the sample should not contain less than five observations.

(*iv*) The hypothetical value μ_0 of μ is a correct value of population mean.

(*v*) The sample values are correctly measured and recorded.

Q. 37. *What are the properties of t-test?*

Ans. (*i*) Student's *t*-test is a robust test. By a robust test we mean a test which is not vitiated much even if all the assumptions made about the test do not fully hold good.

(*ii*) Student's *t*-test for testing H_0: $\mu = \mu_0$ vs, $H_1 : \mu = \mu_1$ for an arbitrary σ from a normal population provides an uniformly most powerful unbiased test.

Q. 38. *A manufacturer of dry cells claimed that the life of their cells is 24.0 hours. A sample of 10 cells had mean life of 22.5 hours with a standard deviation of 3.0 hours. On the basis of available information, test whether the claim of the manufacturer is correct.*

[*Given*: $t_{0.05,\,9} = 2.2623$]

Ans. Assuming that the lifetime of cells is distributed normally. Here we test

$$H_0 : \mu = 24 \text{ vs. } H_1 : \mu \neq 24$$

by student's *t*-test.

$$t = \frac{(24.0 - 22.5) \times 3}{3.0}$$

$$= 1.5$$

The calculated value of *t* is less than the tabulated value of *t* since $t_{0.05,\,9} = 2.262$. Hence we accept H_0, *i.e.*, the claim of the manufacturer is correct.

Q. 39. *Give the procedures for testing the equality of two normal populations mean when the independent samples are drawn from the populations $N(\mu_1, \sigma_1^2)$ and $N(\mu_2, \sigma_2^2)$ in cases, (i) $\sigma_1^2 = \sigma_2^2 = \sigma^2$ (ii) $\sigma_1^2 \neq \sigma_2^2$.*

Ans. Let the two independent small samples of sizes n_1 and n_2 be $x_{11}, x_{12}, \ldots, x_{1n_1}$ and $x_{21}, x_{22}, \ldots, x_{2n_2}$ respectively. The test statistic for testing $H_0 : \mu_1 = \mu_2$ vs. $H_1 : \mu_1 \neq \mu_2$.

Case (i): $\sigma_1^2 = \sigma_2^2 = \sigma^2$ (unknown) is

$$t = \frac{\bar{x}_1 - \bar{x}_2}{s_p\sqrt{\dfrac{1}{n_1} + \dfrac{1}{n_2}}}$$

where $\bar{x}_1 = \dfrac{1}{n_1}\sum_{i=1}^{n_1} x_{1i}, \bar{x}_2 = \dfrac{1}{n_2}\sum_{j=1}^{n_2} x_{2j}$

and
$$s_p^2 = \frac{\sum_i (x_{1i} - \bar{x}_1)^2 + \sum_j (x_{2j} - \bar{x}_2)^2}{(n_1 + n_2 - 2)}$$

$$= \frac{\left\{\sum_i x_{1i}^2 - \dfrac{(\Sigma_i\, x_{1i})^2}{n_1}\right\} + \left\{\sum_j x_{2j}^2 - \dfrac{(\Sigma_j\, x_{2j})^2}{n_2}\right\}}{(n_1 + n_2 - 2)}$$

$$= \frac{(n_1 - 1)s_1^2 + (n_2 - 1)s_2^2}{(n_1 + n_2 - 2)}$$

where s_1^2 and s_2^2 are the variances of the first and second samples respectively.

Statistic *t* has $(n_1 + n_2 - 2)$ d.f.

The test criteria are, reject H_0 if $t \geq t_\alpha, (n_1 + n_2 - 2)$, otherwise accept H_0, where α is the predecided level of significance.

Case (ii): When $\sigma_1^2 \neq \sigma_2^2$ *t*-test for H_0 can be performed by two approaches. One is W.G. Cochran's approximate *t*-test and the other Berhans-Fisher test.

Following usual notations, statistics under Cochran's approximate test is,

$$t = \frac{\bar{x}_1 - \bar{x}_2}{\sqrt{\dfrac{s_1^2}{n_1} + \dfrac{s_2^2}{n_2}}}$$

For making a decision about H_0 *vis-a-vis* H_1 calculated value of *t* is compared with t^* where,

$$t^* = \frac{\dfrac{s_1^2}{n_1} \times t_{\alpha, n_1 - 1} + \dfrac{s_2^2}{n_2} \times t_{\alpha, n_2 - 1}}{\dfrac{s_1^2}{n_1} + \dfrac{s_2^2}{n_2}}$$

Reject H_0 if $t \geq t^*$, otherwise accept H_0.

[*Note*: If $n_1 = n_2 = n$, $t^* = t_\alpha, n - 1$]

Case (iii): When $\sigma_1^2 \neq \sigma_2^2$, it is not possible to get the standard error of $(\bar{x}_1 - \bar{x}_2)$ and hence student's t-test cannot be used directly. Also $\{(n_1 - 1) s_1^2 + (n_2 - 1) s_2^2\}$ is not distributed as $\chi^2 \sigma^2$. In the want of any clear-cut test statistics, W.V. Behrens and later R.A. Fisher suggested an alternate procedure known as Behrens-Fisher test.

Let $\bar{x}_1$, $\bar{x}_2$, be the sample means and s_1^2, s_2^2, the sample variances based on samples of sizes n_1 and n_2 from two normal populations $N(\mu_1, \sigma_1^2)$ and $N(\mu_1, \sigma_2^2)$ respectively where $\sigma_1^2 \neq \sigma_2^2$.

Let us define,

$$t_1 = \frac{\bar{x}_1 - \mu_1}{s_1/\sqrt{n_1}} \text{ and } t_2 = \frac{\bar{x}_2 - \mu_2}{s_2/\sqrt{n_2}}$$

which are distributed with $(n_1 - 1)$ and $(n_2 - 1)$ d.f., respectively. Suppose

$$d = \frac{(\bar{x}_1 - \mu_1) - (\bar{x}_2 - \mu_2)}{\sqrt{\dfrac{s_1^2}{n_1} + \dfrac{s_2^2}{n_2}}}$$

Substitute $\dfrac{s_1}{\sqrt{n_1}} = r \sin\theta$ and $\dfrac{s_2}{\sqrt{n_2}} = r\cos\theta$.

Thus, $r^2 = \left(\dfrac{s_1^2}{n_1} + \dfrac{s_2^2}{n_2}\right)$ and $\tan\theta = \dfrac{s_1}{s_2}\sqrt{\dfrac{n_2}{n_1}}$ using the above relations,

$$(\bar{x}_1 - \mu_1) = \frac{s_1}{\sqrt{n_1}} t_1 \text{ and } \bar{x}_2 - \mu_2 = \frac{s_2}{\sqrt{n_2}} t_2$$

$$d = \frac{\dfrac{s_1 t_1}{\sqrt{n_1}} - \dfrac{s_2 t_2}{\sqrt{n_2}}}{r}$$

$$= \frac{r t_1 \sin\theta - r t_2 \cos\theta}{r}$$

$$= t_1 \sin\theta - t_2 \cos\theta$$

Thus, it is evident that d depends on μ_1 and μ_2 and is independent of σ_1^2 and σ_2^2. If $f_n(t)$ be the p.d.f. of t, the probabilities that the two samples will have values t_1 and t_2, respectively, lying within the specified limits is,

$$\iint f_{(n_1 - 1)}(t_1) f_{n_2 - 1}(t_2) dt_1\, dt_2$$

The integral being over (t_1, t_2) plane.

Let us assume that for some d_0, the region is given by

$$t_1 \sin\theta - t_2 \cos\theta > d_0$$

and determine d_0 such that the double integral is equal to α, the predecided level of significance. For a given α, d_0 will be a function of n_1, n_2 and θ only. Now substituting back, we obtain

$$\frac{\bar{x}_1 - \mu_1}{r} - \frac{\bar{x}_2 - \mu_2}{r} > d_0$$

$$(\bar{x}_1 - \bar{x}_2) - (\mu_1 - \mu_2) > rd_0$$

$$-(\mu_1 - \mu_2) > -(\bar{x}_1 - \bar{x}_2) + rd_0$$

$$(\mu_1 - \mu_2) < (\bar{x}_1 - \bar{x}_2) - rd_0$$

with the help of the above inequality, we can decide about the null hypothesis. If $(\bar{x}_1 - \bar{x}_2) > rd_0$, then $\mu_1 \leq \mu_2$ will have a confidence coefficient less than α. Similarly if $(\bar{x}_1 - \bar{x}_2) < rd_0$, then $\mu_1 \geq \mu_2$ will have a confidence coefficient less that α. The value of d_0 are available in Fisher and Yates tables for different values of θ. For a sufficiently small value of α, we reject H_0 if $|\bar{x}_1 - \bar{x}_2| > rd_0$.

The main objection of Behrens-Fisher test is that $\dfrac{s_1}{s_2}$ has been taken as a constant which is not a correct supposition. But here it is worth pointing out that the power of Beherens-Fisher test is more that the power of Cochran's test.

Q. 40. *Given the statistics of two samples drawn from two normal populations $N(\mu_1, \sigma_1^2)$ and $N(\mu_2, \sigma_2^2)$ as,*

$$n_1 = 6, \bar{x}_1 = 25 \text{ and } s_1^2 = 36.0$$

$$n_2 = 8, \bar{x}_2 = 20 \text{ and } s_2^2 = 25.0$$

Test $H_0 : \mu_1 = \mu_2$ vs. $H_1 = \mu_1 \neq \mu_2$ under two situations (i) $\sigma_1^2 = \sigma_2^2$, (ii) $\sigma_1^2 \neq \sigma_2^2$

[Given: $t_{0.05,\,12} = 2.18$; $t_{0.05,\,13} = 2.16$

$t_{0.05,\,5} = 2.571$; $t_{0.05,\,7} = 2.365$]

Ans. *Situation (i)* $\sigma_1^2 = \sigma_2^2$.

The statistic

$$t = \frac{25-20}{5.44\sqrt{\frac{1}{6}+\frac{1}{8}}}$$

$$= 1.70$$

where

$$s_p^2 = \frac{5\times 36 + 7\times 25}{6+8-2}$$

$$= 29.58$$

$$s_p = 5.44$$

Since $t < 2.18$, the tabulated value of t for 12 d.f. and $\alpha = 0.05$, we accept H_0, *i.e.*, there is no significant difference between the two population means.

Situation (ii): $\sigma_1^2 \neq \sigma_2^2$

First we apply Cochran's test. The test statistic,

$$t = \frac{25-20}{\sqrt{\frac{36}{6}+\frac{25}{8}}}$$

$$= 1.66$$

Value of

$$t^* = \frac{6\times 2.571 + 3.125\times 2.365}{6+3.125}$$

$$= 2.50$$

Since $t = 1.66 < 2.50$. H_0 is accepted.

Now we apply Behrens-Fisher test.

From the given statistics,

$$r^2 = \frac{36}{6} + \frac{25}{8} = 9.125$$

$$\therefore \quad r = 3.02$$

$$\tan\theta = \frac{6}{5}\times\sqrt{\frac{8}{6}} = 1.38$$

$$\theta = \tan^{-1} 1.38 = 60.08°$$

Also $\quad \bar{x}_1 - \bar{x}_2 = 5.$

For $\alpha = 0.05$, d.f. $n_1 - 1 = 5$, $n_2 - 1 = 7$ and $\theta = 60°$, the value of d_0 is 2.50. Thus,

$$rd_0 = 3.02 \times 2.50$$

$$= 7.55$$

$$\bar{x}_1 - \bar{x}_2 = 5 < 7.55$$

Hence, we conclude that there is no significant difference between μ_1 and μ_2.

Q. 41. *When do you use paired t-test and how to apply it?*

Ans. Let us consider two variables X_1 and X_2 which are normally distributed and there exists a correlation ρ between them. In practice, the observation are taken on the same item or the items which are paired before taking the observations. Let the difference between the paired values $X_1 - X_2 = d$. $(X_1 - X_2)$ is distributed with mean μ_d and variance $(\sigma_1^2 + \sigma_2^2 - 2\rho\sigma_1\sigma_2)$.

In paired t-test, we test $H_0 : \mu_D = 0$ vs. $H_1 : \mu_D \neq 0$. The test based on n paired values (x_{11}, x_{21}), (x_{12}, x_{22}), ..., (x_{1n}, x_{2n}) is

$$t = \frac{\bar{d}}{s_d/\sqrt{n}}$$

t has $(n-1)$ d.f.

where, $d_i = x_{1i} - x_{2i}$ for $i = 1, 2, ..., n$.

$$\bar{d} = \frac{1}{n}\sum_{i=1}^{n} d_i \text{ and } s_d^2 = \frac{1}{n-1}\sum_i (d_i - \bar{d})^2$$

Test criteria is, reject H_0 if $|t| \geq t_{\alpha,\, n-1}$, otherwise accept H_0.

Q. 42. *The measurements of diameter of 8 cylindrical rods by vernier calliper and micrometer were as follows:*

Vernier reading (X_1): 2.265 2.267 2.264 2.267
2.268 2.263 2.264 2.258

Micrometer reading: 2.270 2.268 2.269 2.273
(X_2): 2.270 2.270 2.268 2.268

Test whether the difference between measurements of diameter by vernier and micrometer is significant or not. [Given: $t_{7;\,05} = 2.365$]

Ans. The difference $(X_2 - X_1)$,

d: 0.005, 0.001,0.005, 0.006, 0.002, 0.007, 0.004, 0.010

$$\bar{d} = \frac{0.040}{8} = 0.005,$$

$$s_d^2 = \frac{1}{7}\left\{0.000256 - \frac{(0.04)^2}{8}\right\}$$

$$= 0.000008$$

$$\therefore \quad s_d = 0.0028$$

The statistic,

$$t = \frac{0.005 \times \sqrt{8}}{0.0028}$$

$$= 5.05$$

The calculated value of $t = 5.05$ is greater than the tabulated value 2.365 of t for 7 d.f. and $\alpha = 0.05$. Hence, H_0 is rejected. It confirms that there is a significant difference between the readings made by vernier and micrometer at $\alpha = 0.05$.

Q. 43. *How can one test the hypothesis for a hypothetical value of proportion in a class of binomial population on the basis of a sample?*

Ans. The interest lies in testing the hypothesis that the proportion P of items in a class C_1 out of two classes in the population is p_0 or not on the basis of a sample of size n. Here we test,

$$H_0 : P = p_0 \text{ vs. } H_1 : P \neq p_0.$$

H_0 can be tested by Z-test. The condition is that the sample size should be large. For a binomial distribution, to test $H_0 : p = \frac{1}{2}$, n should be 10 or more. Let n_1 be the number of items in the class C_1 and n_2 in class C_2 out of n. Thus $n_1 + n_2 = n$.

Also the proportion of items in C_1 is $\hat{p} = \frac{n_1}{n}$ and in C_2, $\hat{q} = \frac{n_2}{n}$

The test statistic

$$Z = \frac{\hat{p} - p_0}{\sqrt{p_0 q_0 / n}}$$

where, $q_0 = 1 - p_0$ and $Z \sim N(0, 1)$.

The test criteria is reject H_0 if $Z \geq Z_{\alpha/2}$ or $-Z \leq -Z_{\alpha/2}$ where α is the prefixed level of significance. In case, H_1: $P > p_0$, reject H_0 if $Z \geq Z_\alpha$. In case, H_1: $P < p_0$, reject H_0 if $Z < -Z_\alpha$.

Alternative approach: Instead of working with the proportions, it is possible to deal with the number of items (outcomes) belonging to a class associated with p. Taking the number of items x in class C_1, the test statistic for testing H_0 is,

$$Z = \frac{(x + 0.5) - np_0}{\sqrt{n\, p_0\, q_0}} \quad \text{if } x < np_0$$

use $(x - 0.5)$ if $x > np_0$.

The test criteria remain the same as above. Addition of 0.5 to x makes the approximation of binomial to normal distribution more exact.

Q. 44. *In crossing of 30 white dams with brown sires, it is expected that half of the calves will be white and the rest will be brown. But the experiment showed that out of 30 calves, 20 were brown and 10 white. Can it be believed that there will be in general 50 per cent brown calves?*

Ans. Here we have to test $H_0 : p = \frac{1}{2}$ vs. $H_1 : p \neq \frac{1}{2}$.

It means $p_0 = \frac{1}{2}$, $q_0 = \frac{1}{2}$. Also $\hat{p} = \frac{20}{30} = \frac{2}{3}$.

To test H_0, the statistic

$$Z = \frac{2/3 - 1/2}{\sqrt{\left(\frac{1}{2}\times\frac{1}{2}\right)/30}}$$

$$= 1.82$$

The critical value of Z for 5 per cent level of significance is 1.96 which is greater than 1.82. Hence we accept H_0. This reveals that the expectation of 50 per cent brown calves is correct.

Alternatively H_0 is tested by taking the number of calves.

As per the question $x = 20$, $np_0 = 30 \times \frac{1}{2} = 15$, $x > np_0$. The statistic

$$Z = \frac{(20 - 0.5) - 15}{\sqrt{30\times\frac{1}{2}\times\frac{1}{2}}}$$

$$= 1.64$$

Again $Z = 1.64 < 1.96$. We accept H_0.

Q. 45. *How will you test the equality of two proportion of items in the same class on the basis of two independent samples drawn from two populations?*

Ans. Here we are to test $H_0 : P_1 = P_2$ vs. $H_1 : P_1 \neq P_2$ on the basis of two samples of sizes n_1 and n_2 from populations A and B respectively. Let there be two classes C_1 and C_2. The number of items belonging to different classes are displayed in the table below:

Classes

	C_1	C_2	
Sample from A	O_1	O_2	n_1
Sample from B	O'_1	O'_2	n_2
	$O_1 + O'_1$	$O_2 + O'_2$	$n_1 + n_2$

The observed proportions in class C_1 for items from populations A and B are, $p_1 = \frac{O_1}{n_1}$, $q_1 = \frac{O_2}{n_1}$ and $p_2 = \frac{O'_1}{n_2}$, $q_2 = \frac{O'_2}{n_2}$ respectively.

H_0 against H_1 can be tested by the statistic,

$$Z = \frac{|p_1 - p_2|}{\sqrt{\hat{p}\hat{q}\left(\frac{1}{n_1} + \frac{1}{n_2}\right)}}$$

Under H_0, $P_1 = P_2$, $\hat{p} = \frac{O_1 + O'_1}{n_1 + n_2}$, $\hat{q} = 1 - \hat{p}$. The term, $\sqrt{\hat{p}\hat{q}\left(\frac{1}{n_1} + \frac{1}{n_2}\right)}$ is the standard error of $(p_1 - p_2)$.

In case H_0 is doubted to be true, the standard error of $(p_1 - p_2)$ should be restandardised using

$$s_{p_1 - p_2} = \sqrt{\frac{p_1 q_1}{n_1} + \frac{p_2 q_2}{n_2}}$$

The decision about H_0 can be taken in the usual manner.

Q. 46. *A survey was conducted in two types of colonies, one consisting of normal residents and the other of slum dwellings to know whether the prevalence of Tuberculosis (TB) in slum area is more than the normal area.*

A sample of 600 persons in normal area had 28 persons suffering from TB where in a sample of 400 persons in slum area, 96 persons had TB. Do the data support our assertion?

Ans. Here we have to test $H_0 : P_1 = P_2$ vs. $H_1 : P_1 < P_2$. The given information can be tabulated as follows:

Classes

	TB	*No TB*	
Normal area	28	572	600
Slum area	96	304	400
	124	876	1000

From the table,

$$p_1 = \frac{28}{600} 0.047, q_1 = 0.953$$

$$p_2 = \frac{96}{400} = 0.24, q_2 = 0.76$$

Under H_0, $\hat{p} = \frac{124}{1000} = 0.124, \hat{q} = 0.876$

The statistic

$$Z = \frac{|0.047 - 0.24|}{\sqrt{0.124 \times 0.876\left(\frac{1}{600} + \frac{1}{400}\right)}}$$

$$= \frac{0.193}{0.0213}$$

$$= 9.06$$

Here we have to apply the one-tailed test. If 1 per cent level of significance is chosen, the tabulated value of $Z_\alpha = 2.33$ which is less than 9.06. Hence we reject H_0. It means that the prevalence of TB in slum residential area is more than the normal area.

Q. 47. *How can the hypothesis that the variance of a normal distribution has a specified value σ_0^2 be tested?*

Ans. Here we test H_0: $\sigma^2 = \sigma_0^2$. vs. $H_1 : \sigma^2 \neq \sigma_0^2$. Let there be a random sample $x_1, x_2, ..., x_n$. H_0 can be tested by χ^2-test subject to the condition that $n < 30$.

The test statistic

$$\chi^2 = \frac{\Sigma_i (x_i - \bar{x})^2}{\sigma_0^2} \quad \text{for } i = 1, 2, ..., n.$$

$$= \frac{(n-1)\, s^2}{\sigma_0^2}$$

χ^2 has $(n - 1)$ d.f.

The decision criteria is, reject H_0 if $\chi^2 \geq \chi^2_{\alpha/2, (n-1)}$ or $\chi^2 < \chi_{(1-\alpha/2), (n-1)}$, otherwise accept H_0. Where α is the prefixed level of significance.

In case of one-tailed test, *i.e.*, testing H_0: $\sigma^2 = \sigma_0^2$, vs. H_1: $\sigma^2 < \sigma_0^2$, reject H_0 if $\chi^2 \geq \chi^2_{(1-\alpha), (n-1)}$, otherwise accept H_0.

Again for testing $H_0 : \sigma^2 = \sigma_0^2$ vs. H_1: $\sigma^2 > \sigma_0^2$, reject H_0 if $\chi^2 \geq \chi^2_{\alpha, n-1}$, otherwise accept H_0.

Q. 48. *A manufacturer claims that any of his lot of items cannot have a variance more than 1 cm². A sample of 25 items has a variance of 1.2 cm². Test whether the claim of the manufacturer is correct.*

Ans. Here we test H_0: $\sigma^2 = 1$ vs. $H_1 : \sigma^2 \neq 1$.

The test statistic

$$\chi^2 = \frac{24 \times 1.2}{1}$$

$$= 28.8$$

For $\alpha = 0.05$, $\chi^2_{0.05, 24} = 36.41$ which is greater than $\chi^2 = 28.8$. Hence accept H_0. This confirms the claim of the manufacturer.

Q. 49. *Give an appropriate test for testing the hypothesis $H_0 : \sigma = \sigma_0$ vs. $H_1 : \sigma \neq \sigma_0$ of a normal population with unknown variance σ^2.*

Ans. The appropriate test for testing H_0 against H_1 is Z-test. The statistic

$$Z = \frac{s - \sigma}{s / \sqrt{2n}}$$

for large n.

$s/\sqrt{2n}$ is the standard error of the sample standard deviation s.

Decision about H_0 can be taken by the set procedure.

Q. 50. *Give the test statistic for testing the equality of two standard deviations of the normal populations.*

Ans. Let n_1 and n_2 be the sizes of two large samples from two normal populations $N(\mu_1, \sigma_1^2)$ and $N(\mu_2, \sigma_2^2)$. Also σ_1^2 and σ_2^2 are unknowns.

The statistic for testing $H_0 : \sigma_1 - \sigma_2 = 0$ vs. $H_1 : \sigma_1 - \sigma_2 \neq 0$ is,

$$Z = \frac{|s_1 - s_2|}{\sqrt{\frac{s_1^2}{2n_1} + \frac{s_2^2}{2n_2}}}$$

where s_1^2 and s_2^2 are the variance based on large samples. Also $Z \sim N(0, 1)$.

The decision about H_0 is taken in the usual manner.

Q. 51. *What do you understand by the test of goodness of fit?*

Ans. In test of hypotheses or estimation of parameters it is usually assumed that the random variable follows a particular distribution like Binomial, Poisson, normal distribution, etc. But often the need is felt to confirm whether our assumption is true or not. So on the basis of outcomes of a trial or observational data, Chi-square test is performed which measures the discrepancy between the observed frequencies and theoretically determined frequencies from the assumed distribution for the same event. If the discrepancy is not large, it is considered that our assumption about the distribution of the variable is correct, otherwise not.

Here we test H_0: the data have come from the assumed distribution.

vs. H_1: H_0 is not true.

If $O_1, O_2, ..., O_k$ are the observed frequencies and $E_1, E_2, ..., E_k$ are the corresponding expected frequencies, the test statistic

$$\chi^2 = \sum_i \frac{(O_i - E_i)^2}{E_i} \quad \text{for } i = 1, 2, ..., k$$

$$= \sum_i \frac{O_i^2}{E_i} - n$$

χ^2 has $(n - 1)$ d.f.

where $\sum_i O_i = n$.

The expected frequencies are obtained by finding the probability of an event to which an O_i belongs and then by multiplying the probability by n, we get the corresponding E_i. Thus $E_i = np_i$. Here it should be kept in mind that $\Sigma O_i = \Sigma E_i = n$. The decision criteria is, reject H_0 if $\chi^2 \geq \chi^2_{\alpha, k-1}$ otherwise accept H_0.

Q. 52. *Is it necessary to consult χ^2-table to decide about the null hypothesis?*

Ans. No, because if the calculated value of Chi-square is less than or equal to the degrees of freedom for Chi-square, there is no need to consult χ^2-table. In this situation, null hypothesis be accepted as such. The reason being that under the null hypothesis, the expected value of calculated Chi-square is the degree of freedom of χ^2 and only much higher value of χ^2 will lead to rejection of the null hypothesis.

Q. 53. *How to apply the Chi-square test in case of multinomial distribution?*

Ans. A common problem is to test the hypothesis

$$H_0 : p_i = p_{io} \text{ for } i = 1, 2, ..., k$$

where k is the number of classes. Such a problem is often confronted in genetics and sociometery. A geneticist expects a definite ratio of offspring types out of a set of crossing. A sociologist expects certain ratio of occurrences of certain events. In all these problems, H_0 can be tested by Chi-square test.

Suppose O_i represents the observed frequency in the ith class and E_i is the corresponding expected (theoretical or hypothetical) frequency where $E_i = np_{i0}$ under H_0. The value of p_{i0} can be calculated by the ratio of occurrence of frequencies in k-classes given as $r_1 : r_2 : ... : r_k$. If $\Sigma_i r_i = r$, $p_{i0} = \frac{r_i}{r}$ and $E_i = \frac{n}{r} r_i$.

The test statistic

$$\chi^2 = \sum_i \frac{(O_i - E_i)^2}{E_i} \quad \text{for } i = 1, 2, ..., k$$

χ^2 is distributed with $(k - 1)$ d.f.

The decision about H_0 is taken as usual.

Q. 54. *In a breeding experiment, the ratio of offsprings in four classes was expected to be 1 : 3 : 3 : 9. The experiment yielded the data as follows:*

Classes:	*AA*	*Aa*	*aA*	*aa*
No. of offsprings:	8	29	37	102

Test whether the given data is in agreement with the hypothetical ratio.

Ans. Here we have $n = 176$, $r_1 = 1$, $r = 3$, $r_3 = 3$, $r_4 = 9$ and $r = 16$.

The expected frequencies can be worked out as,

$$E_1 = \frac{176}{16} \times 1 = 11, E_2 = \frac{176}{16} \times 3 = 33,$$

$$E_3 = 33, E_4 = \frac{176}{16} \times 9 = 99$$

Thus

$$\chi^2 = \frac{(8-11)^2}{11} + \frac{(29-33)^2}{33} + \frac{(37-33)^2}{33} + \frac{(102-99)^2}{99}$$

$$= 0.818 + 0.485 + 0.485 + 0.091$$

$$= 1.879$$

For $\alpha = 0.05$, $\chi^2_{0.05,\,3} = 7.81$ which is greater than the calculated value of $\chi^2 = 1.879$. Hence, we accept H_0. It suggests that the data support the expected ratio in the four classes.

Q. 55. *What is a contingency table?*

Ans. A contingency table is a two-way table in which the columns are classified according to one criterion or attribute and rows are classified according to the other criterion or attribute. Each cell contains that number of items 0_{ij} possessing the qualities of the ith row and j^{th} column, where $i = 1, 2, ..., m$ and $j = 1, 2, ..., p$. In such a case, the contingency table is said to be of order $(m \times p)$. Each row or column total is known as *marginal total*. Also the sum of row totals $\sum_i R_i$ is equal to the sum of column totals $\sum_j C_j$, *i.e.*, $\sum_i R_i = \sum_j C_j = n$, (the sample size).

Contingency table helps to test the independence of two attributes.

Q. 56. *What is an incomplete contingency table?*

Ans. If in a contingency table, one or more cells are having zero count, then it is an incomplete contingency table.

Q. 57. *What is the difference between structural and random zeros?*

Ans. If there is a zero in *a* cell and this cell count has expected value zero *i.e.* the probability of having any observation in the cell is zero, then such a zero is a structural zero.

On the other hand, if the expected value *i.e.* the probability of having a count in the cell is greater than zero, then the zero present in a cell is a random zero.

Q. 58. *Give a contingency table showing structural and random zeros.*

Ans. Consider the following (3 × 4) contingency table:

Factor B

Factor A	B_1	B_2	B_3	B_4
A_1	0	0	0	0
A_2	5	10	0	11
A_3	9	12	8	10

The expected value of any cell count of first row is zero. Hence such zero counts in the first row are structural zeros. Whereas the zero count in the cell (2, 3) is a random zero.

Technically, the structural and random zeros are to be treated in the same way.

Q. 59. *Is a contingency table only a two-dimensional table?*

Ans. No. A contingency table may be a 3, 4 or more dimensional table. In general, it is a multidimensional table. As an example, we provide a 3 × 2 × 3 hypothetical contingency table below:

Social group	*Sex*	*Employment type*		
		Technical	*Skilled*	*Unskilled*
High	Male	28	15	9
	Female	5	13	11
Middle	Male	34	23	45
	Female	25	18	51
Low	Male	7	12	106
	Female	1	2	61

Q. 60. *What is an explanatory variable in a contingency table?*

Ans. Many times the aim of analysis in a contingency table is to explain the variation in one of the variables through the variation of the other variable. Thus, those variables which are used in a contingency table to explain the variation in the response variable, are called explanatory variables. For example, the variation in alcohol consumption, the response variable, may be explained through the variation in explanatory variables like, social groups, marital status, age groups etc.

Q. 61. *How will you test the independence of two attributes?*

Ans. Suppose n randomly selected items are arranged in a contingency table given below:

	Columns						
Rows	B_1	B_2	...	B_j	...	B_p	Total
A_1	O_{11}	O_{12}	...	O_{1j}	...	O_{1p}	R_1
A_2	O_{21}	O_{22}	...	O_{2j}	...	O_{2p}	R_2
⋮	⋮			⋮		⋮	⋮
A_i	O_{i1}	O_{i2}	...	O_{ij}	...	O_{ip}	R_i
⋮	⋮						⋮
A_m	O_{m1}	O_{m2}	...	O_{mj}	...	O_{mp}	R_m
Total	C_1	C_2	...	C_j	...	C_p	n

Corresponding to each O_{ij}, find the expected frequency E_{ij} under H_0 by the formula,

$$E_{ij} = \frac{R_i \times C_j}{n}$$

Here we test H_0: Attributes A and B are independent.

vs. H_1 : Attributes A and B are associated.

H_0 can be tested by the statistic

$$\chi^2 = \sum_{i=1}^{m}\sum_{j=1}^{p}\frac{(O_{ij} - E_{ij})^2}{E_{ij}}$$

χ^2 has $(m - 1)(p - 1)$ d.f.

The test criteria is, reject H_0 if $\chi^2 \geq \chi^2_{\alpha,(m-1)(p-1)}$ otherwise accept H_0.

Q. 62. *Give the formula for calculating statistic χ^2 in case of contingency table of order (2×2).*

Ans. Suppose the contingency table of order (2×2) is as displayed below:

Rows	Columns		Total
	B_1	B_2	
A_1	a	b	$a + b$
A_2	c	d	$c + d$
Total	$a + c$	$b + d$	$a + b + c + d = n$

The direct formula for calculating the value of statistic-χ^2 is,

$$\chi^2 = \frac{n(ad - bc)^2}{(a+b)(c+d)(a+c)(b+d)}$$

χ^2 has 1 d.f.

Q. 63. *If there are only two classes C_1 and C_2 having frequencies a and b which are hypothesised to occur in the ratio $r_1 : r_2$, how can you calculate the value of statistic-χ^2?*

Ans. Suppose $\frac{r_1}{r_2} = r$. The direct formula for χ^2-statistic to test the validity of the hypothetical ratio $r_1 : r_2$ is,

$$\chi^2 = \frac{(a - rb)^2}{r(a+b)}$$

χ^2 has 1 d.f.

Q. 64. *What is Yates' correction and how to apply it?*

Ans. When the expected frequency in a cell of (2×2) contingency table is small say, less than 5, the continuity of χ^2 distribution is disturbed. To remove this deficiency, Yates in 1934 suggested that 0.5 be added to the small frequency for which the expected frequency is less than 5 and other cell frequencies be adjusted by adding and subtracting 0.5 in such a way that the marginal totals remain the same. After adjustment, the value of χ^2 is calculated in the usual manner.

An alternative formula is suggested which automatically takes care of the adjustments in cell frequencies. The formula is,

$$\chi^2 = \frac{n\left(|ad - bc| - \frac{n}{2}\right)^2}{(a+b)(c+d)(a+c)(b+d)}$$

Here it is worth pointing out that the value of χ^2 after adjustment in cell frequencies by a quantity 0.5 and the value of χ^2 obtained by the alternative formula are equal. Yates' correction is applicable only in case of contingency table of order (2 × 2).

Q. 65. *Following table provides data with regard to stature of the fathers and their first sons at the age of 25 years:*

		Stature of fathers		
		Tall	*Short*	*Total*
Stature of sons	*Tall*	*8*	*2*	*10*
	Short	*7*	*6*	*13*
Total		*15*	*8*	*23*

Test that the stature of sons is independent of the stature of the fathers.

Ans. The expected frequency corresponding to the cell frequency 2 is less than 5. Hence, Yates' correction will have to be applied.

H_0: The stature of son is independent of the stature of father.

vs. H_1: H_0 is not true.

The new configuration of the table under Yates' correction is,

7.5	2.5	10
7.5	5.5	13
15	8	23

The statistic,

$$\chi^2 = \frac{23(7.5 \times 5.5 - 7.5 \times 2.5)^2}{10 \times 13 \times 15 \times 8}$$

$$= 0.746$$

The value of the statistic by the alternative formula is,

$$\chi^2 = \frac{23(|48 - 14| - 11.5)^2}{10 \times 13 \times 15 \times 8}$$

$$= 0.746$$

For $\alpha = 0.05$, $\chi^2_{0.05,\,1} = 3.841$. Since the calculated value of χ^2 is less than tabulated value, we accept H_0. It reveals that the stature of sons is independent of the stature of their fathers.

Q. 66. *What is Dandekar's correction for continuity of χ^2 in a contingency table of order (2 × 2)?*

Ans. V. M. Dandekar's evolved a different correction methods to maintain the continuity of χ^2 when the expected frequency in one or more cells are less than 5 in a contingency table of order (2 × 2). From a (2 × 2) table calculate χ_0^2, χ_{-1}^2, χ_{+1}^2 for the observed configuration and those obtained by decreasing and increasing the smallest frequency by unity respectively. It should be kept in mind that under any change in configuration, the marginal totals remain same. Using the three Chi-square values, calculate the value of corrected χ^2 by the formula,

$$\chi_c^2 = \chi_0^2 - \frac{\chi_0^2 - \chi_{-1}^2}{\chi_{+1}^2 - \chi_{-1}^2}(\chi_{+1}^2 - \chi_0^2)$$

Dandekar's correction, in general is slightly better than Yates' correction, although the Yates' correction is easier to apply.

Q. 67. *For the problem given in Q. No. 65, test H_0 by applying Dandekar's Correction.*

Ans. Here we calculate directly χ_c^2.

$$\chi_0^2 = \frac{23(48 - 14)^2}{10 \times 13 \times 15 \times 8}$$

$$= 1.704$$

$$\chi_{-1}^2 = \frac{23(63 - 6)^2}{10 \times 13 \times 15 \times 8}$$

$$= 4.790$$

$$\chi_{+1}^2 = \frac{23(35 - 24)^2}{10 \times 13 \times 15 \times 8}$$

$$= 0.178$$

$$\chi_c^2 = 1.704 - \frac{1.704 - 4.790}{0.178 - 4.790}(0.178 - 1.704)$$

$$= 2.725$$

Calculated value of $\chi^2 = 2.725$ is less than the tabulated value of $\chi^2_{0.05} = 3.841$. Hence H_0 is accepted. It means that the stature of sons is independent of the stature of their fathers.

Q. 68. *Describe Fisher's exact test for testing the hypothesis of independence of attributes in a (2 × 2) contingency table.*

Ans. Fisher's exact test consists of calculating the probability of the configurations of the contingency table of order (2 × 2) such as

		B		
		B_1	B_2	
A	A_1	a	b	$a+b$
	A_2	c	d	$c+d$
		$a+c$	$b+d$	$a+b+c+d=n$

from smallest observed frequency up to zero by reducing each time the smallest cell frequency by unity keeping the marginal totals fixed. The probability for a configuration say, with d being smallest can be obtained by the formula,

$$p_d = \frac{\binom{a+b}{a}\binom{c+d}{c}}{\binom{n}{a+c}}$$

$$= \frac{(a+b)!(c+d)!(a+c)!(b+d)!}{n!a!b!c!d!}$$

Calculate $P = p_d + p_{d-1} + \ldots\ p_1 + p_0$, which is the probability corresponding to one tail of the distribution. Reject H_0 if $P \leq \alpha$, otherwise accept H_0. Fisher's exact test can be used to test (*i*) independence of attributes (*ii*) the equality of proportions in two classes.

The chief defect of Fisher's exact test is that it involves too much of computation, particularly when the smallest frequency is more than 2.

Q. 69. *Write the purpose of coefficient of contingency, and how is it measured?*

Ans. When the hypothesis of independence of attributes in a contingency table is rejected by performing χ^2-test, it ensures the association between two attributes. One is not satisfied merely with association but is also interested in the strength of association. Hence, there is a desideratum for a measure of the strength of association. For this a measure known as *coefficient of contingency* was evolved by Karl Pearson in 1904. The coefficient of contingency

$$C = \sqrt{\frac{\chi^2}{n + \chi^2}}$$

where n is the sample size. The value of C lies between 0 and 1 and never attains 1. $C = 0$ indicates complete dissociation. A value near to 1 shows a high degree of association. Actually C is calculated only when H_0 is rejected.

Q. 70. *If Chi-square test indicates dependence, how can one detect which cells in a (p × q) contingency table contribute most to departure from independence?*

Ans. For detecting whether the contribution in departure from independence of an individual cell (*i, j*) is significant or not, we commonly find the square root of the individual terms in the Chi-square statistic, *i.e.*, calculate $(O_{ij} - E_{ij})/\sqrt{E_{ij}}$ as an indicator. But such an indicator has no yardstick for claiming which of the indicator is large or small. As a matter of fact, it follows no standard distribution. Hence $(O_{ij} - E_{ij})$ is standardised such that it follows a standard normal distribution – so we use the expression,

$$\frac{O_{ij} - E_{ij}}{\sqrt{E_{ij}(1 - p_{i\cdot})(1 - p_{\cdot j})}}$$

These standardised values are called residuals or more exactly standardised residuals.

If the value of an individual residual is greater than the 97.5 per cent value of standard normal distribution, *i.e.*, 1.96, the contribution of an individual cell is significant otherwise not.

[*Note*: Where p_{ij} is the proportion of frequency in (i, j) cell.]

Q. 71. *What treatment is metted to Chi-square having large degrees of freedom?*

Ans. If the d.f. for χ^2 are 100 or more, then Chi-square can be approximated to a standard normal deviate using the relation,

$$Z = \sqrt{2\chi^2} - \sqrt{2k-1}$$

where k is the d.f. for χ^2 and $Z \sim N(0, 1)$. Here H_0 is tested by one-sided normal deviate test.

Q. 72. *Give a suitable test for testing the homogeneity (equality) of several population variances.*

Ans. Suppose one is interested to test the homogeneity of k population variances, *i.e.*, to test

$H_0: \sigma_1^2 = \sigma_2^2 = \ldots = \sigma_k^2$

vs. H_1 : at least any two of them are not equal.

Out of various test procedures, the most accepted test procedure is one given by M.S. Bartlett in 1937.

Suppose $s_1^2, s_2^2, \ldots, s_k^2$ are the estimated variances of $\sigma_1^2, \sigma_2^2, \ldots, \sigma_k^2$ based on $(n_1 - 1), (n_2 - 1), \ldots, (n_k - 1)$ d.f. respectively. Let s_p^2 is the pooled estimated variance where,

$$s_p^2 = \frac{\sum_{i=1}^{k} (n_i - 1)s_i^2}{\sum_{i=1}^{k} (n_i - 1)}$$

To test H_0, we make use of χ^2-test where

$$\chi^2 = \log_e 10 \left[\log_{10} s_p^2 \sum_{i=1}^{k} (n_i - 1) - \sum_{i=1}^{k} (n_i - 1) X \log_{10} s_i^2\right]$$

$$= 2.3026 \left[\log_{10} s_p^2 \sum_{i=1}^{k} (n_i - 1) - \sum_{i=1}^{k} (n_i - 1) X \log_{10} s_i^2\right]$$

χ^2 has $(k - 1)$ d.f.

It has been proved that χ^2 has an upward bias. Hence a correction factor C is calculated by the formula,

$$C = 1 + \frac{1}{3(k-1)}\left[\sum_{i=1}^{k} \frac{1}{n_1 - 1} - \frac{1}{\sum_{i=1}^{k} (n_i - 1)}\right]$$

Corrected value of Chi-square

$$\chi_c^2 = \chi^2/C$$

Using χ_c^2 distributed with $(k - 1)$ d.f., the decision about H_0 is taken in the usual manner.

Q. 73. *How do you test the equality of variances of two normal populations?*

Ans. Here we want to test

$$H_0 : \sigma_1^2 = \sigma_2^2 \text{ vs. } H_1 : \sigma_1^2 \neq \sigma_2^2$$

Let s_1^2 and s_2^2 be the estimates of σ_1^2 and σ_2^2 based on sample sizes n_1 and n_2 respectively. H_0 can be tested by the F-test where

$$F = \frac{s_1^2}{s_2^2}$$

F has d.f. $(n_1 - 1), (n_2 - 1)$ where s_1^2 is taken to be larger variance.

If $F \geq F_{\{(1-\alpha/2), (n_1 - 1), (n_2 - 1)\}}$, reject H_0, otherwise accept H_0

In case H_1 is one-sided, *i.e.*, H_1: $\sigma_1^2 > \sigma_2^2$, reject H_0 if

$$F \geq F_{(1-\alpha), \{(n_1 - 1), (n_2 - 1)\}}$$

Again if H_1: $\sigma_1^2 < \sigma_2^2$, reject H_0 if

$$F \leq F_{(\alpha), \{(n_1 - 1), (n_2 - 1)\}}$$

The value of statistic F is never negative.

Q. 74. *How will you test the equality of several normal population means?*

Ans. Let there be k normal populations $N(\mu_1, \sigma_1^2)$,

$N(\mu_2, \sigma_2^2), ..., N(\mu_k, \sigma_k^2)$. We have to test

$$H_0 : \mu_1 = \mu_2 = ... = \mu_k$$

vs. H_1: at least two means are not equal.

Under the assumption of homogeneity of variances, *i.e.*, $\sigma_1^2 = \sigma_2^2 = ... = \sigma_k^2$. *F*-test under H_0 can be performed in the following manner. The statistic

$$F = \frac{\text{Between sample variances}}{\text{within sample variances}}$$

Suppose

$Y_{ij} = j^{\text{th}}$ observation in the ith sample for $i = 1, 2, ..., k$ and $j = 1, 2, ..., n_i$.

$n_i = i^{\text{th}}$ sample size

$$\bar{Y}_i = \sum_{j=1}^{n_i} Y_{ij}/n_i = i^{\text{th}} \text{ sample mean.}$$

$$\bar{Y} = \sum_{i=1}^{k} n_i \bar{Y}_i/\Sigma n_i = \text{over all mean.}$$

In notational form,

$$F = \frac{\sum_{i=1}^{k} n_i(\bar{Y}_i - \bar{Y})^2/(k-1)}{\sum_{i=1}^{k}\sum_{j=1}^{n_i} (\bar{Y}_{ij} - \bar{Y}_i)^2 \Big/ \sum_{i=1}^{k} (n_i - 1)}$$

Reject H_0, if $F \geq F_{(1-\alpha),(\nu_1,\nu_2)}$ where $\nu_1 = k - 1$ and

$$\nu_2 = \sum_{i=1}^{k} (n_i - 1).$$

Q. 75. *What do you understand by analysis of variance?*

Ans. Analysis of variance is a device to split the total variance of an experiment or trial into component variances responsible for contributing towards total variance. The gap between total variance and sum of component variances is attributed to experimental (random) error and so is true for degrees of freedom. Analysis of variance utilises F-test. Each component variance is tested against error variance and conclusion is drawn in the same way as we do in *F*-test for equality of two variances or several means. Analysis of variance is abbreviated is ANOVA.

Q. 76. *Give skeleton analysis of variance table.*

Ans. The skeleton ANOVA table is as given below:

Source of variation	*Degrees of freedom*	*Sum of squares*	*Mean sum of squares*	*Variance ratio*
Due to	*d.f.*	*S.S.*	*M.S.*	*F-value*
A				–
B				
⋮				
C				
Error				
Total				

In practice column captions are used only in abbreviated form

Q. 77. *Define Bayes' test.*

Ans. A test T_g of $H_0:\theta = \theta_0$ vs. $H_1: \theta = \theta_1$ is said to be a Bayes' test with regard to a prior distribution $g = P(\theta = \theta_1)$ if for any other test *T*, the following inequality holds.

$$(1-g)R(T_g, \theta_0) + gR(T_g, \theta_1) \leq (1-g) R(T, \theta_0) + gR(T, \theta_1)$$

where $R(T_g, \theta_0)$ and $R(T_g, \theta_1)$ are the risks in choosing the test T_g under H_0 and H_1 respectively. In the same way $R(T, \theta_0)$ and $R(T, \theta_1)$ are the risks in choosing the test *T* under H_0 and H_1, respectively.

Q. 78. *Give in brief the idea of sequential probability ratio test (SPRT).*

Ans. In case of tests based on fixed sample size, it is generally not possible to determine the optimum sample size so that no extra observations are recorded except those necessitated to reach a decision. Moreover, sometimes the sample is too small to arrive at a right decision. To overcome this problem, Professor A. Wald innovated in 1947 sequential probability ratio test. In this test procedure, a decision about H_0 is taken after each successive observation. Hence in SPRT, sample size *n* is a random variable. There are three types of decisions with which an investigator comes across namely, reject H_0, accept H_0 or continue sampling. The process is terminated as soon as a decision either to reject or to accept H_0 is taken. The test procedure is as follows:

Suppose one wants to test $H_0 : \theta = \theta_0$ vs. $H_1 : \theta = \theta_1$. Let $X_1, X_2, ..., X_m$ be the sample selected up to the mth stage where x's are i.i.d. with p.d.f. $f(x ; \theta)$. The test criteria is that for any two numbers A_0 and A_1 such that $A_0 < A_1$ the process of taking observations is continued if the ratio of joint p.d.f. under H_1 to the joint p.d.f. under H_0 satisfies the following inequality.

$$A_0 < \prod_{i=1}^{m} \frac{f(x_i, \theta_1)}{f(x_i, \theta_0)} < A_1$$

H_0 is accepted if $\prod_{i=1}^{m} f(x_i, \theta_1) / f(x_i, \theta_0) \leq A_0$ or rejected if $\prod_{i=1}^{m} f(x_i, \theta_1) / f(x_i, \theta_0) \geq A_1$ and the process of taking observations is terminated. If α and β are the probabilities of rejecting H_0 when it is true and accepting H_0 when H_1 is true, the decision is taken in the following manner:

$$\text{Accept } H_0 \text{ if } \prod_{i=1}^{m} \frac{f(x_i ; \theta_1)}{f(x_i ; \theta_0)} \leq \frac{\beta}{1-\alpha}$$

$$\text{Reject } H_0 \text{ if } \prod_{i=1}^{m} \frac{f(x_i ; \theta_1)}{f(x_i ; \theta_0)} \geq \frac{1-\beta}{\alpha}$$

and continue sampling if

$$\frac{\beta}{1-\alpha} < \prod_{i=1}^{m} \frac{f(x_i ; \theta_1)}{f(x_i ; \theta_0)} < \frac{1-\beta}{\alpha}.$$

It has been proved that the process of taking observations terminates with probability one and on an average there is saving in sample number.

Note: Testing of hypotheses with regard to correlation coefficient(s) and regression coefficient(s) are given in the respective chapters. Analysis of variance is given in the chapter on experimental designs and otherwise also.

SECTION B

Fill in the Blanks

Fill in the suitable word(s) or phrase(s) in the blanks:

1. There can be ________ procedure(s) to test the same hypothesis.
2. The theory of testing parametric hypothesis was first originated by ________ in ________.
3. Besides Neyman, the other pioneer worker in the field of testing of hypothesis was ________.
4. A hypothesis is an ________ about the parameter of a population.
5. The hypothesis which is under test for possible rejection is called ________ hypothesis.
6. A hypothesis contrary to null hypothesis is known as ________ hypothesis.
7. The idea of alternative hypothesis was propounded by ________.
8. The hypothesis $H_0 : \theta = \theta_0$ vs. $H_0 : \theta = \theta_1$ is a ________ hypothesis against ________ alternative hypothesis.
9. The hypothesis $H_0 : \theta > \theta_0$ is a ________ hypothesis.
10. There can be only ________ types of errors in taking a decision about H_0.
11. Type ________ error is more severe than type ________ error.
12. ________ kind of error is minimised for

a prefixed level of ________ kind of error.

13. Probability of first kind of error is called the ________ of the test.

14. Probability of type I error is called ________.

15. Rejecting H_0 when H_0 is true is ________ error.

16. Accepting H_0 when H_0 is false, is a ________ error.

17. Whether a test is one-sided or two-sided depends on ________ hypothesis.

18. The test statistic ________ in case of one-tailed and two-tailed test.

19. If β is the probability of type II error, the power of the test is ________.

20. With usual notation, the function β(θ) is known as ________ function.

21. Level of significance lies between ________ and ________.

22. The choice of level of significance is akin to the ________ of the test.

23. Critical region is also known as ________.

24. A statistical test is a ________ to decide about H_0.

25. A randomised test does not involve any ________.

26. A test in which the decision about a hypothesis H is based on a statistic is called ________ test.

27. A null hypothesis is rejected if the value of a test statistic lies in the ________.

28. There cannot be two ________ regions in any testing problem.

29. One-sided alternative hypothesis leads to one region of ________.

30. The size of a test is equal to the area of the ________.

31. The number of independent values in a set of values is known as ________.

32. Degrees of freedom in a test takes care of the ________.

33. A test which minimises the two types of error is termed as ________ test.

34. Does an ________ test exist in real life?

35. A test T is said to be ________ if there is no other test of which the power is more than that of T.

36. A test T of size α is said to be a ________ test if there is no other test of the same size whose power is more than that of T.

37. Neyman-Pearson lemma provides a ________ test of simple null hypothesis against a simple alternative.

38. Neyman-Pearson lemma helps to determine the size of ________ and ________ errors for the given range of the variable X.

39. With the help of Neyman-Pearson lemma, one can determine the ________ and ________ of a test of testing H_0 against H_1.

40. If the maximum risk of a test T under simple H_0 and H_1 is not more than the maximum risk of any other test T^* under simple H_0 and H_1, the test T is said to be ________ test.

41. If a test procedure T is such that the probability of rejecting H_0 when it is false is at least as much as the probability of rejecting H_0 when it is true, T is said to be an ________ test.

42. Among the class of unbiased tests, a test which is uniformly most powerful is called a ________ test.

43. A critical region corresponding to a UMPU test is the critical region of ________.

44. The name critical region of type A_1 was given by ________.

45. If a critical region is such that the power of the test based on it is never less than its size, the critical region is known as ________ region.

46. If a test procedure δ for testing a hypothesis about a parameter θ is such that its risk is never greater than any other test δ′ for testing the same hypothesis about θ and is

less for some θ, then δ is said to be an _________ test.

47. The term critical function is related to _________ test.

48. A function $\psi_T(x_1, x_2, ..., x_n)$, where T is a test of H_0, is equal to the probability of rejecting H_0 when $x_1, x_2, ..., x_n$ is observed, $\psi_T(x_1, x_2, ..., x_n)$ is called a _________ .

49. The critical value of a test statistic is a _________ point between the region of acceptance and the region of rejection.

50. A normal deviate test does not utilise _________ .

51. A test based on the outcome of tossing of a coin is a _________ test.

52. If the likelihood ratio is λ, the variable $-2 \log \lambda$ is approximately distributed as _________.

53. Student's t-test is applicable in case of _________ samples.

54. Statistic-t is defined as deviation of sample mean from population mean expressed in terms of _________ .

55. The formula for student's-t statistic is _________ .

56. Student's-t is valid in case the variable x follows _________ distribution.

57. t has $(n - 1)$ d.f. when all the n observations in the sample are _________ .

58. The minimum number of observations required for t-test in a sample is _________ .

59. Student's t-test is a _________ test.

60. t-test for a simple null hypothesis against a simple alternative for an arbitrary population standard deviation provides a _________ test.

61. Student's-t test based on two samples of sizes n_1 and n_2 for testing the equality of two normal population means when the populations have same variances has degrees of freedom equal to _________ .

62. Sample variances for testing equality of two normal population means with unequal variances cannot be _________ .

63. Approximate t-test for testing the equality of two normal populations means with unequal variances was given by _________ .

64. Beside Cochran's approximate test for testing $H_0 : \mu_1 = \mu_2$ of two populations $N(\mu_1, \sigma_1^2)$ and $N(\mu_2, \sigma_2^2)$ when $\sigma_1^2 \neq \sigma_2^2$, the other test is _________ test.

65. Behrens and Fisher gave t-test for unequal population variances _________ .

66. Fisher gave the test _________ than Behrens for testing $H_0: \mu_1 = \mu_2$ when $\sigma_1^2 \neq \sigma_2^2$.

67. Behrens was _________ to give t-test for testing $H_0: \mu_1 = \mu_2$ when $\sigma_1^2 \neq \sigma_2^2$.

68. Behrens-Fisher test is also not free from _________ .

69. The power of Behrens-Fisher test is _________ than Cochran's approximate t-test.

70. Paired t-test is applicable only when the observations are _________ .

71. The two variables say, X and Y in paired t-test are _________ .

72. In paired t-test, one test the significance of population _________ .

73. When the population standard deviation is known, the hypothesis about population mean is tested by _________ .

74. If the sample drawn from a population is large, then the hypothesis about μ can be tested by _________ .

75. The validity of a hypothetical value of proportion in a class of dichotomous population can be tested by _________ .

76. By adding ± 0.5 to the number of items belonging to a class in Z-test approximates the binomial distribution to _________ distribution.

77. To test whether the data follow an assumed distribution or not is known as a test of _________ .

78. The value of χ^2-statistic depends on the difference between ________ and ________ frequencies.

79. The value of Chi-square varies from ________ to ________ .

80. The value of coefficient of contingency lies between ________ and ________ .

81. The value of coefficient of contingency never attains the value ________.

82. In a multinomial population with k classes, the degrees of freedom for χ^2 is ________ .

83. In working with a contingency table of order 4 × 5, the d.f. for χ^2 is ________ .

84. The d.f. for χ^2 while dealing with a contingency table of order (2 × 2) is ________.

85. Direct formula for χ^2 in case of contingency table of order (2 × 2) with usual notations is ________ .

86. Direct formula for testing the validity of a hypothetical ratio r for frequencies in two classes is ________ .

87. If in a (2 × 2) contingency table, the expected frequency in a cell is less than 5, ________ of χ^2 distribution is disturbed.

88. For small expected frequency in a 2 × 2 frequency table, ________ suggested a correction for continuity.

89. Dandekar's correction is applicable when the expected frequency in a cell of 2 × 2 contingency table is ________ .

90. In general Dandekar's correction is ________ than Yates' correction.

91. Dandekar's correction is not so frequently used because its ________ is bit complicated.

92. The value of statistic χ^2 under Yates' correction can directly be obtained by the formula ________ .

93. Fisher's test of independence of attributes is exact in the sense that it calculates the ________ of the configurations and no distribution is approximated.

94. Fisher exact test involves too much ________.

95. Coefficient of contingency measures the degree of ________ .

96. When the value of χ^2 is zero, the value of coefficient of contingency is ________ .

97. Coefficient of contingency is calculated only when H_0 is ________ by χ^2-test.

98. The value of coefficient of contingency near unity ensures ________ of association between attributes.

99. Chi-square can be approximated to standard normal distribution only if the d.f. for Chi-square are ________ or more.

100. Homogeneity of several population variances can be tested by ________ test.

101. Bartlett's test utilises ________ test.

102. There is an ________ bias in Bartlett's Chi-square statistic.

103. Equality of two population variances can be tested by ________ .

104. The ratio s_1^2/s_2^2 of two sample variances follows ________ under the hypothesis $\sigma_1^2 = \sigma_2^2$.

105. Equality of several normal populations mean can be tested by ________ .

106. Analysis of variance utilises ________ .

107. Abbreviated form of analysis of variance is ________ .

108. Mean sum of square due to a component factor is nothing but its ________ .

109. Error sum of square is obtained by________.

110. In sequential probability ratio test, sample size is a________ .

111. In SPRT, decision is taken after each ________ observation.

112. Sequential probability ratio test was invented by ________ in ________ .

113. Sequential probability ratio test is based on the functions of ________ .

114. Bayes' test with regard to a given prior distribution utilises ________ .

115. If the difference in sample means of two groups A and B of size 12 each is 5.42 units and the standard deviation of mean difference is 2 units, to test the significance of mean difference, you would prefer to apply _________.

116. Suppose there are two groups A and B of same size. A received special treatment and B is kept as control. Then, the null hypothesis for comparing two groups is _________ .

117. On the basis of a sample of farm workers, the hypothesis that 50 per cent of workers are farm owners can be tested by _________ .

118. Whether five brands of fertilizers have equal mean effect can be tested with the help of _________ .

119. The average life of electric bulbs is 1600 hours with S.D. = 112 hours. It is desired that 95 per cent bulbs should not fall short of the average life by more than 1 per cent, the required sample size is _________ .

[Given: $z_{0.05} = -1.64$]

120. A box contains 10 switches out of which θ are non-defective. Test $H_0 : \theta = 5$ vs. $H_1 : \theta = 4$. Also H_0 will be rejected if the two switches drawn at random with replacement are defective. The size of the test is _________.

121. For the problem given in Q. No. 120, the size of type II error is _________ .

122. The daily consumption of diesel of a transporter is considered to be exponentially distributed. The hypothesis that the average consumption $H_0 : \theta = 1000$ litres/day is to be tested against $H_1 : \theta = 2000$. If the consumption on a randomly selected day is 1500 litres or more, H_0 is rejected. The size of the test is _________ .

123. For the problem in Q. No. 122, the power of the test is _________ .

124. If p is the probability of turning up a head in tossing of a coin. To test $H_0 : p = 0.5$ vs. $H_1 : p = 0.6$, H_0 is rejected if there are 7 or more heads in 10 trials. The size of the test is _________ .

125. For the problem in Q. No. 124, the power of the test is _________.

126. For the problem is Q. No. 124, the size of type II error is _________ .

127. A large population of heights of person is distributed with mean 66 inches and S.D. = 10 inches. A sample of 400 persons had mean height = 62 inches. The data _________ the hypothesis H_0: $\mu = 66$ inches.

128. Two cattle feeds A and B are compared on two groups of cows of the same breed of size 32 and 45. The average increases in milk yield are 10 litres and 15 litres per week with variances 4 and 5 litres^2 respectively. The hypothesis of the same average effect of feeds A and B is _________ at $\alpha = 0.01$.

129. If in a box of 20 transistors, θ are defective. The hypothesis $\theta = 10$ is rejected if any two transistors selected at random with replacement are defective. If H_1: $\theta = 20$, the type II error is _________ .

130. The probability that the sample mean should not differ by population mean by more than $\sigma/2$ units is 0.95 where $\sigma/2$ is the population standard deviation. For the validity of the statement, the sample size should be _________ .

131. Each particle attracts other particle is not a _________ hypothesis.

132. Fifty persons suffered from tuberculosis (TB) in a village. Out of which 20 died. The hypothesis that 50 per cent TB patients die is _________ at 5 per cent level of significance.

133. For the given configuration,

	B_1	B_2
A_1	20	10
A_2	15	15

the value of statistic χ^2 is _________ .

134. Out of two groups consisting of 200 and 300

urban and rural males, 100 and 150 favoured family planning. From the data it is concluded at 95 per cent level that proportion of persons in urban and rural populations favouring family planning is ________ .

135. Suppose the yields of 12 and 8 plots of two varieties of wheat are assumed to be normally distributed as $N(\mu_1, \sigma^2)$ and $N(\mu_2, \sigma^2)$. The average yield from 12 plots is 30 q/ha. with a S.D. = 3.0 q/ha and 8 plots 25 q/ha with a S.D. = 2.0 q/a. After statistical test it is concluded that both the fertilizers are ________ effective at $\alpha = 0.05$.

[Given, $t_{0.05,\ 18} = 2.101$]

136. A sample of 30 items has a variance of 8 units. The hypothesis of the true variance of 10 units is ________ at $\alpha = 0.05$.

137. The variances of daily consumption of electricity in two cities in the month of June were 130 units and 170 units. The statistical test of H_0 that the variances in two cities are equal against H_1 that they are not equal reveals that H_0 is ________ at $\alpha = 0.05$.

138. A sample of 30 items was distributed in a contingency table of order (2 × 2). The value of χ^2 on computation was 7.84. The value of coefficient of contingency is ________ .

139. The interest lies to test $H_0 : p = 1/2$ vs. $H_1 : p = 2/3$ in tossing of a coin. H_0 is rejected if there are more than 4 heads out of 6 tossings. The size of type I error is ________ .

140. For the problem given in Q. No. 139, the size of type II error is ________ .

141. For the problem given in Q. No. 139, the power of the test is ________ .

142. It is desired that the population standard deviation should not differ from sample standard deviation by more than 4 per cent. To be 95.44 per cent confident, the minimum sample size should be ________ .

143. A large population has mean 5 inches and S.D. = 2 inches. A large sample of 400 persons from this population has mean = 3.5 inches. The data ________ the value of population mean.

144. An investigator aspires that the sample standard deviation should not differ from population standard deviation by more than 5 per cent. To be 99.73 per cent confident, the sample size should be ________ .

145. Critical value of t ________ as the sample size increases.

146. A test of hypothesis provides a ________ about the probable truth.

147. Research hypotheses are the ________ which a researcher postulates.

148. The critical value of Chi-square for any level of significance is ________ its degrees of freedom.

149. A contingency table can be ________ .

150. A contingency table having a few empty cells will be called ________ contingency table.

151. A zero in a cell of a contingency table having its expected value zero is called ________ zero.

152. If a cell of a contingency table having zero count has its expected frequency greater than zero, then such a zero count is termed as ________ .

153. If the calculated value of Chi-square statistic is less than its degrees of freedom, then we can straightaway ________ the null hypothesis.

154. Significant contribution of an individual cell towards dependency of attributes can be detected with the help of ________ .

155. Paired t-test is applicable in case of ________ samples only.

156. A value of a standardised residual greater than 1.96 will indicate the ________ contribution of the cell.

157. An insurance company claims that it settles the claims on an average in six days. To test

the validity of the claim, H_0: _________ and H_1: _________ are the only suitable hypothesis.

158. A Dean of a college wants to verify whether the grades awarded by a professor follow the bell-shaped curve. The appropriate test for verification is _________ test.

159. The rejection region in F-test lies on _________ .

160. A government agency claims that only 20 per cent families are below poverty line. Whereas a citizen's body claims that this percentage is much higher. To ascertain about the claims, you will like to apply _________ .

SECTION C

Multiple Choice Questions

Select the correct alternative out of given ones:

1. The idea of testing of hypothesis was first set forth by:
(*a*) R.A. Fisher
(*b*) J. Neyman
(*c*) E.L. Lehman
(*d*) A. Wald

2. In 1933, the theory of testing of hypotheses was propounded by:
(*a*) R.A. Fisher
(*b*) J. Neyman
(*c*) E.L. Lehman
(*d*) Karl Pearson

3. A hypothesis may be classified as:
(*a*) simple
(*b*) composite
(*c*) null
(*d*) all the above

4. The hypothesis under test is:
(*a*) simple hypothesis
(*b*) alternative hypothesis
(*c*) null hypothesis
(*d*) none of the above

5. Whether a test is one-sided or two-sided depends on:
(*a*) alternative hypothesis
(*b*) composite hypothesis
(*c*) null hypothesis
(*d*) simple hypothesis

6. A wrong decision about H_0 leads to:
(*a*) one kind of error
(*b*) two kinds of error
(*c*) three kinds of error
(*d*) four kinds of error

7. Power of a test is related to:
(*a*) type I error
(*b*) type II error
(*c*) types I and II errors both
(*d*) none of the above

8. If θ is the true parameter and β the type II error, the function $\beta(\theta)$ is known as:
(*a*) power function
(*b*) power of the test
(*c*) operating characteristic function
(*d*) none of the above

9. Level of significance is the probability of:
(*a*) type I error
(*b*) type II error
(*c*) not committing error
(*d*) any of the above

10. In terms of type II error β and θ, the true parameter, the function $1 - \beta(\theta)$ is called:
(*a*) power of the test
(*b*) power function
(*c*) OC function
(*d*) none of the above

11. Out of the two types of error in testing, the more severe error is:
(*a*) type I error
(*b*) type II error
(*c*) both (*a*) and (*b*) are equally severe
(*d*) no error is severe

12. Area of the critical region depends on:
(*a*) size of type I error
(*b*) size of type II error
(*c*) value of the statistic
(*d*) number of observations

13. Critical region of size α which minimised β amongst all critical regions of size α is called:
(*a*) powerful critical region
(*b*) minimum critical region
(*c*) best critical region
(*d*) worst critical region

14. A test based on a test statistic is classified as:
(*a*) randomised test
(*b*) non-randomised test
(*c*) sequential test
(*d*) Bayes test

15. Size of critical region is known as:
(*a*) power of the test
(*b*) size of type II error
(*c*) critical value of the test statistics
(*d*) size of the test

16. Degrees of freedom is related to:
(*a*) no. of observations in a set
(*b*) hypothesis under test
(*c*) no. of independent observations in a set
(*d*) none of the above

17. A critical function provides the basis for:
(*a*) accepting H_0
(*b*) rejecting H_0
(*c*) no decision about H_0
(*d*) all the above

18. A test which maximises the power of the test for fixed α is known as:
(*a*) optimum test
(*b*) randomised test
(*c*) Bayes test
(*d*) likelihood ratio test

19. A test T which is at least as powerful as any other test of the same size, is called:
(*a*) best test
(*b*) most powerful test
(*c*) uniformly most powerful test
(*d*) none of the above

20. Neyman-Pearson lemma provides:
(*a*) an unbiased test
(*b*) a most powerful test
(*c*) an admissible test
(*d*) minimax test

21. A test T for which maximum risk under H_0 and H_1 is not more than the maximum risk of any other test T^* under H_0 and H_1 is called:
(*a*) an unbiased test
(*b*) uniformly most powerful test
(*c*) an admissible test
(*d*) minimax test

22. With usual notations the condition for unbiased test is:
(*a*) $\underset{\theta \varepsilon \theta_0}{\text{Sup}}\, P_T(\theta) \leq \underset{\theta \varepsilon \theta_1}{\text{Inf}}\, P_T(\theta)$
(*b*) $\underset{\theta \varepsilon \theta_0}{\text{Sup}}\, P_T(\theta) \geq \underset{\theta \varepsilon \theta_1}{\text{Inf}}\, P_T(\theta)$
(*c*) $\underset{\theta \varepsilon \theta_0}{\text{Sup}}\, P_T(\theta) = \underset{\theta \varepsilon \theta_1}{\text{Inf}}\, P_T(\theta)$
(*d*) none of the above

23. A uniformly most powerful test among the class of unbiased test is termed as:
(*a*) minimax test
(*b*) minimax unbiased test
(*c*) uniformly most powerful unbiased test
(*d*) all the above

24. A test procedure δ for testing a hypothesis about a parameter θ whose risk is not more than the risk of any test procedures δ' for all θ and is definitely less for some θ is called:
(*a*) minimax test
(*b*) admissible test
(*c*) most powerful test
(*d*) optimum test

25. The ratio of the likelihood function under H_0 and under the entire parametric space is called:
(*a*) probability ratio
(*b*) sequential probability ratio

(*c*) likelihood ratio
(*d*) none of the above

26. Student's *t*-test was invented by:
(*a*) R.A. Fisher
(*b*) G.W. Snedecor
(*c*) W.S. Gosset
(*d*) W.G. Cochran

27. Student's *t*-test is applicable in case of:
(*a*) small samples
(*b*) for samples of size between 5 and 30
(*c*) large samples
(*d*) none of the above

28. A population is distributed as $N = (\mu, 10.24)$. A sample of 576 items has a mean 4.7. The value of the statistic Z to test $H_0 : \mu = 5.2$ is:
(*a*) 3.75
(*b*) 28.125
(*c*) –3.75
(*d*) none of the above

29. It was claimed that the average life of dry battery cells is 60 hours. A large sample of 441 cells had mean life 42 hours with a variance of 81 hours^2. Do the data ascertain the claim:
(*a*) the claim is refuted
(*b*) the claim is accepted
(*c*) no decision is possible
(*d*) none of the above

30. A sample of 12 specimen taken from a normal population is expected to have a mean 50 mg/cc. The sample has a mean 64 mg/cc with a variance of 25. To test $H_0 : \mu = 50$ vs. $H_1 : \mu \neq 50$, you will use:
(*a*) Z-test
(*b*) χ^2-test
(*c*) F-test
(*d*) t-test

31. For the problem given in No. 30, the test reveals that for $\alpha = 0.05$, H_0 should be:
[Given $t_{0.05,\,11} = 2.201$]
(*a*) rejected
(*b*) accepted
(*c*) left undecided
(*d*) none of the above

32. Student's *t*-test is applicable only when:
(*a*) the variate values are independent
(*b*) the variable is distributed normally
(*c*) the sample is not large
(*d*) all the above

33. To test H_0: $\mu = \mu_0$ vs. H_1: $\mu > \mu_0$ when the population S.D. is known, the appropriate test is:
(*a*) t-test
(*b*) Z-test
(*c*) Chi-test
(*d*) none of the above

34. For two populations $N(\mu_1, \sigma^2)$ and $N(\mu_2, \sigma^2)$ with σ^2 unknown, the test statistics for testing $H_0 : \mu_1 = \mu_2$ based on small samples with usual notations is:

(*a*) $t = \dfrac{\bar{X} - \bar{X}_2}{\sqrt{\dfrac{1}{n_1} + \dfrac{1}{n_2}}}$

(*b*) $t = \dfrac{\bar{X}_1 - \bar{X}_2}{\sqrt{\sigma^2\left(\dfrac{1}{n_1} + \dfrac{1}{n_2}\right)}}$

(*c*) $t = \dfrac{\bar{X}_1 - \bar{X}_2}{s_p\sqrt{\left(\dfrac{1}{n_1} + \dfrac{1}{n_2}\right)}}$

(*d*) any of the above

35. Test of hypothesis $H_0 : \mu = 70$ vs. $H_1 : \mu > 70$ leads to:
(*a*) one-sided left-tailed test
(*b*) one-sided right-tailed test
(*c*) two-tailed test
(*d*) none of the above

36. Testing $H_0 : \mu = 1500$ against $\mu < 1500$ leads to:
(*a*) one-sided lower tailed test
(*b*) one-sided upper tailed test
(*c*) two-tailed test
(*d*) all the above

37. Testing H_0: $\mu = 100$ vs. $H_1 : \mu \neq 100$ leads to:

(*a*) one-sided upper tailed test
(*b*) one-sided lower tailed test
(*c*) two-tailed test
(*d*) none of the above

38. If there are two populations $N(\mu_1, \sigma_1^2)$ and and $N(\mu_2, \sigma_2^2)$ the two samples from them have means $\bar{X}_1$, $\bar{X}_2$ and variances s_1^2 and s_2^2 based on n_1 and n_2 observations respectively, the hypothesis $H_0 : \mu_1 = \mu_2$ vs. $H_1 : \mu_1 \neq \mu_2$ when $\sigma_1^2 \neq \sigma_2^2$ can be tested by:
(*a*) Cochran's test
(*b*) Behrens-Fisher test
(*c*) both (*a*) and (*b*)
(*d*) neither (*a*) nor (*b*)

39. Cochran's test testing $H_0 : \mu_1 = \mu_2$ for two normal populations with heterogeneous variances is:
(*a*) an exact test
(*b*) an approximate test
(*c*) a random test
(*d*) an unreliable test

40. Behrens-Fisher test for testing $H_0 : \mu_1 = \mu_2$ vs. $H_1 : \mu_1 \neq \mu_2$ for two normal populations with unequal variances is:
(*a*) better than Cochran's test
(*b*) inferior than Cochran's test
(*c*) as powerful as Cochran's test
(*d*) a hoax

41. Paired *t*-test is applicable when the observations in the two samples are:
(*a*) paired
(*b*) correlated
(*c*) equal in number
(*d*) all the above

42. The mean difference between 9 paired observations is 15.0 and the standard deviation of differences is 5.0. The value of statistic *t* is:
(*a*) 27
(*b*) 9
(*c*) 3
(*d*) zero

43. The degrees of freedom for statistic-*t* for paired *t*-test based on *n* pairs of observations is:
(*a*) $2(n - 1)$
(*b*) $n - 1$
(*c*) $2n - 1$
(*d*) none of the above

44. To test an hypothesis about proportions of items in a class, the usual test is:
(*a*) *t*-test
(*b*) *F*-test
(*c*) *Z*-test
(*d*) none of the above

45. To test $H_0 : P = 0.4$ vs. $H_1\ P \neq 0.4$ in binomial population, there are eight persons out of fifteen who favoured a proposal. The value of statistic-*Z* is:
(*a*) 5.813
(*b*) 1.08
(*c*) 7.32
(*d*) none of the above

46. Standard error of the difference of proportions $(p_1 - p_2)$ in two classes under the hypothesis $H_0 : P_1 = P_2$ with usual notations is:
(*a*) $\sqrt{\hat{p}\hat{q}\left(\frac{1}{n_1} + \frac{1}{n_2}\right)}$
(*b*) $\sqrt{\hat{p}\left(\frac{1}{n_1} + \frac{1}{n_2}\right)}$
(*c*) $\hat{p}\hat{q}\sqrt{\frac{1}{n_1} + \frac{1}{n_2}}$
(*d*) $\sqrt{\frac{p_1q_1}{n_1} + \frac{p_2q_2}{n_2}}$

47. Formula for the standard error of the difference between proportions $(p_1 - p_2)$ under the hypothesis $H : P_1 \neq P_2$ with usual notation is:
(*a*) $\sqrt{\hat{p}\hat{q}\left(\frac{1}{n_1} + \frac{1}{n_2}\right)}$

(b) $\hat{p}\hat{q}\sqrt{\frac{1}{n_1}+\frac{1}{n_2}}$

(c) $\hat{q}\hat{q}\left(\frac{1}{n_1}+\frac{1}{n_2}\right)$

(d) $\sqrt{\frac{p_1q_2}{n}+\frac{p_2q_2}{n_2}}$

48. The formula in general for testing the hypothesis for proportions $H_0 : P_1 = P_2$ vs. $H_1 : P_1 \neq P_2$ is:

(a) $Z = \frac{p_1 - p_2}{s_{(p_1-p_2)}}$

(b) $Z = \frac{p_1 - p_2}{s^2_{(p_1-p_2)}}$

(c) $Z = \frac{p_1 - p_2}{s_{p_1} - s_{p_2}}$

(d) none of the above

49. The hypothesis that the population variance has a specified value can be tested by:

(a) *F*-test

(b) *Z*-test

(c) χ^2-test

(d) none of the above

50. The test statistic to be used to test $H_0 : \sigma^2 = C$ vs. $H_1 : \sigma^2 \neq C$ with usual notations is:

(a) $\chi^2 = \frac{(n-1)s^2}{C^2}$

(b) $\chi^2 = \frac{(n-1)s^2}{C}$

(c) $\chi^2 = \frac{ns^2}{C^2}$

(d) all the above

51. Statistic-χ^2 to test $H_0 : \sigma^2 = \sigma_0^2$ is based on a sample of size *n* has degrees of freedom equal to:

(a) $n - 1$

(b) n

(c) $(n + 1)$

(d) none of the above

52. Degrees of freedom for statistic-χ^2 in case of contingency table of order (2×2) is

(a) 3

(b) 4

(c) 2

(d) 1

53. In a multinomial distribution with 4 classes, the degrees of freedom for χ^2 is:

(a) 3

(b) 4

(c) 2

(d) 1

54. Test statistic for testing $H_0 : \sigma = c$ vs. $H_1 : \sigma \neq c$ is:

(a) $z = \frac{s - c}{s/\sqrt{n}}$

(b) $z = \frac{s - c}{s/\sqrt{2n}}$

(c) $z = \frac{s - c}{s/\sqrt{2n}}$

(d) none of the above

55. The hypothesis $H_0: \sigma_1 = \sigma_2$ vs. $H_1 : \sigma_1 > \sigma_2$ can be tested by the statistic:

(a) $Z = \frac{|s_1 - s_2|}{\sqrt{\frac{s_1^2}{n_1}+\frac{s_2^2}{n_2}}}$

(b) $Z = \frac{|s_1 - s_2|}{\sqrt{\frac{s_1}{2n_1+\frac{s_2}{2n_2}}}}$

(c) $Z = \frac{|s_1 - s_2|}{\sqrt{\frac{s_1^2}{2n_1}+\frac{s_2^2}{2n_2}}}$

(d) none of the above

56. Formula for χ^2 for testing a null hypothesis in a multinomial distribution with usual notations is:

(*a*) $\chi^2 = \sum_{i=1}^{k} \frac{(O_i - E_i)^2}{E_i}$

(*b*) $\chi^2 = \sum_{i=1}^{k} \frac{O_i^2}{E_i} - n$

(*c*) $\chi^2 = \sum_{i=1}^{k} \frac{O_i^2}{np_i} - n$

(*d*) all the above

57. The statistic-χ^2 with usual notations in case of contingency table of order $(m \times p)$ is given by the formula:

(*a*) $\chi^2 = \sum_{i=1}^{m} \sum_{j=1}^{p} \frac{(O_{ij} - E_{ij})^2}{E_{ij}}$

(*b*) $\chi^2 = \sum_{i=1}^{m} \sum_{j=1}^{p} \frac{O_{ij}^2 - E_{ij}^2}{E_{ij}}$

(*c*) $\chi^2 = \sum_{i=1}^{m} \sum_{j=1}^{p} \left(\frac{O_{ij} - E_{ij}}{E_{ij}} \right)^2$

(*d*) all the above

58. Degrees of freedom for Chi-square in case of contingency table of order (4×3) are:

(*a*) 12

(*b*) 9

(*c*) 8

(*d*) 6

59. The degrees of freedom for χ^2 in case of dischotomised frequencies are:

(*a*) 4

(*b*) 2

(*c*) 1

(*d*) 0

60. Formula for statistic-χ^2 for the binomial frequencies a and b to occur in a specified ratio $r : 1$ is:

(*a*) $\frac{r(a-b)^2}{r(a+b)}$

(*b*) $\frac{(a-rb)^2}{r(a+b)}$

(*c*) $\frac{(a-rb)^2}{r(a+b)^2}$

(*d*) $\frac{(ar-b)^2}{r(a+b)}$

61. If the binomial frequencies 35 and 9 are expected to occur in the ratio 3:1, the value of statistic Chi-square is approximately equal to

(*a*) 0.48

(*b*) 5.10

(*c*) 1.45

(*d*) none of the above

62. An exact test for testing the independence of attributes in a contingency table of order (2×2) was given by:

(*a*) Karl Pearson

(*b*) Pascal

(*c*) Demoivre

(*d*) R.A. Fisher

63. An exact test for testing the independence of attributes in a contingency table of order (2×2) is based on the calculation of:

(*a*) the value of statistic-χ^2

(*b*) probabilities of configurations

(*c*) the value of statistic-Z

(*d*) none of the above

64. Fisher's exact test can be used to test:

(*a*) the independence of two attribute

(*b*) equality of proportions in two classes

(*c*) both (*a*) and (*b*)

(*d*) neither (*a*) nor (*b*)

65. Fisher's exact test is preferably used when:

(*a*) a cell frequency is smalls

(*b*) all cell frequencies are small

(*c*) both (*a*) and (*b*)

(*d*) none of the above

66. Coefficient of contingency is calculated when:

(*a*) the attributes are independent

(*b*) the attributes are associated

(*c*) both (*a*) and (*b*)

(*d*) neither (*a*) and (*b*)

67. The value of coefficient of contingency lies between:

(*a*) 0 and ∞

(*b*) 0 and 1

(*c*) 0 to 100

(*d*) –1 and +1

68. When the value of coefficient of contingency $C = 0$, it shows:

(*a*) complete dissociation amongst attributes

(*b*) complete association amongst attributes

(*c*) both (*a*) and (*b*)

(*d*) neither (*a*) nor (*b*)

69. When coefficient of contingency $C = 1$, it indicates:

(*a*) high degree of association

(*b*) low degree of association

(*c*) low degree of dissociation

(*d*) nothing

70. For a sample of *n* individuals, formula for coefficient of contingency is

(*a*) $C = \sqrt{\dfrac{\chi^2}{\chi^2 + (n-1)}}$

(*b*) $C = \sqrt{\dfrac{\chi^2}{n\chi^2}}$

(*c*) $C = \dfrac{\chi^2}{\chi^2 + n}$

(*d*) $C = \sqrt{\dfrac{\chi^2}{\chi^2 + n}}$

71. When d.f. for χ^2 are 100 or more, Chi-square is approximated to:

(*a*) *t*-distribution

(*b*) *F*-distribution

(*c*) *Z*-distribution

(*d*) none of the above

72. Homogeneity of several variances can be tests by:

(*a*) Bartlett's test

(*b*) Fisher's exact test

(*c*) *F*-test

(*d*) *t*-test

73. Statistics-χ^2 under Barlett's test has:

(*a*) a downward bias

(*b*) an upward bias

(*c*) zero bias

(*d*) none of the above

74. Equality of two population variances can be tested by:

(*a*) Bartlett's test

(*b*) *F*-test

(*c*) both (*a*) and (*b*)

(*d*) neither (*a*) nor (*b*)

75. Equality of several normal population means can be tested by:

(*a*) Bartlett's test

(*b*) *F*-test

(*c*) χ^2-test

(*d*) *t*-test

76. The ratio of between sample variance and within sample variance follows:

(*a*) *F*-distribution

(*b*) χ^2-distribution

(*c*) *Z*-distribution

(*d*) *t*-distribution

77. Analysis of variance utilises:

(*a*) *F*-test

(*b*) χ^2-test

(*c*) *Z*-test

(*d*) *t*-test

78. Customarily the large variance in the variance ratio for *F*-statistic is taken:

(*a*) in the denominator

(*b*) in the numerator

(*c*) either way

(*d*) none of the above

79. In sequential probability ratio test (SPRT), the sample size is:

(*a*) fixed
(*b*) fixed but small
(*c*) fixed but large
(*d*) a random variable

80. In SPRT, decision about the hypothesis H is taken:
(*a*) after each successive observation
(*b*) after a fixed number of observations
(*c*) at least after five observations
(*d*) when the experiment is over

81. To decide about H_0, SPRT involves:
(*a*) one region only
(*b*) two regions only
(*c*) three regions
(*d*) four regions

82. SPRT was initiated by:
(*a*) R.A. Fisher
(*b*) A. Wald
(*c*) G.W. Snedecor
(*d*) Thomas Bayes

83. The decision criteria in SPRT depends on the functions of:
(*a*) type I error
(*b*) type II error
(*c*) types I and II errors
(*d*) none of the two types of errors

84. If in a contingency table of order (2 × 3), the frequencies are such that $x + y + z = N$ and $x' + y' + z' = N$, the value of statistic-χ^2 is:
(*a*) $(x - x')^2 + (y - y')^2 + (z - z')^2$
(*b*) $\frac{(x - x')^2}{2} + \frac{(y - y')^2}{2} + \frac{(z - z')^2}{2}$
(*c*) $\left(\frac{x - x'}{x + x'}\right)^2 + \left(\frac{y - y'}{y + y'}\right)^2 + \left(\frac{z - z'}{z + z'}\right)^2$
(*d*) $\frac{(x - x')^2}{x + x'} + \frac{(y - y')^2}{y + y'} + \frac{(z - z')^2}{z + z'}$

85. Formula for Chi-square statistic in a 2 × 2 contingency table under Yates' correction is
(*a*) $n\left(|ad - bc| - \frac{n}{2}\right)^2 \Big/ D$
(*b*) $n\left(ab - bc - \frac{n}{2}\right)^2 \Big/ D$
(*c*) $\left(ad - bc - \frac{n}{2}\right)^2 \Big/ D$
(*d*) $n\left(\frac{ad - bc - \frac{n}{2}}{D}\right)^2$

where, $D = (a + b)(b + d)(a + c)(c + d)$.

86. The value of statistic Chi-square for a contingency table

	B_1	B_2
A_1	2	28
A_2	13	7

after Yates' correction is
(*a*) 625/28
(*b*) 4225/252
(*c*) 845/2520
(*d*) none of the above

87. For testing H_0: $\mu_1 = \mu_2$, the value of the statistic $|\bar{x} - \bar{y}| \Big/ \left(\sigma\sqrt{\frac{1}{n_1} + \frac{1}{n_2}}\right)$ lies between 1.96 and 2.58, then H_0 is:
(*a*) rejected at 5% level of significance
(*b*) accepted at 5% level of significance
(*c*) rejected at 1% level of significance
(*d*) any of the above

88. If two samples of size 9 and 11 have means 6.8 and 8.8, and variances 36 and 25 respectively from two populations $N(\mu_1, \sigma^2)$ and $N(\mu_2, \sigma^2)$, the absolute value of statistic t for testing H_0: $\mu_1 = \mu_2$ is:
(*a*) 0.148
(*b*) 1.83
(*c*) 0.81
(*d*) none of the above

89. Assume that the daily sales of petrol follows

exponential distribution. The hypothesis H that the sales of petrol is 1000 litres per day is tested against the hypothesis that it is 1500 litres per day. If the sales on a day is 1200 litres or more, H_0 is rejected, the size of type I error is

(a) $1 - e^{-1.2}$
(b) $e^{1.2}$
(c) $e^{-1.2}$
(d) none of the above

90. For the problem given in Q. No. 89, the size of type II error is:

(a) $1 - e^{-0.8}$
(b) $1 - e^{0.8}$
(c) $e^{-0.8} - 1$
(d) none of the above

91. For the problem given in No. 89, the power of the test is:

(a) $1 - e^{-0.8}$
(b) $e^{-0.8}$
(c) $-e^{-0.8}$
(d) $2 - e^{-0.8}$

92. In tossing of a coin, let the probability of turning up a head be p. The hypotheses are H_0: $p = 0.4$ vs. H_1: $p = 0.6$. H_0 is rejected if there are 5 or more heads in six tosses. Then the size of type I error is:

(a) 0.041
(b) 0.037
(c) 0.029
(d) none of the above

93. For the test given in Q. No. 92, the size of type II error is:

(a) 0.767
(b) 0.762
(c) 0.233
(d) none of the above

94. For the problem given in Q. No. 92, the power of the test is:

(a) 0.767
(b) 0.762
(c) 0.233
(d) none of the above

95. It is desired that the sample standard deviation should not differ from population standard deviation by more than 3 per cent. To have 68.26 per cent confidence, the sample size should not be less than:

(a) 1111
(b) 556
(c) 8889
(d) none of the above

96. Two samples, one from urban and the other from rural adult males of sizes 400 and 600 had standard deviations 165 cm and 175 cm respectively. Test of hypothesis of equality of standard deviations in the two populations at 5 per cent level is:

(a) accepted
(b) rejected
(c) no decision about H_0
(d) none of the above

97. Two samples of size 10 and 8 had sample means 18 cm and 12 cm with variances 25 and 16. Supposing that the samples have been drawn from normal populations $N(\mu_1, \sigma_1^2)$ and $N(\mu_2, \sigma_2^2)$, the value of statistic-t for testing H_0: $\mu_1 = \mu_2$ under $\sigma_1^2 \neq \sigma_2^2$ is

(a) 2.67
(b) 2.75
(c) 1.33
(d) 2.83

98. A manufacturer claims that his items could not have a large variance. 18 of his items has a variance = 0.033. The value of statistic χ^2 to test H_0: $\sigma^2 = 1$ is:

(a) 30.30
(b) 5.55
(c) 0.56
(d) none of the above

99. The variance due to two treatments in an experiment is 480 and the error variance is 60.0 with 14 d.f. Test for the equality of treatments effect reveals that:

[Given $F_{0.05, (1, 14)} = 4.60$]

(*a*) treatments are equally effective

(*b*) treatments differ significantly

(*c*) no conclusion

(*d*) none of the above

100. It is expected that 50 per cent people of a city are cinema goers. A survey of 1600 people revealed that 35 per cent people go to cinema. The value of statistic-Z is:

(*a*) 12.0

(*b*) 6.0

(*c*) 12.58

(*d*) –12.0

101. A normal population has a mean of 0.5 and S.D. = 6.0. The probability that the sample mean of 625 items of a sample will be negative is:

(*a*) 0.0188

(*b*) 0.365

(*c*) 0.4812

(*d*) 0.135

102. The claimed average life of electric bulbs is 2000 hours with a S.D. = 250 hours. To make 95 per cent sure that the bulbs should not fall below the claimed average life by more than 5 per cent, the sample size should be:

(*a*) 24

(*b*) 16

(*c*) 41

(*d*) none of the above

103. Given the sample statistics,

$$n_1 = 400, \bar{x}_1 = 24.50, \quad s_1 = 2.5$$

$$n_2 = 500, \bar{x}_2 = 20.0, \quad s_2 = 2.0$$

The value of test statistic to test H_0: $\mu_1 = \mu_2$, when $\sigma_1^2 = \sigma_2^2$ is:

(*a*) $Z = 44.47$

(*b*) $Z = 8.97$

(*c*) $Z = 30.0$

(*d*) none of the above

104. From the sample statistics given Q. No. 103, the hypothesis H_0: $\sigma_1 = \sigma_2$ is:

(*a*) accepted

(*b*) rejected

(*c*) not possible to be tested

(*d*) none of the above

105. From a population of 200 items with S.D. = 3.0, a sample of size n is drawn. If it is desired that the sample mean differs from population mean by 1 unit or more is controlled at $\alpha = 0.05$, the value of smallest n is:

(*a*) 35

(*b*) 6

(*c*) 12

(*d*) 312

106. An experiment consisted of two storage practices. In the first storage practice, out of 100 fruits 5 were putrefied and in the second, out of 150 fruits, 5 were putrefied. Can it be concluded that the second storage practice is better than first?

(*a*) No

(*b*) Yes

(*c*) not possible to decide

(*d*) none of the above

107. A die is thrown 60 times and number of times the following faces were obtained.

Faces:	1	2	3	4	5	6
No. of times:	14	7	5	8	10	16

Can the die be regarded as fair?

[Given: $\chi^2_{0.05, 5} = 11.07$]

(*a*) The die is not fair

(*b*) The die is fair

(*c*) no conclusion

(*d*) none of the above

108. For the problem given in Q. No. 107, the value of statistic χ^2 is:

(*a*) 1.8

(*b*) 9.0

(*c*) 40.96

(*d*) none of the above

109. For the problem given in Q. No. 107, d.f. for statistic χ^2 are:

(*a*) 6

(*b*) 4

(*c*) 5

(*d*) 1

110. Given the following eight sample values –4, –3, –3, 0, 3, 3, 4, 4, the value of student's *t*-test H_0: $\mu = 0$ is:
(*a*) 2.73
(*b*) 0.97
(*c*) 3.30
(*d*) 0.41

111. If all frequencies of classes are same, the value of χ^2 is:
(*a*) 1
(*b*) ∞
(*c*) zero
(*d*) none of the above

112. The value of statistic χ^2 is zero if and only if:
(*a*) $\sum_i O_i = \sum_i E_i$
(*b*) $O_i = E_i$ for all i
(*c*) E_i is large
(*d*) all the above

113. The range of statistic-χ^2 is:
(*a*) –1 to +1
(*b*) $-\infty$ to ∞
(*c*) 0 to ∞
(*d*) 0 to 1

114. Range of statistic-*t* is
(*a*) –1 to 1
(*b*) $-\infty$ to ∞
(*c*) 0 to ∞
(*d*) 0 to 1

115. Range of the variance ratio *F* is:
(*a*) –1 to 1
(*b*) $-\infty$ to ∞
(*c*) 0 to ∞
(*d*) 0 to 1

116. The mean and S.D. of a set of values are 15 and 5 respectively. Then the value of student's-*t* is calculated to test H_0: $\mu = 10$. If each sample value is increased by 2, the value of *t* will be:
(*a*) decreased
(*b*) increased
(*c*) same
(*d*) all the above

117. A random sample of size 20 from a normal population gives a mean 42 and a variance 25. To test that the population standard deviation is 8, the value of statistic-χ^2 is:
(*a*) 7.42
(*b*) 15.62
(*c*) 51.20
(*d*) none of the above

118. Degrees of freedom for χ^2 in Q. No. 117 is:
(*a*) 20
(*b*) 24
(*c*) 7
(*d*) 19

119. A coin is tossed 400 times and it turns up head 216 times. The hypothesis that the coin is unbiased can be tested by:
(*a*) χ^2 test
(*b*) *Z*-test
(*c*) both (*a*) and (*b*)
(*d*) neither (*a*) nor (*b*)

120. The best critical region consists of:
(*a*) extreme positive values
(*b*) extreme negative values
(*c*) both (*a*) and (*b*)
(*d*) neither (*a*) nor (*b*)

121. Reduction in the size of a test results into:
(*a*) decrease in its power
(*b*) increase in its power
(*c*) no change in its power
(*d*) all the above

122. A sample of 36 measurements shows a standard deviation of 0.07. Test of hypothesis H_0 that the true standard deviation is 0.05 against that it is not at 5 per cent level of significance reveals that:
(*a*) H_0 is accepted
(*b*) H_0 is rejected
(*c*) not possible to test
(*d*) none of the above

123. 25 persons were found suffering from cancer in a city and only 10 saved. Can it be concluded at 95 per cent confidence level that in general 50 per cent person suffering from cancer were saved against that it is less.
(*a*) No

(*b*) Yes
(*c*) no test is available
(*d*) none of the above

124. Statistic $Z \dfrac{\bar{x}-\bar{y}}{\sigma\sqrt{\dfrac{1}{n_1}+\dfrac{1}{n_2}}}$ is used to test the null hypothesis:
(*a*) H_0: $\mu_1 + \mu_2 = 0$
(*b*) H_0: $\mu_1 - \mu_2 = 0$
(*c*) H_0: $\mu = \mu_0$ (a constant)
(*d*) none of the above

125. In a contingency table, the expected frequencies are computed under:
(*a*) null hypothesis H_0
(*b*) alternative hypothesis H_1
(*c*) H_0 and H_1 both
(*d*) no consideration of hypothesis

126. Which one of the following is a research hypothesis?
(*a*) Two population means are equal
(*b*) Intelligent people have more reading habit
(*c*) Population correlation coefficient is zero
(*d*) Two populations follow the same distribution.

127. Which one of the following with usual notations is not a statistical hypothesis?
(*a*) $H : \sigma^2 = \sigma_0^2$
(*b*) $H : \sigma_1^2 > \sigma_1^2$
(*c*) $H : \rho_1 = \rho_2$
(*d*) *H* : People suffering from T.B. belong to the poor section of the society.

128. A contingency table having a zero count is called:
(*a*) a complete contingency table
(*b*) an incomplete contingency table
(*c*) abnormal contingency table
(*d*) none of the above

129. If the calculated value of Chi-square is greater than its degrees of freedom, then
(*a*) null hypothesis be accepted directly
(*b*) null hypothesis be rejected straight-away
(*c*) χ^2-table be consulted to arrive at a decision about the null hypothesis
(*d*) all the above.

130. A zero count in a cell of a contingency table having its expected frequency zero is called:
(*a*) structural zero
(*b*) random zero
(*c*) false zero
(*d*) all the above

131. A zero in a cell of a contingency table having a finite expected value is termed as:
(*a*) structural zero
(*b*) random zero
(*c*) false zero
(*d*) none of the above

132. Calculated value of Chi-square less than its degrees of freedom leads to:
(*a*) acceptance of H_0 directly
(*b*) rejection of H_0 straight away
(*c*) no decision about H_0
(*d*) none of the above

133. For testing that a bivariate random sample has come from an uncorrelated population, the appropriate test is:
(*a*) normal deviate test
(*b*) χ^2-test
(*c*) *F*-test
(*d*) *t*-test

134. A variable which is used in a contingency table to explain the response variable is known as:
(*a*) random variable
(*b*) discrete variable
(*c*) explanatory variable
(*d*) dummy variable

135. In general a contingency table is a:
(*a*) one-dimensional table
(*b*) two-dimensional table
(*c*) three-dimensional table
(*d*) multi-dimensional table

136. The expression for knowing the significant

contribution of a cell in a $(p \times q)$ contingency table with usual notations is:

(a) $(O_{ij} - E_{ij})/\sqrt{E_{ij}}$
(b) $\sqrt{(O_{ij} - E_{ij})/E_{ij}}$
(c) $(O_{ij} - E_{ij})/[E_{ij}(1-p_i)(1-p_j)]^{1/2}$
(d) $(O_{ij} - E_{ij})/E_{ij}p_i \cdot p_j$

137. For testing $H_0 : \sigma = \sigma_0$ in a normal population $N(0, \sigma^2)$, a critical region based on sample $X_1, X_2, ..., X_n$ is $\Sigma X_i^2 < K$. For which alternative hypothesis does this provide uniformly most powerful test?

(a) $\sigma \neq \sigma_0$
(b) $\sigma^2 = \sigma_0^2$
(c) $\sigma < \sigma_0$
(d) $\sigma > \sigma_0$

138. Let $X_1, X_2, ..., X_n$ be a random sample from $N(0, \sigma^2)$. Consider maximum likelihood ratio test for which the critical region is given as $\Sigma X_i^2 > K$. The alternative hypothesis against $H_0 : \sigma = \sigma_0$ which leads to an uniformly most powerful test is:

(a) $\sigma \neq \sigma_0$
(b) $\sigma^2 = \sigma_0$
(c) $\sigma < \sigma_0$
(d) $\sigma > \sigma_0$

139. In testing the equality of several population means by F-test, the assumption is:

(a) populations are continuous
(b) population variances are homogeneous
(c) populations are correlated
(d) all the above

140. The test of goodness of fit of an assumed population means:

(a) testing a hypothesis about its mean
(b) testing a hypothesis about its variance
(c) to make a comparison between observed and expected number of observations
(d) none of the above.

141. Why do we always test null hypothesis H_0, why not alternative hypothesis H_1?

(a) Because H_0 is given before H_1
(b) Because it is to test H_0
(c) Because all test statistics are derived under H_0
(d) Because it has become a tradition

142. For a binomial variate, testing of null hypothesis about expected frequency in a class by Z-test and χ^2-test will lead to:

(a) different conclusions
(b) same conclusion
(c) no conclusion
(d) incompatible results

ANSWERS

Section B

1. more than one **2.** J. Neyman; 1928 **3.** Karl Pearson **4.** assertion **5.** null **6.** alternative **7.** J. Neyman **8.** simple; simple **9.** composite **10.** two **11.** second; first **12.** Second; first **13.** size **14.** level of significance **15.** type I **16.** type II **17.** alternative **18.** remains same **19.** $1 - \beta$ **20.** operating characteristic **21.** 0; 1 **22.** power **23.** region of rejection **24.** rule or procedure **25.** test statistic **26.** non-randomised **27.** critical region **28.** acceptance **29.** rejection **30.** critical region **31.** degrees of freedom **32.** sample size **33.** optimum **34.** optimum **35.** most powerful **36.** uniformly most powerful **37.** most powerful **38.** type I; type II **39.** size; power **40.** minimax **41.** unbiased **42.** UMPU **43.** type A_1 **44.** Neyman and Pearson **45.** unbiased critical **46.** admissible **47.** randomised **48.** critical function **49.** border **50.** degrees of freedom **51.** randomised **52.** Chi-square **53.** small **54.** standard error **55.** $(\bar{x} - \mu)\sqrt{n}/s$ **56.** normal **57.** independent **58.** five **59.** robust **60.** UMPU **61.** $n_1 + n_2 - 2$ **62.** pooled **63.** W.G. Cochran **64.** Behrens-Fisher **65.** separately **66.** later **67.** first **68.** objection or lacuna **69.** more **70.** paired **71.** correlated **72.** mean difference **73.** Z-test **74.** Z-test **75.** Z-test **76.** normal

77. goodness of fit **78.** observed; expected **79.** 0; ∞ **80.** 0; 1 **81.** unity **82.** $k-1$ **83.** 12 **84.** 1 **85.** $n(ad-bc)^2/(a+b)(c+d)(a+c)(b+d)$ **86.** $(a-rb)^2/r(a+b)$ **87.** continuity **88.** Yates **89.** small **90.** better **91.** calculation **92.** $n\left(|ad-bc|-\dfrac{n}{2}\right)^2 \Big/ (a+b)(c+d)(a+c)\times(b\times d)$ **93.** probabilities **94.** computation **95.** association **96.** zero **97.** rejected **98.** high degree **99.** 100 **100.** M.S. Bartlett **101.** Chi-square **102.** upward **103.** *F*-test **104.** *F*-distribution **105.** *F*-test **106.** *F*-test **107.** ANOVA **108.** variance **109.** difference **110.** random variable **111.** successive **112.** A. Wald; 1947 **113.** two types of error **114.** risk function **115.** paired *t*-test **116.** $\bar{X}_A = \bar{X}_B$ **117.** Chi-square or *Z*-test **118.** analysis of variance

119. 132 $\left[\textit{Hint.} \dfrac{-16}{112/\sqrt{n}} = -1.64\right]$ **120.** 1/4

$$\left[\textit{Hint.}\ \alpha = p\ (\text{reject } H_0/H_0) = \frac{\binom{5}{1}\binom{5}{1}}{\binom{10}{1}\binom{10}{1}} = \frac{1}{4}\right]$$

121. 16/25 [*Hint.* $\beta = p$ (reject H_0/H_1)

$$= \frac{\binom{4}{1}\binom{4}{1}}{\binom{10}{1}\binom{10}{1}} + \frac{\binom{4}{1}\binom{6}{1}}{\binom{10}{1}\binom{10}{1}} + \frac{\binom{6}{1}\binom{4}{1}}{\binom{10}{1}\binom{10}{1}} = \frac{16}{25}\Bigg]$$

122. $e^{-1.5}$

$$\left[\textit{Hint.}\ f(x;\theta) = \theta e^{-\theta x} = \int_{1500}^{\infty} \frac{1}{1000} e^{-x/1000}\,dx\right]$$

123. $e^{-3/4}$ [*Hint.* $1-\beta = P$ (reject H_0/H_1)

$$= \int_{1500}^{\infty} \frac{1}{2000} e^{-x/1000}\,dx\Bigg]$$

124. = 0.172 [*Hint.* $\alpha = P(x \geq 7/H_0)$

$$= \frac{1}{2^{10}} \times \sum_{x=7}^{10} \binom{10}{x}\Bigg]$$

125. 0.382 [*Hint.* Power $= \displaystyle\sum_{x=7}^{10} \binom{10}{x}\left(\frac{3}{4}\right)^x \times \left(\frac{2}{5}\right)^{10-x}\Bigg]$

126. 0.618 **127.** do not support **128.** rejected **129.** zero **130.** 16 **131.** statistical **132.** accepted **133.** 1.71 **134.** same **135.** not equally **136.** accepted **137.** accepted **138.** 0.455 **139.** 7/64 **140.** 0.649 **141.** 0.351 **142.** 125 **143.** do not support **144.** 1800 **145.** decreases **146.** decision rule **147.** objectives **148.** greater than **149.** multidimensional **150.** incomplete **151.** structural **152.** random zero **153.** accept **154.** standardised residuals **155.** dependent **156.** significant **157.** $\mu = 6$; $\mu > 6$ **158.** Chi-square test **159.** right tail **160.** *Z*-test

Section C

1. (*b*) **2.** (*d*) **3.** (*d*) **4.** (*c*) **5.** (*a*)
6. (*b*) **7.** (*b*) **8.** (*c*) **9.** (*a*) **10.** (*b*)
11. (*b*) **12.** (*a*) **13.** (*c*) **14.** (*b*) **15.** (*d*)
16. (*c*) **17.** (*d*) **18.** (*a*) **19.** (*c*) **20.** (*b*)
21. (*d*) **22.** (*a*) **23.** (*c*) **24.** (*b*) **25.** (*c*)
26. (*c*) **27.** (*b*) **28.** (*c*) **29.** (*a*) **30.** (*d*)
31. (*a*) **32.** (*d*) **33.** (*b*) **34.** (*c*) **35.** (*b*)
36. (*a*) **37.** (*c*) **38.** (*c*) **39.** (*b*) **40.** (*a*)
41. (*d*) **42.** (*b*) **43.** (*b*) **44.** (*c*) **45.** (*d*)
46. (*a*) **47.** (*d*) **48.** (*a*) **49.** (*c*) **50.** (*b*)
51. (*a*) **52.** (*d*) **53.** (*a*) **54.** (*b*) **55.** (*c*)
56. (*d*) **57.** (*a*) **58.** (*d*) **59.** (*c*) **60.** (*b*)
61. (*a*) **62.** (*d*) **63.** (*b*) **64.** (*c*) **65.** (*c*)
66. (*b*) **67.** (*b*) **68.** (*a*) **69.** (*a*) **70.** (*d*)
71. (*c*) **72.** (*a*) **73.** (*b*) **74.** (*c*) **75.** (*b*)
76. (*a*) **77.** (*a*) **78.** (*b*) **79.** (*d*) **80.** (*a*)
81. (*c*) **82.** (*b*) **83.** (*c*) **84.** (*d*) **85.** (*a*)
86. (*b*) **87.** (*a*) **88.** (*c*) **89.** (*c*) **90.** (*a*)
91. (*b*) **92.** (*a*) **93.** (*a*) **94.** (*c*) **95.** (*b*)
96. (*b*) **97.** (*d*) **98.** (*c*) **99.** (*b*) **100.** (*d*)
101. (*a*) **102.** (*b*) **103.** (*c*) **104.** (*b*) **105.** (*a*)
106. (*b*) **107.** (*b*) **108.** (*b*) **109.** (*c*) **110.** (*d*)
111. (*c*) **112.** (*b*) **113.** (*c*) **114.** (*b*) **115.** (*c*)
116. (*b*) **117.** (*a*) **118.** (*d*) **119.** (*c*) **120.** (*c*)
121. (*a*) **122.** (*b*) **123.** (*a*) **124.** (*b*) **125.** (*a*)
126. (*b*) **127.** (*d*) **128.** (*b*) **129.** (*c*) **130.** (*a*)
131. (*b*) **132.** (*a*) **133.** (*d*) **134.** (*c*) **135.** (*d*)
136. (*c*) **137.** (*c*) **138.** (*d*) **139.** (*b*) **140.** (*d*)
141. (*c*) **142.** (*b*).

SUGGESTED READING

1. Agarwal, B.L., *Basic Statistics*, New Age International, New Delhi, 8th edition, 2024.
2. Arora, S. and Lal, B., *New Mathematical Statistics*, Satya Prakashan, New Delhi, 1989.
3. Crammer, H., *Mathematical Methods of Statistics*, (8th. edn.), Princeton University Press, Princeton, 8th. edn., 1958.
4. Goon, A.M., Gupta, M.K. and Dasgupta, B., *An Outline of Statistical Theory*, The World Press, Calcutta, 2nd. edn., 1980.
5. Gupta, S.C. and Kapoor, V.K., *Fundamentals of Mathematical Statistics*, Sultan Chand & Sons, New Delhi, 9th edn., 1994.
6. Kapur, J.N. and Saxena, H.C., *Mathematical Statistics*, S. Chand, New Delhi, 12th edn., 1984.
7. Kendall, M.G. and Stuart, A., *The Advanced Theory of Statistics*, Vol. 2 (3rd edn.), Charles Griffin, London, 3rd. ed., 1973.
8. Lehmann, E.L., *Testing Statistical Hypotheses*, Wiley Eastern, New Delhi, 1976.
9. Mood, A.M., Graybill, F.A. and Boes, D.C., *Introduction to the Theory of Statistics*, Mc-Graw Hill, Kogakusha, Tokyo, 3rd edn., 1974.
10. Saxena, H.C. and Surendran, P.U., *Statistical Inference*, S. Chand, New Delhi, 2nd edn., 1973.
11. Wilks, S.S., *Mathematical Statistics*, John Wiley, New York, 1962.
12. Zacks, S., *The Theory of Statistical Inference*, John Wiley, New York, 1971.

CHAPTER 12

Nonparametric Statistical Methods

SECTION A

Short Essay Type Questions

Q. 1. *Give a brief account of the need of nonparametric statistical methods.*

Ans. Parametric statistical methods are based on stringent assumptions about the population from which the sample has been drawn. Particularly the assumptions like form of the probability distribution, accuracy of observations, etc., are more common. Also, the parametric methods are applicable primarily to the data which are measured in interval or ratio scale. In practice, however, stringent assumptions are seldom fully valid. Moreover, the measurements are often made on nominal or ordinal scale.

If the assumption do not hold good or the data do not meet the requirement of parametric statistical methods, nonparametric methods come to the rescue of the worker. Nonparametric methods entail very mild assumptions like continuity and symmetry of the distribution. Also most of the nonparametric methods are applicable for ordered statistics.

Q. 2. *Distinguish between nonparametric methods and distribution free methods.*

Ans. Those statistical methods, which are not concerned with the estimation or testing of hypothesis for one or more parameters of probability distribution functions are termed as nonparametric methods.

Those inferences whose validity do not rest on the form of specific probability distribution of the population from which the sample has been drawn are termed as distribution free methods. These two terms are not synonyms. But the statistical methods applied in the two cases are almost same and they are interchangeably used.

Q. 3. *When should the nonparametric methods be preferably used?*

Ans. Nonparametric methods be used when one or more of the following situations exist:

(*i*) The hypothesis does not involve a parameter of the probability function of the population.

(*ii*) The observations are not as accurate as required for a parametric inference. Also when the measurements are on the nominal or ordinal scale.

(*iii*) The assumptions necessary for a validity of a parametric method are suspected to hold good. For example, the assumption of normal population is doubtful.

(*iv*) One wants to avoid complicated analysis of data.

(*v*) One is interested in quick results.

Q. 4. *What are the advantages of nonparametric methods?*

Ans. There are many advantages of nonparametric methods over parametric ones. The advantages can precisely be delineated as under:

(*i*) Any inference based on the parametric analysis which does not uphold the underlying assumptions necessitated for it will be erroneous. In such a situation nonparametric methods can safely be applied.

(*ii*) If the measurement scale of data is nominal or ordinal, nonparametric methods can be used.

(*iii*) In case the measurements are not so accurate as to apply parametric methods, non-parametric methods perform better.

(*iv*) With so-called *dirty data* (contaminated observations, outliers, etc.), many nonparametric methods are appropriate.

(*v*) There is no restriction for minimum size of sample for nonparametric methods for valid and reliable results.

(*vi*) Nonparametric methods require minimum assumption like continuity of the sampled population.

(*vii*) The analysis of data is simple and involves little computation work.

(*viii*) Nonparametric test may be quite powerful even if the sample size is small.

(*ix*) Nonparametric test are inherently robust against certain violation of assumptions.

Q. 5. *What are the disadvantages of non-parametric procedures?*

Ans. Nonparametric procedures are also not free from demerits. Some of the main disadvantages are as follows:

(*i*) Because of the simplicity of nonparametric procedures, they are often used even if appropriate parametric methods are available.

(*ii*) All nonparametric methods are not as simple as they are claimed to be.

(*iii*) It is not possible to determine the actual power of a nonparametric test due to the want of actual situation.

Q. 6. *How can one judge the relative performance of two tests?*

Ans. In many situations there can be more than one test which appear appropriate for the test of a hypothesis. Then there is a need to fix some criteria to choose one out of many alternative tests. The asymptotic relative efficiency (ARE) is a single measure which provides satisfactory results for comparing the performance of two tests based on large samples. The concept of ARE was given by S.J.G. Pitman in 1961, and hence ARE is often named as Pitman efficiency. The calculation of ARE is based on the classical distribution and assumption of the nonparametric tests that have parametric analogues.

The *asymptotic relative efficiency* of test *A* relative to a test *B* can be defined as the limiting value of n_B/n_A where n_B and n_A are the sample sizes required for the tests *A* and *B* to have the same power.

Q. 7. *What is power efficiency?*

Ans. The *power efficiency* of test *A* relative to a test *B* is the ratio of sample sizes n_B/n_A where both the tests are for the same H_0 and H_1 and having same power of the tests *A* and *B*. Since it is difficult to calculate power efficiency, ARE is more frequently used.

Q. 8. *What is meant by tied observations?*

Ans. Under the assumption of continuous distribution, no two observations can be equal. But due to the rounding of figures, precision of measuring instruments, inaccuracy of measurements, etc., some observations seldom occur which are exactly equal in magnitude. Such observations are called *tied observations*. Due to tie among observations, one faces the problem in awarding ranks to them.

Q. 9. *How to surmount the problem of tied observations?*

Ans. There are different approaches to overcome the problem of tied observations. Five important approaches are discussed over here.

(*i*) **Midranks approach.** Under this approach, each group of tied observations is ranked as if they are all distinguishable and then take the average of the ranks of tied values and assign the same average rank to the tied observations of that group. This is the most frequently used methods of breaking the ties. When the mid rank method is used, a correction of ties is often applied in most of the tests and measures of associations.

(*ii*) **Average statistics approach.** If there are K groups of different observations in a set and i^{th} group is of size r_i, there are in all $\prod_{i-1}^{k} r_i!$ possible arrangements of values. Now calculate the test statistic for each arrangement and take their average. Use this average value for taking the decision. Under this approach, the test statistic will have the same mean but smaller variance. This method is generally not used because it usually involves too much computation.

(*iii*) **Least favourable statistic approach.** Instead of averaging the test statistics for all possible arrangements under tied observations, one might choose that statistics value out of all which minimises the probability of rejection. Under this approach, there is least chance of committing type I error.

(*iv*) **Range of probability approach.** In this method one chooses two values of test statistics, the least and most favourable values. But a decision is possible only if both the values fall either inside or outside the region of rejection. If not so, the method fails.

(*v*) **Omitting the tied observations.** This is the simplest but risky approach. In this method one discards all tied values and reduce the sample by that number. If the number of tied observations is small as compared to the sample size, the test is not affected much otherwise, there is a loss of information and the procedure introduces bias towards rejection of the null hypothesis.

Q. 10. *What assumptions are generally made for a nonparametric test?*

Ans. Following assumptions are most commonly made about any nonparametric test:

(*i*) The sample at hand is a random sample drawn from a population whose median is unknown.

(*ii*) All the observations in the sample are independent.

(*iii*) The variable of interest is continuous.

(*iv*) The sampled population is symmetric.

(*v*) The observations are measured at least on ordinal scale.

Q. 11. *What are the basic steps involved in any nonparametric test of hypothesis?*

Ans. Various basic steps involved in a test are:

(*i*) First of all one should look for the assumptions necessary for the validity of a test procedure.

(*ii*) The sample data required should be collected.

(*iii*) The null and alternative hypotheses should be established.

(*iv*) The test statistic or procedure should be decided.

(*v*) The decision criteria should be fixed to decide about the rejection or acceptance of H_0 *vis-a-vis* H_1.

(*vi*) The interpretation to the conclusions drawn should be given.

Q. 12. *What do you understand by ordered statistics?*

Ans. Let $X_1, X_2, \ldots, X_n$ be a random sample from a continuous population with probability of any X's being equal to zero. If $x_{(1)}$ is the smallest X value in $X_1, X_2, \ldots, X_n$ $x_{(2)}$ the next larger value and $x_{(n)}$, the highest, then the set of values $x_{(1)}, x_{(2)}, \ldots, x_{(n)}$ is called the ordered statistics. This is an ascending order. If one wants he can put the observations in descending order as $x_{(n)}, x_{(n-1)}, \ldots, x_{(1)}$. If $x_{(r)}$ denotes the rth ordered value for $r = 1, 2, \ldots, n$, the ordered statistics deals with the properties of $x_{(r)}$. Ordered statistics is extremely useful in nonparametric methods.

The ordered statistics do not possess the same probability distribution as the original variable X. Also the values in the ordered statistics are not independent even if original variate values are independent as is always true in case of random samples.

Q. 13. *Give the names of various nonparametric tests and statistics.*

Ans. The names of the nonparametric tests and statistics are as follows:

One sample nonparametric tests:

(*i*) Kolmogorov-Smirnov test
(*ii*) Ordinary sign test
(*iii*) Wilcoxon signed-rank test
(*iv*) Runs test

Two or more samples nonparametric tests and statistics:

(*i*) Kolmogorov-Smirnov two-sample test
(*ii*) Sign test for paired samples
(*iii*) Wilcoxon paired sample signed-rank test
(*iv*) Median test
(*v*) Wald-Wolfowitz runs test
(*vi*) Mann-Whitney *U*-test
(*vii*) Mcnemar's test
(*viii*) Cochran's *Q*-test
(*ix*) Mood's test for dispersion
(*x*) Moses test for dispersion
(*xi*) Kruskal-Wallis one way analysis
(*xii*) Friedman's method of two way analysis
(*xiii*) Jonckheere Terpstra test
(*xiv*) Page's test
(*xv*) Spearman's rank correlation
(*xvi*) Kendall's correlation coefficient τ
(*xvii*) Coefficient of concordance
(*xviii*) Brown and Mood's test
(*xix*) Mood's test
(*xx*) Theil's test
(*xxi*) Confidence interval
(*xxii*) Confidence band

Q. 14. *Describe briefly Kolmogorov-Smirnov test of goodness of fit in case of one sample.*

Ans. Let $X_1, X_2, ..., X_n$ be a random sample from an unknown continuous population having the cumulative distribution function $F(x)$. Also let the ordered statistics be $x_{(1)}, x_{(2)}, ..., x_{(n)}$. The *K-S* test is based on Glivenko-Cantelli theorem which states that *the step function $S_n(x)$ with jumps occurring at the values of $x_{(1)}, x_{(2)}, ..., x_{(n)}$ of the ordered statistics for the sample approaches the true distribution for all X.* Kolmogorov-Smirnov used this theorem and compared the empirical distribution function $S_n(x)$ of the sample for any value of x with the population c.d.f. under H_0, *i.e.*, $F_0(x)$.

The hypothesis under test is,

$$H_0: F(x) = F_0(x) \text{ vs. } H_1: F(x) \neq F_0(x)$$

where $F_0(x)$ is a completely specified continuous distribution.

To test H_0, the numerical difference $| s_n(x) - F_0(x) |$ is used in *K-S* test. Since the difference depends on x, the *K-S* statistic D_n is taken to be the supremum of such differences, *i.e.*,

$$D_n = \underset{\text{overall } x}{\text{Sup}} \left| s_n(x) - F_0(x) \right|$$

Under H_0, the statistic D_n has a distribution which is independent of the c.d.f. $F(x)$ that defines H_0. The statistic D_n is distribution free.

To take a decision about H_0, the test criteria are, reject H_0 if $D_n \geq D_n$ a (tabulated value), otherwise accept H_0.

Q. 15. *Compare the Chi-square test of goodness of fit with Kolmogorov-Smirnov test.*

Ans. The Chi-square test is also one of the very popular test of goodness of fit. If we compare the two, we find that:

(*i*) χ^2-test is specially meant for categorical data whereas *K-S* statistics are for random samples from continuous populations. However, when the data are categorical, the two tests can interchangeably be used.

(*ii*) Chi-square requires categorical data, whereas the *K-S* statistic utilises each of the *n* observations. Hence, the *K-S* makes better use of available information than Chi-square statistic.

(*iii*) The Kolmogorov-Smirnov statistic is more flexible than Chi-square statistic as it can be used to determine minimum sample size and confidence band.

(*iv*) In *K-S* test, we can use one side test also which is not possible in Chi-square test.

(*v*) The *K-S* test is easier to apply.

(*vi*) The Chi-square test also comes in the category of parametric tests whereas *K-S* test is only a nonparametric test.

Q. 16. *How can you perform ordinary sign test?*

Ans. Let $x_{(1)}, x_{(2)}, ..., x_{(n)}$ be the ordered sample values from a population $F(x)$ and M be its median.

Also $P(X = M) = 0$. Here we test, $H_0 : M = M_0$ vs. $H_1 : M \neq M_0$ where M_0 is the given value of the median and hence $P(X > M_0) = P(X < M_0) = 0.5$.

So we can test $H_0 : P(X > M_0) = P(X < M_0)$

vs. $H_1 : P(X > M_0) \neq P(X < M_0)$

To perform the sign test, find the differences $(X_{(i)} - M_0)$ for $i = 1, 2, \ldots, n$ and consider their signs. Suppose the number of +ve signs is r and negative signs, $(n - r)$. For the purpose of test we consider only positive signs. So r follows binomial distribution. Also the null hypothesis H_0 changes to $p = 0.5$. So the hypothesis under test amounts to testing,

$$H_0 : p = 0.5 \quad \text{vs.} \quad H_1 : p \neq 0.5$$

The test criterion is, reject H_0 if $r \geq r_{\alpha/2}$ where $r_{\alpha/2}$ is the critical value at significance level α. $r_{\alpha/2}$ is the smallest integer which satisfies the conditions,

$$\sum_{r=r_{\alpha/2}}^{n} \binom{n}{r}\left(\frac{1}{2}\right)^r\left(\frac{1}{2}\right)^{n-r} \leq \alpha/2$$

or $r \leq r'_{\alpha/2}$ is the smallest integer such that

$$\sum_{r=0}^{r'_{\alpha/2}} \binom{n}{r}\left(\frac{1}{2}\right)^r\left(\frac{1}{2}\right)^{n-r} \leq \alpha/2$$

For one-sided test use r_α instead of $r_{\alpha/2}$. Rest of the test procedure remains the same.

Large sample case: If $n \geq 25$, normal deviate test is applied to decide about H_0. Z is given by the statistic,

$$Z = \frac{(r + 0.5) - np_0}{\sqrt{np_0q_0}} \quad \text{where } r < np_0$$

$$= \frac{(r - 0.5) - np_0}{\sqrt{np_0q_0}} \quad \text{where } r > np_0$$

where $p_0 = 0.5$ and $q_0 = 1 - 0.5 = 0.5$.

The decision about H_0 is taken in a usual manner as described with parametric tests.

Q. 17. *How to resolve the problem of zero differences in sign test?*

Ans. In practice zero differences seldom occur. To resolve this problem, the best way is to discard zero differences and reduce the sample size by that number. Another way is to count half zeros as positive and half zeros as negative.

Q. 18. *Following are the yields of maize in q/ha recorded from an experiment and arranged in ascending order with median M = 20.*

15.4, 16.4, 17.3, 18.2, 19.2, 20.9, 22.7, 23.6, 24.5.

Test H_0: M = 20 vs. H_1: M ≠ 20 at a = 0.05

[Given: $P(x \leq 4) = 0.50$]

Ans. To test H_0, we find the difference $(X - 20)$ and write their signs.

– – – – – + + + +

Here $n = 9$, $r = 4$

$P(x \leq 4) = 0.5$ is greater than $\alpha = 0.05$. Hence H_0 is not rejected at 5 per cent level of significance.

Q. 19. *How Wilcoxon's signed-rank test differ from sign test and how to perform it?*

Ans. Ordinary sign test was based only on the direction of differences ignoring their magnitudes. But Wilcoxon's signed rank test takes into consideration, the both. This test is more sensitive and powerful than ordinary sign test.

To perform the test for $H_0 : M = M_0$ vs. H_1: $M \neq M_0$, find the differences $d_i = X_{(i)} - M_0$ for $i = 1, 2, \ldots, n$. d_i will be distributed symmetrically about the median zero so that +ve and –ve differences of equal absolute magnitude have equal probabilities of occurrences. The steps of the test are as follows:

Step-1. Arrange the differences in ascending order ignoring the sign and rank them from 1 to n.

Step-2. Now assign the signs to the ranks which the original differences possessed.

Step-3. Suppose the sum of ranks of +ve d_i's is T^+ and that of ranks of –ve d_i's is T^-. For a symmetric distribution, it is expected that T^+ and T^- will approximately be equal.

Also $$T^+ + T^- = \sum_{i=1}^{n} i = \frac{n(n+1)}{2}$$

Choose smaller of the T^+ and T^- for conducting the test. Suppose T^+ is smaller.

Step-4. Denote the rank of $|d_i|$ by $r(|d_i|)$ and a variable Z_i such that,

$$Z_i = \begin{cases} 1 & \text{if } d_i > 0 \\ 0 & \text{if } d_i < 0 \end{cases}$$

Therefore, $$T^+ = \sum_{i=1}^{n} Z_i r(|d_i|)$$

Step-5. If we take the subscript on the original sample such that all $|d_i|$ for $i = 1, 2, \ldots, n$ are ordered statistics replace $r(|d_i|)$ by i and Z_i by $Z_{(i)}$ where

$$Z_{(i)} = \begin{cases} 1 & \text{if } d_i \text{ with rank } i \text{ is +ve} \\ 0 & \text{if } d_i \text{ with rank } i \text{ is -ve} \end{cases}$$

Then, $$T^+ = \sum_{i=1}^{n} i\, Z_{(i)}$$

$Z_{(i)}$ are independent Bernoulli variables but are not identically distributed. $Z_{(i)}$ has mean p_i and variance $p_i q_i$ and Cov $(Z_{(i)}, Z_{(j)}) = 0$ for $i \neq j$. T^+ has mean $\sum_{i=1}^{n} i\, p_i$ and variance $\sum_{i=1}^{n} i\, p_i(1-p_i)$.

Under H_0, $p_i = \frac{1}{2}$ and hence

$$E(T^+) = \frac{1}{2}\sum_{i=1}^{n} i = \frac{n(n+1)}{4}$$

and

$$\text{var}(T^+) = \frac{1}{4}\sum_{i=1}^{n} i^2 = \frac{n(n+1)(2n+1)}{24}$$

If T^- is smaller, same treatment can be given. Let $T = \min(T^+, T^-)$. If T_α is a number such that $P(T < T_\alpha) = \alpha$ (the level of significance). The test criteria for testing

$$H_0: M = M_0 \quad \text{vs.} \quad H_1: M \neq M_0$$

is, find the critical value of T from the table for the sample size n and prefixed level of significance α. If $T^+ < T_\alpha$, reject H_0, otherwise accept H_0. If the alternative hypothesis leads to one-tailed test, the critical value of T from the table be consulted for given α for one-tailed test.

Q. 20. *For the problem given in Q. No. 18, test*

$$H_0: M = 20 \quad \text{vs.} \quad H_1: M > 20.$$

[Given $T_{0.05, 9} = 6$]

Ans. The differences $X_{(i)} - 20$ are:

$-4.6, -3.6, -2.7, -1.8, -0.8, 0.9, 2.7, 3.6, 4.5.$

The ordered sequence of numbers ignoring the sign and their ranks with original signs are as follows:

0.8, 0.9, 1.8, 2.7, 2.7, 3.6, 3.6, 4.5, 4.6

–1, 2, – 3, 4.5, – 4.5, 6.5, – 6.5, 8., – 9

Thus, $T^+ = 21$ and $T^- = 24$

$T^+ = 21 > 6$ (Table value), so we accept H_0. It means the median yield of maize in general is 20 q/ha.

Q. 21. *Define a run in a sequence of symbols.*

Ans. A run is a sequence of symbols followed and preceded by other type of symbols or no symbols. For example, a sequence FMMFFMMMFF of symbols F & M has five runs.

Q. 22. *What indication can one get from the number of runs?*

Ans. The number of runs in a sequence are indicative of randomness. Any set pattern of symbols in a sequence shows lack of randomness. In other words, too many or too less runs show lack of randomness.

Q. 23. *Give runs test for randomness.*

Ans. Let **a** and **b** be the symbols to show the kind of items, individuals or numbers forming a sequence. The hypothesis, H_0 : the symbols occur in random order vs. H_1 : the symbols occur in a set pattern, can be tested by runs test. The test procedure is as follows:

Suppose the sample of size n contains n_1 symbols of one kind say, **a** and n_2 symbols of the other kind say, **b**. Thus $n_1 + n_2 = n$. Also suppose, the number of runs of **a** symbols is r_1 and of **b** symbols r_2 and $r_1 + r_2 = r$.

To decide about H_0, the value of r is compared with the critical number of runs obtained from tables. These tables provide lower and upper critical values of the number of runs. If the observed number of runs in a sample lies in between these critical values, H_0 is not rejected and if outside these critical values, H_0 is rejected.

Q. 24. *Following is a sequence of heads (H) and tails (T) in tossing of a coin 14 times.*

HTTHHHHTHTTHHTH

Test whether the heads, and tails occur in random order. [*Given: For* $\alpha = 0.05$, $r_L = 3$, $r_U = 12$]

Ans. For the given sequence,

The sample size, $n = 14$

No. of heads, $n_1 = 8$

No. of tails, $n_2 = 6$

No. of runs of H, $r_1 = 5$

No. of runs of T, $r_2 = 4$

Thus, $r = 5 + 4 = 9$

Since the observed value of $r = 9$ lies between the critical values 3 and 12, we accept H_0. It means that the heads and tails occur in random order or it can be said that the coin is unbiased.

Q. 25. *How can one use the Kolmogorov-Smirnov test for two sample problem?*

Ans. When two samples are drawn from two continuous populations F_1 and F_2, it is desired to test whether two samples have come from identical populations, *i.e.*, one wants to test,

$$H_0 : F_1(x) = F_2(x) \text{ for all } x$$

$$\text{vs.} \quad H_1 : F_1(x) \neq F_2(x) \text{ for some } x$$

Under the *K-S* test, the decision about H_0 is taken on the basis of the distance between the empirical distributions of the two samples. If $S_{n_1}(x)$ and $S_{n_2}(x)$ are the empirical distributions of two samples of sizes n_1 and n_2 from the populations F_1 and F_2 respectively, the *K-S* statistic is,

$$D_{n_1, n_2} = \max_{\text{over all } x} | S_{n_1}(x) - S_{n_2}(x) |$$

Decision about H_0 is taken by comparing D_{n_1, n_2} with critical value of D for n_1 and n_2 sample sizes and α level of significance from the corresponding table in the usual manner.

Q. 26. *In what way the ordinary sign test can be used for paired samples?*

Ans. Let $(x_1, y_1), (x_2, y_2), ..., (x_n, y_n)$ be the paired sample observations.

Suppose $d_i = x_i - y_i$ for $i = 1, 2, ..., n$.

Here it is assumed that population of d_i's is continuous and obviously $P(d = M_d) = 0$.

The hypothesis to be tested is

$$H_0 : P(d > M_d^0) = P(d < M_d^0)$$

$$\text{vs.} \quad H_1 : P(d > M_d^0) \neq P(d < M_d^0)$$

So in two sample case, instead of dealing with the sample values, one has to deal with the differences d and perform the test in the same way as we do for one sample case.

Q. 27. *How can one apply Wilcoxon's signed-ranked test for matched-paired samples?*

Ans. Under matched-paired samples, the differences d within n paired sample values (x_i, y_i) for $i = 1, 2, ..., n$ are assumed to have come from continuous and symmetric population differences. If M_d^0 is the median of the population of differences and expected to possess a known value M_d^0, we test

$$H_0: M_d = M_d^0 \quad \text{vs.} \quad H_1: M_d \neq M_d^0$$

Now rest of the test procedure remains same as in case of one sample test. Here, our variable is d instead of X.

Q. 28. *How to test the equality of location parameters of two populations by the median test?*

Ans. The median test for testing the equality of location parameters of two populations does not require the restriction of paired observation as we have in matched pair sign test. It is a more general test. If we have random samples $X_1, X_2, ..., X_{n_1}$ and

$Y_1, Y_2, \ldots, Y_{n_2}$ from two populations F_X and F_Y respectively, then we have to test

$$H_0 : F_X(x) = F_Y(x) \quad \text{for all } x$$

vs. $$H_1 : F_X(x) = F_Y(x - \delta) \quad \text{for all } x \text{ and } \delta \neq 0$$

where δ is the shift in the location parameter which is the median. The procedure for median test is as follows:

Step-1. Combine the two samples and arrange the pooled observations in order.

Step-2. Find the median of the combined samples, say it is θ.

Step-3. Count the number of X's and Y's on the left of θ. Suppose there are u X's and v Y's to the left of θ. Obviously there are $(n_1 - u)$ X's and $(n_2 - v)$ Y's not to the left of θ.

Step-4. Calculate the probability of the event that $u + v = t$ observations are on the left of θ. If p is the probability for any observation to be on the left of θ, then $P(u + v = t)$ is

$$f(t) = \binom{n_1 + n_2}{t} p^t (1 - p)^{n_1 + n_2 - 1}$$

for $t = 0, 1, 2, \ldots, (n_1 + n_2)$

Also the conditional distribution of u given t is,

$$f(u \mid t) = \frac{\binom{n_1}{u}\binom{n_2}{v}}{\binom{n_1 + n_2}{t}}$$

for $u = 0, 1, 2, \ldots, n_1$

It is worth noting that $f(u \mid t)$ follows hyper-geometric distribution. This expression gives the conditional probability of u where $t = \dfrac{n}{2}$ for even n and $t = \dfrac{n-1}{2}$ for odd n.

Step-5. The test based on u, the number of X-observations which are less than θ in the combined sample is called median test.

Under H_0, the probability distribution of $U = u$ is,

$$f_U(u) = \binom{n_1}{u}\binom{n_2}{v} \Big/ \binom{n_1 + n_2}{t}$$

for $u = 0, 1, 2, \ldots, n_1$ and $t = \dfrac{n}{2}$.

Step-6. The decision criteria for the test of size α are:

reject H_0 if $u \leq c$ or $u \geq c'$ for $H_1 : \delta \neq 0$

reject H_0 if $u \geq c'_\alpha$ for $H_1 : \delta > 0$

reject H_0 if $u \leq c_\alpha$ for $H_1 : \delta < 0$

where $P(u \leq c) + P(U \geq c') = \alpha$

Also c_α and c'_α are respectively the largest and smallest integers such that $P(U \leq c_\alpha) \leq \alpha$ and $P(U \geq c'_\alpha) \leq \alpha$. The critical values of c, c', c_α and c'_α are also tabulated by Lieberman and Owen in 1961. As an alternative, a simple approach to decide about H_0 is to calculate the probability $f_U(u)$ and compare it with α, the prefixed level of significance. For a two-tailed test $f_U(u) \leq \alpha/2$, reject H_0, otherwise accept H_0.

Again for a one-tailed test, if $f_U(u) \leq \alpha$, reject H_0, otherwise not.

If $n \geq 10$, H_0 can be tested by Z-test. The variable U is distributed with mean $= \dfrac{n_1 t}{n}$ and variance $= \dfrac{n_1 n_2 (n - t)}{n^2 (n - 1)}$. Hence for large n,

$$Z = \frac{U - \dfrac{n_1 t}{n}}{\sqrt{\dfrac{n_1 n_2 (n - t)}{n^2 (n - 1)}}}$$

where $Z \sim N(0, 1)$

Decision about H_0 can be taken in the usual way.

Q. 29. *Is it possible to apply the median test for testing the identicalness of more than two-sampled populations? If yes, how to perform this test?*

Ans. The median test is applicable for testing the identicalness of more than two populations. The procedure for performing the median test is same as in the case of two populations. Let us consider in general k populations and random samples of sizes $n_1, n_2, \ldots, n_k$ from the populations $F_1(x), F_2(x), \ldots, F_k(x)$ respectively.

Here we test

$H_0: F_1(x) = F_2(x) = \ldots = F_k(x)$ in respect of median

vs. H_1 : at least two of them are not same.

As a test procedure, pool all the samples and find the median θ. Then count how many observations for each sample are to the left of θ. Consider a random variable U_i denoting the number of observations which are to the left of θ in the ith sample for $i = 1, 2, \ldots, k$. Supposing

$$r = \sum_{i=1}^{k} u_i = \begin{cases} \dfrac{N}{2} & \text{if } N \text{ is even} \\ \dfrac{N-1}{2} & \text{if } N \text{ is odd} \end{cases}$$

where $N = \sum_i n_i$

Under H_0, all $\binom{N}{r}$ possible sets of observations are equally likely. Hence,

$$f(n_1, u_2, \ldots, u_k \mid r) = \frac{\binom{n_1}{u_1}\binom{n_2}{u_2}\cdots\binom{n_k}{u_k}}{\binom{N}{r}}$$

Under H_0, all u_i should be equal. Hence, if one or more u_i's differ largely from their expected u_i, H_0 should be rejected. But this approach is vague. So the best thing is to calculate the probabilities for observed and extreme values of $u_1, u_2, \ldots, u_k$ and cumulate these probabilities. In practice, if the sum of probabilities so calculated is less than the desired level α, reject H_0, otherwise H_0 is not rejected.

Calculation of probabilities is a tedious job. Hence, an alternative approach is better provided the number of observations N is not less than 25 and no individual sample has less than 5 observations. To test H_0, we apply the Chi-square test. The test statistic for $2K$ categories is

$$q = \sum_{i=1}^{K}\sum_{j=1}^{2} \frac{(f_{ij} - e_{ij})^2}{e_{ij}}$$

where $f_{i1} = u_i$ = no. of observations in the ith sample to the left θ.

and $f_{i2} = n_i - u_i$ = no. of observations in the ith sample not to the left θ.

As a common procedure,

$$e_{i1} = \frac{r}{N} n_i$$

$$e_{i2} = \frac{N-r}{N} n_i$$

Substituting the value of f_{ij} and e_{ij}, the test statistic

$$q = \frac{N^2}{r(N-r)} \sum_{i=1}^{K} \frac{\left(u_i - \frac{r}{N} n_i\right)^2}{n_i}$$

q is approximately distributed as χ^2 with $(K - 1)$ d.f. The decision about H_0 can be taken in the usual manner.

It has been found that there is an upward bias in q as a χ^2-approximation. Hence a correction is incorporated in q, *i.e.*, to multiply q by $\left(\frac{N-1}{N}\right)$. This makes the approximation more virile.

Q. 30. *The blood pressure (systolic) of 6 persons without any medication and of 7 persons after 3 days of medication were as follows:*

B.P. without medication (X): 120, 104, 82, 142, 98, 96

B.P. after 3 days medication (Y): 122, 108, 105, 130, 134, 132, 92.

Test whether the distribution of pulse rate of persons before and after medication is same at $\alpha = 0.05$.

Ans. To test H_0: $F_X(x) = F_Y(x)$ vs. H_1:$F_X(x) =$

$F_Y(x - \alpha)$, we combine the two samples and find the median θ of the combined samples.

<u>82</u>, 92, <u>96</u>, 98, <u>104</u>, 105, 108, <u>120</u>, 122, 130, 132, 134, <u>142</u>.

Here, $\theta = 108$, $n_1 = 6$, $n_2 = 7$, $u = 4$, $v = 2$, $t = 6$

The probability

$$f_U(u) = \frac{\binom{6}{4}\binom{7}{3}}{\binom{13}{6}}$$

$$= 0.184$$

Since $f_U(u) = 0.184 > \alpha/2$, we accept H_0.

This leads to the conclusion that the distribution of pulse rates before and after medication with regard to median are same.

Q. 31. *Describe Wald-Wolfowitz runs test for identicalness of two populations.*

Ans. Wald-Wolfowitz runs test uses the data of two random samples $X_1, X_2, ..., X_m$ and $Y_1, Y_2, ..., Y_n$ of sizes m and n from two populations F_1 and F_2 respectively. The hypothesis under test is

H_0: the populations F_1 and F_2 are identical

vs. H_1 : the two populations F_1 and F_2 differ in any respect whatsoever, the measure of location or dispersion.

Notationally, we test

H_0: $F_X(x) = F_Y(x)$ for all x

vs. H_1 : $F_X(x) \neq F_Y(x)$ for some x

Suppose $m = 5$ and $n = 6$. Let the combined ordered statistic is

XX | YY | X | Y | X | YYY | X.

So there are 7 runs in all.

Suppose the total number of runs in the pooled ordered arrangement of m X's and nY's are denoted by the random variable R. Now to take a decision about H_0, the critical region for Wald-Wolfowitz runs test of level α is given by

$$R \leq r_\alpha$$

where r_α is chosen to the largest integer such that under H_0, $P(R \leq r_\alpha) \leq \alpha$.

The decision rule is, reject H_0 at $\alpha/2 = 0.025$ (say) if the computed value of R is less than or equal to the tabulated value of r for m and n sample sizes.

Large sample approximation: When either m or n is greater than 20, critical value of r is not available in the table. Hence in such a situation, distribution of R can be approximated to normal distribution with,

$$\text{mean } (R) = \frac{2mn}{m+n} + 1$$

and

$$\text{var } (R) = \frac{2mn(2mn - m - n)}{(m+n)^2\,(m+n-1)}$$

Thus, the normal deviate

$$Z = \frac{R - \text{mean}(R)}{\sqrt{\text{var}(R)}}$$

where $Z \sim N(0, 1)$.

The decision about H_0 is taken in the usual manner.

Q. 32. *Explicate Mann-Whitney U-test for testing the identicalness of two populations.*

Ans. Let the two random samples from two populations be $X_1, X_2, ..., X_{n_1}$ and $Y_1, Y_2, ..., Y_{n_2}$. The hypothesis whether the two samples have come from two identical populations can be tested by Mann-Whitney U-test. It is a good substitute for t-test when the conditions imposed on parent populations are not met. This test is based on the criterion of the magnitude of Y's in relation to X's or *vice versa*. Here, we test

$H_0: F_X(x) = F_Y(x)$ for all x

vs. $H_1: F_X(x) \neq F_Y(x)$ for some x.

We may use one-sided test if there is some prior information whether $F_X(x) > F_Y(x)$ or $F_X(x) < F_Y(x)$. Also assume that $F_X(x)$ and $F_Y(x)$ both are continuous. It avoids the chance of tied observations.

Under the Mann-Whitney procedure, combine the data of two samples and arrange them in ascending order. Keep track which observation belongs to which sample. Statistic U is defined as the number of times

Y's precede the X's in the combined sequence of $(n_1 + n_2)$ variate values. Here we define an indicator variable D_{ij} to compute U

$$\text{where, } D_{ij} = \begin{bmatrix} 1 \text{ if } Y_j < X_i \text{ for } i = 1, 2, \ldots, n_1 \\ 0 \text{ if } Y_j > X_i \text{ for } j = 1, 2, \ldots, n_2 \end{bmatrix}$$

$$\text{and} \quad U = \sum_{i=1}^{n_1} \sum_{j=1}^{n_2} D_{ij}$$

Obviously D_{ij} are the Bernoulli variables with $P(D_{ij} = 1) = P(Y < X) = \pi$.

If H_0 is true for all x, $P(X < Y) = P(Y < X) = \frac{1}{2} = \pi$.

Hence, we have to test

$$H_0 : \pi = \frac{1}{2} \text{ for all } x, \text{ vs. } H_1 : \pi \neq \frac{1}{2} \text{ for some } x.$$

Decision about H_0 can be taken by comparing the calculated value of U with the tabulated value of U for sample-sizes n_1 and n_2, and at a level of significance.

Alternative approach: The value of U can also be obtained by considering the sum of the ranks S_2 of Y's (the case when Y precedes X) in the ordered combined sequence. The formula for U is,

$$U = n_1 n_2 + \frac{n_2(n_2 + 1)}{2} - S_2$$

Similarly, if the ranks of X's are counted (the case when X precedes Y), the value of U' can be obtained by the formula,

$$U' = n_1 n_2 + \frac{n_1(n_1 + 1)}{2} - S_1$$

where S_1 is the sum of rank's of X's in the combined sequence of X's and Y's.

It is interesting to point out that the value of U obtained by the use of indicator variable D_{ij} or directly by the formula are same. Also there exists a relation between U and U' which is given as,

$$U' = n_1 n_2 - U$$

This relation helps to obtain U' when U is known and *vice-versa* without redoing the whole calculations and is often required for getting the probabilities under Mann-Whitney U-test or the critical value of U for different values of n_1 and n_2.

Large sample case: If n_1 and n_2 are so large that the tabulated probabilities or critical values of U are not available, then the distribution of U can be approximated to normal distribution with

$$\text{mean } (U) = \frac{n_1 n_2}{2} \text{ and var } (U) = \frac{n_1 n_2 (n_1 + n_2 + 1)}{12}$$

The test statistic is,

$$Z = \frac{U - \frac{n_1 n_2}{2}}{\sqrt{\frac{n_1 n_2 (n_1 + n_2 + 1)}{12}}}$$

where $Z \sim N(0, 1)$

The decision about H_0 can be taken in the usual way.

Q. 33. *Given the score of two groups of persons, the one under placebo and other under drug are as follows:*

Scores under placebo (X)	*Scores under drug (Y)*
10	20
13	14
12	7
15	9
16	17
8	18
6	19
	25
	24

Test that the distributions of scores under placebo and under drug are identical.

Ans. We test

$$H_0 : F_X(x) = F_Y(x) \text{ vs. } H_1 : F_X(x) \neq F_Y(x)$$

The combined ordered sequence is,

	6,	7,	8,	9,	10,	12,	13,	14,
	X	Y	X	Y	X	X	X	Y
ranks	1	2	3	4	5	6	7	8
	15,	16,	17,	18,	19,	20,	24,	25
	X	X	Y	Y	Y	Y	Y	Y
ranks	9	10	11	12	13	14	15	16

Now find D_{ij} in case, Y precedes X.

$D_{i1} = 6, D_{i2} = 5, D_{i3} = 2, D_{i4} = 0, D_{i5} = 0, ...$

$U = \Sigma D_{ij} = 6 + 5 + 2 + 0 + 0 = 13$

For the given question, $n_1 = 7, n_2 = 9$.

The sum of ranks of $Y = S_2 = 95$

$$U = 7 \times 9 + \frac{9(9+1)}{2} - 95$$

$$= 13$$

Here it is shown that the value of U obtained in either way remains same.

The decision about H_0 can be taken by comparing the calculated value of U with the tabulated value of U from the table XIV.b, *Basic Statistics* by B.L. Agarwal. Tabulated value of U for $n_1 = 7$, $n_2 = 9$ and $\alpha = 0.05$ is 12. Since the critical value of U is less than the calculated value, we reject H_0. It leads to the conclusion that distribution of scores under the drug and placebo are not identical.

Q. 34. *How can one perform Mcnemar's test for the significance of change?*

Ans. Mcnemar's test to see the effect of some treatment, training or advertisement which brings about the change in attitude of individuals. This test is particularly useful when the measurements are on nominal or ordinal scale.

Here we test

H_0 : There is no significant change in individuals after the treatment.

vs. H_1 : There is a significant change in individuals after the treatment.

As a test procedure, prepare a (2 × 2) contingency table denoting a positive response by +ve sign and a negative response by – sign. So the table will be of the kind

		After Treat.	
		–	+
Before Treat.	+	A	B
	–	C	D

(1, 1)th and (2, 2)th cells give the number of individuals which showed change, *i.e.* $(A + D)$.

Under null hypothesis, the expected frequencies corresponding to A and D will be $(A + D)/2$ and $(A + D)/2$ respectively. In case of contingency table, χ^2 test is applicable. Here we confine our attention to two cells which indicate a change. Thus the Chi-square test statistic is,

$$\chi^2 = \sum \frac{(O_i - E_i)^2}{E_i}$$

$$= \frac{\left(A - \frac{A+D}{2}\right)^2}{(A+D)/2} + \frac{\left(D - \frac{A+D}{2}\right)^2}{(A+D)/2}$$

$$= \frac{(A-D)^2}{(A+D)}$$

χ^2 has 1 d.f.

When the expected frequency in either cell A or D or both is small, use Yates' correction. Under Yates' correction, the statistic

$$\chi^2 = \frac{(|A-D|-1)^2}{(A+D)}$$

The decision about H_0 is taken in the usual manner.

Q. 35. *An opinion survey was conducted about the GATT treaty from a group of 25 persons, whether they favour (+) it or against (–) it. They were exposed to certain lectures and discussions for a few weeks time. Again their opinion were taken about the GATT treaty. The results were as follows:*

		After Lect. & Discussion	
		–	+
Initially	+	4	5
	–	2	14

Test whether there is a significant change in the opinion of persons. [Given : $\chi^2_{0.05,1} = 3.841$]

Ans. Here we test

H_0 : There is no change in opinion after lectures and discussions.

vs. H_1 : There is a change in opinion after lectures and discussions.

We apply Mcnemar's test and also apply Yates' correction. Thus,

$$\chi^2 = \frac{(|4-14|-1)^2}{(4+14)}$$

$$= \frac{81}{18}$$

$$= 4.50$$

Calculated value of χ^2 = 4.50, which is greater than 3.841. Hence we reject H_0. This leads to the conclusion that the opinion about GATT treaty changed significantly after lectures and discussions.

Q. 36. *Give Mood's test procedure to test the equality of two population dispersions.*

Ans. To test the equality of two variances, *F*-test is most frequently used. But *F*-test is valid when two populations are normally distributed. But often the populations are non-normal. In that situation there is a desideration for some other test. In this endeavour Mood's test is the first test of choice to test,

$$H_0 : \sigma_1 = \sigma_2 \text{ vs. } H_0 : \sigma_1 \neq \sigma_2$$

or $$H_0 : \sigma_1 \leq \sigma_2 \text{ vs. } H_1 : \sigma_1 > \sigma_2$$

or $$H_0 : \sigma_1 \geq \sigma_2 \text{ vs. } H_1 : \sigma_1 < \sigma_2$$

where σ_1 and σ_2 are not necessarily standard deviations but some measure of dispersion, and has to make some more assumptions besides general assumptions like,

(*i*) The data consists of two random samples $X_1, X_2, \ldots, X_{n_1}$ and $Y_1, Y_2, \ldots, Y_{n_2}$ from two populations F_1 and F_2 respectively where $n_1 \leq n_2$.

(*ii*) The data are measured at least on ordinal scale.

(*iii*) The two populations median are equal and populations are identical except possibly for a difference in dispersion measures.

To perform the test, combine both the samples, arrange them in ascending order and rank them. The mood's test statistic is

$$M = \sum_{i=1}^{n_1} \left(r_i - \frac{n+1}{2}\right)^2$$

where r_i is the rank of X_i's in the joint ordered statistics and $n = n_1 + n_2$.

As a matter of fact, the right hand expression in the above statistic is the sum of square of deviations of the rank's of *X*'s from the overall mean rank.

Decision about H_0 is taken by comparing the value of *M* with the tabulated critical value of *M* given by mood in Daniel's book, *Applied Nonparametric Statistics*. This table provides two values of *M*, the one *M*′ and the other *M*″. For a two-sided test, *M*′ is located in the column equal to $\alpha/2$, where α is the predecided level of significance, which is the first entry in the row of n_1 and n_2 and also *M*″ in the column of $(1 - \alpha/2)$, which is the third column entry in the row of n_1 and n_2. Reject H_0 if $M < M'$ or $M \geq M''$, otherwise accept H_0.

For one-sided alternative $\sigma_1 > \sigma_2$, reject H_0 if $M \leq M''$ where M'' is the critical value of *M* which is the third entry in the column of $(1 - \alpha)$ and the row of n_1 and n_2.

Again for one-sided alternative $\sigma_1 < \sigma_2$, reject H_0 if $M \leq M'$ where M' is the critical value of *M* which is the first entry in the column of α and the row of n_1 and n_2.

Q. 37. *For the problem given in Q. No. 30, test that the populations of pulse rate before and after medication are identical with regard to a measure of dispersion. Perform the test at 5 per cent level of significance.*

Ans. Safely it can be assumed that the populations have equal median.

Also, $n_1 = 6$, $n_2 - 7$ and $n_1 < n_2$.

We test $H_0 : \sigma_1 = \sigma_2$ vs. $H_1 : \sigma_1 \neq \sigma_2$

The combined ordered sequence with their ranks is:

Combined ordered Sequence:	<u>82</u>,	92,	<u>96</u>,	<u>98</u>,	<u>104</u>,	105,	108,
Ranks:	(1)	2	(3)	(4)	(5)	6	7

Combined ordered Sequence:	<u>120</u>,	122,	130,	132,	134,	<u>142</u>,
Ranks:	(8)	9	10	11	12	(13)

The value of $M = 102$.

From the table A.9 of Daniel *Applied Nonparametric Statistics*, $M'_{.025,\,(6,\,7)} = 38$ and $M''_{0.975,\,(6,\,7)} = 130$. The calculated value of $M > 38$ and < 130. Hence, we accept H_0. It means that the two populations of blood pressure with and without medication are identical with regard to measure of dispersion.

Q. 38. *Explicate Moses' test for equality of two population dispersion measures.*

Ans. Moses' test is more general than Mood's test in the sense that one has not to assume the equality of medians of the two population. *Secondly*, it is not necessary that $n_1 < n_2$. Rest of the assumptions remain the same.

Here we have to test,

$$H_0 : \sigma_1 = \sigma_2 \text{ vs. } H_1 : \sigma_1 \neq \sigma_2$$

or $$H_0 : \sigma_1 \leq \sigma_2 \text{ vs. } H_1 : \sigma_1 > \sigma_2$$

or $$H_0 : \sigma_1 \geq \sigma_2 \text{ vs. } H_1 : \sigma_1 < \sigma_2$$

Test procedure is totally different from all procedures. In this, we have two independent samples

say, sample $X : X_1, X_2, \ldots, X_{n_1}$

and sample $Y : Y_1, Y_2, \ldots, Y_{n_2}$.

Different steps for the test procedure are:

Step-1. Divide X's at random into sub-samples of arbitrary chosen size k. Discard left over observations. Let the number of these sub-samples is m_1.

Step-2. Repeat step-1 for Y's. Let the number of sub-samples of Y's is m_2.

Step-3. For each sub-sample of X's, calculate the sum of squares of the deviations from mean *i.e.*, $\Sigma(X - \bar{X})^2$.

Step-4. For each sub-sample of Y's, calculate $\Sigma(Y - \bar{Y})^2$.

Now the quantities $\Sigma(X - \bar{X})^2$ and $\Sigma(Y - \bar{Y})^2$ are our variate values with m_1 and m_2 sample sizes randomly. Let them be denoted as $u_1, u_2, \ldots, u_{m_1}$ and $v_1, v_2, \ldots, v_{m_2}$ respectively.

Step-5. Now apply Mann-Whitney test taking u's and v's as two independent samples of sizes m_1 and m_2 respectively.

Step-6. Calculate the statistic,

$$U = S - \frac{m_1(m_1 + 1)}{2}$$

where, S is the sum of ranks of u's.

Step-7. To decide about H_0, compare the calculated value of U with W of Moses table A.8 in Daniel's *Applied Nonparametric Statistics*.

For a two-sided test reject H_0, if $U \leq W_{\alpha/2,\,(m_1,\,m_2)}$ or $U \geq W_{1-\alpha/2,\,(m_1,\,m_2)}$, otherwise accept H_0.

For a one-sided test $H_1 : \sigma_1 > \sigma_2$, reject H_0 in favour of H_1 if $U \geq W_{1-\alpha,\,(m_1,\,m_2)}$, otherwise accept H_0.

For a one-sided hypothesis $H_1 : \sigma_1 < \sigma_2$, reject H_0 in favour of H_1 if $U \leq W_{\alpha,\,(m_1,\,m_2)}$, otherwise accept H_0.

Note: As regards the sub-sample size k, it should be large enough but not more than 10. Also K should be chosen in such a way that m_1 and m_2 are large enough to yield meaningful results.

Q. 39. *In a study on goats, the body weight of 3-month-old 26 goats and of 6-month-old 22 goats were as follows:*

Body weight (in kg) of 3-month-old goats (X): 13.0, 7.5, 8.0, 11.5, 6.4, 9.0, 12.0, 10.5, 12.8, 10.2, 7.6, 10.1, 13.0, 14.0, 7.4, 7.8, 10.5, 9.7, 12.5, 9.2, 9.7, 11.6, 14.4, 12.8, 12.5, 14.5.

Body weight (in kg) of 6-month old goats (Y): 11.3, 11.7, 17.0, 10.0, 9.0, 16.4, 15.3, 15.5, 13.8, 12.7, 14.7, 18.0, 12.5, 13.4, 13.7, 17.7, 13.3, 9.6, 14.7, 17.0, 16.5, 15.3.

Test by Moses' method whether two populations of goats have equal dispersion in weights at 5 per cent level of significance.

Ans. Here we test $H_0 : \sigma_1 = \sigma_2$ vs. $H_1 : \sigma_1 \neq \sigma_2$. Let us take $k = 5$.

So for the given data $m_1 = 5$ and $m_2 = 4$.

Now we draw sub-sample randomly and calculate the sum of squares of the deviations from mean for both the samples.

Sample No.	*Sub-samples (X)*	$\Sigma(X-\bar{X})^2$
1.	10.2, 11.6, 11.8, 7.8, 7.6	21.04
2.	12.5, 9.7, 9.7, 12.0, 7.5	16.29
3.	12.8, 10.2, 13.0, 14.5, 13.0	9.68
4.	6.4, 14.0, 11.5, 8.0, 10.5	35.43
5.	7.5, 9.2, 9.0, 10.5, 12.5	14.05

Sample No.	*Sub-samples (Y)*	$\Sigma(Y-\bar{Y})^2$
1.	11.3, 17.0, 15.3, 16.0, 13.7	19.89
2.	14.7, 18.0, 9.0, 14.7, 13.8	42.01
3.	10.0, 15.5, 16.5, 15.3, 11.7	31.28
4.	13.3, 17.0, 12.5, 9.6, 13.4	27.93

Discarded X-value =10.1

Discarded Y-values = 12.7, 17.7

Combine the quantities $\Sigma(X-\bar{X})^2$ and $\Sigma(Y-\bar{Y})^2$ and arrange them in ascending order. The quantities for $\Sigma(X-\bar{X})^2$ are underlined to keep track.

Combined order statistics:	$\underline{9.68}$,	$\underline{14.05}$,	$\underline{16.29}$,	19.89,	$\underline{21.04}$,
Ranks:	(1)	(2)	(3)	4	(5)
Combined order statistics:	27.93,	31.28,	$\underline{35.43}$,	42.01,	
Ranks:	6	7	(8)	9	

Sum of rank's of u's, *i.e.*, $S = 19$

The test statistic

$$U = 19 - 5(5+1)/2$$
$$= 4$$

Tabulated value of $W_{0.025,(5,\,4)} = 2$

Since $U = 4 > W_{0.025,(5,\,4)}$, we reject H_0. It means that the two populations of goats have unequal measures of dispersion.

Q. 40. *When do you use Cochran's Q-test and how to apply it?*

Ans. Cochran's Q-test is used to test the equality of certain treatments particularly when the observations can be dichotomatised say success coded as 1 and failure coded as 0.

We test

H_0 : The treatments are equally effective

vs. H_1 : All are not equally effective.

In the experiment, the treatments are applied to as many equal size groups of units as the number of treatments. Suppose there are r groups and each group contains k units. The observations can be arranged in a $r \times k$ table as follows:

Groups	*Treatments*						*Total*
	1	*2*	...	*j*	...	*k*	
1	x_{11}	x_{12}	...	x_{1j}	...	x_{1k}	R_1
2	x_{21}	x_{22}	...	x_{2j}	...	x_{2k}	R_2
⋮	⋮						⋮
i	x_{i1}	x_{i2}	...	x_{ij}	...	x_{ik}	R_i
⋮	⋮						⋮
r	x_{r1}	x_{r2}	...	x_{rj}	...	x_{rk}	R_r
Total	C_1	C_2	...	C_j	...	C_k	n

Suppose, $x_{ij} = 1$ if the treatment effect is favourable and

$x_{ij} = 0$ if it is not.

To test H_0, the test statistic

$$Q = \frac{k(k-1)\sum_{j=1}^{k} C_j^2 - (k-1)\,n^2}{kn - \sum_{i=1}^{r} R_i^2}$$

The statistic Q is approximately distributed as χ^2 with $(k-1)$ d.f. Here a precaution is required while approximating the distribution of Q to χ^2. The number of treatments should be at least 4 and total number of observations be at least 24. If it is less than 24, construct the exact distribution of Q or use special tables prepared by Tata and Brown in 1964 available in a monograph at University of Pennsylvania. Also if there are all 0's or 1's in any group (block), delete that group for the purpose of analysis provided the remaining observations are not less than 24.

Q. 41. *Eight groups of a fruit each consisting of 4 fruits were stored, one under four different storage methods. The fruits were examined after a week. If the fruit was putrefied, it was coded as 1 and if not putrefied, then 0. The results of the experiments are presented in the following table:*

	Storage Methods				
Groups	*I*	*II*	*III*	*IV*	*Total*
1	*0*	*1*	*0*	*1*	*2*
2	*1*	*0*	*0*	*0*	*1*
3	*1*	*1*	*0*	*0*	*2*
4	*1*	*1*	*1*	*0*	*3*
5	*0*	*0*	*0*	*1*	*1*
6	*0*	*1*	*0*	*0*	*1*
7	*1*	*0*	*1*	*1*	*3*
8	*0*	*1*	*1*	*0*	*2*
Total	*4*	*5*	*3*	*3*	*15*

Test whether there is any difference in storage methods in respect of putrefication. [*Given:* $\chi^2_{0.05,3} = 7.81$]

Ans. We test,

H_0: All the storage methods are equally good.

vs. H_1 : At least two of them differ significantly.

The test statistic

$$Q = \frac{4(4-1)(4^2+5^2+3^2+3^2)-3\times 15^2}{4\times 15-(2^2+1^2+2^2+3^2+1^2+1^2+3^2+2^2)}$$

$$= \frac{708-675}{60-33}$$

$$= 1.22$$

Since the calculated value $\chi^2 = 1.22 < 7.81$, the tabulated value, H_0 is accepted. It leads to the conclusion that all the storage methods are equally effective.

Q. 42. *Give Kruskal-Wallis method of analysis for one way classification of data.*

Ans. Kruskal-Wall test is one of the most frequently used method in nonparametric statistics for analysing data in one way classification. It is equivalent to one way analysis of variance in parametric methods.

We test the identicalness of k populations (in respect of medians) from which the independent samples have been drawn. There is no restriction on sample sizes.

***Assumptions*:** Kruskal-Wallis test is based on the following assumptions:

1. The observations are independent within and between samples.
2. The variable under study is continuous.
3. The populations are identical except possibly in respect of median.

We test

H_0: All the populations are identical.

vs. H_1 : At least one pair of populations do not have the same median.

Let there be k independent samples from k populations of sizes $n_1, n_2, ..., n_k$. The observations in k samples can always be presented in the tabular form as given below:

Sample Numbers					
1	2	...	*i*	...	*k*
x_{11}	x_{21}	...	x_{i1}	...	x_{k1}
x_{12}	x_{22}	...	x_{i2}	...	x_{k2}
⋮	⋮		⋮		⋮
x_{1n_1}	x_{2n_2}	...	x_{in_i}	...	x_{kn_k}

Assign rank to each observation from 1 to $N = \sum_{i=1}^{n} n_i$ by pooling all the sample observations and writing them in ascending order. The sum of ranks is obviously equal to $\frac{N(N+1)}{2}$. Under H_0, the sum of the ranks would be divided in proportion to sample size among k samples.

For the ith sample of size n_i, the expected sum of ranks is

$$\frac{n_i}{N}\frac{N(N+1)}{2} = \frac{n_i(N+1)}{2}$$

Suppose R_i is the actual sum of ranks of observations in sample i.

To test H_0, Kruskal-Wallis test statistic is a weighted sum of squares of deviations of the sum of ranks of the treatments from the expected sum of ranks, using reciprocals of sample size as the weights. The Kruskal-Wallis statistic in notational form is,

$$H = \frac{12}{N(N+1)}\sum_{i=1}^{k}\frac{1}{n_i}\left[R_i - \frac{n_i(N+1)}{2}\right]^2$$

$$= \frac{12}{N(N+1)}\sum_{i=1}^{k}\frac{R_i^2}{n_i} - 3(N+1)$$

The statistic H is approximately distributed as χ^2 with $(k-1)$ d.f. subject to the condition that n_i should be large, *i.e.*, each n_i should not be less than 5.

The decision about H_0 can be taken in the usual manner.

Note: When $k = 2$, H test reduces to Mann-Whitney U-test. Some people call it Wilcoxon's U-test.

Q. 43. *What adjustment has to be made for ties in Kruskal-Wallis H?*

Ans. If there are a substantial number of ties, one must adjust H for ties. The adjustment factor

$$C = \frac{\Sigma T}{n(n^2-1)}$$

where $T = (t^3 - t)$ for t, the number of tied observations in a group and Σ is overall such groups. The corrected test statistic,

$$H_C = H/C.$$

Q. 44. *Wool yield of three groups of ewe lambs under different feeding regimen (in kg) was as given below:*

Feed 1 (pasture)	*Feed ll Pasture + concentrate*	*Feed lll Pasture + concentrate + minerals*
8.78	5.16	9.92
6.23	9.64	14.74
7.65	6.52	7.93
5.10	5.38	11.90
5.95	6.80	10.77
8.50		7.37
10.20		7.08
		5.67

From the experimental data, test whether the three types of feeds affect the wool yield.

[Given: $\chi^2_{0.05,2} = 5.99$]

Ans. In this problem, we have to test

H_0 : The three feeds are equally effective

vs. H_1 : At least two feeds do not have the same effect on the production of wool.

To test H_0 we first assign ranks to each yield value by pooling them and tabulate them as given below:

	Ranks	*Sums*	*Sample size*
Feed I	14, 6, 11, 1, 5, 13, 17	67	7
Feed II	2, 15, 7, 3, 8	35	5
Feed III	16, 20, 12, 19, 18, 10, 9, 4	108	8
			$N = 20$

The test statistic

$$H = \frac{12}{20 \times 21}\left(\frac{67^2}{7} + \frac{35^2}{5} + \frac{108^2}{8}\right) - 3 \times 21$$

$$= 3.98$$

Calculated $\chi^2 = 3.98 < 5.99$, the tabulated value of χ^2 at 5 per cent level of significance and 2 d.f., we do not reject H_0. It means that the three feeds are equally effective.

Q. 45. *Delineate Friedman's two way analysis of variance by ranks.*

Ans. When the assumptions necessitated for two way analysis of variance in parametric test do not hold good, the data can be analysed by Friedman's nonparametric procedure. The method utilises the ranks within a block. Suppose there are k treatments and r blocks, each block of size k. Each treatment occurs once in each block.

Assumptions for Friedman's test are same as per Kruskal-Wallis test.

The data for r blocks and k treatments can be presented in the following two-way table:

Blocks	Samples (Treatments)			
	1	2	...	k
1	x_{11}	x_{12}	...	x_{1k}
2	x_{21}	x_{22}	...	x_{2k}
⋮	⋮			
r	x_{r1}	x_{r2}	...	x_{rk}

We test

H_0: All treatments have same effect.

vs. H_1: All treatments do not have the same effect.

To test H_0, assign ranks to all observations from 1 to k (lowest to highest) in each block independently. Under H_0, it is expected that the sum of ranks in all columns will almost be the same. It the difference in sum of ranks of the columns is remarkable, it cannot be left to random variation. Hence, we have to delve deep. For this, Friedman gave the following test.

Suppose R_{ij} is the rank of the observation in i^{th} row and j^{th} column for $i = 1, 2, \ldots, r$ and $j = 1, 2, \ldots, k$. So the two-way table for ranks can be displayed as below:

Blocks	Treatments				Total
	1	2	...	k	
1	R_{11}	R_{12}	...	R_{1k}	$k(k+1)/2$
2	R_{21}	R_{22}	...	R_{2k}	$k(k+1)/2$
⋮	⋮			⋮	⋮
r	R_{r1}	R_{r2}	...	R_{rk}	$k(k+1)/2$
Total	R_1	R_2	...	R_k	$rk(k+1)/2$

Friedman's test statistic under H_0 is,

$$F = \frac{12}{rk(k+1)} \sum_{j=1}^{k} R_j^2 - 3r(k+1)$$

The statistic F is approximately distributed as Chi-square with $k - 1$ d.f. Reject H_0, if χ^2_{cal} is greater than or equal to the tabulated value of χ^2 for α level of significance and $(k - 1)$ d.f., otherwise accept H_0.

Q. 46. *What adjustment factor should be used in Friedman's test statistic F when there are ample number of tied observations in blocks?*

Ans. In case of ample number of tied observations within blocks, an adjustment in Friedman's F-statistic has to be made.

The adjustment factor is

$$C = 1 - \sum_{i=1}^{r} \frac{T_i}{rk(k^2 - 1)}$$

where $T_i = \Sigma t_i^3 - \Sigma t_i$, where t_i is the number of tied observations for a given rank in the ith block. The adjusted Friedman's test statistic

$$F_C = F/C.$$

Q. 47. *How can you make multiple comparison in Friedman's test when H_0 is rejected?*

Ans. We can make comparison of all possible pairs of treatment effects by the following relation. For any two treatment rank totals R_j and R'_j for $j \neq j'$, the difference is significant if and only if,

$$| Rj - R'_j | \geq Z\sqrt{\frac{rk(k+1)}{6}}$$

where for α size of the test, Z is the standard normal deviate corresponding to $\alpha/k\,(k-1)$.

Q. 48. *Four technicians determined the percent moisture content of the samples of a powder manufactured by five different companies. Their determinations of moisture contents were as follows:*

Technicians	*Moisture Content (%) Companies*				
	1	*2*	*3*	*4*	*5*
A	*9*	*10*	*8*	*11*	*12*
B	*10*	*11*	*9*	*7*	*12*
C	*9*	*10*	*8*	*12*	*11*
D	*8*	*11*	*7*	*14*	*12*

Test whether the per cent moisture content in the powder of five companies is same.

[*Given:* $\chi^2_{0.05,4} = 9.49$]

Ans. We have to test

H_0: The moisture content in the powder of five companies is same.

vs. H_1: The moisture content in the powder of at least two companies differ significantly.

Since the data are not normal, it is preferable to apply Friedman's method of two-way analysis.

Assigning ranks to each observation for each technician independently, we get the following data of ranks:

Technicians	Companies				
	1	2	3	4	5
A	2	3	1	4	5
B	3	4	2	1	5
C	2	3	1	5	4
D	2	3	1	5	4
Total	9	13	5	15	18

The value of the test statistic

$$F = \frac{12}{4 \times 5 \times 6}(9^2 + 13^2 + 5^2 + 15^2 + 18^2) - 3 \times 4 \times 6$$

$$= \frac{824}{10} - 72$$

$$= 10.4$$

Since the computed value of $F = 10.4$ is greater than the tabulated value of $\chi^2_{0.05,4} = 9.49$, we reject H_0. This shows that the moisture content in the powder of five companies is not same.

Q. 49. *How can you perform the Jonckheere-Terpstra test for ordered alternatives?*

Ans. The Jonckheere-Terpstra test is a test specially designed for testing the null hypothesis of equality of treatment means against ordered alternatives. Notationally we test

$H_0 : \mu_1 = \mu_2 = \ldots = \mu_k$ vs. $H_1 : \mu_1 \leq \mu_2 \leq \ldots \leq \mu_k$

where $\mu_1, \mu_2, \ldots, \mu_k$ are k treatment (sample) means. Assumptions for this test are same as for Kruskal-Wallis test.

The test statistic is

$$J = \sum_{i<j} U_{ij}$$

where U_{ij} is the number of pairs of observations in which an observation X_{ia} under the treatment a is less than of all values under the treatment b. Also we compare all pairs of different treatments in a sequence.

To draw a decision about H_0, compare the value of computed J with the critical value of J for α level of significance, K treatments (populations) and n_1, n_2, ... n_k sample sizes. Reject H_0, if $J \geq J_{\alpha, n_1, n_2, \ldots, n_k}$ otherwise accept H_0.

Note: If two values are equal in a paired comparison, it gets a value 1/2.

Q. 50. *For the problem given in Q. No. 44, test the equality of feeds effect against the assertion that feed I is inferior than feed II and feed II than III.*

Ans. Let the feeds I, II and III mean effects be denoted by τ_1, τ_2 and τ_3 respectively.

Here we have to test

$$H_0 : \tau_1 = \tau_2 = \tau_3 \quad \text{vs.} \quad H_1 : \tau_1 \leq \tau_2 \leq \tau_3$$

To calculate the value of J, compare feeds I and II, I and III and II and III.

$$U_{\text{I, II}} = 1 + 3 + 1 + 5 + 3 + 1 + 0 = 14$$

$$U_{\text{I, III}} = 4 + 7 + 5 + 8 + 7 + 4 + 3 = 38$$

$$U_{\text{II, III}} = 8 + 4 + 7 + 8 + 7 = 34$$

Thus, $\Sigma U_{ij} = 14 + 38 + 34 = 86$

Critical value of J for $\alpha = 0.05$, $k = 3$, $n_1 = 5$, $n_2 = 7$, $n_3 = 8$ from the table A-14 of Daniel's *Applied Nonparametric Statistics*, is 89. Since computed value of $J = 86 < 89$, accept H_0. It means all the feeds are equally effective with regard to the wool yield.

Q. 51. *Discuss Page's test for ordered alternatives in two-way analysis of data.*

Ans. Let T_j be the effect of jth treatment of $j = 1, 2, \ldots, k$.

To test the hypothesis

$$H_0 : \tau_1 = \tau_2 = \ldots = \tau_k \quad \text{vs.} \quad H_1 : \tau_1 \leq \tau_2 \leq \ldots \leq \tau_k$$

Page's test is quite suitable. In this test, ranks are independently assigned to observations within each block. Also care should be taken that the treatments $T_1, T_2, \ldots, T_k$ be written in the same order as they occur in the alternative hypothesis. Page's test statistic is

$$L = 1R_1 + 2R_2 + \ldots + kR_k$$

$$= \sum_{j=1}^{k} jR_j$$

The decision rule is, reject H_0 if the computed value of L is greater than or equal to the critical value of L for α level of significance, the number of treatments k and r, the number of blocks. Consult table A.16 of Daniel's *Applied Nonparametric Statistics*. E.B. Page tables are available only for maximum $k = 8$ and different number of blocks. Hence, for large k, we can apply normal deviate test for which the statistic

$$Z = \frac{L - \left[rk(k+1)^2/4\right]}{\sqrt{r(k^3 - k)^2/144(k-1)}}$$

$Z \sim N(0, 1)$.

The decision about H_0 can be taken in the usual manner.

Q. 52. *For the problem of Q. No. 48, test the equality of moisture content in the powder of five companies, i.e., test H_0: $M_1 = M_2 = \ldots = M_5$ against the ordered alternative H_1: $M_1 \leq M_2 \leq M_3 \leq M_4 \leq M_5$.*

Ans. To test H_0 against H_1, we use the rank sums of the five columns as such. Thus, the test statistic

$$L = 1 \times 9 + 2 \times 13 + 3 \times 5 + 4 \times 15 + 5 \times 18 = 200$$

The critical value of L for $\alpha = 0.05$, $k = 5$ and $r = 4$ is 197. Since the computed value of $L = 200 > 197$, we reject H_0. This reveals that the moisture content in the powder of five companies is not equal.

Q. 53. *How to measure the association between ranks of individuals awarded by two judges or investigators independently?*

Ans. In many situations, the individuals are ranked by two judges or the measurements taken for two variables are assigned ranks within the samples independently. Now it is desired to know the extent of association between the ranks. The method of calculating the association between ranks was given by Charles Edward Spearman in 1906 and is known as *Spearman's rank correlation.* In common parlance, the term *rank correlation* alone stands for Spearman's rank correlation.

If for n individuals, d_i is the difference between ranks of the ith individual for $i = 1, 2, \ldots, n$; the formula for Spearman's rank correlation is,

$$r_S = 1 - \frac{6\Sigma d_i^2}{n(n^2 - 1)}$$

The formula for r_S is based on the usual Pearsonian formula for correlation coefficient. Here it is assumed that no ties occur in the ranks within a sample.

The value of r_S lies between -1 and 1.

Q. 54. *If the ties occur within the samples, how the formula for rank correlation is amended?*

Ans. Often the measurements are taken on individuals and then ranked. In such a situation, sometimes ties do occur. If so, then a correction has to be made in rank correlation. If the number of tied observations in X for a particular rank is t_X. There can be more than one t_X in X-sample units. In the same way we can define t_Y. Now define the following values:

$$T_X = \frac{t_X^3 - t_X}{12}, \; T_Y = \frac{t_Y^3 - t_Y}{12},$$

and
$$\sum x^2 = \frac{n^3 - n}{12} - \sum T_X;$$

$$\sum y^2 = \frac{n^3 - n}{12} - \sum T_Y.$$

Σ is overall groups of tied values.

After incorporating the correction for ties, the amended formula for rank correlation is,

$$r_S' = \frac{\Sigma x^2 + \Sigma y^2 - \Sigma d_i^2}{2\sqrt{\Sigma x^2 \, \Sigma y^2}}$$

Q. 55. *How can the significance of Spearman's rank correlation be tested?*

Ans. Kendall in 1962 derived the frequency function of r_S and gave exact critical value r_S. But the approximate test of r_S which is the same as t-test for Pearsonian correlation coefficient is good enough for all practical purposes. Here we test $H_0 : \rho_S = 0$ vs. $H_1 : \rho_S \neq 0$.

The test statistic

$$t = \left[\frac{(n-2)r_s^2}{1 - r_S^2}\right]^{1/2}$$

$$= \frac{r_S\sqrt{n-2}}{\sqrt{1 - r_S^2}}$$

t has $(n - 2)$ d.f.

The decision about H_0 is taken in the usual way.

Q. 56. *Following are the ranks awarded to seven debators in a competition by two judges:*

Debators	*A*	*B*	*C*	*D*	*E*	*F*	*G*
Ranks by judge I (X)	3	2	1	6	7	4	5
Ranks by judge II (Y)	5	6	3	7	4	2	1

Calculate the rank correlation and test its significance. *[Given: $t_{0.05,5} = 2.571$]*

Ans. First, we find d's which are:

d : -2 -4 -2 -1 3 2 4

Also
$$\sum_{i=1}^{7} d_i^2 = 54$$

Thus,
$$r_S = 1 - \frac{6 \times 54}{7 \times 48}$$

$$= 0.036$$

To test $H_0 : \rho_S = 0$ vs. $H_1 : \rho_S \neq 0$, the statistic

$$t = \frac{0.036 \times \sqrt{7-2}}{\sqrt{1 - (0.036)^2}}$$

$$= \frac{0.080}{0.9993}$$

$$= 0.080$$

Calculated value of $t = 0.080 < 2.571$, hence we accept H_0. It means that there is a dissociation between the ranks awarded by two judges.

Q. 57. *What is Kendall's rank correlation coefficient and how to measure it?*

Ans. Kendall's rank correlation coefficient 'τ' is suitable for the paired ranks as in case of Spearman's rank correlation. The condition is that both the variables X and Y be measured at least on ordinal scale.

One advantage of τ over r_S is that τ can be generalised to a partial correlation coefficient which is not possible in case of r_S.

The procedure for calculating τ consists of the following steps:

Step-1. Arrange the rank of the first set (X) in ascending order and rearrange the ranks of the second set (Y) in such a way that n pairs of rank remain the same.

Step-2. After operating step-1, the ranks of X are in natural order. Now we are left to determine how many pairs of ranks in the set Y are in their natural order and how many are not. A number is said to be in natural order if it is smaller than the succeeding number and is coded as +1, and also if it is greater than its succeeding number then it will not be taken in natural order and will be coded as –1. In this way all $\binom{n}{2}$ pairs of the set (*Y*) will be considered and assigned the values +1 and –1.

Step-3. Find the sum '*S*' of all the coded values.

Step-4. The formula for Kendall's rank correlation coefficient τ is,

$$\tau = \frac{S}{\binom{n}{2}} = \frac{\text{Actual value}}{\text{Max. possible value}}$$

$$= \frac{2S}{n(n-1)}$$

Q. 58. *Give the properties of Kendall's correlation τ.*

Ans. Properties of Kendall's τ are:

(*i*) The range of τ is –1 to 1.

(*ii*) For large *n*, there exists an approximate relation between τ and r_S. The relation is,

$$\tau = \frac{2}{3} r_S$$

(*iii*) If τ = 1, it means that there is perfect correspondence between the rankings awarded by two judges or the rankings based on the scores earned by the individuals.

(*iv*) If τ = – 1, it reveals that the ranking of *X* are just in reverse order of the rankings of *Y*.

(*v*) The distribution of τ approaches to normality more rapidly than r_S.

(*vi*) Calculation of τ is considered more cumbersome than r_S.

(*vii*) An important difference between τ and r_S is that τ provides an unbiased estimate of population rank correlation whereas r_S does not.

(*viii*) The distribution of $\hat{\tau}$ tends to normal more rapidly than r_S. So for moderate size samples, $\hat{\tau}$ may provide a more reliable *z*-test statistic than r_S.

(*ix*) For the same set of data, τ and r_S provide different numerical values but on testing hypothesis about them usually lead to the same conclusion.

Q. 59. *How can the problem of tied observation be resolved while calculating Kendall's rank correlation τ?*

Ans. Many times it is possible to grade two or more individuals differently and hence they receive the same rank. The ranks to the tied observations are assigned by using the midrank method. Also there can be more than one group of tied observations in *X* or *Y* or both. Hence, an adjustment is made in the formula for τ.

The formula after adjustment is,

$$\tau = \frac{S}{\sqrt{\frac{1}{2}n(n-1) - \Sigma T_X}\sqrt{\frac{1}{2}n(n-1) - \Sigma T_Y}}$$

where, $T_X = \frac{t_X(t_X - 1)}{2}$; t_X being the number of tied observations in one group of the variable *X*. Also there may be more than one such group. Similarly $T_Y = \frac{t_Y(t_Y - 1)}{2}$ for the variable *Y*.

Q. 60. *How can the significance of τ be tested?*

Ans. Test of significance of τ means testing H_0 : τ = 0, *i.e.*, no correspondence between the ranks of *X* and *Y*.

If no correspondence exists, then for the natural order of ranks of *X*, all possible corresponding arrangements of *Y* are equally likely. Thus, H_0 can be tested under three alternative hypotheses namely,

H_{A+}: Direct association (consider right tailed probability)

H_{A-}: Inverse association (consider left tailed probability)

H_A : No association (consider two-tailed probability)

For the test of H_0 vs. H_A's of size α, direct tables A.20 of Daniel's *Applied Nonparametric Statistics* have been provided for n and α. This table gives the value of τ^*, the critical value of τ. If computed $\tau \geq \tau^*$ reject H_0, otherwise not.

Because of the symmetry of the distribution of τ, the same table is being used for either right or left tailed probability. As an usual practice, for two-sided test, we consult the table for n and $\alpha/2$.

Also for one-tailed test, consult the table for n and α and get the value of τ^*.

If computed τ is positive and greater than τ^*, reject H_0, otherwise not.

If computed τ is negative and smaller than $-\tau^*$, reject H_0, otherwise not.

Again for large n, the distribution of τ can be approximated to normal distribution. For $n > 10$, τ is taken to be distributed normally with mean,

$$\mu_\tau = 0$$

and variance,
$$\sigma_\tau^2 = \frac{2(2n+5)}{9n(n-1)}$$

Hence,
$$Z = \frac{\tau - 0}{\sqrt{\dfrac{2(2n+5)}{9n(n-1)}}}$$

or in terms of S,

$$Z = \frac{S}{\sqrt{n(n-1)\,(2n+5)/18}}$$

The decision about H_0 is taken in the usual way.

Q. 61. *For the problem given in Q. No. 56, calculate Kendall's rank correlation τ and test its significance.*

Ans. We write below the ranks of X in natural order and ranks of Y correspondingly.

X:	1	2	3	4	5	6	7
Y:	3	6	5	2	1	7	4

For this problem, $n = 7$

For S, take the rank 3 and give + 1 or – 1 value for all pairs with subsequent ranks of Y. $3 < 6$, give a number + 1; $3 < 5$, again + 1; $3 > 2$, give a number – 1 and so on. Then choose 6 and take the pairs (6, 5), (6, 2), (6, 1), (6, 7) and (6, 4) and continue the process till we reach the last pair (7, 4). Proceedings in this manner,

$$\begin{aligned} S &= (+1+1-1-1+1+1) + (-1-1-1+1-1) \\ &\quad + (-1-1+1-1) + (-1+1+1) \\ &\quad + (+1+1) + (-1) \\ &= 2-3-2+1+2-1 \\ &= -1 \end{aligned}$$

Thus,
$$\tau = \frac{-2\times 1}{7\times 6} = -0.048$$

To test the significance of τ, we test

$$H_0 : \tau = 0 \quad \text{vs.} \quad H_1 : \tau \neq 0$$

From the table A.2 of Daniel's *Applied Nonparametric Statistics* for $n = 7$ and $\dfrac{\alpha}{2} = 0.025$, $\tau^* = 0.714$.

Since $-0.048 \not< -0.714$, we accept H_0. It reveals that there is no association amongst the ranks awarded by two judges.

Q. 62. *Give the formula for calculating the Kendall's partial rank correlation coefficient between two variables X and Y eliminating the effect of the third variable Z.*

Ans. The formula for calculating Kendall's partial rank correlation coefficient $\tau_{XY \cdot Z}$ is analogous to formula for partial correlation coefficient $r_{12.3}$. Thus,

$$\tau_{XY \cdot Z} = \frac{\tau_{XY} - \tau_{YZ}\,\tau_{XZ}}{\sqrt{(1-\tau_{YZ}^2)(1-\tau_{XZ}^2)}}$$

where τ_{XY}, τ_{XZ}, τ_{YX}, are Kendall's rank correlations.

The value of $\tau_{XY \cdot Z}$ lies between – 1 and + 1. Similar formulae can be given for $\tau_{XZ \cdot Y}$ and $\tau_{YZ \cdot X}$.

Q. 63. *What is coefficient of concordance and how is it calculated?*

Ans. The measure for knowing the agreement or concordance between k ($k \geq 3$) sets of rankings of the same n individuals awarded by k judges or the same n individuals being measured for k variates and then ranked was given by M.G. Kendall.

As a general discussion, one can easily conceive that if all the k judges are in perfect agreement, the sum of the ranks of n individuals would be $1k, 2k, \ldots, n_k$ and if they totally disagree, then the sum of ranks of individuals would be almost equal. From this, it is evident that the degree of agreement between the ranks awarded by k judges is reflected by the degree of variation between the n sums of ranks. So we find the sum of squares of the deviations of the actual n rank totals from the mean.

Under perfect agreement, the sum of squares of the deviations of the actual n rank totals from the average column total will be constant equal to,

$$KS_t = \sum_{j=1}^{n}\left[jk - \frac{k(n+1)}{2}\right]^2$$

$$= \frac{k^2n(n^2-1)}{12}$$

The actual sum of squares of the deviations of observed columns totals from the average column total is equal to

$$S = \sum_{j=1}^{n}\left[R_j - \frac{k(n+1)}{2}\right]^2$$

where R_j is the sum of actual ranks of the jth individual for $j = 1, 2, \ldots, n$.

The coefficient of concordance

$$W = \frac{S}{kS_t}$$

$$= \frac{12S}{k^2n(n^2-1)}$$

The measure 'W' is called the *Kendall's coefficient of concordance.*

Q. 64. *Mention the properties of coefficient of concordance 'W'.*

Ans. Properties of W are:

(*i*) The value of W lies between 0 and 1. It is apparent that W is the ratio of the two sum of squares, and hence, it cannot be negative and greater than 1 because numerator can not exceed the denominator.

(*ii*) If $W = 0$, it means that there is no agreement between the rankings of the k judges.

(*iii*) If $W = 1$, it means that there is perfect concordance between the rankings of k sets.

(*iv*) A value between 0 and 1 can be interpreted accordingly.

(*v*) There exists a linear relation between average Spearman's rank correlation r_{Sav} and coefficient of concordance W. By average of rank correlation r_{Sav}, we mean the average of r_S of all $\binom{K}{2}$ pairs of rankings. The relation is,

$$r_{Sav} = \frac{kW-1}{(k-1)}$$

(*vi*) W cannot take a value -1 as there is no such thing like perfect discordance when more than two sets of rankings are involved, *i.e.*, the rankings cannot all disagree perfectly.

Q. 65. *What adjustments have to be made in W if the ties occur within samples and across samples?*

Ans. If the ties occur across samples, no adjustment has to be made. But tied ranks do affect the value of W if they occur within a sample. First break the ties by midrank method and then think of the adjustment in the formula for W. If the proportion of ties is small, the effect on W is negligible and no adjustment is required. If the proportion of ties is large, an adjustment in the formula for W has to be made.

Suppose there are t tied ranks in a group and there are more than one group.

Then we find the quantity

$$T = \frac{\Sigma(t^3-t)}{12}$$

where Σ is taken overall groups of tied observations.

Hence, the formula for W corrected for ties is,

$$W = \frac{S}{\frac{1}{12}k^2n(n^2-1) - k\Sigma T}$$

In the above formula, Σ is taken for all T over K set of rankings.

The formula clearly indicates that W will be higher than what it would have been if the correction would have not been implemented.

Q. 66. *How can the significance of coefficient of concordance W be tested?*

Ans. Here we test

H_0: The k sets of rankings are independent

vs. H_1: They are not independent.

To test H_0, the distribution of S has been worked out and the critical values of S have been tabulated for n = 3 to 7, k = 3 to 20 and α = 0.01 and 0.05. (Reference table R, Sidney Siegel).

Again if $n > 7$, the expression 12 $S/kn\ (n + 1)$ is approximately equal to χ^2. Therefore,

$$\frac{12\,S}{kn(n+1)} = k(n-1)W$$

$$\therefore \quad \chi^2 = k(n-1)W$$

χ^2 has $(n - 1)$ d.f. The decision about H_0 can be taken in the usual manner.

Q. 67. *Five tea testers ranked seven brands of tea from 1 to 7, i.e., lowest to best quality tea as given below:*

Testers	*Brands of Tea*						
	B_1	B_2	B_3	B_4	B_5	B_6	B_7
T_1	2	3	4	7	1	5	6
T_2	4	3	6	5	2	1	7
T_3	5	1	3	7	4	6	2
T_4	6	5	7	3	2	4	1
T_5	3	1	4	6	5	2	7
Sums	20	13	24	28	14	18	23

Calculate the coefficient of concordance and test its significance. [*Given:* $\chi^2_{0.05,6} = 12.59$].

Ans. For the given problem, $k = 5$, $n = 7$.

Thus, $\frac{k(n+1)}{2} = \frac{5\times 8}{2} = 20$

$$S = (20-20)^2 + (13-20)^2 + (24-20)^2 + (28-20)^2 + (14-20)^2 + (18-20)^2 + (23-20)^2$$

$$= 0 + 49 + 16 + 64 + 36 + 4 + 9$$

$$= 178$$

Now, $$W = \frac{12 \times 178}{25 \times 7 \times 48}$$

$$= 0.25$$

Now we test, H_0: $W = 0$ vs. H_1: $W \neq 0$

$$\chi^2 = 5 \times 6 \times 0.25$$

$$= 7.5$$

Here χ^2 has 6 d.f.

Computed value of $\chi^2 = 7.50 \leq 12.50$. So we accept H_0. This leads to the conclusion that there is no agreement, between the ranks awarded by the five testers.

Q. 68. *Describe in brief the procedure of fitting a regression line through nonparametric approach.*

Ans. Let the equation of the regression line is,

$$Y = a + bx$$

G.W. Brown and A.M. Mood gave a method for determining 'a' and 'b' based on n paired sample values (X_1, Y_1), (X_2, Y_2), ..., (X_n, Y_n).

We should remember that in nonparametric statistics median is in consideration as mean is in parametric case. A line of best fit will be one for which the median of the deviations about the line is zero for the two groups of pairs formed by considering Y values with X that are less than or equal to the median of X and the other Y values with X that are greater than the median of X.

Various steps to determine *'a'* and *'b'* are as follows:

(1) Plot the paired values on a graph.

(2) Draw a vertical line through the median of X values. If some points fall on this line, shift this line to the right or left in such a way that as nearly as possible, the number of points on either side is equal.

(3) Compute the median of X and Y for both the groups separately. So we have two points, one in each group whose co-ordinates are the median values of X and Y.

(4) Plot both the points obtained in step (3) and join them. This line is our required line.

(5) If the median of the vertical deviations of the points from the line drawn in step (4) is not zero in both the groups, then shift the line to either side maintaining the slope in such a way that the median deviations on both the groups is zero or near zero.

(6) The value of a is the intercept of the final line and $b = (Y_1 - Y_2)/(X_1 - X_2)$ for any two points (X_1, Y_1) and (X_2, Y_2) on the final line.

Q. 69. *Are there any tests available for testing the significance of regression coefficients?*

Ans. Earlier it was believed that nonparametric tests are not available for testing the hypothesis about regression coefficients. But in 1950 and onwards, nonparametric tests were evolved by C.W. Brown, A.M. Mood and H. Theil to test the significance of regression coefficients.

Q. 70. *Discuss Brown and Mood's method of testing hypothesis about the parameters of a simple regression equation.*

Ans. Suppose the regression equation is,

$$Y = \alpha + \beta X + \varepsilon$$

Let $(X_1, Y_1), (X_2, Y_2), ..., (X_n, Y_n)$ be the n paired sample observations and on the basis of these observations we have to test the hypothesis about α and β.

The null hypothesis

$H_0: \alpha = \alpha_0$ and $\beta = \beta_0$ is to be tested against

$H_1: \alpha \neq \alpha_0$ and $\beta \neq \beta_0$

where α_0 and β_0 are the known values of regression constants.

Various steps of Brown and Mood's test procedure are:

Step-1. Plot the points (X_i, Y_i), for $i = 1, 2, ..., n$; as a scatter diagram.

Step-2. Draw the line $Y = \alpha_0 + \beta_0 X$ on the scatter diagram.

Step-3. Draw a vertical line on the X-axis at the median of X values.

Step-4. Count the number of points n_1 which lie above the hypothesised regression line $Y = \alpha_0 + \beta_0 X$ and to the left of the vertical line. Also count the number of points n_2 which lie to the right of vertical line and above the line $Y = \alpha_0 + \beta_0 X$.

Step-5. Once we know n_1, n_2 and n, the test statistic is,

$$\chi^2 = \frac{8}{n}\left\{\left(n_1 - \frac{n}{4}\right)^2 + \left(n_2 - \frac{n}{4}\right)^2\right\}$$

Here the test statistic χ^2 is distributed with 2 d.f. under H_0 and also if n is not too small. The decision about H_0 is taken in the usual manner.

The main feature of this test is that the decision about α and β is taken simultaneously, *i.e.*, both the values α_0 and β_0 are accepted or both are rejected.

Another interesting point of the test is that it does not require the estimates of α and β.

Q. 71. *How can you test the hypothesis about regression coefficient alone by Mood's test?*

Ans. Mostly the interest lies in testing the hypothesis about β alone of the regression line $Y = \alpha + \beta X + \varepsilon$. Hence, Mood evolved the nonparametric test for testing $H_0: \beta = \beta_0$ vs. $H_1: \beta \neq \beta_0$.

The test procedure may be described through the following steps:

Suppose (X_i, Y_i) are the n paired sample observations for $i = 1, 2, ..., n$.

Step-1. Plot the points (X_i, Y_i) as a scatter diagram.

Step-2. Plot the line $Y = a + \beta_0 X$ where a is median of the deviations $(Y_i - \beta_0 X_i)$. The line $Y = a + \beta_0 X$ can easily be fitted by plotting the line $Y = \beta_0 X$ and then drawing a line parallel to $Y = \beta_0 X$ at the intercept point $Y = a$.

Step-3. Draw a vertical line on X-axis through the median of the X-values.

Step-4. Count the number of points n_1 which lie above the line $Y = a + \beta_0 X$ and to the left of the vertical line.

Step-5. Once we know n_1 and n, the test statistic

$$\chi'^2 = \frac{16}{n}\left(n_1 - \frac{n}{4}\right)^2$$

The statistic χ'^2 follows Chi-square distribution with 1 d.f. when n is fairly large say, $n \geq 20$.

Decision about H_0 is taken in the usual way.

Q. 72. *What is Theils method for testing the significance of the regression coefficient in a regression line?*

Ans. Suppose the simple linear regression model is $Y = \alpha + \beta X + \varepsilon$.

Theils proposed the method of testing

$$H_0 : \beta = \beta_0 \text{ vs. } H_1 : \beta \neq \beta_0$$

or $$H_0 : \beta \leq \beta_0 \text{ vs. } H_1 : \beta > \beta_0$$

or $$H_0 : \beta \geq \beta_0 \text{ vs. } H_1 : \beta < \beta_0$$

where β_0 is a known value of regression coefficient β.

Let $(X_1, Y_1), (X_2, Y_2), \ldots, (X_n, Y_n)$ be n pairs of observations on which the test is based.

Theils test is based on Kendall's τ statistic. Kendall's τ is calculated by comparing all possible pairs of the form $(X_i, Y_i - \beta_0 X_i)$ for $i = 1, 2, \ldots, n$.

Various steps of Theils procedure are:

Step-1. Arrange all pairs of modified observations $(X_i, Y_i - \beta_0 X_i)$ in ascending order in respect of X_i alone.

Step-2. Search those pairs of modified observations in which $(Y_i - \beta_0 X_i) < (Y_j - \beta_0 X_j)$ for $i < j$ are in natural order. Let this number of pairs be P also let Q be the number of pairs in which $(Y_i - \beta_0 X_i) > (Y_j - \beta_0 X_j)$ for $i < j$.

Step-3. Find the quantity

$$S = P - Q$$

Step-4. Calculate Kendall τ by the formula,

$$\hat{\tau} = \frac{2S}{n(n-1)}$$

Step-5. To take a decision about H_0, compare $\hat{\tau}$ with the critical value τ^* of τ for n d.f. and $\alpha/2$ level of significance in case of two-sided test available in table A. 20 of Daniel's *Applied Nonparametric Statistics.*

If $|\hat{\tau}| \geq \tau^*$ reject H_0, otherwise accept H_0. Again for one-sided test, obtain the value of τ^* for n and α and take the decision in the same way.

Q. 73. *How can the confidence interval for the population median using sign test be found out?*

Ans. The confidence interval for the population median M with confidence coefficient $(1 - \alpha)$ 100 per cent can be found out in the following manner:

Let $X_{(1)}, X_{(2)}, \ldots, X_{(n)}$ be the ordered sample statistics. We have to determine two extreme values of X say, X_L and X_U such that the probability of M lying between X_L and X_U is $(1 - \alpha)$, *i.e.*, $P(X_L < M < X_U) = 1 - \alpha$.

If there are k positive differences among n differences $(X_i - M)$ for $i = 1, 2, \ldots, n$, then for all k which satisfy the relation,

$$P(k'_{\alpha/2} + 1 \leq k \leq k_{\alpha/2} - 1) = 1 - \alpha$$

iff, $$P\left[X_{(k'_{\alpha/2}+1)} < M < X_{(k_{\alpha/2})}\right] = 1 - \alpha$$

Using the normal approximation with continuity correction, we get the values of $k'_{\alpha/2}$ and $k'_{\alpha/2}$ by the relations,

$$k_{\alpha/2} = \left(n+1+\sqrt{n}Z_{\alpha/2}\right)/2$$

and $$k'_{\alpha/2} = \left(n-1-\sqrt{n}Z_{\alpha/2}\right)/2$$

Once we know $k_{\alpha/2}$ and $k'_{\alpha/2}$ it is trivial to determine the values of $X_{(k'_{\alpha/2}+1)}$ > and $X_{(k_{\alpha/2})}$, which are the lower and upper limits for the confidence interval of *M*.

Q. 74. *Give the idea of confidence band.*

Ans. Kolmogorov-Smirnov statistics D_n is also useful in finding the confidence band for the distribution $F_X(x)$ for all *x*. Making use of *K – S* tables for critical values of $D_{n,\alpha}$ such that

$$P(D_n > D_{n,\alpha}) = \alpha$$

where, $$D_n = \underset{\text{all } x}{\text{Sup}} \,|\, S_n(x) - F_X(x) \,|$$

Therefore, the first statement is equivalent to,

$$P[\underset{\text{all } x}{\text{Sup}} \,|\, S_n(x) - F_X(x) \,| < D_{n,\alpha}] = 1 - \alpha$$

or $$P[S_n(x) - D_{n,\alpha} < F_X(x) < S_n(x) + D_{n,\alpha}] = 1 - \alpha$$

We know $0 \le F_X(x) \le 1$ for all *x*, whereas the above inequality admits the members outside this range which satisfy the inequality.

Supposing,

$$L_n(x) = S_n(x) - D_{n,\alpha}$$
$$U_n(x) = S_n(x) + D_{n,\alpha}$$

The inequality reduces to,

$$P[L_n(x) < F_X(x) < U_n(x)] = 1 - \alpha$$

Thus, the region between $L_n(x)$ and $U_n(x)$ is called the confidence band for $F_X(x)$ with confidence coefficient $(1 - \alpha)$.

SECTION B

Fill in the Blanks

Fill in the suitable word(s) or phrase(s) in the blanks:

1. Nonparametric tests are based on _________ assumptions.
2. Nonparametric statistical methods are applicable even if the measurements are on _________ scale.
3. Nonparametric statistical method are not affected even if the observations are not very _________ .
4. Nonparametric methods and distribution free methods are _________ .
5. Any hypothesis which does not involve the parameters of a probability function will be tested by _________ tests.
6. Nonparametric analysis is _________ as compared to parametric analysis.
7. If the assumptions required for parametric analysis do not hold good, then _________ methods are applicable.
8. Nonparametric methods are appropriate even with _________ data.
9. Generally there is _________ on sample size.
10. The most common assumption in nonparametric statistic is the _________ of the sampled population.
11. Nonparametric methods are not devoid of _________ .
12. The criteria for judging the relative performance of two tests are _________ or _________ .
13. Asymptotic relative efficiency is also known as _________ efficiency.
14. Besides ARE, another measure for comparing the relative performance of two tests is _________ .
15. The same ranks assigned to different units are called _________ .

16. Most frequently used method of breaking the ties is the _________ method.
17. Average statistics approach is useful in _________ the problem of tied observations.
18. Under least favourable approach for coping with the problem of ties, there is least chance of _________ .
19. Range of probability approach in resolving the problem of tied observations is _________ feasible.
20. If the number of observations is large and number of tied values is small, one can _________ the tied values.
21. Before we apply a test it is necessary to establish the _________ .
22. Any test always requires _________ .
23. The decision about any hypothesis is to be taken according to the _________ .
24. When the observations are arranged in ascending or descending order, they are said _________ .
25. The probability function of ordered statistics is _________ as that of original variables.
26. All the observations in ordered statistics are _________ .
27. Kolmogorov-Smirnov test is based on _________ theorem.
28. Kolmogorov-Smirnov statistics can be used to determine _________ or _________ .
29. Ordinary sign test is based on the sign of the deviations from _________ .
30. Sign test utilises _________ distribution.
31. Wilcoxon signed-rank test is based on the _________ as well as _________ of the differences.
32. We use large sample Wilcoxon'x signed-rank test when the sample size is greater than _________ .
33. A set of like symbols followed and preceded by different kind of symbols or no symbols is called a _________ .
34. Runs test is a test of _________ .
35. Too many runs are indicative of _________ .
36. Too few runs are indicative of _________ .
37. Any set pattern of symbols in a sequence shows _________ .
38. Kolmogorov-Smirnov test for two samples is based on the distance between two _________ distributions.
39. Kolmogorov-Smirnov test for two samples is based on the _________ between two empirical distributions.
40. Sign test for paired samples is founded on the _________ between paired values.
41. By median test, one can test the equality of _________ .
42. In median test the variable u, the number of X's to the left of median in the pooled sample for given t, the total number of observations to the left of the median follows _________ distribution.
43. For large samples, the variable U in median test has mean _________ and variance _________ .
44. The critical values for Mann-Whitney U were tabulated by _________ in _________ .
45. Procedures for testing identicalness of two populations by Wald-Wolfowitz runs test and for randomness in one sample population are _________ .
46. By Mann-Whitney *U-test*, one tests the identicalness of _________ .
47. With usual notations, the relation between U and U' is _________ .
48. In case of large samples, Mann-Whitney U is distributed with mean _________ and variance _________ .
49. When m or n in Wald-Wolfowitz runs test are greater than 20, the variable R representing the number of runs follows normal distribution with mean _________ and variance _________ .
50. Mood's test is meant for testing the equality of two populations _________ .

51. In Mood's test, two population medians are taken to be ________ .

52. Regarding sample size, the condition for the validity of Mood's test is ________ .

53. Mood's test statistic M is the ________ of the deviations of ranks of variates of smaller sample from the overall mean rank.

54. Moses' test is meant for testing the equality of two populations ________ .

55. In Moses' test, samples on two variates are divided into ________ of equal size.

56. The corrected sum of squares for sub-samples are taken as ________ in Moses' test.

57. Moses' test utilises ________ test statistic.

58. Mcnemar test for change utilises only ________ frequencies of a (2 × 2) contingency table.

59. The test statistic used in Mcnemar's test follows ________ distribution.

60. When the cell's expected frequency under consideration are small, ________ correction is applied.

61. Cochran's Q-test is used in ________ analysis of data.

62. For Cochran's Q-test, the variate values should be ________ .

63. Cochran's Q-statistic is approximately distributed as ________ .

64. Kruskal-Wallis test is used for analysis of ________ classification of data.

65. Kruskal-Wallis test statistic is a ________ sum of squares.

66. If there are K sampled populations, Kruskal-Wallis statistic H is distributed as Chi-square with ________ d.f.

67. Friedman's nonparametric procedure is meant for ________ analysis of variance.

68. In Friedman's test, on tests the ________ of treatment effects.

69. Jonckheere-Terpştra test is applicable only for ________ .

70. With usual notations, the Jonckheere test statistic is ________ .

71. Page's test is applicable only when the alternative hypothesis is ________ .

72. Following common notations, Page's test statistics is ________ .

73. Rank correlation between sets of ranks was given by ________ .

74. Formula for Spearman's rank correlation is ________ .

75. The range of rank correlation is ________ .

76. Spearman's rank correlation formula has to be ________ for tied values.

77. The significance of rank correlation can be tested by ________ .

78. Kendall's rank correlation τ is based on the ________ of ranks.

79. Kendall's τ can be calculated by the formula ________ .

80. For large sample size n, the relation between τ and r_S is ________ .

81. Kendall's τ lies between ________ .

82. $\tau = 1$ shows ________ correspondence between two sets of rankings.

83. Kendall's τ is ________ by tied ranks.

84. For large n, Kendall's τ follows normal distribution with mean ________ and variance ________ .

85. Coefficient of concordance is a measure of ________ for three or more sets of rankings.

86. Coefficient of concordance was given by ________ .

87. The limits of coefficient of concordance W are from ________ .

88. If the coefficient of concordance $W = 1$, it indicates ________ concordance between k sets of rankings.

89. If $W = 0$, it shows ________ between k sets of rankings.

90. The linear relation between average rank

correlation r_{Sav} and coefficient of concordance is ________ .

91. The value of $W = -1$ ________ exist.

92. $W = -1$ cannot exist because there is noting like ________ between k sets of rankings.

93. Formula for W has ________ for tied ranks.

94. The hypothesis H_0: $W = 0$ can be tested by ________ test.

95. The test statistic for testing H_0 : $W = 0$ is ________ .

96. Statistics-χ^2 with n individuals for testing H_0: $W = 0$ has ________ d.f.

97. ________ test is meant for testing the significance of regression coefficient of a regression line.

98. Both the parameters of a linear regression model can simultaneously be tested by ________ test.

99. Brown and Mood's test applied for testing the significance of regression parameters utilises ________ statistic.

100. Theils test procedure for testing the significance of regression coefficient is based on ________ .

101. The number of runs in the sequence ABBAAABAABBBAAAB is ________ .

102. The residuals in a regression analysis may be positive or negative. The hypothesis whether these positive and negative residuals occur in random order can be tested by ________ .

103. With usual notations, the correction factor in Kruskal-Wallis test statistic H is ________ .

104. With usual notations, the correction factor for tied observations in Friedman's F-statistic is ________ .

105. Friedman's test statistic adjusted for ties with usual notations is ________ .

106. For large number of treatments $k > 8$ and number of blocks r large, Page statistics L is distributed normally with mean ________ and variance ________ .

107. The region between $L_n(x)$ and $U_n(x)$, where $L_n(x) = S_n(x) - D_{n,\alpha}$, and $U_n(x) = S_n(x) + D_{n,\alpha}$ are the terms of Kolmogorov- Smirnov test, is called ________ .

108. The Kolmogorov-Smirnov test is more ________ than Chi-square test.

109. There is no one-sided test in ________ test.

110. Formula tor Kendall's partial rank correlation $\tau_{XZ \cdot Y}$ is ________ .

111. The range or Kendall's partial rank correlation coefficient is ________ .

112. When the number of treatments $k = 2$ in Kruskal-Wallis test, then H reduces to ________ or ________ test.

113. In Moses' test, the size of the sub-sample should not be more than ________ .

114. Following are the ranks awarded by judges I and II to seven contestants.

Contestants:	*A*	*B*	*C*	*D*	*E*	*F*	*G*
Judge I:	1	2	3	4	5	6	7
Judge II:	2	5	4	3	7	1	6

The rank correlation between the rank is ________ .

115. For the problem given in Q. No. 114, Kendall's rank correlation τ is equal to ________ .

116. A tranquilliser was given to 12 patients and their hours of sleep at night were as follows:

Patient No:	1	2	3	4	5	6
Hours of sleep:	3.9	7.6	10.0	6.1	8.2	6.2
Patient No:	7	8	9	10	11	12
Hours of sleep:	10.1	6.5	6.6	8.5	9.2	7.6

It is claimed that the medicine will induce median sleep of 7 hours. The value of Wilcoxon's signed-rank statistic T^+ is ________ .

117. If Kendall's τ's between pairs of variables

X, Y and Z are $\tau_{XY} = 0.58$, $\tau_{XZ} = 0.45$ and $\tau_{YZ} = 0.24$, Kendall's partial rank correlation $\tau_{XY \cdot Z}$ is equal to ________ .

118. Ranks of five students in three subjects graded by three teachers grading 5 as best and 1 as worst were as follows:

	Students				
	A	*B*	*C*	*D*	*E*
Teacher *X*	2	1	3	4	5
Teacher *Y*	5	3	4	1	1
Teacher *Z*	4	2	5	3	1

For the three sets of ranks, the coefficient of concordance W is equal to ________ .

119. Given $W = 0.5$, $K = 3$, $n = 6$, the computed value of χ^2 for testing the significance of W is equal to ________ .

120. If the rank correlation $r_S = 0.40$ based on two sets of eight rankings, the value of statistic t for testing the significance of rank correlation is ________ .

121. An alternative to t-test in nonparametric statistics is ________ .

122. A unbiased estimate of population rank correlation coefficient is ________ .

123. Spearman's rank correlation r_S is ________ estimate of population rank correlation coefficient.

124. Kendall's τ based on moderate sample size tends to ________ .

125. Spearman's r_S and Kendall's τ on testing lead to ________ conclusion.

126. The significance of Kendall's τ is tested by ________ .

127. In fitting a regression line through non-parametric method, the ________ of the deviation about the line is zero.

128. The significance of Spearman's r_S can be tested by ________ .

129. The method of fitting a regression line through nonparametric approach was given by ________ and ________ .

130. Nonparametric approach of fitting a regression line is a ________ method.

SECTION C

Multiple Choice Questions

Select the correct alternative out of given ones:

1. Nonparametric methods are based on:
(*a*) mild assumptions
(*b*) stringent assumptions
(*c*) no assumptions
(*d*) none of the above

2. Most of the nonparametric methods utilise measurements on:
(*a*) interval scale
(*b*) ratio scale
(*c*) ordinal scale
(*d*) nominal scale

3. Ordered statistics is a sequence of:
(*a*) observations
(*b*) ranks
(*c*) natural numbers
(*d*) integers

4. Most commonly used assumption about the distribution of a variable is:
(*a*) continuity of the distribution
(*b*) symmetry of the distribution
(*c*) both (*a*) and (*b*)
(*d*) neither (*a*) nor (*b*)

5. The term dirty data implies:
(*a*) contaminated data
(*b*) inaccurate data
(*c*) data with outliers
(*d*) all of the above

6. The concept of asymptotic relative efficiency was given by:

(*a*) Jean Gibbons
(*b*) E.J.G. Pitman
(*c*) A.M. Mood
(*d*) F. Wilcoxon

7. Relative efficiency in nonparametric tests is the ratio of:
(*a*) power of two tests
(*b*) size of two tests
(*c*) size of the samples
(*d*) all of the above

8. Most frequently used method of breaking the ties is:
(*a*) midrank method
(*b*) average statistics approach
(*c*) to omit tied values
(*d*) most favourable statistic approach

9. Kolmogorov-Smirnov test is based on the theorem given by:
(*a*) N.V. Smirnov
(*b*) A.N. Kolmogorov
(*c*) Kolmogorov-Smirnov
(*d*) Glivenko-Cantelli

10. Kolmogorov-Smirnov test is useful as:
(*a*) a test of goodness of fit
(*b*) a test of identicalness of two populations
(*c*) a measure of confidence band
(*d*) all of the above

11. If the observed and theoretical cumulative distribution functions are,
Observed c.d.f:
0.038, 0.066, 0.093, 0.177, 0.288, 0.316, 0.371
Theoretical c.d.f:
0.036, 0.042, 0.129, 0.159, 0.243, 0.275, 0.238
then the value of *K-S* test statistic D_n is:
(*a*) 0.133
(*b*) 0.002
(*c*) 0.043
(*d*) none of the above

12. Kolmogorov-Smirnov test is a:
(*a*) one left-sided test
(*b*) one right-sided test
(*c*) two-sided test
(*d*) all of the above

13. Ordinary sign test utilises:
(*a*) Poisson distribution
(*b*) binomial distribution
(*c*) both (*a*) and (*b*)
(*d*) neither (*a*) nor (*b*)

14. Ordinary sign test considers the difference of observed values from the hypothetical median value in terms of:
(*a*) signs only
(*b*) magnitude only
(*c*) sign and magnitude both
(*d*) none of the above

15. Wilcoxon's signed-rank test considers the differences $(X_i - M_0)$ by way of:
(*a*) signs only
(*b*) magnitudes only
(*c*) signs and magnitudes both
(*d*) all of the above

16. If there are zero differences in sign test, they may be:
(*a*) discarded
(*b*) treated half of them as positive
(*c*) treated half of them as negative
(*d*) all of the above

17. If in Wilcoxon's-signed rank test, the sample size is large, the statistic T^+ is distributed with mean:
(*a*) $n(n+1)/4$
(*b*) $n(n+1)/2$
(*c*) $n(2n+1)/4$
(*d*) $n(n-1)/4$

18. If the sample size is large in Wilcoxon's signed rank test, the statistic T^+ is distributed with variance:
(*a*) $n(n-1)(2n-1)/24$
(*b*) $n(n+1)(2n+1)/24$
(*c*) $n(2n+1)/12$
(*d*) $n(n-1)(2n+1)/12$

19. The production of lignite in India from 1975 to 1985 in Mn. Tonnes was,
3.03, 4.02, 3.58, 3.30, 2.90, 5.11, 6.31, 6.93, 7.30, 7.80, 8.03

It is expected that the median production of lignite in India is 5 Mn. Tonnes/year. To test $H_0: M = 5.0$, the value of T^- in Wilcoxon's signed rank test is:

(*a*) 28
(*b*) 27
(*c*) 25
(*d*) 26

20. For the data given in Q. No. 19, the number of positive deviations for sign test will be:

(*a*) 5
(*b*) 6
(*c*) 4
(*d*) 7

21. If, there are 10 symbols of two types, equal in number, the maximum possible number of runs is:

(*a*) 8
(*b*) 9
(*c*) 10
(*d*) none of the above

22. If there are 10 symbols of two types, equal in number, the minimum possible number of runs is:

(*a*) 5
(*b*) 3
(*c*) 1
(*d*) none of the above

23. A sequence of symbols shows lacks of randomness if there are:

(*a*) Too many runs
(*b*) Too few runs
(*c*) both (*a*) and (*b*)
(*d*) neither (*a*) nor (*b*)

24. Randomness of a sequence through runs test is adjudged by comparing the observed number of runs with:

(*a*) two critical values
(*b*) one upper critical value
(*c*) one lower critical value
(*d*) none of the above

25. If the number of symbols of either type is large, then one can apply:

(*a*) *t*-test
(*b*) normal deviate test
(*c*) Chi-square test
(*d*) none of the above

26. If the sample size in Wald-Wolfowitz runs test is large, the variate *R* is distributed with mean:

(*a*) $\frac{2m}{m+n}+1$

(*b*) $\frac{2n}{m+n}+1$

(*c*) $\frac{2mn}{n+m}$

(*d*) $\frac{2mn}{m+n}+1$

27. If the sample size in Wald-Wolfowitz runs test is large, the variate *R* is distributed with variance:

(*a*) $\frac{2mn(2mn-m-n)}{(m+n)\,(m+n-1)}$

(*b*) $\frac{2mn(2mn-m-n)}{(m+n)^2\,(m+n-1)}$

(*c*) $\frac{mn(2mn-m-n)}{(m+n)^2\,(m+n-1)}$

(*d*) $\frac{2mn(2mn-m-n)}{(m+n)\,(m+n-1)}$

28. Mann-Whitney test statistic *U* depends on the fact that:

(*a*) how many times *Y*'s precede *X*'s
(*b*) how many times *X*'s precede *Y*'s
(*c*) both (*a*) and (*b*)
(*d*) none of (*a*) and (*b*)

29. The relation between *U* when *Y* precedes *X* and *U*′ when *X* precedes *Y* in Mann-Whitney test is:

(*a*) $U + U' = n_1n_2$
(*b*) $U = n_1n_2 - U'$
(*c*) $U' = n_1n_2 - U$
(*d*) all of the above

30. If n_1 and n_2 in Mann-Whitney test are large, the variable U is distributed with mean:

(*a*) $(n_1 + n_2)/2$

(*b*) $(n_1 - n_2)/2$

(*c*) $n_1n_2/2$

(*d*) n_1n_2

31. If n_1 and n_2 are large in Mann-Whitney test, the variable U is distributed with variance equal to:

(*a*) $n_1n_2(n_1 + n_2 + 1)/12$

(*b*) $n_1n_2(n_1 + n_2 - 1)/12$

(*c*) $n_1n_2(n_1 + n_2)/12$

(*d*) $n_1n_2 (n_1n_2 + 1)/12$

32. The hypothesis tested by Mood's test, is:

(*a*) equality of two standard deviations

(*b*) equality of two mean deviations about median

(*c*) equality of any two measure of dispersion

(*d*) all of the above

33. Mood's test statistic is:

(*a*) sum of squares of the deviations of the ranks of pooled ordered statistic from their mean rank

(*b*) sum of the absolute deviations of the ranks of pooled ordered statistics from their mean

(*c*) sum of square of the deviations of the ranks of pooled sample ranks from their median

(*d*) none of the above

34. Mood's table provides at α level of significance and n_1, n_2 sample sizes:

(*a*) a critical value of M

(*b*) two critical values of M

(*c*) probabilities for Mood's statistic M.

(*d*) none of the above

35. In Mood's test, one can test the hypotheses:

(*a*) $H_0: \sigma_1 = \sigma_2$ vs. $H_1: \sigma_1 \neq \sigma_2$

(*b*) $H_0: \sigma_2 \leq \sigma_2$ vs. $H_1: \sigma_1 > \sigma_2$

(*c*) $H_0: \sigma_1 \geq \sigma_2$ vs. $H_1: \sigma_1 < \sigma_2$

(*d*) all the above

36. In Moses' test for testing the equality of two populations dispersion measure, the size of sub-samples should not be more than:

(*a*) 5

(*b*) 10

(*c*) 15

(*d*) 20

37. In Moses' test for equality of two populations dispersion, the variable for the test statistic is

(*a*) sum of square corrected for mean

(*b*) mean deviation from median

(*c*) mean deviation from mean

(*d*) any of the above

38. In Moses' test, the statistic used for making decision is

(*a*) Mood's M-statistic

(*b*) Wilcoxon's T statistic

(*c*) Mann-Whitney U statistic

(*d*) none of the above

39. Mcnemar test is a test of:

(*a*) change

(*b*) independence

(*c*) association of attributes

(*d*) none of the above

40. With usual notations, Mcnemar χ^2-statistics is:

(*a*) $\left(\frac{A-D}{A+D}\right)^2$

(*b*) $\frac{(A-D)^2}{A+D}$

(*c*) $\frac{|A-D|}{(A+D)^2}$

(*d*) $\frac{|A+D|}{(A-D)^2}$

41. Cochran's Q-test for equality of a number of treatments is applicable for a variable which is:

(*a*) continuous
(*b*) discrete
(*c*) dichotomous
(*d*) all of the above

42. Cochran's Q-test is applicable only if the number of treatments under test are:

(*a*) not more than four
(*b*) not less than four
(*c*) at least two
(*d*) none of the above

43. Cochran's Q-test restricts to the minimum number of observations in the experiment, that number is:

(*a*) 20
(*b*) 24
(*c*) 25
(*d*) 4

44. Kruskal-Wallis analysis of data is meant for:

(*a*) one-way classification
(*b*) two-way classification
(*c*) non-classified data
(*d*) none of the above

45. While performing Kruskal-Wallis test, the ranks are assigned:

(*a*) independently to the observations for each treatment
(*b*) for observations in each block independently
(*c*) by pooling all the observations
(*d*) none of the above

46. The test statistics in the Kruskal-Wallis test is:

(*a*) weighted sum of squares of the deviations of the sum of treatments rank from the expected sum of ranks
(*b*) sum of squares of the deviations of the sum of treatments rank from the expected sum of ranks
(*c*) both (*a*) and (*b*)
(*d*) neither (*a*) nor (*b*)

47. The statistic H under the Kruskal-Wallis test is approximately distributed as:

(*a*) Student's t
(*b*) Snedecor's F
(*c*) Chi-square
(*d*) normal deviate-Z

48. When the number of treatments in Kruskal-Wallis test is two, the statistic H reduces to:

(*a*) Mann-Whitney U statistic
(*b*) Wilcoxon's U statistic
(*c*) both (*a*) and (*b*)
(*d*) neither (*a*) nor (*b*)

49. Kruskal-Wallis H with K treatments and n blocks which is approximated to Chi-square has d.f:

(*a*) $(n - 1)$
(*b*) $(k - 1)(n - 1)$
(*c*) $(k - 1)$
(*d*) $k(n - 1)$

50. If the ties occur in the Kruskal-Wallis test, with usual notations, the correction C for ties is:

(*a*) $\Sigma T/n(n^2 - 1)$
(*b*) $\Sigma T/k(n^2 - 1)$
(*c*) $\Sigma T/kn(n - 1)$
(*d*) none of the above

51. If C is the correction factor for ties in Kruskal-Wallis test statistic H, the corrected test statistic is:

(*a*) $H - C$
(*b*) H/C
(*c*) $H + C$
(*d*) $H \times C$

52. In Friedman's two-way analysis of variance, the observations are ranked in:

(*a*) blocks
(*b*) treatments
(*c*) pooled observations
(*d*) none of the above

53. Friedmen's test statistic F based on an experiment with K treatments and r blocks and R_j ($j = 1, 2, ..., k$) rank totals for treatments is:

(*a*) $F = \frac{12}{rk(k+1)} \sum_{j=1}^{k} R_j^2 - 3k(k+1)$

(*b*) $F = \frac{12}{rk(k+1)} \sum_{j=1}^{k} R_j^2 - 3r(k+1)$

(*c*) $F = \frac{1}{rk(k+1)} \sum_{j=1}^{k} R_j^2 - 3r(k+1)$

(*d*) $F = \frac{12}{rk(k+1)} \sum_{j=1}^{k} R_j^2 - 3r(k+1)$

54. Friedman's-*F* is distributed as:

(*a*) Snedecor's *F*

(*b*) student's *t*

(*c*) Chi-square

(*d*) none of the above

55. Degrees of freedom for Friedman's-*F* distributed as χ^2 based on *k* treatments and *r* blocks are:

(*a*) $(r - 1)$

(*b*) $(k - 1)$

(*c*) $r(k - 1)$

(*d*) $k(r - 1)$

56. Correction factor *C* for tied observations in Friedman's-*F* with usual notations is:

(*a*) $C = 1 - \sum_{i=1}^{r} \frac{T_i^2}{rk(k-1)}$

(*b*) $C = 1 - \sum_{i=1}^{r} \frac{T_i}{rk(k^2-1)}$

(*c*) $C = 1 - \sum_{i=1}^{r} \frac{T_i}{rk(k-1)}$

(*d*) none of the above

57. The quantity T_i in the formula for correction for ties '*C*' with usual notations is:

(*a*) $\Sigma t_i^3 - \Sigma t_i$

(*b*) $\Sigma(t_i^3 - t_i)$

(*c*) both (*a*) and (*b*)

(*d*) neither (*a*) and (*b*)

58. The critical difference for multiple comparisons in Friedman's test with usual notations is:

(*a*) $Z\sqrt{\frac{rk^2(k+1)}{6}}$

(*b*) $Zr\sqrt{\frac{k(k+1)}{6}}$

(*c*) $Zk\sqrt{\frac{r(k+1)}{4}}$

(*d*) $Z\sqrt{\frac{rk(k+1)}{6}}$

59. In an experiment with 4 treatments and 5 blocks, the sum of the ranks for treatments were 12, 15, 6, 17.

Friedman's-*F* based on the given data is equal to:

(*a*) 23.28

(*b*) – 5.6

(*c*) – 68.06

(*d*) 8.28

60. The Jonckheere-Terpstra test for equality of *k* treatments mean is applicable when the alternative hypothesis is:

(*a*) at least two of them are not equal

(*b*) all of them differ from each other

(*c*) ordered in respect of treatment means

(*d*) none of the above

61. Page's test for equality of *k* treatments mean is applicable when the alternative hypothesis is:

(*a*) all treatment means differ from one another

(*b*) ordered

(*c*) at least two treatment means are not equal

(*d*) none of the above

62. With k treatments and R_j, the rank total for j^{th} treatment in a two-way classification, the Page's test statistic L is:

(*a*) $\sum_{j=1}^{k} jR_j$

(*b*) $\sum_{j=1}^{k} R_j/j$

(*c*) $\sum_{j=1}^{k} j^2R_j$

(*d*) none of the above

63. When number of treatments k is large ($k > 8$), the Page's statistic L is distributed as normal variates with mean:

(*a*) $r\,k\,(k + 1)/2$

(*b*) $r\,k\,(k + 1)^2/2$

(*c*) $r\,k\,(r + 1)^2/4$

(*d*) $r\,k\,(k + 1)^2/4$

64. In case of large number of treatments k, Page's statistic L is distributed normally with variance:

(*a*) $r\,(k^3 - k)/144\,(k - 1)$

(*b*) $r\,(k^3 - k)^2/144\,(k - 1)$

(*c*) $r\,(k^2 - k)^3/144\,(r - 1)$

(*d*) none of the above

65. Rank correlation was given by:

(*a*) A.M. Mood

(*b*) M.G. Kendall

(*c*) L.E. Moses

(*d*) C.E. Spearman

66. Rank correlation was invented in the year:

(*a*) 1916

(*b*) 1925

(*c*) 1928

(*d*) none of the above

67. Formula for rank correlation between two sets of ranks with usual notations is:

(*a*) $r_s = 1 - \dfrac{6\sum_i d_i^2}{n(n^2 - 1)}$

(*b*) $r_s = 1 - \dfrac{6\Sigma_i d_i}{n(n^2 - 1)}$

(*c*) $r_s = 1 - \dfrac{6\Sigma_i d_i^2}{n(n - 1)}$

(*d*) all of the above

68. The range of r_s is:

(*a*) –1 to 1

(*b*) 0 to 1

(*c*) $-\infty$ to ∞

(*d*) 0 to ∞

69. If $r_s = 1$, means that:

(*a*) the ranks awarded by two judges are same

(*b*) there is perfect association between the ranks awarded by two judges

(*c*) all difference (d_i's) are zero

(*d*) all of the above

70. If $r_s = 0$, it shows:

(*a*) no rank correlation between the ranks of two sets

(*b*) the ranks of two sets are independent

(*c*) $6\Sigma d_i^2 = n(n^2 - 1)$

(*d*) all of the above

71. When there are only two individuals ranked by two judges, then the possible values of rank correlation r_s are:

(*a*) zero

(*b*) – 1 or + 1

(*c*) 1 or zero

(*d*) 0 and –1

72. When there are three items ranked by two investigators, the only possible values of rank correlation r_s are

(*a*) $-1, -\frac{1}{2}, \frac{1}{2}, 1$

(*b*) $-1, -\frac{1}{2}, 0, \frac{1}{2}, 1$

(c) $-\frac{1}{2}, 0, \frac{1}{2}$

(d) – 1, 0, 1

73. If there are three items and number of judges is two, then the probabilities of occurrence of the values of r_S as $-1, -\frac{1}{2}, \frac{1}{2}, 1$ are, respectively:

(a) $\frac{1}{4}, \frac{1}{4}, \frac{1}{4}, \frac{1}{4}$

(b) $\frac{1}{6}, \frac{1}{3}, \frac{1}{3}, \frac{1}{6}$

(c) $-\frac{1}{6}, -\frac{1}{3}, \frac{1}{3}, \frac{1}{6}$

(d) none of the above

74. When the rank correlation between two sets of ranks awarded by two judges is – 1, then it leads to the conclusion that:

(a) there is complete disassociation between the ranks of two sets

(b) the ranks awarded by one judge are in reverse order of the ranks awarded by the other judge

(c) $3\Sigma d_i^2 = n(n^2 - 1)$

(d) all of the above

75. If the tied values occur in *X* variable as well as in *Y* variable, then the formula for r_S incorporating the correction for ties with usual notations is:

(a) $\dfrac{\Sigma x_i^2 + \Sigma y_i^2 + \Sigma d_i^2}{\sqrt{\Sigma x_i^2 \, \Sigma y_i^2}}$

(b) $\dfrac{\Sigma x_i^2 + \Sigma y_i^2 - \Sigma d_i^2}{\sqrt{\Sigma x_i^2 + \Sigma y_i^2}}$

(c) $\dfrac{\Sigma x_i^2 + \Sigma y_i^2 - \Sigma d_i^2}{2\sqrt{\Sigma x_i^2 \, \Sigma y_i^2}}$

(d) none of the above

76. The significance of rank correlation can be tested by:

(a) χ^2-test

(b) *t*-test

(c) *Z*-test

(d) *F*-test

77. The test statistic for testing the significance of r_S is:

(a) $t = \dfrac{r_S\sqrt{n-2}}{\sqrt{1-r_S^2}}$

(b) $t = \dfrac{r_S\sqrt{n-1}}{\sqrt{1-r_S^2}}$

(c) $t = \dfrac{r_S(n-2)}{\sqrt{1-r_S^2}}$

(d) $t = \dfrac{r_S\sqrt{n-2}}{(1-r_S^2)}$

78. Exact frequency distribution of r_s was derived by:

(a) C. Spearman

(b) M.G. Kendall

(c) Sidney Siegel

(d) none of the above

79. If *S* is the total number of pairs in the rearranged second set that are in natural order minus the number of pairs that are in the unnatural order in a set of *n* rankings, the formula for Kendall's rank correlation is:

(a) $\tau = \dfrac{\text{Actual value}}{\text{Maximum possible value}}$

(b) $\tau = S\Big/\dbinom{n}{2}$

(c) $\tau = \dfrac{2S}{n\,(n-1)}$

(d) all the above

80. The range of Kendall's rank correlation coefficient τ is:

(a) 0 to 1

(b) 0 to ∞

(*c*) – 1 to 1

(*d*) – ∞ to ∞

81. Kendall's rank correlation $\tau = 1$ can be interpreted as:

(*a*) a perfect correspondence between the rankings by the two judges

(*b*) no correspondence between the rankings by the two judges

(*c*) ranks awarded by two judges are in reverse order

(*d*) all of the above

82. If Kendall's rank correlation coefficient $\tau = 0$, it means that:

(*a*) there is a perfect correspondence between the rankings given by two judges.

(*b*) for the natural order of ranks of one set, all possible order of ranks in the other set are all equally likely.

(*c*) rankings of one set are in reverse order of the rankings of the other set.

(*d*) all of the above

83. If Kendall's rank correlation coefficient $\tau = -1$, it physical interpretation can be given as:

(*a*) a perfect correspondence between the rankings of the two sets

(*b*) no correspondence between the rankings of the two sets

(*c*) the ranks in one set are in reverse order of the other set

(*d*) none of the above

84. If t_X and t_Y are the number of tied observations in the set *X* and *Y* out of *n* pairs respectively $T_X = t_X(t_X - 1)/2$ and $T_Y = t_Y(t_Y - 1)/2$, the formula for Kendall's τ adjusted for ties is:

(*a*) $\dfrac{S}{\sqrt{T_X T_Y}}$

(*b*) $\dfrac{S}{\sqrt{\dfrac{n(n-1)}{2} - T_X}\sqrt{\dfrac{n(n-1)}{2} - T_Y}}$

(*c*) $\dfrac{S - T_X - T_Y}{\binom{n}{2}}$

(*d*) none of the above

85. If there are only two individual items that have been ranked by two judges, then Kendall's τ can have only values:

(*a*) – 1 or 0

(*b*) – 1 or 1

(*c*) 0 or 1

(*d*) not calculable

86. If $n = 3$, then Kendall's τ can have the only values as:

(*a*) $-1, -\frac{1}{2}, \frac{1}{2}, 1$

(*b*) $-1, -\frac{1}{3}, \frac{1}{3}, 1$

(*c*) $-\frac{1}{3}, -\frac{1}{2}, \frac{1}{2}, \frac{1}{3}$

(*d*) none of the above

87. If $n = 3$, the probability of occurrence of the values $-1, -\frac{1}{3}, \frac{1}{3}, 1$ of Kendall's rank correlation τ are:

(*a*) $\frac{1}{4}, \frac{1}{4}, \frac{1}{4}, \frac{1}{4}$

(*b*) $\frac{1}{6}, \frac{1}{6}, \frac{1}{3}, \frac{1}{3}$

(*c*) $\frac{1}{3}, \frac{1}{6}, \frac{1}{6}, \frac{1}{3}$

(*d*) $\frac{1}{6}, \frac{1}{3}, \frac{1}{3}, \frac{1}{6}$

88. The approximate relationship between τ and r_s is:

(*a*) $\tau = r_S$

(*b*) $\tau = \frac{2}{5} r_S$

(c) $\tau = \frac{2}{3} r_S$

(d) $\tau = \frac{1}{3} r_S$

89. For large n, τ is distributed as:

(a) $N\left(0, \frac{2(2n+5)}{9n(n-1)}\right)$

(b) $N\left(\mu_\tau, \frac{2(2n+1)}{9n(n-1)}\right)$

(c) $N\left(0, \frac{2(2n+3)}{9n(n+1)}\right)$

(d) none of the above

90. Five students were ranked at their schooling period and college period as follows:

Students:	*A*	*B*	*C*	*D*	*E*
At schooling	2	3	1	5	4
At college	3	4	1	2	5

The Kendall's rank correlation τ between the ranks at schooling and at college is:

(a) $\tau = 7/10$

(b) $\tau = 2/5$

(c) $\tau = -1/5$

(d) none of the above

91. If $\tau = 2/5$, then r_S is approximately equal to:

(a) 2/5

(b) 1

(c) 3/5

(d) none of the above

92. Coefficient of concordance was invented by:

(a) A.M. Mood

(b) C. Spearman

(c) Sidney Siegel

(d) M.G. Kendall

93. Coefficient of concordance is calculated when there are:

(a) three or more sets of rankings

(b) three sets of rankings

(c) at least five sets of rankings

(d) exactly five sets of rankings

94. Formula for coefficient of concordance W with usual notations is:

(a) $W = \frac{12S}{k^2 n(n^2-1)}$

(b) $W = \frac{12S}{n(n^2-1)}$

(c) $W = \frac{6S}{k^2 n(n^2-1)}$

(d) $W = \frac{6S}{kn^2(n-1)}$

95. The value of coefficient of concordance W lies in the range:

(a) -1 to 1

(b) 0 to 1

(c) 0 to ∞

(d) $-\infty$ to 0

96. If $W = 1$, one can conclude that:

(a) there is no concordance between the rankings of various sets

(b) there is perfect concordance between the rankings of various sets

(c) both (a) and (b)

(d) neither (a) nor (b)

97. The value of $W = 0$ leads to the conclusion that:

(a) there is no concordance between the rankings of various sets

(b) there is perfect concordance between the rankings of various sets

(c) both (a) and (b)

(d) none of (a) and (b)

98. The relation between the average rank correlation and coefficient of concordance is:

(a) linear

(b) quadratic

(c) cubic

(d) non-existent

99. If there are t tied ranks in one group of a set and there are more than one such groups in a set, the correction factor is equal to:

(*a*) $\Sigma T = \dfrac{\Sigma t^3 - t}{12}$

(*b*) $\Sigma T = \dfrac{\Sigma t^3 - \Sigma t^2}{12}$

(*c*) $\Sigma T = \dfrac{\Sigma(t^3 - t)}{12}$

(*d*) none of the above

100. The formula for coefficient of concordance W after the adjustment for tied ranks is:

(*a*) $\dfrac{12S}{k^2 n(n^2 - 1) - \Sigma T}$

(*b*) $\dfrac{12S}{\frac{1}{12} k^2 n(n^2 - 1) - \Sigma T}$

(*c*) $\dfrac{S}{\frac{1}{12} k^2 n(n^2 - 1) - k\Sigma T}$

(*d*) none of the above

101. The linear relation between average rank correlation r_{Sav} and coefficient of concordance W is:

(*a*) $r_{Sav} = \dfrac{k(W-1)}{k-1}$

(*b*) $r_{Sav} = \dfrac{kW - 1}{k-1}$

(*c*) $r_{Sav} = \dfrac{(k-1)W}{W-1}$

(*d*) $r_{Sav} = \dfrac{kW}{k-1}$

102. The hypothesis that the k ($k > 2$) sets of rankings of 7 or more individuals are independent can be tested by:

(*a*) χ^2-test

(*b*) t-test

(*c*) Z-test

(*d*) F-test

103. Chi-square statistic for testing the significance of coefficient of concordance W with usual notations is:

(*a*) $\chi^2 = \dfrac{12S}{kn(n+1)}$

(*b*) $\chi^2 = k(n-1)W$

(*c*) both (*a*) and (*b*)

(*d*) none of (*a*) and (*b*)

104. The statistic-χ^2 for testing the significance of W based on n rankings awarded by k judges has degrees of freedom equal to:

(*a*) $k - 1$

(*b*) $n - 1$

(*c*) $kn - 1$

(*d*) $k(n + 1)$

105. In an extempore debate, all the speakers were awarded the same ranks by three judges. In this situation, the value of coefficient of concordance W is equal to:

(*a*) 1

(*b*) 0

(*c*) 1/2

(*d*) none of the above

106. If three items are ranked by three investigators such that the sum of all rows and columns is 6, the coefficient of concordance W is:

(*a*) 1

(*b*) 0

(*c*) 1/2

(*d*) none of the above

107. The null hypothesis under Brown and Mood's test is:

(*a*) $H_0 : \alpha = \alpha_0$

(*b*) $H_0 : \beta = \beta_0$

(*c*) $H_0 : \alpha = \alpha_0, \beta = \beta_0$

(*d*) all the above

108. Brown and Mood's test provides a decision about the:

(*a*) intercept alone

(*b*) slope alone

(*c*) intercept and slope simultaneously

(*d*) none of the above

109. Formula for χ^2-statistic under Brown and Mood's test with usual notations is:

(a) $\chi^2 = \frac{8}{n}\left\{\left(n_1 - \frac{n}{2}\right)^2 + \left(n_2 - \frac{n}{2}\right)^2\right\}$

(b) $\chi^2 = \frac{4}{n}\left\{\left(n_1 - \frac{n}{4}\right)^2 + \left(n_2 - \frac{n}{4}\right)^2\right\}$

(c) $\chi^2 = \frac{n}{8}\left\{\left(n_1 - \frac{n}{4}\right)^2 + \left(n_2 - \frac{n}{4}\right)^2\right\}$

(d) $\chi^2 = \frac{8}{n}\left\{\left(n_1 - \frac{n}{4}\right)^2 + \left(n_2 - \frac{n}{4}\right)^2\right\}$

110. Degrees of freedom for the χ^2-statistic for Brown and Mood's test for regression parameters is:

(a) 1
(b) 2
(c) 4
(d) 8

111. Brown and Mood's test involves the estimated value of:

(a) the intercept α
(b) the slope β
(c) the intercept α and slope β
(d) none of the above

112. The parameter of α simple regression line $Y = \alpha + \beta X$ of which the significance can be tested by Mood's test is:

(a) the intercept α
(b) the slope β
(c) both (a) and (b)
(d) neither (a) nor (b)

113. Mood's test for testing the significance of simple regression coefficient is based on:

(a) Chi-square statistic
(b) Statistic-t
(c) Kendall's τ
(d) none of the above

114. Theil's test is meant for testing the null hypotheses:

(a) $H_0 : \beta = \beta_0$ vs. $H_1 : \beta \neq \beta_0$
(b) $H_0 : \beta \leq \beta_0$ vs. $H_1 : \beta > \beta_0$
(c) $H_0 : \beta \geq \beta_0$ vs. $H_1 : \beta < \beta_0$
(d) all of the above

115. Theil's test for a hypothesis about regression coefficient of a simple linear regression equation is based on:

(a) χ^2-statistic
(b) student-t
(c) Kendall's-τ statistic
(d) none of the above

116. Formula for Kendall's partial correlation coefficient $\tau_{YZ \cdot X}$ is:

(a) $\tau_{YZ \cdot X} = \frac{\tau_{XY} - \tau_{XZ}\,\tau_{XZ}}{\sqrt{1-\tau_{XZ}^2}\,\sqrt{1-\tau_{YZ}^2}}$

(b) $\tau_{YZ \cdot X} = \frac{\tau_{YZ} - \tau_{XZ}\,\tau_{XY}}{\sqrt{1-\tau_{XZ}^2}\,\sqrt{1-\tau_{XY}^2}}$

(c) $\tau_{YZ \cdot X} = \frac{\tau_{XZ} - \tau_{XY}\,\tau_{YZ}}{\sqrt{1-\tau_{XY}^2}\,\sqrt{1-\tau_{YZ}^2}}$

(d) none of the above

117. In nonparametric statistic, usually the confidence interval is found out for:

(a) population median
(b) population mean
(c) both (a) and (b)
(d) neither (a) nor (b)

118. With usual notations of Kolmogorov-Smirnov test, the distribution $F_X(x)$ lying between the limits $Sn(x) \pm D_{n,\alpha}$ with confidence probability $1 - \alpha$ is called:

(a) Confidence interval
(b) Confidence band
(c) Confidence limits
(d) none of the above

119. One sample runs test is better than binomial test in the sense that:

(a) runs test is based on the order of the events
(b) runs test gives information not indicated by the frequency of the events

(*c*) runs test often rejects the hypothesis which would never be rejected by binomial test
(*d*) all the above

120. Wald-Wolfowitz runs test for two samples is affected when the ties occur:
(*a*) within samples
(*b*) between samples
(*c*) either within or between samples
(*d*) all of the above

121. Which of the following tests is analogous to χ^2 test of goodness of fit?
(*a*) Mann-Whitney *U*-test
(*b*) Kolmogorov-Smirnov test
(*c*) Wilcoxon signed rank test
(*d*) Median lest

122. To test the randomness of a sample, the appropriate test is:
(*a*) run test
(*b*) sign test
(*c*) median test
(*d*) Page's test

123. Kolmogorov-Smirnov test is a:
(*a*) one sample test
(*b*) two sample test
(*c*) either one or two sample test
(*d*) neither one nor two sample test.

124. Kruskal-Wallis test differs from that of Friedman test in respect of:
(*a*) hypothesis about treatment effects
(*b*) ranking procedure
(*c*) the distribution of test statistics
(*d*) all of the above

125. In Wilcoxon matched pairs signed rank test for testing the significance of median, possibly the alternative hypothesis is:
(*a*) Median of the population is not zero
(*b*) Median of the population is less than zero
(*c*) Median of the population is greater than zero
(*d*) any one of the above

126. Kendall's τ and Spearman's r_S differ in respect of:
(*a*) their approach towards unity
(*b*) numerical values for the same set of data
(*c*) the unbiasedness of estimates
(*d*) all of the above

127. Kendall's τ and coefficient of concordance *W* have one thing in common that is:
(*a*) both have same range
(*b*) the inventor of both is same
(*c*) both are unbiased estimates of population rank correlation coefficient
(*d*) all of the above

128. Page's test and Friedman test in two-way analysis differ in respect of:
(*a*) the alternative hypothesis
(*b*) their test statistics
(*c*) in their approach towards normality
(*d*) all of the above

129. Cochran's procedure of analysis of data is a generalisation of the technique propounded by:
(*a*) Kruskal-Wallis
(*b*) Friedman
(*c*) Mcnemar
(*d*) Kendall

130. Brown and Mood's method of fitting a regression line is a:
(*a*) graphical method
(*b*) mathematical procedure
(*c*) method of least squares
(*d*) none of the above

ANSWERS

Section B

1. mild **2.** nominal **3.** accurate **4.** not synonymous **5.** nonparametric **6.** easier **7.** nonparametric **8.** dirty **9.** no restriction **10.** continuity **11.** demerits **12.** Asymptotic relative efficiency; Power efficiency **13.** Pitmans **14.** power efficiency **15.** tied ranks **16.** mid rank **17.** surmounting **18.** type I error **19.** not always **20.** discard **21.** hypotheses **22.** sample observations **23.** fixed criteria **24.** ordered statistics

25. not the same **26.** dependent **27.** Glivenko Cantelli **28.** sample size; confidence band **29.** median **30.** binomial **31.** signs; magnitude **32.** 25 **33.** run **34.** randomness **35.** nonrandomness **36.** nonrandomness **37.** lack of randomness **38.** empirical **39.** distance **40.** differences **41.** location parameters **42.** hypergeometric **43.** $n_1\, t/n$; $n_1 n_2(n-t)/n^2(n-1)$ **44.** Lieberman and Owen; 1961 **45.** identical **46.** two populations **47.** $U' = n_1 n_2 - U$ **48.** $n_1 n_2/2$; $n_1 n_2 (n_1 + n_2 + 1)/12$

49. $\dfrac{2mn}{m+n}+1; \dfrac{2mn(2mn-m-n)}{(m+n)^2\,(m+n-1)}$ **50.** dispersions

51. equal **52.** $n_1 \leq n_2$ **53.** sum of squares **54.** dispersion **55.** sub-samples **56.** variate values **57.** Mann-Whitney **58.** two cell **59.** Chi-square **60.** Yates **61.** one way **62.** dichotomous **63.** Chi-square **64.** oneway **65.** weighted **66.** $k-1$ **67.** two way **68.** equality **69.** ordered alternatives **70.** $J = \sum_{i<j} U_{ij}$

71. ordered **72.** $L = \sum_j jR_j$ **73.** C.E. Spearman

74. $1-\dfrac{6\Sigma d_i^2}{n(n^2-1)}$ **75.** -1 to $+1$ **76.** adjusted **77.** *t*-test

78. natural order **79.** $S\Big/\dbinom{n}{2}$ **80.** $\tau = \dfrac{2r_s}{3}$ **81.** -1 to $+1$ **82.** perfect **83.** affected **84.** 0, $2(2n+5)/9n(n-1)$ **85.** association **86.** M.G. Kendall **87.** 0 to 1

88. perfect **89.** no agreement **90.** $r_{Sav} = \dfrac{kW-1}{k-1}$

91. does not **92.** perfect discordance **93.** to be adjusted **94.** Chi-square **95.** $\chi^2 = k(n-1)W$ **96.** $n-2$ **97.** Mood's or Theil's **98.** Brown's and Mood's **99.** Chi-square **100.** Kendall's τ **101.** eight

102. runs test **103.** $\dfrac{\Sigma T}{n(n^2-1)}$ **104.** $1-\dfrac{\Sigma T_i}{rk(k^2-1)}$

105. $1-\dfrac{F}{1-\dfrac{\Sigma T_i}{rk(k^2-1)}}$ **106.** $rk(k+1)^2/4$; $\dfrac{r(k^3-k)^2}{144(k-1)}$

107. confidence band **108.** flexible **109.** Chi-square

110. $(\tau_{XZ} - \tau_{XY}\,\tau_{YZ})\Big/\sqrt{(1-\tau_{XY}^2)(1-\tau_{YZ}^2)}$ **111.** -1 to 1 **112.** Mann-Whitney; Wilcoxon's **113.** 10 **114.** 0.25 **115.** 1/7 **116.** 52.5 **117.** 0.54 **118.** 0.289 **119.** 7.5 **120.** 1.07 **121.** Mann-Whitney *U*-test **122.** Kendall's τ **123.** a biased **124.** normal distribution **125.** same **126.** *Z*-test **127.** median **128.** *t*-est **129.** G.W. Brown; A.M. Mood **130.** graphic

Section C

1. (*a*) **2.** (*c*) **3.** (*a*) **4.** (*a*) **5.** (*d*)
6. (*b*) **7.** (*c*) **8.** (*a*) **9.** (*d*) **10.** (*d*)
11. (*a*) **12.** (*d*) **13.** (*b*) **14.** (*a*) **15.** (*c*)
16. (*d*) **17.** (*a*) **18.** (*b*) **19.** (*d*) **20.** (*b*)
21. (*c*) **22.** (*d*) **23.** (*c*) **24.** (*a*) **25.** (*b*)
26. (*d*) **27.** (*b*) **28.** (*c*) **29.** (*d*) **30.** (*c*)
31. (*a*) **32.** (*c*) **33.** (*a*) **34.** (*b*) **35.** (*d*)
36. (*b*) **37.** (*a*) **38.** (*c*) **39.** (*a*) **40.** (*b*)
41. (*c*) **42.** (*b*) **43.** (*b*) **44.** (*a*) **45.** (*c*)
46. (*a*) **47.** (*c*) **48.** (*c*) **49.** (*c*) **50.** (*a*)
51. (*b*) **52.** (*a*) **53.** (*d*) **54.** (*c*) **55.** (*b*)
56. (*b*) **57.** (*c*) **58.** (*d*) **59.** (*d*) **60.** (*c*)
61. (*b*) **62.** (*a*) **63.** (*d*) **64.** (*b*) **65.** (*d*)
66. (*d*) **67.** (*a*) **68.** (*a*) **69.** (*d*) **70.** (*d*)
71. (*b*) **72.** (*a*) **73.** (*b*) **74.** (*d*) **75.** (*c*)
76. (*b*) **77.** (*a*) **78.** (*b*) **79.** (*d*) **80.** (*c*)
81. (*a*) **82.** (*b*) **83.** (*c*) **84.** (*b*) **85.** (*b*)
86. (*b*) **87.** (*d*) **88.** (*c*) **89.** (*a*) **90.** (*b*)
91. (*c*) **92.** (*d*) **93.** (*a*) **94.** (*a*) **95.** (*b*)
96. (*b*) **97.** (*a*) **98.** (*a*) **99.** (*c*) **100.** (*c*)
101. (*b*) **102.** (*a*) **103.** (*c*) **104.** (*b*) **105.** (*a*)
106. (*b*) **107.** (*c*) **108.** (*c*) **109.** (*d*) **110.** (*b*)
111. (*d*) **112.** (*b*) **113.** (*a*) **114.** (*d*) **115.** (*c*)
116. (*b*) **117.** (*a*) **118.** (*b*) **119.** (*d*) **120.** (*b*)
121. (*b*) **122.** (*a*) **123.** (*c*) **124.** (*b*) **125.** (*d*)
126. (*d*) **127.** (*b*) **128.** (*d*) **129.** (*c*) **130.** (*a*).

SUGGESTED READING

1. Agarwal, B.L., *Basic Statistics*, New Age International, New Delhi, 8th edition, 2024.
2. Daniel, W.E., *Applied Nonparametric Statistics*, Hougton Mifflin Company, Boston, 1978.

3. Gibbon, J.D., *Nonparametric Statistical Inference*, McGraw Hill, Kogakusha, Tokyo, 1971.
4. Gibbon, J.D., *Nonparametric Methods for Quantitative Analysis*, Hold, Rinehart and Winston, New York, 1976.
5. Mood, A.M., Graybill, F.A., Boes, D.C., *Introduction to the Theory of Statistics*, McGraw-Hill Kogakusha, Tokyo, 3rd. edn., 1974.
6. Ostle, B., *Statistics in Research*, Oxford & IBH, New Delhi, 1966.

CHAPTER 13

Regression and Correlation Methods

SECTION A

Short Essay Type Questions

Q. 1. *Give the idea of regression methods.*

Ans. Regression methods are meant to determine the best functional relationship between a dependent variable Y with one or more concomitant or related variable (s) X. The functional relationship of a dependent variable with one or more independent variables is called a *regression equation.* If the relationship between a dependent variable Y and an independent variable X is linear, it is known as *simple regression of* Y on X. The graph of the regression equation in general is known as the *curve of regression.* If the curve is a straight line, it is called the line of *regression.* The functional relationship of a variable Y with other two or more independent variables is termed as *multiple regression.* Often the independent variables are called *regressors* or *explanatory* variables. Also the dependent variable is frequently named as *regressed* or *response* variable.

The aim of regression model is to estimate as best as possible, the dependent variable Y from the independent variable (s) X. Hence, a regression equation is also called a *estimating* or *prediction equation. The line of average relationship* is another name given to the regression line.

In many situations, it is possible to take X as dependent variable and Y as independent variable. If so, the line of regression is of X on Y. For example, the height and weight of persons are the variables in which either can be taken as independent variable and the other as dependent variable. Hence, one can obtain two lines of regression namely the regression line of Y on X and of X on Y. But if the regression of Y on X is linear, it is not necessary that the regression of X on Y is also linear and *vice-versa.*

Q. 2. *What is a regression model?*

Ans. A functional relationship of a dependent variable Y with the independent variable (s) $X_1, X_2, ..., X_k$ involving the parameters $\beta_0, \beta_1, \beta_2, ..., \beta_k$ of the type.

$$Y = \psi(X_1, X_2, ..., X_k \mid \beta_0, \beta_1, \beta_2, ..., \beta_k) + \varepsilon$$

is called a *regression model.*

Where ψ indicates the form of the equation and ε is a random variable distributed with mean 0 and variance σ_e^2 and is known as the residual or error term. Such a regression equation is called mathematical, or statistical or probabilistic model. The main advantage of probabilistic model is that it enables one to draw inferences about the parameter $\beta_0, \beta_1, ..., \beta_k$. As a special case, a function of the type

$$Y = \psi(X_1, X_2, ..., X_k \mid \beta_0, \beta_1, \beta_2, ...; \beta_k)$$

is known as deterministic model.

More specifically, the statistical model for simple linear regression of Y on X is

$$Y = \beta_0 + \beta_1 X + \varepsilon$$

In this equation β_0 is the intercept which the line cuts on the axis of Y and β_1 is the slope of the line and is called the *regression coefficient*. ε is error which is distributed as $N(0, \sigma_e^2)$.

Q. 3. *What are the assumptions made in a linear regression?*

Ans. There are four assumptions made in a linear regression model:

(*i*) For each selected X, Y's are distributed normally and independently about the mean $\mu_{Y/X} = \eta = \beta_0 + \beta_1 X$ and variance $\sigma^2_{Y/X} = \sigma^2_{Y \cdot X}$.

(*ii*) The population of values of Y corresponding to each selected X has mean μ, which lies on the line

$$\mu = \beta_0 + \beta_1(X - \bar{X})$$
$$= \beta_0 + \beta_1 x.$$

(*iii*) The variable X is measured without error and is known exactly.

(*iv*) The homoscedasticity of the variance $\sigma^2_{Y/X}$ is assumed in a linear regression model and is same as σ_e^2.

Q. 4. *Define regression coefficient.*

Ans. The regression coefficient 'β' is a measure of change in dependent (response) variable Y corresponding to an unit change in independent variable X.

β is often written as β_{YX} to indicate that it is the regression coefficient of Y on X. Similarly β_{XY} denotes the regression coefficient of X on y. Often the suffix are omitted and are understood by themselves.

Q. 5. *Who coined the term 'regression'?*

Ans. The linear relation between two variables was named as 'regression' for the first time by the English scientist, Sir Francis Galton.

Q. 6. *What is a scatter diagram?*

Ans. When the pairs of values (X_i, Y_i) for $i = 1, 2, ..., n$ are plotted on a graph paper, the points show the pattern in which they lie. Such a diagram is known as scatter diagram. If these points lie on a straight line, it is expected that there is a linear relationship between X and Y, otherwise not.

Q. 7. *What do you understand by fitting of regression equation?*

Ans. By fitting of a regression equation we mean to estimate the regression parameters $\beta_0, \beta_1, ..., \beta_k$ with the help of sample observational data in such a way that error ε is minimised.

Q. 8. *How can the parameters β_0 and β_1 be estimated?*

Ans. Most commonly adopted method is legendre's least squares approach. Under this approach, the residual sum of squares

$$\sum_i \varepsilon_i^2 = \sum_i (y_i - \beta_0 - \beta_1 x_i)^2$$

where (x_i, y_i) are the n pairs of sample observations for $i = 1, 2, ..., n$.

is minimised by partially differentiating it w.r.t. β_0 and β_1 respectively and equating them to zero. Also replace β_0 and β_1 by their estimates b_0 and b_1 respectively. In this way, we get two equations,

$$\sum_i y_i = nb_0 + b_1 \sum_i x_i$$

$$\sum_i x_i y_i = b_0 \sum_i x_i + b_1 \sum_i x_i^2$$

These equations are known as *normal equations*. Solving these equations, one gets the values of b_0 and b_1 which are,

$$b_0 = \bar{y} - b_1 \bar{x}$$

and $$b_1 = \frac{\sum_i x_i y_i - \frac{(\sum_i x_i)(\sum_i y_i)}{n}}{\sum_i x_i^2 - \frac{(\sum_i x_i)^2}{n}}$$

$$= \frac{\sum_i (x_i - \bar{x})(y_i - \bar{y})}{\sum_i (x_i - \bar{x})^2}$$

$$= \frac{\text{cov}(X, Y)}{\text{var}(X)}$$

$$= \frac{s_{XY}}{s_X^2}$$

$$= r\frac{s_Y}{s_X}$$

If we study whole population, the value of

$$\beta_{YX} = \frac{\sigma_{XY}}{\sigma_X^2} = \rho\frac{\sigma_Y}{\sigma_X}.$$

The estimated regression equation of Y on X is

$$\hat{Y} = (\bar{y} - b_1\bar{x}) + b_1 X$$

or $$(\hat{Y} - \bar{y}) = b_1(X - \bar{x})$$

Note: To obtain the regression equation of X on Y, replace Y by X and X by Y in the whole process.

Q. 9. *Comment on the unbiasedness of regression estimates.*

Ans. Taking the deviations from mean of x values for n pairs of observations, the regression equation can be given as,

$$y_i = \beta_0 + \beta_1 (x_i - \bar{x}) + \varepsilon_i$$

for $i = 1, 2, ..., n$

where $\varepsilon_i \sim N(0, \sigma_e^2)$ and $\bar{x} = \Sigma x_i / n$.

The estimate of β_0, *i.e.*, $b_0 = \bar{y} = \beta_0 + \bar{\varepsilon}$

$$E(b_0) = E(\bar{y}) = E(\beta_0 + \bar{\varepsilon}) = \beta_0$$

since $$E(\bar{\varepsilon}) = \frac{1}{n}E\left(\sum_i \varepsilon_i\right) = 0$$

The estimate of β_1 is,

$$b_1 = \frac{\sum_i y_i(x_i - \bar{x})}{\sum_i (x_i - \bar{x})^2}$$

$$= \frac{\sum_i [\beta_0 + \beta_1(x_i - \bar{x}) + \varepsilon_i](x_i - \bar{x})}{\sum_i (x_i - \bar{x})^2}$$

$$= \beta_1 + \frac{\sum_i (x_i - \bar{x})\varepsilon_i}{\sum_i (x_i - \bar{x})^2}$$

$$E(b_1) = \beta_1.$$

Hence, it has been proved that both the regression estimates are unbiased.

Q. 10. *Give expressions for the variance of estimates of the constants of the regression line $Y = \beta_0 + \beta_1 X + \varepsilon$ and also of estimates of Y on X and X on Y.*

Ans. Let there be n pairs of values (x_i, y_i) for $i = 1, 2, ..., n$ and $\varepsilon_i \sim N(0, \sigma_e^2)$. Then

$$V(b_1) = \frac{\sigma_e^2}{\sum_i (x_i - \bar{x})^2}$$

$$V(b_0) = \frac{\sigma_e^2}{n}$$

Also, $$S_{YX}^2 = \frac{1}{n}\sum_i (Y_i - \bar{Y}_i)^2 = \sigma_y^2(1 - r^2),$$ similarly

$$S_{XY}^2 = \frac{1}{n}\sum_i (X_i - \bar{X}_i)^2 = \sigma_x^2(1 - r^2).$$

Q. 11. *Delineate the properties of regression coefficients.*

Ans. Different properties of regression coefficients are delineated below:

(*i*) The range of regression coefficient is $-\infty$ to ∞.

(*ii*) The correlation coefficient between two variable X and Y is the geometric mean of the two regression coefficients b_{YX} and b_{XY}. This is known as the *fundamental property* of regression coefficients.

Notationally,

$$\beta_{YX} = \rho\frac{\sigma_Y}{\sigma_X} \text{ and } \beta_{XY} = \rho\frac{\sigma_X}{\sigma_Y}$$

$$\beta_{YX}\cdot\beta_{XY} = \rho\frac{\sigma_Y}{\sigma_X}.\rho\frac{\sigma_X}{\sigma_Y}$$

or $\beta_{YX}\cdot\beta_{XY} = \rho^2$

or $\rho = \sqrt{\beta_{YX}\cdot\beta_{XY}}$

For sample, $r = \sqrt{b_{YX}\cdot b_{XY}}$

(*iii*) The signs of regression coefficients and correlation coefficient are always the same. This is known as *signature property of regression coefficient.*

Notationally,

$$\beta_{YX} > 0 \Leftrightarrow \rho > 0 \quad \text{or} \quad \beta_{XY} > 0 \Leftrightarrow \rho > 0$$
$$\beta_{YX} < 0 \Leftrightarrow \rho < 0 \quad \text{or} \quad \beta_{XY} < 0 \Leftrightarrow \rho < 0$$

(*iv*) The arithmetic mean of the two regression coefficients β_{YX} and β_{XY} is greater than or equal to the correlation coefficient between the variables X and Y. This is known as the *mean property* of regression coefficients. Notationally,

$$\frac{1}{2}(\beta_{YX} + \beta_{XY}) \geq \rho$$

(*v*) If one of the regression coefficient in a simple linear regression is greater than unity, the other is less than unity. This is known as the *magnitude property* of regression coefficients. Notationally,

if $\beta_{YX} > 1 \Leftrightarrow \beta_{XY} < 1$

or if $\beta_{XY} > 1 \Leftrightarrow \beta_{YX} < 1$

(*vi*) If the variables X and Y are independent, the regression coefficients are zero. This is known as the *independence property* of regression coefficients. Notationally, if X and Y are independent, then

$$\rho = 0 \Leftrightarrow \sigma_{XY} = \sigma_{YX} = 0 \Leftrightarrow \beta_{YX} = \beta_{XY} = 0$$

(*vii*) Variance of the regression coefficient of Y on X is,

$$V(b_{YX}) = \frac{1}{n}\frac{\sigma_Y^2}{\sigma_X^2}(1-\rho^2)$$

Similarly, $$V(b_{XY}) = \frac{1}{n}\frac{\sigma_X^2}{\sigma_Y^2}(1-\rho^2)$$

Q. 12. *At what point, the two lines of regression intersect?*

Ans. The lines of regression of Y on X and X on Y intersect at the mean value of the variables, *i.e.*, their point of intersection is $(\bar{X}, \bar{Y})$. Obviously, the point $(\bar{X}, \bar{Y})$ satisfy both the equations, $(\hat{Y} - \bar{Y}) = b_{YX}(X - \bar{X})$ and $(\hat{X} - \bar{X}) = b_{XY}(Y - \bar{Y})$.

Q. 13. *If we convert the two variables of a simple regression line into standard deviates, through which point, the two regression lines will pass.*

Ans. The regression lines of Y on X and X on Y will pass through the origin.

Q. 14. *What is the tangent of the angle between the two lines of regression?*

Ans. If ∂ is the angle between the regression lines $(Y - \bar{Y}) = \beta_{YX}(X - \bar{X})$ and $(X - \bar{X}) = \beta_{XY}(Y - \bar{Y})$, then

$$\tan(\theta) = \frac{1-\rho^2}{\rho}\cdot\frac{\sigma_X\sigma_Y}{\sigma_X^2 + \sigma_Y^2}$$

(*i*) If $\rho = \pm 1$, $\tan\theta = 0 \Rightarrow \theta = 0$. This shows, when there is perfect correlation between X and Y, the two lines of regression are coincident.

(*ii*) If $\rho = 0$, $\tan\theta = \infty \Rightarrow \theta = \frac{\pi}{2} = 90°$. This infers, when the variables X and Y are uncorrelated, the two lines of regression are perpendicular to each other. In terms of regression coefficients,

$$\tan(\theta) = \frac{1 - b_{YX} \cdot b_{XY}}{b_{YX} + b_{XY}}$$

(*ii*) The two lines of regression are coincident if $b_{YX} \cdot b_{XY} = 1$.

(*ii*) The two lines of regression are perpendicular to each other if the two regression coefficients are equal in magnitude but opposite in sign, *i.e.*,

$$b_{YX} = -\,b_{XY}$$

Q. 15. *What is the effect of coding on regression coefficient?*

Ans. If we subtract constants c_1 and c_2 from the variables X and Y and then divide them by suitable constants d_1 and d_2 respectively, the variables are said to be coded or linearly transformed. Thus, the coded variables are $X' = \frac{X - c_1}{d_1}$ and $Y' = \frac{Y - c_2}{d_2}$.

It is trivial to prove that the regression coefficient is independent of origin but not of scale. The relation between regression coefficient without and with coding is,

$$\beta_{YX} = \frac{d_2}{d_1}\,\beta_{Y'X'} \text{ and } \beta_{XY} = \frac{d_1}{d_2}\,\beta_{X'Y'}$$

Q. 16. *Where does one require the assumption of normality of ε vis-a-vis the variable Y?*

Ans. The assumption of normality becomes essential while testing the significance of regression parameters or finding their confidence limits.

Also this assumption becomes necessary while testing the significance of regression coefficient by F-test. Under the assumption of normality, the regression mean sum of squares $b \sum_{i=1}^{n} u_i v_i$ is distributed as $\chi_1^2 \sigma_e^2$ with 1 d.f. and residual mean sum of square 'S_e^2' is distributed as $\chi_2^2 \sigma_e^2$ with $(n-2)$ d.f. where $u_i = x_i - \bar{x}$ and $v_i = y_i - \bar{y}$.

Q. 17. *How will you test the significance of regression coefficient?*

Ans. The significance of the regression coefficient can be tested by student's t-test. Here we test,

$$H_0 : \beta_{YX} = 0 \text{ vs. } H_1 : \beta_{YX} \neq 0$$

To test H_0 against H_1, the test statistic is,

$$t = \frac{b_{YX}}{S_b}$$

t has $(n-2)$ d.f.

where b_{YX} is the estimated value of β_{YX} and s_b is the standard error of β_{YX}. s_b can be computed by the formula,

$$s_b = \sqrt{\frac{s_e^2}{\sum_i u_i^2}}$$

where $u_i = x_i - \bar{x}$ and $v_i = y_i - \bar{y}$ for $i = 1, 2, \ldots, n$

Also, $$s_e^2 = \frac{1}{(n-2)}\left\{\sum_i v_i^2 - b_{YX}\sum_i u_i v_i\right\}$$

Substituting the value of b_{YX} and s_b, the value of t is available. On comparing the computed value of t with the tabulated value of t at α level of significance and for $(n-2)$ d.f., the decision about H_0 is taken in the usual way.

Q. 18. *Give a test for testing the significance of the intercept β_0.*

Ans. The test of the hypothesis

$$H_0 : \beta_0 = 0 \text{ vs. } H_1 : \beta_0 \neq 0$$

can be tested by the statistic

$$t = \frac{b_0}{s_{b_0}}$$

where s_{b_0} is the standard error of an estimator b_0. With usual notations.

$$s_{b_0}^2 = s_e^2\left\{\frac{1}{n} + \frac{\bar{x}^2}{\sum_i u_i^2}\right\}$$

The decision about the acceptance or rejection of H_0 is taken in the usual manner.

Q. 19. *Give F-test for testing the significance of the regression coefficient.*

Ans. The hypothesis

$$H_0 : \beta_{YX} = 0 \text{ vs. } H_1 : \beta_{YX} \neq 0$$

can be tested by the test statistics

$$F = \frac{b\sum_i u_i v_i}{s_e^2}$$

F has $(1, n-2)$ d.f.

To decide as to whether the regression coefficient is significant or not, the tabulated value of F for $(1, n-2)$ d.f. and α level of significance and computed value of F are compared. If $F \geq F_{\alpha(1,\, n-2)}$, reject H_0. It means that the value of regression coefficient is significant. Again if $F \leq F_{\alpha(1,\, n-2)}$, accept H_0. It reveals that the value of regression coefficient is non-significant.

Q. 20. *What do you understand by regression function?*

Ans. From minimisation problem it is known that $E\{Y - g(X)\}^2$ is minimum when $g(x) = E\{Y \mid X = x\}$. The graph of this minimum function $Y = g(x)$ is the *regression curve* of Y on X. The random function $g(x)$ is called the *regression function* of Y on X.

The regression curve of the mean of Y on X can be defined as the functional relation $y = E(Y \mid X = x)$. Also $E(Y \mid x) = \alpha + \beta X$ is called the line of regression of Y on X. In the same way, the *regression curve* of the mean of X on Y is defined as the functional relation $x = E\{X \mid Y = y\}$. Also $E(X \mid y) = \alpha' + \beta' Y$ is known as the line of regression of X on Y.

Q. 21. *If $(X, Y) \sim BN(0, 0, \sigma_X^2, \sigma_Y^2, \rho)$, find the correlation between X^2 and Y^2.*

Ans. For the given bivariate normal distribution, the two regression equations, of Y on X and of X on Y are,

$$Y = \rho\frac{\sigma_Y}{\sigma_X} X \text{ and } X = \rho\frac{\sigma_X}{\sigma_Y} Y$$

or

$$Y^2 = \frac{\rho^2\sigma_Y^2}{\sigma_X^2} X^2 \text{ and } X^2 = \rho^2\frac{\sigma_X^2}{\sigma_Y^2} Y^2$$

These equations represent the linear regression equations of Y^2 on X^2 and of X^2 on Y^2 respectively. Thus, the correlation between X^2 and Y^2 is the geometric mean of the regression coefficients, *i.e.*,

$$\text{Corr. Coeff.} = \sqrt{\rho^2\frac{\sigma_Y^2}{\sigma_X^2} . \rho^2\frac{\sigma_X^2}{\sigma_Y^2}}$$

$$= \rho^2$$

Hence, the correlation coefficient between X^2 and Y^2 is ρ^2.

Q. 22. *Give the expression for $(1 - \alpha)$ 100 per cent confidence limits for the regression coefficient β_{YX}.*

Ans. $(1 - \alpha)$ 100 per cent confidence limits for the regression coefficient β_{YX} with usual notations can be given as,

$$b_{YX} \mp s_b \cdot t_{\alpha,\,(n-2)}$$

where $t_{\alpha,\,(n-2)}$ is student's t-value obtained from t-table for a two-tailed test for α level of significance and $(n - 2)$ d.f.

Q. 23. *What formula is used to find the confidence limits for the intercept β_0?*

Ans. Following the usual principle of confidence interval estimation, the formula for $(1 - \alpha)$ 100 per cent confidence limits for the intercept β_0 is,

$$b_0 \mp s_{b_0} \cdot t_{\alpha,\,(n-2)},$$

where $t_{\alpha,\,(n-2)}$ is the tabulated t-value, from a t-table tabulated for two-tailed test, for α level of significance and $(n - 2)$ d.f.

Q. 24. *For the regression equation $\mu_{Y/X} = \beta_0 + \beta_1 X$ estimated as $\hat{Y} = b_0 + b_1 X$, find $(1 - \alpha)$ 100 per cent confidence limits for $\mu_{Y|X} = \eta$ (say).*

Ans. $(1-\alpha)$ 100 per cent confidence limits for η are obtained by the formula,

$$\hat{Y} \mp s_{\hat{Y}} t_{\alpha, (n-2)}$$

where $t_{\alpha, (n-2)}$ the tabulated value of t for two-sided t-table at α level of significance and $(n-2)$ d.f. Also the estimated variance of predicted individual Y for a given X is,

$$s_{\hat{Y}}^2 = s_e^2 \left\{1 + \frac{1}{n} + \frac{(X - \bar{X})^2}{\sum_i u_i^2}\right\}$$

where $u_i = (x_i - \bar{x})$.

Q. 25. *What are the uses of regression analysis?*

Ans. There are many uses of regression analysis. The important ones are given below:

(*i*) In many situations the dependent variable Y is such that it cannot be measured directly. But with the help of some concomitant or auxiliary variables as independent variables in a regression equation, Y can be estimated.

(*ii*) The effect of certain treatments can better be adjudged by estimating the effect of concomitant variables.

(*iii*) The length of a confidence interval of population mean can be deduced by considering the effect of dummy variables.

(*iv*) Regression equation is often used as a prediction equation.

(*v*) To measure the influence of independent variables on the dependent variable which may be having a casual relationship.

Q. 26. *Give five examples where the use of regression analysis can beneficially be made.*

Ans. Five examples of use of regression analysis from different areas are given below:

(*i*) Height of a person at a given age can be estimated by finding the regression of height (Y) on age (X).

(*ii*) The yields of a crop can be predicted for different doses of a fertilizer, of course within the non-toxic doses of fertilizer.

(*iii*) A scientist may be able to estimate the brain size on the basis of certain related external body measurements.

(*iv*) Future demand of food may be predicted with the help of regression models.

(*v*) Certain treatments can be compared accurately by eliminating the effect of certain variables like percentage germination per unit area, number of weeds per unit area, etc.

Q. 27. *How can you test the linearity of regression?*

Ans. To test the linearity of regression, one must have a measure of error other than the residual sum of squares. This can be achieved only by obtaining repeated measures of the dependent variable Y for each value of the independent variable X by repeating the experiment a number of times.

We now assert that the regression line of Y on X is of the form

$$Y_{ij} = \beta_0 + \beta_1(x_i - \bar{x}) + \varepsilon_{ij}$$

for $i = 1, 2, ..., p$

$j = 1, 2, ..., n_i$

ε_{ij} are i.i.d. $N(0, \sigma_e^2)$. Here we are considering the most general case when the data are large and independent. Variates are grouped in different classes.

Let x_i be the median value of the class into which they fall having n_i values. The least squares estimates b_0 and b_1 of β_0 and β_1, respectively, are:

$$b_0 = \frac{\sum_i n_i \bar{y}_i}{n} = \bar{y}$$

$$b_1 = \frac{\sum_i n_i(\bar{x}_i - \bar{x})(\bar{y}_i - \bar{y})}{\sum_i n_i(x_i - \bar{x})^2}$$

$$= \frac{\sum_i n_i\, \bar{y}_i(x_i - \bar{x})}{\sum_i n_i(x_i - \bar{x})^2}$$

where $\sum_i n_i = n,\ \bar{y}_i = \frac{1}{n_i}\sum_j y_{ij}$

and $\bar{x} = \frac{\sum_i n_i\, \bar{x}_i}{n}$

Test of linearity of regression can easily be performed through analysis of variance for one way classification. Thus the ANOVA table is as follows:

Source (i)	*d.f.* (ii)	*S.S.* (iii)	*M.S.* (iv) (iii) ÷ (ii)	*F-value* (v)
Due to regression	1	$b_1^2 \sum_i n_i (x_i - \bar{x})^2$		
Due to deviation from regression	$(p-2)$	$\sum_i n_i (y_i - \bar{y})^2$ $-b_1 \sum_i n_i (x_i - \bar{x})^2$	D	D/E
Between groups	$(p-1)$	$\sum_i n_i (y_i - \bar{y})^2$		
Error	$n-p$	$\sum_i \sum_j (y_{ij} - \bar{y}_i)^2$	E	
Total	$n-1$	$\sum_i \sum_j (y_{ij} - \bar{y})^2$		

If the *F*-value equal to *D*/*E* is greater than or equal to the tabulated value of *F* at α level of significance and for $\{(p-2), (n-p)\}$ d.f., we reject the hypothesis that regression is linear. Otherwise, the hypothesis of linearity is accepted.

Note: It is further emphasised that the significance of regression coefficient has nothing to reveal about the linearity of regression equation.

Q. 28. *What do you understand by weighted regression?*

Ans. If the assumption of homoscedasticity holds no longer, one cannot assume that $\sigma^2_{Y|X}$ is same for all *X*. Hence, the variance $\sigma^2_{Y|X}$ will be dependent of X_i. Let it be denoted by σ_i^2. The variance,

$$\sigma_i^2 = \sigma^2 / w_i$$

where w_i is a known constant and is called the weight of variance for x_i. Often one finds that σ_i^2 is proportional to X_i and hence it looks germane to take $w_i = \frac{1}{X_i}$ or $\sigma_i^2 = \sigma^2 X_i$.

If we consider the regression equation as,

$$Y_{ij} = \beta_0 + \beta_1 X_i + \varepsilon_{ij}$$

for $i = 1, 2, ..., k$

$j = 1, 2, ..., n_i$

Following least square method for estimation of β_0 and β_1, the normal equations are

$$\left(\sum_{i=1}^{k} \frac{n_i}{X_i}\right) b_0 + n b_1 = \sum_{i=1}^{k} \sum_{j=1}^{n_i} \frac{y_{ij}}{X_i}$$

$$n b_0 + \left(\sum_{i=1}^{k} n_i X_i\right) b_1 = \sum_{i=1}^{k} \sum_{j=1}^{n_i} y_{ij}$$

where $\sum_i n_i = n$.

Solving the normal equations it is trivial to get the values of b_0 and b_1.

Q. 29. *The following measurements show the respective heights in inches of ten fathers and their eldest sons:*

Father (X): 67, 63, 66, 71, 69, 65, 62, 70, 61, 72

Son (Y): 68, 66, 65, 70, 69, 67, 64, 71, 60, 63

(i) *Find the regression line of son's height on father's height.*

(ii) *Estimate the height of son for the given height of father as 70 inches.*

(iii) *Test the significance of the regression coefficient β_{YX}.*

(iv) *Calculate 95 per cent confidence limits for β_{YX}.*

(v) *Test the significance of the intercept of the line Y on X.*

(vi) *Find the regression line of X on Y.*

(vii) *At what point the two lines of regression intersect?*

Ans. To fit in the regression lines and test the significance of regression coefficients, etc., we first do the following computations:

$n = 10$, $\Sigma X = 666$, $\Sigma Y = 663$, $\Sigma X^2 = 44490$,

$\Sigma Y^2 = 44061$, $\Sigma XY = 44224$.

$\bar{X} = 66.6$, $\bar{Y} = 66.3$, $\Sigma u_i^2 = 44490 - \frac{(666)^2}{10} = 134.4$

$$\Sigma v_i^2 = 44061 - \frac{(663)^2}{10} = 104.1,$$

$$\Sigma u_i\, v_i = 44224 - \frac{666 \times 663}{10} = 68.2$$

(*i*) The regression coefficient

$$b_{YX} = \frac{68.2}{134.4}$$

$$= 0.507$$

Regression line of son's height on Father's height is,

$$(\hat{Y} - 66.3) = 0.507\,(X - 66.6)$$

$$\hat{Y} = 0.507\,X + 32.53$$

(*ii*) The estimate of son's height for $X = 70$ is,

$$\hat{Y} = 0.507 \times 70 + 32.53$$

$$\hat{Y} = 68.02 \text{ inches}$$

(*iii*) To test

$$H_0 : \beta_{YX} = 0 \text{ vs. } H_1 : \beta_{YX} \neq 0$$

$$s_e^2 = \frac{1}{8}\left\{104.1 - \frac{(68.2)^2}{134.4}\right\}$$

$$= 8.69$$

$$s_b^2 = \frac{8.69}{134.4}$$

$$= 0.0646$$

$$\therefore \quad s_b = 0.2543$$

Thus, the statistic

$$t = \frac{0.507}{0.2543}$$

$$= 1.99$$

Tabulated $t_{0.05,\,8} = 2.306$, which is greater than 1.99. Hence, the regression coefficient is non-significant.

(*iv*) The confidence limits for β_{YX} are,

$$\left.\begin{matrix} b_L \\ b_U \end{matrix}\right] = 0.507 \mp 0.2543 \times 2.306$$

Therefore, $b_L = -0.079$ and $b_U = 1.093$

(*v*) To test

$$H_0 : \beta_0 = 0 \text{ vs. } H_1 : \beta_0 \neq 0$$

we compute,

$$s_{b_0}^2 = 8.69\left\{\frac{1}{10} + \frac{(66.6)^2}{134.4}\right\}$$

$$= 287.66$$

$$\therefore \quad s_{b_0} = 16.96$$

The statistic,

$$t = \frac{32.53}{16.96}$$

$$= 1.918$$

Tabulated $t_{0.05,\,8} = 2.306$, which is greater than 1.918. Hence, the intercept β_0 is non-significant.

(*vi*) For the regression line of X on Y,

$$b_{XY} = \frac{68.2}{104.1}$$

$$= 0.655$$

The regression line of X on Y is,

$$(\hat{X} - 66.6) = 0.655\,(Y - 66.3)$$

$$\hat{X} = 0.655\,Y + 23.174$$

(*vii*) The two lines of regression intersect at the point (66.6, 66.3).

Q. 30. ***What is meant by curvilinear regression?***

Ans. If the test for linearity of regression model reveals that linear fit is inadequate, one is bound to desiderate for some non-linear model. Under this, a scientist often tries one of the following or other function which is non-linear in nature:

(*i*) Second degree curve of parabola,

$$Y = \alpha + \beta X + \gamma X^2$$

(*ii*) Exponential growth curve or compound interest function,

$$Y = a\beta^X$$

(*iii*) Exponential decay model,

$$Y = \alpha\beta^{-X} \text{ for } \beta < 1$$

curves (*ii*) and (*iii*) becomes linear functions by taking logarithm.

(*iv*) Logistic growth curve,

$$\frac{1}{Y} = \alpha\beta^{X} + \gamma \text{ for } \alpha, \beta, \gamma > 0$$

(*v*) Compertz function,

$$\log_e Y = \log_e \gamma + \beta^X \log_e \alpha \text{ for } \alpha, \beta, \gamma > 0$$

(*vi*) Mitscherlich function,

$$Y = \gamma(1 - e^{\alpha - \beta X}) \text{ for } \alpha, \beta, \gamma > 0$$

(*vii*) Cubic Parabola

$$Y = \alpha + \beta X + \gamma X^2 + \delta X^3$$

(*viii*) Equilateral hyperbola, asymptotic to a line parallel to *X*-axis,

$$Y = \frac{1}{\alpha + \beta X}$$

(*ix*) Equilateral hyperbola, asymptotic to a line parallel to *y*-axis.

$$Y = a + b\left(\frac{1}{X}\right)$$

(*x*) Equilateral hyperbola, asymptotic to lines parallel to both the axes,

$$\frac{1}{Y} = a + b\left(\frac{1}{X}\right)$$

(*xi*) The curve with convex or concave bend,

$$\log Y = a + b \log X$$

Convex from above if b is positive,

Concave from above if b is negative.

Q. 31. *What is an orthogonal polynomial and how to fit it?*

Ans. A polynomial ϕ_k in X of degree k is said to be an orthogonal polynomial if corresponding to any other polynomial ϕ_j for $j = 1, 2, \ldots$, the conditions, $\Sigma \phi_j \phi_k = 0$ holds good. The summation (Σ) runs over-all admissible values of X. Here we shall confine our discussion to the orthogonal polynomials in which the X values are equally spaced and the common difference is unity. If it is not unity, it can be made so by dividing each value of X by the common difference. The method of fitting the orthogonal polynomial is as follows.

Let the orthogonal polynomial to be fitted is,

$$Y = \beta_0 + \beta_1 X + \beta_2 X^2 + \ldots + \beta_k X^k$$

The above equation is also called the *parabola of degree k*. Here it is not known what should actually be the value of k or in other words, what should be the degree of the polynomial. One way is to fit in the first degree equation and test the significance of the coefficient of X. If it is significant, add second degree term and test the significance of its coefficient. If it is significant, add third degree term and test the significance of the coefficient of X^3 and continue this process till two consecutive coefficients come out to be non-significant. But this process is very tedious in the sense that every time a fresh calculations have to be made. The tedium of this method can be overcome by using the method of fitting of orthogonal polynomial with X's at equal intervals,

$$\hat{Y} = a_0 + a_1 X + a_2 X^2 + \ldots + a_k X^k$$

can be expressed as,

$$\hat{Y} = a_0 + a_1\phi'_1 + a_2\phi'_2 + \ldots + a_k\phi'_k$$

where ϕ_i's ($i = 1, 2, k$) are orthogonal polynomials and a_i are constants such that,

$$a_0 = \frac{1}{n}\sum_j Y_j = \bar{Y} \text{ and } a_i = \frac{\sum_i Y_i \phi'_i}{\Sigma \phi_i'^2}$$

for $i = 1, 2, \ldots, k$

Elaborately, the orthogonal polynomials are,

$$\phi_1 = (X - \bar{X})$$

$$\phi_2 = (X - \bar{X})^2 - \frac{1}{12}(n^2 - 1)$$

$$\phi_3 = (X - \bar{X})^3 - \frac{1}{20}(3n^2 - 7)(X - \bar{X})$$

A recurrence relation between ϕ_r and ϕ_{r+1} can be established as,

$$\phi_{r+1} = \phi_1 \phi_r - \frac{r^2(n^2-1)}{4(4r^2-1)}\phi_{r-1}$$

The relation between ϕ_r and ϕ'_r is,

$$\phi'_r = \lambda_r \phi_r$$

where λ is the smallest number for which ϕ_r assumes only the integral values. The advantage of the method of orthogonal polynomials is that we can add terms one by one sparingly without redoing the whole calculations. Substituting the values ϕ'_i's, a_0 and a_i's, the orthogonal polynomial is fitted.

The values of ϕ'_i's, λ and $\Sigma\phi^2_i$ can be obtained from Fisher and Yates tables. A part of the table is given below for three values of n:

	$n = 3$		$n = 4$			$n = 5$			
	ϕ_1	ϕ_2	ϕ_1	ϕ_2	ϕ_3	ϕ_1	ϕ_2	ϕ_3	ϕ_4
	–1	1	–3	1	–1	–2	+2	–1	1
	0	–2	–1	–1	3	–1	–1	2	–4
	1	1	1	–1	–3	0	–2	0	6
			3	1	1	1	–1	–2	–4
						2	2	1	1
λ's	1	3	2	1	10/3	1	1	5/6	35/12
$\Sigma\phi^2_{ji}$	2	6	20	4	20	10	14	10	70

The fitted orthogonal polynomial is of the type.

$$\hat{y} = a_0 + a_1\lambda_1(X-\bar{X}) + a_2\lambda_2\left\{(X-\bar{X})^2 - \frac{n^2-1}{12}\right\}$$

$$+\ a_3\lambda_3\left\{(X-\bar{X})^3 - (X-\bar{X})\left(\frac{3n^2-7}{20}\right)\right\} + \ldots$$

Reduction in sum of squares due to first, second, third, ... degree terms can be calculated by the formula for testing the significance of the first, second, third exponents, etc.

Reduction in sum of square due to j^{th} power of X is equal to

$$a_j\left(\sum_i Y_i \phi_{ji}\right)$$

Total sum of squares $= \sum_i (Y_i - \bar{Y})^2$

Sum of squares due to deviation from regression = Total S.S – S.S. due to different exponent terms. Significance of each exponent term can be tested by F-test in an analysis of variance table and the decision about the highest power of the orthogonal polynomial can be taken accordingly.

Q. 32. *How can you fit in a second degree equation (parabola)?*

Ans. A second degree parabola is,

$$Y = \beta_0 + \beta_1 X + \beta_2 X^2 + \varepsilon$$

Suppose (X_i, Y_i) for $i = 1, 2, \ldots, n$ are n paired observations. The regression parameters β_0, β_1 and β_2 can be estimated as b_0, b_1 and b_2 using Legendre's method of least squares. The normal equations under least squares method are:

$$\sum_i Y_i = nb_0 + b_1\Sigma X_i + b_2 \sum_i X_i^2$$

$$\sum_i X_i Y_i = b_0 \sum_i X_i + b_1 \sum_i X_i^2 + b_2 \sum_i X_i^3$$

$$\sum_i X_i^2 Y_i = b_0 \sum_i X_i^2 + b_1 \sum_i X_i^3 + b_2 \sum_i X_i^4$$

Solving these equations, the values of b_0, b_1 and b_2, come out to be,

$$b_1 = \frac{s_{1y}s_{22} - s_{2y}s_{12}}{s_{11}s_{22} - s_{12}^2},\ b_2 = \frac{s_{2y}s_{11} - s_{1y}s_{12}}{s_{11}s_{22} - s_{12}^2}$$

and $\quad b_0 = \bar{Y} = b_1\bar{X} - b_2\bar{X}^2$

where $s_{1y} = \sum_i X_i Y_i - n\bar{X}\bar{Y}$, $s_{2y} = \sum_i X_i^2 Y_i - n\bar{X}^2\bar{Y}$

$$s_{11} = \sum_i X_i^2 - n\bar{X}^2,\ s_{12} = \sum_i X_i^3 - n\bar{X}^3$$

and $\quad s_{22} = \sum_i X_i^4 - n(\bar{X}^2)^2$

Substituting the values of b_0, b_1 and b_2, we obtain the equation of the parabola or second degree polynomial as

$$\hat{Y}' = b_0 + b_1X + b_2X^2$$

CORRELATION

Q. 33. *What do you understand by correlation between two variables?*

Ans. When a bivariate population is under consideration, there is generally a need to study the simultaneous variation between two variables say, X and Y. For example, the variation between heights and weights of persons, demand and price of commodities, circumference of head and marks obtained by students, etc. We know that the variation in a variable X is measured by $E[X - \bar{X})^2$ and in Y by $E(Y - \bar{Y})^2$. Also the joint variation in X and Y is measured as $E(X - \bar{X})(Y - \bar{Y})$. We know, the three terms represent variance of X, Y and covariance between X and Y. So to obtain a measure of relation between X and Y independent of units of measurements. Karl Pearson in 1890 defined a measure of relationship given by the formula,

$$\rho_{XY} = \frac{E(X - \bar{X})(Y - \bar{Y})}{\sqrt{E(X - \bar{X})^2 E(Y - \bar{Y})^2}}$$

$$= \frac{\text{cov}(X, Y)}{\sqrt{\text{var}(X)\,\text{var}(Y)}}$$

$$= \frac{\sigma_{XY}}{\sigma_X \sigma_Y}$$

$$= \frac{\mu_{12}}{\sqrt{\mu_{11}\mu_{22}}}$$

The measure ρ_{XY} is called the *product moment correlation coefficient* or simply *correlation coefficient*. Generally, the suffix XY is not attached to ρ and is understood by itself.

Q. 34. *Define correlation coefficient.*

Ans. Correlation coefficient is a measure of degree or extent of linear relationship between two variables X and Y. The population correlation coefficient is denoted by ρ and its estimate by r.

Q. 35. *Give the formula for sample correlation coefficient r.*

Ans. Let (x_i, y_i) be the n paired sample values. The formula for the sample correlation coefficient r is,

$$r = \frac{\sum_i (x_i - \bar{x})(y_i - \bar{y})}{\sqrt{\sum_i (x_i - \bar{x})^2 \sum_i (y_i - \bar{y})^2}}$$

for $i = 1, 2, ..., n$

$$= \frac{\text{cov}(X, Y)}{\sqrt{v(X)v(Y)}}$$

$$= \frac{s_{XY}}{s_X s_Y}$$

$$= \frac{\sum_i x_i y_i - \frac{(\sum_i x_i)(\sum_i y_i)}{n}}{\sqrt{\left[\sum_i x_i^2 - \frac{(\sum_i x_i)^2}{n}\right]\left[\sum_i y_i^2 - \frac{(\sum_i y_i)^2}{n}\right]}}$$

Q. 36. *What purpose is being served by correlation coefficient?*

Ans. In regression analysis we estimate the value of Y for a given value of X. The estimate is good if the mean sum of squares due to error (deviation from regression) is minimum. We know, the error mean sum of squares is,

$$\sigma_e^2 = \sigma_Y^2 - \frac{\sigma_{XY}^2}{\sigma_X^2}$$

$$= \sigma_Y^2\left(1 - \frac{\sigma_{XY}^2}{\sigma_X^2\,\sigma_y^2}\right)$$

$$= \sigma_Y^2(1 - \rho^2)$$

If $\rho = 0$, there is no purpose of regression of Y on X as $\sigma_e^2 = \sigma_Y^2$. If ρ is high, σ_e^2 will be small and Y can be determined accurately through X. The quantity

ρ^2 is called the *coefficient of determination* and $(1 - \rho^2)$, the *coefficient of non-determination.* Also the quantity $\sqrt{1-\rho^2}$ is called the *coefficient of alienation.*

Q. 37. *Find the limits of* ρ.

Ans. We know that error mean sum of squares,

$$\sigma_e^2 = \sigma_Y^2(1 - \rho^2)$$

Since any sum of squares cannot be negative,

$$1 - \rho^2 \geq 0$$

$$-\rho^2 \geq -1$$

or $$\rho^2 \leq 1$$

or $$\rho \leq \pm 1$$

Thus, the limits of ρ are from -1 to 1 and so is true for r.

Alternative proof. By Schwarz inequality, we know.

$$\{E(x, y)\}^2 \leq E(x^2)\, E(y^2)$$

or $$\left\{\frac{E(x, y)}{\sqrt{E(x^2)E(y^2)}}\right\}^2 \leq 1$$

$$\rho^2 \leq 1$$

or $$-1 \leq \rho \leq 1$$

Q. 38. *Interpret the values of* ρ *as* -1, *1 and 0.*

Ans. If $\rho = 1$, it means that Y is proportional to X which ensures perfect positive linear association. In this case, all points in a scatter diagram lie on a straight line extending from left bottom to the right top. It means as X increases, Y also increases. If $\rho = -1$, it means as X increases, Y decreases. This ensures perfect negative association. In this situation Y is proportional to $\frac{1}{X}$. All the points lie on a straight line extending from left top to the right bottom.

The value $\rho = 0$, confirms the lack of linear association between two variables. In this case, all the points are scattered on a graph and hardly any three points lie in a straight line.

Q. 39. *Discuss the properties of correlation coefficient.*

Ans. The properties of correlation coefficient are:

(*i*) Correlation coefficient is a pure number, *i.e.*, it has no unit.

(*ii*) The correlation coefficient ρ (or r) ranges from -1 to 1.

(*iii*) The correlation between two variables is known as simple correlation or correlation of zero order.

(*iv*) It is not affected by coding (linear transformation) of variables or variate values.

(*v*) The relation between the correlation coefficient 'r' and the regression coefficients b_{YX} and b_{XY} is,

$$r = \sqrt{b_{YX} \cdot b_{XY}}$$

(*vi*) The sign of r will be the same as that of b_{YX} or b_{XY}.

(*vii*) If the two variables are independent, the correlation coefficient between them is zero but the converse is not true.

(*viii*) If ρ (or r) = 0, it shows that the relationship between the variables X and Y is not linear.

(*ix*) The relationship between the correlation coefficient with a regression coefficient is,

$$\beta_{YX} = \rho\frac{\sigma_Y}{\sigma_X};$$

$$\beta_{XY} = \rho\frac{\sigma_X}{\sigma_Y}$$

(*x*) Arithmetic mean of two regression coefficients is always greater than the positive correlation coefficient between the variables. Symbolically,

$$\frac{1}{2}\left(\rho\frac{\sigma_Y}{\sigma_X} + \rho\frac{\sigma_X}{\sigma_Y}\right) \geq \rho$$

$$\sigma_Y^2 + \sigma_X^2 \geq 2\sigma_X\sigma_Y$$

$(\sigma_Y - \sigma_X)^2 \geq 0$

This confirms the property.

(*xi*) If X and Y are two correlated normal variables, the origin of ρ lies in the bivariate normal distribution,

$$f_{X,Y}(x, y) = \frac{1}{2\pi\rho\sigma_X\sigma_Y\sqrt{1-\rho^2}}$$

$$\times\, e^{-\frac{1}{2(1-\rho^2)}\left\{\left(\frac{X-\mu_X}{\sigma_X}\right)^2 - 2\rho\left(\frac{X-\mu_X}{\sigma_X}\right)\left(\frac{Y-\mu_Y}{\sigma_Y}\right)+\left(\frac{Y-\mu_Y}{\sigma_Y}\right)^2\right\}}$$

(*xii*) r^2, the square of correlation coefficient is referred to as *coefficient of determination* and $(1 - r^2)$ as *coefficient of non-determination.*

(*xiii*) The quantity $\sqrt{1-r^2}$ is referred to coefficient of alienation.

Q. 40. *If $r_{XY} = 0$, show by an example that X and Y are not necessarily independent.*

Ans. Consider the following paired observations:

X:	–3	–2	–1	0	1	2	3
Y:	9	4	1	0	1	4	9

For the above data,

$$\Sigma XY = 0,\ \Sigma X = 0,\ \Sigma Y = 28.$$

Therefore, $r_{XY} = 0$

But, the data clearly reveals that, $Y = X^2$, which means X and Y are not independent.

Q. 41. *If the correlation coefficient between two variables is zero, where would the two regression lines lie?*

Ans. The regression line of Y on X, when $\rho = 0$, will be a line parallel to abscissa at the distance of the intercept. Similarly the regression line of X on Y will be parallel to ordinate at a distance of corresponding intercept.

Q. 42. *If the two variables having zero correlation are converted into standard deviates, where shall the two regression lines lie.*

Ans. The regression lines are nothing but the axes. That is the regression line of Y on X, when $\rho = 0$ is the X-axis. Similarly the regression line of X on Y when $\rho = 0$ is the Y-axis Further the two regression lines are perpendicular to each other, *i.e.*, they are at an angle of 90 degrees.

Q. 43. *If there are two standard deviates X and Y having zero correlation, what shall be the slopes of the regression lines of Y on X and of X on Y and also the value of regression coefficients.*

Ans. The slope of both the regression lines will be zero degree. Also both the regression coefficients will be zero.

Q. 44. *If there is a perfect relationship between two variables under consideration for a regression line, what about the position of regression lines?*

Ans. There are two implications which we can think about the regression lines when $\rho = 1$.

(*i*) The two regression lines must coincide with each other. This means we get the same results whether we predict Y from X or predict X from Y.

(*ii*) The regression lines may bisect exactly an angle of 45 degree, *i.e.*, they bisect the alternate quadrants say N–E and S–W.

Q. 45. *If r is simple correlation coefficient between the two variables X and Y based on n paired observations (x_i, y_i) for i = 1, 2, ..., n, the standard error of r is given by the formula,*

S.E. $(r) = \dfrac{1-r^2}{\sqrt{n}}$ and its square, $\dfrac{(1-r^2)^2}{n}$ is called the variance of r.

Q. 46. *Define probable error of the correlation coefficient of r.*

Ans. Probable error of r is an old measure to test its reliability. According to **Secrist**, "The probable error of correlation coefficient is an amount which if added to and subtracted from the mean correlation coefficient, produces amounts within which the chances are that a coefficient of correlation from a series selected at random will fall." The formula for probable error is,

$$\text{P.E.}(r) = 0.6745\ \frac{1-r^2}{\sqrt{n}}$$

Q. 47. *What is the use of probable error?*

Ans. Probable error is useful in roughly having an idea about the significance of coefficient of correlation. If $r < 3$ P.E. (r), the correlation coefficient is definitely not significant. If $r > 6$ P.E., r is definitely significant. This approach is seldom used as t-test is an exact test for testing the significance of correlation coefficient.

Q. 48. *How will you test the significance of the correlation coefficient ρ?*

Ans. The hypothesis,

$$H_0 : \rho = 0 \text{ vs. } H_1 : \rho \neq 0$$

can be tested by t-test where the statistic,

$$t = \frac{r}{s_r}$$

$$= \frac{r\sqrt{n-2}}{\sqrt{1-r^2}}$$

t has $(n-2)$ d.f. The decision about the hypothesis can be taken in the usual manner.

Q. 49. *How can one perform the test for a specified value of population correlation coefficient?*

Ans. The test of the hypothesis

$$H_0 : \rho = \rho_0 \text{ vs. } H_1 : \rho \neq \rho_0$$

can be performed by using Fisher's transformation.

Suppose the estimated value of ρ is r and is based on n pairs of observed values.

Fisher's Z-transformation for the values ρ_0 and r are:

$$Z_r = \frac{1}{2}\log_e\left(\frac{1+r}{1-r}\right) = \tanh^{-1} r$$

$$= 1.1513 \{\log_{10}(1+r) - \log_{10}(1-r)\}$$

Similarly,

$$Z\rho_0 = 1.1513 \{\log_{10}(1+\rho_0) - \log_{10}(1+\rho_0)\}$$

The transformed values of Z corresponding to different values of correlation coefficient can also be obtained from the tables. Fisher told that Z_r is distributed normally with mean Z_{ρ_0} and variance $1/(n-3)$. Also he pointed out that for small n, Z_{ρ_0}, the mean of Z_r is somewhat biased and hence can be improved by using the transformation

$$Z_{\rho_0} = \frac{1}{2}\log_e\left(\frac{1+\rho_0}{1-\rho_0}\right) + \frac{\rho_0}{2(n-1)}$$

The test statistic

$$Z = \frac{Z_r - Z_{\rho_0}}{1/\sqrt{n-3}}$$

$$= (Z_r - Z_{\rho_0})\sqrt{n-3}$$

The decision about H_0 can be taken in the usual way.

Q. 50. *Give the formula for the confidence limits for the population correlation coefficient ρ.*

Ans. Following usual notation, $(1-\alpha)$ 100 per cent confidence limits can be obtained by the formula,

$$\left.\begin{matrix} Z_L \\ Z_U \end{matrix}\right] = Z_r \pm Z_{1-\alpha/2}\frac{1}{\sqrt{n-3}}$$

The limits for ρ can be obtained by retransformation.

Q. 51. *How can the equality of the correlation coefficients of two bivariate populations be tested?*

Ans. The hypothesis

$$H_0 : \rho_1 = \rho_2 \text{ vs. } H_1 : \rho_1 \neq \rho_2$$

can be tested by making use of Fisher's Z-transformation.

Suppose r_1 and r_2 are the estimates of ρ_1, and ρ_2 obtained from the samples of sizes n_1 and n_2, respectively.

Under Fisher's Z-transformation,

$$Z_{r_1} = \frac{1}{2}\log_e\left(\frac{1+r_1}{1-r_1}\right) = \tanh^{-1} r_1$$

and $$Z_{r_2} = \frac{1}{2}\log_e\left(\frac{1+r_2}{1-r_2}\right) = \tanh^{-1} r_2$$

Fisher showed that $(Z_{r_1} - Z_{r_2})$ is distributed with mean

$$\frac{\rho}{2(n_1-1)} - \frac{\rho}{2(n_2-1)}$$

and variance

$$\left(\frac{1}{n_1-3}+\frac{1}{n_2-3}\right)$$

where $\rho_1 = \rho_2 = \rho$ (the common correlation coefficient).

If n_1 and n_2 are not small, the test statistic is,

$$Z = \frac{Z_{r_1} - Z_{r_2}}{\sqrt{\frac{1}{n_1-3}+\frac{1}{n_2-3}}}$$

$Z \sim N(0, 1)$. The decision about H_0 can be taken by the set procedure.

Q. 52. *Give the test for testing the equality of population correlation coefficients of k ($k \geq 3$) bivariate normal populations.*

Ans. Here one has to test the hypothesis,

$$H_0: \rho_1 = \rho_2 = \dots = \rho_k = \rho$$

vs. H_1 : at least two ρ's are not equal.

This hypothesis amounts to testing whether several r's are from the bivariate normal populations having the same correlation coefficient. This also serves the purpose to know whether all the r's can be pooled to obtain an estimate of ρ.

Suppose there are k samples of sizes $n_1, n_2, \dots, n_k$ respectively and sample correlation coefficients are $r_1, r_2, \dots, r_k$ respectively.

Applying Fisher's Z-transformation,

$$Z_{r_i} = \frac{1}{2}\log_e\left(\frac{1+r_i}{1-r_i}\right)$$

for $i = 1, 2, \dots, k$

The transformed values are $Z_{r_1}, Z_{r_2}, \dots, Z_{r_k}$.

Having known these values, calculate the quantities $\sum_i(n_i-3)$, $\sum_i(n_i-3)Z_i$, $\sum_i(n_i-3)Z_i^2$. To test H_0, statistics Chi-square is

$$\chi^2 = \sum_i(n_i-3)Z_i^2 - \frac{\left\{\sum_i(n_i-3)Z_i\right\}^2}{\sum_i(n_i-3)}$$

χ^2 has $(k-1)$ d.f. The decision about H_0 is taken as usual.

Q. 53. *What formula is used for correlation coefficient in case of grouped bivariate population?*

Ans. Certain notation used in the formula are explained below:

(*i*) Suppose there are p groups of X variate and q groups of Y variate.

(*ii*) Let f_{ij} be the frequency corresponding to $(i, j)^{\text{th}}$ cell for $i = 1, 2, \dots, p$ and $j = 1, 2, \dots, q$.

(*iii*) Let R_i $(i = 1, 2, \dots, p)$ represents the frequency of the ith group of X and C_j $(j = 1, 2, \dots, q)$, the frequency of the jth group of Y.

(*iv*) Let dx_i be the coded value for i^{th} group of the variate X and dy_j, the coded value for the jth group of the variate Y.

Having known the above terms, the value of correlation coefficient in the grouped bivariate data can be calculated by the formula,

$$r = \frac{\sum_{i,j} f_{ij}\, dx_i\, dy_j - \frac{(\Sigma_i R_i\, dx_i)(\Sigma_j C_j dy_j)}{n}}{\sqrt{\left\{\sum_i R_i dx_i^2 - \frac{(\Sigma_i R_i dx_i)^2}{n}\right\} \times \left\{\sum_i C_j dy_j^2 - \frac{(\Sigma_j C_j dy_j)^2}{n}\right\}}}$$

where $\sum_{i,j} f_{ij} = n$

Q. 54. *What is coefficient of concurrent deviation, and how is it calculated?*

Ans. It is another measure of correlation which depends only on the signs of the deviations of the variables X and Y at a point of time from its value at the preceding point of time. It does not take into consideration the magnitude of the difference but the direction of deviations, +ve or –ve. The formula for the coefficient of concurrent deviation is,

$$r_c = \pm \sqrt{\pm \frac{2c - n}{n}}$$

where c is the number of positive signs of the product of deviations for X and Y, n the number of deviations. Also the same sign within and outside the square root has to be used. If $(2c - n)$ is negative, use negative sign and *vice-versa*.

Q. 55. *Following are the data of Gross National Product (GNP) and Net National Product (NNP) at current prices from 1971-72 to 1979-80.*

Years:	*1971-72*	*1972-73*	*1973-74*	*1974-75*	*1975-76*
	1976-77	*1977-78*	*1978-79*	*1979-80*	
GNP(X):	*38983*	*42993*	*53501*	*63051*	*66375*
₹ (crore)	*71432*	*69760*	*65842*	*87058*	
NNP(X):	*36999*	*36629*	*38486*	*38958*	*42799*
₹ (crore)	*41566*	*47233*	*54711*	*53468*	

Find the coefficient of concurrent deviation.

Ans. We prepare the following table to calculate r_c:

Years	*GNP (X)*	*NNP (Y)*	*Signs of deviations from previous year for X*	*Signs of deviations from previous year for Y*	*Product of signs of deviations*
1971-72	38983	36999			
1972-73	42993	36629	+	–	–
1973-74	53501	38486	+	+	+
1974-75	63051	38958	+	+	+
1975-76	66375	42799	+	+	+
1976-77	71432	41566	+	–	–
1977-78	69760	47233	–	+	–
1978-79	65842	54711	–	+	–
1979-80	87058	53468	+	–	–
$n = 8$					$c = 3$

Having calculated n and c, the coefficient of concurrent deviation,

$$r_c = \pm \sqrt{\pm \frac{2 \times 3 - 8}{8}}$$

$$= -\sqrt{\frac{1}{4}}$$

$$= -0.5$$

Q. 56. *Give the formula for coefficient of correlation where we can make use of the variance of difference (X – Y).*

Ans. The formula for the coefficient of correlation using the variance of the difference $(X - Y)$ is,

$$\rho = \frac{\sigma_X^2 + \sigma_Y^2 - \sigma_{X-Y}^2}{2\sigma_X \sigma_Y}$$

and its estimate

$$r = \frac{s_X^2 + s_Y^2 - s_{X-Y}^2}{2s_X s_Y}$$

The main feature of this formula is that it does not involve covariance term and the value of r obtained by this formula is same as that obtained by Karl Pearson's formula.

Q. 57. *Yield of foodgrains in kg/ha in Kharif and Rabi seasons from 1975-76 to 1984-85 were as follows:*

Year	*Kharif (X)*	*Rabi (Y)*
1975-76	89	104
1976-77	94	109
1977-78	94	116
1978-79	78	105
1979-80	93	120
1980-81	95	119
1981-82	92	130
1982-83	106	131
1983-84	104	134
1984-85	105	142

Year	X	$X-\bar{X}$	$(X-\bar{X})^2$	Y	$Y-\bar{Y}$	$(Y-\bar{Y})^2$	$Y-X=Z$	$Z-\bar{Z}$	$(Z-\bar{Z})^2$	$(X-\bar{X})\times(Y-\bar{Y})$
1975-76	89	–6	36	104	–17	289	15	–11	121	102
1976-77	94	–1	1	109	–12	144	15	–11	121	12
1977-78	94	–1	1	116	–5	25	22	–4	16	5
1978-79	78	–17	289	105	–16	256	27	1	1	272
1979-80	93	–2	4	120	–1	1	27	1	1	2
1980-81	95	0	00	119	–2	4	24	–2	4	0
1981-82	92	–3	9	130	9	81	38	12	144	–27
1982-83	106	11	121	131	10	100	25	–1	1	110
1983-84	104	9	81	134	13	169	30	4	16	117
1984-85	105	10	100	142	21	441	37	11	121	210
Total	950	00	642	1210	00	1510	260	00	546	803

(*i*) *Find the coefficient of correlation by using variance of differences and also verify that this value is same as that of Pearsonian correlation coefficient.*

(*ii*) *Judge the significance of correlation co-efficient by probable error.*

(*iii*) *Test the significance of the correlation co-efficient by t-test.* [*Given:* $t_{0.05,\,8} = 2.306$]

(*iv*) *Find 95% confidence limits for* ρ.

Ans. To calculate the value of r, we prepare the above table:

$$n = 10, \bar{X} = \frac{950}{10} = 95.0, \bar{Y} = \frac{1210}{10} = 121.0,$$

$$\bar{Z} = \frac{260}{10} = 26.0$$

$$s_X^2 = \frac{642}{9} = 71.33, s_Y^2 = \frac{1510}{9} = 167.78,$$

$$s_{Y-X}^2 = s_Z^2 = \frac{546}{9} = 60.67.$$

(*i*) The coefficient of correlation by the formula,

$$r = \frac{s_X^2 + s_Y^2 - s_{Y-X}^2}{2s_X s_Y}$$

$$r = \frac{71.33 + 167.78 - 60.67}{2\sqrt{71.33 \times 167.78}}$$

$$= \frac{178.44}{218.80}$$

$$= 0.8155$$

Pearsonian correlation coefficient,

$$r = \frac{\Sigma(X-\bar{X})(Y-\bar{Y})}{\sqrt{\Sigma(X-\bar{X})^2 \Sigma(Y-\bar{Y})^2}}$$

$$= \frac{803}{\sqrt{642 \times 1510}}$$

$$= \frac{803}{984.59}$$

$$= 0.8155$$

The above results show that the coefficient of correlation obtained by the formula using the variance of the differences and by Pearsonian formula are exactly the same,

(*ii*) Probable error,

$$\text{P. E.} = 0.6745 \frac{1-(0.8155)^2}{\sqrt{10}}$$

$$= \frac{0.2260}{3.1623}$$

$$= 0.07145$$

Again $6 \times$ P.E. $= 6 \times 0.07145$

$= 0.4287$

Since $0.8155 > 0.4287$, the coefficient of correlation is definitely significant.

(*iii*) To test the hypothesis,

$$H_0 : \rho = 0 \text{ vs. } H_1 : \rho \neq 0$$

The test statistic,

$$t = \frac{0.8155\sqrt{10-2}}{\sqrt{1-(0.8155)^2}}$$

$$= \frac{2.3066}{0.5788}$$

$$= 3.9851$$

Since the calculated value of $t = 3.9851$ is greater than the tabulated value of $t = 2.306$ for $\alpha = 0.05$ and 8 d.f., we reject H_0. It means that the correlation between the per hectare productions of Rabi and Kharif crops is significant.

(*iv*) To find 95 per cent confidence limits for ρ, we first find Z_L and Z_U and then retransform to r.

$$\left.\begin{matrix} Z_L \\ Z_U \end{matrix}\right] = 1.1586 \mp \frac{1.9611}{2.646}$$

$$= 1.1586 \mp 0.7407$$

$$Z_L = 0.4179,\ Z_U = 1.8993$$

$\therefore$ Lower limit of $\rho = 0.4$ (approx.)

Upper limit of $\rho = 0.955$ (approx.)

Q. 58. *How can the correlation coefficient between the two variables X and Y be calculated by the method of least squares?*

Ans. By the method of least squares, we find the estimated value $\hat{Y}$ of Y by simple regression equation. Then find the deviations $d = Y - \hat{Y}$ and Σd^2. Calculate,

$$S_Y^2 = \frac{\Sigma d^2}{N}$$

$$\sigma^2_Y = \frac{1}{N}(Y_i - \bar{Y})^2$$

The formula for coefficient of correlation by the method of least squares is,

$$\rho = \sqrt{1 - \frac{s_Y^2}{\sigma_Y^2}}$$

If we estimate X by the regression of X on Y as $\hat{X}$, the formula is,

$$\rho = \sqrt{1 - \frac{s_X^2}{\sigma_X^2}}$$

where, $s_X^2 = \frac{\Sigma d^2}{N}$ and $\sigma^2_X = \frac{1}{N}(X_i - \bar{X})^2$

Q. 59. *Calculate coefficient of correlation by the method of least squares for the following paired values of X and Y variables. Also verify that this value of r is same as that obtained by Pearson's formula.*

X:	10	12	13	17	18
Y:	5	6	7	9	13

Ans. To calculate the coefficient of correlation by the method of least squares and otherwise, we prepare the following table:

X	$X-\bar{X}$	$(X-\bar{X})^2$	Y	$Y-\bar{Y}$	$(Y-\bar{Y})^2$	$(X-\bar{X}) \times (Y-\bar{Y})$	$\hat{X}$	$X - \hat{X} = d$	d^2
10	–4	16	5	–3	9	12	11	–1	1
12	–2	4	6	–2	4	4	12	0	0
13	–1	1	7	–1	1	1	13	0	0
17	3	9	9	1	1	3	15	2	4
18	4	16	13	5	25	20	19	–1	1
70	00	46	40	00	40	40	70	0	6

Due to convenience of calculation, we have chosen the regression line of X on Y.

The regression coefficient

$$b_{XY} = \frac{40}{40} = 1$$

The regression line is,

$$\hat{X} = 14 + 1\,(Y - 8)$$

$$\hat{X} = Y + 6$$

$$s_X^2 = \frac{6}{5} = 1.2$$

$$\sigma_X^2 = \frac{46}{5} = 9.2$$

$$r = \sqrt{1 - \frac{1.2}{9.2}}$$

$$= \sqrt{0.8696}$$

$$= 0.9325$$

Coefficient of correlation by Pearson's formula is,

$$r = \frac{40}{\sqrt{46 \times 40}}$$

$$= 0.9325$$

Thus, the correlation coefficient by the method of least squares and Pearson's formula is same.

Q. 60. *Discuss correlation ratio and give its measure.*

Ans. Pearsonian correlation is appropriate only if the relation between the variables X and Y is linear. If this relation is non-linear, correlation ratio η^2 of X on Y is a better measure of correlation. A great advantage of correlation ratio is that it is not necessary that there should be only one value of Y for each corresponding value of X. For example, in a group of persons we may find that there are many persons of the same weight but with varying heights. So we have a number of weights and for each weight there are groups of persons of varying heights.

Suppose a value of X_i has n_i values of Y say, Y_{i1}, Y_{i2}, ..., Y_{in_i} for $i = 1, 2, k$. In this way y_{ij} represents the jth observation in the ith group for $j = 1, 2, ..., n_i$. Let the estimate of η^2 be denoted by E^2.

The correlation ratio,

$$E^2 = \frac{\text{Among groups sum of squares}}{\text{Total corrected sum of squares}}$$

$$= \frac{\sum_{i=1}^{k} n_i(\bar{Y}_i - \bar{Y})^2}{\sum_{i=1}^{k}\sum_{j=1}^{n_i} (\bar{Y}_{ij} - \bar{Y})^2}$$

$$= \frac{\sum_{i=1}^{k} n_i \frac{G_i^2}{n_i} - \frac{G^2}{n}}{\sum_{i=1}^{k}\sum_{j=1}^{n_i} Y_{ij}^2 - \frac{G^2}{n}}$$

where $\bar{Y}_i = \frac{1}{n_i}\sum_{j=1}^{n_i} Y_{ij}$ and $G_i = n_i\bar{Y}_i = \sum_{j=1}^{n_i} Y_{ij}$,

$n = \sum_{i=1}^{k} n_i$ and $G = \sum_{i=1}^{k} G_i$ = Total of all values.

Q. 61. *Write the properties of correlation ratio.*

Ans. Properties of correlation ratio are as follows:

(*i*) The range of η^2 (or E^2) is from 0 to 1.

(*ii*) If each group consists of only one observation, then $E^2 = 1$.

(*iii*) If all the observations are in one group, then $E^2 = 0$. Hence one should be wary of the number and size of groups.

(*iv*) Here it is worth pointing out that E^2 is calculated merely from the values of the dependent variable Y. Hence, it hardly matters whether the variable X is quantitative or qualitative. So, the correlation ratio can be used to measure the correlation between a quantitative and a qualitative variable.

(*v*) If ρ is the Pearsonian correlation coefficient, in general $\rho^2 \le \eta^2$. Equality holds only if the regression of X on Y is perfectly linear.

Q. 62. *What is intraclass correlation and how to compute it?*

Ans. Often the need arises to measure similarity among individuals within the classes or groups. For this, a measure known as *intraclass correlation coefficient* is used. Some people seldom call it the *coefficient of homotypic correlation.* For example, one may require to measure the similarity between heights or weights of brothers. Intraclass correlation is denoted by P_I and its estimate by r_I. It can easily be calculated using analysis of variance technique. Suppose there are k groups and each group contains n observations. Let Y_{ij} be the ith observation in the jth group and G_j, the jth group total. Also $G = \sum_{j=1}^{k} G_j$.

ANOVA table for calculating r_I can be presented as follows:

	d.f.	*S.S.*	*M.S.*
Between groups	$k-1$	$\frac{1}{n}\sum_{j=1}^{k} G_j^2 - \frac{G^2}{kn} = G_{XX}$	$\frac{G_{XX}}{k-1} = S_w^2 + nS_b^2 = MS_b$
Within groups	$k(n-1)$	$\sum_{j=1}^{k}\sum_{i=1}^{n} Y_{ij}^2 - \frac{1}{n}\sum_{j=1}^{n} G_j^2 = W_{XX}$	$\frac{W_{XX}}{k(n-1)} = S_w^2 = MS_W$
Total	$kn-1$	$\sum_{j=1}^{k}\sum_{i=1}^{n} Y_{ij}^2 - \frac{G^2}{kn}$	

The formula for intraclass correlation is,

$$r_1 = \frac{S_b^2}{S_w^2 + S_b^2}$$

$$= \frac{MS_b - MS_w}{MS_b + (n-1)MS_w}$$

The value of r_1 (or ρ_1) can be negative if $MS_b = 0$ but never less than $-\frac{1}{n-1}$ and cannot exceed than unity.

Q. 63. *What do you understand by biserial correlation? Also give the formula for calculating it.*

Ans. In studies pertaining to education, psychology and sociology, often one encounters the situations in which one variable (X) is dichotomous according to some qualitative factor and the other variable (Y) has a number of classes 'c' according to some quantitative variate. In this way, there is a $(2 \times c)$ contingency table. In such type of studies Pearsonian correlation is not possible. Hence, a measure of correlation known as *biserial correlation coefficient* is preferably used and is denoted by r_b. The assumptions made for biserial correlation are:

(*i*) Y is almost normally distributed.

(*ii*) The regression of Y on X is linear so that we get a measure of linear association between X and Y.

(*iii*) The mean value of $\bar{Y}_1$ in the minor or smaller category as specified by X lies on the regression line.

Decoding the various quantities as.

p = proportion of units in the major category

q = proportions of units in the minor category

Z = ordinate of the standard normal curve cutting off a tail with area equal to q

$\bar{Y}_2$ = mean of Y in the major category

S_Y = standard deviation of all the Y-values. The biserial correlation coefficient,

$$r_b = \frac{pq(\bar{Y}_2 - \bar{Y}_1)}{ZS_Y}$$

Biserial correlation is analogous to correlation ratio.

Q. 64. *Describe succinctly when should the tetrachoric correlation be used?*

Ans. Tetrachoric correlation is suitable when both the variables *X* and *Y* are dichotomous. This measure of linear association between *X* and *Y is* based on the assumption that the underlying distribution is bivariate normal. Here the actual observations on *X* and *Y* are not available but their distribution of frequencies in a (2 × 2) contingency table are known. A measure of correlation in this situation is called tetrachoric correlation.

Q. 65. *Explicate autocorrelation and its measure.*

Ans. Often in time series data, it has been observed that the figures or consecutive periods are correlated. For example, the area under irrigation in a year is correlated to its previous year irrigated area, the area under high yielding varieties (HYV) in a year is correlated to the previous year area under HYV, etc. In this situation, the assumption of independent errors of linear probabilistic model is refuted, *i.e.*, if the linear model is,

$$Y = \alpha + \beta X + \varepsilon$$

$$E(\varepsilon_i\, \varepsilon_{i'}) \neq 0 \text{ for } i \neq i'$$

The simplest form of autocorrelation is the linear dependence of error on its previous year value. Symbolically,

$$e_t = be_{t-1} + \varepsilon_t$$

This is known as the first order autoregressive scheme. Thus, a measure of linear association between the errors of consecutive periods is given by autocorrelation. Autocorrelation is also known as *serial correlation.* The formula for autocorrelation is

$$r_A = \sqrt{\frac{\Sigma e_t e_{t-1}}{\sqrt{\Sigma e_t^2 \cdot \Sigma e_{t-1}^2}}}$$

Q. 66. *Why are multiple linear regression equations needed?*

Ans. In real life problems, a variate value does not depend only on one independent variable but on many variables. Hence to estimate a dependent variable, it is not enough to include only one independent variable only but many independent variables. For example, the cost of a produced unit depends on the cost of raw material, labour cost, cost of energy, transportation, etc. In this situation, to estimate the cost of production, it is necessary to include all those variables in the regression model which add to the cost of the unit produced.

Q. 67. *Give mathematical model for multiple linear regression and the method for its fitting.*

Ans. A mathematical model with dependent variable *Y* and *k* independent variables $X_1, X_2, ..., X_k$ can be given as,

$$Y = \beta_0 + \beta_1 X_1 + \beta_2 X_2 + ... + \beta_k X_k + e$$

This equation is called *multiple linear regression equation* or *prediction equation* with *Y* as predictant and $X_1, X_2, ..., X_k$ as predictors. In this model *e* is the error term and for all types, e_i are i.i.d. normal variates with mean 0 and variance σ_e^2, *i.e.*, $e \sim N(0, \sigma_e^2)$.

To fit in the regression model, suppose there are *n* composite sample observations which can be presented in the following format:

Composite sample No.	*Variables*						
	Y	X_1	X_2	...	X_j	...	X_k
1	y_1	x_{11}	x_{21}	...	x_{j1}	...	x_{k1}
2	y_2	x_{12}	x_{22}	...	x_{j2}	...	x_{k2}
⋮	⋮	⋮	⋮		⋮		⋮
i	y_i	x_{1i}	x_{2i}	...	x_{ji}	...	x_{kj}
⋮	⋮	⋮	⋮		⋮		⋮
n	y_n	x_{1n}	x_{2n}	...	x_{jn}	...	x_{kn}
Total	$\sum_i y_i$	$\sum_i x_{1i}$	$\sum_i x_{2i}$	...	$\sum_i x_{ji}$	...	$\sum_i x_{ki}$

where $i = 1, 2, ..., n$ and $j = 1, 2, ..., k$. To fit in the regression equation by the method of least squares and supposing that $b_0, b_1, b_2, ..., b_k$ are the estimates of $\beta_0, \beta_1, \beta_2, ..., \beta_k$ respectively, the set of normal equations is,

$$\sum_i y_i = nb_0 + b_1 \sum_i x_{1i} + b_2 \sum_i x_{2i} + ... + b_k \sum_i x_{ki}$$

$$\sum_i x_{1i} y_i = b_0 \sum_i x_{1i} + b_1 \sum_i x_{1i}^2 + b_2 \sum_i x_{1i} x_{2i} + ... + b_k \sum_i x_{1i} x_{ki}$$

$$\sum_i x_{2i} y_i = b_0 \sum_i x_{2i} + b_1 \sum_i x_{1i} x_{2i} + b_2 \sum_i x_{2i}^2 + \ldots + b_k \sum_i x_{2i}\, x_{ki}$$

$$\vdots$$

$$\sum_i x_{ki}\, y_i = b_0 \sum_i x_{ki} + b_1 \sum_i x_{1i} x_{ki} + b_2 \sum_i x_{2i} x_{ki} + \ldots + b_k \sum_i x_{ki}^2$$

In matrix form, the above equations after transposal are,

$$\begin{bmatrix} n & \Sigma x_{1i} & \Sigma x_{2i} & \cdots & \Sigma x_{ki} \\ \Sigma x_{1i} & \Sigma x_{1i}^2 & \Sigma x_{1i} x_{2i} & \cdots & \Sigma x_{1i} x_{ki} \\ \Sigma x_{2i} & \Sigma x_{1i} x_{2i} & \Sigma x_{2i}^2 & \cdots & \Sigma x_{2i} x_{ki} \\ \vdots & & & & \vdots \\ \Sigma x_{ki} & \sum_i x_{1i} x_{ki} & \Sigma x_{2i} x_{ki} & \cdots & \Sigma x_{ki}^2 \end{bmatrix} \begin{bmatrix} b_0 \\ b_1 \\ b_2 \\ \vdots \\ b_k \end{bmatrix} = \begin{bmatrix} \Sigma y_i \\ \Sigma x_{1i} y_i \\ \Sigma x_{2i} y_i \\ \vdots \\ \Sigma x_{ki} y_i \end{bmatrix}$$

$$(X'\,X)_{(k+1)\times(k+1)}\, B_{(k+1)\times 1} = (X'\,Y)_{(k+1)\times 1}$$

If we denote the regression equation as

$$Y = X\beta + e$$

and its estimated equation as

$$Y = XB,$$

then the set of normal equations can be written as,

$$X'\,XB = X'\,Y$$

or

$$B = (X'\,X)^{-1}\,X'\,Y$$

where the matrices $X'\,X$, B and $X'Y$ are as indicated above. The matrix $X'\,X$ is known as the *coefficient matrix.*

From the first normal equation we get,

$$b_0 = \bar{y} - b_1 \bar{x}_1 - b_2 \bar{x}_2 \ldots b_k \bar{x}_k$$

On substituting the value of b_0 and representing the deviation from mean of the respective variables as,

$$x_{ji} - \bar{x}_j = u_{ji} \text{ and } y_i - \bar{y} = v_i$$

The set of normal equations reduces to,

$$\underset{A_{k\times k}}{\begin{bmatrix} \Sigma u_{1i}^2 & \Sigma u_{1i} u_{2i} & \cdots & \Sigma u_{1i} u_{ki} \\ \Sigma u_{1i} u_{2i} & \Sigma u_{2i}^2 & \cdots & \Sigma u_{2i} u_{ki} \\ \vdots & & & \\ \Sigma u_{1i} u_{ki} & \Sigma u_{2i} u_{ki} & \cdots & \Sigma u_{ki}^2 \end{bmatrix}} \underset{B_{k\times 1}}{\begin{bmatrix} b_1 \\ b_2 \\ \vdots \\ b_k \end{bmatrix}} = \underset{Y_{k\times 1}}{\begin{bmatrix} \Sigma u_{1i} v_i \\ \Sigma u_{2i} v_i \\ \vdots \\ \Sigma u_{ki} v_i \end{bmatrix}}$$

In matrix notation, the normal equation are,

$$AB = Y$$

or

$$B = A^{-1}\,Y$$

Suppose A is non-singular and its inverse is

$$A^{-1} = \begin{bmatrix} c_{11} & c_{12} & \cdots & c_{1k} \\ c_{21} & c_{22} & \cdots & c_{2k} \\ \vdots & & & \\ c_{k1} & c_{k2} & \cdots & c_{kk} \end{bmatrix}$$

Matrix A^{-1} is symmetric which means $c_{ij} = c_{ij}$. Hence, the matrix equations leading to the solution of b's are,

$$\begin{bmatrix} b_1 \\ b_2 \\ \vdots \\ b_k \end{bmatrix} = \begin{bmatrix} c_{11} & c_{12} & \cdots & c_{1k} \\ c_{21} & c_{22} & \cdots & c_{2k} \\ \vdots & & & \\ c_{k1} & c_{k2} & \cdots & c_{kk} \end{bmatrix} \begin{bmatrix} \Sigma u_{1i} v_i \\ \Sigma u_{2i} v_i \\ \vdots \\ \Sigma u_{ki} v_i \end{bmatrix}$$

Thus,

$$\begin{aligned} b_1 &= c_{11} \Sigma u_{1i} v_i + c_{12} \Sigma u_{2i} v_i + \ldots + c_{1k} \Sigma u_{ki} v_i \\ b_2 &= c_{21} \Sigma u_{1i} v_i + c_{22} \Sigma u_{2i} v_i + \ldots + c_{2k} \Sigma u_{ki} v_i \\ &\vdots \\ b_k &= c_{k1} \Sigma u_{1i} v_i + c_{k2} \Sigma u_{2i} v_i + \ldots + c_{kk} \Sigma u_{ki} v_i \end{aligned}$$

Substituting the values of $b_0, b_1, \ldots, b_k$, the estimated linear regression equation is,

$$\hat{Y} = \bar{y} + b_1(X_1 - \bar{x}_1) + b_2(X_2 - \bar{x}_2) + \ldots + b_k\,(X_k - \bar{x}_k)$$

From this equation, Y can be predicted for given values of $X_1, X_2, \ldots, X_k$. In multiple linear regression equation, each of β_j (or b_j) is known as *partial regression coefficient*. Its range is from $-\infty$ to ∞.

Definition. Partial regression coefficient β_j is the measure of change in dependent variable Y corresponding to a unit increase in the independent variable X_j whereas the other independent variables are kept fixed.

Note: When $k = 2$, the equation of multiple linear regression reduces to plane of regression.

Q. 68. *How will you test the significance of a partial regression coefficient?*

Ans. To test the hypothesis

$$H_0 : \beta_j = 0 \text{ vs. } H_1 : \beta_j \neq 0$$

for $j = 1, 2, ..., k$

The test statistic is,

$$t = \frac{b_j}{s_{b_j}}$$

Statistic t has $(n - k - 1)$ d.f.

where, $s_{b_j}^2 = s_e^2 c_{jj}$

c_{jj} is the $(j, j)^{\text{th}}$ cell element of A^{-1} and

$$s_e^2 = \frac{\sum_i (Y_i - \hat{Y}_i)^2}{(n-k-1)}$$

$$= \frac{1}{n-k-1}(\Sigma v_i^2 - R^2 \Sigma v_i^2)$$

whereas,

$$R^2 \, \Sigma v_i^2 = b_1 \, \Sigma u_{1i} v_i + b_2 \, \Sigma u_{2i} v_i + ... + b_k \, \Sigma u_{ki} v_i$$

The quantity $R^2 \sum_i v_i^2$ is known as the *regression sum of squares,*

$$s_{b_j} = \sqrt{s_{b_j}^2}$$

Decision about H_0 is taken in the usual way. If H_0 is rejected, it means that the contribution of X_j in estimating Y is significant. If H_0 is accepted, it means that the inclusion of X_j in the equation is redundant.

Q. 69. *How can you test the equality of two partial regression coefficients?*

Ans. Sometime one wants to test whether the contribution of two independent variables X_j and X_l in estimating Y is same or not. Thus, the hypothesis

$$H_0 : \beta_j = \beta_l \quad \text{vs.} \quad H_1 : \beta_j \neq \beta_l$$

for $j \neq l = 1, 2, ..., k$

can be tested by the statistic

$$t = \frac{b_j - b_l}{s_{b_j - b_l}}$$

t has $(n - k - l)$ d.f.

where $s_{b_j - b_l}^2 = s_e^2 (c_{jj} + c_{ll} - 2c_{jl})$.

The decision about H_0 can be taken in the usual manner.

Q. 70. *How can the significance of partial regression coefficient be tested simultaneously?*

Ans. The hypothesis

$$H_0 : \beta_1 = \beta_2 = ... = \beta_k = 0$$

vs. H_1 : at least one of β_j is not zero for $j = 1, 2, ..., k$

can be tested through analysis of variance. The ANOVA table is,

Source	*d.f.*	*S.S.*	*M.S.*	*F-value*
Regression	k	$R^2 \sum_i v_i^2$	$\frac{R^2 \sum_i v_i^2}{k}$	$\frac{(n-k-1)R^2 \sum_i v_i^2}{k(\sum_i v_i^2 - R^2 \sum_i v_i^2)}$
Residual (Deviation from regression)	$(n - k - 1)$	$\sum_i v_i^2 - R^2 \sum_i v_i^2$	$\frac{\sum_i v_i^2 - R^2 \sum_i v_i^2}{(n-k-1)}$	
Total	$n - 1$	$\sum_i v_i^2$		

The statistic F in the last column of ANOVA has $(k, n-k-1)$ d.f. If $F_{Cal} \geq F_{\alpha(k, n-k-1)}$, reject H_0. It means, all β's are not zero. Again if $F_{Cal} < F_{\alpha(k, n-k-1)}$, accept H_0. This indicates that the independent variables $X_1, X_2, ..., X_k$ are not suitable for predicting Y.

Q. 71. *Delineate the term correlation index.*

Ans. The ratio,

$$R^2 = \frac{\text{S.S. due to regression}}{\text{Total corrected S.S.}}$$

$$= \frac{R^2 \sum_i v_i^2}{\sum_i v_i^2}$$

is referred to as *correlation index* or *coefficient of determination as* R^2 is analogous to r^2 in simple linear regression.

Q. 72. *In what ways each potential parameter in a model can be specified?*

Ans. Each potential parameter in a model can be specified in either of the three categories, namely, a free parameter, a fixed parameter or a constrained parameter.

Q. 73. *What is a free parameter?*

Ans. A free parameter is that parameter which is unknown and is thereby to be estimated.

Q. 74. *Define a fixed parameter.*

Ans. A fixed parameter is that parameter which is not free but has a fixed value either 0 or 1.

Q. 75. *Explicate a constrained parameter.*

Ans. A parameter which is unknown but is constrained to be equal to one or more parameters is called a constrained parameter.

Q. 76. *Define multiple correlation coefficient and explain its utility.*

Ans. Multiple correlation coefficient

$$R = +\sqrt{R^2}$$

Definition-1. It may be defined as a measure of linear association of a variable Y (say) with all other X-variables.

Definition-2. Multiple correlation coefficient is the simple correlation between Y and $\hat{Y}$, where $\hat{Y} = \overline{Y} + b_1X_1 + b_2X_2 + ... + b_kX_k$.

The range of R is from 0 to 1.

The value of R is indicative as to whether the linear regression equation is a good fit or not. If R is near to 1, the regression equation is a good fit otherwise not.

Q. 77. *Express multiple correlation coefficient in terms of simple correlation coefficients.*

Ans. If $X_1, X_2, ..., X_k$ are k variables and the sample correlation coefficient between any two variables X_i and X_j for $i, j = 1, 2, ..., k$ is r_{ij}, correlation matrix P consists of the elements which are the simple correlation coefficients among all possible pairs of variables X_i and X_j. Also $r_{ij} - r_{ji}$. Thus, the correlation matrix,

$$P = \begin{bmatrix} 1 & r_{12} & r_{13} & \cdots & r_{1k} \\ r_{21} & 1 & r_{23} & \cdots & r_{2k} \\ r_{31} & r_{32} & 1 & \cdots & r_{3k} \\ \vdots & & & & \\ r_{k1} & r_{k2} & r_{k3} & \cdots & 1 \end{bmatrix}$$

The multiple correlation coefficient of a variable X_j with rest of the variables can be obtained by the formula,

$$R_{j.12...(j-1)(j+1)...k} = \left(1 - \frac{|P|}{P_{jj}}\right)^{1/2}$$

where $|P|$ is the determinant of the correlation matrix P and P_{jj} is the cofactor of r_{jj}.

Here it is revealed that the sign of $|P|$ and P_{jj} will always be the same. Also, $|P| \leq P_{jj}$. If both these conditions do not hold good, the value of R (suffix omitted) will become greater than 1 which is an impossibility.

The range of R is 0 to 1. If $R = 0$, it means X_j has no linear relationship with rest of the variables and

$R = 1$, shows that X_j has perfect linear relationship with the remaining variables. Also $R_{1.23}$, is never less than any of simple correlation coefficients r_{12}, r_{13} and r_{23} *i.e.*, $R_{1.23} \geq r_{12}, r_{13}, r_{23}$.

Q. 78. *If there are three variables X_1, X_2 and X_3, express the multiple correlation coefficient of a variable with the other two.*

Ans. Following usual notations, the formulae for multiple correlation coefficients $R_{1.23}$, $R_{2.13}$, and $R_{3.12}$ in terms of r_{12}, r_{13} and r_{23} are:

$$R_{1.23} = \sqrt{\frac{r_{12}^2 + r_{13}^2 - 2r_{12}r_{13}r_{23}}{1 - r_{23}^2}}$$

$$R_{2.13} = \sqrt{\frac{r_{12}^2 + r_{23}^2 - 2r_{12}r_{23}r_{13}}{1 - r_{13}^2}}$$

$$R_{3.12} = \sqrt{\frac{r_{13}^2 + r_{23}^2 - 2r_{13}r_{23}r_{13}}{1 - r_{13}^2}}$$

Q. 79. *Fit a plane of regression in a trivariate population with the help of correlation coefficients.*

Ans. Let the equation of the plane involving three random variables X_1, X_2 and X_3 be,

$$X_1 = a + b_{12.3}X_2 + b_{13.2}X_3 + e_i$$

Let the means and standard deviations of X_1, X_2 and X_3 be $\bar{X}_1, \bar{X}_2, \bar{X}_3$ and $\sigma_1, \sigma_2, \sigma_3$ respectively. Also r_{12}, r_{13} and r_{23} be the simple correlation coefficients between three pairs of variables. In the above equation $b_{12.3}$ and $b_{13.2}$ are known as the partial regression coefficients. Without loss of generality we can assume that X_1, X_2 and X_3 are measured from their respective means. Thus, the estimates of $b_{12.3}$ and $b_{13.2}$ by the principle of least squares are:

$$b_{12.3} = -\frac{\sigma_1}{\sigma_2}\frac{P_{12}}{P_{11}} \text{ and } b_{13.2} = -\frac{\sigma_1}{\sigma_3}\frac{P_{13}}{P_{11}}$$

where P_{ij} is the cofactor of r_{ij} in the determinant,

$$\begin{vmatrix} 1 & r_{12} & r_{13} \\ r_{12} & 1 & r_{23} \\ r_{13} & r_{23} & 1 \end{vmatrix} \qquad \because \quad r_{ij} = r_{ji}$$

Thus,

$$b_{12.3} = \frac{\sigma_1}{\sigma_2} \cdot \frac{r_{12} - r_{13} - r_{13}r_{23}}{1 - r_{23}^2} = -\frac{P_{12}}{P_{11}} \cdot \frac{\sigma_1}{\sigma_2}$$

$$b_{13.2} = -\frac{\sigma_1}{\sigma_3} \cdot \frac{r_{13} - r_{12}r_{23}}{1 - r_{23}^2} = -\frac{P_{13}}{P_{11}} \cdot \frac{\sigma_1}{\sigma_3}$$

Hence, the equation of plane of regression is,

$$\hat{X}_1 = b_{12.3}X_2 + b_{13.2}X_3$$

Shifting back to the origin, the equation becomes,

$$(\hat{X}_1 - \bar{X}_1) = b_{12.3}(X_2 - \bar{X}_2) + b_{13.2}(X_3 - \bar{X}_3)$$

which is,

$$\hat{X}_1 = a + b_{12.3}X_2 + b_{13.2}X_3$$

where, $a = \bar{X}_1 - b_{12.3}\bar{X}_2 - b_{13.2}\bar{X}_3$

The same equation of the plane can simply be obtained by the determinable equation,

$$\begin{vmatrix} \frac{\hat{X}_1 - \bar{X}_1}{\sigma_1} & \frac{X_2 - \bar{X}_2}{\sigma_2} & \frac{X_3 - \bar{X}_3}{\sigma_3} \\ r_{12} & 1 & r_{23} \\ r_{13} & r_{23} & 1 \end{vmatrix} = 0$$

Expanding the determinant, we get

$$\frac{\hat{X}_1 - \bar{X}_1}{\sigma_1}(1 - r_{23}^2) + \frac{X_2 - \bar{X}_2}{\sigma_2}[-(r_{12} - r_{13}r_{23})]$$

$$+ \frac{(X_3 - \bar{X}_3)}{\sigma_3}(r_{12}\,r_{23} - r_{13}) = 0$$

$$(\hat{X}_1 - \bar{X}_1) + (X_2 - \bar{X}_2)\frac{P_{12}}{P_{11}} \cdot \frac{\sigma_1}{\sigma_2}$$

$$+ (X_3 - \bar{X}_3)\frac{P_{13}}{P_{11}} \cdot \frac{\sigma_1}{\sigma_3} = 0$$

$$\hat{X}_1 = -\frac{P_{12}}{P_{11}}\cdot\frac{\sigma_1}{\sigma_2}X_2 - \frac{P_{13}}{P_{11}}\cdot\frac{\sigma_1}{\sigma_3}X_3 + \left(\bar{X}_1 + \frac{P_{12}}{P_{11}}\cdot\frac{\sigma_1}{\sigma_2}\bar{X}_2 + \frac{P_{13}}{P_{11}}\cdot\frac{\sigma_1}{\sigma_3}\bar{X}_3\right)$$

or $\hat{X}_1 = b_{12.3}X_2 + b_{13.2}X_3 + a$

The determinantal equation can be extended to any number of variables resulting into hyperplane of regression.

[**Notes:** 1. If the population standard deviations are not known, their estimated values can be used.

2. It is simple to use determinantal equation.]

Q. 80. *For a trivariate population with random variables X_1, X_2 and X_3, following results are available:*

Means :	$\bar{X}_1 = 10$,	$\bar{X}_2 = 15$,	$\bar{X}_3 = 20$
Variance:	$V(X_1) = 4$,	$V(X_2) = 9$,	$V(X_3) = 16$
Correlations :	$r_{12} = 0.2$,	$r_{13} = 0.4$,	$r_{23} = 0.6$

(*i*) Fit in the equation of plane of regression.

(*ii*) Estimate X_1 for $X_2 = 10$ and $X_3 = 25$.

Ans. Using the determinantal equation, the plane of regression is,

$$\begin{vmatrix} \frac{X_1-10}{2} & \frac{X_2-15}{3} & \frac{X_3-20}{4} \\ 0.2 & 1 & 0.6 \\ 0.4 & 0.6 & 1 \end{vmatrix} = 0$$

Also from the determinant of the correlation matrix,

$$P = \begin{vmatrix} 1 & 0.2 & 0.4 \\ 0.2 & 1 & 0.6 \\ 0.4 & 0.6 & 1 \end{vmatrix}$$

$P_{11} = 1 - .6^2 = 0.64$, $P_{12} = -(.2 \times 1 - .6 \times .4) = 0.04$

$P_{13} = (.2 \times .6 - 1 \times .4) = -0.28$

Equation of the plane of regression is,

$$(\hat{X}_1 - 10) + (X_2 - 15) \times \frac{0.04}{0.64}\cdot\frac{2}{3} + (X_3 - 20) \times \frac{(-0.28)}{0.64}\cdot\frac{2}{4} = 0$$

$$\hat{X}_1 + 0.04167X_2 - .21875\,X_3 + (-10 - .62505 + 4.375) = 0$$

$$\hat{X}_1 = -0.04167\,X_2 + 0.21875\,X_3 + 6.25$$

For $X_2 = 10$, $X_3 = 25$, estimated value of X_1 is,

$$\hat{X}_1 = -0.04167 \times 10 + .21875 \times 25 + 6.25 = 11.30.$$

Q. 81. *Give necessary and sufficient condition for the regression planes, X_1 on X_2 and X_3; X_2 on X_1 and X_3, and X_3 on X_1 and X_2 to be coincident.*

Ans. The necessary and sufficient condition for the regression planes X_1 on X_2 and X_3; X_2 on X_1 and X_3, and X_3 on X_1 and X_2 to be coincident is,

$$r_{12}^2 + r_{13}^2 + r_{23}^2 - 2r_{12}r_{13}r_{23} = 1$$

Q. 82. *Give the concept and definition of partial correlation coefficient.*

Ans. In a multivariate study, the correlation between any two variables is not free from the influence of other variables. Hence, it becomes necessary to eliminate the common association of other variables to obtain the actual association between the two variables.

To be more specific in its explanation, consider three variables X_1, X_2 and X_3. Now we want to find out the partial correlation between X_1 and X_2 after eliminating the linear effect of X_3 on X_1 and X_2. In this situation, define two residual variables $X_{1.3}$ and $X_{2.3}$ where $X_{1.3} = X_1 - b_{13}X_3$ and $X_{2.3} = X_2 - b_{23}X_3$ and b_{13}, b_{23} are the simple regression coefficients of X_1 on X_3 and X_2 on X_3 respectively. Thus, the partial correlation coefficient between X_1 and X_2 eliminating the influence of X_3 is the simple correlation coefficient between $X_{1.3}$ and $X_{2.3}$. The formula is,

$$r_{12.3} = \frac{\text{cov}(X_{1.3}, X_{2.3})}{\sqrt{\text{var}(X_{1.3})\,\text{var}(X_{2.3})}}$$

Definition. Partial correlation coefficient may be defined as a measure of degree of association between any two variables out of a set of variables eliminating the common association of remaining variables from both of them.

Q. 83. *Give the formula for partial correlation coefficient in terms of simple correlation coefficients.*

Ans. If the correlation matrix for k variables X_1, X_2, ..., X_k is

$$P = \begin{bmatrix} 1 & r_{12} & r_{13} & \cdots & r_{1k} \\ r_{21} & 1 & r_{23} & \cdots & r_{2k} \\ r_{31} & r_{32} & 1 & \cdots & Y_{3k} \\ \vdots & & & & \\ r_{k1} & r_{k2} & r_{k3} & \cdots & 1 \end{bmatrix}$$

The partial correlation coefficient between any two variables X_i and X_j for $i \neq j = 1, 2, ..., k$ can be computed by the formula,

$$r_{ij.12...(i-1)(i+1)...(j-1)(j+1)...k} = \frac{P_{ij}}{\sqrt{P_{ii}P_{jj}}}$$

where, P_{ij}, P_{ii} and P_{jj} are the cofactors of r_{ij}, r_{ii} and r_{jj} respectively in the determinant of the correlation matrix P. The range of partial correlation coefficient is from –1 to 1.

Q. 84. *Express partial correlation coefficient between any two variables eliminating the influence of the third variable out of the variables X_1, X_2 and X_3 in terms of simple correlation coefficients.*

Ans. If r_{12}, r_{13} and r_{23} are the simple correlation coefficients between the variables X_1 and X_2; X_1 and X_3; X_2 and X_3 respectively, the formulae for the partial correlation coefficients are:

$$r_{12.3} = \frac{r_{12} - r_{13}r_{23}}{\sqrt{(1-r_{13}^2)(1-r_{23}^2)}}$$

$$r_{13.2} = \frac{r_{13} - r_{12}r_{23}}{\sqrt{(1-r_{12}^2)(1-r_{23}^2)}}$$

$$r_{23.1} = \frac{r_{23} - r_{12}r_{13}}{\sqrt{(1-r_{12}^2)(1-r_{13}^2)}}$$

Recall $r_{12} = r_{21}$, $r_{13} = r_{31}$ and $r_{23} = r_{32}$. Also the partial correlation coefficients $r_{12.3}$, $r_{13.2}$ and $r_{23.1}$ are called the *first order partial correlation coefficients* as there is only one figure in the suffix to the right of the dot.

Q. 85. *Write the formula for the partial correlation coefficient $r_{12.34}$ in case of multivariate study of the four variables X_1, X_2, X_3 and X_4 in terms of simple correlation coefficients.*

Ans. If r_{12}, r_{13}, r_{14}, r_{23}, r_{24} and r_{34} are the simple correlation coefficients between two variables marked by the respective suffixes and $r_{12.4}$, $r_{13.4}$, $r_{23.4}$, $r_{12.3}$, $r_{14.3}$, and $r_{24.3}$ are the first order partial correlation coefficients, the partial correlation coefficient,

$$r_{12.34} = \frac{r_{12.4} - r_{13.4}r_{23.4}}{\sqrt{(1-r_{13.4}^2)(1-r_{23.4}^2)}}$$

or alternatively,

$$r_{12.34} = \frac{r_{12.3} - r_{14.3}r_{24.3}}{\sqrt{(1-r_{14.3}^2)(1-r_{24.3}^2)}}$$

$r_{12.34}$ or any other likewise partial correlation coefficient is called *second order partial correlation coefficient* as there are two figures in the suffix after the dot. So to calculate second order partial correlation coefficient, one has to compute first order partial correlation coefficients from simple correlation coefficients. Formulae for $r_{13.24}$, $r_{13.24}$, etc., can be written by simply changing the suffixes.

Q. 86. *Expatiate part correlation.*

Ans. Part correlation is the correlation between two variables with variable(s) controlled for in one of the two variables in which the correlation is worked out.

More simply, in partial correlation $r_{12.3}$, the effect of variable 3 is eliminated from both the variables 1 and 2. But if the variable 3 is influencing only one variable, *i.e.*, either variable 1 or variable 2, then we have to eliminate the effect from one variable only and should calculate part correlation.

Formula for part correlation between X_1 and X_2 where X_3 is controlled for in only X_2 is given as,

$$r_{1(2.3)} = \frac{r_{12} - r_{13}r_{23}}{\sqrt{1 - r_{23}^2}}$$

Similarly the formula for part correlation between X_1 and X_2 eliminating the effect of X_3 from X_1 is,

$$r_{2(1.3)} = \frac{r_{12} - r_{13}r_{23}}{\sqrt{1 - r_{13}^2}}$$

Q. 87. *Out of partial correlation and part correlation which one is always greater.*

Ans. Partial correlation will always be greater than the part correlation between the same variables.

Q. 88. *What is spurious or nonsense correlation?*

Ans. If the two variables X and Y are such that it is not possible to explain the casual relationship between them but the correlation, calculated merely on numerical basis, is called *spurious* or *nonsense* correlation. For example, the correlation between the number of students in a country and the number of cattles in that country during the last twenty years is a nonsense correlation.

SECTION B

Fill in the Blanks

Fill in the suitable word(s) or phrase(s) in the blanks:

1. The functional relationship of a dependent variable with independent variable(s) is called ________ .
2. The linear regression equation of Y on X is known as ________ .
3. The graph of regression equation is called ________ of regression.
4. If there are two or more independent variables in a regression equation, it is named as ________ regression.
5. The independent variables in a multiple regression are also termed as ________ .
6. The dependent variable in a regression equation is termed as ________ .
7. The independent variables in a regression equation are often called ________ variables.
8. Other names of regression equation are ________ or ________ equation.
9. If there are two variables X and Y, there can be at most ________ regression lines.
10. A regression model is a ________ relationship between the dependent and independent variables.
11. A regression model may be ________ or ________ .
12. A regression function involving the error term is called a ________ or ________ model.
13. A regression model in which residual term is not involved, called a ________ model.
14. The term regression was introduced by ________ .
15. The paired values plotted on a graph marked by points lead to a ________ diagram.
16. The measure of change in dependent variable corresponding to an unit change in independent variable is called ________ .
17. If the regression coefficient $\beta_{YX} > 1$, then β_{XY} ________ .
18. If the regression coefficient $\beta_{YX} < 1$, then β_{XY} ________ .
19. The regression coefficient β_{YX} is the ________ of the regression line.
20. The constant β_0 is the coefficient of X to the power ________ .

21. In the regression equation $Y = \beta_0 + \beta_1 X$, the constant β_0 is the _________ which the line cuts from Y-axis.

22. The estimated value of β_0 in the regression line is $Y = \beta_0 + \beta_1 X + \varepsilon$ is _________ .

23. The estimated value of β in the regression equation $Y = \alpha + \beta X + \varepsilon$ in terms of variance-covariance is _________ .

24. If $\rho = 1$, the relation between β_{YX} and β_{XY} is _________ .

25. $r = \sqrt{b_{YX} \cdot b_{XY}}$ is known as the _________ property of regression coefficients.

26. The fundamental property of regression coefficients means the relation _________ .

27. The signature property in regression means that the signs of β_{YX}, β_{XY} and ρ are _________ .

28. The arithmetic mean of two regression coefficients is _________ to the correlation coefficient.

29. The property $\frac{1}{2}(\beta_{YX} + \beta_{XY}) \geq \rho$ is known as _________ property of regression co-efficients.

30. If the variables X and Y are independent, the value of regression coefficient is _________ .

31. The two regression lines for the variables X and Y intersect at the point _________ .

32. If $\rho = \pm 1$, the two regression lines are _________ .

33. If $\rho = 0$, the two lines of regression are at an angle of _________ .

34. If the two lines of regression are coincident, the relation between regression coefficients is _________ .

35. If the two lines of regression are perpendicular to each other, then the relation between regression coefficients is _________ .

36. If a constant value 10 is subtracted from each variate value of X and Y, the value of regression coefficient will _________ .

37. If each value of the variate X is divided by 5, then b'_{YX} from coded values will be _________ of the original value of b_{YX}.

38. If each value of both the variables X and Y is divided by 5, then b'_{YX} from coded values will be _________ as b_{YX}.

39. The significance of regression parameters can be tested by _________ .

40. F-test can be used to test the significance of _________ simultaneously.

41. $E(Y \mid X) = \alpha + \beta X$ is called _________ of Y on X.

42. A function $g(x) = E(y/x)$, which minimises $E\{Y - g(x)\}^2$, is called _________ .

43. If the variables (X, Y) are distributed bivariate normally with parameters $(0, 0, \sigma_x^2, \sigma_y^2, \rho)$ the correlation coefficient between X^2 and Y^2 is _________ .

44. The formula for $(1 - \alpha)$ 100 per cent confidence limits for β_{YX} with usual notations is _________ .

45. The formula for $(1 - \alpha)$ 100 per cent confidence limits for β_0 with usual notations is _________ .

46. The assumption of homoscedasticity of the variance $\sigma^2_{Y \mid X}$ is required in _________ of regression coefficients.

47. If the assumption of homoscedasticity of the variance $\sigma^2_{Y \mid X}$ does not hold, one has to go for _________ regression.

48. With the help of regression equation one can measure a variable which is not _________ measurable.

49. Population projections can be obtained with the help of _________ analysis.

50. True effects of certain treatments can be estimated by the use of_________ eliminating the effect of concomitant variables.

51. Least square estimate of β_{YX} is _________ .

52. Least square estimate of β_0 is _________ .

53. If ε of the regression model $Y - \beta_0 + \beta_1 X + \varepsilon$ is distributed as $N(0, \sigma_\varepsilon^2)$, the variance of the estimate b_1 of β_1 is _________ .

54. If the error $\varepsilon \sim N(0, \sigma_\varepsilon^2)$ in $Y = \beta_0 + \beta_1 X + \varepsilon$, the variance of b_0 is _________ where b_0 is an estimate of β_0.

55. The equation $Y = \gamma(1 - e^{\alpha - \beta X})$ for $\alpha, \beta, \gamma >$ 0 represents _________ .

56. $Y = \alpha + \beta X + \gamma X^2$ is the equation of a _________ .

57. The function $\log_e Y = \log_e \gamma + \beta^X \log_e \alpha$ represents _________ curve.

58. The equation $Y = 1/(a + bX)$ represents _________ .

59. The equation for exponential growth curve is _________ .

60. The equation for logistic growth curve is _________ .

61. In orthogonal polynomial, the _________ terms can be added one by one.

62. The method of fitting orthogonal polynomials was given by _________ .

63. The idea of correlation was given by _________ .

64. Karl Pearson defined correlation in the year _________ .

65. Pearson's formula for correlation coefficient ρ_{XY} is _________ .

66. If (X_i, Y_i) are n pairs of observations on the variables X and Y, the formula for correlation coefficient is _________ .

67. The quantity ρ^2 (or r^2) is known as _________ .

68. The quantity $(1 - \rho^2)$, where ρ is the correlation coefficient, is called _________ .

69. If ρ is the correlation coefficient, the $\sqrt{1-\rho^2}$ is termed as _________ .

70. The range of Pearson's coefficient of correlation is _________ .

71. If $\rho_{XY} = 1$, the line on the graph will extend from _________ to _________ .

72. If $\rho_{XY} = -1$, it means that there is a _________ correlation between X and Y.

73. If $\rho = 0$, it depicts _________ association.

74. Correlation coefficient is a _________ number.

75. If each value of data is reduced by 10, the correlation coefficient between coded values is _________ as that of original values.

76. If the variate values of X are divided by 100 and Y values by 1000, the correlation between X and Y from coded values is _________ as that of original values.

77. If each value of X and Y is reduced by 5 and then divided by 10, the correlation between coded values is _________ as that of original observations.

78. The relation between the regression coefficient β_{YX} and correlation coefficient ρ is _________ .

79. The regression coefficient β_{XY} can be expressed in terms of correlation coefficient ρ as _________ .

80. The origin of correlation coefficient lies in _________ distribution.

81. The standard error of sample correlation coefficient r, based on n paired values, is _________ .

82. The formula for probable error with usual notations is _________ .

83. Probable error helps to know the _________ of correlation coefficient.

84. If the sample correlation coefficient is less than thrice the probable error, the correlation coefficient is ________ .

85. If the correlation coefficient r is greater than ________, the correlation coefficient is significant.

86. The test statistic for testing the significance of correlation coefficient ρ is ________ .

87. The test statistic $r\sqrt{n-2}/\sqrt{1-r^2}$ is distributed as ________ .

88. Statistic-t for the test of $H_0: \rho = 0$ based on n paired values has ________ degrees of freedom.

89. The test of hypothesis for a known value of population correlation coefficient can be performed with the help of ________ transformation.

90. The formula for Fisher's transformation from r to Z is ________ .

91. In testing H_0: $\rho = \rho_0$ (a constant value), Z_r is distributed as ________ .

92. For the test of hypothesis H_0: $\rho = \rho_0$, the test statistic with usual notations is ________ .

93. $(1 - \alpha)$ 100 per cent confidence limits for ρ with usual notations can be found indirectly by the formula ________ .

94. The equality of two population correlation coefficients can be tested with the help of ________ transformation.

95. The quantity $\frac{1}{2}\{\log_e(1 + r) - \log_e(1 - r)\}$ in terms of hyperbolic functions is equivalent to ________ .

96. Equality of several population correlation coefficients can be tested by ________ test.

97. Coefficient of concurrent deviations depends only on the ________ of deviations.

98. The magnitude of the deviation of a series at a point of time from its preceding value receives no attention in the calculation of coefficient of ________ .

99. The formula for coefficient of concurrent deviation with usual notations is ________ .

100. The formula for coefficient of correlation using variance of the difference $(X - Y)$ with usual notation is ________ .

101. The value of correlation coefficient by Pearson's formula and the formula using the variance of the differences $(X - Y)$ is ________ .

102. The formula for the coefficient of correlation which does not involve the covariance term is ________ .

103. Correlation ratio is a suitable measure of correlation if the relation between X and Y is ________ .

104. In correlation ratio, for each value of X, there can be ________ values of Y.

105. Correlation ratio is defined as the ratio of ________ sum of squares to the ________ sum of squares.

106. Correlation ratio is usually denoted by ________ and its estimate by ________ .

107. The range of correlation ratio is ________ .

108. If each group consists of only one observation, η^2 is equal to ________ .

109. If all observations are in one group, the value of correlation ratio is ________ .

110. In general η^2 is ________ than ρ^2.

111. $\eta^2 = \rho^2$ only when the relation between the variables X and Y is ________ .

112. Similarity among individuals within the groups can be measured through ________ correlation.

113. If each of the k groups contains n observations, the limits of intraclass correlation coefficient are ________ .

114. If one variable is dichotomous and the other variable has many classes, then a suitable measure of association is ________ correlation.

115. When both the variables X and Y are dichotomous and are presentable in a 2 × 2

contingency table, an appropriate measure of association is ________ correlation.

116. If the consecutive values of a time series of data are correlated, a measure of linear association between the errors of consecutive periods is ________ .

117. Another name of autocorrelation is ________ correlation.

118. A regression equation having two or more independent variables is called ________ .

119. The positive square root of the quantity R^2 is known as ________ correlation.

120. The range of multiple correlation is ________ .

121. Multiple correlation is a measure of ________ association of a variable with other variables.

122. If the value of multiple correlation is near to unity, it indicates that multiple linear regression is a ________ fit.

123. If P is the correlation matrix, the formula for multiple correlation of a variable X with rest of the $(k-1)$ variables is ________ .

124. In case of three variables X_1, X_2 and X_3, the multiple correlation coefficient $R_{1.23}$ in terms of simple correlation coefficients is equal to ________ .

125. If X_1, X_2 and X_3 are three variables, the regression planes X_1 on X_2, X_3 ; X_2 on X_1, X_3 and X_3 on X_1, X_2 are coincident iff ________ .

126. Partial correlation coefficients is a measure of association between two variables ________ the common effect of the rest of the variables.

127. If P is the correlation matrix, the partial correlation coefficient between X_i and X_j eliminating the influence of the rest of the $(k-2)$ variables can be calculated by the formula ________ .

128. Partial correlation coefficient is the simple correlation between ________ variables.

129. The formula for partial correlation coefficient $r_{12.3}$ in terms of simple correlation coefficients is ________ .

130. $r_{12.3}$ is known as ________ order partial correlation coefficient.

131. The formula for $r_{12.34}$ in terms of first order partial correlation coefficient is ________ .

132. $r_{12.34}$ is known as ________ order partial correlation coefficient.

133. The range of partial correlation coefficient is ________ .

134. If the variable $X \sim N(0, 1)$ and $Y = X^2$, cov (X, Y) = ________ .

135. If $X_1 \sim N(5, 4)$ and $X_2 \sim N(10, 9)$, also the variable U and V are defined as $U = 3X_1 + 4X_2$ and $V = 3X_1 - X_2$ then corr (U, V) = ________ .

136. If X and Y are two independent variables and the variables $U = X + Y$ and $V = X - Y$, then corr (U, V) = ________ .

137. If X and Y are two independent variables with variances $V(X) = 25$ and $V(Y) = 15$, the correlation coefficient between $U = X + Y$ and $V = X - Y$ is equal to ________ .

138. If $X_1, X_2, \ldots, X_n$ are n i.i.d. variables, the correlation between X_i and $\bar{X}$ is equal to ________ .

139. If $X_1, X_2, \ldots, X_n$ are i.i.d. variables, the correlation coefficient between $(X_i - \bar{X})$ and $\bar{X}$ is ________ .

140. If $E(XY) = E(X)\,E(Y)$, the correlation coefficient between X and Y is ________ .

141. If X_1, X_2 and X_3 are three variates, each distributed with variance σ^2 and the correlation between any two is r, the mean $\bar{X}$ has variance equal to ________ .

142. Two independent variables are ________ .

143. Correlation coefficient is invariant under the change of ________ and ________ .

144. If the line of regression of Y on X is $Y = 2X + 1$ and of X on Y is $6X = Y - 3$, then corr (X, Y) = ________ .

145. If the lines of regression of Y on X is $4X - 5Y + 33 = 0$ and of X on Y is $20X - 9Y - 107 = 0$, the mean value $\bar{X}$ is ________ and $\bar{Y}$ ________ .

146. If the regression line of Y on X is $2Y = 3X - 6$, the estimated value of Y for given value of $X = 10$ is ________ .

147. The given values, $b_{YX} = \frac{1}{5}$ and $b_{XY} = 10$ are ________ .

148. If the correlation coefficient is zero, the value of regression coefficient is ________ .

149. Both the regression coefficients cannot exceed ________ .

150. If $R_{1.23} = 1$, then $R_{2.13}$ is equal to ________ .

151. The correlation between the number of blinds per year and the production of liquor per year is ________ correlation.

152. If the sum of the product of the deviation of X and Y from their means is zero, the correlation between X and Y is ________ .

153. If the probable error is more than r, the correlation coefficient is ________ .

154. If one regression coefficient is negative, the other would be ________ .

155. The values $r_{12} = 0.6$, r_{13}, $= -0.5$ and $r_{23} = 0.8$ obtained in a certain investigation are ________ .

156. The multiple correlation coefficient in multiple regression analysis is equivalent to simple correlation between a variable Y and ________ .

157. Two regression lines of standard normal deviates pass through the ________ .

158. If $\rho = 0$, the regression line of Y on X will be parallel to ________ at a distance of ________ .

159. The regression line of Y on X, the two uncorrelated standard normal deviates, is ________ .

160. The two regression lines of two uncorrelated standard normal variates are ________ to each other.

161. The slope of regression lines of two standard normal deviates having zero correlation is ________ .

162. If simple correlation coefficient is zero, then regression coefficient is equal to ________ .

163. If $\rho = 1$ between X and Y, then the two regression lines may intersect at an angle of ________ .

164. An unknown parameter in a model likely to be estimated is called a ________ parameter.

165. A parameter of a model, which can take values either zero or unity, is specified as ________ parameter.

166. A parameter in a regression model which is forced to be equal to some other parameter(s) is termed as ________ parameter.

167. A regression equation with a dependent variable and two independent variables is called a ________ .

168. Out of three variables X_1, X_2 and X_3 if X_3 influences either X_1 or X_2, then to find the correlation between X_1 and X_2 eliminating the effect of X_3, one should preferably calculate ________ .

169. The formula for part correlation $r_{1(3.2)}$ is ________ .

170. Part correlation coefficient is always ________ than partial correlation coefficient.

SECTION C

Multiple Choice Questions

Select the correct alternative out of given ones:

1. The term regression was introduced by:
   (*a*) R.A. Fisher
   (*b*) Sir Francis Galton
   (*c*) Karl Pearson
   (*d*) none of the above
2. If X and Y are two variates, there can be at most:
   (*a*) one regression line
   (*b*) two regression lines
   (*c*) three regression lines
   (*d*) an infinite number of regression lines
3. In a regression line of Y on X, the variable X is known as:
   (*a*) independent variable
   (*b*) regressor
   (*c*) explanatory variable
   (*d*) all of the above
4. Regression equation is also named as:
   (*a*) prediction equation
   (*b*) estimating equation
   (*c*) line of average relationship
   (*d*) all of the above
5. Scatter diagram of the variate values (X, Y) gives the idea about:
   (*a*) functional relationship
   (*b*) regression model
   (*c*) distribution of errors
   (*d*) none of the above
6. The estimate of β in the regression equation $Y = \alpha + \beta X + e$ by the method of least squares is:
   (*a*) biased
   (*b*) unbiased
   (*c*) consistent
   (*d*) efficient
7. The formula for the estimate of β in the regression equation $Y = \alpha + \beta X + \varepsilon$ is:
   (*a*) $\text{cov}(X, Y)/V(X)$
   (*b*) $r\sigma_Y/\sigma_X$
   (*c*) $\Sigma(X_i - \bar{X})(Y_i - \bar{Y})/\Sigma(X_i - \bar{X})^2$
   (*d*) all of the above
8. In the regression line $Y = \alpha + \beta X$, β is called the:
   (*a*) slope of the line
   (*b*) intercept of the line
   (*c*) neither (*a*) nor (*b*)
   (*d*) both (*a*) and (*b*)
9. In the regression line $Y = \beta_0 + \beta_1 X$, β_0 is the:
   (*a*) slope of the line
   (*b*) intercept of the line
   (*c*) both (*a*) and (*b*)
   (*d*) neither (*a*) nor (*b*)
10. If β_{YX} and β_{XY} are two regression coefficients, they have:
    (*a*) same sign
    (*b*) opposite sign
    (*c*) either same or opposite signs
    (*d*) nothing can be said
11. The property that β_{YX} and β_{XY} and ρ have same signs, it called:
    (*a*) fundamental property
    (*b*) signature property
    (*c*) magnitude property
    (*d*) none of the above
12. The average of two regression coefficients is always greater than or equal to the correlation coefficient is called:
    (*a*) fundamental property
    (*b*) signature property
    (*c*) magnitude property
    (*d*) mean property
13. If $\beta_{YX} > 1$, then β_{XY} is:
    (*a*) less than 1
    (*b*) greater than 1
    (*c*) equal to 1
    (*d*) equal to 0

14. If $\beta_{YX} < 1$, then β_{XY} is:
(*a*) less than 1
(*b*) greater than 1
(*c*) equal to 1
(*d*) equal to 0

15. The property $\beta_{YX} > 1$ implies that $\beta_{XY} < 1$ is known as:
(*a*) fundamental property
(*b*) signature property
(*c*) magnitude property
(*d*) none of the above

16. If X and Y are independent, the value of regression coefficient β_{YX} is equal to:
(*a*) 0
(*b*) 1
(*c*) ∞
(*d*) any positive value

17. The property if X and Y are independent, then $\beta_{YX} = \beta_{XY} = 0$ is called:
(*a*) fundamental property
(*b*) mean property
(*c*) independence property
(*d*) magnitude property

18. The lines of regression intersect at the point:
(*a*) (X, Y)
(*b*) $(\bar{X}, \bar{Y})$
(*c*) $(0, 0)$
(*d*) $(1, 1)$

19. The coordinates $(\bar{X}, \bar{Y})$ satisfy the lines of regression of:
(*a*) Y on X
(*b*) X on Y
(*c*) both the regression lines
(*d*) none of the two regression lines

20. If $\rho = \pm 1$, the two lines of regression are:
(*a*) coincident
(*b*) parallel
(*c*) perpendicular to each other
(*d*) none of the above

21. If $\rho = 1$, the angle between the two lines of regression is:
(*a*) zero degree
(*b*) ninety degree
(*c*) sixty degree
(*d*) thirty degree

22. If $\rho = 0$, the lines of regression are:
(*a*) coincident
(*b*) parallel
(*c*) perpendicular to each other
(*d*) none of the above

23. If $\rho = 0$, the angle between the two lines of regression is:
(*a*) zero degree
(*b*) ninety degree
(*c*) sixty degree
(*d*) thirty degree

24. If the two lines of regression are perpendicular to each other, the relation between the two regression coefficients is:
(*a*) $\beta_{YX} = \beta_{XY}$
(*b*) $\beta_{YX} \cdot \beta_{XY} = 1$
(*c*) $\beta_{YX} \leq \beta_{XY}$
(*d*) $\beta_{YX} = -\beta_{XY}$

25. If the two lines of regression are coincident, the relation between the two regression coefficients is:
(*a*) $\beta_{YX} = \beta_{XY}$
(*b*) $\beta_{YX} \cdot \beta_{XY} = 1$
(*c*) $\beta_{YX} \leq \beta_{XY}$
(*d*) $\beta_{YX} = -\beta_{XY}$

26. Regression coefficient is independent of:
(*a*) origin
(*b*) scale
(*c*) both origin and scale
(*d*) neither origin nor scale

27. If a constant 50 is subtracted from each of the value of X and Y, the regression coefficient is:
(*a*) reduced by 50
(*b*) $\frac{1}{50}$ th of the original regression coefficient
(*b*) increased by 50
(*c*) not changed

28. If each observation in the set of values (X, Y) is divided by 100, the regression coefficient of Y on X is:

(a) increased by 100
(b) decreased by 100
(c) $\frac{1}{100}$ th of b_{YX}
(d) none of the above

29. If each of X variate is divided by 5 and of Y by 10, then b'_{YX} by coded values is:
(a) same as b_{YX}
(b) half of b_{YX}
(c) twice of b_{YX}
(d) none of the above

30. If each value of X is divided by 2 and of Y is multiplied by 2, then b'_{YX} by coded values is:
(a) same as b_{YX}
(b) twice of b_{YX}
(c) four times of b_{YX}
(d) eight times of b_{YX}

31. If from each value of X and Y, constant 25 is subtracted and then each value is divided by 10, the coded b'_{YX} is:
(a) same as b_{YX}
(b) 2½ times of b_{YX}
(c) 25 times of b_{YX}
(d) 10 times of b_{YX}

32. If each value of X is multiplied by 10 and of Y by 20, b_{XY}, the regression coefficient by coded values is:
(a) same as b_{XY}
(b) half of b_{XY}
(c) four times of b_{XY}
(d) one-fourth of b_{XY}

33. If from each value of Y, a constant value 15 is subtracted and then divided by 2, the regression coefficient b_{XY} through coded values is:
(a) half of b_{XY}
(b) twice of b_{XY}
(c) same as b_{XY}
(d) none of the above

34. Significance of a regression coefficient can be tested by:
(a) t-test
(b) F-test
(c) both (a) and (b)
(d) neither (a) nor (b)

35. The test statistics for testing the significance of regression coefficient is:
(a) $F = b/s_b$
(b) $\chi^2 = b^2/s_b^2$
(c) $Z = b/s_b$
(d) none of the above

36. Residual mean sum of squares in case of regression analysis with usual notations is:
(a) $(\Sigma v_i^2 - b_{YX}\,\Sigma u_i v_i)/(n-1)$
(b) $(\Sigma v_i^2 - b_{YX}\,\Sigma u_i v_i)/(n-2)$
(c) $\left(\Sigma v_i^2 - \frac{\Sigma u_i v_i}{\Sigma u_i^2}\right)(n-2)$
(d) all of the above

37. Standard error of the intercept b_0 in a regression line of Y on X can be obtained by:
(a) $s_e^2\left\{\frac{1}{b} + \frac{\bar{X}^2}{\Sigma u_i^2}\right\}$
(b) $s_e^2\left\{\frac{1}{n} + \frac{\bar{X}^2}{\Sigma u_i^2}\right\}$
(c) $s_e^2\left\{\frac{1}{n-1} + \frac{\Sigma u_i^2}{\bar{X}^2}\right\}$
(d) none of the above

38. The statistic-F for testing H_0: $\beta_{YX} = 0$ in regression analysis has d.f.:
(a) $(n-2)$
(b) $(1, n-2)$
(c) $(1, n-1)$
(d) $(2, n-2)$

39. The statistic-F for testing H_0: $\beta_{YX} = 0$ with usual notations is:
(a) $(b\,\Sigma u_i v_i)/s_e^2$

(*b*) $(b\ \Sigma u_i v_i)/s_b^2$

(*c*) $(b\ \Sigma u_i v_i)/\Sigma u_i^2$

(*d*) $(b\ \Sigma u_i v_i)/\Sigma v_i^2$

40. The random function $g(x) = E\{Y/X = x\}$ is called the:

(*a*) regression curve of Y on X

(*b*) regression line of Y on X

(*c*) regression function Y on X

(*d*) none of the above

41. The functional relation $Y = E(Y/X = x)$ is called:

(*a*) regression line of Y on X

(*b*) regression function of Y on X

(*c*) regression curve of the mean of Y on X

(*d*) all of the above

42. If the correlation coefficient between the variables X and Y is ρ, the correlation coefficient between X^2 and Y^2 is:

(*a*) ρ

(*b*) ρ^2

(*c*) 0

(*d*) 1

43. The confidence limits for the regression coefficient β_{YX} with usual notations can be given by the formula:

(*a*) $b_{YX} \mp s_e \cdot t_{\alpha, n-2}$

(*b*) $b_{YX} \mp s_b^2 \cdot t_{\alpha, n-1}$

(*c*) $b_{YX} \mp s_b \cdot t_{\alpha, n-1}$

(*d*) $b_{YX} \mp s_b \cdot t_{\alpha, (n-2)}$

44. The standard error of $\hat{Y}$, the estimate of $\mu_{Y/X}$ with usual notations is given by the formula:

(*a*) $s_{\hat{Y}}^2 = s_e^2 \left\{ \frac{1}{n} + \frac{(X - \bar{X})^2}{\Sigma u_i^2} \right\}$

(*b*) $s_{\hat{Y}}^2 = s_e^2 \left\{ 1 + \frac{1}{n} + \frac{\Sigma(X - \bar{X})^2}{\Sigma u_i^2} \right\}$

(*c*) $s_{\hat{Y}}^2 = s_b^2 \left\{ 1 + \frac{1}{n} + \frac{(X - \bar{X})^2}{\Sigma u_i^2} \right\}$

(*d*) $s_{\hat{Y}}^2 = s_e^2 \left\{ 1 + \frac{1}{n} + \frac{(X - \bar{X})^2}{\Sigma u_i^2} \right\}$

45. If the assumption of homoscedasticity of $\sigma_{Y/X}^2$ is not true in a linear regression model, one must use:

(*a*) curvilinear regression

(*b*) orthogonal polynomial

(*c*) weighted regression

(*d*) any of the above

46. Regression analysis can be used for:

(*a*) reducing the length of confidence interval

(*b*) for prediction of dependent variate value

(*c*) to know the true effect of certain treatments

(*d*) all of the above

47. b_{YX} as an estimate of β_{YX} is:

(*a*) a consistent estimator

(*b*) unbiased

(*c*) efficient

(*d*) all of the above

48. b_0 as an estimate of β_0 in regression analysis is:

(*a*) asymptotically normal

(*b*) admissible

(*c*) unbiased

(*d*) all of the above

49. To test the linearity of a regression equation, one needs:

(*a*) error S.S. other than residual S.S.

(*b*) residual S.S.

(*c*) both (*a*) and (*b*)

(*d*) neither (*a*) nor (*b*)

50. If in a regression equation $Y = \alpha + \beta X + e$, $e \sim N(0, \sigma_e^2)$ the variance of b, the estimate of β is:

(*a*) $\sigma_e^2/(n-2)$
(*b*) $\sigma_e^2/\Sigma u_i^2$
(*c*) σ_e^2/n
(*d*) none of the above

51. If in a regression equation $Y = \alpha + \beta X + e$, $e \sim N(0, \sigma_e^2)$, the standard deviation of a, the estimate of α, is:
(*a*) σ_e^2/n
(*b*) $\sigma_e^2/\Sigma u_i^2$
(*c*) $\sigma_e/\sqrt{n}$
(*d*) none of the above

52. The function,

$$\frac{1}{Y} = \alpha\beta^X + \gamma \quad \text{for} \quad \alpha, \beta, \gamma > 0$$

represent:
(*a*) logistic growth curve
(*b*) compertz curve
(*c*) equilateral hyperbola
(*d*) exponential growth curve

53. The equation $Y = \alpha\beta^{-X}$ for $\beta < 1$ represents:
(*a*) exponential growth curve
(*b*) exponential decay curve
(*c*) a parabola
(*d*) none of the above

54. The function $Y = a + bX + cX^2 + dX^3$ represents:
(*a*) a hyperbola
(*b*) a exponential curve
(*c*) a parabola
(*d*) all of the above

55. The mathematical function,

$$\frac{1}{Y} = a + b\left(\frac{1}{X}\right)$$

represents:
(*a*) an equilateral hyperbola
(*b*) exponential curve
(*c*) compertz curve
(*d*) none of the above

56. The model

$$Y = \gamma(1 - e^{\alpha-\beta X}) \text{ for } \alpha, \beta, \gamma > 0$$

is known as,
(*a*) equilateral hyperbola
(*b*) compertz curve
(*c*) Mitscherlich function
(*d*) none of the above

57. The mathematical function

$$Y = \gamma\alpha^{\beta^X} \quad \text{for } \alpha, \beta, \gamma > 0$$

represents:
(*a*) an equilateral hyperbola
(*b*) compertz curve
(*c*) Mitscherlich function
(*d*) none of the above

58. The advantage of orthogonal polynomial is:
(*a*) one can fit a polynomial of appropriate degree
(*b*) it saves time of computation
(*c*) easy to fit in the equation
(*d*) all of the above

59. If the correlation between the two variables X and Y is negative, the regression coefficient of Y on X is:
(*a*) positive
(*b*) negative
(*c*) not certain
(*d*) none of the above

60. Given the two lines of regression as, $3X - 4Y + 8 = 0$ and $4X - 3Y = 1$, the means of X and Y are:
(*a*) $\bar{X} = 4, \bar{Y} = 5$
(*b*) $\bar{X} = 3, \bar{Y} = 4$
(*c*) $\bar{X} = \frac{4}{3}, \bar{Y} = \frac{5}{4}$
(*d*) none of the above

61. The idea of product moment correlation was given by:
(*a*) R.A. Fisher
(*b*) Sir Francis Galton

(*c*) Karl Pearson

(*d*) Spearman

62. Correlation coefficient was invented in the year:

(*a*) 1910

(*b*) 1890

(*c*) 1908

(*d*) none of the above

63. The formula for simple correlation coefficient between the variables X and Y with usual notations is:

(*a*) $\text{cov}(X, Y) / \sqrt{V(X)V(Y)}$

(*b*) $\mu_{XY} / \sqrt{\mu_{XX}\,\mu_{YY}}$

(*c*) $\sigma_{XY} / \sigma_X \sigma_Y$

(*d*) all of the above

64. The formula for calculating r from n paired sample values (X_i, Y_i) is:

(*a*) $r = \dfrac{\Sigma(X_i - \bar{X})\,\Sigma(Y_i - \bar{Y})}{\sqrt{\Sigma(X_i - \bar{X})^2 \Sigma(Y_i - \bar{Y})^2}}$

(*b*) $r = \dfrac{\Sigma X_i Y_i}{\Sigma X_i^2\ \Sigma Y_i^2}$

(*c*) $r = \dfrac{\Sigma(X_i - \bar{X})(Y_i - \bar{Y})}{\sqrt{\Sigma(X_i - \bar{X})^2 \Sigma(Y_i - \bar{Y})^2}}$

(*d*) all of the above

65. If ρ is the simple correlation coefficient, the quantity ρ^2 is known as:

(*a*) coefficient of determination

(*b*) coefficient of non-determination

(*c*) coefficient of alienation

(*d*) none of the above

66. If ρ is the simple correlation, the quantity $(1 - \rho^2)$ is called:

(*a*) coefficient of determination

(*b*) coefficient of non-determination

(*c*) coefficient of alienation

(*d*) none of the above

67. If ρ is the correlation coefficient, the quantity $\sqrt{1-\rho^2}$ is termed as:

(*a*) coefficient of determination

(*b*) coefficient of non-determination

(*c*) coefficient of alienation

(*d*) all of the above

68. The unit of correlation coefficients is:

(*a*) kg/cc

(*b*) per cent

(*c*) non-existing

(*d*) none of the above

69. The range of simple correlation coefficient is:

(*a*) 0 to ∞

(*b*) $-\infty$ to ∞

(*c*) 0 to 1

(*d*) -1 to 1

70. If $\rho = 1$, the relation between the two variables X and Y is:

(*a*) Y is proportional to X

(*b*) Y is inversely proportional to X

(*c*) Y is equal to X

(*d*) none of the above

71. If $\rho_{XY} = 0$, the variables X and Y are:

(*a*) linearly related

(*b*) independent

(*c*) not linearly related

(*d*) none of the above

72. If $\rho_{XY} = -1$, the relation between X and Y is of the type:

(*a*) when Y increases, X also increases

(*b*) when Y decreases, X also decreases

(*c*) X is equal to $-Y$

(*d*) when Y increases, X proportionately decreases

73. The correlation between two variables is of order:

(*a*) 2

(*b*) 1

(*c*) 0

(*d*) none of the above

74. The geometric mean of the two regression coefficient b_{YX} and b_{XY} is equal to:

(*a*) r
(*b*) r^2
(*c*) 1
(*d*) none of the above

75. The relation $r = \sqrt{b_{YX} \cdot b_{XY}}$ is known as:
(*a*) mean property of regression coefficients
(*b*) fundamental property of regression coefficients
(*c*) signature property of r
(*d*) none of the above

76. Standard error of the sample correlation coefficient r based on n paired values is:
(*a*) $\dfrac{1+r^2}{\sqrt{n}}$
(*b*) $\dfrac{1-r^2}{n}$
(*c*) $\dfrac{1-r^2}{\sqrt{n}}$
(*d*) none of the above

77. The formula for probable error is:
(*a*) P. E. $= 0.6745\sqrt{\dfrac{1-r^2}{n}}$
(*b*) P. E. $= 0.6745\sqrt{\dfrac{1-r^2}{n-2}}$
(*c*) P. E. $= 0.6745\dfrac{1-r^2}{n}$
(*d*) P. E. $= 0.6745\ \dfrac{1-r^2}{\sqrt{n}}$

78. Probable error is used for:
(*a*) measuring the error in r
(*b*) testing the significance of r
(*c*) both (*a*) and (*b*)
(*d*) neither (*a*) nor (*b*)

79. Significance of a simple correlation coefficient can be tested by:
(*a*) *t*-test
(*b*) *Z*-test
(*c*) χ^2-test
(*d*) *F*-test

80. The test statistic for testing the significance of $\rho = 0$ with usual notations is:
(*a*) $t = \dfrac{r\sqrt{1-r^2}}{\sqrt{n-2}}$
(*b*) $t = \dfrac{r\sqrt{n-2}}{\sqrt{1-r^2}}$
(*c*) $t = \dfrac{r\sqrt{n-2}}{1-r^2}$
(*d*) $t = \dfrac{r^2(1-r^2)}{n-2}$

81. The statistic t for testing the hypothesis $\rho = 0$ based on a sample of size n from a bivariate population has d.f.:
(*a*) n
(*b*) $n-1$
(*c*) $n-2$
(*d*) $n-3$

82. The hypothesis for a specific known value of ρ can be tested by:
(*a*) *t*-test
(*b*) *Z*-test
(*c*) χ^2-test
(*d*) *F*-test

83. The hypothesis $H_0 : \rho = \rho_0$ (a constant) can be tested by making use of the transformation:
(*a*) $Z_\rho = \log_{10}\left(\dfrac{1+\rho}{1-\rho}\right)$
(*b*) $Z_\rho = \log_{10}\left(\dfrac{1-\rho}{1+\rho}\right)$
(*c*) $Z_\rho = \dfrac{1}{2}\log_e\left(\dfrac{1+\rho}{1-\rho}\right)$
(*d*) $Z_\rho = \log_e\left(\dfrac{1-\rho}{1+\rho}\right)$

84. Z_r, the Fisher's transform of the correlation coefficient r based on a sample of size n in the test of H_0: $\rho = \rho_0$ is distributed as:

(a) $N(0, Z_{\rho_0})$

(b) $N(Z_{\rho_0}, 1)$

(c) $N(Z_{\rho_0}, n-3)$

(d) $N\left(Z_{\rho_0}, \frac{1}{n-3}\right)$

85. The test statistic for testing H_0: $\rho = \rho_0$ with usual notations is:

(a) $Z = \frac{Z_r - Z_{\rho_0}}{1/(n-3)}$

(b) $Z = \frac{Z_r - Z_0}{1/(n-3)}$

(c) $Z = \frac{Z_r - Z_{\rho_0}}{1/\sqrt{n-3}}$

(d) none of the above

86. Test statistic for testing $H_0 : \rho_1 = \rho_2$ with usual notations is:

(a) $Z = (Z_{r_1} - Z_{r_2}) \Big/ \sqrt{\left(\frac{1}{n_1 - 3} + \frac{1}{n_2 - 3}\right)}$

(b) $Z = (Z_{r_1} - Z_{r_2}) \Big/ \left(\frac{1}{n_1 - 3} + \frac{1}{n_2 - 3}\right)$

(c) $Z = \frac{Z_{r_1}}{n_1 - 3} + \frac{Z_{r_2}}{n_2 - 3}$

(d) all of the above

87. Homogeneity of three or more population correlation coefficients can be tested by:

(a) t-test

(b) Z-test

(c) χ^2-test

(d) F-test

88. Coefficient of concurrent deviation depends on:

(a) the signs of the deviations

(b) the magnitude of deviation

(c) both (a) and (b)

(d) none of (a) and (b)

89. The formula for coefficient of concurrent deviation with usual notations is:

(a) $\sqrt{\frac{2c-n}{n}}$

(b) $\pm\sqrt{\pm\frac{2c-n}{n}}$

(c) $\pm\sqrt{\frac{2c-n}{n}}$

(d) $\pm\sqrt{-\frac{2c-n}{n}}$

90. Formula for coefficient of correlation by making use of the variance of the difference $(X - Y)$ of the variables X and Y is:

(a) $\rho = \frac{\sigma_X^2 + \sigma_Y^2 + \sigma_{X-Y}^2}{2\sigma_X \sigma_Y}$

(b) $\rho = \frac{\sigma_X^2 + \sigma_Y^2 + \sigma_{X-Y}^2}{\sigma_X \sigma_Y}$

(c) $\rho = \frac{\sigma_X^2 + \sigma_Y^2 - \sigma_{X-Y}^2}{2\sigma_X^2 \sigma_Y^2}$

(d) $\rho = \frac{\sigma_X^2 + \sigma_Y^2 - \sigma_{X-Y}^2}{2\sigma_X \sigma_Y}$

91. The formula for calculating the correlation coefficient by the method of least squares with usual notations is:

(a) $\rho = \sqrt{1 - \frac{S_Y^2}{\sigma_Y^2}}$

(b) $\rho = \sqrt{1 - \frac{S_X^2}{\sigma_X^2}}$

(c) both (a) and (b)

(d) neither (a) nor (b)

92. Correlation ratio is an appropriate measure of relationship between the two variables X and Y only if the functional relationship between them is:

(*a*) linear
(*b*) non-linear
(*c*) parabolic
(*d*) none of the above

93. The value of correlation ratio varies from:

(*a*) –1 to 1
(*b*) –1 to 0
(*c*) 0 to 1
(*d*) 0 to ∞

94. If all the observations lie in one group, the value of correlation ratio E^2 is:

(*a*) 0
(*b*) 1
(*c*) between 0 and 1
(*d*) between –1 and 1

95. If each group consists of one observation only, the value of correlation ratio is:

(*a*) 0
(*b*) 1
(*c*) between 0 to 1
(*d*) between –1 and 1

96. The relation between Pearson's correlation coefficient ρ and correlation ratio η^2 is:

(*a*) $\rho^2 \leq \eta^2$
(*b*) $\rho^2 > \eta^2$
(*c*) $\rho^2 < \eta^2$
(*d*) none of the above

97. If there are k groups and each group consists on n observations, the limits of intraclass correlation are:

(*a*) 0 to 1
(*b*) $\frac{1}{n-1}$ to 1
(*c*) $-\frac{1}{n-1}$ to 1
(*d*) –1 to 1

98. From a given (2 × c) contingency table, the appropriate measure of association is:

(*a*) correlation ratio
(*b*) biserial correlation
(*c*) intraclass correlation
(*d*) tetrachoric correlation

99. When both the variables X and Y are dichotomous, a suitable measure of association between X and Y is:

(*a*) correlation ratio
(*b*) biserial correlation
(*c*) intraclass correlation
(*d*) tetrachoric correlation

100. Another name of autocorrelation is:

(*a*) biserial correlation
(*b*) serial correlation
(*c*) Spearman's correlation
(*d*) none of the above

101. A measure of linear association between the errors of consecutive periods is called:

(*a*) autocorrelation
(*b*) serial correlation
(*c*) both (*a*) and (*b*)
(*d*) neither (*a*) nor (*b*)

102. The idea of multiple regression equation strikes the mind only when:

(*a*) a variable Y depends on two independent variables only
(*b*) a variable Y depend on a number of independent variables
(*c*) the relation between a dependent variable and independent variables is not known
(*d*) all of the above

103. A coefficient of any independent variable in a multiple linear regression equation is known as:

(*a*) partial regression coefficient
(*b*) multiple regression coefficient
(*c*) simple regression coefficient
(*d*) none of the above

104. The ratio of the regression sum of squares to the total sum of square is called:

(*a*) correlation index
(*b*) coefficient of determination
(*c*) both (*a*) and (*b*)
(*d*) neither (*a*) nor (*b*)

105. Significance of the partial regression coefficients can simultaneously be tested by:
(a) t-test
(b) Z-test
(c) χ^2-test
(d) F-test

106. A measure of linear association of a variable say, X_1 with a number of other variables $X_2, X_3, ..., X_k$ is known as:
(a) partial correlation
(b) multiple correlation
(c) simple correlation
(d) autocorrelation

107. The range of multiple correlation coefficient R is:
(a) 0 to 1
(b) 0 to ∞
(c) -1 to 1
(d) $-\infty$ to ∞

108. The range of a partial correlation coefficient is:
(a) 0 to 1
(b) 0 to ∞
(c) -1 to 1
(d) $-\infty$ to ∞

109. If the value of multiple correlation coefficient R is near to 1, it leads to the conclusion that:
(a) there is a lack of linear relationship
(b) linear relation is a good fit
(c) there is a curvilinear relation
(d) all of the above

110. The multiple correlation coefficient $R_{1.23}$ of X_1 with X_2 and X_3 variable is always:
(a) greater than the correlation coefficient of zero order
(b) less than the correlation coefficient of zero order
(c) equal to each of the correlation coefficient of zero
(d) all of the above

111. If P is the correlation matrix, the formula for multiple correlation coefficient $R_{i.12...k}$ in terms of determinants is:
(a) $\left(1-\frac{|P|}{P_{ii}}\right)$
(b) $\left(1-\frac{|P|}{P_{ii}}\right)^2$
(c) $\left(1-\frac{|P|}{P_{ii}}\right)^{1/2}$
(d) $\left(1-\frac{P_{ii}}{|P|}\right)^{1/2}$

112. The formula for multiple correlation coefficient $R_{2.13}$ in terms of simple correlation coefficients r_{12}, r_{13} and r_{23} is:
(a) $\frac{r_{12}^2 + r_{23}^2 - 2r_{12}r_{23}r_{13}}{1-r_{13}^2}$
(b) $\sqrt{\frac{r_{12}^2 + r_{23}^2 - 2r_{12}^2\, r_{13}^2\, r_{23}^2}{1-r_{13}^2}}$
(c) $\sqrt{\frac{r_{12}^2 + r_{23}^2 - 2r_{12}r_{13}r_{23}}{1-r_{13}^2}}$
(d) $\sqrt{\frac{r_{12}^2 + r_{23}^2 - 2r_{12}r_{23}r_{13}}{1-r_{13}^2}}$

113. The necessary and sufficient condition for the three planes, X_1 on X_2, X_3; X_2 on X_1, X_3 and X_3 on X_1, X_2 is:
(a) $r_{12} + r_{23} + r_{13} - 2r_{12}\, r_{13}\, r_{23} = 1$
(b) $r_{12}^2 + r_{13}^2 + r_{23}^2 - 2r_{12}\, r_{13}\, r_{23} = 1$
(c) $r_{12}^2 + r_{13}^2 + r_{23}^2 - 2r_{12}\, r_{13}\, r_{23} = 0$
(d) none of the above

114. In a multivariate study, the correlation between any two variables eliminating the effect of all other variables is called:
(a) simple correlation
(b) multiple correlation

(c) partial correlation

(d) partial regression

115. The range of partial regression coefficient is:

(a) 0 to 1

(b) −1 to 1

(c) 0 to ∞

(d) −∞ to ∞

116. If P is the correlation matrix and $X_1, X_2, ..., X_k$ are k variables, the correlation between X_1 and X_2 eliminating the influence of $X_3, X_4, ..., X_k$ can be calculated by the formula:

(a) $\left(1-\frac{P_{12}}{P_{11}P_{22}}\right)$

(b) $\frac{P_{12}}{P_{11}P_{22}}$

(c) $\sqrt{\frac{P_{12}}{P_{11}P_{22}}}$

(d) $\frac{P_{12}}{\sqrt{P_{11}P_{22}}}$

117. If X_1, X_2 and X_3 are three variables, the partial correlation between X_2 and X_3 eliminating the effect X_1 in terms of simple correlation coefficients is given by the formula:

(a) $r_{23.1} = \frac{r_{23} - r_{12}r_{13}}{\sqrt{(1-r_{12}^2)(1-r_{13}^2)}}$

(b) $r_{23.1} = \frac{r_{32} - r_{21}r_{31}}{\sqrt{(1-r_{21}^2)(1-r_{31}^2)}}$

(c) $r_{23.1} = \frac{r_{32} - r_{12}\, r_{13}}{\sqrt{(1-r_{12}^2)(1-r_{13}^2)}}$

(d) all of the above

118. The partial correlation coefficient $r_{13.2}$ is called:

(a) first order partial correlation

(b) zero order partial correlation

(c) second order partial correlation

(d) none of the above

119. The partial correlation coefficient $r_{12.34}$ is called:

(a) zero order partial correlation

(b) first order partial correlation

(c) second order partial correlation

(d) third order partial correlation

120. The formula for the partial correlation coefficient $r_{13.24}$ is:

(a) $r_{13.24} = \frac{r_{13.4} - r_{12.4}\, r_{23.4}}{\sqrt{(1-r_{12.4}^2)(1-r_{23.4}^2)}}$

(b) $r_{13.24} = \frac{r_{13.2} - r_{14.2}\, r_{34.2}}{\sqrt{(1-r_{14.2}^2)(1-r_{34.2}^2)}}$

(c) both (a) and (b)

(d) neither (a) nor (b)

121. A positive significant correlation between the number of shoes produced and the steel produced per year is:

(a) a nonsense correlation

(b) a spurious correlation

(c) a meaningless correlation

(d) all of the above

122. Given the expected values for variables X and Y as:

$E(X) = 2$, $E(X^2) = 10$, $E(Y) = 3$, $E(Y^2) = 20$ and $E(XY) = 16$

we conclude that:

(a) correlation coefficient will be positive

(b) correlation coefficient will be negative

(c) expected values are incompatible

(d) none of the above

123. If X and Y are two independent variates with variances σ_X^2 and σ_Y^2 respectively, the correlation coefficient between X and $(X - Y)$ is equal to:

(a) $\sigma_{XY} / \sqrt{\sigma_X^2 \sigma_Y^2}$

(b) $\sigma_X / \sqrt{\sigma_X^2 + \sigma_Y^2}$

(c) $\sigma_Y / \sqrt{\sigma_X^2 + \sigma_T^2}$

(d) $\sigma_X \sigma_Y / \sqrt{\sigma_X^2 + \sigma_Y^2}$

124. If ρ is the correlation coefficient between X and Y, the correlation coefficient between $aX + b$ and Y is:

(a) $a\rho$

(b) $a\rho + b$

(c) $a^2 \rho$

(d) ρ

125. If the two regression lines are $Y = \frac{a}{b}X + c$ and $X = \frac{b'}{a'}y + c'$, the relation between ab' and $a'b$ is:

(a) $ab' \le a'b$

(b) $ab' \ge a'b$

(c) $ab' = a'b$

(d) none of the above

126. If the two lines of regression are $x + 2y - 5 = 0$ and $2x + 3y - 8 = 0$, the regression line of Y on X is:

(a) $x + 2y - 5 = 0$

(b) $2x + 3y - 8 = 0$

(c) any of the two lines

(d) none of the two lines

127. If the two lines of regression are $x + 2y - 5 = 0$ and $2x + 3y - 8 = 0$, the means of X and Y are:

(a) $\bar{x} = -3, \bar{y} = 4$

(b) $\bar{x} = 2, \bar{y} = 4$

(c) $\bar{x} = 1, \bar{y} = 2$

(d) none of the above

128. Give the regression lines $X + 2Y - 5 = 0$, $2X + 3Y - 8 = 0$ and $V(X) = 12$, the value of $V(Y)$ is:

(a) 16

(b) 4

(c) $\frac{3}{4}$

(d) $\frac{4}{3}$

129. If the two lines of regression are

$$X = -\frac{1}{18}Y + l;\ Y = -2X + m$$

and the mean of the distribution is at (–1, 2) the values of l and m are:

(a) $l = \frac{8}{9}, m = -5$

(b) $l = \frac{8}{9}, m = -3$

(c) $l = -\frac{10}{9}, m = -4$

(d) $l = -\frac{8}{9}, m = 0$

130. If $Y = mX + 4$ and $X = 4Y + 5$ are the regression lines of Y on X and X on Y, then m lies between the values:

(a) 0 and 1

(b) 0 and 0.5

(c) 0 and 0.25

(d) none of the above

131. Give the following results:

$$\mu_X = 9.2,\ \mu_Y = 16.5,\ \sigma_X = 2.1,$$
$$\sigma_Y = 1.6 \text{ and } \rho_{XY} = 0.84,$$

the regression line of Y on X is:

(a) $Y = X + 7.3$

(b) $Y = 0.64\,X + 10.612$

(c) $Y = 0.4\,X + 12.82$

(d) none of the above

132. If the two lines of regression in a bivariate distribution are $X + 9Y = 7$ and $Y + 4X = 16$, then $\sigma_X : \sigma_Y$ is:

(a) 3 : 2

(b) 2 : 3

(c) 9 : 4

(d) 4 : 9

133. If $\sigma_X = 0.5$, $\sigma_Y = 1.5$ and $\sigma^2_{X-Y} = 1.25$, the coefficient of correlation between X and Y is:
(*a*) 1
(*b*) 1/4
(*c*) 1/2
(*d*) 5/6

134. If $\sigma_X = 0.5$, $\sigma_Y = 1.5$, $\sigma^2_{X-Y} = 1.25$, $\bar{X} = 8$ and $\bar{Y} = 6$, the regression line of Y on X is:
(*a*) $2Y = 5X - 28$
(*b*) $3Y = 2X - 1$
(*c*) $6X = 4 + 42$
(*d*) none of the above

135. If the correlation coefficient between two variables X and Y is very high, the two lines of regression are:
(*a*) far apart
(*b*) coincident
(*c*) near to each other
(*d*) none of the above

136. Regression coefficient is independent of the change of:
(*a*) scale
(*b*) origin
(*c*) both origin and scale
(*d*) neither origin nor scale

137. If the covariance between the two variables is positive, it means that:
(*a*) the variables would change in the same direction
(*b*) the variables would change in the opposite direction
(*c*) the variables would not change
(*d*) none of the above

138. If the correlation between two variables is zero, it implies that:
(*a*) two variable are independent
(*b*) two variables do not have negative correlation
(*c*) the two variables are not linearly related
(*d*) all of the above

139. Correlation between the direction of deviations is calculated by the method of:
(*a*) product moments
(*b*) rank correlation
(*c*) coefficient of concurrent deviation
(*d*) Kendall's τ

140. The correlation between the two variables is unity, there is:
(*a*) perfect correlation
(*b*) perfect positive correlation
(*c*) perfect negative correlation
(*d*) no correlation

141. The quantity R^2 in reference to multivariate study is known as:
(*a*) correlation index
(*b*) coefficient of determination
(*c*) both (*a*) and (*b*)
(*d*) neither (*a*) nor (*b*)

142. Equality of k partial regression coefficient can simultaneously be tested with the help of:
(*a*) t-test
(*b*) χ^2-test
(*c*) Z-test
(*d*) analysis of variance

143. The partial correlation coefficient $r_{12.34}$ can be calculated with the help of:
(*a*) zero order correlation coefficient
(*b*) first order correlation coefficient
(*c*) both (*a*) and (*b*)
(*d*) neither (*a*) nor (*b*)

144. Which of the following relation is correct?
(*a*) $r_{12.34} = r_{13.24}$
(*b*) $r_{12.3} = r_{21.3}$
(*c*) $r_{13} = r_{23}$
(*d*) $r_{12.3} = r_{13.2}$

145. If we transform the variables of a simple regression line into standard normal deviates, then the two regression lines pass through the point:
(*a*) (0, 0)
(*b*) (1, 1)
(*c*) $(\bar{X}, \bar{Y})$
(*d*) $(\hat{X}, \hat{Y})$

146. The correlation between the five paired

measurements (3, 6), $\left(\frac{1}{2}, 1\right)$, (2, 4), (1, 2), (4, 8) for the variables X and Y is equal to:

(*a*) 0
(*b*) 1
(*c*) ½
(*d*) –1

147. On the basis of the following paired values of the variables X and Y,

$$X: 1, -\frac{1}{2}, -\frac{1}{4}, \; 0, \; 1, \; \frac{1}{2}, \frac{1}{4}$$

$$Y: 1, \; \frac{1}{4}, \frac{1}{16}, \; 0, \; 1, \; \frac{1}{4}, \; \frac{1}{16}$$

we can conclude that:

(*a*) the correlation between X and Y is 1.
(*b*) the variable are independent
(*c*) the variables are related
(*d*) the data are incompatible

148. A potential parameter of a model which is unknown and estimated is termed as:

(*a*) fixed parameter
(*b*) free parameter
(*c*) constrained parameter
(*d*) noise parameter

149. A parameter of model which can take the value either 1 or 2 is called:

(*a*) a free parameter
(*b*) non-centrality parameter
(*c*) constrained parameter
(*d*) fixed parameter

150. If an unknown potential parameter of a model is equalised to one or more parameters of the model, then the parameter is classified as:

(*a*) nuisance parameter
(*b*) constrained parameter
(*c*) free parameter
(*d*) non-centrality parameter

151. There are three continuous variables X_1, X_2 and X_3. It is known that the variable X_3 effects the variable X_1 but not X_2. Now to find the correlation between X_1 and X_2 eliminating the effect of X_3, you would work out:

(*a*) partial correlation
(*b*) multiple correlation
(*c*) part correlation
(*d*) simple correlation

152. For the same set of data for three variables X_1, X_2 and X_3 the relation between partial correlation $r_{12.3}$ and part correlation $r_{1(2.3)}$ is:

(*a*) $r_{12.3} > r_{1(2.3)}$
(*b*) $r_{12.3} = r_{1(2.3)}$
(*c*) $r_{12.3} < r_{1(2.3)}$
(*d*) no definite relation

153. Let the correlation coefficient between two variables X and Y be unity. Then the relation between the regression coefficients β_{YX} and β_{XY} that always holds is:

(*a*) $\beta_{YX} > \beta_{XY}$
(*b*) $\beta_{YX} < \beta_{XY}$
(*c*) $\beta_{YX} = \beta_{XY}$
(*d*) $\beta_{YX} \cdot \beta_{XY} = 1$

154. If the correlation between the variable X and Y is 0.5, then the correlation between the variables $2x - 4$ and $3 - 2y$ is:

(*a*) 1
(*b*) 0.5
(*c*) –0.5
(*d*) 0

155. Let the equations of the regression lines be expressed as $2X - 3Y = 0$ and $4Y - 5X = 8$. Then the correlation between X and Y is:

(*a*) $\sqrt{15/8}$
(*b*) $\sqrt{8/15}$
(*c*) $\sqrt{6/15}$
(*d*) $\sqrt{i/15}$

156. An investigator reports that the arithmetic mean of two regression coefficients of a regression line is 0.7 and correlation coefficient is 0.75. Are the results:

(*a*) valid

(*b*) invalid
(*c*) inconclusive
(*d*) none of the above

157. Given the two regression lines $X + 2Y = 5$ and $2X + 3Y = 8$ and $\sigma_Y^2 = 4$, the value of σ_X^2 is:
(*a*) 12
(*b*) $27/4$
(*c*) 6
(*d*) none of the above

158. Given $r_{12} = 0.6$, $r_{13} = 0.5$ and $r_{23} = 0.8$, the value of $r_{12.3}$ is,
(*a*) 0.4
(*b*) 0.72
(*c*) 0.38
(*d*) 0.47

159. If the sum of squares of the differences between ten ranks of two series is 33, then the rank correlation coefficient is:
(*a*) 0.967
(*b*) 0.725
(*c*) 0.80
(*d*) 0.67

160. If Var $(X + Y)$ = Var (X) + Var (Y), then the value of correlation coefficient r_{XY} is:
(*a*) 0
(*b*) 1
(*c*) –1
(*d*) 0.5

161. Let the coefficient of correlation be 0.7, then the coefficient of alienation is:
(*a*) 0.51
(*b*) 0.71
(*c*) 0.49
(*d*) none of the above

162. If Var $(X + Y)$ = Var $(X - Y)$, then the correlation between X and Y is equal to:
(*a*) 1
(*b*) 1/2
(*c*) 1/4
(*d*) 0

163. If $u + 3x = 5$, $2y - v = 7$, $r_{xy} = 0.12$, then the correlation r_{uv} is equal to:
(*a*) –0.12
(*b*) 0.12
(*c*) 0.08
(*d*) 1.0

164. Let the regression lines of Y on X and X on Y are respectively $Y = aX + b$ and $X = cY + d$, then the correlation coefficient between X and Y is:
(*a*) $\sqrt{c/a}$
(*b*) $\sqrt{a/c}$
(*c*) $\sqrt{ac}$
(*d*) $\sqrt{bd}$

165. Let the regression lines of Y on X and X on Y are respectively $Y = \alpha X + \beta$ and $X = \theta Y + \delta$. Then the ratio of the variances of X and Y is:
(*a*) θ/α
(*b*) $\sqrt{\theta/\alpha}$
(*c*) $\sqrt{\theta\alpha}$
(*d*) α/θ

166. If one regression coefficient of the two regression lines is greater than unity, the other will be:
(*a*) > 1
(*b*) 1
(*c*) < 1
(*d*) 1/2

167. If $R_{1.32} = 0$, then all total and partial correlation coefficients involving X_1 are:
(*a*) 0
(*b*) 1
(*c*) –1
(*d*) 1/2

168. The multiple correlation coefficient $R_{1.23}$ as compared to any simple correlation coefficients between the variables X_1, X_2 and X_3 is:
(*a*) less than any r_{12}, r_{13}, r_{23}
(*b*) not less than any r_{12}, r_{13} and r_{23}

(c) always equal to the sum of r_{12}, r_{13}, r_{23}
(d) always equal to the product of r_{12}, r_{13}, r_{23}

169. In a trivariate population $r_{12} = 0.7$, $r_{13} = 0.6$ and $r_{23} = 0.5$, then the value of $R_{1.23}$ is:
(a) 0.74
(b) 0.50
(c) 0.57
(d) 0.84

170. The number of categories in which the potential parameters of a model can be specified are:
(a) one
(b) two
(c) three
(d) four

171. If the correlation coefficient between two variables X and Y is 1, it implies that:
(a) X and Y are inversely proportional
(b) X and Y are directly proportional
(c) X and Y are equal
(d) X and Y are independent

172. If for a bivariate distribution $\sigma_X^2 = \sigma_Y^2$, then how shall the values of β_{YX}, β_{XY} and ρ_{XY} be affected?
(a) All of them will be unity
(b) All of them will be zero.
(c) All of them will be equal
(d) All of them may take any value

ANSWERS

Section B

1. regression equation **2.** regression line **3.** curve **4.** multiple **5.** regressors **6.** response **7.** explanatory **8.** estimating; prediction **9.** two **10.** functional **11.** linear; non-linear **12.** mathematical; probabilistic **13.** deterministic **14.** Sir Francis Galton **15.** scatter **16.** regression coefficient **17.** < 1 **18.** > 1 **19.** slope **20.** zero **21.** intercept, **22.** $\bar{Y} - b_1\bar{X}$ **23.** cov (X, Y)/V(X) **24.** $\beta_{YX} = \dfrac{1}{\beta_{XY}}$ **25.** fundamental **26.** $r = \sqrt{b_{YX} b_{XY}}$ **27.** same **28.** ≥ **29.** mean **30.** zero **31.** $(\bar{X}, \bar{Y})$ **32.** coincident **33.** π/2 **34.** $b_{YX} b_{Xy} = 1$ **35.** $b_{YX} \cdot b_{XY} = 0$ **36.** not alter **37.** one-fifth **38.** same **39.** t-test **40.** regression coefficients **41.** line of regression **42.** regression function **43.** ρ^2 **44.** $b_{YX} \mp s_{b_{YX}} \cdot t_{\alpha, n-2}$ **45.** $b_0 \mp s_{b_0} \cdot t_{\alpha, n-2}$ **46.** testing the significance **47.** weighted **48.** directly **49.** regression **50.** regression analysis **51.** unbiased **52.** unbiased **53.** $\sigma_\varepsilon^2 / \sum_i (x_i - \bar{x})^2$ **54.** σ_ε^2/n **55.** Mitscherlich curve **56.** parabola **57.** compertz **58.** equilateral hyperbola **59.** $Y = \alpha\beta^X$ **60.** $\dfrac{1}{Y} = \alpha\beta^X + \gamma$ **61.** higher degree **62.** R.A. Fisher **63.** Karl Pearson **64.** 1890 **65.** cov $(X, Y)/\sqrt{V(X)V(X)}$ **66.** $\dfrac{\Sigma(x_i - \bar{x})(y_i - \bar{y})}{\sqrt{\Sigma(x_i - \bar{x})^2 \, \Sigma(y_i - \bar{y})^2}}$ **67.** coefficient of determination **68.** coefficient of non-determination **69.** coefficient of alienation **70.** –1 to 1 **71.** left bottom; right top **72.** perfect negative **73.** lack of linear **74.** pure **75.** same **76.** same **77.** same **78.** $\rho\dfrac{\sigma_Y}{\sigma_X}$ **79.** $\rho\dfrac{\sigma_X}{\sigma_Y}$ **80.** bivariate normal **81.** $\sqrt{(1 - r^2)/(n-2)}$ **82.** $0.6745(1 - r^2)/\sqrt{n}$ **83.** significance **84.** nonsignificant **85.** 6 P.E. **86.** $t = \dfrac{r\sqrt{n-2}}{\sqrt{1 - r^2}}$ **87.** student's-t **88.** n – 2 **89.** Fisher's-Z **90.** $Z_r = \dfrac{1}{2}\log_e\left(\dfrac{1+r}{1-r}\right)$ **91.** $N\left(Z_{\rho_0}, \dfrac{1}{n-3}\right)$ **92.** $Z = (Z_r - Z\rho_0)\sqrt{n-3}$ **93.** $Z_r \mp Z_{1-\alpha/2} \times \dfrac{1}{\sqrt{n-3}}$ **94.** Fisher's-Z **95.** $\tanh^{-1} r$ **96.** Chi-square **97.** signs **98.** concurrent deviation **99.** $\pm\sqrt{\pm\dfrac{2c - n}{n}}$ **100.** $(\sigma_X^2 + \sigma_Y^2 - \sigma_{X-Y}^2)/2\sigma_X \sigma_Y$ **101.** same **102.** $(\sigma_X^2 + \sigma_Y^2 - \sigma_{X-Y}^2)/2\sigma_X \sigma_Y$ **103.** non-linear **104.** many **105.** among groups; total **106.** $\eta^2; E^2$ **107.** 0 to 1 **108.** 1 **109.** zero **110.** greater **111.** linear **112.** intraclass **113.** $-\dfrac{1}{n-1}$ to 1 **114.** biserial **115.** tetrachoric **116.** autocorrelation **117.** serial **118.** multiple regression **119.** multiple **120.** 0 to 1 **121.** linear **122.** good **123.** $\left(1-\dfrac{|P|}{P_{ii}}\right)^{1/2}$ **124.** $\sqrt{\dfrac{r_{12}^2+r_{13}^2-2r_{12}r_{13}r_{23}}{(1-r_{23}^2)}}$ **125.** $r_{12}^2 + r_{13}^2 + r_{23}^2 - 2r_{12}r_{13}r_{23} = 1$ **126.** eliminating **127.** $P_{ij}/\sqrt{P_{ii}P_{jj}}$ **128.** residual **129.** $(r_{12}-r_{13}r_{23})/\sqrt{(1-r_{13}^2)(1-r_{23}^2)}$ **130.** first **131.** $(r_{12.3}-r_{14.3}r_{24.3})/\sqrt{(1-r_{14.3}^2)(1-r_{24.3}^2)}$ **132.** second **133.** –1 to 1 **134.** 0 **135.** 0 **136.** $(\sigma_X^2 - \sigma_Y^2)/(\sigma_X^2+\sigma_Y^2)$ **137.** 0.25 **138.** $1/\sqrt{n}$ **139.** 0 **140.** 0 **141.** $\sigma^2(1+2r)/3$ **142.** uncorrelated **143.** origin; scale **144.** $1/\sqrt{3}$ **145.** 13; 17 **146.** 12 **147.** impossible **148.** zero **149.** 1 **150.** 1 **151.** nonsense **152.** zero **153.** nonsignificant **154.** negative **155.** not consistent **156.** its linear estimate $\hat{Y}$ **157.** origin **158.** abscissa; intercept **159.** x-axis **160.** perpendicular **161.** zero **162.** zero **163.** 45° **164.** free **165.** fixed **166.** constrained **167.** plane of regression **168.** part correlation **169.** $(r_{13}-r_{12}r_{23})/\sqrt{1-r_{23}^2}$ **170.** less.

Section C

1. (*b*) **2.** (*b*) **3.** (*d*) **4.** (*d*) **5.** (*a*)
6. (*b*) **7.** (*d*) **8.** (*a*) **9.** (*b*) **10.** (*a*)
11. (*b*) **12.** (*d*) **13.** (*a*) **14.** (*b*) **15.** (*c*)
16. (*a*) **17.** (*c*) **18.** (*b*) **19.** (*c*) **20.** (*a*)
21. (*a*) **22.** (*c*) **23.** (*b*) **24.** (*d*) **25.** (*b*)
26. (*a*) **27.** (*d*) **28.** (*d*) **29.** (*b*) **30.** (*c*)
31. (*a*) **32.** (*b*) **33.** (*b*) **34.** (*c*) **35.** (*d*)
36. (*b*) **37.** (*b*) **38.** (*b*) **39.** (*a*) **40.** (*a*)
41. (*c*) **42.** (*b*) **43.** (*d*) **44.** (*d*) **45.** (*c*)
46. (*d*) **47.** (*b*) **48.** (*c*) **49.** (*c*) **50.** (*b*)
51. (*c*) **52.** (*a*) **53.** (*b*) **54.** (*c*) **55.** (*a*)
56. (*c*) **57.** (*b*) **58.** (*d*) **59.** (*b*) **60.** (*a*)
61. (*c*) **62.** (*b*) **63.** (*d*) **64.** (*c*) **65.** (*a*)
66. (*b*) **67.** (*c*) **68.** (*c*) **69.** (*d*) **70.** (*a*)
71. (*c*) **72.** (*d*) **73.** (*c*) **74.** (*a*) **75.** (*b*)
76. (*c*) **77.** (*d*) **78.** (*b*) **79.** (*a*) **80.** (*b*)
81. (*c*) **82.** (*b*) **83.** (*c*) **84.** (*d*) **85.** (*c*)
86. (*a*) **87.** (*c*) **88.** (*a*) **89.** (*b*) **90.** (*d*)
91. (*c*) **92.** (*b*) **93.** (*c*) **94.** (*a*) **95.** (*b*)
96. (*a*) **97.** (*c*) **98.** (*b*) **99.** (*d*) **100.** (*b*)
101. (*c*) **102.** (*b*) **103.** (*a*) **104.** (*c*) **105.** (*d*)
106. (*b*) **107.** (*a*) **108.** (*c*) **109.** (*b*) **110.** (*a*)
111. (*c*) **112.** (*d*) **113.** (*b*) **114.** (*c*) **115.** (*d*)
116. (*d*) **117.** (*d*) **118.** (*a*) **119.** (*c*) **120.** (*c*)
121. (*d*) **122.** (*c*) **123.** (*b*) **124.** (*d*) **125.** (*a*)
126. (*a*) **127.** (*c*) **128.** (*b*) **129.** (*d*) **130.** (*c*)
131. (*b*) **132.** (*a*) **133.** (*d*) **134.** (*a*) **135.** (*c*)
136. (*b*) **137.** (*a*) **138.** (*c*) **139.** (*c*) **140.** (*b*)
141. (*c*) **142.** (*d*) **143.** (*c*) **144.** (*b*) **145.** (*a*)
146. (*b*) **147.** (*c*) **148.** (*b*) **149.** (*d*) **150.** (*b*)
151. (*c*) **152.** (*a*) **153.** (*d*) **154.** (*c*) **155.** (*b*)
156. (*b*) **157.** (*a*) **158.** (*c*) **159.** (*c*) **160.** (*a*)
161. (*b*) **162.** (*d*) **163.** (*a*) **164.** (*c*) **165.** (*a*)
166. (*c*) **167.** (*a*) **168.** (*b*) **169.** (*c*) **170.** (*c*)
171. ? **172.** ?

SUGGESTED READING

1. Agarwal, B.L., *Basic Statistics*, New Age International Publishers, New Delhi, 8th edition, 2024.
2. Agarwal, B.L., *Comprehensive Research Methodology*, New Age International Publishers, New Delhi, 2014.

3. Anderson, T.W., *An Introduction to Multivariate Analysis*, John Wiley, New York, 1958.
4. Arora, S. and Bansi, L., *New Mathematical Statistics*, Satya Prakashan, New Delhi, 1989.
5. Ezeikiel, M., *Methods of Correlation Analysis*, John Wiley, London, 2nd edition, 1941.
6. Gupta, S.C. and Kapoor, V.K., *Fundamentals of Mathematical Statistics*, Sultan Chand & Sons, New Delhi, 9th edition, 1994.
7. Kapoor, J.N. and Saxena, H.C., *Mathematical Statistics*, S. Chand, New Delhi, 12th edition, 1984.
8. Kendall, M.G. and Stuart, A., *The Advanced Theory of Statistics*, Vol. 2, Griffin, London, 4th edition, 1960.
9. Kshirsagar, A.M., *Multivariate Analysis*, Marcel Decker, New York, 1972.
10. Mood, A.M., Graybill, F.A. and Boes, D.C., *Introduction to the Theory of Statistics*, McGraw Hill Kogakusha, Tokyo, 3rd edition, 1974.
11. Ostle, B., *Statistics in Research*, The Iowa State University Press, Ames, Iowa, 1966.
12. Rao, C.R., *Advanced Statistical Methods in Biometric Research*, John Wiley, New York, 1952.
13. Rao, C.R., *Linear Statistical Interference and its Applications*, Wiley Eastern, New Delhi, 2nd edition, 1973.
14. Seber, G.A.F., *Linear Regression Analysis*, John Wiley, New York, 1977.
15. Snedecor, G.W. and Cochran, W.G., *Statistical Methods*, The Iowa University Press, Ames, Iowa, 6th edition, 1967.

CHAPTER 14

Measures of Association of Attributes

SECTION A

Short Essay Type Questions

Q. *When do you apply association of attributes?*

Ans. Correlation is a suitable measure of association when both the variables belong to a bivariate normal population. But in behavioural sciences one often deals with the variables which are not quantitatively measurable but can be cross-classified with respect to two or more classifications or polytomies such as eye colour, hair style, skin colour, liking of programmes, etc. If an attribute has only two classes, it is said to be *dichotomous,* and if it has many classes, it is called *manifold* classification. Sometimes polytomies may be arising from an underlying continuum. For instance, age may be divided into categories or classes but may be treated as qualitative classes. Hence, the need is often felt as to whether there is some association between different attributes or not. For this, some measures are developed specifically known as measures of association of attributes.

Q. 2. *Give a brief idea of notations and terminology used in classification of attributes.*

Ans. The system adopted to show the presence or absence of a attribute in an unit singly or in combination with other attributes is as follows:

Generally, the presence of an attribute in an individual is indicated by the Latin letters A, B, C, etc., and its absence by the small Latin letter a, b, c, etc., or by Greek letters α, β, γ, etc. Two or more attributes present in an individual or individuals are indicated by the combination of Latin letters AB, AC, BC, ABC, etc. Also the presence of one attribute and the absence of the other will be represented by Ab or $A\,\beta$, aB or αB, ABc or $AB\,\gamma$, abc or $\alpha\,\beta\,\gamma$ etc. Ab represents the presence of A and absence of B in an individual. Similarly, the combination ABc or $AB\,\gamma$ represents the unit which shows the absence of the attribute C and presence of A and B. Likewise any other combination of letters can be interpreted.

Q. 3. *What is meant by the order of classes?*

Ans. The total of all frequencies denoted as N is known as the class of order zero. Whereas the classes A, a, B, b, etc., are called the classes of first order. At the same time, combination of any two letters showing the presence or absence of attributes are called the classes of second order, e.g., AB, Ab, aB, ab (AB, $A\beta$, $\alpha\,B$, $\alpha\,\beta$), etc. Similarly, any combination like ABC, ABc, Abc, aBC, abc (ABC, $AB\,\gamma$, $A\beta\,\gamma$, $\alpha\,BC$, $\alpha\,\beta\,\gamma$), etc., is known as the class of third order and so on. The highest order classes are termed as *ultimate order classes.*

The total number of classes depends upon the number of attributes. For n attributes, the number of classes are 3^n. For $n = 1$, the three classes are A, a, N. For $n = 2$, the nine classes are N, A, a, B, b, AB, Ab, aB, ab and so on.

Q. 4. *How are frequencies represented for various combination of attributes?*

Ans. The number of individual or units belonging to a class is known as its *frequency.* For convenience and clear understanding, the frequency of a class is denoted by the letters in parentheses representing that cell. For example, the frequency of the cell representing the attributes AB is denoted by (AB). Similarly, for the class Ab or $A\beta$, frequency is denoted by (Ab) or $(A\beta)$, for the class ABC, frequency is (ABC), etc.

The frequency of a lower order class can always be expressed in terms of the higher order class frequencies. For three factors, A, B and C, all possible twenty-seven combinations of attributes belonging to different classes in the form of a pedigree can be displayed in the following manner:

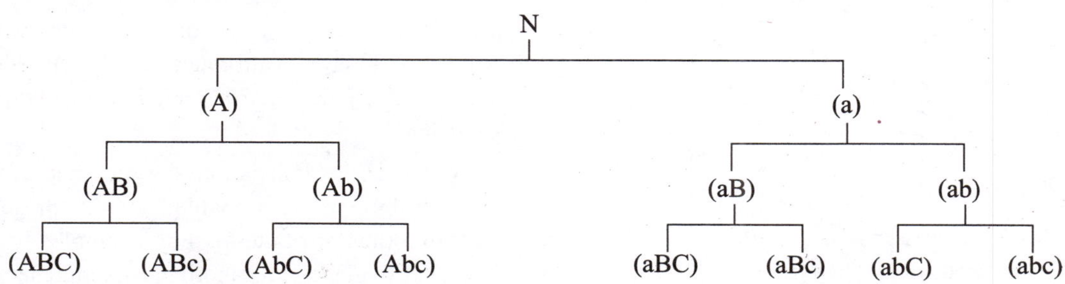

Similarly relations can be given by taking N, B, b and N, C, c.

From the above relations, it is apparent that:

$$(A) = (AB) + (Ab);\ (a) = (aB) + (ab)$$

$$(AB) = (ABC) + (ABc);\ (Ab) = (AbC) + (Abc)$$

$$(aB) = (aBc) + (aBc);\ (ab) = (abC) + (abc)$$

$$N = (A) + (a) = (B) + (b) = (C) + (c)$$

$$N = (AB) + (Ab) + (aB) + (ab)$$

$$N = (ABC) + (ABc) + (AbC) + (Abc) + (aBC) + (aBc) + (abC) + (abc)$$

Similarly other relations can be given.

Also it is obvious from the above relations that no higher order class frequency can exceed the lower order class frequency. For example,

$$(AB) \le (A);\ (AB) \le (B)$$

$$(ABC) \le (AB);\ (ABC) \le (AC);\ (ABC) \le (BC)$$

$$(abc) \le (ab);\ (abc) \le (ac), \text{ etc.}$$

Q. 5. *How can the frequencies for various attributes be displayed in a contingency table?*

Ans. If there are n attributes with dichotomy, there will be 2^n ultimate frequencies each represented by the combination of n letters, capital or small. Thus, the contingency table of order (2×2) for two attributes A and B can be displayed as given below:

	A	a	
B	(AB)	(aB)	(B)
b	(Ab)	(ab)	(b)
	(A)	(a)	(N)

Some of the missing frequencies can be determined with the help of the relations among frequencies.

Q. 6. *You are given,*

$(A) = 90$, $(AB) = 40$, $N = 150$ and $(b) = 80$.

Complete (2×2) contingency table.

Ans. We know,

$$(A) = (AB) + (Ab)$$

$$90 = 40 + (Ab) \text{ or } (Ab) = 50$$

$$(b) = (Ab) + (ab)$$

$$80 = 50 + (ab) \text{ or } (ab) = 30$$

$$N = (B) + (b)$$

$150 = (B) + 80$ or $(B) = 70$

$(B) = (AB) + (aB)$

$70 = 40 + (aB)$ or $(aB) = 30$

$(a) = (aB) + (ab)$

$= 30 + 30 = 60$

Thus, the complete contingency table is,

	A	a	Total
B	40	30	70
b	50	30	80
Total	90	60	150

Q. 7. *Explicate the method of expressing any class frequency in terms of other class frequency.*

Ans. If we define the frequency of an attribute as the attribute multiplied by the total frequency *N*, *e.g.*, $A.N = (A)$, $AB.N = (AB)$, $aB.N = (aB)$, $Abc.N = (Abc)$, etc.

The frequency of any class in terms of the frequencies of other classes can be obtained by writing the attribute as such and its negation as $(1 - X)$, where *X* is an attribute, multiplied by *N*. Here we use the letters for attributes as *operators*. For example,

$$AB\gamma = AB(1 - C)\cdot N = AB \cdot N - ABC \cdot N$$
$$= (AB) - (ABC)$$
$$A\beta\gamma = A(1 - B)(1 - C)\cdot N$$
$$= A \cdot N - AB \cdot N - AC \cdot N + ABC \cdot N$$
$$= (A) - (AB) - (AC) + (ABC)$$
$$(\alpha\beta C) = (1 - A)(1 - B)C \cdot N$$
$$= C \cdot N - AC \cdot N - BC \cdot N + ABC \cdot N$$
$$= (C) - (AC) - (BC) + (ABC)$$

Similarly,

$$(\alpha\beta\gamma) = N - (A) - (B) - (C) + (AB) + (BC) + (AC) - (ABC)$$

and so on.

Q. 8. *What do you understand by inconsistency of data?*

Ans. It is a bare fact that no frequency can be negative. Hence, the data are said to be inconsistent if they lead to any frequency obtained by the relations among frequencies as negative. Also no higher order class can have a greater frequency than the lower order class frequency.

If any frequency of an attribute or combination of attributes is greater than total frequency *N*, the data are inconsistent. Some of the examples of inconsistency of data are as follows:

If given that $(AB) > (A)$, then (Ab) is negative. Hence the data are inconsistent.

If given that $(AB) < (A) + (B) - N$, then (ab) will be negative. So the data are inconsistent.

If $(ABC) > (AB) + (AC) + (BC) - (A) - (B) - (C) + N$ then (abc) will be negative. Obviously, the data are inconsistent.

Some other relations for inconsistency of data are,

$$(ABC) < (AB) + (AC) - A$$
$$(ABC) < (AB) + (BC) - B$$
$$(ABC) < (AC) + (BC) - C$$
$$(AB) + (AC) + (BC) < (A) + (B) + (C) - N$$
$$(AB) + (AC) - (BC) > (A)$$
$$(AB) + (BC) - (AC) > (B)$$
$$(AC) + (BC) - (AB) > (C)$$

etc.

Q. 9. *What kind of associations among attributes are likely to occur?*

Ans. There are three kinds of associations which possibly occur between attributes namely, (*i*) positive association; (*ii*) negative association and (*iii*) no association.

(*i*) In positive association, the presence of one attribute is accompanied by the presence of other attribute(s). For example, health and hygiene, education and intelligence are positively associated.

In case of positive association, the observed frequency of the combined positive attributes is greater than the expected frequencies, *i.e.*,

$$(AB) > \frac{(A)(B)}{N}$$ .Similar relations hold for other attributes.

(*ii*) When the presence of an attribute say, *A* ensures the absence of another attribute say, *B* or *vice-versa*, the attributes *A* and *B* are said to be negatively associated. For instance, the vaccination and occurrence of disease for which the vaccine is meant for, are negatively associated. In this situation, the actual frequency of the cell for combination of attributes is smaller than the expected frequency, *i.e.*, $(AB) < \frac{(A)(B)}{N}$.

(*iii*) If the two attributes are such that the presence or absence of one attribute has nothing to do with the absence or presence of the other, they are said to be independent. For instance, skin colour and intelligence of persons are independent attributes. If the two attributes A and B are independent, then

$$(AB) = \frac{(a)(b)}{N}$$

or $$(ab) = \frac{(a)(b)}{N}$$

etc.

Q. 10. *Name different methods of measures of association.*

Ans. There are mainly five methods of measures of association:

(*i*) Proportion method
(*ii*) Method of probability
(*iii*) Yule's coefficient of association
(*iv*) Coefficient of colligation
(*v*) Coefficient of contingency

Q. 11. *Give proportion method for finding the association between two attributes.*

Ans. Let us consider two attributes A and B. To find out the association between A and B by proportion method, one has to find the proportion of B's in A's and B's in non-A's, *i.e.*, to calculate $\frac{(AB)}{(A)}$ and $\frac{(aB)}{(a)}$. If $\frac{(AB)}{(A)} = \frac{(aB)}{(a)}$, A and B are independent. Again if $\frac{(AB)}{(A)} > \frac{(aB)}{(a)}$, there is a positive association between A and B. On the contrary, if $\frac{(AB)}{(A)} < \frac{(aB)}{(a)}$, then, attributes A and B are negatively associated. It only indicates the kind of association but fail to provide the extent of association.

Q. 12. *How to know the nature of association by the method of probability?*

Ans. The method utilises the probability of occurrence of an attribute or combination of attributes to determine the expected frequencies. The expected frequency is the product of the probability of an event and total number of possible outcomes. For instance, if A and B are two attributes, and N, the total number of cases (outcomes), the expected frequency of the event AB through probability is $\frac{(A)\times(B)}{N}$ or for aB is $\frac{(a)\times(B)}{N}$ etc. To decide about the nature of association, the criteria are as given below:

Observed frequency	*Expected frequency*	*Relation*	*Type of association*
(AB)	$\frac{(A)\times(B)}{N}$	$(AB) = \frac{(A)\times(B)}{N}$	A and B are independent
(AB)	$\frac{(A)\times(B)}{N}$	$(AB) > \frac{(A)\times(B)}{N}$	+ve association
(AB)	$\frac{(A)\times(B)}{N}$	$(AB) < \frac{(A)\times(B)}{N}$	–ve association
(aB)	$\frac{(a)\times(B)}{N}$	$(aB) > \frac{(a)(B)}{N}$	+ve association
(ab)	$\frac{(a)\times(b)}{N}$	$(ab) > \frac{(a)\times(b)}{N}$	+ve association

and so on.

The negative association is also termed as *dissociation.*

This method does not give the idea of degree of association between attributes.

Q. 13. *Give Yule's coefficient of association.*

Ans. Yule's coefficient of association is named after its inventor G. Undy Yule. It is a relative measure of association between two attributes say, A and B. If (AB), (aB), (Ab) and (ab) represent the frequencies of all the four distinct combination of A, B, a and b, Yule's coefficient of association is given by the formula,

$$Q_{AB} = \frac{(AB)(ab) - (Ab)(aB)}{(AB)(ab) + (Ab)(aB)}$$

Q. 14. *Delineate the properties of Yule's coefficient of association.*

Ans.

(*i*) The value of Q_{AB} lies between – 1 and 1.

(*ii*) If $Q = 1$, A and B has perfect positive association. This leads to the following relations:

$$(AB) = (A) \Rightarrow (Ab) = 0$$

$$(AB) = (B) \Rightarrow (aB) = 0$$

(*iii*) If $Q = -1$, A and B possess perfect negative association. This leads to the relation, $(AB) = 0$ or $(ab) = 0$.

(*iv*) If $Q = 0$, A and B are independent. In this situation,

$$(AB)(ab) = (Ab)(aB)$$

(*v*) Any other value between – 1 and 1 gives the idea of degree of association between two attributes.

Q. 15. *Discuss coefficient of colligation and give its relation with Q.*

Ans. Coefficient of colligation as a measure of association was given by Professor Yule. If A and B are two attributes and (AB), (aB), (Ab) and (ab) are the class frequencies, the coefficient of colligation,

$$Y = \frac{1 - \sqrt{\dfrac{(Ab)(aB)}{(AB)(ab)}}}{1 + \sqrt{\dfrac{(Ab)(aB)}{(AB)(ab)}}}$$

The relation between Y and Q_{AB} is,

$$Q_{AB} = \frac{2Y}{1 + Y^2}$$

The range of Y is from – 1 to 1 and can be interpreted in the same way as Q.

Q. 16. *Compare Yule's coefficients Y and Q.*

Ans. Both the coefficients of association Y and Q hold the same properties. But the formula for Q is simple and easily calculable, and hence it is mostly used. Cell frequencies for Q or Y are easily ascertained by preparing a (2×2) contingency table.

Q. 17. *What do you understand by partial association between attributes?*

Ans. The need for partial association arises due to the fact that the association between two attributes may sometimes occurs due to the third attribute rather than the actual association between the two. For instance, the association amongst the prevalence of Tuberculosis (TB) and vaccination may be different in posh colonies and slum area.

The association between any two attributes A and B in the sub-populations say C and c of an universe are called *partial association*. It is usually denoted by $Q_{AB.C}$ and $Q_{AB.c}$.

The formula for partial associations between the attributes A and B in the sub-populations C and c in terms of class frequencies are:

$$Q_{AB.C} = \frac{(ABC)(abC) - (AbC)(aBC)}{(ABC)(abC) + (AbC)(aBC)}$$

$$Q_{AB.c} = \frac{(ABc)(abc) - (Abc)(aBc)}{(ABc)(abc) + (Abc)(aBc)}$$

Similarly the formulae for $Q_{AC.B}$, $Q_{AC.b}$, $Q_{BC.A}$ and $Q_{BC.a}$ can be given simply by interchanging the letters.

Q. 18. *What is illusory association?*

Ans. Sometimes the association between two attributes is not actually the association amongst them but due to some non-ascribable factors. Such an association is known as *illusory association*. This is due to the fact that there is no direct causal relationship between the attributes. Though partial association provides a check to the illusory association but not totally. An illusory association creates lot of confusion, and hence one should be wary of it. For instance, there is a high positive association between white colour people in Europe and sport of skiing. This is an illusory association because it is not the colour associated with skiing but the cold whether which is responsible for white colour people and snow covered hills.

Q. 19. *Compare measure of association and correlation.*

Ans. Association and correlation both have similarities and dissimilarities which are as follows:

(*i*) Both are relative measures.

(*ii*) Both the measures range from – 1 to 1.

(*iii*) Measure of association is based on qualitative factors which are not quantitatively measurable. For instance, level of education and crime. In association no variables are involved.

(*iv*) Correlation measures the relationship (association) between the factors which we can measure quantitatively. In this measure, actually the variables are involved.

(*v*) Measure of association is based merely on frequencies of various polytomies whereas in correlation actual paired measurements are used.

(*vi*) In association, the frequencies of joint attributes should be more than the expected frequency. It has nothing to do with the large or small frequency of the joint attribute.

(*vii*) Correlation is a measure of proportional increase or decrease in the two variables simultaneously.

(*viii*) Association of attributes is measured in terms of total or partial association.

(*ix*) Correlation is measured in terms of simple, multiple and partial correlation coefficient.

Q. 20. *Comment on coefficient of contingency.*

Ans. Coefficient of contingency is connected with the Chi-square statistic. The coefficient of contingency is worked out when Chi-square test confirms the association between attributes. If so, the formula for coefficient of contingency is,

$$C = \sqrt{\frac{\chi^2}{\chi^2 + n}}$$

where, n is the total sample size (sum of all ultimate frequencies) and χ^2, the calculated value of the statistic. C lies between 0 to 1 but never attains the value unity. A value of C near to 1 shows a great degree of association between the two attributes and a value near to zero shows no association.

If we put, $\phi = \chi^2/n$, then

$$C = \sqrt{\frac{\phi}{\phi + 1}}$$

Q. 21. *What is Tschuprow's coefficient?*

Ans. Coefficient of contingency can never attain the value unity. Hence, Tschuprow gave another coefficient which is named after him as Tschuprow's coefficient which is given by the formula,

$$T = \sqrt{\frac{C^2}{(p-1)(q-1)(1-C^2)}}$$

where,

p = Number of rows in the contingency table.

q = Number of columns in the contingency table, and $C^2 = \chi^2/n$.

SECTION B

Fill in the Blanks

Fill in the suitable word(s) or phrase(s) in the blanks:

1. If an attribute has two classes, it is said to be ________ .

2. If an attribute has more than two classes, it is called to possess ________ classification.

3. The number of letters representing a class determines the ________ of the class.

4. The class represented by AC is of _________ order.

5. The total of all frequencies N is of order _________.

6. The order of the class represented by $\alpha\beta\gamma$ is of order _________.

7. If there are two attributes A and B and their negations a and b respectively, the frequency (A) in terms of the second order frequencies is equal to _________.

8. In case of two attributes A and B, the zero order frequency in terms of ultimate frequencies with usual notations is _________.

9. If we are given the frequencies for two attributes A and B as $(Ab) = 65$, $(A) = 55$ and $N = 100$, the given data are _________.

10. In case of consistent data, no class frequency can be _________.

11. If the frequency of the combined attributes is less than the expected frequency, they are _________.

12. If the attributes A and B are independent, the frequency (AB) is equal to _________.

13. If the proportion of B's in A's and of B's in non-A's is same, the attributes A and B are _________.

14. If all A's are B's and all B's are C's, then all A's are _________.

15. If $\frac{(A)}{N} = x$, $\frac{(B)}{N} = 2x$ and $\frac{(C)}{N} = 3x$ and $\frac{(AB)}{N} = \frac{(BC)}{N} = \frac{(AC)}{N} = y$, then neither x nor y can exceed _________.

16. If $(A) = 50$, $(B) = 60$, $(C) = 50$, $(AC) = 20$ and $N = 100$, the upper and lower limit of (BC) are _________ so that the data are consistent.

17. If the attributes A and B are independent, the relation between the frequencies (AB), (Ab), (aB) and (ab) of attributes is _________.

18. If the attributes A and B are independent, the value of (AB) in terms of (A) and (B) is _________.

19. If A and B are independent, Yule's coefficient Q is equal to _________.

20. If A and B are completely associated, then $(AB) =$ _________ and _________.

21. If A and B are two completely dissociated attributes, then $(AB) =$ _________ and/or ab = _________.

22. If two attributes A and B are completely dissociated, the value of Yule's coefficient Q is equal to _________.

23. If two attributes A and B are completely associated, then $(Ab) =$ _________ and/or $(aB) =$ _________.

24. If A and B are two completely associated attributes, Yule's coefficient of association between A and B is equal to _________.

25. If Yule's coefficient $Q = 0$, the coefficient of colligation $Y =$ _________.

26. If Yule's coefficient $Q = -1$, then coefficient of colligation Y is equal to _________.

27. The relation between Yule's coefficient Q and coefficient of colligation Y is _________.

28. If Yule's coefficient $Q = 1$, the coefficient of colligation Y is equal to _________.

29. If the frequencies for combination of two attributes are $(AB) = 40$, $(Ab) = 15$, $(aB) = 70$ and $(ab) = 30$, the value of Yule's coefficient of association Q is _________.

30. If $Q = 0.6$, the coefficient of colligation Y _________.

31. Given the data for two attributes A and B as, $N = 100$, $(ab) = 30$, $(B) = 60$ and $(a) = 70$, the other frequencies of a 2×2 contingency table are _________.

32. From the given data for two attributes as, $N = 60$, $(A) = 15$, $(B) = 40$ and $(AB) = 10$, one concludes that the attributes A and B are _________.

33. Data $(AB) = 20$, $(aB) = 50$, $(Ab) = 10$, $(ab) = 15$ leads to infer that the attributes A and B are __________.

34. For the data given in Q. No. 33, the attributes a and B are __________.

35. In the proportion method, the attributes A and B are independent if __________.

36. In the proportion method, the attributes A and B have frequencies such that $(AB)/(A) < (aB)/(a)$, then A and B are __________.

37. Method of proportion for association of attributes __________ the idea about the degree of association.

38. The signs of coefficient of association Q and coefficient of colligation Y are always __________.

39. The value of coefficient of colligation __________ the value of coefficient of association Q.

40. Formula for Tschuprow's coefficient with usual notations is __________.

41. The coefficient of contingency never __________ unity.

42. Coefficient of contingency never attains the value __________.

43. The association between two attributes in a population is called __________ association.

44. The association between two attributes in a sub-population is known as __________ association.

45. The range of partial association between attributes is __________.

46. The formula for partial association $Q_{BC.A}$ is __________.

47. Partial association eliminates the influence of the __________ attribute from the association between two attributes.

48. If two attributes are such that there exists an association between them even though there is casual relation, such an association is known as __________ association.

49. An association between skin colour and intelligence is an __________ association.

50. Association is meant for __________ whereas correlation is meant for __________.

51. Just like partial association there is also a parallel correlation measure named as __________ correlation.

52. Just like multiple correlation, there is __________ measure in association of attributes.

53. Correlation and association both are __________ measures.

54. Two attributes A and B are said to be positively associated in the population of C's iff __________.

55. If $N = 100$, $(A) = 60$, $(B) = 40$ and $(AB) = 24$, the attributes A and B are __________.

56. If $(A) = 25$, $(AB) = 15$, $(\alpha\beta) = 4$ and $(B) = 24$, the coefficient of association between A and B is __________.

57. Association and correlation are __________.

58. Limits of Yule's coefficient square are __________.

59. If A and B are positively associated, then the attributes α, β showing their absence are __________ positively associated.

60. If every individual that possesses an attribute A also possesses the attribute B, then coefficient of colligation between A and B is equal to __________.

61. If there is a perfect association between two attributes, Yule's coefficient Q is equal to __________.

62. If $\delta = (AB) - \dfrac{(A)(B)}{N}$, then δ in terms of ultimate class frequencies with usual notations is equal to __________.

63. If two attributes A and B are independent then $\dfrac{(A\alpha)}{(A)} = \dfrac{(\alpha B)}{(B)} =$ __________.

64. If A and B are two independent attributes,

the relation between ultimate frequencies is ________.

65. If $\delta = (AB) - \frac{(A)(B)}{N}$, then in case of independence of attributes A and B, δ = ________.

66. If $\delta = (AB) - (AB)_0$ where $(AB)_0 = \frac{(A)(B)}{N}$ then for A and B to be positively associated δ must be ________.

67. If $\delta = (AB) - (AB)_0$, then for two attributes A and B to be negatively associated, δ must be ________.

68. If $(A) = (\alpha) = (B) = (\beta) = \frac{N}{2}$, then (AB) = ________ and $(A\beta)$ = ________.

69. If $N = 500$, $(A) = 300$, $(B) = 250$ and $(AB) = 40$, the data are ________.

SECTION C

Multiple Choice Questions

Select the correct alternative out of given ones:

1. Measures of association usually deal with:
   (*a*) attributes
   (*b*) quantitative factors
   (*c*) variables
   (*d*) numbers
2. The combination AB of attributes is known as the class of
   (*a*) first order
   (*b*) second order
   (*c*) third order
   (*d*) none of the above
3. The total N of all the frequencies is known as the class of:
   (*a*) zero order
   (*b*) first order
   (*c*) second order
   (*d*) third order
4. The notation (ABC) represents:
   (*a*) combination of the attributes A, B and C
   (*b*) cell in a contingency table
   (*c*) the frequency of the class ABC
   (*d*) none of the above
5. The frequency of a class can always be expressed as a sum of frequencies of:
   (*a*) lower order classes
   (*b*) higher order classes
   (*c*) zero order classes
   (*d*) none of the above
6. With two attributes one can have in all:
   (*a*) two class frequencies
   (*b*) four class frequencies
   (*c*) eight class frequencies
   (*d*) nine class frequencies
7. With two attributes, the total number of ultimate class frequencies is:
   (*a*) two
   (*b*) four
   (*c*) six
   (*d*) none of the above
8. With three attributes A, B and C, one obtains in all:
   (*a*) eight class frequencies
   (*b*) nine class frequencies
   (*c*) twenty class frequencies
   (*d*) three class frequencies
9. With three factors X, Y and Z, the number of ultimate frequencies is:
   (*a*) eight
   (*b*) nine
   (*c*) six
   (*d*) eighteen
10. With two attributes A, B and their negation a and b respectively, the frequency (A) in terms of ultimate frequencies is:

(*a*) $(AB) + (ab)$
(*b*) $(AB) + (Ab)$
(*c*) $(ab) + (AB)$
(*d*) none of the above

11. With three attributes *A, B* and *C*, the number of second order class frequencies is:
(*a*) six
(*b*) nine
(*c*) twelve
(*d*) fifteen

12. With three attributes *A, B* and *C*, the number of first order classes is:
(*a*) six
(*b*) nine
(*c*) twelve
(*d*) none of the above

13. In case of two attributes *A* and *B*, the class frequency (αB) in terms of other class frequencies can be expressed as:
(*a*) $(B) + (AB)$
(*b*) $(B) - (AB)$
(*c*) $(Ab) - (B)$
(*d*) $N - (AB)$

14. In case of three attributes *A, B* and *C*, the class frequency $(\alpha\beta\gamma)$ in terms of other class frequencies is:
(*a*) $(AB) + (AC) - (B) - (ABC)$
(*b*) $(ABC) - (B) + (AB) - (BC)$
(*c*) $(ABC) - (A) - (C) + (B)$
(*d*) $(B) - (AB) - (BC) + (ABC)$

15. With three factors *A, B* and *C*, the class frequency $(A\beta\gamma)$ in terms of other class frequencies can be expressed as:
(*a*) $(A) + (BC) - (AB) - (ABC)$
(*b*) $(A) + (AB) + (AC) - (ABC)$
(*c*) $(A) - (AB) - (AC) + (ABC)$
(*d*) $(A) + (AB) + (BC) + (ABC)$

16. With three factors *A, B* and *C*, the frequency $(\alpha\gamma)$ can be expressed in terms of frequencies with positive attributes as:
(*a*) $1 - (A) - (C) + (AC)$
(*b*) $N - (A) - (C) + (AC)$
(*c*) $N + (A) - (C) - (AC)$
(*d*) none of the above

17. With three attributes *A, B* and *C*, the frequency (β) in terms of positive attribute frequencies is:
(*a*) $N - (A) - (B) - (C)$
(*b*) $N - (A) - (C)$
(*c*) $N - (AC)$
(*d*) $N - (B)$

18. The class frequency $(\alpha\beta)$ in terms of frequencies of positive attribute is:
(*a*) $N - (A) - (B) + (AB)$
(*b*) $N - (A) - (B) + (C)$
(*c*) $N - (AB)$
(*d*) $N - (A) - (B)$

19. The class frequency $(\alpha\beta\gamma)$ in terms of positive attributes is:
(*a*) $N + (A) + (B) + (C) - (AB) - (AC) - (BC) + (ABC)$
(*b*) $N - (A) - (B) - (C) + (AB) + (AC) + (BC) + (ABC)$
(*c*) $N - (A) - (B) - (C) - (AB) - (AC) - (BC) + (ABC)$
(*d*) none of the above

20. If for two attributes *A* and *B*, $\frac{(AB)}{(A)} = \frac{(\alpha\beta)}{(\alpha)}$, then *A* and *B* are:
(*a*) independent
(*b*) positively associated
(*c*) negatively associated
(*d*) no conclusion

21. If for two attributes *A* and *B*, $(AB) > \frac{(A)(B)}{N}$, the attribute are:
(*a*) independent
(*b*) positively associated
(*c*) negatively associated
(*d*) none of the above

22. If in case of two attributes *A* and *B*, $(\alpha\beta) < \frac{(\alpha)(\beta)}{N}$, then the attributes are:
(*a*) independent
(*b*) positively associated

(*c*) negatively associated

(*d*) no conclusion

23. If for two attributes *A* and *B*, the relation $(\alpha\beta) = \frac{(\alpha)(\beta)}{N}$ holds, the attributes (α) and (β) are:

(*a*) independent

(*b*) positively associated

(*c*) negatively associated

(*d*) no conclusion

24. If $\frac{(AB)}{(B)} > \frac{(\alpha\beta)}{(\beta)}$, then

(*a*) $\frac{(AB)}{(A)} = \frac{(\alpha\beta)}{(\alpha)}$

(*b*) $\frac{(AB)}{(A)} > \frac{(\alpha\beta)}{(\alpha)}$

(*c*) $\frac{(AB)}{(A)} < \frac{(\alpha\beta)}{(\alpha)}$

(*d*) none of the above

25. With three attributes *A*, *B* and *C*, the frequency (*A*) in terms of ultimate class frequencies is equal to:

(*a*) $(ABC) + (AB\gamma)$

(*b*) $(ABC) + (AB\gamma) + (A\beta C)$

(*c*) $(ABC) + (AB\gamma) + (A\beta\gamma)$

(*d*) $(ABC) + (A\beta\gamma) + (A\beta C) + (AB\gamma)$

26. With three factors *A, B* and *C*, the frequency (A) in terms of second order frequencies is:

(*a*) $(AB) + (A\beta)$

(*b*) $(\alpha\beta) + (\alpha A)$

(*c*) $(\alpha B) + (AB)$

(*d*) none of the above

27. The class frequencies $(A) = 90$, $N = 100$, $(B) = 70$ and $(Ab) = 40$ reveal that the:

(*a*) data are consistent

(*b*) data are inconsistent

(*c*) data are insufficient

(*d*) none of the above

28. Given $(A) = 95$, $(Ab) = 35$, $(B) = 150$, $N = 200$ and $(AB) = 60$, the class frequency (*ab*) is equal to:

(*a*) 35

(*b*) 90

(*c*) 15

(*d*) 105

29. Given that $(AB) = 76$, $(\alpha B) = 228$, $(A\beta) = 13$ and $(\alpha\beta) = 39$, one can conclude that:

(*a*) *A* and *B* are independent

(*b*) *A* and *B* are negatively associated

(*c*) *A* and *B* are positively associated

(*d*) none of the above

30. Give the information $(AB) = 76$, $(A\beta) = 98$, $(\alpha\beta) = 228$ and $N = 300$, one finds that:

(*a*) the data are insufficient to draw any conclusion

(*b*) the data are consistent

(*c*) the data are inconsistent

(*d*) none of the above

31. The following contingency table gives the distribution of 100 selected candidates in a company.

	Graduates	*Non-Graduates*
5 years experience or more	38	29
Less than 5 years experience	22	11

The data reveals that the association between education and experience is:

(*a*) positive

(*b*) negative

(*c*) no association

(*d*) none of the above

32. Of the patients admitted to a hospital consecutively, every fifth patient is treated by new therapy. Out of 100 patients treated by new therapy 20 per cent die, and 30 per cent die who are treated by old therapy. If *A*-new therapy, *a*-old therapy. *B*-die, *b*-alive, then the cell frequencies are:

(*a*) $(AB) = 20$, $(Ab) = 80$, $(aB) = 380$, $(ab) = 120$

(*b*) $(AB) = 30, (Ab) = 30, (aB) = 110, (ab) = 290$

(*c*) $(AB) = 20, (Ab) = 30, (aB) = 30, (ab) = 20$

(*d*) $(AB) = 20, (Ab) = 80, (aB) = 120, (ab) = 280$

33. For three attributes A, B and C given that,

$$(A) = (B) = (C) = \frac{N}{2} \text{ and } (ABC) = (\alpha\beta\gamma),$$

the relation between (ABC), (AB), (AC), (BC) and N is:

(*a*) $(ABC) = (AB) + (AC) + (BC) - N$

(*b*) $(ABC) = (AB) + (AC) + (BC) - \frac{N}{2}$

(*c*) $2\,(ABC) = (AB) + (AC) + (BC) - N$

(*d*) $2\,(ABC) = (AB) + (AC) + (BC) - \frac{N}{2}$

34. For two attributes A and B and their negations a and b, if $\frac{(aB)}{a} < \frac{(AB)}{(A)}$, then A and B are:

(*a*) positively associated

(*b*) negatively associated

(*c*) independent

(*d*) non-conclusive

35. For two attributes A and B with their negations a and b, if $\frac{(aB)}{(a)} > \frac{(AB)}{(A)}$, then A and B are:

(*a*) positively associated

(*b*) negatively associated

(*c*) independent

(*d*) non-conclusive

36. Given the following contingency table for two attributes A and B is as:

	A	α
A	a	b
β	c	d

the formula for Yule's Q is:

(*a*) $Q = (ab - cd)/(ab + cd)$

(*b*) $Q = (ac - bd)/(ac + bd)$

(*c*) $Q = (ad - bc)/(ad + bc)$

(*d*) none of the above

37. If in case of two attributes A and B, the class frequency $(AB) = 0$, the value of Q is:

(*a*) 1

(*b*) –1

(*c*) 0

(*d*) any value between 0 and –1

38. If for two attributes A and B, the class frequency $(ab) = 0$, then Q is equal to:

(*a*) 1

(*b*) –1

(*c*) 0

(*d*) any value between 0 and – 1

39. If for two attributes the class frequency $(Ab) = (aB) = 0$, the value of the coefficient of colligation is:

(*a*) 1

(*b*) –1

(*c*) 0

(*d*) none of the above

40. If for two attributes A and B, the class frequencies hold the relation $(AB)\,(ab) = (Ab)\,(aB)$, then the value of Q is:

(*a*) 1

(*b*) –1

(*c*) 0

(*d*) none of the above

41. If class frequencies between two attributes A and B hold the inequality, $(AB)\,(ab) > (aB)\,(Ab)$, then the value of Q is:

(*a*) 1

(*b*) –1

(*c*) 0

(*d*) any value between 0 and 1

42. If with usual notations for two attributes, the inequality $(AB)\,(ab) < (aB)\,(Ab)$ holds, then:

(*a*) $-1 \le Q \le 1$

(*b*) $-1 \le Q < 0$

(*c*) $0 \le Q \le 1$

(*d*) none of the above

43. If for two factors A and B, the class

frequencies are such that $(AB)\,(ab) = (Ab)\,(aB)$, then:

(*a*) A and B are positively associated
(*b*) A and B are negatively associated
(*c*) A and B are independent
(*d*) none of the above

44. If A and B are positively associated, then:

(*a*) $(AB) > \dfrac{(A)\,(B)}{N}$
(*b*) $(AB) < (A)(B)/N$
(*c*) $(AB) = (A)(B)/N$
(*d*) none of the above

45. If the class frequencies for two attributes hold the relation $(AB)\,(ab) < (Ab)\,(aB)$, then A and B are:

(*a*) positively associated
(*b*) negatively associated
(*c*) independent
(*d*) none of the above

46. If two attributes A and B are such that the class frequencies hold the relation. $(AB)\,(ab) > (Ab)\,(aB)$, then A and B are:

(*a*) positively associated
(*b*) negatively associated
(*c*) independent
(*d*) none of the above

47. If all A's are B's, then the coefficient of association Q is equal to:

(*a*) 1
(*b*) –1
(*c*) 0
(*d*) ∞

48. If for two attributes A and B, all B's are a's, then the coefficient of association Q is equal to:

(*a*) 1
(*b*) –1
(*c*) 0
(*d*) ∞

49. Formula for coefficient of colligation between two attributes A and B with usual notations is:

(*a*) $Y = \dfrac{1+\sqrt{\dfrac{(aB)\,(Ab)}{(AB)\,(ab)}}}{1-\sqrt{\dfrac{(aB)\,(Ab)}{(AB)\,(ab)}}}$

(*b*) $Y = \dfrac{1-\sqrt{\dfrac{(aB)\,(Ab)}{(AB)\,(ab)}}}{1+\sqrt{\dfrac{(aB)\,(Ab)}{(AB)\,(ab)}}}$

(*c*) $Y = \dfrac{1-\dfrac{(aB)\,(Ab)}{(AB)\,(ab)}}{1+\dfrac{(aB)\,(Ab)}{(AB)\,(ab)}}$

(*d*) $Y = \dfrac{1-\sqrt{\dfrac{(AB)\,(ab)}{(Ab)\,(aB)}}}{1+\dfrac{(AB)\,(ab)}{(Ab)\,(aB)}}$

50. The relation between Yule's Q and coefficient of colligation Y is:

(*a*) $Q = Y/(1 + Y^2)$
(*b*) $Q = 2Y/(1 + Y^2)$
(*c*) $Q = Y/(1 + 2Y^2)$
(*d*) $Q = 2Y/(1 + 2Y)$

51. If all A's are B's, the coefficient of colligation is equal to:

(*a*) 0
(*b*) –1
(*c*) 1
(*d*) ∞

52. If the class frequencies in a contingency table are such that the cross products are equal, the coefficient of colligation is equal to:

(*a*) 0
(*b*) –1
(*c*) 1
(*d*) ∞

53. If in a (2×2) frequency table for two attributes *A* and *B*, the frequency of the cell *ab* is zero, the coefficient of colligation is equal to:
(*a*) 0
(*b*) –1
(*c*) 1
(*d*) ∞

54. If $Y = 1$, then it implies that
(*a*) Either (aB) or (Ab) is zero
(*b*) $(aB) = (Ab)$
(*c*) $(aB)(Ab) = 1$
(*d*) all of the above

55. Given the cell frequencies for two attributes as, $(AB) = 90$, $(aB) = 60$, $(Ab) = 180$ and $(ab) = 30$, the coefficient of colligation is:
(*a*) –1
(*b*) 2/3
(*c*) –1/3
(*d*) 0

56. Out of 200 persons of a locality, 100 were vaccinated to prevent TB. Out of 50 patients, 10 were vaccinated. Coefficient of association *Q* between vaccination and prevention from TB is:
(*a*) 5/7
(*b*) 5/11
(*c*) –5/11
(*d*) none of the above

57. Partial Association between two attributes refers to the association:
(*a*) with a third attribute
(*b*) in a third population
(*c*) in a sub-population
(*d*) none of the above

58. Partial association eliminates the influence of:
(*a*) third attribute
(*b*) wrong frequencies
(*c*) wrong calculations
(*d*) none of the above

59. If two attributes have no causative relationship, the association between them is known as:
(*a*) positive association
(*b*) negative association
(*c*) illusory association
(*d*) none of the above

60. Coefficient of contingency is a measure of:
(*a*) independence of attributes
(*b*) dependence of attributes
(*c*) correlation
(*d*) all of the above

61. The numerical value of coefficient of contingency:
(*a*) lies between 0 and 1
(*b*) never attains the value 1
(*c*) can never be negative
(*d*) all of the above

62. Another measure related to coefficient of contingency is:
(*a*) Yule's coefficient
(*b*) coefficient of correlation
(*c*) Tschuprow's coefficient
(*d*) all of the above

63. In an investigation on immunisation of cattle from renderpest disease, the following results were obtained:

	Affected	*Not Affected*
Inoculated	12	26
Not-inoculated	16	6

The value of coefficient of contingency is:
(*a*) $C = 0.33$
(*b*) $C = 0.37$
(*c*) $C = 0.95$
(*d*) none of the above

64. For the problem given in Q. No. 63, Tschuprow's coefficient is:
(*a*) $T = 0.43$
(*b*) $T = 0.10$
(*c*) $T = 0.466$
(*d*) none of the above

65. If for two attributes *A* and *B*, $N = 140$, $(A) = 100$, $(b) = 105$ and $(AB) = 25$, the attributes *A* and *B* are:
(*a*) dependent
(*b*) positively associated
(*c*) negatively associated
(*d*) independent

ANSWERS

Section B

1. dichotomous **2.** manifold **3.** order **4.** second **5.** zero **6.** three **7.** $(AB) + (Ab)$ **8.** $(AB) + (Ab) + (aB) + (ab)$ **9.** inconsistent **10.** negative **11.** dissociated **12.** $(A)(B)/N$ **13.** independent **14.** C's **15.** 1/4 **16.** $15 \le (BC) \le 35$ **17.** $(AB)(ab) = (Ab)(aB)$ **18.** $(A)(B)/N$ **19.** zero **20.** (A); (B) **21.** zero; zero **22.** – 1 **23.** zero; zero **24.** 1 **25.** zero **26.** – 1 **27.** $Q = 2Y/[1 + Y^2]$ **28.** 1 **29.** 0.066 **30.** 1/3 **31.** $(AB) = 20$, $(aB) = 40$, $(Ab) = 10$, $(A) = 30$ and $(b) = 40$ **32.** independent **33.** positively associated **34.** dissociated **35.** $(AB)/(A) = (aB)/(a)$ **36.** negatively associated **37.** does not give **38.** same **39.** never exceeds **40.** $T = \sqrt{\dfrac{C^2}{(1 - C^2)(p-1)(q-1)}}$ **41.** exceeds **42.** unity **43.** total **44.** partial **45.** – 1 to 1 **46.** $\dfrac{(BCA)(bcA) - (BcA)(bCA)}{(BCA)(bcA) + (BcA)(bCA)}$ **47.** third **48.** illusory **49.** illusory **50.** attributes; variables **51.** partial **52.** no **53.** relative **54.** $(ABC) > (AC)(BC)/(C)$ **55.** independent **56.** – 0.2 **57.** not same **58.** from 0 to 1 **59.** not necessarily **60.** 1 **61.** – 1 or 1 **62.** $[(AB)(\alpha\beta) - (\alpha B)(A\beta)]/N$ **63.** $\dfrac{(\alpha\beta)}{(\beta)}$ **64.** $(AB)(\alpha\beta) = (\alpha B)(A\beta)$ **65.** zero **66.** greater than zero or positive **67.** negative or less than zero **68.** $\alpha\beta$; αB **69.** inconsistent.

Section C

1. (a)	**2.** (b)	**3.** (a)	**4.** (c)	**5.** (b)
6. (d)	**7.** (b)	**8.** (c)	**9.** (a)	**10.** (b)
11. (c)	**12.** (a)	**13.** (b)	**14.** (d)	**15.** (c)
16. (b)	**17.** (d)	**18.** (a)	**19.** (d)	**20.** (a)
21. (b)	**22.** (c)	**23.** (a)	**24.** (b)	**25.** (d)
26. (a)	**27.** (b)	**28.** (c)	**29.** (a)	**30.** (c)
31. (b)	**32.** (d)	**33.** (d)	**34.** (a)	**35.** (b)
36. (c)	**37.** (b)	**38.** (b)	**39.** (a)	**40.** (c)
41. (d)	**42.** (b)	**43.** (c)	**44.** (a)	**45.** (b)
46. (a)	**47.** (a)	**48.** (b)	**49.** (b)	**50.** (b)
51. (c)	**52.** (a)	**53.** (b)	**54.** (a)	**55.** (c)
56. (a)	**57.** (c)	**58.** (a)	**59.** (c)	**60.** (b)
61. (d)	**62.** (c)	**63.** (b)	**64.** (a)	**65.** (d)

SUGGESTED READING

1. Agarwal, B.L., *Basic Statistics,* New Age International Publishers, New Delhi, 8th edition, 2024.
2. Ansari, M.A., Gupta, O.P. and Chaudhari, S.S., *Applied Statistics,* Kedar Nath Ram Nath & Co., Meerut, 1979.
3. Arora, S. and Bansi Lal, *New Mathematical Statistics,* Satya Prakashan, New Delhi, 1989.
4. Garg, N.L., *Practical Problems in Statistics,* Ramesh Book Depot, Jaipur, 1978.
5. Goodman, L.A. and Kruskal, W.H., *Measures of Association for Cross Classification,* Springer-Verlag, Berlin, 1979.
6. Gupta, S.C. and Kapoor, V.K., *Fundamentals of Mathematical Statistics,* Sultan Chand & Sons, New Delhi, 9th edn., 1994.
7. Sancheti, D.C. and Kapoor, V.K., *Statistics,* Sultan Chand & Sons, New Delhi, 7th edn., 1991.

CHAPTER 15

Interpolation and Extrapolation

SECTION A

Short Essay Type Questions

Q. 1. *Give the general idea about interpolation and extrapolation.*

Ans. The method of estimating a value of the dependent variable Y corresponding to a given value of X has already been explained in regression analysis. The interpolation and extrapolation come under mathematical approach known as numerical analysis. This approach is nonprobabilistic. If a value of Y is to estimated for a given value of X and it lies within the range of X-values, it is called *interpolation*. If it lies outside the range of its given values, it is known as *extrapolation*. According to **W.M. Harper,** "Interpolation consists in reading a value which lies between two extreme points. Extrapolation means reading a value that lies outside the two extreme points."

Q. 2. *What are the assumptions on which the interpolation and extrapolation are based?*

Ans. Interpolation and extrapolation are based on the following assumptions:

(*i*) There is no violent fluctuation within the given series of data. This makes the interpolation more accurate.

(*ii*) There should be a regularity in variation of variate values.

(*iii*) The dependent and independent variables should have definite mathematical relationship of the type $y = f(x)$.

Q. 3. *What are the uses of interpolation and extrapolation?*

Ans. There are various uses of interpolation and extrapolation, which are delineated below:

(*i*) Mostly the periodic observations or data are collected. But often the need arises for the intermediary periods. Interpolation provides the estimates for such values.

(*ii*) The data are available only for a span of time. But there is often a need of values of the past or future periods. In such a situation extrapolation is helpful in estimating the values outside the series of data.

(*iii*) Often the data for some period or the value of independent variable get lost. In such a situation inverse interpolation comes to our rescue to estimating the missing value.

(*iv*) For planning, one is always curious to know the position of demand in advance. Extrapolation to a great extent fulfils this requirement. For example, we can regulate our production keeping in view the population forecast ten years ahead.

(*v*) For comparison of data, it is necessary that the data should belong to the same reference period. If it is not so, it is necessary that the data be transformed to the same period. Interpolation and extrapolation serves this purpose very well.

Q. 4. *Out of interpolation and extrapolation which one is more frequently used, and why?*

Ans. Interpolation is more frequently used than extrapolation. Also the estimates obtained by interpolation are more accurate than extrapolation because they are free from the unseen and unknown vagaries of the past and the future.

Q. 5. *Name different kinds of approaches for interpolation.*

Ans. There are two kinds of interpolation approaches namely:

(*i*) Graphical method

(*ii*) Algebraic methods.

Q. 6. *Name different algebraic methods.*

Ans. The algebraic methods of interpolation are as follows:

(*i*) Binomial expansion method

(*ii*) Parabolic curve method

(*iii*) Newton's formula for advancing differences

(*iv*) Newton's backward formula

(*v*) Newton's-Gauss forward formula

(*vi*) Newton's-Gauss backward formula

(*vii*) Newton's-method of divided differences

(*viii*) Lagrange's interpolating formula

(*ix*) Stirling's formula

(*x*) Bessels formula

(*xi*) Inverse interpolation.

Q. 7. *On what factors, the accuracy of interpolation and extrapolation depends?*

Ans. Interpolation and extrapolation are simply estimation procedures. To expect absolutely accurate results from them is to deceive ourselves. Anyhow, there are many factors on which the accuracy of interpolation and extrapolation depends. Besides, interpolation is usually more accurate then extrapolation. The factors responsible for accuracy can be summarised as follows:

(*i*) One should have an idea about the fluctuations occurring in a series of data.

(*ii*) The knowledge about the unusual events related to the data be gathered by the analyst.

(*iii*) A proper choice of an interpolation or extrapolation formula in largely responsible for the accuracy of the estimates.

Q. 8. *Describe, in brief, the graphical method of interpolation.*

Ans. In graphical method, the paired variate values of the variables X and Y $(= f(x))$ are plotted on the graph paper after choosing appropriate scales along abscissa and ordinate. The plotted points are joined in sequence through a smooth line or curve. The value of Y for any value of X is estimated by drawing a line at the given point $X = x_0$ parallel to Y-axis so long as it touches the line or curve. From the point of intersection, draw a line parallel to X-axis. The point at which this touches the Y-axis, the corresponding reading on Y-axis is the estimated value of Y for the given value of X.

Graphical method provides a good estimate if the relation between X and Y is linear. But the estimate becomes poorer as the plotted points distort from an exact line or curve.

Graphical method is not frequently used.

Q. 9. *What special terms are used for independent and dependent variate values with reference to interpolation and extrapolation?*

Ans. As for interpolation and extrapolation, the independent variate values x's are called *arguments* and dependent variate values y's which are a function of x, *i.e.*, $y = f(x)$ are known as *entries*.

Q. 10. *How to make use of binomial expansion method for interpolation?*

Ans. If we want to interpolate for y for a given value of x, the method is applicable only when the values of x advance with equal jumps. Let the given paired observations for the two variables be:

x	x_0	x_1	x_2	...	x_i	...	x_n
y	y_0	y_1	y_2	...	y_i	...	y_n

We define the nth finite difference $\Delta^n_{y_0}$ through an operator E such that

$$\Delta^n y_0 = (E - 1)^n y_0'$$

If one entry say y_r corresponding to $(r + 1)^{th}$ argument is missing, then

$$\Delta^n y_0 = (E - 1)^n y_0 = 0$$

$$\Delta^n y_0 = \left[E^n - \binom{n}{1}E^{n-1} + \binom{n}{2}E^{n-2} - \ldots + (-1)^n\right] \times y_0 = 0$$

Now taking $E^i_{y_0} = y_i$, we obtain

$$y_n - \binom{n}{1}y_{n-1} + \binom{n}{2}y_{n-2} - \ldots + (-1)^n y_0 = 0$$

To estimate an unknown value, we choose n as the number of known values of y.

Also we shall have as many equations as the number of unknowns by taking $\Delta^n y_0 = \Delta^n y_1 = \Delta^n y_2 = \ldots = 0$. Solving these equations we obtain the missing values.

Q. 11. *For the following data:*

x:	1	2	3	4
y:	7	?	13	24

find the missing value by binomial expansion method.

Ans. Since 3 values are known, we would take third order finite difference zero. Thus,

$$y_3 - 3y_2 + 3y_1 - y_0 = 0$$

$$24 - 3 \times 13 + 3y_1 - 7 = 0$$

$$y_1 = \frac{22}{3}$$

Q. 12. *Given the values of a variable x and f(x), find the missing values.*

x:	0	1	2	3	4	5
y:	230	220	?	330	?	500

Ans. Since four values are known, we have to take $\Delta^4_{y_0} = 0$ and $\Delta^4_{y_1}$ where,

$$y_0 = f(x_0) \text{ and } y_1 = f(x_1)$$

$$(E - 1)^4 y_0 = y_4 - 4y_3 + 6y_2 - 4y_1 + y_0 = 0$$

$$(E - 1)^4 y_1 = y_5 - 4y_4 + 6y_3 - 4y_2 + y_1 = 0$$

According to the given data,

$$y_0 = 230, y_1 = 220, y_2 = y_2, y_3 = 330, y_4 = y_4, y_5 = 500$$

Substituting the values in the two equations, we get

$$y_4 + 6y_2 = 1970$$

$$4y_4 + 4y_2 = 2700$$

Solving the two equation we obtain the missing values as,

$$y_2 = 259 \text{ and } y_4 = 416$$

Q. 13. *Describe in brief the parabolic method of interpolation and extrapolation.*

Ans. In this method, a polynomial of degree n is always considered when $(n + 1)$ is the number of known entries y or $f(x)$, *i.e.*, we consider the polynomial.

$$y = a_0 + a_1x + a_2x^2 + \ldots + a_nx^n$$

This equation is called the parabola of degree n. Putting the given values of x's and corresponding y's in sequence, we get as many equations as the number of unknown constants $a_0, a_1, \ldots, a_n$. Solving these equations, we obtain the numerical values of a's. Substituting the values of $a_0, a_1, \ldots, a_n$, in the equation of the polynomial, we get the estimating polynomial. Now for any given value of x, y can be estimated. This method is also known as the *method of simultaneous equations*. This method is applicable almost in all situations for interpolation and extrapolation. Extrapolation is good if the situation outside the series, prevails similar to that of within the series, otherwise not.

Q. 14. *Give merits and demerits of the parabolic method of interpolation and extrapolation.*

Ans. Merits of parabolic method are:

(*i*) It is applicable in almost all situations.

(*ii*) The value of entry *y* can be estimated for any argument *x*.

(*iii*) The curve is a good fit if it passes through all the points.

Demerit of parabolic method is:

(*i*) The calculation becomes very lengthy if the interpolation has to be carried out for more than one value.

Q. 15. *Following are the prices per kg of an item during the four years:*

Year:	*1981*	*1984*	*1986*	*1989*
Prices:	*5*	*8*	*11*	*13*

Interpolate the price for the year 1987 by parabolic method.

Solution. Since four years (X) data are given, we have to use a parabolic equation of degree 3. The equation is.

$$y = a_0 + a_1x + a_2x^2 + a_3x^3 \quad ...(A)$$

Ans. Let us code years taking 1984 as origin and fit in the parabolic equation.

Years	*Coded value (x)*	*y*
1981	– 3	5
1984	0	8
1986	2	11
1989	5	13

Substituting the values of *x* and *y* in the third degree equation.

$$5 = a_0 - 3a_1 + 9a_2 - 27a_3 \quad ...(i)$$
$$8 = a_0 + a_1 \times 0 + a_2 \times 0 + a_3 \times 0 \quad ...(ii)$$
$$11 = a_0 + 2a_1 + 4a_2 + 8a_3 \quad ...(iii)$$
$$13 = a_0 + 5a_1 + 25a_2 + 125a_3 \quad ...(iv)$$

Solving the 4 equations for a_0, a_1, a_2 and a_3, we obtain

$$a_0 = 8,\ a_1 = 1.5,\ a_3 = -1/30,\ a_2 = 1/15$$

Substituting the values of a_0, a_1, a_2 and a_3, the parabolic equation is,

$$y = 8 + 1.5x + \frac{1}{15}x^2 - \frac{1}{30}x^3 \quad ...(B)$$

To estimate *y* for 1987, $x = 3$

Putting $x = 3$ in equation (*B*),

$$y = 8 + 1.5 \times 3 + \frac{1}{15} \times 9 - \frac{1}{30} \times 27$$
$$= 12.2$$

The estimated price for the year 1987 is 12.2 which of course lies between 11 and 13.

Q. 16. *What do you understand by finite differences for equal intervals?*

Ans. We consider equal intervals for the independent variable *x* as it makes the differences comparable and workable. The difference between two consecutive values of $y = f(x)$ starting from the origin x_0 are called finite differences. x_0 may be in the beginning of a series or somewhere in its midway or even the last argument. The values preceding to x_0 are suffixed with negative figures and following it by positive figures like – 1, – 2, – 3, ... and 1, 2, 3, ... The finite differences are denoted as,

$$y_1 - y_0 = \Delta y_0,\ y_2 - y_1 = \Delta y_1,\ y_3 - y_2 = \Delta y_2, \ldots$$

and $\quad y_0 - y_{-1} = \Delta y_{-1},\ \Delta y_{-1} - \Delta y_{-2} = \Delta y_{-2}, \ldots$

These are known as first order differences and are placed in between the position of two entries in the next column. Similarly, the differences,

$$\Delta y_{-1} - \Delta y_{-2} = \Delta^2 y_{-2},\ \Delta y_{-2} - \Delta y_{-3} = \Delta^2 y_{-3}, \ldots$$

or $\quad \Delta y_1 - \Delta y_0 = \Delta^2 y_0,\ \Delta y_2 - \Delta y_1 = \Delta^2 y_1, \ldots$ are called the differences of second order and so on.

Finite differences are frequently used in a large number of interpolation formulae.

Q. 17. *What are divided differences?*

Ans. The difference between two consecutive *y*-values divided by the interval length of the *x*-values is called divided difference.

Following usual, notations, the difference

$$\Delta y_i = \frac{y_j - y_j}{x_j - x_i}$$

The higher order divided differences are obtained by taking the differences of the preceding order difference and dividing them by the difference(s) of the corresponding *x*-values (arguments). Divided differences are extremely useful for data having unequally spaced *x*-values.

Argument x	Entry y	I difference Δy	II difference $\Delta^2 y$	III difference $\Delta^3 y$	IV difference $\Delta^4 y$	V difference $\Delta^5 y$
x_0	y_0					
		$y_1 - y_0 = \Delta y_0$				
x_1	y_1		$\Delta y_1 - \Delta y_0 = \Delta^2 y_0$			
		$y_2 - y_1 = \Delta y_1$		$\Delta^2 y_1 - \Delta^2 y_0 = \Delta^3 y_0$		
x_2	y_2		$\Delta y_2 - \Delta y_1 = \Delta^2 y_1$		$\Delta^3 y_1 - \Delta^3 y_0 = \Delta^4 y_0$	
		$y_3 - y_2 = \Delta y_2$		$\Delta^2 y_2 - \Delta^2 y_1 = \Delta^3 y_1$		$\Delta^4 y_1 - \Delta^4 y_0 = \Delta^5 y_0$
x_3	y_3		$\Delta y_3 - \Delta y_2 = \Delta^2 y_2$		$\Delta^3 y_2 - \Delta^3 y_1 = \Delta^4 y_1$	
		$y_4 - y_3 = \Delta y_3$		$\Delta^2 y_3 - \Delta^2 y_2 = \Delta^3 y_2$		
x_4	y_4		$\Delta y_4 - \Delta y_3 = \Delta^2 y_3$			
		$y_5 - y_4 = \Delta y_4$				
x_5	y_5					

In nutshell, divided differences are symmetric functions of their arguments. Also the divided differences are independent of the order of the arguments.

Q. 18. *What kind of difference tables are usually prepared for interpolation?*

Ans. Various kinds of difference tables frequently used for interpolation are:

(*i*) Diagonal difference table

(*ii*) Central difference table

(*iii*) Divided difference table.

Q. 19. *Give the method of preparing a diagonal difference table.*

Ans. In diagonal difference table, the first argument (first x-value) is taken as origin x_0 and corresponding entry (y-value) as y_0. The diagonal difference table with six values is displayed above:

The first differences $\Delta^n y_0$ (n = 1, 2, ...) in columns are called diagonal differences.

Q. 20. *Explain a central difference table.*

Ans. In central difference table, the origin x_0 of the argument lies in the midst of the series and corresponding entry (y-value) is taken as y_0. The central difference table with five values has been prepared and presented below:

Argument x	Entry y	I difference Δy	II difference $\Delta^2 y$	III difference $\Delta^3 y$	IV difference $\Delta^4 y$
x_{-1}	y_{-2}				
		$y_{-1} - y_{-2} = \Delta y_{-2}$			
x_{-2}	y_{-1}		$\Delta y_{-1} - \Delta y_{-2} = \Delta^2 y_{-2}$		
		$y_0 - y_{-1} = \Delta y_{-1}$		$\Delta^2 y_{-1} - \Delta^2 y_{-2} = \Delta^3 y_{-2}$	
x_0	y_0		$\Delta y_0 - \Delta y_{-1} = \Delta^2 y_{-1}$		$\Delta^3 y_{-1} - \Delta^3 y_{-2} = \Delta^4 y_{-2}$
		$y_1 - y_0 = \Delta y_0$		$\Delta^2 y_0 - \Delta^2 y_{-1} = \Delta^3 y_{-1}$	
x_1	y_1		$\Delta y_1 - \Delta y_0 = \Delta^2 y_0$		
		$y_2 - y_1 = \Delta y_1$			
x_2	y_2				

Q. 21. *Discuss a divided difference table.*

Ans. When the argument x does not advance with equal interval, divided difference table has to be prepared for interpolation. The divided difference table is presented below by taking five values only for the purpose of illustration:

(3) Newton's formula of advancing differences can also be used for extrapolation if the interpolation value lies slightly before the first value of x.

Difference table

Prepare diagonal difference table.

Argument x	*Entry* y	*I difference* $\not\Delta y$	*II difference* $\not\Delta^2 y$	*III difference* $\not\Delta^3 y$	*IV difference* $\not\Delta^4 y$
x_0	y_0				
		$\frac{y_1 - y_0}{x_1 - x_0} = \not\Delta y_0$			
x_1	y_1		$\frac{\not\Delta y_1 - \not\Delta y_0}{x_2 - x_0} = \not\Delta^2 y_0$		
		$\frac{y_2 - y_1}{x_2 - x_1} = \not\Delta y_1$		$\frac{\not\Delta^2 y_1 - \not\Delta^2 y_0}{x_3 - x_0} = \not\Delta^3 y_0$	
x_2	y_2		$\frac{\not\Delta y_2 - \not\Delta y_1}{x_3 - x_1} = \not\Delta^2 y_1$		$\frac{\not\Delta^3 y_1 - \not\Delta^3 y_0}{x_4 - x_0} = \not\Delta^4 y_0$
		$\frac{y_3 - y_2}{x_3 - x_2} = \not\Delta y_2$		$\frac{\not\Delta^2 y_2 - \not\Delta^2 y_1}{x_4 - x_1} = \not\Delta^3 y_1$	
x_3	y_3		$\frac{\not\Delta y_3 - \not\Delta y_2}{x_4 - x_2} = \not\Delta^2 y_2$		
		$\frac{y_4 - y_3}{x_4 - x_3} = \not\Delta y_3$			
x_4	y_4				

where $\not\Delta$ ≡ is divided difference.

Q. 22. *Discuss in brief Newton's formula of advancing differences for interpolation.*

Ans. Newton's formula of advancing differences which is also known as Newton-Gregory forward formula for interpolation is explicated below:

Applicability

(1) The formula is applicable when the arguments advance with equal intervals such as x, $x + h$, $x + 2h$, ...

(2) The formula is more appropriate if the interpolating item, *i.e.*, the value of x lies in the beginning of the series.

Formula

Suppose there are n arguments and n corresponding entries such as,

X:	x_0,	$x_0 + h$,	$x_0 + 2h$,	...	$x_0 + (n-1)h$
Y:	y_0,	y_1,	y_2,	...	y_{n-1}

Let x be the argument for which the entry say, y_x is to be estimated. Newton's formula of advancing differences is,

$$y_x = y_0 + \binom{u}{1}\Delta y_0 + \binom{u}{2}\Delta^2 y_0 + \ldots + \binom{u}{n-1}\Delta^{n-1} y_0$$

$$= y_0 + \sum_{r=1}^{n-1} \binom{u}{r} \Delta^r y_0$$

where, $u = \dfrac{x - x_0}{h}$

and $\binom{u}{r} = \dfrac{u(u-1)(u-2)\ldots(u-r+1)}{r(r-1)(r-2)\ldots 3.2.1}$

Substituting the values of different terms in the formula, we get the estimated value of y_x.

Q. 23. *Give Newton's backward formula.*

Ans. This is also known as Newton-Gregory backward formula and is described below:

Applicability

Newton's backward formula is applicable:

(1) When the argument x advances with equal jumps.

(2) When the x-value to be interpolated lies near the end of the series.

(3) For extrapolation also if the extrapolating value x lies slightly beyond the last x-value of the series.

Difference table

Diagonal difference table is used in Newton's backward formula. But the differences used are in the reverse order.

Formula

If there are n arguments and n corresponding entries, Newton's backward formula for the entry y_x to be interpolated for the argument x is,

$$y_x = y_n + \binom{u}{1}\Delta_{y_{n-1}} + \binom{u+1}{2}\Delta^2_{y_{n-2}} + \binom{u+2}{3}\Delta^2_{y_{n-3}} + \ldots$$

$$= y_n + \sum_{r=1}^{n} \binom{u+r-1}{r} \Delta^r y_{n-r}$$

where, $u = \dfrac{x - x_n}{h}$

x_n – last x-value of the series

h – common difference between two consecutive x-values.

Q. 24. *Describe the Newton-Gauss forward formula.*

Ans. The Newton-Gauss forward formula is also known as *Gauss forward polynomial formula*. This is not much different from Newton's formula for advancing differences except that in this formula the origin x_0 is the nearest lower value of x in the series to the given value of x instead of the first value of the series.

Applicability

(1) This formula is preferably used when the interpolating value x lies in the middle of the series or in the upper half of the series.

(2) It is necessary that the arguments x-advance with equal increment.

Difference table

For this formula central difference table has to be used.

Formula

The formula with usual notations is,

$$y_x = y_0 + \binom{u}{1}\Delta y_0 + \binom{u}{2}\Delta^2 y_{-1} + \binom{u+1}{3}\Delta^3 y_{-1} + \binom{u+1}{4}\Delta^4 y_{-2} + \binom{u+2}{5}\Delta^5 y_{-2} + \ldots$$

where, $u = \dfrac{x - x_0}{h}$

and h is the constant interval between x-values. It is trivial to calculate y_x for a given value of x.

Q. 25. *Discuss the Newton-Gauss backward method of interpolation.*

Ans. This method is also known as the *Gauss backward polynomial formula.*

Applicability

(1) This method is applicable when the arguments have equal common difference between arguments.

(2) The value to be interpolated lies near the end of a series.

Difference table

For this formula, central difference table is to be prepared taking origin x_0, the value of x succeeding to the given interpolating value of x in the series.

Formula

The Newton-Gauss backward formula with usual notations is,

$$y_x = y_0 - \binom{u}{1}\Delta_{y-1} + \binom{u+1}{2}\Delta^2_{y_{-1}} - \binom{u+1}{3}\Delta^3_{y_{-2}} + \ldots$$

where, $u = \dfrac{x_0 - x}{h}$

y_x is easily calculable by the above formula.

Q. 26. *Discuss Newton's method of backward differences of interpolation.*

Ans. Newton's backward formula is same as Newton-Gauss forward formula except that it utilises the last leading differences obtained by taking the initial value at the end of the series.

Applicability

(1) This method can be applied only when the x-values are equidistant.

(2) The method is appropriate only when the interpolating value lies at the end of the series.

Difference table

In this method the diagonal difference table is prepared by taking the last value of x in the series as initial value denoted as x_0 and the corresponding entry as y_0. To differentiate from other Newton's method, the differences are shown by inverted delta '∇'.

Formula

The formula for estimating the y-value 'y_x' corresponding to the interpolating value of x is

$$y_x = y_0 + \binom{u}{1}\nabla y_0 + \binom{u+1}{2}\nabla^2 y_0 + \binom{u+2}{3}\nabla^3 y_0 + \ldots$$

$$= y_0 + \sum_{r=1}^{n} \binom{u+r-1}{r}\nabla^r y_0$$

where, $u = \dfrac{x - x_0}{h}$

and h is the common difference between x-values.

Q. 27. *Explicate Newton's method of divided differences.*

Ans. This method is similar to Newton's method of advancing differences. But in this method the condition of equal increment in x-values is not imposed. To workout y_x corresponding to an interpolating value x with Newton's method of divided difference, it is necessary that x-values be arranged in ascending order and corresponding y-values be rearranged accordingly.

Applicability

(1) This formula is used when the x-values are not equally spaced.

(2) The formula gives a more exact estimated y corresponding to a value x if it lies in the upper half of the series.

Difference table

The formula utilises the divided difference table with first x-value as x_0 and corresponding y-value as y_0. The divided differences are denoted by $\not\Delta$.

Formula

Newton's formula of divided differences for estimating y_x corresponding to x is,

$$y_x = y_0 + (x - x_0)\ \not\Delta y_0 + (x - x_0)(x - x_1)\ \not\Delta^2 y_0 + (x - x_0)(x - x_1)(x - x_2)\ \not\Delta^3 y_0 + \ldots$$

This formula includes all terms till all leading differences are exhausted. Substituting the values of all terms, y_x is calculated in the usual way.

Q. 28. *Explain Lagrange's interpolating polynomial.*

Ans. When arguments are unequally spaced, there is a dearth of suitable methods, divided difference method could help in this situation. But Lagrange's interpolating polynomial is another very good formula for interpolation as well as extrapolation.

Applicability

(1) This method has no restriction on the x-variable (argument) whether it should be equally spaced or not.

(2) Lagrange's method can be used for any value of x either for interpolation or extrapolation.

(3) Lagrange's interpolation formula can also be used to estimate the argument x for a given value of y. It means Lagrange's formula can be used for inverse interpolation also.

Difference table

It requires no difference table.

Formula

If $(n + 1)$ known values of y, which are a function of x, *i.e.*, $y = f(x)$ corresponding to $(n + 1)$ arguments, are as follows,

x:	$x_0,$	$x_1,$	$x_2,$	$\ldots,$	x_n
y:	$y_0,$	$y_1,$	$y_2,$	$\ldots,$	y_n

then for estimating y corresponding to a given value of x, the formula is,

$$y_x = \frac{(x-x_1)(x-x_2)(x-x_3)\ldots(x-x_n)}{(x_0-x_1)(x_0-x_2)(x_0-x_3)\ldots(x_0-x_n)}y_0 + \frac{(x-x_0)(x-x_2)(x-x_3)\ldots(x-x_n)}{(x_1-x_0)(x_1-x_2)(x_1-x_3)\ldots(x_1-x_n)}y_1 + \frac{(x-x_0)(x-x_1)(x-x_3)\ldots(x-x_n)}{(x_2-x_0)(x_2-x_1)(x_2-x_3)\ldots(x_2-x_n)}y_2 + \cdots + \frac{(x-x_0)(x-x_1)(x-x_2)\ldots(x-x_{n-1})}{(x_n-x_0)(x_n-x_1)(x_n-x_2)\ldots(x_n-x_{n-1})}y_n$$

Substituting the value of given x and other known values of the arguments and entries, a good estimate of y is obtained. Lagrange's formula is most general formula.

The only demerit of this formula is that it entails heavy computational work.

Q. 29. *Why do we require formulae for central interpolation?*

Ans. Formulae propounded by Newton, Gauss, Lagrange and others are applicable for interpolation in general. But the question remains, how exact is the estimate in a particular situation. Therefore, there is a desideration for better and better formulae. In quest of the same, Stirling and Bessel gave interpolation formulae which are more appropriate for values to be estimated lying in the mid or central part of the given series.

Q. 30. *Enunciate Stirlings formula and its implications.*

Ans. Stirling's formula is applicable only when the values of the arguments x are equidistant. It is most suitable for interpolation near the middle of the tabulated values of the set. Let there be a set of $(2n + 1)$ values of the function $y = f(x)$ as,

$$x_{-n}, x_{-n+1}, \ldots, x_{-2}, x_{-1}, x_0, x_1, x_2, \ldots, x_n$$

$$y_{-n}, y_{-n+1}, \ldots, y_{-2}, y_{-1}, y_0, y_1, y_2, \ldots, y_n$$

The Stirling's formula is,

$$y_x = y_0 + \frac{u}{1!}\frac{\Delta y_0 + \Delta y_{-1}}{2} + \frac{u^2}{2!}\Delta^2_{y_{-1}} + \frac{u(u^2-1^2)}{3!}\frac{\Delta^3_{y_{-1}} + \Delta^3_{y_{-2}}}{2} + \frac{u^2(u^2-1^2)}{4!}\Delta^4_{y_{-2}} + \frac{u(u^2-1^2)(u^2-2^2)}{5!}\frac{\Delta^5_{y_{-2}} + \Delta^5_{y_{-3}}}{2} + \frac{u^2(u^2-1^2)(u^2-2^2)}{6!}\Delta^6_{y_{-3}} + \cdots + \frac{u^2(u^2-1^2)(u^2-2^2)\ldots\{u^2-(n-1)^2\}}{(2n-1)!} \times \frac{\Delta^{2n-1}_{y_{-(n-1)}} + \Delta^{2n-1}_{y_{-n}}}{2}$$

$$+\frac{u^2(u^2-1^2)(u^2-2^2)\ldots\{u^2-(n-1)^2\}}{(2n)!}\Delta^{2n}_{y_{-n}}$$

where,

$$u=\frac{x-x_0}{h} \text{ and } h=x_1-x_0=x_2-x_1=\ldots$$

Q. 31. *Expound Bessel's formula. Let there be a set of (2n + 1) values as given in Q. 30. of the function y =f(x). Bessel's formula is applicable only when the values of the argument x are at equal intervals.*

Ans. The formula expounded by Bessel to interpolate y for a given value of x which lies in the central part of the series is,

$$y_x=\frac{y_0+y_1}{2}+\frac{v}{1!}\Delta y_0+\frac{v^2-\frac{1}{4}}{2!}\frac{\Delta^2 y_0+\Delta^2 y_{-1}}{2}$$

$$+\frac{v\left(v^2-\frac{1}{4}\right)}{3!}\Delta^3 y_{-1}+\frac{\left(v^2-\frac{1}{4}\right)\left(v^2-\frac{9}{4}\right)}{4!}\times$$

$$\frac{\Delta^4 y_{-1}+\Delta^4 y_{-2}}{2}+\frac{v\left(v^2-\frac{1}{4}\right)\left(v^2-\frac{9}{4}\right)}{5!}\Delta^5 y_{-2}$$

$$+\frac{\left(v^2-\frac{1}{4}\right)\left(v^2-\frac{9}{4}\right)\left(v^2-\frac{25}{4}\right)}{6!}\frac{\Delta^6 y_{-2}+\Delta^6 y_{-3}}{2}$$

$$\vdots$$

$$+\frac{\left(v^2-\frac{1}{4}\right)\left(v^2-\frac{9}{4}\right)\ldots\left\{v^2-\frac{(2n-1)^2}{4}\right\}}{(2n)!}\times$$

$$\frac{\Delta^{2n}y_{-(n-1)}+\Delta^{2n}y_{-n}}{2}$$

$$+\frac{v\left(v^2-\frac{1}{4}\right)\left(v^2-\frac{9}{4}\right)\ldots\left\{v^2-\frac{(2n-1)^2}{4}\right\}}{(2n+1)!}\Delta^{2n+1}y_{-n}$$

where,

$$v=\frac{x-x_0}{h}-\frac{1}{2}=u-\frac{1}{2}$$

and

$$h=x_1-x_0=x_2-x_1=\ldots$$

Q. 32. *Make a comparative statement on Stirling's and Bessel's formulae of interpolation.*

Ans. Following points can be specified while comparing Stirling's and Bessel's formulae of interpolation.

1. Both the formulae are applicable for equidistant arguments.
2. Both are preferable for interpolating values near the middle of the series.
3. Stirling used u as in Newton-Gauss formulae whereas Bessel used v which is equal to $\left(u-\frac{1}{2}\right)$.
4. For both the formulae, choose x_0 which makes u and v as small as possible. Preferably u and v should lie between – 0.5 and 0.5.
5. It has been experienced that
   (*i*) Stirling's formula provides more accurate results if the interpolating value lies near the beginning or the end of the central interval and also u lies from –0.25 to 0.25.
   (*ii*) Bessel's formula yields more accurate results when the interpolating value lies near the middle of the central interval and v ranges from – 0.25 to 0.25, *i.e.*, $0.25 \le u \le 0.75$.

Q. 33. *What do you understand by inverse interpolation?*

Ans. When $y = f(x)$ and for a given values of arguments x and corresponding entries y, a value of x is to be estimated for a given value of y, the interpolation is known as inverse interpolation. In other words, if the value of the independent variable x is to be estimated for a given value of the dependent variable y within the series, it is called inverse interpolation.

Q. 34. *Name different methods of inverse interpolation.*

Ans. A few methods of inverse interpolation are:

(*i*) Lagrange's method

(*ii*) Iterative method

(*iii*) Successive approximation method.

Q. 35. *Give a brief account of Lagrange's method for inverse interpolation.*

Ans. Lagrange's method of interpolation can be used for inverse interpolation by writing the formula similar to interpolation replacing y by x and x by y. In this way, the interpolated value x_y for a given value y can be obtained by the formula.

$$x_y = \frac{(y-y_1)(y-y_2)(y-y_3)\ldots(y-y_n)}{(y_0-y_1)(y_0-y_2)(y_0-y_3)\ldots(y_0-y_n)}x_0$$

$$+\frac{(y-y_0)(y-y_2)(y-y_3)\ldots(y-y_n)}{(y_1-y_0)(y_1-y_2)(y_1-y_3)\ldots(y_1-y_n)}x_1$$

$$+\frac{(y-y_0)(y-y_1)(y-y_3)\ldots(y-y_n)}{(y_2-y_0)(y_2-y_1)(y_2-y_3)\ldots(y_2-y_n)}x_3$$

$$\vdots \qquad\qquad \vdots$$

$$+\frac{(y-y_0)(y-y_1)(y-y_2)\ldots(y-y_{n-1})}{(y_n-y_0)(y_n-y_1)(y_n-y_2)\ldots(y_n-y_{n-1})}x_n$$

This formula can be applied in exactly the same manner as for interpolating y.

Q. 36. *Explain iterative method of inverse interpolation.*

Ans. This method obtains an interpolated value in stages. This approach can be adopted for any polynomial formula suitable for a particular problem. Here it is explained by taking Newton's forward polynomial only. We know that Newton's forward polynomial can be written as,

$$y = y_0 + \binom{u}{1}\Delta y_0 + \binom{u}{2}\Delta^2 y_0 + \binom{u}{3}\Delta^3 y_0 + \ldots + \binom{u}{n}\Delta^n y_0$$

$$= y_0 + u\Delta y_0 + \sum_{r=2}^{n}\binom{u}{r}\Delta^r y_0$$

$$u = \frac{y-y_0}{\Delta y_0} - \frac{1}{\Delta y_0}\sum_{r=2}^{n}\binom{u}{r}\Delta^r y_0$$

The above formula is an iteration formula in u. If we know u, it is trivial to know x as $u = \dfrac{x-x_0}{h}$.

Suppose,

$$u_1 = \frac{y-y_0}{\Delta y_0}$$

and
$$I(u) = \frac{1}{\Delta y_0}\sum_{r=2}^{n}\binom{u}{r}\Delta^r y_0$$

$$\therefore \quad u = u_1 - I(u)$$

Let the value of u so obtained be denoted by u'_1 as a first approximation. Use u'_1 to obtain second approximation u'_2 by the formula,

$$u'_2 = u_1 - I(u'_1)$$

Again use u'_2 to get third approximation. Continue the process till almost same value of u is obtained in two successive iterations.

Q. 37. *Explicate the method of successive approximation for inverse interpolation.*

Ans. Under this method choose a polynomial deemed fit for interpolation. Once we have written the polynomial, the successive approximation method can be operated in the following manner. Now we take Newton's forward polynomial to explain the inverse interpolation. The polynomial is,

$$y = y_0 + \binom{u}{1}\Delta y_0 + \binom{u}{2}\Delta^2 y_0 + \binom{u}{3}\Delta^3 y_0 + \ldots + \binom{u}{n}\Delta^n y_0$$

After algebraic manipulation we can write the above polynomial in the form,

$$u = \frac{y-y_0}{\Delta y_0} - \frac{1}{\Delta y_0}\binom{u}{2}\Delta^2 y_0 - \frac{1}{\Delta y_0}\binom{u}{3}\Delta^3 y_0 \ldots - \frac{1}{\Delta y_0}\binom{u}{n}\Delta^n y_0$$

As a first approximation, take

$$u_1 = \frac{y - y_0}{\Delta y_0},$$

neglecting all terms at right hand side involving u. As a second approximation, take $u = u_1$, the value of u obtained under first approximation and include one more term of the right hand side involving second order finite difference. Thus, the second approximated u is,

$$u_2 = \frac{y - y_0}{\Delta y_0} - \frac{1}{\Delta y_0}\binom{u_1}{2}\Delta^2 y_0$$

Repeat the process taking $u = u_2$ and include two terms of right hand side involving $\Delta^2 y_0$ and $\Delta^3 y_0$. Continue the process till all terms of right hand side are involved or two equal values of u under successive approximations are obtained.

SECTION A

Fill in the Blanks

Fill in the suitable word(s) or phrase(s) in the blanks:

1. Interpolation and extrapolation are the parts of ________ analysis.
2. Interpolation and extrapolation approaches are ________.
3. Interpolation and extrapolation formulae assume ________ in the data of the series.
4. For interpolation or extrapolation, the two variables should have ________ relationship.
5. Interpolation is ________ frequently used than extrapolation.
6. Non-algebraic method of interpolation is ________ method.
7. Binomial method for interpolation is applicable when the independent variable x advances with ________.
8. If n values of dependent variable y are known, we take ________ finite difference zero.
9. Parabolic method can be used for ________ as well as ________.
10. Parabolic method of interpolation is applicable in ________.
11. Interpolation helps to estimate the ________ value in a series of data.
12. The estimation for a value beyond the given series of data is called ________.
13. With the help of interpolation and extrapolation, two series can be made ________.
14. The differences between two consecutive dependent variate values are called ________ differences.
15. The finite differences $\left(\Delta^2_{y_2} - \Delta^2_{y_1}\right)$ is called ________ order finite difference.
16. The difference between two consecutive dependent variate values divided by the interval between the corresponding independent variate values is called ________ difference.
17. The independent variate values in interpolation are termed as ________.
18. The dependent variate value in interpolation and extrapolation is called ________.
19. In diagonal difference table, the ________ argument of the series is taken as origin.
20. ________ types of difference tables are usually used in interpolation and extrapolation.
21. In a central difference table, the origin lies in the ________ of the series.
22. Newton's formula for advancing differences is also known as ________ forward formula.
23. Newton's formula for advancing differences is applicable if the interpolating value lies in the ________ of the series.
24. Newton's formula for advancing differences

utilises _________ finite difference of each column of the difference table.

25. In Newton's forward formula, the restriction on arguments is that they should advance with _________.

26. Newton's backward formula is used when the _________ value lies at the end of the series.

27. Newton-Gauss forward formula is also known as _________ polynomial formula.

28. The origin x_0 in difference table in the Newton-Gauss forward formula is the _________ value of x to the given value of x.

29. The relation between operators E and Δ within its usual sense in interpolation is _________.

30. Newton's backward polynomial formula utilises the _________ leading difference of each column.

31. In Newton's backward formula, the origin is the _________ value of the argument in the series.

32. Newton's method of divided differences takes care of the _________ spaced arguments.

33. All the Newton-Gauss formulae are _________ formulae.

34. The $(n + 1)^{th}$ order finite difference of a nth order polynomial is _________.

35. Lagrange's interpolation formula has _________.

36. Lagrange's polynomial is suitable for _________ as well as _________.

37. Lagrange's formula can be used for _________ interpolation also.

38. Lagrange's polynomial for n given entries has _________ terms.

39. Each term of a Lagrange's formula involving n arguments is a polynomial of degree _________.

40. The demerit of Lagrange's formula is that it involves _________ computations as compared to other formulae.

41. If for a given functional relation $y = f(x)$, one estimates x for a given y, it is called _________ interpolation.

42. Lagrange's formula for inverse interpolation given that $y = f(x)$ is a polynomial in _________.

43. Iterative method of inverse interpolation is not confined to _________ formula.

44. Iteration is continued till a _________ value of $u = (x - x_0)/h$ is obtained.

45. In successive approximation, terms are added _________ at each stage.

46. Inverse interpolation is not as accurate as _________.

47. Given $y_0 = 3, y_1 = 12, y_2 = 10, y_3 = 8$ the value of $\Delta^3 y_0$ is equal to _________.

48. Binomial expansion method is based on the theme that if n entries are known, then _________.

49. Given the data,

x:	1	3	5
y:	2	?	15

the missing **y**-value is _________.

50. Given the following values of x and $f(x)$,

x:	30	31	32	33	34
y_x:	0	1	2	3	4

Newton-Gregory forward polynomial is _________.

51. If l_x represents the number living at the age x in a life table, given that

x:	10	15	20	25
l_x:	42	34	25	18

l_x for $x = 22$ by Newton's backward formula is _________.

52. Divided differences are symmetric _________ of their arguments.

53. Divided differences are independent of the _________ of the arguments.

54. Five pairs of values of arguments and entries

would determine _________ degree polynomial.

55. Appropriate formulae for interpolating values near the middle of the series were originated by _________ and _________.

56. Bessel's formula for interpolation is _________ from Stirling's formula.

57. Bessel's and Stirling's interpolation formulae are applicable for _________ arguments only.

58. The relation between u of Stirling's formula and v of Bessel's formula is _________.

59. If the interpolating value lies near the beginning or the end of the central interval, _________ formula yields better results.

60. For Bessel's and Stirling's formulae, x_0 must be chosen in such a way that u and v lie in the interval _________.

61. Better formula for interpolating a value which lies in the middle of the central interval is _________ formula.

62. If $y = a_0 + a_1x + a_2x^2$, then Δ^3y is equal to _________.

63. Formulae for quartiles for grouped frequency distribution are based on _________ formula.

64. Lagrange's formula does not require the construction of _________ table.

65. The differences of the type $\Delta^2_{y_0} = \Delta_{y_1} - \Delta_{y_0}$, $\Delta^2_{y_1} = \Delta_{y_2} - \Delta_{y_1}$, etc., are called the differences of _________ order.

SECTION C

Multiple Choice Questions

Select the correct alternative out of given ones:

1. Interpolation is a technique for:
   (*a*) obtaining most likely missing links
   (*b*) finding relationship between two variables
   (*c*) comparing the two series
   (*d*) none of the above

2. Interpolation approach of estimation is:
   (*a*) probabilistic
   (*b*) non-probabilistic
   (*c*) non-mathematical
   (*d*) none of the above

3. Interpolation means estimating a value which lies:
   (*a*) within the given range of arguments
   (*b*) outside the given range of arguments
   (*c*) outside the range of the dependent variable
   (*d*) none of the above

4. Extrapolation means estimating for a value which lies:
   (*a*) within the two extremes of the given independent variate values
   (*b*) beyond the given highest values of the independent variable only
   (*c*) below the given lowest value of the independent variable only
   (*d*) none of the above

5. Interpolation is not affected by:
   (*a*) violent fluctuations
   (*b*) irregular variations
   (*c*) unforeseen events
   (*d*) none of the above

6. Estimation under interpolation:
   (*a*) is less accurate than extrapolation
   (*b*) is as accurate as extrapolation
   (*c*) is more accurate than extrapolation
   (*d*) none of the above

7. Interpolation and extrapolation are same in the sense that:
   (*a*) both determine most likely estimate
   (*b*) both results into same value
   (*c*) both are complementary to each other

(*d*) all of the above

8. Very many formulae of interpolation and extrapolation are given by:
(*a*) Newton
(*b*) Gregory
(*c*) Gauss
(*d*) all of the above

9. Most general formula for interpolation and extrapolation is due to:
(*a*) Newton and Gauss
(*b*) Newton and Gregory
(*c*) Lagrange
(*d*) all of the above

10. If n entries are known for $(n + 1)$ argument at equal intervals having a missing entry, a non-polynomial estimation method is:
(*a*) Lagrange's method
(*b*) Newton's formula
(*c*) binomial expansion method
(*d*) none of the above

11. Binomial expansion method is based on the principle that with n known entries:
(*a*) n^{th} finite difference $\Delta^n y_0 = 0$
(*b*) we take $(E - I)^n y_0 = 0$
(*c*) $y_n - \binom{n}{1} y_{n-1} + \binom{n}{2} y_{n-2} \cdots + (-1)^n y_0 = 0$
(*d*) all of the above

12. In binomial expression method we always get:
(*a*) n equations
(*b*) as many equations as the number of unknowns
(*c*) two equations
(*d*) $(n + 1)$ equations

13. Graphical method of estimation is:
(*a*) always very accurate
(*b*) sometimes very accurate
(*c*) never accurate
(*d*) none of the above

14. Graphical method can be used for:
(*a*) interpolation only
(*b*) extrapolation only
(*c*) interpolation and extrapolation both
(*d*) none of the above

15. Graphical method of interpolation is:
(*a*) simple
(*b*) non-algebraical
(*c*) not fully reliable
(*d*) all of the above

16. For the given $(n + 1)$ paired values, parabolic method means fitting of a polynomial:
(*a*) of degree n
(*b*) of degree 2
(*c*) of degree $(n + 1)$
(*d*) of degree 3

17. Parabolic method of interpolation is also known as:
(*a*) method of orthogonal polynomials
(*b*) method of simultaneous equations
(*c*) both (*a*) and (*b*)
(*d*) neither (*a*) nor (*b*)

18. Parabolic method of estimation is good for:
(*a*) interpolation
(*b*) extrapolation
(*c*) interpolation as well as extrapolation
(*d*) none of the above

19. A polynomial of degree n is known as:
(*a*) a parabola of degree n
(*b*) a parabola of degree $(n + 1)$
(*c*) a parabola
(*d*) none of the above

20. Interpolation is helpful in estimating:
(*a*) missing value(s) of a series
(*b*) an intermediary value for a given argument
(*c*) the argument for a given entry
(*d*) all of the above

21. Which of the following relation amongst finite differences is not correct?
(*a*) $\Delta^3 y_{-1} - \Delta^3 y_{-2} = \Delta^4 y_{-2}$
(*b*) $\Delta^2 y_{-1} - \Delta^2 y_0 = \Delta^3 y_0$
(*c*) $\Delta y_2 - \Delta y_1 = \Delta^2 y_1$
(*d*) $y_2 - y_1 = \Delta y_1$

22. Divided differences are useful when:
(*a*) arguments are equally spaced
(*b*) arguments are unequally spaced
(*c*) arguments advance with unit intervals
(*d*) all of the above

23. A finite difference table is said to be diagonal difference table if:
(*a*) the origin x_0 is the first argument in a series
(*b*) the origin x_0 is the last argument of the series
(*c*) the origin x_0 is an intermediary value of the series
(*d*) none of the above

24. A finite difference table is said to be a central difference table if:
(*a*) the origin x_0 is the first argument in a series
(*b*) the origin x_0 is the last argument of the series
(*c*) the origin x_0 is an intermediary value of the series
(*d*) none of the above

25. Newton's formula of advancing differences for interpolation with usual notations and n pairs of values is:
(*a*) $y_x = y_0 + \sum_{r=1}^{n-1} \binom{u}{r} \Delta^r y_0$
(*b*) $y_x = \sum_{r=0}^{n} \binom{u}{r} \Delta^r y_0$
(*c*) $y_x = \sum_{r=1}^{n} \binom{u}{r} y_0^r$
(*d*) all of the above

26. Newton's formula of advancing differences for interpolation is applicable if:
(*a*) the interpolation value lies in the beginning of the series
(*b*) the arguments advance with constant interval
(*c*) both (*a*) and (*b*)
(*d*) neither (*a*) nor (*b*)

27. Newton's formula of advancing differences is also known as:
(*a*) Newton-Gregory forward formula
(*b*) Gauss forward formula
(*c*) Lagrange's formula
(*d*) none of the above

28. Newton's backward formula is used when the interpolating value lies:
(*a*) in the middle of the series
(*b*) at the end of the series
(*c*) in the beginning of the series
(*d*) none of the above

29. The Newton-Gauss forward formula and Newton's formula of advancing differences differ in respect of:
(*a*) the choice of origin x_0
(*b*) finite difference table
(*c*) use of finite differences
(*d*) all of the above

30. The Newton-Gauss backward formula is to be applied when:
(*a*) the interpolating value of argument lies in the middle of the series
(*b*) the interpolating value of argument lies at the end of the series
(*c*) the interpolating value of argument lies anywhere in the series
(*d*) none of the above

31. Newton's method of backward differences differs from the Newton-Gauss backward formula in the sense that:
(*a*) it takes last argument of series as origin x_0
(*b*) it utilises the last finite differences
(*c*) the finite differences are denoted by inverted delta (∇)
(*d*) all of the above

32. Newton's formula of backward differences with usual notations is:
(*a*) $y_x = y_0 + \sum_{r=1}^{n} \binom{u}{r} \Delta^r y_0$
(*b*) $y_x = y_0 + \sum_{r=1}^{n-1} \binom{u+r}{r} \nabla^r y_r$

(*c*) $y_x = y_0 + \sum_{r=1}^{n} \binom{u+r-1}{r} \nabla^r y_0$

(*d*) none of the above

33. Newton's method of divided differences is preferred when:

(*a*) the arguments are not equally spaced

(*b*) when the interpolating value of the argument lies in the upper half of the series

(*c*) both (*a*) and (*b*)

(*d*) none of (*a*) and (*b*)

34. Standard notation for divided difference is:

(*a*) Δ

(*b*) ∇

(*c*) $\not\Delta$

(*d*) D

35. Divided difference method can be used when the given independent variate values are:

(*a*) at equal intervals

(*b*) at unequal intervals

(*c*) not well defined

(*d*) all of the above

36. Lagrange's formula is useful for:

(*a*) interpolation

(*b*) extrapolation

(*c*) inverse interpolation

(*d*) all of the above

37. Lagrange's polynomial for interpolation can be used even if:

(*a*) the given arguments are not equally spaced

(*b*) extrapolation is to be done

(*c*) inverse interpolation is to be done

(*d*) all of the above

38. If $(n + 1)$ pairs of arguments and entries are given, Lagrange's formula is:

(*a*) a polynomial of degree n in x

(*b*) a polynomial of degree n in y

(*c*) a polynomial in x in which each term has degree n

(*d*) a polynomial with highest degree 1

39. The method of inverse interpolation is:

(*a*) iterative method

(*b*) Lagrange's method

(*c*) successive method of approximation

(*d*) all of the above

40. Iterative method of inverse interpolation utilises:

(*a*) Newton's forward formula only

(*b*) Newton's backward formula only

(*c*) any suitable polynomial formula

(*d*) none of the above

41. In iterative method of inverse interpolation:

(*a*) the value of u is estimated successively

(*b*) the value of x is directly estimated

(*c*) the value of y is directly estimated

(*d*) all of the above

42. Method of successive approximation utilises:

(*a*) a polynomial formula as a whole

(*b*) terms of a polynomial formula successively

(*c*) only the terms independent of u

(*d*) only the terms involving u

43. Given the following data:

Income per day not exceeding (₹) :	10	18	20	28	40
Workers :	12	32	68	80	100

To interpolate number of workers for income not exceeding ₹ 30 per day, the suitable method is:

(*a*) Newton's backward formula

(*b*) Lagrange's formula

(*c*) binomial expansion method

(*d*) Gauss's backward formula

44. Given the profits of a firm in lakh rupees and the number of firms as follows:

Profits	*No. of firms*
100-150	25
150-200	30
200-250	28
250-300	16

The appropriate formula for estimating the number of firms with profit below 180 lakh is:

(*a*) Newton's formula of advancing differences
(*b*) Lagrange's formula
(*c*) Newton-Gauss forward formula
(*d*) all of the above

45. Given the following frequency distribution of marks:

Marks	*No. of students*
20-30	3
30-40	10
40-50	?
50-60	15
60-70	8

An appropriate method of estimating the missing frequency is:

(*a*) Newton-Gauss formula
(*b*) binomial expansion formula
(*c*) Lagrange's formula
(*d*) all of the above

46. The missing value for the following data:

x:	5	10	15	20
y:	2	5	?	8

by the binomial expansion method is:

(*a*) 7
(*b*) – 7
(*c*) 3
(*d*) 25/3

47. Given the profits for the last three years as,

Years	1991	1992	1993
Profits (lakh ₹)	15	18	24

the expected profit during the year 1994 by parabolic method is:

(*a*) 27
(*b*) 48
(*c*) 33
(*d*) 21

48. If the temperature of three dates of June, 1994 were as follows:

Dates:	1	10	25
Temp. (°C):	33	38	46

The estimated temperature for 20th June, 1994 by divided difference method is:

(*a*) 43.37
(*b*) 42.37
(*c*) 43.73
(*d*) 39.0

49. If $y = f(x)$ and the values of $f(x)$ for given x are, $f(1) = 14, f(2) = 12, f(5) = 6$ and $f(8) = 21, f(7)$ is:

(*a*) 2
(*b*) 12
(*c*) – 8
(*d*) none of the above

50. If the observed values of x and function u_x are:

x:	2	6	8	9
u_x:	198	150	102	93

The interpolating function u_x is:

(*a*) $x^3 - 4x^2 + 80x + 102$
(*b*) $x^3 - 18x^2 + 80x + 294$
(*c*) $x^3 - 18x^2 + 80x + 102$
(*d*) none of the above

51. The most suitable formula for estimating a value lying in the central part of a series is:

(*a*) Lagrange's formula
(*b*) Stirling's formula
(*c*) Newton-Gauss forward formula
(*d*) Newton-Gauss backward formula

52. Interpolation formulae are based on the fundamental assumption that the data can be expressed as:

(*a*) a linear function
(*b*) a quadratic function
(*c*) a polynomial function
(*d*) none of the above

53. The relationship between u of Stirling's formula and v in Bessel's formula for interpolation is:

(*a*) $u = v + 1$
(*b*) $u = v - 1$

(*c*) $u = v - \frac{1}{2}$

(*d*) $u = v + \frac{1}{2}$

54. Interpolation provides good estimates of missing values if and only if:

(*a*) the change of values is consistent

(*b*) the series does not refer to abnormal periods

(*c*) the arguments are equidistant

(*d*) all of the above

55. Bessel's and Stirling's interpolation formulae yield good estimates if the values of u and v in general lie between:

(*a*) – 1 and +1

(*b*) – 0.5 and 1

(*c*) – 0.5 and 0.5

(*d*) 0 and 1

56. If there are consecutive missing values in a series, their estimation is:

(*a*) not possible

(*b*) not reliable

(*c*) a complicated problem

(*d*) all of the above

57. Bessel's interpolation formula is most appropriate to estimate for a value in a series which lies:

(*a*) at the end

(*b*) in the beginning

(*c*) in the middle of the central interval

(*d*) outside the series

58. The problems of interpolation are simpler than prediction because:

(*a*) interpolation has fewer restrictions than prediction

(*b*) interpolation is based on more stringent restrictions than prediction

(*c*) there are no restriction in case of interpolation

(*d*) all of the above

59. Stirling's and Bessel's interpolation formulae for interpolation are applicable in case of:

(*a*) equidistant arguments

(*b*) for all types of series

(*c*) arguments increasing by one only

(*d*) arguments decreasing by one only

60. If the arguments in a series are not at equal interval, the proper formula that can be used for interpolation is:

(*a*) Bessel's formula

(*b*) Lagrange's formula

(*c*) Stirling's formula

(*d*) Newton's formula

61. If Δy_x is constant, then y_x may be:

(*a*) constant

(*b*) at equal intervals

(*c*) both (*a*) and (*b*)

(*d*) none of the above

62. The third differences of a cubic $\Delta^3 y$ function are:

(*a*) constant

(*b*) not constant

(*c*) variables

(*d*) none of the above

63. Which formula is appropriate for central interpolation?

(*a*) Bessel's formula

(*b*) Stirling's formula

(*c*) both (*a*) and (*b*)

(*d*) neither (*a*) nor (*b*)

64. If the interpolating value lies near the middle of the central interval, then the most exact formula is:

(*a*) Bessel's interpolation formula

(*b*) Lagrange's interpolation formula

(*c*) Stirling's interpolation formula

(*d*) Newton-Gauss interpolation formula

65. If the interpolating value lies near the beginning or the end of the central interval, then the most exact formula is:

(*a*) Newton-Gauss formula

(*b*) Newton-Gregory formula

(*c*) Bessel's formula

(*d*) none of the above

ANSWERS

Section B

1. Numerical **2.** non-probabilistic **3.** no fluctuations **4.** definite **5.** more **6.** graphical **7.** equal jumps **8.** n^{th} **9.** interpolation; extrapolation **10.** all situations **11.** missing **12.** extrapolation **13.** comparable **14.** finite **15.** third **16.** divided **17.** arguments **18.** entry **19.** first **20.** Three **21.** midst **22.** Newton-Gregory **23.** beginning **24.** first **25.** equal increment **26.** interpolating **27.** Gauss forward **28.** just lower **29.** $E - 1 = \Delta$ **30.** last **31.** last **32.** unequally **33.** polynomial **34.** constant **35.** no restrictions **36.** interpolation; extrapolation **37.** inverse **38.** n **39.** $n - 1$ **40.** heavy **41.** inverse **42.** y variable **43.** single **44.** stable **45.** one by one **46.** interpolation **47.** 11 **48.** $\Delta^n y_0 = 0$ **49.** 6.5 **50.** $30 + x$ **51.** 19.63 **52.** functions **53.** order **54.** fourth **55.** Bessel; Stirling **56.** different **57.** equidistant **58.** $v = u - \frac{1}{2}$ **59.** Stirling's **60.** – 0.5 and 0.5 **61.** Bessel's **62.** zero **63.** interpolation **64.** difference **65.** second.

Section C

1. (*a*)	**2.** (*b*)	**3.** (*a*)	**4.** (*d*)	**5.** (*d*)
6. (*c*)	**7.** (*a*)	**8.** (*d*)	**9.** (*c*)	**10.** (*c*)
11. (*d*)	**12.** (*b*)	**13.** (*b*)	**14.** (*c*)	**15.** (*d*)
16. (*a*)	**17.** (*b*)	**18.** (*c*)	**19.** (*a*)	**20.** (*d*)
21. (*b*)	**22.** (*b*)	**23.** (*a*)	**24.** (*c*)	**25.** (*a*)
26. (*c*)	**27.** (*a*)	**28.** (*b*)	**29.** (*d*)	**30.** (*b*)
31. (*d*)	**32.** (*c*)	**33.** (*c*)	**34.** (*c*)	**35.** (*b*)
36. (*d*)	**37.** (*d*)	**38.** (*a*)	**39.** (*d*)	**40.** (*c*)
41. (*a*)	**42.** (*b*)	**43.** (*b*)	**44.** (*d*)	**45.** (*b*)
46. (*a*)	**47.** (*c*)	**48.** (*a*)	**49.** (*b*)	**50.** (*c*)
51. (*b*)	**52.** (*c*)	**53.** (*d*)	**54.** (*d*)	**55.** (*c*)
56. (*a*)	**57.** (*c*)	**58.** (*a*)	**59.** (*a*)	**60.** (*b*)
61. (*c*)	**62.** (*a*)	**63.** (*c*)	**64.** (*a*)	**65.** (*d*)

SUGGESTED READING

1. Agarwal, B.L., *Basic Statistics*, New Age International Publishers, New Delhi, 8th edition, 2024.
2. Gerald, C.F., *Applied Numerical Analysis*, Addison-Wesley Publishing Co., Philippines, 1970.
3. Hilderband, F.B., *Introduction to Numerical Analysis,* Tata McGraw-Hill Publishing Co., New Delhi, 1974.
4. Johnson, L.W. and Riefs, R.D., *Numerical Analysis*, Addison-Wesley Publishing Co., Philippines, 1977.
5. Maron, M.J., *Numerical Analysis*, Macmillan Publishing Co., New York, 1982.
6. Nielson, K.L., *Methods in Numerical Analysis*, Macmillan Publishing Co., New York, 1956.
7. Scarborough, J.B., *Numerical Mathematical Analysis*, John Hopkins University Press, Baltimore, 1950.

CHAPTER 16

Time Series Analysis

SECTION A

Short Essay Type Questions

Q. 1. *What is a time series?*

Ans. A time series is a set of observations measured at time or space intervals arranged in chronological order. For instance, the yearly demand of a commodity, weekly prices of an item, food production in India from year to year, etc. Many economists and statisticians have defined time series in different words. Some of them are quoted below:

Wessel and Wellet: When quantitative data are arranged in the order of their occurrence, the resulting statistical series is called a time series.

Moris Hamburg: A time series is a set of statistical observations arranged in chronological order.

Patterson: A time series consists of statistical data which are collected, recorded or observed over successive increments.

Ya-lun-Chou: A time series may be defined as a collection of magnitudes belonging to different time periods, of some variable or composite of variables such as production of steel, per capita income, gross national product, price of tobacco or index of industrial production.

Cecil H. Meyers: A time series may be defined as a sequence of repeated measurements of a variable made periodically through time.

Werner Z. Hirsch: A time series is a sequence of values of the same variate corresponding to successive points of time.

Spiegel: A time series is a set of observations taken at specified times, usually at equal intervals. Mathematically, a time series is defined by the values Y_1, Y_2, ... of a variable Y (temperature, closing price of a share, etc.) at time t_1, t_2 ... . Thus, Y, is a function of t symbolised by $Y = F(t)$.

Q. 2. *What purpose is served by time series analysis?*

Ans. The analysis of time series has been found useful to economists and business persons, in particular, and also to scientists, sociologists, etc. It has also found its utility in meteorology, seismology, oceanography, geomorphology, etc., in earth sciences; electrocardiograms, electroencephotograms in medical sciences and problem of estimating missile trajectories. Time series analysis helps in understanding the following phenomena:

(*i*) It helps in knowing the real behaviour of the past.

(*ii*) It helps in predicting the future behaviour like demand, production, weather conditions, prices, etc.

(*iii*) It helps in planning the future operations.

(*iv*) Analysis of time series helps to compare the present accomplishments with the past performances.

(*v*) Two or more times series can be compared belonging to the same reference period.

Q. 3. *Throw light on the main drawbacks of the time series analysis.*

Ans. The drawbacks of the time series analysis can be summarised as follows:

(*i*) The conclusions drawn on the basis of time series analysis are not cent per cent true.

(*ii*) Time series analysis is unable to fully adjust the influences affecting a time series like customs, climate, policy changes, etc.

(*iii*) The complex forces affecting a time series existing at certain period may not be having the same complex forces in future. Hence, the forecasts may not hold true.

Q. 4. *What is the need of editing of data before time series analysis?*

Ans. The data have to be critically examined and adjusted for various factors before the analysis of time series, otherwise many discrepancies are likely to arise leading to wrong conclusions. For example, the production for January could be more than February. In reality, it may be due to more number of days in January than in February.

Q. 5. *Give various adjustments usually practised during editing of data meant for analysis of a time series.*

Ans. Various adjustments normally incorporated in a time series data are as follows:

(*i*) *Calendar variation.* One should be wary of the type of variable dealing with before implementing the adjustments for calendar variation. Production of a unit per month has to be adjusted for 30 days a month for comparability. But series should not be adjusted for salary as employees are paid on a monthly basis irrespective of the number of days in a month.

(*ii*) *Price variation.* Production or sales are to be adjusted for price variation by the formula.

$$q = v/p$$

where, q – quantity of sales or production in a specified period

v – sales in terms of amount

p – price per unit in the reference period.

If this adjustment is not done, increased prices will lead to the conclusion that production or sales have increased (decreased), though in reality it is not so.

(*iii*) *Population variation.* Demand or consumption of a commodity is directly related to the population of a particular area. If the demand doubles and population also doubles, it should not be taken that demand has increased. It is simply the effect of the number of consumers and not that of increased demand. As a matter of fact, demand is the same.

(*iv*) *Miscellaneous changes.* For comparison of two time series, it is necessary that the data pertaining to certain period should have been measured in the same units. If they are not, they should be converted to the same unit of measurements. Also, the articles, which are to be compared in terms of prices, should be adjusted for their standard and durability. For example, synthetic fibre clothes are more durable than cotton fibre clothes. Hence, their prices be adjusted for their durability in terms of time period.

Q. 6. *Name various components of a time series.*

Ans. There are four components or elements of a time series, namely:

(*i*) Secular Trend–*T*

(*ii*) Seasonal Variation–*S*

(*iii*) Cyclical Variation–*C*

(*iv*) Irregular Variation–*I*

Q. 7. *What do you understand by secular trend?*

Ans. Term trend implies *secular trend.* It measures long-term changes occurring in a time series without bothering about short-term fluctuations occurring in between. In short, secular trend measures smooth and regular long-term movements of a time series delineating the increasing, decreasing or stagnant trend over a long span of time. The graph showing trend is a straight line running from left bottom to right top, left top to right bottom or parallel to abscissa depicting growth, decline or stagnation, respectively. In some situations curvilinear trend is also studied.

Q. 8. *Give the idea of seasonal variation.*

Ans. Short-term fluctuations observed in a time series data, particularly in a specified period usually within a year, are called seasonal variations. For instance, certain items have more sale in a particular season like ice cream in summer, rain coats in rainy season and woollens in winter season. Similarly, first week of a month records greater sale of grocery than the last week of a month. Certain items have tremendous sale on festivals only in a particular month. All such variation in a time series come under seasonal variation. Seasonal variations are more akin to climatic and weather conditions.

Q. 9. *What is meant by cyclic variation?*

Ans. Cyclic variation relates to periodic changes, particularly in business. A cycle consists of more than a year period. The cycles in a time series depict the prosperity and recession, ups and downs, booms and slumps of a business. A complete cycle usually has four constituents namely, *prosperity, recession, depression* and *recovery.* Cycles related to business are termed as *business cycles* or *trade cycles.* The length of business cycles varies from one business to the other. The graph of cyclic variation is a curve having alternately convexity and concavity.

Cycles are never regular in periodicity and amplitude. Hardly any time series has strict cycles. Hence, in practice, statisticians and economists often use the term *undulations* or *oscillations* instead of cycles.

Since a cycle covers a long span of time, the data required for the depiction of cycles should be recorded for a large number of years (periods).

Q. 10. *What factors are generally responsible for the occurrence of cycles?*

Ans. A large number of factors are responsible for the occurrence of cycles. But a few important ones are given below:

(*i*) Likes and dislikes of the people change after a certain period and they cause cycles in business phenomenon.

(*ii*) Production of certain items is stopped and new items are produced. Again old items are adopted. Such changes form cycles.

(*iii*) Social customs change from time to time resulting into business cycles.

(*iv*) New scientific and technological developments affect the production and consumption of items which create cycles.

Q. 11. *Discuss irregular variation in the context of time series.*

Ans. Irregular variations or the so-called *random variations* are irregular in the sense that it is not possible to think of their time of occurrence, direction and magnitude. These variation usually occur due to epidemics, earthquakes, floods, wars, accidents, etc. Another name given to irregular variations is *residual variations.* This name is derived in the sense that all those variations which cannot be subsumed in trend, seasonal and cyclic variations, are assigned to irregular variations.

Q. 12. *Discuss mathematical models for a time series analysis.*

Ans. In a traditional or classical time series analysis, the most commonly assumed mathematical model is the *multiplicative model.* Here, it is assumed that any particular observation Y at time t is as a result of the product of the effect of the four components of a time series namely. Trend (T), seasonal variation (S), cyclic variation (C) and the irregular variation (I), *i.e.,*

$$Y = T \times S \times C \times I$$

Further the multiplicative model does not assume the independence of the four components of the time series. It is appropriate for projections.

Some people believe that the observation Y is as a result of additive effect of the components T, S, C and I, *i.e.,*

$$Y = T + S + C + I$$

The additive model is based on the assumption that the four components are independent of each other. Additive model is rarely used as it is not appropriate for future events.

Some people have also advocated the use of mixed models. A mixed model is a mathematical relation which is expressed as a combination of multiplicative and additive components of a time series. They may be combined in a number of ways. Such types of models are hardly used. Some of the examples of mixed models are given below:

$$Y = T + S \times C + I$$
$$Y = T + S \times C \times I$$
$$Y = T + S + C \times I$$
$$Y = T \times C + S \times I$$

Q. 13. *What are the essential requirements for proper analysis of a time series?*

Ans. The essential requirements for proper analysis of a time series are:

(*i*) Data should be available for a long period.

(*ii*) The value should have been available as far as possible at equal interval of time. If not, they have to be adjusted.

(*iii*) The time periods should be definite according to calendar.

(*iv*) The data should consist of a homogeneous set of values in respect of units of measurements and time scale.

Q. 14. *Give the names of different methods of measuring trend.*

Ans. Various methods of measuring trend are:

(*i*) Free-hand or graphic method

(*ii*) Semi-average method

(*iii*) Moving average method

(*iv*) Least square method

Q. 15. *How to find out the trend and trend value by the free-hand method?*

Ans. The free-hand method is the simplest method of ascertaining trend. In this method, points (t_1, y_1) (t_2, y_2) ..., (t_n, y_n) are plotted on a graph paper taking time t on abscissa and variate values y on the ordinate by choosing suitable scales. Then a free-hand straight line is drawn in between the points with the help of a transparent scale such that half of the points are above the line and half below it. The angle of the line gives the idea about increasing, decreasing or stagnant trend of the phenomenon under consideration. Also the y-coordinate of a point on the line at any point of time gives the *trend value*.

The main drawback of free-hand method is that it solely depends on the judgement of the investigator or the scientist.

Q. 16. *Explicate semi-average method of determining trend.*

Ans. In this approach, the series is divided into halves. Then average is found out for each half of the series. The average values are plotted on the graph paper against the mid-points of the corresponding each half series. The line joining these two plotted points gives trend line. The direction of line indicates about rising, falling or constant trend of business movements.

If the number of years in a series is odd, the middle year (period) is excluded at the time of dividing the series into halves and then either included in both the series or excluded totally depending on whether the left over half series contains an even or odd number of years respectively.

The semi-average method gives good results when the trend is almost linear.

Q. 17. *What are the merits and demerits of the semi-average method?*

Ans.

Merits:

(*i*) It has no subjectively,

(*ii*) For one series, there is only one trend line.

Demerits:

(*i*) It is affected by extreme values, if present in time series data.

(*ii*) It does not ensure the elimination of seasonal and cyclic variations.

(*iii*) This method is appropriate, if the data are given for a long period.

Q. 18. *Discuss in brief the moving average method for ascertaining the trend.*

Ans. The moving average method is an improvement over semi-average method as short-term fluctuation are eliminated by it. Different steps of moving average method are as follows:

Step-1. To obtain the moving average, a group of beginning years (periods), which constitute a business cycle, is chosen for calculating the average. This average is placed in front of the middle of the years (periods) of the group averaged.

Step-2. Now delete first year (period) value from the group and add a succeeding year value in the group. Find the average of the reconstituted group and place it in front of the middle year of this group.

Step-3. If the number of years (periods) in a group is odd, there is no problem of locating the middle year. But if the number of years (periods) in the group is even, no single year is middle year. Hence, to overcome this difficulty, the average of the averages in pairs is calculated and placed against the mid-year of the two. In this way, moving averages are set against years.

Step-4. Keep on repeating step-2 till all years data are exhausted.

Step-5. These moving averages themselves constitute a time series.

Step-6. Plot the moving averages on a graph paper taking years (periods) along abscissa and moving averages along ordinate by choosing the proper scales.

Step-7. Join all the plotted points in the sequence of time periods. The resulting graph provides the trend.

Q. 19. *What are the advantages and disadvantages of the moving average method?*

Ans.

Advantages:

(*i*) The greatest advantage of this method is that it eliminates the short-term fluctuations.

(*ii*) It reduces the effect of extreme values.

(*iii*) Extending the series by some more ensuing years does not require to redo the whole computations but can add some more trend values by calculating additional moving averages.

Disadvantages:

(*i*) A few years in the beginning and at the end of the series are left over without the moving averages being entered against them. Hence, no points are plotted against these years causing a loss of information.

(*ii*) Since there are no points plotted for a few beginning and end years, the moving-average method is not appropriate for projections.

(*iii*) There is hardly any time series having regular cycles. But they are always taken to be regular. This introduces an error.

(*iv*) Normally, a small number of years (periods) in a group for moving average is preferred. But many a times greater number of years are included in groups which deflates the magnitude of oscillations in a time series. Greater the degree of deflation, less realistic is the resulting trend. In such a situation, moving averages anticipate faster changes than they actually occur.

(*v*) This method is not fully mathematical.

(*vi*) There is no strict rule through which one decides the number of years (periods) in a group. Hence, the element of subjectivity is introduced in this method. So, for the same time series there can be a number of trends.

Q. 20. *How do you fit a trend line by the method of least squares?*

Ans. Let us consider the linear trend equation as,

$$Y = \alpha + \beta X + \varepsilon$$

As per the least square principle, we will estimate the parameters α and β in such a manner that the error ε is minimised. In this endeavour, we minimise the quantity,

$$Q = \sum_i \varepsilon_i^2 = \sum_i (Y_i - \alpha - \beta X_i)^2$$

where i runs overall periods of time series 1 to n. Differentiating Q partially with respect to α and β and equating to zero, we get two normal equations. Also we replace α and β by a and b, their least square estimates.

Thus we have,

$$\sum_i Y_i = na + b \sum_i X_i$$

$$\sum_i X_i Y_i = a \sum_i X_i + b \sum_i X_i^2$$

Solving these normal equations we get,

$$a = \bar{Y} - b\bar{X}$$

$$b = \frac{\sum X_i Y_i - \frac{(\Sigma X_i)(\Sigma Y_i)}{n}}{\sum X_i^2 - \frac{(\Sigma X_i)^2}{n}}$$

Substituting the values of a and b in the trend equation we obtain the trend line as,

$$Y = a + bX$$

In this equation, the variable X stands for the periods and Y for corresponding dependent variable.

Usually, the variables X is coded in such a manner that ΣX_i is zero. This reduces the values of a and b as,

$$a = \bar{Y}$$

and $$b = \frac{\Sigma X_i Y_i}{\Sigma X_i^2}$$

Q. 21. *Write the merits and demerits of the least square method of finding the trend.*

Ans.

Merits:

(*i*) The method is mathematically sound.

(*ii*) The algebraic sum of the deviations of actual values from trend values is zero.

(*iii*) The sum of squares of the deviations, $\Sigma(Y - \hat{Y})^2$ is minimum.

(*iv*) The least square method is devoid of all kinds of subjectivity.

(*v*) The estimates a and b are unbiased.

(*vi*) The estimates a and b have minimum variance.

(*vii*) The trend by this method gives very accurate interpolated value.

Demerits:

(*i*) Trend line by least square method is not very appropriate for projections unless and until the same situation continues to prevail during the period of extrapolation as they do within the series period.

(*ii*) It has been assumed that Y is only a linear function of time period X which may not be true in many situations.

Q. 22. *How can the shift of origin be incorporated in trend equation?*

Ans. When the origin is shifted, the value of b remains unchanged. What we have to determine is the value of the intercept 'a' by putting $x \pm k$ in place of x in the given trend equation? k is the number of periods by which the origin is shifted and is negative if the origin is shifted backward and positive, if the origin is shifted forward.

Q. 23. *How can you convert annual-trend equation to monthly-trend equation?*

Ans. If the annual data are reduced to monthly data, a divisor 12 is introduced. Hence, the annual-trend equation,

$$Y = a + bX$$

is converted to monthly-trend equation by dividing a by 12 and b by 12 × 12, where X represents increments from month to month. Thus, the required equation is,

$$Y = \frac{a}{12} + \frac{b}{12 \times 12} X$$

Q. 24. *How can the annual-trend equation be converted to quarterly-trend equation?*

Ans. In the annual-trend equation $Y = a + bX$, required to be converted to quarterly-trend equation,

the converted $a = \frac{3}{12}a$ and converted $b = \frac{3}{12 \times 12} b$.

Hence, the quarterly-trend equation is,

$$\hat{Y} = \frac{a}{4} + \frac{b}{48} X$$

where, X unit: one quarter, Y unit: Quarterly values.

Q. 25. *How will you convert the annual-trend equation to half-yearly trend equation?*

Ans. The annual-trend equation, $\hat{Y} = a + bX$ converted to half-yearly trend equation will be,

$$\hat{Y} = \frac{a}{2} + \frac{b}{24} X$$

Note: If the trend equation is computed from the annual monthly averages, there has to be no change in a and single operation divisor has to be used for b.

Q. 26. *Comment on curvilinear trend.*

Ans. The trend of the dependent variable Y on time X is not always linear, *i.e.*, the increase or decrease in Y does not occur at a constant rate with the elapse of time. Hence, one has to look for a curvilinear trend. Some of the frequently encountered curves are, (*i*) second or third degree parabola; (*ii*) exponential curve and (*iii*) compertz curve, etc.

Q. 27. *How to fit in a second degree trend equation?*

Ans. The equation of a second degree parabola (quadratic trend) is,

$$Y = a + bX + cX^2$$

The curve can be fitted by the method of least squares. Following the usual procedure, we get three normal equations:

$$\Sigma Y = \Sigma a + b\,\Sigma X + c\,\Sigma X^2$$
$$\Sigma XY = a\,\Sigma X + b\,\Sigma X^2 + c\,\Sigma X^3$$
$$\Sigma X^2Y = a\,\Sigma X^2 + b\,\Sigma X^3 + c\,\Sigma X^4$$

Summation (Σ) runs overall pairs of observations.

Solving the three equations, we obtain the values of a, b and c, substituting the values of the constants a, b and c, we get the second degree parabola.

The shape of the second degree curve depends on the values of b and c.

If $b > 0$, $c > 0$, the curve is concave from left bottom to right top.

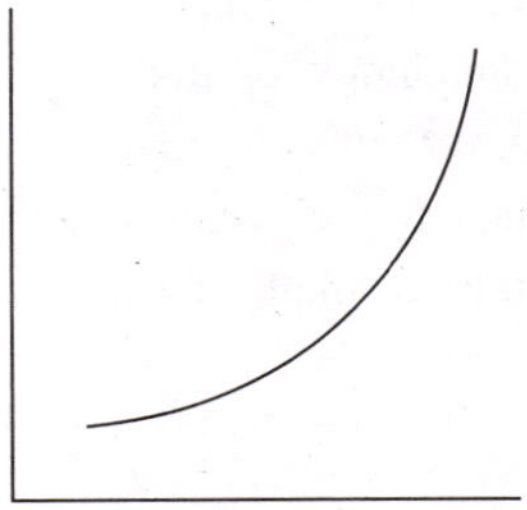

Fig. 16.1

If $b > 0$, $c < 0$, the curve is convex from left bottom to right top.

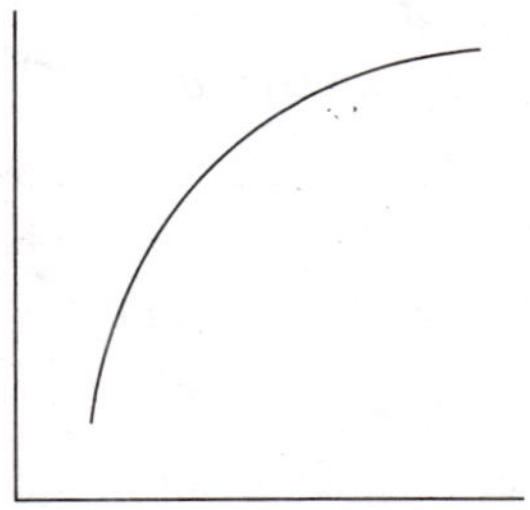

Fig. 16.2

If $b < 0$, $c < 0$, the curve is convex from left top to right bottom.

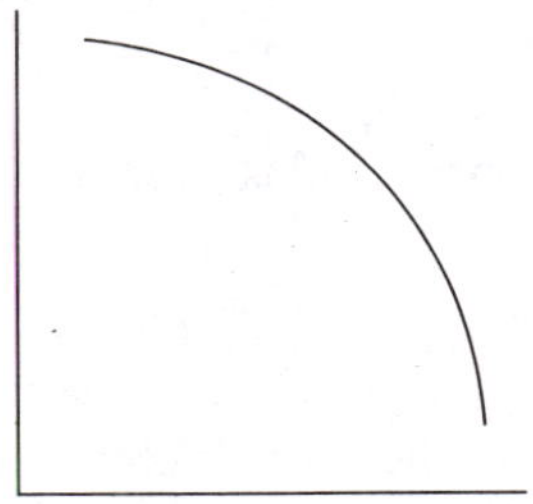

Fig. 16.3

If $b < 0$, $c > 0$, the curve is concave from left top to right bottom.

Fig. 16.4

Q. 28. *Give the equation of an exponential curve and method for its fitting.*

Ans. Exponential curve is also called *geometric trend.* The equation of the curve is,

$$Y = ab^X.$$

If we plot the time series data as such, it will be a curve with upward trend provided $b > 1$ and with downward trend for $b < 1$. Since X occurs in power of b, it is called *exponential curve.*

It is difficult to fit in the equation as such but by taking logarithm of the equation, it becomes trivial to fit it. The log transformed equation is,

$$\log Y = \log a + X \log b,$$

which is a linear equation in log Y and X. The values of log a and log b can be computed by the formulae,

$$\log a = \frac{1}{n} \sum \log Y - \bar{X} \log b$$

$$\log b = \frac{\Sigma X \log Y - (\Sigma X)(\Sigma \log Y)/n}{\Sigma X^2 - (\Sigma X)^2 /n}$$

where summation (Σ) runs overall pairs of values. Taking antilog of log a and log b, we obtain the values of a and b. On substituting the values of a and b in the equation of the exponential curve, the trend equation of the curve is obtained.

Q. 29. *Write a short note on compertz curve with its relevance in time series analysis.*

Ans. The curve is useful in actuarial studies and sometimes in business forecasting and population projections. The equation of the compertz curve is,

$$Y = ab^{c^X}$$

Taking logarithm of the equation, it is transformed to,

$$\log Y = \log a + c^X \log b$$

The equation can be fitted by Cowden's method with a little modification.

Q. 30. *How can a best model for a time series be selected?*

Ans. For a time series, many linear or curvilinear models may appear to be suitable. Now the question arises which one should be taken as best fitted model. The easiest way to adjudge is to compute the quantity $Q = \sum_i (y_i - \hat{y}_i)^2$ for each model, where y_i the actual value in the time series and y_i is its estimated value. As a matter of fact, the quantity Q is residual sum of squares. The model yielding the minimum value of Q is the best and should be selected.

Q. 31. *What methods are generally used for measuring the seasonal variation?*

Ans. To isolate seasonal variation, one must eliminate trend, cyclic and irregular variations from the time series data and he is left with seasonal variation, *i.e.*, $S = Y/T \times C \times I$ *or* $S = Y - T - C - I$. Various methods of measuring seasonal variations are based on this very idea. Different methods are:

(*i*) Simple average method

(*ii*) Ratio to trend method

(*iii*) Ratio to moving average method

(*iv*) Link relative method.

Q. 32. *Discuss the simple average method for measuring seasonal variation.*

Ans. The simple average method of measuring seasonal variation is suitable when trend and cycles are not present, if any, have negligible effect on the time series.

We all know that a season is a part of the year, may the seasons be half-yearly, quarterly, monthly, weekly, etc. To calculate seasonal indices, first find out the average of each period (season) and then the average of the averages (grand average). The seasonal index for any period (season) in case of multiplicative model is calculated by the formula,

$$\frac{\text{Average of a season (period)}}{\text{Grand average}}$$

Calculate seasonal index for all the periods (seasons). If $\bar{X}_1, \bar{X}_2, ..., \bar{X}_k$ are the seasonal averages based on the periodic data for all years and $\bar{X}$ is the grand average, then the seasonal indices for multiplicative model are, $\frac{\bar{X}_1}{\bar{X}} \times 100, \frac{\bar{X}_2}{\bar{X}} \times 100, ..., \frac{\bar{X}_k}{\bar{X}} \times 100.$

Also for additive model they are, $(\bar{X}_1 - \bar{X}), (\bar{X}_2 - \bar{X}), ..., (\bar{X}_k - \bar{X})$.

As a check to the calculations, one should ensure that the sum of the seasonal indices in multiplicative model is 100 × *k*. If *k* is the number for quarterly data, it is 400. Also for additive model, the sum of the seasonal indices in zero. If it is suspected that the trend is present, the seasonal indices are to be adjusted for trend through regression approach.

Q. 33. *Give the merits and demerits of the simple average method.*

Ans.

Merits:

(*i*) It is the easiest method to compute seasonal indices.

(*ii*) It gives good results if trend and cyclic variation have negligible or no effect on the time series. Which is rarely true. Hence, this method is seldom used.

Demerits:

(*i*) It is not appropriate as it does not remove the cyclic and irregular variations.

(*ii*) Simple average method becomes quite cumbrous if the seasonal indices so obtained are to be adjusted for trend.

Q. 34. *Delineate the procedure of computing seasonal indices by ratio to trend method.*

Ans. This method provides seasonal indices free from trend as it assumes that seasonal variation for a given period is a constant fraction of trend. Different steps in ratio to trend method are:

Step-1. Estimate the trend values for each period (quarter or month) by establishing a trend line (or parabola) by the method of least squares.

Step-2. Divide each originally given seasonal (quarterly or monthly) value by the corresponding trend value and multiply it by 100 to convert it into percentage. The indices so obtained are free from trend.

Step-3. Now to obtain the seasonal indices free from cyclic or irregular variations, we proceed in this manner. Find the median (mean) of ratio to trend values for each season for any number of years. The median is preferred over mean if there are some extreme values. In this way irregular variations are removed. These median (mean) values represent seasonal indices. Mean removes the random effects. Mean removes the random effects better than median. Hence, one should choose median or mean after a careful examination of the data.

Step-4. If the seasons are quarters, the sum of seasonal indices in case of multiplicative model should be 400, and if months, it should be 1,200. But often the sum is not exactly what it should be. Hence, the seasonal indices are adjusted by multiplying each of them by (400/sum of seasonal indices) or (1200/sum of seasonal indices) as the case may be.

Q. 35. *Give plus points and limitations of ratio to trend method.*

Ans.

Plus points:

(*i*) The method is based on sound and logical footings.

(*ii*) It utilises the complete information.

(*iii*) If periods are of short duration, it gives very good results.

(*iv*) It is easy to compute and understand.

Limitations:

(*i*) If there are pronounced cyclical swings in the time series data, a linear or curvilinear trend does not give good trend values. In such a situation ratio to moving average method performs better than ratio to trend method.

Q. 36. *How can the ratio to moving average method be applied for computing the seasonal indices?*

Ans. The ratio to moving average method is also known as *percentage to moving average method.* This method is the most popular and best on the ground that on taking the 12-month moving average in a monthly data or 4-quarter moving average in a quarterly data, the trend and cyclic variations are removed by dividing the actual data by the moving average entered against it. These ratio are generally given in percentages. So these percentages contain only the seasonal and irregular variations. These percentages (ratios) are averaged for each period (month or quarter) over the years. This removes the influence of irregular variations from the data. The isolated average values so obtained measure the seasonal variation.

Different steps involved in calculating seasonal indices are:

Step-1. Find 12-month (4-quarter) moving average and enter it against the central position of the 12-month (4-quarter) data. This will remove the influences of seasonal and irregular variations, *i.e.*, these moving average will be containing trend and cyclic variations ($T \times C$).

Step-2. Express the original data for each month or quarter as the percentage ratio of the moving average entered against it, *i.e.*, (Y/moving average) × 100 which is equivalent to $(T \times S \times C \times I)/T.C = S \times I$.

Step-3. Find the median or average for each period (month or quarter) over the years to eliminate irregular variations. These average or median values for periods represent the seasonal indices.

Step-4. These indices must average to hundred. If not so, the seasonal indices are adjusted to eliminate the discrepancy. The adjustment factor is 1200/(Total of 12-month indices) for monthly data or 400/(Total of 4-quarter indices) for quarterly data.

Q. 37. *What are specific seasonal index and typical seasonal index.*

Ans. The seasonal indices for each month or quarter of different years are called specific seasonals and the averages of specific seasonals for months or quarters for a number of years are known as typical seasonals.

Q. 38. *Discuss good and bad points of the ratio to moving average method.*

Ans.

Good points:

(*i*) Ratio to moving average method is based on most logical approach and yields most satisfactory results.

(*ii*) This method is superior to ratio to trend method.

(*iii*) This method has more flexibility.

Bad point: The only drawback of this method is that seasonal indices for half of the beginning periods of the first year and half of the periods of the last year are not calculable.

Q. 39. *Elucidate the link-relative method of measuring seasonal indices of a time series.*

Ans. The link-relative method was propounded by Karl Pearson and hence this is also called as *Karl Pearson's method.* This method involves most complicated calculations. That is why this is least used. Anyway, various steps for measuring seasonal indices by link relative method are given below:

Step-1. For each monthly or quarterly figure, calculate link relatives by the following formula:

$$\text{Link relative} = \frac{\text{Current season's figure}}{\text{Preceding season's figure}} \times 100$$

Obviously, there will be no link relative for the first season's figure. Also in the calculation of the link relative, preceding monthly or quarterly figure is taken as base. Calculation of link relatives eliminates the influence of the trend.

Step-2. Find the mean or median for each season (month or quarter) whichever is considered appropriate. Generally median is calculated as it eliminates the influence of irregular variations.

Step-3. Convert the link relatives into chain relatives. Take chain relative for first season (quarter or month) as 100. Abbreviating link relative as L.R. and chain relative as C.R., the formula for chain relative can be given as,

C.R. for I period = 100

C.R. for i^{th} period

$$= \frac{\text{L.R. for } i^{th} \text{ period} \times \text{C.R. for } (i-1)^{th} \text{ period}}{100}$$

where i varies overall periods (month or quarters).

Step-4. The chain relative for the first season (I month or I quarter) is calculated on the basis of the last season by the formula,

C.R for I period =

$$\frac{\text{Median for } I \text{ period} \times \text{C.R. for the last period}}{100}$$

The chain relative for I period from the above formula will have a different value as it would have been by the previous formula. Hence it needs some adjustment. The adjustment factor c is worked out by the formula,

$$c = \frac{100 - \text{C.R. for } I \text{ period}}{\text{Number of periods}}$$

For monthly data, no. of periods = 12 and for quarterly data, no. of periods = 4. The corrections for chain relatives for $I, II, III, \ldots$, periods are $0 \times c$, $1 \times c$, $2 \times c$, ..., etc. The quantities are added to $I, II, III, \ldots$, periods chain relatives, respectively. In this way, we obtain the adjusted chain relatives. Find the average of the adjusted chain relatives by the formula,

$$\text{Av. of adjusted C.R.} = \frac{\text{Sum of adj. C.R.}}{\text{no. of periods}}$$

Seasonal index by the link-relative method is,

$$\text{Seasonal index} = \frac{\text{Adjusted C.R.}}{\text{Average of Adj. C.R's}} \times 100$$

Please check that the sum of the seasonal indices is equal to 100 × no. of seasons.

Q. 40. *What are the methods of measuring cyclic variations?*

Ans. Six methods of measuring cyclic variations are as follows:

(*i*) Residual method

(*ii*) First difference method

(*iii*) Percentage ratio method

(*iv*) Direct method

(*v*) Reference cycle analysis method

(*vi*) Harmonic analysis method.

Q. 41. *How can one isolate cyclic variations by residual method?*

Ans. The name of the method is itself indicative of the procedure. First we remove seasonal variation from the data and then trend. In this way the values obtained contain only cyclic and irregular variations. As a matter of fact, the two variations are almost inseparable. In this way, the cyclic and irregular variations are obtained as the residuals of the observed values in terms of percentages. So the name follows. Symbolically,

For an additive model,

$$Y = T + S + C + I$$

$$Y - T - S = C + I$$

and for a multiplicative model,

$$\frac{Y}{S \times T} = C \times I$$

This method yields good results only if the trend and seasonal are perfectly measurable. The irregular fluctuations can be identified by an examination of the periods and corresponding observed values. If irregular fluctuations are present, they may be removed logically or applying the moving average method on $C \times I$ values.

Q. 42. *How can the first difference method be applied to identify and measure cyclic variations?*

Ans. The first difference method is applicable only when the yearly data are given. We know that yearly data are devoid of seasonality. Hence one needs to remove secular trend from the given time series data to obtain cycles.

In this method the differences of a year from its preceding year are calculated with signs. These differences are available for second year and onwards. The differences are plotted on the graph paper taking years on abscissa and differences along ordinate.

Joining the points we get the cycles present in the time series. The graph provides a clear picture of cycles through troughs and crests.

Q. 43. *Discuss the percentage ratio method for measurement of cyclic variations.*

Ans. This method is applicable for yearly data only. In this method, divide each year's observed value by its preceding year value and multiply it by hundred to get the values in percentages. Plot these values on the graph paper against their corresponding years. The convex and concave portions of the graph give clear picture of the cycles.

This method is equivalent to the first difference method in the sense that here we find relative changes in values, whereas in the first difference method we work out actual changes. Both the methods leads to almost the same results. In both the methods, one misses the value for the first year of the time series.

Q. 44. *How do you identify cycles in a time series by direct method?*

Ans. This method is founded on calculating the per cent variation each month or quarter with respect to preceding year's same month or quarter. These percentages show upward changes in case of rising cycles and downward changes in case of declining cycles. Some businessmen adopt this techniques because of its simplicity.

Q. 45. *Discuss in brief the reference cycle analysis method for the measurement of cyclic variations.*

Ans. The reference cycle analysis method for identifying cycles had been developed by National Bureau of Economic Research, USA and used for more than 1000 time series analysis. This method is appropriate for analysing past series only.

Under this method, the index of variation in each series is computed with regard to a given reference date, whereas the reference dates are the dates of the peaks and troughs of business cycles. Obviously, if the reference date is a peak year, the economic series will show a downward falling index till the cycle takes a turn and *vice-versa*.

Q. 46. *Give advantages and disadvantages of the reference cycle analysis method.*

Ans.

Advantages:

(*i*) The main advantage of this method is that it facilitates a comparative assessment of the changes in various economic time series.

(*ii*) It is also possible through this analysis to find out which series has a lead or lag in the process of upward or downward swing, as the case may be. This method is frequently used in business forecasting.

(*iii*) Though the method appears to be cumbersome, it has proved to be simple and effective for comparing the cyclic variations of the individual series with those of general business.

(*iv*) This method is devoid of the errors which could have been introduced, in case the trend is not properly estimated.

Disadvantages: The foremost shortcoming of this method is that it cannot be applied to the current time series because no cycles can be studied in this way until it is completed.

Note: The above discussion gives only the approach of the method. The details are kept out.

Q. 47. *Express succinctly the harmonic analysis method of determining the cyclic component of a time series.*

Ans. The harmonic analysis method is a sophisticated mathematical device of determining cyclic component of a time series. This method is based on expressing any function Y_t in the form of a Fourier series, a series of sums of sines and cosines of the angles $2\pi/\lambda$ where λ is the period of oscillations. λ can better be determined by periodogram analysis.

Note: The mathematical details of the method are omitted.

Q. 48. *How can the irregular influences be measured?*

Ans. The name, irregular influences implies that there is nothing definite about their occurrence and amplitude. Hence, no mathematical methods have been evolved to isolate and measure them. The only way in the residual method, *i.e.*, to eliminate trend, seasonality and cyclic variation, if any, from the series and thus, the residual fluctuations in the series are regarded as the irregular variations.

As a matter of fact, cycles themselves are quite erratic in nature and are almost inextricably mixed with irregular variations and hence the two are measured together. Mathematically,

$$I = \frac{Y}{T \times S \times C}$$

and for an additive model,

$$I = Y - T - S - C$$

Q. 49. *Define an autoregressive series.*

Ans. If the value of a series at any time t is itself a linear function of its own values at times $t - 1$, $t - 2$, ..., $t - k$, it is known as autoregressive series. Mathematically an autoregressive series is represented by the recurrence relation,

$$Y_t = a_1 Y_{t-1} + a_2 Y_{t-2} + ... + a_k Y_{t-k} + \varepsilon_t$$

where ε_t are known as disturbance terms such that ε_t are identically and independently distributed as normal variates having the mean 0 and variance σ^2. Such a series is called an autoregressive series.

SECTION B

Fill in the Blanks

Fill in the suitable word(s) or phrase(s) in the blanks:

1. A time series is a set of values arranged in _________ order.
2. The definition, "A time series consists of statistical data which are collected, recorded or observed over successive increments was given by _________.
3. The definition, "A time series is a sequence of values of some variate corresponding to successive points of time" was given by _________.
4. A time series helps to know the _________ of the past business phenomenon.
5. Time series helps to _________ the ups and down of a business phenomenon.
6. Two or more time series can be compared by _________ analysis.
7. The conclusions drawn from time series analysis are _________ true.
8. Time series analysis is not capable to adjust all shorts of _________ affecting the series.
9. A time series consists of at the most _________ components.
10. The component representing the long-term fluctuations of a time series is called _________.
11. Adjustment of data before analysis is called _________ of data.
12. The adjustment for the number of days of a month is known as _________ adjustment.
13. Production or sales of a commodity expressed in terms of its value need adjustment for _________.
14. The data with regard to the demand or consumption are to be adjusted for increasing or decreasing _________.
15. Monthly fluctuation observed in a time series data are termed as _________ variation.
16. Quarterly fluctuations observed in a time series represent _________ variation.
17. Periodic changes in a business time series are called _________.
18. Monthly data are made comparable by multiply each monthly value by _________.
19. Monthly data in a leap year are adjusted by multiplying each monthly value by _________.

20. A complete cycle consists of a period of _________ and _________.

21. A complete cycle passes through _________ stages of business phenomenon.

22. Likes and dislikes, social customs and new scientific changes affect the _________.

23. The abrupt changes observed in a time series data are attributed to _________ variations.

24. There are _________ types of mathematical models given for a time series.

25. The multiplicative model of a time series is given as _________.

26. The additive model of a time series is expressed as _________.

27. Most frequently used mathematical model of a time series is _________ model.

28. Mixed model of a time series is _________ used.

29. Sometimes used mathematical model for a time series is _________ model.

30. The method of ascertaining secular-trend which involves no calculations is _________ method.

31. The method which determines secular trend with the help of two points only is known as _________ method.

32. The semi-average method does not ensure elimination of _________ and _________ variations.

33. The moving-average method eliminates _________.

34. The trend obtained by moving average method is not necessarily a _________.

35. The moving-average method suffers with the lacuna that some _________.

36. The moving-average method is not appropriate for _________.

37. Number of periods included in a group for moving averages depends on _________ in a time series data.

38. The moving-average method is not fully _________.

39. Least square method of fitting a trend line is same as fitting of a _________ line.

40. Least square method of fitting a trend is _________.

41. Least square trend line provides most accurate _________ value.

42. The trend by least square method may be _________ or _________.

43. Parabolic trend is a _________.

44. Exponential trend is also known as _________.

45. The mathematical equation of the exponential curve is _________.

46. Mathematical equation of the compertz curve is _________.

47. The simple average method of measuring seasonal variation is suitable only when _________ and _________ have negligible effect.

48. The sum of the seasonal indices in a multiplicative model is _________.

49. For additive model, the sum of the seasonal indices is _________.

50. The simple average method does not remove the effects of _________ and _________ variations.

51. Seasonal index by the simple average method is the ratio of _________ to _________.

52. Irregular variations from trend free seasonal indices are removed by taking the _________ or _________ of the seasons.

53. In case of pronounced cyclical swings, ratio to trend is _________ than ratio to the moving-average method.

54. Ratio to trend method yields good results if the periods are of _________.

55. Ratio to the moving-average method is considered to be the _________ for ascertaining seasonal indices.

56. Moving averages remove _________ and _________ variations.

57. Moving averages contain only _________ and _________ variations.

58. Dividing the original data for a season by the corresponding moving average, one is left with _________ variations only.

59. Indices for irregular variations are adjusted by finding out their _________ or _________.

60. Ratio to the moving-average method has more _________ than any other method.

61. Link relative method for measuring seasonal indices was expounded by _________.

62. Link relative means the ratio of a value to its _________ value.

63. Link relatives for calculating seasonal indices are converted into _________.

64. Cyclic variations are interwoven with _________ variations.

65. Residual method of measuring cyclic variations means removal of _________ and _________ from the series.

66. Yearly data is devoid of _________.

67. The first difference method for cyclic indices involves the calculation of difference of a yearly value from its _________ year value.

68. The percentage-ratio method for measuring cyclic variations measures _________.

69. Direct method for isolating cycles measures relative change of each month to its preceding year's _________ value.

70. The reference cycle analysis method for identifying cycles was invented by _________.

71. The reference cycle analysis method for determining cycles cannot be applied to _________.

72. The reference cycle analysis method is mostly used for business _________.

73. The harmonic analysis method of determining cycles utilises _________.

74. The only way of isolating irregular variations is to remove _________ from the time series.

75. An autoregressive series is a _________ of values of a time series at time t with values at previous time intervals.

76. First difference method for isolating cyclic variations is applicable on _________ only.

77. Deseasonalisation data means eliminating _________ from the series.

78. A monthly or quarterly trend equation can be converted into _________ trend equation.

79. An overall tendency of rise and fall in a time series represents _________.

80. Cyclic movement in a time series occur due to _________.

81. Short-term fluctuations in a time series are represented by _________ components.

82. A polynomial representing a trend equation of the type $Y = a + bX + cX^2$ is called a _________.

83. In a trend line $Y = a + bX$, the constant b represents the _________.

84. Value of b in $Y = a + bX$ remains same with the change of _________.

85. The trend line obtained by the method of least squares is known as the _________.

86. Ratio to trend method is used to estimate _________ in a time series.

87. Lockups and strike in a factory affecting the production represent _________ component of a time series.

88. Increase in population in India represents the _________ component of a time series.

89. The harmonic analysis method is meant for ascertaining _________.

90. Given the trend equation $\hat{Y} = 108 + 2.88\,X$, with origin 1980 and yearly data given from 1980 to 1992, the monthly trend equation is _________.

91. Given the trend equation $\hat{Y} = 108 + 2.88\,X$ with 1980 as origin and yearly data from 1980 to 1992, the estimated value for 1985 is _________.

92. Given the exponential curve $Y = 31.5\ (1.5)^X$, the equation of the curve by shifting the origin backward by two years is ________.

93. Given the trend equation $\hat{Y} = 122.5 + 7.2\ X$ with 1985 as origin and yearly data, the trend equation after shifting the origin to 1980 is ________ and to 1988 is ________.

94. Given the monthly trend equation $\hat{Y} = 9.4 + 2.4X$ with January as origin, the annual trend equation is ________.

95. If the actual sales of an item for the month of October 1990 is ₹ 785 and the seasonal index for October is 128.4, the estimated sales for October 1990 is ________ and based on this information, the estimate of the annual sales is ________.

96. Given the parabolic trend equation as $Y = 25 + 10X + 3X^2$ based on year to year data and 1980 as origin, the equation of the parabola with 1984 as origin will be ________.

97. Given the trend equation $\hat{Y} = 96 + 4X$ with origin 1987 and X unit = 1 year, the trend equation after shifting the origin to 1985 is ________ and to 1st Jan. 1990 is ________.

98. If the annual trend equation with 1984 as origin is $\hat{Y} = 112.8 + 6.48X$, the monthly trend equation is ________.

99. Given the equation $\hat{Y} = 54 + 3.6X$ with 1981 as origin and $X = \frac{1}{2}$ year and Y units in terms of annual production, the monthly trend equation is ________.

100. All seasonal variations are periodic but all periodic variations are not ________.

101. The monthwise seasonal indices of different years are called ________.

102. Cyclical fluctuations helps the business executives in framing ________ and establishing ________.

103. Appropriateness of various models can be decided by comparing ________.

104. The names in which the periodic movements can be classified are ________ and ________ fluctuations.

105. The averages of specific seasonals for a number of years are known as ________.

SECTION C

Multiple Choice Questions

Select the correct alternative out of given ones:

1. A time series is a set of data recorded:

(*a*) periodically

(*b*) at time or space intervals

(*c*) at successive points of time

(*d*) all of the above

2. The time series analysis helps:

(*a*) to compare the two or more series

(*b*) to know the behaviour of business

(*c*) to make predictions

(*d*) all of the above

3. A time series is unable to adjust the influences like:

(*a*) customs and policy changes

(*b*) seasonal changes

(*c*) long-term influences

(*d*) none of the above

4. A time series consists of:

(*a*) two components

(*b*) three components

(*c*) four components

(*d*) five components

5. The forecasts on the basis of a time series are:

(*a*) cent per cent true

(*b*) true to a great extent

(*c*) never true

(*d*) none of the above

6. The component of a time series attached to long-term variations is terms as:
(*a*) cyclic variation
(*b*) secular trend
(*c*) irregular variation
(*d*) all of the above

7. The component of a time series which is attached to short-term fluctuations is:
(*a*) seasonal variation
(*b*) cyclic variation
(*c*) irregular variation
(*d*) all of the above

8. A lock-out in a factory for a month is associated with the component of a time series:
(*a*) irregular movement
(*b*) secular trend
(*c*) cyclic variation
(*d*) none of the above

9. The general decline in sales of cotton clothes is attached to the component of the time series:
(*a*) secular trend
(*b*) cyclical variation
(*c*) seasonal variation
(*d*) all of the above

10. The sales of a departmental store on Dushera and Diwali are associated with the component of a time series:
(*a*) secular trend
(*b*) seasonal variation
(*c*) irregular variation
(*d*) all of the above

11. The consistent increase in production of cereals constitutes the component of a time series:
(*a*) secular trend
(*b*) seasonal variation
(*c*) cyclical variation
(*d*) all of the above

12. Secular trend is indicative of long-term variation towards:
(*a*) increase only
(*b*) decrease only
(*c*) either increase or decrease
(*d*) none of the above

13. Linear trend of a time series indicates towards:
(*a*) constant rate of change
(*b*) constant rate of growth
(*c*) change in geometric progression
(*d*) all of the above

14. Method of least squares to fit in the trend is applicable only if the trend is:
(*a*) linear
(*b*) parabolic
(*c*) both (*a*) and (*b*)
(*d*) neither (*a*) nor (*b*)

15. Seasonal variation means the variations occurring within:
(*a*) a number of years
(*b*) parts of a year
(*c*) parts of a month
(*d*) none of the above

16. Salient factors responsible for seasonal variation are:
(*a*) weather
(*b*) social customs
(*c*) festivals
(*d*) all of the above

17. Cyclic variations in a time series are caused by:
(*a*) lockouts in a factory
(*b*) war in a country
(*c*) floods in the states
(*d*) none of the above

18. Irregular variations in a time series are caused by:
(*a*) lockouts and strikes
(*b*) epidemics
(*c*) floods
(*d*) all of the above

19. Trend in a time series means:
(*a*) long-term regular movement
(*b*) short-term regular movement
(*c*) both (*a*) and (*b*)
(*d*) neither (*a*) nor (*b*)

20. The terms prosperity, recession, depression

and recovery are in particular attached to:

(*a*) secular trend
(*b*) seasonal fluctuations
(*c*) cyclic movements
(*d*) irregular variations

21. A linear trend shows the business movement of a time series towards:

(*a*) growth
(*b*) decline
(*c*) stagnation
(*d*) all of the above

22. Cycles in a time series are regular in:

(*a*) periodicity
(*b*) amplitude
(*c*) both (*a*) and (*b*)
(*d*) neither (*a*) nor (*b*)

23. The factors responsible for the occurrence of business cycles are:

(*a*) likes and dislikes of people
(*b*) social customs
(*c*) scientific and technological developments
(*d*) all of the above

24. An additive model of time series with the components T, S, C and I is:

(*a*) $Y = T + S + C \times I$
(*b*) $Y = T + S \times C \times I$
(*c*) $Y = T + S + C + I$
(*d*) $Y = T + S \times C + I$

25. A multiplicative model of a time series with components T, S, C and I is:

(*a*) $Y = T \times S \times C \times I$
(*b*) $T = Y/(S \times C \times I)$
(*c*) $C \times I = Y/(S \times T)$
(*d*) all of the above

26. A mixed model of a time series with components T, S, C and I is:

(*a*) $I = Y/S \times C \times T$
(*b*) $Y = T + S \times C + I$
(*c*) $Y = T + S + C + I$
(*d*) none of the above

27. Most frequently used mathematical model of a time series is:

(*a*) additive model
(*b*) multiplicative model
(*c*) mixed model
(*d*) all of the above

28. A method full of subjectivity to find out the trend line is:

(*a*) semi-average method
(*b*) moving average method
(*c*) free-hand method
(*d*) all of the above

29. Semi-average method of finding trend is appropriate if the data are available for a:

(*a*) long period
(*b*) short period
(*c*) long and short period both
(*d*) none of the above

30. A group for moving average consists of:

(*a*) 5-years period
(*b*) 3-years period
(*c*) a period which forms a cycle
(*d*) none of the above

31. Moving average method of fitting trend in a time series data removes the effect of:

(*a*) long-term movements
(*b*) short-term movements
(*c*) cyclic variations
(*d*) none of the above

32. Moving average method of ascertaining trend is not suitable for:

(*a*) finding trend values
(*b*) projections
(*c*) both (*a*) and (*b*)
(*d*) neither (*a*) nor (*b*)

33. Moving average method suffers from:

(*a*) the loss of information
(*b*) the element of subjectivity
(*c*) the decision about the number of years in groups
(*d*) all of the above

34. Least square method of fitting a trend is:

(*a*) most exact
(*b*) least exact
(*c*) full of subjectivity
(*d*) mathematically unsound

35. Least square estimates of parameter of a trend line:

(*a*) have minimum variance

(*b*) are unbiased

(*c*) can exactly be obtained

(*d*) all of the above

36. If the origin in a trend equation is shifted forward by three years, X in the equation $Y = a + bX$ will be replaced by:

(*a*) $X - 3$

(*b*) $X + 3$

(*c*) $3X$

(*d*) none of the above

37. If the origin in the trend equation $Y = a + bX$ is shifted backward by two years, the variable X in the trend equation will be replaced by:

(*a*) $(X - 2)$

(*b*) $(X + 2)$

(*c*) $X/2$

(*d*) none of the above

38. If the trend line with 1975 as origin is $Y = 20.6 + 1.68X$, the trend line with 1971 as origin is:

(*a*) $Y = 20.6 + 6.72X$

(*b*) $Y = 13.88 + 1.68X$

(*c*) $Y = 34.61 + 1.68X$

(*d*) none of the above

39. Given the trend equation $Y = 118.5 + 2.2X + 1.4X^2$ with origin 1980, the trend equation with origin 1981 is:

(*a*) $Y = 117.7 - 0.6X + 1.4X^2$

(*b*) no change in the equation

(*c*) $Y = 122.1 + 5X + 1.4X^2$

(*d*) none of the above

40. Given the annual trend with 1981 as origin and X unit = one year and Y = annual demand as

$Y = 148.8 + 7.2X$,

the monthly trend equation is:

(*a*) $Y = 12.4 + 0.05X$

(*b*) $Y = 12.4 + 0.6X$

(*c*) $Y = 148.8 + 0.6X$

(*d*) none of the above

41. For the equation given in Q. No. 40, the quarterly trend is:

(*a*) $Y = 12.4 + 1.8X$

(*b*) $Y = 37.2 + 0.15X$

(*c*) $Y = 37.2 + 0.2X$

(*d*) $Y = 12.4 + 0.2X$

42. The equation $Y = \alpha\beta^X$ represents:

(*a*) compertz curve

(*b*) exponential curve

(*c*) logarithmic curve

(*d*) none of the above

43. The equation, $Y = a + bX + cX^2 + dX^3$ represents:

(*a*) hyperbola

(*b*) cardiod

(*c*) cubic parabola

(*d*) none of the above

44. The equation, $Y = \alpha\beta^{\gamma^X}$ stands for:

(*a*) compertz curve

(*b*) exponential curve

(*c*) both (*a*) and (*b*)

(*d*) neither (*a*) nor (*b*)

45. Simple average method is used to calculate:

(*a*) trend values

(*b*) cyclic variations

(*c*) seasonal indices

(*d*) none of the above

46. In case of multiplicative model, the sum of seasonal indices is:

(*a*) 100 times the number of seasons

(*b*) zero

(*c*) 100

(*d*) any of the above

47. Simple average method for finding out seasonal indices is good when:

(*a*) the time series is free from trend

(*b*) the time series has no cyclic effect

(*c*) the time series has no trend and cyclic variations

(*d*) the series has all the components of the time series present

48. Simple average method for seasonal indices of a time series is applicable in case of:

(*a*) multiplicative model only
(*b*) additive model only
(*c*) multiplicative as well as additive model
(*d*) none of the above

49. In ratio to trend method for seasonal indices, the indices become free from trend component of the time series by:
(*a*) subtracting the trend value for each corresponding value
(*b*) taking the ratio of each seasonal value to the corresponding trend value
(*c*) taking the ratio of each trend value to the corresponding seasonal value
(*d*) none of the above

50. In ratio to trend method the median of the trend free indices for each period represents:
(*a*) the seasonal indices
(*b*) cyclic variation
(*c*) irregular variation
(*d*) none of the above

51. Ratio to trend method for seasonal indices provides good results if:
(*a*) the periods are of long duration
(*b*) the periods are given six monthly
(*c*) the periods are of short duration
(*d*) all the above situations

52. The best method for finding out seasonal variation is:
(*a*) simple average method
(*b*) ratio to moving average method
(*c*) ratio to trend method
(*d*) none of the above

53. In ratio to moving average method for seasonal indices, the ratio of an observed value to the moving average remove the influence of:
(*a*) trend
(*b*) cyclic variation
(*c*) trend and cyclic variation both
(*d*) none of the above

54. The moving averages in a time series are free from the influences of:
(*a*) seasonal and cyclic variations
(*b*) seasonal and irregular variations
(*c*) trend and cyclical variations
(*d*) trend and random variations

55. Link relatives in a time series remove the influence of:
(*a*) the trend
(*b*) cyclic variation
(*c*) irregular variations
(*d*) all of the above

56. Cyclic variations are interwoven with:
(*a*) trend
(*b*) seasonal variations
(*c*) irregular variations
(*d*) all of the above

57. Residual method for measuring cycles in a time series consists of:
(*a*) removing the trend from the series
(*b*) removing the seasonal variation from the series
(*c*) removing the influences of trend, seasonal and irregular variations
(*d*) none of the above

58. First difference method for isolating cycles is applicable if observations pertain to:
(*a*) yearly data
(*b*) quarterly data
(*c*) monthly data
(*d*) any data

59. Graphically cycles of a time series are identifiable through:
(*a*) troughs and crests
(*b*) concave and convex portions
(*c*) cups and crests
(*d*) all of the above

60. In percentage ratio method of measuring cyclic variations one finds:
(*a*) actual changes
(*b*) relative changes
(*c*) per cent ratio changes
(*d*) all of the above

61. Reference cycle analysis method of measuring cyclic variations was developed by:
(*a*) Delhi school of economics
(*b*) National Bureau of Economic Research, U.S.A

(c) Indian Council of Economic Research
(d) none of the above

62. Reference cycle analysis method of measuring cyclic variations is useful in:
(a) business forecasting
(b) comparing cyclic variations with those of general business
(c) making the comparative assessment of the changes in various economic time series
(d) all of the above

63. Reference cycle analysis method of measuring cycles is applicable to:
(a) current time series
(b) past time series
(c) both (a) and (b)
(d) neither (a) nor (b)

64. Harmonic analysis method is based on the function y_t expressed in the form of:
(a) Taylor's function
(b) Harmonic series
(c) Fourier series
(d) none of the above

65. The left over variation in a time series, after eliminating the influences of trend, seasonal and cyclic variations, is assigned to:
(a) irregular variation
(b) random variation
(c) residual variation
(d) all of the above

66. If the value of a series at any time t is a function of its values at some previous time intervals, such a time series is known as:
(a) autoregressive series
(b) Fourier series
(c) Harmonic series
(d) none of the above

67. Value of b in the trend line $Y = a + bX$ is:
(a) always positive
(b) always negative
(c) both positive or negative
(d) none of the above

68. A time series consists of:
(a) long-term changes
(b) short-term variations
(c) irregular variations
(d) all of the above

69. A time series is affected by:
(a) economic factors
(b) non-economic factors
(c) both (a) and (b)
(d) neither (a) nor (b)

70. A cycle in a time series is represented by the difference between:
(a) two successive peaks
(b) the end points of a convex portion
(c) the mid-points of a trough and the crest
(d) none of the above

71. Cyclic changes are affected by:
(a) climate
(b) self-generating unspecified factors
(c) festivals
(d) all of the above

72. For the given five values 15, 24, 18, 33, 42, the three years moving averages are:
(a) 19, 22, 33
(b) 19, 25, 31
(c) 19, 30, 31
(d) none of the above

73. Irregular variations are:
(a) regular
(b) cyclic
(c) episodic
(d) all of the above

74. Trend cannot be:
(a) linear
(b) non-linear
(c) S-shaped in a short duration
(d) none of the above

75. A trend is linear iff:
(a) growth or decay rate is constant
(b) growth or decay follow geometric law
(c) change is constant in the beginning but stops after some time
(d) none of the above

76. Method of least squares for determining trend is used when
(a) trend is known

(*b*) trend is curvilinear only
(*c*) the value Y is not a function of time t
(*d*) none of the above

77. To which component of the time series, the term recession is attached?
(*a*) Trend
(*b*) Seasonals
(*c*) Cycles
(*d*) Random variation

78. If the slope of the trend line is positive, it shows:
(*a*) rising trend
(*b*) declining trend
(*c*) stagnation
(*d*) any of the above

79. The equation of the parabolic trend is,

$$Y = 46.6 + 2.4X - 1.3X^2$$

If the origin is shifted backward by three years the equation of the parabolic trend will be:
(*a*) $Y = 27.7 - 5.4X - 1.3X^2$
(*b*) $Y = 51.1 - 5.4X - 1.3X^2$
(*c*) $Y = 27.7 + 10.2X - 1.3X^2$
(*d*) none of the above

80. If the equation of exponential trend with 1989 as origin is

$$Y = 15\ (1.8)^X,$$

the equation of the exponential trend with 1991 as origin will be:
(*a*) $Y = 15\ (1.8)^{X^2}$
(*b*) $Y = 48.6\ (1.8)^X$
(*c*) $Y = 4.62\ (1.8)^X$
(*d*) $Y = 15/(1.8)^X$

81. Out of a number of models fitted to a time series data, the best model can be adjudged by:
(*a*) the estimates of the parameters
(*b*) the value of residual sum of squares
(*c*) the shape of the curves
(*d*) all the curves

82. The seasonal indices for each month or quarter of different years are called:
(*a*) chain relatives
(*b*) link relatives
(*c*) typical seasonals
(*d*) specific seasonals

83. Time series analysis helps to:
(*a*) understand the behaviour of a variable in the past
(*b*) predict the future behaviour of a variable
(*c*) plan future operations
(*d*) all of the above

84. The averages of the specific seasonals for months or quarters for a number of years of a time series are known as:
(*a*) erratic fluctuations
(*b*) mean seasonals
(*c*) typical seasonals
(*d*) all of the above

85. In spite of merits of least square method for trend, the limitation is that:
(*a*) predictions based on trend ignore other components of time series
(*b*) this method is not applicable for a number of growth curves which follow business trends
(*c*) both (*a*) and (*b*)
(*d*) neither (*a*) nor (*b*)

ANSWERS

Section B

1. Chronological **2.** Patterson **3.** Werner Z. Hirsch **4.** real behaviour **5.** predict **6.** time series **7.** not absolutely **8.** influences **9.** four **10.** secular trend **11.** editing **12.** calendar **13.** prices **14.** population **15.** seasonal **16.** seasonal **17.** cycles **18.** 30.417/No. of days in the month **19.** 30.5/No. of days in the month **20.** prosperity; recession **21.** four **22.** cycles **23.** irregular **24.** three **25.** $Y = T \times S \times C \times I$ **26.** $Y = T + S + C + I$ **27.** multiplicative **28.** hardly **29.** additive **30.** free-hand **31.** semi-average

32. seasonal; cyclic 33. short-term fluctuations 34. straight line 35. information is lost 36. projections 37. cycles 38. mathematical 39. regression 40. most exact 41. interpolated 42. linear; curvilinear 43. n^{th} degree polynomial 44. geometric trend 45. $Y = ab^X$ 46. $Y = ab^{c^X}$ 47. trend; cycles 48. 100 × No. of seasons 49. zero 50. cyclic; irregular 51. periodic average; grand average 52. mean; median 53. inferior 54. short duration 55. best 56. seasonal; irregular 57. trend; cyclic 58. seasonal × irregular 59. median; mean 60. flexibility 61. Karl Pearson 62. preceding 63. chain relatives 64. irregular 65. trend; seasonals 66. seasonality 67. preceding 68. relative changes 69. same month 70. National Bureau of Economics Research, U.S.A 71. current time series 72. forecasting 73. Fourier series 74. T, S and C 75. linear function 76. yearly data 77. seasonal component 78. yearly 79. secular trend 80. business cycles 81. S, C and I 82. parabola 83. slope 84. origin 85. line of best fit 86. seasonal indices 87. irregular 88. trend 89. cycles 90. $\hat{Y} = 9 + 0.24X$ 91. 122.40 92. $Y = 14 (1.5)^X$ 93. $\hat{Y} = 86.5 + 7.2X$; $\hat{Y} = 144.1 + 7.2X$ 94. $\hat{Y} = 271.2 + 345.6X$ 95. ₹ 611.37; 7336.44 96. $\hat{Y} = 113 + 34X + 3X^2$ 97. $\hat{Y} = 88 + 4X$; $\hat{Y} = 106 + 4X$ 98. $\hat{Y} = 9.4 + 0.045X$ 99. $\hat{Y} = 4.5 + 0.5X$ 100. seasonal variations 101. specific seasonals 102. policies; level of business activity 103. residual sum of squares 104. seasonal; cyclical 105. typical seasonals.

Section C

1. (d)	2. (d)	3. (a)	4. (c)	5. (b)
6. (b)	7. (d)	8. (a)	9. (a)	10. (b)
11. (a)	12. (c)	13. (a)	14. (c)	15. (b)
16. (d)	17. (d)	18. (d)	19. (a)	20. (c)
21. (d)	22. (d)	23. (d)	24. (c)	25. (d)
26. (b)	27. (b)	28. (c)	29. (a)	30. (c)
31. (b)	32. (b)	33. (d)	34. (a)	35. (d)
36. (b)	37. (a)	38. (b)	39. (c)	40. (a)
41. (b)	42. (b)	43. (c)	44. (a)	45. (c)
46. (a)	47. (c)	48. (c)	49. (b)	50. (a)
51. (c)	52. (b)	53. (c)	54. (b)	55. (a)
56. (c)	57. (c)	58. (a)	59. (d)	60. (c)
61. (b)	62. (d)	63. (b)	64. (c)	65. (d)
66. (a)	67. (c)	68. (d)	69. (c)	70. (a)
71. (d)	72. (b)	73. (c)	74. (c)	75. (a)
76. (d)	77. (c)	78. (b)	79. (a)	80. (c)
81. (b)	82. (d)	83. (d)	84. (c)	85. (c)

SUGGESTED READING

1. Agarwal, B.L., *Basic Statistics,* New Age International Publishers, New Delhi, 8th edition, 2024.
2. Anderson, T.W., *The Statistical Analysis of Time Series,* John Wiley, New York, 1958.
3. Berenson, M.L. and Levine, D.M., *Business Statistics,* Prentice Hall, Englewood Cliff, 1979.
4. Byrkit, D.R., *Elementary Business Statistics,* D. Von Nostrand Co., New York, 1979.
5. Enns, P.G., *Business Statistics,* Richard D. Irwin, Illinois, 1985.
6. Fuller, W.A., *Introduction to Statistical Time Series,* John Wiley & Sons, New York, 1976.
7. Hadley, G., *Introduction to Business Statistics,* Holden-Day, 1968.
8. Hannan, E.J., *Multiple Time Series,* John Wiley & Sons, New York, 1970.
9. Richard, L.E., Lacava, J., *Business Statistics* (*Why and When*), McGraw-Hill Book Co., 1978.
10. Sancheti, D.C. and Kapoor, V.K., *Statistics,* Sultan Chand & Sons, New Delhi, 7th edn., 1991.

CHAPTER 17

Index Numbers

SECTION A

Short Essay Type Questions

Q. 1. *What is the rationale behind index numbers?*

Ans. Economic phenomenon is dynamic in nature. Hence, one wants to know the state of economic activity at a particular time, space or situation as compared to some other time period, place or situation, particularly in respect of the value of products and services. In this endeavour, one finds a special type of average which provides a measure of relative changes from time to time or place to place. Index numbers are also known as economic barometers because they reveal the state of inflation or deflation.

Q. 2. *Define index numbers.*

Ans. An index number is a measure of relative change in the value added by a variable or a group of related variables over time or space. Many economists and statisticians have defined index numbers in their own way. Some of them are quoted below:

Irving Fisher: The purpose of index number is that it shall fairly represent, so far as one single figure can, the general trend of the many diverging ratios from which it is calculated.

John I. Griffin: An index number is a quantity which by reference to a base period, shows by its variations, the changes in the magnitude over a period of time. In general, index numbers are used to measure changes over time in magnitudes which are not capable of direct measurement.

Wessel, Willet and Simone: An index number is a special type of an average that provides a measurement of relative change from time to time or place to place.

Clark and Schkade: An index number is a percentage relative that compares economic measure, in a given period with those some measures at a fixed time period in the past.

A.M. Tuttle: An index number is a single ratio (usually in percentages) which measures the combined (*i.e.*, averaged) change of several variables between two different times, places or situations.

L.R. Conor: In its simplest form it represents a special case of an average, generally a weighted average, compiled from a sample of items judged to be representative of the whole.

A.L. Bowley: Index numbers are used to measure the changes in some quantity which we cannot observe directly.

M.M. Blair: Index numbers are the signs and guide posts along the business highway that indicate to the businessman how he should drive or manage his affairs.

Q. 3. *What are the characteristics of an index number?*

Ans. Following characteristics of index numbers are observed almost in all cases:

(*i*) Index numbers are expressed in percentages which make it feasible to compare any two or more index numbers.

(*ii*) They are of comparable nature at any two timings or places or any other situation.

(*iii*) Index numbers are a sort of averages, usually weighted averages, which always pertain to two periods, one is known as the base period and the other, the current period. The two are always comparable with each other.

(*iv*) Index numbers measure changes in some quantities which cannot be observed directly.

Q. 4. *What are the uses of index numbers?*

Ans. Various uses of index numbers are as follows:

(*i*) ***An aid to framing of policies:*** Fixing of wages and dearness allowance is mainly based on consumer price index. Many other economic policies are guided by index numbers like volume of trade, fixing of wholesale and retail prices, etc.

(*ii*) ***To find trend:*** Index numbers measure the changes from time to time which enable us to study the general trend of the economic activity under consideration. As a measure of average change in an specified group, the index number may be used for forecasting.

(*iii*) ***To assess the purchasing power of money:*** The consumer price index helps in computing the real wages of a person. If a person was getting ₹ 300 per month in 1960 and ₹ 3000 per month in 1990, his real wages have increased or decreased – can be assessed with the help of index number.

(*iv*) ***For adjusting national income:*** Index numbers are used for deflating the net national product (NNP) or net national income (NNI) converted at current prices. The deflated net national product or income represent the NNP or NNI at constant prices under inflationary conditions.

(*v*) ***A measure of comparative changes:*** The main purpose of index number is to measure the relative temporal or cross-sectional changes at a point of time over some previous time. All those phenomena which cannot be measured directly like consumer price index, price index, price level, etc., are measured with the help of index numbers.

Q. 5. *Delineate the limitations and/or lecunae of index numbers.*

Ans. Index numbers are extensively used in economic analysis. They are not devoid of lecunae and limitations. The some are discussed below:

(*i*) ***The errors of sampling:*** Since index numbers are based on sample data, all those errors which are involved in sampling procedure creep in the construction of index numbers. So, the index numbers may not present the true picture.

(*ii*) ***Subjectivity in the construction of index numbers:*** There is no definite rule which makes one to decide about the base year, number of commodities, weights, sampling procedure, etc. All this depends on the purpose of index numbers and the person making decisions. So, an element of subjectivity is involved in the construction of index numbers.

(*iii*) ***Adjustment for changes:*** With rapid scientific advancement, change in outlook, taste and quality of material, it is difficult to make exact adjustments in the construction of indices. Hence, index numbers may not be the true measure of change.

(*iv*) ***Formula error:*** All formulae known so far for index numbers suffer from one or the other deficiency. For example, Laspeyre's formula generate an upward bias in index number, whereas Paasche's formula a downward bias. So, the choice of a formula is a problem as it may introduce bias in index number.

(*v*) ***Choice of the type of average:*** Index numbers are a special kind of averages. Since various averages possess different virtues and limitations, it is not possible to say that a particular average is absolutely good for index number. Of course, arithmetic and geometric means are frequently used.

(*vi*) ***Errors in collection of data:*** After all index numbers are calculated from the data collected through surveys. If the data are not collected accurately regarding prices, consumption, production, etc., the index number will definitely be misleading.

Q. 6. *What type of index numbers are usually calculated?*

Ans. Index numbers are constructed in economic activity covering a wide range of aspects. Different kinds of usually constructed index numbers are:

(*i*) ***Price index numbers:*** These are the mostly used index numbers which measure the general change in the retail or wholesale prices of a commodity or a group of commodities at current period as compared to some previous period known as base year.

(*ii*) ***Quantity index numbers:*** This is another important measure of index number which measures the changes occurring in the quantity of goods demanded, consumed, produced, imported or exported, etc.

(*iii*) ***Consumer price index:*** In common parlance it is also known as *cost of living index*, though the two are not exactly the same. Consumer price index is a special kind which is constructed for the prices of only the essential items. Such a list of items is known as *basket*.

(*iv*) ***Value index:*** This compares the total value of certain item(s) at a point of time as compared to a base period. We know that the total value is the product of the price and quantity. This type of index is used in sales of a company, foreign trade, etc.

(*v*) ***Diffusion index:*** It reveals the changes in a group of time series indicating the turning point of an economic cycle.

Q. 7. *Discuss various problems involved in the construction of index numbers.*

Ans. No index number is an all-purpose index number. Hence, there are many problems involved in the construction of index numbers, which are to be tackled by an economist or statistician. They are briefly discussed below:

(*i*) ***Purpose of the index number:*** The first and foremost objective is to clearly delineate the purpose of index number for which it is going to be constructed. All other factors involved in the construction of index numbers mostly depend on the purpose. If the purpose is not stated clearly and unambiguously, the index number will do no good as an economic barometer.

(*ii*) ***Selection of base period:*** All index numbers are constructed in reference to a period against which the comparisons are to be made. Such a reference period is known as *base period*. The index for base period is always taken to be 100. As a matter of fact, the base primarily depends upon the purpose of the index number. Still there are certain requirements for an ideal base period.

(*a*) It should be a normal period in the sense that it should be free from epidemics, earthquakes, war, etc. A perfect normal period is not easy to obtain, hence 2-3 years average is sometimes taken as a base year.

(*b*) The base period should not be a distant past as the technology and circumstances changes with lapse of time.

(*iii*) ***Collection of data:*** Data are to be collected on the items which are to be included in the construction of index numbers. The choice of items totally depends on the purpose of index number. The information – usually the prices, consumption or demand – should be collected carefully from the units selected in the sample.

(*iv*) ***Selection of weights:*** All items do not carry the same importance with regard to their consumption or requirement. For instance, butter is less important than milk, fruits are less important than vegetables, etc. Hence, the items are to be weighted according to their relative importance. Sometimes people use unweighted indexes but rarely so.

(*v*) ***Choice of the average:*** An index number is a special type of average. Hence, which type of average should be used, need thoughtful consideration. Usually, three types of averages are used given in order of their priority:

(1) Geometric mean (G.M.)

(2) Arithmetic mean (A.M.)

(3) Median

(1) *Geometric mean* is the most preferred one because:

(*a*) index numbers deal with ratios and proportions.

(*b*) index numbers give equal weights to equal ratio of changes,

(*c*) extreme values do not receive undue weights,

(*d*) geometric mean based indices are reversible.

(2) *Arithmetic mean* is unduly affected by extreme values. Still it is widely used because of easiness of computations.

(3) *Median ignores* completely the extreme values. But, it is seldom used.

(*vi*) ***Selection of formula:*** The choice of a formula for index number depends on the purpose of index number and the data available. Anyhow, Irving Fisher has expounded a formula, which is considered as an ideal one and satisfies time reversal and factor reversal tests. Still no formula can be regarded as best because a formula may be very good in one situation and deficient in the other.

Q. 8 *Discuss in general the basis of formulae evolved for index numbers.*

Ans. Two types of formulae are in existence for index numbers namely, (*i*) unweighted formulae, (*ii*) weighted formulae.

Unweighted formulae have very little use because of their limitations. Hence, weighted formula basically requires three things:

(*i*) The data regarding the items (for which the index number is to constructed) for the base and current periods. Usually the data are with regard to prices and quantities.

(*ii*) The information necessitated for the weights.

(*iii*) The kind of average to be used.

Q. 9. *Explain the notations commonly used in index number formulae.*

Ans. Commonly we use the following notations:

p_{ji} – the price of the ith commodity (item) in the jth year.

q_{ji} – the quantity of the ith commodity (item) in j^{th} year.

v_{ji} – the value of the ith commodity (item) in the jth year which is equal to $p_{ji} \times q_{ji}$.

In general, $j = 0, 1, 2, \ldots, k$ and $i = 1, 2, \ldots, n$ (the number of commodities under consideration).

For a base year, $j = 0$ and current year, $j = 1$

P_{01} – The price index of the current period 1 as compared to based period 0.

Q_{01} – The quantity index for the current period 1 as compared to base period 0.

Q. 10. *Give the unweighted price index number.*

Ans. The unweighted price index number for n items for the current year 1 and base year 0 is given by the formula,

$$P_{01} = \frac{\sum_i p_{1i}}{\sum_i p_{0i}} \times 100$$

for $i = 1, 2, \ldots, n$

This formula has hardly got any utility because:

(*i*) different items generally have different units of measurements, *e.g.*, wheat ₹ per kg, cloth ₹/m, milk ₹ per litre and hence cannot be pooled.

(*ii*) the relative importance of different items is totally ignored.

Q. 11. *Briefly discuss the unweighted quantity index.*

Ans. An unweighted quantity index for n commodities can be computed by the formula,

$$Q_{01} = \frac{\sum_i q_{1i}}{\sum_i q_{0i}} \times 100$$

for $i = 1, 2, \ldots, n$.

This index suffers from the drawbacks that:

(*i*) different items included in the quantity index having different units of measurements like petrol in litres, cereals in quintal, electric bulbs in numbers, etc., and hence cannot be combined to get an aggregated quantity.

(*ii*) all items carry equal importance (weights) in this formula which is not admissible.

Q. 12. *Explicate Laspeyre's price and quantity index numbers.*

Ans. Laspeyre's index is also known as *base year method* index. In Laspeyre's price index, the base year quantities (consumption, demand, production etc., corresponding to the prices of the items are taken as weights. Laspeyre's, a French economist gave the following aggregative price index L_{01} in 1871. For n items, Laspeyre's formula for price index number is,

$$L_{01} = \frac{\sum_i p_{1i}\, q_{0i}}{\sum_i p_{0i}\, q_{01}} \times 100$$

for $i = 1, 2, \ldots, n$.

Similarly for quantity index number, base year prices are taken as weights. Laspeyre's formula for quantity index number is,

$$L^q_{01} = \frac{\sum_i q_{1i}\, p_{0i}}{\sum_i q_{0i}\, p_{0i}} \times 100$$

for $i = 1, 2, \ldots, n$

Anyhow Laspeyre's indices have an upward bias.

Q. 13. *Discuss Paasche's price and quantity index numbers.*

Ans. Paasche's index is also known as given (current) year method index. Paasche, a German statistician expounded the index number formula in 1874 with the plea that the weights should be of the given year. It is denoted by P_{01}.

Paasche's price index formula is,

$$P^p_{01} = \frac{\sum_i p_{1i}\, q_{1i}}{\sum_i p_{0i}\, q_{1i}} \times 100$$

for $i = 1, 2, \ldots, n$

Similarly, Paasche's quantity index number is,

$$P^q_{01} = \frac{\sum_i q_{1i}\, p_{1i}}{\sum_i q_{0i}\, p_{1i}} \times 100$$

for $i = 1, 2, \ldots, n$

where n is the number of items selected for index numbers. Paasche's indices possess a downward bias.

Q. 14. *Give your choice between Laspeyre's and Paasche's formulae along with your comments.*

Ans. Both the formulae stand at their sound logic and anyone cannot be outrightly rejected at the cost of the other. All the more, if the base year and the given year are not much distant (not more than 2-3 years), both the formulae almost lead to the same index number and it makes little difference which one is chosen. But usually, the base period and given period are quite distant apart. Hence, some mid-way has to be found out. In the desideration of the same, the economists and statisticians have suggested many formulae.

Q. 15. *Give the Drobish-Bowley price index formula.*

Ans. The Drobish-Bowley price index formula is simply the arithmetic mean of the Laspeyre's and Paasche's formula which was expounded in 1901.

$$P^{DB}_{01} = \frac{1}{2}(L + P) = \frac{1}{2}\left(\frac{\sum_i p_{1i}\, q_{0i}}{\sum_i p_{0i}\, q_{0i}} + \frac{\sum_i p_{1i}\, q_{1i}}{\sum_i p_{0i}\, q_{1i}}\right) \times 100$$

for $i = 1, 2, \ldots, n$

Drobish-Bowley pleaded that the arithmetic mean of L and P is good because the over-estimate of L is compensated by the underestimate of P.

Q. 16. *What is geometric cross formula?*

Ans. The geometric cross formula for price index is also known as *Walsh price index*. He gave this formula in 1901.

$$P^W_{01} = \sqrt{L \times P} = \sqrt{\frac{\sum_i p_{1i}\, q_{0i}}{\sum_i p_{0i}\, q_{0i}} + \frac{\sum_i p_{1i}\, q_{1i}}{\sum_i p_{0i}\, q_{1i}}} \times 100$$

for $i = 1, 2, \ldots, n$.

Walsh formula is one of the most accepted formula. In 1920, Irving Fisher called it an ideal formula for index numbers. Still it is not universal and all purpose index formula.

Q. 17. *Delineate arithmetically crossed-weight formula.*

Ans. Marshall and Edgeworth emphasised the use of the combined or average quantities of base and current periods as weights for price index. Irving Fisher advocated that this system of weighting yields a good index number. The arithmetically crossed weight formula is,

$$P_{01}^{ME} = \frac{\sum_i p_{1i}(q_{0i}+q_{1i})}{\sum_i p_{0i}(q_{0i}+q_{1i})} \times 100$$

for $i = 1, 2, \ldots, n$

Q. 18. *Give geometrically crossed-weight formula.*

Ans. In the Marshall-Edgeworth price index formula, one may even use the geometric mean of the quantities of the base and current years as weights. Hence, the price index formula is.

$$P_{01}^{ME} = \frac{\sum_i p_{1i}\sqrt{q_{0i}\, q_{1i}}}{\sum_i p_{0i}\sqrt{q_{0i}\, q_{1i}}} \times 100$$

for $i = 1, 2, \ldots, n$

Q. 19. *Discuss Kelly's fixed weight formula.*

Ans. Truman L. Kelly preferred the fixed weights for price index as it is not necessary to use the base year and/or current year quantities as weight. These may be any logically ascertained quantities. But to be more sound, the average of any two or more year's quantities may be taken as weight. The choice of the type of average (A.M. or G.M.) lies with the investigator.

The greatest advantage of Kelly's fixed weight system is that the change in base year does not require to determine the new weights. The fixed weight index is quite popular in U.S.A. in the construction of whole-sale price index of the Bureau of Labour.

Note: Formulae for quantity index numbers can conveniently be obtained from price index numbers by replacing p by q and q by p.

Q. 20. *What is meant by average of price relatives?*

Ans. The average of the price indices calculated for each individual commodity at a given year '1' relative to a base year '0' is known as the average of the price relatives. Usually, the average is either arithmetic mean or geometric mean. Price index based on arithmetic mean is,

$$P_{01} = \frac{1}{n}\sum_{i=1}^{n}\left(\frac{p_{1i}}{p_{0i}}\right) \times 100$$

Price index based on geometric mean is,

$$P_{01} = \left[\prod_{i=1}^{n}\left(\frac{p_{1i}}{p_{0i}}\right)\right]^{1/n} \times 100$$

F.Y. Edgeworth pleaded for the use of harmonic mean as well. But it is seldom used.

Q. 21. *Give the formulae for weighted average of price relatives.*

Ans. Commonly, the indices are obtained through weighted price relatives. If $w_1, w_2, \ldots, w_n$ are the weights for n items price relatives, the formula for price index based on arithmetic mean of weighted price relatives is,

$$P_{01} = \frac{1}{\sum_i w_i}\sum_i w_i\left(\frac{p_{1i}}{p_{0i}}\right) \times 100$$

for $i = 1, 2, \ldots, n$

If w_i is taken as the base year value, *i.e.*, $w_i = p_{0i}\, q_{0i}$, the above formula reduces to Laspeyre's formula and if current year values, *i.e.*, $w_i = p_{0i} \cdot q_{1i}$, the above formula is changed to Paasche's formula.

Again the formula for price index based on geometric mean of weighted price relatives is,

$$P_{01} = \left[\prod_i\left(\frac{p_{1i}}{p_{0i}}\right)^{w_i}\right]^{1/\sum_i w_i} \times 100$$

for $i = 1, 2, \ldots, n$

Q. 22. *How can one judge the adequacy of a formula?*

Ans. All formulae stand at equal footing based on their own logic. Now the question arises, how to choose one out of many. To have some definite idea about their exactness, Irving Fisher and some other statisticians and economists put forth some tests or criteria which conform to their reasonalability. A test satisfying all the tests can be considered as best. But no formula satisfies all the tests.

Q. 23. *What is formula error?*

Ans. The difference between the price (quantity) indices due to Laspeyre's and Paasche's is known as formula error. If the difference between the two is negligible, the formula error is also insignificant. Let the difference be denoted by D. Then,

$$D = P_{01}^{La} - P_{01}^{Pa}$$

or,

$$D = Q_{01}^{La} - Q_{01}^{Pa}$$

Q. 24. *What is meant by sampling error in reference to index numbers, and how to check it?*

Ans. Index numbers are often constructed for n selected items out of the total number of N items produced or used. Hence, some error creeps in due to sampling of items. If P_{01}^{n} is the price index based on n sampled items and P_{01}^{N} on total N items, the quantity $(P_{01}^{n} - P_{01}^{N})$ is called the sampling error of the price index number. A similar expression $(Q_{01}^{n} - Q_{01}^{N})$ represents the sampling error of the quantity index number.

Sampling error can be reduced firstly by selecting a random sample of items. But in practice a purposive sample is mostly taken including the items of vital importance and excluding the remaining ones. Another way is to include as many items as possible to reduce the gap between P_{01}^{n} and P_{01}^{N}.

Q. 25. *Explicate homogeneity error in reference to index numbers.*

Ans. The accuracy of an index number to a great extent depends on the number of binary items. Hence, the error caused by the consideration of only the binary items omitting the unique items present in the base and current periods is known as *homogeneity error*. The extent of homogeneity error may be measured through R-test.

If N_0 and N_1 are the number of items in the base and current periods respectively and N_{01} is the number of binary items, then a real number R is defined as,

$$R = \frac{N_0 + N_1 - 2N_{01}}{N_0 + N_1}$$

The numerator in the above formula gives the number of unique items and $(N_0 + N_1)$ in the denominator is the total number of items in both the periods considered separately. If there is no unique item, $N_0 + N_1 - 2N_{01} = 0$ and hence, $R = 0$. Again, if there is no binary, $N_{01} = 0$ and hence, $R = 1$.

This shows R lies between 0 and 1.

A value of R equal to zero or near 0 is preferred, and this can be achieved by taking the base year not far from the current year.

A large value of R is indicative of substantial homogeneity error.

Q. 26. *What is meant by unit test?*

Ans. It is to verify that the index number is independent of the units of measurements in which the prices and quantities have been measured. This test is satisfied by all formula for index numbers except simple aggregative index.

Q. 27. *Discuss time reversal test.*

Ans. Irving Fisher argued that an index formula would be accurate if it maintains time consistency, i.e., the product of price indices by reversing bases is unity. Mathematically,

$$P_{01} \times P_{10} = 1$$

If the relation does not hold, the discrepancy $(P_{01} \times P_{10} - 1)$ was termed as joint error. Thus, the measure of joint error

$$E_1 = P_{01} \times P_{10} - 1$$

It is trivial to prove that Fisher's ideal formula satisfies time reversal test.

Q. 28. *Explain the factor reversal test.*

Ans. The factor reversal test was originated by Irving Fisher with the logic that a formula which correctly reflects price changes would also reflect quantity changes. Thus, the two results multiplied together should give the true value ratio. Notationally,

$$P_{01} \times Q_{01} = V_{01}$$

where, V_{01} is the ratio of the values of a fixed number of articles in the given year to the base year,

i.e., $$V_{01} = \frac{\Sigma p_{1i} q_{1i}}{\Sigma p_{0i} q_{0i}}$$

We can also write,

$$\frac{P_{01} \times Q_{01}}{V_{01}} = 1$$

If any formula does not satisfy this relation, the error

$$E_2 = \frac{P_{01} \times Q_{01}}{V_{01}} - 1$$

is called the joint error.

It can easily be verified that only Fisher's ideal formula satisfies factor reversal test and none else. That is why Fisher's formula is an ideal one.

Q. 29. *What is circular test and what does is signify?*

Ans. This test is an extension of time reversal test and is based on the shiftability of the base period. In this test, we find the price indices by taking the preceding year as base year, and the first year price index is worked out by taking the last year as base. If we have data for $(k + 1)$ years at hand and calculate price indices as $P_{01}, P_{12}, P_{23}, \ldots, P_{(k-1)k}$ and P_{k0}, then for the circular test to hold true, the following relation be satisfied.

$$P_{01} \times P_{12} \times P_{23} \times \ldots \times P_{(k-1)k} \times P_{k0} = 1$$

or, $$P_{01} \times P_{12} \times P_{23} \times \ldots \times P_{(k-1)k} = P_{0k}$$

The circular test is satisfied only by the indices:

(*i*) based on geometric mean of price relatives,

(*ii*) obtained from Kelly's fixed weight method.

Even Fisher's ideal formula does not satisfy circular test.

Q. 30. *What do you understand by test of proportionality?*

Ans. If all sub-indices are equal to P, then total index should also be equal to P.

Q. 31. *What is meant by test of definiteness?*

Ans. If one of the sub-indices is zero or infinity, then the total index must not be zero or infinity or indeterminate.

Q. 32. *What is being ensured through test of commensurability?*

Ans. If the unit of measurement of commodity is changed, the value of the index must not change.

Q. 33. *How can one find indices by the chain-base method?*

Ans. If there are k consecutive year's data at hand and each time we consider the same n items to be included in the construction of indices, the chain-base method consists of calculating the price index for each year taking the preceding year as base. This brings the homogeneity error to almost zero level.

In this method, we can use any appropriate index number formula. All such year-to-year indices are called *link relatives*. The beauty of this method is that the index for any year to zero base year can be obtained by multiplying all the indices worked out so far. Notationally, a link relative for the jth year is,

$$P_{(j-1)j} = \frac{\sum_i p_{ji}\, q_{(j-1)i}}{\sum_i p_{(j-1)i}\, q_{(j-1)i}}$$

for $i = 1, 2, \ldots, n$

$j = 1, 2, \ldots, k$

Putting, $j = 1, 2, \ldots, k$, we get the formula for all link relatives.

Various indices of the series by chain base method can be obtained by the following relations:

$$P_{01} = P_{01} \qquad \text{(as a first link)}$$

$$P_{02} = P_{01} P_{12}$$

$$P_{03} = P_{01} P_{12} P_{23} = P_{02} P_{23}$$

$$\vdots$$

$$P_{0k} = P_{01} P_{12} P_{23} \ldots P_{(k-1)k} = P_{0(k-1)} P_{(k-1)k}$$

with the help of the above relations, a general formula can be given as,

$$\text{Chain index} = \frac{\text{Previous year chain index} \times \text{Current year link relative}}{100}$$

Q. 34. *Give the relation of converting the chain index number to fixed-base index number.*

Ans. The formula for converting the chain-base

index number (C.B.I.) into fixed-base index number (F.B.I.) is,

$$\text{Current year F.B.I} = \frac{\text{Current year C.B.I} \times \text{Previous year F.B.I}}{100}$$

Q. 35. *Give the advantages and limitations of chain-base indices.*

Ans.

Advantages:

(*i*) Often in business, the interest lies in making the comparisons with the preceding year rather than a distant past. This purpose is very well served by the link relatives.

(*ii*) In the chain-base method, introduction of new items and deletion of old ones can be done without hazards and hassles. Because of this facility, the chain-base index numbers are used in consumer and wholesale price indices.

(*iii*) The chain-base method brings the homogeneity error to almost zero.

(*iv*) Weights can be adjusted whenever required. Such a flexibility is not available with any other number.

(*v*) Index numbers calculated by the chain-base method are to a great extent, free from the effect of seasonal variations as compared to other types of index numbers.

Limitation: The chain-base indices are not suitable for long range comparisons.

Q. 36. *When one comes across the problem of base shifting and how can it be tackled?*

Ans. When we are given indices in the form of time series with respect to a base year, one often requires the indices to a base year other than the base year they are referred to. In such a situation, the problem of base shifting arises. The need is felt when:

(*i*) the given indices are referred to a long-back base period and one wants the indices based on recent base period.

(*ii*) If two given series of indices with different base periods are to the compared, one of them has to be converted to the base period of the other series. This makes the two series comparable.

One way of tackling the problem of base shifting is to get required data and recalculate everything. But such a process is cumbrous and time consuming.

An easy but approximate method to obtain the indices to the new base is to take the index number of the new base period as 100 and then express the index number of the original base as the percentage of the index number to be adopted as new base.

Index number recasted to the new base is,

$$\text{New base index No.} = \frac{\text{Old index No. of current year}}{\text{Index No. of new base year}} \times 100$$

Q. 37. *Following are the wholesale price index numbers from 1975 to 1980 to base 1970.*

Year:	*1975*	*1976*	*1977*	*1978*	*1979*	*1980*
Index Nos:	*175.8*	*172.4*	*185.4*	*185.0*	*206.2*	*246.8*

Find the wholesale price indices to the base 1977.

Ans. The wholesale index numbers to the base 1977 are:

Year	*By formula*	*Index numbers*
1975	$\frac{175.8}{185.4} \times 100$	94.82
1976	$\frac{172.4}{185.4} \times 100$	92.99
1977	$\frac{185.4}{185.4} \times 100$	100
1978	$\frac{185.0}{185.4} \times 100$	99.78
1979	$\frac{206.2}{185.4} \times 100$	111.22
1980	$\frac{246.8}{185.4} \times 100$	133.12

Q. 38. *What do you understand by splicing of index numbers and how to implement it?*

Ans. In economic phenomenon, a new series of indices is constructed banishing the old one. This is done owing to major changes in quantity weights. But in new series, the base period is always the last year (period) of the old series. But to make the two series comparable the indices are required with the base of the old series. So, it is a sort of base shifting. Hence, the combining of two series of indices into one is known as *splicing*.

If an old series is connected with the new one, it is known as *forward splicing*. In this type of splicing all index numbers are converted to the base of the old series. The formula for forward splicing is,

Forward Spliced Index No.

$$= \frac{\text{Old index No. of the new base year} \times \text{index No. for the given year}}{100}$$

There can be *backward splicing* also. In this, the new series is connected with the old one in the sense that the indices of the old series are converted to the base of the new series. The formula for backward splicing is,

Backward Spliced Index No.

$$= \frac{\text{Index No. to be spliced}}{\text{Old index No. of the new base year}} \times 100$$

Q. 39. *The following table gives the index numbers of wholesale prices from 1972-73 to 1981-82 to the base 1970-71 in column (ii) and from 1982-83 to 1988-89 to the base 1981-82 in column (iii).*

Ans. Forward and backward spliced index numbers are given in columns (*iv*) and (*v*) along with computations, respectively.

(*i*) *Year*	(*ii*) *Index No. base 1970-71*	(*iii*) *Index No. base 1981-82*	(*iv*) *Forward spliced Index No.*	(*v*) *Backward spliced Index No.*
1972-73	111		111	$111 \times \frac{100}{264} = 42$
1973-74	142		142	$142 \times \frac{100}{264} = 54$
1974-75	178		178	$178 \times \frac{100}{264} = 67$
1975-76	166		166	$166 \times \frac{100}{264} = 63$
1976-77	167		167	$167 \times \frac{100}{264} = 63$
1977-78	184		184	$184 \times \frac{100}{264} = 70$
1978-79	181		181	$181 \times \frac{100}{264} = 69$
1979-80	207		207	$207 \times \frac{100}{264} = 78$
1980-81	238		238	$238 \times \frac{100}{264} = 90$

(*Contd.*)

Table Contd.

(i) Year	*(ii)* Index No. base 1970-71	*(iii)* Index No. base 1981-82	*(iv)* Forward spliced Index No.	*(v)* Backward spliced Index No.
1981-82	264	100	$264\times\frac{100}{100}=264$	100
1982-83		107	$264\times\frac{107}{100}=282$	107
1983-84		118	$264\times\frac{118}{100}=312$	118
1984-85		126	$264\times\frac{126}{100}=333$	126
1985-86		126	$264\times\frac{126}{100}=333$	126
1986-87		137	$264\times\frac{137}{100}=362$	137
1987-88		153	$264\times\frac{153}{100}=404$	153
1988-89		160	$264\times\frac{160}{100}=422$	160

Q. 40. *What is meant by deflating the index numbers and how can it be done?*

Ans. Deflating the index number means, making allowance in indices for the effect of changes in price levels. If the present price of a commodity is doubled as compared to a base year, the purchasing power for that commodity is reduced to half. In this way, money value of our earning changes with the rise or fall in prices of commodities or consumer price index. Hence using deflation technique, the real wages, money income index number and real income index number can be calculated by the following formulae. Real wage or real income

$$=\frac{\text{Income of the year (money wage)}}{\text{Price index of the current year}}\times 100$$

Money Income Index No.

$$=\frac{\text{Real Income}}{\text{Income of base year}}\times 100$$

Real Income Index No.

$$=\frac{\text{Money Income Index No.}}{\text{Consumer Price Index No.}}\times 100$$

Real income is also known as deflated income. This technique is widely used in deflating value series or value indices, rupee sales, inventories, income wages, etc. Also,

$$\text{Purchasing power of money}=\frac{1}{\text{Price index}}\times 100$$

Q. 41. *Per capita income of a person from 1980-81 to 1986-87 and the consumer prices index with 1980-81 as base were as follows:*

Year	Income per capita (₹)	Index Nos.
1980-81	1627	100
1981-82	1851	103.5
1982-83	1993	103.4
1983-84	2290	109.4
1984-85	2494	110.9
1985-86	2735	113.8
1986-87	2970	115.6

Find real wages and real income indices.

Year	*Per capita income* (₹)	*Index No.*	*Real wage*	*Money Income Index No.*	*Real Income Index No.*
1980-81	1627	100	$\frac{1627}{100}\times 100 = 1627$	$\frac{1627}{1627}\times 100 = 100$	$\frac{100}{100}\times 100 = 100$
1981-82	1851	103.5	$\frac{1851}{103.5}\times 100 = 1788.40$	$\frac{1788.40}{1851}\times 100 = 96.6$	$\frac{96.6}{103.5}\times 100 = 93.3$
1982-83	1993	103.4	$\frac{1993}{103.5}\times 100 = 1927.47$	$\frac{1927.47}{1993}\times 100 = 96.7$	$\frac{96.7}{103.4}\times 100 = 93.5$
1983-84	2290	109.4	$\frac{2290}{109.4}\times 100 = 2093.24$	$\frac{2093.20}{2290}\times 100 = 91.4$	$\frac{91.4}{109.4}\times 100 = 83.5$
1984-85	2494	110.9	$\frac{2494}{110.9}\times 100 = 2248.87$	$\frac{2248.87}{2494}\times 100 = 90.2$	$\frac{90.2}{110.9}\times 100 = 81.3$
1985-86	2735	113.8	$\frac{2735}{113.8}\times 100 = 2403.34$	$\frac{2403.34}{2735}\times 100 = 87.9$	$\frac{87.9}{113.8}\times 100 = 77.2$
1986-87	2970	115.6	$\frac{2970}{115.6}\times 100 = 2560.34$	$\frac{2560.34}{2970}\times 100 = 86.2$	$\frac{86.2}{115.6}\times 100 = 74.6$

Ans. The real wages and real income indices are given in the above table along with computations:

Q. 42. *What is consumer price index (CPI)?*

Ans. The consumer price index is a measure of average percentage change in prices at a particular time as compared to a base period for a section of the population for which it is referred. In a simple way, it tells the per cent increase or decrease in the amount required to purchase certain commodities and services of the fixed standard at a point of time as compared to some base period. CPI is constructed on weekly basis.

Earlier '*cost of living index*' was the term used in place of consumer price index. But on the recommendation of the international conference of labour statisticians held under the auspices of international labour organisation, the term cost of living index was changed to *consumer Price Index* or *Retail Price Index*. There is a little difference between the two. Cost of living is affected by the standard of living, taste, quality of items, types of services utilised, etc. Whereas consumer price index considers only one major aspect of cost of living index for consuming a basket from time to time.

Q. 43. *What purpose is served by consumer price index?*

Ans. The purposes of consumer price index are summarised below:

(*i*) It helps to fix dearness allowance to compensate the rise (or fall) in prices of commodities of common utility.

(*ii*) Purchasing power of money is evaluated through this measure.

(*iii*) It reflects on the real income of a group of people for whom it has been constructed.

(*iv*) The consumer price index works as a guideline in determining various economic policies like wage policy, fixing of prices, taxation, house rent allowance, etc.

(*v*) It enables one to make comparison of the cost of living at a particular time or place as compared to any other time or place for the similar class of people.

Q 44. *Discuss succinctly the various steps involved in the construction of consumer price index.*

Ans. As a matter of fact, the construction of consumer price index is as good as any other price index. Because it is a special purpose price index, it needs some specific considerations. The same are highlighted below:

(*i*) ***Selection of items***: The items which are most commonly used by the section of the people, for whom CPI is required, are included in the basket. The basket of goods for middle class people consists of the following items:

(*a*) *Food items:* Wheat, rice, pulses, meat, milk, edible oils, condiments and spices, sugar, tea, etc.

(*b*) *Smoking and intoxicants*: Cigarettes, bidi, betels, liquors, tobacco, etc.

(*c*) *Fuel and light*: Firewood, coke, coal, kerosene, electricity, cooking gas, etc.

(*d*) *Services*: medical, barber charges, entertainment, transport, postal expenses, etc.

(*e*) *House rent:* House rent or rental value of the self occupied house.

(*f*) *Miscellaneous*: Soaps, hair oil, cream, powder, crockery, utensils, etc.

Presently the total number of items included in the basket is 110. While including the commodities, their quality or brand has to be specified.

(*ii*) ***Adjustment for quality changes***: Due to technological advancement and new inventions, new products of better quality enter the market. Hence, adjustments should be made in the prices of such items. This makes the comparison of prices at two occasions more realistic.

(*iii*) ***Collection of price data***: Price data should be collected from the retailers who are patronised by the majority of consumers. Also, the prices be adjusted to the same units at two periods under reference. For instance, price of cloth per yard in base period be adjusted to the price of cloth per meter in current period, rate of rice per cent in the base year be adjusted to ₹ per kg, etc.

(*iv*) ***Fixing of weights for CPI***: Assigning weights to prices is the usual practice in calculating the price indices. In consumer price index, the weights are the percentages of expenditure of each item of the goods and services of the basket to the total expenditure. In the calculation of consumer price index, weights are assigned to each individual item of a group first and then to the groups like food items, clothing, house, fuel, etc. The whole structure of weights is known as *weighting diagram*.

(*v*) ***Selection of base period***: Generally the base period for consumer price index is the year declared by the government. The weighting diagram is based on the budget enquiry conducted in the declared base year. In practice, the weighting diagram determined once remains fixed for 10 to 15 years, depending on the life of a series.

(*vi*) ***Imputation of expenditure***: There are many items on which the expenditure is incurred in a family but those items do not belong to the basket. The expenditure due to such items are distributed amongst the items of the basket so that the total articles are taken into account. For instance, curd and cheese are included with milk, maize, jawar and bajra are added to cereals. This process of adjusting the weights is known as *imputation of weights*.

(*vii*) ***Selection of formula for consumer price index***: The computation of CPI is based on Laspeyre's formula. There are two approaches which are discussed below:

(*a*) *Weighted aggregate expenditure method*: In this method, the prices of various items are weighted with the respective quantities consumed in the base year. Thus, with usual notations

$$\text{CPI} = \frac{\sum_i p_{1i}\, q_{0i}}{\sum_i p_{0i}\, q_{0i}}$$

for $i = 1, 2, \ldots, n$.

This formula faces the problem that quantitative weights cannot be assigned for the services utilised. Hence, this formula can be used when the basket includes only consumable articles.

(*b*) *Family budget method*: This method is also known as *method of weighted relatives*. The computation of CPI under family budget method runs into two steps. As a first step, the price index is calculated for each group separately. In the second step, the weighted average of the group indices is computed which is nothing but CPI.

In the first step, we calculate price relatives in percentages for individual items of a groups, *i.e.*, $p_{1i}/p_{0i} \times 100$. Each price relative is weighted by the weight w_i, which is usually in terms of percentage of expenditure. So, we calculate the quantity, $\left(\frac{p_{1i}}{p_{0i}} \times 100\right) w_i$. Then find the weighted average for a group say, j^{th} group G^j, over all the items of the group for i running from 1 to n_i. So the CPI for the jth group is,

$$G^j_{01} = \frac{\sum\limits_i \left(\frac{p_{1i}}{p_{0i}} \times 100\right) w_{ij}}{\sum\limits_i w_{ij}}$$

As a second step, the group index numbers (G^j_{01}) are multiplied by the respective group weights. The sum of these products divided by the sum of group weights provides the consumer price index. Generally, the CPI is obtained on monthly basis and is known as *general index* for the mid of that month. The formula for general CPI is,

$$P_{01} = \frac{\sum\limits_j G^j_{01}\, w_j}{\sum\limits_j w_j}$$

where j varies over all groups.

Q. 45. *What does a consumer price index reflect?*

Ans. A consumer price index does not reflect on a particular family budget but it tells about the price changes experienced by families on an average. To be more specific, if the effect of price changes experienced by all the families of the population are pooled and averaged, the average experience would be reflected by consumer price index.

Q. 46. *Differentiate between explicit and implicit weights.*

Ans. Explicit weights are those weights which can be expressed with definiteness, e.g., the quantities consumed or produced. In most of the studies explicit weights are used.

Sometimes items are assigned weights according to their importance. Such weights are known as implicit weights. Suppose, two varieties of wheat are marketed. One variety is four times in demand than the other. So, it will receive four times the weight than the weight for other variety. But such a weighting system is seldom used.

Q. 47. *In what respects the wholesale price index differs from the general price index?*

Ans. The wholesale price index is basically not much different from the general price index except for some special considerations given below:

(*i*) The wholesale price index gives an indication of price movement in all markets except retail markets.

(*ii*) The wholesale price index quotations are taken only from wholesale dealers on each Friday.

(*iii*) The price quotations are collected from officials as well as non-official sources.

(*iv*) The wholesale price index does not include items pertaining to services like barber charges, repairing, etc.

(*v*) In the wholesale price index, the commodity weights are determined by the estimates of commodity value of domestic production and the value of imports inclusive of import duty during the base year. In general, price index, weighting system and collection of price data are not exactly so.

Q. 48. *How is the wholesale price index worked out?*

Ans. Once the data required for prices and weights are collected, the commodity indices are obtained as the average of the price relatives; sub-groups or groups indices are calculated as the weighted arithmetic mean of commodity indices. Finally, the general wholesale price index or *all commodities* index is obtained as the weighted average of the group indices.

Q. 49. *What series of the wholesale price indices are issued so far?*

Ans. The first series of the wholesale price index was issued by the Economic Advisor, Ministry of Commerce and Industry in January, 1947 with the year ending August, 1939 as base year.

The second wholesale price index series was issued in April 1956 with 1952-53 as base year. This series was based on 112 commodities classified into six groups namely, food; liquor and tobacco; fuel and power, light and lubricants; industrial raw material; intermediate products; finished products. For this series, 555 price quotations were collected from 183 official and non-official markets. In this series, the base year was 1952-53, but weights were based on 1948-49 information.

On the recommendation of Wholesale Price Index Revision Committee, a new series of wholesale price indices with base 1961-62 were issued. This series covered 139 commodities and price data were collected through 774 quotations. This series added two new groups namely, chemicals; machinery and transport equipments.

The next series was issued in January 1977 with 1970-71 as base year. This series was comprised of 360 commodities and 1295 price quotations.

A new series of wholesale price indices with 1981 -82 as base year had been released in July, 1989 to replace old series with 1970-71 as base. This series comprised of 447 items and 2371 price quotations.

It is a continuous process so long as the needs, trends and prices continue to change.

Q. 50. *What do you understand by the index of industrial production?*

Ans. The index of industrial production (IIP) measures the changes in the level of industrial production in a given period as compared to a base period. Here, it should be kept in mind that it measures the changes in the quantum of production and not in values. The data for IIP includes the production of private and public sectors.

The formula for computing IIP for the current year 1 as compared to a base year 0 is,

$$IIP_{01} = \frac{\left(\sum_i \frac{q_{1i}}{q_{0i}}\right) w_i}{\sum_i w_i} \times 100$$

where i varies over all items of industrial production.

w_i's represent the weights based on the relative importance of different outputs.

The index of industrial production throws light on the industrial development of a country and also the availability of industrial goods.

Q. 51. *What series of index of industrial productions have been issued?*

Ans. The revised series of index of industrial production were constructed by the Central Statistical Organisation, Government of India, New Delhi with base 1980-81. The industries were classified into four categories namely, basic industries; capital goods industries; intermediate goods industries and consumer goods industries. The weights were assigned to different industrial groups according to the reports published by the *Annual Survey of Industries*.

Q. 52. *How index numbers are related to gross national product?*

Ans. The gross national product (GNP) at factor cost is the value of the product at factor cost attributable to the factors of production supplied by the normal residents of the country prior to deduction of the consumption of the fixed capital. The gross national product is equal to the value of the gross domestic product (GDP) at factor cost plus the factor income from abroad.

The gross national product enables one to determine the degree by which the physical goods and services have grown (or deflated) over time. The increase in the value of goods and services due to price rise should be eliminated. If this is not done, there can be a deceleration in the production of quantity of goods and services but the value of GNP gets higher due to inflation. Hence to determine the real economic growth, one should use price index number to deflate to GNP value. This is achieved by dividing GNP for the current year by an adjustment factor, known as *deflator index number*. This is how price index number is attached with gross national product.

Q. 53. *What is the difference between the net national product and the gross national product?*

Ans. The Net national product is the value of the product at factor cost attributable to the factors of production by the normal residents of a country after deducting the consumption of the fixed capital. Whereas in the gross national product it is prior to the deduction of the consumption of the fixed capital.

Q. 54. *Given the following information,*

Groups	Weights	Group indices
Food	48	320
Fuel and lighting	12	180
Clothing	10	210
House rent	20	250
Miscellaneous	10	150

find the consumer price index.

Ans. The consumer price index.

$$P_{01} = \frac{\sum_j G_{01}^j w_j}{\sum_j w_j}$$

$$= \frac{320 \times 48 + 180 \times 12 + 210 \times 10 + 250 \times 20 + 150 \times 10}{48 + 12 + 10 + 20 + 10}$$

$$= \frac{26120}{100}$$

$$= 261.2$$

Q. 55. *Given the sum of the products of prices and quantities for the current year 1 and base year 0 for five items as,*

$$\Sigma p_0 q_0 = 782, \Sigma p_0 q_1 = 1008, \Sigma p_1 q_0 = 1084, \Sigma p_1 q_1 = 1329$$

On the basis of the given information show that the data satisfies time reversal test.

Ans. For Fisher's ideal formula,

$$P_{01} = \sqrt{\frac{1084}{782} \times \frac{1329}{1008}} \times 100$$

$$= 135.19$$

and,

$$P_{10} = \sqrt{\frac{1008}{1329} \times \frac{782}{1084}} \times 100$$

$$= 73.97$$

For the time reversal test,

$$P_{01} \times P_{10} = \frac{135.19 \times 73.97}{100 \times 100}$$

$$= 1.00$$

Hence, the given data satisfies the time reversal test.

Q. 56. *For the information given in Q. No. 55, show that the data satisfies factor reversal test.*

Ans. Fisher's ideal index number,

$$P_{01} = \sqrt{\frac{1008}{782} \times \frac{1329}{1008}} \times 100$$

$$= 135.19$$

and Fisher's ideal quantity index number

$$Q_{01} = \sqrt{\frac{1008}{782} \times \frac{1329}{1084}} \times 100$$

Thus,

$$P_{01} Q_{01} = \sqrt{\frac{1084}{782} \times \frac{1329}{1008} \times \frac{1008}{782} \times \frac{1329}{1084}} \times 100$$

$$= \frac{1329}{782}$$

$$= \frac{\sum_i p_{1i} q_{1i}}{\sum_i p_{0i} q_{0i}}$$

$$= V_{01}$$

Hence, the given data satisfies factor reversal test.

Q. 57. *In the section of middle class people in cities A and B, a survey revealed that the expenditure in city A for food and other items was in the ratio of 60 : 40 and that in the city B it was in the ratio of 50 : 50. If the consumer price index for city A in 1991 is 350 and that of city B 300, then find the price indices for the groups (i) food, and (ii) other items.*

Ans. Let the CPI for food group is x and other items groups y.

Making use of the formula for CPI, for city A,

$$\frac{60x + 40y}{60 + 40} = 350$$

and for city B,

$$\frac{50x + 50y}{50 + 50} = 300$$

Solving the two equations we get, $x = 550$ and $y = 50$. It means that the price index for food is 550 and other items 50.

Q. 58. *The prices and quantities consumed for three items A, B and C during the base year 0 and current year 1 were as follows:*

Commodity	Base year		Current year	
	Price p_0	Quantity q_0	Price p_1	Quantity q_1
A	2	6	3	4
B	3	5	5	6
C	5	4	6	7

For the given data prove that,

$$\frac{L(p)}{L(q)} = \frac{P(p)}{P(q)}$$

Ans. From the given data we get,

$$\sum_i p_{0i} q_{0i} = 47, \sum p_{0i} q_{1i} = 51, \sum p_{1i} q_{0i} = 67, \sum p_{1i} q_{1i} = 84,$$

$$L(p) = \frac{\sum_i p_{1i}\, q_{0i}}{\sum_i p_{0i}\, q_{0i}} = \frac{67}{47}$$

$$L(q) = \frac{\sum_i q_{1i}\, p_{0i}}{\sum_i q_{0i}\, q_{0i}} = \frac{51}{47}$$

$$P(p) = \frac{\sum_i p_{1i}\, q_{1i}}{\sum_i p_{0i}\, q_{1i}} = \frac{84}{51}$$

$$P(q) = \frac{\sum_i q_{1i}\, p_{1i}}{\sum_i q_{0i}\, p_{1i}} = \frac{84}{67}$$

Now,

$$\frac{L(p)}{L(q)} = \frac{67/47}{51/47} = \frac{67}{51}$$

$$\frac{P(p)}{P(q)} = \frac{84/51}{84/67} = \frac{67}{51}$$

Therefore, $$\frac{L(p)}{L(q)} = \frac{P(p)}{P(q)}$$

SECTION B

Fill in the Blanks

Fill in the suitable word(s) or phrase(s) in the blanks:

1. Index numbers are known as _________.
2. Index numbers measure changes over time in magnitudes which are not capable of _________.
3. An index number is a special type of _________.
4. Index numbers are expressed in _________.
5. Index numbers always involve _________ periods or places.
6. Index numbers help in framing of _________.
7. The trend of economic activity can be studied with the help of _________.
8. Index numbers can be used for _________.
9. Index numbers help to assess the _________.
10. Price indices are _________ used.
11. Consumer price index is also known as _________.

12. Diffusion index reveals the changes in a group of _________.
13. Value index is used in the _________.
14. The base period should preferably be _________.
15 Use of weights in index numbers makes them _________.
16. Weights depend on _________ of the items.
17. In the computation of index numbers, most preferred type of average is _________.
18. Most commonly used average for index numbers is _________.
19. Geometric mean gives _________ weight to equal ratios of changes.
20. Geometric mean-based indices are _________.
21. In most of the situations, index numbers are the _________ averages.
22. The ideal formula for index number is due to _________.
23. Formula for unweighted price index number has _________ utility.
24. Unweighted quantitative index for n items can be calculated by the formula _________.
25. Laspeyre's price index uses the _________ quantities as weights.
26. Laspeyre's index is also known as _________ index.
27. Laspeyre's gave the aggregative index formulae in _________.
28. Laspeyre was a _________.
29. Paasche was a _________.
30. Paasche's indices use weights derived from the _________.
31. Paasche's index is also called _________ index.
32. Paasche expounded the formula for index number in _________.
33. Paasche's formula for price index is _________.
34. Paasche's formula for quantity index is _________.
35. The Drobish-Bowley price index is the _________ of L and P.
36. Geometric cross formula for price index is _________.
37. Fisher's ideal index number is the _______ of Laspeyre's and Paasche's index numbers.
38. Marshall and Edgeworth formula for price index utilises the _______ from the base and current years as weights.
39. Geometrically crossed-weight formula was given by _______.
40. The fixed weight system for index numbers was propounded by _______.
41. The difference between Laspeyre's and Paasche's indices is known as _______.
42. The difference between the index numbers based on n-sampled items and all the N items is known as _________.
43. The error caused by considering only the binary items is called _______.
44. The value of homogeneity error lies between _______ and _________.
45. When the homogeneity error $R = 0$, it means that there is _________ item.
46. When the homogeneity error $R = 1$, it shows that there is _________ item.
47. _______ the value of homogeneity error R, better it is.
48. Greater the value of homogeneity error R, _________ it is.
49. If the relation $P_{01} \times P_{10} = 1$ holds, it means that the price indices satisfy _______ test.
50. The quantity $(P_{01} \times Q_{01} - 1)$ is known as _______.
51. Fisher's ideal formula satisfies _______ and _______ tests.
52. The condition for factor reversal test to hold good is _______.
53. The quantity $\left(\frac{P_{01} \times Q_{01}}{V_{01}} - 1\right)$ is known as _______.

54. The condition for the circular test to hold good with usual notations is _________.

55. Circular test is satisfied only by the indices based on _________.

56. Indices base on Kelly's fixed weight method satisfy _________ test.

57. Circular test _________ satisfied by Fisher's ideal formula.

58. The relation between price indices of the type $P_{02} = P_{01}\ P_{12}$ comes from _______ method.

59. In the chain-base method, we find indices in respect of _______ as base period.

60. The indices obtained sequentially with preceding year as base are known as _______.

61. In the chain-base method, addition and deletion of items is _______.

62. In the chain-base method, weights can _______ be adjusted on any stage.

63. Indices calculated by the chain-base method are free from _______.

64. The chain-base indices are not suitable for _______ comparisons.

65. Base shifting is required to make the two series of indices _______.

66. Combining of two series of indices with different base periods into one series with common base period is known as _______.

67. If an old series is connected with a new series of index numbers, it is known as _______.

68. If a new series of index numbers is connected with an old one, it is called _______.

69. Deflation of index numbers helps to determine _______.

70. Consumer price index indicates _______ in prices of items of a basket at a point of time as compared to a base period.

71. Cost of living index is same in general sense as _______.

72. Purchasing power of money can be assessed through _______.

73. Consumer price index is mostly used for framing _______.

74. Dearness allowance of a certain cadre of people is fixed on the basis of _______.

75. Cost of living at two different cities can be compared with the help of _______.

76. Consumer price index helps to evaluate _______ of money.

77. The list of items included in the computation of consumer price index is known as _______.

78. For consumer price index, the price data should be collected from _______.

79. Weights used in the computation of consumer price index are usually the _______ on each item and groups.

80. Inclusion of expenditure on items not included in the basket in the calculation of consumer price index is known as _______.

81. The most popular method of computing consumer price index as _______.

82. Consumer price index tells about _______ experienced by the population on an average.

83. Weights which can be expressed with definiteness are called _______.

84. The price movement in all the markets except retailers is indicated by _______.

85. The industrial development of a country is reflected by _______.

86. The gross national product value is deflated through _______.

87. The adjustment factor used to deflate the gross national product is known as _______.

88. The production of a country at factor cost by the residents of a country after deducting the consumption of fixed capital is known as _______.

89. Family budget method is also known as _______.

90. An upward bias is given by _______ formula.

91. Paasche's index number gives _______ bias.

92. Unit test ensures the independence of index numbers from _______.

93. The consumer price index for April, 1985 was 125. The food index was 120 and for other items 135. The percentage of total weight given to food is _______.

94. If the salary of a person in the base year is ₹ 2000 per annum and in the current year ₹ 5000. The CPI is 325, then the allowance required to maintain the same standard of living is ₹ _______.

95. If the percentage of expenditure on five groups of commodities is 30, 15, 25, 20 and 10 and group indices 190, 180, 140, 120 and 100, then the consumer price index is _______.

96 The total expenditure of a family is ₹ 2500 per month and he spends ₹ 1000 on food, ₹ 300 on clothing, ₹ 800 per month on rent and has no record of expenditure on light and miscellaneous groups. If the group indices are 190, 180, 140, 120 and 100 and CPI as 160, the family expenditure on light and miscellaneous items are ₹. _______ and ₹ _______ respectively.

97. Fisher's ideal formula does not satisfy _______ test.

98. Weighted geometric mean of relatives with fixed weights does not satisfy _______ test.

99. Weighted arithmetic mean of price relatives with fixed weights satisfies _______ of the time reversal, factor reversal and circular tests.

100. Simple arithmetic mean of price relatives does not satisfy _______ tests.

101. If all the sub-indices are equal to a value P and total index is also equal to P, then it is satisfying the test of _______.

102. Unit test is not satisfied by _______ index.

103. If on changing the unit of measurement of commodities, the index number remains same, then is said to fulfil the requirement of the test of _______.

104. Splicing is very useful for comparison between _______ and _______ index numbers.

105. Test of definiteness ensures that if a subindex is zero or infinity, then the total index must not be _______ or _______.

SECTION C

Multiple Choice Questions

Select the correct alternative out of given ones:

1. Index numbers reveal the state of:
(*a*) inflation
(*b*) deflation
(*c*) both (*a*) and (*b*)
(*d*) neither (*a*) nor (*b*)

2. Index numbers are also known as:
(*a*) economic barometers
(*b*) signs and guide posts
(*c*) both (*a*) and (*b*)
(*d*) neither (*a*) nor (*b*)

3. Index number is a:
(*a*) measure of relative changes
(*b*) a special type of an average
(*c*) a percentage relative
(*d*) all of the above

4. Index numbers are expressed:
(*a*) in percentages
(*b*) in ratios
(*c*) in terms of absolute value
(*d*) all of the above

5. Index numbers help:
(*a*) in framing of economic policies
(*b*) in assessing the purchasing power of money
(*c*) for adjusting national income
(*d*) all of the above

6. The error(s) involved in the construction of index numbers is/are:
(*a*) error of sampling
(*b*) formula error
(*c*) error in collected data
(*d*) all of the above

7. Element of subjectivity is involved in index numbers due to:
(*a*) choice of base year
(*b*) selection of weights
(*c*) choice of commodities
(*d*) all of the above

8. Most commonly used index number is:
(*a*) Diffusion index number
(*b*) price index number
(*c*) value index number
(*d*) none of the above

9. One of the limitations in the construction of index numbers is:
(*a*) the choice of the type of average
(*b*) choice of investigators
(*c*) choice of variables to be studied
(*d*) all of the above

10. Consumer price index number is constructed for:
(*a*) a well defined section of people
(*b*) all the people
(*c*) factory workers only
(*d*) all of the above

11. Diffusion index reveals the changes in:
(*a*) elite
(*b*) industrial production
(*c*) a group of time series
(*d*) none of the above

12. The first and fore most step in the construction of index numbers is:
(*a*) choice of base period
(*b*) choice of weights
(*c*) to delineate the purpose of index numbers
(*d*) all of the above

13. Base period for an index number should be:
(*a*) a year only
(*b*) a normal period
(*c*) a period at distant past
(*d*) none of the above

14. Data for index numbers should be collected from:
(*a*) the retailers
(*b*) the wholesale dealers
(*c*) the selected group of persons
(*d*) none of the above

15. Most preferred type of average for index numbers is:
(*a*) arithmetic mean
(*b*) geometric mean
(*c*) harmonic mean
(*d*) none of the above

16. Most frequently used index number formulae are:
(*a*) weighted formulae
(*b*) unweighted formulae
(*c*) fixed weight formulae
(*d*) none of the above

17. The unweighted price index formula based on *n* items is:
(*a*) $\sum_{i=1}^{n} p_{1i}/p_{0i}$
(*b*) $\sum_{i=1}^{n} \frac{p_{1i}}{p_{0i}} \times 100$
(*c*) $\frac{\sum_{i=1}^{n} p_{1i}}{\sum_{i=1}^{n} p_{0i}} \times 100$
(*d*) none of the above

18. Unweighted price index formula is:
(*a*) most frequently used
(*b*) seldom used
(*c*) the best
(*d*) all of the above

19. Laspeyre's index formula uses the weights of the:
(*a*) base year
(*b*) current year

(c) average of the weights of a number of years

(a) none of the above

20. Laspeyre's index numbers possess:

(a) downward bias

(b) no bias

(c) upward bias

(d) none of the above

21. Laspeyre's gave the aggregative price index formula in the year:

(a) 1901

(b) 1871

(c) 1874

(d) none of the above

22. Laspeyre's index number is also known as:

(a) fixed base index

(b) given year method index

(c) base year method index

(d) none of the above

23. The weights used in Paasche's formula belong to:

(a) the base period

(b) the given period

(c) to any arbitrary chosen period

(d) none of the above

24. Paasche was:

(a) an English mathematician

(b) a French economist

(c) a German statistician

(d) none of the above

25. Paasche's index number was invented in the year:

(a) 1871

(b) 1901

(c) 1874

(d) 1918

26. Drobish-Bowley gave the formula for price index in:

(a) 1910

(b) 1901

(c) 1801

(d) 1871

27. Paasche's price index formula with usual notations for n items is:

(a) $\left[\sum_{i=1}^{n} p_{1i}q_{1i} \Big/ \sum_{i=1}^{n} p_{0i}q_{1i}\right]\times 100$

(b) $\left[\sum_{i=1}^{n} p_{1i}q_{1i} \Big/ \sum_{i=1}^{n} p_{0i}q_{0i}\right]\times 100$

(c) $\left[\sum_{i=1}^{n} p_{0i}q_{1i} \Big/ \sum_{i=1}^{n} p_{1i}q_{1i}\right]\times 100$

(d) $\left[\sum_{i=1}^{n} p_{1i}q_{0i} \Big/ \sum_{i=1}^{n} p_{0i}q_{1i}\right]\times 100$

28. Paasche's quantity index formula for n items is:

(a) $\left(\sum_{i=1}^{n} p_{1i}q_{1i} \Big/ \sum_{i=1}^{n} p_{0i}q_{1i}\right)\times 100$

(b) $\left(\sum_{i=1}^{n} p_{1i}q_{1i} \Big/ \sum_{i=1}^{n} p_{0i}q_{0i}\right)\times 100$

(c) $\left(\sum_{i=1}^{n} p_{0i}q_{1i} \Big/ \sum_{i=1}^{n} p_{1i}q_{1i}\right)\times 100$

(d) $\left(\sum_{i=1}^{n} p_{1i}q_{1i} \Big/ \sum_{i=1}^{n} p_{1i}q_{0i}\right)\times 100$

29. The Drobish-Bowley price index formula is the:

(a) geometric mean of Laspeyre's and Paasche's price index formulae

(b) arithmetic mean of Laspeyre's and Paasche's price index formulae

(c) Weighted mean of Laspeyre's and Paasche's price index formulae

(d) none of the above

30. The price index as the arithmetic mean of Laspeyre's and Paasche's indices was expounded by:

(a) Kelly

(b) Irving Fisher

(c) Drobish and Bowley

(d) Walsh

31. The geometric mean of Laspeyre's and Paasche's price indices is also known as:

(a) Fisher's price index
(b) Kelly's price index
(c) Drobish-Bowley price index
(d) Walsh price index

32. Geometric cross formula for index number is known as:
(a) Walsh ideal formula
(b) Fisher's ideal formula
(c) Bowley's standard formula
(d) none of the above

33. Fisher named the geometric cross formula as an ideal index formula in the year:
(a) 1901
(b) 1910
(c) 1920
(d) 1950

34. Marshall and Edgeworth price index number formula utilises the weights as:
(a) quantities of the base year
(b) quantities of the given year
(c) combined quantities of base and given year
(d) any of the above

35. Kelly emphasised on the use of weights for price index number belonging to the:
(a) base period
(b) current period
(c) average of the base and current periods quantities
(d) any logically ascertained quantities

36. The weighted price relatives with selective weights can be reduced to:
(a) Laspeyre's formula
(b) Paasche's formula
(c) both (a) and (b)
(d) neither (a) nor (b)

37. The difference between the quantity indices due to Laspeyre and Paasche is called:
(a) formula error
(b) sampling error
(c) homogeneity error
(d) none of the above

38. The difference between the index numbers based on *n* selected items and total numbers of items is called:
(a) formula error
(b) sampling error
(c) homogeneity error
(d) none of the above

39. Sampling error in respect of index numbers can be reduced by:
(a) taking a random sample of items
(b) including large number of items
(c) both (a) and (b)
(d) neither (a) nor (b)

40. Binary items are those in reference to index numbers which belong to:
(a) current period
(b) base period
(c) the base and current periods together
(d) none of the above

41. The ratio of the unique items to the total number of items is a measure of:
(a) formula error
(b) homogeneity error
(c) sampling error
(d) none of the above

42. The range of homogeneity error in reference to index numbers is:
(a) 0 to 1
(b) 0 to ∞
(c) – 1 to 1
(d) – ∞ to ∞

43. Most preferred value of homogeneity error '*R*' in reference to index numbers is:
(a) 1
(b) 0
(c) ∞
(d) – 1

44. If the index number is independent of the units of measurements, then it satisfies:
(a) times reversal test
(b) factor reversal test
(c) unit test
(d) all of the above

45. The condition for the time reversal test to hold good with usual notations is:
(a) $P_{01} \times P_{10} = 1$
(b) $P_{10} \times P_{01} = 0$

(*c*) $P_{01}/P_{10} = 1$

(*d*) $P_{01} + P_{10} = 1$

46. The discrepancy ($P_{01} \times P_{10} - 1$) is termed as:

(*a*) joint error

(*b*) homogeneity error

(*c*) formula error

(*d*) none of the above

47. Factor reversal test was invented by:

(*a*) Walsh

(*b*) A.L. Bowley

(*c*) John I. Griffin

(*d*) Irving Fisher

48. The condition for the factor reversal test to be satisfied with usual notations is:

(*a*) $P_{01} \times Q_{01} = V_{01}$

(*b*) $\frac{P_{01} \times Q_{01}}{V_{01}} = 1$

(*c*) $\frac{P_{01} \times Q_{01}}{V_{01}} - 1 = 0$

(*d*) all the above

49. The condition for the price indices to satisfy the circular test for four years data is:

(*a*) $P_{01} P_{12} P_{23} P_{30} = 1$

(*b*) $P_{01} P_{12} P_{23} P_{34} = 1$

(*c*) $P_{01} + P_{12} + P_{23} = P_{43}$

(*d*) $P_{12} + P_{23} + P_{34} = 1$

50. Circular test for prices indices is satisfied by the formula:

(*a*) based on geometric mean of price relatives

(*b*) obtained by Kelly's fixed weight method

(*c*) both (*a*) and (*b*)

(*d*) neither (*a*) nor (*b*)

51. Fisher's ideal formula does not satisfy:

(*a*) time reversal test

(*b*) circular test

(*c*) factor reversal test

(*d*) unit test

52. Year-to-year indices in the chain-base method are called:

(*a*) chain indices

(*b*) link relatives

(*c*) fixed base indices

(*d*) all of the above

53. The relation between fixed base indices P_{01}, P_{02}, P_{03} and the chain base indices P_{01}, P_{12}, P_{23} is:

(*a*) $P_{03} = P_{01} P_{12} P_{23}$

(*b*) $P_{03} = P_{02} P_{23}$

(*c*) $P_{01} P_{12} = P_{02} P_{23}$

(*d*) all of the above

54. Indices calculated by the chain-base method are almost free from:

(*a*) homogeneity error

(*b*) seasonal variations

(*c*) rigidity of weights

(*d*) all of the above

55. When the indices given for a number of years are to be worked out to a new base period, this phenomenon is known as:

(*a*) splicing

(*b*) base shifting

(*c*) both (*a*) and (*b*)

(*d*) neither (*a*) nor (*b*)

56. Combining of two index number series having different base periods into one series with common base period is known as:

(*a*) splicing

(*b*) base shifting

(*c*) both (*a*) and (*b*)

(*d*) neither (*a*) nor (*b*)

57. If the old series is connected, with the new series of index numbers, it is known as:

(*a*) base sifting

(*b*) backward splicing

(*c*) forward splicing

(*d*) none of the above

58. If the new series is connected with the old series, it is known as:

(*a*) base shifting

(*b*) backward splicing

(*c*) forward splicing
(*d*) all of the above

59. Deflation of index numbers is meant for calculating:
(*a*) real wages
(*b*) money income index
(*c*) real income index number
(*d*) all of the above

60. Purchasing power of money is estimated by the formula:
(*a*) Price index × 100
(*b*) $\dfrac{\text{Money income}}{\text{Consumer price index}} \times 100$
(*c*) $\dfrac{100}{\text{price index}}$
(*d*) $\dfrac{\text{price index}}{100}$

61. Consumer price index reflects on the price changes experienced by:
(*a*) an individual
(*b*) a particular family
(*c*) all families of a population
(*d*) all of the above

62. An appropriate method for working out consumer price index is:
(*a*) weighted aggregate expenditure method
(*b*) family budget method
(*c*) price relatives method
(*d*) none of the above

63. For consumer price index, price quotations are collected from:
(*a*) retailers
(*b*) wholesale dealers
(*c*) fair price shops
(*d*) government depots

64. In computation of consumer price index, usually the weights used are:
(*a*) quantities consumed by the families
(*b*) percentages of expenditure
(*c*) quantities of production
(*d*) all of the above

65. The quantities of items consumed or produced taken as weights come under the category of:
(*a*) implicit weights
(*b*) explicit weights
(*c*) fixed weights
(*d*) none of the above

66. The weights assigned according to the relative importance of the items are known as:
(*a*) implicit weights
(*b*) explicit weights
(*c*) fixed weights
(*d*) all of the above

67. The wholesale price index is different from consumer price index in respect of:
(*a*) collection of price quotations
(*b*) weights
(*c*) inclusion of services
(*d*) all of the above

68. Index of industrial production measures the changes in:
(*a*) the quantum of production
(*b*) the value of products
(*c*) the demand of industrial goods
(*d*) none of the above

69. In determining the real economic growth, the price index number is used to:
(*a*) evaluate the value of national products
(*b*) deflate the GNP value
(*c*) both (*a*) and (*b*)
(*d*) neither (*a*) nor (*b*)

70. Net national product (NNP) and gross national product (GNP):
(*a*) are different
(*b*) measure the value of national production
(*c*) evaluate the value of national product at factor cost
(*d*) all of the above

71. The values of gross national product (GNP) and net national product (NNP) follow the relation:
(*a*) GNP = NNP
(*b*) GNP < NNP

(*c*) GNP > NNP
(*d*) GNP ≥ NNP

72. Factor reversal test permits the interchange of:
(*a*) base periods
(*b*) price and quantity
(*c*) weights
(*d*) none of the above

73. The consumer price index in 1990 increases by 80 per cent as compared to the base 1980. A person in 1980 getting ₹ 60,000 per annum should now get:
(*a*) ₹ 1,08,000 per annum
(*b*) ₹ 72,000 per annum
(*c*) ₹ 54,000 per annum
(*d*) none of the above

74. If a family spends on food, housing and clothing in the ratio of 5 : 3 : 2 and experiences the rise in prices of these heads by 40, 30 and 20 per cent respectively, the family budget will be increased by:
(*a*) 33 per cent
(*b*) 30 per cent
(*c*) 27 per cent
(*d*) none of the above

75. If the index number for 1990 to the base 1980 is 250, the index number for 1980 to the base 1990 is:
(*a*) 4
(*b*) 40
(*c*) 400
(*d*) none of the above

76. If Laspeyre's price index is 324 and Paasche's price index 144, then Fisher's ideal index is:
(*a*) 234
(*b*) 180
(*c*) 216
(*d*) none of the above

77. If the consumer price index for 1994 is 800, then the purchasing power of a rupee is:
(*a*) 0.125 paise
(*b*) 12.5 paise
(*c*) 8 paise
(*d*) none of the above

78. The consumer price index numbers for 1981 and 1982 to the base 1974 are 320 and 400 respectively. The consumer price index for 1981 to the base 1982 is:
(*a*) 125
(*b*) 80
(*c*) 128
(*d*) none of the above

79. The index number for 1985 to the base 1980 is 125 and for 1980 to the base 1985 is 80. The given indices satisfy:
(*a*) time reversal test
(*b*) factor reversal test
(*c*) circular test
(*d*) all of the above

80. The price relatives for three commodities are 125, 120 and 130 with their respective weights 5, *w* and 8. If the price index for the set is 1125.25, the value of *w* is:
(*a*) 6
(*b*) – 7
(*c*) 7
(*d*) none of the above

81. If the group indices are 80, 120 and 125 and their respective group weights are 60, 20 and 20, the consumer price index is:
(*a*) 108.33
(*b*) 97.00
(*c*) 98.49
(*d*) none of the above

82. Which index satisfies factor reversal test?
(*a*) Paasche's index
(*b*) Laspeyre's index
(*c*) Fisher's ideal index
(*d*) Walsh price index

83. If a sub-index is zero, then the total index must:
(*a*) be zero
(*c*) be infinity
(*d*) indeterminate
(*d*) not be zero

84. If the unit of measurement of a commodity changes, the value of index number:
(*a*) also changes
(*b*) remains same

(c) increases

(d) decreases

85. If all the sub-indices are equal to P, then the total index will be:

(a) equal to P

(b) equal to 100

(c) equal to 1

(d) equal to 0.

86. The property, that on changing the unit of measurement of a commodity, the index number does not change, is called:

(a) test of equality

(b) test of homogeneity

(c) test of commensurability

(d) test of proportionality

87. The property that a sub-index is zero or infinity but the total index is not zero or infinity is known as:

(a) test of randomness

(b) factor reversal test

(c) test of definiteness

(d) none of the above

88. The property that in case of all sub-indices being P resulting into total index equal to P, is termed as:

(a) test of randomness

(b) test of proportionality

(c) test of definiteness

(d) test of commensurability

89. Index numbers are the special type of:

(a) averages

(b) percentage relatives

(c) ratios

(d) all of the above

90. The index that indicates the progress or recession of an economic cycle in a group of time series is:

(a) value index

(b) quantitative index

(c) diffusion index

(d) all of the above

ANSWERS

Section B

1. economic barometers **2.** direct measurement **3.** average **4.** percentages **5.** two **6.** policies **7.** index numbers **8.** forecasting **9.** real wages **10.** frequently **11.** cost of living index **12.** time series **13.** sales of company **14.** normal period **15.** better representative **16.** relative importance **17.** geometric mean **18.** arithmetic mean **19.** equal **20.** reversible **21.** weighted **22.** Irving Fisher **23.** little **24.** $\left[\sum_i q_{1i} \Big/ \sum_i q_{0i}\right] \times 100$ **25.** base year **26.** base year method **27.** 1871 **28.** French economist **29.** German statistician **30.** Current period **31.** given year method **32.** 1874 **33.** $\left[\sum_i p_{1i}\, q_{1i} \Big/ \sum_i p_{0i}\, q_{1i}\right] \times 100$ **34.** $\left[\sum_i q_{1i}\, p_{1i} \Big/ \sum_i q_{0i}\, p_{1i}\right] \times 100$ **35.** arithmetic mean **36.** $\sqrt{L \times P}$ **37.** geometric mean **38.** combined quantities **39.** Marshall and Edgeworth **40.** Kelly's **41.** formula error **42.** sampling error **43.** homogeneity error **44.** 0; 1 **45.** no unique **46.** no binary **47.** Lesser **48.** poorer **49.** time reversal **50.** joint error **51.** time reversal; factor reversal **52.** $P_{01} \times Q_{01} = V_{01}$ **53.** joint error **54.** $P_{01}\, P_{12}\, P_{23} \cdots P_{(k-1)k}\, P_{k0} = 1$ **55.** geometric mean **56.** circular **57.** is not **58.** chain base **59.** preceding period **60.** link relatives **61.** easily feasible **62.** easily **63.** seasonal variations **64.** long range **65.** comparable **66.** splicing **67.** forward splicing **68.** backward splicing **69.** real wages **70.** rise or fall **71.** consumer price index **72.** consumer price index **73.** wage policy **74.** consumer price index **75.** consumer price index **76.** purchasing power **77.** basket **78.** retailers **79.** percentages of expenditure **80.** imputation of expenditure **81.** family budget method **82.** price changes **83.** explicit weights **84.** wholesale price index **85.** index of industrial production **86.** price index number **87.** deflator index number **88.** net national product **89.** method of weighted relatives **90.** Laspeyre's **91.** downward **92.** units of measurements

93. 66.67% $\left[\text{Hint: } \frac{120x + (100 - x)\,135}{100} = 125\right]$

94. 1500 $\left[\text{Hint: } \frac{325}{100} \times 2000 = 6500; \text{ Amt. reqd.} = (6500 - 5000)\right]$

95. 153 per cent **96.** 200; 200 **97.** circular **98.** factor reversal **99.** none **100.** time and factor reversal **101.** proportionality **102.** simple aggregative index **103.** commensurability **104.** new; old **105.** zero; infinite

Section C

1. (*c*)	**2.** (*c*)	**3.** (*d*)	**4.** (*a*)	**5.** (*d*)
6. (*d*)	**7.** (*d*)	**8.** (*b*)	**9.** (*a*)	**10.** (*a*)
11. (*c*)	**12.** (*c*)	**13.** (*b*)	**14.** (*d*)	**15.** (*b*)
16. (*a*)	**17.** (*c*)	**18.** (*b*)	**19.** (*a*)	**20.** (*c*)
21. (*b*)	**22.** (*c*)	**23.** (*b*)	**24.** (*c*)	**25.** (*c*)
26. (*b*)	**27.** (*a*)	**28.** (*d*)	**29.** (*b*)	**30.** (*c*)
31. (*d*)	**32.** (*b*)	**33.** (*c*)	**34.** (*c*)	**35.** (*d*)
36. (*c*)	**37.** (*a*)	**38.** (*b*)	**39.** (*c*)	**40.** (*c*)
41. (*b*)	**42.** (*a*)	**43.** (*b*)	**44.** (*c*)	**45.** (*a*)
46. (*a*)	**47.** (*d*)	**48.** (*d*)	**49.** (*a*)	**50.** (*c*)
51. (*b*)	**52.** (*b*)	**53.** (*d*)	**54.** (*d*)	**55.** (*b*)
56. (*a*)	**57.** (*c*)	**58.** (*b*)	**59.** (*d*)	**60.** (*c*)
61. (*c*)	**62.** (*b*)	**63.** (*a*)	**64.** (*b*)	**65.** (*b*)
66. (*a*)	**67.** (*d*)	**68.** (*a*)	**69.** (*b*)	**70.** (*d*)
71. (*c*)	**72.** (*c*)	**73.** (*a*)	**74.** (*a*)	**75.** (*b*)
76. (*c*)	**77.** (*b*)	**78.** (*b*)	**79.** (*a*)	**80.** (*c*)
81. (*b*)	**82.** (*c*)	**83.** (*d*)	**84.** (*b*)	**85.** (*a*)
86. (*c*)	**87.** (*c*)	**88.** (*b*)	**89.** (*d*)	**90.** (*c*)

SUGGESTED READING

1. Agarwal, B.L., *Basic Statistics,* New Age International Publishers, New Delhi, 8th edition, 2024.
2. Berenson, M.L. and Levine D.M., *Basic Business Statistics*, Prentice Hall, Englewood Cliffs, 1979.
3. Chou, Ya Lu, *Statistical Analysis with Business and Economics, Applications*, Holt, Rinehart and Winston, New York, 1975.
4. Enns, P.G., *Business Statistics*, Richard D. Irwin, Illinois, 1985.
5. Gupta, S.C. and Kapoor, V.K., *Fundamentals of Applied Statistics*, Sultan Chand & Sons, New Delhi, 1993.
6. Mudgett, B.D., *Index Numbers*, John Wiley, New York, 1951.
7. Richards, L.E. and Lacava, J.J., *Business Statistics*, McGraw Hill Book Company, New York, 1978.
8. Spurr, W.A., Kellogg, L.S. and Smith, J.H., *Business and Economic Statistics*, Richard D. Irwin, Illinois, 1954.
9. Summers, G.W., Peters, W.S., and Armstrong, C.P., *Student Supplement for Basic Statistics, An Introduction*, Wadsworth Publishing Company, California, 1977.

Chapter 18

Business Forecasting

SECTION A

Short Essay Type Questions

Q. 1. *What do you understand by business forecasting?*

Ans. The success of any business depends on its future estimates. On the basis of these estimates, a businessman plans his production, stocks, selling markets, expansion of plants, arrangement of additional funds, curtailment of loans, etc. Forecasting is different from prediction and projections. Regression analysis, analysis of time series, extrapolation, index numbers are some of techniques through which the predictions and projections are made. Whereas forecasting is a method of foretelling the course of business activity based on the analysis of past and present data mixed with the consideration of ensuing economic policies and circumstances. Forecasting means forewarning. Forecasts based on statistical analysis are much more reliable than a mere guess work.

Many economists and statisticians defined forecasting according to their own perceptions. Some of them are quoted below.

(*i*) **Charles W. Elliot:** All business proceed on beliefs or judgements of probabilities and not on certainties.

(*ii*) **H.J. Wheldon:** Business forecasting is not so much the estimation of certain figures of sales, production, profits, etc., as the analysis of known data, internal and external, in a manner which will enable policy to be determined to meet probable future conditions to the best advantage.

(*iii*) **Leo Barness:** The aim of forecasting is to establish, as accurate as possible, the probable behaviour of economic activity based on all data available and to set policies in terms of these probabilities.

(*iv*) **Neter and Wasserman:** Business forecasting refers to the statistical analysis of the past and current movements in a given time series, so as to obtain clues about the future pattern of the movements.

(*v*) **T.S. Lewis and R.A. Fox:** Forecasting is using the knowledge we have at one time to estimate what will happen at some future movement of time.

Q. 2. *What are the main aspects of business forecasting and their role?*

Ans. Two main aspects of business forecasting are:

(*i*) Historical analysis

(*ii*) Analysis of current economic conditions.

(*i*) ***Historical analysis:*** To understand the future course of business activity, it becomes necessary to analyse the past data and circumstances. Analysis of past data is very well carried through analysis of time series which separately tell about the four components of time series namely, trend, seasonals, cyclic variation and irregular variation.

Trend clearly reveals the happenings of the past and indicate towards the future trend of business activity. Study of seasonal variations discloses the likely changes in near future whereas the study of cyclic variations depicts the state of business, *i.e.*, whether the business is passing through the state of prosperity, decline, depression or recovery.

(*ii*) ***Analysis of current economic conditions:*** The forecasting is very much affected by the changes in governmental economic policies, industrial policies, taxation, traditions, fashion, import and export, war, etc. *Hence, the study of all such factors is necessary for* forecasting.

For a reliable business forecast, it becomes essential to study the above two aspects.

Q. 3. *Give the names of different methods of business forecasting.*

Ans. There are three basic categories of business forecasting methods:

(*i*) Naive method

(*ii*) Barometric methods

(*iii*) Analytical methods

Each of these categories covers a number of methods which are used for business forecasting.

(*i*) ***Naive method:*** It contains only the economic rhythm theory.

(*ii*) ***The barometric methods cover:***

(*a*) Specific historical analogy

(*b*) Lead-lag relationship

(*c*) Diffusion index

(*d*) Action-reaction theory.

(*iii*) ***The analytical methods contain:***

(*a*) The factor listing method

(*b*) Cross-cut analysis theory

(*c*) Exponential smoothing

(*d*) Econometric methods.

Q. 4. *How are the forecasts made under economic rhythm theory?*

Ans. The economic rhythm theory implies the forecasts made by the manufacturer himself regarding production, sales, dividends, etc. In this method, the manufacturer analyses the time series data of his own firm or company and forecasts on the basis of projections so obtained. The forecasts based on this method are applicable only for the individual firm for which the data are analysed. The forecasts under this method are not very reliable as no subjective matters are being considered.

Q. 5. *Name the forecasting agency which believes in economic rhythm theory and delineate its functioning.*

Ans. Standard and Poor's Trade and Securities Service; New York, believes in economic rhythm theory. The institute analyses data for forecasting according to the existing situations with a fresh outlook.

Q. 6. *What is the theme behind specific historical analogy method of business forecasting?*

Ans. The method is based on the famous dictum, 'history repeats itself'. Under this method, a period from past bearing similarity to the present economic situation is selected and a study is made how the business movement took place under the circumstances. The same sort of business movements are considered to occur now, of course with certain amount of adjustment looking to some special circumstances.

Q. 7. *How does the lead-lag relationship theory help in business forecasting?*

Ans. The Lead-Lag theory of forecasting is also known as *sequence theory.* This theory of forecasting is based on the principle that changes in business occur in succession, not simultaneously. For instance, the decrease in exchange rate causes the increase in wholesale prices which eventually increase the retail prices and consequently the salaries and wages. Thus, the impact of inflation on wholesale and retail prices and wages is not simultaneous but in phases one after the other with certain lag of time. This shows that the variables governing the business activity have a lead-lag relationship. Under this theory, an effort is made to determine the lag of time between the movement of business cycles.

The lead-lag relationships are usually developed by the critical inspection of graphs of various series and the correlation studies.

Q. 8. *In what manner did Harward index of general business conditions consist of three prediction curves, (a) speculation, the leading series, (b) business, the coincident series and (c) money, the lagging series.*

Ans. The rise and fall of the speculation curves was used to forecast the movement of business cycles. It is worth pointing out that the speculation curve and money curve have movements in opposite directions. It means that the upturn of speculation curve is accompanied by the downturn of the money curve. Such a situation marks the boom in business within few months while a reverse situation is an indication of the recession in business.

Q. 9. *What are the indicators involved in lead-lag approach of business forecasting?*

Ans. Three types of indicators are involved in lead-lag approach of business forecasting:

First, the lead indicators are price indices of equity shares, bank reserves, exchange rate of currency, borrowing from financial agencies, creation of new companies, etc.

Secondly, the coincident indicators are employment, industrial production index, gross national product at current prices, business profits, total freight traffic, etc.

Third, the lag indicators are personal income payments, total sales from retail stores, business loans (quarterly), interest rates, inventories of finished products, etc.

Q. 10. *What are the limitations of lead-lag approach of business forecasting?*

Ans. There are many limitations in lead-lag method of business forecasting which are as follows:

(*i*) It is not always possible to correctly interpret the movement of indicator variables because of the variability of timing and presence of irregular movements in the series.

(*ii*) Selection of indicators is also a problem as no thumb-rule is available. Many times some indicators fail to signal at all.

(*iii*) It is difficult to forecast the amplitude of the cycles.

(*iv*) The lead-lag method is a supplement to the methods of forecasting, not beyond it.

Q. 11. *Which forecasting agencies make use of the lead-lag method?*

Ans. *The National Bureau of Economic Research, Massachusetts* has carried out most careful and comprehensive work on the lead-lag relationship as initiated by the Harward Committee of Economic Research in the early twenties of twentieth century. It publishes a weekly report.

The Econometric Institute and the Index Number Institute, New York analyse data and measure trends, cycles, their lead and lag about each other or phase differences, the systematic patterns of residuals and econometric relationships.

The institute publishes a forecasting bulletin, *economic measures.*

Q. 12. *Discuss the diffusion index method of business forecasting.*

Ans. The diffusion index method is based on the principle that different factors, affecting business, do not attain their peaks or troughs simultaneously. There is always a time lag between them. This method has the convenience that one has not to identify which series has a lead and which a lag. The diffusion index depicts the movement of broad group of series as a whole without bothering about the individual series. The diffusion index shows the percentage of a given set of series as expanding in a time period. It should be carefully noted that the peaks and troughs of the diffusion index are not the peaks and troughs of the business cycles. All series do not expand or contract concurrently. Hence, if more than 50 per cent are expanding at a given time, it is taken that the business is in the process of booming and *vice-versa.*

The graphic method is usually employed to work out the diffusion index. The diffusion index can be constructed for a group of business variables like prices, investments, profits, etc.

Q. 13. *In what manner the action-reaction theory is applied in business forecasting?*

Ans. Newton's third law of motion has been applied to the theory of economics. Enough confidence has been posed in action-reaction theory as it has been observed that in business activity, there is always a recession after prosperity and prosperity after recession. This process continues eternally.

Babson found that the area covered by a time series or index of activity curve above the line is approximately as much as it is below the line of normal activity. Of course, the span of the period of prosperity and recession are usually not the same.

Q. 14. *Which business forecasting organisation utilises action-reaction theory and what are its publications?*

Ans. *The Business Statistics Organisation,* Washington, one of the oldest organisations of the USA founded by *Roger W. Babson* formerly known as *Babson's Statistical,* Organisation, utilises action-reaction theory. It has its affiliated organisation in Canada named as Babson's Canadian Reports Ltd., Toronto, Ontario.

The publications of this organisation are:

(*i*) Investment and Barometer (Weekly)

(*ii*) Confidential Barometer Letter (Weekly)

(*iii*) Business Inventory – Commodity Price Forecasts (Monthly).

(*iv*) Babson's Washington Forecasts.

Q. 15. *What is the basis of business forecasting by the factor listing method?*

Ans. Under the factor listing method, various factors which are likely to influence the business are identified by the analyst. Each factor is analysed to assess whether the probable impact of the factor upon aggregate business activity is favourable or not. No mathematical tool is applied for the analysis of data. Inferences are drawn regarding the effect of each factor on the business and then aggregated, merely by his own judgement, to forecast the likely state of business in near future.

Q. 16. *What are the merits and demerits of the factor listing method?*

Ans.

Merits:

(*i*) This method is not dependent on any mathematical treatment.

(*ii*) There is no restriction on the number of variables to be included in the process of forecasting.

(*iii*) Due weightage can be given to each factor according to its importance in explaining the business condition without any hassles.

(*iv*) A judgement of likely turning points through dominating variables is always easy and handy.

Demerits:

(*i*) The main drawback of the factor listing method is that it is totally subjective. Hence, a decision about the state of business condition will vary from person to person.

(*ii*) The results are not precise as no mathematical analysis of data is involved.

Q. 17. *Delineate the cross-cut analysis method of business forecasting.*

Ans. The cross-cut analysis theory is just opposite to historical analogy theory. Cross-cut analysis theory claims that past cycles cannot be the guide for future cycles as the factors like technological advancement, government policies, demand, availability of inputs, styles, fads, etc., change with the lapse of time. Hence, a thorough analysis of all the factors under present situations has to be done and an estimate of the composite effect of all factors is being made. This method takes into account the views of managerial staff, economists, consumers, etc., prior to the forecast. The forecast about future state of business is made on the basis of the overall assessment of the effect of all the factors.

Q. 18. *What are the drawbacks of cross-cut analysis method?*

Ans. There are two main drawbacks of the crosscut analysis method:

(*i*) The people do not express their views sincerely and plainly.

(*ii*) It is very difficult to analyse each variable separately and then to pool their effect for a business forecast.

Q. 19. *Which forecasting agency follows the principle of cross-cut analysis and how it operates?*

Ans. The Brookmire Economic Service, New York emphasises the theory of cross-cut (cross-section) analysis. Their belief is that domination of one cycle may have little or no effect on the next cycle. The forecasts of this service are based on this principle. The Brookmire Economic Service has the following publications:

(*i*) *Brookmire bulletin*

(*ii*) *Brookmire special report* (Weekly).

Q. 20. *How is the method of opinion polling used for the purpose of business forecasting?*

Ans. The device of opinion poll for business forecasting makes use of the survey reports and opinions obtained through surveys. The theme behind this method is that the present attitudes of the people towards business can be real guide for evaluating the real change in business conditions in near future. For this purpose, opinions are invited from business experts, persons in strategic positions, the sales forces and consumers. The information so obtained is analysed for business forecasts.

The forecasts made by the opinion polling method are simple and least expensive. Opinion polling method is suitable for short-term business forecasts.

Q. 21. *How does the method of exponential smoothing help in business forecasting?*

Ans. It is a mathematical device for improving trend by moving average method. Under exponential smoothing, the weights assigned to various items are in geometric progression. Greater weights are assigned to recently observed values and smaller weights to distant past observations.

Suppose the weights in geometric series are:

$$1, (1 - w), (1 - w)^2, ..., (1 - w)^{n-1}$$

where, $0 < w < 1$

and, n = No. of observations.

The weighted average till the current period t for n observations $X_t, X_{t-1}, ..., X_{t-(n-1)}$ is,

$$\bar{X}_t = \frac{1 \cdot X_t + (1-w)X_{t-1} + (1-w)^2 X_{t-2} + ... + (1-w)^{n-1} X_{t-(n-1)}}{1 + (1-w) + (1-w)^2 + ... + (1-w)^{n-1}}$$

Similarly,

$$\bar{X}_{t+1} = \frac{1 \cdot X_{t+1} + (1-w)X_t + (1-w)^2 X_{t-1} + ... + (1-w)^{n-1} X_{t-(n-2)}}{1 + (1-w) + (1-w)^2 + ... + (1-w)^{n-1}}$$

Taking n large and neglecting higher powers of w and $(1 - w)$, doing certain algebraic manipulations, the following relationship between the next period forecast value $\bar{X}_{t+1}$ and current forecast value $\bar{X}_t$ can be established.

$$\bar{X}_{t+1} = wX_{t+1} + (1 - w)\bar{X}_t$$

i.e., New forecast = w × observation + $(1 - w)$ × old forecast $\bar{X}_{t+1}$, the smoothed value at the next period is itself an average smoothed value. Now to make a forecast for each successive period, these smoothed values are used to find out a change in each period. w is called the *smoothing* coefficient and $w/(1 - w)$ the *trend factor.*

Since only one w is used as smoothing coefficient in the above procedure, it is called *single parameter exponential* smoothing.

The forecast for the first period is usually taken from some old forecast if available and if not, it is often assumed.

The quantity $(\bar{X}_t - \bar{X}_{t-1})$ is called the error. Thus, the forecast for the period t is the preceding average $\bar{X}_{t-1}$ plus w times the error. The trend coefficient which is required for preparing the forecast is calculated by the formula.

(Trend coeff.) $\theta_1 = w$ × change in smoothed value + $(1 - w)$ × preceding trend coefficient

The forecast F_t is obtained by the relation,

F_t = *Smoothed value + Trend factor × Trend coeff.*

Also error in forecast,

$$E_t = X_t - F_t$$

Q. 22. *How to choose the value of weight w in exponential smoothing procedure for business forecasting?*

Ans. There is no rule which governs to choose the value of *w*. It is usually chosen arbitrarily. Of course, some tips may be given to choose the value of *w*. If the fluctuations in production, sales, demand, etc., appear to be random, a smaller value of *w* be chosen. Also, in case the actual value turns down but the forecast does not turn down, a larger value of *w* is more suitable and *vice-versa*.

Q. 23. *Can there be more than one parameter w in the exponential smoothing method of forecasting?*

Ans. It has been observed that whenever there is a pronounced upward trend in the actual value of a time series, the forecast resulting from the single parameter exponential smoothing procedure is consistently low. To overcome this difficulty, a second smoothing constant is chosen from trend itself. Even more than two smoothing constants can be chosen.

Q. 24. *What is the role of econometric methods in business forecasting?*

Ans. Econometric methods involve economics, statistics and mathematics. The econometric methods are used to analyse an econometric system which are useful in economic theory. Usually, in econometric methods an inter-relationship is established between a number of variables in an economic system.

Q. 25. *What type of variables are involved in economic methods?*

Ans. Two types of variables are involved in economics system namely, (*i*) endogeneous variables, and (*ii*) exogeneous variables.

(*i*) *Endogenous variables* are those which belong to the economic system itself. For example, the production, stocks, interest, rent, prices, money reserves, employment, wages, etc.

(*ii*) *Exogenous variables* are those which do not belong to the economic system but they do affect it. For instance, politics, customs, life style, nature, environment, etc.

Q. 26. *Name three forecasting agencies which do not believe in any single theory for the purpose of forecasting.*

Ans. Three forecasting agencies which do not believe in any single theory for the purpose of forecasting are:

(*i*) Standard and Poor's Trade and Securities Service, New York.

(*ii*) Moody's Investors Service, New York.

(*iii*) International Statistical Bureau, New York.

Q. 27. *What are the publications of standard and Poor's Trade and Securities Services, New York.*

Ans. Standard and Poor's Trade and Securities Service New York, publishes the following weekly and monthly bulletins.

(*i*) *Industry Surveys – Trends and Projections*

(*ii*) *The Outlook*

(*iii*) *The stock guide*

(*iv*) *Basic Statistics* – a set of statistical bulletins

(*v*) *Basic Surveys* – irregular reports.

Q. 28. *What bulletins are published by Moody's Investors Service?*

Ans. Moody's Investors Service, New York publishes two regular bulletins as given below:

(*i*) *Moody's stock survey*

(*ii*) *Moody's Bond survey.*

Q. 29. *Is there any regular publication of the International Statistical Bureau, New York?*

Ans. Yes, The International Statistical Bureau, New York has a solo weekly publication entitled. *Business and Investment.*

Q. 30. *What is the position of forecasting agencies in India?*

Ans. There are no professional forecasting agencies as such in India. But some big companies have established separate corporate planning and forecasting cells. To name a few, the companies are;

Imperial Chemical Industries, Dunlop India, Indian Textile Corporation, Hindustan Levers, Metal Box, Texamco and Coal India Ltd.

Q. 31. *In what sense does forecasting differ from prediction and projection?*

Ans. A forecast is an estimate for some future period, partly based on past and present data and partly on subjective estimates arising out of experience and judgement of the forecaster. Whereas prediction is an estimate based on the analysis of past data for a point outside the series and projection is a prediction based on certain assumptions.

SECTION B

Fill in the Blanks

Fill in the suitable word(s) or phrase(s) in the blanks:

1. The success of a business depends on ________.
2. Forecasting is different from ________ and ________.
3. Forecasting involves ________ as well as ________ factors.
4. Forecasts based on statistical analysis are ________.
5. Forecasting means ________.
6. The statement, "All business proceeds on beliefs or judgement of probabilities and not on certainties" was given by ________.
7. Historical analysis is an aspect of ________.
8. Consideration of industrial policies, taxation, import and export for forecasting comes under ________.
9. Naive method of forecasting follows ________.
10. Forecasts made under the economic rhythm theory are applicable for ________.
11. Specific historical analogy for forecasting comes under the category of ________ methods.
12. Forecasts made under the economic rhythm theory are based on ________ data.
13. Specific historical analogy method for forecasting is based on the adage ________.
14. The lead-lag theory of forecasting is also known as ________.
15. The theory based on the principle that changes in business occur in succession is called ________.
16. Wages are increased in succession of ________.
17. The lead-lag theory for forecasting is utilised by ________
18. The Harward index of general business conditions consisted of ________ series.
19. Speculation curve is used to forecast the ________.
20. Speculation and money curves move in ________ directions.
21. Upturn of speculations curve and downturn of money curves marks the ________ in business.
22. Price indices and bank reserves work as ________ in lead-lag approach of forecasting.
23. Employment and industrial production index are known as ________ indicators in lead-lag approach for forecasting.
24. Personal income and total sales are called ________ indicators in lead-lag approach for forecasting.
25. In the lead-lag approach, it is difficult to forecast the ________ of the cycles.
26. The lead-lag relationship approach of forecasting is followed by ________.
27. Diffusion index depicts the movement of ________ as a whole without bothering about the individual series.

28. In diffusion index, one finds the ________ of series of a set which are expanding at a given time.
29. If more than 50 per cent series out of a set of series are expanding at a given time, it is considered that the business is in the process of ________ .
30. ________ method is used to construct the diffusion index for a group of business variables.
31. In action-reaction theory as applied to business forecasting, prosperity follows ________ and vice-versa.
32. The span of the period of prosperity and recession in business activity are usually ________.
33. The action-reaction theory for forecasting is followed by ________ .
34. The factor listing method means identifying ________ which are likely to influence the business activity.
35. The factor listing method involves ________.
36. Main drawback of the factor listing method is ________ .
37. The cross-cut analysis theory is just opposite to ________ .
38. Under the cross-cut analysis forecasts are made on the basis of overall assessment of ________ .
39. In the cross-cut analysis method, it is ________ to pool the effect of all factors for forecasting.
40. The cross-cut analysis method of forecasting is adopted by ________ .
41. The opinion polling method for forecasting relies on the ________ of the people.
42. The opinion polling method is suitable for ________ business forecasts.
43. Exponential method for forecasting is to improve ________ by ________ .
44. ________ weights are assigned to recent observations and ________ weight to distant past observations.
45. The difference between the forecast values $\bar{X}_{t+1}$ and $\bar{X}_t$ at the time periods $(t + 1)$ and t is called ________ .
46. If w is the smoothing coefficient in exponential smoothing method of forecasting, the quantity $w/(1 - w)$ is called ________ .
47. Whenever there is a pronounce upward trend in the actual values of a time series, the forecast resulting from the single parameter exponential smoothing procedure is consistently ________ .
48. In econometric methods an ________ is established between a number of variables in an economic system.
49. The variables which belong to the economic system itself are called ________ .
50. The variables like customs, politics which do not belong to economic system but do affect it are called ________ .

SECTION C

Multiple Choice Questions

Select the correct alternative out of given ones:

1. Business forecasts are made on the basis of:
   (*a*) present data
   (*b*) past data
   (*c*) policies and circumstances
   (*d*) all of the above

2. Forecasting enables a businessman:
   (*a*) to set policies for future business
   (*b*) to know his future
   (*c*) to be certain about profits
   (*d*) none of the above

3. One of the main aspects of business forecasting is:
   (*a*) government policies
   (*b*) taxation
   (*c*) historical analysis
   (*d*) all of the above
4. Analysis of current economic conditions helps in:
   (*a*) prediction
   (*b*) projection
   (*c*) maximising profits
   (*d*) none of the above
5. Historical analysis is a means to:
   (*a*) know the future profits
   (*b*) forecasting
   (*c*) prediction
   (*d*) all of the above
6. Forecasting based on the economic rhythm theory is applicable:
   (*a*) to individual company
   (*b*) for business in general
   (*c*) to governmental business
   (*d*) all of the above
7. The forecast under the economic rhythm theory are:
   (*a*) reliable
   (*b*) not reliable
   (*c*) certain
   (*d*) none of the above
8. The economic rhythm theory comes under the category of:
   (*a*) analytical methods
   (*b*) naive method
   (*c*) barometric methods
   (*d*) none of the above
9. Under specific historical analogy theory, the forecasts are made through:
   (*a*) lead-lag relationship
   (*b*) regression models
   (*c*) as past resembling situation
   (*d*) all of the above
10. The lead-lag relationship theory of forecasting is also known as:
   (*a*) action-reaction theory
   (*b*) sequence theory
   (*c*) cross-cut analysis theory
   (*d*) none of the above
11. The lead-lag theory expounds that the changes in business activity occur:
   (*a*) in succession
   (*b*) simultaneously
   (*c*) in times to come
   (*d*) none of the above
12. The leading, coincident and lagging series are utilised by the Harward index of general business conditions under:
   (*a*) cross-cut analysis
   (*b*) specific historical analogy
   (*c*) lead-lag theory
   (*d*) none of the above
13. Price indices of equity shares and bank reserves come under the category of:
   (*a*) lead indicators
   (*b*) lag indicators
   (*c*) coincident indicators
   (*d*) all of the above
14. Employment and gross national product in respect of forecasting are:
   (*a*) lead indicators
   (*b*) coincident indicators
   (*c*) lag indicators
   (*d*) none of the above
15. Personal income and business loans in forecasting are used as:
   (*a*) lead indicators
   (*b*) coincident indicators
   (*c*) lag indicators
   (*d*) all of the above
16. The lead-lag approach of business forecasting fail to:
   (*a*) forecast the amplitude of business cycles
   (*b*) interpret the movement of indicator variables
   (*c*) act as a complete method of forecasting
   (*d*) all of the above
17. The forecast by National Bureau of Economic Research, Massachusetts, are based on:
   (*a*) action-reaction theory
   (*b*) economic rhythm theory

(*c*) lead-lag theory
(*d*) none of the above

18. The forecasts made by Moody's Investors Service; New York, are based on:
(*a*) the action-reaction theory
(*b*) specific historical analogy
(*c*) lead-lag relationship
(*d*) none of the above

19. The diffusion index method of forecasting makes use of:
(*a*) the movement of individual series
(*b*) broad group of series
(*c*) some selected series
(*d*) none of the above

20. Under the diffusion index method, business is considered in the process of booming iff:
(*a*) more than 50 per cent series are expanding
(*b*) less than 50 per cent series are expanding
(*c*) exactly 50 per cent series are expanding
(*d*) none of the above

21. The business forecasts under the action-reaction theory are based on the principle that:
(*a*) prosperity follows recession
(*b*) recession follows prosperity
(*c*) both (*a*) and (*b*)
(*d*) neither (*a*) nor (*b*)

22. The action-reaction theory for business forecasting was expounded by:
(*a*) Roger W. Babson
(*b*) Brookmire
(*c*) Harward
(*d*) none of the above

23. Under the factor listing method for forecasting, one has to identify:
(*a*) lead factor
(*b*) all factors which are likely to influence the business
(*c*) past time series
(*d*) none of the above

24. The factor listing method makes forecasts by utilising:
(*a*) index numbers
(*b*) extrapolation
(*c*) no mathematical tool
(*d*) none of the above

25. The merit(s) of the factor listing method of business forecasting is/are:
(*a*) it is independent of mathematical juglery
(*b*) it has no restriction on the number of variables to be studied
(*c*) it gives due weightage to different factors
(*d*) all of the above

26. The demerit(s) of the factor listing method of business forecasting is/are:
(*a*) it is fully subjective
(*b*) it is fully mathematical
(*c*) it is easy to identify dominating variables
(*d*) none of the above

27. The cross-cut analysis of business forecasting makes use of the:
(*a*) past series
(*b*) present situation
(*c*) both (*a*) and (*b*)
(*d*) neither (*a*) nor (*b*)

28. The cross-cut analysis method of forecasting faces the difficulty that:
(*a*) the people do not express their views clearly
(*b*) all variables cannot be analysed individually and then pooled
(*c*) both (*a*) and (*b*)
(*d*) neither (*a*) nor (*b*)

29. The method of cross-cut analysis for forecasting is followed by the agency:
(*a*) The Brookmire Economic Service, New York
(*c*) Standard and Poor's Trade and Securities Service, New York.
(*c*) Babson's Statistical Organisation, Washington
(*d*) all of the above

30. Forecasts made by the method of opinion polling are suitable for:

(*a*) short-term business forecasts
(*b*) long-term business forecasts
(*c*) business in general
(*d*) all of the above

31. Exponential smoothing method of business forecasting utilises weights which are:
(*a*) in arithmetic progression
(*b*) fixed
(*c*) in geometric progression
(*d*) arbitrarily chosen

32. If *w* is chosen as smoothing coefficient in exponential smoothing method of forecasting, then the trend factor is:
(*a*) $w/(1 + w)$
(*b*) $w/(1 - w)$
(*c*) $1/w$
(*d*) $w/(w - 1)$

33. Exponential smoothing method of forecasting can involve:
(*a*) only one smoothing coefficient
(*a*) up to two smoothing coefficients
(*a*) an infinite number of smoothing coefficients
(*d*) none of the above

34. The variables prices, production and wages in an economic system are called:
(*a*) endogenous variables
(*b*) exogenous variables
(*c*) random variables
(*d*) none of the above

35. The variables like politics and lifestyle in an economic system are known as:
(*a*) endogenous variables
(*b*) exogenous variables
(*c*) discrete variables
(*d*) none of the above

36. Standard and Poor's Trade and Securities Service, New York publishes the bulletin(s):
(*a*) The Outlook
(*b*) The Stock Guide
(*c*) Basic Statistics
(*d*) all of the above

37. The publication entitled, 'Business and Investment' is published by:
(*a*) Moody's Investors Service, New York
(*b*) International Statistical Bureau, New York
(*c*) The Brookmire Economic Service, New York
(*d*) none of the above

38. Econometric methods involve:
(*a*) economics and mathematics
(*b*) economics and statistics
(*c*) economics, statistics and mathematics
(*d*) none of the above

39. Business forecasting agencie(s) is/are established in India by:
(*a*) Imperial Chemical Industries
(*b*) Indian Textile Corporation
(*c*) Hindustan levers
(*d*) all of the above

40. There is no difference between forecasting and:
(*a*) prediction
(*b*) projection
(*c*) guessing
(*d*) none of the above

ANSWERS

Section B

1. future estimates **2.** prediction, projection **3.** quantitative; qualitative **4.** more reliable **5.** Forewarn **6.** Charles W. Elliot **7.** business forecasting **8.** analysis of current economic conditions **9.** economic rhythm theory **10.** individual company **11.** barometric **12.** his own **13.** history repeats itself **14.** sequence theory **15.** lead-lag relationship theory **16.** inflation **17.** Harward index of general business conditions **18.** three **19.** business cycles **20.** opposite **21.** boom **22.** lead indicators **23.** coincident **24.** lag **25.** amplitude **26.** National Bureau of Research, Massachusetts **27.** broad group of series **28.** percentage

29. booming **30.** Graphic **31.** recession **32.** not equal **33.** The business statistics organisation, Washington (Babson's Statistical Organisation) **34.** various factors **35.** mathematical tool **36.** total subjectivity **37.** historical analogy theory **38.** all factors **39.** difficult **40.** The Brookmire Economic Service, New York **41.** present attitude **42.** short-term **43.** trend; moving average method **44.** Greater; smaller **45.** error **46.** trend factor **47.** low **48.** inter-relationship **49.** endogenous variables **50.** exogenous variables

Section C

1. (*d*)	**2.** (*a*)	**3.** (*c*)	**4.** (*d*)	**5.** (*b*)
6. (*a*)	**7.** (*a*)	**8.** (*b*)	**9.** (*c*)	**10.** (*b*)
11. (*a*)	**12.** (*c*)	**13.** (*a*)	**14.** (*b*)	**15.** (*c*)
16. (*d*)	**17.** (*c*)	**18.** (*d*)	**19.** (*b*)	**20.** (*a*)
21. (*c*)	**22.** (*a*)	**23.** (*b*)	**24.** (*c*)	**25.** (*d*)
26. (*a*)	**27.** (*b*)	**28.** (*c*)	**29.** (*a*)	**30.** (*a*)
31. (*c*)	**32.** (*b*)	**33.** (*d*)	**34.** (*a*)	**35.** (*b*)
36. (*d*)	**37.** (*b*)	**38.** (*c*)	**39.** (*d*)	**40.** (*d*)

SUGGESTED READING

1. Agarwal, B.L., *Basic Statistics,* New Age International Publishers, New Delhi, 8th edition, 2024.
2. Anderson, O.D., *Forecasting: Preceedings of the Institute of Statisticians Annual Conference, Cambridge,* North Holland Publishing Company, Amsterdam, New York, 1976.
3. Chou, Y.L., *Applied Business and Economic Statistics,* Holt, Rinehart and Winston, New Delhi, 1963.
4. Firth, M., *Forecasting Methods in Business and Management,* Edward Arnold, London, 1977.
5. Frisbee, I.N. and Riggleman, J.R., *Business Statistics,* McGraw-Hill International Book Company, New York, 1951.
6. Lapin, L.L., *Quantitative Methods for Business Decisions,* Harcourt Brace Jovanovich, New York, 1981.
7. Levin, R.I., Lirkpatrick, A. and Rubin, D.S., *Quantitative Approach to Management,* McGraw-Hill International Book Company, New York, 5th edn., 1982.
8. Nelson, C.R., *Applied Time Series Analysis for Management Forecasting,* Holden Day, San Francisco, 1973.
9. Richard, L.E., and Lacava, J.J., *Business Statistics,* McGraw-Hill Book International Company, New York, 1978.
10. Wheel, W., and Makridakis, S., *Forecasting Methods and Applications*, John Wiley, London, 1978.

CHAPTER 19

Statistical Techniques in Quality Control

SECTION A

Short Essay Type Questions

Q. 1. *What is meant by quality of a product?*

Ans. Every article or product is required for a specific purpose. If it fully serves the purpose, it is of good quality otherwise not. It means that if an article or material meets the specifications required for its rightful use, it is good quality, and if not, then the quality of the article is considered to be poor.

Q. 2. *What role does statistical quality control play in maintaining the quality of a product?*

Ans. There is hardly any control on the quality of products produced by the nature and hence the statistical quality control remains confined to articles produced by the industry. Variation in items produced in any manner is inevitable. This variation occurs due to two types of causes namely (*i*) chance factors and (*ii*) assignable causes.

(*i*) ***Chance factors:*** Some deviations from the desired specification is bound to occur in the articles produced, howsoever efficient, the production process may be. If the variations occurs due to some inherent pattern of variation and no causes can be assigned to it, it is called chance or random variation. Chance variation is tolerable and does not materially affect the quality of a product. In such a situation, the process is said to be under statistical control.

(*ii*) ***Assignable causes:*** If the articles show marked deviation from the given specifications of a product, the utility of articles is in jeopardy. In that situation, one has to make a search for the causes responsible for the large variation in the product. The causes due to faulty process and procedure are known as *assignable causes.* The variation due to assignable causes is of non-random nature.

Hence, the role of statistical quality control is to collect and analyse relevant data for the purpose of detecting whether the process is under control or not. If not, what can possibly be the reason for the fault(s).

Q. 3. *What do you understand by control charts in statistical quality control?*

Ans. Control charts are the devices to describe the patterns of variation. The control charts were developed by the physicist, Dr. Walter A. Shewhart of Bell Telephone Company in 1924.

Control Chart delimits the range or band in which the basic variability is within tolerance limits and beyond this range or band, the variability is due to some assignable causes. The range or band ascertained by the control chart is little broader than the natural tolerance range. The most frequently used control charts are for mean $\overline{X}$, the range *R*, the root mean square σ, number of defects *c*, etc. In general, a control chart consists of three lines namely, (*i*) central line (CL) depicting the desired standard or level of the process, (*ii*) upper control limit (UCL) and (*iii*) the lower control limit (LCL) as shown in Fig. 19.1.

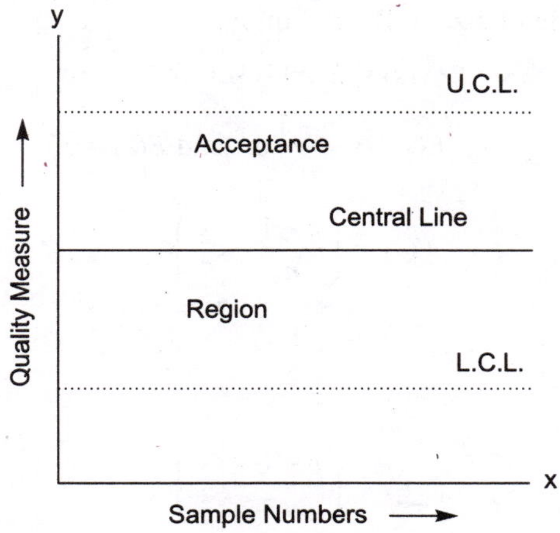

Fig. 19.1. Control chart in general.

Q. 4. *What benefits are expected out of the use of control charts?*

Ans. Control charts are meant to uncover whether the basic variability of a manufacturing process is within its natural tolerance or beyond tolerance range due to assignable causes.

If the variability is due to assignable causes, the causes can be discovered and faults can be removed. This brings the process under control. Once the process is under control, one can feel confident that the product will meet the specifications.

Q. 5. *Delineate the main tools for statistical quality control.*

Ans. There are four closely associated tools for statistical quality control as given below:

(*i*) ***Shewhart's control charts for variables:*** Such charts consider measurable data on quality characteristics which are usually continuous in nature. Such type of data utilises $\overline{X}$, *R* and σ charts.

(*ii*) ***Shewhart control charts for fraction defectives:*** Such charts are used when the units are classified as defective or non-defective. The control charts meant for fraction defectives are known as *p*-charts.

(*iii*) ***Shewhart control charts for number of defects per unit:*** In this situation one deals with discrete variables which are the counts of the number of defects per unit. Control charts used in this situation are called *c*-charts.

(*iv*) ***Acceptance sampling procedure:*** Acceptance inspection has to be carried out by the manufacturer or by the buyer. It is not only difficult but rather impossible in many cases to inspect all the items produced or purchased. Hence, sampling inspection is the only device left over at hand. Moreover, it has many advantages over 100 per cent inspection. Some acceptance sampling procedures are evolved which are superior than traditional sampling procedure.

Q. 6. *What is the rationale behind setting of control limits?*

Ans. Let μ and σ be the population mean and standard deviation respectively. By the property of normal distribution curve we know that 99.73 per cent units full within the $\mu \pm 3\,\sigma$ limits. Hence, 3σ limits are usually used for control charts. If the population constants are not known, their estimated values are used to set-up the control limits.

Suppose we have taken *k* samples of size *n*. Let, the mean of the ith sample is $\overline{X}_i$ and standard deviation S_i for $i = 1, 2, \ldots, k$. The process is considered to be under control if the mean values $\overline{X}_i$ fall within $\mu \pm 3\,\sigma$ limits.

Q. 7. *How are the control limits set-up for mean?*

Ans. In many situations the specifications of the units produced are known and also the variation which can be tolerated. Suppose μ′, the mean and σ′, the standard deviation are the known specifications. In this situation, the control limits for mean are given by the formula,

$$\mu' \pm 3\frac{\sigma'}{\sqrt{n}}$$

where n is the size of the samples on which the sample means $\bar{X}_i$ are based for plotting the points.

The upper control limit,

$$\text{U.C.L.} = \mu' + A\sigma'$$

The central limit,

$$\text{C.L.} = \mu'$$

The lower control limit,

$$\text{L.C.L.} = \mu' - A\sigma'$$

where, $A = \dfrac{3}{\sqrt{n}}$

In case the standard values μ' and σ' are not known, one has to use their estimated value. The control limits based on subgroups are called *trial control limits.* If $\bar{X}_i$, is the mean of the ith sample based on n observations for $i = 1, 2, \ldots, k$, the estimated value $\bar{X}$ for μ is,

$$\bar{X} = \frac{1}{k}\sum_{i=1}^{k} \bar{X}_i$$

and $\bar{S}$, the overall mean of all the sample standard deviation s_i is,

$$\bar{S} = \frac{1}{k}\sum_{i=1}^{k} s_i$$

whereas the estimated value of σ is $\bar{S}/c_2$. Thus, the upper, central and lower control limits are,

$$\text{U.C.L.}_{\bar{X}} = \bar{X} + A_1\bar{S}$$

$$\text{C.L.}_{\bar{X}} = \bar{X}$$

and, $\text{L.C.L.}_{\bar{X}} = \bar{X} - A_1\bar{S}$

where, $A_1 = \dfrac{3}{\sqrt{n}\,c_2} = \dfrac{A}{c_2}$; $c_2 = \sqrt{\dfrac{2}{n}}\,\dfrac{\left(\dfrac{n-2}{2}\right)!}{\left(\dfrac{n-3}{2}\right)!}$

and, $A = \dfrac{3}{\sqrt{n}}$

The values of A_1 for different values of n are being tabulated and available in Appendix table XV of *Basic Statistics* by B.L. Agarwal.

Q. 8. *Set the control limits for σ-chart.*

Ans. In many situations, the quality characteristics of a product is preferably the standard deviation. So, for this σ-chart is to be used. The control limits for σ-chart can be set in the following manner.

Let s be the sample standard deviation based on sample of size n. By definition,

$$v(s) = E(s^2) - [E(s)]^2$$

$$E(s^2) = \frac{n-1}{n}\sigma^2 \text{ and } E(s) = c_2\sigma$$

$$\therefore \quad V(s) = \left(\frac{n-1}{n} - c_2^2\right)\sigma^2$$

where, $= c_3^2\,\sigma^2$

$$\text{S.D}(s) = c_3\sigma$$

where, $c_3^2 = \left(\dfrac{n-1}{n} - c_2^2\right)$

Thus, the control limits for σ-chart are,

$$\begin{aligned}
\text{U.C.L.}_s &= E(s) + 3\text{ S.E. }(s) \\
&= (c_2 + 3\,c_3)\sigma \\
&= B_2\sigma \\
\text{C.L.}_s &= c_2\sigma \\
\text{L.C.L.}_s &= E(s) - 3\text{ S.E. }(s) \\
&= (c_2 - 3c_3)\sigma \\
&= B_1\sigma
\end{aligned}$$

where, $B_1 = c_2 - 3c_3$, $B_2 = c_2 + 3c_3$ when σ is not known, its estimated value has to be used in setting up the control limits for σ-chart. If $\bar{S}$ is the mean standard deviation obtained from k-samples of size n by the formula,

$$\bar{S} = \frac{1}{k}\sum_{i=1}^{k} s_i$$

then, $\hat{\sigma} = \bar{S}/c_2$

Thus taking, $\hat{\sigma} = \bar{S}/c_2$, the trial control limits for σ-chart are,

$$\text{U.C.L.}_s = (c_2 + 3c_3)\frac{\bar{S}}{c_2}$$

$$= \left(1 + 3\frac{c_3}{c_2}\right)\bar{S}$$

$$= B_4\bar{S}$$

$$\text{C.L.}_s = c_2 = \frac{\bar{S}}{c_2} = \bar{S}$$

$$\text{L.C.L.}_S = (c_2 - 3c_3)\frac{\bar{S}}{c_2} = \left(1 - \frac{3c_3}{c_2}\right)\bar{S} = B_3\bar{S}$$

where, $B_4 = \left(1 + \frac{3c_3}{c_2}\right) = \frac{B_2}{c_2}$, $B_3 = \left(1 - \frac{3c_3}{c_2}\right) = \frac{B_1}{c_2}$

Values of B_1, B_2, B_3 and B_4 and c_2 have already been tabulated and can be seen in appendix table XV of *Basic Statistics* by B.L. Agarwal.

Q. 9. *What is the theme behind the use of R-chart in statistical quality control?*

Ans. Statisticians experience has revealed that in case of small samples, the range and standard deviation vary concurrently in the same direction. Generally, small samples are used in quality control. Hence, the control limits for standard deviation (σ) can be replaced by the control limits for range (R). Thus, the charts constructed by making use of range are known as R-charts.

The main advantage of R-charts is that it is easier to calculate R than σ. Of course, there is a little loss of efficiency in replacing σ by R. But looking to the convenience, a little loss in efficiency is acceptable.

Q. 10. *How do you set the control limits for R-charts in statistical quality control?*

Ans. We know that,

$$E(R) = d_2\sigma$$
$$S.D.(R) = d_3\sigma$$

If $\bar{R}$ is the mean of R_i's, the ranges of k samples and σ_R is the standard error of R for $i = 1, 2, ..., k$. Also if σ' is known value of σ, then $d_2 = \bar{R}/\sigma'$.

Thus, $\bar{R} = d_2\sigma'$ or $\sigma' = \bar{R}/d_2$.

Case (i): When the range R' and standard error of R', $\sigma_{R'}$ are known values of R and σ_R respectively, the control limits for R' are given as,

$$\text{U.C.L.}_{R'} = E(R') + 3S.D.(R')$$
$$= d_2\sigma_{R'} + 3d_3\sigma_{R'}$$
$$= (d_2 + 3d_3)\,\sigma_{R'}$$
$$= D_2\sigma_{R'}$$
$$\text{C.L.}_{R'} = d_2\sigma_{R'}$$

Similarly, $\text{L.C.L.}_{R'} = (d_2 - 3d_3)\,\sigma_{R'} = D_1\sigma_{R'}$

where, $D_1 = d_2 - 3d_3$ and $D_2 = d_2 + 3d_3$

Case (ii): When the population range R is not known, we make use of the sample mean range $\bar{R}$.

For $\bar{X}$ chart, the control limits are,

$$\text{U.C.L.}_{\bar{X}} = \bar{X} + 3\sigma_{\bar{X}}$$
$$= \bar{X} + 3\sigma/\sqrt{n}$$
$$= \bar{X} + 3\frac{\bar{R}}{d_2\sqrt{n}}$$
$$= \bar{X} + A_3\bar{R}$$
$$\text{C.L.}_{\bar{X}} = \bar{X}$$

Also, $\text{L.C.L.}_{\bar{X}} = \bar{X} - A_3\bar{R}$

where, $A_3 = 3/(d_2\sqrt{n})$

For R chart, the control limits are,

$$\text{U.C.L.}_R = E(R) + 3\,S.D.(R)$$
$$= d_2\sigma + 3d_3\sigma$$
$$= \left(1 + 3\frac{d_3}{d_2}\right)\bar{R}$$
$$= D_4\bar{R}$$
$$\text{C.L.}_R = \bar{R}$$

Also, $\text{L.C.L.}_R = \left(1 - 3\frac{d_3}{d_2}\right)\bar{R}$

$$= D_3\bar{R}$$

where, $D_4 = 1+\frac{3d_3}{d_2}$ and $D_3 = 1-\frac{3d_3}{d_2}$

The values of d_1, d_2, A_3, D_3, and D_4 are given in appendix table XV of *Basic Statistics* by B.L. Agarwal.

Q. 11. *Discuss the behaviour of $\bar{X}$-charts in relation to R-charts.*

Ans. The behaviour of $\bar{X}$-charts in relation to *R*-charts can be spelled out as follows:

(*i*) $\bar{X}$-chart should not be prepared unless *R*-chart shows that the process is under control.

(*ii*) Once $\bar{X}$-chart shows that the process is under control, then *R*-chart should not be prepared as it will always reveal that the process is under control.

(*iii*) $\bar{X}$-charts reveal the variability between rational subgroups whereas *R*-chart discover the assignable causes within groups.

(*iv*) Since $\bar{X}$-chart and *R*-chart discover assignable causes between and within samples respectively, both type of charts be prepared. In this situation, there are meagre chances of assignable causes not being detected.

Q. 12. *Compare R-chart versus σ-chart.*

Ans. For comparing *R*-charts with σ-charts, following points can be put forth:

(*i*) The range and standard deviation fluctuate simultaneously in the same direction particularly in case of small samples. Hence *R*-charts and σ-chart lead to similar conclusions.

(*ii*) Since it is easy to calculate range as compared to standard deviation, *R*-charts are frequently used.

(*iii*) If the sample sizes are large, σ-charts should be used.

(*iv*) *R*-charts are economical as compared to σ-charts.

Q. 13. *How can the control charts be prepared?*

Ans. The control charts can be prepared in the following manner:

(*i*) Draw axes on a graph paper.

(*ii*) Calculate upper, lower and central limits.

(*iii*) Central line be drawn on the graph paper as a smooth line at a distance of central limit parallel to *X*-axis. Upper and lower control limits be indicated through broken lines at their respective distances parallel to abscissa.

(*iv*) Sample numbers be taken along *X*-axis.

(*v*) The variate values like means, ranges or standard deviations be taken along *Y*-axis on a suitable scale.

(*vi*) Sample values be plotted against respective sample numbers on the graph and points be marked accordingly.

Q. 14. *How can the Shewhart control charts be interpreted to draw meaningful conclusions?*

Ans. The Shewhart control charts are meant mainly to detect whether the process is under control or not. Still many more conclusions are being drawn from these charts which are given below:

(*i*) If all the points lie within control limits, the process is considered under control. Also, a point or more lying outside the control limits is a clear indication of the lack of process control due to assignable causes. The faults be detected and corrected.

(*ii*) Although all the points may be in control limits, still the patterns of points reveal some assignable causes. One such situation is a run of seven or more points above or below the central line. A run of points above the central line is indicative of the process spread and reflects undesirable situation. Whereas a run below the control line is a mark of desirable situation with regard to variability.

(*iii*) The sample points close to central line in $\bar{X}$ and *R* charts indicate systematic differences within samples and also point out for improper selection of samples and biases in measurements.

(*iv*) The upward and downward trends also indicate assignable causes even through the process is under control.

(*v*) Cyclic pattern of sample points in the control charts indicate towards assignable causes even though the process is under control. Such a pattern occurs due to material and machines.

Q. 15. *A dry-cells producing factory wanted to test the life of cells produced daily. The cells will be considered satisfactory if their life is 25 hours. For this, a sample of 5 cells was drawn on 12 consecutive days. The results were as follows:*

Days (Subgroups)	*Life of cells (in hours)*				
	1	*2*	*3*	*4*	*5*
1.	27.0	28.0	25.5	26.5	23.0
2.	23.5	27.5	26.0	27.0	29.0
3.	27.5	27.0	28.0	26.5	24.5
4.	28.0	26.5	27.5	28.5	27.0
5.	27.5	24.5	25.0	26.0	27.5
6.	26.5	26.0	27.0	27.5	26.0
7.	21.0	22.0	28.0	26.5	25.0
8.	25.5	24.5	25.0	27.5	27.5
9.	28.0	26.5	30.0	29.5	27.0
10.	25.0	27.0	26.5	24.5	23.0
11.	22.0	26.5	27.5	23.5	25.5
12.	26.0	28.0	27.0	30.0	29.0

(*i*) *Calculate 3 σ-limits of control chart for* $\bar{X}$ *when the value of mean of the universe is 25 hours and standard deviation is 2 hours.*

(*ii*) *Set-up the control limits for* $\bar{X}$ *-chart when the standard values for mean and S.D. are not known. Also, prepare the control chart and comment whether the process is under control or not.*

(*iii*) *Construct σ-chart when the specified values for standard deviation are not known.*

(*iv*) *Draw a range chart when standard values are not specified.*

[Given that for n = 5; $A = 1.342$, $A_1 = 1.596$, $A_2 = 0.577$, $c_2 = 0.8407$, $B_1 = B_3 = 0$, $B_2 = 1.756$, $B_4 = 2.089$, $d_2 = 2.326$, $D_1 = D_3 = 0$, $D_2 = 4.918$, $D_4 = 2.115$*]*

Ans.

(*i*) Given that $\mu' = 25$ and $\sigma' = 2$, 3-sigma limits for $\bar{X}$ -chart are,

$$\mu' \pm 3\sigma'/\sqrt{n}$$

$$\text{U.C.L.}_{\bar{X}} = 25 + \frac{3\times 2}{\sqrt{5}}$$

$$= 27.68$$

$$\text{C.L.}_{\bar{X}} = 25$$

$$\text{L.C.L.}_{\bar{X}} = 25 - 2.68$$

$$= 22.32$$

(*ii*) To construct trial control limits for $\bar{X}$, σ and *R* charts, we prepare the following calculation table.

Days (Subgroups)	*Total*	$\bar{X}$	*s*	*R*
1.	130	26.0	1.90	5.0
2.	133	26.6	2.04	5.5
3.	133.5	26.7	1.35	3.5
4.	137.5	27.5	0.79	2.5
5.	130.5	26.1	1.39	3.0
6.	133.0	26.6	0.65	1.5
7.	122.5	24.5	2.96	7.0
8.	130.0	26.0	1.41	3.0
9.	141.0	28.2	1.52	3.5
10.	126.0	25.2	1.60	4.0
11.	125.0	25.0	2.24	5.5
12.	140.0	28.0	1.58	4.0
Total	1582.0	316.4	19.43	48.0
Mean	26.37	26.37	1.62	4.0

The control limits for $\bar{X}$-chart, when standard values not known, are

$$\bar{X} \pm A_1\bar{S}$$

From the above table $\bar{X} = 26.37$ and $\bar{s} = 1.62$.

Also given that, $A_1 = 1.596$ Thus,

$$\text{U.C.L.}_{\bar{X}} = 26.37 + 1.596 \times 1.62$$

$$= 26.37 + 2.586$$

$$\text{L.C.L.}_{\overline{X}} = 26.37 - 2.586$$

$$= 23.784$$

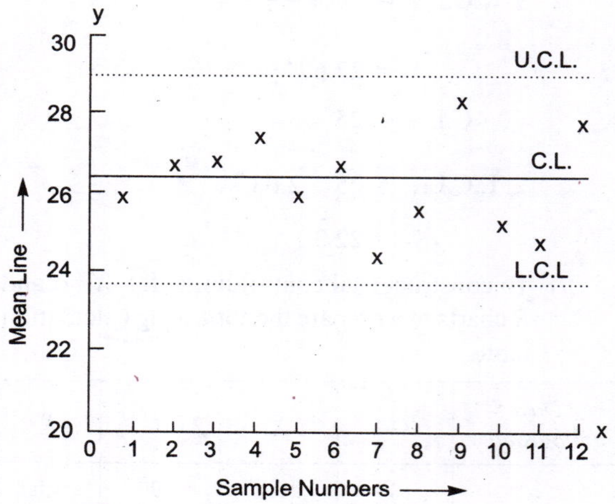

Fig. 19.2. $\overline{X}$-chart

Since no point falls outside the control limits, we conclude that the process is under control.

(*iii*) When the specific value for standard deviation is not given, the control limits are,

$$U.C.L._{\overline{X}} = B_4\overline{S}$$

$$= 2.089 \times 1.62$$

$$= 3.38$$

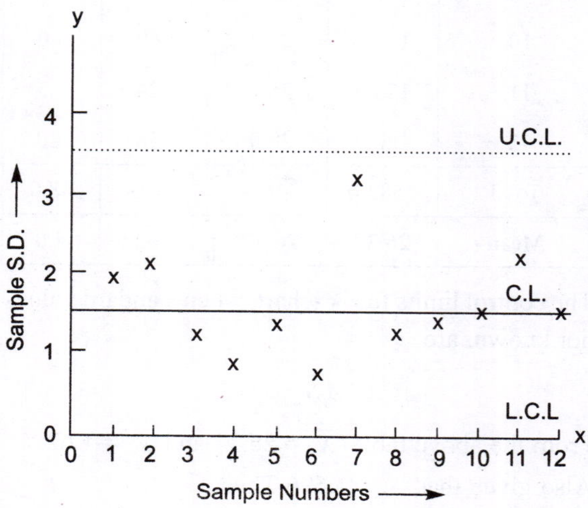

Fig. 19.3. σ-chart

$$\text{C.L.}_s = \overline{S} = 1.62$$

$$\text{L.C.L.}_s = B_3\overline{S} = 0$$

(*iv*) The control limits for *R*-chart, when the standard value of range is not known, are

$$\text{U.C.L.}_R = D_4\overline{R}$$

$$= 2.115 \times 4.0$$

$$= 8.46$$

$$\text{C.L.}_R = \overline{R} = 4.0$$

$$\text{L.C.L.}_R = D_3\overline{R} = 0$$

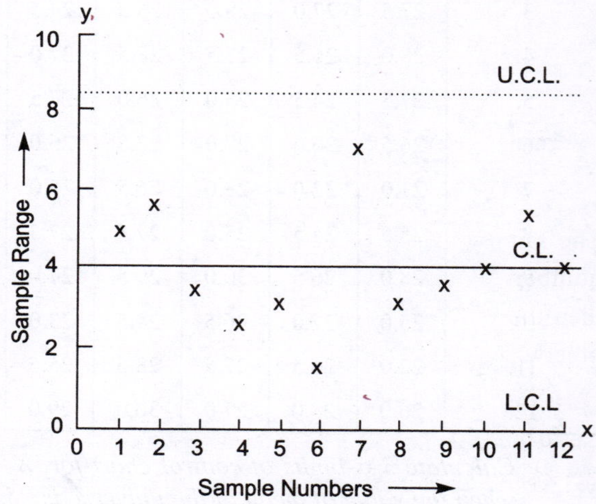

Fig. 19.4. *R*-chart

Since the mean ranges of all the subgroups lie within the control limits and no particular pattern is observed, it is inferred that the process is very well under control.

Q. 16 *When should the control charts for fraction defectives be prepared?*

Ans. In many situations, one is interested in the units possessing certain desired specifications. If the units do not possess all those specifications, they are classified as defective. In this way, the variable is dichotomised and thus follows binomial distribution. Hence, the mean and standard deviation of a binomial distribution are applicable.

If the lot contains a proportion of defectives which is acceptable to the producer, the process is under control, otherwise not. It safeguards against falling of reputation of the firm. So the control charts are to be prepared for fraction defectives.

Q. 17. *How will you prepare the control charts for fraction defectives?*

Ans.

Case (*i*): The charts prepared for fraction defectives are known as *p*-charts. Let *P* be the proportion of defectives in the population and p' be its given standard value. If we have selected samples from each lot of size *n,* then 3-sigma control limits can be given as,

$$\text{U.C.L.}_{p'} = p' + 3\sigma_{p'}$$

$$= p' + 3\sqrt{\frac{p'q'}{n}}$$

$$\text{C.L.}_{p'} = p'$$

$$\text{LC.L.}_{p'} = p' - 3\sqrt{\frac{p'q'}{n}}$$

The sample values of *p* are plotted against sample numbers. If the points lie within control band, then the process is considered to be under control, otherwise not.

Case (*ii*): When the standard value of *P* is not given, it has to be estimated through sample fraction defectives. Let *k* samples be drawn at regular intervals from the lots in an specified period. Suppose d_i is the number of defectives in the ith sample of size n_i for $i = 1, 2, \ldots, k$. The fraction defective p_i in the ith sample is,

$$p_i = \frac{d_i}{n_i}$$

Also the estimate of the population fraction defective *P* is,

$$\bar{p} = \sum_{i=1}^{k} d_i \Big/ \sum_{i=1}^{k} n_i$$

Generally, a sample of equal size is preferred in statistical quality control. Therefore, taking $n_1 = n_2 = \ldots = n_k = n$,

$$\bar{p} = \frac{1}{nk}\sum_{i=1}^{k} d_i$$

$$= \frac{1}{k}\sum_{i=1}^{k} p_i$$

It is trivial to verify that $\bar{p}$ is an unbiased estimate of *P*.

Again 3-sigma control limits for fraction defective by using $\bar{p}$, the estimated value of *P* based on the samples of equal size *n* are,

$$\text{U.C.L.}_p = \bar{p} + 3\sqrt{\frac{\bar{p}\,\bar{q}}{n}}$$

$$\text{C.L.}_p = \bar{p}$$

$$\text{L.C.L.}_p = \bar{p} - 3\sqrt{\frac{\bar{p}\,\bar{q}}{n}}$$

where, $\bar{q} = 1 - \bar{p}$

Sample *p*-values are plotted on the graph against sample numbers. If any plotted point lies outside the control limits, the process is considered to be out of control, otherwise not.

The points lying above the upper control limit are called *high spots,* and below the lower control limit *low spots*. High spots show a deterioration in the process, whereas low spots may be due to slackness.

Q. 18. *How can one decide the sample size for fraction defective charts (p-charts)?*

Ans. To make an effective use of *p*-chart, some fraction defectives be observed in the sample which can be rejected. If the quality of the product is good, there are meagre chances of defective items and hence to get defective item(s), a large sample is to be drawn. For instance, for 0.1 per cent defectives to be detected in the process at least a sample of 1,000 items has to be selected. If this is not done and we take a sample of 10 items and a defective appears in this sample, it will lead to 10 per cent of the items rejectable which is not really the case.

In short, better is the quality, the larger must be the size of the sub-samples. In other words, smaller the sample sizes, less sensitive is the *p*-chart to detect the changes in quality level or to indicate the assignable causes of variation.

Q. 19. *Formulate control limits for number of defectives.*

Ans. If p_i is the proportion of defectives in the ith sample of size n for $i = 1, 2, \ldots, k$, the number of defectives,

$$d_i = np_i$$

and,
$$\bar{p} = \frac{1}{nk}\sum_{i=1}^{k} d_i$$

3-sigma trial control limits for number of defectives are,

$$\text{U.C.L.}_d = d + 3\sigma_d = n\bar{p} + 3\sqrt{n\bar{p}(1-\bar{p})}$$

$$\text{C.L.}_d = n\bar{p}$$

$$\text{L.C.L.}_d = d - 3\sigma_d = n\bar{p} - 3\sqrt{n\bar{p}(1-\bar{p})}$$

If the standard value p' of p is given, the control limits for number of defectives are,

$$\text{U.C.L.}_{d'} = d' + 3\sigma_{d'} = np' + 3\sqrt{n\,p'\,q'}$$

$$\text{C.L.}_{d'} = d' = np'$$

$$\text{L.C.L.}_{d'} = d' - 3\sigma_{d'} = np' - 3\sqrt{n\,p'\,q'}$$

where, $d' = np'$ and $p' = 1 - q'$

Here the points are plotted for the number of defectives and sample number. The decision about process control is taken in the usual manner.

Q. 20. *When should the control charts for number of defects be constructed?*

Ans. The control charts for number of defects per unit are constructed in situations where the chances of defects are large and the actual occurrence tends to be small. For instance, the number of woven defect in per sq. m. of cloth, blemishes in a fool-scap sheet of paper, number of defects per fan, etc. In such situations, the variable C, denoting the number of defects, follows Poisson distribution.

An item is defective even for the minutest deviation from its specifications or standardised fabrication. But mere classification whether an item is defective or non-defective is not enough. It also matters how many defects per unit occur. Hence, it seems germane to construct control charts for number of defects.

Q. 21. *Give control limits for C-charts, i.e., the number of defects charts in case of samples of equal size.*

Ans. Here we consider first the number of defects c per sample which follow Poisson distribution.

If the Poisson variate c is distributed with parameter λ and λ' is its given specified value, then the control limits are,

$$\text{U.C.L.}_c = \lambda' + 3\sqrt{\lambda'}$$

$$\text{C.L.}_c = \lambda'$$

$$\text{L.C.L.}_c = \lambda' - 3\sqrt{\lambda'}$$

If the value of λ is not given, it has to be estimated through samples. If C_i is the number of defects in the ith sample for $i = 1, 2, \ldots.\ k$, the estimated value of λ say $\bar{C}$ is,

$$\hat{\lambda} = \bar{C} = \frac{1}{k}\sum_{i=1}^{k} C_i$$

Let the mean of the defects counted in samples usually of size 25 or more be $\bar{C}$. Obviously its variance will also be $\bar{C}$. Hence 3-sigma trial control limits for number of defects are:

$$\text{U.C.L.}_c = \bar{C} + 3\sqrt{\bar{C}}$$

$$\text{C.L.}_c = \bar{C}$$

$$\text{L.C.L.}_c = \bar{C} - 3\sqrt{\bar{C}}$$

The values of $\bar{C}$ for various samples are plotted against the sample numbers. The conclusions about process control are taken in the usual manner, *i.e.*, if any point lies outside the control limits, it is inferred that the process is not under control, otherwise it is under statistical quality control.

If we consider 'C' as the number of defects per unit and its established value C' is known, then 3-sigma control limits will be,

$$\text{U.C.L.}_{c'} = C' + 3\sqrt{C'/n}$$

$$\text{C.L.}_{c'} = C'$$

$$\text{L.C.L.}_{C'} = C' - 3\sqrt{C'/n}$$

Again if C' is not known, the value of C is to be estimated. Let this value be $\bar{C}$. For k samples of equal size n,

$$\bar{C} = \frac{1}{nk}\sum_i C_i$$

for $i = 1, 2, \ldots, k$

Thus, 3-sigma control limits are,

$$\text{U.C.L.}_C = \bar{C} + 3\sqrt{\bar{C}/n}$$

$$\text{C.L.}_C = \bar{C}$$

$$\text{L.C.L.}_C = \bar{C} - 3\sqrt{\bar{C}/n}$$

Here, we take the standard deviation of $\bar{C}$ as the under root of $\bar{C}$ divided by the square root of the sample size n since $\bar{C}$ cannot be taken to follow Poisson distribution. Hence, C-charts for average number of defects per sample are better.

Q. 22. *Sixteen boxes of electric switches each containing 20 switches were randomly selected from a lot of switch boxes and inspected for the number of defects per box. The number of defects per box were as follows:*

Box No.	*No. of defects*	*Box No.*	*No. of defects*
1	12	10	12
2	15	11	16
3	9	12	13
4	14	13	19
5	18	14	18
6	26	15	14
7	8	16	21
8	6		
9	11		

Calculate 3-sigma limits for C-chart and draw conclusion.

Ans. First we calculate average number of defects per sample, *i.e.*,

$$\bar{C} = \frac{1}{k}\sum_{i=1}^{16} C_i$$

$$= \frac{232}{16}$$

$$= 14.5$$

The upper control limit for C-chart is,

$$\text{U.C.L.}_c = 14.5 + 3\sqrt{14.5}$$

$$= 14.5 + 3 \times 3.81$$

$$= 25.93$$

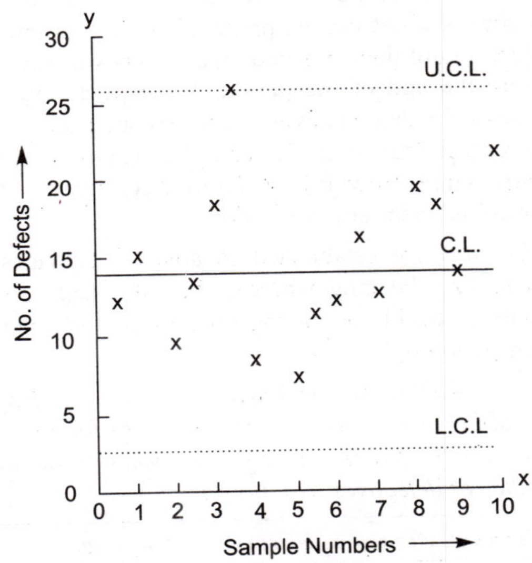

Fig. 19.5. *C*-chart

Central limit for C-chart is,

$$\text{C.L.}_c = 14.5$$

Lower control limit for C-chart is,

$$\text{L.C.L.}_c = 14.5 - 11.43$$

$$= 3.07$$

One point lies above the upper control limit and hence, the process is not under control.

Q. 23. *Give five situations in which C-charts can be used.*

Ans. Five situations in which C-charts can be used are given below:

(*i*) Number of missing rivettes in the assembly of an aircraft.

(*ii*) Number of weak points in a coil of insulated electric wire.

(*iii*) Number of air bubbles observed per square metre in a sheet of glass.

(*iv*) Number of defects per television set.

(*v*) Number of defects per metre in a hand woven cloth.

Q. 24. *What conspicuous advantage is there having an established value in advance of the parameter used in a control chart?*

Ans. The practical aspect of a given standard value and an estimated value used in a chart is that no control chart can be prepared for the estimated value(s) until the estimated value is known, *i.e.*, not before the end of the period. Whereas a standard value established in advance enables one to compute the control limits everyday and plot the points on the control chart. Now, it is trivial to check whether the process is under control or not.

So, a value established in advance provides a day-to-day checking whereas the estimated values enable to decide about the process control after a fixed period only.

Q. 25. *A TV voltage stabilizer manufacturer checks the quality of 50 units of his product daily for 15 days and finds the fraction of non-conforming units and number of defectives as follows:*

Days	*Fraction defectives*	*No. of defectives*
1	0.10	5
2	0.20	10
3	0.06	3
4	0.04	2
5	0.16	8
6	0.02	1
7	0.08	4
8	0.06	3
9	0.02	1
10	0.16	8
11	0.12	6
12	0.14	7
13	0.08	4
14	0.10	5
15	0.06	3

(*i*) *Construct 3-sigma trial control limits for fraction defectives.*

(*ii*) *Construct 3-sigma trial control limits for np-chart.*

Ans.

(*i*) 3-sigma trial control limits for fraction defectives can be established in the following manner:

The estimated value,

$$\bar{p} = \frac{1}{15}\sum_{i=1}^{15} p_i$$

$$= \frac{1.4}{15} \quad \text{since} \sum_{i=1}^{15} p_i = 1.4$$

$$= 0.093$$

and, $1-\bar{p} = 0.907$

3-sigma control limits for fraction defectives are,

$$\text{U.C.L.} = \bar{p} + 3\sqrt{\frac{\bar{p}\,\bar{q}}{n}}$$

$$= 0.093 + 3\sqrt{\frac{0.093 \times 0.907}{50}}$$

$$= 0.093 + 0.123$$

$$= 0.216$$

$$\text{C.L.} = 0.093$$

$$\text{L.C.L.} = 0.093 - 0.123$$

$$= -\,0.03 = 0$$

No sample value of fraction defectives is beyond control limits and hence the product conforms to statistical quality control.

(*ii*) Now we find 3-sigma trial control limits for *np*-chart.

Total number of defectives = 70

Average fraction defective,

$$\bar{p} = \frac{70}{50 \times 15}$$

$$= 0.093$$

$$n\bar{p} = 50 \times 0.093 = 4.65$$

$$3\hat{\sigma}_{np} = 3\sqrt{n\bar{p}\,(1-\bar{p})}$$

$$= 3\sqrt{4.65 \times 0.907}$$

$$= 6.161$$

3-sigma trial control limits for *np*-chart are,

$$\text{U.C.L.}_{np} = n\bar{p} + 3\hat{\sigma}_{np}$$

$$= 4.65 + 6.161$$

$$= 10.811$$

$$\text{C.L.}_{np} = 4.65$$

$$\text{L.C.L.}_{np} = 4.65 - 6.161$$

$$= -1.51 = 0$$

Control limits for *np*-chart lead to the result that the process is under statistical quality control.

Q. 26. *What are the advantages of statistical quality control?*

Ans. Statistical quality control methods are extensively used in industrial production process because of number of advantages as given below:

(*i*) ***Reduction in cost:*** Control charts are based on sampling inspection. Hence, there is reduction in cost. Also a lot of time is saved.

(*ii*) ***Greater efficiency:*** Because of the availability of time due to little inspection time, a greater efficiency is maintained in the process of inspection.

(*iii*) ***Timely detection of faults:*** Since the samples are inspected quickly, there is timely detection of faults. Hence, if the process is out of control, the faults can be removed. This protects against heavy losses.

(*iv*) ***Adherence to specifications:*** Statistical quality control enables a manufacturer to adhere to quality specification of a product as the assignable causes are soon detected and the process is brought under control.

(*v*) ***The only possibility:*** In situations where the units are destroyed or perished during the process of inspection, cent per cent inspection of items is not possible. Hence, the samples from the lots can only be inspected to adjudge the quality of the product. For example, the life of electric bulbs, life of cells, tensile strength of wire, etc.

(*vi*) ***Basis for specifications:*** Process control provides the basis of deciding the specifications of a product. There is no use of fixing the specifications which cannot be maintained.

(*vii*) ***To ascertain the impact of change in process or personnel:*** Statistical quality control enables the manufacturer to ascertain whether the changes brought in the process or technical persons have brought an improvement in the product or not.

(*viii*) ***Basis for satisfaction:*** The engineers may expect a total adherence to specifications whereas the operators may emphasise their performance satisfactory in spite of large variation. But the controversy is resolved if the process is under control.

(*ix*) ***Protection against losses:*** Statistical quality control provides protection against losses to the manufacturers as well as consumers.

Q. 27. *What are the limitations of statistical quality control?*

Ans. Statistical quality control should not be considered a panacea against all evils of production process. Many factors are involved which are not covered by statistical quality control. A production is not a part of statistical quality control but it is the other way round.

Q. 28. *Briefly differentiate between natural, specification and modified control limits.*

Ans. If μ and σ are the process mean and standard deviation respectively, the limits $\mu \pm 3\sigma$ are called the *natural tolerance limits.* The width of tolerance band is 6σ and is known as natural tolerance. If μ and σ are not known, they are estimated by $\hat{\mu} = \bar{X}$ and $\hat{\sigma} = \dfrac{\bar{R}}{d_2}$ or $\hat{\sigma} = \dfrac{\bar{S}}{c_2}$ and the control limits are constructed.

The *specification limits* are those which are desired by the consumer. Let the upper specification limit (U.S.L) and lower specification limit (L.S.L) be denoted by X_{max} and X_{min} respectively for some quality characteristic. A comparison of tolerance limit with the specification limits leads to the following inferences:

(*a*) If $X_{max} - X_{min} > 6\sigma$, there is a likelihood of better product. In this case specification limits lie outside the natural tolerance limits.

(*b*) If $X_{max} - X_{min} = 6\sigma$, this is an ideal situation. In this situation, the product will meet the specifications.

(*c*) If $X_{max} - X_{min} < 6\sigma$, a process under statistical control does not ensure that the product will meet the specifications.

Modified control limits give the relationship between specification limits and $\bar{X}$ values in $\bar{X}$-chart used to allow a shift in process levels within permissible limits.

For the samples (sub-groups) of size *n*, the maximum and minimum values of upper and lower control limits for $\bar{X}$ which are known as upper rejection limit (U.R.L) and lower rejection limit (L.R.L) respectively are given as,

$$URL_{\bar{X}} = USL - 3\sigma' + \frac{3\sigma'}{\sqrt{n}}$$

$$LRL_{\bar{X}} = LSL - 3\sigma' - \frac{3\sigma'}{\sqrt{n}}$$

where σ' is the specified known value of standard deviation.

The upper and lower rejection limits are known as *modified control limits.*

In case of rejection limits we do not have a line but a central band in which the product will conform to specifications. The upper and lower edges of the central band are given by USL – $3\sigma'$ and LSL + $3\sigma'$.

Q. 29. *What do you understand by acceptance sampling plan?*

Ans. It looks germane to inspect each and every item produced by a manufacturing unit and make sure about the quality specifications before releasing it for sale. But cent per cent inspection has its own weaknesses.

Firstly, due to fatigue of checking a large number of items, the efficiency of inspection goes down and hence one cannot expect that no defective or nonconforming item will not be left out after inspection.

Secondly, cent per cent inspection is an impossibility in cases where the produce or items are perished under inspection such as inspection for life of electric bulbs, life of battery cells, combustibility of coke, etc.

Thirdly, the time and cost are other two important economic factors which deter a manufacturer from 100 per cent inspection. So the acceptance or rejection of a lot is usually based on the inspection of samples drawn from the lots at regular intervals during the manufacturing process. Usually people call it *acceptance sampling plan.* Thus, under acceptance sampling plan one takes the decision whether a lot is to be accepted or rejected.

Q. 30. *When should the cent per cent inspection be preferred?*

Ans. In spite of many factors against cent per cent inspection, it is still preferred under special situations such as:

(*i*) a defective item may cause danger to life.

(*ii*) a defect may stop the whole function of a system.

(*iii*) the lot size is small.

(*iv*) the incoming quality is very poor.

Q. 31. *State the situations when no inspection is called for quality control.*

Ans. There are many situations which call for no inspection. If the process is such that the items are of high quality and there is hardly any chance of defective item, the product may be sold without inspection.

Q. 32. *What purposes are served by sampling inspection plans?*

Ans. Broadly, three purposes are served by sampling inspection plans.

(*i*) It enables to know whether the process is producing the product which meets the quality specification or not.

(*ii*) It reveals whether the finished product is good for marketing or not.

(*iii*) It minimizes the risk of the consumer and protects the producer from future losses.

Q. 33. *Compare sampling inspection by attributes with inspection by variables.*

Ans. The acceptance or rejection of a lot is based on inspection of a sample drawn from a submitted lot. Usually, the decision is based on the number or proportion of defectives present in the sample according to attributes under consideration. But the item can also be classified as defective or non-defective on the basis of measurable quality characteristics as well. For instance, an item heavier than a fixed weight or shorter than a fixed length can be classified as defective. Hence, the inspection by attributes contrasted with inspection by variables is given below:

(*i*) Inspection by variables has one major advantage over inspection by attributes that it needs fewer items for inspection for a given degree of accuracy.

(*ii*) The decision about the acceptance or rejection of a lot is more reliable if based on inspection by variable than by attributes for the fixed sample size.

(*iii*) The main advantage of inspection by attributes over inspection by variables is that it requires less accuracy of measurement, less skill, less time and less sophisticated instrument for measurements.

(*iv*) The calculations involved in deciding about the lot are much less in case of inspection by attributes as compared to inspection by variables.

(*v*) In case of inspection by attributes, selection and installation of sound sampling plans is easier than by variables.

(*vi*) Sampling inspection plan for variables do exists but are not so prevalent as for attributes.

(*vii*) Inspection plans by attributes are more economical than for variables. Thus, the lower cost of inspecting each item by attributes offsets the increase in sample size.

(*viii*) Per cent defective is usually an appropriate measure and its appropriateness is not affected by shifting between variables and attributes. Hence, inspection by attributes has been in vogue.

Q. 34. *What types of decision procedures are usually used for acceptance or rejection of a lot? Give a brief description.*

Ans. Two types of sampling inspection procedures are normally used, (*i*) sampling inspection by attributes and (*ii*) sampling inspection by variables.

Both the inspection types lead to the same conclusion. But the sampling inspection by attributes is mostly practised. Hence, we discuss only acceptance sampling by attributes. In this type of inspection, items are classified as defective or non-defective. Also, the acceptance or rejection of a lot depends on fraction defectives in the sample. The decision about the lot can be of two types, (*i*) acceptance-rejection type, (*ii*) acceptance-rectification type. In the first type, the lot is either accepted or rejected. If the lot is accepted, then the defective items in the sample are replaced by non-defectives and then the lot is passed for marketing. Whereas if the lot is rejected, it will cause heavy losses to the manufacturer. Hence, to reduce losses, the second decision procedure, *i.e.*, acceptance-rectification plan is adopted. In this plan, each and every unit of the lot is inspected and the defectives found in the lot are replaced by the non-defectives and the lot is released for sale.

Q. 35. *How will you distinguish between a major and minor defect?*

Ans. A defect of an item is called *major* if the defect will cause a failure of the item to function for which it is meant. Again, a defect of an item is called *minor* if the defect impairs the efficiency or shorten the life of the item.

Q. 36. *Define a producer and producer's risk.*

Ans. A producer is a person who produces goods for the purpose of consumption by others.

Producer's risk lies in rejecting a lot even though this is of desirable quality. Suppose the process is set for a fraction defective $\bar{p}$. The *average fraction defective* $\bar{p}$ is known as *producer's process average.* The probability of rejecting a lot having 100 $\bar{p}$ as the process average per cent defectives is known as producer's risk P_p. Symbolically,

P_p = Prob (rejecting a lot having 100 $\bar{p}$ defectives)

$= \alpha$

Q. 37. *Define a consumer and consumer's risk.*

Ans. A consumer is a person who purchases goods for his own consumption and not for sales to others directly or indirectly.

There is always a risk that a person gets a lot having an undesirable proportion of defectives. Such a risk is known as *consumer's risk.* If P_t is the proportion of defectives in the lot which can be tolerated, the probability of accepting a lot with fraction defectives P_t is known as consumer's risk and is denoted by P_c. Thus,

$$P_c = \text{Prob (accepting a lot having } P_t \text{ defectives)} = \beta$$

Dodge and Roming suggested that β can be taken as 10 per cent, *i.e.*, 0.1.

Q. 38. *What do you understand by acceptance quality level (A.Q.L)?*

Ans. The percentage of defective items, in an inspection lot which under sampling plan leads to the acceptance of 95 per cent of the submitted lots for inspection, having that percentage of defectives, is known as A.Q.L.

Let p_1 be the small fraction defective in the lot which is such that one is not to reject the lot more than a small number of times, then p_1 is known as the *acceptance quality level.* Usually,

$$P \text{ (rejecting a lot of quality level } p_1) = 0.05$$

$$P \text{ (accepting a lot of quality level } p_1) = 0.95$$

A lot having this quality is considered satisfactory.

Q. 39. *What is meant by lot tolerance percentage defective (L.T.P.D)?*

Ans. Lot tolerance percentage defective say, p_t denotes the quality of the lot which is not acceptable to the consumer. A lot, having p_t or more proportion of defectives, is not acceptable to the consumer. Thus, 100 p_t, is called *lot tolerance percentage defective.* In a way, p_t is the quality level at which the lot is rejected by the consumer and is also called *rejecting quality level* (R.Q.L). Customarily this percentage defective is about 10 per cent.

Q. 40. *Explain the meaning of average outgoing quality (A.O.Q).*

Ans. Average percentage of defectives remaining in the product finally accepted is known as *average outgoing quality.* Let it be denoted by *p*. Also, the maximum average percentage of defective items in a product finally accepted is known as average outgoing quality limit (A.O.Q.L).

Suppose, a sample of *n* items is drawn from a lot of size *N* and P_a is the probability of accepting a lot of average quality level *p,* then

$$\text{A.O.Q.L} = \frac{p(N-n)\,P_a}{N}$$

If the sampling fraction *n/N* is negligible, then,

$$\text{A.O.Q.L} = p \cdot P_a$$

Q. 41. *What does average total inspection mean?*

Ans. Average total inspection relates to rectification of inspection plan. Average number of items inspected per inspection lot under a particular sampling plan is known as *average total inspection* (A.T.I).

Q. 42. *What is blind sampling?*

Ans. Drawing items from a lot or process without any regard to their quality is called *blind sampling.*

Q. 43. *Give the definitions of average sample number (ASN) and ASN curve.*

Ans. Average sample number is the expected size of the sample required to arrive at a decision about the acceptance or rejection of a lot under sampling inspection plan. This depends on *p*, the actual proportion of defectives present in the lot.

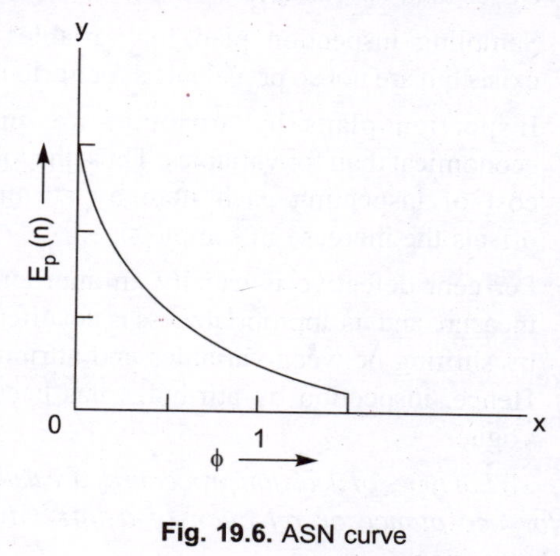

Fig. 19.6. ASN curve

The graph of the average sample numbers 'E_p (n)' against proportion 'p' of defectives is known as *ASN curve.*

A sampling plan resulting into the lowest *ASN* curve is considered better than any other sampling plan provided all other factors are kept constant.

Q. 44. *Delineate operating characteristic (OC) curve of a sampling plan.*

Ans. Let a large number of lots containing a given fraction defective p are submitted to a given plan and out of these lots, a proportion of lots, 'L_p' is accepted. Obviously, this proportion differs from one plan to the other. Now, it becomes necessary to know what proportion of lots under each plan will be accepted for each possible quality p of submitted lots. It is evident that a plan is unsuitable if it accepts too many lots of unsatisfactory quality or rejects too many lots of satisfactory quality. This information is very well represented by *OC* curve of the plan. The *OC* curve is plotted by taking p along abscissa and L_p along ordinate. A typical *OC* curve is shown below:

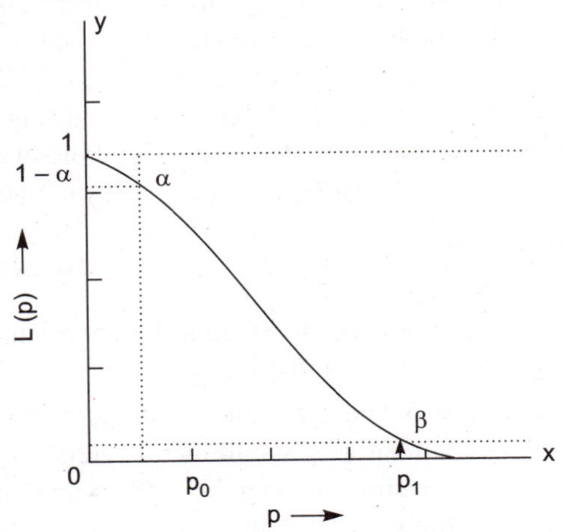

Fig. 19.7. Operating characteristic curve

Here, it is emphasised that the *OC* curve should not be taken to show the probability that an accepted lot will be of quality p but it gives the probability of accepting a lot of quality p.

In short, a curve showing the proportion (percentage) of submitted lots that will be accepted on the basis of sampling plan for each percentage of defectives items in the lots under consideration is known as *OC* curve.

More steep is the *OC* curve, better it is as this provides greater protection to consumer. In nutshell, it can be said that the *OC* curve of an acceptance sampling plan reveals the ability of the plan to distinguish between good and bad lots.

In the Fig. 19.7, p_0 is the *limiting acceptable quality and* p_1 *the limiting admissible* quality, α is the producer's risk and β is the consumer's risk.

Q. 45. *Discuss sampling inspection plans in reference to statistical quality control.*

Ans. There are various sampling inspection plans which can be grouped into three classes, viz. – single, double and sequential sampling plans. A plan which is good for some product and/or a supplier may not be good for the other. So, there is great need for selecting a plan best suited for a product and supplier in question. A plan is suitable in the sense that it holds certain properties as given below:

(*i*) The sampling plan ensures that the lots of high quality will be accepted and those of poor quality will be rejected.

(*ii*) The amount of inspection required under the plan is neither very high nor too low.

(*iii*) The plan encourages the producer to improve the quality of the product if it is not up to the mark.

(*iv*) The plan is not too much complicated so that it cannot be administered and operated with ease.

Q. 46. *Delineate single sampling inspection plan and its implications.*

Ans. A sampling plan in which a decision about the acceptance or rejection of a lot is based on one sample that has been inspected.

Suppose that, the lot consists of N items having a proportion of defectives as P and in all D defectives, *i.e.*, $D = NP$. A sample of size n is drawn from the submitted lot which contains d defectives. Let c be the maximum allowable number of defectives in the sample, c is known as *acceptance number.* The quantities n and c can either be determined by *lot quality* protection approach or by an *average quality protection* approach.

The procedure to arrive at a decision about the acceptance or rejection of a lot is as follows:

(*i*) Select a random sample of size n from the submitted lot.

(*ii*) Inspect each and every unit included in the sample and classify them as defective or non-defective. Suppose the number of defectives in the sample is d.

The criteria for the acceptance or rejection of the lot is,

(*a*) If $d \le c$, the lot is accepted. In this case, all the defective items in the sample are replaced by non-defectives and the lot is released for marketing.

(*b*) If $d > c$, the lot is rejected. In this situation, inspect the whole lot and replace all defectives found in the lot by the non-defectives and release the lot for sale.

In single sampling plan, the variable d follows the hypergeometric distribution. Various probabilities under this plan can be worked out by the following formulae:

I. The probability of obtaining d defectives in a sample of size n from the lot is,

$$P_d = \frac{\binom{NP}{d}\binom{N-NP}{n-d}}{\binom{N}{n}}$$

II. The probability of accepting the lot having not more than c defectives in the sample of n items is,

$$P_a = \sum_{d=0}^{c} \frac{\binom{NP}{d}\binom{N-Np}{n-d}}{\binom{N}{n}}$$

III. The consumer risk when the lot having the proportion of defectives p_t is accepted.

$$P_c = \sum_{d=0}^{c} \frac{\binom{NP_t}{d}\binom{N-Np_t}{n-d}}{\binom{N}{n}}$$

IV. The producer's risk when the lot containing a proportion $\bar{p}$ of defectives is rejected.

$$P_p = \sum_{d=c+1}^{n} \frac{\binom{N\bar{p}}{d}\binom{N-N\bar{p}}{n-d}}{\binom{N}{n}}$$

$$= 1 - \sum_{d=0}^{n} \frac{\binom{N\bar{p}}{d}\binom{N-N\bar{p}}{n-d}}{\binom{N}{n}}$$

From the above expressions we draw the following conclusions:

(*a*) Usually, P is not known, hence it is taken as $\bar{p}$.

(*b*) Consumer's risk does not depend on p, the process average fraction defectives, whereas producer's risk does depend on $\bar{p}$.

(*c*) In certain situations, depending upon the values of N, n and p, the variable d may follow binomial or Poisson's distributions. The probabilities have to be worked out by the formulae deduced for these distributions. The thumb rules for approximating the hypergeometric distribution to Poisson and binomial distributions are:

(*i*) If $p < 0.1$ and also $\frac{n}{N} < 0.01$, hyper geometric distribution be approximated to Poisson distribution.

(*ii*) If N and n are large and np or $N - NP$ is relatively small, then hypergeometric distribution can be approximated to binomial distribution. Numerically, if $p < 0.10$, hypergeometric distribution tends to binomial distribution.

Q. 47. *What distinction is being made by Dodge and Roming between Type A and Type B OC curves?*

Ans. Dodge and Roming distinguished between Type A and Type B OC curves as:

(*i*) Type A OC curves give the probabilities of different fraction defectives as a function of the lot quality of finite lots. In principle, such curves should be established by hypergeometric probabilities.

(*ii*) Type *A* curves are usually desirable in evaluating consumer's risk with regard to individual lots.

(*iii*) Type *B OC* curve gives the probability of acceptance of a lot as a function of the product quality as if the lots were infinite.

(*iv*) Type *B OC* curve based on binomial probabilities provide exact results.

(*v*) Type *B OC* curves are generally appropriate in evaluating producer's risk.

(*vi*) If we plot Type *A* and Type *B OC* curves on the same graph, Type *A OC* curve always falls below the type *B OC* curve.

Q. 48. *Explain the double sampling inspection plan.*

Ans. The double sampling scheme was originated by Dodge and Roming. A sampling plan when a decision about the acceptance or rejection of a lot has not been reached after single sample inspection from a submitted lot, a decision will always be reached when the second sample from the same lot has been inspected.

Suppose there is an inspection lot of N items and a sample of n items is drawn and every item in the sample is inspected for its quality. Let there be two numbers c_1 and c_2 such that the number of defectives 'd' in the sample is less than or equal to 'c_1' ($d \leq c_1$), the lot is accepted and if $d \geq c_2$, the lot is rejected. But if $c_1 < d < c_2$, no decision can be taken. In this situation, a second sample of size n_2 ($n_2 \geq n_1$) is drawn from the same lot and again all its items are inspected for the number of defectives. At this stage we consider jointly the sample of size $(n_1 + n_2)$ and number of defectives as a whole. If it contains the defectives less than c_2, the lot is accepted and if c_2 or more, the lot is rejected. In case, the lot is rejected under the double sampling plan, inspect the whole lot and replace all defectives by non-defectives and release the lot for sale.

Q. 49. *Explicate sequential sampling inspection plan.*

Ans. The phrase sequential sampling is normally used for the type of sampling procedure in which the decision is taken after the inspection of each selected item in sequence and no limit is specified for the sample size. This type of sampling plan is also known as *item-by-item* sampling plan. In sequential sampling, sample size 'n' is itself a random variable.

In a decision problem under sequential sampling scheme, the total decision space is divided into three regions namely, (*i*) acceptance region, (*ii*) rejection region, and (*iii*) the region of continuance.

In sequential sampling, items are selected and inspected one by one sequentially and after each inspection, a decision is taken. About the acceptance or rejection of the lot or continuance of the process of sampling and inspection according to the position of the point lying in the acceptance, rejection or continuance region respectively. Sequential sampling requires minimum amount of inspection. Hence, it is often preferred. It has been proved that the sequential sampling process terminates with probability one. The theory of sequential analysis was originally given by Abraham Wald in 1947.

Q. 50. *Give the idea of sequential probability ratio test (S.P.R.T.).*

Ans. Suppose p is the unknown proportion of defectives in the lot. Now, we consider two values of p say, p_0 and p_1 with $p_0 < p_1$. Usually in quality control problems, p_0 = A.Q.L and p_1 = L.T.P.D. A producer will not reject the lot if $p \leq p_0$ and a consumer will not like to accept the lot if $p \geq p_1$. At the same time, the producer and consumer will not be able to take a decision if $p_0 < p < p_1$.

Let type I and type II errors be defined as,

P (rejecting the lot when $p \leq p_0$) = α (Type I error)

P (accepting the lot when $p \geq p_1$) = β (Type II error)

In terms of *OC* function it is desired that,

$$L(p) \geq 1 - \alpha \quad \text{when, } p \leq p_0$$

$$L(p) \leq \beta \quad \text{when, } p \geq p_1$$

Dr A. Wald gave S.P.R.T for testing,

$$H_0 : p = p_0 \text{ vs. } H_1 : p = p_1$$

Let the result X_i of the inspection of ith item be denoted by Bernoulli's variable as,

$x_i = 1$ if the item is found to be defective,

and $x_i = 0$ if the item is found to be non-defective.

Suppose the sequential sampling continues till the m items are inspected. So, we have variates x_1, x_2, …, x_m which are independently and identically distributed with probability mass function $f(x, p)$. So the probability mass function,

$$f(x, P) = \prod_{i=1}^{m} p^{x_i} (1-p)^{1-x_i}$$

Under H_1, the probability mass function (p.m.f.) for the sample x_1, x_2, …, x_m is,

$$P_{1m} = \prod_{i=1}^{m} p_1^{x_i} (1-p_1)^{1-x_i}$$

and under H_0, the p.m.f. is,

$$P_{0m} = \prod_{i=1}^{m} p_0^{x_i} (1-p_0)^{1-x_i}$$

Thus, the likelihood ratio λ_m is given as,

$$\lambda_m = \frac{\prod_{i=1}^{m} f(x_i, p_1)}{\prod_{i=1}^{m} f(x_i, p_0)}$$

$$= \frac{p_1(m)}{p_0(m)}$$

$$= \frac{\prod_{i=1}^{m} P_1^{x_i} (1-p_1)^{1-x_i}}{\prod_{i=1}^{m} P_0^{x_i} (1-p_0)^{1-x_i}}$$

$$= \frac{P_1^{\Sigma x_i} (1-p_1)^{m-\Sigma x_i}}{P_0^{\Sigma x_i} (1-p_0)^{m-\Sigma x_i}}$$

Supposing that out of m units inspected, d_m are defective. Then,

$$\lambda_m = \frac{p_1(m)}{p_0(m)}$$

$$= \frac{P_1^{d_m} (1-p_1)^{m-d_m}}{P_0^{d_m} (1-p_0)^{m-d_m}}$$

The decision about the acceptance, rejection or continuance of sampling process is taken according to the following rules.

Accept the lot if

$$\lambda_m \le \frac{\beta}{1-\alpha}$$

Reject the lot if

$$\lambda_m \ge \frac{1-\beta}{\alpha}$$

Continue sampling if

$$\frac{\beta}{1-\alpha} < \lambda_m < \frac{1-\beta}{\alpha}$$

Now, substituting for λ_m in terms of the p.m.f., the inequalities can be expressed as:

Accept the lot provided,

$$\left(\frac{p_1}{p_0}\right)^{d_m} \left(\frac{1-p_1}{1-p_0}\right)^{m-d_m} \le \frac{\beta}{1-\alpha}$$

Taking logarithm we get,

$$d_m \left\{\log\frac{p_1}{p_0} - \log\frac{1-p_1}{1-p_0}\right\} \le m\log\frac{1-p_0}{1-p_1} + \log\frac{\beta}{1-\alpha}$$

$$\text{or } d_m \le \frac{m\log\frac{1-p_0}{1-p_1} + \log\frac{\beta}{1-\alpha}}{\log\frac{p_1}{p_0} - \log\frac{1-p_1}{1-p_0}}$$

$$d_m \le \frac{\log\frac{\beta}{1-\alpha}}{\log\frac{p_1}{p_0} - \log\frac{1-p_1}{1-p_0}} + m\frac{\log\frac{1-p_0}{1-p_1}}{\log\frac{p_1}{p_0} - \log\frac{1-p_1}{1-p_0}}$$

Suppose R.H.S. of the inequality is denoted by a_m. Thus, accept the lot if

$$d_m \le a_m$$

Similarly reject the lot if

$$d_m \ge r_m$$

where

$$r_m = \frac{\log \frac{1-\beta}{\alpha}}{\log \frac{p_1}{p_0} - \log \frac{1-p_1}{1-p_0}} + m \frac{\log \frac{1-p_0}{1-p_1}}{\log \frac{p_1}{p_0} - \log \frac{1-p_1}{1-p_0}}$$

Continue sampling if

$$a_m < d_m < r_m$$

Q. 51. *How can sequential sampling plan be implemented graphically under S.P.R.T.?*

Ans. We know a_m and r_m represent straight lines which are parallel to each other as the coefficient of m in both lines is same. In other words, both the lines have slope equal to

$$\left\{\log \frac{1-p_0}{1-p_1}\right\} \Big/ \left\{\log \frac{p_1}{p_0} - \log \frac{1-p_1}{1-p_0}\right\}$$

On a graph paper, represent m on abscissa and cumulative number of defectives d_m on ordinate choosing suitable scales. Draw the lines a_m and r_m in the first quadrant of the graph as shown in the figure below.

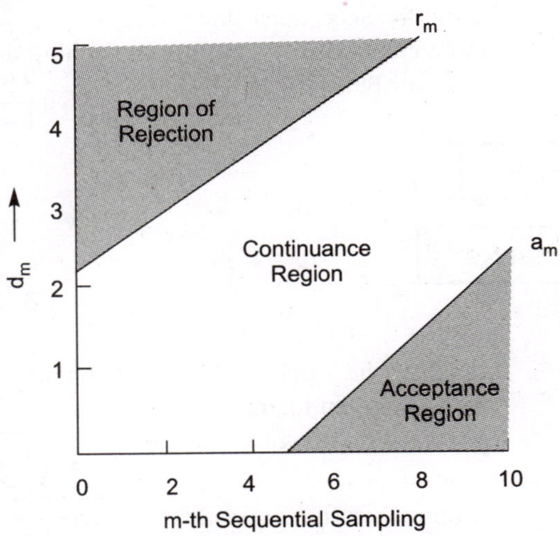

Fig. 19.8. Decision space diagram

Start from plotting the first sample point. If it lies on or below the line a_m, accept the lot. If the plotted point lies on or above the line r_m, reject the lot. In either situation terminate the sampling process as a decision is reached. If the point lies between a_m and r_m, the process of sampling and inspection continues. Again select another item and inspect it. Plot the point and see where does this point lies. The process is continued till a decision is taken about the acceptance or rejection of the lot.

Q. 52. *Give OC function of a sequential probability ratio test.*

Ans. The *OC* function of a S.P.R.T. for testing H_0: $p = p_0$ vs. $H_1 : p = p_1$ is given by

$$L(p) = \frac{\left(\frac{1-\beta}{\alpha}\right)^h - 1}{\left(\frac{1-\beta}{\alpha}\right)^h - \left(\frac{\beta}{1-\alpha}\right)^h} \qquad (1)$$

The value of h is obtained by the equation,

$$p\left(\frac{p_1}{p_0}\right)^h + (1-p)\left(\frac{1-p_1}{1-p_0}\right)^h = 1 \qquad (2)$$

It is cumbersome to solve equation (2) for h. Hence, we rearrange the equation (2) for p in terms of h, *i.e.*,

$$p = \frac{1 - \left(\frac{1-p_1}{1-p_0}\right)^h}{\left(\frac{p_1}{p_0}\right)^h - \left(\frac{1-p_1}{1-p_0}\right)^h} \qquad (3)$$

Now to draw an *OC* curve, we calculate p for different arbitrary chosen values of h. For these values of h, calculate $L(p)$ from (1). Plot the points $[p, L(p)]$ on graph and draw *OC* curve. As a norm, at least five points be plotted to have correct shape of the curve.

It is now trivial to verify that when there is no defective, *i.e.*, $p = 0$, then $L(0) = 1$. Also, when all are defective items, *i.e.*, $p = 1$, then $L(1) = 0$.

Q. 53. *What do you understand by expected sample size of a sequential sampling plan and how to determine it?*

Ans. We know that in sequential sampling plan, the sample size n is a random variable and hence it can be determined with the help of the probability function $f(x, p)$. Expected sample size is also known as average sample number (A.S.N.). The expected sample size or A.S.N, of a S.P.R.T. for testing $H_0 : p = p_0$ vs. $H_1 : p = p_1$ where, A.Q.L. = p_0 and L.T.D.P. = p_1, can be determined by the formula,

$$E(n) = \frac{L(p)\log \frac{\beta}{1-\alpha} + \{1 - L(p)\}\log \frac{1-\beta}{\alpha}}{E(z)} \qquad (1)$$

$$\text{where, } E(z) = p \log \frac{p_1}{p_0} + (1-p)\log \frac{1-p_1}{1-p_0} \qquad (2)$$

Formula (1) is known as A.S.N. function. A good idea for A.S.N. curve can be had by suitably choosing five points which are easy to locate corresponding to the values $p = 0, 1, p_0, p_1$ and

$$\left[\left\{\log \frac{1-p_0}{1-p_1}\right\} \Big/ \left\{\log \frac{p_1}{p_0} + \log \frac{1-p_0}{1-p_1}\right\}\right]$$

Q. 54. *Make comparative statement on single, double and sequential sampling plans.*

Ans. Single and double sampling are equally good in respect of operating characteristic and A.S.N. But, double sampling results into 25-33 per cent saving in sampling whereas sequential sampling on the average requires 33-50 per cent less inspection of sampling units as compared to single sampling.

Q. 55. *What problems are faced in case of sampling inspection for variables as compared to fraction defectives?*

Ans. The methods developed for fraction defectives are also applicable for variables.

But the defects will be due to different measurements like length, width, diameter, chemical composition, etc. Hence, different charts have to be prepared for each variable separately and then the results are to be pooled to arrive at a conclusion about the acceptance or rejection of a lot. When the results are contradictory to one another, it is very difficult to reach a single decision. The ideas can be summarised as follows:

(*i*) For a given sample size, better quality protection is usually obtained in case of inspection by variables than by attributes.

(*ii*) Smaller samples may be used with variables than with attributes.

(*iii*) The variables criterion is given more weight to attain the desired quality protection.

(*iv*) Errors of measurements are better surfaced with variables information.

(*v*) The use of variables as a decision criteria about the acceptance and rejection of a lot is more cumbersome and time consuming than with attributes.

SECTION B

Fill in the Blanks

Fill in the suitable word(s) or phrase(s) in the blanks:

1. Variation in the measurements of items produced under any system is ________ .
2. The variation due to ________ factors is tolerable.
3. Statistical quality control takes care of the variation due to ________ causes.
4. Through statistical quality control, one finds whether the process is under ________ or not.
5. Whether the variability in the manufactured items is within tolerance limits or not can be ascertained through ________ .
6. Control charts ________ the ________ within which the variability is tolerable.
7. A control chart contains ________ lines.
8. Most frequently used five control charts are ________ charts.
9. In control charts we establish ________ limits.
10. Control limits utilise the constant factors given by ________ .

11. Control charts for mean utilise factors _________ due to Shewhart.

12. Control limits for σ-charts involve the factors _________ evolved by Shewhart.

13. In case of small samples, range and _________ vary concurrently in the same direction.

14. Control limits in *R*-charts for statistical quality control involve Shewhart constants _________.

15. $\bar{X}$-charts discover assignable causes _________ samples.

16. *R*-charts uncover assignable causes _________ samples.

17. If $\bar{X}$-chart reveals that the process is under control, there is no need of preparing _________.

18. *R*-charts are economical than _________ .

19. In case of large samples, _________ charts should preferably be used.

20. A peculiar pattern of points within the control limits of quality control charts is indicative of _________ .

21. Cyclic pattern of sample points within the control limits occurs due to _________ and _________.

22. In case of fraction defective, the variable under consideration is _________ .

23. The variance of the fraction defectives is obtained by the variance of _________ distribution.

24. If better is the quality of the product, _________ is the sample size required.

25. Control charts for number of defects are prepared when occurrence per item is _________ as compared to the number of defective items.

26. Number of defects follows _________ distribution.

27. Control charts for process control result into saving of _________ and _________ .

28. Sampling inspection results into _________ in the process of inspection than total inspection.

29. Sampling inspection protects against _________ to the producer.

30. When the items are perished under the process of quality checking, _________ inspection is the only way out for quality control.

31. Sampling inspection enables one to compare two _________ .

32. The control limits delimited by the consumer are known as _________ limits.

33. The limits $\mu \pm 3\sigma$, with known μ and σ, are called _________ limits in statistical quality control.

34. Cent per cent inspection is a must in cases where single defective item is _________ .

35. No inspection is called for when items are of _________ .

36. Sampling inspection reduces the risk of the _________ .

37. Sampling inspection protects the producer from _________ .

38. Sampling inspection by attributes is more prevalent than by _________ .

39. The decision about the lot under sampling inspection is of _________ types.

40. A defect in an item may be classified as _________ or _________ .

41. If a defect stops the function of an item, it is known as _________ defect.

42. A defect in an item reducing its efficiency is classified as _________ defect.

43. The average fraction defective is also termed as _________ average.

44. Producer's risk is referred to _________ error.

45. Consumer's risk is akin to _________ error.

46. Sampling inspection by variables requires _________ inspection as compared to inspection by attributes for the same information.

47. The decision based on inspection by variables is ________ reliable than by attributes.

48. Sampling plans for variables do ________ .

49. The average fraction defective $\bar{p}$ is known as ________ .

50. The probability of rejecting a lot $\bar{p}$ defectives is known as ________ .

51. The probability of accepting a lot with fraction defectives p_t is known as ________ .

52. Inspection by attributes is ________ and ________ as compared to inspection by variables.

53. Inspection by attributes is in ________ .

54. The per cent defectives in a lot below which only the lot is acceptable is known as ________ .

55. The minimum quality level at which the lot is rejected is called ________ .

56. Average percentage of defectives remaining in an outgoing lot is known as ________ .

57. The percentage of maximum defective items finally accepted in a lot is known as ________ .

58. Drawing units from a lot or process irrespective of their quality is known as ________ .

59. The expected sample size required to arrive at a decision about the lot is called the ________ .

60. The average sample number depends on the ________ present in the lot.

61. The graph drawn for proportion defectives and average sample number is known as ________ .

62. The sampling inspection plan resulting into the lowest A.S.N. curve is ________ .

63. Operating characteristic (*OC*) curve depicts the probability of ________ a lot of quality p.

64. More steep is the *OC* curve, ________ it is.

65. *OC* curve is a device which reflects on the quality of a sampling plan to differentiate between ________ .

66. A sampling inspection plan is good if it can correctly decide about the ________ or ________ of the lot.

67. A good sampling inspection plan requires an ________ number of inspection of items.

68. A sampling inspection plan is considered satisfactory if it is not ________ .

69. The probability of obtaining d defectives in a sample of size n from a lot having N items with p as proportion of defectives is ________ .

70. The curve depicting the probabilities of different fraction defectives as a function of the lot quality of finite lots is called ________ .

71. The curve giving the probability of acceptance of a lot as a function of the product quality of infinite lots is categorised as ________ .

72. Type *A OC* curve helps to evaluate ________ of individual lots.

73. Type *B OC* curve usually evaluate ________ .

74. Type *A OC* curve utilises ________ probabilities.

75. Type *B OC* curve is based on ________ probabilities.

76. Type *B OC* curve always lies ________ the Type *A OC* curve if plotted on the same graph.

77. If the number of defectives in a sample lies between the acceptance and rejection limits, we make use of ________ .

78. In sequential sampling decision about the acceptance or rejection of a lot is taken after the selection of ________ .

79. Sequential sampling plan requires ________ amount of inspection.

80. The theory of sequential sampling plan was originally given by ________ .

81. Sequential analysis was developed in the year ________ .

82. In a sequential decision problem, the total space is divided into ________ regions.

83. The lines dividing the space into region of acceptance, rejection and continuance are obtained through ________ .

84. The lines dividing the space into three regions in S.P.R.T. are always ________ .

85. The graph of the points [p, L (p)] under S.P.R.T. provides ________ .

86. In sequential sampling plan, the sample size is a ________ .

87. The expectation of the sample size n in sequential sampling is known as ________ .

88. In double sampling plan, there is a ________ per cent saving in sampling inspection as compared to single sampling plan.

89. In sequential sampling, the sampling inspection is reduced by ________ per cent as compared to single sampling plan.

90. Sampling inspection by variables provides ________ protection than by attributes.

91. Errors of measurements are more prominent in sampling inspection by ________ than by ________ .

92. To ensure that the proportion of defective items in the manufactured product is not beyond certain limits is called ________ .

93. Control on the quality of the product by critical examination at strategic points is called ________.

94. The control charts help to achieve ________.

95. Sampling inspection plans are meant for ________ .

96. Sampling inspection plans were pioneered by ________ .

97. The inspection of 25 aircrafts revealed that there are 350 missing rivets in all. The appropriate control chart in this situation which can be prepared is ________ .

98. A list shows the number of non-conforming items in each of the 25 samples, each sample consisting of 40 items. The appropriate statistical control chart in this situation is ________.

99. The number of mistakes committed by a mechanic in 20 samples of assembled radios are 25. The lower control limit for c-chart from the given data is ________ .

100. A factory produces 300 articles per day. After inspecting 3,000 articles on 30 consecutive days, 270 articles were non-conforming to the specification. The upper control limit for p-chart is ________ .

SECTION C

Multiple Choice Questions

Select the correct alternative out of given ones:

1. Variation in the items produced in a factory may be due to:
   (*a*) chance factors
   (*b*) assignable causes
   (*c*) both (*a*) and (*b*)
   (*d*) none of the above

2. Chance or random variation in the manufactured product is:
   (*a*) controlable
   (*b*) not controlable
   (*c*) both (*a*) and (*b*)
   (*d*) none of the above

3. Chance variation in respect of quality control of a product is:
   (*a*) tolerable
   (*b*) not effecting the quality of a product
   (*c*) uncontrolable
   (*d*) all of the above

4. The causes leading to vast variation in the specifications of a product are usually due to:
   (*a*) random process
   (*b*) assignable causes

(c) non-traceable causes
(d) all of the above

5. Variation due to assignable causes in the product occurs due to:
(a) faulty process
(b) carelessness of operators
(c) poor quality of raw material
(d) all of the above

6. The faults due to assignable causes:
(a) can be removed
(b) cannot be removed
(c) can sometimes be removed
(d) all of the above

7. Control charts in statistical quality control are meant for:
(a) describing the pattern of variation
(b) checking whether the variability in the product is within the tolerance limits or not
(c) uncovering whether the variability in the product is due to assignable causes or not
(d) all of the above

8. Control charts consist of:
(a) three control lines
(b) upper and lower control limits
(c) the level of the process
(d) all of the above

9. Main tools of statistical quality control are:
(a) shewhart charts
(b) acceptance sampling plans
(c) both (a) and (b)
(d) none of the above

10. Trial control limits for mean with usual notations are:
(a) U.C.L. = $\bar{X} + A_1\bar{S}$, C.L. = $\bar{X}$ and L.C.L. = $\bar{X} - A_1\bar{S}$
(b) U.C.L. = $\bar{X} + A_1\bar{S}$, C.L. = $A_1\bar{S}$ and L.C.L. = $\bar{X} - A_1\bar{S}$
(c) U.C.L. = $\bar{X} + A_2\bar{S}$, C.L. = $\bar{X}$ and L.C.L. = $\bar{X} - A_2\bar{S}$
(d) none of the above

11. The trial control limits for σ-chart with $\bar{S}$ as mean standard deviation and usual constant factors are:
(a) U.C.L. = $\bar{S} + B_1\bar{S}$, C.L. = $\bar{S}$ and L.C.L. = $\bar{S} - B_4\bar{S}$
(b) U.C.L. = $B_4\bar{S}$, C.L. = B_4 and L.C.L. = $B_3\bar{S}$
(c) U.C.L. = $B_4\bar{S}$, C.L. = $\bar{S}$ and L.C.L. = $B_3\bar{S}$
(d) U.C.L. = $B_3\bar{S}$, C.L. = $\bar{S}$ and L.C.L. = $B_4\bar{S}$

12. The relation between expected value of R and S.D. σ with usual constant factors is:
(a) $E(R) = d_1\sigma$
(b) $E(R) = d_2\sigma$
(c) $E(R) = D_1\sigma$
(d) $E(R) = D_2\sigma$

13. The control limits for R-chart with a known specified range R' and usual constant factors are:
(a) $\text{U.C.L.}_{R'} = (d_2 + 3d_3)\sigma_{R'}$, $\text{C.L.}_{R'} = d_2\sigma_{R'}$ and $\text{L.C.L.}_{R'} = (d_2 - 3d_3)\,\sigma_{R'}$
(b) $\text{U.C.L.}_{R'} = D_2\,R'$, $\text{C.L.}_{R'} = d_2\sigma_{R'}$ and $\text{L.C.L.}_{R'} = D_1\sigma_{R'}$
(c) either (a) or (b)
(d) neither (a) nor (b)

14. When the value of the population range R is not known, then for $\bar{X}$-chart, the trial control limits with usual constant factors are:
(a) U.C.L. = $\bar{X} + A_3\bar{R}$, C.L. = $\bar{X}$ and L.C.L. = $\bar{X} - A_2\bar{R}$
(b) U.C.L. = $\bar{X} + A_3\bar{R}$, C.L. = $\bar{X}$ and L.C.L. = $\bar{X} - A_3\bar{R}$

(c) U.C.L. = $A_3\bar{R}$, C.L. = $\bar{X}$ and L.C.L. = $A_2\bar{R}$

(d) U.C.L. = $\bar{X} + A_3\bar{R}$, C.L. = $\bar{X}$ and L.C.L. = $\bar{X} - A_3\bar{R}$

15. The trial control limits for *R*-chart with usual constant factors are:

(a) U.C.L. = D_4R, C.L. = R and L.C.L. = D_3R

(b) U.C.L. = $D_4\bar{R}$, C.L. = $\bar{R}$ and L.C.L. = $D_3\bar{R}$

(c) U.C.L. = $D_4\bar{R}$, C.L. = $\bar{R}$ and L.C.L. = $D_4\bar{R}$

(d) all of the above

16. *R*-charts are preferable over σ-charts because:

(a) *R* and S.D. fluctuate together in case of small samples

(b) *R* is easily calculable

(c) *R*-charts are economical

(d) all of the above

17. The Shewhart control charts are meant:

(a) to detect whether the process is under statistical quality control

(b) to find the assignable causes

(c) to reflect the selection of samples

(d) all of the above

18. 3-sigma control limits of defectives having a given value of fraction defectives p' are:

(a) U.C.L. = $p' + \sqrt{\dfrac{3p'q'}{n}}$, C.L. = p' and L.C.L. = $p' - \sqrt{\dfrac{3p'q'}{n}}$

(b) U.C.L. = $p' + \dfrac{1}{3}\sqrt{\dfrac{p'q'}{n}}$, C.L. = p' and L.C.L. = $p' - \dfrac{1}{3}\sqrt{\dfrac{p'q'}{n}}$

(c) U.C.L = $p' + 3\sqrt{\dfrac{p'q'}{n}}$, C.L. = p' and L.C.L. = $p' - 3\sqrt{\dfrac{p'q'}{n}}$

(d) all of the above

19. 3-sigma trial control limits with p' as mean number of defectives based on a sample of size *n* are:

(a) U.C.L. = $n\bar{p} + \sqrt{n\bar{p}(1-\bar{p})}$, C.L. = $\bar{p}$ and L.C.L. = $n\bar{p} - \sqrt{n\bar{p}(1-\bar{p})}$

(b) U.C.L. = $n\bar{p} + 3\sqrt{n\bar{p}(1-\bar{p})}$, C.L. = $n\bar{p}$ and L.C.L. = $n\bar{p} - 3\sqrt{n\bar{p}(1-\bar{p})}$

(c) U.C.L. = $n\bar{p} + 3\sqrt{n\bar{p}(1-\bar{p})}$, C.L. = $\bar{p}$ and L.C.L. = $\bar{p} - 3\sqrt{n\bar{p}(1-\bar{p})}$

(d) none of the above

20. 2-sigma trial control limits for *c*-chart for equal size samples are given as:

(a) U.C.L. = $\bar{C} + 3\sqrt{\bar{C}}$, C.L. = $\bar{C}$ and L.C.L. = $\bar{C} - 3\sqrt{\bar{C}}$

(b) U.C.L. = $\bar{C} + \sqrt{2\bar{C}}$, C.L. = $2\bar{C}$ and L.C.L. = $\bar{C} - \sqrt{2\bar{C}}$

(c) U.C.L. = $\bar{C} + \sqrt{2\bar{C}}$, C.L. = $\bar{C}$ and L.C.L. = $\bar{C} - 2\sqrt{\bar{C}}$

(d) U.C.L. = $\bar{C} + 2\sqrt{\bar{C}}$, C.L. = C and L.C.L. = $\bar{C} - 2\sqrt{\bar{C}}$

21. A control chart based on known parameter values is:

(a) more advantageous than the one based on estimated values

(*b*) complicated than that of the control chart based on estimated values
(*c*) less reliable than the control chart based on estimated values
(*d*) all of the above

22. If μ and σ are the process mean and S.D., then the control limits $\mu \pm 3\sigma$ are known as:
(*a*) modified control limits
(*b*) natural control limits
(*c*) specified control limits
(*d*) none of the above

23. The control limits delimited by the consumer are called:
(*a*) modified control limits
(*b*) natural control limits
(*c*) specified control limits
(*d*) none of the above

24. For the subgroups of size *n*, the upper and lower control limits for rejection of a lot are termed as:
(*a*) modified control limits
(*b*) natural control limits
(*c*) specified control limits
(*d*) none of the above

25. Acceptance sampling plans are preferable due to:
(*a*) the economy in inspection
(*b*) protection to perishable items
(*c*) increased efficiency in the inspection of items
(*d*) all of the above

26. Cent per cent inspection is preferable when:
(*a*) a defective item may cause danger to life
(*b*) a defective item may stop the function as a whole
(*c*) the incoming items are of very poor quality
(*d*) all of the above

27. One may require no inspection of items if:
(*a*) the demand of item is too much
(*b*) the items produced are of very high quality
(*c*) the inspection cost is very high
(*d*) all of the above

28. The sampling inspection procedures adopted in statistical quality control are of:
(*a*) three types
(*b*) two types
(*c*) mixed types
(*d*) none of the above

29. The decision about the lot under sampling inspection procedures can be of:
(*a*) two types
(*b*) three types
(*c*) no use
(*d*) none of the above

30. Sampling inspection procedure by variables as compared to by attributes is:
(*a*) more prevalent
(*b*) not practised
(*c*) less prevalent
(*d*) all of the above

31. A defect in an item is classified as minor if:
(*a*) it stops the function of the process
(*b*) it is easily detectable
(*c*) it impairs the life of the system
(*d*) all of the above

32. A defect in an item is classified as major if:
(*a*) its stops the function of the process
(*b*) it is not detectable
(*c*) it shortens the life of the system
(*d*) all of the above

33. The probability of rejecting a lot having $\overline{p}$ as the process average defective is known as:
(*a*) consumer's risk
(*b*) type II error
(*c*) producer's risk
(*d*) all of the above

34. The probability of accepting a lot with fraction defective P_t is known as:
(*a*) consumer's risk
(*b*) type I error
(*c*) producer's risk
(*d*) none of the above

35. The decision about the acceptance or rejection of a lot by variables is:
(*a*) less reliable than by attributes

(b) more reliable than by attributes
(c) not feasible
(d) none of the above

36. Sampling inspection by variables requires:
(a) fewer inspection than by attributes
(b) greater inspection than by attributes
(c) equal inspection to that of by attributes
(d) none of the above

37. Inspection by attributes over inspection by variables requires:
(a) less time
(b) less skill
(c) less calculations
(d) all of the above

38. The small fraction of defectives p_1, on the basis of which a lot is not rejected except for a small number of times, is called:
(a) lot tolerance percentage defective (LTPD)
(b) rejecting quality level (RQL)
(c) acceptance quality level (AQL)
(d) none of the above

39. If the percentage defective p_t, or more in a lot is not acceptable to the consumer, then it is known as:
(a) let tolerance percentage defective (LTPD)
(b) rejecting quality level (RQL)
(c) both (a) and (b)
(d) none of the above

40. The maximum limit of percentage defectives in a finally accepted product is called:
(a) acceptance quality level (AQL)
(b) average outgoing quality limit (AOQL)
(c) lot tolerance percentage defective (LTPD)
(d) all of the above

41. Drawing items from a lot without giving any heed to their quality is known as:
(a) random sampling
(b) purposive sampling
(c) systematic sampling
(d) blind sampling

42. The expected sample size required to arrive at a decision about the lot is called:
(a) a random variable
(b) average sample number (ASN)
(c) both (a) and (b)
(d) none of the above

43. The graph of the proportion of defectives in the lot against average sample number is:
(a) *OC* curve
(b) A.S.N. curve
(c) power curve
(d) all of the above

44. The lowest A.S.N. curve of a sampling plan as compared to any other sampling plan under similar conditions is considered:
(a) better
(b) inferior
(c) useless
(d) none of the above

45. A curve showing the probability of accepting a lot of quality p is known as:
(a) *OC* curve
(b) A.S.N. curve
(c) Compertz curve
(d) none of the above

46. *OC* curve reveals the ability of the sampling plan to distinguish between:
(a) good and bad lots
(b) good and bad sampling plans
(c) good and bad product
(d) all of the above

47. A sampling plan is good for use provided:
(a) it ensures correct decision about the acceptance or rejection of a lot
(b) it requires an adequate number of inspections
(c) it is not complicated
(d) all of the above

48. The decision about the acceptance or rejection of a lot through a single sampling plan is reached by considering:
(a) number of defectives in the sample and acceptance number
(b) the acceptance quality level
(c) lot tolerance percentage defective
(d) all of the above

49. Type A and Type B OC curves differ from one another in respect of:

(a) hypergeometric and binomial probabilities

(b) finite and infinite sizes of the lots

(c) consumer's and producer's risks

(d) all of the above

50. In a double sampling plan, a decision about the acceptance or rejection of a lot:

(a) will never reach

(b) will always reach

(c) will sometimes reach

(d) none of the above

51. The decision in a sequential sampling scheme is taken:

(a) after inspecting the sample as a whole

(b) after selection and inspection of items one by one

(c) both (a) and (b)

(d) none of the above

52. In a decision problem under sequential sampling scheme, the total decision space is divided into:

(a) two regions namely, acceptance and rejection regions

(b) n equally spaced regions consisting of alternating acceptance and rejection regions

(c) three regions namely, the regions of acceptance, rejection and continuance

(d) none of the above

53. If p is the unknown proportion of defectives in the lot and p_0 and p_1 are two values such that $p_0 < p_1$. Also

$$\alpha = P\,(\text{reject the lot} \mid p \leq p_0)$$

$$\beta = P\,(\text{accept the lot} \mid p \geq p_1)$$

Then the operating characteristic function $L(p)$ takes the values as:

(a) $L\,(p) = 1 - \alpha$ when, $p \leq p_0$ and $L\,(p) = \beta$ when, $p = p_1$

(b) $L\,(p) = 1 - \alpha$ when, $p < p_0$ and $L\,(p) = \beta$ when, $p \geq p_1$

(c) $L\,(p) = 1 - \alpha$ when, $p \geq p_0$ and $L\,(p) = 1 - \beta$ when, $p \geq p_1$

(d) $L\,(p) = 1 - \alpha$ when, $p \leq p_0$ and $L\,(p) = 1 - \beta$ when, $p \geq p_1$

54. In a sequential probability ratio test, the criterion for acceptance of the lot with usual notations is:

(a) $\lambda_m \leq \dfrac{\beta}{1-\alpha}$

(b) $\lambda_m \geq \dfrac{\beta}{1-\alpha}$

(c) $\lambda_m \leq \dfrac{1-\beta}{\alpha}$

(d) $\lambda_m \geq \dfrac{1-\beta}{\alpha}$

55. In sequential probability ratio test, the lot is rejected if (with usual notations), the following inequality holds:

(a) $\lambda_m \leq \dfrac{1-\beta}{\alpha}$

(b) $\lambda_m \geq \dfrac{1-\beta}{\alpha}$

(c) $\lambda_m \leq \dfrac{\beta}{1-\alpha}$

(d) $\lambda_m \geq \dfrac{\beta}{1-\alpha}$

56. An inspector continues his inspection of items selected one after the other so long as the following inequalities hold:

(a) $\lambda_m > \dfrac{\beta}{1-\alpha}$ and $\lambda_m < \dfrac{1-\beta}{\alpha}$

(b) $\dfrac{\beta}{1-\alpha} < \lambda_m$ and $\dfrac{1-\beta}{\alpha} > \lambda_m$

(c) $\dfrac{\beta}{1-\alpha} < \lambda_m < \dfrac{1-\beta}{\alpha}$

(d) all the above

57. In sequential probability ratio test, the lines dividing the total space into regions are:

(*a*) perpendicular to each other
(*b*) passing through the origin
(*c*) parallel to each other
(*d*) all the above

58. When there is no defective in the lot, the *OC* function for $p = 0$ is:
(*a*) $L(0) = 0$
(*b*) $L(0) = 1$
(*c*) $L(0) = \infty$
(*d*) none of the above

59. When the lot contains all defectives, the *OC* function for $p = 1$ is:
(*a*) $L(p) = 0$
(*b*) $L(p) = 1$
(*c*) $L(p) = \infty$
(*d*) none of the above

60. If P (reject a lot | p_0) = α and P (accept a lot | p_1) = β in case of S.P.R.T. for testing $H_0 : p = p_0$ vs. $H_1 : p = p_1$, the *O.C.* function:
(*a*) $L(p_0) = 1 - \beta$
(*b*) $L(p_0) = \alpha$
(*c*) $L(p_0) = \beta$
(*d*) $L(p_0) = 1 - \alpha$

61. In a sequential sampling plan, the sample size is:
(*a*) a discrete random variable
(*b*) a continuous random variable
(*c*) both (*a*) and (*b*)
(*d*) neither (*a*) nor (*b*)

62. Expected sample size of S.P.R.T. is called:
(*a*) discrete random variable
(*b*) continuous random variable
(*c*) average sample number
(*d*) all the above

63. Which of the following statement is correct?
(*a*) Single sampling plan requires maximum inspection
(*b*) In doubling sampling plan, there is 25-33 per cent saving in sampling inspection as compared to single sample plan.
(*c*) In double sampling plan there is 33-50 per cent saving in sampling inspection as compared to single sampling plan
(*d*) all the above

64. A sequential sampling plan is:
(*a*) an infinite process
(*b*) the process requiring much more sampling units than a fixed size sample
(*c*) a process in which sampling terminates with probability one
(*d*) all the three

65. Which of the following statement is/are correct?
(*a*) Sampling inspection by variables provides better quality protection than by attributes
(*b*) Sampling inspection by variables require less inspection than by attributes
(*c*) Errors of measurements are better surfaced in sampling inspection by variables than by attributes
(*d*) all the above

ANSWERS

Section B

1. inevitable **2.** chance **3.** assignable **4.** control **5.** control charts **6.** delimit; control band **7.** three **8.** $\bar{X}$, R, σ, p and c **9.** 3-sigma **10.** Shewhart **11.** A, A_1 and A_2 **12.** c_2, B_1, B_2, B_3 and B_4 **13.** standard deviation **14.** d_2, D_1, D_2, D_3 and D_4 **15.** between **16.** within **17.** *R*-chart **18.** σ-charts **19.** σ **20.** assignable causes **21.** material; machines **22.** dichotomous **23.** binomial **24.** larger **25.** large **26.** Poisson **27.** money; time **28.** greater efficiency **29.** losses **30.** sampling **31.** manufacturing processes **32.** specification **33.** natural **34.** fatal **35.** high quality **36.** purchaser **37.** future losses **38.** variables **39.** two **40.** major; minor **41.** major **42.** minor **43.** producer's process **44.** Type I **45.** Type II **46.** lesser **47.** more

48. exist 49. producer's process average 50. producer's risk 51. consumer's risk 52. convenient; economical 53. vogue 54. L.T.P.D. 55. R.Q.L. 56. A.O.Q. 57. A.O.Q.L. 58. blind sampling 59. Average sample number 60. proportion of defectives 61. A.S.N. curve 62. best 63. accepting 64. better 65. good and bad lots 66. acceptance; rejection 67. adequate 68. complicated

69. $\binom{Np}{d}\binom{N-Np}{n-d}\bigg/\binom{N}{n}$ 70. Type *A OC* curve

71. Type *B OC* curve 72. Consumer's risk 73. producer's risk 74. hypergeometric 75. binomial 76. above 77. second example 78. each item in sequence 79. minimum 80. A. Wald 81. 1947 82. three 83. S.P.R.T. 84. parallel 85. *OC* curve 86. random variable 87. average sample number 88. 25-33 89. 35-50 90. better 91. variables; attributes 92. process control 93. product control 94. process control 95. product control 96. Dodge and Roming 97. *c*-chart 98. *p*-chart 99. zero 100. 0.14

Section C

1. (*c*)	2. (*b*)	3. (*d*)	4. (*b*)	5. (*d*)
6. (*a*)	7. (*d*)	8. (*a*)	9. (*c*)	10. (*a*)
11. (*c*)	12. (*b*)	13. (*c*)	14. (*d*)	15. (*b*)
16. (*d*)	17. (*d*)	18. (*c*)	19. (*b*)	20. (*a*)
21. (*a*)	22. (*b*)	23. (*c*)	24. (*a*)	25. (*d*)
26. (*d*)	27. (*b*)	28. (*b*)	29. (*a*)	30. (*c*)
31. (*c*)	32. (*a*)	33. (*c*)	34. (*a*)	35. (*b*)
36. (*a*)	37. (*d*)	38. (*c*)	39. (*c*)	40. (*b*)
41. (*d*)	42. (*b*)	43. (*b*)	44. (*a*)	45. (*a*)
46. (*a*)	47. (*d*)	48. (*a*)	49. (*d*)	50. (*b*)
51. (*b*)	52. (*c*)	53. (*b*)	54. (*a*)	55. (*b*)
56. (*d*)	57. (*c*)	58. (*b*)	59. (*a*)	60. (*d*)
61. (*a*)	62. (*c*)	63. (*d*)	64. (*c*)	65. (*d*)

SUGGESTED READING

1. Agarwal, B.L., *Basic Statistics*, New Age International Publishers, New Delhi, 8th edition, 2024.
2. Albert, H.B. and Henry, P.G., *Sampling Inspection by Variable,* McGraw-Hill Book Company, New York, 1950.
3. Burr, I.W., *Engineering Statistics and Quality Control,* McGraw-Hill Book Company, New York, 1963.
4. Cowden, D.J., Statistical Method in Quality Control, Asia Publishing House, Bombay, 1960.
5. Duncan, A.J., *Quality Control and Industrial Statistics,* Richard. D. Irwin, Homewood, 1953.
6. Ekambram, S.K., *The Statistical Basis of Acceptance Sampling,* Asia Publishing House, Bombay, 1963.
7. Gnedenko, B.V. Belyayav, Yu. K. and Solovyev, A.D., Mathematical Methods of Reliability Theory, Academic Press, New York, 1969.
8. Grant, E.L. and Leavenworth, R.S., *Statistical Quality Control,* McGraw-Hill Book Company, International Student Edition, Singapore, 6th print, 1985.
9. Gupta, S.C., and Kapoor, V.K., *Fundamentals of Applied Statistics,* Sultan Chand and Sons, New Delhi, Reprint, 1993.
10. *Mannual on Quality Control of Materials*, American Society for Testing and Materials, Philadelphia.

CHAPTER 20

Vital and Population Statistics

SECTION A

Short Essay Type Questions

Q. 1. *What events are covered under vital statistics?*

Ans. Vital statistics maintains the records of marriage, divorce, adoption, legitimation, recognition, annulment and legal separation, live births, deaths, foetal deaths, still births, sickness, etc. It is a part of demography.

Q. 2. *Which records are maintained under population statistics?*

Ans. Population statistics usually mean the maintenance of records of population of countries, regions or community and distribution of population at a point of time. It also encompasses the population growth, immigration, emigration, fecundity, education, etc.

Q. 3. *Are vital statistics and population statistics totally different?*

Ans. No, vital statistics and population statistics in general sense are interchangeable and cover all the topics under either head. In practice, no clear-cut distinction is made between the two headings.

Q. 4. *Define vital statistics.*

Ans. Vital statistics mean the data pertaining to the vital events of a population under reference, especially with regard to births, deaths, marriages, health, migration, etc. In the present times, vital statistics not only consider the number of people but also the quality of human life. Here the vital statistics defined by certain authors are quoted.

1. ***Arthur Newsholme*:** The branch of biometry which deals with data and the laws of human mortality, morbidity and demography.
2. ***Arthur Newsholme*:** Vital statistics may be interpreted in two ways—in a broader sense it refers to all types of population statistics collected by whatever mode, while in a narrower sense if refers only to the statistics derived from the registration of births, deaths and marriages.
3. ***B. Benjamin*:** Vital statistics are conventionally, numerical records of marriage, births, sickness and deaths by which the health and growth of a community may be studied.

Q. 5. *What are the differences between population census and vital statistics?*

Ans. The differences between census and vital statistics are delineated below:

(*i*) Census consists of the complete enumeration of the population of a country or a region under reference and collecting information about the individuals with regard to age, sex, marital status, religion, occupation and other socio-economic aspects. While vital statistics collects information about special events like births, deaths, marriages, health, annulment, divorce, etc.

(*ii*) Census is like a still picture of the population of a country whereas vital statistics presents a motion picture of the vital events of a population in space and time.

(*iii*) Population census is a sort of human inventory, while vital statistics provide the analysis of a population with regard to deaths, births, fecundity, growth rates, death rates, etc.

(*iv*) Population census is conducted at a definite interval of time, mostly ten years, whereas the collection of vital statistics is a continuous process.

(*v*) Information for population census is to be supplied necessarily by legislation. But in many countries, information about vital events is not compulsorily registered under the act.

Q. 6. *What are various uses of vital statistics for a country?*

Ans. Various uses of vital statistics for a country are as follows:

1. ***Analysis of demographic trends.*** Vital statistics reflect on the changing pattern of the population pertaining to the intercensual years. It reveals regarding death rates, birth rates, fecundity, virility of races, etc. The vital rates enable to measure the growth of population.
2. ***Legal value.*** The records regarding births, marriages, deaths, citizenship, etc., are legal documents. They help to protect their rights in property, insurance, etc.
3. ***Help in planning of health services.*** On the basis of vital statistics, governments decide about family planning, number of maternity homes and hospitals, etc.
4. ***Planning of medical research and eradication of diseases.*** The data regarding the causes of deaths enables the governments and social bodies to plan for medical research for the treatment and eradication of diseases.
5. ***Use in public administration.*** Population estimation and projection, birth and mortality rates are the basic tools in the hands of the administration for maintaining the regular supply of foodgrains, light and water, etc. These data also help to prepare electoral rolls, to create jobs, etc.
6. ***Useful to actuaries.*** Mortality rates help to estimate life expectancy, which is the back bone of various insurance schemes of all life insurance companies.
7. ***Basis for social reforms.*** The data with regard to marriages, separation, divorce, legitimation, annulment, etc., reveal the existing state of society. On the basis of this information social evils can be reformed so that social security, social justice, economic independence can be created for each section of the society.

Q. 7. *Give a brief historical background of collection of vital statistics.*

Ans. Before Christ, ecclesiastical societies in Egypt, Greek and Rome used to collect data regarding births, deaths and marriages. In the year 720, Japan made arrangements for the registration of births, deaths and marriages, etc. The registration of vital information also started in the European countries particularly America, Canada and England.

In India, vital statistics are registered and collected under Births, Deaths and Marriages Registration Act, 1886. But under this Act, the supply of information of the vital events was not a binding. But some States made it compulsory under their own legislation like the governments of Tamil Nadu and West Bengal.

The central government of India started a central registration system under an Act known as Birth-Death Registration Act, 1969. In villages, collection of vital statistics is the responsibility of the Head of villages, Patwaris, Lekhpals and chowkidars.

In cities, registration work is taken care of by the municipalities.

In spite of the act and administrative support, there is a lot of incompleteness in the information which has made the estimates and results dubious.

Q. 8. *What are the weaknesses of registration of vital statistics in India?*

Ans. The registration system of vital events in India suffers with many lacunae which are enunciated below:

(*i*) ***Incompleteness of reporting.*** First, in spite of the Act, the registration of births, deaths and marriages is incomplete due to slackness of registering authorities. *Secondly*, the Act has not been implemented sincerely. *Thirdly* most of the marriages in India are sacramental. Hence, hardly any of them are being entered in the registration offices. *Fourthly*, people are not serious about reporting of the events in registration offices.

(*ii*) ***Lack of uniformity.*** Different systems and rules for registration of vital statistics exist in different States of India. This has created many discrepancies.

(*iii*) ***Voluntary registration.*** As per the Births, Deaths and Marriages Registration Act of India, the registration of births, deaths and marriages is voluntary. Hence, a large number of births, deaths and marriages are not registered creating a big gap in information. Some States have made the registration compulsory but it has not been implemented effectively.

(*iv*) ***Incomplete coverage.*** About $\frac{3}{4}$th part of the population of India is covered under the registration scheme. So the information is obviously incomplete.

(*v*) ***Lack of accuracy.*** The information supplied to the registration authorities with regard to births, deaths and marriages is often inadequate due to carelessness of the reporting personnel and registration authorities. Also there is no system to check the correctness of information.

(*vi*) ***Lack of training.*** The reporting and registration authorities are not fully trained. So they are not sincere to their jobs. This has brought in lot of inaccuracy and incompleteness in vital statistics.

Q. 9. *What steps have been taken to improve the registration system of vital statistics?*

Ans. Since pre-Independence many steps had been taken to improve the quality and completeness of vital statistics. They are summarily presented below:

(*i*) Bhor Committee in 1946 recommended that:

(*a*) a office of the 'Registrar General of Vital and Population statistics' be created at the centre and Registrar's offices at the state level.

(*b*) The registration of vital events be made compulsory.

(*c*) Educated and trained personnel be engaged in the job of registration.

(*d*) The area allotted to them be such that they can visit their areas at least once in a week.

(*ii*) In 1948, the government of India formed a vital statistics committee to consider the recommendations of the Bhor committee. Further, it suggested that the information about the age of the mother on the day of delivery, order of birth, age on the day of death of a person, reason for death, etc., should also be registered.

(*iii*) In 1952, a national register of citizens was opened to have comprehensive list of citizens of India.

(*iv*) To have an estimate of births and death rates in the States, a sample census system was implemented.

(*v*) A number of demographic surveys are being conducted in different parts of the country to reveal many interesting aspects of vital statistics.

(*vi*) In 1969, the government of India passed Registration of Births and Deaths Act. This Act has a number of provisions.

Q. 10. *What are the provisions of Registration of Births and Deaths Act, 1969?*

Ans. The different provisions of Registration of births and Deaths Act are:

(*a*) The central government will appoint a Registrar General at the apex to issue necessary instructions from time to time and to coordinate the work of the registrars of the states.

(*b*) A Chief Registrar will be appointed in each State who shall be responsible for carrying the registration of vital statistics in the state and will submit a report every year.

(*c*) A district registrar will be appointed in each district who will be responsible to chief registrar.

(*d*) The responsibility of handing over the information about births and deaths to the registering offices lies with the head of the family in the house, medical officer in the hospital and maternity home, Jailor in the prison, chief manager in the hotel, police officer of the area, etc.

(*e*) Any person failing in his duty to supply the required information is liable to be fined.

Q. 11. *What are the different methods of collection of vital statistics?*

Ans. There are five methods usually followed for collection of vital statistic namely,

(*i*) Registration method

(*ii*) Census enumeration method

(*iii*) Survey method

(*iv*) Sample registration method

(*v*) Analytical method.

Q. 12. *What procedure is followed to collect vital statistics through registration system?*

Ans. The registration of vital events like births, deaths, marriages, etc., is compulsory in India and several other countries through an Act. In India, the Act is known as 'The Registration of Births, deaths Act, 1969.' Unfortunately, the act is not enforced strictly.

In case of birth, the information with regard to date of birth, place, name of the father, sex of the new born, nationality, religion and occupation of the parents has to be supplied to the registering authority of the area.

In case of death, the information in respect of date of death, name of the deceased, father's/husband's name, actual address, place of death, age, sex, marital status, nationality, religion and cause of death are to be reported to the registration authority of the area.

The responsibility of reporting lies as per provisions of the Act.

Q. 13. *What is the approach behind census enumeration method for registration of vital statistics?*

Ans. A census is a comprehensive profile of the population of a country. Census operation is carried out almost in all countries of the world once in ten years. In a census operation, the heads of the people of a country in all habitational areas are counted along with additional information about their age, sex, marital status, occupation, religion, and other socio-economic factors as deemed necessary from time to time. The census operation is carried out in a limited period of about five days.

The main drawback of the census method is that it provides information for the census year only and not beyond it.

Q. 14. *How does survey method help in completing the vital statistics?*

Ans. There are many regions where the registration offices/officers either do not exist or are not functioning effectively. In such areas, surveys are conducted from time to time to collect data for vital statistics. These surveys add to the completeness of vital statistics.

Q. 15. *What purpose is served by sampling registration system (S.R.S.) in respect of vital statistics?*

Ans. Vital rates are required from time to time to have a clear picture about fertility, growth and death rates. Such an information for a particular period is usually not available during the intercensal year. Hence, for any period, rates are obtained through sampling registration system. These rates help in monitoring the ongoing family planning and welfare programmes and also to plan further to achieve the desired objectives.

Q. 16. *Explain sampling registration system for collecting vital statistics.*

Ans. Sample registration of births and deaths is carried out in almost all parts of the country by selecting a fairly large sample under the aegis of Registrar General and Census Commissioner. Sampling registration system came into operation in July, 1968 in urban areas and in 1967 in rural areas. Under this scheme, a large number of census blocks are randomly selected in rural and urban areas separately as sampling units. The sample covers less than one per cent of the population. Regular information about births, marriages and deaths is collected by the appointed recorders. Also periodic enumeration is done for each family in the selected blocks by a team of investigators. The anomalies found in the daily records and periodic (half-yearly) enumeration are removed by revisiting the families in doubt by a new team of investigators.

Presently, the scheme of permanent house marking has been in operation so as to maintain full coverage at the time of half-yearly checking. Once the survey is complete, all old sampling units are replaced by new ones based on the frame of the latest census.

Following factors are studied under sampling registration system:

At all-India level

(*a*) Infant mortality.

(*b*) Age specific mortality rates in rural areas.

(*c*) Sampling variability of vital rates.

At state level

(*a*) Differences in birth rates in respect of education, religion and parity.

(*b*) Extent of institutional and domiciling event.

(*c*) Sex ratio of vital statistics.

(*d*) Seasonality in birth and death rates.

The main advantage of S.R.S. is that it provides estimates for rural and urban areas separately. A series of estimates every six month enable the planners to revise or continue their programmes accordingly.

Q. 17. *What are the lacunae of sample registration system?*

Ans. The sampling registration system fails to record:

(*i*) volume of migration in the sample areas.

(*ii*) age and sex composition

(*iii*) errors in matching

Q. 18. *What do you understand by analytical methods for estimating vital statistics or rates?*

Ans. Ad-hoc surveys cannot be conducted as soon as we desire to know the vital statistics or rates for any period in between two censal years. All the more such surveys are time consuming and too expensive. Also many errors creep in due to sampling and non-sampling errors. Many a times, the information becomes obsolete by the time sample estimates are available. Hence, analytical methods, which are nothing but the mathematical devices to get the estimates from the available data, are generally useful. These methods are based on certain assumptions and thus provide good estimates provided the assumptions hold true. The most prominent of all assumptions is that population grows at a constant rate.

Q. 19. *Give the formula for estimating the population of region or place in a given intercensal year.*

Ans. Knowing well the following information,

P_0 – population of the region in the previous census

P_1 – population of the region in the succeeding census

N – number of gap years between two census

n – number of gap years between the given year and the previous census

The interpolation formula for the population estimate $\hat{P}_t$ in the year t is,

$$\hat{P}_t = P_0 + \frac{n}{N}(P_1 - P_0)$$

The above formula provides very good estimate provided the population grows at a constant rate throughout the intercensal years.

Q. 20. *What algebraic formula will be applied to estimate the population for an intercensal year 't' having known the number of births, deaths and migrants?*

Ans. If the information about,

P_0 – the population in the previous census say 0 year

B – number of births between 0 and t

D – number of deaths between 0 and t

i – number of immigrants between 0 and t

E – block of emigrants from 0 to t

is available, the estimate P_t of the population for the year 't' is obtained by the formula,

$$\hat{P}_t = P_0 + (B - D) + (I - E)$$

The estimate from the above formula is very good provided the figures for P_0, B, D, I and E are exact.

Q. 21. *How can one estimate population by compound interest formula?*

Ans. Malthus believed that population increases in geometric progression if unchecked. Hence, the population of any year 't' after the previous census year 0 can be estimated if we know the population P_0 and growth rate r. The population estimate $\hat{P}_t$ can be computed by the formula,

$$\hat{P}_t = P_0(1 + r)^n$$

where n is the gap between 0 and t years. If r is not known, but the population P_0 for the previous census and P_n for the succeeding census are known, r can be calculated by the formula.

$$r = \sqrt[n]{\frac{P_n}{P_0}} - 1$$

where n represents the number of gap year between two censuses.

Q. 22. *Give the formula to estimate the population for the mid-period of the two censuses?*

Ans. If P_1 and P_2 are the populations at the two consecutive censuses, the estimated population P_{1-2} for the mid-period is easily calculable by the formula,

$$P_{1-2} = \sqrt{P_1 \times P_2}$$

Q. 23. *What is meant by vital rates in general?*

Ans. All vital events of life in a population under reference are of prime importance and are thus enumerated in the form of frequencies such as, n_1 births have taken place in a year, n_2 persons have died in a year, n_3 persons have married in a year, etc. These frequencies are not well interpretable from statistical point of view. Hence, the data are analysed statistically and expressed in the form of vital rates. In general vital rates can be expressed as.

$$\text{Vital rate of an event} = \frac{\text{No. of persons in a population covered under the event}}{\text{Total number of persons in the population under reference}}$$

vital rates are usually expressed on the basis of per thousand (%). Hence, the above ratio is multiplied by 1000.

Q. 24. *What are the measures of mortality to express death rates?*

Ans. Broadly there are three types of death rates which can be used to know about depletion of population. They are:

(*i*) Crude death rate (C.D.R.)

(*ii*) Specific death rate (S.D.R.)

(*iii*) Standardised death rate (S_T.D.R.)

Q. 25. *How can one calculate the crude death rate (C.D.R.)?*

Ans. The Crude death rates are the simplest type of death rates. This is defined as the ratio of the number of deaths occurred in a specified period to the population under reference in the same period multiplied by 1000. In practice, the period is usually one year. So the formula can be given as,

$$\text{C.D.R.} = \frac{\text{No. of deaths in the year}}{\text{Annual mean population}} \times 1000$$

C.D.R., if not expressed as per thousand person but as simple ratio, it is equivalent to the probability of death of a person during the year under consideration. The death rate so calculated is crude in the sense that it gives equal weightage to all age group persons which is not true.

Q. 26. *In what sense specific death rates are better than the crude death rates?*

Ans. The experience tells that the deaths are not uniformly distributed in all sections of the population. They do differ in different age groups or according to sex, occupation or social status. Hence, it becomes necessary to know the mortality rates for various age groups or in women of child bearing age, etc. As an instance, we know that infant deaths are more than deaths in adolescence.

The child welfare societies will be interested in knowing mortality rates in children of 1 to 10 years age. A women welfare organisation would be interested to know the death rate of women in the reproductive age group of 15 to 45 years and so on. Hence, specific death rates reveal categorically more than that what crude death rates do.

Q. 27. *How can you calculate the specific death rate for a specific section of the population?*

Ans. The death rate for a particular segment of the population is known as specific death rate. It can, in general, be calculated by the formula,

$$\text{S.D.R.} = \frac{\text{No. of deaths in the specified section of a population in a given period}}{\text{Average total population of the specified section in the same period}}$$

$$= \frac{D_s}{P_s} \times 1000$$

Usually the given period is one year.

Q. 28. *Define and discuss age specific death rates.*

Ans. The death rates calculated for the population consisting of the specified age group is called age specific death rate (age—S.D.R.). Let the number of deaths in the age group x to $(x + n)$ in a given period $= {}_nD_x$.

Total number of persons in the same period in the age group x to $(x + n) = {}_nP_x$.

Then the age specific death rate (Age – S.D.R.) per thousand person for the age x to $(x + n)$ is,

$$\text{Age S.D.R.} = \frac{{}_nD_x}{{}_nP_x} \times 1000$$

(*i*) If $x > 0$ and $(x + n) < 1$ year, then, the Age – S.D.R. is known as infant mortality rate. Thus, infant mortality is the number of child deaths under one year of age per 1000 live births.

(*ii*) The age – S.D.R. of the children under one month of age are called neo-natal mortality rate.

(*iii*) The death rate due to child birth among the women of child bearing age, *i.e.*, 15-49 years during a given year in a region is known as *maternal mortality* rate.

(*iv*) If the death rates are calculated for male and female populations separately, they represent the specific death rates.

(*v*) Age specific death rate per thousand males can be calculated by a similar formula as above for male population only in the age group x to $x + n$ as,

$$\text{Age} - \text{S.D.R}_m = \frac{{}_n^mD_x}{{}_n^mP_x} \times 1000$$

Similarly for females,

$$\text{Age} - \text{S.D.R}_f = \frac{{}_n^fD_x}{{}_n^fP_x} \times 1000$$

The main drawback of age specific death rates is that they are not capable to throw light on mortality conditions prevailing in two different regions.

Q. 29. What purpose is served by standardised death rates, and how are they calculated?

Ans. We know that many socio-economic factors do effect the death rates. Hence, to compare the death rates of two regions or communities, heterogeneity factors such as educational level, income, occupation, etc., be removed. In this way, the population is standardised. If the death rates are calculated by pooling death rates of different categories of populations of a region, they are known as *standardised death rates*.

To calculate the standardised death rate, firstly the death rate for each group or category obtained separately for each region is multiplied by the respective population of that group or category of the standard region and summed up. This sum is divided by the total population of the standard groups. The formula for standardised death rate can be given as,

$$S_T\text{.D.R.} = \frac{\Sigma_x p_x^s D_x}{\Sigma_x P_x^s} \times 1000$$

for, $x = 1, 2, \ldots$

where, p_x^s – population of standard group x

D_x – S.D.R. for the group x.

Standardised death rates for each region are calculated on the basis of standard population. In this way, $\Sigma_x p_x^s$ for each region remains the same for S_T.D.R. Standardised death rates are logically suitable for comparing the death rates of two different regions.

Q. 30. *The population and number of deaths according to age and sex during the years 1988 and 1992 were as follows:*

Age group (Years)	*1988*						*1992*					
	Population			*No. of deaths*			*Population*			*No. of deaths*		
	Male	*Female*	*Total*	*Male*	*Female*	*Total*	*Male*	*Female*	*Total*	*Male*	*Female*	*Total*
< 1	12680	10255	22935	1864	1569	3433	14720	11358	26078	2208	1840	4048
1–4	12711	10284	22995	750	977	1727	14633	11351	25984	717	840	1557
5–14	12523	10200	22723	551	510	1061	14878	11479	26357	610	551	1161
15–24	12690	10327	23017	533	568	1101	14638	11318	25956	688	747	1435
25–34	12706	10353	23059	648	528	1176	14830	11338	26168	875	805	1680
35–44	12600	10347	22947	756	507	1263	14838	11404	26242	1009	593	1602
45–59	12696	10322	23018	1003	609	1612	14713	11338	26051	2001	907	2908
≥ 60	12668	10277	22945	6562	5015	11577	14749	11364	26113	6637	5091	11728
Total	101274	82365	183639	12667	10283	22950	117999	90950	208949	14745	11374	26119

(*i*) *Calculate the crude death rate for the year 1988 and 1992 separately.*

(*ii*) *Calculate specific death rates for males and females for the two years 1988 and 1992 separately.*

(*iii*) *Calculate age specific death rates for the years 1988 and 1992 separately.*

(*iv*) *Calculate standardised death rate taking the population of 1988 as standardised population and compare the death rates of the two years.*

Ans. From the given data, the crude death rate for 1988 is,

$$\text{C.D.R.} = \frac{22950}{183639} \times 1000$$

$$= 125‰$$

The crude death rate for the year 1992 is,

$$\text{C.D.R.} = \frac{26119}{208949} \times 1000$$

$$= 125‰$$

(*ii*) Specific death rates for males and females in the year 1988 are,

$$S.D.R_M = \frac{12667}{101274} \times 1000$$

$= 125$ males ‰

$$S.D.R_F = \frac{10283}{82365} \times 1000$$

$= 124.85$ female ‰

Specific death rates for males and females in the year 1992 are,

$$S.D.R_M = \frac{14745}{117999} \times 1000$$

$= 124.96$ males ‰

$$S.D.R_F = \frac{11374}{90950} \times 1000$$

$= 125.06$ females ‰

(*iii*) Age specific death rates for the year 1988 and 1992 are calculated and displayed in the table given below:

Age group (Years)	1988	1992
	Age Specific death rate (D_x^a) (per thousand)	Age Specific death (D_x^b) rate (per thousand)
< 1	$\frac{3433}{22935} \times 1000 = 149.68$	$\frac{4048}{26078} \times 1000 = 155.22$
1 – 4	$\frac{1727}{22995} \times 1000 = 75.10$	$\frac{1557}{25984} \times 1000 = 59.92$
5 – 14	$\frac{1061}{22723} \times 1000 = 46.69$	$\frac{1161}{26357} \times 1000 = 44.05$
15 – 24	$\frac{1101}{23017} \times 1000 = 47.83$	$\frac{1435}{25956} \times 1000 = 55.28$
25 – 34	$\frac{1176}{23059} \times 100 = 51.00$	$\frac{1680}{26168} \times 1000 = 64.20$
35 – 44	$\frac{1263}{22947} \times 1000 = 55.04$	$\frac{1602}{26242} \times 1000 = 61.05$
45 – 59	$\frac{1612}{23018} \times 1000 = 70.03$	$\frac{2908}{26051} \times 1000 = 111.63$
≥ 60	$\frac{11577}{22945} \times 1000 = 504.55$	$\frac{11728}{26113} \times 1000 = 449.12$

(*iv*) The calculation table for obtaining the standardised death rates is prepared first. The standardised death rate for the year 1988 is, (see table on page 528)

$$S_T.D.R. = \frac{22949537.45}{183639}$$

$= 124.97$

The standardised death rate for the year 1992 is, (see table on page 528)

$$S_T.D.R. = \frac{22967018.90}{183639}$$

$= 125.07$‰

Comparison of the standardised death rates for the years 1988 and 1992 reveals that the death rate in 1992 is higher than in 1988.

Q. 31. *Define crude birth rate.*

Ans. Crude birth rate (C.B.R.) is the ratio of the number of live births during the year to the total mean population during the same year. To express it per thousand persons, this ratio is multiplied by 1000. As a formula,

$$C.B.R. = \frac{\text{Total No. of live-births during a year}}{\text{Total mean population during the same year}} \times 1000$$

Crude birth rate is hardly able to reveal any exhumating facts about fertility. Hence, one has to resort to some specific fertility rates.

Q. 32. *Name different types of fertility rates.*

Ans. Normally, six types of fertility rates have been defined.

(*i*) General fertility rate (G.F.R.).

(*ii*) Age specific fertility rate (A.S.F.R.).

(*iii*) General marital fertility rate (G.M.F.R.).

(*iv*) Age specific marital fertility rate (A.S.M.F.R.).

(*v*) Total marital fertility rate (T.M.F.R.).

(*vi*) Total fertility rate (T.F.R.).

Q. 33. *What is general fertility rate, and how can it be determined?*

Age group (Year)	*Standard population*	*1988*		*1992*	
	P_x^a	*S.D.R.* D_x^a	$P_x^a \times D_x^a$	*S.D.R.* D_x^b	$P_x^a \times D_x^b$
< 1	22935	149.68	3432910.80	155.22	3559970.70
1-4	22995	75.10	1726924.50	59.92	1377860.40
5-14	22723	46.69	1060936.87	44.05	1000948.15
15-24	23017	47.83	1100903.11	55.28	1272379.76
25-34	23059	51.00	1176009.00	64.20	1480387.80
35-44	22947	55.04	1263002.88	61.05	1400914.35
45-59	23018	70.03	1611950.54	111.63	2569499.34
≥ 60	22945	504.55	11576899.75	449.12	10305058.40
Total	183639		22949537.45		22967018.90

Ans. General fertility rate gives the rate of births per thousand women of child bearing age of a country or region in a given year without giving any cognizance to any other factor. In India, the child bearing age is 15-49 years. G.F.R. is obtained as the annual number of births divided by the mid-year population of women of child bearing age. In the formulaic form,

$$\text{G.F.R.} = \frac{\text{Annual number of births}}{\text{Mid-year population of women of age 15-49 of the region in the given year}} \times 1000$$

General fertility rates do not provide adequate basis for effective planning with regard to reducing the population growth and family welfare schemes.

Q. 34. *In what sense are age-specific fertility rates better than general fertility rate, and how to calculate them?*

Ans. Population explosion is the most horrifying problem today before the world. Hence, to bring down the population growth, one has to study it very minutely. We know that the fertility of women is not the same for all age groups. Hence, it seems germane to find out the marital status and age-specific fertility rates.

Age-specific fertility rate may be defined as, the number of births during a given period (usually a calender year) to women of a specified age or age group divided by the average number of women of that age or age group living during that period (usually by the mid-year). In the formulaic form,

$$\text{A.S.F.R.} = \frac{\text{No. of live births to the women of age group } x \text{ to } (x+n) \text{ during a year}}{\text{Average No. of women in the same age group during that year}}$$

Q. 35. *What information do we gather from general marital fertility rates?*

Ans. The births are confined to married women only barring exceptions of births to unmarried or widow women. Hence, for family planning, emphasis has to be laid to married women only. For this it looks very logical to study the fertility rates among married women only.

General marital fertility rate can be defined as the number of offsprings born alive during a period (usually a year) per thousand married women of child bearing age. It can be formulated as,

$$\text{G.M.F.R.} = \frac{\text{No. of births during a year to married women}}{\text{Mid-year population of married women during that year of age 15-49 years}} \times 1000$$

G.M.F.R. do not provide classified fertility rates of married women, particularly, in respect of age. Hence, the information through G.M.F.R. is not complete.

Q. 36. *How are age specific marital fertility rates more helpful in family planning programmes, and how are they calculated?*

Ans. It is a known fact that fecundity varies with age. For example, in Indian women fecundity is maximum in the age group 25-29 and is little less in the age group 20-24 also after 29 year of age it goes down. Hence, for the success of family planning schemes, it becomes necessary to study age-specific marital fertility rates.

A.S.M.F.R. is defined as, the number of children born alive during a given period (usually a calender year) per thousand married women of a particular age or age group. As a formula,

$$\text{A.S.M.F.R.} = \frac{\text{No. of live births to married women during a year in the age group } x \text{ to } (x+n)}{\text{Mid-year population of married women during that year in the same group}} \times 1000$$

Q. 37. *What is total marital fertility rate, and how can it be calculated?*

Ans. Total marital fertility rate gives the total number of live births that would have taken place per thousand married women, had the current schedule of age-specific marital fertility rates been applicable for the entire child bearing period. For the age group x to $(x + n)$ years, the total marital fertility rate,

$$\text{T.M.F.R.} = \text{A.S.M.R.R.} \times n$$

where, n is the interval in years.

Q. 38. *Define and formulate total fertility rate.*

Ans. Total fertility rate is a measure which gives approximately the magnitude of 'complete family size' that is the total number of children, a women would bear on an average in the lifetime assuming no mortality and no adoption of family planning measures. In short, the sum of age-specific fertility rates over all ages of the child bearing period. Formula for total fertility rate in the age group x to $(x + n)$ is,

$$\text{T.F.R.} = \text{Sum of A.S.F.R.} \times n$$

To obtain the total fertility rate per woman, the above value of T.F.R. has to be divided by 1000.

Q. 39. *What do you understand by measurement of population growth?*

Ans. Population growth mainly depends on the sex of the newly born children, *i.e.,* the population growth rate increases if the majority of births consists of girls. Thus, fertility rates fail to reflect on the rate of population growth because they do not take into consideration the sex of the newly born children. Therefore, to measure the rates of population growth, it becomes necessary to take into account the female births and their mortality before they reach the child bearing age. The rate of population growth are measured in terms of reproduction rates.

Q. 40. *Name different measures of population growth.*

Ans. Various measures of population growth are as follows:

(*i*) Crude rate of national increase

(*ii*) Vital index

(*iii*) Gross reproduction rate (G.R.R.)

(*iv*) Net reproduction rate (N.R.R.)

(*v*) Replacement index.

Q. 41. *Explicate the method of obtaining the crude rate of natural increase.*

Ans. Crude rate of natural increase is equal to the difference between crude birth rate (C.B.R.) and crude death rate (C.D.R.). This difference is also known as *survival rate.* Symbolically,

$$\text{Crude rate of natural increase} = \text{C.B.R.} - \text{C.D.R.}$$

In case, the total number of births (ΣB), the total number of deaths (ΣD) and the mid-year population (ΣP) for a given year are known, then

$$\text{Crude rate or natural increase} = \frac{\Sigma B - \Sigma D}{\Sigma P}$$

Q. 42. *What is meant by vital index of population, and how can it be measured?*

Ans. Vital index of population was propounded by Dr. Rayond Pearl. Vital index is measured as the ratio of births to deaths in a given year expressed in terms of percentages. In the formulaic form,

$$\text{Vital Index} = \frac{\text{Births in a year}}{\text{Deaths in the same year}} \times 100$$

Vital index is not a good measure of population growth as it does not take into consideration the number of female births and deaths in the year under reference.

Q. 43. *Discuss gross reproduction rate.*

Ans. Population growth is dependent on the number of female births who are actually the future mothers. Hence, population growth is certainly a function of the fertility rates restricted to the female births. According to the 'demographic book', published the United Nations in 1954, *"The gross reproduction rate indicates the average number of daughters who would be borned to a group of girls beginning life together in a population where none died before the upper limit of child bearing age and where the given set of fertility rates was in operation."*

The gross reproduction rate is based on the assumptions:

(*i*) No female children die till they attain the upper limit of child bearing age which is 49 years in India.

(*ii*) Female population remains stagnant in spite of migration.

(*iii*) The current fertility rates continue to hold during the entire period of child bearing age.

The above assumptions are not relevant in real life. Hence, gross reproduction rate does not depict a true picture.

Q. 44. *Give the formula for gross reproduction rate.*

Ans. Gross reproduction rate can be calculated in either of the following ways.

(*a*) If S_{ix} is the fertility rate at age x restricted to female births $\sum_{x=0}^{n} S_{ix}$ is equal to G.R.R. where n is the upper child bearing age.

(*b*) Another formula for gross reproduction rate is,

$$\text{G.R.R.} = \frac{\text{No. of female live births}}{\text{Total number of live births}} \times \text{Total fertility rate}$$

(*c*) Also, the gross reproduction rate can be calculated by making use of the current age specific fertility rate, under the assumption of no mortality, by the formula.

$$\text{G.R.R.} = \frac{\text{No. of daughters expected to be borned to 1000 newly borned girls}}{1000}$$

Gross reproduction rates are not accurate because mortality of females and migration in all age groups are inevitable.

Q. 45. *What improvement is brought out by net reproduction rate over gross reproduction rate?*

Ans. Gross reproduction rate gives the idea about the replacement of one generation to the next. But it overestimates the next generation because it omits the mortality of newly born female infants till they attain their maximum child bearing age. This makes G.R.R. quite artificial. The other factors like migration, divorce, unmarried women do affect the reproduction rate but are negligible as compared to the extent of mortality. The United Nations Demographic Year Book 1954 defined net reproduction rate as, *"The net reproduction rate may be interpreted as the number of daughters that would be produced by women throughout their lifetime if they were exposed at each age to the fertility and mortality rates on which the calculation is based."*

From the above discussion it is apparent that NRR gives the number of females produced per woman who continue to survive till their maximum reproduction age.

Q. 46. *In what ways, can the net reproduction rate be calculated?*

Ans. Various approaches to calculate net reproduction rate are as follows:

(*a*) The calculation of net reproduction rate by making use of life-tables. If B_g is the number of girls horned to P_2 women of the age group x to $(x + n)$ and S is the survival rate (p_x) per woman which is obtained by the life table for each age group, then

$$\text{N.R.R.} = \sum_{\text{all age group}} \left(\frac{B_g}{P_g} \times S \right) \times \text{class interval of the age group}$$

(*b*) Net reproduction rate can directly be calculated by the formula,

$$\text{N.R.R.} = \frac{\text{No. of female babies expected to be borned to 1000 newly born females on the basis of current fertility and mortality rates}}{1000}$$

(*c*) George Barclay gave the formula for net reproduction rate in terms of life table notations as,

$$\text{N.R.R.} = \underset{x=15}{\overset{49}{S}} b_x \frac{L_x}{L_0}$$

where,

S – Stands for summation just as Σ.

b_x – rate of female births per person at age x.

L_x – No. of persons-years lived at age x per woman borned to the original cohort

L_0 – Original cohort

x – varies from 15 to 49 years of age, *i.e.*, the child bearing age.

(*d*) In common parlance,

$$\text{N.R.R.} = \frac{\Sigma(\text{No. of female births} \times \text{\% survival rate})}{100}$$

Q. 47. *Comment on the values of net reproduction rate.*

Ans. The experience gives some ideas about the values of N.R.R. and their importance as follows:

(*i*) Normally N.R.R. varies from 0 to 5.

(*ii*) N.R.R. can not exceed G.R.R. as N.R.R. takes into account the mortality

(*iii*) N.R.R. will he equal to G.R.R. if all the newly borned female children survive till their maximum child bearing age.

(*iv*) If N.R.R. = 1, the female population will exactly replace itself into new generation and population remains constant.

(*v*) If N.R.R. < 1, this will result into the reduction in the number of mothers and will thus cause reduction in population.

(*vi*) If N.R.R. > 1, there will be a greater number of mothers in the next generation which will tend to increase the population.

Q. 48. *What are the drawbacks of net reproduction rate?*

Ans. Beside many good qualities of N.R.R. over G.R.R., it is not devoid of drawbacks such as:

(*i*) N.R.R. are based on the constant rates of fertility and mortality over generation which is not true to the real life phenomenon.

(*ii*) N.R.R. do not take into account the number of emigrants or immigrants. Many times, the number is so large that it affects the reproduction rate.

(*iii*) A.S.F.R.'s are also not so constant as they are taken to be for the purpose of N.R.R.

Q. 49. *The population and its distribution by sex and number of births in a tehsil in 1991 and survival rates are given in the table below:*

From the given data, calculate

(*i*) *General fertility rate*

(*ii*) *Age specific fertility rate*

(*iii*) *Total fertility rate*

(*iv*) *Gross reproduction rate*

(*v*) *Net reproduction rate*

assuming no mortality.

Group	Population	Males	Females	Male births	Female births	Total births	Survival rate
15–19	11832	6145	5687	65	60	125	0.91
20–24	10538	5214	5324	144	132	276	0.90
25–29	9375	4655	4720	135	127	262	0.84
30–34	7843	3910	3933	82	81	163	0.87
35–39	7270	3600	3670	62	56	118	0.85
40–44	6315	3290	3025	12	15	27	0.83
45–49	5394	2793	2601	3	3	6	0.82
Total	58567	29607	28960	503	474	977	

Ans.

(*i*) $\text{G.F.R.} = \dfrac{\text{Annual No. of live births}}{\text{Av. female population of 15-49 years age}} \times 1000$

$= \dfrac{977}{28960} \times 1000$

= 33.73‰

(*ii*) Age specific fertility rates are calculated as follows:

Age group	No. of women	Total births	ASFR per thousands
15–19	5687	125	$\dfrac{125}{5687} \times 1000 = 21.98$
20–24	5324	276	$\dfrac{276}{5324} \times 1000 = 51.84$
25–29	4720	262	$\dfrac{262}{4720} \times 1000 = 55.51$
30–34	3933	163	$\dfrac{163}{3933} \times 1000 = 41.44$
35–39	3670	118	$\dfrac{118}{3670} \times 1000 = 32.15$
40–44	3025	27	$\dfrac{27}{3025} \times 1000 = 8.92$
45–59	2601	6	$\dfrac{6}{2601} \times 1000 = 2.31$

(*iii*) total fertility rate = Sum of ASFR × n

= 214.15 × 5

= 1070.75

n = 5, since we have to take continuous age groups.

(*iv*) $\text{G.R.R.} = \dfrac{\text{No. of female live births}}{\text{Total no. of live births}} \times \text{Total fertility rate}$

$= \dfrac{474}{977} \times 1070.75$

= 519.48

(*v*) $\text{N.R.R.} = \sum_{\text{all age groups}} \left(\dfrac{B_g}{P_g} \times S \right) \times$ class interval of age groups

$$= \left(\frac{60}{5687} \times 0.91 + \frac{132}{5324} \times 0.90 + \frac{127}{4720} \times 0.84 + \frac{81}{3933} \times 0.87 + \frac{56}{3670} \times 0.85 + \frac{15}{3025} \times 0.83 + \frac{3}{2601} \times 0.82 \right) \times 5$$

= (0.0096 + 0.0223 + 0.0226 + 0.0179 + 0.0130 + 0.0041 + 0.0009) × 5

= 0.0904 × 5

= 0.452 per woman.

or, N.R.R. = 452‰ women.

Q. 50. *What is replacement index, and what purpose does it serve?*

Ans. Replacement index is defined as, the proportion of observed child-woman ratio of actual population to the child-woman ratio from life-table stationary population.

Sometimes the trend of population growth is indicated by replacement index R. Replacement index is seldom used in practice.

Q. 51. *Formulate replacement index.*

Ans. In this index, child-woman ratio is the ratio of the number of children of age less than 5 years (0-4 years), *i.e.*, $\sum_{x=0}^{4} P_x$ to the number of women of child bearing age (15-49 years), *i.e.*, $\sum_{15}^{49} P_f$.

Thus the replacement index,

$$R = \frac{\sum_{x=0}^{4} P_x}{\sum_{15}^{49} P_f}$$

$$= R_a/R_s$$

where,

R_a – child-woman ratio in actual population

R_s – child-woman ratio in stationary population.

Q. 52. *Express net migration rate and its importance.*

Ans. Net migration rate (N.M.R.) is the ratio of the annual net migration to the annual mean population. When this ratio is multiplied by 1000, it gives the net migration rate per thousand. Thus,

$$\text{N.M.R.} = \frac{\text{Annual net migration}}{\text{Annual mean population}} \times 1000$$

$$= \frac{\text{overseas immigration} - \text{overseas emigration}}{\text{Annual mean population}} \times 1000$$

Net migration rate conveys about the population augmentation and depletion through net migration during a given year.

Q. 53. *Give the concept of a life-table.*

Ans. A life-table comprises of a set of values showing how a group of infants born on the same day and giving under similar conditions would gradually die out. In other words, a life-table summarises the mortality or longevity of any cohort.

George Barclay expressed life-table as, "*The table is a life history of a hypothetical group or cohort or people, as it is diminished gradually by deaths. The record begins at birth of each member and continues till all have died.*"

O. 54. *What is revealed by a life-table?*

Ans. A life-table reveals the following aspects:

(*i*) Beside death rate, life-table is another device of describing mortality in a population under consideration. That is why some people call life-table as *mortality table*.

(*ii*) As a matter of fact, a life-table exhibits the numbers living and dying at each age on the basis of experience of a cohort.

(*iii*) It also gives the probability of dying and living separately at each age. The probability to dying manifests the mortality rate. Obviously, the probability of living evinces survival rate.

(*iv*) The life-table provides the expectation of life at any age x. In other words, a life-table essentially presents the mortality at all ages in a tabular form.

Q. 55. *On what assumptions or factors is the construction of life-table based?*

Ans. The factors or assumptions in the construction of life-table are as given below:

(*i*) Mortality rates are not same in all age groups. Hence, life-tables utilise only the age specific mortality rates.

(*ii*) The deaths are uniformly distributed between two consecutive birth days.

(*iii*) The mortality rates differ widely for male and female populations. Hence, life-tables for males and females are constructed separately. Not only this, the experience shows that the pattern of mortality for different races, occupational groups, regions, etc., are different. Hence, life-tables are prepared separately for different cohorts.

(*iv*) The cohort is closed to migration. In other words, the change in population occurs only due to deaths.

(*v*) The cohort originates with a standard number of births say 1,00,000, 10,000, 1,000, etc. This number is known as the *radix* of the table.

Q. 56. *What is the historical background of life-tables?*

Ans. Ulpians life-tables consisting of a series of values diminishing with increasing age appeared first. But the manner in which they were constructed and their purpose was not clear.

Life-table in the real sense came into existence and popularity at the end of eighteenth century for the purpose of life assurance. This enabled the acturies to calculate the insurance risks and premium rate. In recent years, life-table approaches are being increasingly utilised even to follow up studies of chronic diseases of hospital patients, chalking out welfare programmes for different cohorts, etc.

Q. 57. *What are various uses of life-table?*

Ans. A life-table mainly displays the death rate between two consecutive birth days and expectation of life at any age of a cohort. The information revealed by a life-table has applications in many fields and hence its uses can be summarised as given below:

(*i*) Life-tables are of great use to actuaries to estimate the insurance risks and premiums.

(*ii*) Life-tables help to construe the population projections by age and sex.

(*iii*) Life-table is used to calculate accurate fertility rates.

(*iv*) Life-table clearly depicts the distribution of people according to sex which helps a great deal in planning of education, employment and workforce.

(*v*) Life-table helps to check the accuracy of census figures, registration of deaths, births, etc.

(*vi*) The computation of net reproduction rate and true rate of natural increase is easily made by the use of life-tables.

(*vii*) It helps to assess the impact of family planning programmes on population growth.

(*viii*) How far, the better medical aid, high standard of living and new scientific inventions have increased the span of life, can be evaluated through life-tables.

Q. 58. *How can a life-table be constructed?*

Ans. A life-table starts with a convenient cohort size like 1,00,000 or 10,000 known as radix. The record of a life-table begins at the birth of each member and continues till all have died. It is worth pointing out that a life-table diminishes gradually.

A life-table consists of eight columns which are as given below:

Columns:

(1) x = The age in years

(2) l_x = No. of persons living at the age x.

(3) d_x = No. of persons dying between the ages x and $(x + 1)$.

$$= l_x - l_{x+1}$$

(4) q_x = Prob. of dying of a person between the ages x and $(x + 1)$.

(5) P_x = Prob. of living of a person between the ages x and $(x + 1)$.

(6) L_x = No. of person living between x and $(x + 1)$.

$$L_x = \frac{l_x + l_{x+1}}{2}$$

$$= l_x - \frac{1}{2}dx$$

(7) T_x = No. of persons living above the age x

$$l_x + l_{x+1} + \ldots = L_x + T_{x+1}$$

(8) e_x^0 = Expectation of life at age x.

$$= T_x / l_x$$

Q. 59. *Given the age returns for the two ages x = 9 years and x + 1 = 10 years with a few life-table values as, l_9 = 75,824, l_{10} = 75,362, d_{10} = 418 and T_{10} = 49,53,195. Give the complete life-table for two ages of persons.*

Columns							
1	*2*	*3*	*4*	*5*	*6*	*7*	*8*
x	l_x	d_x	q_x	p_x	L_x	T_x	e_x
9	75824	462	0.00609	0.99391	75593	5028788	66.32
10	75362	418	0.00555	0.99445	75153	4953195	65.72

Ans. Using the relations between different columns of the life-table we get the following completed life-table:

Calculations:

$$d_9 = 75824 - 75362 = 462$$

$$q_9 = \frac{462}{75824} = 0.00609,\ q_{10} = \frac{418}{75362} = 0.00555$$

$$p_9 = 1 - 0.00609 = 0.99391,\ p_{10} = 1 - 0.00555 = 0.99445$$

$$L_9 = 75362 - \frac{1}{2} \times 462 = 75593$$

$$L_{10} = 75362 - \frac{1}{2} \times 418 = 75153$$

$$T_9 = 4953195 + 75593 = 5028788$$

$$e_9^0 = \frac{5028788}{75824} = 66.32$$

$$e_{10}^0 = \frac{4959195}{75362} = 65.72$$

Q. 60. *Can the unemployment rates be calculated just like death rates?*

Ans. The unemployment rates like crude unemployment rate, age-specific unemployment rates and standardised unemployment rates can be obtained in a similar manner as we calculate various death rates.

Q. 61. *The following statistics are available about a standard population and a local population:*

Calculate:

(*i*) the crude rate of unemployment in the total area.

(*ii*) the standardised rate of unemployment in the local area.

	Age group (years)			
Standard Population (A)	20–30	30–40	40–50	50 & above
Population	300	350	400	450
Unemployment %	150	120	80	60
Local population (B)				
Population	250	300	350	400
Unemployment %	200	120	60	40

Ans. The unemployment rates can be calculated by preparing the following table given on next page:

Total population = 1500 + 1300 = 2800

Total no. of unemployed = 146 + 123 = 269

For total area,

$$\text{C.U}_E\text{.R} = \frac{269}{2800} \times 1000$$

$$= 96.07\%$$

$$S_T \text{ rate of unemployment} = \frac{144000}{1500}$$

$$= 96.00\%$$

Q. 62. *Under what conditions a population is said to be a stationary population?*

Ans. If the size of a population is constant and its composition according to age and sex also remains constant over time, then such a population is known as stationary population.

The constancy in population for size and composition is maintained if,

Age Group	S_T. Population			Local Population			
	Population	No. of Unemployed	Age Sp. UE rate ‰	Population	No. of Unemployed	Age. Sp. UE rate ‰	Age. Sp. UE rate × S_T. Population
20–30	300	45	150	250	50	200	60,000
30–40	350	42	120	300	36	120	42,000
40–50	400	32	80	350	21	60	24,000
50–	450	27	60	400	16	40	18,000
Total	1500	146		1300	123		144,000

(*i*) births and deaths are equal in number and are uniformly distributed over the year.

(*ii*) either there is no migration or the emigration and immigration are equal during the year.

Q. 63. *What is the concept of a stable population?*

Ans. The concept of stable population was given by A.J. Lotka. If a population increases (decreases) at a constant rate, *i.e.*, the rates of births and deaths remain constant, the population is said to be *stable.* Further, a stable population holds the following properties:

(*i*) It has a fixed age and sex distribution over time.

(*ii*) Population is closed for migration either way.

Q. 64. *How does a stable population differ from stationary population?*

Ans. The fine differences between stable and stationary population are:

(*i*) In stable populations, its size changes at constant rate whereas in stationary population, its size remains constant.

(*ii*) If the births and deaths over time are equal, the stable and stationary population are equivalent.

Q. 65. *Does a life-table depicts the life history of an actual cohort?*

Ans. Most life-tables do not represent the life history of any actual cohort. Instead a life-table synthesises the life history of a cohort from the mortality rates by age during some years or short base period and thus represent short segments of the experience of many cohorts. In view of this, a life-table based on the experiment of actual cohort is sometimes specifically called a *generation life-table* or *fluent life-table.*

Q. 66. *What do you understand by abridged life-table?*

Ans. A life-table is the description of life expectancy at all ages at an interval of one year. Whereas an abridged life-table consists of all columns of a life-table for ages distant apart usually 5 to 10 years or for age groups usually of width 5 to 10 years. In this way there is tremendous cut in size of life-tables, and hence, such life-tables are named as *abridged life-table.*

Q. 67. *Name three methods of construction of abridged life-tables.*

Ans. Three principle methods of construction of abridged life-tables are:

(*i*) Reed Merrel method

(*ii*) Greville's method

(*iii*) King's method.

Q. 68. *How can one represent and determine various columns of an abridged life-table?*

Ans. An abridged life-table for an age interval of *n* years consists of the following columns:

(*i*) The age advances from x to $(x + n)$

(*ii*) l_x – the number of persons living at the initial age of the interval x to $(x + n)$ out of a cohort l_0.

(*iii*) q_x – the probability of dying of a person in age group x to $(x + n)$.

$$_nq_x = \frac{l_x - l_{x+n}}{l_x}$$

$$= 1 - \frac{l_{x+n}}{l_x}$$

(*iv*) $_nd_x$ – the number of deaths in the interval x to $(x + n)$, *i.e.*,

$$_nd_x = l_x \times {_nq_x}$$

(*v*) $_np_x$ – the probability of living of a person between the age x and $(x + n)$ and can be given as,

$$_np_x = \frac{l_{x+n}}{l_x}$$

$$= 1 - {_nq_x}$$

(*vi*) $_nL_x$ – the number of persons of the life-table stationary population in the interval x to $(x + n)$ years and can be obtained as,

$$_nL_x = \int_0^n l_{x+t}dt$$

(*vii*) T_x – the number of persons living after the age x.

(*viii*) e_x^0 – the expectation of life at the age x and is given as,

$$e_x^0 = \frac{T_x}{l_x}$$

Q. 69. *In what way, does the construction of an abridged life-table differ from a complete life-table?*

Ans. The main difference lies in finding the value of $_nq_x$ because $_nq_x$ is often not a smooth function of x and shows irregular variation because of the larger interval instead of one year. Hence, a standardised value of $_nq_x$ is determined for usage. The value of $_nq_x$ is standardised either by Compertz law or Makeham's law or by some other rule. Also a suitable interval n should be chosen and proper grouping of age be done.

In an abridged life-table, the class interval n is more than one year and is usually 5 to 10 years.

Q. 70. *Discuss the term, 'central mortality rate', and give the formula for its calculations.*

Ans. The central mortality rate is the probability of dying of a person, whose exact age is not known but lies between the age x and $(x + 1)$, within one year following the attainment of that age. Let us denote,

m_x – the central mortality rate.

d_x – the number of deaths between x and $(x + 1)$ years.

L_x – the average size of the cohort in the interval x to $(x + 1)$.

l_x – the cohort size at the age x.

The central mortality rate,

$$m_x = \frac{\text{No. of deaths in the interval } x \text{ to } (x+1)}{\text{Average size of the cohort in the interval}}$$

$$= \frac{dx}{L_x}$$

$$= \frac{d_x}{l_x - \frac{1}{2}d_x}$$

$$= \frac{2d_x/l_x}{2 - d_x/l_x}$$

$$= \frac{2q_x}{2 - q_x}$$

or,

$$q_x = \frac{2m_x}{2 + m_x}$$

Q. 71. *Discuss force of mortality.*

Ans. In the construction of life-tables, we have confined to initial population l_x at an age x where x is an integral number. But death does not occur only at the end of a year alone but at any time during the year. Thus, l_x is a continuous function of x. Hence, the rate of decrease in l_x can be given by the differential, $\frac{d}{dx}l_x$.

In view of the above fact, the force of mortality may be defined as, *the ratio of the rate of decrease in l_x to the initial population l_x.*

Symbolically,

$$\mu_x = -\frac{d}{dx} lx / l_x$$

$$= -\frac{1}{l_x}\frac{d}{dx} l_x$$

$$= -\frac{d}{dx}(\log l_x)$$

Q. 72. *Give the relation between central mortality rate and force of mortality.*

Ans. Central mortality rate gives the probability of a person dying between the age x and $(x + 1)$. Hence, locating at the mid of the year, the relation between central mortality rate m_x and force of mortality is,

$$m_x = \mu_x + \frac{1}{2}$$

Q. 73. *What is the approach of Reed-Merrel towards constructing the abridged life-table?*

Ans. The Reed-Merrel method of constructing abridged life-table is based on central mortality rate. If ${}_nP_x^z$ and ${}_nd_x^z$ are the average population size and the number of deaths in the age interval x to $(x + n)$ in the calender year z, then

$${}_nm_x^z = \frac{{}_nd_x^z}{{}_nP_x^z}$$

and,

$${}_nq_x^z = \frac{2n({}_nm_x^z)}{2 + n({}_nm_x^z)}$$

Also, ${}_np_x = 1 - {}_nq_x$, $l_{x+n} = l_x \times {}_np_x$

Once we known ${}_nq_x$, it is trivial to construct the abridged life-table.

Q. 74. *In what manner the abridged life-table is constructed by Greville's method?*

Ans. Greville's made use of the age specific central mortality rate ${}_nm_x$ for estimating the death ${}_nq_x$ in the age interval x to $(x + n)$ years. The formula for the estimation of ${}_nq_x$ propounded by Greville is,

$${}_nq_x = \frac{2n({}_nm_x)}{1 + {}_nm_x\left[n + \frac{n^2}{6}({}_nm_x - \log_e C)\right]}$$

The above formula involves C which is estimated by making assumption that ${}_nm_x$ follows the Compertz (exponential) law,

$${}_nm_x = BC^x$$

Also following usual notations, the other constituents of the abridged life-table are estimated as follows:

An approximation to ${}_nL_x$ based on numerical quadrature is,

$${}_nL_x = \frac{n}{2}(l_x + l_{x+n}) + \frac{n}{24}(nd_{x+n} - nd_{x-n})$$

If l_x vanishes at the age $w + n$, then

$${}_nL_x = \frac{l_w}{{}_nm_w}$$

and thus,

$$T_x = {}_nL_x + {}_nL_{x+n} + \ldots + {}_nL_w$$

$$= {}_nL_x + T_{x+n}$$

Obviously, the last column of the life-table is,

$$e_x^0 = \frac{T_x}{l_x}$$

Q. 75. *In what manner are the central mortality rate and subsequently the death rate under Kings method for preparing an abridged life-table used?*

Ans. Central morality rate can be calculated precisely provided the population P_x^0 and the number of deaths D_x^0 for the central age in the age interval $\{x, x + n\}$ can be estimated precisely from the known values of population and deaths ${}_nP_x$ and ${}_nD_w$ respectively in the age group x to $(x + n)$. Under the assumption that P_x^0 and D_x^0 be approximated by a second degree parabola. G. King estimated them by the formula,

$$P_x^0 = \frac{1}{n}({}_nP_x) - \frac{1}{24n}\left(1 - \frac{1}{n^2}\right)\Delta^2({}_nP_x)$$

$$D_x^0 = \frac{1}{n}({}_nD_x) - \frac{1}{24n}\left(1 - \frac{1}{n^2}\right)\Delta^2({}_nD_x)$$

Once we know P_x^0 and D_x^0, the central mortality rate,

$$m_x = \frac{D_x^0}{P_x^0} \text{ for } x = x_0, x_0 + n, x_0 + 2n, \ldots$$

and,

$$q_x = \frac{2m_x}{2 + m_x}$$

Also

$$P_x = 1 - q_x$$

where x_0 is the initial age from where to start.

Other constituents of the abridged life-table are given as,

$$l_{x+n} = l_x({}_nP_x)$$

$$l_{x+2n} = l_{x+n}({}_nP_{x+n})$$

where as ${}_nP_x$ is computed by the relation,

$$\log({}_nP_x) = \sum_{i=1}^{n-1} \log P_{x+i}$$

The value of ${}_nP_x$ can be improved by using interpolation technique. King denoted the number of years lived by the radix l_x during the interval $(x + n)$ by T^*_{xn}. Under the assumption that deaths are distributed uniformly over the year x to $x + n$, $T^*_{x.n}$ is given as,

$$T^*_{x.n} = L_x + L_{x+1} + \ldots + L_{x+n-1}$$

$$= \sum_{i=1}^{n-1} l_{x+i} - \frac{1}{2}(l_x - l_{x+n})$$

Finally e_x^0, the expectation of life at the age x by the persons living in the interval $(x, x + n)$ is obtained by the formula,

$$e_x^0 = \frac{T^*_{x.n}}{l_x}$$

The construction of abridged life-tables by King's method involves many approximations and lengthy calculations.

SECTION B

Fill in the Blanks

Fill in the suitable word(s) or phrase(s) in the blanks:

1. Vital statistics is a part of _________ .
2. The terms, vital statistics and population statistics in a wider sense are _________ .
3. The branch of biometry which deals with the data and laws of human mortality, morbidity and demography is known as _________ .
4. The definition that statistics derived from the registration of births, deaths and marriages is called vital statistics is due to _________ .
5. The credit of defining vital statistics as the numerical records of marriages, births, sickness and deaths by which the health and growth of a community may be studied goes to _________ .
6. Population census is a sort of _________ .
7. Vital statistics provide the _________ of a population.
8. Population census is usually conducted at an interval of _________ .
9. Collection of vital statistics is a _________ .

10. In life insurance, vital statistics is utilised by the ________ .
11. Vital statistics can be a guide to bring about the ________ .
12. Family planning very much depend upon ________ .
13. Often the medical research programmes are based on ________ .
14. Vital statistics in post-Independent India are collected through an act passed in ________ .
15. For the first time in India, the Act for collecting vital statistics was enforced in ________ .
16. Most of the marriages in India are ________.
17. Registration system for vital events is operative in about ________ part of India.
18. Pre-Independence committee to improve upon the registration system of vital events was ________ committee.
19. The national register of citizens in India was opened in the year ________ .
20. To estimate the birth and death rates at the States level, ________ system was implemented.
21. For the proper collection of vital statistics, the government of India created the post of ________.
22. A census is a ________ of the population of a country.
23. Census provides information for the ________ only.
24. Survey method helps in completing the ________ statistics.
25. Sampling registration system helps to monitor the ________ at any time.
26. Sampling registration system came into operation in rural areas in the year ________ .
27. Sampling registration system started in urban areas in ________ .
28. For collecting information about vital events under sampling registration system, the sampling units are ________ .
29. Collection of information on infant mortality is subjected to ________ .
30. The greatest advantage of sampling registration system is that it provides estimates separately for ________ and ________ areas.
31. Sampling registration system fails to record the volume of ________ .
32. Age and sex composition ________ available under sampling registration system.
33. The formula for estimating the population of a country for an intercensal year with usual notations is ________ .
34. The most common assumption for estimating the population is that the population grows ________ .
35. The growth rate of population in between two census years is calculable by the formula ________ .
36. If P_1 and P_2 are the populations in two successive censuses, the mid-period population is equal to ________ .
37. Vital rates are customarily expressed on ________ basis.
38. Crude death rate per person is equivalent to the ________ of ________ of a person during the said period.
39. Crude death rate gives ________ to the death of persons of all ages.
40. Specific death rate is ________ than crude death rate.
41. Specific death rates fail to throw light on ________ of two regions.
42. Standardised death rate is the ________ rate of various categories of a population.
43. Crude birth rate fails to bring out any ________ facts about fertility of a population.
44. Child bearing age of woman in India is ________ years.
45. General fertility rate is based on women of ________ .
46. General fertility rates are not able to pinpoint for ________ .

47. Age specific fertility rates create better ground for _________ .

48. General marital fertility rate is confined to birth rate of children borned to _________ women only.

49. Most fertile period of women can be ascertained by calculating _________ .

50. The total number of children that could have borned to 1000 married women during their entire child bearing period is known as _________ .

51. The sum of age specific fertility rates multiplied by n in the age interval x to $(x + n)$ provides the estimate of _________ .

52. The rate of increase of population mainly depends on the _________ of the new-born.

53. Measures of population growth are the function of _________ and their _________.

54. Population growth is measured in terms of _________.

55. The ratio of births to deaths in a year is called _________.

56. Gross reproduction rate is a _________ number.

57. Gross reproduction rate is based on fictitious assumption that _________ till the age of 49 years.

58. Number of daughters expected to be borned to 1000 newly borned girls is equivalent to _________ per thousand.

59. The number of females produced per woman who survive till their full reproduction age is nothing but _________.

60. When the mortality of newly borned girls is zero, the net reproduction rate is same as _________.

61. Gross reproduction rate cannot be _________ net reproduction rate.

62. If NRR = 1, then the female population will exactly _________ .

63. If NRR < 1, the population will in general tend to _________ .

64. If NRR > 1, the population of a country will very likely _________ .

65. The assumption of constant fertility and mortality in the calculation of NRR is practically _________ .

66. NRR based on current fertility and mortality rates _________ the future growth in reality.

67. Migrants are _________ in the calculation of net reproduction rates.

68. Replacement index is _________ used in practice as a measure of population growth.

69. The ratio of the total number of births to the total deaths in a given region during a given year is called _________ .

70. The range of vital index is _________ to _________ .

71. The value of vital index greater than 1 is indicative of _________ .

72. Vital index less than 1 shows a _________ in population.

73. The measure for population change merely due to migration is _________ .

74. The number living and dying at each age on the basis of the experience of a cohort are exhibited by _________ .

75. The probability of dying manifests the _________ .

76. The probability of living reveals the _________ rate.

77. The expectation of life at any age can be obtained from a _________ .

78. Life-tables are prepared _________ for male and female populations.

79. Age-specific mortality rates are the back bone of _________ .

80. Life-tables are _________ of the consideration of migrations.

81. The standard number of births originating a cohort is called _________ of the life-table.

82. A life-table shows the pattern in which the population _________ gradually.

83. The life-table continues till all people _________.

84. The life-table appearing first are due to _________.

85. The extensive use of life-tables is made by _________.

86. Life-table can also be utilised in medical science for follow up studies of _________.

87. Accuracy of census figures can be checked with the help of _________.

88. The impact of family planning programmes can be assessed through _________.

89. The overall impact of developed medical aid on life expectancy can be evaluated from _________.

90. A life-table contains _________ columns in all.

91. The calculation of unemployment rates can be done parallel to _________.

92. A population of constant size having the same sex composition over time is called a _________ population.

93. If the births and deaths, immigrants and emigrants are equal in number, the size of population remains _________.

94. A population with varying size but having a constant rate of growth or depletion is called a _________ population.

95. A stable population has a fixed _________ ratio over time.

96. A stable population is closed for _________.

97. If the birth and death rates over time are equal and no migration takes place, the _________ and _________ populations are equal.

98. An abridged life-table usually consists of ages at distance of _________ years.

99. In an abridged life-table, the distance between ages is _________ one year.

100. The main difference in the construction of a complete life-table and an abridged life-table lies in determining _________.

101. Central mortality rate is the probability of _________ of a person whose _________ age is not known but lies in the interval x and $(x + 1)$.

102. Merrel's method of construction of abridged life-table is mainly based on _________.

103. Greville mainly utilises _________ in the construction of abridged life-table.

104. Greville's approximation to ${}_nL_x$ for abridged life-tables is based on _________.

105. King estimated the population and number of deaths for construction of abridged life-table for the central age in the interval $\{x, (x + n)\}$ by approximating to _________.

106. Out of Merrell's, Greville's and King's methods of construction of abridged life-tables, maximum approximations are involved in _________ method.

107. A life-table based on actual cohort is called _________ life-table.

108. The death rate of 15.4 of a posh city A and the death rate of 12.9 of a suburb B is _________ of salubrity of the later.

SECTION C

Multiple Choice Questions

Select the correct alternative out of given ones:

1. Vital statistics is mainly concerned with:
   (*a*) births
   (*b*) deaths
   (*c*) marriages
   (*d*) all of the above

2. Population statistics mainly display the records pertaining to:
   (*a*) foetal deaths

(*b*) population of regions
(*c*) morbidity
(*d*) all of the above

3. Complete count of the heads of people of a country is known as:
(*a*) census
(*b*) vital statistics
(*c*) demography
(*d*) none of the above

4. Vital statistics throws light on:
(*a*) changing pattern of the population during intercensal period
(*b*) virility of races
(*c*) growth of population
(*d*) all of the above

5. The registration of births, deaths and marriages are:
(*a*) a fancy of society
(*b*) a part of medical research
(*c*) a legal document
(*d*) all of the above

6. Vital statistics is greatly utilised by:
(*a*) acturies
(*b*) planners
(*c*) social reformers
(*d*) all of the above

7. In India, the collection of vital statistics started for the first times in:
(*a*) 720
(*b*) 1886
(*c*) 1969
(*d*) 1946

8. The registration of vital statistics in India suffers from:
(*a*) incomplete reporting
(*b*) incomplete coverage
(*c*) lack of accuracy
(*d*) all of the above

9. To improve upon the registration of vital statistics in India, the central government appointed a committee in 1948 known as:
(*a*) Bhor Committee
(*b*) Rath Committee
(*c*) Arthur Committee
(*d*) none of the above

10. Registration of vital statistics is organised at the apex by:
(*a*) Director General
(*b*) Registrar General
(*c*) Census Commissioner
(*d*) all of the above

11. At state level, the registration of vital statistics is carried by:
(*a*) Director of Economics & Statistics
(*b*) Chief Returning Officer
(*c*) Chief Registrar
(*d*) none of the above

12. In post-Independence India, the registration of Births and Deaths Act was passed in:
(*a*) 1948
(*b*) 1959
(*c*) 1969
(*d*) 1979

13. Vital statistics is obtained through:
(*a*) census operation
(*b*) registration system
(*c*) survey method
(*d*) all of the above

14. Sampling registration system of births and deaths came into operation in rural areas in the year:
(*a*) 1967
(*b*) 1968
(*c*) 1969
(*d*) none of the above

15. Sampling registration system for recording births and deaths in urban areas started in the year:
(*a*) 1967
(*b*) 1968
(*c*) 1969
(*d*) none of the above

16. The advantage of sampling registration system is that:
(*a*) it has full coverage
(*b*) it is more accurate
(*c*) it provides the estimate for rural and urban areas separately
(*d*) all of the above

17. The sampling registration system fails to record:
(a) age and sex composition
(b) birth rates
(c) death rates
(d) all of the above

18. The most important assumption, on which the analytical methods are based, is that:
(a) the population is stagnant
(b) the population grows at a constant rate
(c) there is no time lag
(d) none of the above

19. Having known the population of the two consecutive censuses, the formula for population estimate $\hat{P}_t$ in the intercensal year t with usual rotations is:

(a) $\hat{P}_t = P_0 + \frac{N}{n}(P_1 - P_0)$

(b) $\hat{P}_t = P_1 + \frac{n}{N}(P_1 - P_0)$

(c) $\hat{P}_t = P_0 + \frac{n}{N}(P_1 - p_0)$

(d) $\hat{P}_t = P_0 + \frac{N}{n}(P_0 - P_1)$

20. If P_1 and P_2 are the populations at two censuses conducted at an interval of five years, then the rate of population growth 'r' can be estimated by the formula:

(a) $r = \sqrt[10]{\frac{P_2}{P_1}} - 1$

(b) $r = \sqrt[5]{\frac{P_1}{P_2}} - 1$

(c) $r = \sqrt[5]{\frac{P_2}{P_1}} - 1$

(d) $r = \sqrt[n]{\frac{P_2}{P_1}} - 1$

21. If we have the last census population, migration, births and deaths data for a region in a given period, the population at the time t can be estimated by the formula (using usual notations) as:

(a) $\hat{P}_t = P_0 + (B - D) + (I - E)$

(b) $\hat{P}_t = (B - D) + (I - E)$

(c) $\hat{P}_t = P_0\{(B - D) + (I - E)\}$

(d) none of the above

22. Having known the last census population 'P_0' and growth rate 'r', the population after n years based on compound interest formula will be:

(a) $\hat{P}_t = P_0 (1 + r)^n$

(b) $\hat{P}_t = P_0 (1 + n)^r$

(c) $\hat{P}_t = P_0/(1 + r)^n$

(d) $\hat{P}_t = P/(1 + r)^n$

23. If P_1 and P_2 are the population at an interval of 10 years, the population just after five years will be:

(a) $\frac{1}{2}(P_1 + P_2)$

(b) $\sqrt{P_1 \times P_2}$

(c) $\frac{1}{2}\left(\frac{1}{P_1} + \frac{1}{P_2}\right)$

(d) $\sqrt{P_1 + P_2}$

24. Vital rates are customarily expressed as:
(a) percentages
(b) per thousand
(c) per million
(d) per trillion

25. Crude death rate, expressed simply as a ratio, provides:
(a) the probability of babies borned and died during the year under reference
(b) the probability of a foetal death during the year under reference

(*c*) the probability of dying of a person during the year under reference
(*d*) all of the above

26. The child bearing age in India is:
(*a*) 20-24 years
(*b*) 20-29 years
(*c*) 15-49 years
(*d*) 13-48 years

27. The fertility of a woman in India is maximum in the age group:
(*a*) 15-20
(*b*) 20-24
(*c*) 25-29
(*d*) 15-29

28. The death rate obtained for a segment of a population is known as:
(*a*) specific death rate
(*b*) crude death rate
(*c*) standardised rate
(*d*) vital index

29. The age-specific death rate for the babies of age less than one year is specifically called:
(*a*) neonatal death rate
(*b*) infant mortality rate
(*c*) maternal mortality rate
(*d*) foetal death rate

30. The death rate of babies under one month is known as:
(*a*) neonatal mortality rate
(*b*) infant mortality rate
(*c*) maternal mortality rate
(*d*) foetal death rate

31. The death rate of women due to delivery of children is termed as:
(*a*) neonatal mortality rate
(*b*) infant mortality rate
(*c*) maternal mortality rate
(*d*) foetal death rate

32. Age-specific mortality rates fail to reveal:
(*a*) mortality conditions
(*b*) age distribution of persons
(*c*) sex ratio
(*d*) all of the above

33. Standardised death rates are particularly useful for:
(*a*) comparing the death rates in males and females
(*b*) comparing the death rates of two regions
(*c*) both (*a*) and (*b*)
(*d*) neither (*a*) and (*b*)

34. Fertility rates mainly depend on:
(*a*) total female population
(*b*) total population
(*c*) female population of child bearing age
(*d*) number of newly borned babies

35. Adequate basis for family planning is provided by:
(*a*) general fertility rate
(*b*) age specific marital fertility rate
(*c*) total marital fertility rate
(*d*) total fertility rate

36. Total fertility rates provides the basis for:
(*a*) the expected maximum family size
(*b*) population projection
(*c*) population increase in a desired period
(*d*) all of the above

37. Population growth is mainly concerned with:
(*a*) total number of births
(*b*) number of male births
(*c*) number of female births
(*d*) none of the above

38. Fertility rates provide an adequate basis for:
(*a*) population growth
(*b*) family planning
(*c*) checking the infant mortality
(*d*) all of the above

39. Survival rate, in general, is measured through:
(*a*) the difference in crude birth and death rates
(*b*) the ratio of the difference in total births and total deaths to the mean population
(*c*) both (*a*) and (*b*)
(*d*) neither (*a*) nor (*b*)

40. The ratio of births to the total deaths in a year is called:
(*a*) survival rate
(*b*) total fertility index

(*c*) vital index
(*d*) population death rate

41. Vital index for ascertaining population growth is:
(*a*) a good measure
(*b*) a rough measure
(*c*) useless
(*d*) none of the above

42. The vital index for population growth was propounded by:
(*a*) B. Benjamin
(*b*) G. Barcley
(*c*) A. Newsholmes
(*d*) Rayond Pearl

43. Gross reproduction rate is gross in the sense that:
(*a*) its basis is hypothetical
(*b*) it is based on clumsy grounds
(*c*) it is based on unrealistic assumptions
(*d*) all of the above

44. The main drawback of gross reproduction rate is:
(*a*) assumption of no mortality of female children till their fecundity age
(*b*) non-consideration of divorces
(*c*) the neglect of the number of unmarried women
(*d*) all of the above

45. Net reproduction rate is more viable than gross reproduction rate because:
(*a*) it takes into account fertility rates as well as mortality rates
(*b*) it makes use of life-tables
(*c*) it utilises survival rate
(*d*) all of the above

46. The relation between N.R.R. and G.R.R. is:
(*a*) N.R.R. and G.R.R. are usually equal
(*b*) N.R.R. can never exceed G.R.R.
(*c*) N.R.R. is generally greater than G.R.R.
(*d*) none of the above

47. N.R.R. = 1 leads one to conclude that:
(*a*) female population will exactly replace itself
(*b*) population remain constant
(*c*) there is no mortality in female births till their child bearing age
(*d*) all of the above

48. The value of N.R.R. < 1 is indicative of:
(*a*) increase in population
(*b*) reduction in population
(*c*) constancy in population
(*d*) all of the above

49. A value of N.R.R. > 1 will result into:
(*a*) increase in population
(*b*) negative increase in population
(*c*) zero increase in population
(*d*) none of the above

50. A deep consideration of N.R.R. brings forth that:
(*a*) its basis of using constant fertility and mortality rates is not very appropriate
(*b*) migrants are not the subjects of N.R.R. which is not correct
(*c*) A.S.F.R. are taken as constant for N.R.R. which is not true in real life
(*d*) all of the above

51. The ratio of the number of children of age less than five years to the total number of women of 15-49 years age is called:
(*a*) net reproduction rate
(*b*) vital index
(*c*) gross reproduction rate
(*d*) replacement index

52. The ratio of annual net migration to the annual mean population provides:
(*a*) vital index
(*b*) net migration rate
(*c*) population growth rate
(*d*) none of the above

53. Life-table has also been named as:
(*a*) mortality table
(*b*) survival table
(*c*) life expectancy table
(*d*) all of the above

54. A life-table is a profile of human population which exhibits:
(*a*) probability of dying at each age
(*b*) numbers living and dying

(c) expectation of life at each age
(d) all of the above

55. A life-table is a compendium which:
(a) foretells about each individual
(b) forecasts the year of death of each individual
(c) provides the age of each individual of the population
(d) none of the above

56. Construction of life-tables is based on the assumption that:
(a) age specific death rates are constant at all ages
(b) death rates are uniformly distributed between two birth days
(c) mortality rates are same for male and female populations
(d) all of the above

57. Life-tables are usually constructed:
(a) jointly for male and female populations
(b) separately for male and female populations
(c) both (a) and (b)
(d) neither (a) and (b)

58. The standard number of births 10,000 originating a life-table is known as:
(a) a cohort
(b) initial population
(c) radix
(d) all of the above

59. A life-table is most utilised by:
(a) life insurance companies
(b) general insurance companies
(c) employment exchanges
(d) all of the above

60. Life-table is a mean of:
(a) monitoring the family planning programmes
(b) checking the census figures
(c) giving population projections
(d) all of the above

61. Normally a life-table is constructed for an age interval of:
(a) five years
(b) five to 10 years
(c) one year
(d) none of the above

62. Which leader amongst the following attained the maximum age of a life-table?
(a) Mao Tse-tung of China
(b) Karl Marx of Germany
(c) Morarji Desai of India
(d) Macmillan of U.K.

63. A life-table consists of:
(a) seven columns
(b) eight columns
(c) nine columns
(d) none of the above

64. Unemployment rates are similar to:
(a) death rates
(b) survival rates
(c) migration rates
(d) none of the above

65. A population have constant size and composition is called a:
(a) stable population
(b) stationary population
(c) continuous population
(d) discrete population

66. A population maintaining a constant growth rate is said to be a:
(a) stable population
(b) stationary population
(c) mobile population
(d) none of the above

67. The probability of dying of a person of age between x and $(x + 1)$ years is known as:
(a) age-specific death rate
(b) infant mortality rate
(c) central mortality rate
(d) none of the above

68. A life-table constructed for an age interval of 5 to 10 years is specifically known as:
(a) grouped life-table
(b) interval life-table
(c) abridged life-table
(d) none of the above

69. An abridged life-table can be constructed by the method suggested by:
(*a*) Reed Merrel
(*b*) Greville
(*c*) G. King
(*d*) all the above

70. Reed Merrel method of construction of abridged life-tables utilises:
(*a*) age specific mortality rates
(*b*) central mortality rates
(*c*) both (*a*) and (*b*)
(*d*) neither (*a*) nor (*b*)

71. Greville's method for estimating death rate in the age interval of x to $(x + n)$ years utilises:
(*a*) Compertz law
(*b*) exponential law
(*c*) both (*a*) and (*b*)
(*d*) neither (*a*) nor (*b*)

72. G. King's abridged life tables are based on the calculation of:
(*a*) central mortality rate
(*b*) the number of persons and deaths for the central age in the interval $\{x, x + n\}$
(*c*) both (*a*) and (*b*)
(*d*) neither (*a*) and (*b*)

73. A life-table based on the experience of actual cohort is called:
(*a*) generation life-table
(*b*) fluent life-table
(*c*) both (*a*) and (*b*)
(*d*) neither (*a*) and (*b*)

74. The probability of living of a person in the age group x to $(x + n)$ can be obtained by the formula:
(*a*) l_{x+n}/l_x
(*b*) $(l_x - l_{x+n})/l_x$
(*c*) $(l_x - l_{x+n})/l_{x+n}$
(*d*) l_x/l_{x+n}

75. The central mortality rate 'm_x' in terms of q_x is given by the formula:
(*a*) $2q_x/(2 + q_x)$
(*b*) $2q_x/(2 - q_x)$
(*c*) $q_x/(2 + q_x)$
(*d*) $q_x/(2 - q_x)$

76. If l_x is the number of persons living at the age x and L_x the number of persons living in the mid of x and $(x + 1)$ years, then the relation between l_x and L_x is:
(*a*) $L_x = \frac{1}{2}(l_x + l_{x+1})$
(*b*) $L_x = \frac{x}{2} + l_x$
(*c*) $L_x = l_{x+\frac{1}{2}}$
(*d*) none of the above

77. The relation between the central mortality rate 'm_x' and force of mortality 'μ_x' is:
(*a*) $m_x = \mu_x + \frac{1}{2}$
(*b*) $m_x = \frac{1}{2}\mu_{x+1}$
(*c*) $m_x = \frac{1}{2}(\mu_x + \mu_{x+1})$
(*d*) none of the above

78. The ratio of the rate of decrease in initial population l_x at age x to l_x is known as:
(*a*) nominal annual rate of mortality
(*b*) force of mortality
(*c*) central mortality rate
(*d*) all the above

79. The probability q_x of dying of a person between the age interval x and $(x + 1)$ and m_x, the central mortality rate are related as:
(*a*) $q_x = 2m_x/(2 - m_x)$
(*b*) $q_x = m_x/(2 + m_x)$
(*c*) $q_x = 2m_x/(2 + m_x)$
(*d*) none of the above

80. If l_x, the initial population at age x in an abridged life-table vanishes at the age $w + n$, then with usual notation:
(*a*) ${}_nL_w = l_x/m_x$
(*b*) ${}_nL_x = l_w/{}_nm_w$
(*c*) ${}_nL_w = l_x/m_x$
(*d*) ${}_nL_w = l_x/{}_nm_x$

ANSWERS

Section B

1. demography **2.** interchangeable **3.** vital statistics **4.** Arthur Newsholme **5.** Benjamin **6.** human inventory **7.** analysis **8.** ten years **9.** continuing process **10.** acturies **11.** social reforms **12.** vital statistics **13.** vital statistics **14.** 1969 **15.** 1886 **16.** sacramental **17.** three-fourth **18.** Bhor **19.** 1952 **20.** sample census **21.** Registrar General **22.** Comprehensive profile **23.** census year **24.** vital **25.** programmes **26.** 1967 **27.** 1968 **28.** census blocks **29.** all India level **30.** rural; urban **31.** migration **32.** is not **33.** $p_0 + \frac{n}{N}(P_1 - P_0)$ **34.** at a constant rate **35.** $\sqrt[5]{P_n/P_0} - 1$ **36.** $\sqrt{P_1 \times P_2}$ **37.** per thousand **38.** probability; death **39.** equal weightage **40.** more informative **41.** mortality conditions **42.** pooled death **43.** exhumating **44.** 15-49 **45.** all ages **46.** family planning **47.** family planning **48.** married **49.** A.S.F.R. **50.** T.M.F.R. **51.** T.F.R. **52.** sex **53.** female births; mortality **54.** reproduction rates **55.** vital index **56.** normative **57.** no female child dies **58.** gross reproduction rate **59.** net reproduction rate **60.** gross reproduction rate **61.** less than **62.** replace itself **63.** decrease **64.** increase **65.** not valid **66.** fail to estimate **67.** not involved **68.** rarely **69.** vital index **70.** 0 ; ∞ **71.** population growth **72.** depletion **73.** net migration rate **74.** life-table **75.** mortality rate **76.** survival **77.** life-table **78.** separately **79.** life-tables **80.** devoid **81.** radix **82.** diminishes **83.** have died **84.** Ulpian **85.** acturies **86.** chronic diseases **87.** life-tables **88.** life-tables **89.** life-tables **90.** eight **91.** death rate **92.** stationary **93.** constant **94.** stables **95.** sex **96.** migration **97.** stationary; stable **98.** 5 to 10 **99.** more than **100.** ${}_nq_x$ **101.** dying; exact **102.** central mortality rate **103.** age specific central mortality rate **104.** numerical quadrature **105.** second degree parabola **106.** King's **107.** generation or fluent **108.** no evidence.

Section C

1. (*d*) **2.** (*b*) **3.** (*a*) **4.** (*d*) **5.** (*c*)
6. (*d*) **7.** (*b*) **8.** (*d*) **9.** (*a*) **10.** (*b*)
11. (*c*) **12.** (*c*) **13.** (*d*) **14.** (*a*) **15.** (*b*)
16. (*d*) **17.** (*a*) **18.** (*b*) **19.** (*c*) **20.** (*c*)
21. (*a*) **22.** (*a*) **23.** (*b*) **24.** (*b*) **25.** (*c*)
26. (*c*) **27.** (*c*) **28.** (*a*) **29.** (*b*) **30.** (*a*)
31. (*c*) **32.** (*d*) **33.** (*b*) **34.** (*c*) **35.** (*b*)
36. (*d*) **37.** (*c*) **38.** (*b*) **39.** (*a*) **40.** (*c*)
41. (*b*) **42.** (*d*) **43.** (*d*) **44.** (*a*) **45.** (*d*)
46. (*b*) **47.** (*d*) **48.** (*b*) **49.** (*a*) **50.** (*d*)
51. (*d*) **52.** (*b*) **53.** (*a*) **54.** (*d*) **55.** (*d*)
56. (*b*) **57.** (*b*) **58.** (*c*) **59.** (*a*) **60.** (*d*)
61. (*c*) **62.** (*c*) **63.** (*b*) **64.** (*a*) **65.** (*b*)
66. (*a*) **67.** (*c*) **68.** (*c*) **69.** (*d*) **70.** (*b*)
71. (*a*) **72.** (*c*) **73.** (*c*) **74.** (*a*) **75.** (*b*)
76. (*c*) **77.** (*a*) **78.** (*b*) **79.** (*c*) **80.** (*b*)

SUGGESTED READING

1. Agarwal, B.L., *Basic Statistics,* New Age International Publishers, New Delhi, 8th edition, 2024.
2. Barcely, G.W., *Techniques of Population Analysis,* John Wiley & Sons, Inc., New York, 7th reprint, 1966.
3. Benjamin, B., *Elements of Vital Statistics,* George Allen and Unwin Ltd., London, 1959.
4. Benjamin, B., *Demographic Analysis,* George Allen and Unwin Ltd., London, 1968.
5. Cassen, R.H., *India: Population, Economy, Society,* The Macmillan Company of India, Delhi, 1979.
6. *Census of of India*, 1991, Publications.
7. Cox, PR., *Demography,* Vikas Publishing House, Delhi, 1979.
8. Gupta, S.C. and Kapoor, V.K., *Fundamentals of Applied Statistics,* Sultan Chand & Sons, New Delhi, reprinted, 1993.
9. Kohli, K.L., *Mortality in India* (Statewise study) Sterling Publishers, Delhi, 1961.
10. Nafis Sadik, *Population Policies and Programmes,* United Nations Population Fund, New York University Press, New York, 1991.
11. *Vital Statistics of India for 1959*, Ministry of Home Affairs, India, 1961.

Chapter 21

Basic Experimental Designs

SECTION A

Short Essay Type Questions

Q. 1. *What is an experimental design?*

Ans. Any person has often total or partial ignorance about certain factors or treatments underlying a phenomenon and is desirous to confirm it by way of certain experimentation or trial. The effect of factors or treatments can be ascertained or compared only if they are set completely free to show their effects on the subjects while all other factors which are likely to affect the treatments or factors under study, are kept under control.

Thus, the plan in which an experiment has to be conducted so that all situations, except that of treatments or factors are kept under control as much as possible, are known as experimental design. These designs may be for engineering, chemical industry, crop experiments, etc. For instance, an experiment may be conducted to see the effect of different fertilisers. In this situation, the field has to be divided into a number of plots of equal size and same shape, homogeneous in respect of soil fertility, irrigation, crop, seed, plant protection umbrella, crop management, etc., and each plot receives the fertilizer treatment randomly. The variability in crop yield or any other criterion measure can enable the investigator to distinguish between fertilizers. Such a plan of experiment is known as *design of experiment.*

Q. 2. *How do you define an experimental unit?*

Ans. A subject or a group of objects or the total material to which a treatment is applied in a trial in a single replication is known as an experimental unit. For instance, a plot in field trial in agricultural experiments, a rat or a rabbit in a biological experiments, a cow or a horse in an experiment in animal sciences, a group of insects in entomological experiment, etc.

Q. 3. *Define a treatment in reference to an experiment.*

Ans. A treatment is a substance or a known factor which is administered or allocated to one or more experimental units to estimate its effect pertaining to certain characters or for comparing it with others. Application of *fertilizers* to field plots, testing *feeds* on cows, administering *medicines* to patients are a few of the examples of treatments which are applied to experimental units. Whereas *dates of sowing, crop geometries* to see their effect on the yield of crop, *breed* of poultry birds for their meat quality, etc., are the treatments which are attached to the experimental units. An experimental unit may receive a simple treatment or a combination of treatments.

Q. 4. *What are the requirements of a good experimental design?*

Ans. There are three requirements of a good design namely:

(*a*) Randomization

(*b*) Replication

(*c*) Local control.

Q. 5. *What do you understand by randomization in experimental designs?*

Ans. The allocation of treatments to experimental units in such a manner that an experimental unit has equal chance of receiving any of the treatments is called randomization. The total number of units in an experiment is always equal to the sum of the replicates of all the treatments selected.

Randomization is appropriately implemented with the help of random number tables.

Q. 6. *What is the role of randomization in the process of experimentation?*

Ans. There are definitely many advantages of assigning the treatments randomly to the experimental units. They are summarily discussed below:

(*i*) Randomization eliminates the human biases. May these biases be introduced advertently or inadvertently.

(*ii*) Randomization makes the experiment free from any systematic influences of environment.

(*iii*) The process of randomization enables to apply mathematical theories which would have otherwise not been possible.

(*iv*) One of the important assumption for the analysis of variance of data is that the experimental errors are independent. It this assumption is violated, the validity of *F*-test or *t*-test is always doubtful. But a proper randomization introduces the independence in the assignment of treatments to the experimental units which in turn creates independence amongst the observations. *Thus, randomization may be considered a device to effectively make the experimental errors independent.*

In short, randomization makes tests valid in the analysis of experimental data.

(*v*) R.A. Fisher in 1949 stated that randomization in experimental designs is one of the required conditions to attach a probability statement to the estimated treatment difference.

Q. 7. *What is meant by replication, and what purpose dose it serve in experimental designs?*

Ans. Repetition of a treatment on a number of experimental units under similar conditions is called the *replication* of the treatment. As a matter of fact, many purposes are served by the use of replications in an experiment.

(*i*) Replications are essential to obtain a valid estimate of the experimental error variance.

(*ii*) Replications are necessarily required to attach a probability statement with estimated treatment differences.

(*iii*) The larger number of replications reduces the standard error of the treatment mean(s). But one cannot take more than certain number of replications because of the management problems and limitation of resources.

(*iv*) Replications enable the experimenter to infer whether the differences in treatment means are actually more than the sampling fluctuations. If the variation among treatments is more by a certain quantity as compared to sampling fluctuation, then they are considered to be significantly different, otherwise not.

(*v*) Replications of a treatment also compensate for the inadvertent favour or disfavour received by a particular treatment from one unit to the other. For example, a treatment may be favoured due to better soil fertility in one plot and be handicapped in the other plot due to poor soil fertility. In this way, average performance of the treatment is better assessed by way of replications.

Q. 8. *What do you understand by local control and in what way does it increase the efficiency of an experimental designs?*

Ans. Local control is a device to maintain greater homogeneity of experimental units within a block of an experiment or as a whole. This is achieved by considering the natural factors likely to influence the treatment effects inherent within the experimental units. For instance, soil fertility of field is a factor which affects the plant growth and yield. So all the neighbouring plots having the same soil fertility should constitute a block. The soil fertility of land can be assessed by conducting an uniformity trial on the field prior to actual field experiment and making fertility contour map on the basis of fertility gradient. These contours help to form blocks. In animal experiments, local control means the animals of the same litter, breed, age, weight, lactation, etc., be grouped together to constitute a block.

Local control is also called as *error control* by some workers. It contributes a lot in increasing the efficiency of an experiment. A few points in favour of local control are highlighted below:

(*i*) With the help of fertility map one can form blocks of contiguous plots which are homogeneous in the real sense.

(*ii*) Local control reduces the experimental error.

(*iii*) Local control is meant to make designs more efficient.

(*iv*) It makes any test of significance more sensitive and powerful.

(*v*) A reduction in experimental error consequently helps the investigator to detect the small real difference between treatment means.

Q. 9. *Discuss and define experimental error.*

Ans. It is always an endeavour of the experimenter to control all factors which can effect the independent performance of the treatments and the choice of the design depends which can most likely to fulfil this objective. But, in spite of all efforts, there are always certain extraneous factors which are beyond the control of the experimenter. *Thus, the error caused by the extraneous factors which are beyond the control of human approach is known as experimenter error.* For instance, germination of seed, plant growth, number of pods or ears per plant, response to feed by the animal, taste of a person, etc., are the factors beyond human control. All such factors add towards experimental error.

The reduction in experimental error provides smaller standard error for a treatment mean or for the difference between two treatment means which results in detecting small differences between treatment means. In this way the efficiency of the experiment increases.

Q. 10. *What factors are responsible for determining the number of replications?*

Ans. There are mainly nine factors which are responsible for determining the number of replications.

(*i*) Extent of precision required.

(*ii*) Heterogeneity of experimental material.

(*iii*) Availability of resources.

(*iv*) Size of experimental units.

(*v*) Required degrees of freedom of experimental error.

(*vi*) The relative cost of experimental units.

(*vii*) The extent and nature of competition among experimental units.

(*viii*) The number and nature of the treatments.

(*ix*) The fraction to be sampled.

Q. 11. *How does the extent of precision work as a criterion for ascertaining the number of replications in an experiment?*

Ans. The extent of precision desired by an investigator means to spell out the magnitude of the treatment differences which are expected to be detected through the experiment. As a general rule, if the differences between treatment means are expected to be large, then a low degree of precision is required. Hence, in this situation, a small number of replications are enough. On the contrary, if the differences between treatment means are likely to be small, a large number of replications are to be taken.

Keeping in view the above ideas, if we know the magnitude '*d*' of the difference between two treatment means to be detected, an estimate of the error means square '*s*' based on some previous experiment or some empirical study, then the number of replications can be determined by the formula,

$$r = \frac{2t_{\alpha}^2 s^2}{d^2}$$

where, t_α is the tabulated t-value at α level of significance (usually $\alpha = 0.05$) and for the degrees of freedom associated with s^2.

The number of replications estimated from the above formula have only 50 per cent chance of detecting the specified difference '*d*'. Of course, this chance is too low. Hence for improvement, some other methods are propounded namely, Harris-Horvitz-Mood method, Tukey's method, Tang's methods, etc.

Q. 12. *What idea can be had after looking the variability in experimental material?*

Ans. If the experimental units are more heterogeneous, greater number of replications are required in an experiment and if, homogeneous, a small number of replications will suffice to have reliable inferences.

Q. 13. *How does the availability of resources bind a researcher in choosing the number of replications?*

Ans. Many times, theoretically an experiment may require a large number of replications but the resources do not permit it. The word resources implies availability of treatment material (seeds, chemicals etc.), technical persons, equipment and more so the number of experimental units. In animal experiments, the availability of desired number of animals which are all alike to form a replicate is a great problem. Hence we have to confine to a small number of replicates.

Even if many resources are at the disposal of the investigator, one cannot take too many replications unnecessarily for the reason that it increases the cost of the experiment and also adds the error due to management problems.

Q. 14. *In what way does the size of experimental units matter in deciding the number of replicates in an experiment?*

Ans. *First,* the question of size and shape of the experimental units is usually related to field experiments. In some cases, it may also be concern with the number of insects in a group forming an experimental unit, litter, pen or cage size and shape etc. But here they are out of context. Therefore, the question of size and shape of experimental units in relation to number of replicates for experimental plots in the field is discussed.

If the field size and the number of treatments is fixed, the number of replicates will be easily determined. The size of units also depends upon the type of power equipment or hand operated equipment to be used. Use of seed drill, combine, etc., required large size plots whereas hand operated equipments can easily be managed with small size plots.

Mathematically, an empirical relationship between plot size 'x' and plot variance 'V_x' developed by Fairfield Smith helps to determine the plot size. The relationship is,

$$\log V_x = \log V_1 - b' \log x$$

where V_1 is the variance among plots of size unity and b' is the regression coefficient indicating the relationship between adjacent individuals or units. Hence, the value of b' lies between 0 and 1 except for the situation of inter-experimental unit competition. Many improvements in Fairfield Smith's formula were suggested later which are not discussed.

Q. 15. *How do the degrees of freedom for experimental error lead to decide the minimum number of replications in an experimental design?*

Ans. As a general rule, more is the number of replications, better it is. But the problem is to decide about the least number of replications. This can be very well decided by considering the information available from the data. If s^2 is estimate of the error variance based on n degrees of freedom, then R.A. Fisher found that the amount of information available from the experimental data is given by the formula,

$$\left(\frac{n+1}{n+3}\right)\left(\frac{1}{s^2}\right)$$

whereas, if the error variance σ^2 is known, the information is equal to $1/\sigma^2$.

The coefficient of $\frac{1}{s^2}$, *i.e.*, $\left(\frac{n+1}{n+3}\right)$ increases rapidly so long as the value of n increases from 1 to 11 but stablizes to a great extent. when, n = 12 or more.

Hence, to have a stable information, the number of replications should be such that the available degrees of freedom for error variance are at least 12.

Q. 16. *How does the cost of the experimental units play its role in deciding the number of replications?*

Ans. Obviously, when the cost per unit is high, one would like to take minimum number of replications and if low, a large number of replications may preferably be taken keeping all other factors responsible for replications constant. In this situation, two designs with unequal number of replications may yield the same amount of information as the cost for additional replications in one experiment may be compensated by lesser per unit cost and vice-versa on a per unit information basis. Thus, if s^2 is the error mean square based on n df taking r replications in the design and c, the cost per replicate, the information available by the experimental data is,

$$\left(\frac{c}{s^2}\right)\left(\frac{n+1}{n+3}\right)$$

Also, the relative efficiency of design 1 over design 2 for fixed cost is,

$$E_{12} = \left(\frac{c_1}{s_1^2}\right)\left(\frac{n_1+1}{n_1+3}\right) \Big/ \left(\frac{c_2}{s_2^2}\right)\left(\frac{n_2+1}{n_2+3}\right)$$

Since n_1 and n_2 depend on the number of replications one can choose r keeping in view the cost such that $E_{12} = 1$.

Q. 17. *Define relatively efficiency of one design over the other:*

Ans. The relative efficiency of design 1 over design 2 is the ratio of the inverse of the error mean square of design 1 to the inverse of the error means square of design 2, *i.e.*

$$E_{12} = \frac{1/\sigma_1^2}{1/\sigma_2^2} = \frac{\sigma_2^2}{\sigma_1^2}$$

Q. 18. *How does sampling in experimental units have bearing on the number of replications?*

Ans. If the plot size in an experiment is large and it is not possible to harvest the entire plot for the study of certain characters, a sample from experimental units is often selected. Therefore, an experiment should be planned in such a way that the plot size and required number of replicates should result in the required degree of precision in spite of sampling. Yates and Zacopanay suggested that for the cereal crops, the sampling rate should be about 6 per cent of the plot. Also they worked out that the loss of information due to sampling as compared to complete harvesting was about one-third.

Q. 19. *What is meant by analysis of variance of experimental data?*

Ans. The measurements are taken on each experimental unit pertaining to character of interest and its variance is calculated. This total variance is due to various factors involved in the experiment. The purpose of analysis of variance is to split the total variance into component variances and to test the hypothesis about these component factors. The main interest lies in estimating and comparing pairwise treatment or testing contrasts (comparisons) among treatments.

The component variance are always displayed and tested in an analysis of variance table abbreviated as ANOVA table. An analysis of variance table contains five columns as depicted below.

The sources of variance are various components *A, B, C,...* and also the experimental error which are responsible for total variation.

The skeleton ANOVA table is as given below:

Source of variation	*Degrees of freedom*	*Sum of squares*	*Mean sum of squares*	*F-value*
		OR		
Source of variation	*d.f.*	*S.S.*	*M.S.*	*F-value*
A				
B				
C				
...				
Error				

The analysis of variance enables one to know whether the variance due to a component factor is significantly more than the variance due to experimental error or not. Here it should be kept in mind that mean sum of square due to component is nothing but the variance due to that component. Also the ratio of two component variances is distributed as F with corresponding d.f. Also often the interest lies in particular comparisons (contrasts) of treatments and to test their significance. This can also be tested by analysis of variance. For comparing pairwise treatments, further tests have to be carried out.

Q. 20. *How do we decide the component factors responsible for variation in an experiment?*

Ans. The measurement, generally the yield, in crop experiments or likewise any other character measured is as a result of many factors which are usually taken to be of additive nature. For instance, the yield of a cereal in an experiment having k treatments applied in each of the r blocks of k plots which are homogeneous within themselves but likely to be heterogeneous between themselves can be represented by following linear statistical model,

$$y_{ij} = \mu + \tau_i + \beta_j + \varepsilon_{ij}$$

for $i = 1, 2, ..., k$

$j = 1, 2, ..., r$

where

y_{ij} – yield of the plot receiving i^{th} treatment of jth block.

μ – true mean effect, *i.e.*, the mean yield which would have been even without the ith treatment and j^{th} block effects.

τ_i – true effect of the ith treatment.

β_j – true effect of the jth block.

ε_{ij} – error, *i.e.*, true effect of the experimental unit receiving i^{th} treatment in j^{th} block.

In the above model it is assumed that μ is a constant and ε_{ij} are identically and independently distributed normal variates with mean zero and variance σ_e^2, *i.e.*, $\varepsilon_{ij} \sim N(0, \sigma_e^2)$. But the specification of the model is based on the nature of treatment τ_i. Thus, the components of variance in the ANOVA table come from statistical model. Here the factors are μ, τ, β and ε.

Q. 21. *Is there any method of testing the additivity of a statistical model?*

Ans. Yes, if there is any doubt about the additivity of components in a statistical model, it can be tested by a test suggested by J.W. Tukey in 1949. The procedure is a part of error sum of squares and has one degrees of freedom. This sum of square tend to be inflated if there is non-additivity. This sum of square is tested against error mean square by F-test. If F-value is significant, it is indicative of non-additivity. In this situation, the investigator should think of alternative model for it.

Q. 22. *What are different types of statistical model for experimental designs?*

Ans. Statistical models for experimental designs are classified into three types namely,

(*i*) fixed effect model (Model-I)

(*ii*) random effect model (Model-II)

(*iii*) mixed effect model (Model-Ill)

The specification of the model emerges with the idea that either the effect of treatments (factors) is of fixed or random nature. Also there are some experiments in which certain effects are of fixed type and others of random nature. Such experiments lead to mixed effect model.

Q. 23. *Explicate fixed effect model.*

Ans. A fixed effect model is also known as *analysis of variance model or Model I*. In this model, the investigator is concerned to draw inferences about t treatments involved in the experiment. If we take the model for a design in which k treatments are randomly assigned to n homogeneous units whereas i^{th} treatment is replicated r_i times such that $\sum_{i=1}^{k} r_i = n$.

Then the statistical model with usual notations is,

$$y_{ij} = \mu + \tau_i + \varepsilon_{ij} \quad (1)$$

for $i = 1, 2, ..., k$

$j = 1, 2, ..., r_i$

In case, the main interest likes only in estimating the

effect of k treatments included in the experiment, the above model is a fixed effect model. For this model, the assumption is that $\sum_{i=1}^{k} \tau_i = 0$. For instance, the investigator's study is confined to the effect of k fertilizers or fertilizer doses, he has to choose a fixed effect model. Model (1) is suited to completely randomized design.

Q. 24. *Elucidate the random effect model.*

Ans. The random effect model is also known as *component of variance model* or *Model II*. This model is suitable for an experiment in which a researcher is interested to draw inferences about the population of treatments of which only a sample of k treatments is selected. For an experiment involving k treatments randomly allocated to n experimental units such that i^{th} treatment is replicated r_i times and $\sum_{i=1}^{k} r_i = n$, the model is,

$$y_{ij} = \mu + \tau_i + \varepsilon_{ij}$$

for $\quad i = 1, 2, ..., k$

$\quad j = 1, 2, ..., r_i$

The above model is suitable for a completely randomized design. The model can be extended to other designs as well. In this model, $\tau_i \sim N(0, \sigma^2_\tau)$ besides the basic assumptions that μ is a constant and $\varepsilon_{ij} \sim N(0, \sigma^2_e)$. For example, if a breeder is interested in assessing the performance of certain varieties, then these varieties have to be taken as a random sample as they have come from a population of varieties. The random effects can belong to finite or infinite population. In random effect model, the main emphasis is on estimating and testing the variability among the effects of different treatments.

Q. 25. *Explain mixed effect model.*

Ans. Mixed effect model is also known as Model III. If an experiment involves two factors, say, A and B where A has a levels and B has b levels, then the statistical model can be given as,

$$y_{iju} = \mu + \alpha_i + \beta_j + \varepsilon_{iju} \qquad (1)$$

for, $\quad i = 1, 2, ..., a$

$\quad j = 1, 2, ..., b$

$\quad u = 1, 2, ..., n$

where n is the number of experimental units.

Also, if we consider the treatments as combinations of a levels of factor A and b levels of factor B, then the statistical model for completely randomized design having n experimental units can be written as,

$$y_{iju} = \mu + \alpha_i + \beta_j + (\alpha\beta)_{ij} + \varepsilon_{iju} \qquad (2)$$

for, $\quad i = 1, 2, ..., a$

$\quad j = 1, 2, ..., b$

$\quad u = 1, 2, ..., n$

Models (1) and (2) are suitable for completely randomized design.

In the above models α_i is the effect of ith level of A and β_j is the effect of jth level of B and in model (2), $(\alpha\ \beta)_{ij}$ is the interaction effect of ith level of A with j^{th} level of B.

The above models will be called a mixed model if the factor A is fixed and B is random or the factor A is random and B is fixed.

When A is fixed and B is random, then the assumptions are,

$$\sum_{i=1}^{a} \alpha_i = 0, \ \sum_{i=1}^{a} (\alpha\beta)_{ij} = 0 \text{ but } \sum_{j=1}^{b} (\alpha\beta)_{ij} \neq 0$$

and, $\qquad \beta_j \sim \text{NID}(0, \sigma^2_\beta)$

when A is random and B is fixed, then the assumptions are

$$\sum_{j=1}^{b} \beta_j = 0, \ \sum_{j=1}^{b} (\alpha\beta)_{ij} = 0 \text{ but } \sum_{i=1}^{a} (\alpha\beta)_{ij} \neq 0$$

and, $\qquad \alpha_j \sim \text{NID}(0, \sigma^2_\alpha)$

Note. The above models (1) and (2) will be called fixed effect model if both α_i and β_j are unknown constants and random effect model if α_i and β_j are random variables.

Q. 26. *Name various methods applicable to test*

the significance of differences between all pairs of treatment means involved in an experiment.

Ans. When the F-value for treatments comes out to be significant, it reveals that treatment means are not equal. But the question remains unanswered, which of them differ significantly with one another and which do not. Various tests have been evolved for comparing differences among treatment means by a number of statisticians as named below. These tests are known as *multiple range* tests.

(*i*) Least significant difference (1sd) test or multiple t-test.

(*ii*) Student-Newman-Kuel test.

(*iii*) Duncan's multiple range test.

(*iv*) Tukey's test.

Q. 27. *How can one compare the differences in a set of paired treatment means with the help of least significant difference?*

Ans. Firstly a standard value is calculated which is the minimum difference required to be significant between any two treatment means in a set of treatments. In principle, the formula for least significant difference is,

$$lsd = \sqrt{\frac{2s_e^2}{r}} \times t_{.05, v}$$

where s_e^2 is the error mean square associated with v d.f. and r, the replication of treatments and $t_{.05, v}$ is the t-value at 5 per cent level of significance and v d.f. Compare the absolute differences between the treatment means with the value of *lsd*. If the difference between any two means remains less than *lsd*, it is non-significant and as soon as a difference comes out greater than or equal to *lsd*, it becomes significant.

Least significant difference is considered appropriate for small number of treatment means. As a matter of fact, type I error increases as the number of treatment means increases. Type I error associated with the largest and smallest treatment mean pair for five treatments is 27 per cent, for ten treatments it is 59 per cent and for twenty treatments, it is 86 per cent.

Q. 28. *What is Student-Newman-Kuel's test for comparing the ordered treatment means?*

Ans. This test takes care of the distance between two means in an ordered set of treatment means. This test is similar to *lsd* test except that for every pair of treatment means, a separate value of 'q' for percentage points depending on the level of significance α and the distance between the ordered means and v d.f. for error is used instead of t.

The value,

$$q_{\alpha, n, v} = \frac{\bar{x}_{max} - \bar{x}_{min}}{S_{\bar{x}}}$$

where, $$S_{\bar{x}} = \sqrt{\frac{s_e^2}{r}}$$

and r is the number of replications for each treatment.

The difference between two extreme treatment means in the ordered set $(\bar{x}_n - \bar{x}_1)$ is compared with W_n where,

$$W_n = q_{\alpha, n, v} \cdot \sqrt{2}\, s_{\bar{x}}$$

Similarly for $\bar{x}_{n-1}$ vs. $\bar{x}_1$,

$$W_{n-1} = q_{\alpha, n-1, v} \sqrt{2}\, s_{\bar{x}}$$

$$\vdots$$

and for $\bar{x}_2$ vs. $\bar{x}_1$,

$$W_2 = q_{\alpha, 2, v} \sqrt{2}\, s_{\bar{x}}$$

and so on.

The values of $q_{\alpha, n, v}$ can either be calculated or can be read from Table-29 of *Biometrika Tables for Statistician*, Vol. 1, Cambridge Univ. Press, 1954 by E.S. Pearson and H.O. Hartley.

The test can easily be performed by preparing a two way difference table by taking the treatment means along rows in descending order and along columns in ascending order. If $W_n \geq q_{\alpha, n, v} \sqrt{2}\, s_{\bar{x}}$, then the difference between two means is significant, otherwise not.

Q. 29. *Give Duncan's multiple range test for comparing the paired treatment means.*

Ans. Duncan's multiple range test makes use of a least significant difference value for each pair of treatment means. The treatment means are arranged in order and the least significant value for comparing two treatment means situated at a distance *n* in an ordered set and α level of significance calculated by the formula,

$$D_{\alpha, n} = s_{\bar{x}} \times \text{(Dunchan's significant range value for } \alpha \text{ level, } n \text{ distance and } v \text{ error d.f.)}$$

Duncan's significant ranges can be seen in the table given in *Biometrics,* 11, 1–42, 1995 by D.B. Duncan.

For each pair situated at different distances, a different Duncan's least significant value is obtained and compared with the difference in the two treatment means. If this difference is greater than or equal to Duncan's least significant value $D_{\alpha, n}$, then the two treatments are taken to differ significantly in their effects. All possible pairs of Treatment means can conveniently be compared by preparing a two way difference table by taking the treatment means in ascending order along rows and in descending order along columns. In this table all differences are covered by the upper diagonal and diagonal elements.

The greatest advantage of Duncan's multiple range test lies in the fact that it allows the experimenter to commit fewer *Type II error* and more *Type I error* than *lsd* and Newman-Kuel's test.

D.B. Duncan showed that the level of significance for *k*-treatments changes according to the following formula.

$$\alpha_k = 1 - (1 - \alpha)^{k-1}$$

Q. 30. *What is special with Tukey's test?*

Ans. It is a multiple range test similar to *lsd* test except that Tukey utilised honestly significant difference (*hsd*) test or the *w*-procedure. This is one approach out of many discussed by Tukey. The value of honestly significant difference is equal to $W_n = k$ of Newman-Kuel multiple range test. Any two treatment means having a difference more than honestly significant difference (*hsd*) are said to be significantly different, otherwise not. *hsd* for *n* treatments is equal to $q_{\alpha, n} . s_{\bar{x}}$, where $q_{\alpha, n}$ is same as Student-Newman-Kuels critical value.

Q. 31. *Discuss Contrasts.*

Ans. A researcher is not only interested in comparing pairwise treatment means but is often interested in certain specific functions of treatments known as *contrasts.* Here it is to point out that the term *comparison* is equally and frequently used for contrasts.

If there are *k* treatment totals, $T_1, T_2, ..., T_k$ where the treatment T_i is replicated r_i times for $i = 1, 2, ...,$ *k*, then a linear combination Z_w of *k* treatment totals defined as,

$$Z_w = l_{w1} T_1 + l_{w2} T_2 + l_{wk} T_k$$

is said to be a contrast iff,

$$r_1 l_{w1} + r_2 l_{w2} + ... + r_k l_{wk} = 0$$

or,

$$\sum_{i=1}^{k} r_i l_{wi} = 0$$

Since most of the theory of contrasts has been developed by taking equireplicate treatments, we also consider that each treatment is replicated *r* times. Hence the linear combination z_w among *k* treatment totals is said to be a contrast iff

$$l_{w1} + l_{w2} + ... + l_{wk} = 0$$

or,

$$\sum_{i=1}^{k} l_{wi} = 0$$

For instance, linear combinations among three quantities T_1, T_2 and T_3 like, $T_1 - 2T_2, + T_3$; $T_1 - T_3$; $T_3 - T_1$; $T_1 - T_2$ are contrasts. Similarly for treatments T_1, T_2, T_3 and T_4, the linear combinations like, $T_1 + T_2 - T_3 - T_4$; $-3T_1 - T_2 + T_3 + 3T_4$; $T_1 - T_2 - T_3 + T_4$, etc., are contrasts. In the same way, for five quantities T_1, T_2, T_3, T_4 and T_5, the linear combinations like, $-2T_1 - T_2 + T_4 + 2T_5$; $T_1 - T_3$; $T_1 - 2T_2 + T_5$, etc., are contrasts. An arbitrary contrast does not reveal anything worth-while to the researcher. Hence, the interest lies in a particular set of contrasts known as orthogonal contrasts or a contrast depicting a specially known effect of treatment combination.

Q. 32. *Distinguish between pairwise and non-pairwise contrasts.*

Ans. A linear combination of $K\ (\geq 3)$ treatments, in which all coefficients are zero except two coefficients whose sum is also zero, is called a pairwise contrast. Any contrast among K treatments with more than two non-zero coefficients is a nonpairwise contrast.

Q. 33. *Differentiate between a priori and posteriori contrasts.*

Ans. A contrast which is constructed for testing its significance with specific purpose before the analysis of data is called *a priori* or *planned* contrast. On the other hand, a contrast constructed following a significant F-test is called *a posteriori* or *post hoc* or *unplanned* contrast.

Q. 34. *What are orthogonal contrasts?*

Ans. Two contrast Z_w and $Z_{w'}$ among k equireplicate treatment totals $T_1, T_2, ..., T_k$ say,

$$Z_w = l_{w1}T_1 + l_{w2}T_2 + ... + l_{wk}T_k \quad (1)$$

and

$$Z_{w'} = l_{w'1}T_1 + l_{w'2}T_2 + ... + l_{w'k}T_k \quad (2)$$

are said to be orthogonal iff,

$$l_{w1}\, l_{w'1} + l_{w2}\, l_{w'2} + ... + l_{wk} l_{w'k} = 0$$

i.e.,

$$\sum_{i=1}^{k} l_{wi}\, l_{w'i} = 0 \quad (3)$$

Out of k treatments, there can be utmost $(k - 1)$ orthogonal contrasts. The idea of orthogonal contrasts emerged from orthogonal polynomial. If we have k treatments, an orthogonal polynomial of order $(k - 1)$ can at most be fitted. For instance, if $k = 4$, we can at the maximum fit a cubic,

$$E(y) = a + bx + cx^2 + dx^3 \quad (4)$$

between the response variable y and the treatment levels x of a treatment or factor which are equidistant.

Instead of fitting the equation (4), we fit in the polynomial,

$$E(y) = \beta_0\mu_0 + \beta_1\mu_1 + \beta_2\mu_2 + \beta_3\mu_3 \quad (5)$$

In polynomial (5), $u_0 = 1$ and u_i for $i = 0, 1, 2, 3$, are polynomials of order i in x. Elaborately,

$$u_1 = a_1 + b_1\, x;\ u_2 = a_2 + b_2x + c_2x^2;$$

$$u_3 = a_3 + b_3\, x + c_3x^2 + d_3x^3$$

These polynomials are orthogonal if $\Sigma u_i u_{i}' = 0$ for each pair (i, i') for $i \neq i'$. Now let us consider four levels of a factor as 30, 60, 90, 120. May it be fertilizer does, temperature, timings, concentrations of a chemical compound, etc. Now consider $u_1 = a_1 + b_1x$. The condition for u_1 to be an orthogonal polynomial is $\Sigma u_0\, u_1 = 0$. Since $u_0 = 1$, $\Sigma u_1 = 0$.

Thus,

$$\Sigma u_1 = ka_1 + b_1\Sigma x \quad (6)$$

$$0 = 4a_1 + 300\, b_1 \quad (7)$$

Equation (7) is a single equation in two unknowns a_1 and b_1. The solution of (7) which results into the smallest integral values of u_1 for the four values of x are $a_1 = -5$, $b_1 = \dfrac{1}{15}$. Putting these values in $u_1 = a_1 + b_1\, x$

or,

$$u_1 = \frac{x - 75}{15}$$

when $x = 30,\ u_1 = -3.$

$x = 60,\ u_1 = -1$

$x = 90,\ u_1 = 1$

$x = 120,\ u_1 = 3$

Thus, the contrast,

$$-3T_1 - T_2 + T_3 + 3T_4 \quad (I)$$

represents the linear effect.

Now we consider the quadratic,

$$u_2 = a_2 + b_2u_1 + c_2\, u_1^2$$

The orthogonality conditions are,

$$\Sigma u_0\, u_2 = 0 \text{ and } \Sigma u_1\, u_2 = 0$$

The condition $\Sigma u_0\, u_2 = 0$ gives the equation,

$$\Sigma u_0 u_2 = \Sigma u_0 a_2 + b_2 \Sigma u_0 u_1 + c_2 \Sigma u_0 u_1^2 \quad (8)$$

$$0 = \Sigma a_2 + b_2 \Sigma u_1 + c_2 \Sigma u_1^2$$

$$= 4a_2 + b_2 \times 0 + 20c_2$$

$$0 = a_2 + 5c_2$$

or, $$a_2 = -5c_2 \quad (9)$$

The condition $\Sigma u_1 u_2 = 0$ gives the equation,

$$\Sigma u_1 u_2 = a_2 \Sigma u_1 + b_2 \Sigma u_1^2 + c_2 \Sigma u_1^3$$

$$0 = a_2 \times 0 + b_2 \times 20 + c_2 \times 0$$

$$20b_2 = 0$$

or, $$b_2 = 0 \quad (10)$$

From (9), we have the choice that $a_2 = -5$, $c_2 = 1$.

Thus,

$$u_2 = -5 + u_1^2$$

$$u_1 = -3, u_2 = 4$$

$$u_1 = -1, u_2 = -4$$

$$u_1 = 1, u_2 = -4$$

$$u_1 = 3, u_2 = 4$$

So the contrast is,

$$4T_1 - 4T_2 - 4T_3 + 4T_4.$$

A better choice of contrast with minimum coefficient is,

$$T_1 - T_2 - T_3 + T_4 \quad \text{(II)}$$

which represents the quadratic effect.

Now consider the cubic,

$$u_3 = a_3 + b_3 u_1 + c_3 u_1^2 + d_3 u_1^3 \quad (11)$$

The conditions for orthogonality are,

$$\Sigma u_0 u_3 = 0, \Sigma u_1 u_3 = 0, \Sigma u_2 u_3 = 0$$

The condition $\Sigma u_0 u_3 = 0$ gives,

$$0 = \Sigma a_3 + b_3 \times 0 + c_3 \Sigma u_1^2 + d_3 \times 0$$

or, $$4a_3 + 20c_3 = 0 \quad (12)$$

since, $u_0 = 1, \Sigma u_1 = \Sigma u_1^3 = 0, \Sigma u_1^2 = 20$

The condition $\Sigma u_1 u_3 = 0$ gives,

$$0 = a_3 \times 0 + b_3 \times 20 + c_2 \times 0 + d_3 \times 164$$

or, $$20b_3 + 164 d_3 = 0 \quad (13)$$

The condition $\Sigma u_2 u_3 = 0$ gives,

$$\Sigma(a_2 + b_2 u_1 + c_2 u_1^2) u_3 = 0$$

$$a_2 \Sigma u_3 + b_2 \Sigma u_1 u_3 + c_2 \Sigma u_1^2 u_3 = 0$$

or, $$\Sigma u_1^2 u_3 = 0 \quad (14)$$

Since, $u_0 = 1, \Sigma u_0 u_3 + \Sigma u_3 = 0, \Sigma u_1 u_3 + 0, c_2 = 1.$

$$\Sigma u_1^2 u_3 = a_3 \Sigma u_1^2 + b_3 \Sigma u_1^3 + c_3 \Sigma u_1^4 + d_3 \Sigma u_1^5$$

$$0 = 20a_3 + 0 + 164c_3 + d_3 \times 0$$

or, $$20a_3 + 164c_3 = 0 \quad (15)$$

Equation (15) has easiest solution as $a_3 = 0$, $c_3 = 0$ and equation (13) gives,

$$b_3 = -\frac{41}{5} d_3 \quad (16)$$

Equation (16) is satisfied for $d_3 = 5$, $b_3 = -41$.

Thus, $$u_3 = -41u_1 + 5u_1^3 \quad (17)$$

$$u_1 = -3, u_3 = -12$$

$$u_1 = -1, u_3 = 36$$

$$u_1 = 1, u_3 = -36$$

$$u_1 = 3, u_3 = 12$$

Thus, the contrast giving the cubic effect is,

$$-12T_1 + 36T_2 - 36T_3 + 12T_4$$

or the better choice of cubic contrast with minimum coefficients is,

$$-T_1 + 3T_2 - 3T_3 + T_4 \quad \text{(III)}$$

In a similar manner we can derive linear, quadratic, cubic, quartic, ... contrasts for any number of treatments.

Q. 35. *Give the sets of linear, quadratic, cubic and quartic contrasts in case of 3, 4 and 5 treatments whichever possible in each case.*

Ans. Let T_1, T_2, T_3, T_4 and T_5 be five equispaced treatments in increasing order doses. The orthogonal contrasts representing linear, quadratic, cubic and quartic effects of treatments are as tabulated below:

3-Treatments

Table–1

Treats.	*Lin. contrast coeffs.*	*Quad. contrast coeffs.*
T_1	1	1
T_2	0	–2
T_3	–1	1

4-Treatments

Table–2

Treats.	*Lin. contrast coeffs.*	*Quad. contrast coeffs.*	*Cubic contrast coeffs.*
T_1	–3	1	–1
T_2	–1	–1	3
T_3	1	–1	–3
T_4	3	1	1

5-Treatments

Table–3

Treats.	*Lin. contrast coeffs.*	*Quad. contrast coeffs.*	*Cubic contrast coeffs.*	*Quartic contrast coeffs.*
T_1	–2	2	–1	1
T_2	–1	–1	2	–4
T_3	0	–2	0	6
T_4	1	–1	–2	–4
T_5	2	2	1	1

Q. 36. *How can one detect the contrast that represents the linear, quadratic, cubic effects, etc.?*

Ans. If the first order Newton's differences of the coefficients of a contrast are same, then it represents a linear effect, if second order differences are equal, it represents a quadratic effect, if third order differences are equal, it represents a cubic effect and so on.

Q. 37. *How can the sum of squares due to a contrast be calculated?*

Ans. If,

$$Z_w = l_{w1}T_1 + l_{w2}T_2 + \ldots + l_{wk}T_k$$

is a contrast among k treatment totals whereas i^{th} treatment is replicated r_i times for $i = 1, 2, \ldots, k$, then sum of square due to the contrast Z_w is,

$$Z_w^2/(r_1 l_{w1}^2 + r_2 l_{w2}^2 + \ldots + r_k l_{wk}^2)$$

$$= \frac{Z_w^2}{\sum_{i=1}^{k} r_i l_{w1}^2}$$

In case, each treatment is replicated r times, then the sum of square due to the contrast Z_w is,

$$Z_w^2 \Big/ r \sum_{i=1i}^{k} l_{wi}^2$$

If there are in all $(k – 1)$ orthogonal contrasts Z_1, Z_2, ..., Z_{k-1}, then the total of sum of squares due to $(k – 1)$ orthogonal contrasts each having 1 d.f. is equal to the treatment sum of squares having $(k – 1)$ d.f.

Q. 38. *What are the formulae used to calculate the standard error of a contrast among k treatment means?*

Ans. Let,

$$Z'_w = l_{w1}\,\bar{y}_1 + l_{w2}\,\bar{y}_2 + \ldots + l_{wk}\,\bar{y}_k$$

is a contrast among k treatment means where the treatment T_i is replicated r_i times. The standard error of the contrast Z_w is obtained by the formula,

$$\sigma_{z'_w} = \sigma\sqrt{\frac{l_{w1}^2}{r_1} + \frac{l_{w2}^2}{r_2} + \frac{l_{wk}^2}{r_k}}$$

where σ^2 is the actual error mean square. Generally σ^2 is not known and hence σ is substituted by s_e, the square root of error mean square.

If each treatment is replicated r times, then the standard error of the contrast Z'_w is equal to,

$$\sigma_{z'_w} = \frac{\sigma}{\sqrt{r}}\sqrt{l_{w1}^2 + l_{w2}^2 + \ldots + l_{wk}^2}$$

and its estimate,

$$\hat{\sigma}_{z'_w} = \frac{s_e}{\sqrt{r}}\sqrt{l_{w1}^2 + l_{w2}^2 + \ldots + l_{wk}^2}$$

Q. 39. *In what way are contrasts helpful in the analysis of experimental data?*

Ans. Contrasts have great utility in the analysis of experimental data as given below:

(*i*) A researcher can see the effect of a specified combination of treatments conceived prior to analysis of the data.

(*ii*) We can calculate the linear, quadratic, cubic effects, etc., of treatments through contrasts.

(*iii*) All main effects and interactions in a 2^n factorial experiment can be represented by a set of orthogonal contrasts.

(*iv*) The treatment sum of square can be partitioned into component sum of squares each having one degree of freedom through orthogonal contrasts.

(*v*) Contrasts provide much more information about treatments than a simple *F*-test of equality of treatment means.

Q. 40. *What is the classification made for experimental designs?*

Ans. The experimental designs (plans) have been divided into two classes namely,

(*i*) systematic designs (*ii*) randomized designs.

Q. 41. *What are systematic designs?*

Ans. Experimental plans, which are devoid of randomization process, are categorised as *systematic designs*. In these type of designs all the treatments, being repeated a fixed number of times, are assigned together on adjacent experimental units sequentially one after the other in any direction. For instance, if there are four treatments *A, B, C,* and *D* and each treatment is replicated three times, then a systematic design may be set in any of the following manner.

A	*B*	*C*	*D*
A	*B*	*C*	*D*
A	*B*	*C*	*D*

Plan (*i*)

A	*A*	*A*
B	*B*	*B*
C	*C*	*C*
D	*D*	*D*

Plan (*ii*)

ABCD	*ABCD*	*ABCD*

Plan (*iii*)

The history of agricultural field research using systematic designs dates back to 1834.

Q. 42. *What are the disadvantages of systematic designs?*

Ans. The main disadvantages of systematic designs are:

(*i*) One cannot rule out the possibility of personal biases.

(*ii*) Systematic errors are introduced due to correlation among adjacent experimental plots.

(*iii*) It is not possible to have valid estimates of variances as no probability is involved. This makes the analysis of experimental data meaningless.

Due to the above disadvantages, systematic designs are out of context.

Q. 43. *What are the advantages of systematic designs?*

Ans. The advantages of systematic designs are delineated below:

(*i*) There is an ease of operation particularly in crop experiments.

(*ii*) It enables the experimenter to make an intelligible placement of various treatments to experimental units.

(*iii*) Systematic designs make sampling of experimental area easier and better.

(*iv*) The chances of drifting the influence of one treatment over the other are reduced.

Q. 44. *When do you call an experimental design a randomized design?*

Ans. Experimental designs in which the treatments are allocated randomly to the experimental units come under the category of randomized designs and are classified as completely randomized design, randomized block design, Latin square design, split plot design, cross over design, progeny row trial, family block design, etc.

Q. 45. *Characterise a completely randomized design.*

Ans. Any design in general is characterised by the nature of grouping of experimental units and the manner in which the treatments are randomly allocated to the experimental units.

Completely randomized design is the one in which all the experimental units are taken in a single group which are homogeneous as far as possible. For example, all the field plots constituting the group are having the same soil fertility, soil depth, soil texture, soil moisture, etc.; all the cows forming a group are of the same breed, same age, same weight, same lactation, etc. Suppose there are k treatments and the treatment T_i is replicated r_i times. So we require $\sum_{i=1}^{k} r_i = n$ units. Assign K treatments randomly to n experimental units such that the treatment T_i occupies r_i units or plots. Such a design is called a *completely randomised design* (CRD). This design is also seldom called a *non-restrictional design.* Completely randomized design is most suitable for laboratory experiments, pot experiments, green house experiments, and sometimes for poultry and animal experiments.

To specify more elaborately, suppose there are four treatments T_1, T_2, T_3 and T_4 which are replicated 4, 3, 3 and 5 times, respectively. Then the layout of the completely randomized design having 15 plots (units) and 4 treatments, using a one digited random number table is as displayed below:

T_2(1)	T_2(10)	T_2(11)
T_3(2)	T_4(9)	T_3(12)
T_4(3)	T_4(8)	T_1(13)
T_1(4)	T_1(7)	T_1(14)
T_3(5)	T_4(6)	T_4(15)

Layout of a CRD

Q. 46. *What are the merits of a completely randomized design?*

Ans. A completely randomized design possesses many virtues which are delineated below:

(*i*) Its layout is very easy.

(*ii*) There is complete flexibility in this design, *i.e.*, any number of treatments and replicates for each treatment can be taken.

(*iii*) Whole experimental material can be utilised in this design.

(*iv*) This design yields maximum degrees of freedom for experimental error.

(*v*) The analysis of data is simplest as compared to any other design.

(*vi*) Missing observation(s) creates no problem in analysis of data. The analysis is carried out in the usual manner neglecting the missing plot as if it was not there in the experiment. This does not break any assumption or rule of analysis of variance.

(*vii*) Completely randomized designs are specially suitable in situations where an appreciable fraction of the units is likely to be destroyed during experimentation or is likely to fail to respond.

Q. 47. *What are the demerits of a completely randomized design?*

Ans. Completely randomized design suffers from many lacunae which are as follows:

(*i*) The design is suitable for a small number of treatments.

(*ii*) It is difficult to find homogeneous experimental units in all respects.

(*iii*) Completely randomized design is seldom suitable for field experiments as compared to other experimental designs.

Q. 48. *Give statistical model for completely randomized design with one observation per unit.*

Ans. The appropriate statistical model for a completely randomized design with k treatments and r_i replications of the treatment T_i is,

$$y_{ij} = \mu + \tau_i + \varepsilon_{ij} \qquad (1)$$

for, $i = 1, 2, ..., k$

$j = 1, 2, ..., r_i$

Also $\sum_{i=1}^{k} r_i = n$ = total number of experimental units.

In the above model,

μ – true mean effect.

τ_i – true effect of the ith treatment.

ε_{ij} – true effect of the jth unit receiving i^{th} treatment and all other extraneous factors so called, the experimental error.

μ is assumed to be a constant and $\varepsilon_{ij} \sim$ NID $(0, \sigma_e^2)$.

The statistical model will represent Model-I if researcher's interest lies only in k treatments included in the experiment and in this situation $\sum_{i=1}^{k} \tau_i = 0$.

Again if the interest lies in the population of treatments of which k treatments are a random sample, then $\tau_i \sim$ NID $(0, \sigma_\tau^2)$ and statistical model (1) represents Model-II.

Q. 49. *Give skeleton analysis of variance table for completely randomized design under Model-I and Model-II.*

Ans. The analysis of variance under Model-I and Model-II differ in respect of the hypotheses and expected mean squares as given below.

Table–4

Source of variation	*d.f.*	*S.S.*	*M.S.*	*F-value*	*Model-I Expected M.S.*	*Model-II Expected M.S.*
Treatment	$k-1$	T_{yy}	$\frac{T_{yy}}{k-1} = T_y$	T_y/E_y	$\sigma_e^2 + \sum_{i=1}^{k} r_i\tau_i^2/(k-1)$	$\sigma_e^2 + n_0\sigma_\tau^2$
Error	$n-k$	E_{yy}	$\frac{E_{yy}}{n-k} = E_y$		σ_e^2	σ_e^2
Total	n–1					

Under Model-I, the null hypothesis,

$$H_0: \tau_1 = \tau_2 = ... = \tau_k = 0$$

is tested against

$$H_1: \text{all } \tau\text{'s are not equal to zero.}$$

Under Model-II, the null hypothesis

$$H_0: \sigma_\tau^2 = 0$$

is tested against

$$H_1: \sigma_\tau^2 \neq 0$$

The expected mean squares are only the source which enable the investigator to adopt a correct procedure for estimating the parameters and/or testing the hypotheses about parameters.

Note. These concepts are applicable for all designs and their models.

Now we give below the analysis of variance table for completely randomized design with extra columns, one giving the expected mean squares for Model-I and the other for Model-II. Such an analysis of variance is always applicable for *one way classification.*

where, $$n_0 = \left[\sum_{i=1}^{k} r_i - \sum_{i=1}^{k} r_i^2 \Big/ \sum_{i=1}^{k} r_i\right]\Big/(k-1)$$

If, $r_1 = r_2 = ... = r_k = r$

then, $n_0 = r$

The expected mean squares in the ANOVA Table-4 clearly reveal that the experimental error is appropriate to test the hypothesis about treatments under Model-I as well as Model-II. Since the exact rest is available for testing H_0, the statistical model is said to be *completely specified.*

Q. 50. *Give the method of calculating sum of squares for the observations of a completely randomized design with k treatments and i^{th} treatment being replicated r_i times.*

Ans. Let the observation y_{ij} be the jth observation of ith treatment in a completely randomized design as tabulated ahead:

Calculations,

C.F. $= y^2 ../n$ where $\sum_{i=1}^{k} r_i = n =$ Total no. of observations

	Treatments					
	T_1	T_2	...	T_i	...	T_k
	y_{11}	y_{21}	...	y_{i1}	...	y_{k1}
	y_{12}	y_{22}	...	y_{i2}	...	y_{k2}
	$\vdots$	$\vdots$		$\vdots$		$\vdots$
	y_{1r_1}	y_{2r_2}	...	y_{ir_i}	...	y_{kr_k}
Total	$y_{1\cdot}$	$y_{2\cdot}$	...	$y_{i\cdot}$	...	$y_{k\cdot}$ $y_{\cdot\cdot}$

$$\text{Treatment S.S.} = \frac{y_{1.}^2}{r_1} + \frac{y_{2.}^2}{r_2} + \ldots \frac{y_{k.}^2}{r_k} - \frac{y_{..}^2}{n}$$

$$= \sum_{i=1}^{k} \frac{y_{i.}^2}{r_i} - \text{C.F.}$$

$$\text{Total S.S.} = \sum_{i=1}^{k} \sum_{j=1}^{r_i} y_{ij}^2 - \text{C.F.}$$

$$\text{Error S.S.} = \sum_{i=1}^{k} \sum_{j=1}^{r_i} y_{ij}^2 - \sum_{i=1}^{k} \frac{y_{i.}^2}{r_i}$$

Q. 51. *Given the following data obtained from a completely randomized design with four treatments, analyse the given data and draw conclusion about the equality of treatment effects.*

Treatments			
T_1	T_2	T_3	T_4
20.9	23.7	13.2	5.8
12.4	14.4	10.2	6.1
10.1	9.0	5.1	4.8
4.2			1.5

Ans. Here we test,

$$H_0: \tau_1 = \tau_2 = \tau_3 = \tau_4$$

vs. H_1: at least two of them are not equal.

Treatment Total,

$$T_1 = 47.6,\ T_2 = 47.1,\ T_3 = 28.5,\ T_4 = 18.2$$

and $G = 141.4$

Number of replications for treatments T_1, T_2, T_3 and T_4 are, $r_1 = 4$, $r_2 = r_3 = 3$ and $r_4 = 4$ respectively and $n = 14$.

$$y_{..} = 141.4,\ \text{C.F.} = \frac{(141.4)^2}{14} = 1428.14$$

$$\text{Total S.S.} = (20.9^2 + 12.4^2 + \ldots + 1.5^2) - \text{C.F.}$$
$$= 1960.70 - 1428.14$$
$$= 532.56$$

Treatment S.S.

$$= \frac{47.6^2}{4} + \frac{47.1^2}{3} + \frac{28.5^2}{3} + \frac{18.2^2}{4} - \text{C.F.}$$
$$= 1659.47 - 1428.14$$
$$= 231.33$$

$$\text{Error S.S.} = 532.56 - 231.33$$
$$= 301.23$$

ANOVA Table

Source of Variation	*d.f.*	*S.S.*	*M.S.*	*F-value*
Treatments	3	231.33	77.11	2.56
Error	10	301.23	30.12	
Total	13	532.56		

Tabulated value of $F_{.05\,(3,\,10)} = 3.71$ which is greater than the calculated value of $F = 2.56$.

Hence, we accept H_0 which means that the four treatments are equally effective.

Q. 52. *Is there any equivalence between the analysis of data in completely randomized design with two treatments and student's t-test?*

Ans. Yes, in analysis of variance with two treatments we test H_0: $\tau_1 = \tau_2$ under Model-I by F-test and in student t-test, we test H_0: $\mu_1 = \mu_2$ where $\mu_1 = \tau_1 + \mu$ and $\mu_2 = \tau_2 + \mu$.

Q. 53. *What do you understand by sub-sampling in experimental designs?*

Ans. If more than one determinations are made on each experimental unit pertaining to the same character, such a process of collecting data is known as sub-sampling. For example, one may be interested in determining the nitrogen uptake in plants and may take a sample of five plants in a plot at various positions and determine the nitrogen uptake for each sample; one may be interested in knowing the infestation of insects per plant and may select samples of 3 plants at five positions in a plot and count the number of insects on each sampled plant. All such type of studies in experimental designs are called *sub-sampling.*

Q. 54. *What changes are undergone in the analysis of data of a completely randomised design with sub-sampling?*

Ans. If n_{ij} determinations are made on the jth experimental unit receiving the ith treatment and h_{iju} is the uth sample taken from j^{th} unit receiving the ith treatment, the model for CRD with usual notations is,

$$y_{iju} = \mu + \tau_i + \varepsilon_{ij} + \eta_{iju}$$

for $i = 1, 2, ..., k$

$j = 1, 2, ..., r_i$

$u = 1, 2, ..., n_{ij}$

The ANOVA table contains one more source of variation than the usual one, *i.e.,* sampling error. ANOVA table for CRD for Model-I and Model-II is presented below (Table 5) with two additional columns giving expected mean squares.

$$m_2 = \frac{\sum_{i=1}^{k}\left(\sum_{j=1}^{r_i} n_{ij}^2 \Big/ \sum_{j=1}^{r_i} n_{ij}\right) - \sum_{i=1}^{k}\sum_{j=1}^{r_i} n_{ij}^2 \Big/ N}{k-1}$$

$$m_3 = \frac{N - \sum_{i=1}^{k}\left(\sum_{j=1}^{r_i} n_{ij}\right)^{\!2}\Big/ N}{k-1}$$

In case, an equal number of determinations say, m are made from each experimental unit, then the expected mean squares in the above ANOVA table clearly reveal that treatment M.S. be tested against experimental error.

Q. 55. *Can the value of F be less than unity? If so, what are its implications?*

Ans. The expected mean squares lead us to conclude that F-value in ANOVA table for component factors is never less than unity. But in actual working it is quite probable that F-value turns out to be less than unity. If it happens, we should review our whole process rather than concluding that H_0: $\tau_i = 0$ or $H_0 : \sigma_\tau^2 = 0$ is accepted.

If $F_{\alpha;(\nu_1,\nu_2)}$ is so small that $F' = 1/F_{\alpha;(\nu_1,\nu_2)}$ is significant, what should we conclude at this juncture?

Table–5

Source of variation	*d.f.*	*S.S.*	*M.S.*	*F-value*	*Model-I Expected M.S.*	*Model-II Expected M.S.*
Treatments	k-1	T_{yy}	T	T/E	$\sigma_\eta^2 + m_2\sigma_e^2 + \sum_{i=1}^{k}\left(\sum_{j=1}^{r_i} n_{ij}\right)^2 \frac{\tau_i^2}{k-1}$	$\sigma_\eta^2 + m_2\sigma_e^2 + m_3\sigma_\tau^2$
Exptl. error	n-k	E_{yy}	E		$\sigma_\eta^2 + m_1\sigma_e^2$	$\sigma_\eta^2 + m_1\sigma_e^2$
Sampling error	N-n	S_{yy}	S_y		σ_η^2	σ_η^2
Total	N-1					

where, $\sum_{i=1}^{k}\sum_{j=1}^{r_i} n_{ij} = N$ and $\sum_{i=1}^{k} r_i = n$

$$m_1 = \frac{N - \sum_{i=1}^{k}\left(\sum_{j=1}^{r_i} n_{ij}^2 \Big/ \sum_{j=1}^{r_i} n_{ij}\right)}{\sum_{i=1}^{k}(r_i - 1)}$$

We have no hypothesis at our disposal which can be rejected on the basis of the value of F'. In this situation, it looks germane that the postulated statistical model be rejected as such. Now, we should further make a thorough search for the following anomalies:

(*i*) We should confirm whether the postulated linear model is true to the existing situation or not.

(*ii*) Check whether the proper randomization had been adopted or not.

(*iii*) One must check whether observations follow the law of normality or not.

(*iv*) We must test whether the variances of subclasses are homogeneous or not.

Q. 56. *What do you understand by crossed classification?*

Ans. If every level of a factor *A* can be used in combination with every level of the other factor *B*, then such a situation is known as *crossed classification.* Here the factors have crossed each other and their interactions are the sub-classes or cells wherein the data arise. Even if the data for some cell does not exist, even then it remains crossed classification as it does not rule out the feasibility of the existence of that cell. For instance, one may be interested to know the effect of 3 levels of fertilizers on 4 varieties of wheat. Here we have 12 cells and will be able to get the effects of fertilizer levels, varieties and their interactions.

Q. 57. *When is a classification called nested or hierarchical classification?*

Ans. When we have a set of sampled units and from each sampled unit, a sub-sample is taken and from sub-sampled unit, a number of determinations are taken. *Such a process of repeated sampling and sub-sampling within each sampling unit is called nested or hierarchical classification.* For example, we may select some plant from a field, from each plant we may select a few leaves and on each leave we may do three estimations of calcium content. Such a classification will lead to nested or hierarchical classification.

When we consider the factors in an experiment in which all levels of a actor occur within each single level of some other factor, we should call these factors as *nested factors.* As an instance, in a plant breeding experiment if a researcher takes '*s*' species and n_i strains within each specie and study r_{ij} individuals per strain, the factors involved in this manner are called nested factors. As an other example, if we may take *s* sires, each sire is mated to a set of *d* dams and study r_{ij} siblings of *ds* sire-dam combinations, the factors involved in this experiment are called nested factors. "In short, the effects of a factor which are restricted to a single level of the other factor are said to be nested within that factor.

Q. 58. *Discuss the model for a two-factor nested design and its peculiarity and the analysis of variance table.*

Ans. Consider a two-factor experiment in which the factor *B* is nested under factor *A*. Let there be *a* levels of a factor *A* and *b* levels of factor *B*. The statistical model for such a design with *n* determinations on each unit is as follows:

$$y_{iju} = \mu + \alpha_i + \beta_{j(i)} + \varepsilon_{iju} \qquad (1)$$

for $i = 1, 2, ..., a$

$j = 1, 2, ..., b$

$u = 1, 2, ..., n$

where,

μ – true mean effect

α_i – true effect of the jth level of *A*

$\beta_{j(i)}$ – true effect of the jth level of *B* nested under i^{th} level of *A*.

The peculiar feature of this nested experiment is that the interaction effect of *A* and *B* cannot be evaluated. Analysis of variance Table-6 for the above model of the nested design is given on page 568.

Mean square for *A* is to be tested against *B* or *E* will depend on the model specification.

Q. 59. *Describe a randomized complete block design.*

Ans. In common parlance, randomised complete block design is spoken as *randomized block design* (R.B.D.). The word *complete* is implicit.

If experimental units show one way variation, the effect of this kind of heterogeneity is taken care of by grouping the experimental units into blocks in such a way that the units are homogeneous within a block but there is every possibility of heterogeneity amongst blocks.

Each block consists of as many experimental units as the number of treatments.

Source of Variation	d.f.	S.S.	M.S.	F-value
Among A's	$a-1$	$\frac{1}{nb}\sum_i y_{i..}^2 - \frac{y_{...}^2}{abn} = A_{yy}$	$\frac{A_{yy}}{a-1} = A_y$	A_y/B_y or E_y
Among B's within A's	$a(b-1)$	$\sum_i\left\{\sum_j \frac{y_{ij.}^2}{n} - \frac{y_{i..}^2}{nb}\right\} = B_{yy}$	$\frac{B_{yy}}{a(b-1)} = B_y$	B_y/E_y
Experimental error (with determinations)	$ab(n-1)$	$\sum_i\sum_j\left\{\sum_u y_{iju}^2 - \frac{y_{ij.}^2}{n}\right\} = E_{yy}$	$\frac{E_{yy}}{ab(n-1)} = E_y$	
Total	$abn-1$	$\sum_i\sum_j\sum_u y_{iju}^2 - \frac{y_{...}^2}{abn}$		

The treatments are allocated randomly to the experimental units within each block independently such that each treatment occurs once. So each treatment is replicated as many times as the number of blocks or the number of blocks are chosen to be equal to the number of replications for the treatments.

In this design all treatments are equireplicated. Sometimes blocks are also termed as replications.

Randomized block designs are used in field experiments where the soil fertility is varying in one direction. Blocks are always formed in a direction perpendicular to fertility gradient. In animal experiments, litters, pens or cages may be taken as blocks each containing similar animals within the pen and they may differ from pen to pen. An oven may form one block maintained at one temperature, while other one may form the other block maintained at some other temperature, etc.

Randomized block design is a *one restrictional design.*

As a word of caution, one should form the groups or blocks in respect of the observable character or variable which is most likely to influence the character(s) under study.

The layout of a randomised block design with five treatments and four blocks can be of the kind given ahead:

Block-1	Block-2	Block-3	Block-4
A	B	E	C
C	D	D	A
D	A	B	D
E	C	A	E
B	E	C	B

Q. 60. *Enumerate the advantages of a randomized complete block design over a C.R.D.*

Ans. Randomized complete block design is superior to completely randomized design in many respects as delineated below:

(*i*) Blocking reduces the sum of squares due to experimental error. So it increases the efficiency of the design as compared to C.R.D.

(*ii*) The design is feasible with any number of treatments and blocks subject to the basic requirements of the design. For instance, there should be at least two blocks to provide an estimate of error variance and a test of significance.

(*iii*) The number of replicates should be enough to contribute at least 12 d.f. to error.

(*iv*) Control treatments can easily be included without causing any complications in the analysis of data.

(*v*) The statistical analysis is simple and less time consuming.

(*vi*) The problem of one or two missing observations can easily be tackled.

(*vii*) W.G. Cochran found that error mean square for R.B.D. was 60 per cent to that of C.R.D. error mean square.

(*viii*) Completely randomized design require ten replicates to get the same amount of information as we get from six replicates in randomized complete block design.

Q. 61. *Are there any drawbacks of randomized block design?*

Ans. Randomized block design suffers from certain weaknesses as no design is perfect in itself. The weaknesses are as follows:

(*i*) It cannot accommodate a large number of treatments since in this situation, the homogeneity of groups or blocks is always in jeopardy.

(*ii*) In many situations, the criterion for blocking or grouping is not easily selectable.

(*iii*) Usually the blocks are not as homogeneous as they are taken to be.

Q. 62. *Discuss the statistical model for randomized block design with one observation per experimental unit.*

Ans. Linear statistical model for randomized block design having k treatments and b blocks with one observation per experimental unit is,

$$y_{ij} = \mu + \tau_i + \beta_j + \varepsilon_{ij} \qquad (1)$$

for $i = 1, 2, ..., k$

$j = 1, 2, ..., b$

where, μ – the true mean effect *i.e.* a constant

τ_i – the true effect of the ith treatment

β_j – the true effect of the jth block

ε_{ij} – the true effect of the experimental unit receiving the ith treatment in j^{th} block.

Also, $\sum_{j=1}^{b} \beta_j = 0$ and $\varepsilon_{ij} \sim$ NID $(0, \sigma_e^2)$

Linear equation (1) with respect to the treatment effect τ_i will represent the Model-I if $\sum_{i=1}^{k} \tau_i = 0$ and Model-II if $\tau_i \sim$ NID $(0, \sigma_\tau^2)$

Q. 63. *Present the analysis of variance table for a randomized block design with k treatments and b blocks with one observation per experimental unit.*

Ans. The analysis of variance table for a randomized block design having k treatments and b blocks in case of one observation per experimental unit is given below with two additional columns giving the expected mean squares under Model-I and Model-II.

From the ANOVA Table-7 it is easily deducible that:

(*i*) the experimental error mean square is appropriate to perform F-test for blocks as well as for treatments.

Table - 7

Source of variation	*d.f.*	*S.S.*	*M.S.*	*F-value*	*Model-I Expected M.S.*	*Model-II Expected M.S.*
Blocks	$b-1$	B_{yy}	$\frac{B_{yy}}{b-1} = B_y$	B_y / E_y	$\sigma_e^2 + k \sum_{j=1}^{b} \frac{\beta_j^2}{b-1}$	$\sigma_e^2 + k\sigma_\beta^2$
Treatments	$k-1$	T_{yy}	$\frac{T_{yy}}{k-1} = T_y$	T_y / E_y	$\sigma_r^2 + b \sum_{i=1}^{b} \frac{\tau_i^2}{k-1}$	$\sigma_e^2 + b\sigma_\tau^2$
Experimental Error	$(b-1) \times (k-1)$	E_{yy}	$\frac{E_{yy}}{(b-1)(k-1)} = E_y$		σ_e^2	σ_e^2
Total	$bk-1$					

(*ii*) the error degrees of freedom are the product of the blocks and treatments degrees of freedom.

Q. 64. *For the observations of a randomized block design with k treatments and b blocks presented below, give the formulae for calculating the sum of squares required for analysis of variance of data.*

Table - 8

Treatments	*Blocks*						*Total*
	B_1	B_2	...	B_j	...	B_b	
T_1	y_{11}	y_{12}	...	y_{1j}	...	y_{1b}	$y_{1.}$
T_2	y_{21}	y_{22}	...	y_{2j}	...	y_{2b}	$y_{2.}$
⋮	⋮	⋮	⋮	⋮	⋮	⋮	⋮
T_i	y_{i1}	y_{i2}	...	y_{ij}	...	y_{ib}	$y_{i.}$
⋮	⋮	⋮	⋮	⋮	⋮	⋮	⋮
T_k	y_{k1}	y_{k2}	...	y_{kj}	...	y_{kb}	$y_{k.}$
Total	$y_{.1}$	$y_{.2}$	...	$y_{.j}$	...	$y_{.b}$	$y_{..}$

Ans. S.S. due to correction for mean, *i.e.*, correction factor (C.F.) = y^2/bk.

$$\text{Block S.S.} = \frac{1}{k}\{y_{.1}^2 + y_{.2}^2 + ... + y_{.b}^2\} - \frac{y_{..}^2}{bk}$$

$$= \frac{1}{k}\sum_{j=1}^{b} y_{.j}^2 - \frac{y_{..}^2}{bk}$$

$$\text{Treatment S.S.} = \frac{1}{b}\{y_{1.}^2 + y_{2.}^2 + ... + y_{k.}^2\} - \frac{y_{..}^2}{bk}$$

$$= \frac{1}{b}\sum_{i=1}^{k} y_{i.}^2 - \frac{y_{..}^2}{bk}$$

$$\text{Total S.S.} = \sum_{i=1}^{k}\sum_{j=1}^{b} y_{ij}^2 - y^2_{..}/bk$$

Error S.S. = Total S.S. – Block S.S. – Treat S.S.

$$= \sum_{i=1}^{k}\sum_{j=1}^{b} y_{ij}^2 - \frac{1}{k}\sum_{j=1}^{b} y_{.j}^2 - \frac{1}{b}\sum_{i=1}^{k} y_{i.}^2 + y^2_{..}/bk$$

Q. 65. *How can the relative efficiency of a randomized block design relative to a completely randomized design be calculated?*

Ans. Consider a R.B.D. with k treatments and b blocks. Also let B and E be the block and Error M.S. respectively. The relative efficiency (R.E.) of R.B.D. relative to C.R.D. utilising the same experimental material is,

$$\text{R.E.} = \frac{\left(\frac{n_2+1}{n_2+3}\right)\frac{1}{\text{Error M.S. for RBD}}}{\left(\frac{n_1+1}{n_1+3}\right)\frac{1}{\text{Error M.S. for CRD}}}$$

$$= \frac{(n_1+3)(n_2+1)\times \text{Error M.S. for CRD}}{(n_1+1)(n_2+3)\times \text{Error M.S. for RBD}}$$

where $n_1 = k(b-1)$, $n_2 = (k-1)(b-1)$.

Error mean square E_1 of a C.R.D. with the same experimental material as in R.B.D. is equal to,

$$E_1 = \frac{(b-1)B_y + b(k-1)E_y}{(bk-1)}$$

Thus,

$$\text{R.E.} = \frac{\{(k-1)(b-1)+1\}\{k(b-1)+3\}E_1}{\{(k-1)(b-1)+3\}\{k(b-1)+1\}E}$$

Q. 66. *In what way can the analysis of data of a randomized block design having one missing value be carried out?*

Ans. If during the process of experimentation, the response value from one experimental unit is lost for whatsoever reason, it cannot be neglected as the data do not conform to the pattern which was originally postulated. Hence, the missing value is estimated first and then analysis of variance is carried out in the usual manner with a little modification that one d.f. is reduced from total d.f. which results into the reduction of one d.f. for error.

F.E. Allan and J. Wishart were the first who proposed a formula in 1930 to estimate the missing value. The same formula was reaffirmed by F. Yates in 1933 proving that their formula is one which Yates obtained on minimising error sum of square. The method of estimating one missing value is very simple. Substitute x for the missing value and analyse the data as if all observations were present. Obviously, the error sum of square shall be involving x. This sum of square is minimised as it is always our endeavour to minimize error variance. With this aim, differentiate error sum of square with respect to x and equate it to zero. Solving the equation for x, we obtain the estimated value of x.

Suppose the missing value is occurring for the ith treatment in j^{th} block of a randomized block design having k treatments and b blocks.

Let $y'_{i.}$ be the total of all available values for the ith treatment and $y'_{.j}$, the total of the jth block of available value and $y'_{..}$ be total of all observations ignoring the missing value. The estimated value for the missing observation by the method of least squares is,

$$\hat{x} = \frac{by'_{.j} + ky'_{i.} - y'_{..}}{(k-1)(b-1)}$$

After inserting the value for the missing observation, the analysis of variance is carried out in the usual manner with three modifications.

(*i*) Reduce the total d.f. by one which consequently reduces error d.f. by one.

(*ii*) It has been found that there is an upward bias in treatment sum of square obtained after inserting the missing value. Hence, a correction is suggested for this bias. A quantity,

$$C_{TT} = \frac{(ky'_{i.} + y'_{.j} - y'_{..})^2}{k(k-1)(b-1)^2}$$

$$= \frac{\{y'_{.j} - (k-1)\hat{x}\}^2_{..}}{k(k-1)}$$

is subtracted from the treatment sum of square. This correction rules out the possibility of treatments being declared significant when actually they are not.

(*iii*) Also the standard error of the difference between a treatment mean having the missing value and any other treatment mean is equal to,

$$\text{S.E}'. = \sqrt{s_e^2\left\{\frac{2}{b} + \frac{k}{b(b-1)(k-1)}\right\}}$$

where s_e^2 is the error mean square.

Q. 67. *What procedure should be adopted for analysis of data of a randomised block design having more than one missing value?*

Ans. Many formulae were developed by various workers to estimate the missing values in various situations. But, the one usually adopted is the iterative method due to F. Yates in 1933. Under this procedure one missing value is substituted by x and the rest missing values by guess estimate which is generally the mean of all available values. The value of x is estimated by the formula for one missing value which with usual notations is,

$$\hat{x} = \frac{by'_{.j} + ky'_{i.} - y'_{..}}{(b-1)(k-1)}$$

As a next step substitute the estimated value for all missing values except one out of the remaining missing values and repeat the process. The process is continued till all missing values are estimated. In this way we obtain one set of estimated values. Repeat the whole process until the estimated values are established for each of the unit having missing value. The experience tells that it generally requires three cycles of estimation.

Another suitable approach is to estimate the missing value through analysis of covariance technique. Analysis of covariance is carried out by considering the values of the dummy variables. Let us consider the case of two or more missing values. In this situation, a value 0 is assigned to the dummy variable for which the observations are present and –1 to the missing plots. Also all missing values are taken to be zero during analysis of covariance. The estimation of missing values through analysis of covariance is due to *M.S. Bartlett*.

Q. 68. *Grain yield per plant (gms) of maize of nine varieties in a randomized block design were as* *tabulated below:*

Varieties	*Rep. I*	*Rep. II*	*Rep. III*
V_1	21.0	20.0	19.5
V_2	19.0	18.0	18.5
V_3	18.5	18.0	18.9
V_4	27.5	X	27.0
V_5	31.0	32.5	32.6
V_6	31.5	30.5	32.0
V_7	25.3	25.0	26.6
V_8	39.0	40.0	38.5
V_9	39.0	38.5	40.0

Analyse the experimental data having one missing value and interpret the result.

Ans. Variety totals, replication totals and grand total are first calculated which are as follows:

$V_1 = 60.5$, $V_2 = 55.5$, $V_3 = 55.4$, $V_4' = 54.5$, $V_5 = 96.1$, $V_6 = 94.0$, $V_7 = 76.9$, $V_8 = 117.5$, $V_9 = 117.5$;

$R_1 = 251.8$, $R_2' = 222.5$, $R_3 = 253.6$ and $G' = 727.9$

The estimate of the missing value X is obtained by the formula,

$$\hat{X} = \frac{k\tau_i' + b\beta_j' - G'}{(k-1)(b-1)}$$

where $y_{i.}' = \tau_i'$; $y_{.j}' = \beta_j'$, $G' = y_{..}'$

Here $k = 9$, $b = 3$, $\tau_i' = 54.5$, $\beta_j' = 222.5$ and $G' = 727.9$

$$\hat{X} = \frac{9\times 54.5 + 3\times 222.5 - 727.9}{(9-1)(3-1)}$$

$$= \frac{430.10}{16}$$

$$= 26.9$$

Now we calculate the sum of squares.

$$\text{C.F.} = \frac{(727.9 + 26.9)^2}{27}$$

$$= 21100.85$$

$$\text{Total S.S.} = \sum_i \sum_j y_{ij}^2 - \text{C.F.}$$

$$= 22686.48 - 21100.85$$

$$= 1585.63$$

$$\text{Replication S.S.} = \frac{1}{9}\sum_{j=1}^{3} R_j^2 - \text{C.F.}$$

$$= 21101.84 - 21100.85$$

$$= 0.99$$

$$\text{Treat. S.S.} = \frac{1}{3}\sum_{i=1}^{9} V_i^2 - \text{C.F.}$$

$$= 22677.65 - 21100.85$$

$$= 1576.80$$

$$\text{Error S.S.} = 1585.63 - 1576.80 - 0.99$$

$$= 7.84$$

Correction for treatment S.S.,

$$C_{TT} = \frac{(kT_i' + B_j' - G')^2}{k(k-1)(b-1)^2}$$

$$= \frac{(9\times 54.5 + 222.5 - 727.9)^2}{9\times 8\times 4}$$

$$= 0.77$$

Thus, the corrected treatment S.S.

$$= 1576.80 - 0.77$$

$$= 1576.03$$

Analysis of variance table

Source of Variance	*d.f.*	*S.S.*	*M.S.*	*F-value*
Replications	2	0.99	0.495	< 1 (NS)
Treatments	8	1576.03	197.00	343.61**
Error	15	8.61	0.574	
Total	25	1585.63		

NS : Non-significant.

**Significant at 1 per cent level of significance.

(*a*) The standard Error of the difference between two-treatment means not involving the missing value,

$$\text{S.E}_d = \sqrt{\frac{2s_e^2}{r}} = \sqrt{\frac{2\times 0.574}{3}}$$

$$= 0.619\text{/plant}$$

(*b*) Standard error of the difference between two treatment means, one with missing value and an other mean is,

$$\text{S.E}_d = \sqrt{s_e^2\left[\frac{2}{b}+\frac{k}{b(b-1)(k-1)}\right]}$$

$$= \sqrt{0.574\left(\frac{2}{3}+\frac{9}{3\times 2\times 8}\right)}$$

$$= 0.70\text{/plant}$$

Critical difference for the two treatment means not involving the treatment having missing value,

$$\text{C.D}_1 = \text{S.E}_d \times t_{0.05\times 15}$$
$$= 0.619 \times 2.131$$
$$= 1.319$$

Critical difference for the two-treatment means out of which one-treatment (variety) has a missing value,

$$\text{C.D}_2 = 0.70 \times 2.131$$
$$= 1.492$$

There is a highly significant difference between varieties since the calculated value of $F = 343.61$ is greater than the tabulated value of F at $\alpha = 0.01$ and (8, 15) d.f., *i.e.*, 4.00. Now we find which of the pairs of treatment means differ significantly. The variety means are arranged in ascending order and displayed below. Now comparing the difference between variety means by the appropriate critical difference (C.D.) value, the varieties which do not differ significantly are underlined.

$\bar{V}_2$	$\bar{V}_3$	$\bar{V}_1$	$\bar{V}_7$	$(\bar{V}_4)$	$\bar{V}_6$	$\bar{V}_5$	$\bar{V}_8$	$\bar{V}_9$
18.5	18.5	20.17	25.63	27.13	31.33	32.03	39.17	39.17

Q. 69. *Give statistical model and analysis of variance table for the analysis of data of a randomized block design under sub-sampling.*

Ans. In many situations, two or more determinations are made for the same characteristic on each experimental unit. Such a process of obtaining several observations on each unit is termed as sub-sampling.

The appropriate statistical model for a randomized block design with k treatments and b blocks in which n observations are taken on each experimental unit is,

$$y_{iju} = \mu + \tau_i + \beta_j + \varepsilon_{ij} + \eta_{iju}$$

for $i = 1, 2, ..., k$

$j = 1, 2 ..., b$

$u = 1, 2, ..., n$

The analysis of variance table for the above model adopting standard notations is as given in Table-9. The ANOVA table contains an extra column meant for depicting the expected mean squares under Model-I.

Expected mean squares in the above ANOVA table clearly reveal that experimental error is appropriate to test the hypothesis $H_0 : \tau_i = 0$ and $H_0 : \beta_j = 0$ for treatment effects and block effects respectively.

Note. (1) The sum of squares can be calculated in the usual manner.

(2) Under model-II, the expected mean square for blocks and treatments will be $\sigma_n^2 + n\sigma_e^2 + kn\,\sigma_\beta^2$ and $\sigma_n^2 + n\sigma_e^2 + bn\,\sigma_\tau^2$ respectively and all other terms remain the same.

Q. 70. *How can be sampling error be utilised in the test of significance about treatments?*

Ans. A.E. Paull in 1950 (Ann. Math. Stat.) initiated the idea of *preliminary test of significance* (P.T.S.) concerning the hypothesis $H_0' : \sigma_e^2 = 0$. Here experimental error mean square is tested against

Table - 9

Source of variation	*d.f.*	*S.S.*	*M.S.*	*F-value*	*Expected M.S.*
Blocks	$b-1$	B_{yy}	$\frac{B_{yy}}{b-1}=B_y$	B_y/E_y	$\sigma_\eta^2+n\sigma_e^2+kn\sum_{j=1}^{b}\frac{\beta_j^2}{b}-1$
Treatments	$k-1$	T_{yy}	$\frac{T_{yy}}{k-1}=T_y$	T_y/E_y	$\sigma_\eta^2+n\sigma_e^2+bn\sum_{i=1}^{k}\frac{\tau_i^2}{k-1}$
Experimental Error	$(b-1)(k-1)$	E_{yy}	$\frac{E_{yy}}{(b-1)(k-1)}=E_y$		$\sigma_\eta^2+n\sigma_e^2$
Sampling Error	$bk(n-1)$	S_{yy}	$\frac{S_{yy}}{bk(n-1)}=S_y$		σ_η^2

sampling error mean square by F-test. In case H_0' is accepted, it is always preferable to pool the sum of squares due to experimental error and sampling error and dividing this pooled sum of square by their pooled degrees for freedom. Now use this new pooled mean square for testing H_0: $\tau_i = 0$. Again if H_0' is rejected, then do not pool the two error sum of squares and test $H_0: \tau_i = 0$ against experimental error M.S. In this way, we have performed a F-test for testing the significance of experimental error variance against sampling error variance prior to testing the final hypothesis. Such a test is referred to as *preliminary test of significance.*

Now one pertinent question arises: What would happen if we always pool the two errors or never pool them? Why depend on P.T.S.? To reply these questions, we will follow Paull. Supposed the researcher decides to always pool the two mean squares without performing P.T.S. This will work well if per chance $H_0' : \sigma_e^2 = 0$ is true. In case, H_0' is not true and pooling is done, in that situation, the pooled mean square in final F-test tend to be too small and the final F-test produces a significant result even though $H_0 : \tau_i = 0$ is true. Such a result is very misguiding. Quoting Paull, "a test which the research worker thinks is being made at the 5 per cent level might actually be at, say, the 47 per cent level." Thus a P.T.S. guards against such an eventuality.

Another advantage of a P.T.S. is that it increases the power of the final F-test relative to the never pool test. So a P.T.S. is a good tool in the hands of a researcher. Of course it is preferable to perform a P.T.S. at some higher level of significance than 5 per cent as the situation may call for. However, a researcher will not go far wrong if he decides to follow the rule of never pooling rather than always pooling. So pooling be done only when P.T.S. permits, otherwise not.

Q. 71. *Discuss a Latin square design.*

Ans. A Latin square is a balanced two-way classification scheme. This arrangement was originally presented through Latin letters. So it is called a *Latin square.* When these letters represent some treatments of an experiment it is known as *Latin square design.* A Latin square design of a 3 × 3 arrangement can be of the type as,

A	*B*	*C*		*A*	*C*	*B*
C	*A*	*B*		*B*	*A*	*C*
B	*C*	*A*		*C*	*B*	*A*

Arrangement (*a*)   Arrangement (*b*)

A Latin square design of order four exhibits the following type of balance of the letters (treatments).

A	*B*	*C*	*D*		*C*	*D*	*A*	*B*
B	*C*	*D*	*A*		*D*	*A*	*B*	*C*
C	*D*	*A*	*B*		*A*	*B*	*C*	*D*
D	*A*	*B*	*C*		*B*	*C*	*D*	*A*

Arrangement (*c*)   Arrangement (*d*)

In the same way, Latin square arrangements of any order can be given.

A Latin square design holds the following properties:

(*i*) Number of rows, columns and treatments are all equal.

(*ii*) Each letter (treatment) occurs once and only once in each row and in each column.

(*iii*) Each row and each column is a complete block.

(*iv*) A letter in $(i, j)^{th}$ position also occurs in $(j, i)^{th}$ position.

(*v*) A Latin square with p rows and p columns is called a $p \times p$ Latin square or a Latin square of order p.

(*vi*) Two Latin squares are said to be *conjugate* if one can be obtained by interchanging rows and columns of the other. Arrangements (*a*) and (*b*) are *conjugate* Latin squares whereas (*c*) and (*d*) are not.

(*vii*) A Latin square is said to be *self-conjugate square* if the arrangement of letters in rows and columns is same, e.g.,

$$\begin{matrix} A & B & C \\ B & C & A \\ C & A & B \end{matrix}$$

(*viii*) A Latin square in which the letters (numerals) in first row and first column occur in alphabetical (numerical) order is said to be in *standard form* or a *reduced Latin square.*

(*ix*) Latin square design is a two restrictional design.

(*x*) The sets of Latin squares formed by permuting each of the three factors, rows, columns and treatments (not necessarily all different) are called *adjugate sets*.

Q. 72. *How many Latin squares can be formed with p letters.*

Ans. With p letters there will be in all $p!\,(p-1)!$ arrangements for every one standard square (self conjugate) including the standard square itself.

So if there are 4 standard Latin squares of order 4×4, there will be in all $4 \times 4!\,(4-1)! = 576$ Latin squares.

Q. 73. *What is the importance of Latin square design?*

Ans. There are many situations in which two-directional variation has to be controlled to have valid estimates or comparisons of treatments. Such type of control is well maintained through a Latin square design. For example, a land shows a fertility gradient in two perpendicular directions. In this situation, two way variation in fertility is well taken care of by considering the variation along rows and columns in a Latin square design. In an animal feed experiment, all cows of the same breed may be taken along rows and same lactation along columns. Latin square designs are frequently used in field, greenhouse, industrial, laboratory, medical, psychology, educational, animal experiments, etc.

Q. 74. *What are the advantages of a Latin square design?*

Ans. The advantages of a Latin square design over C.R.D. and R.B.D. are:

(*i*) A Latin square design is able to control two way variability which is not possible in C.R.D. or R.B.D. This brings reduction in error mean square.

(*ii*) The analysis of data does not entail any complications.

(*iii*) The estimation and analysis in case of missing data is simple.

(*iv*) Analytical procedures are available for the analysis of data when two or more rows, columns or treatments are missing. These cases were dealt by F. Yates and R.W. Hale in 1939 (J. Roy. Stat. Soc.)

(*v*) A 4×4 Latin square is as efficient as a randomized block design with five replications and an equal number of treatments.

Q. 75. *What are the dements of a Latin square design?*

Ans. Some of the drawbacks of the Latin square design are given below:

(*i*) Latin square design can accommodate a limited number of treatments. As a practice, more than ten treatments are seldom used.

(*ii*) A Latin square for less than five treatments does not provide adequate degrees of freedom for experimental error.

(*iii*) A Latin square design of order 2, 3, and 4 may not be as efficient as a C.R.D. or R.B.D. with same number of replications.

Q. 76. *Elucidate mutually orthogonal Latin squares.*

Ans. Two Latin squares are said to be orthogonal if one square is superimposed over the other, the same pair of symbols occur once and only once in the composite square. Consider the following two squares of order three.

A	B	C
B	C	A
C	A	B

Square (*a*)

α	β	γ
γ	α	β
β	γ	α

Square (*b*)

If square (*a*) is superimposed over the square (*b*) or vice-versa, the composite square is as given below:

Aα	Bβ	Cγ
Bγ	Cα	Aβ
cβ	Aγ	Bα

Square (*c*)

Square (*c*) is such that each pair of Greek and Latin letters has occurred only once. Hence, squares (*a*) and (*b*) are mutually orthogonal. Square (*c*) is known as *Greaco-Latin square.*

In a 3 × 3 Greaco-Latin Square, the degrees of freedom will be partitioned as 2 d.f. each for rows, columns, Greek letters and Latin letters which totals to 8 d.f. Also there are nine experimental units in all leading to eight d.f. for total. So no more orthogonal Latin squares can exist. In this way for a 3 × 3 Latin square, there can only be two orthogonal Latin squares. Now we give a general rule for the existence of the possible number of mutually orthogonal Latin squares.

"For a Latin square of order p, where p is a prime number or a power of the prime number, there can be at the most a set of (p – 1) mutually orthogonal Latin squares (MOLS)".

In a set of MOLS, any two Latin squares are orthogonal to each other. For example, a complete set of orthogonal Latin squares of order 4 × 4 is given below:

I

A	B	C	D
B	A	D	C
C	D	A	B
D	C	B	A

II

A	B	C	D
C	D	A	B
D	C	B	A
B	A	D	C

III

A	B	C	D
D	C	B	A
B	A	D	C
C	D	A	B

Q. 77. *Give the layout of a 4 × 4 Greaco-Latin square with Greek letters α, β, γ, δ and Latin letters A, B, C and D.*

Ans. A Greaco-Latin square of order 4 × 4 can be as given below:

A α	B β	C γ	D δ
B δ	A γ	D β	C α
C β	D α	A γ	B γ
D γ	C δ	B α	A β

The above Greaco-Latin square is one arrangement out of 144 possible arrangements.

Q. 78. *Give statistical model and analysis of variance table for a Latin square of side k.*

Ans. Statistical model for a Latin square of side *k* with one observation per unit based on the assumptions:

(*i*) the row, column and treatment effects are additive.

(*ii*) the treatment effects do not interact with the row or column effects.

(*iii*) the errors are independently and identically distributed normally with mean 0 and a constant variance.

$$y_{ij(u)} = \mu + \rho_i + \gamma_j + \tau_u + \varepsilon_{ij(u)}$$

for $i = 1, 2, ..., k$

$j = 1, 2, ..., k$

$u = 1, 2, ..., k$

where μ is a true mean, ρ_i, γ_j and τ_u are the true effect of the ith row, j^{th} column and u^{th}

Table - 10

Source of variation	d.f.	S.S.	M.S.	F-value	Expected mean square	
					Model-I	Model-II
Rows	$k-1$	R_{yy}	$\frac{R_{yy}}{k-1}=R_y$	R_y/E_y	$\sigma_e^2+k\sum_i\frac{\rho_i^2}{k-1}$	$\sigma_e^2+k\sigma_\rho^2$
Columns	$k-1$	C_{yy}	$\frac{C_{yy}}{k-1}=C_y$	C_y/E_y	$\sigma_e^2+k\sum_j\frac{\gamma_j^2}{k-1}$	$\sigma_e^2+k\sigma_\gamma^2$
Treatments	$k-1$	T_{yy}	$\frac{T_{yy}}{k-1}=T_y$	T_y/E_y	$\sigma_e^2+k\sum_u\frac{\tau_u^2}{k-1}$	$\sigma_e^2+k\sigma_\tau^2$
Experimental error	$(k-1)\times(k-2)$	E_{yy}	$\frac{E_{yy}}{(k-1)(k-2)}=E_y$		σ_e^2	σ_e^2
Total	k^2-1	$\Sigma\Sigma y_{ij}^2-\text{C.F.}$				

treatment placed in $(i, j)^{\text{th}}$ position, respectively.

Under Model-I, the assumptions are,

$$\sum_{i=1}^{k}\rho_i=\sum_{j=1}^{k}\gamma_j=\sum_{u=1}^{k}\tau_u=0$$

Under Model-II, the assumptions are,

$$\rho_i\sim N(0,\sigma_\rho^2),\ \gamma_j\sim N(0,\sigma_\gamma^2),\ \tau_u\sim N(0,\sigma_\tau^2)$$

The analysis of variance table based on model (1) along with two extra columns for expected mean squares under Model-I and Model-II is as displayed above (Table-10).

Q 79. *How can the sum of squares for analysis of variance of a Latin square design of order k be calculated?*

Ans. Let R_i, C_j and T_u be the totals of the ith row j^{th} column and u^{th} treatment for $i, j, u = 1, 2, ..., k$. Also suppose G is the total of all the k^2 observations. Thus, the expressions for the sum of squares are:

$$\text{Sum of square due to } \mu = \text{C.F.} = \frac{G^2}{k^2}$$

$$\text{Row S.S.} = \frac{1}{k}(R_1^2+R_2^2+...+R_k^2)-\text{C.F.}=R_{yy}$$

$$\text{Column S.S.} = \frac{1}{k}(C_1^2+C_2^2+...C_k^2)-\text{C.F.}=C_{yy}$$

$$\text{Treatment S.S.} = \frac{1}{k}(T_1^2+T_2^2+...+T_k^2)-\text{C.F.}=T_{yy}$$

$$\text{Total S.S.} = \sum_i\sum_j y_{ij}^2-\text{C.F.}$$

$$\text{Error S.S.} = \text{Total S.S.} - R_{yy} - C_{yy} - T_{yy}$$

Q. 80. *How can the data with a single missing value of a k × k Latin square design be analysed?*

Ans. To analyse the data of a $k \times k$ Latin square design having one missing value, we first estimate the missing value by minimizing the error mean square as suggested by F. Yates in 1933 (Emp. J. Exp. Agr.). Under this procedure, substitute x for the missing value and analyse the data as if all observations are present. Obviously, the error sum of square involves x. To minimize the error variance, differentiate the expression for it with respect to x and equate it to zero. Solving this equation for x, we obtain the estimated value of x. Supposing that R', C' and T' are the totals for the row, column and treatment having the missing value and G' is the total of (k^2-1) available values, the estimated value of x is,

$$\hat{x}=\frac{k(R'+C'+T')-2G'}{(k-1)(k-2)}$$

Substitute the missing value and analyse the data in the usual manner with the following modifications.

(*i*) Decrease 1 d.f. from total d.f. which results into the decrease of 1 d.f. for error.

(*ii*) There is an upward bias in the treatment sum of squares. So, subtract the correction factor,

$$C_{TT} = \left\{\frac{(k-1)T' + R' + C' - G'}{(k-1)(k-2)}\right\}^2$$

from the calculated treatment sum of square. This provides the corrected treatment sum of square for use.

(*iii*) The standard error of the difference of the treatment mean having the missing value and any other treatment mean is.

$$\text{S.E.}' = \sqrt{s_e^2\left\{\frac{2}{k} + \frac{1}{(k-1)(k-2)}\right\}}$$

S.E.′ should be used while comparing such treatment means,

(*iv*) S.E. for any two treatments not having missing value is $\sqrt{2s_e^2/k}$.

Q. 81. *Give the expression for the relative efficiency of a Latin square design of order k over a completely randomized design.*

Ans. If we designate *R*, *C* and *E* for the row, column and error mean squares respectively, the relative efficiency of a Latin square of order *k* over completely randomized design using the same experimental material can be obtained by the expression,

$$\text{R.E.} = \frac{R + C + (k-1)E}{(k+1)E}$$

Q. 82. *How can we measure the relative efficiency of a Latin square design of side k relative to a randomized complete block design?*

Ans. If *R* and *E* denote the row and error mean square in a Latin square design respectively, the efficiency of a Latin square design of side *k* relative to a randomized complete block design using the same experimental material and taking the columns as blocks can be measured by the formula,

$$\text{R.E.} = \frac{R + (k-1)E}{kE}$$

If rows are used as blocks and *C* is the column mean square, then

$$\text{R.E.} = \frac{C + (k-1)E}{kE}$$

Q. 83. *A company wants to purchase cars for its own use. He has to select the make of the car out of the four makes A, B, C and D available in the market. For this he tries four cars of each make by assigning the cars to four drivers to run on four different routes. For this, he chooses a Latin squares design. The efficiency of cars is measured in terms of time in hours. The layout and time consumed is as given below:*

Routes	*Drivers*			
	1	*2*	*3*	*4*
1	18 (*C*)	12 (*D*)	16 (*A*)	20 (*B*)
2	26 (*D*)	34 (*A*)	25 (*B*)	*X* (*C*)
3	15 (*B*)	22 (*C*)	10 (*D*)	28 (*A*)
4	30 (*A*)	20 (*B*)	15 (*C*)	9 (*D*)

Analyse the experimental data and draw conclusions.

Ans. First we estimate the missing value by the formula,

$$\hat{x} = \frac{k(R' + C' + T') - 2G'}{(k-1)(k-2)}$$

From the given data,

$R' = 85$, $C' = 57$, $T' = 55$, $G' = 300$ and $k = 4$.

$$\hat{x} = \frac{4(85 + 57 + 55) - 2 \times 300}{3 \times 2}$$

$$= 31.33$$

$$= 31$$

Substituting the missing value, following values are obtained.

Row totals: $R_1 = 66$, $R_2 = 116$, $R_3 = 75$, $R_4 = 74$

Column totals: $C_1 = 89$, $C_2 = 88$, $C_3 = 66$, $C_4 = 88$

Car Makes totals: $A = 108$, $B = 80$, $C = 86$, $D = 57$

Treatment (cars) means: $\bar{A} = 27$, $\bar{B} = 20$, $\bar{C} = 21.5$, $\bar{D} = 14.25$

Grand total: $G = 331$

Now we calculate the sum of squares (S.S.).

$$\text{S.S. due to true mean} = \text{C.F.} = \frac{(331)^2}{16} = 6847.56$$

$$\text{Total S.S.} = (18^2 + 12^2 + ... + 9^2) - \text{C.F.} = 7741 - 6847.56 = 893.44$$

$$\text{S.S. due to routes} = \frac{1}{4}(66^2 + 116^2 + 75^2 + 74^2) - \text{C.F.}$$

$$= 7228.25 - 6847.56 = 380.69$$

S.S. due to Drivers

$$= \frac{1}{4}(89^2 + 88^2 + 66^2 + 88^2) - \text{C.F.}$$

$$= 6941.25 - 6847.66 = 93.69$$

$$\text{S.S. due to cars} = \frac{1}{4}(108^2 + 80^2 + 86^2 + 57^2) - \text{C.F.}$$

$$= 7177.25 - 6847.66 = 329.69$$

$$\text{S.S. due to error} = 893.44 - (380.69 + 93.69 + 329.69) = 89.37$$

Correction factor for bias in treatment S.S.,

$$C_{TT} = \frac{\{(k-1)T' + R' + C' - G'\}^2}{(k-1)^2 (k-2)^2}$$

$$= \frac{(3 \times 55 + 85 + 57 - 300)^2}{9 \times 4}$$

$$= 1.36$$

Corrected S.S. due to cars = 329.69 – 1.36 = 328.33

ANOVA Table

Source of variation	*d.f.*	*S.S.*	*M.S.*	*F-value*
Routes	3	380.69	126.89	6.99*
Drivers	3	93.69	31.23	1.72
Cars	3	328.33	109.44	6.03*
Error	5	90.73	18.15	
Total	14			

Tabulated value, $F_{.05\,(3,\,5)} = 5.41$

There is a significant difference among routes and cars as the calculated value is greater than the tabulated F-value of 5.41.

(*a*) Standard error of the difference between two treatment (car makes) means not involving the missing value $= \sqrt{\frac{2s_e^2}{k}}$

$$\text{S.E}_d = \sqrt{\frac{2 \times 18.15}{4}} = 3.01$$

(*b*) Standard error of the difference between two-treatment (car makes) means, one of which involves the missing value

$$= \sqrt{s_e^2 \left\{\frac{2}{k} + \frac{1}{(k-1)(k-2)}\right\}}$$

$$\text{S.E}'_d = \sqrt{18.15\left(\frac{2}{4} + \frac{1}{3 \times 2}\right)} = 3.48$$

Critical difference for two-treatment means not having missing value = $S.E_d \times t_{.05, 5}$

$$\text{C.D.} = 3.01 \times 2.571$$
$$= 7.74$$

Critical difference for the treatment C versus any other treatment = $S.E_d' \times t_{.05, 5}$

$$\text{C.D.} = 3.48 \times 2.571$$
$$= 8.94$$

Comparing the treatment means by the appropriate C.D. values, non-significant differences are underlined.

D	*B*	*C*	*A*
14.25	20	21.5	27

Result: Car D is significantly better than Car A. Rest all other cars are at par.

Q. 84. *What is meant by group of Latin squares and why are they required?*

Ans. It has been observed that a single 3 × 3 Latin square provides only 2 degrees of freedom for error, which is much less than required. Hence, a group of Latin squares is often used to have a sufficient degrees of freedom for error. In groups of experiments, generally lower order Latin squares are used, *i.e.*, 2 × 2 or 3 × 3 Latin squares.

For a group of Latin squares, either we have to take two or more Latin squares at the same experimental site or one Latin square at several locations. In both the situations, the Latin squares considered together for the purpose of analysis of data are said to be a group of Latin squares.

Q. 85. *Give the analysis of variance table for a group of m Latin squares of side k.*

Ans. The analysis of variance table for a group of m Latin squares of side k with usual notations will be as follows (Table-11).

The sum of squares in the following ANOVA table for various components can be calculated in the usual manner.

Q. 86. *Elucidate cross-over design.*

Ans. Balanced designs are often required in situations where number of experimental units are less than the number of treatments. To fulfil the requirement of balancing in such a case, several

Table-11

Source of Variation	*d.f.*	*S.S.*	*M.S.*	*F-value*
Squares (Locations)	$(m-1)$	S_{yy}	$\frac{S_{yy}}{m-1} = S_y$	S_y/E_y
Rows within squares	$m(k-1)$	R_{yy}	$\frac{R_{yy}}{m(k-1)} = R_y$	R_y/E_y
Columns within squares	$m(k-1)$	C_{yy}	$\frac{C_{yy}}{m(k-1)} = C_y$	C_y/E_y
Treatments	$(k-1)$	T_{yy}	$\frac{T_{yy}}{k-1} = T_y$	T_y/E_y
Treat. × squares	$(m-1)(k-1)$	T_{syy}	$\frac{T_{syy}}{(m-1)(k-1)} = T_{sy}$	T_{sy}/E_y
Residual within squares or Experimental Error	$m(k-1)(k-2)$	E_{yy}	$\frac{E_{yy}}{m(k-1)(k-2)} = E_y$	
Total	$mk^2 - 1$			

cycles in respect of periods are usually taken. The cross-over design is one such balanced design. Such balanced designs are covered under various names, *cross-over design, switch back design, reversal design, change over design*, etc. All these designs amount to same type of designs.

The cross-over designs are more appropriate for small number of treatments say, 2 or 3. For the construction of this design, the condition is that the number of replicates must be a multiple of the number of treatments.

The cross-over designs are suitable for the problems in which the treatments have carry-over or residual effect. Because this design is capable of measuring the direct effects of treatments by giving a proper rest period between two applications of treatments. Also with the help of this design one is able to measure direct as well as residual effects. In animal and biological experiments, the cross-over designs are frequently used. To remove inter-subject variability for the comparison of bio-availability due to drugs, the cross-over designs are often used.

Q. 87. *Give the layouts and analysis of variance tables for the cross-over design.*

Ans. Below we give two types of layouts of a cross-over design with two treatments and six subjects. In the layout (*a*), subjects are taken as replicates and in the layout (*b*), we make three Latin squares of order 2.

Rows	*Subject (Replicates)*					
	I	*II*	*III*	*IV*	*V*	*VI*
Period 1	*B*	*A*	*B*	*B*	*A*	*A*
Period 2	*A*	*B*	*A*	*A*	*B*	*B*

(*a*) Cross-over design

	Columns					
	Square I		*Square II*		*Square III*	
Row 1	*B*	*A*	*A*	*B*	*A*	*B*
Row 2	*A*	*B*	*B*	*A*	*B*	*A*

(*b*) 3 sets of 2 × 2 Latin squares

In both the layouts given above, each treatment occurs equal number of times in each row and a treatment is followed by the other treatment equal number of times. The difference between the two types of arrangements is apparent from the following break-up in ANOVA tables.

The cross-over design gives more degrees of freedom for error than a set of Latin squares. But the set of Latin squares gives an additional information. So, if the number of treatments is four or more, it is inadvisable to use a cross-over design in place of sets of Latin squares.

ANOVA: Cross-over design

Table - 12

Source of Variation	*d.f.*
Columns	5
Rows (Pd. 1 vs. Pd. 2)	1
Treatments	1
Error	4
Total	11

Three sets of Latin squares

Table - 13

Source of Variation	*d.f.*
Squares	2
Columns within squares	3
Rows within squares	3
Treatments	1
Error	2
Total	11

Q. 88. *What is meant by a factorial experiment?*

Ans. In many experiments, our interest does not confine in the effect of a factor alone but in its effect at various levels also. Further, the interest lies in estimating the effect of the levels of a factor at different levels of the other factor(s). The experiments, in which the effect of a number of levels of a factor is to be assessed in combination with levels of other factor(s) simultaneously are called *factorial experiments*. The name factorial experiment was given by F. Yates in 1926 (J. Ministry. Agr.). Before this, such experiments were called '*complex experiments*'. Here one should bear in mind that a factorial experiment is not a factorial design.

Q. 89. *What are symmetrical and asymmetrical factorials?*

Ans. Each factorial experiment involves the combinations of two or more factors each at two or more levels taken as treatments. If all factors have equal number of levels, they are called symmetrical factorial and otherwise asymmetrical factorial. For instance, an experiment with combination of 3 levels of nitrogen and 3 levels of phosphorous is a symmetrical, 3^2-factorial experiment and experiment with combinations of 3 levels of nitrogen and 2 levels of phosphorous is an asymmetrical, 3×2 factorial experiment.

A p^n-factorial means a symmetrical factorial experiment with n factors each at p levels. Also a $p_1 \times p_2 \times p_3 \times \ldots \times p_k$ factorial is an asymmetrical experiment with k factors each at the levels $p_1, p_2, p_3, \ldots, p_k$ respectively where all p's are not equal.

Q. 90. *What effects are measured in factorial experiments?*

Ans. Two types of effects are measured in factorial experiments namely (*i*) main effects (*ii*) interaction effect(s).

(*i*) The *main effect* of a factor may be defined as a measure of change in response due to change in the level of the factor averaged over all levels of all other factors in a factorial experiment.

(*ii*) The *interaction* between two factors may be defined as the failure of a factor to give the same response at various levels of the other factor(s).

In general, an interaction is an additional effect due to the combined effect of two or more factors.

Also the interaction AB between two factors A and B is same as BA. Further, the interaction between two factors is known as first order interaction, between three factors as second order interaction and so on.

Q. 91. *Write the set of orthogonal contrasts for main effects and interactions in* (*i*) 2^2 *factorial,* (*ii*) 2^3 *factorial.*

Ans. (*i*) Suppose A and B are two factors each at two levels 0 and 1. Let a_1 and a_0 denote the levels of factor A and similarly b_1 and b_0, the levels of factor B. For simplicity, we denote the higher level a_1 of A by a, lower case letter and its lower level a_0 by 1, *i.e.*, by its absence. In the same manner, b_1 by b and b_0 by, 1, *i.e.*, its absence. The contrasts can be specified for main effects and interaction as given below.

$$A = (a_1 - a_0)(b_1 + b_0)$$
$$= (a - 1)(b + 1)$$
$$= ab - b + a - (1)$$

Similarly,

$$B = (a_1 + a_0)(b_1 - b_0)$$
$$= (a + 1)(b - 1)$$
$$= ab + b - a - (1)$$

and

$$AB = (a_1 - a_0)(b_1 - b_0)$$
$$= (a - 1)(b - 1)$$
$$= ab - a - b + (1)$$

In a concised manner, the contrasts for main effects A, B and the interaction AB can be written as given below supposing that the factors with levels given in columns are attached with the signs for the corresponding factors.

Effects	*(1)*	*a*	*b*	*ab*
A	−	+	−	+
B	−	−	+	+
AB	+	−	−	+

Here it is worth pointing out that the coefficients for the contrast AB can be easily obtained by multiplying the coefficients of A and B contrasts.

(*ii*) In a manner similar to 2^2 factorials, the set of contrasts for main effects and interactions in 2^3 factorials can be given as follows:

Effects	*(I)*	*a*	*b*	*ab*	*c*	*ac*	*bc*	*abc*
A	−	+	−	+	−	+	−	+
B	−	−	+	+	−	−	+	+
AB	+	−	−	+	+	−	−	+
C	−	−	−	−	+	+	+	+
AC	+	−	+	−	−	+	−	+
BC	+	+	−	−	−	−	+	+
ABC	−	+	+	−	+	−	−	+

Q. 92. *Explain simple effect in a* 2^n *factorial experiment.*

Ans. Any factor at its lower level denoted by level 0 is called the first level of that factor and the higher level denoted by level 1 is called the second level of that factor.

The simple effect of a factor say 'A' is the difference measured at the second and first level of that factor at the same level of the other factors either first or second. For example, in a 2^2 factorial, the simple effect of A at the first level of B is $[(a) - (1)]$ and at the second level of B is $[(ab) - (b)]$.

Also it is trivial to verify that,

$$(a) - (1) = A - AB$$

$$(ab) - (b) = A + AB$$

Similarly, simple effect of B at the first level of A is $[(b) - (1)]$ and at the second level of A is $[(ab) - (a)]$. Also,

$$(b) - (1) = B - AB$$

$$(ab) - (a) = B + AB$$

The simple effect of the interaction AB is the difference of the simple effect A at the second and first levels of B or the difference of the simple effect of B at the second and first level of A, *i.e.*, the difference of the simple effect $(ab) - (b)$ and $(a) - (1)$ or $(ab) - (a)$ and $(b) - (1)$ which is equal to $2\ AB$.

In a similar manner in 2^3 factorial arrangement, the simple effect of A is calculated for each of the four combinations of the factor not containing a, *i.e.*, (1), b, c and bc. To be more specific, the simple effect of A,

at first level of B and C $= (a) - (1)$

at second level of B and C $= (abc) - (bc)$

at second level of B $= (ab) - (b)$

at second level of C $= (ac) - (c)$

Similarly, all other simple effects in a 2^3 factorial arrangement can be expressed.

Q. 93. *How can the estimates and sum of squares for the main effects and interactions be obtained through contrasts in 2^n factorial experiments?*

Ans. If we denote the total response measured due to a treatment in 2^n factorial arrangement by enclosing the treatment combination in parentheses, the estimate of a main effect and an interaction in 2^n factorials can be obtained by dividing the value of the contrast by $2^{n-1} \times r$, where each treatment is replicated r times. We can say that the estimate of the effect of any factor is the average of the simple effects.

For instance, the effect A in a 2^2 factorial is the average of the simple effects $(a) - (1)$ and $(ab) - (b)$. It can also be understood in this way.

$$A - AB = (a) - (1)$$

$$A + AB = (ab) - (b)$$

Adding these two simple effects, we get

$$2A = (ab) + (a) - (b) - (1)$$

or

$$A = \frac{1}{2}\ [(ab) + (a) - (b) - (1)]$$

So is true for other effects.

The right hand contrast in the bracket represents A and its divisor is 2 which is equal to 2^{2-1}. Further, 2^{n-1} is multiplied by r if each total is based on r replications. The same holds true for all other factors.

The sum of squares for any effect is equal to the square of the contrast value divided by $2^n \times r$. For example, if the total response values from 3 replication in an experiment for the treatment combinations are; $(1) = 15$, $(a) = 35$, $(b) = 25$, $(ab) = 20$, then the estimates of the effects are,

$$A = \frac{1}{2 \times 3}\ [(ab) + (a) - (b) - (1)]$$

$$A = \frac{1}{6}(20 + 35 - 25 - 15)$$

$$= 2.5$$

$$B = \frac{1}{2 \times 3}[(ab) - (a) + (b) - (1)]$$

$$= \frac{1}{6}[20 - 35 + 25 - 15]$$

$$= -5/6$$

$$AB = \frac{1}{2 \times 3}[(ab) - (a) - (b) + (1)]$$

$$= \frac{1}{6}(20 - 35 - 25 + 15)$$

$$= -25/6$$

Sum of squares can be calculated as,

$$\text{S.S. due to } A = \frac{1}{4 \times 3}\ [(ab) + (a) - (b) - (1)]^2$$

$$= \frac{1}{12} \times 15^2$$

$$= 18.75$$

$$\text{S.S. due to } B = \frac{1}{4 \times 3} [(ab) - (a) + (b) - (1)]^2$$

$$= \frac{1}{12} \times 5^2$$

$$= 25/12$$

$$\text{S.S. due to } AB = \frac{1}{4 \times 3} [(ab) - (a) - (b) + (1)^2$$

$$= \frac{1}{12} \times 25^2$$

$$= 625/12$$

Q. 94. *How can one estimate the effects and calculate the sum of squares in case of p^n experiments with the help of modulo technique?*

Ans. The contrasts can be written in a p^n factorial experiment for the main effects and interactions when $p = 2$ but it is not possible for $p > 2$. So a general approach has been discussed known as *modulo technique*. We define the modulo value as $x = m$ mod p. It means when x is divided by p, the remainder is m where m can take values from 0 to $p - 1$ and 0, 1, 2, ..., $p - 1$ are members of family modulo p. So any number p or a multiple of p is 0, *i.e.*, p, $2p$, $3p$, p^2, ..., are all reduced to zero. Similarly, $p + 1$, $2p + 1$, $3p + 1$, ... are all reduced to 1 and $p + 2$, $2p + 2$, $3p + 2$, ... are reduced to 2 and so on. The estimation and calculation of sum of squares for main effects and interactions in case of 2^2 and 3^2 factorials are discussed below which can be extended for any p^n system.

Suppose A and B are two factors each at two levels 0 and 1 in a 2^2 factorial. Also suppose each treatment is replicated r times. We work out total responses for the factors and their interaction(s) at the levels 0 and 1. Dividing the differences between higher and lower level responses by $2r$, we obtain the estimates due to main effects and interaction(s) and dividing the squares of the differences by $4r$, we obtain the sum of squares due to the factors and all their interaction.

Let the level of A be denoted by i and of B by j. Thus we have four treatment combinations (ij) levelled as 00, 01, 10, 11. The response due to factor combinations at the higher levels and lower levels reduced to modulo 2 are:

$$(A)_0 = 00 + 01 \qquad \text{For} \quad i = 0 \text{ mod } 2$$

$$(A)_1 = 10 + 11 \qquad i = 1 \text{ mod } 2$$

$$(B)_0 = 00 + 10 \qquad j = 0 \text{ mod } 2$$

$$(B)_1 = 01 + 11 \qquad j = 1 \text{ mod } 2$$

$$(AB)_0 = 00 + 11 \qquad i + j = 0 \text{ mod } 2$$

$$(AB)_1 = 01 + 10 \qquad i + j = 1 \text{ mod } 2$$

The estimates of the main effects and interaction are:

$$(A)_1 - (A)_0 = \frac{1}{2r} (10 + 11 - 00 - 01)$$

$$(B)_1 - (B)_0 = \frac{1}{2r} (01 + 11 - 00 - 10)$$

$$(AB)_0 - (AB)_1 = \frac{1}{2r} (11 + 00 - 01 - 10)$$

Note. The treatment combinations in parentheses are same as contrasts for A, B and AB.

On putting the total response value for corresponding treatment combinations, the sum of squares for,

$$A = \frac{1}{4r}[(A)_1 - (A)_0]^2 = \frac{(A)_1^2 + (A)_0^2}{2r} - \frac{[(A)_1 + (A)_0]^2}{4r}$$

$$B = \frac{1}{4r}[(B)_1 - (B)_0]^2 = \frac{(B)_1^2 + (B)_0^2}{2r} - \frac{[(B)_1 + (B)_0]^2}{4r}$$

$$AB = \frac{1}{4r}[(AB)_1 - (AB)_0]^2 = \frac{(AB)_1^2 + (AB)_0^2}{2r} - \frac{[(AB)_1 + (AB)_0]^2}{4r}$$

Now we consider a 3^2 factorial experiment. Suppose A and B are two factors each at three levels 0, 1 and 2. Nine treatment combinations are 00, 01, 02, 10

11, 12, 20, 21 and 22. The factor combinations for responses at three levels reduced to modulo 3 are:

$$(A)_0 = 00 + 01 + 02 \quad \text{For} \quad i = 0 \text{ mod } 3$$
$$(A)_1 = 10 + 11 + 12 \quad i = 1 \text{ mod } 3$$
$$(A)_2 = 20 + 21 + 22 \quad i = 2 \text{ mod } 3$$
$$(B)_0 = 00 + 10 + 20 \quad j = 0 \text{ mod } 3$$
$$(B)_1 = 01 + 11 + 21 \quad j = 1 \text{ mod } 3$$
$$(B)_2 = 02 + 12 + 22 \quad j = 2 \text{ mod } 3$$
$$(AB)_0 = 00 + 12 + 21 \quad i + j = 0 \text{ mod } 3$$
$$(AB)_1 = 01 + 10 + 22 \quad i + j = 0 \text{ mod } 3$$
$$(AB)_2 = 02 + 11 + 20 \quad i + j = 2 \text{ mod } 3$$

The sum of the responses at factor levels to obtained can be summarized in a 3 × 3 table as follows:

	b_0	b_1	b_2	*Total*
a_0	X_{00}	X_{01}	X_{02}	$X_{0.}$
a_1	X_{10}	X_{11}	X_{12}	$X_{1.}$
a_2	X_{20}	X_{21}	X_{22}	$X_{2.}$
Total	$X_{.0}$	$X_{.1}$	$X_{.2}$	$X_{..}$

The nine treatments represented by all possible combinations has 8 d.f. which has a break up as 2 d.f. for *A*, 2 d.f. for *B* and 4 d.f. for *A* × *B*. The main effects *A* and *B* may be linear or quadratic effects with 1 d.f. each and the interaction *A* × *B* can be splitted into two parts *AB* and AB^2 with 2 d.f. for each.

Note: Here it should be noted that A^2B is same as AB^2 reduced to modulo 3, *i.e.*, $(A^2 B)^2 = A^4 B^2 = AB^2$. Also $A^2 B^2$ is equivalent to *AB* *i.e.* $(A^2 B^2)^2 = A^4 B^4 = AB$.

It is known that for three treatments (3 levels), the linear contrast will be represented by – 1, 0, 1 and quadratic contrast by 1, –2, 1.

Let us assume that in the above two way table each value X_{ij} $(i, j = 0, 1, 2)$ is a total of *r* individual responses for nine treatment combination. The linear and quadratic effects for the factors *A*, *B*, and their interaction effects can be calculated as explicated below:

Note. One is not required to prepare both parts of the table given below. One may prepare only the right half or left half table.

The divisors for the estimates of the effect will be 3*r*. Moreover the divisors for the sum of squares will be as tabulated on page 586.

	A_l –1 0 1	A_q 1 –2 1		B_l –1 0 1	B_q 1 –2 1
b_0	$X_{20} - X_{00}$	$X_{20} - 2X_{10} + X_{00}$	a_0	$X_{02} - X_{00}$	$X_{02} - 2X_{01} + X_{00}$
b_1	$X_{21} - X_{01}$	$X_{21} - 2X_{11} + X_{01}$	a_1	$X_{12} - X_{10}$	$X_{12} - 2X_{11} + X_{10}$
b_2	$X_{22} - X_{02}$	$X_{22} - 2X_{12} + X_{02}$	a_2	$X_{22} - X_{20}$	$X_{22} - 2X_{21} + X_{20}$
Total	$X_{2.} - X_{0.} = A_l$	$X_{2.} - 2X_{1.} + X_{0.} = A_q$	Total	$X_{.2} - X_{.0} = B_l$	$X_{.2} - 2X_{.1} + X_{.0} = B_q$
$(-1, 0, 1)\ B_l$	$(X_{22} - X_{02}) - (X_{20} - X_{00}) = A_l B_l$	$(X_{22} - 2X_{12} + X_{02}) - (X_{20} - 2X_{10} + X_{00}) = A_q B_l$	$(-1, 0, 1)\ A_l$	$(X_{22} - X_{20}) - (X_{02} - X_{00}) = A_l B_l$	$(X_{22} - 2X_{21} + X_{20}) - (X_{02} - 2X_{01} + X_{00}) = A_l B_q$
$(1, -2, 1)\ B_q$	$(X_{22} - X_{02}) - 2(X_{21} - X_{01}) + (X_{20}) - X_{00}) = A_l B_q$	$(X_{22} - 2X_{12} + X_{02}) - 2\,(X_{21} - 2X_{11} + X_{01}) + (X_{20} - 2X_{10} + X_{00}) = A_q B_q$	$(1, -2, 1)\ A_q$	$(X_{22} - X_{20}) - 2(X_{12} - X_{10}) + (X_{02} - X_{00}) = A_q B_l$	$(X_{22} - 2X_{21} + X_{20}) - 2\,(X_{12} - 2X_{11} + X_{10}) + (X_{02} - 2X_{01} + X_{00}) = A_q B_q$

Effect	*Divisors*	*S.S.*
A_l	$3r\{(-1)^2 + 0^2 + 1^2\} = 6r$	$A_l^2/6r$
B_l	$3r\{(-1)^2 + 0^2 + 1^2\} = 6r$	$B_l^2/6r$
A_q	$3r\{1^2 + (-2)^2 + 1^2\} = 18r$	$A_q^2/18r$
B_q	$3r\{1^2 + (-2)^2 + 1^2\} = 18r$	$B_q^2/18r$
A_lB_l	$r\{(-1)^2 + 0^2 + 1^2\}\{(-1)^2 + 0^2 + 1^2\} = 4r$	$(A_l B_l)^2/4r$
A_lB_q	$r\{(-1)^2 + 0^2 + 1^2\}\{1^2 + (-2)^2 + 1^2\} = 12r$	$(A_l B_q)^2/12r$
A_qB_l	$r\{1^2 + (-2)^2 + 1^2\}\{(-1)^2 + 0^2 + 1^2\} = 12r$	$(A_q B_l)^2/12r$
A_qB_q	$r\{1^2 + (-2)^2 + 1^2\}\{1^2 + (-2)^2 + 1^2] = 36r$	$(A_q B_q)^2/36r$

Q. 95. *Give the method, of calculating sum of squares for factorial effects in general.*

Ans. In general method, one prepares 2-way, 3-way, 4-way tables and calculate the sum of squares due to main effects and interaction(s) with the help of these tables.

For 2^2 factorial experiment say, laidout in randomized block design with r blocks, the total for four treatment combinations are as tabulated below:

	b_0	b_1	*Total*
a_0	X_{00}	X_{01}	$X_{0.}$
a_1	X_{10}	X_{11}	$X_{1.}$
Total	$X_{.0}$	$X_{.1}$	$X_{..}$

$$S.S. \text{ due to } A = \frac{1}{2r}(X_{0.}^2 + X_{1.}^2) - \frac{X_{..}^2}{4r}$$

$$S.S. \text{ due to } B = \frac{1}{2r}(X_{.0}^2 + X_{.1}^2) - \frac{X_{..}^2}{4r}$$

$$S.S. \text{ due to } AB = \frac{1}{r}(X_{00}^2 + X_{01}^2 + X_{10}^2 + X_{11}^2) - \frac{X_{..}^2}{4r}$$

$$- \text{S.S. (A)} - \text{S.S. (B)}$$

Let us consider the data of a 2^3 factorial experiment. For this data prepare two way tables for A & B, A & C and B & C. From these tables calculate the sum of squares due to A, B, C, AB, AC and BC in the usual manner. The sum of square for ABC interaction is obtained by calculating treatment sum of square and subtracting from it the sum of squares due to all main effects and first order interactions.

For a $p_1 \times p_2 \times p_3$ asymmetrical factorial with factors A, B and C prepare two way tables for A and B of order $p_1 \times p_2$, A and C of order $p_1 \times p_3$ and B and C of order $p_1 \times p_3$. From these tables calculate the sum of squares for the main effects and interactions as we do for 2^2 factorials. The divisor in calculating sum of squares is equal to the number of individual experimental units in a value which is squared. The sum of square for ABC is obtained by calculating the treatment sum of square and subtracting from this the sum of squares due to main effects and first order interactions.

Q. 96. *Give Yates' method of analysis of data of a 2^n factorial experiment.*

Ans. Yates' method is a mechanical approach to calculate the effects and sum of squares due to various factors and their interactions in a 2^n factorial only. This method has emerged as a result of thorough study of the nature of contrasts.

Various steps involved in Yates' method are as follows:

(*i*) In column (1), write all treatment combinations in a sequence introducing the letters a, b, c, etc., in turn.

(*ii*) In column (2), give the total responses corresponding to the treatment combinations given in column (1).

(*iii*) In column (3), in the upper half write the sums of the values of column (2) taken in pairs and in the lower half write the difference of pairs even minus odd, *e.g.*, (2nd-1st), (4th-3rd) and so on.

(*iv*) Repeat step (*iii*) on the values of column (3) to obtained column (4).

(*v*) Process of pairwise adding and subtracting is continued in as many columns as n, the number of factors.

(*vi*) The last column containing sums and differences gives effect totals. One may verify that these effect totals are same as those obtained from contrasts.

(*vii*) To obtain factorial effect means, the effect total are divided by $2^{n-1} \times r$, whereas the effect total for (1) is divided by $2^n \times r$ giving grand mean.

(*viii*) To obtain the sum of squares due to factorial effects, square of each effect total is divided by $2^n \times r$. Yates' method does not require writing of any contrasts or formation of tables etc. The method is very quick and handy.

Q. 97. *In an experiment with three fertilizers N, P and K each at two levels 0 and 1, the yield data (kg/plot) due to eight treatment combinations of a R.B.D. with three replications is give below:*

Treats.	Rep. I	Rep. II	Rep. III
(1)	40	53	38
n	35	59	18
p	40	69	43
np	64	78	52
k	71	72	58
nk	26	31	19
pk	43	45	27
npk	51	62	40

Calculate the treatment mean effects and sum of squares by Yate's method.

Ans. To calculate the mean effects and sum of squares due to various effects by Yate's method we prepare the following table.

Treats. Col. 1	Treat. Totals Col. 2	Col. 3	Col. 4	Effect Totals Col. 5	Effect means	S.S. due to effects
(1)	131	243	589	1134	94.50	53581.50
n	112	346	545	–64	–5.33	170.67
p	152	277	23	94	7.83	368.17
np	194	268	–87	224	18.67	2090.67
k	201	–19	103	–44	–3.67	80.67
nk	76	42	–9	–110	–9.17	504.17
pk	115	–125	61	–112	–9.33	522.67
npK	153	38	163	102	8.50	433.50

The last two columns give the estimates of the effect means and sum of squares respectively.

Q. 98. *Comment on the designs to be used in case of factorial experiments.*

Ans. The layout of a factorial experiment can be done in any design namely, completely randomized design, randomized complete block design, Latin square design, split plot design and incomplete block designs. The analysis of data will be carried out in the usual manner. The only difference in analysis of variance table is that the treatment sum of square is further splitted up in main effects and interactions sum of squares. If all the contrasts are orthogonal, the total of the sum of squares due to main effects and interactions is equal to the treatment sum of square.

Q. 99. *Write down the statistical model for a two-factor factorial experiment with a levels of A, b levels of B respectively laid out in completely randomized design. Also give analysis of variance table with expected mean squares.*

Ans. The statistical model for a two factor factorial with a levels of A, b levels of B and r replications in a completely randomized design with one observation per experimental unit is,

$$y_{ijk} = \mu + \alpha_i + \beta_j + (\alpha\beta)_{ij} + \varepsilon_{ijk} \quad (1)$$

For $i = 1, 2, ..., a$

$j = 1, 2, ..., b$

$k = 1, 2, ..., r$

ANOVA Table-14

(i) Source of Variation	(ii) d.f.	(iii) S.S.	(iv) M.S.	(v) Expected M.S. Model-I (A and B fixed)	(vi) Expected M.S. Model-II (A and B random)
Treatments	$ab-1$	T_{yy}	$\frac{T_{yy}}{ab-1}=T_y$		
A	$a-1$	A_{yy}	$\frac{A_{yy}}{a-1}=A_y$	$\sigma_e^2+rb\sum_{i=1}^{a}\alpha_i^2/(a-1)$	$\sigma_e^2+r\,\sigma_{\alpha\beta}^2+rb\sigma_\alpha^2$
B	$b-1$	B_{yy}	$\frac{B_{yy}}{b-1}=B_y$	$\sigma_e^2+ra\sum_{j=1}^{b}\beta_j^2/(b-1)$	$\sigma_e^2+r\,\sigma_{\alpha\beta}^2+ra\sigma_\beta^2$
AB	$(a-1)\times(b-1)$	$(AB)_{yy}$	$\frac{(AB)_{yy}}{(a-1)(b-1)}=AB_y$	$\sigma_e^2+r\sum_{i=1}^{a}\sum_{j=1}^{b}\frac{(\alpha\beta)_{ij}^2}{(a-1)(b-1)}$	$\sigma_e^2+r\,\sigma_{\alpha\beta}^2$
Experimental error	$ab(r-1)$	E_{yy}	$E_{yy}/ab(r-1)=E_y$	σ_e^2	σ_e^2
Total	$abr-1$	$\sum_i\sum_j y_{ijk}^2 - C.F.$			

(vii) Expected M.S. Model-III (A fixed, B random)	(viii) Expected M.S. Model-III (A random, B fixed)
$\sigma_e^2+r\sigma_{\alpha\beta}^2+rb\sum_{i=1}^{a}\frac{\alpha_i^2}{a-1}$	$\sigma_e^2+rb\sigma_\alpha^2$
$\sigma_e^2+ra\sigma_\beta^2$	$\sigma_e^2+r\sigma_{\alpha\beta}^2+ra\sum_{j=1}^{b}\frac{\beta_j^2}{b-1}$
$\sigma_e^2+r\sigma_{\alpha\beta}^2$	$\sigma_e^2+r\sigma_{\alpha\beta}^2$
σ_e^2	σ_e^2

where μ is the true mean effect, α_i is the true effect of the ith level of A, β_j is the true effect of the jth level of B, $(\alpha\beta)_{ij}$ is the true interaction effect of the ith level of A and j^{th} level of B and ε_{ijk} is the true effect of the kth experimental unit subject to (i, j) treatment combination. Also $\varepsilon_{ij} \sim NID(0, \alpha_e^2)$.

The analysis of variance table with expected mean squares when the model (1) is fixed, random or mixed is displayed above (Table-14).

The expected mean squares in the above table reveal that in case of Model-II, the effects A and B should be tested against the interaction AB mean square by F-test and interaction AB should be tested against error mean square by F-test. Similarly for Model-III (A fixed, B random), M.S. for A be tested against AB M.S. and B M.S. and AB M.S. against error M.S. Again in Model-III (A random, B fixed), M.S. for B be tested against AB M.S. and A M.S. and AB M.S. be tested against error M.S.

Q. 100. *Set-up statistical model for a two-factor factorial experiment in a randomized block design. Also give analysis of variance table with expected mean squares.*

Ans. Suppose there are two factors A and B at levels a and b respectively and r blocks. The appropriate model for the two-factor factorial experiment in randomized block design is,

ANOVA Table-15

Source of Variation	*d.f.*	*S.S.*	*M.S.*	*Expected M.S. Model-I (A and B fixed)*	*Expected M.S. Model-II (A and B random)*	*Expected M.S. Model-III (A fixed, B random)*	*Expected M.S. Model-III (A random, B fixed)*
Blocks	$(r-1)$	R_{yy}	$\frac{R_{yy}}{r-1} = R_y$				
Treatments	$(ab-1)$	T_{yy}	$\frac{T_{yy}}{ab-1} = T_y$				
A	$(a-1)$	A_{yy}	$\frac{A_{yy}}{a-1} = A_y$	$\sigma_e^2 + rb \sum_{i=1}^{a} \frac{\alpha_i^2}{a-1}$	$\sigma_e^2 + r\sigma_{\alpha\beta}^2 + rb\sigma_\alpha^2$	$\sigma_e^2 + r\sigma_{\alpha\beta}^2 + rb \sum_{i=1}^{a} \frac{\alpha_i^2}{a-1}$	$\sigma_e^2 + rb\sigma_\alpha^2$
B	$(b-1)$	B_{yy}	$\frac{B_{yy}}{b-1} = B_y$	$\sigma_e^2 + ra \sum_{j=1}^{b} \frac{\beta_j^2}{b-1}$	$\sigma_e^2 + r\sigma_{\alpha\beta}^2 + ra\sigma_\beta^2$	$\sigma_e^2 + ra\sigma_\beta^2$	$\sigma_e^2 + r\sigma_{\alpha\beta}^2 + ra \sum_{j=1}^{b} \frac{\beta_j^2}{b-1}$
AB	$(a-1) \times (b-1)$	$(AB)_{yy}$	$\frac{(AB)_{yy}}{(a-1)(b-1)} = (AB)_y$	$\sigma_e^2 + r \sum_{i=1}^{a} \sum_{j=1}^{b} \frac{(\alpha\beta)_{ij}^2}{(a-1)(b-1)}$	$\sigma_e^2 + r\sigma_{\alpha\beta}^2$	$\sigma_e^2 + r\sigma_{\alpha\beta}^2$	$\sigma_e^2 + r\sigma_{\alpha\beta}^2$
Experimental error	$(r-1) \times (ab-1)$	E_{yy}	$\frac{E_{yy}}{(r-1)(ab-1)} = E_y$	σ_e^2	σ_e^2	σ_e^2	σ_e^2
Total	$rab-1$	$\sum_{i=1}^{a} \sum_{j=1}^{a} \sum_{k=1}^{r} y_{ijk}^2$ – C.F.					

$$y_{ijk} = \mu + \alpha_i + \beta_j + (\alpha\beta)_{ij} + \varepsilon_{ijk}$$

For $i = 1, 2, ..., a$

$j = 1, 2, ..., b$

$k = 1, 2, ..., r$

μ, α_i, β_j, $(\alpha\beta)_{ij}$ carry their usual meaning and ρ_k is the true effect of the kth block and $\varepsilon_{ijk} \sim$ NID $(0, \alpha_e^2)$.

The analysis of variance table for the above model is presented in Table-15 with additional columns for expected mean squares under three models, (see in the table on the last page).

After making a critical view of the expected mean squares under various models, it is trivial to decide when should the main effects *A* and *B* be tested against experimental error and when against interaction *AB* mean square. Also interaction *AB* has to be tested against experimental error in all situations.

Q. 101. *Give general rules for writing the expected mean squares in case of factorial experiments with one observation per unit.*

Ans. There is no end to models for varying number of factors involved in factorial experiments and the respective ANOVA tables. Expected mean squares are of prime importance as they enable one to decide about an appropriate test for factors involved and their interactions. Hence, it looks pertinent to give general rules for writing expected mean squares.

Here we denote any main effect or an interaction by a letter *U* in general. The method of writing the expected mean squares is as follows:

(*i*) The expected mean square for any effect *U* always includes the term σ_e^2 (error mean square) with coefficient unity.

(*ii*) In fixed effect model (Model-I), the expected mean square due to a fixed effect *U* is σ_e^2 plus the sum of square due to the effect *U* divided by its degrees of freedom and this expression is multiplied by *r* times the levels of all factors except itself.

(*iii*) In case of random effect model, the expected mean square due to a factor *U* is σ_e^2 plus σ_u^2 and add all variance terms of the interactions with *U* whereas each variance except σ_e^2 is multiplied by *r* times the levels of the factors not present in *U*.

(*iv*) In case of mixed effect model, expected mean square due to a fixed effect *U* contains σ_e^2, mean sum of square due to *U* multiplied by *r* times the levels of all factors except *U* and all variance terms of the interaction of *U* with random effects only each multiplied by *r* times the product of levels of factors that do not appear in the interaction under consideration.

(*v*) In case of mixed model, expected mean square due a random factor *U* contains σ_e^2, the variances due to *U* and its interactions with random effects multiplied by *r* times the product of the levels of factors that did not appear in suffix to σ^2.

Q. 102. *What do you understand by confounding?*

Ans. We know that in randomized block design, a block should usually not contain more than 20 plots of medium size and a Latin square design of order more than 10 is not commendable. Factorial experiments are usually conducted in randomized block design and seldom in Latin square and other designs. In factorial experiments, the treatment combinations increase rapidly as the number of factors increases or levels of factors increase. Large number of treatment combinations in factorial experiments become incompatible to be accommodated in randomized blocks as their homogeneity is in jeopardy. Hence, there arises the need of a device which can retain the feature of factorial arrangement and reduce the block size so as to maintain their homogeneity. To fulfil these objectives, there is a device known as *confounding*. In confounding, each block is subdivided into two or more blocks of suitable size known as incomplete blocks by sacrificing the information about a factorial effect usually higher order interaction(s).

Through confounding some factors, which are not confounded, are estimated and tested with high precision and some factor(s) which are confounded lose their identity as they are inextricably mixed with block differences. We know, second and higher order interactions are of little or no importance from their physical interpretation point of view, hence they are primarily chosen for confounding. Confounding is a device of reducing block size applicable only in factorial experiments.

Q. 103. *Differentiate between complete and partial confounding.*

Ans. If the same effect is confounded in all the replicates, it is known as *complete confounding.* This effect is generally of little or no value to the experimenter. For example, in a 3-factor factorial experiment, the second order interaction ABC is generally of least interest. So it is confounded in all replications.

Again if an experimenter is not prepared to sacrifice an effect totally, he chooses to confound one effect in one replicate and the other in other replicate(s). In this process total information is not lost about any effect. The effect which is confounded in one replicate is being estimated and tested on the basis of the replicates in which it is not confounded. This system of confounding is known as *partial confounding.* For example, in a 2^3 factorial, one confounds AB in first replicate, AC in second replicate and BC in the third replicate. The whole set may be repeated more than once.

Q. 104. *When do you call the partial confounding as balance and unbalanced confounding?*

Ans. When all effects of the same order are confounded with incomplete blocks differences equal number of times, the confounding is said to be *balanced confounding* or more specifically *balanced partial confounding.* For instance, AB, AC and BC are confounded in first, second and third replication respectively and there are three such sets of replications.

On the other hand if the effects of certain order are confounded an unequal number of times in the replications, this system of confounding is known as *unbalanced partial confounding.*

Q. 105. *How can complete confounding be operated in a 2^n factorial to reduce the block size to half-replicate?*

Ans. In a 2^n factorial, the block size in randomized block design can be reduced to half by confounding one effect which is of no interest or least interest. In practice, one chooses the highest order interaction. The procedure is very simple. Write the contrast for the effect which is to be confounded. All those treatment combinations with positive sign are randomly assigned in one half replicate (block) and those with negative coefficients in the other half. The same entries of the blocks are repeated in other replications with a fresh randomization within blocks.

We give below the layout of a 2^3 factorial with factors A, B and C each at two levels 0 and 1. The effect ABC is confounded to obtain the blocks of size four units.

$$ABC = (a - 1)(b - 1)(c - 1)$$
$$= abc + a + b + c - ab - ac - bc - (1)$$

Rep. I		*Rep. II*		*Rep. III*	
Bl. 1	*Bl. 2*	*Bl. 3*	*Bl. 4*	*Bl. 5*	*Bl. 6*
a	(1)	*c*	*ab*	*b*	*bc*
abc	*ab*	*b*	*ac*	*c*	(1)
b	*ac*	*abc*	*bc*	*a*	*ac*
c	*bc*	*a*	(1)	*abc*	*ab*

Q. 106. *In what manner, can the blocks of two units in 2^3 factorial in a randomized block design be obtained through confounding?*

Ans. In a 2^3 factorial, there are eight factorial effects. *First,* we confound one effect to reduce the blocks to the size of 4 units. Again we confound another effect to get the blocks of two units. When we confound second effect, we will always find that the four entries within a block will now have two entries with positive sign and two with negative signs. So each block of four units will further be splitted up into two blocks each containing two units.

Here one should be wary of the fact that when we confound two treatment effects to reduce the blocks into one-fourth size, their generalised interaction is automatically confounded. Hence, one should not choose two treatment effects whose generalised interaction is a main effect or some other effect of greater interest. For instance, if we choose to confound first ABC then AB, then the generalized interaction, $ABC \times AB = A^2 B^2 C = C$ (powers reduced to modulo 2), which is a main effect, is automatically confounded. An automatically confounded effect means that the effect will be same as the block differences in confounded design. So it is preferable to confound two first order interactions here say, AB and AC are confounded.

The contrast AB is,

$$AB = (a-1)(b-1)(c+1)$$
$$= abc + c + ab + (1) - b - a - bc - ac$$

Blocks reduced to half in two replications are,

Rep. I

Bl. (i)	*Bl. (ii)*
abc	a
c	b
(1)	bc
ab	ac

Rep. II

Bl. (iii)	*Bl. (iv)*
c	bc
(1)	b
ab	ac
abc	a

The contrast AC is,

$$AC = (a-1)(b+1)(c-1)$$
$$= abc + (1) - c - ab + b + ac - a - bc$$

Rep. I

Bl. 1	*Bl. 2*	*Bl. 3*	*Bl. 4*
abc	c	b	bc
(1)	ab	ac	a

Rep. II

Bl. 5	*Bl. 6*	*Bl. 7*	*Bl. 8*
(1)	c	ac	bc
abc	ab	b	a

Now we check up how BC is confounded. The contrast for BC is as given below:

$$BC = (a+1)(b-1)(c-1)$$
$$= abc + (1) - b - ac + a + bc - c - ab$$
$$= Bl.\ 1 - Bl.\ 3 + Bl.\ 4 - Bl.\ 2\ (Rep.\ I)$$

In this way BC is also confounded.

Q. 107. *Give general rule for confounding effects in a 2^n factorial to reduce the blocks to size of 2^{n-k} units.*

Ans. In a 2^n factorial to have 2^k blocks of 2^{n-k} units each, one has to confounding k effects subject to the restriction that none of them is a generalized interaction of the others amongst themselves. In this situation, $(2^k - k - 1)$ effects are automatically confounded.

Q. 108. *Give the layout of a partially confounded design in 2^3 factorial in which the effects ABC, AC and BC are confounded in three replicates.*

Ans. The layout of a 2^3 factorial experiment in which ABC, AC and BC are confounded in three replicates is as given below.

The contrasts are,

$$ABC = (a-1)(b-1)(c-1)$$
$$= (abc + a + b + c) - (ac + bc + ac + (1))$$
$$AC = (a-1)(b+1)(c-1)$$
$$= (abc + b + ac + (1)) - (a + c + ab + bc)$$
$$BC = (a+1)(b-1)(c-1)$$
$$= (abc + a + bc + (1)) - (ab + ac + b + c)$$

Thus, the layout is,

Rep. I

Bl. 1	*Bl. 2*
a	ac
abc	(1)
b	ab
c	bc

Rep. II

Bl. 3	*Bl. 4*
abc	a
b	ab
(1)	bc
ac	c

Rep. III

Bl. 5	*Bl. 6*
(1)	b
a	ab
bc	c
abc	ac

Effects confounded

ABC *AC* *BC*

Q. 109. *How can we implement confounding in a 3^n factorial design?*

Ans. In 3^n factorials, the effects can be confounded with the help of modulo technique. Here we have an additional advantage that the same interaction effect can be subdivided into components each with two degrees of freedom. So by confounding one component in one replication and the other in second replication, etc., the confounded effect can be estimated through its components from other replications barring its own replication.

In 3^n factorial, confounding can be carried through modulo technique easily. Supposing that in 3^2 factorial experiment in randomized block design, the interaction effect $A \times B$ is confounded to form blocks of size 3 units. Interaction $A \times B$ has 4 d.f. which can be subdivided into components AB and AB^2, each with 2 d.f.

Nine treatment combinations 00, 01, 02, 10, 11, 12, 20, 21, 22 can be sorted out to confound AB in one replication such that $i + j = 0$ mod 3, $i + j = 1$ mod 3 and $i + j = 2$ mod 3 where i represents the level of A and j the level of B. Similarly in the second replication, AB^2 is confounded where the blocks contain the treatment combinations satisfying the conditions $i + 2j = 0$ mod 3, $i + 2j = 1$ mod 3 and $i + 2j = 2$ mod 3. Following the technique, the design is as given below:

Rep. I

Bl. 1	*Bl. 2*	*Bl. 3*
00	10	02
12	01	20
21	22	11

AB confounded

Rep. II

Bl. 4	*Bl. 5*	*Bl. 6*
11	10	20
00	21	12
22	02	01

AB^2 confounded

This technique can be extended to 3^n $(n \geq 3)$ factorials in general.

Q. 110. *How can one carry out the balanced confounding in asymmetrical factorials?*

Ans. Let us consider in general an asymmetrical factorial with k factors at levels $p_1, p_2, ..., p_k$, respectively. Suppose that the total number of treatment combinations $p_1 \times p_2 \times ... \times p_k = P$. We want to obtain a block of size R units. Now determine a quantity Q which is equal to P/R such that Q is either a prime number or a prime power, *i.e.*, $Q = s^m$, where s is a prime number and m is an integer.

All factors in the asymmetrical factorial possessing s levels are called *real factors* and each factor having the levels other than s is called a *factor of asymmetry*.

Now for the construction of a confounded balanced design, the asymmetrical factorial is converted into a symmetrical factorial s^n by adding certain factors each at levels 's' to the factors of asymmetry. These additional factors are called *pseudo factors*. The levels of real and pseudo factors are denoted by the elements of the Galois field s (modulo technique). For distinction we will denote the real factors by A, B, C, ... and factors of asymmetry by X, Y, Z, ... and pseudo factors corresponding to X by $X_1, X_2, X_3, ...$ and for Y by $Y_1, Y_2, Y_3, ...,$ and so on.

The decision about the number of pseudo factors depends on the value of s and the factors having levels other than s. Suppose the factor F_i has levels p_i less than s. Then convert the asymmetrical factorial to symmetrical factorial as s^m by choosing a single pseudo factor for each $X, Y, Z, ...$ as $X_1, Y_1, Z_1, ...$ For those factors where p_i is greater than s, choose as many pseudo factors for X, Y, etc., as required like $X_1, X_2, ...; Y_1, Y_2, ...,$ etc., to convert the asymmetrical factorial into a symmetrical factorial with factors each having s levels. From the factorial combinations delete all those combinations of pseudo factors which are non-existing in the asymmetrical factorial experiment. Now form incomplete blocks of required size by modulo technique. Also reduce the number of pseudo factors to the number of factors of asymmetry by jointly considering their level combinations to a single level. In this way, we get a confounded design for an asymmetrical factorial.

Q. 111. *Give the layout of a balanced confounded design of an asymmetrical factorial 2 × 2 × 3 with blocks of size 4 units and two replications.*

Ans. No. of combinations, $P = 2 \times 2 \times 3 = 12$

Block size, $R = 4$

$$Q = \frac{P}{R} = \frac{12}{4} = 3$$

There is one real factor say, A at 3 levels and two factors of asymmetry as X and Y each at 2 levels. Since, the levels of the factors X, Y with levels equal to 2 are less than 3, we convert the asymmetrical factorial 2 × 2 × 3 into a 3^3 factorial with pseudo factors X_1 and Y_1 each at 3 levels 0, 1, 2. Out of 27 combinations of X, Y, A, delete all those combinations in which the level of X_1 and/or Y_1 is 2. In this way we are left with 12 treatment combinations of the asymmetrical factorial. The entries of three blocks are determined by modulo technique taking $(X_1\ Y_1\ A)_{I_1+I_2+I_3=0 \bmod 3}$, $(X_1\ Y_1\ A)_{I_1+I_2+I_3=1 \bmod 3}$, $(X_1\ Y_1\ A)_{I_1+I_2+I_3=2 \bmod 3}$, where I_1, I_2 and I_3 denote the levels of X_1, Y_1 and A, respectively. The layout will be as given below:

Treatment Combinations of 3^3 factorial are,

0 0 0	1 0 0	2 0 0
0 0 1	1 0 1	2 0 1
0 0 2	1 0 2	2 0 2
0 1 0	1 1 0	2 1 0
0 1 1	1 1 1	2 1 1
0 1 2	1 1 2	2 1 2
0 2 0	1 2 0	2 2 0
0 2 1	1 2 1	2 2 1
0 2 2	1 2 2	2 2 2

Confounded design with two replications is given below:

Rep. I			Rep. II		
Bl. 1	*Bl. 2*	*Bl. 3*	*Bl. 4*	*Bl. 5*	*Bl. 6*
000	001	002	012	010	110
012	010	011	111	100	011
102	100	101	102	001	002
111	112	110	000	112	101
(*XYA*) 0 mod 3	1 mod 3	2 mod 3	0 mod 3	1 mod 3	2 mod 3

Q. 112. *What shall be the block entries of a 3 × 2 × 2 balanced confounded design with blocks of six units in three replications saving the complete confounding of an interaction?*

Ans. Number of combinations, $P = 3 \times 2 \times 2 = 12$

Block size, $R = 6$

$$Q = \frac{P}{R} = \frac{12}{6} = 2$$

Therefore, $s = 2$. So there are two real factors A and B each at 2 levels and there is one factor of asymmetry say, X at three levels. Since $(p_1 = 3) > (s = 2)$, we will have to take two pseudo factors X_1 and X_2 and convert 3 × 2 × 2 factorial into 2^4 factorial. The four factors are X_1, X_2, A and B. There will be in all 16 treatment combinations in order of these factors. But we require only 12 combinations for the asymmetrical factorial 3 × 2 × 2. Hence, from sixteen combinations, delete four combinations in which the levels of $X_1 X_2$ are 11. The treatment combinations in the order X_1, X_2, A and B are,

0	0	0	0	1	0	0	0
0	0	0	1	1	0	0	1
0	0	1	0	1	0	1	0
0	0	1	1	1	0	1	1
0	1	0	0	1	1	0	0
0	1	0	1	1	1	0	1
0	1	1	0	1	1	1	0
0	1	1	1	1	1	1	1

Making use of the remaining 12 treatment combinations, we give the entries of three replications confounding the effect $X_1 AB$ in replication I, $X_2 AB$ in replication II and $X_1X_2 AB$ in replication III.

Rep. I		Rep. II	
Bl. 1	*Bl. 2*	*Bl. 3*	*Bl. 4*
0000	0001	0000	0001
0011	0010	0011	0010
0100	0101	0101	0100
0111	0110	0110	0111
1010	1000	1000	1001
1001	1011	1011	1010
$(X_1\ AB)_{0 \bmod 2}$	$(X_1\ AB)_{1 \bmod 2}$	$(X_2\ AB)_{0 \bmod 2}$	$(X_2\ AB)_{1 \bmod 2}$

Rep. III

Bl. 5	*Bl. 6*
0000	0001
0011	0010
0101	0100
0110	0111
1010	1000
1001	1011

$(X_2X_2\,AB)_{0 \bmod 2}\ (X_1X_2\,AB)_{1 \bmod 2}$

The above layout involves four factors, two real factors A, B and two pseudo factors X_1 and X_2 for the factor of asymmetry X. Now we amalgamate the levels of X_1X_2 into a single level to get the confounded design for the factors X, A and B. For this we recode the level combinations of X_1 and X_2 as 00 to 0, 01 to 1 and 10 to 2. In this way, we get the required balance confounded design as given below:

Rep. I		*Rep. II*		*Rep. III*	
Bl. 1	*Bl. 2*	*Bl. 3*	*Bl. 4*	*Bl. 5*	*Bl. 6*
000	001	000	001	000	001
011	010	011	010	011	010
100	101	101	100	101	100
111	110	110	111	110	111
210	200	200	201	210	200
201	211	211	210	201	211

Q. 113. *Give the concept of fractional replication.*

Ans. The idea of fractional replication was propounded by D.J. Finney in 1945. Some workers later instituted it as *fractional factorials*. A factorial experiment conducted in a single replicate by utilising a selected few treatment combinations with the interest of estimating only lower order effects with a reasonable degree of precision under the assumption of absence of higher order interactions is known as fractional replication.

Q. 114. *What do you understand by orthogonal fractional factorial designs?*

Ans. Regular fractional factorial plans for symmetrical factorials which make possible the estimation of all relevant effects with zero correlation are called orthogonal fractional factorial designs. The regular fractions are always orthogonal but the converse is not true.

(Box and Hunter defined the regular fraction as a fraction whose treatment combinations form a subgroup.)

Q. 115. *Clarify the idea of fractional replication through an example.*

Ans. To clarify the idea of fractional replication, we consider a 2^3 factorial experiment for the sake of brevity and simplicity though this is not an ideal example in the present context. Conduct the experiment with ½ replicate having the treatment combinations of positive signs in the contrast for the interaction ABC. From the experimental results, the main effects and interactions can be delineated as given below.

Treatment Combinations	*Main effects and interactions*						
	A	*B*	*C*	*AB*	*AC*	*BC*	*ABC*
a	+	–	–	–	–	+	+
b	–	+	–	–	+	–	+
c	–	–	+	+	–	–	+
abc	+	+	+	+	+	+	+

On the basis of above set of contrasts, we specifically reveal the following points:

(*i*) The contrast(s) which is/are used to split a replicate into a divisible fraction is/are called *defining contrast*(*s*). In this example, *ABC* is the defining contrast. It cannot be estimated at all.

(*ii*) From the above set of contrast, it is clear that the effect *A* is same as *BC*, *B* is same as *AC* and *C* is same as *AB*. In this way, the effects *A* and *BC*, *B* and *AC*, *C* and *AB* are inseparable. Hence, the effects which are estimated by the same contrast are called *aliases*. Here main effects and first order interactions are inextricably mixed. Aliases are the generalized interactions of an effect with the defining contrast(s).

The above ideas can be extended to higher order factorial experiments.

Q. 116. *Enucleate resolution of fractional factorial designs.*

Ans. G.E.P. Box and J.S. Hunter in 1961 introduced the term 'resolution'. Resolution simply means classification of fractional factorial designs. Box and Hunter's definition was confined to symmetrical factorials and involved defining contrast(s) or identity groups of interactions. [Identity group of inter-action(s) means the interaction(s) which is/are confounded to obtain fractional replication.] A fractional factorial design is of resolution – R if the smallest interaction in the identity group consists of R factors.

S.R. Webb in 1968 extended the definition of resolution which was applicable to all types of fractional factorials. According to him, a fractional factorial design is of resolution $(2R + 1)$ if the estimation of all effects up to R-factors interaction (including main effects) is possible, whereas all effects involving $(R + 1)$ or more factor are assumed negligible. In the example given in Q. 11, $R = 1$. Hence, this design is of resolution-III. Further, a fractional factorial design is of resolution $2R$ if it allows the estimation of all effects up to $(R – 1)$ – factor interactions (including main effects) whereas all effects involving $(R + 1)$ or more factors are assumed to be absent. Thus, for a design of resolution-IV, all main effects are estimable whereas second and higher order interactions are supposed to be negligible or absent.

Q. 117. *Elucidate the structure of a split plot design.*

Ans. There are many experiments in which certain treatments require large size plot areas or fields whereas some other treatments can efficiently be managed in small plot areas. For instance, an experimenter may take irrigation as treatment and fertiliser as other treatment. In this situation, it is difficult to confine irrigation in small size plot as to stop seepage from plot to plot is a tedious task whereas fertilizers can be applied in small size plots without any difficulty. Hence, one would prefer to take irrigation in large size plots known as *whole plots or main plots* and fertilizer in small size plots within a whole plot known as *sub-plots*. There are as many subplots in a whole plot as the number of treatments to be assigned to sub-plots. Suppose there are p level of a factor A which requires large size experimental units and q levels of a factor B which can easily be managed in small experimental units. There has to be as many replicates as the resources permit or which fulfil the minimum requirement for error degrees of freedom. In this situation, we will assign treatment A to main-plots taking p main-plots in each replication and divide each main-plot into subplots for accommodating each level of factor B. The treatments are allocated randomly in main-plots as well as in sub-plots independently in all replications. The structural layout of a split plot design with $p = 4$ and $q = 5$ and three replications is given below:

Rep. I				*Rep. II*				*Rep. III*			
a_3	a_2	a_1	a_0	a_2	a_1	a_0	a_3	a_1	a_0	a_3	a_2
b_1	b_0	b_1	b_2	b_0	b_1	b_2	b_4	b_4	b_4	b_2	b_3
b_4	b_2	b_3	b_1	b_3	b_2	b_4	b_3	b_0	b_2	b_0	b_0
b_0	b_4	b_2	b_3	b_2	b_4	b_0	b_0	b_3	b_0	b_3	b_1
b_3	b_3	b_4	b_4	b_1	b_3	b_1	b_1	b_2	b_1	b_4	b_4
b_2	b_1	b_0	b_0	b_4	b_0	b_3	b_2	b_1	b_3	b_1	b_2

In 1937, F. Yates carrier out such experiments with two factors at Rothamsted. Such designs were used in agriculture and hence, were named *split plot design*. Nowadays, split plot design is frequently used in chemical industry, animal and various biological experiments. For example, ovens may be taken as whole-plots maintained at different temperatures as main plot treatments and various baking powders mixed-up with the duff in different trays as sub-plot treatments; various pastures may be taken as main plots and different breeds of cows as sub-plots, etc.

Several variations of split plot design are feasible such as double split or split-split plot design, split block or strip plot design etc.

Q. 118. *Throw light on the special features of a split plot design.*

Ans. Split plot design has many special features which are expounded below:

(*i*) The split plot design is similar to partially hierarchical design.

(*ii*) Split plot design is frequently used in industrial experiments and hence it is preferable to use the word *nested design* there in place of split plot design. In split plot design sub-plot treatments are nested within main-plot treatment.

(*iii*) It is a confounded design in which the main-plot treatments are confounded with whole-plots.

(*iv*) Interblock information can be utilised in the analysis of data.

(*v*) Increased precision is attained on the sub-plot treatments and interactions of sub-plot × main-pot treatments as compared to the main-plot treatments alone.

(*vi*) It is quite feasible to use two, three or more splits in split plot design known as double split, triple split or multiple split plot design.

(*vii*) If there are *m* splits in a split plot design, there will be $(m + 1)$ error terms in its analysis of variance.

Q. 19. *Give statistical model and appropriate analysis of variance table for split plot design.*

Ans. Here we consider an experiment with two factors, *A* as whole-plot treatment and *B* as sub-plot treatment at levels *p* and *q* respectively, laid-out in split plot designs. The statistical model is,

$$y_{iju} = \mu + \alpha_i + \beta_j + (\alpha\beta)_{ij} + \rho_u + \delta_{ui} + \varepsilon_{iju}$$

For $i = 1, 2, ..., p$

$j = 1, 2, ..., q$

$u = 1, 2, ... r$

where, μ – overall mean effect.

α_i – effect of the ith level of factor *A* (main-plot treatment).

β_j – effect of the ith level of factor *B* (sub-plot treatment).

$(\alpha\beta)_{ij}$ – the interaction effect of ith level of *A* and j^{th} level of *B*.

ρ_u – the effect of uth replicate.

δ_{ui} – a random error component associated with a_i in the uth replicate.

ε_{iju} – a random error component associated with iju^{th} sub-plot.

y_{iju} – response measure due to i^{th} level of *A* and j^{th} level of *B* in u^{th} replicate.

From the above model, it is apparent that there are two error terms, one associated with main plot and other with sub-plots.

Let the summary table of observations y_{iju} from *r* replications be as follows:

Table. Main × Sub plot treatments responses summed over all replications

	Factor B						
Factor A	b_1	b_2	...	b_j	...	b_q	*Total*
a_1	$y_{11.}$	$y_{12.}$	...	$y_{1j.}$	...	$y_{1q.}$	$y_{1..}$
a_2	$y_{21.}$	$y_{22.}$	...	$y_{2j.}$	...	$y_{2q.}$	$y_{2..}$
$\vdots$	$\vdots$						$\vdots$
a_i	$y_{i1.}$	$y_{i2.}$	...	$y_{ij.}$	...	$y_{iq.}$	$y_{i..}$
$\vdots$	$\vdots$						$\vdots$
a_p	$y_{p1.}$	$y_{p2.}$	...	$y_{pj.}$	...	$y_{pq.}$	$y_{p..}$
Total	$y_{.1.}$	$y_{.2.}$	...	$y_{.j.}$	...	$y_{.q.}$	$y_{...}$

Also the replication total will be $y_{..1}, y_{..2}, y_{..r}$. The total for each main plot is $y_{i.u}$ for $i = 1, 2, ..., p$ and $u = 1, 2, ..., r$.

ANOVA Table-16 for the above design is given on Page 598.

From the above ANOVA table, we come to the following conclusions:

(*i*) Degrees of freedom for Error (*a*) will always be less than the degrees of freedom for Error (*b*).

(*ii*) Error (*b*) mean square should be less than Error (*a*) mean square. If not, we should pool the two errors and analysis be carried out as if it were a factorial experiment in randomized block design.

Q. 120. *Give expected mean squares for various component factors in ANOVA table of a split plot design with two factors.*

ANOVA Table-16

Source of variation	*d.f.*	*S.S.*	*M.S.*	*F-value*
Main-plot				
Replicate	$r-1$	$\frac{1}{pq}\sum_{u=1}^{r} y_{..u}^2 - \frac{y_{....}^2}{rpq} = R_{yy}$	$\frac{R_{yy}}{r-1} = R_y$	R_y/E_{ya}
A	$p-1$	$\frac{1}{rq}\sum_{i=1}^{r} y_{i..}^2 - \frac{y_{....}^2}{rpq} = A_{yy}$	$\frac{A_{yy}}{p-1} = A_y$	A_y/E_{ya}
Eroor (a)	$(r-1)(p-1)$	$\frac{1}{q}\sum_{i=1}^{p}\sum_{u=1}^{r} y_{i.u}^2 - \frac{1}{pq}\sum_{u=1}^{r} y_{.u}^2 - \frac{1}{rq} \times \sum_{i=1}^{p} y_{i..}^2 + \frac{y_{....}^2}{rpq} = E_{yya}$	$\frac{E_{yya}}{(r-1)(p-1)} = E_{ya}$	
Sub-plot				
B	$q-1$	$\frac{1}{rp}\sum_{j=1}^{q} y_{.j.}^2 - \frac{y_{....}^2}{rpq} = B_{yy}$	$\frac{B_{yy}}{q-1} = B_y$	B_y/E_{yb}
$A \times B$	$(p-1)(q-1)$	$\frac{1}{r}\sum_{i=1}^{p}\sum_{j=1}^{q} y_{ij.}^2 - \frac{1}{rq}\sum_{i=1}^{p} y_{i..}^2 - \frac{1}{rp} \times \sum_{j=1}^{q} y_{.j.}^2 + \frac{y_{....}^2}{rpq} = (AB)_{yy}$	$\frac{(AB)_{yy}}{(p-1)(q-1)} = (AB)_y$	$(AB)_y/E_{yb}$
Error (b)	$p(r-1)(q-1)$	By difference $= E_{yyb}$	$\frac{E_{yyb}}{p(r-1)(q-1)} = E_{yb}$	
Total	$rpq-1$	$\sum_i\sum_j\sum_u y_{iju}^2 - y_{...}^2/rpq$		

Ans. Let there be two factors A and B with levels p and q respectively. Also the factor A is main-plot treatment and B, the sub-plot treatment. The layout contains r replications. The expected mean squares, under statistical model

$$y_{iju} = \mu + \alpha_i + \beta_j + (\alpha\beta)_{ij} + \rho_u + \delta_{ui} + \varepsilon_{iju}$$

For $i = 1, 2, ..., p$

$j = 1, 2, ... q$

$u = 1, 2, ..., r$

for the split plot design with usual notation, are given in skeleton ANOVA Table-17 (Page 599).

Q. 121. *Discuss the nature of the experimental error in split plot design.*

Ans. Let us consider an split plot experiment with two treatments A and B where the treatment A is applied to the main plot. Also suppose i represents the level of A, j the level of B in the ith main plot and u^{th} replication.

In this design we assume that any two subunits within the same main-plot are correlated with a correlation coefficient ρ and in two different main-plots are independent. Also suppose the error ε_{iju} is distributed as $N(0, \sigma^2)$. Symbolically,

$$E(\varepsilon_{iju} \, . \, \varepsilon_{ij'u}) = \rho\sigma^2 \quad \text{for } j \neq j'$$

and $$E(\varepsilon_{iju} \, . \, \varepsilon_{i'j'u}) = 0 \quad \text{for } i \neq i'$$

ANOVA Table - 17

Source of Variation	*d.f.*	*Expected M.S. Model-I (A and B fixed)*	*Expected M.S. Model-II (A and B random)*
Whole Plot			
Rep.	$r-1$	$\sigma_\varepsilon^2 + q\sigma_\delta^2 + pq\sigma_\rho^2$	$\sigma_\varepsilon^2 + q\sigma_\delta^2 + pq\sigma_\rho^2$
A	$p-1$	$\sigma_\varepsilon^2 + q\sigma_\delta^2 + \frac{rq}{p-1}\sum_{i=1}^{p}\alpha_i^2$	$\sigma_\varepsilon^2 + q\sigma_\delta^2 + rq\,\sigma_\alpha^2$
Error (a)	$(r-1)(p-1)$	$\sigma_\varepsilon^2 + q\sigma_\delta^2$	$\sigma_\varepsilon^2 + q\sigma_\delta^2$
Sub-Plot			
B	$q-1$	$\sigma_\varepsilon^2 + \frac{rp}{q-1}\sum_{j=1}^{q}\beta_j^2$	$\sigma_\varepsilon^2 + r\sigma_{\alpha\beta}^2 + rp\,\sigma_\beta^2$
$A \times B$	$(p-1)(q-1)$	$\sigma_\varepsilon^2 + \frac{r}{(p-1)(q-1)}\sum_{i=1}^{p}\sum_{j=1}^{q}(\alpha\beta)_{ij}^2$	$\sigma_\varepsilon^2 + r\sigma_{\alpha\beta}^2$
Sub-plot error (b)	$p(r-1)(q-1)$	σ_ε^2	σ_ε^2
Total	$rpq-1$		

Considering an experiment with two sub-units per unit in a split plot design, the error variance of a unit is,

$$E(\varepsilon_{i1u} + \varepsilon_{i2u})^2 = E(\varepsilon_{i1u}^2) + E(\varepsilon_{i2u}^2) + 2E(\varepsilon_{i1u} \cdot \varepsilon_{i2u})$$
$$= \sigma^2 + \sigma^2 + 2\rho\sigma^2$$
$$= 2\,\sigma^2\,(1+\rho)$$

If there are q sub-units per unit, the corresponding error variance of a unit total works-out to be $\sigma^2\{1 + (q-1)\,\rho\}$.

Again, the error variance of the effect of B is equal to the variance of the difference between two sub-units within a unit, *i.e.*,

$$E(\varepsilon_{i1u} - \varepsilon_{i2u})^2 = E(\varepsilon_{i1u}^2) + E(\varepsilon_{i2u}^2) - 2E(\varepsilon_{i1u}\ \varepsilon_{i2u})$$
$$= 2\sigma^2\,(1-\rho)$$

This expression remains the same even if there are q sub-units per unit.

Q. 122. *The layout of a split plot design, in which the irrigations (I) at four levels are assigned to main-plots and fertilizers (F), the combination of N, P, K each at 2 levels are allocated to sub-plots, is given below. Grain yields of maize per plant in gms is also given along with the treatment combinations:*

Rep. I				*Rep. II*			
I_0	I_1	I_3	I_2	I_3	I_2	I_0	I_1
(000) 31.0	(001) 33.0	(110) 32.0	(100) 31.3	(110) 26.7	(011) 32.3	(100) 30.7	(110) 31.5
(010) 29.0	(010) 28.7	(111) 28.8	(011) 24.7	(001) 24.7	(000) 33.7	(101) 31.7	(000) 32.7
(011) 23.3	(101) 25.7	(000) 25.0	(110) 30.0	(010) 25.2)	(110) 30.0	(111) 29.3	(001) 29.7
(100) 28.6	(110) 30.0	(010) 29.3	(101) 31.0	(101) 27.8	(010) 32.7	(110) 32.7	(010) 32.7
(101) 25.0	(100) 24.6	(001) 25.0	(111) 27.0	(011) 27.5	(111) 33.0	(000) 27.3	(011) 30.2
(110) 29.0	(111) 27.0	(011) 29.0	(001) 26.3	(100) 28.2	(101) 35.3	(001) 26.3	(100) 35.8
(001) 26.7	(011) 28.0	(100) 28.0	(010) 30.0	(111) 24.3	(001 32.7)	(010) 30.0	(101) 30.8
(111) 26.7	(000) 27.3	(101) 27.3	(000) 27.0	(000) 27.3	(100) 35.0	(011) 34.0	(111) 35.7

Rep. III

I_1	I_2	I_3	I_0
(001)	(000)	(111)	(011)
30.0	29.0	29.5	30.0
(010)	(001)	(000)	(100)
29.3	26.7	28.0	29.0
(011)	(010)	(110)	(101)
33.0	30.7	31.8	28.7
(100)	(011)	(001)	(110)
29.7	29.7	29.7	28.3
(101)	(100)	(101)	(111)
26.3	24.7	25.5	29.3
(110)	(101)	(010)	(001)
31.0	29.3	30.2	28.7
(111)	(110)	(100)	(000)
29.7	33.7	28.3	31.3
(000)	(111)	(011)	(010)
38.0	31.0	30.2	27.0

Analyse the experimental data and draw conclusions.

Ans. For main-plot analysis we prepare the following two way table and calculate sum of squares.

	I_0	I_1	I_2	I_3	*Total*
R_1	219.3	224.3	227.3	224.4	895.3
R_2	242.0	259.1	264.7	211.7	977.5
R_3	232.3	247.0	234.8	233.2	947.3

Total	693.6	730.4	726.8	669.3	2820.1

$$\text{C.F.} = (2820.1)^2/96 = 82843.38$$

$$\text{S.S. (I)} = \frac{1}{24}(693.6^2 + 730.4^2 + 726.8^2 + 699.3^2) - \text{C.F.}$$

$$= \frac{1990765.85}{24} - 82843.38 = 105.20$$

$$\text{S.S. due to Replications} = \frac{1}{32}(895.3^2 + 977.5^2 + 947.3^2) - \text{C.F.}$$

$$= \frac{265444.63}{32} - 82843.38$$

$$= 108.04$$

$$\text{Main-plot S.S.} = \frac{1}{8}(219.3^2 + 224.3^2 + ... + 234.8^2 + 233.2^2) - \text{C.F.}$$

$$= \frac{665488.99}{8} - 82843.38$$

$$= 342.74$$

$$\text{Error (a) S.S.} = 342.74 - 105.20 - 108.04$$

$$= 129.50$$

For sub-plot analysis, we prepare the following table:

S.S. due to sub-plot treats. (F)

$$= \frac{1}{12}(357.6 + 353.9^2 + ... + 351.9^2 + 351.3^2) - \text{C.F.}$$

S.S. for factorial effects by Yates' method

		I_0	I_1	I_2	I_3	*Total*	*(i)*	*(ii)*	*(iii)*	*Mean effect*	*S.S.*
(1)	000	89.6	98.0	89.7	80.3	357.6	711.5	1433.0	2820.1	29.38	82843.37
n	100	88.3	90.1	91.0	84.5	353.9	721.5	1387.1	12.5	0.26	1.63
p	010	86.0	90.7	93.4	84.7	354.8	683.9	8.2	29.3	0.61	8.94
np	110	90.0	92.5	93.7	90.5	366.7	703.2	4.3	10.1	0.21	1.06
k	001	81.7	92.7	85.7	79.4	339.5	–3.7	10.0	45.9	0.96	21.94
nk	101	85.4	82.8	95.6	80.6	344.4	11.9	19.3	–3.9	–0.08	0.16
pk	011	87.3	91.2	86.7	86.7	351.9	4.9	15.6	9.3	0.19	0.90
npk	111	85.3	92.4	91.0	82.6	351.3	–0.6	–5.5	–21.1	–0.44	4.64

$$= \frac{994591.81}{12} - 82843.38$$

$$= 39.27$$

$$\text{S.S. } (I \times F) = \frac{1}{3} (89.6^2 + 98.0^2 + ... + 91.0^2 + 82.6^2) - \text{C.F.} - \text{S.S.}(I) - \text{S.S. }(F)$$

$$= \frac{249200.69}{3} - 82843.38 - 105.20 - 39.27$$

$$= 79.05$$

$$\text{Total S.S.} = (31.0^2 + 33.0^2 + ... + 30.2^2 + 27.0^2) - \text{C.F.}$$
$$= 83648.95 - 82843.38$$
$$= 805.57$$

$$\text{Error (b) S.S.} = 805.57 - 79.05 - 39.27 - 342.74$$
$$= 344.51$$

ANOVA Table

Source of variation	*d.f.*	*S.S.*	*M.S.*	*F-value*
Main-plot				
Replications	2	108.04	54.02	2.50
Irrigation (I)	3	105.20	35.07	1.62
Error (a)	6	129.50	21.58	
Sub-plot				
Fertilizer (F)	7	39.27	5.61	0.91
N	1	1.63	1.63	0.26
P	1	8.94	8.94	1.45
NP	1	1.06	1.06	0.17
K	1	21.94	21.94	3.57
NK	1	0.16	0.16	0.03
PK	1	0.90	0.90	0.15
NPK	1	4.64	4.64	0.75
I × F	21	79.05	3.76	0.61
Error (b)	56	344.51	6.15	
Total	95	805.57		

Comparing the calculated *F*-values given in ANOVA table below for various component factors with the respective *F*-values as, $F_{.05, (2, 6)} = 5.14$; $F_{.05, (3, 6)} = 4.76$; $F_{.05, (7, 56)} = 2.17$; $F_{.05, (1, 56)} = 4.00$; and $F_{.05, (21, 56)} = 1.74$, we find that all treatments and their interactions are non-significant. Also there is no significant difference among the replications as well.

Q. 123. *What are the variations usually exploited in split plot design?*

Ans. Many variations in split plot design are exploited depending on the number and nature of the treatments. A few are given below:

(*i*) When there are more than two factors and the factors require different size experimental units, then double, triple or more splits are utilised as per the number of factors.

(*ii*) In some situations if the number of replicates are as many as the levels of the main-plot factor *A* and the experimental conditions are conducive, then the levels of *A* in whole plots can be taken in a Latin square design. This sort of arrangement has certain added advantages.

(*iii*) Another variation of the split plot design is to arrange the sub-plots in a Latin square design for the same level of the whole plot treatment provided the number of replications is a multiple of the levels of the sub-plot treatment.

(*iv*) When both the factors require large size experimental units, one has to choose split block (strip plot) design.

(*v*) When sub-plot treatments are factorials, it is many times beneficial to confound certain interactions(s) within the main plots. This helps in reducing the size of the main plot which may otherwise be unpalatable.

ANOVA Table-18

Source of Variation	*d.f.*	*S.S.*	*M.S.*	*F-value*
Whole-plot				
Replications	$r-1$	R_{yy}	$R_{yy/(r-1)} = R_y$	R_y/E_{ya}
A	$p-1$	A_{yy}	$A_{yy/(p-1)} = A_y$	A_y/E_{ya}
Error (a)	$(r-1)(p-1)$	E_{yya}	$E_{yya/(r-1)(p-1)} = E_{ya}$	
Sub-plot				
B	$q-1$	B_{yy}	$B_{yy/(q-1)} = B_y$	B_y/E_{yb}
$A \times B$	$(p-1)(q-1)$	$(AB)_{yy}$	$(AB)_{yy/(p-1)(q-1)} = (AB)_y$	$(AB)_y/E_{yb}$
Error (b)	$p(r-1)(q-1)$	E_{yyb}	$E_{yyb/p(r-1)(q-1)} = E_{yb}$	
Sub-subplot				
C	$m-1$	C_{yy}	$C_{yy/(m-1)} = C_y$	C_y/E_{yc}
$A \times C$	$(p-1)(m-1)$	$(AC)_{yy}$	$(AC)_{yy/(p-1)(m-1)} = (AC)_y$	$(AC)_y/E_{yc}$
$B \times C$	$(q-1)(m-1)$	$(BC)_{yy}$	$(BC)_{yy/(q-1)(m-1)} = (BC)_y$	$(BC)_y/E_{yc}$
$A \times B \times C$	$(p-1)(q-1)(m-1)$	$(ABC)_{yy}$	$(ABC)_{yy/(p-1)(q-1)(m-1)} = (ABC)_y$	$(ABC)_y/E_{yc}$
Error (c)	$pq(m-1)(r-1)$	E_{yyc}	$E_{yyc/pq(m-1)(r-1)}$	

Q. 124. *Give ANOVA table for a split-split plot design.*

Ans. Let there be three factors A, B and C involved in the experiment having levels p, q and m, respectively. Suppose the factor A is allocated to whole plots, B to sub-plots and C to sub-subplots. Also there are r replications in the experiment laid-out in split-split plot design. ANOVA table-18 for the split-split plot design will be as displayed on top.

Q. 125. *Give the field layout of a split-split plot design involving three treatments A, B and C having 4, 3 and 2 levels respectively in two replications.*

Ans. Suppose the factor A is allocated in main plots, B in sub-plots and C in sub-subplots. Then the layout of the split-split plot experiment is as given alongside.

Rep. I

a_1	a_2	a_3	a_0
$c_0 \vdots c_1$ b_1 $\vdots$	$c_0 \vdots c_1$ b_0 $\vdots$	$c_0 \vdots c_1$ b_1 $\vdots$	$c_0 \vdots c_1$ b_1 $\vdots$
$c_0 \vdots c_1$ b_0 $\vdots$	$c_1 \vdots c_0$ b_2 $\vdots$	$c_0 \vdots c_1$ b_2 $\vdots$	$c_1 \vdots c_0$ b_0 $\vdots$
$c_1 \vdots c_0$ b_2 $\vdots$	$c_1 \vdots c_0$ b_1 $\vdots$	$c_0 \vdots c_1$ b_0 $\vdots$	$c_0 \vdots c_1$ b_2 $\vdots$

Rep. II

a_3	a_1	a_0	a_2
$c_1 \vdots c_0$ b_1 $\vdots$	$c_0 \vdots c_1$ b_2 $\vdots$	$c_1 \vdots c_0$ b_0 $\vdots$	$c_1 \vdots c_0$ b_1 $\vdots$
$c_0 \vdots c_1$ b_0 $\vdots$	$c_1 \vdots c_0$ b_0 $\vdots$	$c_0 \vdots c_1$ b_2 $\vdots$	$c_1 \vdots c_0$ b_2 $\vdots$
$c_1 \vdots c_0$ b_2 $\vdots$	$c_1 \vdots c_0$ b_1 $\vdots$	$c_0 \vdots c_1$ b_1 $\vdots$	$c_0 \vdots c_1$ b_0 $\vdots$

Q. 126. *Give the field plan and skeleton ANOVA table of a split plot experiment in which the main plot treatment A is at 3 levels and sub-plot treatment B at 4 levels. Further, the main plot factor level are allocated in a Latin square arrangement.*

Ans. The field plan of a split plot design with three replications where factor A at 3 levels is allocated in main plots in a Latin square arrangement and B at 4 levels in sub-plots is as given below:

Rep. I

a_1	a_2	a_0
b_1	b_2	b_0
b_0	b_1	b_1
b_2	b_3	b_3
b_3	b_0	b_2

Rep. II

a_2	a_0	a_1
b_1	b_3	b_2
b_2	b_0	b_1
b_0	b_1	b_3
b_3	b_2	b_0

Rep. III

a_0	a_1	a_2
b_2	b_1	b_2
b_3	b_3	b_1
b_0	b_0	b_3
b_1	b_2	b_0

The break-up of degrees of freedom in ANOVA table for the above design is depicted below:

Source of variation	*d.f.*
Main-plots	
Rows	2
Columns	2
A	2
Error (a)	2
Sub-plot	
B	3
$A \times B$	6
Error (b)	18
Total	35

Q. 127. *How will you prepare the field plan for a split plot experiment having three replications in which the main plot treatment A at 4 levels is in randomized complete block arrangement and split plot treatment B at 3 levels is in a Latin square arrangement? Also give the break-up of degrees of freedom for this design.*

Ans. The plan of a split plot design taking subplot treatment in a Latin square arrangement within same level of main-plot treatment is as follows:

Rep. I

Order	a_3	a_2	a_1	a_0
1	b_1	b_1	b_0	b_2
2	b_0	b_2	b_1	b_0
3	b_2	b_0	b_2	b_1

Rep. II

Order	a_2	a_1	a_0	a_3
1	b_2	b_1	b_1	b_2
2	b_0	b_2	b_2	b_1
3	b_1	b_0	b_0	b_0

Rep. III

Order	a_1	a_0	a_3	a_2
1	b_2	b_0	b_0	b_0
2	b_0	b_1	b_2	b_1
3	b_1	b_2	b_1	b_2

The break-up of degrees of freedom for the above design will be as presented below.

Source of variation	*d.f.*
Whole-plots	
Replications	2
A	3
Error (a)	6
Sub-plots	
B	2
$A \times B$	6
Orders within plots	8
Error (b)	8
Total	35

Q. 128. *When two factorial treatments require large plots, suggest a suitable experimental design and give its layout plan.*

Ans. Suppose there are two sets of treatments, say, A at 4 levels and B at 3 levels. Also both the treatments are such that they require large size plots due to operational problems, *e.g.*, depth of ploughing and irrigation, spacing and seed rate, etc. In such cases, a design analogous to split plot design is appropriate named as *split block design* or *strip plot design*. In this design, the field is cut into strips for one set of treatments superposed over the strips for the other set of treatments at right angles. Respective treatments are allocated randomly to the strips. The field layout of split block design with 3 replications is displayed below:

Rep. I

	a_1	a_0	a_3	a_2
b_0				
b_2				
b_1				

Rep. II

	a_2	a_3	a_0	a_1
b_2				
b_0				
b_1				

Rep. III

	a_3	a_2	a_0	a_1
b_2				
b_0				
b_1				

Q. 129. *What shall be the break-up of the degrees of freedom of a split block design?*

Ans. Let there be two factors A and B at levels p and p respectively. The treatments are allocated in strips at right angles. Also assume that there are r replications. The break-up of degrees of freedom due to various components is as follows:

Source of variation	*d.f.*
Replications	$r - 1$
A	$p - 1$
Error (a)	$(r - 1)(p - 1)$
B	$q - 1$
Error (b)	$(r - 1)(q - 1)$
$A \times B$	$(p - 1)(q - 1)$
Error (c)	$(r - 1)(p - 1)(q - 1)$
Total	$rpq - 1$

Q. 130. *What are the merits of a split plot design?*

Ans. There are several merits of a split plot design which are delineated below:

(*i*) Treatments requiring large experimental units are easily accommodated without hampering other treatments.

(*ii*) Greater precision is attained on sub-plot treatment and interaction as compared to randomized complete block design.

(*iii*) The precision of split plot design as a whole over randomized block design can be increased by taking whole plot treatment levels in a Latin square arrangement.

(*iv*) The design is very convenient for agricultural experiments where treatments like ploughing, spacing, irrigation, etc., are involved.

(*v*) It saves lot of area which would have otherwise been required in any other design.

Q. 131. *Mention the demerits of a split plot design.*

Ans. Demerits of a split plot design are mentioned below:

(*i*) The precision of whole plot treatment is less as compared to their precision if they were tried in randomized block design.

(*ii*) If there is any missing observation, the analysis becomes much more complex as compared to randomized block design.

(*iii*) The calculation of standard errors for different pairs of treatment means is quite cumbersome. Moreover, there are too many standard errors.

(*iv*) The increased accuracy obtained on the sub-plot treatment and interaction is attained at the cost of main plot treatment.

(*v*) The degrees of freedom for error variance for both the sets of comparisons is less relative to a parallel randomized block design. Hence, randomized block design is superior for all sets of comparisons.

Q. 132. *Give the possible layouts of a confounded split plot design in which the sub-unit treatments are 2^3 factorials and also the unit treatment has two levels. Also compare these layouts.*

Ans. The layout of a confounded 2×2^3 split plot design with factor A at 2 levels in main units and factors B, C and D in sub-units confounding an effect can possibly be arranged in two ways. Since, the highest order interaction is most preferred to be confounded, we confound BCD in sub-units. This obviously reduces the sub-unit size from 8 units to 4 units. First we give two layouts:

Arrangement (i)

Block I		*Block II*	
a_0	a_0	a_1	a_1
c	*bd*	(1)	*b*
d	(1)	*bc*	*bcd*
bcd	*cd*	*cd*	*d*
b	*bc*	*bd*	*c*

Arrangement (ii)

Block I		*Block II*	
a_0	a_1	a_0	a_1
c	*cd*	*bd*	*d*
bcd	*bd*	(1)	*c*
b	(1)	*cd*	*bcd*
d	*bc*	*bc*	*b*

If we compare arrangements (*i*) and (*ii*) we find that;

(1) in arrangement (*i*), the factorial combinations with positive and negative signs are at the same level of A in sub-units.

(2) arrangement (*i*) leads to more accurate estimation of effect A and sub-plot treatments except that of BCD and $ABCD$.

(3) in arrangement (*ii*), we have gone a step further. The sub-unit treatments which have opposite signs in the contrast BCD are placed under a_0 and a_1 in the same sub-block.

(4) in arrangement (*ii*), $ABCD$ is completely confounded with sub-blocks whereas BCD is orthogonal with sub-blocks just like A.

(5) arrangement (*ii*) enables to obtain more precise estimators of A and BCD as compared to (*i*) at the cost of the information of $ABCD$.

(6) arrangement (*ii*) is more appropriate than (*i*) in view of the above points.

Q. 133. *What are the commonly used designs to have incomplete blocks when no factorial treatments are at hand.*

Ans. There is a series of balanced incomplete block (B.I.B) designs and partially balanced incomplete block (P.B.I.B.) designs which accommodate only a limited number of treatments in a block. These designs have been constructed to estimate the effects and test their significance efficiently. Their construction and analysis part are more complicated than basic experimental designs.

Note. B.I.B. and P.B.I.B. designs are kept out of the scope of this chapter.

SECTION B

Fill in the Blanks

Fill in the suitable word(s) or phrase(s) in the blanks:

1. Design of experiments is a branch of ________ .

2. The plan of an experiment which controls all factors as far as possible except the treatments in known as ________ .

3. The designs of experiments were originated mainly for ________ .

4. A subject receiving a treatment in an experiment is called _________ .
5. A substance or a factor attached to an experimental unit to know its effects is termed as _________ .
6. The allocation of treatments to experimental units with equal probability is known as _________ .
7. Through random assignment of treatments to experimental units, one eliminates _________ .
8. Systematic influences likely to occur in an experiment can be removed through _________ .
9. The process of randomization in experiment validates the use of _________ theories.
10. The assumption of independence of errors in experimentation holds good because of _________ .
11. For the validity of probability statements about treatment differences, _________ is a must in experimental designs.
12. The number of times a treatment is repeated in an experiment is called its _________ .
13. Replications provide a valid estimate of _________ .
14. Greater the number of replications in an experiment, _________ it is.
15. The average performance of a treatment is better reflected through _________ .
16. Greater homogeneity within the block in an experiment is better maintained through _________ .
17. In fields, the homogeneity of land is adjudged through _________ .
18. Experimental error is the error caused by _________ .
19. Smaller the experimental error, more _________ is the design.
20. For a greater precision of detecting treatment differences, _________ replications are required.
21. Large number of replications be taken if the experimental unit are _________ .
22. The number of replications should be such that it provides at least _________ degrees of freedom for experimental error.
23. Number of replications depends on the _________ among experimental units.
24. If sub-sampling is involved, _________ replications be taken in the experiment.
25. The mathematical formula for determining the number of replications with usual notations is _________ .
26. An empirical relation between plot size and plot variance was developed by _________ .
27. The information available from an experiment having the error variance s^2 based on n d.f. is equal to _________ .
28. The formula for information from an experiment was propounded by _________ .
29. The relative efficiency of a design over other design is the ratio of the _________ of their error variances.
30. If 6 per cent sampling is done from each plot in cereal crops, the loss of information due to sampling is _________ as compared to complete harvesting.
31. In analysis of variance, the total variance is splitted into _________ .
32. Statistical model always involves _________ and _________ besides treatment and other effects.
33. Errors in a statistical model are always taken to be distributed as _________ .
34. Statistical models for experimental designs are classified into _________ types.
35. Statistical model considered for all designs is an _________ model.
36. The validity of the additive nature of a statistical model can be tested by the test given by _________ .
37. Other names given to fixed effect model are _________ or _________ .

38. Random effect model is also called ________ or ________ .

39. If the interest of a researcher is confined in the treatments involved in the experiment, the appropriate statistical model for it is a ________ model.

40. If the inferences are to be drawn about the population of treatments of which they are the sample, the type of statistical model is ________ .

41. If A is a fixed effect having p levels, then $\sum_{i=1}^{p} \alpha_i$, is equal to ________ .

42. A commonly used approach to test the significance of differences between pairs of treatment means is the ________ method.

43. The formula for least significant difference with usual notations is ________ .

44. Student-Newman Kuel's test takes care of the ________ between two means in an ordered set of treatment means.

45. The chance of committing Type II error is ________ and of Type I error is ________ in Duncan's multiple range test as compared to least significant difference test.

46. Tukey utilized ________ or the ________ .

47. A linear combination of k treatments, in which the sum of the coefficients of the treatments is zero, is called a ________ or ________ .

48. The linear combination $T_1 - 3T_2 + T_3$ of three treatments is ________ .

49. The linear combination $-3T_1 - T_2 + T_3 + 3T_4$ of four treatments is a ________ .

50. If the sum of the cross product of the corresponding coefficients of two contrasts each involving k treatments is zero, they are said to be ________ contrasts.

51. The idea of orthogonal contrasts emerged from ________ .

52. Sum of square due to a contrast $Z_w = T_1 - T_2 - T_3 + T_4$, where each treatment total is a sum of 4 observations is ________ .

53. Among k treatments, there can at most be ________ orthogonal contrasts.

54. Each contrast has ________ d.f.

55. Orthogonal contrasts among three treatments enable to estimate ________ and ________ effects.

56. Contrasts provide ________ information about treatments than F-test alone in analysis of variance.

57. There are ________ categories of experimental designs.

58. The experimental designs not involving any randomization process are called ________ designs.

59. The estimates obtained from systematic designs are ________ .

60. Systematic designs can cause ________ errors.

61. Personal biases cannot be ruled out in ________ designs.

62. Systematic designs make sampling of area ________ .

63. In systematic designs, the chances of drifting of one treatment effect over the other are ________ .

64. The experiments in which the treatments are allocated to the units through a random process are called ________ designs.

65. A completely randomized design is used when all experimental units are ________ .

66. When all experimental units are homogeneous, the most suitable design for an experiment is ________ .

67. Completely randomized design yields ________ degrees of freedom for error.

68. Missing observation in a completely randomized design creates ________ .

69. If the experimental units are likely to fail to respond, ________ is a suitable design.

70. Completely randomized design is not suitable for ________ experiments.

71. If an exact *F*-test for treatments, based on the statistical model of an experiment is available in ANOVA, the model is said to be ________ .

72. Analysis of data of a completely randomized design with two treatments and a *t*-test for their equality are ________ .

73. Taking more than one observation on each experimental unit with regard to the same character is known as ________ .

74. The analysis of variance under sub-sampling involves two error components in ANOVA table namely ________ and ________ errors.

75. If in ANOVA table, *F*-value for treatments comes out to be less than unity, it creates doubt on the validity of the ________ .

76. *F*-value in ANOVA table smaller than one may occur if the observations are not distributed ________ .

77. If the experimental units are subjected to one way variation, then one may prefer to use ________ design.

78. Each block in a randomised block design is a ________ .

79. Each treatment occurs ________ in a block of randomized complete block design.

80. There are as many units in a block as the number of ________ in a randomized block design.

81. When every level of a factor is tried with every level of the other factor, then such an arrangement is called ________ classification.

82. The process of repeated sampling and sub-sampling is known as ________ or ________ classification.

83. If all levels of a factor are tried at each single level of the other factor, the later factor is ________ in the former factor.

84. In a randomized block design, blocks are formed in ________ direction to fertility gradient.

85. Usually randomized block design in field experiments is ________ efficient than completely randomized design.

86. According to Cochran, the error mean square of a randomized block design is ________ per cent to that of an equivalent completely randomized design.

87. For an equal amount of information in completely randomized design ________ replication are equivalent to ________ replications in randomized block design.

88. In a randomized block design, too many treatments ________ accommodated in a block.

89. If there are *t* treatments and *m* blocks in a randomized block design, the error degrees of freedom in ANOVA table be ________ .

90. Statistical model for a randomized block design under Model-I is a ________ model.

91. Error sum of squares ________ be negative.

92. The formula for one missing value in a randomized block design with *k* treatments and *b* blocks following usual notations is ________ .

93. If there are two missing values in a randomized block design with 4 blocks and 5 treatments, the error degrees of freedom will be ________ .

94. Missing value in a randomized block design causes an ________ bias in the treatment sum of square.

95. In case of sub-sampling in a randomized design, the pooling of sampling and experimental errors depends on the result of ________ .

96. In case of sub-sampling in experiments, the analysis of data is safer if the investigator decides for ________ pooling rather than ________ pooling.

97. A Latin square design is a ________ two way classification scheme.

98. A Latin square design controls ________ heterogeneity.

99. A Latin square design is a ________ restrictional design.

100. The number of treatments, rows and columns in a Latin square design are ________ .

101. Each treatment occurs ________ in a row or a column in a Latin square design.

102. Each row and each column is a ________ in a Latin square design.

103. The number of rows or columns denote the ________ of a Latin square.

104. Two Latin squares L_1 and L_2 are called ________ if L_1 is superimposed over L_2, then each pair of letters occurs only once in the composite square.

105. If there is a Latin square of order p, then there can at most be ________ orthogonal Latin squares.

106. Error mean square in the analysis of data of a Latin square is ________ than the error mean square in case of RBD and CRD with the same experimental material.

107. A Latin square design of order 4 is as efficient as a randomized block design with ________ replications for the same treatments.

108. A 3 × 3 Latin square design is ________ efficient than a randomized block design with 3 replications.

109. A composite Latin square design using Latin and Greek letters is called ________ design.

110. The main assumption of a Latin square design is that treatment effects ________ with the row and column effects.

111. The additive model for a Latin square design is a ________ model.

112. The formula for estimating a missing value in a Latin square design having k treatments with usual notations is ________ .

113. There is an ________ bias in treatment sum of square of a Latin square being analysed with a missing value.

114. Relative efficiency of a Latin square of order k over completely randomized design with usual notation can be calculated by the formula ________ .

115. Relative efficiency of a Latin square design with k treatments as compared to randomized block design utilizing the same material can be obtained by the formula ________ .

116. To have sufficient degrees of freedom for error from lower order Latin square, the alternative is to consider a ________ Latin squares.

117. If we consider m Latin squares of order k in an experiment, the degrees of freedom for error is ________ .

118. Another name of cross-over design is ________ or ________ or ________ design.

119. Cross-over design is suitable for ________ number of treatments.

120. Change over designs is capable of estimating ________ and ________ effects.

121. Cross-over designs are frequently used in experiments on ________ .

122. In cross-over design each treatment is followed by the other treatments ________ number of times.

123. An experiment involving two or more factors at various levels is called a ________ experiment.

124. A factorial experiment, with equal number of levels of all factors, is called a ________ factorial experiment.

125. An experiment involving 5 levels of nitrogen, 4 levels of phosphorous and 3 levels of potash is ________ factorial experiment.

126. The factorial experiments were also called ________ experiments.

127. The name factorial experiment is due to ________ .

128. In factorial experiments, one estimates ________ and ________ effects.

129. The measure of change in the response due to change of level of a factor averaged over all levels of other factors is called ________ .

130. The failure of a factor to give the same response at different levels of the other factor is known as ________ .

131. The additional effect due to combined effect of two or more factors is the ________ effect.

132. The interaction effect of the factors N and P is ________ as that of factors P and N.

133. In a 2^n factorial, each main and interaction effect can be expressed as a ________ .

134. In a 2^n factorial, the contrasts for main effects and interaction(s) are ________ to each other.

135. In a 2^n factorial, the lower level of a factor is called its ________ .

136. In a 2^n factorial, the higher level of a factor is known as ________ .

137. If A and B are two factors each at 2 levels, the simple effect of A at the first level of B is ________ .

138. Given two factors A and B each at 2 levels, the simple effect B at the second level of A is ________ .

139. In a 2^2 factorial with factors A and B, the simple effect of B, $(b) - (1)$ is equivalent to ________ .

140. The interaction between two factors A and B each at two levels is the ________ of simple effects of A at second and first levels of B.

141. Sum of squares for main effects and interaction(s) in 2^n factorial can easily be calculated with the help of ________ technique.

142. The sum of squares in a 3^n factorial can easily be calculated with the help of ________ technique.

143. In a 3^n experiment with factors A and B, the interaction $A \times B$ has ________ d.f.

144. In a 3^2 factorial, the interaction $A \times B$ can further be splitted up as ________ and ________ .

145. In a 3^3 factorial, the interaction component A^2B^2C is equivalent to the interaction component ________ .

146. The statistical model for a two factor factorial is a ________ model.

147. The technique of reducing the block size in factorial experiments by sacrificing one or more effects is known as ________ .

148. Preferably ________ interaction is chosen for confounding.

149. The method of confounding to reduce block size is applicable only for ________ experiments.

150. If the same effect is confounded in all the replications, it is known as ________ .

151. If the same effect is not confounded in all the replicates, it is known as ________ .

152. In 2^n factorials, confounding can easily be carried out with the help of ________ .

153. If p^n factorial ($p > 2$), confounding can conveniently be carried out through ________ .

154. When the effects of the same order are confounded an equal number of times in all the replications of a factorial experiment, it is known as ________ .

155. In a 2^4 factorial, the effects ABC and BCD are confounded to obtain the blocks of size 4 units, the effect ________ is automatically confounded with the blocks.

156. The product of any two interactions in a p^n factorial reduced to mod p is known as ________ .

157. Confounding in asymmetrical factorials is carried with the help of ________ factors.

158. The additional factors required to convert the asymmetrical factorial into a symmetrical factorial for the purpose of confounding are called ________ factors.

159. When different factors require different size of units, one should go for ________ design.

160. The large size plots used for one factor in split plot design are called ________ plots.

161. The small size plots within each main plot are called ________ .

162. Split plot design is a confounded design in which the ________ treatments are confounded.

163. Split plot design in agriculture was first used at ________ in ________ .

164. Nowadays split plot design is frequently used in ________ industry.

165. In industrial experiments, split plot design is used under the name ________ design.

166. Split plot design is akin to ________ design.

167. In split plot design, increased precision is attained on ________ and ________ .

168. The d.f. for main-plot error variance is ________ than sub-plot error.

169. Mostly the main-plot error variance is ________ than sub-plot error variance in the analysis of data of a split plot design.

170. In a nested model ________ effect cannot be estimated.

171. A split plot design can entertain more than ________ splits.

172. A split plot design having two splits is called ________ design.

173. Main plot or sub-plot treatments can be arranged in ________ besides randomized block arrangement.

174. If both the treatments of a factorial experiment require large size plots, then one must prefer ________ design.

175. In a strip plot design, maximum precision is attained on ________ effect.

176. Main plot size can be reduced through ________ of ________ treatments.

177. Statistical model for split plot design for fixed and random effects is a ________ model.

178. In a split plot design with A at 5 levels in main-plots and 4 levels of B in sub-plots having 3 replications, the sub-plot error d.f. will be ________ .

179. Randomized block design is ________ to split plot design for all sets of comparisons.

180. Experimental designs is a vast subject in the theory of ________ .

181. The number of Latin squares which can be formed out of p letters is ________ .

182. Purpose of local control is to reduce ________ .

183. Analysis of variance techniques is applied for testing the equivalence of a set of two or more population ________ .

184. Latin square model assumes that there is ________ between treatments and rows or column groupings.

185. The design where only replication and randomization are used is ________ .

186. In experimental designs randomization is necessary to make the ________ valid.

187. A design in which the main effect is confounded is ________ design.

188. A design in which three sources of variation can be eliminated is ________ design.

189. Factorial experiments are necessary in order to study ________ .

190. Another name of fractional replication design is ________ design.

191. The credit of introducing fractional replication designs goes to ________ .

192. Fractional replication designs are in vogue since ________ .

193. The number of replications(s) in a fractional factorial experiment is/are ________ .

194. The interaction effect used to form the fractional replication is called ________ .

195. The factorial effects represented by the same contrast are called ________ .

196. If in a symmetrical factorial, identity group consists of R-factors, then the fractional factorial is of ________ .

197. If the estimation of all effects up to R-factors is possible and the effects with more than

R-factors are assumed negligible, then the fractional factorial design is of resolution ________.

198. A fractional factorial design is of resolution 2R if it makes possible the estimation of all ________ factor effects and ________ or more factor effects are taken to be zero.

199. Fractional factorial designs are used in ________ and ________ experiments.

200. Systematic designs in agricultural field research were used as early as in the year ________.

201. The contrast $T_1 - 2T_2 + T_3$ is a ________ contrast.

202. The contrasts $T_1 - T_3$; $T_2 - T_3$; $T_1 - T_2$ among three treatments are ________ contrasts.

203. Out of 4 treatments, these can be at most ________ pairwise contrasts.

204. The decision to test the quadratic and cubic effects of four fertilizers at the planning level of trial leads to testing of ________ contrasts.

205. The contrasts constructed after the treatments were found significant are known as ________ contrasts.

SECTION C

Multiple Choice Questions

Select the correct alternative out of given ones:

1. An experimental design is:
   (*a*) a map
   (*b*) a plan of experiment
   (*c*) an architect
   (*d*) all of the above

2. An experimental unit in a research work is:
   (*a*) an animal
   (*b*) a field plot
   (*c*) a group of insects
   (*d*) all of the above

3. A medicine is a treatment applied to:
   (*a*) a patient
   (*b*) a field plot
   (*c*) both (*a*) and (*b*)
   (*d*) neither (*a*) nor (*b*)

4. The factors like spacing, date of sowing and breeds are often used as:
   (*a*) experimental unit
   (*b*) treatments
   (*c*) replicates
   (*d*) none of the above

5. Randomization is a process in which the treatments are allocated to the experimental units:
   (*a*) at the will of the investigator
   (*b*) in a sequence
   (*c*) with equal probability
   (*d*) none of the above

6. Randomization in an experiment helps to eliminate:
   (*a*) systematic influences
   (*b*) human biases
   (*c*) dependence among observations
   (*d*) all of the above

7. Randomization is a process which enables the experimenter to:
   (*a*) apply mathematical theories
   (*b*) make probability statements
   (*c*) treat errors independent
   (*d*) all of the above

8. Replication in an experiment means:
   (*a*) the number of blocks
   (*b*) total number of treatments
   (*c*) the number of times a treatment occurs in an experiment
   (*d*) none of the above

9. Replications in an experiment eliminate:
   (*a*) human bias
   (*b*) competition among neighbouring plots

(c) heterogeneity among blocks
(d) none of the above

10. Randomizations in an experiment provide:
(a) the estimate of experimental error
(b) impetus to the treatments
(c) a check to the variation in soil fertility
(d) none of the above

11. Number of replications in an experiment is based on:
(a) the precision required
(b) experimental material available
(c) heterogeneity of experimental material
(d) all of the above

12. The factors responsible for deciding the number of replications in an experiment are:
(a) the desire of the experimenter
(b) minimum degrees of freedom required for experimental error
(c) shape of experimental units
(d) all of the above

13. The decision about the number of replications is taken in view of:
(a) size of experimental units
(b) competition among experimental units
(c) fraction to be sampled
(d) all of the above

14. The formula for determining the number of replications '*r*' with usual notations is:
(a) $r = 2t_\alpha^2 s^2/d^2$
(b) $r = \sqrt{2}t_\alpha s^2/d^2$
(c) $r = t_\alpha^2 s^2/d^2$
(d) $r = 2t_\alpha s/d$

15. Local control is a device to maintain:
(a) homogeneity among blocks
(b) homogeneity within blocks
(c) both (a) and (b)
(d) neither (a) and (b)

16. Local control in the field is maintained through:
(a) uniformity trials
(b) randomization
(c) natural factors
(d) all of the above

17. Local control in experimental designs is meant to:
(a) increase the efficiency of the design
(b) reduce experimental error
(c) to form homogeneous blocks
(d) all the above

18. Experimental error is due to:
(a) experimenter's mistakes
(b) extraneous factors
(c) variation in treatment effects
(d) none of the above

19. Experimental error is necessarily required for:
(a) testing the significance of treatments effects
(b) comparing treatment effects
(c) calculating the information released from an experiment
(d) all of the above

20. Errors in a statistical model are always taken to be:
(a) independent
(b) distributed as $N(0, \sigma_e^2)$
(c) both (a) and (b)
(d) neither (a) and (b)

21. If s^2 is the estimate of error variance in an experiment based on *n* degrees of freedom, the information gathered from the experiment is equal to:
(a) $\dfrac{n+3}{n+1}\dfrac{1}{s^2}$
(b) $\dfrac{n+1}{n+3}\dfrac{1}{s^2}$
(c) $\dfrac{n+3}{n+1}s^2$
(d) $\left(\dfrac{n+1}{n+3}\cdot\dfrac{1}{s}\right)^2$

22. The information from an experiment stabilizes when error degrees of freedom is at least:
(*a*) 6
(*b*) 8
(*c*) 10
(*d*) 12

23. If σ_1^2, is the error variance of design-1 and σ_2^2 of design-2 utilizing the same experiment material, the efficiency of design 1 over 2 is
(*a*) $\frac{1}{\sigma_1^2} \Big/ \frac{1}{\sigma_2^2}$
(*b*) $\frac{1}{\sigma_2^2} \Big/ \frac{1}{\sigma_1^2}$
(*c*) σ_1^2/σ_2^2
(*d*) none of the above

24. If sampling is adopted from plots in an experiment, the loss of information due to sampling as compared to complete harvesting is:
(*a*) negligible
(*b*) one-third
(*c*) two-third
(*d*) none of the above

25. Analysis of experimental data means:
(*a*) estimation of treatment effects
(*b*) dividing the total variance into component variances
(*c*) testing of hypothesis about the parameters involved in the experimental model
(*d*) all of the above

26. A statistical model is a mathematical relationship between the:
(*a*) response measure and the factors responsible for the response
(*b*) response measure and the treatment effects
(*c*) both (*a*) and (*b*)
(*d*) neither (*a*) and (*b*)

27. A statistical model is categorized into:
(*a*) one type
(*b*) two types
(*c*) three types
(*d*) four types

23. The categorization of a statistical model is based on:
(*a*) assumption about the experimental error
(*b*) the nature of treatments
(*c*) characteristics of the response variable
(*d*) all of the above

29. If the conclusions are to be drawn for the treatments in general, then the statistical model shall be known as:
(*a*) analysis of variance model
(*b*) component of variance model
(*c*) mixed effect model
(*d*) none of the above

30. If the researcher's interest is confined in the treatments only involved in the experiment, then the statistical model in this situation will be categorized as:
(*a*) analysis of variance model
(*b*) component of variance model
(*c*) mixed effect model
(*d*) none of the above

31. If an experiment involves two or more treatments in which some treatments are fixed and the others are of random nature, one should choose:
(*a*) analysis of variance model
(*b*) component of variance model
(*c*) mixed effect model
(*d*) none of the above

32. In a fixed effect model, the hypothesis about the treatments under test is:
(*a*) $\sigma_\tau^2 = 0$
(*b*) $\tau_i = 0$
(*c*) $\Sigma\, \tau_i = 0$
(*d*) none of the above

33. In case of a random effect model, the

hypothesis which is to be tested with regard to the treatments is:

(a) $\sigma_\tau^2 = 0$
(b) $\tau_i = 0$
(c) $\Sigma\tau_i^2 = 0$
(a) $\Sigma\tau_i = 0$

34. For a fixed effect model
$y_{ij} = \mu + \alpha_i + \beta_j + (\alpha\beta)_{ij} + \varepsilon_{ij}$,
the assumptions are:
(a) $\Sigma\alpha_i = 0, \Sigma\beta_j = 0, \Sigma(\alpha\beta)_{ij} = 0$
(b) $\sigma_\alpha^2 = 0, \sigma_\beta^2 = 0$ and $\sigma_{\alpha\beta}^2 = 0$
(c) $\sigma_i \sim N(0, \sigma_\alpha^2), \beta_j \sim N(0, \sigma_\beta^2)$ and $(\alpha\beta)_{ij} \sim N(0, \sigma_{\alpha\beta}^2)$
(d) none of the above

35. If a model is such that it provides an exact test about the treatments, then it is called:
(a) unspecified model
(b) incompletely specified model
(c) completely specified model
(d) none of the above

36. If a statistical model fails to provide an exact test about the treatment effects, the model is classified as:
(a) unspecified model
(b) incompletely specified model
(c) completely specified model
(d) none of the above

37. Which of the pairs of treatment means differ significantly out of a set of treatment means, can be ascertained by:
(a) least significant difference test
(b) student-Newman Kuel's test
(c) Duncan's multiple range test
(d) all of the above

38. Out of many multiple range test, the test which is considered superior is:
(a) student-Newman Kuel's test
(b) Duncan's multiple range test
(c) Tukeys' test
(d) none of the above

39. A linear combination of treatments is said to be a contrast iff:
(a) the sum of the treatment effects is zero
(b) all the coefficients of the treatments are unity
(c) the sum of the coefficients of the treatments is zero
(d) the number of positive and negative coefficients is same

40. Two contrasts of the same treatments are said to be orthogonal iff:
(a) they are at right angles
(b) both of them have same coefficients of the treatments
(c) both of them have equal coefficients but opposite in sign
(d) the sum of the cross product of the coefficients of the same treatments is zero

41. Which of the following is a contrast?
(a) $3T_1 + T_2 - 3T_3 + T_4$
(b) $T_1 + 3T_2 - 3T_3 + T_4$
(c) $-3T_1 - T_2 + T_3 + 3T_4$
(d) $T_1 + T_2 + T_3 - T_4$

42. Which of the following is not a contrast among three treatments?
(a) $T_1 + 2T_2 - T_3$
(b) $T_1 - T_3$
(c) $T_1 - 2T_2 + T_3$
(d) $-T_1 + 2T_2 - T_3$

43. The maximum possible number of orthogonal contrasts among four treatments is:
(a) four
(b) three
(c) two
(d) one

44. With the help of contrasts, one can estimate the:
(a) linear effect
(b) quadratic effect

(*c*) cubic effect
(*d*) all of the above

45. The contrast representing the quadratic effect among four treatments is:
(*a*) $-3T_1 - T_2 + T_3 + 3T_4$
(*b*) $-T_1 + 3T_2 - 3T_3 + T_4$
(*c*) $T_1 - T_2 - T_3 + T_4$
(*d*) none of the above

46. The contrast representing the linear effect among four treatments is:
(*a*) $T_1 - 2T_2 + T_3$
(*b*) $T_1 - T_2 - T_3 + T_4$
(*c*) $-T_1 + 3T_2 - 3T_3 + T_4$
(*d*) none of the above

47. The cubic effect among five treatments can' be estimated by the contrast:
(*a*) $-T_1 + 2T_2 - 2T_4 + T_5$
(*b*) $2T_1 - T_2 - 2T_3 - T_4 + 2T_5$
(*c*) $-2T_1 - T_2 + T_4 + 2T_5$
(*d*) none of the above

48. Sum of square due to a contrast, $Z_w = l_{w1}T_1 + l_{w2}T_2 + ... + l_{wk}T_K$ is calculable by the formula:
(*a*) $\left(Z_w / r \sum_i l_{wi}\right)^2$
(*b*) $Z_w^2 / r \sum_i l_{wi}^2$
(*c*) $Z_w^2 / r \sum_i l_{wi}$
(*d*) none of the above

49. Each contrast among k treatments has:
(*a*) $(k - 1)$ d.f.
(*b*) one d.f.
(*c*) k d.f.
(*d*) none of the above

50. An experimental design which is devoid of any randomization process is known as:
(*a*) systematic design
(*b*) non-randomized design
(*c*) purposive design
(*d*) all of the above

51. The experiments in which the treatments are allocated to experimental units through a random process are categorized as:
(*a*) completely randomized design
(*b*) partially randomized design
(*c*) randomized design
(*d*) all of the above

52. A completely randomized design is also known as:
(*a*) unsystematic design
(*b*) non-restrictional design
(*c*) single block design
(*d*) all of the above

53. Completely randomized designs are suitable in the situation(s) when:
(*a*) all experimental units are homogeneous
(*b*) the units are likely to be destroyed during experimentation
(*c*) some units are likely to fail to response
(*d*) all of the above

54. Completely randomized designs are mostly used in:
(*a*) field experiments
(*b*) experiments on animals
(*c*) pot experiments
(*d*) all of the above

55. Missing observation in a completely randomized design is to be:
(*a*) estimated
(*b*) deleted
(*c*) guessed
(*d*) none of the above

56. In a completely randomized design with t treatments and n experimental units, error degrees of freedom is equal to:
(*a*) $n - t$
(*b*) $n - t - 1$
(*c*) $n - t + 1$
(*d*) $t - n$

57. Statistical model for a completely randomized design under Model-I and Model-II is:
(*a*) unspecified
(*b*) completely specified

(*c*) incompletely specified
(*d*) none of the above

58. The process of determining more than one observation on each experimental unit pertaining to the same character is known as:
(*a*) multiple recording
(*b*) sub-sampling
(*c*) repeated observations
(*d*) none of the above

59. In case of sub-sampling in a completely randomized design, the treatment mean square is tested against:
(*a*) experimental error M.S.
(*b*) sampling error M.S.
(*c*) pooled error M.S.
(*d*) none of the above

60. If *F*-value for treatments comes out to be less than one, it may be due to:
(*a*) improper randomization
(*b*) non-normality of response measure
(*c*) selection of wrong statistical model
(*d*) all of the above

61. If every level of a factor is taken at every level of the other factor in an experiment, it is known as:
(*a*) crossed classification
(*b*) nested classification
(*c*) hierarchical classification
(*d*) all of the above

62. When all levels of a factor are woven within each level of some other factor, it is known as:
(*a*) nested classification
(*b*) hierarchical classification
(*c*) both (*a*) and (*b*)
(*d*) neither (*a*) nor (*b*)

63. If a plant breeder includes *s* species and *n* strains within each specie, he has to analyse the data according to:
(*a*) fixed effect model
(*b*) nested model
(*c*) mixed model
(*d*) none of the above

64. The following layout,

A	*B*	*C*	*D*
A	*C*	*B*	*D*
B	*A*	*C*	*C*
A	*A*	*B*	*C*

meets the requirements of a:
(*a*) completely randomized design
(*b*) randomized block design
(*c*) Latin square design
(*d*) none of the above

65. The layout,

A	*C*	*A*	*B*
C	*B*	*C*	*D*
B	*A*	*D*	*A*
D	*D*	*B*	*C*

stands for:
(*a*) cross-over design
(*b*) randomized block design
(*c*) Latin square design
(*d*) none of the above

66. In the field layout of a randomized block design, the blocks are formed in the direction:
(*a*) parallel to fertility gradient
(*b*) perpendicular to fertility gradient
(*c*) diagonally to fertility gradient
(*d*) none of the above

67. Randomized block design is a:
(*a*) three restrictional design
(*b*) two restrictional design
(*c*) one restrictional design
(*d*) no restrictional design

68. A randomized block design has:
(*a*) two way classification
(*b*) one way classification
(*c*) three way classification
(*d*) no classification

69. In the analysis of data of a randomized block design with *b* block and *v* treatments, the error degrees of freedom are:
(*a*) $b(v-1)$
(*b*) $v(b-1)$
(*c*) $(b-1)(v-1)$
(*d*) none of the above

70. Error sum of squares in RBD as compared to CRD using the same material is:

(*a*) more
(*b*) less
(*c*) equal
(*d*) not comparable

71. According to W.G. Cochran, error mean square in case of RBD as compared to CRD utilising same experimental material is:

(*a*) 60 per cent
(*b*) 80 per cent
(*c*) 40 per cent
(*d*) none of the above

72. The ratio of the number of replications required in CRD and RBD for the same amount of information is:

(*a*) 6 : 4
(*b*) 10 : 6
(*c*) 10 : 8
(*d*) 6 : 10

73. The formula for obtaining a missing value in randomized block design by minimizing the error mean square was given by:

(*a*) W.G. Cochran
(*b*) T. Wishart
(*c*) F. Yates
(*d*) J.W. Tukey

74. The formula for estimating one missing value in a randomized block design having b blocks and k treatments with usual notations is:

(*a*) $\dfrac{bT' + kB' - G'}{(b-1)(k-1)}$

(*b*) $\dfrac{bB' + bT' - G'}{(b-1)(k-1)}$

(*c*) $\dfrac{bT' + kT' - kG'}{(b-1)(k-2)}$

(*d*) $\dfrac{bB' + kT' - G'}{(b-1)(k-1)}$

75. In a randomized block design with 4 blocks and 5 treatments having one missing value, the error degrees of freedom will be:

(*a*) 12
(*b*) 11
(*c*) 10
(*d*) 9

76. A missing value in an experiment is estimated by the method of:

(*a*) minimizing the error mean square
(*b*) analysis of covariance
(*c*) both (*a*) and (*b*)
(*d*) neither (*a*) and (*b*)

77. When there occurs a missing value in an experiment, treatment sum of square has:

(*a*) an upward bias
(*b*) a downward bias
(*c*) no bias
(*d*) none of the above

78. In case of sub-sampling in a randomized block design, if preliminary test reveals a non-significant difference between experimental error and sampling error, one should prefer:

(*a*) to pool the two errors
(*b*) not to pool the two errors
(*c*) may or may not pool the two errors
(*d*) none of the above

79. The idea of preliminary test of significance was propounded by:

(*a*) T.A. Bancroft
(*b*) A.E. Paull
(*c*) F. Yates
(*d*) none of the above

80. In the want of preliminary test of significance in case of sub-sampling in the analysis of data of an experiment, it is always preferable:

(*a*) not to pool the two errors
(*b*) to pool the two error
(*c*) to use sampling error
(*d*) to use any one of the errors

81. In a Latin square design, number of rows, columns and treatments are:

(*a*) all different
(*b*) always equal

(*c*) not necessarily equal
(*d*) none of the above

82. A Latin square design is a:
(*a*) one restrictional design
(*b*) two restrictional design
(*c*) three restrictional design
(*d*) non-restrictional design

83. A Latin square design possesses:
(*a*) one way classification
(*b*) two way classification
(*c*) three way classification
(*d*) no way classification

84. If the entries in rows of a Latin square are same as its columns, the Latin square is called:
(*a*) conjugate
(*b*) self-conjugate
(*c*) orthogonal
(*d*) symmetric

85. If two Latin squares are such that one can be obtained by interchanging the rows of one with columns of the other, then the Latin squares are said to be:
(*a*) conjugate
(*b*) self-conjugate
(*c*) orthogonal
(*d*) asymmetric

86. If two Latin squares are such that when one is superimposed over the other, each pair of letters occurs only once, the two Latin squares are said to be:
(*a*) conjugate
(*b*) self-conjugate
(*c*) orthogonal
(*d*) reduced

87. A Latin square in which the letters occur in alphabetical order is called a:
(*a*) conjugate Latin square
(*b*) reduced Latin square
(*c*) orthogonal Latin square
(*d*) none of the above

88. A Latin square design controls:
(*a*) two way variation
(*b*) three way variation
(*c*) multiway variation
(*d*) no variation

89. Completely randomized or randomized block design is better than a Latin square design with same number of replications as in Latin square of order:
(*a*) two
(*b*) three
(*c*) four
(*d*) all of the above

90. A Greaco-Latin square is a composite square of two Latin squares which are:
(*a*) adjugate to one another
(*b*) conjugate to each other
(*c*) orthogonal to each other
(*d*) all of the above

91. For a Latin square of order p, there can at most be:
(*a*) p orthogonal Latin squares
(*b*) $(p - 1)$ orthogonal Latin squares
(*c*) $p - 2$ orthogonal Latin squares
(*d*) p^2 orthogonal Latin squares

92. While analysing the data of a $k \times k$ Latin square, the error d.f. in analysis of variance is equal to:
(*a*) $(k - 1)(k - 2)$
(*b*) $k(k - 1)(k - 2)$
(*c*) $k^2 - 2$
(*d*) $k^2 - k - 2$

93. The formula for estimating one missing value in a Latin square of order k with usual notations is:
(*a*) $(R' + C' + T' - G')/(k - 1)(k - 2)$
(*b*) $[k(R' + C' + T') - 2G']/(k - 1)(k - 2)$
(*c*) $k(R' + C' + T' - 2G')/(k^2 - 1)$
(*d*) $k(R' + C' + T' - 2G')/(k - 1)^2(k - 2)^2$

94. The formula for calculating the bias in the treatment sum of square introduced due to the estimation of a missing value in a Latin square of order k with usual notations is:
(*a*) $[(kT' + R' + C' - G')/(k - 1)(k - 2)]^2$

(b) $[(kT' + kR' + kC' - 2G')/(k - 1)(k - 2)]^2$

(c) $[\{(k - 1)T' + R' + C' - G'\}/(k - 1)(k - 2)]^2$

(d) $[\{(k - 1)T' + kR' + kC' - 2G'/(k - 1)(k - 2)]^2$

95. For lower order Latin square, adequate degrees of freedom for error can be obtained by taking:

(a) a group of Latin squares at a time
(b) a Latin square at two locations
(c) both (a) and (b)
(d) neither (a) and (b)

96. Cross-over design is suitable for measuring:

(a) direct treatment effect
(b) treatments' residual effect
(c) both (a) and (b)
(d) neither (a) nor (b)

97. Cross-over design is also named as:

(a) change over design
(b) switch back design
(c) reversal design
(d) all of the above

98. Error degrees of freedom for a change over design are more when the subjects are taken in:

(a) replicates
(b) a group of Latin squares
(c) any order
(d) all of the above

99. The experiments, in which the effects of the levels of a factor are considered at various levels of the other factor are called:

(a) symmetrical experiments
(b) rotational experiments
(c) factorial experiments
(d) all of the above

100. An experiment having several factors with equal number of levels is known as:

(a) complex experiment
(b) symmetrical factorial experiment
(c) asymmetrical experiment
(d) all the above

101. Two types of effects measured in a factorial experiment are:

(a) main and interaction effects
(b) simple and complex effects
(c) both (a) and (b)
(d) neither (a) nor (b)

102. The additional effect gained due to combined effect of two or more factors is known as:

(a) main effect
(b) interaction effect
(c) either of (a) or (b)
(d) neither of (a) or (b)

103. The experiments with various factors having unequal number of levels are called:

(a) asymmetrical factorials
(b) symmetrical factorials
(c) typical factorials
(d) none of the above

104. An experiments, in which all factors have different number of levels, is known as:

(a) asymmetrical factorial
(b) typical factorial
(c) pseudo factorial
(d) real factorial

105. All contrast, representing the effects of a 2^n factorial, are:

(a) linear contrasts
(b) orthogonal contrasts
(c) both (a) and (b)
(d) neither (a) nor (b)

106. The main and interaction effects in a 2^n-factorial can easily be estimated with the help of:

(a) simple effects
(b) contrasts
(c) both (a) and (b)
(d) neither (a) and (b)

107. If the responses for treatments in a factorial experiment with factors A and B each at two levels from three replications are, $a_0b_0 = 18$, $a_1b_0 = 17$, $a_0b_1 = 25$ and $a_1b_1 = 30$, the sum of square for the interaction AB is equal to:

(a) 4

(*b*) 3
(*c*) 6
(*d*) 675

108. The main and interaction effect's sum of squares in a p^n factorial system in general can easily be calculated with the help of:
(*a*) contrasts
(*b*) modulo technique
(*c*) both (*a*) and (*b*)
(*d*) neither (*a*) nor (*b*)

109. If there is a factor at four levels in a factorial experiment, one can find its:
(*a*) linear effect
(*b*) quadratic effect
(*c*) cubic effect
(*d*) all of the above

110. The quadratic effect of a factor X at three levels 0, 1 and 2 can be estimated by the contrast:
(*a*) $X_0 - X_2$
(*b*) $X_0 + X_2 - 2X_1$
(*c*) $X_1 + X_2 - 2X_0$
(*d*) $X_0 + X_1 - 2X_2$

111. The general approach for estimating the main and interaction effects and sum of squares due to them in any factorial experiment is:
(*a*) modulo technique
(*b*) contrasts method
(*c*) multiway table
(*d*) all of the above

112. In a 2^n factorial, all effects and their sum of squares can be obtained directly at a stretch by:
(*a*) Yates' method
(*b*) modulo technique
(*c*) both (*a*) and (*b*)
(*d*) neither (*a*) nor (*b*)

113. In Yates' method of analysis of data of a factorial experiment, implicit approach is:
(*a*) the modulo technique
(*b*) the utilization of orthogonal contrasts
(*c*) the utilization of multiway tables
(*d*) none of the above

114. Expected mean squares in an ANOVA table are the source which reveal:
(*a*) whether an exact test for a factor exists
(*b*) which factor be tested against which error term
(*c*) whether an exact test for a factor does not exist.
(*d*) all of the above

115. The method of confounding is a device to reduce the size of:
(*a*) experiments
(*b*) replications
(*c*) blocks
(*d*) all the above

116. If the same factorial effect is confounded in all the replications, it is known as:
(*a*) partial confounding
(*b*) complete confounding
(*c*) conservative confounding
(*d*) none of the above

117. The effect, which is confounded in all the blocks in an experimental design:
(*a*) is estimated more precisely
(*b*) is estimated less precisely
(*c*) cannot be estimated
(*d*) none of the above

118. If different effects are confounded in different blocks, it is said to be:
(*a*) complete confounding
(*b*) partial confounding
(*c*) balanced confounding
(*d*) none of the above

119. If all effects of the same order are confounded with incomplete blocks differences, it is said to be:
(*a*) complete confounding
(*b*) partial confounding
(*c*) balanced confounding
(*d*) none of the above

120. If interaction AB is confounded in a 2^3 factorial experiment, the entries of two blocks in a replicate will be:

(*a*) *Bl.* 1: *b*, *ac*, *bc*, *a*
Bl. 2: (1), *ab*, *c*, *abc*
(*b*) *Bl.* 1: (1), *ab*, *a*, *b*
Bl. 2: *abc*, *c*, *bc*, *ac*
(*c*) *Bl.* 1: (1), *ab*, *ac*, *bc*
Bl. 2: *abc*, *a*, *b*, *c*
(*d*) *Bl.* 1: *abc*, *bc*, *ac*, *c*
Bl. 2: *ab*, *a*, *b*, (1)

121. If the interactions *AB* and *BC* are confounded with incomplete blocks in a 2^n factorial experiment, then automatically confounded effect is:
(*a*) *ABC*
(*b*) *AC*
(*c*) *A*
(*d*) *C*

122. If *k* effects are confounded in a 2^n factorial to have 2^k blocks of size 2^{n-k} units, the number of automatically confounded effect is:
(*a*) $2^k - k$
(b) $k^2 - k - 1$
(c) $2^k - k - 1$
(*c*) none of the above

123. The factors, having the levels equal to the quotient which is obtained on dividing the total number of treatment combinations of as asymmetrical factorial by the incomplete block size are called:
(*a*) pseudo factors
(*b*) real factors
(*c*) the factor(s) of asymmetry
(*d*) none of the above

124. The factors which are used to convert the asymmetrical factorial into symmetrical factorial for the purpose of confounding are termed as:
(*a*) pseudo factors
(*b*) real factors
(*c*) the factors of asymmetry
(*d*) none of the above

125. The factors, not having the level(s) equal to the quotient which is obtained on dividing the total number of treatment combinations by the incomplete block size, are called:
(*a*) pseudo factors
(*b*) real factors
(*c*) the factors of asymmetry
(*d*) none of the above

126. Confounding in asymmetrical factorials is carried out with the help of:
(*a*) contrasts
(*b*) modulo technique
(*c*) graphics
(*d*) all of the above

127. When the treatments require different size plot for experimentation, frequently adopted design is:
(*a*) confounded design
(*b*) split plot design
(*c*) Latin square design
(*d*) none of the above

128. Split plot design is a sort of:
(*a*) confounded design
(*b*) partially nested design
(*c*) both (*a*) and (*b*)
(*d*) neither (*a*) and (*b*)

129. A split plot design can involve only:
(*a*) two factors
(*b*) three factors
(*c*) both (*a*) and (*b*)
(*d*) neither (*a*) nor (*b*)

130. Large size plots receiving the treatments in a split plot design are called:
(*a*) main plots
(*b*) whole plots
(*c*) both (*a*) and (*b*)
(*d*) neither (*a*) nor (*b*)

131. A split plot design can be extended to:
(*a*) double split only
(*b*) triple split only
(*c*) multiple split
(*d*) none of the above

132. Split plot design was first used in experiments on:
(*a*) agriculture
(*b*) industry
(*c*) animals
(*d*) all of the above

133. In a split plot design, more precision is attained for:
(*a*) main plot treatment
(*b*) sub-plot treatment
(*c*) block differences
(*d*) all of the above

134. In a split plot design, more error degrees of freedom is obtained for:
(*a*) main plots
(*b*) sub-plots
(*c*) replicates
(*d*) none of the above

135. In a split plot design, smaller error mean square is obtained for:
(*a*) main plot error
(*b*) sub-plot error
(*c*) experimental error
(*d*) none of the above

136. If there is a double split plot design, the analysis of variance table will contain:
(*a*) two error components
(*b*) three error components
(*c*) four error components
(*d*) one error components

137. In a split plot design with factor A at p levels in main-plots, factor B at q levels in subplots and r replications, the degrees of freedom for sub-plot error is equal to:
(*a*) $(q - 1)(r - 1)$
(*b*) $q(p - 1)(r - 1)$
(*c*) $(p - 1)(q - 1)(r - 1)$
(*d*) $p(q - 1)(r - 1)$

138. For a split plot design with factor A in main plots at 4 levels, factor B in sub-plots at 3 levels and having 3 replications, sub-plot error degrees of freedom will be:
(*a*) 24
(*a*) 27
(*c*) 16
(*d*) 12

139. For a split plot experiment conducted with 5 concentrations of an insecticide in main plots and 4 varieties of gram in sub-plots and having 3 replications, main plot error degrees of freedom will be:
(*a*) 8
(*b*) 10
(*c*) 24
(*d*) 6

140. Model-I of a split plot design is:
(*a*) an incompletely specified model
(*b*) a completely specified model
(*c*) an unspecified model
(*d*) none of the above

141. For a double split plot design with 4 levels of main plot treatment, 3 levels of sub-plot treatment and 2 levels of sub-subplot treatment and 2 replications, the error sub-subplot error degrees of freedom is:
(*a*) 48
(*b*) 36
(*c*) 24
(*d*) 12

142. When two treatments at various levels involved in an experiment require large size plots, the appropriate experimental design is:
(*a*) split plot design
(*b*) strip plot design
(*c*) Latin square design
(*d*) any one of the above

143. Split plot design for all sets of comparisons as compared to a randomized block design with the same experimental material is:
(*a*) superior
(*b*) inferior
(*c*) equally good
(*d*) none of the above

144. In a split-split plot design, maximum precision is attained on:
(*a*) whole plot treatment
(*b*) sub-plot treatment
(*c*) sub-subplot treatment
(*d*) none of the above

145. A split block experiment is conducted with 5 level of irrigation (I) and 4 levels of an insecticide (M) for foliar spray. The experiment contained 3 replications. The error

degrees of freedom for the interaction effect will be:

(a) 24
(b) 30
(c) 32
(d) 40

146. The precision of whole-plot treatment can be increased by assigning the treatments to whole plots:

(a) randomly
(b) in randomized block arrangement
(c) in a Latin square arrangement
(d) all of the above

147. The accuracy of estimates after confounding in sub-plots increases:

(a) for main-plot treatments
(b) for all sub-plot treatments
(c) for all sub-plot treatments except those which are confounded
(d) for no treatments

148. In a 3^3 factorial with factors A, B and C each at 3 level, the interaction A^2BC^2 is same as the interaction:

(a) ABC
(b) AB^2C
(c) AB^2C^2
(d) A^2BC

149. The analysis of variance of an experimental data is based on the assumption(s) that:

(a) the response variable is distributed normally
(b) the errors are independent
(c) the errors are homoscedastic
(d) all of the above

150. If in a randomized block design having five treatments and 4 replications, a treatment is added, the increase in error degrees of freedom will be:

(a) 1
(b) 2
(c) 3
(d) 4

151. If in a Latin square design with five treatments, a treatment is added, the increase in error degrees of freedom will be:

(a) 2
(b) 4
(c) 6
(d) 8

152. If two levels of a main plot treatment are increased, the degrees of freedom for main-plot error in a split plot design with three replications will be increased by:

(a) 2
(b) 4
(c) 6
(d) 8

153. If two levels of a sub-plot treatment are increased, the main-plot error in a split plot design with two replications will be:

(a) increased
(b) decreased
(c) same
(d) none of the above

154. If one level of main plot treatment is increased in a split plot design having its p levels, q levels of sub-plot treatment and r replications, then the sub-plot error degrees of freedom will be increased by:

(a) r
(b) $(r-1)(p-1)$
(c) $(r-1)(q-1)$
(d) $(p-1)(q-1)$

155. If two levels of a sub-plot treatment are increased in a split plot design, the main plot error degrees of freedom will be increased by:

(a) 0
(b) 1
(c) 2
(d) none of the above

156. If in a split plot design with two treatments A and B at levels 4 and 3 respectively and three replications, a level of each treatment is dropped, then the total degrees of freedom will be reduced by:

(a) 8
(b) 10

(*c*) 12
(*d*) 18

157. If in a split plot design with treatment A at 4 levels in main-plots, B at 3 levels in subplots and 3 replications, one level of both the treatments is reduced, then the sub-plot error degrees of freedom will be decreased by:
(*a*) 6
(*b*) 8
(*c*) 10
(*d*) 12

158. If in a split plot design with two factors, A in main-plots and B in sub-plots at levels p and q respectively and r replications, a replication is discarded, then the sub-plot error degrees of freedom will be decreased by:
(*a*) rpq
(*b*) $p(q-1)$
(*c*) $(p-1)q$
(*d*) $(r-1)(p-1)(q-1)$

159. If in a split plot design with two factors, A in main plots and B in sub-plots at levels p and q respectively and r replications, a replication is rejected, then the main-plot error degrees of freedom will be decreased by
(*a*) $r-1$
(*b*) $(p-1)$
(*c*) $q-1$
(*d*) $r(p-1)$

160. If in a strip plot design with factors A and B at levels p and q respectively and r replications, a level of both the factors is dropped, then the total degrees of freedom will be reduced by
(*a*) $r(p-1)(q-1)$
(b) $r(p+q-1)$
(*c*) $r(p+q-2)$
(*d*) $r(pq-1)$

161. In randomized block design we always have:
(*a*) No. of blocks = No. of treatments
(*b*) No. of blocks > No. of treatments
(*c*) No. of blocks < No. of treatments
(*d*) none of the above

162. Local control helps to:
(*a*) reduce the no. of treatments
(*b*) increase the no. of plots
(*c*) reduce the error variance
(*d*) increase the error d.f.

163. In one way classification with more than two treatments, the equality of treatment means is tested by:
(*a*) t-test
(*b*) χ^2-test
(*c*) F-test
(*d*) none of the above

164. The degrees of freedom for F-ratio in a 6×6 Latin square design is:
(*a*) (5, 15)
(*b*) (5, 20)
(*c*) (6, 15)
(*d*) (6, 20)

165. In a 5×5 Latin square with one missing value, the totals of row, column and treatment having the missing value are 25, 40, 35 respectively and the total of all the available observations is 100. The estimate of the missing value is:
(*a*) 15
(*b*) 20
(*c*) 25
(*d*) 30

166. The concept of fractional replication was first expounded by:
(*a*) F. Yates
(*b*) D.J. Finney
(*c*) C.R. Rao
(*d*) G.E.P. Box

167. Fractional replication came into existence for the first time in the year:
(*a*) 1961
(*b*) 1950
(*c*) 1945
(*d*) 1937

168. Another name given to fractional replications is:
(*a*) balanced confounded design
(*b*) fractional factorial design

(*c*) partially confounded design
(*d*) nested design

169. Orthogonal fractional factorial designs are those which estimate:
(*a*) all effects with same precision
(*b*) all relevant effects with zero correlation
(*c*) confounded effects
(*d*) only main effects

170. The effect which is utilised to divide a replicate into a fraction is called:
(*a*) defining contrast
(*b*) alias
(*c*) confounded effect
(*d*) all of the above

171. The effects which are represented by the same contrast in a fractional factorial are called:
(*a*) defining contrast
(*b*) aliases
(*c*) both (*a*) and (*b*)
(*d*) neither (*a*) nor (*b*)

172. In a fractional replication as a 1/2 replicate in a 2^3 factorial with defining contrast *ABC* and entries *a*, *b*, *c* and *abc*, the alias to *A* is:
(*a*) *ABC*
(*b*) *AB*
(*c*) *AC*
(*d*) *BC*

173. If a researcher forms a 1/2 replicate in a factorial design with treatment combinations *a*, *b*, *c* and *abc*, the interaction which cannot be estimated at all is:
(*a*) *ABC*
(*b*) *AB*
(*c*) *AC*
(*d*) *BC*

174. In a 2^5 factorial in 1/4 replicate in a fractional factorial design with defining contrasts *ABC*, *CDE* and *ABCD*, the aliases of the main effect *A* are:
(*a*) *ACDE, ABD, ACD*
(*b*) *BC, ACDE, BCD*
(*c*) *ADE, ABE, BCD*
(*d*) none of the above

175. The idea of resolution of fractional factorial designs was introduced by:
(*a*) F.Yates
(*b*) D.J. Finney
(*c*) Box and Hunter
(*d*) S.R.Webb

176. The idea of 'Resolution' of fractional factorial designs was initiated in the year:
(*a*) 1945
(*b*) 1960
(*c*) 1961
(*d*) 1968

177. The definition of resolution of fractional factorials given by Box and Hunter is applicable to:
(*a*) symmetrical factorials
(*b*) asymmetrical factorials
(*c*) 2^3 factorials only
(*d*) all of the above

178. The definition of resolution applicable to all types of fractional factorials was given by:
(*a*) C.R. Rao
(*b*) W.T. Federer
(*c*) O. Kempthorne
(*d*) S.R.Webb

179. General definition of resolution of fractional factorial designs was given in the year:
(*a*) 1950
(*b*) 1945
(*c*) 1968
(*d*) 1961

180. The fractional factorial design in which the main effects are estimable whereas all interactions are assumed negligible is to resolution:
(*a*) 2
(*b*) 3
(*c*) 4
(*d*) 5

181. If a fractional factorial design is such that the main effects can be estimated and 3 or more factor interactions are of zero magnitude, while the others are of no interest, then this design is classified as:

(*a*) Resolution-IV design
(*c*) Resolution-V design
(*b*) Resolution-VI design
(*d*) Resolution-VII design

182. A fractional factorial design in which mean, main effects and first order interactions are estimable and second and higher order interactions are presumed to be negligible is a design of:
(*a*) Resolution-III
(*b*) Resolution-IV
(*c*) Resolution-V
(*d*) none of the above

183. The total of sum of squares (S.S.) due to all orthogonal contrasts in 2^n-factorial experiment is equal to:
(*a*) replication S.S.
(*b*) treatment S.S.
(*c*) total S.S.
(*d*) error S.S.

184. In experimental designs, randomization is necessary to make the estimates:
(*a*) valid
(*b*) accurate
(*c*) precise
(*d*) biased

185. The name of the design in which main effect is confounded is:
(*a*) Latin square design
(*b*) cross-over design
(*c*) split plot design
(*d*) none of the above

186. The pairwise contrast among three treatments is:
(*a*) $T_1 + T_2 - 2T_3$
(*b*) $2T_1 + T_2 - 3T_3$
(*c*) $T_1 + T_3 - 2T_2$
(*d*) $T_3 - T_1$

187. A non-pairwise contrast among four treatments is:
(*a*) $3T_1 + T_2 - T_3 - 3T_4$
(*b*) $3T_1 + T_2 + T_3 - 3T_4$
(*c*) $T_1 + T_2 - 2T_3 + T_4$
(*d*) $T_1 - T_4$

188. For two treatments there can be in all:
(*a*) one contrast
(*b*) two contrasts
(*c*) three contrasts
(*d*) no contrast

189. A contrast constructed while interpreting the results will be categorised as:
(*a*) posteriori contrast
(*b*) planned contrast
(*c*) biased contrast
(*d*) orthogonal contrast

190. A decision of testing the quadratic, cubic and quadratic effects of five fertilizers at the beginning of experimentation will lead to construction of:
(*a*) posteriori contrasts
(*b*) post hoc contrasts
(*c*) a priori contrasts
(*d*) non-orthogonal contrasts

ANSWERS

Section B

1. statistics **2.** design of experiment **3.** field experiments **4.** experimental unit **5.** treatment **6.** randomization **7.** human bias **8.** randomization **9.** mathematical **10.** randomization **11.** randomization **12.** replications **13.** experimental error **14.** better **15.** replications **16.** local control **17.** fertility maps **18.** extraneous factors **19.** efficient **20.** more **21.** heterogeneous **22.** twelve **23.** competition **24.** more **25.** $(\sqrt{2}t_\alpha . s/d)^2$ **26.** Fairfield Smith **27.** $\frac{n+1}{n+3} \cdot \frac{1}{s^2}$ **28.** R.A. Fisher **29.** inverse **30.** one-third **31.** component variances **32.** true mean effect; error term **33.** $N(o, \sigma_e^2)$ **34.** three **35.** additive **36.** J.W. Tukey **37.** analysis of variance model; Model-I **38.** component of variance model; Model-II **39.** fixed effect **40.** Model-II **41.** zero **42.** least significant difference **43.** $\sqrt{2\frac{s_e^2}{r}} \times t_{.05, \nu}$ **44.** distance **45.** more; less

46. honestly significant difference; *w*-procedure **47.** contrast; comparison **48.** not a contrast **49.** contrast (comparison) **50.** orthogonal **51.** orthogonal polynomial **52.** $Z_w^2/16$ **53.** $k-1$ **54.** one **55.** linear; quadratic **56.** more **57.** two **58.** systematic **59.** not valid **60.** systematic **61.** systematic **62.** easy **63.** reduced **64.** randomized **65.** homogeneous **66.** CRD **67.** maximum **68.** no problem **69.** CRD **70.** field **71.** completely specified **72.** equivalent **73.** sub-sampling **74.** experimental; sampling **75.** postulated model **76.** normally **77.** randomized complete block **78.** complete replicate **79.** once **80.** treatments **81.** crossed **82.** nested; hierarchical **83.** nested **84.** perpendicular **85.** more **86.** sixty **87.** ten; six **88.** cannot be **89.** $(t-1)(m-1)$ **90.** completely specified **91.** can never **92.** $(bB'+kT'-G')/(k-1)(b-1)$ **93.** 10 **94.** upward **95.** preliminary test of significance (PTS) **96.** never; always **97.** balanced **98.** two way **99.** two **100.** equal **101.** once **102.** complete block **103.** order **104.** orthogonal **105.** $p-1$ **106.** less **107.** five **108.** less **109.** Greaco-Latin square **110.** do not interact **111.** completely specified **112.** $k(R'+C'+T')-2G'/(k-1)(k-2)$ **113.** upward **114.** $\{R+C+(k-1)E\}/(k+1)E$ **115.** $\{R+(k-1)E\}/kE$ or $\{C+(k-1)E/kE$ **116.** group **117.** $m(k-1)(k-2)$ **118.** change over; reversal; switch back **119.** small **120.** direct; residual **121.** animals **122.** equal **123.** factorial **124.** symmetrical **125.** asymmetrical **126.** complex **127.** F. Yates **128.** main; interaction **129.** main effect **130.** interaction **131.** interaction **132.** same **133.** contrast (comparison) **134.** orthogonal **135.** first level **136.** second level **137.** $(a)-(1)$ **138.** $(ab)-(a)$ **139.** $B-AB$ **140.** difference **141.** contrasts (comparisons) **142.** modulo **143.** four **144.** AB; AB^2 **145.** ABC^2 **146.** Completely specified **147.** confounding **148.** higher order **149.** factorial **150.** complete confounding **151.** partial confounding **152.** contrasts (comparisons) **153.** modulo technique **154.** balanced confounding **155.** AD **156.** generalized interaction **157.** real **158.** pseudo **159.** split plot **160.** whole (main) **161.** sub-plots **162.** main-plot **163.** Rothamsted; 1937 **164.** chemical **165.** nested **166.** partially hierarchical **167.** sub-plot treatment; interaction **168.** less **169.** more **170.** interaction **171.** one **172.** double split or split-split plot **173.** Latin square **174.** strip plot or split block **175.** interaction **176.** confounding; sub-plot **177.** completely specified **178.** 30 **179.** superior **180.** statistics **181.** $p!\,(p-1)!$ **182.** error variance **183.** means **184.** no interaction **185.** completely randomized design (CRD) **186.** estimates or tests **187.** split plot **188.** Greaco-Latin square **189.** interaction effects **190.** fractional factorial **191.** D.J. Finney **192.** 1945 **193.** one **194.** defining contrast **195.** aliases **196.** resolution-R **197.** $2R+1$ **198.** $(R-1)$; $(R+1)$ **199.** agricultural; industrial **200.** 1834 **201.** non-pairwise **202.** pairwise **203.** 12 **204.** *a priori* or planned **205.** *posteriori* or unplanned or post hoc.

Section C

1. (*b*)	2. (*d*)	3. (*a*)	4. (*b*)	5. (*c*)
6. (*b*)	7. (*d*)	8. (*c*)	9. (*d*)	10. (*a*)
11. (*d*)	12. (*b*)	13. (*d*)	14. (*a*)	15. (*b*)
16. (*a*)	17. (*d*)	18. (*b*)	19. (*d*)	20. (*c*)
21. (*b*)	22. (*d*)	23. (*a*)	24. (*b*)	25. (*d*)
26. (*a*)	27. (*c*)	28. (*b*)	29. (*b*)	30. (*a*)
31. (*c*)	32. (*b*)	33. (*a*)	34. (*a*)	35. (*c*)
36. (*b*)	37. (*d*)	38. (*b*)	39. (*c*)	40. (*d*)
41. (*c*)	42. (*a*)	43. (*b*)	44. (*d*)	45. (*c*)
46. (*d*)	47. (*a*)	48. (*b*)	49. (*b*)	50. (*a*)
51. (*c*)	52. (*b*)	53. (*d*)	54. (*c*)	55. (*b*)
56. (*a*)	57. (*b*)	58. (*b*)	59. (*a*)	60. (*d*)
61. (*a*)	62. (*c*)	63. (*b*)	64. (*a*)	65. (*b*)
66. (*b*)	67. (*c*)	68. (*a*)	69. (*c*)	70. (*b*)
71. (*a*)	72. (*b*)	73. (*c*)	74. (*d*)	75. (*b*)
76. (*c*)	77. (*a*)	78. (*a*)	79. (*b*)	80. (*a*)
81. (*b*)	82. (*b*)	83. (*c*)	84. (*b*)	85. (*a*)
86. (*c*)	87. (*b*)	88. (*a*)	89. (*d*)	90. (*c*)
91. (*b*)	92. (*a*)	93. (*b*)	94. (*c*)	95. (*a*)
96. (*c*)	97. (*d*)	98. (*a*)	99. (*c*)	100. (*b*)
101. (*a*)	102. (*b*)	103. (*a*)	104. (*a*)	105. (*c*)
106. (*b*)	107. (*b*)	108. (*b*)	109. (*d*)	110. (*b*)
111. (*c*)	112. (*a*)	113. (*b*)	114. (*d*)	115. (*c*)
116. (*b*)	117. (*c*)	118. (*b*)	119. (*c*)	120. (*a*)
121. (*b*)	122. (*c*)	123. (*b*)	124. (*a*)	125. (*c*)
126. (*b*)	127. (*b*)	128. (*c*)	129. (*a*)	130. (*c*)
131. (*c*)	132. (*a*)	133. (*b*)	134. (*b*)	135. (*b*)
136. (*b*)	137. (*d*)	138. (*c*)	139. (*a*)	140. (*b*)

141. (*d*)	**142.** (*b*)	**143.** (*b*)	**144.** (*c*)	**145.** (*a*)	**166.** (*b*)	**167.** (*c*)	**168.** (*b*)	**169.** (*b*)	**170.** (*a*)
146. (*c*)	**147.** (*c*)	**148.** (*b*)	**149.** (*d*)	**150.** (*c*)	**171.** (*b*)	**172.** (*d*)	**173.** (*a*)	**174.** (*b*)	**175.** (*c*)
151. (*d*)	**152.** (*b*)	**153.** (*c*)	**154.** (*c*)	**155.** (*a*)	**176.** (*c*)	**177.** (*a*)	**178.** (*d*)	**179.** (*c*)	**180.** (*b*)
156. (*d*)	**157.** (*b*)	**158.** (*b*)	**159.** (*b*)	**160.** (*b*)	**181.** (*a*)	**182.** (*c*)	**183.** (*b*)	**184.** (*a*)	**185.** (*c*)
161. (*d*)	**162.** (*c*)	**163.** (*c*)	**164.** (*b*)	**165.** (*c*)	**186.** (*d*)	**187.** (*a*)	**188.** (*b*)	**189.** (*a*)	**190.** (*c*)

SUGGESTED READING

1. Cochran, W.G. and Cox. G.M., *Experimental Designs*, Asia Publishing House, Bombay, 1959.
2. Das, M.N. and Giri, N.C., *Design and Analysis of Experiments*, Wiley Eastern Ltd., Publishers, New Delhi, 1979.
3. Fedrer, W.T., *Experimental Design*, Oxford & IBH Publishing Co., New Delhi, Indian edn., 1967.
4. Kempthorne, O., *The Design and Analysis of Experiments*, Wiley Eastern Ltd., Publishers, New Delhi, 2nd edn., 1974.
5. Mead, R., *The Design of Experiments*, Cambridge University Press, New York, 1990.
6. Montgomery, D.C., *Design and Analysis of Experiments,* John Wiley & Sons, New York, 1984.
7. Ostle, B., *Statistics in Research*, Oxford & IBH Publishing Co., New Delhi, Indian edn., 1966.
8. Panse, V.G. and Sukhatme, P.V., *Statistical Methods for Agricultural Workers*, I.C.A.R., New Delhi, 1978.
9. Peter, W.M. John, *Statistical Design and Analysis of Experiments*, The Macmillan Co., New York, 1971.
10. Quenouille, M.H., *The Design and Analysis of Experiment,* Charles Griffin and Co. Ltd., London, 1953.
11. Scheffe, H., *The Analysis of Variance*, John Wiley & Sons, New York, 1959.
12. Searle, S.R., *Linear Models*, John Wiley & Sons, New York, 1971.
13. Snedcor, G.W. and Cohran, W.G., *Statistical Methods,* Oxford & IBH Publishing Co., Calcutta, 1968.
14. Winer, B.J., *Statistical Principles in Experiment* Design, McGraw-Hill Book Company, New York, 1962.

CHAPTER 22

Multivariate Statistical Methods

SECTION A

Short Essay Type Questions

Q. 1. *What is multivariate Statistic?*

Ans. Multivariate statistics is a form of statistics that encompasses the two or more outcome variables. The multivariate Statistics have application in a variety of multivariate analysis.

Q. 2. *How do you express and organize multivariate data?*

Ans. Multivariate data arise when a researcher takes measurements for two or more variables *i.e.* $p \geq 2$ (characters or factors) on distinct items, objects or individuals, so called statistical units, are categorized as multivariate data. These variables are known as multivariate random variables if they follow some multivariate Probability distribution. Let us consider p variables and n items on each variable. Then the data can be organized in the form of a matrix $\boldsymbol{X}$ of order $(n \times p)$ as follows:

$$\boldsymbol{X} = \begin{bmatrix} x_{11} & x_{12} & \cdots & x_{1j} & \cdots & x_{1p} \\ x_{21} & x_{22} & \cdots & x_{2j} & \cdots & x_{2p} \\ \vdots & \vdots & \vdots & \vdots & \vdots & \vdots \\ x_{i1} & x_{i2} & \cdots & x_{ij} & \cdots & x_{ip} \\ \vdots & \vdots & \vdots & \vdots & \vdots & \vdots \\ x_{n1} & x_{n2} & \cdots & x_{nj} & \cdots & x_{np} \end{bmatrix}$$

Where the element x_{ij} of the matrix represent the jth variable of the ith item. In the above $(n \times p)$ matrix, i^{th} row vector represents p values of the ith item and j^{th} column vector typifies n values of the ith variable. In all p column vectors provide total values for all items.

Q. 3. *How can the multivariate continuous distribution of p random variables be defined.*

Ans. Let the set of $(p \times 1)$ random vector be denoted as $(X_1', \ldots, X_j', \ldots, X_p')$. The joint continuous distribution function denoted as $F_X(x')$ is expressed as $F_X(x_1', x_2', \ldots, x_j', \ldots, x_p')$ $= P[X_1 \leq x_1', X_2 \leq x_2', \ldots, X_p' \leq x_p']$. The above expression is an extension of univariate distribution function.

Now the density function of X is given as

$$f_x(x') = f_x(x_1', x_2', \ldots, x_j', \ldots, x_p'). \text{ Where}$$

$$F_X(x') = \int_{-\infty}^{\infty}\int_{-\infty}^{\infty}\cdots\int_{-\infty}^{\infty} f_X(x_1', x_2', \ldots, x_p')\, dx_1' dx_2' \cdots dx_p'$$

The mean vector μ and variance-covariance matrix are given as,

$$\underset{\sim}{\mu} = \begin{bmatrix} \mu_1 \\ \mu_2 \\ \vdots \\ \mu_p \end{bmatrix}; \ \Sigma = \begin{bmatrix} \sigma_1^2 & \sigma_{12} & \cdots & \sigma_{1p} \\ \sigma_{21} & \sigma_2^2 & \cdots & \sigma_{2p} \\ \vdots & \vdots & \vdots & \vdots \\ \sigma_{p1} & \sigma_{p2} & \cdots & \sigma_p^2 \end{bmatrix}$$

$$\Sigma = \begin{bmatrix} \sigma_1^2 & \rho_{12}\sigma_1\sigma_2 & \cdots & \rho_{1p}\sigma_1\sigma_p \\ \rho_{12}\sigma_1\sigma_2 & \sigma_2^2 & \cdots & \rho_{2p}\sigma_2\sigma_p \\ \vdots & \vdots & \vdots & \vdots \\ \rho_{1p}\sigma_1\sigma_p & \rho_{2p}\sigma_2\sigma_p & \cdots & \sigma_p^2 \end{bmatrix}$$

In case of random sample of n objects or individuals, mean vector and var-cov matrix are,

$$\underset{\sim}{\bar{x}} = \begin{bmatrix} \bar{x}_1 \\ \bar{x}_2 \\ \vdots \\ \bar{x}_p \end{bmatrix}; \ S = \begin{bmatrix} s_1^2 & s_{12} & \cdots & s_{1p} \\ s_{21} & s_2^2 & \cdots & s_{2p} \\ \vdots & \vdots & \vdots & \vdots \\ s_{p1} & s_{p2} & \cdots & s_p^2 \end{bmatrix}$$

Multivariate Probability Distributions

Q. 4. *What is the utility of probability distribution in multivariate statistical analysis?*

Ans. Multivariate statistics is concerned with multivariate probability distributions in the sense that how can they be used to represent the distribution of the observed data and as a part of inference, estimation and testing of hypothesis of vectors of parameters, particularly when many different quantities are of interest out of same analysis. All multivariate tests depend on one or more multivariate probability distributions.

Q. 5. *Why multiple regression is not considered as a part of multivariate statistics?*

Ans. Multiple regression is not usually considered as a part of multivariate statistics because regression analysis is carried out by considering univariate conditional distribution of a single dependent variable for a number of given independent variables.

Q. 6. *Give the concept of logistic regression.*

Ans. Logistic regression is a statistical technique for analyzing a data set in which there are two or more independent variables that determine an outcome which shall be a binary variable usually coded as 1 for one factor and 0 for the other like males as 1 and females as 0.

Q. 7. *Discuss succinctly multivariate normal distribution.*

Ans. This is one of the most used distributions in multivariate statistical techniques. The reason is that the assumption of normality is common to parametric inferential statistics. Such an assumption is based on multivariate central limit theorem. This holds good even if the number of discrete data (ranks) may be thirty or more.

The random vector X $(p \times 1)$ has a p-dimensional multivariate normal distribution if the probability density function with usual notations is,

$$f(x) = \frac{1}{(2\pi)^{\frac{p}{2}} \Sigma^{\frac{1}{2}}} \exp^{[(-\frac{1}{2})(\underset{\sim}{x}-\underset{\sim}{\mu})'\Sigma^{1}(\underset{\sim}{x}-\underset{\sim}{\mu})]}$$

Where, $E(x) = \mu$ and $E(\underset{\sim}{x}-\underset{\sim}{\mu})(\underset{\sim}{x}-\underset{\sim}{\mu})' = \Sigma$

Suppose $(\underset{\sim}{x}-\underset{\sim}{\mu})'\Sigma^{-1}(\underset{\sim}{x}-\underset{\sim}{\mu}) = c^2$. This is known as Mahalanobis squared distance between $\underset{\sim}{x}$ and $\underset{\sim}{\mu}$. The expression for c^2 describes the surface of an ellipsoid centered at $\underset{\sim}{\mu}$.

Q. 8. *What are the properties associated with a random vector **X** following a multivariate normal distribution?*

Ans.

1. Linear combinations of the components of X follow multivariate normal distribution.
2. All subsets of components of X follow multivariate normal distribution.
3. If the covariance between components is zero, then it is implied that the components are independent.
4. The conditional distribution of the components of X are also multivariate normal.

5. The equidensity contours of the components of a nonsingular multivariate normal distribution are ellipsoids centered at the mean.
6. If the components of X are independent with equal variances, the contours are spheres.
7. If the covariance Σ is not of full rank, multivariate normal distribution is degenerate and does not have a density.
8. A multivariate normal distribution $N_p(\underset{\sim}{\mu}, \Sigma)$ follows $c_p^2(\alpha)$which is the quantile function of probability α of chi-squared distribution for which a probability density function exists.

Q. 9. *Discuss succinctly bivariate normal distribution.*

Ans. It is a particular case of multivariate normal distribution when $p = 2$. It is called bivariate normal distribution. In a two dimensional nonsingular case [p = rank (Σ) = 2]. The p.d.f. of a vector (X, Y) with

$$\underset{\sim}{\mu} = \begin{pmatrix} \mu_x \\ \mu_y \end{pmatrix} \text{ and } \Sigma = \begin{bmatrix} \sigma_x^2 & \rho\sigma_x\sigma_y \\ \rho\sigma_x\sigma_y & \sigma_y^2 \end{bmatrix} \text{ is}$$

$$f_{X,Y} = \frac{1}{2\pi\sigma_x\sigma_y\sqrt{1-\rho^2}} \text{Exp}\left[\left(\frac{x-\mu_x}{\sigma_x}\right)^2 - 2\rho(x-\mu_x)(y-\mu_y) + \left(\frac{y-\mu_y}{\sigma_y}\right)^2\right]$$

Where, ρ stands for the correlation coefficient between X and Y.

Q. 10. *What are the special features akin to bivariate normal distribution?*

Ans. It almost holds all properties of multivariate normal distribution. Broadly some important features are:

1. Two normally distributed random variables need not necessarily be jointly bivariate normal.
2. When $p = 2$, prediction interval of the vector having two elements, defines the interior of an ellipse and follows exponential distribution with mean equal to zero.

Note: For all other properties of bivariate normal distribution, please consult Chapter 8.

Q. 11. *Elucidate Wishart distribution.*

Ans. ***Definition:*** Wishart distribution is a generalization of multi-dimensions of the chi-square distribution or in case of non-integer d.f. of the gamma distribution.

If the sample variance-covariance matrix S, based on a ($n \times p$) data matrix as an estimate of Σ from a N_p (0, Σ) population, is given as:

$$S = \frac{1}{n-1}\sum_{i=1}^{n}(x_i - \underset{\sim}{\bar{x}})(x_i - \underset{\sim}{\bar{x}})'$$

The distribution of the term $A = (n-1)\,S$ is called the Wishart distribution. The probability density function of A under the assumption that $|A| > 0$ is,

$$W_{n-1}(A|\Sigma) = \frac{|A|^{(n-p-2)/2}\, e^{-\frac{1}{2}Tr[A\Sigma^{-1}]}}{2^{np/2}\pi^{p(p-1)/4}|\Sigma|^{n/2}\prod_{i=1}^{p}\Gamma(n-i+1)/2}$$

Let $(x_i - \underset{\sim}{\bar{x}}) = z_i$, Then $A = \sum z_i z_i'$.

Properties

1. If $A_1 = \sum_{i=1}^{n_1} z_i z_i'$ and $A_2 = \sum_{j=1}^{n_2} z_j z_j'$, and $n = n_1 + n_2$, then the distribution of $(A_1 + A_2)$ is a Wishart distribution as $W_n(A_1 + A_2|\Sigma)$.
2. If A is distributed as $W_{n-1}(A|\Sigma)$, then CAC' is distributed as $W_{n-1}(CAC'|C\Sigma C')$, where C is a nonsingular triangular matrix in which each scalar quantity $c_{ij} = 0$ for $i > j$.
3. If the mean $\overline{X}, N_p\left(\underset{\sim}{\mu}, \frac{1}{n}\Sigma\right)$ is known to have $\underset{\sim}{\mu} = \mathbf{0}$, then the data matrix X (n, p) has a covariance matrix $X'X$. This is the point where the Wishart distribution comes into existence

since $X'X = \sum_{u=1}^{n} x_u x_u'$ has Wishart distribution $W_p(\Sigma, n)$.

4. When $p = 1$, then $X \sim N_1(0, \sigma^2)$ and thus one dimensional Wishart distribution follows chi-square distribution.
5. If $M = W_p(\Sigma, m)$ and $a\ \Sigma\ R^p$ with $a'\Sigma a = 0$, then the distribution of $\dfrac{a'Ma}{a'\Sigma a}$ is χ^2_m.
6. If $M = W_p(\Sigma, m)$, then $E(M) = n\Sigma$.
7. If M_i's are independent $W_p(\Sigma, n_i)$ for $i = 1, 2, \ldots, k$, $M = \sum_{i=1}^{k} M_i$ follows $W_p(\Sigma, n)$ where $n = \sum_{i=1}^{k} n_i$.
8. Wishart distribution is a generalization of chi-square. In particular case, $W_1(\sigma^2, n) = \sigma^2\chi^2_n$.
9. The empirical covariance S has a $\frac{1}{n} W_p(\Sigma, n-1)$ distribution.

Q. 12. *Clarify the concept of Hotelling's T^2 distribution.*

Ans. Hotelling's T^2 is a multivariate analog of student's t-distribution in univariate distribution. We know, to test H_0: $\mu = \mu_0$ against H_1: $\mu \neq \mu_0$ based on a sample $x_1, x_2, \ldots, x_n$, the statistic t is,

$$t = \frac{\bar{x} - \mu}{s/\sqrt{n}}$$

And its square is,

$$t^2 = \frac{n(\bar{x} - \mu_0)^2}{s^2}$$

Or

$$t^2 = n(\bar{x} - \mu_0)'(s^2)^{-1}(\bar{x} - \mu_0)$$

For rejecting H_0 in favor of H_1 at significance level α, the test criterion is,

$$n\ (\bar{x} - \mu_0)'(s^2)^{-1}(\bar{x} - \mu_0) > t^2_{n-1,\ \alpha/2}$$

and otherwise accept H_0.

Now if p variables are considered simultaneously and one wants to determine whether $(p \times 1)$ vector μ of means of a multivariate normal distribution has a plausible value as $(p \times 1)$ vector μ_0, Harold Hotelling's T^2 is a good option. Generalizing the monovariate t^2 to multivariate case, the statistic,

$$T^2 = n(\underset{\sim}{\bar{x}} - \mu_0)' S^{-1} (\underset{\sim}{\bar{x}} - \mu_0)$$

Where, S^{-1} is the inverse of the variance-covariance matrix S of order $(p \times p)$.

$$S_{ij} = \frac{1}{n-1} \sum_{i=1}^{n} (x_{ij} - \bar{x}_j)(x_{ij'} - \bar{x}_{j'})$$

For $\quad j, j' = 1, 2, \ldots, p$

$$\bar{x}_j = \frac{1}{n} \sum_{i=1}^{n} x_{ij}; \bar{x} = \frac{1}{p'} \sum_{j=1}^{p} \bar{x}_j \text{ and}$$

$$\underset{\sim}{\mu_0} = \begin{pmatrix} \mu_{10} \\ \mu_{20} \\ \vdots \\ \mu_{p0} \end{pmatrix} \quad \text{also } S_{jj'} = S_{j'j}$$

Thus, using the above terms,

$$T^2 = \sqrt{n}(\underset{\sim}{\bar{x}} - \bar{x}_j)' \left[\frac{\sum_{i=1}^{n} (x_{ij} - \bar{x}_j)(x_{ij'} - \bar{x}_{j'})}{n-1} \right]^{-1} \sqrt{n}(\underset{\sim}{\bar{x}} - \bar{x}_j)$$

No exclusive statistical percentage point tables are required for T^2 test, since T^2 follows F-distribution.

The Statistic T^2 is equivalent to $\dfrac{(n-1)p}{n-p} F_{p,(n-p)}$ where $n > p$. Reject H_0 at significance level α if

$$T^2 > \frac{(n-1)p}{n-p} F_{p,(n-p);\alpha}$$

and otherwise accept H_0.

Q. 13. *How Hotelling's T^2 is related to Wishart random matrix?*

Ans. The relation between T^2 and Wishart random matrix $W_{p,\ n-1}(\Sigma)$ is

$$T^2_{p,\, n-1} = N_p(0,\Sigma)'\left[\frac{1}{n-1}W_{p,n-1}(\Sigma)\right]^{-1} N_p(0,\Sigma)$$

Q. 14. *Give the confidence region for the mean of a p-dimensional normal distribution.*

Ans. A 100 (1 – α) % confidence region of a *p*-dimensional normal distribution is an ellipsoid determined by all μ such that

$$n(\underset{\sim}{\bar{x}}-\underset{\sim}{\mu})' S^{-1}(\underset{\sim}{\bar{x}}-\underset{\sim}{\mu}) \le \frac{p(n-1)}{n-p} F_{p,\, n-p}(\alpha)$$

Where n is the sample size and $X_1, X_2, \ldots, X_n$ are the vectors of p sample observations.

Q. 15. *What purpose is served by Mahalanobis distance measure?*

Ans. Mahalanobis distance is a measure of divergence or distance between groups in terms of multiple characteristics to be considered simultaneously. It plays an important role where classification problem arises. For example, one is interested to check the affinities or dissimilarity between ethnic groups or species, medical diagnosis, geographical studies including the structure and development of the crust and interiors of the earth, fossils form, type of rocks, numerical taxonomy, etc. Mahalanobis used his distance measure in anthropological and craniometrical studies in 1930.

Q. 6. *Give the sample version of Mahalanobis distance and its explanation.*

Ans. The experience reveals that population data or parameters are unknown. When sample version of Mahalanobis distance D is given in square term D^2 as an estimate of population distance square Δ^2, because the distribution of D^2 is easily approximated to F-distribution.

Let G_1 and G_2 be the two population groups with mean vectors μ_1 and μ_2 respectively and Σ, the nonsingular variance-covariance matrix. Suppose from each group G_1 and G_2, a random sample of sizes n_1 and n_2 is drawn. Also suppose that p characteristics are measured on each unit in both the samples. Let the sample vector means of two samples be $\underset{\sim}{\bar{x}}_1$ and $\underset{\sim}{\bar{x}}_2$ and variance-covariance matrices S_1 and S_2 respectively.

Then the estimated Mahalanobis distance D^2 is

$$D^2 = \frac{1}{p}(\underset{\sim}{\bar{x}}_1-\underset{\sim}{\bar{x}}_2)' S^{-1}(\underset{\sim}{\bar{x}}_1-\underset{\sim}{\bar{x}}_2)$$

Where, $$S = \frac{(n_1-1)S_1+(n_2-1)S_2}{n_1+n_2-2}$$

Q. 17. *Is D^2 is an unbiased estimate of Δ^2?*

Ans. Bose and Roy in 1938 proved that D^2 is not an unbiased estimate of Δ^2, since $E(D^2) = \Delta^2 + \frac{2}{\bar{n}}$

where, $\bar{n}$ is the harmonic mean of n_1 and n_2 *i.e.*,

$$\bar{n} = \frac{2n_1n_2}{n_1+n_2}$$

Thus, the unbiased estimate of Δ^2 is

$$D_2^2 = D^2 - \frac{2}{\bar{n}'}$$

Since usually Σ^{-1} is unknown, D_2^2 is called unstudentized D^2 and if D^2 is known it is called studentized D^2.

Q. 18. *How the distribution of D^2 is obtained?*

Ans. There exist a relation between T^2 and D^2 such as

$$T^2 = \frac{n_1n_2}{n_1+n_2}D_2^2$$

And we know that the distribution of Hotelling's T^2 is,

$$\frac{T^2}{n_1+n_2-2}\cdot\frac{n_1+n_2-p-1}{p} \approx F(\upsilon_1,\upsilon_2)$$

Where, $\upsilon_1 = p$ and $\upsilon_2 = n_1 + n_2 - p - 1$

In this way the distribution of D_2^2 is obtained indirectly.

Q. 19. *What are the drawbacks of Mahalanobis D^2 and their rectifications?*

Ans.

1. The main drawback of Mahalanobis approach is that the sample points are distributed about

the center of mass in a spherical manner. But mostly the distributions are not spherical say, usually ellipsoidal. In that situation, one would expect the probability of the test point belonging to the set to depend on not only the distance, but also on the direction. In some positions, the test points will be closer wherever the axis is short. When the axis is long, the set points will be farther from the centre.

To do away with this problem, the Mahalanobis distance is simply expressed as the distance of the test point from the center of mass divided by the width of the ellipsoid in the direction of the test point.

2. Mahalanobis D^2 is an overestimate of population counterpart Δ^2. To eliminate the bias, D^2 should be decreased by the quantity $\frac{2}{\bar{n}}$.

Q. 20. *Discuss succinctly Wilks' Lambda distribution.*

Ans. Wilks' Lambda distribution given by Samuel S. Wilks is multivariate generalization of the univariate *F*-distribution. It is related to Wishart distribution variables and may be defined as follows: If $A \sim W_p(\Sigma, m)$ and $B \sim W_p(\Sigma, n)$.

Where, p is the number of characteristics under study and Σ is the variance-covariance matrix. In the context of maximum likelihood ratio test m is d.f. for the sample drawn for the variable A and n is the d.f. for B. So $(m + n)$ is the total d.f. for $(A + B)$. A and B are independent with $m \geq p$. Then Wilks' Λ is given as,

$$\frac{|A|}{|A+B|} \approx \Lambda(p;\, m,\, n)$$

For large m, Bartlett's approximation (1954) is most often used where Λ is approximated to chi-square distribution with np d.f. Thus,

$$\left(\frac{p+n+1}{2} - m\right)\log \Lambda(p; m, n) \sim \chi^2_{np}$$

Q. 21. *How can Wilks' Λ be worked out in case of k populations?*

Ans. Let there be k populations each with p variables. Suppose from each of the k populations, the samples of sizes $n_1, n_2, \ldots, n_k$ are drawn randomly respectively. Also let us denote k sample means as $\bar{x}_{i1}, \bar{x}_{i2}, \ldots, \bar{x}_{ik}$ and S_{hij} as the sum of square and cross-product for the hth population between the variables i and j for $i, j = 1, 2, \ldots, p$. Suppose $\sum_{h=1}^{k} n_h = n$ and also $\bar{x}_1, \bar{x}_2, \ldots, \bar{x}_p$, be the overall p mean values after combining all the samples.

The corrected sum of products amongst k sample means are obtained by the formula,

$$B_{ij} = \sum n_h \bar{x}_{ih} \bar{x}_{jh} - n\bar{x}_i \bar{x}_j$$

Where $\bar{x}_i$ and $\bar{x}_j$ are the overall sample means for the ith and j^{th} variables.

In terms of totals,

$$B_{ij} = \sum_{h=1}^{k} \frac{T_{hi} T_{hj}}{n_h} - \frac{T_i \times T_j}{n}$$

All notations have their usual meaning in terms of totals.

Sum of products within samples is,

$$W_{ij} = S_{ij} - B_{ij}$$

or

$$S_{ij} = W_{ij} + B_{ij}$$

Let the determinants of W_{ij} and $W_{ij} + B_{ij}$ Be denoted by $|W|$ and $|W + B|$ respectively.

Statistic Wilks' Lambda is,

$$\Lambda = \frac{|W|}{|W+B|}$$

The value of Λ lies between 0 and 1.

Again the statistic $-m \log_e \Lambda$ follows χ^2 distribution with $p(k - 1)$ d.f.

Q. 22. *What relationship exists between Wilks' Lambda and F-statistic?*

Ans. The relationship between Wilks' Lambda and *F*-statistic is,

$$\frac{\upsilon s + 2\lambda}{2r} \cdot \frac{1-\Lambda^{1/s}}{\Lambda^{1/s}} = F_{2r,\,(\upsilon s+2\lambda)}$$

Where,

$$\upsilon = n - \frac{p+k}{2},\ \lambda = \sqrt{\frac{p^2(p-1)^2 - 4}{p^2 + (p-1)^2 - 5}}$$

And $$r = \frac{p(k-1)}{2}$$

Q. 23. *How one can interpret the results by way of the value of Wilks' Λ?*

Ans. We know, $0 \le \Lambda \le 1$. The value of Λ near to 1 indicates no difference between group means and a value nearing 0 points out that group means differ from each other.

Also F-value can be a decisive factor about the test of equality of group means. If $F_{cal} > F_{2r,\,(\upsilon s+2\lambda)}$, it is concluded that group means are not equal, otherwise they are equal.

Multivariate Analysis of Variance

Q. 24. *What is the concept of multivariate analysis of variance?*

Ans. Multivariate analysis of variance (MANOVA) is an extension of analysis of variance (ANOVA). In ANOVA only one metric dependent variable is involved whereas in MANOVA, two or more metric dependent variables are measured simultaneously.

ANOVA examines group (treatment or manipulation) differences on the basis of a single dependent variable whereas MANOVA examines the group differences across multiple dependent variables simultaneously. MANOVA is more suitable when the dependent variables are correlated; otherwise ANOVA on each of the dependent variable separately is more appropriate.

Q. 25. *What null hypothesis is tested in multivariate analysis of variance?*

Ans. Let there be K groups of individuals and on each group, a set of p variables $x_1, x_2, \ldots, x_p$ is denoted by the vector $\underset{\sim}{x}$.

Also suppose k samples $x_{i1g}, x_{i2g}, \ldots, x_{ipg}$ for $i = 1, 2, \ldots, n_g$ and $g = 1, 2, \ldots, k$ are drawn from k groups. The null hypothesis,

$$H_0 = \begin{pmatrix} \mu_{11} \\ \mu_{21} \\ \vdots \\ \mu_{p1} \end{pmatrix} = \begin{pmatrix} \mu_{12} \\ \mu_{22} \\ \vdots \\ \mu_{p2} \end{pmatrix} = \cdots = \begin{pmatrix} \mu_{1k} \\ \mu_{2k} \\ \vdots \\ \mu_{pk} \end{pmatrix}$$

or $H_0 : \underset{\sim}{\mu}_1 = \underset{\sim}{\mu}_2 = \cdots = \underset{\sim}{\mu}_k$ Vs. $H_1 : H_0$ is not correct can be tested by Wilks' Λ statistic as given in question No. 20. If there are only two groups, Hotelling's T^2 can be used for the test of difference across two groups.

Q. 26. *What purpose is served by multivariate analysis of variance?*

Ans. The main purpose of MANOVA is that it enables a researcher to test the group differences with two or more metric dependent variables. If the independent variables are nonmetric and the dependent variables are metric and correlated, then MANOVA is an appropriate technique of detecting the group differences. In MANOVA, the null hypothesis to be tested is the equality of vectors of means of multiple correlated metric dependent variables across groups.

As an example, an advertisement (Ad) of face cream was exposed to three groups of people namely, adolescent, juvenile and adults. Suppose each group consist of 30 respondents of each category and are asked to rate face cream out of 10 points in respect of fragrance, anti-aging effect, wrinkles, moisturizing effect and fairness. Because five preference variables are correlated; MANOVA should be conducted to test the difference among groups. Here preferences work as a criterion variables and groups as dependent variable.

Q. 27. *Discuss the procedure and implications of multivariate analysis of variance.*

Ans. MANOVA procedure was developed by S.S. Wilks in 1932. The technique of MANOVA could not be frequently used due to the complexities of calculations. But the availability of computer software packages has changed the analysis to point and click era. So MANOVA has become a common analysis procedure in medical, anthropological, agricultural researches, etc. Earlier it was considered that one should take groups of equal size. But it makes no difference while analyzing data using software package. Most commonly available softwares are SPSS and SAS.

Principal Component Analysis

Q. 28. *What does principal component analysis imply?*

Ans. Principal Component analysis (PCA) considers the total variance present in the data. PCA is performed when primarily the purpose is to determine the minimum number of **factors** that account for the maximum amount of variance of the data for the subsequent uses. Maximum variance means not less than 70–80% of the total variance. These factors are called the principal components. Here it is worth pointing out that principal component analysis and factor analysis are somewhat intermingled.

A principal component is defined as a linear combination of optimally weighted variables. In all, principal components are those uncorrelated linear combinations that extract variance as large as possible. They are orthogonal as well.

Q. 29. *How to determine the principal components?*

Ans. Let X be a vector of p variables, $X_1, X_2, \ldots, X_p$ each having 0 mean. a' be a row vector. Then the set of p equations in matrix notation can be given as,

$$Y = AX$$

Where, A is of order $(p \times p)$ and Y and X are of order $(p \times 1)$. Let Σ be the variance-covariance matrix $\{\sigma_{ij}\}$ for $i, j = 1, 2, \ldots, p$.

As per definition principal components are linear combinations $Y_1, Y_2, \ldots, Y_p$ that are uncorrelated and their variances are large in descending order. Confining to the coefficient vectors of unit length such that they are orthogonal as well, $a_i' a_i = 1$. Now the first linear component Y_i will be one that maximizes Var $(a_i' X)$ subject to $a'a = 1$ and cov $(a_i X, a_j X) = 0$ for $j < i$.

The variance of $a'X$ is

$$E(a'X)^2 = E(a'XX'a) = a'E(XX')a = a'\Sigma a$$

To obtain the normalized linear combinations $a'X$ having maximum variance, we must consider a vector a subject to the condition $a'a = 1$. Following Lagrange's multiplier λ approach, a function, $\Psi = a'\Sigma a - \lambda(a'a - 1)$ is maximized.

Differentiating Ψ partially with respect to a and equating to zero, we get

$$\frac{\partial \Psi}{\partial a} = 2\Sigma a - 2\lambda a = 0$$

or $\quad |\Sigma - \lambda I| = 0$ Since $a \neq 0$

$|\Sigma - \lambda I| = 0$ is a polynomial of degree p. It will have p eigenvalues and let them be $\lambda_1, \lambda_2, \ldots, \lambda_p$ written in descending order. Now to decide how many principal components are required, it is found out on the basis of amount of variance explained by the formula,

$$\text{Variance explained} = \frac{\lambda_1 + \lambda_2 + \ldots + \lambda_k}{p} \times 100\%$$

Where k is that minimum number of higher order eigenvalues λ ($\lambda \leq p$) which cover at least 70–80% of total variance.

The values of a's for the k principal components are obtained during the analysis on computer. This method of finding the principal components is known as **extraction method**.

Q. 30. *Summarize the features of principal component analysis.*

Ans. The features of the principal component analysis are:

- A variable reduction method.
- Used when the variables are highly correlated.
- Used to reduce the observed variables to a number of principal components which take into account (70–80)% of the total variance present in the observed values.
- A large sample procedure.

- One starts with as many principal components as the number of observed variables in the analysis. The first principal component is identified which contains maximum part of the variance present in the data. Then move to the second principal component which has next largest amount of variance left out in the data. In this way, the process is continued so long at least 70% of total variance is retained whereas the remaining principal components are neglected. As given in Question 28, eigenvalues help to retain/reject the principal components.
- All principal components are orthogonal.

Factor Analysis

Q. 31. *What is the purpose of factor analysis?*

Ans. The purpose of factor analysis (*FA*) is to explain the correlation among a set of variables in terms of few underlying but unobservable random quantities known as factors. Factors also represent the underlying dimensions (constructs) that summarize or account for the set of observed variables. The terms *Principal FA*, *Common FA* and *Exploratory FA* are also used for factor analysis.

From the real life problems point of view, there are research problems in which one has to consider many measures that cannot be measured directly such as intelligence, memory, liking, etc., but are measured through other variables. In factor analysis main interest lies in underlying (latent) factors. In nutshell, in factor analysis observed variables are expressed as a linear combination of the factors.

Q. 32. *Delineate the basic approach of common factor analysis.*

Ans. Consider the observed random variable X with p components, mean vector $\underset{\sim}{\mu}$ and covariance matrix Σ. Let the factor model that X is a linear dependent variable upon k unobservable common factors $F_1, F_2, \ldots, F_k$. The model has p random errors $e_1, e_2, \ldots, e_p$. The factor analysis model in matrix form is,

$$X - \mu = LF + \underline{e}$$

Where, $X - \mu = \begin{bmatrix} X_1 - \mu_1 \\ X_2 - \mu_2 \\ \vdots \\ X_p - \mu_p \end{bmatrix}$ and $e = \begin{bmatrix} e_1 \\ e_2 \\ \vdots \\ e_p \end{bmatrix}$

$$L = \begin{bmatrix} l_{11} & l_{12} & \cdots & l_{1k} \\ l_{21} & l_{22} & \cdots & l_{2k} \\ \vdots & \vdots & \vdots & \vdots \\ l_{p1} & l_{p2} & \cdots & l_{pk} \end{bmatrix} \text{ and } F = \begin{bmatrix} F_1 \\ F_2 \\ \vdots \\ F_k \end{bmatrix}$$

$$E(F) = \mathbf{0}, \text{ Cov } (F F') = E(F F') = I$$

$$E(e) = 0, \text{ Cov } (\underline{e}) = E(ee')$$

and $$\Psi = \begin{bmatrix} \Psi_1 & 0 & \cdots & 0 \\ 0 & \Psi_2 & \cdots & 0 \\ \vdots & \vdots & \cdots & \vdots \\ 0 & 0 & \cdots & \Psi_p \end{bmatrix}$$

$$\Sigma = \text{Cov}(X) = LL' + \Psi$$

$$\text{Cov } (X, F) = L \text{ or Cov } (X_i, F_j) = l_{ij}$$

The position of the ith variable contributed to the k common factors is called the ith *communality.*

$$\text{Var } (X_i) = \sigma_{ii} = l_{i1}^2 + l_{i2}^2 + \ldots + l_{ik}^2 + \Psi_i$$

$(l_{i1}^2 + l_{i2}^2 + \ldots + l_{ik}^2)$ is called the **communality** and is denoted by h_i^2. l_{ij} is called the **factor loading** and Ψ_i is known as **specific variance**. Here Varimax method will only be discussed. Since all values of h_i^2 will not be equal, normalize the values l_{ij} by h_i^2. This approach is known as *normalized Varimax rotation.* Now the variable is l_{ij}^2 / h_{ij}^2.

Onward factor analysis can be carried out using principal components.

Factor score: Once the factors are determined, then the composite score for each respondent can be estimated. These scores are said to be *factor scores.*

Q. 33. *How to determine the number of principal components?*

Ans. There is no definite rule or formula for it. Yet a popular approach to determine the number of principal components or factors is the **Scree plot**. This is a graphical approach in which a graph is plotted taking eigenvalues along ordinate (Y-axis) and the eigenvalue number in descending order along abscissa (X-axis). The points are joined by line segments in order. This graph has a typical shape in which there is a sharp downward trend upto certain values of λ_i and then the remaining part becomes almost horizontal. Overall shape of the graph is similar to a scythe or hockey stick. In this way, the graph has an elbow at the turning point. The value of i corresponding to this point determine the number of factors or principal components.

A *prior criterion* may be another approach in which a researcher knows beforehand how many factors are to be there. Percentage of variance may be the criterion in which one considers the factor wise cumulative variance and stops at the mth factor as soon as around 70% variance is retained.

Q. 34. *In what respects principal component analysis differs from factor analysis?*

Ans. Basically principal component analysis and factor analysis are similar procedures which are set to reduce the number of original variables. Still they are different in many respects as follows:

1. In PCA, the components are obtained as linear combinations of the original variables. In FA, the original variables are expressed as the linear combinations of underlying factors.
2. In PCA, the objective is to explain as large as possible the proportion of total variance present in the original variables *i.e.*, 70% with minimum number of components whereas FA explains the covariances or correlations between the variables.
3. PCA is used to reduce the number of original variables to a smaller number of components whereas FA is used to know what constructs are underlying the data?
4. For the same set of data, PCA is constructed to determine factors to be extracted in a factor analysis study.
5. The computer software package like SPSS, MINITAB are available to PCA and FA. Sometimes, the packages conflate and the two analyses can thus be run simultaneously. Anyhow, in MINITAB, you can enter the raw data or a correlation matrix alone to run Factor analysis.

Discriminant Analysis

Q. 35. *What does discriminant analysis signify?*

Ans. Discriminant analysis is a statistical technique employed to model a relationship between categorical criterion (dependent) variable on a nominal or nonmetric scale and one or more continuous independent variables, so called predictor variables. Discriminant analysis is conducted only when the groups are known a priori.

In simple words, discriminant analysis is a method by which combinations are determined between criterion variable (which may be dichotomous or multichotomous) and continuous independent variables. It was first developed by R. A. Fisher in 1936 in case of two groups.

Q. 36. *What are the assumptions underlying discriminant analysis?*

Ans. There are many assumptions which the variables should follow for exact discriminant function analysis.

1. The observed data should be free from outliers.
2. The size of the smallest group should be larger than the number of predictor variables.
3. Predictor variables are normal for each level of the grouping variables. It is also assumed that the sample data are from a multivariate normal distribution.
4. Variances among group variables are same across levels of predictors.
5. Linear discriminant function analysis should be conducted when covariances are equal

otherwise, quadratic discriminant function analysis be conducted.

6. Predictor variables should be independent as far as possible to avoid the problem of multicollinearity.
7. Participants are assumed to be selected randomly. This may imply that a participant's score on variables is assumed to be independent of the score of all other participants.

Q. 37. *For what purposes, can discriminant function analysis be used?*

Ans. Discriminant analysis works by forming one or more linear combinations of predictors, each function creating a new *latent variable*. These functions are known as *discriminant functions*.

Discriminant function analysis is to discriminate between two or more known groups on the basis of multivariate observations. Discriminant analysis is used in many areas of research such as biology, medical sciences, education, psychology, plant breeding, sociology and so on. It is also used to test whether the two population groups significantly differ from one another based on *p*-variables. Discriminant function analysis can also be used to ascertain whether an observation X having *p*-variables belongs to which of the group out of many known groups.

Q. 38. *Usually what test statistics are involved in discriminant analysis technique?*

Ans.

1. To test the hypothesis of zero difference between two groups *p*-variables mean vectors $\underset{\sim}{\mu}_1 - \underset{\sim}{\mu}_2$, first Mahalanobis D_p^2 is calculated. Then the distribution of D_p^2 is approximated to F-distribution and thereby the test is performed.
2. Another test is based on likelihood ratio test. The test is known as Wilks' Lambda test given in 1932 by S.S. Wilks. This test was later extended by M.S. Bartlett in 1934. The basic idea behind this test is to choose coefficients of linear compound in such a manner that the ratio of mean squares due to within samples $|W|$ and combined variance-covariance matrix $|W + B|$ is minimum. Thus,

$$\Lambda = \frac{|W|}{|W + B|}$$

Then F-distribution based on Λ is determined and test is performed in the usual manner.

Q. 39. *How to obtain discriminant scores?*

Ans. In a discriminant function, the unstandardized coefficients are multiplied by the corresponding variate values. The sum of these products results into a constant value termed as discriminant score. For each group member, we will get a separate value of discriminant score.

Q. 40. *Define canonical correlation.*

Ans. Canonical correlation measures the degree of relationship between the discriminant scores and the groups. It is a measure of association between the single discriminant function and the set of dummy variables that define the group membership. Usually the group measures are nonmetric, so they are coded as 0 and 1 and hence they are called dummy variables.

To formulate canonical correlation, we would be interested to find a measure of association between two groups of variables. Let one group of *p*-variables be denoted by vector $\underset{\sim}{X}_1$ of order $(p \times 1)$ and the other group of *q* variables be represented by $\underset{\sim}{X}_2$ of order $(q \times 1)$. Also for some theoretical reasons, assume $p \le q$. For the random vectors we denote the vectors and variance-covariance matrix as follows:

$$E(\underset{\sim}{X}_1) = \underset{\sim}{\mu}_1, \ \mathrm{Cov}(\underset{\sim}{X}_1) = \Sigma_{11}$$

$$E(\underset{\sim}{X}_2) = \underset{\sim}{\mu}_2, \ \mathrm{Cov}(\underset{\sim}{X}_2) = \Sigma_{22}$$

$$\mathrm{Cov}\,(\underset{\sim}{X}_1, \underset{\sim}{X}_2) = \Sigma_{12} = \Sigma_{21}$$

Σ_{12} or Σ_{21} contains $p\ q$ elements, which measure the association between $\underset{\sim}{X}_1$ and $\underset{\sim}{X}_2$. If p and q are large, interpretation of the elements of Σ_{12} becomes arduous. So linear combinations of the two sets are separately formed that are of interest for comparative or predictive purposes. Suppose such linear combinations be represented as,

$$Z_1 = a'\underset{\sim}{X}_1 \text{ and } Z_2 = b'\underset{\sim}{X}_2$$

Thus, $\quad \text{Var}(Z_1) = a'\Sigma_{11}a, \text{ Var}(Z_2) = b'\Sigma_{22}b$

$$\text{Cov}(Z_1, Z_2) = a'\Sigma_{12}b$$

We will find a and b such that the correlation between Z_1 and Z_2,

$$\text{Corr}(Z_1, Z_2) = \frac{a'\Sigma_{12}b}{\sqrt{a'\Sigma_{11}a}\sqrt{b'\Sigma_{22}b}}$$

is as large as possible.

The first pair of canonical variable is the pair of linear combinations $[Z_1^{(1)}, Z_2^{(1)}]$ having unit variances which maximize Corr (Z_1, Z_2). The other pair of canonical variables is the pair of linear combinations $[Z_1^{(2)}, Z_2^{(2)}]$ among all choices that are uncorrelated with the former pair of canonical variables. The process continues till all such pairs are exhausted.

Q. 41. *How to classify an observation X whose identity is unknown?*

Ans. Consider an observation X with p-component variables which can belong to one group out of many groups. We can ascertain its identity by using discriminant analysis. For the sake of brevity as well as ease in understanding the methodology, we consider only two groups π_1 and π_2. Let the distribution of X into two groups be $N(\underset{\sim}{\mu}_1, \Sigma)$ and $N(\underset{\sim}{\mu}_2, \Sigma)$ where $\underset{\sim}{\mu}_1$ and $\underset{\sim}{\mu}_2$ are two vectors of means and Σ is the common covariance matrix. Fisher's discriminant criterion for the square of the distance between two groups is

$$\frac{\underset{a}{Max}(a'\underset{\sim}{\mu}_1 - a'\underset{\sim}{\mu}_2)^2}{a'\Sigma a}$$

Observation X will be classified to π_1 or π_2 to whomsoever it is nearest. After certain algebraic manipulations, the classification criteria are:

Assign X to π_1 if

$$X'\Sigma^{-1}(\underset{\sim}{\mu}_1 - \underset{\sim}{\mu}_2) > \frac{1}{2}(\underset{\sim}{\mu}_1 + \underset{\sim}{\mu}_2)\Sigma^{-1}(\underset{\sim}{\mu}_1 - \underset{\sim}{\mu}_2)$$

where X' is a row vector of the variate values of X.

and categorize X to π_2 if

$$X'\Sigma^{-1}(\underset{\sim}{\mu}_1 - \underset{\sim}{\mu}_2) < \frac{1}{2}(\underset{\sim}{\mu}_1 + \underset{\sim}{\mu}_2)\Sigma^{-1}(\underset{\sim}{\mu}_1 - \underset{\sim}{\mu}_2)$$

Cluster Analysis

Q. 42. *Explain cluster analysis.*

Ans. Cluster analysis is a body of techniques concerned with developing of natural groupings of a set of objects based on some criterion of nearness of the p-variables describing the objects. The groups are formed in such a manner that maximize the similarities of objects within the groups (intra groups) and minimize the likeness of objects between groups (inter groups).

In other words, cluster analysis is a tool for structure generation particularly when hardly anything is known about the nominal variable that is to be identified. Also the number of clusters is not known.

Q. 43. *What is the difference between cluster analysis and factor analysis?*

Ans. Cluster analysis is obverse of factor analysis. Cluster analysis is a technique of reducing the number of objects by grouping them into some clusters each containing a limited number of similar objects. On the other hand, factor analysis is the method of reducing the number of original variables.

Q. 44. *In what areas can cluster analysis be used?*

Ans. Various areas in which cluster analysis can be used are as follows:

(*a*) Taxonomy.

(*b*) Market segmentation.

(*c*) Higher level image processing: Object recognition.

(*d*) Search of similar gene profiles.

(*e*) Specification of syndromes.

(*f*) Visualization of complex graphs.

(*g*) Text categorization in information retrieval.

Q. 45. *What is Euclidean distance measure?*

Ans. Suppose there are n objects (respondents) and each object is measured on p-variables. Then np observations can be presented by a matrix of order $n \times p$, the matrix has n rows and p columns. The elements of the rth and s^{th} row shall be as $(x_{r1}, x_{r2}, ..., x_{ri}, ..., x_{rp})$ and $(x_{s1}, x_{s2}, ..., x_{si}, ..., x_{sp})$. The Euclidean distance between r^{th} and s^{th} objects is given as the square root of the sum of the squared differences between corresponding p variate values. Symbolically, the Euclidean distance,

$$D(r, s) = \sqrt{(x_{r1} - x_{s1})^2 + (x_{r2} - x_{s2})^2 + ... + (x_{rp} - x_{sp})^2}$$

The most used measure of similarity is the Euclidean distance.

Q. 46. *What are the different procedures of clustering? Describe each of them concisely.*

Ans. There are two categories of clustering procedures;

Hierarchical methods: These methods proceed sequentially resulting into a nested arrangement of objects on respondents in groups. In this process, clustering proceeds from left to right forming various clusters. The groups once joined are never separated. The procedure starts from n clusters and ends in one cluster. Hierarchical procedure is characterized by a Hierarchy or a tree like structure. This hierarchical process is called *agglomerative clustering* as all objects start out as a separate cluster and start merging into bigger clusters and ultimately reduced to one cluster. In general terms, the process starts from branches of a tree and move upto the trunk of the tree. If the agglomerative process is reversed *i.e.*, it moves from trunk to branches, then it is called *divisive clustering procedure*.

Linkage methods: Agglomerative methods that involve the distance between the objects for clustering are called *linkage methods*.

Single linkage method is one that is based on the minimum distance between objects or the nearest neighbor rule.

Complete linkage method is based on the maximum distance between the objects or the farthest neighbor approach.

Average linkage method is based on the average distances between all pairs of objects, where one member of the pair is from each of the clusters.

Centroid method is based on the distances between two clusters measured as the sum of square of the differences between cluster centroid for all the p variables of each cluster. Symbolically, if $(\bar{x}_{r1}, \bar{x}_{r2}, ..., \bar{x}_{ri} ..., \bar{x}_{rp})$ and $(\bar{x}_{s1}, \bar{x}_{s2}; ..., \bar{x}_{si}, ..., x_{sp})$ are the means of the rth and s^{th} clusters of sizes n_r and n_s, then the square of the Euclidean distance between the two centroids is given as,

$$d^2 (r, s) = \sum_{i=1}^{p} (\bar{x}_{ri} - \bar{x}_{si})^2$$

Clusters, whose centroids are nearest, are merged to form a new cluster.

Wald's method of clustering is based on the principle of minimizing the 'loss of information' due to merger of two groups. Consider k clusters arbitrarily. Let ESS_k is the sum of square of the deviations of every object in the kth cluster centroid. The total sum of square of the deviations for k clusters is, $ESS = ESS_1 + ESS_2 + ... + ESS_k$.

First the union of every possible pair of clusters is considered. The two clusters which on combining result into least increase of ESS are joined. This process continues till all the clusters are combined into one group. It is a hierarchical precursor to nonhierarchical method.

Nonhierarchical method

If the number of items or objects is large, each one described by p-variables, hierarchical clustering involving Euclidean distances becomes arduous. Hence, nonhierarchical methods are much more compatible.

k-means method of clustering is quite popular and in vogue due to availability of software packages. This method is composed of three steps as follows:

1. Specify the number of clusters arbitrarily and assign items to them deliberately.
2. Calculate the centroid of a cluster for all the p-variables. Similarly obtain the centroid of each cluster for all the p-variables.

The centroid of a cluster is considered as the center of all values in the cluster.

3. Compute the Euclidean distances of each observed value of the kth cluster C_k from its centroid for all the clusters by

$$D(X_{kp}, C_k) = \sqrt{(X_{k1}-\bar{X}_{k1})^2+(X_{k2}-\bar{X}_{k2})^2+...+(X_{kp}-\bar{X}_{kp})^2}$$

$D(X_{kp}, C_k)$ is the deciding factor to which item an observation say *a* belongs. Item a will be reallocated to the cluster for which $D(X_{kp}, C_k)$ is minimum. Now move to the next observation of current cluster. Continue this process until no more assignment takes place. *K*-means procedure is very lengthy and sensitive to outliers. *K*-means do not necessarily find the solution for a given level of clustering.

Sequential threshold method, *Parallel threshold method* and *Optimizing partitioning method* are some other nonhierarchical methods which are seldom used.

Q. 47. *What is a dendogram and how is this constructed?*

Ans. Dendogram is a tree like configuration in hierarchical clustering employed to interpret the output of a cluster analysis that indicates the groups of clusters formed at various similarity levels. In such a tree like diagram it is also possible to show the proximity value at each step without details. The shape of a dendogram is given below taken from the book "Comprehensive Research Methodology" (2014) by B.L. Agarwal, New Age International Publishers, New Delhi, and Figure 16.4.

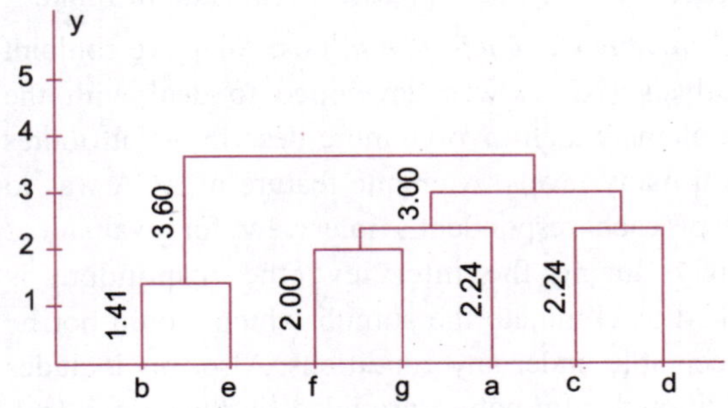

Dendogram

Conjoint Analysis

Q. 48. *On what concept conjoint analysis is based?*

Ans. Conjoint analysis is a popular technique in marketing research which marketers use to determine what features a new product should have and how should it be priced. Conjoint analysis became popular because it was a less expensive and more flexible way to cope with these issues than concept testing. The complexity of analysis has been further eased out due to availability of computer software packages. Conjoint analysis was first time used in 1970 and since then it has become a strong tool of marketing research.

Q. 49. *For what motives conjoint analysis is appropriate?*

Ans. Conjoint analysis is primarily a technique used for identification of the problem and dimensions of the product to be studied. What concerns a marketer is to know about the mindset of the customers what do they prefer? Whether the customers will prefer to purchase a product of high quality or a low priced product. Instead a marketer wants to collect more revenue with trade-off between quality and price and services. One may try for peak profitability by maintaining high quality and high price.

Q. 50. *Define some important terms used in conjoint analysis.*

Ans. **Stimulus:** Specific set of levels and the factors to be evaluated by the respondent.

Stimuli: All pairwise comparisons or factorial combinations of attribute levels are known as stimuli.

Factor: A specific attribute or characteristic of the product or service is regarded as factor.

Part worth: Estimate from conjoint analysis of the overall utility or preference associated with each level of each factor used to evaluate the product or service.

Utility: This is the subjective preference which the consumers attach to the levels of each attribute. Utilities for a combination of various levels of attributes are added under additive model.

Q. 51. *Specify the conjoint variate.*

Ans. The conjoint variate is a linear combination of effects of the factors on a dependent variable. In the conjoint variate, a researcher specifies the factors (independent variables) and the values marked as levels. The information provided by a respondent is the dependent measure.

Q. 52. *Delineate the concept of decompositional model in reference to conjoint analysis.*

Ans. In conjoint analysis a researcher is required to know only a respondent's overall performance or rating for a stimulus. The value of each attribute is a priori decided by the researcher. In this manner, conjoint analysis can decompose the value of each attribute using only the overall performance measure. Hence, conjoint analysis employs decompositional model.

Q. 53. *Is conjoint analysis flexible with regard to model specification?*

Ans. Of course, conjoint analysis does not adhere to the linear relationship between the factors on a dependent variable. It does not assume that the levels are related at all, conjoint analysis can easily handle nonlinear relationships.

Q. 54. *What is the principle lying behind conjoint analysis?*

Ans. The principle behind conjoint analysis starts from breaking a product or services down into its constituents, so called attributes and levels like appearance, size, price, etc. Once the full profile of combinations is ready, a proper statistical analysis is chosen. Now the information is collected and the data so obtained are statistically analyzed to find out the customers' preference. The results of analysis enable a manufacturer and marketer to evaluate on the following basis:

(*a*) Decide how the responses can be aggregated. An analyst has three choices; (*i*) use individual responses, (*ii*) pool all responses into a single utility function, (*iii*) segmentation of respondents who have almost similar responses.

(*b*) Often the part-worth model is one of the simpler approaches to express the utilities of the various attributes which are under consideration. The others are linear models and ideal point quadratic models.

In a full profile design, the utility data are available for each respondent. The question that perplexes a researcher is as to which product design would be most popular in the market or more subtly which one would be most profitable. Such modeling produce as result which product would be preferred most by each individual respondent based on their individual scores. Grouping these respondents, it becomes possible to estimate the market share in this competitive market. Market share means share of preference.

Q. 55. *What methodologies are frequently used for conjoint analysis?*

Ans. There are quite many methodologies that are used for conjoint analysis. However, a few of them which are frequently used are delineated succinctly.

Conjoint analysis models are subjected to changes by the amount and kind of data collected in the task of data collection. Greater detailed data increase the size, complexities and time of evaluation of the task.

Two attributes trade-off analysis: Initially conjoint analysis was considered for two attributes and having a few levels. Their combinations were taken and arranged in two way table. For instance, each attribute has three levels, and then there will be a 3 × 3 table having nine cells. The respondents are asked to rank each combinations from 1 to 9 as per their preferences. But in this process, respondents loose their patience and make cognitive demands. It is simple yet it is time consuming and perplexing. So sometimes the respondents do not express the real state of mind.

Adaptive model conjoint analysis: Adaptive conjoint analysis (ACA) was developed to deal with the problems which involve more descriptive attributes with many levels. A unique feature of ACA was to adapt each respondent's interview for evaluation. Early during the interview, the respondent is asked to eliminate the stimuli which would not be acceptable under any conditions. Also this includes additional information provided by the respondent. This is known as *self-explicated conjoint analysis*.

The attitudes are then presented for evaluation. The choice pairs are presented in an order that increasingly focuses on determining the utility associated with each attribute. The most widely known example of ACA is from saw-tooth software.

Choice based conjoint analysis: In choice based conjoint analysis, the respondent is to make a choice of a single full profile stimulus from a set of stimuli, known as choice set instead of ranking or rating such stimulus separately. The choice phenomenon is thought to simulate an actual buying situation, thereby mimicking actual shopping behaviour.

Full profile conjoint analysis: In full profile conjoint analysis, the respondent is asked to provide ranks or rating to each stimulus of a full profile. Full profile means all combinations of all attributes and their levels. For instance, a bread is described with two levels each; size (small, big), color (white, brown) and price (₹ 12, ₹ 20). Full profile will consist of 8 combinations. The respondent preference ratings for the product description are obtained to know the most preferred stimulus by conducting full profile analysis.

There are some other types of conjoint analysis depending upon the various forms of sets of stimulus of a full profile. But they are not presented here as it is just an introductory chapter.

Q. 56. *What kind of conjoint analysis is superior: adaptive or choice based?*

Ans. The choice of a conjoint analysis depends on what the researcher is interested in retrieving the data forms. If you are looking for data which mimics the purchase process, then choice base conjoint analysis is more adequate. A computer based iterative conjoint method designed for situations where the number of attributes exceeds than what can suitably be used for choice based conjoint analysis, adaptive conjoint analysis is preferable.

Q. 57. *Is there any restrain about maximum levels of options to ask in the choice task?*

Ans. Yes, the likely number is 2 levels for each attribute/feature. The standard is to stick to not more than 1–4 levels per feature or attribute. In some unavoidable situation, one may go upto 5 levels but not more than that. Otherwise the conjoint analysis task will become too complicated and its interpretation will be another problem.

Q. 58. *Express concisely the procedure of conjoint analysis.*

Ans. Conjoint analysis can be carried in any number of algorithms to estimate utility functions. These utility functions indicate the perceived value of the feature and how sensitive consumers' perceptions and preferences are to changes in product attributes.

The actual mode of analysis will depend on the design of the task and profiles rated or ranked by the respondents. Design of a new product is to be chosen according to the requirement of the market. For full profile, regression model may be appropriate. In regression model, independent variables are the preferences of the interviewed persons for the fictive product. For choice based task, maximum likelihood estimation or logistic regression may be used. Also hierarchical Bayesian procedures may be used for choice based data to estimate individual level from more limited choice based designs.

Factor and other values are defined by the researcher in advance. Various combinations of the factor values yield fictive products that are being ranked by the interviewed person. With conjoint analysis it is possible to derive metric partial utilities, from the ranking results. The sum of the partial utilities yields the total metric utilities.

Computer assistance for conjoint analysis is:

SPSS Training Analysis demo in YOU Tube
IBM SPSS Conjoint V.22
Conjoint Analysis – SAS:
Conjoint Analysis creating an orthogonal design use: SPSS V.17

Q. 59. *What are the advantages of conjoint analysis?*

Ans. Some main advantages of conjoint analysis are:

1. It is possible to derive metric partial utilities via ranks.
2. Estimate of psychological trade-offs that consumer make when evaluating several attributes together can be made.

3. To measure preferences at individual as well as on total basis is possible.
4. Segmentation of respondents is possible.
5. It is possible to know realistic choice.

Q. 60. *What are the disadvantages of conjoint analysis?*

Ans. There are many lacunae of conjoint analysis such as,

1. Respondents are unable to articulate attitudes towards fictive products while they would have hardly paid any attention to such issues.
2. Designing of conjoint studies can be complex.
3. Poorly designed studies may over-value/ under-value the performances of the interviewed persons.
4. It does not reflect the number of items per purchase. So it can mislead about market share.
5. If the number of combinations of attributes and their levels are large in number, then the respondents may not be able to rank or rate them properly.

Multidimensional scaling

Q. 61. Expound the terms inextricably linked with multidimensional scaling.

Ans. Multidimensional scaling (MDS) technique involves many terms which are used in a different sense than their literal meaning. The important ones are elucidated below.

Object: Any stimulus which can be assumed or compared by a respondent including tangible entities is termed as object.

Dimensions: It alludes to the features of an object. The dimensions are said to be *objective* if the measures of an object are quantifiable such as price, weight, consumption of petrol per km, etc. On the other hand, if an individual evaluates an object on the basis of his/her own perceptions like look, taste, smell, etc., then such measures are known as subjective dimensions.

Thus, an attempt is made to locate an object in multidimensional space where the number of dimensions corresponds to the number of features which an individual has used in forming his judgment.

Perceptual map: Multidimensional scaling is a procedure for representing the preferences and perceptions of a respondent by way of visual display. Perceived relationship represented as points among products or stimuli are plotted in a multidimensional space. Such a configuration is known as *perceptual map*. Practically it is same as *spatial map*.

Initial dimensionality: Prior to starting a multidimensional scaling procedure, a researcher must specify how many dimensions (features) are involved in the data. This helps in selecting the best spatial map for the data.

Index of fit: Squared correlation index (R^2) are interpreted as indicating the proportion of variance of the disparities that can be accounted by the MDS procedure. It measures how well the raw data fit the MDS procedure.

Similarity judgment: This refers to the ratings of all possible pairs of stimuli or brands in terms of their similarity using a Likert type scale.

Preference rankings: Preference rankings are provided by the respondents to brands or stimuli from most preferred to least preferred *i.e.*, for n stimuli from 1 to n.

Aggregate analysis: A MDS approach in which the perceptual map is developed on the basis of evaluations of objects by a group of respondents as a whole. This composite perceptual map is prepared by a computer software package as it is almost beyond the reach of a researcher to do it manually.

Disaggregate analysis: This is a MDS approach in which a researcher generates perceptual map on a respondent basis. This is not a practically feasible approach. So one should use aggregated approach in which the results of respondents are combined.

Compositional method: This is a method of generating perceptual map by considering overall similarity or preferences from evaluations of separate attributes given by each respondent. Actually most common approach of compositional methods are factor analysis and discriminant analysis.

Decompositional method: This is MDS technique of perceptual mapping in which the respondent provides an overall evaluation of similarity or preference between objects. This set of overall evaluations is then decomposed into a set of dimensions which represents best differences of objects.

Ideal point: This is a point in a perceptual map that represents the most preferred combination of attributes. This implies that the points nearest to farthest to the ideal point shall be less to least preferable.

Q. 62. *What is multidimensional scaling technique?*

Ans. Multidimensional scaling is an approach for measuring respondents' perceptions of similarity of objects and their preferences among its objects and plotting these relationships in a multidimensional space. In other words, the purpose of MDS is to transform consumer judgment in marketing research of overall similarity or preferences for objects, brands, stores, products, etc., into distances represented in the form of a perceptual map.

After preparing perceptual map, use MDS technique to estimate the relative position of each object in multidimensional space. Also identify and interpret the axes of multidimensional space in terms of objective attributes. The perceptual/spatial map in multidimensional space places objects at smaller distances which are more similar or preferred than those which are less similar. The distances change according to the order of preferences.

Q. 63. *What are the purposes of multidimensional scaling?*

Ans.

1. Multidimensional scaling technique is mostly used by the marketers for promoting their products, brands, stores, services, etc. MDS uses only an individual or aggregate measure of perceptions or preferences. Firstly one should choose a set of objects about which similarity or preferences are to be analyzed. The researcher must ensure that all objects in the set are comparable. Thus, implicit assumptions are that the common characteristics, metric or nonmetric, are present and can be used by the respondent for evaluation. As a guideline, a researcher must use more than four times the number of objects than the number of dimensions as desired. for instance, for one dimension choose 5 objects and for two dimensions, choose at least 9 objects and so on. For ranking similarity of pairs of objects, one will use 10 pairs of objects in case of one dimension and 36 pairs of objects in case of two dimensions. Precisely MDS is the multivariate treatment of the data through simultaneous consideration of multiple categorical variables.
2. The crux of the multidimensional scaling analysis lies in the perceptual/spatial map produced in the process. These maps can be utilized to draw main conclusions about the market products as follows:
   - (*i*) The main purpose of MDS analysis is to obtain a spatial map that fits the input data involving minimum number of dimensions.
   - (*ii*) It reveals salient features of the product perceived or preferred by the respondents/ buyers.
   - (*iii*) The order of the combination of attributes most preferred and second best preferred and so on given by the respondents is obtained.
   - (*iv*) The products and services which can be considered as substitute are discerned.
   - (*v*) The products can be differentiated from one another that are not alike.
   - (*vi*) The viable segments of consumers that exist in the market can be ascertained having relative homogeneous perceptions.
   - (*vii*) The weaknesses of a market that can be utilized to venture a new product in the market are divulged.
   - (*viii*) Though similarity judgments and/or ratings of brands are obtained by the

researcher, still supplied attributes may be found by using regression method. The axes can be labeled to the attributes to which they are most aligned.

(*ix*) Stress measure indicates towards the fit of a MDS solution. Lesser the stress, better fit is the solution and vice-versa.

Q. 64. *How to take decision about the number of dimensions in a MDS solution?*

Ans. Actually it is a hard task to decide the number of dimensions. As the number of dimensions increases, the interpretation of results becomes more tedious. Still some norms are given.

1. *Prior knowledge:* The researcher may have some idea on the basis of his past experience and choose the number of dimensions beforehand.
2. *Practical view:* Since it is cumbersome to interpret the configurations on a spatial map in more than three dimensions, one may restrict to two or three dimensions.
3. *Elbow criterion:* A graph is plotted for number of combinations and stress. Number of combinations is taken along abscissa and stress along ordinate. The points are joined by line segments. The graph so obtained is examined. The point at which an elbow or a sharp bend occurs, indicate the appropriate number of dimensions.

Q. 65. *What sort of conclusions can be drawn from interpretation of results of a MDS solution?*

Ans. It is almost impossible to conduct a multidimensional scaling analysis manually. So a researcher has to determine a MDS solution using a computer program.

The spatial configuration provides some insight into how the respondents evaluate the stimuli in terms of a (small) number of potentially unknown dimensions. While interpreting the results, one should know whether the program is run for metric MDS or nonmetric MDS or both combined. For a data matrix consisting of dissimilarities rating such an assumption will be too strong as the proximities are given in terms of Euclidean distances. On the other side, nonmetric MDS assumes that the order of proximities is meaningful. As already mentioned, a common approach to decide how many dimensions to use is the Scree plot to obtain an elbow point. Another criterion for deciding the number of dimensions can be the clarity of the final perceptual map configuration. One can apply validation methods to assess the reliability of results. These methods are not discussed because of brevity of the space. Example of MDS by SPSS software package can be studies from books given in the references.

Correspondence Analysis

Q. 66. *Give the genesis of correspondence analysis.*

Ans. The discussion of MDS revealed that it was based on decompositional approaches. Now the questions arises how about compositional MDS. In this chapter we have studied principal component analysis and factor analysis as compositional techniques but not for perceptual mapping. So correspondence analysis (CA) is evolved which utilizes both the earlier techniques and MDS for perceptual mapping under compositional approach.

Q. 67. *What are the distinctive characteristics of correspondence analysis?*

Ans. In this computer age, correspondence analysis is a popular technique for dimension reduction and perceptual mapping. It is also called as *Optimal scaling, homogeneity analysis* or *reciprocal averaging*. CA has the following distinctive aspects.

1. CA can be used for nominal data *e.g.*, frequency count for preferences for objects across a set of attributes.
2. CA is the compositional technique as it is based on the association between objects and a set of descriptive characteristics or attributes specified by the researcher.
3. CA provides perceptual maps in a single step. The relationship between objects and the variables is the sole objective of CA.
4. The main benefit of CA is that the input data can be presented in the form of a contingency table indicating a qualitative association between rows and columns *e.g.*, brand and attributes in joint space.

Q. 68. *What is the underlying principle of correspondence analysis?*

Ans. Correspondence analysis is an exploratory data analysis technique designed to analyze two way and multi-way table containing some measure of correspondence between rows and columns. CA remarkably simplifies complex data yielding a simple, yet exhaustive analysis. The multivariate nature of CA can reveal relationship that would have not been detected in a series of pair wise comparisons of variables. CA provides graphical display of row and column point in biplots which help in depicting structural relationship among variable categories and objects. The only restriction to carry out CA is the requirement of a rectangular data matrix having no negative entry. The usual procedure for analyzing a cross tabulation is to determine the probability of global association between rows and columns. The significance of association is tested by chi-square test. But this does not yield any result about the significance of individual associations between row and column pairs of the data matrix. Rather CA shows how the variables are related, not just a relationship exists.

Practically it is almost impossible to conduct correspondence analysis humanly. So this is always carried out on a computer using any one of the available computer software packages *e.g.*, in SAS, STAT.PROC CORRESP and SPSS V.19.

Q. 69. *What are the requirements for a proper correspondence analysis?*

Ans. There are three main requirements that should be satisfied for proper results from CA.

1. The data matrix should be large enough so that simple statistical analysis cannot uphold the structure.
2. The variables are homogeneous so that it is possible to show only row and column categories in two dimensions which account for the greatest proportion of deviations from independence.
3. The data matrix is a priori amorphous *i.e.*, its structure is either unknown or negligibly understood.

Q. 70. *Give in brief the procedure of correspondence analysis so as to explain the interpretation of results.*

Ans. Correspondence analysis is applied to contingency table. Its main purpose is to transform a table of numerical information into a graphical display in which each row and column is depicted as a point. CA shows how the variables are related, not that a relationship exists. The procedure is as follows:

Prepare the original data matrix *i.e.*, a contingency table of order $(p \times q)$ having frequencies n_{ij} for $i = 1, 2, \ldots, p$ and $j = 1, 2, \ldots, q$.

$$\text{Rows}\ \overset{\text{Columns}}{\begin{bmatrix} n_{11} & n_{12} & \cdots & n_{1j} & \cdots & n_{1q} \\ n_{21} & n_{22} & \cdots & n_{2j} & \cdots & n_{2q} \\ \vdots & \vdots & \vdots & \vdots & \vdots & \vdots \\ n_{i1} & n_{i2} & \cdots & n_{ij} & \cdots & n_{iq} \\ \vdots & \vdots & \vdots & \vdots & \vdots & \vdots \\ n_{p1} & n_{p2} & \cdots & n_{pj} & \cdots & n_{pq} \end{bmatrix}}$$

Obtain each row profile by dividing each row element by the corresponding row total *i.e.*, $n_{ij}/n_{\circ j}$ for all i and j.

Similarly, obtain each column profile by dividing each column element by the corresponding total *i.e.*, $n_{ij}/n_{\circ j}$ for all i and j. The sum of each row profile and that of each column profile will be 1.

Another concept of *CA* is the concept of mass. The mass of ith row is $n_{i\bullet}/n$ and for j^{th} column $n_{j\bullet}/n$.

The correspondence matrix, $P = \frac{1}{n}[N(p\times q)]$. P shows how one unit of mass is distributed across the cells. The marginal totals of P provide the corresponding row and column mass.

Now we discuss another term *cloud* of points of $N(p)$, which is the set of elements of points $i \in p$, whose coordinates are the components of the profile and whose mass is $n_{i\bullet}/n$. Similarly for the cloud of points $N(q)$, the mass is $n_{j\bullet}/n$.

Now measure weighted Euclidean distances to show the distances between profile points. Here weighting stands for the weighting of the dimensions of the space, definitely not of profiles. Distances between i and i' rows for $i \neq i' = 1, 2, \ldots, p$ is

$$d^2(i, i') = \sum_{j=1}^{q} \frac{1}{n_{.j}} \left(\frac{n_{ij}}{n_{i.}} - \frac{n_{i'j}}{n_{i'.}} \right)^2$$

Similarly distances between j and j' columns for $j \neq j' = 1, 2, \ldots, q$ is

$$d^2(i, i') = \sum_{i=1}^{p} \frac{1}{n_{i.}} \left(\frac{n_{ij}}{n_{.j}} - \frac{n_{ij'}}{n_{.j'}} \right)^2$$

The distances so obtained are called the chi-square distances. The value of chi-square for the given contingency table can be calculated in the usual manner. The quantity χ^2/n is known as the *total inertia* of the contingency table.

The significant value of χ^2 ensures whether there is dependency between rows and columns. Now examine the eigenvalues and percentage of inertia. The next step is to see that what percentage of inertia is explained by two dimensions *i.e.*, the minimum number of dimensions which is most desirable. If the inertia is 80% or more, the two dimensions are satisfactory. Otherwise, one proceeds for three dimensions. The main idea behind CA is to find optimal representation of a contingency table in low dimensional space.

Dimensionality of the solution is achieved by examining the eigenvalues and percentage of inertia. CA determines the principal axes of inertia and for each axis the corresponding eigenvalue is same as the inertia of the cloud in the direction of the axis. The eigenvalues (λ, m) corresponding to the principal axes, which are perpendicular to each other, are in descending order of magnitude *i.e.*, $\lambda_1 > \lambda_2 > \ldots > \lambda_m$. These values show how closely each profile vector lies or correlates with principal axes.

Lastly, graphical representation of contingency table in the asymmetric map, rows and columns are plotted. The quality of representation is judged from the squared correlation given in the output. Physical interpretation will depend on the values obtained and the problem under consideration. Moreover, different software packages find values by different approaches, though they lead to the same conclusion.

Q. 71. *Is correspondence analysis influenced by the presence of outlier points?*

Ans. Outlier points afflict CA. Seldom, a row or column profile is rare in its set of points that it has a minor role in the determination of higher axes. This situation can be detected easily by considering the points contribution to the axes. When a point has a large contribution at a large principal coordinate at major principal axes, then it is called an *outlier*. Outlier points should be treated as supplementary variables to avoid their influence.

SECTION B

Fill in the Blanks

Fill in the suitable word(s) or phrase(s) in the blanks:

1. The statistics which encompasses the simultaneous observations analysis of two or more outcome variables at a time is known as ____________.

2. Multivariate data are usually presented in the form of ____________.

3. Multivariate procedures involve more than one ____________ or ____________ variables.

4. The statistical process of simultaneously analyzing multiple independent variables with multiple dependent variables is known as ____________.

5. ____________ is a numerical representation of the distribution of a trait in the population.

6. When subjects are classified into three or more groups, then ____________ is used.

7. In case of multivariate data, the classification or prediction of subjects into two groups is conducted through ________.

8. The technique applied to studies with two or more related dependent variables having control over the correlation between them is ____________________.

9. If every linear combination of k-components of a random vector of k-variables ($k \geq 2$) has univariate normal distribution, the random vector is said to follow ____________________.

10. The quantity $(x - \mu)'\Sigma^{-1}(x - \mu) = c^2$ (say) is known as ________________ between x and μ.

11. If linear combinations of the components of multivariate normal variable X are independent with equal variance, then the contours are ____________.

12. Generalized multiple dimensions of the chi-square distribution having integral number of degrees of freedom follows ____________.

13. The empirical covariance

$$S = \frac{1}{n}\sum_i (x_i - \bar{x})(x_i - \bar{x})' \text{ follows Wishart}$$

distribution ________________.

14. The statistic for Hotelling's-T^2 for a vector of p-variables with mean vector μ_0 and covariance matrix S is given as

$T^2 =$ ____________________________.

15. The statistic T^2 is approximated to ________.

16. P.C. Mahalanobis used his squared distance measure in ______________ studies.

17. The relation between Mahalanobis D^2 and Hotelling's-T^2 is ______________.

18. Two normally distributed random variables are ____________________ jointly bivariate normal.

19. Expected value of Mahalanobis D^2 is __________________ following usual notations.

20. Wilks' Lambda statistic is the ratio of two ________________________.

21. To test the hypothesis, Statistic Wilks' Λ is approximated to _______________ statistic.

22. Multivariate analysis of variance is performed to test __________________ across ____________________________________ variables simultaneously.

23. Multivariate analysis of variance is more appropriate when the dependent variables are ______________________.

24. The hypothesis which is tested in multivariate analysis of variance is the equality of ____________________________.

25. Multivariate analysis of variance was developed by_________________ in __________.

26. The linear combination of a set of original variables that are uncorrelated and their variances are in descending order are called ____________________________.

27. Principal component analysis is used when the variables are __________correlated.

28. Principal component analysis is a variable _________________ process.

29. Principal component analysis is a _____________ sample process.

30. All Principal components are ___________.

31. The underlying dimensions or constructs that summarize for the set of nonmetric variables represent the _______________.

32. A few underlying but unobservable random variables that describe the variation among many variables are called _______________.

33. As compared to Principal component analysis, the underlying model in Factor analysis specifies a small number of ________________.

34. Factor analysis is mainly concerned with explaining the __________________.

35. Principal component analysis is primarily concerned with explaining the _______________ of the original variables.

36. The graphical method of determining the number of Principal components or factors is ___________________.

37. In Factor analysis the observed variables are expressed as linear combinations of ____________________ variables.

38. An approach to Factor analysis that estimates the factors based only on common variance is known as ________ analysis.

39. The portion of the variance of the ith variable contributed to the k common factors is called ________.

40. Most commonly used software package to run Principal component analysis and Factor analysis is ________.

41. The composite score worked out for each respondent separately is called ________.

42. ____ to ____ per cent of total variance explained by Principal components is considered satisfactory.

43. A plot of the eigenvalues against the number of factors in order of extraction is named as ________.

44. A statistical technique employed to model the relationship between a dichotomous categorical criterion variable and a set of p ($p \geq 2$) predictor variables is called ________ analysis.

45. A fixed question in which a respondent is to choose one out of two alternatives responses on a subject is known as ________ question.

46. Discriminant analysis was developed by ________ in ________.

47. For discriminant analysis, the size of the smallest group should be greater than the number of ________ variables.

48. Sample data are assumed to have been drawn from a ________ population in multivariate analysis.

49. Predictor variables should almost be ________ ________.

50. Each linear combination of predictor variables in discriminant analysis creates a new ________.

51. A linear combination of predictor variables in discriminant analysis is called ________ ________.

52. Discriminant function analysis can be used for ________ of an observation whose group identity is unknown.

53. The measure of degree of association between the discriminant scores and the groups is known as ________.

54. Whether the two population groups significantly differ or not can be tested through ________.

55. Null hypothesis of no difference between two groups p-variables mean vectors can be tested by ________ approximated to ________.

56. Likelihood ratio test to test the significance of difference of mean vectors of two population groups employs ________ test.

57. The sum of the product of unstandardized coefficients and the corresponding variate values in a discriminant function yields ________.

58. The computer software packages ________ and ________ for discriminant function analysis are available.

59. A measure of association between a discriminant function and the set of dummy variables that define the group membership is called ________.

60. Linear discriminant function analysis should be carried out when covariances are ________, otherwise, ________ discriminant function.

61. Discriminant analysis is conducted only when the groups are ________ known.

62. The data should be free from ________.

63. A body of techniques concerned with forming natural groupings of objects based on the relationship of the p ($p \geq 2$) variables describing the objects is known as ________.

64. Discriminant analysis and cluster analysis both are ________ techniques.

65. In cluster analysis there is no ________ information about the groups.

66. Cluster analysis can be used for the ____ ________ of the market.

67. The information obtained on the objects or cases combined at each stage of a hierarchical clustering process is termed as ________ .

68. The cluster centers are initial starting point in ____________ clustering.

69. A clustering procedure characterized by the development of a tree like structure is called ______________ clustering.

70. Cluster analysis is a technique to reduce the ________________ whereas factor analysis reduces ______________ .

71. The distance between two objects measured as the square root of the sum of the squared differences between corresponding p-variate ($p \geq 2$) values is called ________________ .

72. Hierarchical clustering process where all objects start out in one jumbo cluster and then this cluster is splitted into smaller and smaller clusters is known as __________ .

73. Agglomerative methods that involve the distance between the objects for clustering are called ____________ .

74. The clustering method based on furtherest neighbor approach between objects is called ______________ method.

75. The clustering based on minimum distance between the objects is termed as ____________ method.

76. The clustering process based on the average distance between all pairs of objects, where one member of the pair from each of the clusters is involved is called ________ method.

77. The method of clustering based on the principle of minimizing loss of information due to the merger of groups was proposed by ______________ .

78. Nonhierarchical method that involves the Euclidean distance is ________ method.

79. A tree like figure employed to portray the output of a cluster analysis is known as ______________ .

80. A statistical technique that is used to determine the relative importance of salient attributes is ______________ .

81. Conjoint analysis technique can be applied to an ____________ or a ____________ .

82. Conjoint analysis not only determine the preferences for each attribute but also the __________ which the individuals attach to the level of attributes.

83. Conjoint analysis can accommodate either a metric or a nonmetric ____________ .

84. Conjoint analysis can use only a __________ predictor variable.

85. A set of levels of attributes likely to be evaluated by an individual is termed as ________________ .

86. An individual judgment with regard to his preference representing the holistic worth of a specified object is called its __________ .

87. Overall combinations of all levels of attributes in a systematic manner are known as ______________ .

88. Estimates of utility associated with each level of each factor used to evaluate the product under conjoint analysis is known as ________________ .

89. A specified attribute or characteristic of the product is called a __________ .

90. The process of interview in which a respondent is not ready to accept certain stimuli under any condition and may give some additional information at his own, is known as __________ method in a conjoint procedure.

91. The interview method in which a respondent is to choose a choice set out of sets of stimuli is known as __________ conjoint analysis.

92. In a full profile conjoint analysis, the respondents are to provide preferences as ____________ or ____________ .

93. When the number of attributes exceeds than what is required for choice based conjoint

analysis, then ____________ analysis is preferable.

94. Conjoint analysis is carried out to estimate ____________.

95. The perceived value of the features and sensitiveness of consumers' perceptions and preferences with regard to changes in product attributes are indicated by ____________.

96. In conjoint analysis, for full profile ________ model is more appropriate.

97. The sum of partial utilities provide ____________.

98. A linear combination of effects of the factors on a dependent variable is termed as ____________.

99. Conjoint analysis employs ____________ model.

100. For choice based conjoint analysis ____________ estimator or ____________ may preferably be used.

101. Conjoint analysis does not confine to linear relationship between factors on a dependent variable, rather it can handle ____________.

102. A series of procedures for displaying the perception and preferences of respondents by means of visual display is ____________ scaling.

103. Any stimulus which can be evaluated or compared by a respondent including tangible entities is called ____________ in multi-dimensional scaling.

104. Visual representation of a respondent's perception in two or more dimensions is called ____________ or ____________.

105. The number of features of an object which it alludes is called its ____________.

106. A point in the spatial map which represents the most preferred combination of attributes is known as ____________.

107. The ratings of all possible pairs of stimuli in terms of their similarity using Likert type scale is called ____________.

108. Squared correlation index measured under multidimensional scaling procedure is known as ____________.

109. The number of objects that a researcher must choose for three dimensions is ______.

110. For ranking similarity of pairs of objects for three dimensions, one must use ______ pairs of objects.

111. Multidimensional scaling ____________ which products and services can be considered as substitutes.

112. Multidimensional scaling can ____________ products which are not alike.

113. A good fit of a multidimensional scaling solution can be judged by ____________.

114. Lesser the ____________, better is the multidimensional scaling solution.

115. The main purpose of multidimensional scaling solution is to obtain a perceptual map that represents the original data involving ____________ of dimensions.

116. Multidimensional scaling reveals the salient features of a product ____________ or ____________ by the respondents.

117. The order of stimuli in respect of ____________ given by the respondents is revealed by multidimensional scaling solution.

118. One of the most commonly used method for deciding the number of dimensions is ____________.

119. Correspondence analysis is based on ____________ approach.

120. Correspondence analysis utilizes principal component analysis, ____________, and ____________.

121. The other names of correspondence analysis are ____________ and ____________.

122. Correspondence analysis is based on ____________ attributes.

123. Correspondence analysis can also be carried on ____________ data.

124. Correspondence analysis displays graphically the ______________ between variable categories and objects.

125. The data matrix as required for correspondence analysis is ______________.

126. Most easily available computer software packages for correspondence analysis are __________ and __________.

127. If the inertia in correspondence analysis is 80% or more, then ______________ are satisfactory.

128. The eigenvalues say, (λ, m) in correspondence analysis represent the ______________.

129. Weighted Euclidean distances in correspondence analysis are calculated to show the distance between ______________.

130. The main purpose of correspondence analysis is to transform a contingency table of numerical data into ______________.

131. The expression $(\underset{\sim}{x} - \underset{\sim}{\mu})' \Sigma^{-1} (\underset{\sim}{x} - \underset{\sim}{\mu})$ in normal density function describes the surface of an ______________ centered at μ.

132. If the covariance matrix Σ is singular, then the ______________ of the distribution does not exist.

133. Multivariate analysis of covariance is appropriate when the dependent variables are ______________.

134. The increase in heterogeneity on combining of two clusters indicates that a ______________ structure exists when they are separate.

135. Out of various forms of similarity measures, the most preferred similarity measure is ______________.

SECTION C

Multiple Choice Questions

Select the correct alternative out of given ones:

1. Multivariate statistics exists only when the number of variables to be studied simultaneously is:
   (*a*) at least five
   (*b*) three or more
   (*c*) two or more
   (*d*) in any number

2. Multivariate technique to reduce the number of variables is:
   (*a*) factor analysis
   (*b*) principal component analysis
   (*c*) both (*a*) and (*b*)
   (*d*) neither (*a*) nor (*b*)

3. When two factors are studied simultaneously having various levels of each factor, then the data can systematically be displayed through:
   (*a*) frequency distribution
   (*b*) a two way table
   (*c*) a matrix
   (*d*) both (*b*) and (*c*)

4. Multiple variables are said to be multivariate random variables if they follow:
   (*a*) law of large numbers
   (*b*) some probability distribution
   (*c*) law of inertia
   (*d*) central limit theorem

5. Why multiple regression is not considered a multivariate statistical method?
   (*a*) Because it involves only one dependent variable.
   (*b*) Because the number of independent variables is not fixed.
   (*c*) Because the relation between dependent and independent variables is not necessarily linear.
   (*d*) All of the above

6. Multivariate normal distribution is most commonly used in multiple statistical methods, because:
   (*a*) it is easier than other distributions

(*b*) its assumption holds due to multiple central limit theorem in all cases
(*c*) this distribution holds for all types of variables
(*d*) it converges to unity

7. The quantity $(\underset{\sim}{x} - \underset{\sim}{\mu})' \Sigma^{-1} (\underset{\sim}{x} - \underset{\sim}{\mu})$ involved in multivariate normal density function represents:
(*a*) multivariate normal density
(*b*) dispersion matrix
(*c*) exponential series
(*d*) Mahalonobis squared distance

8. The expression present in the density function describing the shape of a multivariate normal distribution is:
(*a*) $\dfrac{1}{(2\pi)^{1/2}\, \Sigma^{1/2}}$
(*b*) $e^{-\frac{1}{2}(\underset{\sim}{x}-\underset{\sim}{\mu})' \Sigma^{-1} (\underset{\sim}{x}-\underset{\sim}{\mu})}$
(*c*) $(\underset{\sim}{x} - \underset{\sim}{\mu})' \Sigma^{-1} (\underset{\sim}{x} - \underset{\sim}{\mu})$
(*d*) all of the above

9. If the covariance between the components of X of a multivariate normal variate is zero, then it is implied that:
(*a*) the components are independent
(*b*) the conditional distribution is multivariate normal
(*c*) linear combinations of components are normally distributed
(*d*) all of the above

10. If S is the covariance matrix as an estimate of Σ from a $N_p(0, \Sigma)$, then $A = (n - 1) S$ follows:
(*a*) chi-square distribution
(*b*) Mahalanobis D^2 distribution
(*c*) Wishart distribution
(*d*) Hotelling's T^2 distribution

11. Let $(x_i - \bar{x}) = z_i$ and the quantities $A_1 = \sum_{i=1}^{n_1} z_i z_i'$ and $A_2 = \sum_{j=1}^{n_2} z_j z_j'$. Also suppose $n = n_1 + n_2$. The quantity $A_1 + A_2$ follows:
(*a*) Gamma distribution
(*b*) Chi-square distribution with n d.f.
(*c*) multivariate normal distribution $N_p(n, \Sigma)$
(*d*) Wishart distribution $W_n(A_1 + A_2 \mid \Sigma)$

12. If the covariance matrix Σ of multivariate normal distribution is not of full rank, then:
(*a*) multivariate normal distribution is degenerate
(*b*) density of multivariate normal distribution does not exist
(*c*) both (*a*) and (*b*)
(*d*) none of the above

13. Logistic regression is based on:
(*a*) two or more independent variables
(*b*) a binary dependent variable
(*c*) logit transformation
(*d*) all of the above

14. The distribution of two normally distributed variables is:
(*a*) necessarily a bivariate normal distribution
(*b*) not necessarily a bivariate normal distribution
(*c*) exponential distribution
(*d*) a gamma distribution

15. In case of bivariate normal distribution, the prediction interval of a vector having two elements defines:
(*a*) a circle
(*b*) the outer of an ellipse
(*c*) the interior of an ellipse
(*d*) none of the above

16. If $M = W_p(\Sigma, m)$ and $a \; \varepsilon R^p$ with $a'\Sigma a \neq 0$, then $\left(\dfrac{a'Ma}{a'\Sigma a}\right)$ follows:
(*a*) Wishart distribution $W_p(\mathbf{0}, m)$
(*b*) chi-square distribution with m d.f.
(*c*) one dimensional Wishart distribution $W_1(\sigma^2, m)$
(*d*) none of the above

17. Wishart distribution $W_1(\sigma^2, n)$ follows:
(*a*) $\sigma^2 \chi^2$ distribution
(*b*) $N(0, \sigma^2)$ distribution

(c) $\frac{e^{-n}\sigma^2}{n}$ distribution

(d) all of the above

18. Hotelling's T^2 is a generalization of:

(a) univariate student's t to multivariate

(b) test of one mean to two or more means simultaneously

(c) involvement of univariate normal to multivariate normal variables

(d) all of the above

19. Hotelling's T^2 statistic with usual notations is:

(a) $T^2 = n(\underset{\sim}{\bar{x}} - \underset{\sim}{\mu})' \Sigma^{-1} (\underset{\sim}{\bar{x}} - \underset{\sim}{\mu})$

(b) $T^2 = \frac{1}{n}(\underset{\sim}{\bar{x}} - \underset{\sim}{\mu})' S^{-1} (\underset{\sim}{\bar{x}} - \underset{\sim}{\mu})$

(c) $T^2 = n(\underset{\sim}{\bar{x}} - \underset{\sim}{\mu})' S^{-1} (\underset{\sim}{\bar{x}} - \underset{\sim}{\mu})$

(d) $T^2 = (\underset{\sim}{\bar{x}} - \underset{\sim}{\mu})' \Sigma^{-1} (\underset{\sim}{\bar{x}} - \underset{\sim}{\mu})$

20. Hotelling's T^2 can be approximated to Statistic F with usual notations as test criterion following the inequality for rejection as:

(a) $T^2 > F_{p,(n-p);\alpha}$ for $n > p$

(b) $T^2 < F_{p,(n-p);\alpha}$ for $n > p$

(c) $T^2 > \frac{(n-1)}{(n-p)} F_{p,(n-p);\alpha}$ for $n > p$

(d) $T^2 > \frac{(n-p)}{(n-1)} F_{p,(n-p);\alpha}$ for $n > p$

21. A relation between Hotelling's T^2 and Wishart random matrix:

(a) exists

(b) does not exist

(c) is as one is reciprocal of the other

(d) is as one is directly proportional to the other

22. Mahalanobis distance measure is used to identify the dissimilarity between:

(a) ethnic groups

(b) fossils forms

(c) numerical taxonomy

(d) all of the above

23. Mahalanobis distance is measured in square terms as D^2 because:

(a) its calculation is simple

(b) its distribution can indirectly be approximated to F

(c) parameters are known

(d) population data are easily available

24. For two samples of sizes n_1 and n_2 from two groups G_1 and G_2 respectively and studying p characteristics on each unit in both the samples, the correct expression for D^2 with usual notations is:

(a) $\frac{1}{p}(\underset{\sim}{\bar{x}}_1 - \underset{\sim}{\bar{x}}_2)' S^{-1} (\underset{\sim}{\bar{x}}_1 - \underset{\sim}{\bar{x}}_2)$

(b) $\frac{1}{n}(\underset{\sim}{\bar{x}}_1 - \underset{\sim}{\bar{x}}_2)' \Sigma^{-1} (\underset{\sim}{\bar{x}}_1 - \underset{\sim}{\bar{x}}_2)$

(c) $\frac{1}{p}(\underset{\sim}{\bar{x}}_1 - \underset{\sim}{\bar{x}}_2)' \Sigma^{-1} (\underset{\sim}{\bar{x}}_1 - \underset{\sim}{\bar{x}}_2)$

(d) none of the above

25. In Mahalanobis approach, the sample points are more likely distributed about the center of mass:

(a) of a sphere

(b) of a parabola

(c) of an ellipsoid

(d) of a cube

26. Mahalanobis D^2 as an estimate of population parameter Δ^2 is:

(a) an unbiased estimate

(b) a biased estimate

(c) an expected value of D^2

(d) none the above

27. Wilks' Lambda distribution is the generalization of the univariate:

(a) χ^2-distribution

(b) F-distribution

(c) Gamma-distribution

(d) none of the above

28. Wilks' Λ statistic in case of two populations is the ratio of:

(a) two Wishart distributed variables

(b) a Wishart to Chi-square distributed variables

(c) two F-distributed variables

(d) a F-distributed to Hotelling's T^2 variables

29. The distribution of Wilks' Λ in case of two populations can be approximated to:

(a) F-distribution

(b) multivariate normal distribution

(c) χ^2-distribution

(d) all of the above

30. The distribution of Wilks' Λ in case of more than two populations can be approximated to:

(a) F-distribution

(b) Gamma distribution

(c) χ^2-distribution

(d) Hotelling's T^2 distribution

31. Wilks' Λ statistic can be equated to:

(a) F-statistic

(b) t-statistic

(c) χ^2-statistic

(d) all of the above

32. The range of Wilks' Λ is:

(a) –1 to 1

(b) 0 to 1

(c) $-\infty$ to $+\infty$

(d) –1 to 0

33. To arrive at a decision of no difference between group means, the value of Wilks' Λ is:

(a) nearly 1

(b) nearly 0

(c) nearly –1

(d) any value >1

34. Zero value of Wilks' Λ indicates that:

(a) there is no difference between group means

(b) there is difference between group means

(c) the groups are independent

(d) no decision about group means can be drawn

35. Correct relation between p-variate Hotelling's T^2 and Wishart random matrix is:

(a) $T^2_{p,n-1} = N_p(0, \Sigma)' \left[\frac{1}{n} W_{p,n}(\Sigma)\right] N_p(0, \Sigma)$

(b) $T^2_{p,n} = N_p(\mu, \Sigma)' \left[\frac{1}{n} W_{p,n}(\Sigma)\right] N_p(\mu, \Sigma)$

(c) $T^2_{p,n-1} = N_p(0, \Sigma)' \left[\frac{1}{n-1} W_{p,n-1}(\Sigma)\right]^{-1} N_p(0, \Sigma)$

(d) $T^2_{p,n-1} = N_p(0, \Sigma)' \left[\frac{1}{n-1} W_{p-1,n-1}(\Sigma)\right]^{-1} N_p(0, \Sigma)$

36. If in the bivariate normal distribution of the variables X and Y, ρ = 0, then:

(a) the joint p.d.f. of X and Y is the product of the individual p.d.f. of X and Y

(b) the joint p.d.f. of X and Y is the average of the p.d.f. of X and Y

(c) the joint p.d.f. vanishes

(d) none of the above

37. S in the expression for Mahalanobis D^2 stands for:

(a) the sum of the two variance-covariance matrices

(b) the average of the two variance-covariance matrices

(c) the pooled variance-covariance matrix of the two matrices

(d) the difference between the two sample variance-covariance matrices

38. Confidence interval for a vector of means μ of p-variate normal distribution is:

(a) a sphere

(b) an ellipsoid

(c) hyperboloid

(d) paraboloid

39. If all the p-variables are independent, then the variance-covariance matrix will be:

(a) a unit matrix

(b) a diagonal matrix

(c) a null matrix

(d) an inverse matrix

40. A statistical analysis is said to be a multi-variate data analysis if it involves:

(a) at least two dependent variables

(b) at least two independent variables

(*c*) one dependent and two or more independent variables
(*d*) all related variables

41. Multivariate analysis of variance to test the difference across group means is more appropriate when the dependent variables are:
(*a*) independent
(*b*) binary
(*c*) correlated
(*d*) on nominal scale

42. When in a multivariate data set the dependent variables are not associated, then to test the difference across group means, more appropriate procedure for analysis is:
(*a*) multivariate analysis of variance
(*b*) analysis of variance for each variable separately
(*c*) pair wise analysis of variance
(*d*) all of the above

43. Three groups of 30 ladies namely, adolescent, young and middle aged are to give scores out of 20 to 5 brands of soap in respect of hardness, foams, antibacterial effect, odor and price. You are to test whether the groups differ significantly. What type of analysis would you prefer?
(*a*) Multivariate analysis of variance
(*b*) Discriminant analysis
(*c*) Factor analysis
(*d*) Principal component analysis

44. If there are two groups and a set of multiple criterion variables, then what test can be employed to test the group differences?
(*a*) Wilks' Λ test
(*b*) Hotelling's T^2
(*c*) both (*a*) and (*b*)
(*d*) neither (*a*) nor (*b*)

45. If there are three or more groups and a set of multiple criterion variables, then the appropriate test for testing the groups mean differences is:
(*a*) Hotelling's T^2
(*b*) Wilks' Λ test
(*c*) both (*a*) and (*b*)
(*d*) none of the above

46. Multivariate analysis of variance technique can be applied in the areas:
(*a*) anthropology
(*b*) marketing
(*c*) medical
(*d*) all of the above

47. Multivariate analysis of variance technique was proposed by:
(*a*) R.A. Fisher in 1935
(*b*) A. Wald in 1944
(*c*) S.S. Wilks in 1932
(*d*) W.G. Cochran in 1956

48. Principal components possess the characteristic as:
(*a*) a set of optimally weighted linear combination of variables
(*b*) a set of uncorrelated linear combinations
(*c*) a set of orthogonal linear combinations
(*d*) all of the above

49. The extraction method of obtaining a set of principal components utilizes the property of:
(*a*) orthogonality
(*b*) equality
(*c*) orthonormality
(*d*) none of the above

50. During the process of obtaining the principal components by extraction method involving p variables, the number of eigenvalues can be:
(*a*) greater than p
(*b*) can be utmost p
(*c*) cannot be more than 3
(*d*) none of the above

51. The variance of principal components during the process varies:
(*a*) in descending order
(*b*) in ascending order
(*c*) in equal proportion
(*d*) in haphazard manner

52. For determining principal components by extraction method, the eigenvalues are selected:
(*a*) in ascending order
(*b*) in descending order
(*c*) in ascending and descending order alternately
(*d*) all of the above

53. The ratio of the sum of eigenvalues to p in p-variables principal component analysis provides:
(*a*) the proportion of variance extracted
(*b*) correlation value between components
(*c*) both (*a*) and (*b*)
(*d*) none of the above

54. Principal component analysis is used when:
(*a*) the number of variables is large
(*b*) the variables are highly correlated
(*c*) a large size sample is possible
(*d*) all of the above

55. Principal component analysis is meant for:
(*a*) reducing the number of observed variables
(*b*) increasing the number of variables
(*c*) to reduce the correlation between variables
(*d*) to reduce the variance among variables

56. Factor analysis is also named as:
(*a*) common factor analysis
(*b*) principal factor analysis
(*c*) exploratory factor analysis
(*d*) all of the above

57. Factor analysis explains the correlation among a set of variables in terms of:
(*a*) certain underlying unobservable quantities
(*b*) multinomial variables
(*c*) physical quantities
(*d*) none of the above

58. Unobservable random quantities in a multivariate analysis are known as:
(*a*) superficial variables
(*b*) outliers
(*c*) factors
(*d*) anorexic

59. Factor analysis is a technique in which the observed variables are expressed in terms of:
(*a*) a factor
(*b*) linear combination of factors
(*c*) correlations
(*d*) distances

60. Unobservable random quantities stand for:
(*a*) intelligence
(*b*) preference
(*c*) memory
(*d*) all of the above

61. The portion of the variance of ith variable contributed to the k common factors is called:
(*a*) common variance
(*b*) specific variance
(*c*) communality
(*d*) error variance

62. The composite scores determined for each individual from the factors obtained in factor analysis are called:
(*a*) factor scores
(*b*) respondent scores
(*c*) component scores
(*d*) all of the above

63. The graph plotted by taking eigenvalues along ordinate and their sequence number along abscissa helps to determine:
(*a*) the factors
(*b*) the number of factors
(*c*) the sample size
(*d*) the number of variables

64. The number of factors or components can be determined with the help of:
(*a*) a priori criterion
(*b*) Scree plot
(*c*) percentage of variance
(*d*) all of the above

65. Principal component analysis and factor analysis both are:
(*a*) variable reduction process
(*b*) variance reduction process
(*c*) both (*a*) and (*b*)
(*d*) neither (*a*) nor (*b*)

66. Principal component analysis explains as large as possible with minimum number of components:
(*a*) the correlation between original variables
(*b*) proportion of variance between variables
(*c*) covariance between variables
(*d*) all of the above

67. Factor analysis accounts for:
(*a*) covariance between the variables
(*b*) correlation between the variables
(*c*) both (*a*) and (*b*)
(*d*) neither (*a*) nor (*b*)

68. Principal component analysis reduces the number of variables in the form of:
(*a*) components
(*b*) factors
(*c*) constructs
(*d*) none of the above

69. Factor analysis reduces the number of variables in the form of:
(*a*) components
(*b*) normalized rotation
(*c*) constructs
(*d*) all of the above

70. For a data set, principal component analysis can be used to determine:
(*a*) number of variables to be used
(*b*) factors to be extracted
(*c*) factor scores
(*d*) none of the above

71. Discriminant analysis is a technique of modeling a relationship between:
(*a*) a continuous dependent variable and independent continuous variable
(*b*) a categorical criterion variable and independent continuous variable
(*c*) a nominal dependent variable and a binary variable
(*d*) a normal variable and multinomial variables

72. For good discriminant analysis which of the following condition is preferable?
(*a*) The size of the smallest group should be greater than the number of predictor variables.
(*b*) Predictor variables must be independent.
(*c*) Sample data are from a multivariate normal distribution.
(*d*) all of the above

73. What restriction is imposed on variance among group variables for discriminant analysis?
(*a*) Variance should be same across levels of predictors.
(*b*) Variance should be heterogeneous across levels of predictors.
(*c*) No restriction is imposed on variances.
(*d*) Variances across predictors' levels should be unity.

74. If the predictor variables are not independent, then what sort of problem may arise?
(*a*) Nonsampling error.
(*b*) Multicollinearity.
(*c*) Simultaneous estimation.
(*d*) Cross validation.

75. Linear function of predictors creating a new latent variable is known as:
(*a*) logistic regression
(*b*) principal component
(*c*) a factor
(*d*) discriminant function

76. To ascertain the group identity of an individual observation X having p-variables, the proper statistical analysis technique is:
(*a*) principal component analysis
(*b*) factor analysis
(*c*) discriminant analysis
(*d*) multivariate analysis of variance

77. The hypothesis of zero difference between two groups mean vectors can be tested using:
(*a*) Mahalanobis D^2 test
(*b*) F-test
(*c*) Wilks lambda
(*d*) all of the above

78. If in an unstandardized discriminant function, the coefficients are multiplied by the corresponding variate values, one gets:
(*a*) discriminant score
(*b*) factor score

(*c*) both (*a*) and (*b*)
(*d*) neither (*a*) nor (*b*)

79. Wilks' lambda statistic is based on the principle of:
(*a*) least square
(*b*) Lagrange's multiplier
(*c*) likelihood ratio
(*d*) variance ratio

80. Linear discriminant function analysis can be used when:
(*a*) the variances are equal
(*b*) the covariances are equal
(*c*) the covariances matrix is nonsingular
(*d*) none of the above

81. When in a variances-covariances matrix, variances are equal in discriminant analysis, then use:
(*a*) linear function
(*b*) polynomial function
(*c*) quadratic function
(*d*) cubic function

82. Discriminant function is a good fit if observed data are free from:
(*a*) observation error
(*b*) sampling error
(*c*) outliers
(*d*) all of the above

83. A measure of association between a discriminant function and a set of dummy variables that define the group membership is known as:
(*a*) multivariate correlation
(*b*) multicollinearity
(*c*) canonical correlation
(*d*) biserial correlation

84. An observation was left out unnoted in the data tables of two groups. Now to identify to which group it belongs can be ascertained using:
(*a*) cluster analysis
(*b*) discriminant analysis
(*c*) factor analysis
(*d*) any of the above

85. Cluster analysis is a statistical technique for:
(*a*) reducing the number of objects
(*b*) forming natural groups
(*c*) maximizing likeness within groups
(*d*) all of the above

86. Each cluster in cluster analysis contains:
(*a*) a few similar objects
(*b*) a few similar variables
(*c*) a few similar factors
(*d*) a few similar functions

87. Cluster analysis technique is useful in the area of:
(*a*) marketing
(*b*) Taxonomy
(*c*) search of gene profile
(*d*) all of the above

88. The most commonly used measure of similarity between objects is:
(*a*) direct distance measurement
(*b*) Euclidean distance
(*c*) projective distance
(*d*) none of the above

89. Hierarchical clustering method involves:
(*a*) agglomerative methods
(*b*) linkage methods
(*c*) centroid method
(*d*) all of the above

90. Agglomerative methods start with clustering:
(*a*) as many clusters as the number of objects
(*b*) as many clusters as the number of variables
(*c*) only one cluster
(*d*) two clusters

91. If a researcher starts with one cluster and then splits it into a number of clusters, then this procedure is called:
(*a*) Wald's method of clustering
(*b*) *K*-means method of clustering
(*c*) divisive clustering method
(*d*) all of the above

92. Single linkage method is based on:
(*a*) minimum distance between objects
(*b*) maximum distance between objects

(*c*) average distance between pairs of objects
(*d*) squared distance between objects

93. Linkage method is:
(*a*) complete linkage method
(*b*) single linkage method
(*c*) average linkage method
(*d*) all of the above

94. Clustering method based on loss of information due to merging of two clusters was given by:
(*a*) K. Walsh
(*b*) A. Wald
(*c*) G. Milligan
(*d*) W.S. Searle

95. The shape of a dendogram is similar to:
(*a*) a tree like configuration
(*b*) a lattice configuration
(*c*) both (*a*) and (*b*)
(*d*) neither (*a*) nor (*b*)

96. Nonhierarchical clustering method is preferable over Hierarchical method when:
(*a*) number of variables is large
(*b*) number of objects is large
(*c*) distance between objects is large
(*d*) the variate values are large

97. Centroid method of clustering utilizes:
(*a*) Euclidean distance between variables
(*b*) square of the distance between paired variables
(*c*) sum of the square of the differences between clusters centroids
(*d*) sum of the differences between clusters centroids

98. Conjoint analysis deals with the marketing problem such as:
(*a*) features of a new product
(*b*) pricing of a new product
(*c*) preference of customers about a new product
(*d*) all of the above

99. The data for conjoint analysis are collected for the facts such as:
(*a*) respondent's subjective evaluations
(*b*) attribute levels
(*c*) stimuli
(*d*) all of the above

100. Adaptive conjoint analysis can entail the cases of:
(*a*) absolute rejection of a stimulus
(*b*) additional information of the respondent
(*c*) both (*a*) and (*b*)
(*d*) neither (*a*) nor (*b*)

101. If addition or rejection of stimuli is incorporated in adaptive conjoint analysis, then it is named as:
(*a*) part-worth analysis
(*b*) self-explicated conjoint analysis
(*c*) utility based conjoint analysis
(*d*) specific respondent analysis

102. If the respondent is asked to select a choice set from a set of stimuli, then a respondent conducts:
(*a*) adaptive model conjoint analysis
(*b*) choice based conjoint analysis
(*c*) utility based conjoint analysis
(*d*) specific object conjoint analysis

103. Full profile means:
(*a*) all attributes taken together
(*b*) taking all attributes at their respective levels
(*c*) taking all possible combinations of attributes and their levels
(*d*) none of the above

104. Ranking or rating the full profile in a marketing research, a researcher should choose to carry out:
(*a*) factor analysis
(*b*) principal component analysis
(*c*) choice based conjoint analysis
(*d*) full profile conjoint analysis

105. Estimated overall utility associated with each level of each factor is known as:
(*a*) conjoint task
(*b*) part-worth
(*c*) main effect
(*d*) hybrid conjoint analysis

106. An individual subjective preference judgment providing overall worth of a specific object is called:
(*a*) part-worth
(*b*) utility
(*c*) stimulus
(*d*) trade-off

107. In a full profile conjoint analysis regression model, the dependent variable is:
(*a*) objective attributes
(*b*) preference given by the respondent
(*c*) perceived values
(*d*) partial utilities

108. Conjoint analysis facilitates a researcher to know:
(*a*) metric partial utilities
(*b*) segments of respondents
(*c*) realistic choice
(*d*) all of the above

109. A study based on conjoint analysis may be misleading if:
(*a*) the number of stimuli is too large
(*b*) a proper statistical design is not employed
(*c*) both (*a*) and (*b*)
(*d*) neither (*a*) nor (*b*)

110. In a full profile conjoint analysis regression model, the independent variable to be taken is:
(*a*) objective attributes
(*b*) fictive responses
(*c*) consumers' perceptions
(*d*) levels of attributes

111. If a manufacturer wants high profitability by maintaining high quality and high price, then it is termed as:
(*a*) choice set
(*b*) utility
(*c*) trade-off
(*d*) segmentation

112. Multidimensional scaling analysis is conducted to obtain a spatial map that fits input data involving:
(*a*) minimum number of objects
(*b*) maximum number of products
(*c*) minimum number of dimensions
(*d*) all of the above

113. Multidimensional scaling analysis can be utilized for the purpose of:
(*a*) differentiating the products from one another
(*b*) viable segmentation of consumers
(*c*) knowing the weaknesses of a market
(*d*) all of the above

114. Multidimensional scaling can be used to obtain the information such as:
(*a*) salient features of a product
(*b*) the rank order of the combination of attributes
(*c*) substitutes of products
(*d*) all of the above

115. For multidimensional scaling analysis, the number of objects should at least be:
(*a*) two times the number of dimensions
(*b*) three times the number of dimensions
(*c*) four times the number of dimensions
(*d*) five times the number of dimensions

116. How well the raw data fits to the multi-dimensional scaling procedure is ascertained by:
(*a*) initial dimensionality
(*b*) index of fit
(*c*) preference ranking
(*d*) decompositional method

117. For obtaining a best spatial map, a researcher must decide in multidimensional scaling procedure:
(*a*) number of respondents
(*b*) number of products
(*c*) number of dimensions
(*d*) number of objects

118. The procedure of preparing a perceptual map by multidimensional scaling analysis based on the evaluation of a group of respondents is called:
(*a*) compositional method
(*b*) similarity judgment
(*c*) aggregate analysis
(*d*) none of the above

119. The method of selecting the number of dimensions before-hand in multidimensional scaling analysis is called:
(*a*) initial dimensionality
(*b*) prior selection
(*c*) both (*a*) and (*b*)
(*d*) none of the above

120. If all pairs of stimulus are rated in terms of their similarity using Likert scale, then the process is known as:
(*a*) paired rating
(*b*) similarity judgment
(*c*) pairwise judgment
(*d*) preference rating

121. When the stimuli or brands are ranked in order by the respondents according to their preferences, the procedure is known as:
(*a*) preference ranking
(*b*) nominal scale ranking
(*c*) sematic scale ranking
(*d*) none of the above

122. A point in perceptual map which represents the most preferred combination of attributes is called:
(*a*) centroid
(*b*) central point
(*c*) index of fit
(*d*) ideal point

123. Perceived relationship displayed by points as a graph among products or stimuli plotted on a multidimensional space is termed as:
(*a*) spatial map
(*b*) perceptual map
(*c*) both (*a*) and (*b*)
(*d*) none of the above

124. Any stimulus which can be assessed by a respondent known as:
(*a*) feature
(*b*) object
(*c*) dimension
(*d*) scaling

125. Stress measure indicates towards:
(*a*) the fit of a multidimensional scaling solution
(*b*) the fit of a spatial map
(*c*) validity of multidimensional scaling procedure
(*d*) reliability of preference data

126. Number of dimensions to retain in a multidimensional scaling solution is based on:
(*a*) researcher's experience
(*b*) limitation of interpretation
(*c*) elbow criterion
(*d*) all of the above

127. The number of features which an individual uses in making his judgment corresponds to:
(*a*) number of dimensions
(*b*) number of brands
(*c*) number of objects
(*d*) number of services

128. A specific set of levels having only one level of each factor to be evaluated by the respondent is called:
(*a*) stimuli
(*b*) stimulus
(*c*) factorial set of combinations
(*d*) all of the above

129. All possible combinations of factors or features at two or more levels are called:
(*a*) stimulus
(*b*) factorial set
(*c*) bridging design
(*d*) stimuli

130. The procedure of measuring respondents' perception of similarity and preference of the objects and plotting the relationship in a multidimensional space is known as:
(*a*) conjoint analysis
(*b*) multidimensional scaling
(*c*) canonical analysis
(*d*) correspondence analysis

131. Multidimensional scaling analysis is based on:
(*a*) compositional approach
(*b*) aggregate analysis
(*c*) decompositional approach
(*d*) all of the above

132. Correspondence analysis procedures for perceptual mapping entail:

(*a*) factor analysis
(*b*) principal component analysis
(*c*) multidimensional scaling
(*d*) all of the above

133. Correspondence analysis is based on:
(*a*) compositional approach
(*b*) decompositional approach
(*c*) hierarchical methods
(*d*) part-worths

134. The other name given to correspondence analysis is:
(*a*) optimal scaling
(*b*) homogeneity analysis
(*c*) reciprocal averaging
(*d*) all of the above

135. The main requirement for proper correspondence analysis is that:
(*a*) the data should be large
(*b*) the variables should be homogeneous
(*c*) the data matrix is a priori amorphous
(*d*) all of the above

136. The input data in case of correspondence analysis can be presented in the form of:
(*a*) a frequency distribution
(*b*) a contingency table
(*c*) a frequency table
(*d*) percentages

137. The unique objective of correspondence analysis is to establish a relationship between:
(*a*) rows and columns of a contingency table
(*b*) objects and variables
(*c*) both (*a*) and (*b*)
(*d*) neither (*a*) nor (*b*)

138. Correspondence analysis can be used for:
(*a*) nominal data
(*b*) data on Likert scale
(*c*) data on ratio scale
(*d*) number of features

139. Correspondence analysis is conducted for the purpose of:
(*a*) dimension reduction
(*b*) perceptual mapping
(*c*) both (*a*) and (*b*)
(*d*) none of the above

140. The sum of each row profile and that of column profile of input data contingency table in the process of correspondence analysis is:
(*a*) *n*, the sample size
(*b*) 1
(*c*) $1/n$
(*d*) any positive value

ANSWERS

Section B

1. multivariate statistics **2.** matrix **3.** dependent; outcome **4.** multivariate analysis **5.** Variance **6.** discriminant analysis **7.** logistic regression **8.** MANOVA **9.** multivariate normal distribution **10.** Mahalanobis squared distance **11.** spheres **12.** Wishart distribution **13.** $\frac{1}{n}W_p(\Sigma, n-1)$ **14.** $n(\underset{\sim}{\bar{x}}-\underset{\sim}{\mu}_0)' S^{-1}(\underset{\sim}{\bar{x}}-\underset{\sim}{\mu}_0)$ **15.** *F*-statistic **16.** Anthropological **17.** $T^2 = \frac{n_1 n_2}{n_1+n_2} D^2$ **18.** not necessarily **19.** $\Delta^2 + \frac{2}{n}$ **20.** Wishart statistics **21.** chi-square **22.** group differences; multiple dependent **23.** correlated **24.** vectors of group means **25.** S.S. Wilks; 1932 **26.** principal components **27.** highly **28.** reduction **29.** large **30.** orthogonal **31.** factors **32.** factors **33.** common factors **34.** covariance **35.** variance **36.** scree plot **37.** unobserved **38.** common factor **39.** communality **40.** SPSS **41.** factor score **42.** 70–80 **43.** scree plot **44.** discriminant **45.** dichotomous **46.** R.A. Fisher; 1936 **47.** predictors **48.** multinomial normal **49.** independent **50.** latent variable **51.** discriminant function **52.** classification **53.** canonical correlation **54.** discriminant analysis **55.** Mahalanobis – D_p^2; F-statistics **56.** Wilks lambda **57.** discriminant score **58.** SPSS; SAS **59.** canonical correlation **60.** equal; quadratic **61.** a priori **62.** outliers **63.** cluster analysis **64.** classification **65.** a priori **66.** segmentation **67.** agglomeration schedule **68.** nonhierarchical **69.** hierarchical **70.** number of objects; number of variables **71.** Euclidean distance **72.** divisive clustering **73.** linkage methods **74.** complete linkage **75.** single linkage **76.** average linkage· **77.** A. Wald **78.** *k*-means **79.** dendogram **80.** conjoint analysis **81.** individual; group of individuals **82.** utilities **83.** dependent variable **84.** categorical **85.** stimulus **86.** utility **87.** stimuli **88.** part-worth **89.** factor **90.** self-explicated **91.** choice based **92.** rankings; ratings **93.** adaptive conjoint **94.** utility function **95.** utility functions **96.** regression **97.** total metric utilities **98.** conjoint variate **99.** decompositional **100.** likelihood ratio; logistic regression **101.** nonlinear relationship **102.** multidimensional **103.** object **104.** spatial map; perceptual map **105.** dimensions **106.** ideal point **107.** similarity judgment **108.** index of fit **109.** 13 **110.** 78 **111.** discern **112.** differentiate **113.** stress measure **114.** stress **115.** minimum number **116.** perceived; preferred **117.** preferences **118.** elbow criterion **119.** compositional **120.** factor analysis; multidimensional scaling **121.** optimal scaling; homogeneity analysis **122.** descriptive **123.** nominal **124.** structural relationship **125.** amorphous **126.** SAS; SPSS V.19 **127.** two dimensions **128.** principal axes **129.** profile points **130.** graphical display **131.** ellipsoid **132.** density **133.** correlated **134.** more natural **135.** distance measure

Section C

1. (*c*)	**2.** (*c*)	**3.** (*d*)	**4.** (*b*)	**5.** (*a*)
6. (*b*)	**7.** (*d*)	**8.** (*c*)	**9.** (*d*)	**10.** (*c*)
11. (*d*)	**12.** (*c*)	**13.** (*d*)	**14.** (*b*)	**15.** (*c*)
16. (*b*)	**17.** (*a*)	**18.** (*d*)	**19.** (*c*)	**20.** (*c*)
21. (*a*)	**22.** (*d*)	**23.** (*b*)	**24.** (*a*)	**25.** (*c*)
26. (*b*)	**27.** (*b*)	**28.** (*a*)	**29.** (*c*)	**30.** (*c*)
31. (*a*)	**32.** (*b*)	**33.** (*a*)	**34.** (*b*)	**35.** (*c*)
36. (*a*)	**37.** (*c*)	**38.** (*b*)	**39.** (*b*)	**40.** (*a*)
41. (*c*)	**42.** (*b*)	**43.** (*c*)	**44.** (*b*)	**45.** (*b*)
46. (*d*)	**47.** (*c*)	**48.** (*d*)	**49.** (*c*)	**50.** (*b*)
51. (*b*)	**52.** (*a*)	**53.** (*a*)	**54.** (*d*)	**55.** (*a*)
56. (*d*)	**57.** (*a*)	**58.** (*c*)	**59.** (*b*)	**60.** (*d*)
61. (*c*)	**62.** (*a*)	**63.** (*b*)	**64.** (*d*)	**65.** (*a*)
66. (*b*)	**67.** (*c*)	**68.** (*b*)	**69.** (*c*)	**70.** (*b*)
71. (*b*)	**72.** (*d*)	**73.** (*a*)	**74.** (*b*)	**75.** (*d*)
76. (*c*)	**77.** (*b*)	**78.** (*a*)	**79.** (*c*)	**80.** (*b*)
81. (*c*)	**82.** (*d*)	**83.** (*c*)	**84.** (*b*)	**85.** (*d*)
86. (*a*)	**87.** (*d*)	**88.** (*b*)	**89.** (*d*)	**90.** (*a*)
91. (*c*)	**92.** (*a*)	**93.** (*d*)	**94.** (*b*)	**95.** (*a*)
96. (*b*)	**97.** (*c*)n	**98.** (*d*)	**99.** (*d*)	**100.** (*c*)
101. (*b*)	**102.** (*b*)	**103.** (*c*)	**104.** (*c*)	**105.** (*b*)
106. (*b*)	**107.** (*b*)	**108.** (*d*)	**109.** (*c*)	**110.** (*a*)
111. (*c*)	**112.** (*c*)	**113.** (*d*)	**114.** (*d*)	**115.** (*c*)
116. (*b*)	**117.** (*c*)	**118.** (*c*)	**119.** (*a*)	**120.** (*b*)
121. (*a*)	**122.** (*d*)	**123.** (*c*)	**124.** (*b*)	**125.** (*a*)
126. (*d*)	**127.** (*a*)	**128.** (*b*)	**129.** (*d*)	**130.** (*b*)
131. (*c*)	**132.** (*d*)	**133.** (*a*)	**134.** (*d*)	**135.** (*d*)
136. (*b*)	**137.** (*b*)	**138.** (*a*)	**139.** (*c*)	**140.** (*b*)

SUGGESTED READING

1. Agarwal, B. L., *Comprehensive Research Methodology*, New Age International, Publishers, New Delhi, 2015.
2. Anderson, T. W., *An Introduction to Multivariate Analysis*, John Wiley, New York, 1958.
3. Borg, I., and Groenen, P. J. F., *Modern Multidimensional Scaling: Theory and Application*, Springer-Verlag, New York, 2nd edition, 2005.

4. Hair Joseph F. Jr., and et al., *Multivariate Data Analysis,* Pearson Education, New Delhi, 6th edition, 2004.
5. Jobson, J. D., Applied *Multivariate Data Analysis,* Vol.-I, Springer-Verlag, New York, 1991.
6. Jobson, J. D., Applied *Multivariate Data Analysis,* Vol.-II, Springer-Verlag, New York, 1992.
7. Johnson, Richard A., and Wichern Dean W., *Applied Multivariate Statistical Analysis,* Prentice Hall, New Jersey, 5th edition, 2009.
8. Morrison, Donald, F., *Multivariate Statistical Methods,* McGraw Hill, New York, 1990.
9. Rao, C. R., *Advanced Statistical Methods in Biometric Research*, John Wiley, New York, 1952.
10. Rencher, A. C., *Methods of Multivariate Analysis*, 2nd edition, John Wiley, New York, 2002.

Some Important Terms

Terminology used frequently in the field of Probability and Statistics is compiled here from various sources.

t-Distribution: A continuous distribution with a specific type of bell-shaped curve with its mean equal to 0 and standard deviation equal to $\sqrt{df/(df-2)}$.

z-Value or z-Score: The units of the standard normal distribution that are denoted by z.

β-Beta: The probability of not rejecting a null hypothesis when it actually is false. (The probability of committing a Type II error).

σ (Sigma): The significance level of a test of hypothesis that denotes the probability of rejecting a null hypothesis when it actually is true. (The probability of committing a Type I error).

α-Alpha: The probability that the statistical test will incorrectly reject the null hypothesis.

μ_d: The mean of the paired differences for the population.

σ_d: The standard deviation of the paired differences for the population.

d: The difference between two matched values in two samples collected from the same source. It is called the paired difference.

$\overline{d}$: The mean of the paired differences for a sample.

Absolute Dispersion: The actual variation or dispersion is called the absolute dispersion.

Absolute Error: The difference, without sign, between the actual value and a statistically determined model value.

All those value that would not be rejected with $p = 0.05$.

Alpha: The probability that the statistical test will incorrectly reject the null hypothesis.

Alternative Hypothesis: A claim about a population parameter that will be true if the null hypothesis is false.

Analysis of Variance (ANOVA): A statistical technique used to test whether the means of three or more populations are equal.

Array: An array is an arrangement of raw numerical data in ascending or descending order of magnitude.

Average: Another name for the mean. The sum of all the data values divided by the number of data values.

Bar Graph: A graph made of bars whose heights represent the frequencies of respective categories.

Bernoulli Trial: Consider a process that consists of a sequence of n independent trials, where the outcome of each trial is a success or a failure. These are called Bernoulli trials.

Beta: The probability of making a *Type II error* when making a statistical hypothesis test. One minus this probability is power, the probability of correctly rejecting the null hypothesis.

Biased Estimator: See unbiased estimator.

Bimodal Distribution: A distribution that has two modes.

Binomial Experiment: An experiment that contains n identical trials such that each of these n trials has only two possible outcomes, the probabilities of these two outcomes remain constant for each trial, and the trials are independent.

Binomial Parameters: The total trails n and the probability of success p for the binomial probability distribution.

Binomial Probability Distribution: The probability distribution that gives the probability of x successes in n trials when the probability of success is p for each trial of a binomial experiment.

Box Plot: The box represents the middle 50% of the data values; that is, the data values from the first to third quartiles. The line or dot in the middle of the box denotes the median. Whiskers – lines extending from the box – extend either to the limits of the data or to a maximum length equal to 1.5 times the length of the box. In the latter case, points beyond the lines indicate outliers.

Box-and-Whisker Plot: A plot that shows the center, spread and skewness of a data set by drawing a box and two whiskers using the median, the first quartile, the third quartile, and the smallest and the largest values in the data set between the lower and the upper inner fences.

Categorical Variable: The values of a categorical variable are discrete categories. Usually the categories cannot be ordered from *highest* to *lowest* in any meaningful way. Rather, the categories just define different groups. Gender and religions are examples of categorical variables. Compare *continuous variable.* See also variable.

Census: A survey conducted by including every element of the population.

Central Limit Theorem: The theorem from which it is inferred that for a large sample size $(n \geq 30)$, the shape of the sampling distribution of $\bar{x}$ is approximately normal. Also, by the same theorem, the shape of the sampling distribution of $\hat{p}$ is approximately normal for a sample for which $np > 5$ and $nq > 5$.

Chebyshev's Theorem: For any number k greater than 1, at least $(1 - 1/k^2)$ of the values for any distribution lie within k standard deviations of the mean.

chi-square Distribution: A distribution, with degrees of freedom as the only parameter, that is skewed to the right for small *df* and looks like a normal curve for large *df.*

chi-square Test: A statistical test for determining whether two categorical variables are related.

Class Boundary: The midpoint of the upper limit of one class and the lower limit of the next class.

Class Frequency: The number of values in a data set that belongs to a certain class.

Class Length: (See class size)

Class Midpoint or Mark: The class midpoint or mark is obtained by dividing the sum of the lower and upper limits (or boundaries) of a class by 2.

Class Size: The size or width of a class interval is the difference between the lower and upper class boundaries. It is also referred to as the class width, class size, or class length.

Class: An interval that includes all the values in a (quantitative) data set that fall within two numbers, the lower and upper limits of the class.

Classical Probability Rule: The method of assigning probabilities to outcomes or events of an experiment with equally likely outcomes.

Cluster Sampling: The sampling technique under which the population is divided into clusters and a sample is chosen from one or a few clusters.

Cluster: A subgroup (usually geographical) of the population that is representative of the population.

Coefficient of Determination: A measure that gives the proportion (or percentage) of the total variation in a dependent variable that is explained by a given independent variable.

Coefficient of Variation: A measure of relative variability that expresses standard deviation as percentage of the mean.

Combinations: The number of ways x elements can be selected from n elements.

Complementary Events: Two events that are taken together include all the outcomes for an experiment but do not contain any common outcomes.

Compound Event: An event that contains more than one outcome of an experiment. It is also called a *composite event.*

Conditional Probability: The probability of an event subject to the condition that another event has already occurred.

Confidence Interval: All the values for a parameter that would not be rejected if they were used as the null hypothesis in a statistical test of that parameter. A 95% confidence interval includes.

Confidence Level: Confidence level, denoted by $(1 - \alpha)$ 100%, states how much confidence we have that a confidence interval contains the true population parameter. This may be thought of as the probability that a given assertion is true. More precisely a statement is true at C confidence level if it is true for fraction C of all notional populations that give the same sampling result as the one actually observed.

Confidence Limit: Stated at C confidence level, the C confidence limits are the endpoints of the C confidence interval.

Consistent Estimator: A sample statistic with a standard deviation that decreases as the sample size increases.

Contingency Coefficient: Quantifies the degree of relationship between two categorical variables.

Continuity Correction Factor: Addition of 0.5 and/or subtraction of 0.5 from the value(s) of x when the normal distribution is used as an approximation to the binomial distribution, where x is the number of successes in n trials.

Continuous Data: Data, which can be described by a continuous variable, are called continuous data.

Continuous Random Variable: A random variable that can assume any value in one or more intervals. A random variable whose values are countable.

Continuous Variable: A variable, which can theoretically assume any value between two given values, is called a continuous variable, otherwise it is called a discrete variable.

Control Group: The group on which no condition is imposed.

Controllable Factor: A design variable that is considered to influence the response and is included in the experiment. The experimenters can control its level.

Convenient Sample: A sample in which the most accessible members of the population are selected.

Covariance: Assesses the degree to which two variables co-vary or vary together. If the two variables are independent then the covariance will equal zero. It is computed as the mean of the products of the mean deviations for each variable.

Critical Value or Critical Point: One or two values that divide the whole region under the sampling distribution of *s* sample statistic into rejection and non-rejection regions.

Cross-Section Data: Data collected on different elements at the same point in time or for the same period of time.

Cumulative Frequency: The cumulative frequency of a class is the frequency of the class divided by the total frequency of all classes and is generally expressed as a percentage.

Cumulative Frequency Distribution: The total frequency of all values less than the upper class boundary of a given class interval is called the cumulative frequency. A table representing such cumulative frequencies is called a cumulative frequency distribution, cumulative frequency table or simply a cumulative distribution.

Cumulative Percentage: The cumulative relative frequency multiplied by 100.

Cumulative Probability: The sum of the probabilities from the minimum possible value up to **a** certain value.

Cumulative Probability Distribution: By cumulating probabilities we obtain cumulative probability distribution, which are analogous to cumulative relative frequency distributions. The function associated with this distribution is often called a distribution function.

Cumulative Relative Frequency: The cumulative frequency of a class divided by the total number of observations.

Curve Fitting: The general problem of finding equations of approximating curves, which fit gives sets of data, is called curve fitting.

Data or Data Set: Collection of observations or measurements on a variable.

Degrees of Freedom (*df*): The number of observations that can be chosen freely. For the estimation of μ using the *t*-distribution, the degrees of freedom are $n - 1$.

Degrees of Freedom for a Simple Linear Regression Model: Sample size minus 2, that is, $n - 2$.

Dependent Events: Two events for which the occurrence of one changes the probability of the occurrence of the other.

Dependent Variable: The variable to be predicted or explained.

Descriptive Statistics: Collection of methods that are used for organising, displaying and describing data using tables, graphs and summary measures.

Designed Experiment: A study in which the experiment controls the assignment of elements to different treatment groups.

Deterministic Model: A model in which the independent variable determines the dependent variable exactly. Such a model gives an exact relationship between two variables.

Discrete Data: Data, which can be described by a discrete variable, are called discrete data.

Discrete Probability Distribution: Of a variation x can assume a discrete set of values with respective probabilities where we can say that a discrete probability distribution for x has been defined.

Discrete Random Variable: A random variable whose values are countable.

Discrete Variable: A variable that can have only certain discrete values. The same as a categorical variable.

Dispersion: The degree to which numerical data tend to spread apart an average value is called the variation or dispersion of the data. The different measure of valuation or dispersion available is the range, mean deviation, semi-interquartile range, and the standard deviation.

Distribution Function: A function giving, for every value x, the probability that a random variable X is lower than equal to x.

Dot Plot: A simple graph in which each observation is represented by a dot at its score.

Efficient Estimator: If the sampling distributors of the two statistics have the same mean (or expectation) the statistic with the smaller variance is called an efficient estimator of the mean while the other statistic is called an inefficient estimator.

Element or Member: A specific subject or object included in a sample or population.

Empirical Rule: For a specific bell-shaped distribution, about 68% of the observations fall in the interval $(\mu - \sigma)$ to $(\mu + \sigma)$, about 95% fall in the interval $(\mu - 2\sigma)$ to $(\mu + 2\sigma)$, and about 99.7% fall in the interval $(\mu - 3\sigma)$ to $(\mu + 3\sigma)$.

Equally Likely Outcomes: Two (or more) outcomes or events that have the same probability of occurrence.

Error: The amount of variation in the response caused by factors other than controllable factors included in the experiment.

Estimate: The value of a sample statistic that is used to find the corresponding population parameter.

Estimated or Predicted Value of *y*: The value of the dependent variable, denoted by $\hat{y}$, that is calculated for a given value of x using the estimated regression model.

Estimation: Estimation is the process of analysing a sample result in order to predict the corresponding value of the population parameter. The sample statistic that is used to estimate a population parameter.

Estimator: The sample statistic that is used to estimate a population parameter.

Event: A collection of one or more outcomes of an experiment.

Expected Frequencies: The frequencies for different categories of a multinomial experiment or for different cells of a contingency table that are expected to occur when a given null hypothesis is true.

Experiment: A process with well-defined outcomes that, when performed, results in one and only one of the, outcomes per repetition.

***F*-Distribution:** A probability distribution for ratios of variances. Most commonly used in *analysis of variance* to compare the ratio of the variance of the means from a number of groups were the same.

Factorial *n*: Factorial n, denoted by $n!$ is simply defined as $n! = n\,(n-1)\,(n-2)\ldots 1$.

Factorial: Denoted by the symbol "!"

First Quartile: The value in a ranked data set such that about 25% of the measurements are smaller than this value and about 75% are larger. It is the median of the values that are smaller than the median of the whole data set.

Frequency Distribution: A tabular arrangement of data by classes put together with the corresponding class frequencies is called a frequency distribution or frequency table.

Frequency Polygon: A frequency polygon is a line graph made by connecting the mid points of the bars in a histogram by straight lines.

Frequency: The number of times a certain data value occurs in the set of observations.

Gaussian Distribution: Another name for the *normal distribution*.

Goodness-of-Fit Test: A test of the null hypothesis that the observed frequencies for an experiment follow a certain pattern or theoretical distribution.

Grouped Data: Data organised and summarised in a frequency-distributed manner are called grouped data.

Histogram: A graph in which classes are marked on the horizontal axis and frequencies, relative frequencies, or percentages are marked on the vertical axis. Bars that are drawn adjacent to each other represent the frequencies, relative frequencies, or percentages or various classes.

Hypothesis Test: A test of whether or not the null hypothesis should be rejected based on the data.

Hypothesis: A hypothesis is an assertion made about a population.

Impossible Event: An event that cannot occur.

Independent Events: Two events for which the occurrence of one does not change the probability of occurrence of the other.

Independent or Explanatory Variable: The variable included in a model to explain the variation in the dependent variable.

Independent Samples: Two samples drawn from two populations such that the selection of one does not affect the selection of the other.

Independent Variable: In an experiment, the levels of independent variables are controlled by the experimenter. Independent variables serve as inputs. Compare *dependent variable.*

Inefficient Estimator: See efficient estimator.

Inferential Statistics: Collection of methods that help make decisions about a population based on sample results.

Interaction: Two factors are said to have interaction with each other if the influence of one on the response function is dependent on the value of the other.

Intercept: In the following equation for a line such as a regression model, the parameter a is the intercept.

y-intercept: The point at which the regression line intersects the vertical **axis** on which the dependent variable is marked. It is the value of y when x is zero.

Interquartile Range (IQR): The difference between the third Quartile (Q_3) and the first quartile (Q_1). The IQR indicates the range of scores spanned n by the middle half of the data values. The box in a box plot represents the IQR.

Intersection of Events: Intersection of events is given by the outcomes that are common to two (or more) events.

Interval Estimate: An estimate of a population parameter given by two numbers between which the parameter may be considered to lie is called an interval estimate of the parameter.

Joint Probability: The probability that two (or more) events occur together.

Judgment Sample: A sample that includes the elements of the population selected based on the judgment and prior knowledge of an expert.

Kruskal-Wallis Test: A non-parametric statistical procedure for comparing medians across groups.

Kurtosis: Kurtosis is the degree of peaked ness of a distribution relative to a normal distribution.

Large Sample: The samples of size greater than 30 are called large samples.

Law of Large Numbers: If an experiment is repeated again and again, the probability of an event obtained from the relative frequency approaches the actual or theoretical probability.

Least-Squares Estimates of *a* and *b*: The values of *a* and *b* that are calculated by using the sample data.

Least-Squares Method: The method used to fit a regression line through a scatter diagram such that the error sum of squares is a minimum.

Least-Squares Regression Line: A regression line obtained by using the least squares method.

Left-Tailed Test: A test in which the rejection region lies in the left tail of the distribution curve.

Level of Significance: The maximum probability in testing a hypothesis is with which type I error is considered to be in risk is called the level of significance of the test.

Linear Correlation Coefficient: A measure of the strength of the linear relationship between two variables.

Linear Regression Model: A regression model that gives a straight-line relationship between two variables.

Lower Inner Fence: The value in a data set that is 1.5 × IQR below the first quartile.

Lower Outer Fence: The value in a data set that is 3.0 × IQR below the first quartile.

Lower Quartile: The lowest 25% of the scores are equal to or less than the lower quartile score. Often represented as Q1; equal to the 25th *percentile.*

Marginal Probability: The probability of one event or characteristic without consideration of any other event.

Maximum Error of Estimate: The quantity that is subtracted from and added to the value of a sample statistic to obtain a confidence interval for the corresponding population parameter.

Maximum: The largest data value in a set of observations.

Mean of a Discrete Random Variable: The mean of a discrete random variable *x* is the value that is expected to occur per repetition, on average, if an experiment is performed a large number of times. The mean of a discrete random variable is also called its *expected value.*

Mean of $\hat{p}$: The mean of the sampling distribution of $\overline{x}$, denoted $\mu\overline{x}$, is equal to the population mean μ.

Mean Square Between Samples or MSB: A measure of the variation among means of samples taken from different populations.

Mean Square Within Samples or MSW: A measure of the variation within data of all samples taken from different populations.

Mean: The average of the data values, that is, the sum of all the data values divided by the number of data values. The mean makes the *sum of squared errors* as small as possible.

Measure of Dispersion: Measures that give the spread of a distribution. The range, variance and standard deviation are three such measures.

Measures of Central Tendency: Measures that describe the centre of a distribution. The mean, median and mode are three of the measures of central tendency.

Measures of Position: Measures that determine the position of a single value in relation to other values in a data set. Quartiles, percentiles, and percentile rank are examples of measures of position.

Median Absolute Deviation (MAD): The median of all the absolute errors or deviations. The MAD describes the spread of the data values away from the model value.

Median: The middle data value in a set of observation. To find the median, reorder the data from smallest to largest and find the middle observation; that is the median. If there is an even number of observations, then there will be two middle values; in that case, the average of those two middle values is the median. The median is also the 50th *percentile.*

Minimum: The lowest data value in a set of observations.

Mode: A value (or values) that occurs with highest frequency in a data set.

Model: Specifies a predicted or representative value of reach observation in a data set. Simple models are the mean or the median for a set of observations. More complex models are, for example, regression lines.

Multimodal Distribution: A distribution that has more than two modes.

Multinomial Experiment: An experiment with *n* trials for which (1) the trials are identical, (2) there are more than two possible outcomes per trial, (3) the trials are independent and (4) the probabilities of various outcomes remain constant for each trial.

Multiple Regression Model: A regression model that contains two or more independent variables.

Mutually Exclusive Events: Two or more events that do not contain any common outcome and, hence, cannot occur together.

Negative Relationship between Two Variables: The value of the slope in the regression line and the correlation coefficient between two variables are both negative.

Nominal Variable: Same as *categorical variable.* Levels of these variables are *noms* or *names.* For example, the names for the levels of the gender variable are *male* and *female.*

Non-linear (simple) Regression Model: A regression model that does not give a straight-line relationship between two variables.

Non-parametric Statistics: Statistical methods that make no assumption that the data are from a *normal distribution.*

Non-random Sample: A sample in which some members of the population may have no chance of being selected.

Non-sampling Errors: The errors that occur during the collection, recording, and tabulation of data.

Non-sampling or Systematic Error: The errors that occur in the collection, recording and tabulation of data.

Normal Distribution: The probability distribution that describes or approximates the distribution of many variables. Most observations in a normal distribution occur near the mean.

Normal Probability Distribution: The probability distribution of a continuous random variable that, when plotted, gives a specific bell-shaped curve. The parameters of the normal distribution are the mean μ and the standard deviation σ.

Null Hypothesis: The hypothesis that nothing is happening in the data that would not be expected by chance. Some null hypotheses are (a) the means of two groups are equal, (b) the slope in a simple regression is zero, (c) the correlation between two variables is zero, and (d) the classification of the data according to one nominal variable is independent of the classification of that data according to a second nominal variable.

Number of Degrees of Freedom: The number of degrees of freedom (n) of a statistic generally is defined as the number N of the independent observatory in the sample (sample size) minus the number k of population parameters estimated from the sample observations.

Observation or Measurement: The value of a variable for an element.

Observation Study: A study in which the assignment of elements to different treatment is voluntary and the researcher simply observes the results of the study.

Observation: A person, place, or thing for which a data value is available or is measured.

Observed Frequencies: The frequencies actually obtained from the performance of an experiment.

Observed Value of z or t: The value z or t calculated for a sample statistic such as the sample mean or the sample proportion.

Ogive: A curve drawn for a cumulative frequency distribution.

One-Way ANOVA: The analysis of variance technique that analyses one variable only.

One-Tailed Test: A test in which there is only one rejection region, either in the left tail or in the right tail of the distribution curve.

Ordinal Variable: A variable whose values indicate only rank and not the distance between values. For example, in a race, an ordinal variable would indicate who was first, second, third, etc., but would not give the time or distance between the racers.

Outcome: An outcome is one particular result of an experiment.

Outlier: An extreme or a typical value that is very different from other data values in the set of observations.

Outliers or Extreme Values: Values that is very small or very large relative to the majority of the values in a data set.

Paired or Matched Samples: Two samples drawn in such a way that they include the same elements and two data values are obtained from each element, one for each sample. Also called dependent samples.

Parameter: An unknown value in a model that is estimated from the data. Examples: mean, median, intercept, and slope.

Percentage: The percentage for a class or category is obtained by multiplying the relative frequency of that class or category by 100.

Percentile Rank: The percentile rank of a value gives the percentage of values in the data set that are smaller than this value.

Percentile: The Pth percentile data value is the score that is equal to or greater than $P\%$ of all the data values. For example, the score equal to the 25th percentile is equal to or greater than one quarter of all the data values (and is also the first *quartile*). The 50th percentile necessarily is the median. Ninety-nine values that divide a ranked data set into 100 equal parts.

Permutations: A permutation of n different objects taken r at a time is an arrangement of r out of the n objects with no special attention given to the order of arrangement. The number of combinations of n objects taken r at a time is denoted by ${}^nP_r$ and is given by ${}^nP_r = \dfrac{n!}{(n-r)!}$.

Pie Chart: A circle divided into portions that represent the relative frequencies or percentages of different categories or classes.

Point Estimate: An estimate of a population parameter given by a single number is called a point estimate of the parameter.

Poisson Parameter: The average occurrences, denoted by λ, during an interval for a Poisson probability distribution.

Poisson Probability Distribution: The probability distribution that gives the probability of x occurrences in an interval when the average occurrences in that interval are λ.

Polygon: A graph formed by joining the midpoints of the tops of successive bars in a histogram by straight lines.

Population Distribution: The probability distribution of the population data.

Population or Target Population: The collection of all elements whose characteristics are being studied.

Population Parameters for a Simple Regression Model: The values of A and B for the regression model $y = A + Bx + \in$ that are obtained by using population data.

Population Parameters: The estimation of unknown population quantities (such as population mean, variance, etc.) often called population parameters from a knowledge of corresponding sample quantities (sample mean variance, etc.), often

Population Proportion p: The ratio of the number of elements in a population with a specific characteristic to the total number of elements in the population.

Population: A population consists of all the individuals or objects in a well-defined group about which information is desired to answer a question.

Positive Relationship between Two Variables: The value of the slope in the regression line and the correlation coefficient between two variables are both positive.

Power: The probability that a statistical test will reject the *null hypothesis* given that some specific alternative model is true. Equivalently, the probability that a *Type II error* will be avoided.

Prediction Interval: The confidence interval for a particular value of y for a given value of x.

Probabilistic or Statistical Model: A model in which the independent variable does not determine the dependent variable exactly.

Probability: The probability of an event occurring in an experiment equals the proportion of times the event occurs if the experiment is repeated a very large (infinite) number of times.

Probability Distribution of a Discrete Random Variable: A list of all the possible values that a discrete random variable can assume and their corresponding probabilities.

Probability Distribution: A distribution that determines the probability that a random variable takes any given value or belongs to a given set of values.

Qualitative or Categorical Variable: A variable that cannot assume numerical values but is classified into two or more categories.

Quantitative Data: Data generated by a quantitative variable.

Quartiles: Summary measures that divide all the scores into four quarters. One-fourth of the data values are equal to or less than the first or *lower quartile* (Q_1), one half of the values are equal to or less than the second quartile (Q_2), also known as the *median),* and three fourths of all the data values are equal to or less than the third or *upper quartile* (Q_3).

Quota Sample: A sample selected in such a way that each group or subpopulation is represented in the sample in exactly the same proportion as in the target population.

Random Error Term (∈): The difference between the actual and predicted value of *y*.

Random Sample: A sample drawn in such a way that each element of the population has same chance of being included in the sample.

Random Sampling: Each member of a population, which has an equal chance of being included, is called random sampling.

Random Variable: A variable, denoted by *x*, whose value is determined by the outcome of a random experiment. Also called a *chance variable.*

Randomisation: The procedure under which elements are assigned to different (treatment and control) groups at random.

Range: The difference between the largest and smallest numbers is called the range of the data.

Ranks: Data values, which indicate only the order of the observations. See *ordinal variable.*

Raw Data: Data recorded in the sequence in which they are collected and before they are processed.

Relative Cumulative Frequency: The relative cumulative frequency or percentage cumulative frequency is the cumulative frequency divided by the total frequency.

Relative Dispersion: Relative dispersion is defined as the ratio of absolute dispersion and the average value.

Relative Frequency: The frequency of a class or category divided by the sum of all frequencies.

Representative Sample: A sample that contains the characteristics of the corresponding population.

Right-Tailed Test: A test in which the rejection region lies in the right rail of the distribution curve.

Sample: A selection of observations from a larger population of all possible observations. Ideally, the sample is selected randomly from the population.

Sample Point: An outcome of an experiment.

Sample Proportion *p*: The ratio of the number of elements in a sample with a specific characteristic to the total number of elements in that sample.

Sample Space: A sample space is the set of all possible outcomes of an experiment. These outcomes are also called the elements of the sample space.

Sample Statistics: See population parameters.

Sample Survey: A survey that includes elements of a sample.

Sampling Distribution: The probability distribution of the statistic one would get by sampling over and over again.

Sampling Distribution of $\bar{x}$: The probability distribution of all the values of $\bar{x}$ calculated from all possible samples of the same size selected from a population.

Sampling Distribution of $\hat{p}$: The probability distribution of all the values of *p* calculated from all possible samples of the same size selected from a population.

Sampling Error: The difference between the values of a sample statistic calculated from a random sample and the value of the corresponding population parameter. This type of error occurs due to chance.

Sampling Frame: The list of elements of the target population that is used to select a sample.

Sampling or Chance Error: The difference between the results obtained from a sample survey and the result that would be obtained from the census.

Scatter Diagram or Scattergram: A plot of the paired observations of x and y.

Scatter Plot, Scattergram: A two-variable plot in which each point represents the levels of an observation on each variable. Often the variable on the horizontal axis is to be used to predict the variable on the vertical axis. Scatter plots are useful for viewing *correlations* and for *simple regression.*

***z*-Score Formula:** The difference between the observation and the mean, divided by the standard deviation. That is,

S_d: The standard deviation of the paired differences for a sample.

Second Quartile: Middle or second of the three quartiles that divide a ranked data set into four equal parts. About 50% of the values in the data set are smaller and about 50% are larger than the second quartile. The second quartile is the same as the median.

Selection Error: The error that occurs because the sampling frame is not representative of the population. Significance Level: The pre-specified probability of a Type I error below which the null hypothesis is considered to be so rare as to be implausible.

Significant: When the probability of obtaining a statistical value is below the significance level, the statistic is said to be *statistically significant.*

Simple Event: An event that contains one and only one outcome of an experiment. It is also called an *elementary event.*

Simple Linear Regression: A regression model with one dependent and one independent variable that assumes a straight-line relationship.

Simple Random Sample: A sample chosen in such a way that each element of the population has the same probability of being included in the sample.

Sixtieth Percentile: The sixtieth percentile is larger than 60% of the scores (and smaller than 40%).

Skewed: A skewed distribution is not symmetric. That is, it has different shapes on each side of the median.

For example:

Skewed-to-the-Left Histogram: A histogram with a longer tail on the left side.

Skewed-to-the-Right Histogram: A histogram with a longer tail on the right side.

Skewness: Skewness is the degree of asymmetry or departure symmetry of a distribution. Of the frequency curve of a distribution has a longer tail to the right of the central maximum than to the left, the distribution is said to be skewed to the right or 5 to have positive skewness. Of the reverse is true, it is called skewed to the left or to have negative skewness.

Slope: The coefficient of x in a regression model that gives the change in y for a change of one unit in x.

Small Samples: The samples of site lesser than 30 are called small samples.

SSB: The sum of squares between samples. Also called the sum of squares of the factor or treatment.

SSE (error sum of squares): The sum of the squared differences between the actual and predicted values of y. It is the portion of the SST that is not explained by the regression model.

SSR (regression sum of squares): The portion of the SST that is explained by the regression model.

SST: The total sum of squares given by the sum of SSB and SSW.

SST (total sum of squares): The sum of the squared differences between actual y value and $\bar{y}$.

SSW: The sum of squares within samples. Also called the sum of squares of errors.

Standard Deviation: A measure of spread that is given by the positive square root of the variance.

Standard Deviation of *x*: The standard deviation of the sampling distribution of $\bar{x}$, denoted by $\sigma_{\bar{x}}$, is equal to $\sigma/\sqrt{n}$ when $n/N \leq 05$.

Standard Deviation of a Discrete Random Variable: A measure of spread for the probability distribution of a discrete random variable.

Standard Deviation of Errors: A measure of spread for the random errors.

Standard Deviation of $\hat{p}$: The standard deviation of the sampling distribution of $\hat{p}$, denoted by $\sigma_{\hat{p}}$, is equal to $\sigma/\sqrt{n}$ when $n/N \leq 05$.

Standard Error: The standard deviation of the sampling distribution for any given statistic.

Standard Error of Mean: The standard deviation of the sampling distribution of the mean.

Standard Normal Distribution: The normal distribution with $\mu = 0$ and $\sigma = 1$. The units of the standard normal distribution are denoted by *z*.

Statistic: A summary measure calculated for sample data.

Statistics: Statistics deals with scientific methods for collecting, organising, summarising, presenting and analysing data, as well as drawing valid conclusions and making reasonable decisions based on such analysis.

Statistical Hypothesis: Assumptions or guesses made which may or may not be true, are called statistical hypotheses and in general are statements about the probability distributions of the populations.

Stem-and-Leaf Display: A display of data in which each value is divided into two portions, a stem and a leaf.

Stratified Random Sampling: The sampling technique under which the population is divided into different strata and a sample is chosen from each stratum.

Stratum: A subgroup of the population whose members are identical with regard to the possession of a characteristic.

Subjective Probability: The probability assigned to an event based on the information and judgment of a person.

Sure Event: An event that is certain to occur.

Survey: Collecting data on the elements of a population or sample.

Symmetric: A symmetric distribution has the same shape on each side of the median. The normal distribution is an example of a symmetric distribution. Compare *skewed.*

Symmetric Histogram: A histogram that is identical on both sides of its central point.

Systematic Random Sampling: Sampling method used to choose a sample by selecting every *k*th unit from the list.

Target Population: The collection of all subjects of interest.

Target Value: A value that a product is expected to posses. Most often this value is different from what a single unit actually does exhibit. For a 9 volt transistor battery the target value is 9 volts.

Test of Homogeneity: A test of the null hypothesis that the proportions of elements that belong to different groups in two (or more) populations are similar.

Tests of Hypothesis: Procedures, which will enable to decide whether to accept or reject hypothesis or to determine whether observed samples differ significantly from expected results are called tests of hypothesis; tests of significance, or rules of decision.

Test of Independence: A test of the null hypothesis that attributes of a population is not related.

Test Statistic: The value of z or t calculated for a sample statistic such as the sample mean or the sample proportion.

Third Quartile: Third of the three quartiles that divide a ranked data set into four equal parts. About 75% of the values in a data set are smaller than the value of the third quartile and about 25% are lager. It is the median of the values that are greater than the median of the whole data set.

Tree Diagram: A diagram in which each outcome of an experiment is represented by a branch of a tree.

Trimmed Mean: The k% trimmed mean is obtained by dropping k% of the smallest values and k% of the largest values from the given data and then calculating the mean of the remaining $(100 - 2k)$% of the values.

Two-Tailed Test: A two-tailed test considers whether the null hypothesis might be wrong in either direction; that is, it allows the possibility that the true parameter might be either above or below the value of the null hypothesis. Compare *one-tailed test.*

Type I Error: An error that occurs when a true null hypothesis is rejected.

Type II Error: An error that occurs when a false null hypothesis is not rejected.

Unbiased Estimator: Of the mean of the sampling distribution of a statistic equals to the corresponding population parameters, the statistic is called an unbiased estimator of the parameters, and otherwise it is called a biased estimator.

Uniform or Rectangular Histogram: A histogram with the same frequency for all classes.

Unimodal Distribution: A distribution that has only one mode.

Union of Two Events: All outcomes that belong either to one or to both events.

Upper Inner Fence: The value in a data set that is 1.5 × IQR above the third quartile.

Upper Outer Fence: The value in a data set that is 3.0 × IQR above the third quartile.

Upper Quartile: The 75th *percentile.* The observation that is greater than or equal to 75% of the observations and less than 25% of the observations. Sometimes designated by Q_3.

***p*-Value:** The smallest significance level at which a null hypothesis can be rejected.

Variable: A characteristic, trait, attribute, or measurement that can take on different values. A variable must vary, having at least one value for some observations and another value for other observations.

Variables, Factors, or Parameters: These words are used synonymously to indicate the controllable factors in an experiment. In the case of a plastic molding experiment, molding temperature, injection pressure, set time, etc., are factors.

Variance: The typical or average squared error. For a population, the sum of squared errors is divided by n the number of observations. More often, interest is in the sample estimate of the variance in which case the sum of squared errors is divided by $n - 1$.

Venn Diagram: A picture that represents a sample space or certain events.

***y*-intercept:** The point at which the regression line intersects the vertical axis on which the dependent variable is marked. It is the value of y when x is zero.

❑❑❑